SIPRI Yearbook 1994

sipri

Stockholm International Peace Research Institute

SIPRI is an independent international institute for research into problems of peace and conflict, especially those of arms control and disarmament. It was established in 1966 to commemorate Sweden's 150 years of unbroken peace.

The Institute is financed mainly by the Swedish Parliament. The staff and the Governing Board are international. The Institute also has an Advisory Committee as an international consultative body.

The Governing Board is not responsible for the views expressed in the publications of the Institute.

sipri

Stockholm International Peace Research Institute
Pipers väg 28, S-170 73 Solna, Sweden
Cable: SIPRI
Telephone: 46 8/655 97 00
Telefax: 46 8/655 97 33

SIPRI Yearbook 1994

sipri

Stockholm International Peace Research Institute

OXFORD UNIVERSITY PRESS
1994

Oxford University Press, Walton Street, Oxford OX2 6DP
Oxford New York
Athens Auckland Bangkok Bombay
Calcutta Cape Town Dar es Salaam Delhi
Florence Hong Kong Istanbul Karachi
Kuala Lumpur Madras Madrid Melbourne
Mexico City Nairobi Paris Singapore
Taipei Tokyo Toronto
and associated companies in
Berlin Ibadan

Oxford is a trade mark of Oxford University Press

Published in the United States
by Oxford University Press Inc., New York

© SIPRI 1994

Yearbooks before 1987 published under title
'World Armaments and Disarmament:
SIPRI Yearbook [year of publication]'

British Library Cataloguing in Publication Data

Data available
ISSN 0953–0282
ISBN 0–19–829182–5

Library of Congress Cataloging in Publication Data

Data available
ISSN 0953–0282
ISBN 0–19–829182–5

Typeset and originated by Stockholm International Peace Research Institute
Printed and bound in Great Britain by
Biddles Ltd., Guildford and King's Lynn

Contents

Part I. Global and regional security and conflicts, 1993

Report to Ministers by the NACC Ad Hoc Group on Co-operation in Peacekeeping—
French Proposal for a Pact on Stability in Europe—Russian President Boris Yeltsin's
letter to US President Bill Clinton—Treaty on European Union (provisions on European
security)—Decisions of the Rome CSCE Council Meeting—Legal Capacity and
Privileges and Immunities—CSCE and the New Europe: Our Security is Indivisible—
Declaration of the Heads of State and Government participating in the Meeting of the
North Atlantic Council, 11 January 1994—Partnership for Peace: Invitation and
Framework Document

Part II. Weapons and technology proliferation, 1993

Part III. Military expenditure, arms production and trade, 1993

Part IV. Arms control and disarmament, 1993

Statement of the Democratic People's Republic of Korea on Withdrawal from the Non-Proliferation Treaty—Non-Proliferation Treaty: Democratic People's Republic of Korea. Letter dated 2 April 1993 to the Secretary-General of the Conference on Disarmament by the Representatives of the Depositary Governments transmitting a statement issued on 1 April 1993—Speech by State President F. W. de Klerk, to Parliament, 24 March 1993, regarding the Non-Proliferation Treaty—Joint Statement by the President of the Russian Federation and the President of the United States of American on Non-proliferation of Weapons of Mass Destruction and the Means of Their Delivery—IAEA Board of Governors Reviews Agency's Inspections in the Democratic People's Republic of Korea

Annexes

Preface

This is the 25th edition of the *SIPRI Yearbook*. The first edition was published in 1969. Then Director Robert Neild described the tasks of this periodical publication as 'to produce a factual and balanced account of a controversial subject—the arms race and attempts to stop it'. It was at a time when there was 'no authoritative international source which provided—in one place—an account of recent trends in world military expenditure, the state of the technological arms race, and the success or failure of recent attempts at arms limitation or disarmament'.

Over the past 25 years the world has changed; so has the *SIPRI Yearbook*. Competent journals have found the *SIPRI Yearbook* 'indispensable' and 'the world's most exhaustive annual survey of military matters' and 'a classic in security policy'.

SIPRI has built its reputation as an unbiased source of data and military statistics, using open sources and open methodology. The credit goes mainly to those who rightly determined the tasks and functions that the Institute and its *Yearbook* were to fulfil. A particular debt is owed to the SIPRI 'founding parents'—Gunnar and Alva Myrdal—and the former directors—Robert Neild, Frank Barnaby, Frank Blackaby and Walther Stützle.

In presenting the 25th edition of the *SIPRI Yearbook* to the reader, I would also like to pay homage to the two prominent persons who passed away in January 1994 and who in various ways influenced the research profile of the Institute, namely, Ambassador Dr Inga Thorsson, who in 1988–91 served as Chairman of the SIPRI Governing Board, and former Norwegian Minister of Foreign Affairs Johan Jørgen Holst. In his address to SIPRI's 25th Anniversary Conference, Johan, a creative and innovative scholar and politician, said: 'Arms control needs not only to be rewritten, it needs to be re-orchestrated in order to contribute to shaping a new order of common security'. This *Yearbook* fully confirms the validity of his postulate.

The structure of recent *Yearbooks* differs from that of the first editions. Part I of this volume deals with conflict developments and regional security issues. The *Yearbook* is no longer confined to world armaments and disarmament matters but embraces a broader notion of international security. Most of the chapters were prepared at the Institute; seven chapters were contributed by prominent experts whom I would like to thank. We are also grateful to the external reviewers for their valuable comments and opinions.

The editorial work was done under the leadership of Connie Wall, whose skill, experience and organizational abilities facilitated rapid production of the book. Other competent and experienced editors—Billie Bielckus, Jetta Gilligan Borg, Eve Johansson and Don Odom—worked with enthusiasm and devotion. My thanks go to Ragnhild Ferm and Shannon Kile, whose close co-operation with the editors contributed to the accuracy. I would also like to thank Gerd Hagmeyer-Gaverus for programming and other computer support and the secretaries—Christina Barkstedt, Cynthia Loo, Marianne Lyons and Miyoko Suzuki. All the maps were prepared by Billie Bielckus and the index by Peter Rea, UK.

Dr Adam Daniel Rotfeld
Director
June 1994

Acronyms

ABACC	Argentinian–Brazilian Agency for Accounting and Control of Nuclear Materials	AWACS	Airborne warning and control system
		BA	Budget authority
ABM	Anti-ballistic missile	BCC	Bilateral Consultation Commission
ACE	Allied Command Europe (NATO)	BMD	Ballistic missile defence
ACM	Advanced cruise missile	BMDO	Ballistic Missile Defense Organization
ACV	Armoured combat vehicle	BW	Biological warfare/weapons
ADM	Atomic demolition munition	BWC	Biological Weapons Convention
AFAP	Artillery-fired atomic projectile	CARICOM	Caribbean Common Market
AIFV	Armoured infantry fighting vehicle	CAS	Committee on Assurances of Supply
ALCM	Air-launched cruise missile	CBM	Confidence-building measure
AMF	Allied Mobile Force	CBW	Chemical and biological warfare/weapons
ANC	African National Congress		
APC	Armoured personnel carrier	CD	Conference on Disarmament
ASAT	Anti-satellite	CEE	Central and Eastern Europe
ASEAN	Association of South-East Asian Nations	CEP	Circular error probable
ASLCM	Advanced sea-launched cruise missile	CFE	Conventional Armed Forces in Europe
ASM	Air-to-surface missile	CFSP	Common Foreign and Security Policy
ASUW	Anti-surface warfare	C^3I	Command, control, communications and intelligence
ASW	Anti-submarine warfare		
ATBM	Anti-tactical ballistic missile	CIO	Chairman-in-Office
ATC	Armoured troop carrier	CIS	Commonwealth of Independent States
ATTU	Atlantic-to-the-Urals (zone)		

CMEA	Council for Mutual Economic Assistance (as COMECON)	EFA	European Fighter Aircraft
		EFTA	European Free Trade Area
COCOM	Coordinating Committee (on Multilateral Export Controls)	ELINT	Electronic intelligence
		ELV	Expendable launch vehicle
COMECON	Council for Mutual Economic Assistance (as CMEA)	EMP	Electromagnetic pulse
		EMU	Economic and Monetary Union
CORRTEX	Continuous reflectometry for radius versus time experiments	Enmod	Environmental modification
		EPU	European Political Union
CPC	Conflict Prevention Centre	ERW	Enhanced radiation (neutron) weapon
CPI	Consumer price index		
CSBM	Confidence- and security-building measure	EU	European Union
CSCE	Conference on Security and Co-operation in Europe	EUCLID	European Cooperative Long-term Initiative on Defence
CSO	Committee of Senior Officials	EURATOM	European Atomic Energy Community
CTB(T)	Comprehensive test ban (treaty)	FAO	Food and Agriculture Organization
CTOL	Conventional take-off and landing	FBR	Fast-breeder reactor
		FBS	Forward-based system
CW	Chemical warfare/weapons	FOC	Full operational capability
CWC	Chemical Weapons Convention	FOTL	Follow-on to Lance
CWFZ	Chemical weapon-free zone	FROD	Functionally related observable difference
DEW	Directed-energy weapon		
DOD	Department of Defense (US)	FROG	Free-rocket-over-ground
		FSC	Forum for Security Co-operation
DOE	Department of Energy (US)	FY	Fiscal year
DST	Defence and Space Talks		
EC	European Community	G7	Group of Seven (leading industrialized nations)
ECOWAS	Economic Community of West African States	G-21	Group of 21 (formerly 21 non-aligned states)
ECU	European Currency Unit	GATT	General Agreement on Tariffs and Trade

GBR	Ground-based radar	JCC	Joint Consultative Commission
GCC	Gulf Co-operation Council	JCG	Joint Consultative Group
GDP	Gross domestic product	JCIC	Joint Compliance and Inspection Commission
GLCM	Ground-launched cruise missile	JSG	Joint Strategy Group
GNP	Gross national product	LDC	Less developed country
GPALS	Global Protection Against Limited Strikes	LDDI	Less developed defence industry
GPS	Global Protection System	LEU	Low-enriched uranium
HACV	Heavy armoured combat vehicle	MAD	Mutual assured destruction
HCNM	High Commissioner on National Minorities	MARV	Manœuvrable re-entry vehicle
HEU	Highly enriched uranium	MBT	Main battle tank
HLTF	High Level Task Force	MD	Military District
HLWG	High Level Working Group	MIC	Military–industrial complex
IAEA	International Atomic Energy Agency	MIRV	Multiple independently targetable re-entry vehicle
ICBM	Intercontinental ballistic missile	MLRS	Multiple launch rocket system
IEPG	Independent European Programme Group	MOU	Memorandum of Understanding
IFV	Infantry fighting vehicle	MRF	Multi-role fighter
IMF	International Monetary Fund	MRV	Multiple re-entry vehicle
		MSC	Military Staff Committee
INF	Intermediate-range nuclear forces	MTCR	Missile Technology Control Regime
INFCIRC	Information circular	MTM	Multinational technical means (of verification)
IOC	Initial operational capability		
IPM	International plutonium management	NACC	North Atlantic Cooperation Council
IPS	International plutonium storage	NATO	North Atlantic Treaty Organization
IRBM	Intermediate-range ballistic missile	NBC	Nuclear, biological and chemical (weapons)

NIC	Newly industrializing country	OMG	Operational Manœuvre Group
NMP	Net material product	OOV	Object of verification
NNA	Neutral and non-aligned (states)	OPANAL	Agency for the Prohibition of Nuclear Weapons in Latin America
NNWS	Non-nuclear weapon state		
NPG	Nuclear Planning Group	OPCW	Organisation for the Prohibition of Chemical Weapons
NPT	Non-Proliferation Treaty		
NRRC	Nuclear Risk Reduction Centre	OSI	On-site inspection
		OSIA	On-Site Inspection Agency
NSG	Nuclear Suppliers Group	PFP	Partnership for Peace
NST	Nuclear and Space Talks	PLA	People's Liberation Army
NSWTO	Non-Soviet WTO	PLO	Palestine Liberation Organization
NTI	National trial inspection		
NTM	National technical means (of verification)	PNE(T)	Peaceful Nuclear Explosions (Treaty)
		PTB(T)	Partial Test Ban (Treaty)
NTS	Nevada test site	R&D	Research and development
NWFZ	Nuclear weapon-free zone	RDT&E	Research, development, testing and evaluation
NWS	Nuclear weapon state		
OAS	Organization of American States	RMA	Restricted Military Area
		RPV	Remotely piloted vehicle
OAU	Organization of African Unity	RV	Re-entry vehicle
OBDA	Official budget defence allocation	SACEUR	Supreme Allied Commander, Europe
ODA	Official development assistance	SALT	Strategic Arms Limitation Talks
ODIHR	Office for Democratic Institutions and Human Rights	SAM	Surface-to-air missile
		SCC	Standing Consultative Commission
OECD	Organisation for Economic Co-operation and Development	SDI	Strategic Defense Initiative
		SDIO	SDI Organization
O&M	Operation and maintenance	SICBM	Small ICBM
OMB	Office of Management and Budget (US)		

SLBM	Submarine-launched ballistic missile	UNDP	United Nations Development Programme
SLCM	Sea-launched cruise missile	UNIKOM	United Nations Iraq–Kuwait Observation Mission
SLV	Space launch vehicle		
SNDV	Strategic nuclear delivery vehicle	UNOSOM	United Nations Operation in Somalia
SNF	Short-range nuclear forces	UNPROFOR	United Nations Protection Force
SRAM	Short-range attack missile		
SRBM	Short-range ballistic missile	UNSCOM	United Nations Special Commission on Iraq
SSBN	Nuclear-powered, ballistic-missile submarine	UNTAC	United Nations Transitional Authority in Cambodia
SSD	Safety, Security and Dismantlement (Talks)	UNTAG	United Nations Transition Assistance Group
SSGN	Nuclear-powered, guided-missile submarine	UNTEA	United Nations Temporary Executive Authority
SS(M)	Surface-to-surface (missile)	VCC	Verification Co-ordinating Committee
SSN	Nuclear-powered attack submarine	V/STOL	Vertical/short take-off and landing
START	Strategic Arms Reduction Talks/Treaty	WEU	Western European Union
SVC	Special Verification Commission	WTO	Warsaw Treaty Organization (Warsaw Pact)
SWS	Strategic weapon system		
TASM	Tactical air-to-surface missile		
TEL	Transporter–erector–launcher		
THAAD	Theatre High Altitude Area Defence		
TLE	Treaty-limited equipment		
TNF	Theatre nuclear forces		
TTB(T)	Threshold Test Ban (Treaty)		
UNCED	United Nations Conference on Environment and Development		

Glossary

RAGNHILD FERM and CONNIE WALL

ABM Treaty

The 1972 Anti-Ballistic Missile Treaty, signed by the USSR and the USA in the SALT I process, which prohibits the development, testing and deployment of sea-, air-, space- or mobile land-based ABM systems. *See also* Ballistic missile defence.

Anti-ballistic missile (ABM) system

Weapon system designed to defend against a ballistic missile attack by intercepting and destroying ballistic missiles and their warheads in flight.

Arab League

Established in 1945. The members of the League of Arab States are Algeria, Bahrain, Djibouti, Egypt, Iraq, Jordan, Kuwait, Lebanon, Libya, Mauritania, Morocco, Oman, Palestine, Qatar, Saudi Arabia, Somalia, Sudan, Syria, Tunisia, the United Arab Emirates and Yemen. The League has a permanent delegation to the UN.

Association of South-East Asian Nations (ASEAN)

Established in 1967. The member states are Brunei, Indonesia, Malaysia, the Philippines, Singapore and Thailand.

ATTU zone

The Atlantic-to-the-Urals zone, stretching from the Atlantic Ocean to the Ural Mountains, which comprises the entire land territory of the European NATO states, former WTO states, and European former Soviet republics with the exception of the Baltic states. *See also* CFE Treaty, CFE-1A Agreement.

Balkan states

States in south-eastern Europe bounded by the Adriatic, Aegean and Black seas: Albania, Bosnia and Herzegovina, Bulgaria, Croatia, Greece, Macedonia (Former Yugoslav Republic of), Romania, Slovenia, Turkey and Yugoslavia (Serbia and Montenegro).

Balladur Plan

See Pact for Stability in Europe.

Ballistic missile

A missile which follows a ballistic trajectory (part of which may be outside the earth's atmosphere) when thrust is terminated.

Ballistic missile defence (BMD)

Systems capable of intercepting and destroying nuclear weapons in flight, for defence against a ballistic missile attack. The now defunct US Strategic Defense Initiative (SDI) was a programme for space-based systems. In May 1993 the Strategic Defense Initiative Organization (SDIO) was renamed the Ballistic Missile Defense Organization (BMDO), signifying the end of the 'Star Wars' era and a re-emphasis of US missile-defence programmes from strategic to theatre defences. *See also* ABM Treaty, Anti-ballistic missile system, Ballistic missile, Theatre Missile Defense Initiative.

Baltic states	Three former Soviet republics in north-eastern Europe which border on the Baltic Sea: Estonia, Latvia and Lithuania.
Binary chemical weapon	A shell or other device filled with two chemicals of relatively low toxicity which mix and react while the device is being delivered to the target, the reaction product being a super-toxic chemical warfare agent, such as nerve gas.
Biological weapon (BW)	A weapon containing living organisms, whatever their nature, or infective material derived from them, which are intended for use in warfare to cause disease or death in man, animals or plants, and which for their effect depend on their ability to multiply in the person, animal or plant attacked, as well as the means of their delivery.
Central Asia	Of the former Soviet republics, this term refers to Kazakhstan, Kyrgyzstan, Tajikistan, Turkmenistan and Uzbekistan (as well as the Central Asian part of Russia).
Central and Eastern Europe (CEE)	The CEE refers to Bulgaria, the Czech Republic, Hungary, Poland, Romania and Slovakia. The CEE region sometimes also includes the European former Soviet republics—Armenia, Azerbaijan, Belarus, Georgia, Moldova, the European part of Russia and Ukraine—and sometimes also the Baltic states. *See also* Central Europe, Eastern Europe.
Central Europe	This region includes Austria, the Czech Republic, Germany, Hungary, Poland and Slovakia. *See also* Central and Eastern Europe.
CFE Treaty	The Treaty on Conventional Armed Forces in Europe, negotiated in the CSCE process, was signed in 1990 by NATO and WTO countries and entered into force on 9 November 1992. It sets ceilings on treaty-limited equipment (TLE) in the ATTU zone. In 1992 the former Soviet republics with territory in the ATTU zone signed the Agreement on the Principles and Procedures of Implementation of the CFE Treaty (Tashkent Agreement), confirming the allocation of TLE on their territories. Also in 1992, the NATO states, Armenia, Azerbaijan, Belarus, Bulgaria, Czechoslovakia, Georgia, Hungary, Kazakhstan, Moldova, Poland, Romania, Russia and Ukraine signed the Final Document of the Extraordinary Conference of the States Parties to the CFE Treaty (Oslo Document), making these states parties to the modified CFE Treaty. *See also* Treaty-limited equipment, ATTU zone.
CFE-1A Agreement	The 1992 Concluding Act of the Negotiation on Personnel Strength of Conventional Armed Forces in Europe entered into force simultaneously with the CFE Treaty. All the CFE Treaty parties are parties to the CFE-1A Agreement, which sets limits on the number of military personnel permitted in the ATTU zone. *See also* ATTU zone, CFE Treaty.

Chemical weapon (CW)   Chemical substances—whether gaseous, liquid or solid—which might be employed as weapons in combat because of their direct toxic effects on man, animals or plants, and the means of their delivery.

Chemical Weapons Convention (CWC)   The multilateral Convention on the Prohibition of the Development, Production, Stockpiling and Use of Chemical Weapons and on their Destruction was opened for signature on 13 January 1993. It bans all chemical weapons world-wide, imposes a wide spectrum of inspections to verify the ban, outlaws any use of these weapons and imposes a strict ban on all activities to develop new chemical weapons. The CWC will not enter into force until 180 days after the date of the deposit of the 65th instrument of ratification, but no earlier than two years after its opening for signature (i.e., no earlier than 13 January 1995).

Common Foreign and Security Policy (CFSP)   *See* European Union and Western European Union.

Commonwealth of Independent States (CIS)   Organization of 12 former Soviet republics, established in Dec. 1991. *See* table of members below.

Comprehensive test ban (CTB)   A proposed ban on all nuclear weapon explosions in all environments, negotiated in the Conference on Disarmament.

Conference on Disarmament (CD)   Multilateral arms control negotiating body, based in Geneva, composed of 37 states (excluding Yugoslavia) representing all the regions of the world and including the permanent members of the UN Security Council. The CD reports to the UN General Assembly. It has been proposed to expand the membership of the CD.

Conference on Security and Co-operation in Europe (CSCE)   The CSCE opened in 1973, with the participation of European states plus the USA and Canada, and in 1975 adopted a Final Act. Follow-up meetings were held in Belgrade (1977–78), Madrid (1980–83), Vienna (1986–89) and Helsinki (1992). Summit Meetings were held in Paris (1990) and Helsinki (1992). The 1994 Follow-up and Summit Meetings will be held in Budapest. The main CSCE institutions are: the Council of Foreign Ministers, the Committee of Senior Officials (CSO), the Secretariat, the Conflict Prevention Centre (CPC), the Office for Democratic Institutions and Human Rights (ODIHR), the Parliamentary Assembly, the Forum for Security Co-operation (FSC), the Chairman-in-Office (CIO), the High Commissioner on National Minorities (HCNM), the Court [on Conciliation and Arbitration] and the Permanent Committee of the CSCE. *See* table of members below.

Confidence- and Security-Building Measure (CSBM)   A measure to promote confidence undertaken by a state. A CSBM is militarily significant, politically binding and verifiable. *See also* Conference on Confidence- and Security-Building Measures and Disarmament in Europe, Vienna Documents 1990 and 1992 on CSBMs.

Conventional weapon	Weapon not having mass destruction effects. *See also* Weapon of mass destruction.
Council of Europe	Established in 1949, with its seat in Strasbourg and 32 members, it is open to all European states. Its main aims are defined in the European Convention on Human Rights (1950) and the Convention for the Protection of Human Rights and Fundamental Freedoms (1953). Among its special bodies is the European Court of Human Rights.
Counter-proliferation	Measures or policies to prevent the proliferation or enforce the non-proliferation of weapons of mass destruction.
Cruise missile	A guided weapon-delivery vehicle which sustains flight at subsonic or supersonic speeds through aerodynamic lift, generally flying at very low altitudes to avoid radar detection, sometimes following the contours of the terrain. It can be air-, ground- or sea-launched and deliver a conventional, nuclear, chemical or biological warhead.
De-Targeting Agreement	US–Russian agreement, signed on 14 January 1994, to 'de-target' strategic nuclear missiles (that is, the missiles will no longer contain information targeting them on the territory of the other party) that are under their respective commands by 30 May 1994. (A Russian–British De-Targeting Agreement was signed on 15 February 1994.)
Eastern Europe	This region includes Albania, Armenia, Azerbaijan, Belarus, Bulgaria, the Czech Republic, Georgia, Hungary, Moldova, Poland, Romania, Slovakia and Ukraine, as well as the European part of Russia. *See also* Central and Eastern Europe.
European Union (EU)	Organization of 12 West European states. In 1991 the texts of draft treaties on an Economic and Monetary Union and a European Political Union were agreed at the European Community (EC) summit meeting in Maastricht, the Netherlands. The Treaty on European Union (Maastricht Treaty) was signed in 1992 and entered into force on 1 November 1993. The main organs of the EU are the European Commission, the European Parliament, the European Council, the Council of Ministers and the European Court of Justice. An EU 'common foreign and security policy' was established in the Maastricht Treaty, *inter alia* to preserve peace, strengthen international security, develop and consolidate democracy, the rule of law and respect for human rights and freedoms, and work as a cohesive force in international relations. *See also* Western European Union, and table of members below.
First-strike capability	Theoretical capability to launch a pre-emptive attack on an adversary's strategic nuclear forces that eliminates the retaliatory, second-strike capability of the adversary.

Fissile material production ban

Proposals were made in 1993 for the negotiation of a multilateral convention to ban the production of fissile material for nuclear weapons or other nuclear explosive devices. The cut-off was recognized in a UN General Assembly resolution in December 1993 as a significant contribution to nuclear non-proliferation in all its aspects.

Group of Seven (G7)

The group of seven leading industrialized countries: Canada, France, Germany, Italy, Japan, the UK and the USA.

INF Treaty

The 1987 US–Soviet Treaty on the Elimination of Intermediate-Range and Shorter-Range Missiles obliged the USA and the USSR to destroy all land-based missiles with a range of 500–5500 km (intermediate-range, 1000–5500 km; and shorter-range, 500–1000 km) and their launchers by 1 June 1991. The INF Treaty was implemented before this date. *See also* Theatre nuclear forces.

Intercontinental ballistic missile (ICBM)

Ground-launched ballistic missile capable of delivering a warhead to a target at ranges in excess of 5500 km.

Intermediate-range nuclear forces (INF)

Theatre nuclear forces with a range of from 1000 km up to and including 5500 km.

International Atomic Energy Agency (IAEA)

With headquarters in Vienna, the IAEA is endowed by its Statute, which entered into force in 1957, with the twin purposes of promoting the peaceful uses of atomic energy and ensuring that nuclear activities are not used to further any military purpose. It plays a role in verification of the NPT, the Treaty of Tlatelolco and UNSCOM activities, and is proposed to play a new role in future multilateral agreements.

Joint Consultative Group (JCG)

Established by the CFE Treaty to promote the objectives and implementation of the CFE Treaty by reconciling ambiguities of interpretation and implementation.

Kiloton (kt)

Measure of the explosive yield of a nuclear weapon equivalent to 1000 tons of trinitrotoluene (TNT) high explosive. (The bomb detonated at Hiroshima in World War II had a yield of about 12–15 kilotons.)

Launcher

Equipment which launches a missile. ICBM launchers are land-based launchers, which can be either fixed or mobile. SLBM launchers are missile tubes on submarines.

Lisbon Protocol

See START I Treaty.

Maghreb states

The North African states of Algeria, Libya, Mauritania, Morocco and Tunisia, members of the Arab Maghreb Union, founded in 1989.

Megaton (Mt)

Measure of the explosive yield of a nuclear weapon equivalent to 1 million tons of trinitrotoluene (TNT) high explosive.

Minsk Group	Group of 10 states acting together in the CSCE: Belarus, the Czech Republic, France, Germany, Italy, Russia, Slovakia, Sweden, Turkey and the USA. The group was set up to organize a conference on political settlement of the Nagorno-Karabakh conflict.
Multiple independently targetable re-entry vehicles (MIRV)	Re-entry vehicles, carried by a nuclear ballistic missile, which can be directed to separate targets along separate trajectories (as distinct from MRVs). A missile can carry two or more RVs.
Multiple re-entry vehicle (MRV)	Re-entry vehicle, carried by a nuclear missile, directed to the same target as the missile's other RVs.
Mutual assured destruction (MAD)	Concept of reciprocal deterrence which rests on the ability of the nuclear weapon powers to inflict intolerable damage on one another after receiving a nuclear attack. *See also* Second-strike capability.
National technical means of verification (NTM)	The technical intelligence means used to monitor compliance with treaty provisions which are under the national control of individual signatories to an arms control agreement.
Non-strategic nuclear forces	*See* Theatre nuclear forces
Nordic countries	Countries in Northern Europe, including Iceland, Finland and the Scandinavian countries Denmark, Norway and Sweden.
North Atlantic Cooperation Council (NACC)	Created in 1991 as a NATO institution for consultation and co-operation on political and security issues between NATO and the former WTO states and former Soviet republics. *See* table of members below.
North Atlantic Treaty Organization (NATO)	A defence alliance established in 1949 by the North Atlantic Pact concluded between the USA, Canada and a number of West European states. Since 1966, NATO Headquarters have been in Brussels. *See* table of members below.
NPT	The multilateral Non-Proliferation Treaty, which entered into force in 1970 and established a regime to prevent the proliferation of nuclear weapons while guaranteeing the peaceful uses of nuclear energy. Under the NPT, non-nuclear weapon states parties undertake to conclude safeguards agreements with the IAEA to prevent the diversion of nuclear energy from peaceful to weapon use.
Nuclear Risk Reduction Centres (NRRC)	Established by the 1987 US–Soviet NRRC Agreement. The two centres, which opened in Washington and Moscow in 1988, exchange information by direct satellite link in order to minimize misunderstandings which might carry a risk of nuclear war. Notifications concerning exchange of information about nuclear explosions under the 1974 Threshold Test Ban Treaty, the 1976 Peaceful Nuclear Explosions Treaty and the Protocols to the two treaties shall also be submitted through the two NRRCs.

Open Skies Treaty	A treaty signed by 25 CSCE states in 1992, permitting flights by unarmed military or civilian surveillance aircraft over the territory of the signatory states, in the area 'from Vancouver to Vladivostok'. Not in force on 1 June 1994.
Organisation for Economic Co-operation and Development (OECD)	Established in 1961 to replace the Organization for European Economic Co-operation (OEEC). With the accession of Canada and the USA, it ceased to be a purely European body. OECD objectives are to promote economic and social welfare by co-ordinating policies. *See* table of members below.
Organization of African Unity (OAU)	Established in 1963 as a union of 32 African states.
Organization of American States (OAS)	Group of states in the Americas, established in 1890. Thirty-five countries are members (Cuba has been excluded from participation since 1962) and 29 countries from other continents are permanent observers.
Oslo Document	*See* CFE Treaty.
Pact for Stability in Europe	A proposal presented to the French Council of Ministers on 9 June 1993 and to the European Union on 22 June 1993 by Prime Minister Edouard Balladur of France (also referred to as the Balladur Plan), for inclusion in the framework of the EU Common Foreign and Security Policy. The objective is to contribute to stability by preventing tension and potential conflicts connected with borders and minorities. It would consist of bilateral agreements between individual countries and the EU. It is proposed to be open to the EU states, other states 'interested in stability in Europe', and the 'countries of Northern, Central and Eastern Europe concerned'. The task of the inaugural Conference held in Paris in May 1994 was to set up round tables. *See also* European Union.
Paris Documents	A set of five documents adopted at the 1990 Paris CSCE summit meeting. They include the CFE Treaty, the Joint Declaration of Twenty-Two States, the Charter of Paris for a New Europe, the Supplementary Document to give new effect to certain provisions contained in the Charter, and the Vienna Document 1990. New CSCE institutions were set up in the Paris Documents.
Partnership for Peace (PFP)	The NATO programme for co-operation with democratic states in the East, in such areas as military planning, budgeting and training, under the authority of the North Atlantic Council. It provides for enhanced co-operation to prepare for and undertake multilateral crisis-management activities such as peace-keeping. The January 1994 NATO summit meeting approved a Framework Document and issued an Invitation to NACC and other CSCE states, welcoming an evolutionary expansion of NATO membership. Subscribing states must provide Presentation Documents to NATO, identifying the steps they will take to achieve the PFP goals, and develop with NATO individual Partnership Programmes. *See* table below.

Peaceful nuclear explosion (PNE)

Application of a nuclear explosion for non-military purposes such as digging canals or harbours or creating underground cavities.

Re-entry vehicle (RV)

That part of a ballistic missile which carries a nuclear warhead and penetration aids to the target, re-enters the earth's atmosphere and is destroyed in the terminal phase of the missile's trajectory. A missile can have one or several RVs; each RV contains a warhead.

Safe and Secure Dismantlement (SSD) Talks

A nuclear arms control forum established in 1992 to institutionalize co-operation between the USA and former Soviet republics with nuclear weapons on their territories, in the safe and environmentally responsible storage, transportation, dismantlement and destruction of former Soviet nuclear weapons. Talks have resulted in bilateral agreements between the USA and some of these states for US funding to assist in the destruction of their nuclear weapons.

Second-strike capability

Ability to receive a nuclear attack and launch a retaliatory blow large enough to inflict intolerable damage on the opponent. *See also* Mutual assured destruction.

Short-range nuclear forces (SNF)

Nuclear weapons, including artillery, mines, missiles, etc., with ranges up to 500 km. *See also* Tactical nuclear weapon, Theatre nuclear forces.

Stability Pact

See Pact for Stability in Europe.

START I Treaty

The 1991 US–Soviet Treaty on the Reduction and Limitation of Strategic Offensive Arms, which reduces US and Soviet offensive strategic nuclear weapons to equal aggregate levels over a seven-year period. It sets numerical limits on deployed strategic nuclear delivery vehicles (SNDVs)—ICBMs, SLBMs and heavy bombers—and the nuclear warheads they carry. In the 1992 Protocol to Facilitate the Implementation of the START Treaty (the Lisbon Protocol), Belarus, Kazakhstan and Ukraine pledge to accede to the START Treaty, to eliminate all strategic weapons on their territories within the seven-year START Treaty reduction period and to join the NPT as non-nuclear weapon states in the shortest possible time. In separate formal letters addressed to the US President, the leaders of Belarus, Kazakhstan and Ukraine pledge to 'guarantee' the elimination of all nuclear weapons located on their territories. The START I Treaty was not in force on 1 June 1994.

START II Treaty

The 1993 US–Russian Treaty on Further Reduction and Limitation of Strategic Offensive Arms, which requires the USA and Russia to eliminate their MIRVed ICBMs and sharply reduce their strategic nuclear warheads to no more than 3000–3500 each (of which no more than 1750 may be deployed on SLBMs) by 1 January 2003 or no later than 31 December 2000 if the USA and Russia reach a formal agreement committing the USA to help finance the elimination of strategic nuclear weapons in Russia. It will not enter into force until the START I Treaty enters into force.

Strategic nuclear weapons	ICBMs, SLBMs and bomber aircraft carrying nuclear weapons of intercontinental range (usually over 5500 km).
Submarine-launched ballistic missile (SLBM)	A ballistic missile launched from a submarine, usually with a range in excess of 5500 km.
Tactical nuclear weapon	A short-range nuclear weapon which is deployed with general-purpose forces along with conventional weapons. *See also* Short-range nuclear forces; Theatre nuclear forces.
Tashkent Agreement	*See* CFE Treaty.
Theater Missile Defense Initiative	A 1993 initiative of President Clinton to develop and test theatre, or tactical, missile defence systems, without harming the objectives of the ABM Treaty. *See also* ABM Treaty.
Theatre nuclear forces (TNF)	Nuclear weapons with ranges of up to and including 5500 km. In the 1987 INF Treaty, nuclear missiles are divided into intermediate-range (1000–5500 km) and shorter-range (500–1000 km). The USA and USSR eliminated their TNF under the INF Treaty. Also called non-strategic nuclear forces. Nuclear weapons with ranges up to 500 km are called short-range nuclear forces. *See also* Short-range nuclear forces.
Throw-weight	The sum of the weight of a ballistic missile's re-entry vehicle(s), dispensing mechanisms, penetration aids, and targeting and separation devices.
Toxins	Poisonous substances which are products of organisms but are inanimate and incapable of reproducing themselves as well as chemically induced variants of such substances. Some toxins may also be produced by chemical synthesis.
Treaty-limited equipment (TLE)	The five categories of equipment on which numerical limits are established in the 1990 CFE Treaty: battle tanks, armoured combat vehicles, artillery, combat aircraft and attack helicopters.
Vienna Documents 1990 and 1992 on CSBMs	The Vienna Document 1990 on CSBMs, included in the set of Paris Documents, repeated many of the provisions in the 1986 Stockholm Document and expands several others. It established a communications network and a risk reduction mechanism. The Vienna Document 1992 on CSBMs builds on the Vienna Document 1990 and supplements its provisions with new mechanisms and constraining provisions.
Visegrad Group	The Czech Republic, Hungary, Poland and Slovakia. (The name comes from a meeting in 1991 of the leaders of these countries held in the Hungarian town of Visegrad.)
Warhead	That part of a weapon which contains the explosive or other material intended to inflict damage.

Warsaw Treaty Organization (WTO)	The WTO, or Warsaw Pact, was established in 1955 by a Treaty of friendship, co-operation and mutual assistance. The WTO was dissolved in 1991.
Weapon of mass destruction	Nuclear weapon and any other weapon which may produce comparable effects, such as chemical and biological weapons.
Western European Union (WEU)	Established in the 1954 Protocols to the 1948 Treaty of Brussels of Collaboration and Collective Self-Defence among Western European States. Within the EU common foreign and security policy (CFSP) and at the request of the EU, the WEU is to elaborate and implement EU decisions and actions which have defence implications *See* table of members below.
Yield	Released nuclear explosive energy expressed as the equivalent of the energy produced by a given number of tons of trinitro-toluene (TNT) high explosive. *See also* Kiloton, Megaton.

Conventions in tables

. .	Data not available or not applicable
–	Nil or a negligible figure
( )	Uncertain data
m.	million
b.	billion (thousand million)
$	US $, unless otherwise indicated

Membership of the major international organizations with security functions, as of 1 June 1994

Country	CSCE 1973	NATO 1949	NACC 1991	WEU 1954	PFP 1993	EU 1993	CIS 1991
Albania	1991		1992		•		
Armenia	1992		1992				•
Austria	•						
Azerbaijan	1992		1992		•		•
Belarus	1992		1992				•
Belgium	•	•	•	•		•	
Bosnia and Herzegovina	1992						
Bulgaria	•		•	b	•		
Canada	•	•	•				
Croatia	1992						
Cyprus	•						
Czech Republic	1993[a]		1993[a]	b	•		
Denmark	•	•	•	b		•	
Estonia	1991		•	b	•		
Finland	•		c		•		
France	•	•[d]	•	•		•	
Georgia	1992		1992		•		•
Germany	•[e]	1955[f]	•	•[f]		•[f]	
Greece	•	1952	•	g			
Holy See	•						
Hungary	•		•	b	•		
Iceland	•	•	•	b			
Ireland	•			b		•	
Italy	•	•	•	•		•	
Kazakhstan	1992		1992		•		•
Kyrgyzstan	1992		1992		•		•
Latvia	1991		•	b	•		
Liechtenstein	•						
Lithuania	1991		•	b	•		
Luxembourg	•	•	•	•		•	
Malta	•						
Moldova	1992		1992		•		•
Monaco	•						
Netherlands	•	•	•	•		•	
Norway	•	•	•	b			
Poland	•		•	b	•		
Portugal	•	•	•	1988		•	
Romania	•		•	b	•		
Russia	•		•				•
San Marino	•						
Slovakia	1993[a]		1993[a]	b	•		
Slovenia	1992			•	•		
Spain	•	1982[d]	•	1988		•	
Sweden	•				•		
Switzerland	•						
Tajikistan	1992		1992				•
Turkey	•	1952	•	b			
Turkmenistan	•		1992		•		•
UK	•	•	•	•		•	
Ukraine	1992		1992		•		•
USA	•	•	•				
Uzbekistan	1992		1992				•
Yugoslavia	•[h]						

CSCE   Conference on Security and Co-operation in Europe
NATO   North Atlantic Treaty Organization
NACC   North Atlantic Cooperation Council
WEU   Western European Union
PFP   Partnership for Peace
EU   European Union
CIS   Commonwealth of Independent States

A • in the column for membership in an organization indicates that the country is one of the original members, that is, since the date given in the column heading for establishment of the organization. A year in the column indicates the year in which a country that is not an original member joined the organization.

[a] The former state of Czechoslovakia was an original member of the CSCE and NACC.

[b] Iceland, Norway and Turkey are associate members of the WEU (they may express views but not block decisions). Denmark and Ireland are observers. Bulgaria, the Czech Republic, Estonia, Hungary, Latvia, Lithuania, Poland, Romania and Slovakia are associate partners.

[c] Finland has observer status at NACC.

[d] France and Spain are not in the integrated military structures of NATO.

[e] The original members of the CSCE were the former Federal Republic of Germany (West Germany) and the German Democratic Republic (East Germany). After unification in 1991, Germany assumed the membership of this organization.

[f] The original member of NATO, the WEU and the EC was the former Federal Republic of Germany (West Germany). After unification of West Germany and East Germany in 1991, Germany assumed the membership of these organizations.

[g] Greece was accepted as a member of the WEU at the WEU Council meeting in Nov. 1992, pending ratification by all WEU state parliaments.

[h] As from 7 July 1992, Yugoslavia is suspended from the CSCE.

Introduction: the search for a new security system

ADAM DANIEL ROTFELD

The end of the East–West confrontation initiated an essential transformation of the international system. We are still, however, at the initial stages of the process of reshaping it. Neither a 'new world order' nor any other universal security system has yet emerged. Moreover, it is difficult to envisage today the essence of a new system or what its tenets, norms and working procedures will be.

I. After bipolarity: new developments

Peace, development and democracy became more closely interrelated in 1993 than ever before. As UN Secretary-General Boutros Boutros-Ghali has put it: 'Without peace, there can be no development, and there can be no democracy. Without development, the basis for democracy will be lacking and societies will tend to fall into conflict. And without democracy, no substantial development can occur; without such development, peace cannot long be maintained'.[1] In 1993 there were undoubted achievements in all these domains.

In the first month of the year, two major accords were signed: the US–Russian START II Treaty and the multilateral Chemical Weapons Convention (CWC). Under the terms of the START II Treaty the two great powers will reduce their respective numbers of nuclear warheads to 3000–3500 by the year 2003. Three months later, newly elected President Bill Clinton and Russian President Boris Yeltsin agreed that negotiations on a comprehensive test ban (CTB) should start at an early date[2] and reaffirmed their determination to strengthen the 1968 Non-Proliferation Treaty (NPT) and make it of unlimited duration. In 1993 only one nuclear explosion was conducted, the lowest annual number since 1959, as all the nuclear powers except China observed unilaterally declared testing moratoria. However, to be viable, a CTB treaty 'should be universal, verifiable and of indefinite duration'.[3] In July, the Group of Seven (G7) leading industrialized nations reiterated in Tokyo the objective of universal adherence to the NPT as well as their determination to extend the duration of the Treaty in 1995. The positive developments include accession to the NPT by Belarus and by Kazakhstan half a year later. There was also international support for negotiation of a ban on the production of fissile

---

[1] Boutros-Ghali, B., *Report on the Work of the Organization from the Forty-seventh to the Forty-eighth Session of the General Assembly* (United Nations: New York, Sep. 1993), p. 3.
[2] Boutros-Ghali noted in his report that among the achievements is the decision by the Conference on Disarmament to give its *Ad Hoc* Committee on a Nuclear Test Ban a mandate to negotiate a CTB treaty.
[3] See note 1, p. 162.

material for nuclear weapons. Another event of great significance was the establishment of the UN Register of Conventional Arms; SIPRI's 25 years of monitoring the arms trade contributed to its establishment and the results of its first year of reporting were the subject of a special assessment by SIPRI.[4] Only the end of the cold war made it possible for governments to release substantive information about arms transfers.

However, instability continued to be the most pronounced feature of international politics, with no organizing principle like that of cold war bipolarity in evidence. Positive developments—such as the peace process in the Middle East and the end of apartheid in South Africa—were accompanied by serious setbacks. One serious concern was North Korea's announcement on 12 March 1993 that it would withdraw from the NPT to 'defend its supreme interests'.[5] Neither of the START treaties has entered into force. Some anxiety surrounds the efforts to institutionalize and prepare for implementation of the CWC.

The end of the bipolar system brought an apparent return to a system of common values among a majority of states. Such notions as the right of nations to self-determination and democracy re-emerged. The breakdown of totalitarian regimes in Central and Eastern Europe and of apartheid in South Africa allowed such notions as human dignity and liberty to flourish; however, it brought with it a fear of responsibility and an 'escape from freedom', to use Erich Fromm's expression. The ghosts of various forms of nationalism and tribalism are reawakening and ethnic, national and religious conflicts are breaking out. The war in Bosnia and Herzegovina has been waged for nearly three years, new conflicts have erupted in the Caucasus and Tajikistan, and tensions continue in many other parts of the world. On the one hand, the time is ripe for practical implementation of the aims and principles of the UN Charter and the use of the instruments and procedures it envisaged. This opportunity was seized on an unprecedented scale and the United Nations heightened its profile, particularly in preventive diplomacy and peacekeeping. On the other hand, the means available to it often proved ineffective or unsuitable.

II. In search of new principles and norms

Basic questions have emerged regarding the new role for the United Nations. The main dilemma is whether international action can only be taken on the initiative and under the leadership of one of the global powers, or whether the UN as an organization can do so itself. In other words, who can police the world?[6] This raises the question not only of a new structure for international politics but also, and even more importantly, of the changing substance of international politics. In a nutshell, changes should not only concern forms,

---

[4] Laurance, E. J., Wezeman, S. T. and Wulf, H., *Arms Watch: SIPRI Report on the First Year of the UN Register of Conventional Arms*, SIPRI Research Report No. 6 (Oxford University Press: Oxford, 1993).

[5] See appendix 15A in this volume.

[6] Urquhart, B., 'Who can police the world?' *New York Review*, May 1994, p. 33.

norms and tenets but also touch upon the crux of the matter. There is an urgent need to redetermine the interrelationship of such principles of contemporary international order as sovereignty, the equal rights of states and non-intervention, on the one hand, and the right of the international community to intervene in the face of genocide and massive abuses of human rights on the other, either when state authorities perpetrate acts of aggression against their own societies or when they can no longer ensure security to populations deprived of basic rights and being killed in conflicts formerly treated as being 'essentially' within the 'domestic jurisdiction' of a state.[7]

This issue has come to the fore at a time when the risk of global war or intentional nuclear attack has been reduced almost to zero and when local, intra-state conflicts have emerged as the main threat.[8] The latter changed in character and grew in intensity; inter-state conflicts, incited in the past by bloc divisions and ideological antagonisms between the communist East and the democratic West, slowly faded away. All the conflicts in 1993 were internal and most were over territory.

Threats and traditional security preoccupations have changed, as have the tasks facing security decision makers and the priorities and hierarchy of outstanding matters. In the past, security was as a rule identified with the East–West military balance. The role of arms control stemming from this perception was to remove the asymmetry of military potential between the blocs and negotiate reductions in the level of armed forces and armaments and, at the same time, build mutual confidence based on openness, transparency and predictability. This political philosophy facilitated agreements between the superpowers on strategic nuclear forces and multilateral agreements on reductions of conventional armed forces in Europe. Since East–West relations were of a decisive character in international politics, it was assumed that the issues of local conflicts and tensions would be practically settled within the respective blocs. Problems of the developing countries, including rising levels of armaments in states not belonging to the blocs, were not placed high on the list of priorities.

The situation has changed radically after the cold war. First, security policy is no longer perceived anywhere as being synonymous with arms control and disarmament. Second, in the hierarchy of security policy tasks, the matter of warding off intra-state conflicts has come to the fore. Third, the breakup of the USSR and the bipolar system has given a new dimension to the problem of proliferation of weapons of mass destruction.

The fundamental change of geopolitical circumstances has transformed the agenda for a new international security system. Co-operative security is the most desirable and adequate concept for the challenges ahead. 'Co-operative engagement is a strategic principle that seeks to accomplish its purposes through institutional consent rather than through threats of material or physi-

---

[7] Charter of the United Nations, Article 2, para. 7.
[8] See chapter 2 in this volume.

cal coercion.'[9] The important thing is that a new global system is being formed not as a result of war, in the wake of which victors impose on the vanquished a new order and rules of conduct, but through negotiations and agreement on common goals, norms, institutions and procedures.

What should be the basic rules of the new system? In the 1950s, Clark and Sohn presented six principles to guide the search for an effective international security system.[10] Their project illustrated certain weaknesses typical of model-based systems. Authors of such propositions, guided by idealistic motives, seek to have political reality fall in line with the logic of the proposed solutions. At the same time they assume that maintaining peace only concerns inter-state relations. In reality, the major conflicts since the end of the cold war have had a domestic character. All the 34 major armed conflicts in 1993 were of an intra-state nature. The most devastating wars in Afghanistan, Angola, Azerbaijan, Bosnia and Herzegovina, Georgia, Somalia, Sri Lanka, Tajikistan and in many other countries could have been interpreted according to conservative criteria as being the internal affairs of sovereign nation-states, outside the competence of any international organization. The view that 'until there is *complete* disarmament under world law there can be no assurance of genuine peace'[11] is similarly divorced from political reality. More realistic than the pacifist approach is the injunction 'to devise agreed-upon measures to prevent war and to do so primarily by preventing the means for successful aggression from being assembled'.[12]

The new security system will emerge as a result of various, often contradictory, practical solutions rather than of a coherent, overall design. It will be contingent upon a process of trial and error rather than on implementation of logical theoretical propositions. Such concepts generally seek new institutional solutions. The crucial point, however, is that not only the structures but also the substance of international security has changed. Creating successor institutions often gives the appearance of action but fails to solve problems. There is no lack of institutions; moreover, their superfluity is costly, they often duplicate each other's tasks and do not facilitate optimizing the process of conflict prevention, management or resolution. The same applies to norms and procedures. Sir Brian Urquhart has rightly noted:

There is, in fact, already an immense body of international law on virtually all aspects of human activity, but we are nowhere near a functioning international legal regime to carry that law out. Each new experiment in international action should also contribute legal precedents and principles for future action. These elements must eventually become the basis for an acceptable and universally accepted international legal system, properly monitored and, if necessary, enforced.[13]

[9] Nolan, J. E. *et al.*, 'The concept of cooperative security', in ed. J. E. Nolan, *Global Engagement: Cooperation and Security in the 21st Century* (Brookings Institution: Washington, DC, 1994), pp. 4–5.
[10] Clark, G. and Sohn, L. B., *World Peace Through World Law* (Harvard University Press: Cambridge, Mass., 1958).
[11] Note 10, p. xii.
[12] Note 9, p. 5.
[13] Note 6, p. 33.

A system based on pragmatic solutions and precedents, which involves the gradual adjustment of various institutions to new needs, is taking shape. It would be wrong if a state or a group of states strove to put bonds on the international community as a whole, trammelling the freedom of states to determine their own security interests. However, it is desirable to determine the framework and directions of the development of the emerging system.

The basis of cold war security was mutual deterrence. The foundation of a new system should be mutual reassurance, which 'requires an ability to initiate and maintain co-operation among sovereign states on matters . . . traditionally conceived of as the heart of sovereignty: decisions about what is needed to maintain and preserve national security'.[14] This is the essence of co-operative security: it presupposes normative and institutional constraints on sovereignty and non-intervention which since the time of Grotius have been treated as the cornerstone of international law and order. Unlike various concepts of 'world government' presented by Clark and Sohn, the system of co-operative security implies 'general acceptance of and compliance with binding commitments limiting military capabilities and actions'.[15] The main actors within this system are nation states, not trans- or supranational structures; the system assumes arms control and limitation, not universal and complete disarmament; the regime must be negotiated and accepted, not imposed. Instead of mistrust, deterrence and enforcement, the co-operative system rests on (a) confidence based on openness, transparency and predictability; (b) co-operation and reassurance; and (c) legitimacy which depends on the acceptance by members that 'the military constraints of the regime in fact substantially ensure their security'.[16] Many of these elements function within existing security structures, primarily the UN system and the Conference on Security and Co-operation in Europe (CSCE) but also NATO (the Partnership for Peace programme), the Western European Union (WEU) 'associated partnership' with Central and East European states, the European Union (EU) and the 'common foreign and security policy' and in many other multilateral security institutions and organizations. The co-operative security system is *in statu nascendi*, in the process of taking shape; but the process is not automatic and a tremendous effort is needed to establish the regime. The difficulty is that the regime can be likened to a boat that 'will have to be built while it is sailing'.[17] The best relative progress can be noted in the sphere of arms control and reductions of armed forces and armaments, particularly in Europe.[18] It is worth asking where the arms control process is heading in the post-cold war period.

[14] Handler Chayes, A. and Chayes A., 'Regime architecture: elements and principles', in Nolan (note 10), p. 65.

[15] Note 14, p. 66.

[16] Note 14, p. 112.

[17] Note 14, p. 112.

[18] Catherine M. Kelleher is right when she asserts: 'In the early 1990s, Europe is by every measure the best test bed for cooperative security. In no other region has there been more progress toward mutual regulation of military capabilities and operations, toward mutual reassurance and the avoidance of tension and uncertainty. The core elements of cooperative security have been practiced in Europe, in West but also East, for at least a half decade—including offensive force limitations, defensive restructuring, confidence-building operational measures, overlapping organizational arrangements facilitating trans-

III. The new role of arms control

In the bipolar world, negotiations on arms control and disarmament were seen as the main channel of political dialogue between East and West, with arms reductions playing a secondary role. These talks were designed mainly to eliminate disparities and asymmetries, and to promote openness, transparency and predictability. The agreements reached were to a great extent a barometer of tension versus *détente* in the international climate. Now arms control developments have assumed their real dimension and proportion. The agreements reached restored the balance between the two opposing blocs, one of which soon disappeared. Irrespective of their operational value in the new security landscape, the agreements introduced specific limitations, procedures and rules of conduct in relations between states. Their main goal was to reduce the danger of the outbreak of a major war between the two antagonistic groupings. In the new situation, the question arises whether and to what extent the implementation of the negotiated arms control accords promotes the prevention or resolution of potential or current intra-state conflicts.

A new conceptual framework is required for arms control and disarmament as instruments of security and stability. There is a need to define the nature of the institutional framework and the 'division of labour' between different structures and negotiation forums. Another basic question is how to define new 'needs' and 'requirements'. How can renationalization of defence policies be prevented? How can the proliferation of nuclear weapons and missiles, old and new technologies, and conventional arms be limited or prevented? How can the existing non-proliferation regimes (both nuclear and conventional) be sustained and strengthened? What should be done to curb the proliferation of missiles and major and small conventional weapons? What kind of new confidence- and security-building measures are required? How can the new military imbalances and risks which have emerged as a result of the new politico-military environment be eliminated? This volume sets out to find answers to these and other questions.[19] For example, in Europe is it worth considering the concept of an arms control and disarmament agency and examining the extent to which it might be instrumental in monitoring implementation of and verifying compliance with multilateral agreements? At first such an agency could either be completely autonomous or act independently within the framework of the CSCE. The prime organizational objective would be to ensure the rapid acquisition and transfer of pertinent information, with due regard to appropriate confidentiality. This might simplify and facilitate the future arms control process in Europe.

In the realm of global arms control the effective prevention of the proliferation of weapons of mass destruction has come to the fore.[20] The concept of counter-proliferation discussed intensively in 1993 may, from the viewpoint

parency and cooperative verification, and joint controls on the proliferation of military technology'. See Kelleher, C. M., 'Cooperative security in Europe', in Nolan (note 9), p. 293.

[19] See chapters 7, 8, 9 and 14 in this volume.

[20] See chapters 15 and 16 in this volume.

of building a co-operative security system, prove counter-productive. Instead of co-operativeness, confrontation could easily return.

The Chemical Weapons Convention—the first multilateral disarmament agreement providing for the elimination of an entire category of mass-destruction weaponry under international verification—proves that negotiations, however protracted and difficult, are the only effective method of getting rid of such weapons.[21] While the post-cold war climate has permitted agreement on reductions of US and Russian nuclear weapons, it remains for China, France and the UK to set limits on their nuclear weapons as well. However, experience shows that there are no short cuts to disarmament.

IV. Options for the future

In crisis situations, especially when armed conflicts break out, there are no easy options. International military intervention or peace enforcement should be considered as an exceptional tool to restore peace, bringing only limited results; it cannot be seen as a universal remedy. As Lawrence Freedman has noted:

Most conflicts can be understood as power struggles, with one group seeking to improve its position *vis-à-vis* another group or groups . . . Any external interference, whether it be in setting rules for the conduct of the conflict, easing suffering, brokering a settlement or intervening on one side, will influence the balance of power. When that external interference ceases there will always be a tendency for local factors to dominate once again. Thus intervention has to be recognized, not as being directed towards a specific end, but as being part of the process, though undoubtedly a process with defined stages.[22]

Relationships between preventive diplomacy and the use of military means are complex and defy accurate definition. Two extreme views are rather widespread: the conviction that all conflicts can be solved by political means, and the opposite opinion that, when means of diplomacy fail, military intervention can eventually restore peace. Both extremes are grounded on illusion. In civil, ethnic and religious wars, as shown by the unsuccessful mediation and intervention in Abkhazia, Afghanistan, Bosnia and Herzegovina, Nagorno-Karabakh or Tajikistan, the traditional instruments of diplomacy and classical peacekeeping operations have been poorly suited to the task. In other cases, as in Namibia, Cambodia and Eritrea, they have worked well. In fact, all these types of UN activity (preventive diplomacy, peacekeeping and peace enforcement) are by definition intertwined[23] and have been performed simul-

---

[21] As of 9 May 1994, the Chemical Weapons Convention was signed by 157 states, after 23 years of negotiation. So far it has been ratified by only 6 states, none of which is a great power. See also chapter 17 in this volume.

[22] Freedman, L., 'The politics of military intervention within Europe', ed. L. Freedman *et al.*, *War and Peace: European Conflict Prevention*, Chaillot Papers No. 11, Oct. 1993, pp. 41–42.

[23] In the understanding of the UN Secretary-General, preventive diplomacy is an action 'to prevent existing disputes from escalating into conflicts and to limit the spread of the latter when they occur'. See note 1, p. 96. See also Boutros-Ghali, B., *An Agenda for Peace: Preventive Diplomacy, Peacemaking*

taneously, some in parallel with the activities of other security structures, such as NATO and the CSCE. Most prominent were UN operations in Cambodia, El Salvador, Somalia and the former Yugoslavia.[24]

Armed conflicts that are not wars between states generally leave little room for compromise or, consequently, for mediation; here peacekeeping operations prove less useful because the parties to those conflicts do not follow the basic rules, namely, that peacekeeping forces must remain impartial and neutral. It does not mean that the international community is helpless.

V. Yearbook findings

The conclusions from the analyses and documents published in this volume are the following:

1. Multilateral efforts in 1993 to prevent, manage and resolve international conflict reached a new intensity, but also confronted difficulties for which they were ill-prepared in the euphoria of the immediate post-cold war years.[25] While success in Cambodia symbolized the possibilities, failure in the former Yugoslavia and Somalia testified to the inadequacy of means for containing wars in or bringing peace to those countries. There was a growing recognition that, while the international community might be more willing than ever before to consider peace indivisible and to widen its definition of threats to the peace, there are limits to what can be achieved with the multilateral instruments and resources currently available to it. The United Nations began a long process of reform and restructuring to cope with the new demands being made on it, while regional organizations played an increasingly important role.

2. Regional security systems are gaining in importance. Increasingly, they are no longer confined to Europe.[26] The regional dialogue that has emerged in the Asia–Pacific region in the past decade, in both economic and security areas, is a significant global security development. As the fastest growing region of the world in economic and trade terms, it is heartening that Asia–Pacific is moving towards discussion of its region-wide security problems in a co-operative framework rather than using the arms it is increasingly able to afford. Although the original ideas on regional co-operative structures for Asia–Pacific came from its periphery—Australia, Canada and the USSR—it is the Association of South-East Asian Nations (ASEAN) that has provided most of the regionalist momentum in the past few years. In contrast, North-East

---

and Peace-keeping, Report of the Secretary-General, UN document A/47/277 (S/24111), 17 June 1992; the text of the report is reprinted in SIPRI, SIPRI Yearbook 1993: World Armaments and Disarmament (Oxford University Press: Oxford, 1993), appendix 2A, pp. 66–80. Peacekeeping entails the deployment of military or police personnel (often civilians as well) in the field with the consent of all the parties concerned. It should be understood 'as an impartial and consent-based set of activities covering a wide range of tasks but not designed to impose solutions or promote specific objectives by coercive means'. See Berdal, M. R., 'Fateful encounter: the United States and UN peacekeeping', Survival, vol. 36, no. 1 (spring 1994), p. 30. The concept of peace enforcement in practice covers peacekeeping activities which do not necessarily involve the consent of all parties concerned. See chapter 1 in this volume.

[24] See chapter 1 and appendices 1A and 1B in this volume.

[25] See chapter 1 in this volume.

[26] See chapter 7 in this volume.

Asia, lacking subregional structures and plagued by major continuing security challenges, has been largely passive—with the important and relatively recent exception of Japan.[27]

3. The collapse of the bipolar system permitted a fundamental breakthrough in the search for peace in the Middle East. The agreement between Israel and the Palestine Liberation Organization (PLO) in September should be seen as one of the most spectacular events of 1993. It would be hard to overestimate the contribution of the late Johan Jørgen Holst, former Norwegian Minister of Foreign Affairs, to this achievement. After five major wars, the present peace process has come closer than any other effort over the past 50 years to resolving the fundamental Palestinian problem.[28] Equally spectacular was South Africa's release from the bonds and borders of apartheid.

4. The former USSR remained the scene of domestic conflict and instability. The economic dependence of the other countries of the Commonwealth of Independent States (CIS) upon Russia and the increasing role of the Russian Army in the political arena, following the struggle for power in Russia in September–October 1993, have led to the drawing up of neo-imperialist concepts of Russia's role in Europe and in the world.[29]

5. SIPRI continues to monitor military technology and international security, and this *Yearbook* includes a case study of India. Military research and development (R&D) in India is not progressing as rapidly as observers had predicted. Indian military R&D programmes have reached some immediate goals, but the anticipated technological momentum that would allow India to move from limited import substitution to indigenous innovation has not been created. Reports that sophisticated conventional or nuclear weapons are easily or inevitably within the grasp of India, or even countries with lesser scientific resources, should therefore be viewed with scepticism.[30]

Non-lethal weapons are analysed in a case study of new technology developments.[31] These weapons are by no means new. Since the 1991 Persian Gulf War there has been a renewed effort, especially in the USA, to develop them for use in situations where less than lethal force is required or desirable. They include such technologies as high-power microwave weapons able to disable unprotected electronic systems, advanced portable lasers for use against sensors and personnel as well as chemical and biological agents capable of degrading the performance of equipment and/or personnel.

6. The chapter on chemical armaments and disarmament examines whether the overwhelming initial support for the CWC has affected the behaviour of states and whether there are any signs of proliferation being reversed. It is estimated that the destruction of the US stockpile by 2004 will cost over $8.6 billion. Russia is still faced with the challenge of completing its draft CW

---

[27] See chapters 4 and 5 in this volume.
[28] See chapter 3 in this volume.
[29] See chapter 6 in this volume.
[30] See chapter 10 in this volume.
[31] See chapter 11 in this volume.

destruction programme.[32] The analysis of the CWC[33] contains an overview of the achievements, problems and main trends related to the involvement of industry, national implementation and the foreseeable ratification process. Some historical and new arms control developments in biological weapons are also discussed.[34]

7. While military spending is declining in nearly all countries, they can hardly be said to be enjoying a genuine peace dividend. In most countries there is a tendency to cut arms procurement more rapidly than defence spending in general. The key issue of conditionality is also discussed: whether foreign aid should continue to be given to countries with high military spending or whether donors should attach conditions.[35]

8. Another crucial aspect of security traditionally analysed by SIPRI is that of arms production and trade. The most recent data show that the dominant trend in the global arms industry continues to be towards rationalization and concentration in the primary centres of arms production. Combined sales by the top 100 arms-producing companies in the Organisation for Economic Co-operation and Development (OECD) countries and the developing world fell by 5 per cent between 1991 and 1992. It is now widely acknowledged that export sales cannot compensate for the reduced domestic demand now facing many companies. In 1993 the international flow of major conventional weapons levelled off after a period of rapid decline since 1987. While the USA remained the dominant supplier, accounting for 48 per cent of total deliveries, Russia increased its share of the global total to 21 per cent in 1993. Arms transfer control may become easier after capacities in the arms industry have been reduced to a more sustainable level.[36]

The changes ushered in five years ago did not lead to wholesale rejection of the norms, procedures and institutions which underlay the global system during the cold war. Although not suited to the new reality, they still function and are being adjusted to the new circumstances. Rethinking the values of the international security system means rethinking both the structure and the substance of world politics. There is a need to re-evaluate the meaning of sovereignty, self-determination and non-intervention as part of the basic principles of international law. The new rules should be instrumental in preventing or containing internal conflicts through agreed international action; in rebuffing any attempt to legitimize a concept of special rights or spheres of interests for great powers; and in consolidating and strengthening non-proliferation. To build a new co-operative security regime, including organization of multinational forces to protect all members of the system against any aggression, implies, as a *conditio sine qua non,* the right to legitimized intervention. Standing idly by would be tantamount to appeasement and an invitation to break the law.

[32] See chapter 9 in this volume.
[33] See chapter 17 in this volume
[34] See chapter 18 in this volume.
[35] See chapter 12 in this volume.
[36] See chapter 13 in this volume.

Part I. Global and regional security and conflicts, 1993

Chapter 1. Multilateral conflict prevention, management and resolution

Chapter 2. Major armed conflicts

Chapter 3. The Middle East: the peace and security-building process

Chapter 4. South-East Asia and the new Asia–Pacific security dialogue

Chapter 5. North-East Asia and multilateral security institutions

Chapter 6. Conflict developments on the territory of the former Soviet Union

Chapter 7. Europe: towards a new regional security regime

1. Multilateral conflict prevention, management and resolution

TREVOR FINDLAY*

I. Introduction

If 1992 witnessed the zenith of post-cold war optimism about the prospects for preventing and resolving international conflict through multilateral action, 1993 saw its nadir. The year reinforced the stark realities which Bosnia and Herzegovina had already made clear in 1992 by revealing international impotence in the face of multiple challenges: continuing ethnic fratricide in the former Yugoslavia, a disastrous United Nations peace-enforcement mission in Somalia, a political stand-off in Haiti, ethnic blood-letting in Burundi, civil chaos in Zaire and Tajikistan, and the wholesale resumption of war in Afghanistan and Angola.[1] The United Nations and the international community scored considerable successes in restoring Cambodia to democratic governance, helping Eritrea gain independence, deploying to the Former Yugoslav Republic of Macedonia the first ever UN conflict prevention force and saving thousands of lives through humanitarian relief operations in Somalia and Bosnia; but these tended to be overwhelmed, at least in popular perception, by a continuing failure to end the war in Bosnia and Herzegovina and tame the Somali warlords. Multilateral organizations such as the European Union (EU) and the Conference on Security and Co-operation in Europe (CSCE) fared no better than the UN in relation to the former Yugoslavia and were only marginally more effective in other European conflicts: Georgia was besieged on two fronts, while the Nagorno-Karabakh conflict raged on unabated.[2]

The year's major peacemaking achievement—the historic accord between Israel and the Palestine Liberation Organization—emerged not from the UN or some other formal multilateral organization but from the secret good offices of a single country, Norway, building on the efforts of an *ad hoc* negotiation forum, the International Conference on the Middle East, initiated largely by the United States.[3] The transition of South Africa towards majority rule and tentative moves towards peace in Northern Ireland, meanwhile, were almost

---

[1] See chapter 2 in this volume.
[2] See chapter 6 in this volume.
[3] See chapter 3 in this volume.

* Olga Hardardóttir and Paul Claesson of the SIPRI Project on Peacekeeping and Regional Security assisted in researching this chapter.

exclusively the work of the parties involved, rather than the result of international intervention.

In addition to tackling ongoing conflicts and crises, the international community continued to grapple with conceptual issues relating to the prevention, management and resolution of conflicts between and within states. The debate revealed that the establishment of new norms, institutional arrangements and practices will take years. None the less the United Nations, prompted by the Secretary-General's *Agenda for Peace*,[4] began reforming its own capacities and procedures, despite rising demands on its services and worsening penury. Preventive diplomacy came into vogue, not just at the UN but in regional organizations, most notably the CSCE and the Organization of African Unity (OAU). The CSCE and the North Atlantic Treaty Organization (NATO) began serious examination of their roles in future peacekeeping operations.

Section II of this chapter reviews the debate on Secretary-General Boutros Boutros-Ghali's *An Agenda for Peace* one year after its release. Section III examines the role and activities of the United Nations in conflict prevention, management and resolution in 1993, with the exception of UN peacekeeping and peace-enforcement operations which, because of their size and complexity, are considered separately in sections IV and V. Regional involvement in conflict prevention, management and resolution in 1993 is considered in section VI.

II. *An Agenda for Peace* one year on

Debate continued throughout 1993 over the *Agenda for Peace*, a blueprint for enhancing the UN role in the maintenance of peace and security after the cold war.[5] Issued in June 1992 at the request of the Security Council, the document was widely greeted as an earnest of the new Secretary-General's willingness to transform his lumbering organization into one fit to meet the challenges of the 21st century. While an early consensus emerged on the merits of the conflict prevention measures proposed, his peacemaking, peacekeeping and peace-enforcement ideas did not fare as well.

Closer examination of the document in various UN forums[6] and in capitals produced political misgivings on the part of some states and revealed concep-

---

[4] Boutros-Ghali, B., *An Agenda for Peace: Preventive Diplomacy, Peacemaking and Peace-keeping*, Report of the Secretary-General, UN document A/47/277 (S/24111), 17 June 1992; the text of the report is reprinted in SIPRI, *SIPRI Yearbook 1993: World Armaments and Disarmament* (Oxford University Press: Oxford, 1993), appendix 2A, pp. 66–80.

[5] For a highly informative study of the origins and progress to date of *An Agenda for Peace,* see Cox, D., 'Exploring *An Agenda for Peace*: issues arising from the Report of the Secretary-General', *Aurora Paper 20* (Canadian Centre for Global Security: Ottawa, 1993). See also Hill, R., 'Preventive diplomacy, peace-making and peace-keeping', *SIPRI Yearbook 1993* (note 4), pp. 45–60.

[6] Within the UN system the document was considered in detail by the Security Council, the General Assembly (including in an informal open-ended working group chaired by Egypt), the Special Committee on the Charter of the United Nations and the Special Committee on Peace-keeping Operations (Committee of 34). An inter-departmental task force within the UN Secretariat was also established to propose further measures for implementing the document. For Committee of 34 views, see its report 'Comprehensive Review of the Whole Question of Peace-keeping Operations in all their Aspects', UN document

tual confusion to others. The developing states, led most vocally by Brazil, India, Pakistan, Malaysia and Mexico, were fearful of the implications of the concept of peace enforcement for their sovereignty, especially in civil war situations. This appeared to be inconsistent with the fact that several of them—notably India, Malaysia and Pakistan—not only supported UN peace-keeping missions involving enforcement elements, as in Somalia and the former Yugoslavia, but also contributed substantial numbers of troops.[7] Of the critics only Mexico has consistently declined to contribute troops to peace-keeping operations.[8]

Some developing states also expressed concern that the new focus on preventing, managing and resolving conflicts would distract the UN from its traditional concern with social and economic development. The critics provided no evidence that the UN was actually diverting resources from one area to the other—in fact, funding for all areas was increasing. Moreover, *An Agenda for Peace* had explicitly recognized the need 'in the largest sense, to address the deepest causes of conflict: economic despair, social injustice and political oppression'.[9] None the less Boutros-Ghali was asked to draft an 'Agenda for Development'.[10] The developing world did not present a united front on such issues, however, Egypt and Indonesia being particularly influential in balancing the views of the more radical.

A more fundamental, if publicly unarticulated, concern of the developing world was that *An Agenda for Peace,* in allegedly reflecting the preoccupations of the industrialized countries, was further evidence that the UN had become a tool of the West. Notwithstanding the fact that Boutros-Ghali was himself from a developing state and that most of his document was directed at solving problems plaguing the developing world, *An Agenda for Peace* was viewed as flawed because it failed to address the underlying UN power structure—specifically the composition and role of the Security Council (see section III).

Western reaction to *An Agenda for Peace* combined enthusiasm for the UN finally engaging in fundamental reform with a surprising cautiousness about some of the Secretary-General's more innovative suggestions. In regard to the proposed standby 'peace-enforcement units',[11] for instance, only France was supportive, having already offered the UN 1000 troops on 48 hours' notice.

A/48/173, 25 May 1993. For General Assembly resolutions on the subject see Resolutions 47/120A, 18 Dec. 1992 and 47/120B, 8 Oct. 1993. For public reactions of the Security Council see Notes by the President of the Security Council, 30 Nov. 1992 (S/24872), 30 Dec. 1992 (S/25036), 29 Jan. 1993 (S/25184), 26 Feb. 1993 (S/25344), 31 Mar. 1993 (S/25493), 30 Apr. 1993 (S/25696) and 28 May 1993 (S/25859). The working group approach to follow-up work on *An Agenda for Peace* has not been very effective; it has produced much paperwork but has been slow and cumbersome.

[7] Malaysia had troops in Somalia and Bosnia and Herzegovina, while India and Pakistan had troops in Somalia.

[8] Mexico has only contributed observers to two missions, UNMOGIP in 1949 and, more recently, ONUSAL in El Salvador.

[9] Boutros-Ghali (note 4), para. 16.

[10] Although requested by the General Assembly (in resolution 47/181 of 22 Dec. 1992) to be ready for the 48th session of the Assembly in 1993, the Agenda for Development was not to be tabled until early 1994. See Resolution A/48/689, 29 Nov. 1993, p. 1, for details.

[11] Boutros-Ghali (note 4), para. 44.

The traditional providers of peacekeeping contingents, while wary of the Secretary-General's peace-enforcement ideas, were however quick to volunteer proposals for streamlining and bolstering the UN's traditional peacekeeping efforts.[12]

Scholarly and some governmental responses to *An Agenda for Peace* pointed to conceptual flaws in the document. As Australian Foreign Minister Gareth Evans told the General Assembly, these would be only of academic interest were it not for the fact that the UN might act in the real world on the basis of these flaws unless clarifications were made.[13] The difficulties mostly revolve around definitions of *preventive diplomacy, peacemaking, peacekeeping* and *peace-building*.

Preventive diplomacy was defined by the Secretary-General as: 'action to prevent disputes from arising between parties, to prevent existing disputes from escalating into conflict and to limit the spread of the latter when they occur'.[14] It was not clear, however, what he regarded as the difference between a dispute and a conflict, although he gave the impression that by conflict he meant armed conflict. This highlighted a fundamental difficulty in *An Agenda for Peace*—its failure to clearly distinguish between conflict, in the sense of a dispute between parties, and armed conflict. Disputes are endemic in the international system, both between states and within them. It is simply not possible, nor desirable, to completely eradicate them.[15] The aim of the international community should then be to prevent escalation of disputes into destructive modes of behaviour, the most extreme of which is armed conflict.

As examples of preventive diplomacy Boutros-Ghali cited confidence-building measures, fact finding, early warning, preventive deployment and demilitarized zones. The term *diplomacy,* however, seems far too narrow to encapsulate not only his own examples (especially preventive deployments of troops and demilitarized zones) but the whole range of measures, diplomatic and non-diplomatic, available to the international community for preventing armed conflict. These include:[16] (*a*) fact finding and observation;[17] (*b*) 'good offices'; (*c*) mediation; (*d*) negotiation; (*e*) international legal measures such as the International Court of Justice (ICJ); (*f*) para-legal instruments such as arbitration and conciliation; (*g*) preventive deployments; (*h*) peacekeeping;

---

[12] Australia presented the most comprehensive response, in the form of the so-called Blue Book tabled at the General Assembly in Sep. 1993 by Foreign Minister Gareth Evans. See Evans, G., *Co-operating for Peace: The Global Agenda for the 1990s and Beyond* (Allen & Unwin: Sydney, 1993). The book seeks to clarify conceptual issues, suggest criteria for different types of UN intervention in conflict situations and propose priority areas for further UN reform.

[13] Evans, G., 'The United Nations: Cooperating for Peace', Address to the UN General Assembly by Senator Gareth Evans, Australian Minister for Foreign Affairs, 27 Sep. 1993, p. 6.

[14] Boutros-Ghali (note 4), para. 20.

[15] For a useful discussion of the positive (and negative) functions of conflict, see Tillett, G., *Resolving Conflict: A Practical Approach* (Sydney University Press: Sydney, 1991), chapter 1.

[16] For a comprehensive examination of the options available to the UN and its member states in the peaceful settlement of disputes, see United Nations, *Handbook on the Peaceful Settlement of Disputes Between States* (UN Office of Legal Affairs, Codification Division: New York, 1992).

[17] See Declaration on Fact-finding by the United Nations in the Field of the Maintenance of International Peace and Security, annexed to General Assembly Resolution 46/59, 9 Dec. 1991.

and (*i*) peace enforcement (including sanctions, embargoes and military action). Boutros-Ghali's preventive diplomacy might have been better described as 'conflict prevention and resolution measures'.

In contrast to preventive diplomacy, the Secretary-General defined *peacemaking* as 'action to bring hostile parties to agreement, essentially through such peaceful means as those foreseen in Chapter VI of the Charter of the United Nations'.[18] Again, it was not clear what he meant by 'hostile', although presumably it was parties engaged in armed combat. Moreover, all of the measures he then mentioned, including mediation, negotiation, 'good offices', arbitration and conciliation, and 'amelioration through assistance' (otherwise known as economic and humanitarian aid), are the same measures that can be used for preventing the outbreak of armed conflict in the first place.

Most tools of conflict prevention, management and resolution can in fact be used at any point in the 'conflict spectrum'. For instance, negotiations can take place before the outbreak of armed conflict or after it has ended. Enforcement measures can be used to resolve a dispute forcibly (for instance, that between Libya and those seeking justice in relation to the Lockerbie airliner bombing) or after armed conflict has erupted (as in the case of the former Yugoslavia). The division of these techniques into categories as in *An Agenda for Peace* is misleading.

The Secretary-General caused further conceptual confusion by including in his peacemaking repertoire the use of military force, including by 'peace-enforcement units' under Security Council authorization and the Secretary-General's command. Most analysts would regard the use of force not as peacemaking but as peace enforcement.

Compounding the confusion, Boutros-Ghali defined *peacekeeping* as 'the deployment of a United Nations presence in the field, *hitherto with the consent of all the parties concerned*, normally involving United Nations military and/or police personnel and frequently civilians as well'.[19] He subsequently declared that peace enforcement should be regarded as peacekeeping activities which 'do not necessarily involve the consent of all the parties concerned'.[20] Both statements appeared to confuse military operations under Chapter VII of the UN Charter, designed to enforce peace, with so-called 'Chapter $6^1/_2$' peacekeeping operations, which have traditionally scrupulously avoided using force, evinced impartiality and relied on consent of the parties.[21] While some peacekeeping operations have included enforcement elements, Boutros-Ghali's statements on the issue simply beg the question of whether peacekeeping forces can have an enforcement component without irretrievably tarnishing their impartiality and jeopardizing their entire mission. As veteran UN

---

[18] Boutros-Ghali (note 4), para. 20.

[19] Boutros-Ghali (note 4), para. 20 (emphasis added).

[20] Boutros-Ghali, B., *Report on the Work of the Organization from the Forty-seventh to the Forty-eighth Session of the General Assembly* (United Nations: New York, Sep. 1993), p. 96.

[21] Foreign Affairs Committee, House of Commons, *The Expanding Role of the United Nations and its Implications for United Kingdom Policy*, third report, vol. 1 (Her Majesty's Stationery Office: London, 23 June 1993), p. ix.

peacekeeping head, former Under Secretary-General Sir Brian Urquhart contends, 'The moment a peacekeeping force starts killing people it becomes a
part of the conflict it is supposed to be controlling and thus a part of the problem'.[22] This is not just a definitional problem but has been the most controversial issue for the UN in three of its most elaborate post-cold war peacekeeping missions—in Cambodia, Somalia and the former Yugoslavia[23]—and
one which the United Nations has yet to come to grips with.

Further definitional murkiness resulted from the Secretary-General's inclusion of new UN activities in the field, such as the conduct and supervision of
elections, the clearance of land mines, and the protection and promotion of
human rights, in a separate section on post-conflict *peace-building* (which
used to be known as post-war reconstruction and development). This unac-
countably neglected the role that such activities have in multi-purpose *peacekeeping* missions, both in resolving conflict and in laying the groundwork for
a lasting peace. The UN Transitional Assistance Group (UNTAG) in Namibia
and the UN Transitional Authority in Cambodia (UNTAC),[24] for instance,
were not operating in post-conflict situations but helping restore peace to
societies still in conflict.

Some of the conceptual difficulties found in *An Agenda for Peace* appeared
to stem from the woolly thinking of the Security Council, which tasked the
Secretary-General with preparing a report on the rather selective menu of
'*preventive diplomacy, peacemaking and peacekeeping*' rather than the comprehensive agenda of conflict prevention, management and resolution. (This
did not, however, stop the Secretary-General from discussing *peace-building*
and *peace enforcement.*)

What has become increasingly clear, and as the Secretary-General himself
has acknowledged, is that the various UN activities outlined in *An Agenda for
Peace* form part of a complex continuum of peace operations.[25] They inter-
twine and may be performed simultaneously or at varying points in the peace
process. Distinctions that seem clear and obvious in theory may dissolve in the
field, where the sole criterion must be whether the particular combination of
techniques works. Observer missions, for instance, can be seen as a conflict
prevention technique, a type of peacekeeping activity or a confidence-building
measure in a post-conflict situation. Preventive diplomacy can occur at any
stage of a conflict, either before the outbreak of armed clashes or after they
have begun, in order to prevent escalation to full-scale war. Humanitarian
intervention can be carried out during a conflict, such as in former Yugoslavia,
or after it, as in the case of the Kurds of Iraq. Peace negotiations can take
place at any point in the conflict spectrum.

Despite criticisms of and disagreements with *An Agenda for Peace*, the
document, prepared at short notice and in a situation of rapid change, stimu-

---

[22] Quoted in Meister, S., 'Crisis in Katanga', *Soldiers for Peace*, Supplement to *MHQ: Quarterly
Journal of Military History*, vol. 5, no.1 (autumn 1992), p. 54.

[23] See appendix 1A for case studies of these missions.

[24] Acronyms for all current UN missions are elucidated in appendix 1A.

[25] Boutros-Ghali (note 20), p. 96.

lated debate and thinking on the UN's role. Moreover, it commendably attempted, for the first time, to integrate all UN activities into a single vision—the attainment and preservation of international peace and security. On a practical level, it launched a long-awaited reform process aimed at improving the UN's conflict prevention, management and resolution capabilities.

III. The United Nations' role in conflict prevention, management and resolution in 1993

The Secretary-General and the Secretariat

One of the preoccupations of the Secretary-General and the Secretariat during the year was the establishment of an efficient UN early-warning system. There is a new awareness that conflict prevention, management and resolution can only be achieved if adequate and timely early-warning information is available. In the UN case there has been not so much a lack of information as an inability to process and interpret it. Although its Office of Research and Collection of Information (ORCI) was abolished early in Boutros-Ghali's tenure as a cost-cutting measure, the Secretary-General, encouraged by the General Assembly, subsequently commissioned a task force to make recommendations on establishing a UN early-warning system. Meanwhile, the USA has donated an intelligence-processing system to enable the Secretariat better to receive, process and disseminate information provided by member states.[26]

An inter-agency early-warning mechanism for detecting mass population displacements has already been established in the UN Department for Humanitarian Affairs.[27] The UN has also established 'Interim Offices' in the former Soviet republics (Armenia, Azerbaijan, Belarus, Georgia, Kazakhstan, Ukraine and Uzbekistan) in part to enable it to monitor conflict situations there.[28] There are plans to establish similar offices in Cambodia, Eritrea and Russia.

While the UN should continue to enhance its information-gathering and -processing capabilities, there are obstacles to its ever being able to become as efficient and effective as national intelligence agencies (which themselves are far from infallible). First, there is sensitivity among developing states about the possibility of the UN using 'intelligence' about them to their detriment, for example in a peace-enforcement operation. Hence the UN avoids the term 'intelligence' in favour of 'information'. Second is the reluctance of the technologically advanced states to turn over much vital information to the UN lest their sources, capabilities (both human and technical) and national security be compromised. However, a precedent has been set in the case of the UN Spe-

---

[26] The Joint Deployable Intelligence Support System is located in the Department of Peace-Keeping Operations (DPKO). See Berdal, M., International Institute for Strategic Studies, *Whither UN Peacekeeping?*, Adelphi Paper no. 281 (Brassey's: London, 1993), p. 55.

[27] Boutros-Ghali (note 20) p. 101.

[28] Boutros-Ghali (note 20), p. 32.

cial Commission (UNSCOM), which received US intelligence information about Iraq to aid its search for that country's weapons of mass destruction and delivery capabilities.[29] A case more relevant to early warning has been US willingness to provide satellite intelligence to the International Atomic Energy Agency to bolster attempts to dissuade North Korea from developing nuclear weapons. Finally, there is opposition to UN intelligence-gathering capabilities because of more amorphous concerns about the UN becoming the precursor of an all-seeing, all-knowing world government.

The situations in Angola, Bosnia and Herzegovina, and Sudan in 1993 were, however, reminders that early warning is useless unless there is a willingness to act appropriately on the basis of the information available. Often it is the UN Secretary-General who is best placed to act, at least in the first instance, using quiet or even secret diplomacy in a good offices, goodwill or fact-finding capacity. Staff drawn from the Secretariat or prominent states-persons may be used in situations where the Secretary-General is unable to be personally involved or where prolonged diplomacy is required. To handle the increased demand for such services, the UN is for the first time imparting pre-ventive and peacemaking diplomacy skills to its staff.[30]

The scale of UN diplomacy in attempting to prevent, manage and resolve conflict is impressive. Boutros-Ghali reported to the General Assembly in September 1993 that more than 100 missions of representation, fact-finding and goodwill offices to various countries have been undertaken on his behalf since he began his term of office on 1 January 1992.[31] In 1992–93 more fact-finding missions were dispatched than in any previous such period in the UN's history.[32]

In 1993 some of these missions were of an unprecedented character. The Secretary-General described as a 'significant breakthrough' the dispatch of UN civilian observers to assist a member state—South Africa—in 'purely a domestic matter, containing the level of violence'.[33] The theory behind this type of mission is that the mere presence of foreign observers can help prevent or quell violence. In 1992 the UN also dispatched fact-finding missions for the first time to former Soviet republics—Armenia and Azerbaijan, Georgia and Abkhazia, Moldova and Tajikistan.[34] Another precedent was set in 1993 when the Secretary-General dispatched a goodwill mission to Zaire to offer UN assistance in resolving a domestic political stand-off that had not yet resulted in significant armed conflict. This was conflict prevention at its purest, although it also clearly amounted to interference in the internal affairs of a

[29] See chapter 19 in this volume.

[30] In Sep. 1993 in Austria, the UN Institute for Training and Research (UNITAR), in co-operation with the International Peace Academy, held its first Fellowship Programme in Peacemaking and Preventive Diplomacy for international and national civil servants (information from the Programme Co-ordinator, Dr Connie Peck).

[31] Boutros-Ghali (note 20), p. 97.

[32] Boutros-Ghali, B., 'An Agenda for Peace: one year later', *Orbis*, vol. 37, no. 3 (summer 1993), p. 325.

[33] First established in 1992, the UN Observer Mission in South Africa currently comprises 49 observers. See Boutros-Ghali (note 20), pp. 97–98.

[34] Boutros-Ghali (note 20), pp. 110–11, 115–17, 134–35 and 137–39.

sovereign UN member state. The case illustrates one of the dilemmas the UN faces in attempting to nip potential armed conflict in the bud.

The Security Council

The Security Council, as the principal organ of the UN entrusted with maintaining international peace and security, has a vital role in conflict prevention, management and resolution. Since the end of the cold war it has become increasingly effective, at least in tackling a wider variety and number of conflicts, broadening its definition of what constitutes a threat to international peace and security and being willing to take, on occasions, decisive action. A key development has been a dramatic fall in the use of the veto by the five permanent members—China, France, Russia, the UK and the USA.[35]

The Council can take a variety of conflict prevention, management and resolution initiatives, including fact finding and observation, the imposition of sanctions and the dispatch of peacekeeping and peace-enforcement missions (see sections IV and V). The Council can also follow up the Secretary-General's conflict-prevention initiatives, in particular by authorizing expanded missions, some of which acquire a UN acronym and separate funding as a 'peacekeeping' operation.[36] For instance, in 1993 the Council followed up the Secretary-General's Georgia–Abkhazia fact-finding missions by establishing the UN Observer Mission in Georgia (UNOMIG).[37]

In 1992–93 the workload of the Council intensified further, the 20-member body meeting in almost continuous session.[38] According to Boutros-Ghali, 'what has emerged is a pattern of operations akin to that of a task force dealing with situations as they arise, on an almost continuing basis'.[39]

Security Council reform

For the developing countries the unrepresentativeness of the Council (particularly the absence of Brazil, India, Indonesia and Nigeria from permanent membership) and the existence of the veto power are a continuing bone of

[35] Evans (note 12), p. 21.
[36] The designation of a UN mission with an acronym is somewhat arbitrary, nor does it qualify the mission as a peacekeeping mission in the sense that it involves deployments of troops. Missions with acronyms run the gamut from observation operations to full-scale comprehensive peacekeeping and peace-enforcement operations. In one instance, the 1990 UN Mission to Verify the Election in Haiti (ONUVEH), the government involved specifically requested, for political reasons, that the mission not be called a peacekeeping mission. See Durch, W. J., *The Evolution of UN Peacekeeping* (The Henry L. Stimson Center: Washington, DC, 1993), p. 35. Acquiring an acronym usually means that the mission has been authorized by the Security Council and funded separately from the normal UN budget, but there are exceptions. The 1947 UN Special Committee on the Balkans (UNSCOB) was established by the General Assembly and funded out of the regular UN budget. Small observer missions like UNTSO in the Middle East continue to be funded out of that budget. The mission in Cyprus, UNFICYP, is however funded by voluntary contributions (see Durch, p. 45). See also appendix 1A, note 13.
[37] Boutros-Ghali (note 20), p. 117.
[38] From 1 Jan. 1992 to 31 Aug. 1993 it held 359 sessions of consultations of the whole, totalling some 428 hours, as well as 247 formal meetings which adopted 137 resolutions and issued 144 statements. See Boutros-Ghali (note 20), pp. 11–12.
[39] Boutros-Ghali (note 20), pp. 11–12.

contention. Not only does the current arrangement lack balance and equity (Germany and Japan are also strongly pressing for permanent membership) but it also tarnishes the legitimacy of Security Council decisions. The problem, in the view of the developing states, has been exacerbated by the Council's authorization of the US-led Operation Desert Storm against Iraq, the imposition of sanctions on Libya over the Lockerbie bombing, the failure to lift the arms embargo against the Muslim-led government of Bosnia and Herzegovina and the absence of action against Israel for its flouting of Security Council resolutions.

Although the developing states represented on the Council participate fully in Council debates and sometimes help frustrate Western policy, they none the less sense the operation of a 'closet veto', whereby the USA, France and the UK use their political, military and financial clout to ultimately get their own way.[40]

During 1993 delicate consultations over the Council's future composition were conducted in the Special Committee on the Charter of the United Nations and in the context of planning for the UN's 50th anniversary celebrations in 1995.[41] However, abolition of the veto is extremely unlikely, whatever the decision about the composition of the Council.

Criteria for UN intervention

Debate over criteria for Security Council authorization of UN intervention in situations of armed conflict grew intense in 1993, inflamed by the perceived lack of criteria involved in Council decisions to intervene in Somalia and former Yugoslavia. President Bill Clinton, in his address to the General Assembly in September, said that the UN had to 'know when to say no', not just because peacekeeping may be inappropriate in particular circumstances, but because the UN cannot possibly cope with all conflicts.[42] Boutros-Ghali himself on several occasions pleaded that the UN was unable, given limitations on its finances and human resources, to respond to every request for intervention or assistance. Britain's UN Ambassador, Sir David Hannay, suggested that if the UN could not say no, it should at least learn to say 'yes, but' and spell out conditions for its involvement.[43] Some observers argued that the UN may be wise to let particular conflicts continue until they were ripe for intervention, rather than waste resources and effort in perhaps making situations worse. Lord Owen argued, for instance, that in feeding all sides in Bosnia and Herzegovina the UN had prolonged the war.[44] Others claimed that

[40] *The Economist*, 12 June 1993, p. 45.

[41] Boutros-Ghali (note 4), paras 40, 115 and 116. The Preparatory Committee for the Fiftieth Anniversary of the United Nations is dealing with Security Council reform in the context of a celebratory UN declaration which would stand alongside the Charter (information provided by the Committee Chairman, Australian Ambassador to the UN, Mr Richard Butler).

[42] 'Confronting the challenges of a broader world', address to the UN General Assembly by President Bill Clinton, 27 Sep. 1993, *US Department of State Dispatch*, vol. 4, no. 39 (27 Sep. 1993), p. 652.

[43] Note 40, p. 44.

[44] *Financial Times*, 12–13 Mar. 1994, p. 2.

knee-jerk resort to peacekeeping represented a failure on the part of the Security Council to address the root causes of conflict, a case in point being Somalia.

In an attempt to address some of these issues the Security Council in May 1993 announced its criteria for establishing peacekeeping operations (jumbled in with some guidelines for its own behaviour) in the last of its series of notes on *An Agenda for Peace*. These criteria were:

• A clear political goal and a precise mandate subject to periodic review and to change in its character or duration only by the Council itself
• The consent of the government and, where appropriate, the parties concerned, save in exceptional circumstances
• Support for a political process or for the peaceful settlement of the dispute
• Impartiality in implementing Security Council decisions
• Readiness of the Security Council to take appropriate measures against parties which do not observe its decisions
• The right of the Security Council to authorize all means necessary for United Nations forces to carry out their mandate
• The inherent right of peacekeepers to use force in self-defence
• An emphasis on the need to find a political solution so that peace-keeping operations do not continue in perpetuity.[45]

In addition the Council stressed that peacekeeping operations 'should not be a substitute for a political settlement nor should they be expected to continue in perpetuity'.[46]

However, while the existence of set criteria can lead to a more orderly and comprehensive decision-making process, in the final analysis decisions on UN intervention will be made on political grounds, particularly since contributions by member states to such interventions will themselves be made on political grounds. Moreover, it will be the 'exceptional circumstances' that will place the most stress on the Security Council's criteria.

Preventive deployments

Amid all the hand-wringing about definitional issues arising from *An Agenda for Peace*, one innovative addition to the UN arsenal of conflict prevention techniques mentioned in that document was quietly inaugurated by the Security Council in 1993—the preventive deployment of 1000 UN troops to Macedonia to deter the spread of the Balkans war to that former Yugoslav republic.[47]

---

[45] Note by the President of the Security Council, UN document S/25859, 28 May 1993, p. 1.
[46] See note 45.
[47] See appendix 1B for details.

Table 1.1. Cases before the International Court of Justice, 1993

• Application of the Convention on the Prevention and Punishment of the Crime of Genocide (Bosnia and Herzegovina v. Yugoslavia (Serbia and Montenegro))

• Maritime Delimitation in the Area between Greenland and Jan Mayen (Denmark v. Norway)

• Territorial Dispute (Libya/Chad)

• Aerial Incident of 3 July 1988 (Iran v. USA)

• Certain Phosphate Lands in Nauru (Nauru v. Australia)

• East Timor (Portugal v. Australia)

• Maritime Delimitation between Guinea-Bissau and Senegal

• Maritime Delimitation and Territorial Questions between Qatar and Bahrain

• Questions of Interpretation and Application of the 1971 Montreal Convention arising from the Aerial Incident at Lockerbie (Libya v. United Kingdom)

• Questions of Interpretation and Application of the 1971 Montreal Convention arising from the Aerial Incident at Lockerbie (Libya v. USA)

• Oil Platforms (Iran v. USA)

• Gabcikovo–Ngyamaros Project (Hungary/Slovakia)

Source: Boutros-Ghali, B., *Report on the Work of the Organization from the Forty-seventh to the Forty-eighth Session of the General Assembly* (United Nations: New York, Sep. 1993), pp. 17–19. Cases listed as one party versus another are those in which one party has brought to the ICJ a case against another party, the others are cases where both parties jointly seek a Court ruling.

Also in 1993 the Security Council expanded the mandate of the UN Iraq–Kuwait Observation Mission (UNIKOM), deployed on the Iraq–Kuwait border, from one of border monitoring to one designed to deter, and if necessary deal with, small-scale Iraqi incursions.[48]

Although *An Agenda for Peace* attempted to categorize preventive deployments separately from peacekeeping, it could be argued that they are a type of peacekeeping, the only difference being that they keep the peace before armed conflict has occurred, rather than afterwards. Many so-called traditional peacekeeping operations have a preventive deployment character—including those in Cyprus, India–Pakistan and the Middle East. On the other hand such deployments, if located only on one side of a border, as in Macedonia, may not have the consent of all parties—a traditional prerequisite of peacekeeping—and may therefore be perceived as partial.[49]

---

[48] Boutros-Ghali (note 20), p. 122; and *UN Chronicle*, vol. 30, no. 3 (Sep. 1993), p. 40. Following the Gulf operation the UN established UNIKOM to monitor the Iraq–Kuwait border. Since it had its basis in a Chapter VII enforcement action this peacekeeping operation is 'an unusual blend of "traditional" peacekeeping and enforcement'. See Foreign Affairs Committee (note 21), p. xii. The force was intended to be bolstered by a mechanized infantry battalion, but to date no UN member state has volunteered such a contingent.

[49] This did not stop the UN Emergency Forces (UNEF I and II) in the Sinai, deployed only on the Egyptian side of the border because of Israeli opposition, being regarded as peacekeeping operations.

International legal mechanisms

International legal mechanisms for resolving international conflicts peacefully, thereby preventing the outbreak of armed conflict, have existed for decades, but have remained under-utilized, largely because states have been unwilling to surrender jurisdiction over their sovereign affairs to an international tribunal. In *An Agenda for Peace* Boutros-Ghali pleaded for greater resort to be had to the ICJ in the Hague in the peaceful settlement of disputes, including the so-called 'chambers' jurisdiction or informal mediation by the court. In 1993, probably more coincidentally than in response to his plea, the Court had before it a record 12 cases. Three have since been resolved, the court handing down judgements in the Denmark versus Norway and Libya/Chad cases, while Australia and Nauru reached a settlement outside the court and agreed to discontinue proceedings in their Certain Phosphate Lands case.[50] The UN Decade of International Law which starts in the year 2000 is being seen as an opportunity to encourage all states to accept the general jurisdiction of the ICJ.

IV. UN peacekeeping operations

Peacekeeping, the deployment of multinational military and/or civilian forces in the field, can be used to prevent, manage or resolve conflict. It can prevent an outbreak or resumption of hostilities, manage localized outbreaks of conflict or constitute part of a comprehensive peace settlement. In Boutros-Ghali's categorization, peacekeeping can be a part of preventive diplomacy, peacemaking or peace-building.

Peacekeeping missions were the most controversial aspects of UN operations in 1993. The world media at times gave the impression that the entire enterprise was on the verge of collapse, citing the operations in Somalia and the former Yugoslavia as prime examples.[51] The débâcle in Mogadishu in particular brought charges of UN incompetence and, combined with the embarrassing failures of its own contingent, a reconsideration by the USA of its future role in UN peacekeeping missions.[52] The UNPROFOR mission in the former Yugoslavia, while criticized on a number of grounds, was just one struggling element in an unfolding political and military tragedy, where none of the players wrapped itself in glory.[53] The Angola mission, UNAVEM II, went seriously wrong, partly because it was under-resourced. It was placed in limbo when brutal civil war resumed following UN-sponsored elections in September 1992.[54] The UN Mission for the Referendum in Western Sahara

---

[50] Information obtained from the Legal Department, Swedish Ministry of Foreign Affairs, Stockholm. See also International Court of Justice, *Reports of Judgments, Advisory Opinions and Orders* (International Court of Justice: The Hague, 1993).

[51] See, for instance, Bellamy, C., 'UN peace missions are a "shambles"', *The Independent*, 13 Oct. 1993, p. 12; Elliot, M., 'Somalia: anatomy of a fiasco', *Newsweek*, 18 Oct. 1993, pp. 6–15; and Krauthammer, C., 'The immaculate intervention', *Time*, 26 July 1993, p. 60.

[52] See case study in appendix 1B.

[53] See case study in appendix 1B.

[54] *UN Chronicle*, vol. 30, no. 3 (Sep. 1993), pp. 27–29.

(MINURSO)[55] also remained on hold as disagreements between the parties derailed plans for a referendum on independence.[56] The UN failed both to return democratically elected President Jean-Bertrand Aristide to power in Haiti and to land a limited peacekeeping mission (the UN Mission in Haiti, UNMIH) at Port-au-Prince in the face of determined opposition by armed civilians mobilized by the Haitian military.[57]

On the positive side, however, Cambodia became the UN's first major post-cold war success story, albeit one that soon faded from the news headlines.[58] A UN mission also quietly assisted Eritrea in achieving its long-held goal of independence by monitoring its April 1993 referendum (the UN Observer Mission to Verify the Referendum in Eritrea, UNOVER).[59] The UN also began tackling the daunting task of returning Mozambique to peace and democracy with a 6000-strong force of troops and civilian police (the UN Operation in Mozambique, ONUMOZ) deployed by June 1993.[60] The UN Observer Mission in El Salvador (ONUSAL) and that in Nicaragua and Honduras (the UN Observer Group in Central America, ONUCA) continued to be largely successful, although their tasks remained far from complete.[61] Towards the end of 1993 the situation in El Salvador showed worrying signs of deterioration in the lead-up to the campaign for the March 1994 elections.[62]

In 1993 UN peacekeeping continued its exponential quantitative expansion. Six new missions were established: in Somalia, Uganda/Rwanda, Georgia, Liberia, Haiti and Rwanda (which absorbed the Uganda/Rwanda mission).[63] At its peak in 1993 the UN had nearly 80 000 troops deployed in 18 operations, more than at any time in its history.[64] The UN peacekeeping budget was expected to have grown from an already unprecedented $1.4 billion in 1992 to $3.6 billion in 1993.[65]

The costs of UN peacekeeping operations are, however, a pittance compared with military spending. The ratio of military expenditures to peacekeeping contributions, calculated for selected countries, range from 182 000 : 1 for Ethiopia to Japan's 574 : 1.[66] Peacekeeping costs also pale in comparison with peace-enforcement operations. While the enforcement action against Iraq

[55] MINURSO is the Spanish acronym for Mision de las Naciones Unidas para el Referendum del Sahara Occidental.

[56] Durch (note 36), pp. 33–34; and *Financial Times*, 28 Oct. 1993, p. 6.

[57] *UN Chronicle*, vol. 30 , no. 4 (Dec. 1993), pp. 20–22; and *International Herald Tribune*, 12 Oct. 1993.

[58] See the case study in appendix 1B.

[59] *UN Chronicle*, vol. 30, no. 3 (Sep. 1993), p. 39.

[60] See note 59, pp. 25–26.

[61] See Baranyi, S. and North, L., 'Stretching the limits of the possible: United Nations peacekeeping in Central America', *Aurora Paper 15* (Canadian Centre for Global Security: Ottawa, Dec. 1992).

[62] Farah, D., 'El Salvador's peace process is seen losing its momentum', *Boston Sunday Globe*, 21 Nov. 1993; and Reid, M., 'UN investigates return of Salvador death squads', *The Guardian*, 11 Nov. 1993, p. 6.

[63] See appendix 1A for details.

[64] *United Nations Peace-keeping Operations*, Background Note (United Nations Information Centre for the Nordic Countries: Copenhagen, Oct. 1993).

[65] Boutros-Ghali (note 20), p. 34.

[66] Ogata, S. and Volcker, P., *Financing an Effective United Nations*, Report of the Independent Advisory Group on UN Financing (Ford Foundation, New York, Apr. 1993), pp. 32–33.

during the Persian Gulf War cost an estimated $40 billion, UNOSOM II in Somalia cost an estimated $1.2 billion in its first 12 months,[67] while UNTAC in Cambodia cost a mere $1.5 billion in total.[68]

UN operations also escalated in complexity, combining elements of traditional peacekeeping (such as separating combatants along a contested frontier) with, in Boutros-Ghali's terms, peacemaking, peace-building and, for the first time since the Congo operation in the 1960s, peace enforcement. Some of this growing complexity was planned, the result of ambitious peace-building operations as in Cambodia. Complexity also came with deteriorating conditions in Bosnia and Herzegovina, forcing ever more ingenious techniques on the UN to achieve delivery of humanitarian aid. The requirements of peace enforcement in a civil war situation in Somalia added further complexity. In Haiti the UN attempted unsuccessfully to inaugurate a new type of peacekeeping mission, designed to provide military and police training to assist in the democratization and demilitarization of Haitian society. As Boutros-Ghali put it, 'peacekeeping has to be reinvented every day'.[69]

The expanded repertoire of UN peacekeeping operations in 1993 included:

1. Election observation (Eritrea and Liberia) and organization (Cambodia);
2. Humanitarian assistance and securing safe conditions for its delivery (Bosnia and Herzegovina, Somalia and Kurdish areas of Iraq);
3. Observation and separation of combatants along a more or less demarcated boundary (Croatia, southern Lebanon, Cyprus, India–Pakistan, Kuwait–Iraq, Israel–Syria and Israel–Egypt);
4. Disarmament of military and paramilitary forces (Cambodia, Somalia and El Salvador);
5. Promotion and protection of human rights (Cambodia and El Salvador);
6. Mine clearance, training and mine awareness (Afghanistan and Cambodia);
7. Military and police training (Cambodia and Haiti);
8. Boundary demarcation (Kuwait–Iraq border);
9. Civil administration (Cambodia);
10. Provision of assistance to and repatriation of refugees (the former Yugoslavia, Cambodia and Somalia);
11. Reconstruction and development (Cambodia and Somalia).

Some of these functions were combined in large, multi-function operations as in Angola, Cambodia, El Salvador, Mozambique, Somalia and the former Yugoslavia.

[67] Evans (note 12), p. 119.
[68] *Jane's Defence Weekly*, 5 Feb. 1994, p. 16.
[69] Boutros-Ghali (note 20), p. 101.

Operational problems

During 1993 the qualitative and quantitative expansion of UN field operations placed an enormous strain on the capacity of the UN to establish, administer and service the multiplicity of field operations. Procurement, logistics and supply, personnel and finance were all strained to breaking point. Part of the problem remained that the UN did not have its own holdings of supplies, apart from a small stock of equipment held at an air base at Pisa, Italy.[70] It therefore continued to procure from external contractors, usually at very short notice, most of the equipment needed for each mission (although towards the end of 1993 it began to recycle equipment from one mission to the next).[71] Despite this situation, a Secretariat proposal to establish stocks of basic military equipment was dropped when member states refused to contribute $15 million to fund it.[72]

Traditionally, the UN's procurement system, including its budgetary procedures, has been extraordinarily slow and complex. Until the General Assembly's Advisory Committee on Administrative and Budgetary Questions (ACABQ) and Fifth Committee approve each mission budget, the Secretariat cannot expend significant funds.[73] Furthermore, insufficient financial delegation is given to mission commanders to procure supplies and equipment locally or regionally; all purchasing orders and requisitions must be channelled through New York.[74] Commanders have traditionally spent valuable time devising creative ways to subvert this cumbersome system.

Co-ordination of UN agencies in the field also remained problematic throughout 1993. In Cambodia, Bosnia and Herzegovina and Somalia, civil–military relations were at times 'strained'.[75] Serious problems were also identified in the relationship between the UN's multiple humanitarian agencies and its political and peacekeeping structures.[76] Jan Eliasson, Under Secretary-General for Humanitarian Affairs, was frustrated in his attempts to improve co-ordination even among the humanitarian agencies themselves.[77]

The failures of peacekeeping in 1993 were for the most part not operational, however, but political. They ranged from failure at the highest level, the Security Council, which lacked the political will to implement its decisions on

---

[70] Durch (note 36), p. 67.

[71] Equipment from the Cambodia mission was sent to Liberia. See *Phnom Penh Post*, 11–24 Feb. 1994, p. 17; United Nations, 'UN Peacekeeping Operations Information Notes', update no. 2, 1993, p. 108.

[72] *Wall Street Journal Europe*, 29 Dec. 1993, p. 1.

[73] Berdal (note 26), p. 34. The Fifth Committee is the General Assembly's committee on finance, membership of which is open to all UN members, unlike the ACABQ which has a limited, elected membership of 16.

[74] Berdal (note 26), p. 34.

[75] Berdal (note 26), p. 15.

[76] Weiss, T. G., *et al.*, *Humanitarian Action in the Former Yugoslavia: The UN's Role, 1991–1993*, Occasional Paper 18 (Thomas J. Watson Institute for International Studies: Providence, R.I., 1994).

[77] *The Independent*, 24 Nov. 1993, p. 13. Moreover, he has not been mandated to deal with Bosnia and Herzegovina, which is the exclusive responsibility of the UN High Commissioner for Refugees (UNHCR). One observer likened this to 'being the England football manager and responsible for everything but the matches'.

former Yugoslavia and Somalia, through to the failure of guerrilla groups like Cambodia's Khmer Rouge and Angola's UNITA (União Nacionale para a Independência Total de Angola) to seize the opportunity offered by UN intervention to give their nations a new beginning. There is little the UN can do when warring parties have no real desire for peace.

Peacekeeping reforms

In response to heightened expectations and demands,[78] problems in the field and widespread criticism, the United Nations began a series of reforms of its peacekeeping operations, especially focused on its headquarters in New York.

The Secretariat's Department of Peace-keeping Operations (DPKO), established in March 1992 and headed after March 1993 by Under Secretary-General Kofi Annan, has been continually reorganized and expanded.[79] After declining in 1988–89 from around 12 to 8 professional officers, it has grown since 1991 to around 25 civilian professionals and an equal number of military officers, the latter mostly on secondment from governments. The target is to almost double the number of professionals in the division to 80 or 90. The Department has been organized into geographical divisions for the first time (Africa, Asia/Middle East and Europe/Latin America) to make tracking and co-ordination of operations in particular regions easier, although this may have the perverse effect of detracting from efforts to improve vertical integration in UN peacekeeping decision-making.[80]

A major, long-advocated reform and potentially the most significant was the integration of the Field Operations Division into the DPKO.[81] This promised to attenuate administrative and communication difficulties and bureaucratic rivalry caused by the previous physical and administrative separation of the operational and policy-making arms of UN peacekeeping. According to F. T. Liu of the International Peace Academy in New York, the old arrangement had had two negative effects: it downplayed the importance of logistical support, which is essential for successful peacekeeping operations, and it weakened the Secretary-General's control in this area.[82]

---

[78] The Security Council called for proposals from the Secretary-General to enhance UN peacekeeping capabilities, including: strengthening and consolidation of the peacekeeping and military structure of the Secretariat; the feasibility of maintaining a limited revolving reserve of equipment commonly used in peacekeeping or humanitarian operations; elements for inclusion in national military or police training programmes for peacekeeping operations, including the feasibility of multinational peacekeeping exercises; refinement of standardized procedures to enable forces to work together more effectively; developing non-military elements of peacekeeping operations; and measures designed to place peacekeeping operations on a more solid and durable financial basis (UN Security Council Resolution S/25859, 28 May 1993).

[79] The following details were obtained in an interview conducted by the author with Ms Hisako Shimura, Director, Department of Peace-keeping Operations, UN, New York, 23 Nov. 1993.

[80] Berdal, M., 'Peacekeeping after the cold war: new opportunities and challenges', paper presented to the SIPRI/Friedrich-Ebert-Stiftung conference on 'Challenges for the New Peacekeepers', Bonn, 21–22 Apr. 1994, p. 9.

[81] The Field Operations Division was absorbed into a new Office of Planning and Support in the DPKO.

[82] Liu, F. T., 'United Nations peace-keeping: management and operations', *Occasional Papers on Peace-keeping*, no. 4, International Peace Academy, New York, 1990, p. 11.

Another much needed reform was the establishment of a 'Situation Centre' (formerly 'Room') for UN peace operations in a modest building across from the UN in New York.[83] While it initially had only one fax and an open-line telephone and was assigned only to UNOSOM II and UNPROFOR, the Centre is a precursor to a global situation room for both early warning and for handling all UN field operations. Unfortunately the US Congress in 1993 rejected an Administration request for $10 million to finance a more sophisticated UN command centre.[84]

To improve the future availability of peacekeeping forces, a Standby Forces Planning Team, comprising seven military officers seconded from member states, led by a French colonel, visited national capitals during 1993 to elicit pledges of contributions of military force components which will be placed on standby availability for future UN operations. The task force was also asked to define the various components of UN forces (for example, 'helicopter squadron', 'mechanized unit') to introduce some standardization into contributions.[85]

The military advice available to UN headquarters was substantially boosted by expansion of the Office of the Military Advisor (MILAD) in the DPKO to more than 40 officers,[86] including secondment of a de-mining expert, a civilian police adviser and a military officer responsible for training and co-ordination.[87] To facilitate long-range planning for its overseas operations a Policy and Analysis Cell (comprising one person) was also established.

In addition to these initiatives taken by the UN itself, member states took up other reform issues. New Zealand, a non-permanent member of the Security Council, and Ukraine initiated the establishment of an *Ad Hoc* Committee of the UN General Assembly to negotiate an international convention on the safety and security of peacekeepers, 'with particular responsibility for attacks on such personnel'.[88]

---

[83] *Wall Street Journal Europe*, 29 Dec. 1993, p. 5.

[84] *International Herald Tribune*, 23 Sep. 1993, p. 6.

[85] Memoranda of Understanding will be negotiated with contributors of personnel, *matériel* and funding.

[86] Berdal (note 26), p. 54.

[87] Initiatives of the Training and Coordination Office in 1993 included:
  1. A *Peacekeeping Training Manual* (based on the Nordic model);
  2. Six training videos and handbooks (published by the UN Institute for Training and Research, UNITAR);
  3. A draft training curriculum for UN military observers;
  4. A study commissioned from the Washington-based Henry L. Stimson Centre on 'Training for Peacekeeping: Alternative Means of Strengthening Current Standards';
  5. An analysis of the role of regional organizations in peacekeeping;
  6. The drafting of a military operations (milops) handbook; and
  7. The drafting of a Code of Conduct for military and civilian peacekeepers.

[88] General Assembly Resolution 48/37. The first round of negotiations were scheduled for 28 Mar.– 8 Apr. in New York. For details see 'Safety of United Nations Troops and Personnel', statement by Ambassador Colin R. Keating, Permanent Representative of New Zealand to the United Nations, to Parliamentarians for Global Action, The Hague, 20–22 Jan. 1994. Draft conventions were tabled by New Zealand (A/C.6/48/L.2) and Ukraine (A/C.6/48/L.3) (information from the New Zealand Embassy, The Hague).

The UN's financial crisis

Throughout 1993 the United Nations remained in severe financial crisis, a consequence of exponential growth in the demands made of the organization and a failure by almost all UN member states to pay their share of UN expenses in full and on time. By the end of 1993 only 19 member states had fully paid their assessed contributions to the regular budget and to peacekeeping operations.[89]

In August Boutros-Ghali revealed that the UN had cash reserves for less than two months' operations and warned that all UN activities were at risk.[90] By October arrears for normal UN operating expenses amounted to $794 million, while arrears for peacekeeping operations (which are assessed separately) were $1.6 billion.[91] The largest UN debtors overall were the USA, Russia, Ukraine, South Africa and Belarus.[92] The largest peacekeeping debtors were: Russia, the USA, Ukraine, Italy, Spain, South Africa, Japan, France, Belarus and Germany.[93]

There were many different reasons for states being in debt. The former Soviet republics were in financial crisis, South Africa had accumulated debts during its ostracism by the General Assembly over apartheid, while Germany was gradually paying off the former German Democratic Republic's debt for its assessed contribution to UNIFIL in Lebanon.[94] Almost all UN members experience difficulty paying their assessed dues because their budgetary processes do not coincide with those of the UN and because their dues for peacekeeping operations can be assessed at any time during the financial year.

Several peacekeeping missions experienced severe cash shortages during 1993, for which temporary advances were made from the Peace-keeping Reserve Fund established by the General Assembly in December 1992.[95] Other cash shortfalls were overcome by internal borrowing from UN funds with a cash surplus. Dick Thornburgh, a former US Attorney-General, author of a critical report on the UN after a year as Under Secretary-General for Management, described UN peacekeeping as a financial bungee jump, undertaken in the blind faith that funding would eventuate.[96] As a consequence of

---

[89] Boutros-Ghali (note 20), p. 34; and *Jane's Defence Weekly*, 5 Feb. 1994, p. 15. The operations of the UN are funded by its member states according to a 'scale of assessment' which for the richest states is proportional to their gross national product (GNP), but which for the poorer is heavily discounted for their paucity of GNP and high external debt. Peacekeeping contributions are assessed separately for each new mission, the contribution of the poorer states being even more heavily discounted in such assessments. See Durch (note 36), p. 45.

[90] Boutros-Ghali (note 20), pp. 34–35.

[91] *Time*, 4 Oct. 1993, p. 45.

[92] See note 91.

[93] *Wall Street Journal Europe*, 29 Dec. 1993, p. 1. By Feb. 1994 all but Brazil, Russia, Ukraine and the USA of the 15 major contributors had paid their past assessed contributions (both regular and for peacekeeping) in full. See United Nations, 'Status of Contributions to the Regular Budget and Peace-Keeping Operations as at 28 February 1994', UN Information Centre for the Nordic Countries, Copenhagen, 28 Feb. 1994.

[94] United Nations (note 93).

[95] Boutros-Ghali (note 20), p. 34.

[96] Note 40, p. 44.

the escalating cost of existing missions, all new peace operations established in 1993 were given relatively small budgets of $100 million or less.[97]

In August 1993, responding to charges of financial irregularities, waste and laxness which the United States in particular has used as a reason for not paying its dues, Boutros-Ghali established the position of Assistant Secretary-General for Inspections and Investigations to head an independent office incorporating previously separate UN units dealing with audit, management advisory services, evaluation and monitoring.[98] An Integrated Management Information System (IMIS) was also established to enhance monitoring and audit capabilities through electronic audit trails.[99] It is not clear what effect these new measures will have, as the main problem remains the unpaid dues of member states and the under-funded nature of many of the UN's efforts.

In February a report entitled *Financing an Effective United Nations*, commissioned by the UN and prepared by an international advisory group of experts co-chaired by Shijuro Ogata and Paul Volcker, was published by the Ford Foundation.[100] It recommended reforms to UN financing, none of which was implemented in 1993. These included the payment of assessed dues in four instalments rather than one lump sum, the imposition of interest charges on late payments and charging states with above-average per capita gross national product (GNP), except for Security Council permanent members, at the same rate for peacekeeping as for their contributions to the regular UN budget.

Ending dysfunctional missions

Stimulated by Security Council concern, the year saw growing debate over how the UN should end those missions of long duration which, although effective in stemming or ending violence, have contributed over time to stultification of the peace process. The outstanding examples of such missions were to be found in Cyprus, Kashmir and the Middle East. In the case of Cyprus, national contributions to UNFICYP, established in 1974, have been whittled down and in some cases completely withdrawn because of frustration over the 20-year political stalemate between the Greek Cypriot and Turkish Cypriot communities. To its credit the UN has actively sought a settlement for years, its efforts in 1993 including the appointment of former Canadian Foreign Minister Joe Clark as the Secretary-General's Special Representative and the initiation of confidence-building measures between the two communities.[101]

Meanwhile the various long-standing UN operations in the Middle East were likely to be affected by the peace process that gained momentum in 1993.[102] In particular there was speculation that the UN Disengagement

[97] *Jane's Defence Weekly*, 5 Feb. 1994, p. 16.

[98] Boutros-Ghali (note 20), p. 25. Former UN auditor, Mohammed Aly Niazi, an Egyptian, was appointed to the position; see also note 91, p. 45.

[99] Boutros-Ghali (note 20), p. 25.

[100] Ogata and Volcker (note 66).

[101] Boutros-Ghali (note 20), pp. 112–14.

[102] See chapter 3 in this volume.

Observer Force (UNDOF) on the Golan Heights between Israel and Syria might be replaced by a US buffer force in the event of a Syria–Israel peace agreement.[103] The UN Truce Supervision Organization (UNTSO), largely overtaken by previous wars, cease-fires and peacekeeping operations, continued to suffer from 'political benign neglect', in part because it remained a training ground for peacekeepers used in more important UN missions.[104]

Another old UN mission, the UN Military Observer Group in India and Pakistan (UNMOGIP), has been present along the Line of Control in contested Kashmir since 1949.[105] In 1993 India continued both to provide facilities for UNMOGIP and to dispute its legal basis on the grounds that the original 1949 cease-fire line had been obliterated by subsequent India–Pakistan wars. It is not clear how long the Security Council will continue to support this $7 million per year operation, although UNMOGIP's supporters claim that it signals continued UN interest in Kashmir and a rejection of India's claim that the issue is purely its own internal affair.[106]

Peacekeeping and human rights

The UN attracted unprecedented criticism in 1993 over its human rights record in relation to peacekeeping, both in allegedly failing to promote and enforce human rights as part of its comprehensive peacekeeping missions and, more disturbing, failing to comply with such standards in its own activities. Amnesty International accused the UN of a 'disastrous' neglect of human rights in six African countries where peacekeeping missions were under way—Angola, Liberia, Mozambique, Rwanda, Somalia and Western Sahara. It deplored the killing of Somali civilians during UN military operations and the detention of Somalis without charge or trial or access to lawyers or relatives. Amnesty noted that 'the UN has so far failed to build essential measures for human rights protection and promotion consistently into its peacekeeping activities'.[107] According to Human Rights Watch: 'while severe human rights abuses often play a critical part in fuelling armed conflict and aggravating humanitarian crises, they have been given a low priority by the officials who oversee UN field operations. This lost agenda handicaps the UN in its new and ambitious undertakings, as it sells short one of the central ideals on which the UN was founded.'[108]

While some of the reports of UN failings in the human rights area may have been exaggerated or misreported, human rights organizations have done the international community a service by alerting the UN to the need to pay greater attention to the issue as it vastly expands its activities in the field.

---

[103] *The Independent*, 13 Jan. 1994, p. 15.

[104] Ghali, M., 'United Nations Truce Supervision Organization', ed. Durch (note 36), p. 100.

[105] United Nations, Fact Sheet on UNMOGIP, PS/DPI/9/Rev. 2, Sep. 1992.

[106] See Birgisson, K. Th., 'United Nations Military Observer Group in India and Pakistan', ed. Durch (note 36), p. 238.

[107] Amnesty International, 'Peace-keeping and Human Rights' (summary), London, Jan. 1994, p. 1 .

[108] Human Rights Watch, *The Lost Agenda: Human Rights and UN Field Operations* (Human Rights Watch: New York, 1993), p. 1.

National efforts and difficulties

More peacekeepers served in UN operations in 1993 than in any previous year. The number of UN member states participating was also unprecedented. Among them were the forces of all five permanent members of the UN Security Council—a development that has only been possible since the end of the cold war. There were also a number of countries participating for the first time in peacekeeping operations in 1993, including the Republic of Korea, Romania, Saudi Arabia, Turkey, Uganda and the United Arab Emirates.

The performance of national contingents came under unprecedented scrutiny during 1993. While most served with dedication and enthusiasm, there were disturbing allegations about the behaviour of, among others, Bulgarians and Tunisians in Cambodia, Ukrainians and Kenyans in the former Yugoslavia and Italians in Mozambique.[109] A UN investigation of UNPROFOR contingents revealed evidence of black marketeering and theft by some troops, while clearing others of allegations that they had run brothels.[110] A combination of poor training and equipment, low pay, lax disciplinary structures and the high-stress environment were undoubtedly contributing factors to the poor performance of some peacekeeping contingents.

On the positive side, by the end of 1993 over 20 UN member states had introduced peacekeeping training into their military training programmes, some of which are open to participants from other states.[111] The Nordic countries (Denmark, Finland, Norway and Sweden) remained the most advanced, each training a particular component of their joint Nordic peacekeeping contingents as well as their own infantry battalions and foreign peacekeepers.[112] In 1993 Australia established a Peacekeeping Centre which will train both Australian and New Zealand peacekeepers.[113] Several US military academies and war colleges incorporated peacekeeping components into their training courses. The USA and Russia concluded a bilateral agreement committing them to co-operate in peacekeeping exercises.[114] Ichiro Ozawa, the Diet's most influential member, proposed the establishment of a standing Japanese UN peacekeeping unit,[115] while think-tanks closely associated with the Association of South-East Asian Nations (ASEAN) governments floated the idea of an ASEAN peacekeeping centre with its own earmarked troops.[116]

---

[109] *International Herald Tribune*, 26–27 Feb. 1994.

[110] *The Independent*, 24 Jan. 1994, p. 8.

[111] *Jane's Defence Weekly*, 5 Feb. 1994, p. 13.

[112] The Nordic countries (Denmark, Finland, Norway and Sweden, but not Iceland) usually contribute peacekeepers as part of an integrated Nordic battalion (Nordbatt). Denmark trains Nordbatt military police, Finland trains observers, Norway provides logistics and transport training, and Sweden trains staff officers. See Durch (note 36), p. 71. In 1969 Finland established the world's first comprehensive UN training facility at Niinisalo to prepare Nordic and other peacekeepers, often under simulated conditions. See Greenberg, K. E., 'The essential art of empathy', *Soldiers for Peace*, Supplement to *MHQ: Quarterly Journal of Military History*, vol. 5, no.1 (autumn 1992), p. 40.

[113] Fetherston, B., 'Australian defence policy: peacekeeping', *Pacific Research*, Aug. 1993, p. 37.

[114] *Jane's Defence Weekly*, 19 June 1993, p. 19.

[115] Ozawa, I., *Blueprints for Building a New Japan* (Kodansha: Tokyo, 1993), cited in note 91, p. 78.

[116] *The Age* (Melbourne), 17 Jan. 1994, p. 7.

There was, however, growing evidence of 'peacekeeping fatigue' among states contributing to UN operations. As Boutros-Ghali reported to the General Assembly in September: 'In June 1992, I was able to report that Member States were keen to participate in peace-keeping operations and that military observers and infantry were invariably available. This is no longer generally the case. Difficulties which were previously encountered only when specialized units were sought now arise also in the case of infantry and military as well as police observers.'[117] By the end of the year the Kuwait–Iraq mission had been waiting six months for 4000 more peacekeepers, while Bosnia and Herzegovina had been waiting for 8000 more since May 1992.[118] An appeal from Burundi for assistance after an outbreak of tribal massacres elicited stony silence from the Security Council.[119]

Many states, especially the United States and other Western countries, evinced a greater cautiousness about contributing to peacekeeping operations in part because of frustration with the performance of the UN in establishing and running such operations, especially in Somalia and former Yugoslavia.

Some governments were responding to public sentiment. Russian opinion polls revealed that 85 per cent of respondents opposed Russian involvement in peacekeeping in the former Yugoslavia and Somalia.[120] In the UK, while 48 per cent supported the British presence in Bosnia and Herzegovina under the existing mandate, only 34 per cent supported sending British troops to Somalia.[121] In Canada polls indicated that 57 per cent of respondents favoured withdrawal of Canadian peacekeepers from the former Yugoslavia.[122]

Others with relatively small military forces became concerned that their normal defence activities were beginning to suffer. Australia withdrew its United Task Force (UNITAF) contingent from Somalia rather than contributing it to UNOSOM II, in part because of its heavy peacekeeping commitments elsewhere, notably Cambodia and Western Sahara. Developed states with larger armed forces were being asked to contribute more troops and equipment to peacekeeping operations at a time when budget cut-backs resulting from the end of the cold war were leading to a downsizing of their military capabilities. The UK and Canada found themselves in this situation. On the other hand, some military establishments, seeing peacekeeping as the wave of the future, began using such operations to push for increased budgetary allocations.

Some developing countries, such as Fiji and Tunisia, expressed reluctance to continue contributing to peacekeeping unless they received large back payments owed to them by the UN. Others could not afford to provide contingents without assistance from other countries with equipment and transport.

---

[117] Boutros-Ghali (note 20), p. 103.

[118] *Wall Street Journal Europe*, 29 Dec. 1993, p. 1.

[119] *Wall Street Journal Europe*, 29 Dec. 1993, p. 5.

[120] Russia International Affairs, Foreign Broadcast Information Service, *Daily Report–Central Eurasia (FBIS-SOV)*, FBIS-SOV-93-185, 27 Sep. 1993, p. 16.

[121] Caines, R. (ed.), *Key Note Market Review: Industry Trends and Forecasts* (Key Note for UK Defence Industry: Middlesex, 1993), pp. 137–38.

[122] *The Guardian*, 17 Feb. 1994, p. 5.

Many contributing states became concerned at the possibility of politically unsustainable fatalities and other casualties among peacekeeping forces. The death toll among peacekeepers in 1993 was the highest in UN history, Somalia being the greatest contributor.[123] National concern over peacekeeping casualties was not necessarily a function of numbers, since while Pakistan sustained the greatest losses, those incurred by US and Italian forces caused the greatest domestic political difficulties for their respective governments. The Spanish public reportedly accepted with equanimity the high death toll among Spanish soldiers serving in former Yugoslavia.[124] In Cambodia the loss of a single Japanese volunteer almost precipitated a Japanese withdrawal, such was the pressure of public opinion. Japan subsequently turned down a request to provide troops for the preventive deployment force in Macedonia.[125] As Canadian General Maurice Baril, the DPKO's chief military adviser, put it: 'the message is that countries won't send their sons and daughters to die unless a vital national interest is at stake. And it's hard to show that humanitarian relief is a vital national interest.'[126]

Despite bitter constitutional wrangles and court proceedings in 1993 Germany contributed troops to a peacekeeping mission for the first time in its history (this was also its first deployment of troops abroad since World War II). This began inauspiciously, when the Indian troops the Germans were meant to support in Somalia failed to arrive, and ended in precipitate withdrawal following the disastrous events in Mogadishu. Although lightly armed and under instructions not to engage in combat, German soldiers killed a Somali intruder in January 1994—the first casualty of German military action since World War II, prompting calls at home for an immediate withdrawal.[127] While the German peacekeepers did not themselves suffer casualties and they accomplished an impressive range of civic action tasks around their base town of Belet Uen, they left Somalia frustrated at the inconclusiveness of the UNOSOM II mission.[128]

Even Canada, the only country to have participated in all UN peacekeeping missions, and with a national commitment to peacekeeping outstripping all but the Nordic states, felt the pinch. It withdrew its contingent from UNFICYP in Cyprus in frustration at the lack of progress in settling the dispute which gave rise to the peacekeeping operation in the first place. (It was replaced by Argentinian troops, operating alongside the British for the first time since the 1982 Falklands/Malvinas War, a fine demonstration of one of the collateral benefits of peacekeeping).[129] Towards the end of 1993 debate raged over whether Canadian troops should be withdrawn from Bosnia and Herzegovina,

---

[123] Boutros-Ghali (note 20), p. 178.

[124] *The Guardian*, 17 Feb. 1994, p. 5.

[125] *The Independent*, 26 Jan. 1994, p. 11.

[126] *Wall Street Journal Europe*, 29 Dec. 1993, p. 5.

[127] *The Independent*, 22 Jan. 1994, p. 11.

[128] Richburg, K. B., 'Satisfaction as Bonn's Somalia role ends', *International Herald Tribune*, 10 Mar. 1994, pp. 1 and 6.

[129] A counter example is the refusal of Indian and Pakistani contingents in UNOSOM II to serve in the same geographical locations.

especially after drunk Bosnian Serb fighters terrorized 11 Canadian peace-keepers.[130]

The role of the United States

While US involvement in peacekeeping operations is not absolutely essential—the operation in Cambodia for instance succeeded without a major US contribution on the ground—US support and involvement can nevertheless be fundamental to success when a rapid response is required, as UNITAF in Somalia demonstrated. Where peace enforcement is mandated, US involvement is probably essential.

In 1993 the USA made a record financial, material and personnel contribution to UN peacekeeping operations, with 300 troops in Macedonia, more than 4000 in UNOSOM II in Somalia, and numerous other contributions ranging from provision of observers and equipment to airlift[131] and communications. As in Namibia, the USA often also assisted in unheralded ways, particularly in emergency situations, to ensure the success of peacekeeping operations.[132]

The Clinton Administration was initially enthusiastic about 'assertive' or 'muscular' multilateralism, whether in the form of peacekeeping or peace enforcement, even to the extent of envisaging placing US troops under UN command. During his election campaign Clinton had supported the establishment of a small, permanent UN rapid deployment force.[133] However, after the traumatic events in Mogadishu in 1993, including the deaths of several US soldiers, the Administration, under pressure from public opinion and Congress, retreated from its previous position. It not only announced a withdrawal from Somalia, but resiled from a previous offer to contribute half of a UN force to supervise a peace settlement in Bosnia and Herzegovina.

By the end of 1993 the Administration had toughened its general criteria for US involvement in multilateral peacekeeping and peace enforcement, proposing a three-tiered approach.[134] US approval of a UN mission and contribution to its funding would depend on there being a genuine threat to international security, a major humanitarian disaster requiring urgent action, a sudden threat to an 'established democracy' or a gross violation of human rights. The USA would also ask whether there was a shared international interest in proceeding with such a mission, whether there was an agreed cease-fire in cases of monitoring missions, whether estimated force requirements were reliable and if there existed a clear plan for ending the operation.

US involvement on the ground in a UN mission would entail additional considerations: including US national interests, domestic political support, a clearly defined end-point and the likelihood that the mission would not suc-

---

[130] *The Guardian*, 17 Feb. 1994, p. 5.

[131] Until recently the USA did not charge the UN for the airlift services it provided.

[132] In the case of Namibia the USA helped convince SWAPO guerrillas to return to their bases in Angola and not disrupt the election. See Durch (note 36), pp. 23–24.

[133] *International Herald Tribune*, 23 Sep. 1993, pp. 1 and 6, and 20–21 Nov. 1993, p. 3. As of late Feb. 1994 the draft Presidential Decision Directive had not yet received formal presidential approval.

[134] *International Herald Tribune*, 20–21 Nov. 1993, p. 3, and 31 Jan. 1994, p. 3.

ceed without US help. For the USA to agree to participate in a mission involving substantial use of force, it would need to identify a vital national or allied interest and a clear commitment to win, among other factors.

Under the new policy the USA would be ready to place its forces under the day-to-day operational control of foreign commanders in a UN mission on a case-by-case basis, but it would never surrender ultimate command authority over the discipline and administration of US forces.[135] US Ambassador to the UN, Madelaine Albright, told the Senate Foreign Relations Committee in October that US contributions to future UN peacekeeping operations would most likely take the form of 'logistics, intelligence, public affairs, and communications, rather than combat'.[136]

Critics argued that the new criteria were deliberately designed to rule out US participation in any but the most innocuous of UN peace operations and that as the remaining superpower the USA had a special responsibility to the international community to set an example and exert leadership in multilateral endeavours. Others wondered about the morality of letting other countries' forces undertake the riskiest peacekeeping tasks, while the USA took the safer supportive roles. Pakistan's Foreign Minister bluntly asked: 'Are Pakistani personnel's lives cheaper than those that came from the West?'[137] In response, Administration spokespersons were at pains to stress that the new policy would establish guidelines rather than strict criteria. But they also admonished those who expected the USA to become the world's 'policeman'.[138] Whatever the practical import of the new policy the USA will in future pay closer attention to whether its national interests are served by support for and participation in UN peacekeeping or peace-enforcement operations.

Much will depend on Congress. While congressional support for US involvement in peacekeeping and peace enforcement became progressively less steady as 1993 wore on, Congress failed to pass resolutions that would have limited the President's authority to send US troops on peacekeeping missions to Somalia, Bosnia and Herzegovina, and Haiti and which would have mandated that US peacekeeping troops always remain under US command.[139]

Congressional opposition to UN funding was more effective. In October it voted only $401.6 million for the US contribution to all peacekeeping operations for fiscal year 1993–94, compared with the assessed contribution of around $1.23 billion.[140] It also cancelled the 1994 instalment of a five-year Bush Administration plan to pay off US accumulated debts by 1995. Finally, Congress cut 10 per cent from the US contribution to the UN regular budget

---

[135] *International Herald Tribune*, 20–21 Nov. 1993, p. 3.

[136] *Atlantic News*, no. 2564 (22 Oct. 1993), p. 4.

[137] *International Herald Tribune*, 14 Mar. 1993, p. 2.

[138] For example, in an address by Ms Sarah Sewall, Deputy Assistant Secretary of Defense for Peacekeeping and Peace Enforcement Policy, to the US Naval War College workshop on 'Beyond Traditional Peacekeeping', Newport, R.I., 23 Feb. 1994.

[139] *Financial Times*, 22 Nov. 1993, p. 8.

[140] *International Herald Tribune*, 23–24 Oct. 1993, p. 3; *Congressional Quarterly*, vol. 51, no. 42 (23 Oct. 1993), p. 2889.

until the Secretary-General appointed an inspector-general to fight waste and corruption.

These decisions will lead to rapidly accumulating US debts to the UN just when the Administration was beginning to reduce them. By October 1993 the USA had paid all its regular budget arrears except for $284.5 million of its 1993 assessment. Its outstanding debt for peacekeeping stood at just $166.6 million. Future US indebtedness may be somewhat eased if the Administration (as mandated by Congress) obtains a cut in the US share of peacekeeping costs from 31.7 per cent to 25 per cent.[141]

V. UN peace enforcement

The two principal means which the UN Charter envisages the UN using to 'enforce' peace are sanctions and the threat or use of military force.[142] Both were used in 1993, sometimes in combination. 'Enforce' is used here in the sense of coercing a state or sub-state group to do something it would otherwise not wish to do or to refrain from doing something it does wish to do. The difference between an enforcement activity and a non-enforcement activity turns on the question of consent. If the consent of all the parties involved is not forthcoming then the action taken is necessarily an enforcement activity.

The clearest case of peace enforcement through military means is its use to redress a violation of a member state's sovereignty, the most recent example being the UN's authorization of the use of force against Iraq in order to liberate Kuwait. In this, as in other cases of peace enforcement, it is not 'peace' that is being enforced so much as the will of the international community or more narrowly that of the UN Security Council. Ironically to some, the level of violence might actually increase during a peace-enforcement operation. At the other end of the spectrum, the mere threat of violence, or even of sanctions, may be sufficient to achieve the enforcement goal.

Sanctions

Sanctions may be imposed either by the Security Council, in which case they can be either mandatory or voluntary for UN member states, or by the General Assembly, which can only recommend that UN members impose sanctions.

Throughout 1993 mandatory Security Council sanctions of some description imposed in previous years remained in place against Bosnia and Herzegovina, Croatia, Iraq, Liberia,[143] Libya, Macedonia, Somalia, South Africa and the Federal Republic of Yugoslavia. With the exception of Iraq, the former Yugoslavia and Libya these sanctions were in the form of arms and/or

---

[141] *Financial Times*, 22 Nov. 1993, p. 8.
[142] Sanctions are described in Article 41 of the Charter as 'measures not involving the use of armed force'. They may include 'complete or partial interruption of economic relations and of rail, sea, air, postal, telegraphic, radio and other means of communication and the severance of diplomatic relations'.
[143] Boutros-Ghali (note 20), p. 127.

petroleum embargoes.[144] While a non-compulsory 'moratorium' on petroleum products (deliberately not described as a form of 'sanctions' to avoid a Chinese veto) was imposed on Cambodia's Khmer Rouge in November 1992 because of its non-compliance with the Paris Peace Accords,[145] this appears to have lapsed after the UN peacekeeping mission, UNTAC, left the country in November 1993.

During 1993 sanctions were also imposed on Haiti and, for the first time ever, against a warring faction, Angola's UNITA.[146] An arms and petroleum products embargo was placed on Haiti and the overseas economic assets of the de facto authorities frozen,[147] while a petroleum and arms embargo was placed on UNITA.[148]

General Assembly sanctions against South Africa were dropped in October 1993 in recognition of its moves to end apartheid.[149] No other states were the subject of General Assembly sanctions.

In 1993, as sanctions became the Security Council's 'enforcement measure of choice' and as their limitations became more apparent, criticism increased.[150] One criticism which gained greater plausibility from the cases of Iraq, former Yugoslavia and Haiti, was that sanctions have unintended consequences, hurting not just the governments whose policies they are directed at, but innocent people, particularly the most vulnerable sectors of society— women, children, the sick, the poor and the elderly.[151] This argument was cynically used by some governments in 1993 to pressure the UN to lift sanctions. Iraq, which continued to refuse a UN offer to sell Iraqi oil to raise funds for social welfare purposes, was particularly vocal in this regard.[152] Neighbouring 'front-line' states also suffer the unintended consequences of sanctions, as Bulgaria, Romania and other neighbours of former Yugoslavia bitterly complained. A second criticism of sanctions is that they are an easy, largely cost-free option for the Security Council to take when it is unable or unwilling to adopt more dramatic measures, such as military action. A final argument is that they simply do not work, or at least not quickly enough. It was almost impossible to make them watertight, as the case of former Yugoslavia illustrated. Advocates of sanctions responded that the pain inflicted by sanctions did not have to be overwhelming, simply persuasive. There were cases, moreover, such as sporting sanctions against South Africa imposed

---

[144] See Evans (note 12) for details.

[145] UN Security Council Resolution 792, 30 Nov. 1992.

[146] *UN Chronicle*, vol. 30, no. 4 (Dec. 1993), p. 58.

[147] Boutros-Ghali (note 20), p. 118; Evans (note 12); and Werleigh, C. A., 'Haiti and the halfhearted', *Bulletin of the Atomic Scientists*, Nov. 1993, p. 20. The embargoes were suspended on 27 Aug. but reimposed when the Haitian settlement fell apart.

[148] Crocker, C. A., 'Yes, Angola's outrageous spectacle can be stopped', *International Herald Tribune*, 14 Oct. 1994, p. 4.

[149] UN Resolution A/RES/48/1, 12 Oct., 1993.

[150] See Special Issue, 'Sanctions: do they work?', *Bulletin of the Atomic Scientists*, vol. 49, no. 9 (Nov. 1993); and General Accounting Office, *'Economic Sanctions: Effectiveness as Tools of Foreign Policy'*, GAO report GAO/NSIAD-92-106 (GAO: Washington, DC, 1992).

[151] For details of the Haiti case see Booth, C., 'The bad embargo joke', *Time*, 21 Mar. 1994, p. 34.

[152] *The Economist*, 19 Feb. 1994, p. 48.

through the Gleneagles Agreement, where sanctions were arguably quite effective.[153]

There appeared, however, to be an emerging consensus in 1993 that sanctions should be more carefully targeted and used less indiscriminately than in the past if the UN is to avoid being seen as violating its own humanitarian precepts.[154] While Boutros-Ghali recommended in *An Agenda for Peace* that a system be established to assist states confronted with the unintended consequences of sanctions, little had been done by the end of 1993.[155]

Use of military force

In 1993 the UN itself used military force in a peace-enforcement operation (in contrast to simply authorizing it, as in the case of Operation Desert Storm against Iraq) for the first time since its Congo mission in the early 1960s. As in the Congo, this took place in the context of a traditional peacekeeping operation, UNOSOM II in Somalia, which was expanded beyond its original goals—not as a pure peace-enforcement operation. Events during the year in Somalia, Yugoslavia and Cambodia reinforced the impression that, as a US Institute for Peace report noted, 'The traditional distinction between peacekeeping and peace enforcement for new, largely internal conflicts is eroding.'[156]

In Somalia, in a civil war situation, when UNOSOM I failed to protect the delivery and distribution of humanitarian aid, both UNITAF (a non-UN force) and UNOSOM II were authorized to use force to carry out such a mission. The latter was also authorized to use force to disarm the Somali factions. Hence these peacekeeping missions contained both extended 'second-generation' characteristics and enforcement elements. In contrast, in Cambodia UNTAC was not authorized to use military force except in self-defence and to protect the electoral process. There were however elements of enforced peacemaking invested in the head of UNTAC, notably the power to override the decisions of the Supreme National Council and to enforce human rights standards, including the arrest of violators.

In former Yugoslavia the peace-enforcement elements in UNPROFOR's evolving mandate in 1993 included the right to use military means to enforce the no-fly zone over Bosnia and Herzegovina, declared by the Security Council in October 1992, and to protect humanitarian relief convoys, the UN Protected Areas (UNPAs) in Croatia and the so-called 'safe areas' around several Bosnian cities and towns. In practice, however, UNPROFOR, throughout 1992 and 1993, relied exclusively on the threat of force, eschewing its use

---

[153] Evans (note 12), p. 136.
[154] For a fuller discussion of the effectiveness of arms embargoes, see chapter 13 in this volume.
[155] Boutros-Ghali (note 4), para. 41.
[156] Wurmser, D. and Dyke, N. B., 'The professionalization of peacekeeping', A Study Group Report (US Institute of Peace: Washington, DC, Aug. 1993), p. ix.

except in self-defence in very localized situations—and even then extremely selectively.[157]

It is in civil war situations that the question of the use of force by peace-keepers arises most urgently but in which the use of force is so problematic. In such conflicts:

1. Peacekeeping forces are under greater physical risk because of the lack of centralized government authority.

2. The impartiality and international identity of a peacekeeper is not universally recognized.

3. 'Interposition' is often impossible because of constant cease-fire violations, the lack of front lines and the denial of right of freedom of manœuvre for peacekeepers.

4. The peacekeeping operation is unable to fulfil its fundamental objectives relating to military arrangements and security for the population.[158]

Major General Indar Jit Rikhye, former commander of the UN Emergency Force (UNEF I) in the Sinai and military adviser to past UN secretaries-general, advocates broadening peacekeeping mandates and capabilities to enable peacekeeping forces to better protect themselves.[159] This does not mean, he says, that peacekeeping should evolve into enforcement actions, but rather that 'self-defence' be redefined to include effective defence of the mission. It may also be possible to use limited force when all significant parties agree on the cease-fire or settlement but unauthorized groups such as renegade units or bandits create a security problem. For instance in Bosnia and Herzegovina, British Coldstream Guards, reportedly with the tacit approval of the local Croat commander, attacked 'freelance' Croat fighters after they fired shots at a UN convoy.[160] Any enforcement measures beyond that, such as enforced disarmament of all or some of the parties to a conflict, as in Somalia, transforms a peacekeeping mission into a peace-enforcement one, for which an appropriate mandate, rules of engagement and much more capable forces are required. In essence the United Nations force then becomes a party to the conflict and must act as if it were at war. To fail to do so is to risk the lives of its peacekeepers, jeopardize the success of the mission and damage the credibility of the UN. While consent of the parties may be overlooked at a tactical level, at the strategic level its establishment or re-establishment is essential to successful peacekeeping.

Boutros-Ghali's proposal for establishment of 'peace-enforcement units' and experience in several missions during the year touched off a debate in

---

[157] Reportedly the first occasion on which UNPROFOR troops used force in self-defence was in Nov. 1992, when a group of British soldiers on a reconnaissance mission in central Bosnia and Herzegovina returned fire after they drove into a gun battle near Tuzla; *Canberra Times*, 9 Nov. 1992. In Mar. 1994 NATO used military force for the first time in its 45-year history when US aircraft enforcing the no-fly zone shot down three Bosnian Serb aircraft engaged in bombing raids on Muslim areas in Bosnia and Herzegovina; *Time*, 14 Mar. 1994, pp. 26–27.

[158] Berdal (note 26), p. 31.

[159] Rikye, I. J. (Maj. Gen.), 'Lessons of experience', *Soldiers for Peace*, supplement to *MHQ: Quarterly Journal of Military History*, vol. 5, no. 1 (autumn 1992), p. 60.

[160] Bellamy, C., 'British troops get tough with Croat attackers', *The Independent*, 25 Feb. 1994, p. 12.

1993 about force options for the United Nations itself.[161] Former UN Under Secretary-General Sir Brian Urquhart reversed his previous long-standing position by advocating, in an article in the *New York Review of Books*, a 'highly trained international volunteer force, willing, if necessary, to fight hard to break the cycle of violence at an early stage in low-level but dangerous conflicts, especially ones involving irregular militias and groups'.[162] In subsequent editions of the *Review* [163] and elsewhere[164] critics pointed to the costs and political difficulties associated with such an idea and the danger that it would lead to escalation requiring deployment of a much larger force. At least one observer suggested using the Ghurkas as a UN force.[165] Consensus appeared to coalesce around the less risky option—which the UN began implementing—of governments, in a comprehensive, planned fashion, earmarking standby military capabilities of all types for rapid assignment to the UN when needed.

VI. The role of regional organizations

Like the UN, regional organizations were often restrained by the cold war from resolving regional conflicts. With the breakdown of bipolarity, some of these organizations have begun examining afresh the political, practical and financial benefits of becoming directly involved in conflict prevention, management and resolution in their regions, especially as the UN has struggled to handle all contingencies.

Conflict prevention and resolution

In *An Agenda for Peace* Boutros-Ghali supported a greater role for regional organizations in preventing and resolving regional conflicts, partly on the assumption that regional states know their region best, but also as a form of burden-sharing. In 1993 the UN increasingly involved regional organizations in the negotiation of peace settlements, In Somalia it co-operated with the OAU, the League of Arab States and the Organization of the Islamic Conference in attempting to draw the Somali factions into a peace settlement. The UN and the Organization of American States (OAS) jointly appointed Dante Caputo as Special Envoy for Haiti and both mandated the International Civilian Mission in Haiti which they attempted to deploy in March 1993. Negotia-

---

[161] The Trilateral Commission, an independent, non-governmental body formed in 1973 by citizens of Europe, Japan and North America to foster co-operation between the three regions, also supported the idea of a peace enforcement force. See Trilateral Commission, *Keeping the Peace in the Post-Cold War Era: Strengthening Multilateral Peacekeeping* (Trilateral Commission: New York, Mar. 1993).

[162] Urquhart, B., 'For a UN volunteer military force', *New York Review of Books*, 10 June 1993, p. 3.

[163] See 'A UN volunteer military force—four views', *New York Review of Books*, 24 June 1993, pp. 58–60; and 'A UN volunteer force—the prospects', *New York Review of Books*, 15 July 1993, pp. 52–56.

[164] See, e.g., Rosenfeld, S. S., 'For the UN, a volunteer peace force', *International Herald Tribune*, 12 July 1993, p. 8.

[165] Altbach, P. G., 'Ghurkas as the UN peace-keepers', *Times of India*, 26 Nov. 1993, p. 12.

tions on a Bosnian peace settlement were conducted jointly by co-chair-persons Thorvald Stoltenberg (successor to Cyrus Vance) and Lord Owen, representing the UN and EU respectively.

The Conference on Security and Co-operation in Europe and the European Union

Outside the UN system the most impressive conflict-prevention and resolution machinery, at least on paper, remained that of the CSCE. It has a Conflict Prevention Centre in Vienna, a Valletta Mechanism for Peaceful Settlement of Disputes, an Emergency Mechanism for calling CSCE meetings during crises, an Office for Democratic Institutions and Human Rights in Warsaw and a High Commissioner for National Minorities. It will soon also have an Arbitration Court in Geneva. Most of these remained grossly under-utilized in 1993.

From 1992 the CSCE mounted an impressive series of rapporteur, fact-finding and good offices missions to the new states that emerged from the collapse of the USSR. These included so-called Long-Term Missions to Estonia, Georgia, Latvia, Moldova and Tajikistan.[166] Meanwhile the CSCE's High Commissioner for National Minorities proved to be a quiet success in helping prevent the outbreak or escalation of communal conflict involving minorities, such as Russian-speakers in the Baltic states.[167]

The CSCE's modest successes in these areas were overshadowed in 1993 by its continuing failure in the former Yugoslavia, despite having been engaged in Balkan politics from at least 1989. In September 1992, the CSCE dispatched observer missions to the region—its so-called Missions of Long Duration to Kosovo, Sanjak and Vojvodina—but these were withdrawn in July 1993 when the Federal Republic of Yugoslavia refused to renew the agreement permitting them to stay.

The CSCE Spillover Mission to Skopje (Macedonia) had been the first international conflict prevention presence in that country. The CSCE also dispatched Sanctions Assistance Missions to Albania, Bulgaria, Croatia, Hungary, Macedonia, Romania and Ukraine. These were neither conflict-prevention nor conflict-resolution efforts but measures in support of a form of peace enforcement—sanctions—against Serbia and Montenegro. Moreover, none of these initiatives could disguise the CSCE's abject failure to prevent or significantly contribute to resolving the Yugoslav imbroglio.

The European Union, for its part, deployed a 300-person Monitoring Mission in 1992 to oversee the implementation of cease-fire agreements signed by

---

[166] Rapporteur missions have been dispatched to Albania; Armenia and Azerbaijan; Ukraine, Moldova and Belarus; Turkmenistan, Uzbekistan and Tajikistan; Kazakhstan and Kyrgyzstan; Georgia; and Bosnia and Herzegovina. Fact-finding missions have been sent to Kosovo, the region of the Georgia–Ossetia conflict, and Georgia. Various other short-term missions have been dispatched to Kosovo, Vojvodina and Sanjak; Nagorno-Karabakh; Macedonia; Yugoslavia and Croatia; Azerbaijan and Armenia; Moldova; Romania; Ukraine; Russia; Estonia; and Latvia. List compiled from informal CSCE Secretariat indexes, CSCE documents and *Survey of CSCE Long-Term Missions and Sanctions Assistance Missions,* CSCE Conflict Prevention Centre, Vienna, 20 Dec. 1993.

[167] Huber, K. J., 'The CSCE and ethnic conflict in the East', Radio Free Europe/Radio Liberty, *RFE/RL Research Report,* vol. 2, no. 31 (July 1993), p. 32.

Serbia with Slovenia and Croatia. It played a useful reporting and conflict-dampening role.[168] However, although it is not a security organization, the EU, being more coherent and better-resourced than the CSCE, also bore responsibility for Europe's failure to prevent the Yugoslav conflict.[169]

The Organization of African Unity

One of the few regional organizations outside Europe with any substantial record in peace operations, the OAU has been involved in observer missions in over 20 of its member states. These have been mostly for election-monitoring purposes, some of them under UN auspices.

In 1993 the OAU was involved with the UN in facilitating peace negotiations on Liberia, Rwanda and Somalia.[170] Its biggest success in 1993 was in securing a peace agreement between the Uganda-based Rwandan Patriotic Front and the Rwandan Government, brokered with Tanzanian assistance and signed at Arusha on 4 August.[171] An OAU Neutral Military Observer Group—with technical and financial assistance from the UN, Belgium, France, Germany and the United States—was already in place to monitor a 1992 cease-fire agreement.[172] In June 1993 the UN established the UN Observer Mission Uganda/Rwanda (UNOMUR) to monitor the Uganda/Rwanda border to verify that no infiltration of military assistance was occurring.[173] In October the Security Council integrated UNOMUR into a new, expanded UN Mission for Rwanda (UNAMIR), to help implement the Arusha Peace Agreement.[174]

In an attempt to become more systematic and professional, and prompted by the realization that conflict prevention is cheaper and, if done by Africans, politically less fraught than international intervention as in Somalia, the OAU in 1993 established an embryonic Conflict Prevention, Management and Resolution Mechanism in Addis Ababa.[175] The mechanism comprises a secretariat as its working arm and a central organ with representatives of all OAU

---

[168] Sjajkowski, B., 'European Community Monitoring Mission', *Encyclopedia of Conflicts, Disputes and Flashpoints in Eastern Europe, Russia and the Successor States* (Longman: Harlow, 1993), p. 112.

[169] Some argue that, worse than this, the then EC helped ignite the conflict by hastening the dissolution of Yugoslavia through premature recognition of the independence of its components.

[170] In Jan. 1994 the warring army factions in Lesotho heeded an OAU call for a cease-fire and negotiations, while the government called for deployment of an African peacekeeping force in the country. *The Guardian*, 26 Jan. 1994, p. 6.

[171] Ocaya-Lakidi, D., 'Regional conflicts, regional coalitions and security cooperation in Africa and the Middle East: the roles of the UN and the US military', paper presented to the 1993 Topical Symposium on 'Military Coalitions and the United Nations: implications for the US Military', National Defense University, Washington, DC, 2–3 Nov. 1993, p. 20. This cease-fire broke down in early 1994, resulting in massive tribal blood-letting.

[172] Boutros-Ghali (note 20), p. 136.

[173] Boutros-Ghali (note 20), p. 136.

[174] Report of the Secretary-General on the UN Assistance Mission for Rwanda, UN Security Council document S/26927, 30 Dec. 1993.

[175] OAU document AHG/Decl.3 (XXXIX) Rev. 1, 'Declaration of the Assembly of Heads of State and Government on the Establishment Within the OAU of a Mechanism for Conflict Prevention, Management and Resolution', Assembly of Heads of State and Government, 29th Ordinary Session, 28–30 June, 1993, Cairo. A previous OAU Commission on Conflict Resolution was a complete failure.

members meeting mostly at ambassadorial level.[176] It is intended at this stage to fulfil essentially an early-warning function as well as helping organize OAU good offices and observer missions. Funding, as in all OAU activities, remains a critical barrier to success.

The first undertaking of the OAU Centre was to organize a good offices mission to the Congo. Being solely an OAU initiative this was described as a significant breakthrough. In addition Togo requested assistance in supervising, rather than simply monitoring, its election, another unprecedented African initiative.

Despite these activities, however, the OAU has been singularly unsuccessful to date in either foreseeing, preventing or resolving armed conflicts in Angola, Burundi, Liberia, Mozambique, Somalia, Sudan, Western Sahara, Zaire and elsewhere on the conflict-ridden African continent. The tendency has been to leave it to the international community as a whole, through the UN, to shoulder the major responsibility.

The Organization of American States

The OAS, lacking its own conflict prevention and resolution mechanisms, was in 1993 for the most part involved in such activities in league with the UN, rather than on its own. Haiti was the prime example. The OAS continued to play a role in promoting peace in Nicaragua and El Salvador as it had done for many years through the Contadora process.[177] In 1993 several OAS members—Colombia, Mexico and Venezuela—along with Spain formed a so-called Group of Friends to work with the UN in promoting agreement between the parties in the longest-running war in Central America, the Guatemalan Government and the Unidad Revolucionaria Nacional Guatemalteca.[178]

Peacekeeping and peace enforcement

Peacekeeping missions conducted by regional organizations have so far not been common. One difficulty is a simple lack of capacity. Most regional organizations do not possess the organizational, technical or financial capabilities to mount such operations. NATO is the sole exception, although it does not regard itself as a regional organization under the UN Charter. Moreover, while regional peacekeepers may have the advantage of being familiar with the climate, terrain, politics, social and economic conditions and culture of their region, their very proximity to the conflict in question and one or more of the parties involved may render them inappropriate as peacekeepers.

[176] The following is based on oral presentations at the Executive Seminar on Conflict Prevention and Conflict Resolution, Uppsala, Sweden, 23–29 Sep. 1993 (organized by the Department of Peace and Conflict Research, Uppsala University) by Mr Christopher Bakwesegha and Ms Adwoa Coleman, respectively Head and Chief of Research, Division of Conflict Management, Organization of African Unity, Addis Ababa. See also Ocaya-Lakidi (note 171), pp. 24–26.

[177] See Goldblat, J. and Millán, V., 'The Central American crisis and the Contadora search for regional security', SIPRI, SIPRI Yearbook 1986: World Armaments and Disarmament (Oxford University Press: Oxford, 1986).

[178] Boutros-Ghali (note 20), p. 117.

The Economic Organization of West African States

The disadvantages of regional peacekeeping were graphically illustrated by the only purely regional peacekeeping operation under way in 1993—that mounted by the Economic Organization of West African States (ECOWAS) in Liberia. The so-called ECOWAS Ceasefire Monitoring Group (ECOMOG) was established in 1990. After negotiation of the Yamoussoukro IV Accord in October 1991 it was expanded into a self-described 'peacekeeping/peace-enforcement' operation. The bulk of the force—12 naval vessels and three infantry battalions—was Nigerian, with smaller contributions from Ghana, Guinea, Sierra Leone, Gambia, Mali and Senegal (later withdrawn).[179] Accused of being a tool of Nigerian foreign policy, the force became a party to the civil war when it undertook enforcement action against the National Patriotic Front of Liberia (NPFL) led by Charles Taylor.[180] It also suffered from changing and unclear mandates, the lack of support of all ECOWAS members (especially Côte d'Ivoire and Burkina Faso) and a succession of different (Nigerian) commanders.[181] By mid-1993 there had been significant casualties among the ECOMOG forces.

On 25 July 1993, after talks in Geneva and Benin jointly sponsored by the UN, the OAU and ECOWAS, the Cotonou Peace Agreement was signed by the parties to the Liberian conflict. It envisaged a cease-fire, establishment of an interim government, demobilization and disarmament of the faction's armed forces and an election in 1994.[182] The process would be monitored by an expanded ECOMOG, including troops from East African countries—Tanzania, Uganda and Zimbabwe—to dilute its domination by Nigeria (a key demand of the NPFL).[183] The UN Security Council subsequently authorized a UN Observer Mission in Liberia (UNOMIL) and an advance team of 30 military advisers to participate in the work of the accord's Joint Ceasefire Monitoring Committee.[184] The UN mission, comprising 300 military and 200 civilian personnel,[185] became the first UN peacekeeping mission undertaken in co-operation with a mission established by another organization.[186]

According to the OAU, future African peacekeeping missions, although not ruled out, are not a priority given the expense involved and African nations' sensitivities about their sovereignty—even in the face of national calamity. The OAU itself had its fingers burned when its peacekeeping force in Chad, deployed in 1991, was withdrawn a year later suffering acute shortages of

---

[179] Oladimejji, Capt. O. A., 'Behold, African peacekeepers', *US Naval Institute Proceedings*, Mar. 1993, p. 66.

[180] Ankomah, B., 'UN: taking sides in Liberia', *New African*, no. 313 (Nov. 1993), pp. 16–17.

[181] Alao, A., 'ECOMOG in Liberia—The anaemic existence of a mission', *Jane's Intelligence Review*, Sep. 1993, pp. 429–30.

[182] United Nations, 'UN Peace-Keeping Operations Information Notes', update no. 2, 1993, p. 106.

[183] Alao (note 180), p. 431.

[184] Boutros-Ghali (note 20), p. 129.

[185] In Mar. 1994 a government comprising all the warring factions was installed in the capital, Monrovia, after which disarmament of the factional forces was to commence. *The Australian*, 9 Mar. 1994, p. 7.

[186] United Nations (note 181), p. 105.

expertise, logistics and finance.[187] African states have contributed successfully to UN peacekeeping missions over the years, however, particularly Nigeria, Ghana, Senegal, Tunisia, Kenya and Egypt. In 1993 African states were represented in each of the largest multi-dimensional UN peacekeeping operations—UNTAC, UNPROFOR and UNOSOM II.

The CSCE, NATO, the North Atlantic Cooperation Council and the Western European Union

In the 1992 Helsinki Document the CSCE promised itself a peacekeeping role in future conflicts but established a policy so hedged with qualifications and conditions as to make such a role unlikely to eventuate in the near future.[188] Moreover the CSCE would have to rely on NATO or the WEU since it has no military forces of its own. NATO undertook in 1992 to provide such forces to the CSCE on a 'case by case basis'.[189] Since this may not be a comforting prospect to non-NATO members of the CSCE, especially those formerly in the Soviet bloc, NATO began planning for task forces of NATO and non-NATO troops to conduct joint exercises to be ready to move quickly on peacekeeping or humanitarian relief missions.[190] Work on the practicalities of joint peacekeeping operations was also included as a goal of the North Atlantic Cooperation Council (NACC, comprising NATO member states and former WTO states[191]) and the Partnership for Peace arrangement offered to all the former Soviet republics and Soviet bloc states of Eastern Europe by NATO in 1993.[192] However, by the end of the year NATO's political authorities had yet to agree on guidance for determining conditions, procedures and policies for NATO involvement in peacekeeping operations.[193]

Meanwhile, the fact that France still does not participate in the military structure of NATO and harbours ambitions for a peacekeeping role for the Paris-based Western European Union (WEU) does not augur well for the unity of future attempts at European peacekeeping operations. Continuing US reluctance, despite earlier undertakings, to commit itself to providing peacekeeping

[187] Berdal (note 26), p. 68.
[188] Helsinki Document 1992: The Challenges of Change, Helsinki, 10 July 1992, Helsinki Decisions, chapter III, reproduced in appendix 5A in SIPRI, *SIPRI Yearbook 1993: World Armaments and Disarmament* (Oxford University Press: Oxford, 1993), pp. 198–200.
[189] NATO press communiqué, M-NACC-1 (92)53, Oslo, 5 June 1992.
[190] *International Herald Tribune*, 7 Jan. 1994, p. 1.
[191] *NATO Review*, Dec. 1993, pp. 27–30.
[192] See chapter 7 in this volume.
[193] This was despite its Military Committee's agreement on strategic guidance in *NATO Military Planning for Peace Support Operations*, NATO Military Committee document, Apr. 1993; the establishment of a peacekeeping office at Supreme Headquarters Allied Powers Europe (SHAPE); and the North Atlantic Assembly's Oct. 1993 report on co-operation in peacekeeping and peace enforcement. See Rader, S., 'NATO and Peacekeeping', paper presented to SIPRI/Friedrich-Ebert-Stiftung conference on 'Challenges for the New Peacekeepers', Bonn, 21–22 Apr. 1994; and North Atlantic Assembly, Defence and Security Committee, Sub-Committee on Defence and Security Cooperation Between Europe and North America, *Co-operation in Peacekeeping and Peace Enforcement*, AK230, DSC/DC (93), 6 Oct. 1993.

troops to Bosnia and Herzegovina in the event of a peace settlement there, further calls into question NATO's future peacekeeping role in Europe.[194]

Notwithstanding these difficulties, NATO, at its ministerial meetings in December 1992 and June 1993, also expressed a willingness to participate in UN peace operations.[195] In 1993 its involvement in support of UN, WEU and EU peacekeeping and peace-enforcement operations in former Yugoslavia increased. It was already helping enforce the no-fly zone over Bosnia and Herzegovina and sanctions against Serbia and Montenegro by providing fighter aircraft, reconnaissance and airborne warning aircraft and naval vessels in the Adriatic in co-operation with the WEU.[196] After July 1993, NATO member states, operating within the NATO framework, for the first time provided protective air cover for UNPROFOR troops and to deter air attacks against UN Protected Areas and Safe Areas.[197] NATO also provided staff and equipment for UNPROFOR's Bosnia and Herzegovina Command headquarters in Kiseljak. In early 1993 NATO became involved in planning for peace-enforcement measures that the Security Council was threatening to take against Bosnian Serb positions and supply elements in central Bosnia and Herzegovina. France, the Netherlands, the UK and the USA stationed aircraft in Italy and on aircraft-carriers in the Adriatic for this purpose. No raids were authorized in 1993.[198] With its involvement in Yugoslavia NATO crossed a Rubicon: although originally conceived as a defensive alliance to protect its members from attack, NATO for the first time operated out-of-area, in defence of broader security values.

The Commonwealth of Independent States[199]

Peacekeeping agreements were signed by the Commonwealth of Independent States (CIS) member states at their 1992 Kiev and Tashkent summits, but by the end of 1993 no coherent peacekeeping doctrine had been agreed upon and no standing peacekeeping force (as envisaged) yet established.[200]

There were, however, three Russian-led military deployments in conflict zones in the CIS area which described themselves as peacekeeping operations, but which were notable, in contrast to UN operations, for their domination by one state and by their preparedness to use force (although they had so far been relatively restrained in using it).[201] These missions were located in South Ossetia, eastern Moldova and Tajikistan.

[194] Drozdiak, W. and Williams D., 'US role in Europe shrinks in wake of Yugoslav War', *International Herald Tribune*, 27 Dec. 1993, p. 1.

[195] Annan, K., 'UN peacekeeping operations and cooperation with NATO', *NATO Review*, Oct. 1993, p. 6.

[196] *Aviation Week & Space Technology*, 7 Dec. 1992, p. 62.

[197] Annan (note 194), p. 6; and Berdal (note 26), pp. 69–70.

[198] In contrast, in 1994 NATO has used force on several occasions to enforce the no-fly zone and to protect UNPROFOR and safe havens.

[199] For further details on the security situation of Russia and the CIS, see chapter 6 in this volume.

[200] See Greene, J. M., 'The peacekeeping doctrines of the CIS', *Jane's Intelligence Review*, Apr. 1993, p. 159.

[201] Hill, J. and Jewett, P., 'Back in the USSR: Russia's intervention in the internal affairs of the former Soviet republics and the implications for United States policy toward Russia', Strengthening Demo-

In the Trans-Dniester Republic in Moldova, Russia had almost 2000 peace-keeping troops—with the letters MS (the Russian abbreviation for Peace Forces) on their sleeves, headgear and equipment to distinguish them from the 14th Russian Army also stationed in that republic.[202] The Russians, along with contributions from the Trans-Dniester Republic and Moldova, were under the supervision of the CSCE as part of a trilateral 'Moldova Joint Force'. Meanwhile, in South Ossetia, the 'South Ossetia Joint Force' was deployed, comprising units from Russia, Georgia and North Ossetia.[203] It was intended to co-ordinate its activities with the CSCE mission to Moldova. In these two cases the Russian peacekeepers were reported to be largely successful in maintaining their neutrality between the warring parties.[204]

In Tajikistan, Russian peacekeepers were drawn from the approximately 18 000 Russian frontier troops engaged in assisting the government forces fight rebel groups. Although they were combined in a joint peacekeeping force—the 'Tajikistan Buffer Force'—with units from Uzbekistan and Kazakhstan, the CIS 'cover' for the operation was more symbolic than real.[205] Since there was no cease-fire and Russia was officially supportive of the Tajik Government, some observers regarded this operation as more a case of peace enforcement or low-intensity conflict than peacekeeping.[206]

Given the legacies of Russian and Soviet history, all three Russian 'peace-keeping' efforts were perceived in some quarters as part of the problem rather than part of the solution. In terms of the traditional peacekeeping ethos—impartiality, consent of the conflicting parties and non-use of force except in self-defence—some questioned whether such missions could be described as peacekeeping at all. For instance, in Georgia some Russian officials supported Abkhazian territorial claims and Russian military equipment was supplied both to the separatists and the government.[207]

Throughout 1993 Russia repeatedly asked for its 'peacekeeping operations' in the CIS to be given blanket endorsement by the UN and the CSCE, in part to secure financial assistance for such efforts.[208] In an interview with *Izvestia* in October Foreign Minister Andrey Kozyrev increased suspicions of Russian motives by declaring that if Russia did not intervene in its 'near abroad' it would be in danger of 'losing geographical positions that took centuries to

cratic Institutions Project (John F. Kennedy School of Government, Harvard University: Cambridge, Mass., Jan. 1994); and Greene (note 199), p. 156.

[202] *International Herald Tribune*, 30 Nov. 1993, pp. 1 and 8.

[203] *International Herald Tribune*, 30 Nov. 1993, pp. 1 and 8; and *Defence & Economy*, 16 June 1993, p. 871.

[204] See Greene (note 199), p. 159.

[205] *International Herald Tribune*, 30 Nov. 1993, pp. 1 and 8; and Radio Free Europe/Radio Liberty, *RFE/RL News Briefs*, vol. 2, no. 2 (1993), p. 9 and vol. 2, no. 11 (1993), pp. 8–9. Border troops from Kyrgyzstan which were originally part of the force were withdrawn in Apr. 1993, apparently because of inadequate training for mountain terrain. See *RFE/RL News Briefs*, vol. 2, no. 16 (1993), p. 9.

[206] Trenin, D., 'Russians as peacemakers', paper presented to the SIPRI–Friedrich-Ebert-Stiftung conference on 'Challenges for the New Peacekeepers', Bonn, 21–22 Apr. 1994.

[207] *New Times International*, no. 48 (1993), pp. 25–26. On 13 Jan. 1994 Georgia and Abkhazia signed an accord calling for deployment of an international peacekeeping force authorized by the Security Council to monitor their cease-fire. *Financial Times*, 14 Jan. 1994, p. 3.

[208] See *New Times International* (note 206).

conquer'.[209] At the UN General Assembly in September, while denying that Russia had 'neo-imperialistic' ambitions, Kozyrev firmly rejected the involvement of any outside power in peacekeeping in these areas.[210] The US view is that Russian peacekeeping operations in the 'near abroad' should only be conducted with the agreement of the international community and the country involved and, preferably, in conjunction with troops from other CIS member states.[211] In December the CSCE postponed giving its endorsement to Russian peacekeeping missions, instead requesting its secretariat to draft guidelines for approving such missions.[212]

Other peacekeeping missions

The only other multilateral organization involved in peace operations in 1993 was the Commonwealth,[213] which had observers in South Africa monitoring political violence and the electoral process, along with those from the OAU, the UN and the EU.[214] In addition an *ad hoc* multilateral mission, the Multinational Force and Observers (MFO), remained in the eastern Sinai under the 1979 Egypt–Israel peace treaty.[215] Finally, a relic of the Korean War, the Neutral Nations Supervisory Commission (NNSC) for Korea, remained stoically in place to supervise the 1953 Armistice Agreement and cease-fire line along the 38th parallel.[216]

VII. Conclusions

Multilateral efforts in 1993 to prevent, manage and resolve international conflict reached a new intensity, but also confronted difficulties that the euphoria of the immediate post-cold war years had ill-prepared them for. While success in Cambodia symbolized the possibilities, failure in former Yugoslavia and Somalia were grim reminders that much work needed to be done. Conceptual issues, especially the relationship between peacekeeping and peace enforcement, continued to be tackled, including in ongoing debate over Boutros-Ghali's *An Agenda for Peace*. The United Nations began a long process of reform and restructuring to cope with the new demands being made on it, while regional organizations struggled to overcome some of their traditional limitations and share the burden. In addition to signs of peacekeeping fatigue among member states there were also encouraging moves to professionalize

---

[209] Cited in Hill and Jewett (note 200), p. 6.

[210] *International Herald Tribune*, 30 Sep. 1993, p. 8.

[211] *International Herald Tribune*, 30 Nov. 1993, pp. 1 and 8.

[212] *Financial Times*, 12 Dec. 1993, p. 2.

[213] The Commonwealth of Nations, formerly the British Commonwealth, comprises mostly former British colonies and dominions.

[214] Commonwealth Secretariat, *International Election Observer's Manual* (Commonwealth Secretariat: London, Apr. 1994), p. 8.

[215] Ghali, M., 'United Nations truce supervision organization: 1948–present', ed. Durch (note 36), p. 97.

[216] 'International Peacekeeping Operations 1947–1993', *Defense & Economy*, no. 1277 (16 June 1993), p. 870. Its participants were Czechoslovakia, Poland, Sweden and Switzerland.

and co-ordinate national peacekeeping contributions. Above all there was a growing recognition that, while the international community might be more willing than ever before to consider peace indivisible and to widen its definition of threats to the peace, there were limits to what could be achieved with the multilateral instruments and resources currently available to it.

Appendix 1A. International observer and peacekeeping operations, 1993

PAUL CLAESSON

This table lists international observer and peacekeeping operations terminated (in *italic*), initiated (in **bold**) or continuing in 1993, by international organization and by starting date. Cost figures are in current US $m. Purely civilian and electoral observation missions are excluded.

Acronym/ (Legal instrument[1])	Name/type of mission (UN)[7] (O: observer) (PK: peacekeeping)	Location	Start date	Countries contributing troops, military observers (mil. obs) and/or civilian police in 1993[2]	Troops/ Mil. obs/ Civ. police[3]	Deaths:[4] To date / In 1993	Cost: Yearly[5] / Unpaid[6]
United Nations (UN)[7] (UN Charter, Chapters VI and VII)	(20 operations)		June 1948	(79 countries; contingents on rotation)	66 679[8] / 2 250 / 1 032	1 027 / 168	3 600[9] / 1 220[10]
UNTSO (UNSC 50)	UN Truce Supervision Organization (O)	Egypt/Israel/ Lebanon/Syria	June 1948	Argentina, Australia, Austria, Belgium, Canada, Chile, China, Denmark, Finland, France, Ireland, Italy, Netherlands, New Zealand, Norway, Russia, Sweden, Switzerland, USA	– / 216 / –	28 / –	31 / –
UNMOGIP (UNSC 91)	UN Military Observer Group in India and Pakistan (O)	India/Pakistan (Kashmir)	Jan. 1949	Belgium, Chile, Denmark, Finland, Italy, Norway, Sweden, Uruguay	– / 37 / –	6 / –	7 / –
UNFICYP (UNSC 186)	UN Peace-keeping Force in Cyprus (PK)	Cyprus	Mar. 1964	**Argentina**, Australia, Austria, *Canada*, *Denmark*, Finland, Hungary, Ireland, Sweden, UK[11]	1 174 / 12 / 35	165 / 6	45[12] / 197
UNDOF (UNSC 350)	UN Disengagement Observer Force (O)	Syria (Golan Heights)	June 1974	Austria, Canada, *Finland*, Poland	1 027 / –[13] / –	31 / –	36[14] / 33
UNIFIL (UNSC 425, 426)	UN Interim Force in Lebanon (PK)	Lebanon (Southern)	Mar. 1978	Fiji, Finland, France, Ghana, Ireland, Italy, Nepal, Norway, Poland, Sweden	5 241 / –[15] / –	193 / 3	146 / 232
OSGAP (UNSG 12 Mar. 1990[16])	Office of the Secretary-General in Afghanistan and Pakistan (O)	Afghanistan/ Pakistan	Mar. 1990	Austria, Canada, Denmark, Fiji, Finland, Ghana, Ireland, Nepal, Poland, Sweden	– / 10[17] / –	– / –	·· / ··

Acronym/ (Legal instrument)[1]	Name/type of mission (O: observer mission) (PK: peacekeeping)	Start date	Location	Countries contributing troops, military observers (mil. obs) and/or civilian police in 1993[2]	Troops/ Mil. obs/ Civ. police[3]	Deaths:[4] To date / In 1993	Cost: Yearly[5] / Unpaid[6]
UNIKOM (UNSC 689)	UN Iraq-Kuwait Observation Mission (O)	Apr. 1991	Iraq/Kuwait (Khawr ʿAbd Allah waterway and UN DMZ[18])	Argentina, Austria, Bangladesh, Canada, China, Denmark, Fiji, Finland, France, Ghana, Greece, Hungary, India, Indonesia, Ireland, Italy, Kenya, Malaysia, Nigeria, Norway, Pakistan, Poland, Romania, Russia, Senegal, Singapore, Sweden, Thailand, Turkey, UK, USA, Uruguay, Venezuela[19]	367[20] / 254 / –	1 / –	75 / 31
UNAVEM II (UNSC 696)	UN Angola Verification Mission II (O)	June 1991	Angola	*Algeria*, Argentina, Brazil, Canada, Colombia, *Congo*, *Egypt*, Guinea-Bissau, Hungary, India, Ireland, Jordan, *Malaysia*, Morocco, Netherlands, *New Zealand*, Nigeria, Norway, *Senegal*, Slovakia, Spain, Sweden, *Former Yugoslavia*, Zimbabwe	14[21] / 46 / 23	3 / 2	37[22] / 30[23]
ONUSAL (UNSC 693, 729)	UN Observer Mission in El Salvador (O)	July 1991	El Salvador	Argentina, Austria, Brazil, Canada, Chile, Colombia, Ecuador, France, Guyana, India, Ireland, Italy, Mexico, Spain, Sweden, Venezuela	4[24] / 30 / 276	2 / 1	35 / 26[25]
MINURSO (UNSC 690)	UN Mission for the Referendum in Western Sahara (O)	Sep. 1991	Western Sahara	Argentina, Australia, Austria, Bangladesh, Belgium, Canada, China, Egypt, France, Germany, Ghana, Greece, Guinea, Honduras, Ireland, Italy, Kenya, Malaysia, Nigeria, Pakistan, Poland, Russia, Switzerland, Togo, Tunisia, USA, Venezuela	101[26] / 225 / 21	4 / 2	37 / 20
UNPROFOR (UNSC 743, 776, 795)	UN Protection Force (PK)	Mar. 1992	Former Yugoslavia (Croatia; Bosnia and Herzegovina; Macedonia[27])	Argentina, Australia, Bangladesh, Belgium, Brazil, Canada, Colombia, Czech Rep., Denmark, Egypt, Finland, France, Ghana, *India*, **Indonesia**, Ireland, Jordan, Kenya, Luxembourg, **Malaysia**, Nepal, Netherlands, New Zealand, Nigeria, Norway, **Pakistan**, Poland, Portugal, Russia, Slovakia, Spain, Sweden, Switzerland, Tunisia, Ukraine, UK, USA, Venezuela	25 694[28] / 587 / 675	59 / 30	1 020[29] / 325
UNTAC (UNSC 745)	*UN Transitional Authority in Cambodia* (PK)	*Mar. 1992*[30]	*Cambodia*	*Algeria, Argentina, Australia, Austria, Bangladesh, Belgium, Brunei, Bulgaria, Cameroon, Canada, Chile, China, Colombia, Egypt, Fiji, France, Germany, Ghana, Hungary, India, Indonesia, Ireland, Italy, Japan, Jordan, Kenya, Malaysia, Morocco, Namibia, Nepal, Netherlands, New Zealand, Nigeria, Norway, Pakistan, Philippines, Poland, Russia, Senegal, Singapore, Sweden, Thailand, Tunisia, UK, USA, Uruguay*	*9 354*[31] / .. / *3 600*	*55* / *28*	*741* / *409*[32]

Operation	Name / type	Location	Date	Contributing countries							
UNOSOM I (UNSC 751)	*UN Operation in Somalia I (PK)*	*Somalia*	*Apr. 1992[33]*	*Australia, Austria, Bangladesh, Belgium, Canada, Czechoslovakia, Egypt, Fiji, Finland, Indonesia, Jordan, Morocco, New Zealand, Norway, Pakistan, Zimbabwe*	500	50		–	–	108[34]	:
ONUMOZ (UNSC 797)	UN Operation in Mozambique (PK)	Mozambique	Dec. 1992	Argentina, Bangladesh, Botswana, Brazil, Canada, Cape Verde, China, Czech Rep., Egypt, Guinea-Bissau, Hungary, India, Italy, Japan, Malaysia, Netherlands, Portugal, Russia, Spain, Sweden, Uruguay, Zambia	6 325[35]	341	–	6	6	290	92
UNOSOM II (UNSC 814)	UN Operation in Somalia II (PK)	Somalia	May 1993	Argentina, Australia, Bangladesh, Belgium, Botswana, Canada, Egypt, France, Germany, Greece, Hungary, India, Indonesia, Ireland, Italy, Jordan, Kuwait, Malaysia, Morocco, Namibia, Nepal, New Zealand, Nigeria, Norway, Pakistan, Romania, Saudi Arabia, Sweden, South Korea, Tunisia, Turkey, Uganda, UAE, USA, Zambia, Zimbabwe	25 747[36]	–		81	81	947	142[37]
UNOMUR (UNSC 846)	UN Observer Mission Uganda–Rwanda (O)	Uganda/Rwanda (Border area)	June 1993[38]	Bangladesh, Botswana, Brazil, Canada, Hungary, Netherlands, Senegal, Slovakia, Zimbabwe	–	78	–	–	–	4[39]	:
UNOMIG (UNSC 849, 858)	UN Observer Mission in Georgia (O)	Georgia (Abkhasia)	Aug. 1993	Denmark[40]	–	5[41]	–	–	–	23	
UNOMIL (UNSC 866)	UN Observer Mission in Liberia (O)	Liberia	Sep. 1993	Austria, Bangladesh, China, Congo, Czech Rep., Egypt, Guinea-Bissau, Hungary, Jordan, Kenya, Malaysia, Pakistan, Poland, Slovakia, Uruguay	65[42]	260	–	–	–	40[43]	:
UNMIH (UNSC 867)	UN Mission in Haiti (PK)	Haiti	Sep. 1993	_[44]	–[45]	–	–	–	–	50	:
UNAMIR (UNSC 872)	UN Mission for Rwanda (PK)	Rwanda	Oct. 1993	Austria, Bangladesh, Belgium, Canada, Congo, Fiji, Ghana, Guyana, Mali, Netherlands, Poland, Senegal, Togo, Tunisia, Uruguay, Zimbabwe[46]	1 012[47]	166	2	–	–	98	:

Acronym/ (Legal instrument[1])	Name/type of mission (O: observer mission) (PK: peacekeeping)	Location	Start date	Countries contributing troops, military observers (mil. obs) and/or civilian police in 1993[2]	Troops/ Mil. obs/ Civ. police[3]	Deaths:[4] To date In 1993	Cost: Yearly[5] Unpaid[6]
Conference on Security and Co-operation in Europe (CSCE)[48] (5 operations[49])							
(CSO 14 Aug. 1992[50])	CSCE Missions of Long Duration (O)	Fed. Rep. of Yugoslavia[51]	Sep. 1992[52]	..	– / 20[53] / –	– / –	1.9[54] / ..
(CSO 18 Sep.1992[55])	CSCE Spillover Mission to Skopje (O)	Former Yugoslav Rep. of Macedonia	Sep. 1992	..	– / 7[56] / –	– / –	0.7[57] / ..
(CSO 6 Nov. 1992[58])	CSCE Mission to Georgia (O)	Georgia (S. Ossetia; Abkhasia)	Dec. 1992	..	– / 10[59] / –	– / –	0.8[60] / ..
(CSO 4 Feb. Moldova 1993[61])	**CSCE Mission to Moldova** (O)	**Moldova**	**Apr. 1993**	..	– / **8** / –	– / –	**0.4**[62] / –
(CSCE 1 Dec. 1993[63])	**CSCE Mission to Tajikistan** (O)	**Tajikistan**	–[64]	..	– / **4** / –	– / –	..
Other			(9 operations)				
NNSC (Armistice agreement[65]) (O)	Neutral Nations Supervisory Commission	North Korea/ South Korea	July 1953	Czech Republic, Poland, Sweden, Switzerland	– / 4 / –	– / –	.. / ..
MFO (Protocol to treaty[66]) (O)	Multinational Force and Observers in the Sinai	Egypt (Sinai)	Aug. 1982	Australia, Canada, Colombia, Fiji, France, Italy, Netherlands, New Zealand, Norway, Uruguay, USA	c. 2 100 / .. / ..	.. / ..	56[67] / ..
ECOMOG (ESMC 7 Aug. 1990[68]) (PK)	ECOWAS[69] Cease-Fire Monitoring Group	Liberia	Aug. 1990	Gambia, Ghana, Guinea, Mali, Nigeria, Senegal, Sierra Leone	c. 8 000[70] / .. / ..	.. / ..	80 / ..

Acronym (mandate)	Name (type)[1]	Location	Start date	Contributing countries[2][3]	No. of troops	No. of mil. observers	No. of civ. police	Deaths[4]	Cost (US $ m.)
ECMM (Brioni Agreement[71])	European Community Monitoring Mission[72] (O)	Former Yugoslavia	July 1991	Belgium, Canada, Czech. Rep., Denmark, France, Germany, Greece, Ireland, Italy, Netherlands, Poland, Portugal, Sweden, Slovakia, Spain, UK	–	152	–	6	24[73]
NMOG (Cease-fire agreement[74])	Rwanda Neutral Military Observer Group[75] (O)	Rwanda	July 1992	Nigeria, Mali, Senegal, Zimbabwe	–	130[76]	–	..	8
– (Bilateral agreement[77])	'South Ossetia Joint Force'[78] (PK)	Georgia (S. Ossetia)	July 1992	Georgia, Russia, North Ossetia	1 453[79]	–	–	2	19[80]
– (Bilateral agreement[81])	'Moldova Joint Force'[82] (PK)	Moldova (Trans-Dniester)	July 1992	Moldova, Russia, 'Trans-Dniester Republic'	3 995[83]	–	–	7	12[84]
UNITAF (UNSC 794)	Unified Task Force[85] (PK)	Somalia	Dec. 1992[86]	*Australia, Belgium, Botswana, Canada, Egypt, France, Germany, India, Italy, Kuwait, Morocco, New Zealand, Nigeria, Norway, Pakistan, Saudi Arabia, Sweden, Tunisia, Turkey, UAE, UK, USA, Zimbabwe*	c. 37 000[87]	–	–	..	..[88]
– (CIS 22 Jan. 1993[89])	CIS 'Tajikistan Buffer Force'[90] (PK)	Tajikistan (Afghan border)	Mar. 1993	**Kazakhstan, Kyrgyzstan, Russia,[91] Uzbekistan**	c. 1 500[92]	–	–	..	..[93]

[1] CIS = Commonwealth of Independent States; CSCE = Conference on Security and Co-operation in Europe; CSO = CSCE Council of Senior Officials; ECOWAS = Economic Community of West African States; ESMC = ECOWAS Standing Mediation Committee; OAU = Organization of African Unity; UNSC = UN Security Council; UNSG = Office of the UN Secretary-General. Acronyms refer to resolution adopted (UNSC) or date of decision taken by respective body or organization.

[2] Countries ending their participation in the course of 1993 in italics. Countries participating for the first time in 1993 in bold.

[3] Civilian observers and international and local civilian staff are not included.

[4] Number of mission fatalities. To date: from beginning of conflict until last reported date for 1993.

[5] Approximate or estimated annual cost.

[6] Approximate value of outstanding contributions to operation fund at the close of 1993 budget period (closing date varies from operation to operation).

[7] Unless otherwise noted, UN data on contributing countries and on number of troops, military observers and civilian police are as of 31 Dec. 1993; on deaths as of 14 Oct. 1993; and on costs as of 31 Oct. 1993.

[8] Operational strength varies from month to month because of rotation.

[9] 16 of the 20 UN peacekeeping operations ongoing in 1993 are financed from their own separate accounts on the basis of legally binding assessments on all member states in accordance with Article 17 of the UN Charter. UNTSO and UNMOGIP are funded through the UNTSO, UNDOF and UNIFIL budgets and through special allocations from the UN regular budget. OSGAP is funded from the UN regular budget. UNFICYP was until 15 June 1993 financed by voluntary contributions (see note 12). Since the mandates of

most forces are renewed periodically on different dates, UN annual cost estimates for comparative purposes are approximate.

[10] Outstanding contributions to UN peacekeeping operations as of 28 Feb. 1994.

[11] Restructuring and reorganization of UNFICYP commenced on 16 Nov. 1992. Troop strengths have been cut by approximately 28%; operational sectors have been cut from 4 to 3; and permanently occupied observation posts have been cut from 51 to 39. The Danish battalion was withdrawn and Austrian, Canadian and British contingents reduced in Dec. 1992. Further reductions followed in 1993. The Canadian battalion was withdrawn in June 1993, and was replaced in Sep. by an Argentinian battalion.

[12] Estimated 1993 cost. Prior to 15 June 1993, force costs were met by the governments providing the military contingents, and by voluntary contributions received for this purpose by the UN; land-use costs by the Government of Cyprus; and administrative, logistic and other extraordinary costs by the UN. The voluntary contributions from member states have consistently fallen short of costs accrued by the UN. As a result, reimbursement claims from the troop-contributing countries have been paid only up to Dec. 1981. General Assembly Resolution 47/236 (1993) established that for the period beginning 16 June 1993 the costs not covered by voluntary contributions will be borne by the UN member states in accordance with Article 17 of the UN Charter. The Government of Cyprus has pledged to cover, on a continuing basis, one-third of the annual operation cost. More than half of the expected annual cost has been pledged in voluntary contributions for the period beginning 16 June 1993.

[13] Supplemented by seconded UNTSO military observers.

[14] Initially financed from special account established for UNEF II (Second UN Emergency Force, Oct. 1973–July 1979). At the termination of UNEF II, the account remained open for UNDOF.

[15] Supplemented by 57 UNTSO military observers. In the course of 1992 the strength of UNIFIL was reduced by 10%.

[16] The decision to establish the mission was taken by the UN Secretary-General, with reference to UNSC 647 (1990), to UN General Assembly Resolution 44/15 (1989) and to consultations with the signatories to the Agreement on the Settlement of the Situation Relating to Afghanistan and Pakistan, signed at Geneva on 14 Apr. 1988 (letter to the President of the UNSC dated 12 Mar. 1990). The decision was upheld by the UNSC (letter from the President of the UNSC to the Secretary-General dated 15 Mar. 1990).

[17] Temporarily detached, with the concurrence of the respective governments, from UNTSO, UNDOF and UNIFIL.

[18] UNSC 687 (1991) established a demilitarized zone (DMZ) stretching about 200 km along the Iraq–Kuwait border, extending 10 km into Iraq and 5 km into Kuwait.

[19] Additional logistic support from Chile and Switzerland.

[20] Initially supplemented by 5 infantry companies drawn from UNFICYP and UNIFIL (withdrawn by the end of June 1991). Authorized strength: 3345 troops and 300 military observers. In response to incidents along the DMZ, UNSC 806 (1993) calls for a phased deployment of additional troops to strengthen UNIKOM.

[21] Authorized strength: 718 troops, 350 military observers and 126 civilian police.

[22] For the period 1 Nov. 1992–15 Sep. 1993.

[23] Total approximate value of outstanding contributions to UNAVEM I (Jan. 1989–June 1991) and UNAVEM II.

[24] Authorized strength: approximately 1000 troops, military observers and civilian police.

[25] Total approximate value of outstanding contributions to ONUCA (UN Observer Group in Central America, Nov. 1989–Jan. 1992) and ONUSAL.

[26] Authorized strength: 1700 troops and military observers and 300 civilian police.

[27] Force divided into three separate operational commands: UNPROFOR I (Croatia); UNPROFOR II (Bosnia and Herzegovina); and UNPROFOR III (Macedonia).

[28] Authorized strength: 26 595 troops, 578 military observers and 716 civilian police. Deployments were as of 31 Oct. 1993: UNPROFOR I: 12 610 troops, 240 military observers and 600 civilian police; UNPROFOR II: 11 120 troops, 311 military observers (including 76 posted at airfields in Serbia and Montenegro to monitor compliance with 'no-fly' zone) and 45 civilian police; UNPROFOR III: 1005 troops, 20 military observers and 25 civilian police.

[29] Military personnel, equipment and logistic support for UNPROFOR protection of humanitarian convoys in Bosnia and Herzegovina are provided at no cost to the UN by the contributing countries.

[30] UNTAC was terminated 15 Nov. 1993. By UNSC Resolution 880 (1993), the period of withdrawal of the UNTAC mine clearance and training unit was extended to 30 Nov. 1993, and of military police and medical components to 31 Dec. 1993. Also by UNSC Resolution 880, a team of 20 liaison officers was established, for a single period

of six months, with a mandate to report on matters affecting security in Cambodia, to maintain liaison with the Government in dealing with residual military matters relating to the Paris Agreements. These liaison officers are separate from UNTAC. On 21 Nov. 1993, the Secretary-General informed the UNSC that he proposed to form the Military Liaison team of 20 military officers from contributions offered by 15 nations: Austria, Bangladesh, Belgium, China, France, India, Indonesia, Malaysia, New Zealand, Pakistan, Poland, Russia, Singapore, Thailand and Uruguay.

[31] Number of all military personnel, including troops and observers, as of 30 Sep. 1993.

[32] Total approximate value of outstanding contributions to UNAMIC (UN Advance Mission in Cambodia, Nov. 1991–Mar. 1992) and UNTAC.

[33] Absorbed by UNOSOM II on 4 May 1993.

[34] Total appropriation by the UN General Assembly for UNOSOM I (1 May 1992–30 Apr. 1993).

[35] Authorized strength: 7000–8000 military and civilian personnel.

[36] Authorized strength: 28 000 troops. In addition, there remained in 1993 following the termination of UNITAF approximately 17 700 troops in the US Joint Task Force in Somalia, which did not form part of UNOSOM II and were not under the operational command of the UNOSOM II Force Commander. This number includes the Quick Reaction Force, which was deployed in support of UNOSOM II.

[37] Total approximate value of outstanding contributions to UNOSOM I and UNOSOM II.

[38] Integrated into UNAMIR in Jan. 1994.

[39] Estimated cost for period June–Dec. 1993.

[40] The following other countries expressed their willingness in principle to make the necessary personnel available: Austria, Bangladesh, the Czech Republic, Germany, Greece, Poland, Sierra Leone, Sweden and Switzerland.

[41] Authorized strength: 88 military observers.

[42] Authorized strength: 65 troops (20 military medical staff and 45 military engineers) and 303 military observers.

[43] A portion of the cost may be defrayed by using certain surplus equipment and supplies from UNTAC.

[44] Deployment was halted following an incident on 11 Oct. 1993 in which armed civilians, unimpeded by the security forces of the acting military government, prevented the landing of a ship carrying an UNMIH advance unit of 220 military personnel. Military personnel are to be provided by Argentina, Canada and USA. Civilian police personnel are to be provided by Algeria, Austria, Canada, France, Indonesia, Madagascar, Russia, Senegal, Spain, Switzerland, Tunisia and Venezuela.

[45] Authorized strength: 700 military personnel and 567 civilian police.

[46] The following countries participate in UNAMIR but did not contribute personnel in 1993: Argentina, Ecuador, Egypt, Malawi, Nigeria, Pakistan, Russia and Tanzania.

[47] Authorized strength: 2217 troops, 331 military observers and 60 civilian police personnel. The mission also incorporated elements of NMOG II (see note 76).

[48] While serving a peacekeeping role, and numbering some military observers, the CSCE missions are not military operations. Figures on number of staff are total for mission, and include both military and civilian staff in 1993.

[49] In addition to the five missions listed here, the CSCE maintained in 1993 two long-term missions in Estonia and in Latvia. The CSCE also maintained a Sanctions Assistance Mission (SAM) in each of the following countries: Albania, Bulgaria, Croatia, Hungary, Former Yugoslav Republic of Macedonia, Romania and Ukraine. The function of the SAMs is to oversee the implementation operation of the sanctions and embargoes imposed on the republics of former Yugoslavia in accordance with relevant UN Security Council Resolutions, in particular UNSC 713, 757, 787 and 820. They were in 1993 staffed by 126 customs officers from various CSCE member states.

[50] The decision to establish the mission was taken at the 15th CSO meeting, 14 Aug. 1992. The mission was authorized by the Government of the Federal Republic of Yugoslavia (Serbia and Montenegro) through an MOU of 28 Oct. 1992. The mandate was extended to 28 June 1993 through a Protocol to the MOU signed on 29 Apr. 1993.

[51] Kosovo, Sandzak and Vojvodina.

[52] The mission was withdrawn after the expiration of the MOU on 28 June 1993. For the remainder of 1993 the mission was non-operative but not terminated.

[53] Authorized strength: 40.

[54] Total budget adopted for the period 1 Sep. 1992–31 Aug. 1993.

[55] The decision to establish the mission was taken at the 16th CSO meeting, 18 Sep. 1992. The mission was authorized by the Government of the Former Yugoslav Republic of Macedonia through Articles of Understanding (corresponding to an MOU) agreed by an exchange of letters on 7 Nov. 1992.

[56] Authorized strength: 8 members. Supplemented by 2 ECMM monitors under the operational command of the CSCE Head of Mission.

[57] Total budget adopted for the period 18 Sep. 1992–31 Dec. 1993.

[58] The decision to establish the mission was taken at the 17th CSO meeting, 6 Nov 1992. The mission was authorized by the Government of Georgia through an MOU of 23 Jan. 1993 and by the 'Leadership of the Republic of South Ossetia' by an exchange of letters on 1 Mar. 1993.

[59] Authorized strength: 11 members, including the Personal Representative of the CSCE Chairman-in-Office.

[60] Total budget adopted for the period 1 Dec. 1992–31 Dec. 1993.

[61] The decision to establish the mission was taken at the 19th CSO meeting, 4 Feb. 1992. The mission was authorized by the Government of Moldova through an MOU of 7 May. An 'Understanding of the Activity of the CSCE Mission in the Pridnestrovian Region of the Republic of Moldova' came into force on 25 Aug. 1993 by an exchange of letters between the Head of Mission and the 'President of the Pridnestrovian Moldovan Republic'.

[62] Total budget adopted for the period 20 Apr. 1993–31 Dec. 1993.

[63] Decisions of the Rome Council Meeting (CSCE/4–C/Dec. 1), Decision I.4, 1 Dec. 1993.

[64] Not deployed in 1993.

[65] Agreement concerning a military armistice in Korea, signed at Panmunjom on 27 July 1953 by the Commander-in-Chief, UN Command; the Supreme Commander of the Korean People's Army; and the Commander of the Chinese People's Volunteers. Entered into force on 27 July 1953.

[66] 1981 Protocol to Peace Treaty between Egypt and Israel of 26 Mar. 1979. Established following withdrawal of Israeli forces from Sinai. Deployment began 25 Apr. 1982.

[67] Funded by Egypt, Germany (since 1992), Israel, Japan (since 1989) and the USA.

[68] The decision to establish the force was taken by the ECOWAS Standing Mediation Committee (ESMC) at its first session on 7 Aug. 1990. The ESMC was composed of representatives of Gambia, Ghana, Guinea, Nigeria, Sierra Leone and Mali.

[69] Economic Community of West African States membership: Benin, Burkina Faso, Cape Verde, Côte d'Ivoire, Gambia, Ghana, Guinea, Guinea-Bissau, Liberia, Mali, Mauretania, Niger, Nigeria, Senegal, Sierra Leone and Togo.

[70] Initial deployment numbered 2500 troops. Troop figure reached c. 10 000 (incl. 5000 Nigerian and 1500 Ghanaian troops) in autumn 1991, and c. 16 000 in spring 1992.

[71] The mission was established through the Brioni Agreement, signed at Brioni (Croatia) on 7 July 1991 by representatives of the EC and the governments of Croatia, the Federal Republic of Yugoslavia (Serbia and Montenegro) and Slovenia. The mission mandate was confirmed by the EC foreign ministers meeting in The Hague on 10 July 1991. The mission was authorized by the governments of Croatia, the Federal Republic of Yugoslavia (Serbia and Montenegro) and Slovenia through an MOU of 13 July 1991.

[72] While established by the EC, the mission is maintained with the co-operation of the CSCE, and includes the participation of monitors from five CSCE countries not members of the EC/EU: Canada, the Czech Republic, Poland, Slovakia and Sweden.

[73] Not including national expenditures.

[74] Cease-fire agreement between the Rwandan Government and the Rwanda Patriotic Front, mediated by the Tanzanian Government and the OAU, concluded July 1992.

[75] Elements of NMOG II (see note 76) were incorporated into UNAMIR in August 1993 under the terms of the Arusha peace accord, mediated by the Tanzanian Government and the OAU and signed in Arusha, Tanzania, on 4 Aug. 1993 by representatives of the Rwandan Government and the Rwanda Patriotic Front.

[76] Initial deployment: 55. Replaced 1 Aug. 1993 by an expanded force (NMOG II) of 250 military observers.

[77] Agreement on the Principles Governing the Peaceful Settlement of the Conflict in South Ossetia, signed on 24 June 1992 by Georgia and Russia. According to the terms of the Agreement, a four-party Joint Monitoring Commission was established with representatives from Russia, Georgia and North and South Ossetia. Also according to the terms of the Agreement, the Force Commander is a Russian. NB: 'The Russian-dominated peacekeeping effort currently under way in South Ossetia [and] Moldova cannot be

described accurately as CIS peacekeeping operations, owing to the fact that peacekeeping agreements for the operation were bilateral, were undertaken by CIS and non-CIS states, or came into being before general CIS peacekeeping agreements had been implemented.' Crow, S., 'Russia promotes CIS as an international organization', *RFE/RL Research Report*, vol. 3, no. 11 (18 Mar. 1994), p. 35, note 11.

[78] Figures provided by the Embassy of the Russian Federation in Stockholm, 15 Feb. 1994.

[79] Including 503 Russian troops. According to July press reports, initial deployment involved c. 1000 Russian troops, c. 200 Georgian troops and c. 600 North Ossetian troops. Authorized strength: 2000 troops plus 1000 reserve troops.

[80] Fatality figures apply to Russian troops only.

[81] Agreement on the Principles Governing the Peaceful Settlement of the Armed Conflict in the Trans-Dniester region, signed on 21 July 1992 by representatives of the governments of Moldova and Russia. NB: not a CIS operation (see note 77).

[82] Figures provided by the Embassy of the Russian Federation, Stockholm, 15 Feb. 1994.

[83] Including five Russian battalions, numbering 1778 troops, three Moldavian battalions and three battalions of the 'Trans-Dniester Republic'.

[84] Fatality figures apply to Russian troops only.

[85] Multi-state force established on the initiative of the USA on the invitation of the UN Security Council (UNSC 794). Under US command, with liaison with UNOSOM.

[86] UNITAF terminated 4 May 1993. Bulk of US troops withdrawn; command of remaining troops, and mission mandate, transfered to UNOSOM II.

[87] Peak figure, including 24 000 US military personnel.

[88] Financed through voluntary contributions, in cash and kind, by UN member states. Bulk of cost borne by the USA.

[89] CIS collective security agreement on Tajikistan's border with Afghanistan signed at Minsk on 22 Jan. 1993 by representatives of the governments of Kazakhstan, Kyrgyzstan, Russia, Tajikistan and Uzbekistan. Signed with reference to Part III, Articles 11 and 12, of the Charter of the Commonwealth of Independent States, also adopted at the Heads of State Meeting at Minsk on 22 Jan. 1993. These provisions are based on the Agreement on Groups of Military Observers and Collective Peacekeeping Forces in the CIS, signed at Kiev on 20 Mar. 1992. The operation in Tajikistan is the first application of the procedures provided for in this Agreement.

[90] The mandate of the CIS operation is limited specifically to guarding the Afghan border. Russian and other CIS forces stationed or operating elsewhere in Tajikistan do not form part of the CIS peacekeeping operation.

[91] The Russian contribution to the CIS force was drawn from Russia's 201st Motor Rifle Division, numbering some 18 000 troops in Tajikistan in 1993, by far the largest military force in the country. The CIS forces were supplemented in 1993 by some 3000 Tajik border guards, effectively under Russian command.

[92] Initial deployment included a battalion each from Kyrgyzstan (286 troops), Russia (430 troops), Uzbekistan (350 troops) and Kazakhstan (unreported number of troops).

[93] According to a cost-sharing agreement signed by the participating countries on 24 Sep. 1993, operation costs are shared as follows: Kyrgyzstan 10%; Tajikistan 10%; Kazakhstan 15%; Uzbekistan 15%; Russia 50%.

Sources: SIPRI peacekeeping and regional security data base. UN material provided by the UN Department of Public Information in New York and by the UN Information Centre for the Nordic Countries in Copenhagen (special thanks to Rea Hoberg). Material pertaining to Russian participation in peacekeeping operations in the former USSR provided by the Embassy of the Russian Federation in Stockholm. Material relating to the Commonwealth provided by the Commonwealth Secretariat, London.

Appendix 1B. Case studies on peacekeeping: UNOSOM II, UNTAC and UNPROFOR

PAUL CLAESSON and TREVOR FINDLAY*

I. UNOSOM II

In December 1992 the UN Security Council took the historic step of authorizing, for the first time, a multilateral military mission by its member states solely for humanitarian purposes.[1] A Unified Task Force (UNITAF), led by the United States, arrived in a blaze of publicity later that month to establish a secure environment for the delivery of humanitarian assistance to Somalia, suffering from famine induced by drought and prolonged by warfare. Clans and sub-clans[2] battled for control of the country, which had been left without a government after President Siyad Barre fled in January 1991. A collapse of civil society, law and order, and government services made Somalia the model 'failed state'. The multinational force, which numbered 24 000 US troops and 13 000 of other nationalities at its peak in February 1993,[3] replaced UN Operation in Somalia (UNOSOM I), a small UN mission, comprising 550 Pakistani troops,[4] which had been unable to establish control beyond Mogadishu airport.

UNITAF was highly successful in creating the conditions for the safe delivery of humanitarian assistance to Somalis in need. Deaths from famine dropped dramatically by March 1993 and the rudiments of a civil society were being reconstructed, especially outside Mogadishu. Despite urgings by UN Secretary-General Boutros-Ghali, UNITAF did not attempt to systematically disarm the Somali factions, even though many observers regarded that step as crucial for returning Somalia to peace. UNITAF commanders argued that disarmament was impossible given the vast number of weapons present in the country, the pervasive gun culture and the fact that Somali law had traditionally not banned private ownership of weapons. In fact, limited disarmament of the factions did take place, particularly focused on the so-called 'technicals', four-wheel drive vehicles mounted with an array of weapons, which had terrorized the Somali capital. US forces on several occasions deliberately attacked factional forces to achieve these limited disarmament goals.

Negotiations conducted by the US Special Envoy to Somalia, Ambassador Robert Oakley, succeeded in producing, in December 1992, an agreement between two of the most powerful sub-clans, led by Ali Mahdi Mohamed and General Mohamed Farah

---

[1] For a full account of the background to the UN intervention in Somali see Sahnoun, M., 'Somalia: the missed opportunities', ed. J. Goodby, SIPRI, *Regional Security after the Cold War* (Oxford University Press: Oxford, forthcoming 1994).

[2] For an explanation of the Somali tribal structure see Sahnoun (note 1).

[3] *Africa Watch*, vol. 5, no. 2 (7 Mar. 1993), p. 14.

[4] The Security Council had authorized the deployment of 4200 troops for UNOSOM I but the Secretariat had been unsuccessful in persuading states to contribute the additional numbers (see letter of UN Secretary-General Boutros-Ghali to the Security Council, 29 Nov. 1992).

---

* Paul Claesson wrote the case study on UNPROFOR (the former Yugoslavia), while Trevor Findlay wrote those on UNOSOM II (Somalia) and UNTAC (Cambodia).

Aideed, to halt hostilities and pull back their weapons from a type of 'green line' dividing Mogadishu.[5]

With conditions in Somalia improving but still unstable, the UN was however obliged in early 1993 to organize a replacement force for UNITAF. The mission had been conceived in the twilight of the Bush presidency as a limited-term operation. The Clinton Administration shared President Bush's fears, reflecting the legacy of the Viet Nam War and perhaps also the bombing of marines at the US Embassy in Beirut in 1983, about the USA becoming bogged down in a quagmire or suffering politically unacceptable casualties.

In May 1993, UNOSOM II, with a smaller, less coherent force under UN command and with a more ambitious mandate, replaced UNITAF. It was the first explicitly authorized UN peace-enforcement mission since the Congo operation (ONUC) in the early 1960s. Its mission was to: continue the restoration of peace, stability and law and order; assist in the re-establishment of the Somali police force; provide security and assistance in the repatriation of refugees and the resettlement of displaced persons; assist in the development of a mine clearance programme; monitor the arms embargo and facilitate disarmament; and assist in the provision of relief and in the economic development of Somalia. The USA retained key positions in UNOSOM II, providing both the mission's overall head, the Special Representative of the UN Secretary-General, retired Admiral Jonathan Howe, and the deputy military commander, Major General Thomas Montgomery. The USA also contributed 4000 troops, left in Somalia after the departure of UNITAF. Montgomery doubled as tactical commander of a small US Quick Reaction Force which was intended to carry out some operations on behalf of UNOSOM II. The force commander was from Turkey, a NATO ally of the USA.[6]

Trouble began when UNOSOM II, as mandated, attempted the systematic disarmament of the factions in the capital.[7] Action was focused on the faction led by General Mohammed Farrah Aideed, based in south Mogadishu, which refused to surrender its weapons, permit UN access to its territory and desist from harassing UN and non-governmental humanitarian efforts. A major crisis occurred when Somali gunmen on 5 June ambushed and killed 23 Pakistani peacekeepers and wounded 54—the highest single day toll in UN peacekeeping history.[8] A controversial UN investigation later implicated the Aideed faction. UNOSOM II subsequently took stronger action against the faction, including bombing raids on its command, control and supply headquarters and radio station. A reward was posted for Aideed's arrest as UNOSOM forces attempted to find and detain him. The USA reinforced its presence with 400 Rangers and a handful of Delta Force commandoes to help capture Aideed. These forces were entirely outside the UN chain of command—the Ranger Task Force took its orders

---

[5] *Africa Watch* (note 3), p. 6. These talks built on previous efforts by Mohamed Sahnoun, Special Representative of the Secretary-General for Somalia, a group of regional states (Djibouti, Eritrea, Ethiopia, Kenya and Sudan), the President of Ethiopia, Meles Zinawi, and the Swedish Life and Peace Institute, which organized a conference in the Seychelles in Oct. 1992. See Sahnoun (note 1).

[6] Berdal, M., International Institute for Strategic Studies, *Whither UN Peacekeeping?*, Adelphi Paper no. 281 (Brassey's: London, 1993), p. 73.

[7] For a useful explanation of the roots of the UN's conflict with Aideed see Farer, T., 'United States Military Participation in UN Operations in Somalia: Roots of Conflict with General Mohamed Farah Aideed and a Basis for Accommodation and Renewed Progress', testimony for submission to the Committee on Armed Services, US House of Representatives, US Congress, 14 Oct. 1993.

[8] *Independent*, 8 June 1993, p. 15.

directly from US Special Forces Headquarters in Florida.[9] Aideed's response was further attacks on UNOSOM forces, including one on 3 October, which killed 15 peacekeepers, among them 12 US soldiers.[10] One US soldier was captured but later released, while the body of another was dragged through the streets of Mogadishu. Hundreds of Somalis, civilians and factional fighters, were killed in these peace-enforcement operations, turning Somali public opinion, to the extent it could be gauged, against the UN presence.[11]

Public and congressional outrage in the United States led the USA quickly to reconsider its Somali policy and eventually its entire peacekeeping and peace-enforcement policy.[12] It subsequently announced that US troops would be withdrawn by March 1994—regardless of the situation on the ground. Following the US lead all other Western contributors—Belgium, France, Germany, Italy, Spain and Sweden—announced that they would withdraw by March. Italy had already clashed with the UN when the Italian force commander, General Bruno Loi, insisted on clearing UN military instructions with Rome.[13] Boutros-Ghali sought his removal. Italy in turn accused the UN of incompetence and blamed it for not seeking Italian advice (Italy being the former colonial power) in dealing with the Somali factions.

Faced with these difficulties the Security Council set March 1995 as the cut-off point for UNOSOM II.[14] Although the aim was to signal that the Council did not see its Somalia operation as open-ended, its effect was to remove a major incentive for the Somali factions to reach a political settlement. Both the USA and the UN dropped their goal of capturing Aideed and facilitated his participation in peace talks sponsored by Ethiopia and Eritrea. Their forces also ended their attempted forcible disarmament of the factions, bunkered down in fortified areas and sharply curtailed their presence on the streets of Mogadishu. While outside Mogadishu conditions continued by and large to improve, inside the city law and order began to deteriorate again, with international aid agencies once more targeted. Inter-factional skirmishes resumed, including in the previously relatively peaceful southern port of Kismayu. After holding several key Aideed supporters in custody for several months without charge and without legal proceedings being instituted, the UN released them in January 1994 to facilitate the outcome of peace talks.[15] UNOSOM's mandate meanwhile was overhauled; coercive disarmament was abandoned.[16]

US troops began their staged withdrawal in mid-December.[17] Although two of the remaining large troop contributors, India and Pakistan, decided to remain, the UN was forced by the Western abandonment of UNOSOM II to seek contributions from other developing states, particularly from Africa, for a scaled-down force of only 15 000.

[9] Information from Mats Berdal, International Institute for Strategic Studies (IISS), London.

[10] See Atkinson, R., 'US expedition in Somalia: the making of a disaster' and 'Somalia: the battle that changed US policy', *International Herald Tribune,* 1 and 2 Feb. 1994.

[11] Makinda, S., 'Seeking peace from chaos: Humanitarian intervention in Somalia', Occasional Paper (US International Peace Academy: New York, 1993), p. 81. While no reliable figures exist, at least 300 Somalis were killed, while total casualties may have been 1000.

[12] Ocaya-Lakidi, D., 'Regional conflicts, regional coalitions and security cooperation in Africa and the Middle East: the roles of the UN and the US military', paper presented at 1993 Topical Symposium on 'Military coalitions and the United Nations: Implications for the US Military', National Defense College, Washington, DC, 2–3 Nov. 1993, p. 5.

[13] *The Independent,* 17 July 1993, p. 10.

[14] Security Council Resolution 865, 22 Sep. 1993.

[15] *The Independent,* 19 Jan., 1994, p. 12.

[16] See Security Council Resolution S/1994/12, 6 Jan. 1994.

[17] *International Herald Tribune,* 18–19 Dec. 1993, p. 5.

Egypt, Morocco, Nigeria, Tunisia, Uganda and Zimbabwe were reportedly considering participating, subject to the availability of UN funds.[18]

The experience of Somalia—in which an estimated 800 largely urban guerrillas were able to frustrate and severely harass a UN force of up to 28 000—caused a fundamental reconsideration of the feasibility of UN peace enforcement in a civil war situation, particularly as a component of a peacekeeping operation. In Somalia the UN had abandoned both its impartiality and its aloofness and become a party to the civil war. Several lessons should be drawn from the experience.

One is that purely military solutions should not be attempted in such situations; political negotiations must be given the best possible chance. As Okaya-Lakidi notes, 'Military action is not irrelevant to peace enforcement, even to peacemaking when used as a form of *compellence*; but the US military [and the UN have] yet to work out the appropriate doctrine for this.'[19]

A second lesson is that forces operating under UN command must either obey orders from UN commanders or withdraw. A related issue is the inherent difficulty of a multilateral UN force operating in the same theatre as an independent national force (in Somalia's case the US force) also engaged in peacekeeping/peace enforcement, a dilemma also faced in the former Yugoslavia by UNPROFOR and NATO. Either the national force must be under UN command or co-ordination between them must be extraordinarily tight. Ultimately, however, the UN must have overriding authority in view of the vulnerability of its lightly armed peacekeepers on the ground.

A third lesson from Somalia is that if there is to be an enforcement operation the UN force must be properly equipped for such a mission. In some respects the UN used too little and too much force in Somalia—too little in the early days when a show of force might have hastened disarmament and too much indiscriminate force when pursuing Aideed.

A final lesson from Somalia, one reiterated by outgoing UNOSOM II Commander Lt General Cevik Bir in an open letter to Boutros-Ghali, is that a well-conceived plan and timetable are essential.[20] Unlike the more successful mission in Cambodia, the Somali operation from the outset lacked a strategic plan, other than the goal of safely delivering humanitarian aid. One result was differences within the UN Secretariat about the balance of military and humanitarian efforts.[21]

Blame for the failures in Somalia does not, however, lie solely with the UN. The United States was highly influential in UNOSOM II. In keeping its Quick Response Force under its own command, the USA militarized the operation and helped propel the UN towards a policy of forcibly seeking to capture General Aideed.[22] Although Boutros-Ghali was strongly in favour of this strategy, reportedly out of personal animus towards Aideed, Admiral Howe and the US Ambassador to Somalia, April Glaspie,[23] were also leading advocates, as was the State Department. (The UNITAF commanders and the US military adviser in Somalia were opposed.)

Moreover, the United States had declined to systematically disarm the factions when it was in charge of UNITAF, but helped craft a Security Council mandate which

---

[18] *International Herald Tribune*, 7 Jan. 1994, p. 2.

[19] Okaya-Lakidi (note 12), p. 14.

[20] *Jane's Defence Weekly*, 29 Jan. 1994, p. 6.

[21] Under Secretary-General for Humanitarian Affairs Jan Eliasson pointed out that for every dollar spent on the humanitarian operation, $10 went to the military. *The Independent*, 24 Nov. 1993, p. 13.

[22] See Ocaya-Lakidi (note 12), pp. 7–15.

[23] Cockburn, P., 'Glaspie faulted over Somali role', *The Independent*, 22 Sep. 1993, p. 12.

authorized UNOSOM II, with fewer and less capable forces, to do so. It then criticized the UN when it failed in this task, despite the fact that it was US Rangers who had blundered in their attempts to capture Aideed.

The other members of the Security Council were also exerting strong pressure for tough tactics in Somalia.[24] Confusingly, both for UNOSOM forces and the UN Secretariat, by the end of 1993 there had been 12 Security Council resolutions on Somalia, the last of which completely overturned its predecessor by dropping the peace-enforcement operations against General Aideed.[25]

The failure in Mogadishu should also be placed in context. Elsewhere UNOSOM II made commendable progress. Somalia continued to be free of the starvation and hunger that were prevalent in 1992. Law and order were largely re-established in the countryside. Progress was made in establishing local government councils (although some would argue that these were artificial structures at cross-purposes with Somali tradition and culture which would collapse once the UN withdrew) and in training a Somali police force. Somalia's provincial cities were relatively calm and orderly.

However, with the commencement of the withdrawal of the Western components of UNOSOM II after December and the adoption of the mission's new low profile, lawlessness and clan warfare were beginning to return to Mogadishu, the clans reportedly re-arming for the future struggle for power. The hard-won gains of the year in Somalia, such as they were, remained in grave jeopardy as 1993 ended.[26]

II. UNTAC

The UN operation in Cambodia, carried out by the UN Transitional Authority in Cambodia (UNTAC) in 1992–93, was at the time the UN's largest, most ambitious and most expensive ever. Although it did not entirely extinguish the Cambodian civil war, it de-escalated and de-internationalized it, politically isolating the Khmer Rouge and permitting the Cambodian people for the first time in almost 40 years to choose their government in a comparatively free, fair and democratic manner.[27] This undertaking was carried out in fulfilment of the 1991 Paris Peace Accords,[28] designed to end Cambodia's civil war. The Accords provided for a cease-fire between the four Cambodian 'factions',[29] the withdrawal of foreign forces (the Vietnamese) from Cambodian terri-

---

[24] According to the UN's chief military adviser, Canadian General Maurice Baril, 'There was a lot of war paint in the Council—a feeling that enough is enough. Nobody ever stood up and said, "This peace enforcement is bull. It won't fly"' (*Wall Street Journal Europe*, 29 Dec. 1993, p. 5).

[25] *Wall Street Journal Europe*, 29 Dec. 1993, p. 5.

[26] A peace accord signed between elders of the main Somali clans on 16 Jan. 1994 seemed unlikely to hold. Richburg, K., '60 die in Somalia as West pulls back and chaos returns', *International Herald Tribune*, 14 Feb. 1994, p. 1.

[27] For an excellent up-to-date history of Cambodia see Chandler, D. P., *A History of Cambodia*, 2nd edn (Westview Press: Boulder, Colo., 1993).

[28] The Paris Peace Accords (UN documents A/46/608, S/23177, 30 Oct. 1991) signed on 23 Oct. 1991 in Paris by the four contending Cambodian factions, the five permanent members of the Security Council and 12 other interested regional states, comprised: (*a*) the Final Act of the Paris Conference on Cambodia; (*b*) the Agreement on a Comprehensive Political Settlement of the Cambodia Conflict, with Annexes; (*c*) the Agreement Concerning the Sovereignty, Independence, Territorial Integrity and Inviolability, Neutrality and National Unity of Cambodia; and (*d*) the Declaration on the Rehabilitation and Reconstruction of Cambodia.

[29] The four Cambodian parties were: the Hun Sen Government, the so-called State of Cambodia (SOC); the Party of Democratic Kampuchea (PDK) (widely known as the Khmer Rouge); the republican Khmer People's National Liberation Front (KPNLF); and FUNCINPEC, the Front Uni National Pour Un

tory, the cessation of external military assistance, the disarmament, cantonment and demobilization of military forces and their eventual incorporation into a new national army, and the release of all prisoners of war and civilian political prisoners. Elections would be held for a Constitutional Assembly which would write a new constitution before becoming Cambodia's new National Assembly. A new government would be drawn from the Assembly's ranks.

The role of UNTAC in this process was unprecedented in the history of UN peace operations.[30] Although commonly called a 'peacekeeping' mission and although it included elements of traditional UN peacekeeping operations such as cease-fire monitoring, UNTAC was charged with implementing something much more ambitious: a comprehensive, staged plan to bring peace, democracy, constitutionality, reconciliation and reconstruction to Cambodia. To this end UNTAC would 'directly control' those government activities that could most influence the outcome of an election—foreign affairs, defence, finance, public security and information—and 'supervise and control' any other elements deemed necessary. UNTAC had seven key components: military, police, human rights, electoral, civil administration, repatriation and reconstruction.

The Accords also established a Supreme National Council (SNC), comprising the Cambodian factions, under the chairmanship of then Prince Sihanouk, to embody Cambodian sovereignty during the transitional period. The SNC was required to delegate to UNTAC 'all powers necessary' to implement the Paris Accords, and to advise UNTAC on policy. If the SNC was unable to provide agreed advice, the head of UNTAC, the Special Representative of the Secretary-General, Yasushi Akashi, had the power to act as he saw fit.[31]

Despite these unprecedented powers, UNTAC was dogged from the outset by the non-cooperation of two of the 'factions', the Khmer Rouge and the Hun Sen Government. The guerrilla group repeatedly violated the cease-fire, refused to allow UNTAC into its jungle bastions, declined to permit its forces to be disarmed and cantoned and decided not to participate in the elections. It demanded unreasonable proof that there were no Vietnamese forces left in Cambodia and the virtual dismantling of the Hun Sen Government before it would co-operate. It also began massacring Vietnamese Cambodians in an attempt to drive them from the country and to appeal to long-standing Khmer antagonism towards Viet Nam. For its part the Hun Sen Government failed to fully co-operate with UNTAC's attempts to assert administrative oversight over its operations, especially its security forces. In addition to harassing (in scores of cases murdering) its electoral opponents, especially pro-Royalist FUNCINPEC candidates, government forces, like the Khmer Rouge, also violated the cease-fire and committed human rights violations.

Faced with these developments the UN Security Council abandoned disarmament and cantonment, imposed (largely symbolic) 'embargoes' on the Khmer Rouge and switched the role of UNTAC military forces to one of protecting and helping prepare for the elections, which the Council decided should proceed. Electoral enrolment had

Cambodge Indépendent, Neutre, Pacifique et Coopératif (the United National Front for an Independent, Neutral, Peaceful and Co-operative Cambodia).

[30] Although the UN had in the past been responsible for former colonial territories under the trusteeship system, as in Namibia, or those in transition from the suzerainty of one power to another, as in West Irian, this 'supervision and control' of a sovereign, independent, UN member state was unprecedented.

[31] Ratner, S. R., 'The Cambodia settlement agreements', *American Journal of International Law*, vol. 87, no. 1 (Jan. 1993), p. 12.

gone well (4.6 million people,[32] over 90 per cent of eligible voters, had enrolled), repatriation of 350 000 refugees from the Thai–Cambodian border had been accomplished relatively smoothly and electoral rallies and information flow were contributing to the electoral momentum. None the less, the Council's decision to proceed with the election without the disarmament of all the factions and without the creation of a neutral and safe political environment was a high-risk strategy.

Yet the elections were a triumph. Almost 90 per cent of enrolled electors voted enthusiastically and peacefully in the 23–28 May ballot, an astonishing result given the political environment, poor transportation and infrastructure and driving rains in many parts of the country.[33] Such momentum was created early in the election, and so powerful and moving was the signal from the Cambodian people that they genuinely wanted peace and national reconciliation through democratic means, that by the end of the polling period even elements of the Khmer Rouge were voting. Militarily, the week was one of the quietest since UNTAC's arrival. On 29 May a relieved Akashi proclaimed the elections 'free and fair'.[34]

The outcome was a close finish between FUNCINPEC, led by Prince Sihanouk's son Prince Ranariddh, which gained 58 seats in the 120-seat Constituent Assembly, and the Hun Sen Government's Cambodian People's Party (CPP), which gained 51.[35] The remainder went to two minor parties. After initial difficulties, including a threatened territorial secession by one of the CPP's factions, a provisional government was formed by all the parties which had gained seats. Bizarre even by Cambodian standards, it was headed by two Prime Ministers, Prince Ranariddh and Hun Sen, erstwhile enemies. Amazingly the Constituent Assembly was able to complete its drafting and approval of a new Cambodian Constitution by the required date in September. It established a democratic, constitutional monarchy, with Prince Sihanouk returning to the throne as head of state. At the end of September, on schedule, the Constituent Assembly became the National Assembly, the provisional government became the new Cambodian Government, to which the SNC formally handed back sovereignty, and King Sihanouk ascended the throne.[36] The mandate of UNTAC was formally ended, its last personnel leaving by November.[37]

The key to the success of the Cambodian operation was clearly the May elections. They created a sense of national purpose, isolated the Khmer Rouge and produced an essentially two-party parliamentary system which was then transformed, Cambodian-style, into a government of national unity. Within UNTAC responsibility for this outcome lies largely with the efficiency and dedication of the UNTAC Electoral Component.[38] UN volunteers, low-paid, enthusiastic amateurs from many countries, were highly successful in enrolling voters and disseminating electoral information in remote and hazardous areas. The military's role in protecting and facilitating the election process was also crucial. Critical to the success of the mission as a whole was the support given at key junctures by the five permanent members of the UN Security Council and

[32] *Phnom Penh Post*, 29 Jan.–11 Feb. 1993, p. 16.

[33] Akashi, Y., 'The challenge of peace-keeping in Cambodia: lessons to be learned', speech to the School of International and Public Affairs, Columbia University, New York, 29 Nov. 1993, p. 6.

[34] *Phnom Penh Post*, 6–12 June 1993, p. 3.

[35] *Phnom Penh Post*, 18 June–1 July 1993, p. 4.

[36] *Phnom Penh Post*, 24 Sep.–7 Oct. 1993, p. 1.

[37] The UN retained some personnel in Cambodia after Nov. but they were no longer under UNTAC auspices. See appendix 1A, note 31.

[38] See Hayes, M., 'UN advance team sets stage for elections', *Phnom Penh Post*, 24 July 1992, p. 1.

regional states (especially Australia, France, Indonesia and Japan). Finally, Prince Sihanouk's role at precarious moments in the peace process must be acknowledged, especially his arrival in Phnom Penh the day before the elections and his pivotal role in the formation of the new Cambodian coalition government and the reaching of agreement on a new constitution. He continued to play a central, if capricious, role in holding the fractious coalition government together in the crucial months after the elections.

One factor in the success of the Cambodia mission was that it operated, unlike the coincident missions in Somalia and the former Yugoslavia, according to a staged plan. However a major flaw of UNTAC was its late deployment, a situation which emboldened the Cambodian factions to violate the Paris Accords and jeopardized the entire mission.[39] This was in part the result of lack of experience and capacity at the UN Secretariat in New York in handling the planning for and logistics of a mission of such complexity. Criticism should also be directed at the international community and the Security Council for not equipping the Secretariat with a greater capacity before entrusting such a mission to it.

UNTAC has also been criticized for not asserting its authority forcefully from the moment it was established. Deployed late and piecemeal, it failed to take advantage of the elements of surprise, unfamiliarity of the combatants with the UN, the deterrent effect of its technical capabilities (especially its mobility and communications) and the moral and political authority inherent in its mandate.

The UNTAC civilian police (CivPol) component was widely perceived as disastrous. A large number of very small units from a wide range of countries resulted in language difficulties, an enormous diversity of styles and ethical standards, and poor disciplinary structures. The CivPol element in any peacekeeping mission is critical to good relations with the local populace and must be the subject of greater UN attention.

Another lesson to be learned from Cambodia is that the protection of human rights should be paramount in cases where government authority has collapsed (as in Somalia) or when an attempt is being made to establish a neutral political environment for electoral purposes. In Cambodia the UN did well in propagating human rights information and encouraging the establishment of local human rights groups, but was much less successful in detecting, arresting and prosecuting human rights violators.[40] In seeking to rescue so-called failed states the UN may have to supply an entire legal system or at least significant components.

The UN and the Paris negotiators also failed to realize the importance of de-mining to the peace process. Without extensive de-mining (Cambodia probably being the most heavily mined country on earth[41]) repatriation and resettlement efforts were jeopardized, electioneering was rendered more difficult and scores of Cambodians continued

[39] Warner, N., 'Cambodia: lessons of UNTAC for future peacekeeping operations', paper presented at Australian Government/International Peace Academy seminar on 'UN Peacekeeping at the Crossroads', Canberra, 21–24 Mar. 1993, p. 4.

[40] See Asia Watch, 'Political control, human rights, and the UN mission in Cambodia', New York, Sep. 1992 and 'Cambodia: human rights before and after the elections', Asia Watch, vol. 5, no. 10 (May 1993) and the UN response, 'Statement by the Director of UNTAC Human Rights Component on Political Violence', Phnom Penh, 23 May 1993.

[41] See Asia Watch and Physicians for Human Rights, Land Mines in Cambodia: The Coward's War (Asia Watch and Physicians for Human Rights: New York, Sep. 1991); and Aitkin, S., Getting The Message About Mines: Towards a National Public Information Strategy and Program on Mines and Mine Safety, vol. 1 (UNESCO Cambodia: Phnom Penh, Sep. 1993).

to be maimed and killed during the peace process. The UN is now seized of this problem and is beginning long-range planning for future de-mining programmes.

The United Nations and the international community could however be well pleased with UNTAC, a complex multilateral operation which to date has brought stability, constitutional legality, a good measure of democracy and, finally, optimism to Cambodia for the first time in decades.

III. UNPROFOR

The UN Protection Force (UNPROFOR) in the former Yugoslavia was established in early 1992 as an interim measure to create the conditions of peace and security required for the European Community (EC)-initiated negotiation of an overall settlement of the Yugoslav crisis. Within its first year of operation it had already evolved into three distinct missions: a traditional disengagement mission in contested areas of Croatia; a major humanitarian support mission in Bosnia and Herzegovina; and a much smaller observation mission in Macedonia.[42] While UNPROFOR's tasks multiplied, mainly in response to the rapidly deteriorating situation in Bosnia and Herzegovina, the resources at its disposal lagged behind and the political process on which it relied for authority and direction all but disintegrated. Developments in 1993 reflect this discrepancy of resolve between the UN forces on the ground and their national and international political leaderships.

While the EC and the UN both assumed an early and active role in the search for a peaceful settlement, initial friction between the two bodies set a lasting precedent of disunity, contradictory policies and disrupted initiatives in the international community's response to the conflicts. Efforts to reach a negotiated settlement, by the UN/EC-sponsored International Conference on the Former Yugoslavia (ICFY) in Geneva, failed three times in the course of 1993.[43] Reflecting the persistent unwillingness of the warring parties to reconcile their territorial claims, the failures also reveal discord between the EC and the USA on the mediating effort and on the envisaged terms of a settlement. While the EC, represented by ICFY Steering Committee Co-Chairman Lord Owen,[44] pursued in the first instance a policy of containment,[45] the USA, acting

---

[42] In 1993 Macedonia was accepted as a member state of the United Nations under the name of the Former Yugoslav Republic of Macedonia (FYROM). For a discussion of the evolution of the three UNPROFOR commands, see Eknes, Å., *Blue Helmets in a Blown Mission? UNPROFOR in Former Yugoslavia*, NUPI Research Report no. 174 (Norwegian Institute of International Affairs: Oslo, Dec. 1993), pp. 16–33. For UNPROFOR 1993 deployment figures, see appendix 1A.

[43] The initial EC effort, in the framework of the 1991–92 EC Conference on Yugoslavia chaired by Lord Carrington, was closely linked with that of the Conference on Security and Co-operation in Europe (CSCE), and included the establishment of a 337-man EC Monitoring Mission (ECMM). Lord Carrington resigned on the eve of the joint EC/UN London Conference on the Former Yugoslavia (26–27 Aug. 1992) following a dispute with UN Secretary-General Boutros Boutros-Ghali over negotiating authority. For an assessment of the initial EC/CSCE effort, see Gow, J. and Smith, J. D. D., *Peace-making, Peace-keeping: European Security and the Yugoslav Wars*, London Defence Studies no. 11 (Centre for Defence Studies: London, May 1992). For a discussion of the history, mandate, structure and activities of the ECMM, see Schmidl, E. A., "'Eisverkäufer" im Feuer: die EG-Beobachtermission im ehemaligen Jugoslawien (ECMM) seit 1991'['"Ice-cream salesman" in the fire: the EC Observer Mission in the former Yugoslavia'], *Österreichische Militärische Zeitschrift*, vol. 32, no. 1 (Jan./Feb. 1994), pp. 41–50. For material on the London Conference, initiating the joint UN/EC effort in the context of the ICFY, see 'Material relating to the London Conference (August 26–27, 1992) and the crisis in the former Yugoslavia', *US Department of State Dispatch*, vol. 3, Supplement no. 7 (Sep. 1992).

[44] The other Co-Chairman was former US Secretary of State Cyrus Vance, acting in his capacity as UN Secretary-General Javier Pérez de Cuellar's (later Boutros Boutros-Ghali's) Special Representative. Vance

through the UN Security Council, pursued at times a more assertive policy, in response to domestic as well as international pressures to attain greater concessions from the Bosnian Serbs.[46]

The lack of progress in Geneva left the UNPROFOR Bosnia-Herzegovina Command without a peacekeeping mandate. At the same time, the continuing spread and escalation of the conflict, and the need to co-ordinate UNPROFOR activities with those of the UN High Commission for Refugees (UNHCR), the International Red Cross and other humanitarian relief efforts, meant that the UN Security Council was continuously called on to respond. By August 1993, 42 resolutions and 15 mandate enhancements had been adopted since UNPROFOR was established by UN Security Council (UNSC) Resolution 743 of 21 February 1992[47] to help implement the so-called Vance Plan.[48] With a peacekeeping budget already strained beyond its limits, the UN lacked the means to back these resolutions with a commensurate increase in forces and logistic support.[49] The UN member states were also reluctant to commit more forces to Bosnia and Herzegovina out of fear of escalating the conflict. In the words of one analyst, this 'placed impossible demands on UNPROFOR and has generated legitimate criticisms from field personnel to the effect that the Security Council treats resolutions as if they are "self-executing"'.[50]

UNPROFOR in Croatia

By the time of the UN-brokered January 1992 cease-fire agreement,[51] Serb forces had occupied about one-third of Croatian territory. Under the terms of the Vance Plan, a UN peacekeeping force was deployed to conflict areas in Croatia's Slavonia and

was succeeded on 1 May 1993 in both capacities by Norwegian Foreign Minister Thorvald Stoltenberg. On 3 Dec. 1993, Yasushi Akashi, until recently the Secretary-General's Special Representative for Cambodia, replaced Stoltenberg as Special Representative for the former Yugoslavia. While Stoltenberg retained the ICFY Co-Chairmanship, Akashi was appointed UNPROFOR Chief of Mission.

[45] Criticized by many as a policy of 'peace at any price', legitimizing and consolidating Bosnian Serb territorial claims, the EC's position reflected the unwillingness of its member states in 1993 to commit more troops to enforce a settlement. At an emergency meeting on the former Yugoslavia requested by Lord Owen at the EC summit meeting in Copenhagen on 20 June, the use of military force was ruled out by all EC member states. See Lambert, S., 'Owen seeks new mandate', *The Independent*, 21 June 1993, p. 1.

[46] These included pressures to revoke the UN arms embargo on the republics of former Yugoslavia (UNSC Resolution 713 of 25 Sep. 1991) as it applies to the Bosnian Government, and pressures for outright US intervention. For a discussion of the UN arms embargo, see chapter 13, section VIII, in this volume.

[47] Berdal (note 6), p. 31.

[48] The Vance Plan was named after Cyrus Vance, the main architect of the UN-brokered settlement for Croatia.

[49] 'With outstanding contributions to UN peace-keeping accounts totalling $1260 million in mid-June and unpaid assessments amounting to some $2236 million, it was "highly probable that in the coming months the Organization will not be able to meet its day-to-day obligations"'. *Report of the Secretary-General Pursuant to Security Council Resolution 838* (1993), UN document S/26018, 1 July 1993, p. 7, citing the Secretary-General's report to the General Assembly of 24 June 1993, UN document A/C.5/47/13/Add. 1. Appendix 1A, last column, gives approximate values of outstanding contributions to UN peacekeeping operations in 1993.

[50] Berdal (note 6), p. 31.

[51] The Jan. 1992 agreement was the 15th cease-fire negotiated by Vance since his appointment as Special Representative in Oct. 1991.

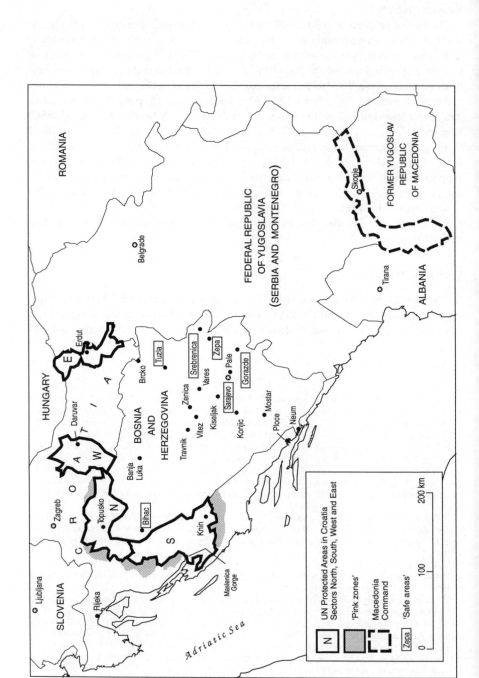

Figure 1B. The former Yugoslavia

Krajina,[52] claimed and controlled by Yugoslav National Army (YNA) and Krajina Serb paramilitary forces. The original mandate involved the deployment of some 14 000 troops and military observers to oversee the demilitarization of specially designated 'United Nations Protected Areas' (UNPAs), later expanded to include the monitoring of so-called 'pink zones' of predominantly ethnic Serb settlement, within Croatia's borders. In March 1992 Force Headquarters were established in Sarajevo, capital of neighbouring Bosnia and Herzegovina, which until then had remained relatively free of violence. By May 1992, 12 UNPROFOR battalions had been deployed to the four designated UNPAs within the Serb-occupied areas shown in figure 1B.[53] While all YNA units were gradually withdrawn to Serbia, many troops, some heavily armed, remained in Croatia, transferred to local Serb police forces.[54]

The resulting stalemate remained unresolved at the close of 1993, partly as a result of the formulation of the 1992 accord. The Vance Plan is ambiguous on the role of UNPROFOR in Croatia and the future status of the UNPAs. In the Croatian view, the role of the UN forces is to disarm the Serbs, facilitate the return of Croatian refugees and gradually enable the Croatian authorities to reassert their authority in Serb-held areas. In the Serb view, the role of the UN forces is to guarantee the security of the Serb enclaves and to safeguard the autonomy of the local Serb population. As UNPROFOR's authority swayed under the strain of having to supervise a peace agreement which it had neither the mandate nor the resources to enforce, the Serb position was strengthened. UNPROFOR failed not only to resettle Croatian refugees or re-establish Croatian local administration but could not even extend its own authority within the UNPAs, which remained under the control of local Serb forces.[55]

These tensions notwithstanding, political rather than military considerations dominated Croatian–Serbian relations in 1993, leaving UNPROFOR somewhat outside the equation. On 22 January 1993, Croatian forces broke the cease-fire agreement and launched an attack on Serb positions controlling the Maslenica Gorge, in an attempt to re-establish the severed road link to Dalmatia, cut off from the rest of Croatia by Serb-held southern Krajina. While the territorial issue was given much prominence, the planned February presidential election in Croatia seems to have been a more important factor behind President Franjo Tudjman's decision to launch the attack.[56] Similarly, in subsequent months both Belgrade and Zagreb recognized that complementary interests in Bosnia and Herzegovina argued against allowing their disagreements over the UNPAs to take precedence over the Geneva peace talks, especially following the collapse of the Croat–Bosnian alliance in Bosnia and Herzegovina in April. In the autumn of 1993, following the demise of the Owen–Stoltenberg Peace Plan (see below), the

---

[52] Slavonia, between the Drava and Sava rivers in north-eastern Croatia, borders on Hungary to the north, on Bosnia and Herzegovina to the south and on the former Yugoslav Autonomous Province of Vojvodina (incorporated by Serbia in 1989) to the east. Krajina (Serbo-Croat: border) is a name applied to areas on both sides of the Croatian–Bosnian border. In Croatia it applies to the area along the eastern border (roughly corresponding to UNPAs N and S, see figure 1B) historically settled by Serbs.

[53] For a summary of the UNPROFOR deployment to Croatia, see Shoup, P., 'The UN force: a new actor in the Croatian–Serbian crisis', *RFE/RL Research Report*, vol. 1, no. 13 (27 Mar. 1992), pp. 17–22.

[54] Vego, M., 'The army of Serbian Krajina', *Jane's Intelligence Review*, vol. 5, no. 10 (Oct. 1993), pp. 442–44; Moore, P., 'A return of the Serbian–Croatian conflict', *RFE/RL Research Report*, vol. 2, no. 42 (22 Oct. 1993), p. 17.

[55] Moore, P., 'The shaky truce in Croatia', *RFE/RL Research Report*, vol. 2, no. 21 (21 May 1993), p. 46.

[56] See Moore, P., 'Croatia and Bosnia: a tale of two bridges', *RFE/RL Research Report*, vol. 3, no. 1 (7 Jan. 1994), p. 112.

convergence of Serb and Croat interests in settling their respective territorial disputes with the Bosnian Government at the latter's expense set the tone for the continued talks.[57]

UNPROFOR in Bosnia and Herzegovina

By the time the first contingents were in place in Croatia in April 1992, war had spread to Bosnia and Herzegovina. Sarajevo immediately became the target of shelling by Bosnian Serb forces, placing the UNPROFOR command in the front line of the new conflict. By June 1992 the situation in Bosnia and Herzegovina had deteriorated to such a degree that UN humanitarian intervention became compelling. With UNSC Resolutions 761 of 29 June and 770 of 13 August 1992, UNPROFOR's mandate and strength were enlarged to ensure the security and functioning of Sarajevo's international airport and the delivery of humanitarian assistance to Sarajevo and its environs. With UNSC Resolution 776 of 14 September 1992, its mandate was further enlarged to protect the delivery by the UNHCR and other relief agencies of humanitarian supplies throughout Bosnia and Herzegovina.

Diplomatic efforts

Following the London Conference in August 1992,[58] Vance and Owen initiated, in the context of the Geneva peace talks, the search for a long-term solution for Bosnia and Herzegovina. On 2 January 1993, the three warring parties met face to face in Geneva for the first time since March 1992. As a basis for negotiation, Vance and Owen presented the parties with a map dividing Bosnia and Herzegovina into 10 autonomous provinces, with special status for Sarajevo. The Bosnian Serbs, controlling about 70 per cent of the Republic's territory at the time, were allotted 43 per cent.[59] The proposal was quickly accepted by Bosnian Croat leader Mate Boban. The Bosnian Government, under President Alija Izetbegovic, objected that the plan amounted to the endorsement of 'ethnic cleansing', but succumbed to strong US pressure to accept a slightly modified draft following a six-point US initiative by the new Clinton Administration, presented by US Secretary of State Warren Christopher on 10 February. This included a declaration of US preparedness to participate in the implementation and enforcement of a settlement that left the door open to the use of military force.[60] Izetbegovic signed the plan on 25 March. The Bosnian Serbs, under Radovan Karadzic, succumbed, after several months of hard negotiations, to pressures from the international community and, not the least, from Serbian President Slobodan Milosevic, and signed the agreement following a special meeting in Athens on 1–2 May. How-

---

[57] Sheridan, M., 'Muslims denounce Bosnia carve-up', *The Independent*, 24 June 1993, p. 1; Tanner, M., 'Serbs and Croats meet for secret peace talks', *The Independent*, 3 Nov. 1993, p. 12; Silber, L. and Tett, G., 'Bosnian foes peer into the abyss', *Financial Times*, 3 Sep. 1993, p. 3; 'Two factions report on pact for partition of Bosnia', *International Herald Tribune*, 22 Dec. 1993, p. 1; Moore (note 56), p. 113.

[58] See note 43.

[59] For a summary of the plan, including a map of the proposed division, see 'Bosnia and Herzegovina: peace negotiations', *IBRU Boundary and Security Bulletin*, vol. 1, no. 1 (Apr. 1993), pp. 2–3.

[60] Other key provisions in the US initiative were: the redrawing of provincial boundaries; the strengthening of the central authority of the Bosnian Government; and the establishment of a war crimes commission. See 'New steps toward conflict resolution in the former Yugoslavia', *US Department of State Dispatch*, vol. 4, no. 7 (15 Feb. 1993), pp. 81–82.

ever, the plan was subsequently rejected by the Assembly of Serbs in Bosnia and Herzegovina, meeting in the Bosnian Serb 'capital' of Pale on 5 May.[61]

The diplomatic failure to carry through the momentum of the Athens meeting was augmented by the failure of the UN to agree to deploy new forces in Bosnia and Herzegovina, to begin what the Russian Foreign Minister, Andrei Kozyrev, in a joint statement with Lord Owen, called a 'progressive implementation' of the Vance–Owen Plan.[62] This depended on the presence of US troops, but an emergency meeting in Washington of the foreign ministers of France, Russia, Spain, the UK and the USA resulted in a virtual abdication of US responsibility. On 22 May, the five ministers agreed on a 'Joint Action Program', formulated as a policy instrument for the UN Security Council, that limited any enforcement provisions to apply only to the military protection of the six 'safe areas' established by UNSC Resolutions 819 and 824 (see below), in effect killing the Vance–Owen Plan.[63] In part this turn-about reflected US disagreement with the EC over the arms embargo against the Bosnian Government. According to an unnamed EC source, '[t]he Europeans obtained America's agreement to ditch its proposal to arm the Muslims. The US obtained the European's agreement to ditch Vance–Owen.'[64]

On 27 July a new round of negotiations began in Geneva. In the new proposal presented by Stoltenberg and Owen, Bosnia and Herzegovina would be declared a 'union' of three republics, with a Serb republic controlling 52.8 per cent of the territory, a 'Muslim' republic controlling 30.0 per cent (including Sarajevo) and a Croat republic controlling 17.2 per cent. While the Serb republic would form a contiguous whole with borders abutting Serbia and Serb-controlled areas of Croatia, and the Croat republic would consist of two areas with borders abutting Croatia, the 'Muslim' republic would consist of a land-locked patchwork of six distinct parts: a main area centred on Zenica and Tuzla; a Krajina enclave in the west centred on Bihac; two eastern enclaves centred on Srebrenica/Zepa and on Gorazde; and the Sarajevo and Mostar areas, under UN and EC control, respectively. Special agreements with Croatia would guarantee free transit for the 'Muslim' republic to the Croatian seaports of Rijeka and Ploce, and a corridor arrangement with the Serb republic would provide access to the river port at Brcko. Disputes with the Croats over access to the Adriatic,[65] with the Serbs over access to the eastern enclaves and to the Sava River,[66] and dissatisfaction over the dis-

[61] 'Tragedy continues with "no sign of abatement"', *UN Chronicle*, vol. 30, no. 3 (Sep. 1993), p. 16.

[62] 'Kozyrev notes "unprecedented" consensus on Vance–Owen Plan' (transcript), Moscow Mayak Radio Network, 16 May 1993, and 'Seeks "progressive implementation"' (transcript), Moscow ITAR-TASS World Service, 16 May 1993, both in Foreign Broadcast Information Service, *Daily Report–Central Eurasia (FBIS-SOV)*, FBIS-SOV-93-093, 17 May 1993, pp. 10–11.

[63] For the text of and Secretary of State Christopher's commentary on the 'Joint Action Program', see *US Department of State Dispatch*, vol. 4, no. 21 (24 May 1993), pp. 368–70. See also Lambert (note 45).

[64] Savill, A. and Brown, C., 'Owen reviews role as Bosnia mediator', *The Independent*, 25 May 1993, p. 1.

[65] While the Bosnian Croat side agreed to a transit road policed by an international access authority, and the Croatian Government agreed to sell the Bosnian Government land for a sovereign port on the Dalmatian coast, Croatian President Tudjman refused to relinquish control over Bosnia and Herzegovina's Neum corridor, long held by Croat militias, even though Croatia has no legal claim to the territory. See Sheridan, M., 'Negotiations founder on Bosnian demands', *The Independent*, 3 Sep. 1993, p. 10; Moore (note 56), p. 113.

[66] See Traynor, I., 'Bosnian peace talks collapse', *The Guardian*, 2 Sep. 1993, p. 16.

tribution of territory led the Bosnian Government to reject the proposed terms for a settlement.[67]

In late November, France and Germany presented a third proposal for a settlement, involving the gradual lifting of UN economic sanctions on the rump Federal Republic of Yugoslavia (Serbia and Montenegro) in return for more territory to the 'Muslim' republic. The proposal was given a guarded reception by the other EU governments, torn between the need to take action to head off a humanitarian disaster and the danger of becoming embroiled in the civil war.[68] The negotiations foundered on disagreement over territory, and over the settlement on Sarajevo concluded in the previous round.[69]

UNPROFOR deployments and activities in 1993

While the failure of the successive peace plans was reflected in the changing geography of the conflict, the lack of progress towards a settlement meant that the various diplomatic initiatives had little impact on UNPROFOR's activities on the ground. While mission headquarters were moved to Zagreb in May 1992, after the initial Serb attack on Sarajevo, an UNPROFOR presence was re-established in the city in June, with Egyptian, French and Ukrainian units. Command headquarters for Bosnia and Herzegovina were established at Kiseljak, some 35 km to the west. A 7000-strong multinational force of mainly NATO units redeployed under national command formed the bulk of the Bosnia-Herzegovina Command, which in staffing, equipment and command structure effectively became a NATO operation.[70] National contingents were deployed as follows: British, with Belgian and Dutch transport units, at Vitez; Spanish at Mostar; French and Portuguese at Bihac; Danish and Norwegian at Kiseljak; and Canadian and Dutch at Banja Luka. Later in 1993 a Nordic battalion, comprising Danish, Norwegian and Swedish troops, was deployed to Tuzla, and a Malaysian battalion was deployed to Konjic, on the Sarajevo–Mostar road (see figure 1B).

A 'no-fly zone', banning unauthorized military flights in the airspace of Bosnia and Herzegovina, was established by UNSC Resolution 781 of 9 October 1992. At the request of the UN Secretary-General, NATO air forces, including a multinational Airborne Warning and Control System (AWACS) force as well as a Western European Union (WEU) air/sea force operating in the Adriatic, were tasked with monitoring

---

[67] While Stoltenberg and Owen stressed that the proposal was a compromise, in effect it confirmed Serb territorial gains. Most of the 'ethnically cleansed' areas, before the war largely populated by Muslims or Croats, were allocated to the Serb republic. See 'Bosnia Hercegovina: Geneva agreements', *IBRU Boundary and Security Bulletin*, vol. 1, no. 3 (Oct. 1993), pp. 2–4. Bosnian protests followed consultations between President Izetbegovic and Charles Redman, US President Bill Clinton's special envoy. According to Redman, it was the US view that the proposal was unfair to the Muslims and that it had to be changed in their favour. According to press reports, he again told Izetbegovic that the USA did not rule out lifting the arms embargo. See Sheridan (note 65), p. 10; Graham, G., 'US blames failure on Croats and Serbs', *Financial Times*, 3 Sep. 1993, p. 3. For a critical appraisal of the package of terms contained in the Owen–Stoltenberg Plan, including a map of a proposed flyover complex for the Brcko corridor, see Zumach, A., 'How the West forced Izetbegovic to sign', *Balkan War Report*, no. 21 (Aug./Sep. 1993), pp. 6–7.

[68] 'European Union proposal on Bosnia assessed', *Wireless File*, 26 Nov. 1993, p. 2; Barber, L., 'Franco-German plan to end Bosnian war', *Financial Times*, 9 Nov. 1993, p. 2.

[69] *IBRU Boundary and Security Bulletin* (note 67), p. 2.

[70] Command headquarters in Kiseljak were established from a section of a NATO Army Group HQ (NORTHAG in Germany), transferred with all necessary support elements. However, despite the links to NATO, the Command was and is not a NATO force. Officers were disengaged from NATO service and re-engaged as national officers before assuming their new commands. Eknes (note 42), pp. 25–26.

compliance with the ban.[71] The ban had primarily a symbolic function, given the limited contribution by air forces to the fighting on the ground.[72]

In the first months of 1993, UNPROFOR's efforts targeted mainly eastern and northern Bosnia and Herzegovina, where Bosnian Serb forces engaged in an aggressive policy of 'ethnic cleansing'. UNSC Resolution 819 of 16 April condemned the Serbian aggression and declared the besieged, predominantly Muslim, town of Srebrenica in eastern Bosnia a 'safe area', but calls made to increase the UNPROFOR presence in Bosnia and Herzegovina met with little enthusiasm. UNSC Resolution 824 of 6 May expanded the number of 'safe areas' to six (to include Bihac, Gorazde, Sarajevo, Tuzla and Zepa, all under siege and bombardment by Bosnian Serb forces), again to little or no avail, as UNPROFOR was given neither the mandate nor the resources to defend the areas with armed force. In April the uneasy alliance between local Croat forces and forces loyal to the Bosnian Government collapsed, as fighting shifted to central and southern Bosnia and Herzegovina. During the summer and autumn, fighting occurred on two fronts. To the east and north of Sarajevo, Serb forces were continuing the siege of the city and of the eastern Muslim enclaves, and were massing forces around the strategic Brcko corridor linking Serbia with the Serb-controlled areas in western Bosnia and in Croatia, as Bosnian Government forces pushed north to gain access to the Sava River. To the west and south of Sarajevo, Bosnian Government forces were laying siege to Croat enclaves around Vares, Vitez and Travnik, and were pushing south toward territory held by forces of the self-proclaimed Croat 'Republic of Herzeg-Bosna'. Croat forces laid violent siege, with heavy bombardment, to the partly Muslim city of Mostar, claimed as the 'capital' of 'Herzeg-Bosna'.[73] UNPROFOR forces in the area witnessed extreme acts of violence. The Croat massacre of Muslim peasants in the village of Stupni Do, near Vares, in October was only one in a series of atrocities committed by all three sides during the year. In several instances, notably in Mostar, local UNPROFOR units served a passive role as hostages, protecting by their presence the local population from shelling. Spanish and British construction units attempted, in vain, to repair and maintain the Sarajevo–Mostar road, an essential route for aid convoys to and from Sarajevo, Mostar and the Adriatic coast.

---

[71] Couvault, C., 'Russian instability draws NATO's attention', *Aviation Week & Space Technology*, 23 Nov. 1992, pp. 28–29; Couvault, C., 'NATO seeks upgrades, presses air/sea blockade', *Aviation Week & Space Technology*, 7 Dec. 1992, pp. 62–63; 'NATO support for the "no-fly" zone in the former Yugoslavia', *US Department of State Dispatch*, vol. 3, no. 52 (28 Dec. 1992), pp. 925–26. For a description of the NATO/WEU operation in the Adriatic ('Sharp Guard'), see Assembly of the Western European Union, 'An operational organisation for WEU: naval co-operation—part one: Adriatic operations, Report submitted on behalf of the Defence Committee by Mr Marten and Sir Keith Speed, Joint Rapporteurs', Document 1396, 9 Nov. 1993, *Proceedings*, thirty-ninth ordinary session, second part, Nov.–Dec. 1993, vol. II: Assembly documents (WEU: Paris, 1994), pp. 241–42.

[72] Despite the NATO/WEU air presence, the 'no-fly zone' was continuously violated. Between Nov. 1992, when monitoring began, and June 1993, 624 flights were recorded as apparent violations. *UN Chronicle* (note 61). Croatian supply flights into Bihac and Bosnian Serb aircraft operating out of Banja Luka accounted for most of these violations. However, according to testimony by Rear Admiral Mike W. Cramer, US Navy, Director of Current Intelligence, Office of the Joint Chiefs of Staff, 'even if the coalition were to completely enforce the no fly zone with no planes flying . . . it would not make an appreciable military difference'. See *Joint Chiefs of Staff Briefing on Current Military Operations in Somalia, Iraq, and Yugoslavia*, Hearing before the Committee on Armed Services, US House of Representatives, 103rd Congress (US Government Printing Office: Washington, DC, 1993), pp. 76–77.

[73] For a summary of the military situation at the year's end, see Collinson, C., 'Bosnia this winter—a military analysis', *Jane's Intelligence Review*, vol. 5, no. 12 (Dec. 1993), pp. 547–50.

The issue of enforcement came to a head in July–August, as the bombardment of Sarajevo increased in concert with the Serb diplomatic offensive in Geneva. While NATO prepared for UN-sanctioned air strikes against Serb artillery positions around the city, UNPROFOR argued that such strikes would put UN forces on the ground at grave risk of retaliatory attack.[74] The notion of air strikes found critics on both sides of the intervention debate, one side arguing that such strikes would only serve to defuse criticism of the USA and its NATO allies for not putting more forces on the ground,[75] the other insisting that they risked precipitating the West into an unwanted, full-scale military intervention.[76] Wary of the Somali experience, the latter view held sway as the West again pinned its hopes on the Geneva talks.

UNPROFOR in Macedonia

Under UNSC Resolution 795 of 11 December 1992, a separate Macedonian command was set up with headquarters in the capital city of Skopje to monitor the Republic's borders with the Federal Republic of Yugoslavia (Serbia and Montenegro) and Albania. Although formally part of UNPROFOR, it is in effect a separate operation, deployed at the invitation of the Macedonian Government to prevent a southward spread of the Yugoslav conflict. Initial deployment of 147 Canadian military observers began on 6 January 1993. These were replaced on 2 March by a Nordic battalion, numbering 700 Danish, Finnish, Norwegian and Swedish troops. In July these were supplemented by some 300 US Marines, for a complete force of about 1000 troops.

While not large enough to prevent even a small-scale cross-border incursion, the force (particularly in its inclusion of US troops) was intended to demonstrate that the Security Council regarded Macedonian sovereignty seriously. So far this unprecedented UN mission has achieved its goal, although it is not clear what the UN would do if it fails. Some observers claim that the deployment is simply an attempt by the Council to assuage its guilt over its lack of action in the main Yugoslav arena—Bosnia and Herzegovina. Others allege that it has worked so far simply because Serbia has been preoccupied with its involvement in Croatia and in Bosnia and Herzegovina. Others point to the danger that in authorizing preventive deployments on only one side of a border the UN risks abandoning its neutrality.

Conclusions

While the disengagement operation in Croatia presented the UN with a task much in keeping with traditional UN peacekeeping efforts elsewhere, such as UNMOGIP in Kashmir, UNFICYP in Cyprus or UNDOF in Syria,[77] UNPROFOR's mandate in Bosnia and Herzegovina in 1993 involved neither the implementation, monitoring or enforcement of a negotiated peace settlement, nor the protection of the civilian population—an omission puzzling to the local population and to Western public opinion alike. The failure of the warring parties to reach such an agreement, and the unwilling-

[74] 'Air strikes may cause more problems, UN chief warns', *Sydney Morning Herald*, 31 July 1993; Giovanni, J. and Adams, J., 'Sarajevo's besiegers sneer at international disarray', *Sunday Times*, 8 Aug. 1993, p. 13.

[75] Eyal, J., '. . . Or will air strikes only make it worse?', *Sunday Times*, 8 Aug. 1993, p. 12.

[76] O'Brien, C. C., 'Two UNs at war with each other', *The Independent*, 14 Aug. 1993, p. 18.

[77] See appendix 1A for details on these operations.

ness of the UN, the EC, NATO or the USA to commit their political authority and suf-ficient troops to enforce a peace, meant that UNPROFOR was forced to operate in Bosnia and Herzegovina without a medium- or long-term plan. With limited resources, its mission was instead to attend to a growing number of localized, short-term tasks, leaving its commanders with little room for manœuvre. At the same time, the military situation on the ground was far from simple. It involved in the first instance support of relief efforts during, and in the midst of, a tripartite war, involving largely irregular forces not always responsive to national or even local authorities.[78] In the words of one analyst, 'the principal military lesson from Bosnia . . . is that in the midst of continuing civil war any kind of support operation by the military is exceptionally difficult'.[79]

One strategy pursued by the UNHCR to partly overcome these difficulties was to airdrop supplies into Sarajevo and other besieged areas. In stark contrast to relief efforts using land convoys, which were dogged by road blocks, sniper fire, inhospit-able terrain and bureaucratic and diplomatic snags, the airdrop campaign was an undeniable—if largely unrecognized—success. Between July 1992 and February 1994, NATO transport aircraft operating under UNHCR supervision out of airfields in Germany and Italy delivered in nearly 11 000 flights more than 100 000 t of supplies, at a cost of about $124 million. According to UNHCR officials, had it not been for the airdrops, Sarajevo would have faced starvation.[80] Sadly, the success of the UNHCR airdrop campaign only highlights the failure of UNPROFOR in its main task in Bosnia and Herzegovina: to provide protection and support for UNHCR and other agencies' aid convoys and other relief efforts on the ground.

Inevitably, the unsatisfactory military situation in Bosnia and Herzegovina led to friction between the UN Headquarters in New York and the UNPROFOR commands in Zagreb and Kislejak. This was exacerbated by the Secretary-General's irritation over the tendency of Force commanders to pay more heed to their governments than to him.[81] Nothing illustrates better this tension than the 'waltz of the generals', the rapid turnover of Force commanders, that in late 1993 became the mission command's haunting *leitmotif*.[82] Disagreements between the Secretary-General's office and previ-ous UNPROFOR commanders—Lieutenant General Lars-Eric Wahlgren of Sweden and General Philippe Morrillon of France—led to their replacement. Wahlgren's suc-cessor as UNPROFOR Commander, French General Jean Cot, was summarily dis-missed by Boutros-Ghali in January 1994 for having openly criticized the Secretary-General's decision not to cede air-strike authority to military commanders on the ground.[83] In February 1994 it was announced that French Lt General Bertrand de Lapresle would replace Cot as UNPROFOR Commander. According to a press report

---

[78] Whether or not claims by local military authorities, that unresponsive forces are irregular, can be trusted is debatable. See Williams, I., 'United Nations: the Security Council's rubber-stamp resolutions', *Balkan War Report*, no. 21 (Aug./Sep. 1993), p. 27.

[79] Berdal (note 6), p. 22.

[80] The recovery rate of parcels delivered by airdrop has been estimated at 20–100%, depending on the accuracy of the drop and the ability of the besieged townspeople to scavenge under fire. Atkinson, R., 'Feeding Bosnia by air: one program that worked', *International Herald Tribune*, 18 Mar. 1994, p. 1.

[81] Eknes (note 42), pp. 35–40, 42; Traynor, I., 'UN military and political chiefs fall out over resumption of convoys to Bosnia', *The Times*, 16 Nov. 1993, p. 9.

[82] See Isnard, J., 'Valse des généraux à l'ONU', *Le Monde*, 21 Jan. 1994, pp. 1, 3.

[83] 'Commander of UN Force removed', *Jane's Defence Weekly*, 29 Jan. 1994, p. 11. While the issue of air-strike authority was the immediate cause for Cot's dismissal, relations between him and the UN politi-cal leadership, in particular Stoltenberg, had been strained for some time. Buchan, D., 'Friction with UN fails to deter French', *Financial Times*, 12 Jan. 1994, p. 2; 'France recalls UN general', *The Independent*, 19 Jan. 1994, p. 10.

citing French military sources, de Lapresle represented a 'last chance' to improve relations between UNPROFOR and UN Headquarters.[84] Morrillon's successor as UNPROFOR Commander in Bosnia and Herzegovina, Belgian General Francis Briquemont, resigned in January 1994 in frustration over lack of resources and support from UN headquarters. He had commented that he no longer bothered to read UN resolutions because he lacked the troops and resources to carry them out.[85] Briquemont's successor, British General Sir Michael Rose, signalled a greater willingness to make do with what there was, but also indicated his agreement in principle with Cot on the issue of air strike authority.[86] While Rose's 'can-do' attitude raised expectations of a more resolute handling of UNPROFOR's limited mandate in Bosnia and Herzegovina, the essential problem remained unresolved. The main theme of the 'generals' waltz' was not the authority of the UNPROFOR commanders but the credibility of the mission itself.

[84] 'De Lapresle to head UNPROFOR', *Jane's Defence Weekly*, 5 Feb. 1994, p. 3.

[85] Tett, G., 'Red tape tangles up UN troops in Bosnia', *Financial Times*, 12 Jan. 1994, p. 2.

[86] Bellamy, C., 'British commander takes over in Bosnia', *The Independent*, 25 Jan. 1994, p. 10.

2. Major armed conflicts

PETER WALLENSTEEN and KARIN AXELL

I. Introduction

In 1993, 34 major armed conflicts were waged in 28 locations around the world. In comparison to 1992, when there were 33 major armed conflicts in 29 conflict locations, these figures show a slight increase in the number of conflicts but a slight decrease in the number of conflict locations.[1] All the conflicts in 1993 were intra-state conflicts.

A 'major armed conflict' is defined here as prolonged combat between the military forces of two or more governments, or of one government and at least one organized armed group, and incurring the battle-related deaths of at least 1000 people during the entire conflict.[2] A conflict 'location' is the territory of a state. Since certain countries are the location of more than one conflict, the number of conflicts reported is greater than the number of conflict locations.[3]

The two new locations for major armed conflicts in 1993 were Georgia and Algeria, while three locations—India–Pakistan, Laos and Mozambique—were dropped from the list (see section II).

New conflicts arose in some locations, for instance in Bosnia and Herzegovina (with a new conflict between the Bosnian Government and Bosnian Croat forces) and in South Africa (where old conflicts between the South African Government and anti-apartheid forces became transmuted into one between the new Transitional Executive Council and the Freedom Alliance).

Appendix 2A provides information on the locations, contested incompatibilities, warring parties, and figures for active armed forces and deaths incurred in the conflicts. Major armed conflicts resulting in over 1000 battle-related deaths in 1993 alone were recorded in 13 locations: Afghanistan, Algeria, Angola, Azerbaijan, Bosnia and Herzegovina, Colombia, Georgia, India, Peru, South Africa, Sri Lanka, Tajikistan and Turkey. The conflict in Angola was the most devastating war in terms of human costs, with a high number of civilian war-related casualties. The conflicts in Azerbaijan and Georgia escalated most rapidly in 1993, resulting in both governments having

---

[1] In the *SIPRI Yearbook 1993*, 30 conflict locations were recorded for calendar year 1992. However, Chad was subsequently reclassified as a minor conflict and therefore excluded from the list of conflict locations for both 1991 and 1992. See Amer, R., Heldt, B., Landgren, S., Magnusson, K., Melander, E., Nordquist, K.-Å., Ohlson, T. and Wallensteen, P., 'Major armed conflicts', *SIPRI Yearbook 1993: World Armaments and Disarmament* (Oxford University Press: Oxford, 1993), chapter 3.

[2] See appendix 2A in this volume for definitions of the criteria. See also Heldt, B. (ed.), *States in Armed Conflict 1990–91* (Department of Peace and Conflict Research, Uppsala University: Uppsala, 1992), chapter 3, for the full definitions.

[3] Some countries are also the location of minor armed conflicts, but the table in appendix 2A presents only the major armed conflicts in those countries.

Table 2.1. Regional distribution of conflict locations with at least one major armed conflict, 1989–93[a]

Region	1989	1990	1991	1992	1993
Africa	9	10	10	7	7
Asia	11	10	8	11	9
Central and South America	5	5	4	3	3
Europe	2	1	2	4	5
Middle East	5	5	5	4	4
Total	**32**	**31**	**29**	**29**	**28**

[a] Note that the figures for 1989–92 which appeared in the *SIPRI Yearbook 1993* (table 3.1, p. 86) have been revised.

Source: Uppsala Conflict Data Project.

to relinquish control over substantial amounts of territory and in an increase in casualties.

Table 2.1 shows the decline in the number of conflict locations during the past five years, 1989–93. In terms of the regional distribution of conflict locations, Europe is the only region with an upward trend, with a sharp rise from two conflicts in 1989 to five in 1993. In Asia, the number of conflict locations fell in 1993, with no reports of conflict activity in the Indian–Pakistani and Laotian conflicts, even though no solutions to the incompatibilities were found. In Central and South America, three protracted conflicts continued—in Colombia, Guatemala and Peru.

All the major armed conflicts waged in 1993 were intra-state, concerning openly declared contested 'incompatibilities' of control over either government or particular areas or regions (territory). In 1993, 19 of the 34 major armed conflicts were over territory, as shown in table 2.2, confirming the tendency since 1991 for territorial issues to gain increasing salience as a source of conflict; 1993 marks the first year in which conflicts over autonomy or independence markedly outnumbered conflicts over the type of political system or government composition. Of the newer conflicts, several concerned territorial issues. The dissolution of Yugoslavia and the Soviet Union continued to produce major armed conflicts over borders and the extension of the state (in Azerbaijan, Bosnia and Herzegovina, and Georgia). The conflicts in Algeria and Tajikistan clearly concerned government issues, whereas the new developments in South Africa concerned a mixture of territorial and government issues. Demands for a White state and Zulu autonomy arose in response to fears of an African National Congress (ANC)-dominated majority government.

Interestingly, most of the incompatibilities in Africa and Central and South America in the period 1989–93 concerned control over government, whereas issues of territory dominated in other regions. Even in disputes over government, ethnic distinctions may be important despite the conflict issues being expressed in the struggle for government control.

Table 2.2. Regional distribution, number and type of contested incompatibilities in the major armed conflicts, 1989–93[a]

Region	1989 Govt	1989 Terr	1990 Govt	1990 Terr	1991 Govt	1991 Terr	1992 Govt	1992 Terr	1993 Govt	1993 Terr
Africa	7	3	8	3	8	3	6	1	6	2
Asia	6	8	5	10	3	8	5	9	4	7
Central and South America	5	–	5	–	4	–	3	–	3	–
Europe	1	1	–	1	–	2	–	4	–	6
Middle East	1	4	1	4	2	5	2	3	2	4
Total	*20*	*16*	*19*	*18*	*17*	*18*	*16*	*17*	*15*	*19*
Total	**36**		**37**		**35**		**33**		**34**	

[a] Note that the figures for 1989–92 which appeared in the *SIPRI Yearbook 1993* (table 3.2, p. 87) have been revised. The total number of conflicts for 1993 does not necessarily correspond to the number of conflict locations in table 2A, appendix 2A, since there may be more than one major armed conflict in each location.

Source: Uppsala Conflict Data Project.

The conflicts in Bosnia and Herzegovina particularly captured the attention of the international community. Despite international peace efforts, the number of casualties continued to rise. Bosnian Serbs and Bosnian Croats initially made considerable territorial gains, later meeting determined government resistance, with the Bosnian Government regaining some territory towards the end of the year. Bosnia and Herzegovina was the internationally recognized state, and the peace efforts in 1993 were aimed at restoring the country as one unit, albeit with considerably diffused authority for the central government. The contested incompatibility thus concerned territorial control within this state. In that sense, it was an intra-state conflict. However, supplies and personnel were clearly coming in across borders for all sides. It is inconceivable that Bosnian Serb advances could have been made without support from Serbia. There were also reports of the participation of regular troops from Croatia. Bosnian Serbs and Bosnian Croats also continue to contest each other's territory within Bosnia and Herzegovina.

II. Changes in the table of conflicts for 1993

Conflicts recorded in 1992 that did not appear in 1993

Three conflict locations for 1992 did not reappear in 1993: India–Pakistan, Laos and Mozambique. In Mozambique, a mediated peace accord brought the civil war to an uneasy peace, which was supported by UN peacekeeping operations. In contrast, there were no political agreements among the parties in the Indian–Pakistani and Laotian conflicts. However, neither were there reports of direct conflict activity.

New conflict locations in 1993

In 1993 the new conflict locations of Algeria and Georgia were recorded. Algeria witnessed the rise of Islamic militancy after the government cancellation of the 1991 elections which would have brought Islamic parties to power. In Georgia, troops fighting for the independence of Abkhazia evicted government soldiers from the region. While both conflicts were active in 1992, they did not cross the 1000-deaths threshold until 1993.

Inter-state tensions

Although no major armed conflict between states was reported in 1993, there was continued tension along some contested international borders. The Iraq–Kuwait border and the India–Pakistan Line of Control in Kashmir were the scenes of minor hostilities although in neither case was there regular military action.[4] The United Nations was active along both frontiers, with an observation mission supervising the new border between Iraq and Kuwait and being given a strengthened mandate to prevent minor border incursions, while UN military observers continued monitoring the lines in Kashmir.

Involvement of foreign forces in conflicts

In 1993 foreign troops were involved militarily in a number of conflict locations. Troops from Russia intervened in several conflicts emanating from the dissolution of the Soviet Union,[5] and troops from Croatia and Serbia in conflicts emanating from the dissolution of the former Yugoslavia. Armenian troops were also involved in the Nagorno-Karabakh conflict in Azerbaijan. Russian troops were directly involved in the fighting in Georgia and Tajikistan, in both cases supporting government forces against internal rebels; the Russian presence was in accordance with agreements between the governments. Neither Armenia, Croatia nor Serbia admitted regular military involvement outside their borders.

Conflicts with lowered intensity and peace efforts

In a number of major armed conflicts there was an abatement in military intensity in 1993 compared to 1992. This was true for the conflicts in Guatemala, Liberia, Myanmar, the Philippines and Somalia.

In Guatemala, conflict activities continued at a low level during the year. Peace talks broke down in April 1993 but were resumed in January 1994. The parties to the conflict in Liberia signed a peace agreement in July, and the number of deaths was significantly reduced compared to 1992. In the case of Myanmar, the Government was apparently trying to improve its international

---

[4] For details, see chapter 1 in this volume.

[5] For the conflicts on the territory of the former Soviet Union, see chapter 6 in this volume.

image by refraining from conducting its normal dry-season offensive. Nine different rebel groups concluded agreements with the Government, and remaining groups were under pressure to do the same. In the Philippines, where the Government reached agreements with right-wing military rebels and was interested in negotiating with the New People's Army (NPA), the NPA was internally divided on the issue. In the case of Somalia, the heavy international presence initially had an impact in reducing the level of fighting. In Cambodia, despite the presence of an international peacekeeping operation (UNTAC), fighting continued between the Khmer Rouge and the Cambodia Government.[6]

The year 1993 was also one of steps towards peace in three of the world's most protracted conflicts.

In South Africa, progress was made through direct negotiations, leading to an agreement in November between 21 parties. A new constitution was approved, granting equal rights to the entire population, and an interim government (the Transitional Executive Council) was formed, including the ANC and the Nationalist Party, to guide the country to its first democratic elections. A second case of *rapprochement* occurred between Israel and the Palestine Liberation Organization (PLO).[7] With the mediatory assistance of the Norwegian Foreign Ministry, Israel and the PLO negotiated an autonomy and recognition agreement that was signed in Washington in September 1993. There was also movement in the conflict in Northern Ireland, where the British and the Irish Prime Ministers issued a statement opening the door for direct talks with Sinn Fein, the political wing of the Irish Republican Army (IRA). The agreement was contingent on the IRA renouncing terrorism and observing a cease-fire. In all three cases, it remains to be seen if the developments will have an impact on the intensity of the conflicts. In none of these cases have the peace efforts had any major influence on reducing the number of casualties during the year.

[6] See also appendix 1B in this volume.
[7] See also chapter 3 in this volume.

Appendix 2A. Major armed conflicts, 1993

KARIN AXELL, BIRGER HELDT, ERIK MELANDER, KJELL-
ÅKE NORDQUIST, THOMAS OHLSON and CARL ÅSBERG*

The following notes and sources apply to the locations listed in table 2A:[1]

[a] The stated general incompatible positions. 'Govt' and 'Territory' refer to contested incompatibilities concerning government (type of political system, a change of central government or in its composition) and territory (control of territory [inter-state conflict], secession or autonomy), respectively.

[b] 'Year formed' is the year in which the incompatibility was stated. 'Year joined' is the year in which use of armed force began or recommenced.

[c] The non-governmental warring parties are listed by the name of the parties using armed force. Only those parties which were active during 1993 are listed in this column.

[d] The figures for 'No. of troops in 1993' are for total armed forces (rather than for army forces, as in the *SIPRI Yearbooks 1988–1990*), unless otherwise indicated by a note (*).

[e] The figures for deaths refer to total battle-related deaths during the conflict. 'Mil.' and 'civ.' refer, where figures are available, to *military* and *civilian* deaths, respectively; where there is no such indication, the figure refers to total military and civilian battle-related deaths in the period or year given. Information which covers a calendar year is by necessity more tentative for the last months of the year. Experience has also shown that the reliability of figures improves over time; they are therefore revised each year.

[f] The 'change from 1992' is measured as the increase or decrease in the number of battle-related deaths in 1993 compared with the number of battle-related deaths in 1992. Although based on data that cannot be considered totally reliable, the symbols represent the following changes:

+ +	increase in battle deaths of > 50%
+	increase in battle deaths of > 10 to 50%
0	stable rate of battle deaths (+ or – 10%)
–	decrease in battle deaths of > 10 to 50%
– –	decrease in battle deaths of > 50%

n.a.   not applicable, since the major armed conflict was not recorded for 1992.

Note: In the last three columns ('Total deaths', 'Deaths in 1993' and 'Change from 1992'), '. .' indicates that no reliable figures, or no reliable disaggregated figures, were given in the sources consulted.

---

[1] Note that although some countries are also the location of minor armed conflicts, the table lists only the major armed conflicts in those countries. Reference to the tables of major armed conflicts in previous *SIPRI Yearbooks* is given in the list of sources.

* Birger Heldt was responsible for the data for the conflict locations of Liberia, Rwanda, Sudan and Northern Ireland. Erik Melander was responsible for Azerbaijan, Croatia, Georgia, Tajikistan, and Bosnia and Herzegovina. Thomas Ohlson was responsible for Angola and South Africa. Kjell-Åke Nordquist was responsible for Colombia, Guatemala, Peru and Israel. Carl Åsberg was responsible for India; Ashok Swain and Sarbajit Pattnaik provided assistance in the case of India. Karin Axell was responsible for the remaining conflict locations. Ylva Nordlander and Kajsa Larsson provided assistance in the data collection.

Sources: For additional information on these conflicts, see chapters in previous editions of the *SIPRI Yearbook*: Amer, R., Heldt, B., Landgren, S., Magnusson, K. Melander, E., Nordquist, K-Å., Ohlson, T. and Wallensteen, P., 'Major armed conflicts', *SIPRI Yearbook 1993: World Armaments and Disarmament* (Oxford University Press: Oxford, 1993), chapter 3; Heldt, B., Wallensteen, P. and Nordquist, K.-Å., 'Major armed conflicts in 1991', *SIPRI Yearbook 1992* (Oxford University Press: Oxford, 1992), chapter 11; Lindgren, K., Heldt, B., Nordquist, K-Å. and Wallensteen, P., 'Major armed conflicts in 1990', *SIPRI Yearbook 1991* (Oxford University Press: Oxford, 1991), chapter 10; Lindgren, K., Wilson, G. K., Wallensteen, P. and Nordquist, K.-Å., 'Major armed conflicts in 1989', *SIPRI Yearbook 1990* (Oxford University Press: Oxford, 1990), chapter 10; Lindgren, K., Wilson, G. K. and Wallensteen, P., 'Major armed conflicts in 1988', *SIPRI Yearbook 1989* (Oxford University Press: Oxford, 1989), chapter 9; Wilson, G. K. and Wallensteen, P., 'Major armed conflicts in 1987', *SIPRI Yearbook 1988* (Oxford University Press: Oxford, 1988), chapter 9; and Goose, S., 'Armed conflicts in 1986, and the Iraq–Iran War', *SIPRI Yearbook 1987* (Oxford University Press: Oxford, 1987), chapter 8.

The following journals, newspapers and news agencies were consulted: *Africa Confidential* (London); *Africa Events* (London); *Africa Reporter* (New York); *Africa Research Bulletin* (Oxford); *AIM Newsletter* (London); *Asian Defence Journal* (Kuala Lumpur); *Asian Recorder* (New Delhi); *Balkan War Report* (London); *Burma Focus* (Oslo); *Burma Issues* (Bangkok); *Conflict International* (Edgware); *Dagens Nyheter* (Stockholm); Dialog Information Services Inc. (Palo Alto); *The Economist* (London); *Facts and Reports* (Amsterdam); *Far Eastern Economic Review* (Hong Kong); *Financial Times* (Frankfurt); *The Guardian* (London); *Horn of Africa Bulletin* (Uppsala); *Jane's Defence Weekly* (Coulsdon, Surrey); *Jane's Intelligence Review* (Coulsdon, Surrey); *The Independent* (London); *International Herald Tribune* (Paris); *Kayhan International* (Teheran); *Keesing's Contemporary Archives* (Harlow, Essex); *Latin America Weekly Report* (London); *Le Monde Diplomatique* (Paris); *Mexico and Central America Report* (London); *Middle East International* (London); *Moscow News* (Moscow); *Newsweek* (New York); *New Times* (Moscow); *New York Times* (New York); *RFE/RL (Radio Free Europe/Radio Liberty) Research Report* (Munich); *Pacific Report* (Canberra); *Pacific Research* (Canberra); *S.A. Barometer* (Johannesburg); *Selections from Regional Press* (Institute of Regional Studies: Islamabad); *Southern African Economist* (Harare); *Southern Africa Political & Economic Monthly* (Harare); *SouthScan* (London); *Sri Lanka Monitor* (London); *The Statesman* (Calcutta); *Svenska Dagbladet* (Stockholm); *Teheran Times* (Teheran); *The Times* (London); *World Aerospace & Defense Intelligence* (Newtown, Conn.).

Table 2A. Table of conflict locations with at least one major armed conflict in 1993

Location	Incompat- ibility[a]	Year formed/ year joined[b]	Warring parties[c]	No. of troops in 1993[d]	Total deaths[e] (incl. 1993)	Deaths in 1993	Change from 1992[f]
Europe							
Azerbaijan	Territory	1988/1990	Govt of Azerbaijan vs. Republic of Nagorno-Karabakh, Armenia	42 600 10 000 20 000	4 000– 10 000	> 2 000	+ +
Bosnia and Herzegovina*	Territory	1992/1992	Govt of Bosnia and Herzegovina vs. Serbian Republic (of Bosnia and Herzegovina), Serbian irregulars, Yugoslavia	60 000 80 000 136 500	20 000– 50 000	10 000– 30 000	+
	Territory	1991/1993	vs. Republic of Herzeg-Bosna, Croatia	50 000 103 500			
Croatia	Territory	1990/1990	Govt of Croatia vs. Serbian Republic of Krajina, Yugoslavia	103 500 16 000 136 500	6 000– 10 000*	100–500	+ +

* Fighting between the Army of the Serbian Republic of Bosnia and Herzegovina and the Bosnian Croat Defence Council (or Bosnian HVO, the armed forces of the Croat Republic of Bosnia and Herzegovina) is not included as a conflict since neither of these parties is a national government.

* This figure includes the fighting during 1991 in which not only the two parties participated (see *SIPRI Yearbook 1992*, chapter 11).

Georgia	Territory	1992/1992	Govt of Georgia vs. Republic of Abkhazia	20 000 5 000	2 500	2 000	+ +
United Kingdom	Territory	1969/1969	Govt of UK vs. Provisional IRA	274 800 200–400	3 100*	86	0

Provisional IRA: Provisional Irish Republican Army.
* Approximately half of these deaths were related to the conflict between the Govt of the UK and the IRA. The remaining deaths were nearly exclusively caused by sectarian violence by other paramilitary organizations.

Middle East

Iran	Govt 1970/1991 Territory 1972/1979		Govt of Iran vs. Mujahideen e-Khalq vs. KDPI	473 000*	..	50–200	..

KDPI: Kurdish Democratic Party of Iran.
* Including the Revolutionary Guard.

Iraq	Govt 1980/1991 Territory 1977/1980 1961/1980		Govt of Iraq vs. SAIRI* vs. PUK, DPK	350 000–400 000 10 000** 36 000***	..	..	..

SAIRI: Supreme Assembly for the Islamic Revolution in Iraq.
PUK: Patriotic Union of Kurdistan.
DPK: Democratic Party of Kurdistan.
* Most of the Shia rebels belong to this group.
** Total strength of Shia rebels.
*** Total strength of both Kurdish groups.

Location	Incompatibility[a]	Year formed/ year joined[b]	Warring parties[c]	No. of troops in 1992[d]	Total deaths[e] (incl. 1993)	Deaths in 1993	Change from 1992[f]
Israel	Territory	1964/1964	Govt of Israel vs. PLO* vs. Non-PLO groups**	176 000	1948–; >12 300	...	...

* The Palestine Liberation Organization (PLO) is an umbrella organization; armed action is carried out by member organizations. The main groups represented on the Executive Committee are Al-Fatah, PFLP (Popular Front for the Liberation of Palestine; George Habash), DFLP (Democratic Front for the Liberation of Palestine; Branch of Nayef Hawatmeh), DFLP (Democratic Front for the Liberation of Palestine; Branch of Yassar Abed Rabbo), ALF (Arab Liberation Front), PPSF (Palestine Popular Struggle Front; Samir Ghosheh), PLP (Palestinian Liberation Front; Mahmoud Abul Abbas) and PPP (Palestinian People's Party, formerly PCP Palestinian Communist Party). Apart from these groups, 10 other members of the Executive Committee are not affiliated with any particular political party, ideology or organization.
** Examples of these groups are Hamas and PFLP–GC (Popular Front for the Liberation of Palestine–General Command).

Turkey	Territory	1974/1984	Govt of Turkey vs. PKK	600 000 7 000–10 000	9 200– 10 500	3 000	0

PKK: or Apocus, Kurdish Worker's Party.

Asia

Afghanistan	Govt	1978/1978 1992/1992	Govt of Afghanistan vs. Hezb-i-Islami, Hezb-i-Wahdat vs. Uzbek militia (Dostum)	... ...	>1 000 000 Apr. 1992– Dec. 1993: >10 000	2 000– 3 000	...
Bangladesh	Territory	1971/1982	Govt of Bangladesh vs. JSS/SB	107 000 2 000–5 000	1975–; 3 000–3 500	<25	...

JSS/SB: Parbatya Chattagram Jana Sanghati Samiti (Chittagong Hill Tracts People's Co-ordination Association/Shanti Bahini (Peace Force).

Cambodia	Govt	1979/1979	Govt of Cambodia vs. PDK	135 000 8 000–10 000	>25 500*	...	...

PDK: Party of Democratic Kampuchea (Khmer Rouge).
* For figures for battle-related deaths in this conflict prior to 1979, see *SIPRI Yearbook 1990*, p. 405, and note *p*, p. 418. Regarding battle-related deaths in 1979–89, that is, not only involving the Govt and PDK, the only figure available is from official Vietnamese sources, indicating that 25 300 Vietnamese soldiers died in Cambodia. An estimated figure for the period 1979–89, based on various sources, is >50 000, and for 1989 >1000. The figures for 1990, 1991 and 1992 were lower.

India		Govt of India	1 265 000	33 600***	> 3 000****	—
	Territory	. ./. .	vs. Kashmir insurgents*	..		
	Territory	. ./1981	vs. Sikh insurgents**	..		
	Territory	. ./1992	vs. ATTF	..		
		. ./1992	vs BSF	..		
		1982/1988	vs. ULFA	..		
		1978/. .	vs. NSCN	..		
		. ./1991	vs. PLA	..		

ATTF: All Tripura Tribal Force.
BSF: Bodo Security Force.
ULFA: United Liberation Front of Assam.
NSCN: National Socialist Council of Nagaland.
PLA: People's Liberation Army.
* A number of groups are active, some of the most important being the Jammu and Kashmir Liberation Front (JKLF) and the Hizbul Mujahideen.
** A number of groups are active, some of the most important being the Khalistan Liberation Force (KLF) and the Khalistan Commando Force (KCF).
*** Only the Kashmir and Punjab conflicts. Of these deaths, approximately 25 200 were killed in the Sikh conflict and at least 8200 in the Kashmir conflict.
**** Of these, 2600 were killed in the Kashmir conflict.

Indonesia		Govt of Indonesia	279 900	15 000–	—
	Territory	1975/1975	vs. Fretilin	150–200	16 000 (mil.)	< 50

Fretilin: Frente Revolucionária Timorense de Libertação e Independência (Revolutionary Front for an Independent East Timor).

Location	Incompat-ibility[a]	Year formed/ year joined[b]	Warring parties[c]	No. of troops in 1992[d]	Total deaths[e] (incl. 1993)	Deaths in 1993	Change from 1992[f]
Myanmar	Territory	1948/1948	Govt of Myanmar vs. KNU	286 000 4 000	1948–49: 3 000 1950: 5 000 1981–84: 400–600 yearly 1985–87: 1 000 yearly 1988: 500–3 000	..	..
The Philippines*	Govt	1968/1986	Govt of the Philippines vs. NPA	106 500 8 400–12 500	21 000– 25 000**	523***	—
Sri Lanka	Territory	1976/1983	Govt of Sri Lanka vs. LTTE	110 800 7 000	> 26 000	> 2 000	..
Tajikistan	Govt	1991/1992	Govt of Tajikistan, Russia, Uzbekistan vs. Popular Democratic Army	2 000–3 000 2 030 000 40 000	20 000– 50 000	16 000– 20 000	0

KNU: Karen National Union.

NPA: New People's Army.
*   Clashes between the Moro National Liberation Front (MNLF) and the Govt have been reported. However, it is unclear whether MNLF controls the groups that carry out these attacks. MNLF has split into several factions.
**   Official military sources claim that 6 500 civilians were killed during 1985–91.
***   523 is the figure for total insurgency activity for the first six months of 1993.

LTTE: Liberation Tigers of Tamil Eelam.

Africa

Location		Year formation/ Year joined	Warring parties	Mil. forces 1993	Total deaths	Deaths in 1993	Change from 1992
Algeria	Govt	1992/1992 1993/1993	Govt of Algeria vs. FIS* vs. GIA	139 000 10 000–15 000** ..	1 700–3 000	1 100–2 400	++
Angola	Govt	1975/1975	Govt of Angola vs. UNITA	>50 000* >45 000*	>36 000 (mil.)** >86 000 (civ.)**	4 000 (mil.)** 16 000 (civ.)**	++
Liberia	Govt	1989/1989	Govt of Liberia, ECOMOG vs. NPFL	200–400 15 000–17 000 10 000	20 000*	<2 000	–
Rwanda	Govt	1987/1990	Govt of Rwanda vs. FPR	40 000 10 000–15 000	5 500	<1 000	..

FIS: Front Islamique du Salut, *Jibhat al-Inqath* (Islamic Salvation Front).
GIA: Groupe Islamique Armé (Armed Islamic Group). It is unclear whether there are ties between GIA and FIS.
* Several armed Islamic groups are brought together under the command structure of the FIS military wing.
** Total strength of all armed militants.

UNITA: União Nacional para a Independência Total de Angola (National Union for the Total Independence of Angola).
* Troop estimates refer to end-1993. Both sides recruited heavily throughout the year. UN estimates govt forces 65–70% demobilized prior to Sep. 1992 elections, while UNITA's demobilization rate is estimated at only 25%.
** When estimating all war-related deaths, incl. victims of war-induced starvation or disease, the UN suggests 450 000–500 000 deaths in Angola in Oct. 1992–Dec. 1993. During most of 1993, the UN estimates 1000 war-related deaths per day.

ECOMOG: Economic Community of West African States Monitoring Group.
NPFL: National Patriotic Forces of Liberia.
* Excluding 1993. Note that this figure includes the fighting in 1990–91 (incurring 15 000 deaths) in which other than only the two parties participated.

FPR: Front Patriotique Rwandais (Rwandan Patriotic Front).

Location	Incompatibility[a]	Year formed/ year joined[b]	Warring parties[c]	No. of troops in 1992[d]	Total deaths[e] (incl. 1993)	Deaths in 1993	Change from 1992[f]
Somalia	Govt	1991/1991	Govt of Somalia* vs. USC faction/SNA	.. ..	..	..	..

USC: United Somali Congress.
SNA: Somali National Alliance.
* There was no effective central government in Somalia in 1993; 'Govt of Somalia' here represents the issue over which the parties fought.

Location	Incompatibility[a]	Year formed/ year joined[b]	Warring parties[c]	No. of troops in 1992[d]	Total deaths[e] (incl. 1993)	Deaths in 1993	Change from 1992[f]
South Africa	Govt	1948/1961	Govt of South Africa vs. ANC	70 000	1984-93: 18 900*	4 400*	0
		1963/1992	vs. PAC	..			
		1977/1992	vs. AZAPO	..			
	Govt/ Territory**	1990/1993	vs. FA	..			

ANC: African National Congress (armed wing: MK, Umkhonto we Sizwe).
PAC: Pan-Africanist Congress (armed wing: APLA, Azanian People's Liberation Army).
AZAPO: Azanian People's Organisation (armed wing: AZANLA, Azanian National Liberation Army).
FA: Freedom Alliance (Conservative Party, Inkatha Freedom Party, Afrikaner VolksFront, and the leaders of the homeland governments of Bophuthatswana and Ciskei).
* Victims of 'political violence', according to Jan. 1994 statistics from the South African Human Rights Commission.
** The nature of the incompatibility changed as the actors in the negotiation process, including the Nationalist Party government and the ANC, agreed upon and in Dec. effectuated a partial transition of political power from the government to the Transitional Executive Council (TEC), pending the outcome of the Apr. 1994 elections. The incompatibility thus shifted to being between those in favour of the negotiated path to democracy, as laid down in the interim constitution adopted in Dec. 1993, and those against it. The new incompatibility includes claims for autonomy and secession by various groups that do not accept the content of the interim constitution.

Location	Incompatibility[a]	Year formed/ year joined[b]	Warring parties[c]	No. of troops in 1992[d]	Total deaths[e] (incl. 1993)	Deaths in 1993	Change from 1992[f]
Sudan	Territory	1980/1983	Govt of Sudan vs. SPLA (Garang faction)*	72 800	37 000– 40 000 (mil.)**	..	..

SPLA: Sudanese People's Liberation Army.
*   There were no reports on fighting between the Riek Machar faction and the Govt of Sudan.
**   Figure for 1991.

Central and South America

Location	Year formed/joined	Warring parties	No. of troops	Total deaths	Deaths in year	
Colombia	1949/1978	Govt of Colombia vs. FARC	139 000	..*	1 500 (mil.)	0
	1965/1978	vs. ELN	8 000**			
Guatemala	1967/1968	Govt of Guatemala vs. URNG	43 900	<2 800 (mil.)	<200	– –
			800–1 100	<43 500 (civ.)		
Peru	1980/1981	Govt of Peru vs. Sendero Luminoso	115 000	>28 000	<1 700	–
	1984/1986	vs. MRTA	5 000–8 000			
			500			

FARC: Fuerzas Armadas Revolucionarias Colombianas (Revolutionary Armed Forces of Colombia).
ELN: Ejército de Liberación Nacional (National Liberation Army).
*   In the last three decades the civil war of Colombia has claimed a total of some 30 000 lives.
**   Total forces of all anti-government guerrillas.

URNG: Unidad Revolucionaria Nacional Guatemalteca (Guatemalan National Revolutionary Unity).

Sendero Luminoso: Shining Path.
MRTA: Movimiento Revolucionario Tupac Amaru (Tupac Amaru Revolutionary Movement).

3. The Middle East: the peace and security-building process

RICHARD EISENDORF

I. Introduction

1993 will stand as a landmark in the history of the Middle East. It was a year of historic local diplomatic initiatives in a new international environment. The most important development of the year was the signing on 13 September of the Declaration of Principles by Israel and the Palestine Liberation Organization (PLO), the result of secret negotiations held in Norway since January 1993. This was followed by the signing of an Israeli–Jordanian Common Agenda on 14 September.[1] Throughout 1993, the official peace talks between Israel and Jordan, Lebanon, the Palestinians and Syria provided a framework in which bilateral relations and multilateral issues of Middle East security, economic co-operation, water resources and the environment, among other issues, continued to be discussed. The year ended with continuing negotiation on implementation of the Israel–PLO agreement and an expected resumption of bilateral and multilateral negotiations concerning other fronts.

Although the Declaration represents significant progress in the peace process, the final outcome of negotiations is still unclear. Several promising signs, including discussions addressing regional co-operation on the social, environmental and economic levels, indicate that the steps already taken towards achieving peace will yield lasting results, but the road ahead still presents many obstacles. On one level, there are numerous practical administrative issues to be resolved; on another level, there are serious unresolved tensions which have plagued the region for generations and will continue to exist in the region.

II. Principal issues

Israel and the Palestinians

Since the establishment of the state of Israel in 1948, the core Arab–Israeli conflict has been over control of a relatively small piece of land. Successive attempts to negotiate a settlement of Arab–Israeli conflicts did not resolve the crucial issue of establishing a Palestinian homeland, the lack of which gives rise to the 'Palestinian problem'. The recent talks, which may indeed lead to a successful resolution, have come closer than any other to realizing this goal,

---

[1] The complete texts of the Israeli–PLO Declaration of Principles and the Israeli–Jordanian Common Agenda are reproduced in appendix 3A.

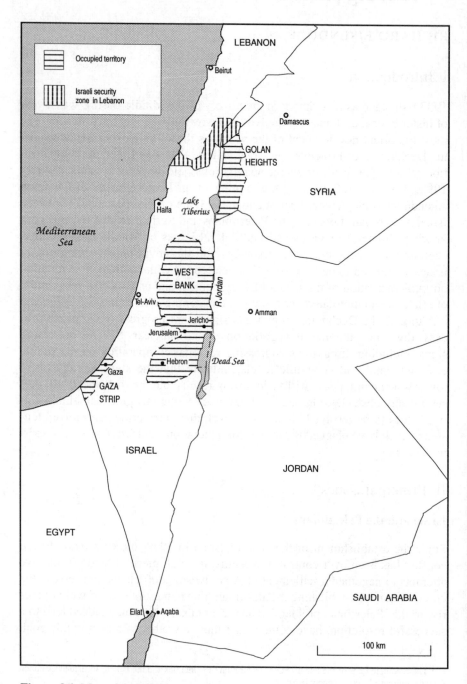

Figure 3.1. Map of the Middle East region

even if to a far more limited degree than would have been acceptable in the past.

The principal issues under negotiation between Israel and the Palestinians include: (a) the definition of the territory that is to be included in a settlement; (b) the degree of autonomy of a Palestinian administrative body; (c) the security structures to be established in the autonomous Palestinian territories and in Israel; and (d) a timetable for both implementing the Declaration and negotiating issues still under contention. The Declaration of Principles not only provides a detailed outline for an agreement between Israel and the PLO; it is also a declaration of the signatories' commitment to resolve outstanding issues in direct bilateral discussions. Although it has been characterized as a 'sellout' by some and as offering more than the Balfour Declaration gave Israel by others,[2] it stands as a monumental achievement.

Israel and Syria

On the Israeli–Syrian front, the primary issue is control of the Golan Heights. Lost to Israel in the 1967 Arab–Israeli War, the Golan is considered a strategic asset by both Israel and Syria. The territory overlooks much of southern Syria and northern Israel, as well as southern Lebanon, giving its occupiers a geo-strategic advantage over its neighbours.[3] Syria insists on its return to Syrian sovereignty as a prerequisite for normalizing relations with Israel. Israel under Likud Prime Minister Yitzhak Shamir was adamantly opposed to relinquishing the Golan: Israel, in fact, took steps in 1981 formally to annex the terri-tory.[4] When Prime Minister Yitzhak Rabin assumed office in July 1992, how-ever, Israeli negotiators acknowledged that United Nations Security Council Resolution 242, which calls for Israeli withdrawal from territory occupied during the 1967 War,[5] applies to all fronts in the Arab–Israeli conflict—a message which has been read to mean that the Golan is negotiable territory. Syria historically has linked its position regarding the Golan to a compre-hensive Arab–Israeli peace settlement. Syrian President Hafez al-Assad has defined a 'just and comprehensive' settlement as one which achieves 'Israel's total withdrawal from all Arab occupied land, primarily Jerusalem, the Golan

[2] Nusseibeh, S., 'Battle of the egos', *Jerusalem Report*, no. 13 (Jan. 1994), p. 19. The Balfour Declaration was the 1917 communication that demonstrated British support for the establishment of a Jewish national homeland in Palestine. It also required that safeguards be reached for the rights of non-Jewish communities in Palestine.

[3] Muslih, M., 'The Golan: Israel, Syria and strategic calculations', *Middle East Journal,* vol. 47, no. 4 (autumn 1993), pp. 611–32.

[4] Migdalovitz, C., The Middle East Peace Conference, CRS Issue Brief (Library of Congress, Congressional Research Service: Washington, DC, 1 Dec. 1993), p. 9. The Begin Government extended Israeli law over the Golan Heights in a *de facto* act of annexation, but no other country, including the USA, recognized it as legal or binding.

[5] Tomeh, G., 'UN resolution 242: stating the principles of a just and lasting peace in the Middle East', *The United Nations Resolutions on Palestine and the Arab–Israeli Conflict,* vol. 1, 1947–1974 (Institute for Palestine Studies: Washington, DC, 1975), p. 143.

Heights and southern Lebanon'.[6] Israel on the other hand has consistently sought to address the different fronts separately, long avoiding an international conference in which all Arab–Israeli issues would be open to inquiry.

Israel and Jordan

Since the Arab–Israeli War of 1973, Israeli–Jordanian relations have been less contentious than other fronts in the conflict. Official Jordanian policy advocates creative solutions to problems of regional security and has shown more flexibility *vis-à-vis* the Israeli–Palestinian problem.[7] Although Israel has long favoured a joint Jordanian–Palestinian solution, Jordan formally disengaged from the West Bank in 1988, giving Palestinians greater responsibility in the territory and in their relations with Israel. In spite of this, neither Israel nor Jordan abandoned the idea of confederation in which Jordan would have administrative links to a Palestinian entity. As it is neither a military nor an economic power in the region, Jordan poses less of a physical threat to Israel. Its importance in the peace process lies in its relationship with the Palestinians. As a country with a population of about 60 per cent Palestinian origin[8] (official Jordanian figures give 40 per cent[9]) and close geographical, institutional and familial links to the West Bank, Jordan will no doubt have a significant relationship with a future Palestinian entity. Official Israeli–Jordanian talks have fared well, but they take a back seat to those with the Palestinians and Syria, partly because Jordan aims to be part of a comprehensive settlement and partly, perhaps more importantly, because Jordan does not have the confidence to make a separate peace with Israel.

Israel and Lebanon

Since the start of the civil war in 1977, Lebanon has been a battleground on which many of the Middle East's conflicts are played out. Syria's presence and enduring influence in Lebanon, Israel's control of its self-declared security zone in the south and the numerous militias divided along sectarian lines have created a Lebanon without a central sovereign authority. Viewed by

---

[6] 'Saudi, Syria say comprehensive Mideast peace vital', Reuter, 19 Oct. 1993.

[7] Before the beginning of the official Arab–Israeli peace talks, Jordanian Crown Prince Hassan, brother and likely successor of King Hussein, presented a concept for a 'Helsinki-type' approach to the Middle East in a number of speeches to international audiences. He proposed an alternative definition of the term 'security' which addresses the root causes of conflict, including questions of demography, human rights, the environment and ideology. The speeches outline a plan which identifies democracy, security and prosperity as interrelated elements of stability in the Middle East. See El Hassan Bin Talal, 'Looking beyond the Gulf War: reconciliation and reconstruction', Paper presented at the National Conference in Response to the Gulf War, Tamalpais Institute, San Francisco, Calif., 23 Mar. 1991; Hassan, 'After war what?', Paper presented at the International Development Conference, Washington, DC, 1991.

[8] Tal, L., 'The Israeli–PLO accord: is Jordan doomed?' *Foreign Affairs*, vol. 72, no. 5 (Nov./Dec. 1993), p. 55.

[9] Muasher, M., 'Implications of the accord for Jordan's demographic, economic and political interests', *Jordan: Issues and Perspectives*, no. 16 (Nov./Dec. 1993), p. 14.

many as a virtual pawn of Syria, Lebanon's fate is inextricably linked to the dynamics of the Israeli–Syrian relationship.[10]

Lebanese officials have declared a readiness to settle with Israel on the basis of UN Security Council Resolution 425, which calls for Israeli withdrawal from southern Lebanon.[11] Israel, which has maintained a military presence in southern Lebanon since its invasion in 1982, is most concerned about the Iranian-backed Hizbollah, the strongest force of resistance in Lebanon, which the Lebanese Government has been unable to control. Prime Minister Rabin has declared that Israel has no territorial interest in Lebanon, characterizing Israel's problem with Lebanon as 'limited to security'.[12] He has outlined a plan by which Lebanon would disarm Hizbollah and bring it under control for a period of time. Given a stable northern border, Rabin has declared, Israel would withdraw its forces from southern Lebanon.[13]

Lebanon is positioned between two more powerful states, neither of which sets a high priority on its interests, and settlement for Lebanon is strongly dependent on the outcome of Israeli–Syrian conflicts.

III. The international and regional context

The Arab–Israeli conflict has led to five wars and numerous diplomatic initiatives to resolve the long-standing disputes in the region. The most recent initiative, the Arab–Israeli talks begun in Madrid in 1991, was the result of international diplomatic efforts as well as of developments on the international and regional stage.

The Middle East Peace talks began with an international conference in Madrid from 30 October 1991 to 1 November 1991 with the structure of a two-track approach. One track convenes bilateral meetings between Israel on the one part and Syria, Lebanon and a joint Jordanian–Palestinian delegation on the other. The second track, initiated at a conference held on 28–29 January 1992 in Moscow, addresses regional issues in multilateral meetings. Five working groups were formed to address the questions of arms control, the environment, economic development, refugees and water. These meetings are attended by representatives of each of the principal countries and the Palestinians, as well as representatives from a host of other Arab and European states, China, Japan, Russia, the USA, Canada and Australia. The multilateral talks supplement the bilateral by delving deeper into some issues, and they provide an opportunity for outside powers to help foster an atmosphere for the

[10] Norton, A., [in] 'Security zones in South Lebanon', *Journal of Palestine Studies*, vol. 23, no. 1 (autumn 1993), p. 76.

[11] UN Security Council Resolution 425, 19 Mar. 1978 (UN document S/12610, 19 Mar. 1978), reproduced in *Yearbook of the United Nations 1978*, vol. 32, p. 312; Nader, G., 'Prime Minister Rafiq B. Hariri of Lebanon', *Middle East Insight*, vol. 9, no. 2 (Jan./Feb. 1993), pp. 21–23, an interview.

[12] Rabin, Y., 'Israeli Prime Minister calls for "An Era of Peace" in the Middle East', *Middle East Insight*, vol. 10, no. 1 (Nov./Dec. 1993), p. 18, excerpts from an address by Yitzhak Rabin delivered on 16 Nov. 1993.

[13] Rabin (note 12), p. 18.

development of peace. From the start, Syria and Lebanon have boycotted the multilateral meetings.

It is valuable to consider the events of 1993 in the context of changes in the regional and international environment which led up to them. These developments include (a) the collapse of the Soviet Union and with it Soviet support for Syria, Iraq and the PLO, among others, (b) the alliances formed in the 1991 Persian Gulf War and the resulting impact of the war on the region, (c) the shift in Israeli domestic politics, and (d) the rise of Islamist groups in the West Bank and the Gaza Strip. As discussed below, each of these factors had far-reaching effects on the entire region, including the Arab–Israeli and Arab–Palestinian conflicts.

Collapse of the Soviet Union

The dissolution of the Soviet Union had serious implications for the region, particularly for the PLO and those Arab states which had maintained close ties to Moscow. Soviet support of the hard-line Arab states and US support of Israel and moderate Arab states gave the Middle East supra-regional importance as a battleground for superpower conflicts. With the decline of Moscow's support, the hard-line states and the PLO lost more than economic aid: they also lost political patronage in the international arena. The new Russian state assumed a new role when it aligned itself with the USA in sponsorship of the Arab–Israeli peace talks.

The Persian Gulf War

The Gulf War gave rise, for the first time in the region's history, to an Arab–US coalition aligned against another Arab state. The Iraqi invasion of Kuwait and the inter-Arab conflict that followed confirmed for Arabs and for the world at large the decline of Arab nationalism and its further weakening as a unifying force in the Arab world. Since 1948, the Palestinian cause had been the *cause célèbre* of the Arab world and Israel had come to symbolize the root of all the region's troubles. In the Gulf War, interests of security and political and economic alliances took precedence over these long-held associations.

Seeking to make the war into an ideological battle, Iraq turned its guns against Israel. The Arab–US coalition remained intact, however, and Israel did not respond to Iraq's attacks. It was clear that the once unified alliance of the Arab states against Israel had begun to crumble.[14]

The alliance of PLO Chairman Yasser Arafat with President Saddam Hussein in this war had detrimental effects on the PLO. As a result, the PLO

---

[14] Joffé, G., 'Iraq and Kuwait: the invasion, the war and the aftermath', *The Middle East and North Africa, 1993* (Europa Publications, Ltd.: London, 1992), pp. 14–19.

and Palestinians became outcasts as Gulf funds were cut,[15] and amid accusations that they had colluded with the invading Iraqi forces more than 250 000 Palestinians were expelled from the Gulf region.[16] The PLO, known for its 'cradle to grave' economic and social services, faced serious economic crisis by late 1991. As an indication, the budget of the Palestine Union of Charitable Organizations, which receives funding from the PLO and other Arab and international sources, was cut by approximately 70 per cent.[17] Other PLO-funded institutions reported similar cuts, while social services and subsidies were also reduced.[18] One result of the economic crisis was that the PLO suffered a dramatic loss of popular political support.

Election of the Israeli Labour Government

After almost one year of the peace negotiations, the Israeli Labour Party won the June 1992 election and formed a coalition government. In contrast to Shamir's intention to let the talks drag on without resolution,[19] one of Yitzhak Rabin's campaign promises was to settle the Palestinian question within nine months. Labour's victory opened the door to new possibilities. Even before the election, the idea of 'Gaza first', by which Israel would withdraw from Gaza unilaterally or as part of a negotiated settlement, had already been gaining currency in Labour circles. Such a plan was not accepted by Likud.

Another factor distinguishing Rabin's Labour Party was its position on Israeli settlements in the West Bank and Gaza. At a time when domestic economic concerns were paramount, with a severe housing shortage and 11.5 per cent unemployment (about 40 per cent among new immigrants),[20] the government's expenditure on settlements was becoming increasingly unpopular and economically untenable. Determined to improve Israel's economic well-being and under pressure from the international community, one of Rabin's first steps upon taking office was to stop the building of new settlements in the West Bank and Gaza. While projects already under way continued, the Rabin government gave less indication of continued support for them.

---

[15] Kuwait, Saudi Arabia and the United Arab Emirates cut all aid to Fatah (Arafat loyalists in the PLO) but resumed funding at a reduced level in 1993. See Gazit, S. (ed.), *The Middle East Military Balance: 1992–1993* (Westview Press: Boulder, Colo., 1993), p. 351.

[16] Peretz, D., *Palestinians, Refugees and the Middle East Peace Process* (United States Institute of Peace Press: Washington, DC, 1993), p. 102.

[17] Gubser, P., 'Middle East trip report: 25 Oct.–14 Nov. 1990' (American Near East Refugee Aid: Washington, DC, Nov. 1990), pp. 6–7.

[18] Abu Taomeh, K., 'Intifadah on a shoestring', *Jerusalem Report*, 11 Mar. 1993, p. 25. PLO-affiliated newspapers and journals were reportedly forced to cut their budgets by 30–40% in early 1991 in response to worsening economic conditions, and some Palestinian welfare services were reportedy cut by as much as 75%.

[19] Susser, L., 'Rabin's master plan', *Jerusalem Report*, 16 July 1992, p. 12.

[20] Carnegy, H., 'Rabin will be no pushover for the peace process', *The Guardian,* 25 June 1992, p. 4.

Islamic radicalism

The decline of the secular nationalist PLO contributed to the emergence of politically oriented Islamic organizations in the West Bank and Gaza. Hamas, founded with the start of the *intifada*, was one of the most popular of the groups claiming adherents among a growing portion of the Palestinian population. Part of Hamas' appeal arose from the PLO's own inability to improve the Palestinians' situation after years of upheaval. In 1988, the PLO had declared its commitment to a negotiated settlement and renounced the use of violence.[21] The Islamists, on the other hand, remained committed to armed struggle, which appealed to the young population of the territories, many of whom identified with the Islamists' image of strength and resistance.[22] The conflict between the secular, moderate PLO and the theologically based, more radical Hamas continues, with an estimated 40–60 per cent of Gazans and 25–40 per cent of West Bank Palestinians sympathetic to the Islamist groups.[23]

The rise of Islamic extremism in the territories had a dual effect on Israeli diplomacy. On the one hand, it fuelled reductionist claims that the Palestinians are bent on the destruction of Israel. On the other hand, it forced Israel to look more closely at internal Palestinian dynamics. Israel's refusal to enter into negotiations with the PLO for years had indirectly played into the hands of the Islamists, contributing to their popularity. Compared to the Islamists, the PLO represented a more moderate position and, although Israel was loath to deal directly with the PLO, there was little alternative. The local leadership in the territories lacked authority to negotiate, and Hamas was a far less appealing option. By entering into secret negotiations with the PLO in Norway, Rabin was taking advantage of Arafat's weakened position and, paradoxically, was arguably negotiating with the only Palestinian who could strike a deal.

IV. The official peace negotiations

In 1993, two rounds of bilateral talks took place in Washington. The ninth round was held from 27 April to 13 May and the tenth from 15 to 30 June. These meetings, taking place in ignorance of the secret talks that were going on between Israel and the PLO, worked to narrow the differences on all fronts in the Arab–Israeli conflict. For over a year the bilateral and multilateral talks had served to identify areas of difference between the parties, but had produced no tangible results.

Since the breakdown of the previous round in December 1992, the atmosphere had been tense. Round eight stopped short when Arab delegations

---

[21] Mark, C., Palestinians and Middle East Peace: Issues for the US, CRS Issue Brief (Library of Congress, Congressional Research Service: Washington, DC, 17 Dec. 1993), p. 14.

[22] Wilkinson, P., 'Hamas—an assessment', *Jane's Intelligence Review,* July 1993, p. 313. A poll held in late 1991 found that only 55% of Palestinian youths supported the peace negotiations. See Peretz (note 16), p. 38.

[23] Wilkinson (note 22).

walked out after Israel expelled 415 suspected Hamas activists to southern Lebanon. The Arab states, eager to resume talks and cognizant of the threat of Islamists to their own societies, condemned the expulsion but did little more. Palestinians sided with Hamas in condemning the expulsion and refused to return to the negotiating table without a satisfactory resolution. In the end, helped by Egyptian President Hosni Mubarak, the Palestinians and Israel came to a compromise. Israel agreed to a timetable for the return of the expelled Palestinians,[24] and Faisal Husseini became the head of the Palestinian negotiating team. Husseini's Jerusalem residency and overt ties to the PLO had previously kept him off the delegation and relegated him to an advisory capacity. As one of the most popular Palestinians in the territories, his promotion to chief negotiator was a boon for the Palestinians. In addition to satisfying them, this agreement also averted UN-invoked sanctions against Israel by securing a US commitment to block such a move.[25] All parties agreed to return to the negotiating table for the ninth round of bilateral talks in April 1993.

The Israeli–Palestinian track

When the make-up of the Palestinian delegation was established before the opening of the Madrid conference, it was agreed that representatives must be residents of the West Bank or Gaza, excluding Jerusalemites and members of the PLO. After a stand-off between Israeli and Palestinian negotiators in the second round of talks, this formula was modified. Two joint delegations were formed, one with nine Palestinians and two Jordanians, the other with nine Jordanians and two Palestinians. Still without direct PLO representation, this formula was again modified when Faisal Husseini became leader of the Palestinian team. After the revelation of the secret Norway talks at the end of 1993, Israel and the PLO formally opened direct bilateral negotiations.

In the early months of 1993, Israel sealed off the West Bank and Gaza after an increasing number of attacks within Israel. Israelis were feeling the tension before the closure as day after day brought reports of incidents in different cities and towns throughout Israel. The closure also cut East Jerusalem off from the rest of the West Bank. For the Palestinians, this sparked concern that Israel was making policy by creating facts on the ground, and they hardened their negotiating stance on Jericho. [26]

As the first talks of 1993 began, the Israeli and Palestinian delegations established working groups on water and land, self-government and human rights better to address some of their outstanding differences. A comparison of a proposed 10-point declaration of principles presented by the Palestinians in this meeting with Israel's draft proposal on interim self-government arrange-

---

[24] 'The reporter', *Jerusalem Report,* 13 Jan. 1994, p. 4. By the end of 1993, all the deportees were brought back except 18 who chose to remain in Lebanon, fearing imprisonment if they returned.
[25] Susser, L., 'More please', *Jerusalem Report,* 25 Feb. 1993, p. 20.
[26] Migdalovitz (note 4), p. 8.

ments presented at the December 1992 round of talks highlights many of these differences.[27]

Concerning jurisdiction, the Palestinians sought authority over all of the West Bank and Gaza as defined by the pre-1967 borders, while Israel insisted on retaining control of Jerusalem and direct authority over Israeli settlements and main thoroughfares. Both sides agreed to the formation of a legislative body or 'self-government authority'. However, whereas the Palestinian plan called for a body with about 180 delegates and full executive, judicial and legislative powers,[28] Israel envisioned only a 12- to 20-member council with limited legislative powers. The Palestinian negotiators called for the Israeli civil administration and military government to be disbanded, while Israel insisted on maintaining the military government and subordinating a Palestinian political authority to it. Concerning a timetable for implementation, the Palestinians would have liked to see negotiations on the final status of a Palestinian authority start within 18 months, but the Israelis preferred them to begin three years after the establishment of Palestinian self-rule. Recalling the age-old differences Israelis and Palestinians have over the implementation of UN Security Council Resolutions 242 and 338,[29] in their proposal Palestinians emphasize Israeli withdrawal from *all* the territories occupied in 1967. Israelis have insisted on talking about the principle of exchanging land for peace, interpreting the resolutions to be referring to *some* of the territories occupied in 1967.

Towards the end of the ninth round, the USA sought to synthesize the Israeli and Palestinian positions in a draft statement of principles, but this brought no further progress in the talks. At the 10th round of talks, Israeli and Palestinian negotiators continued to work on a declaration of principles. They made little progress and were deadlocked over whether the issue of Jerusalem would be addressed in the interim or the final status negotiations. The Palestinians wanted to discuss Jerusalem in the interim phase, and Israel refused to discuss the issue at all.[30] Another proposal presented by US negotiators to bridge Israeli and Palestinian positions did little to bring the parties closer together.

[27] The text of the Israeli plan and a discussion of differences appear in *Peacewatch Anthology: Analysis of the Arab–Israeli Peace Process from the Madrid Peace Conference to the Eve of President Clinton's Inauguration* (Washington Institute for Near East Policy: Washington, DC, 1993), pp. 161–69. The points of disagreement are also discussed in Susser, L., 'Back to the shuttle? Israel hopes the personal touch of a visiting US envoy can end the peace talks stalemate', *Jerusalem Report*, 3 June 1993, p. 17.

[28] Israeli negotiator Itamar Rabinovich, in a speech to Arab journalists on 14 Apr. 1993, pointed out that '180 is the number of representatives from the West Bank and Gaza in the Palestine National Conference', the PLO's governing authority. See Rabinovich, I., 'The prospects for peace', *Middle East Insight*, vol. 9, no. 3 (May/June 1993), p. 28.

[29] UN Security Council Resolution 242, 22 Nov. 1967 (UN document S/8247, 22 Nov. 1967), reproduced in *Yearbook of the United Nations 1967*, vol. 21, pp. 257–58; UN Security Council Resolution 338, 22 Oct. 1973 (UN document S/11036, 22 Oct. 1973), reproduced in *Yearbook of the United Nations 1973*, vol. 27, p. 213; Tomeh (note 5), pp. 143, 151.

[30] Migdalovitz (note 4) p. 8.

The Israeli–Syrian track

Before 1993, little progress was made in talks between Israel and Syria. Although they are reported to have been working on a draft declaration of principles, their negotiations produced no tangible results. A text of a Syrian-proposed statement of principles, printed in an Arabic weekly in late 1992, reinforces Syria's public positions on the questions of the Golan and Middle East peace. It restates Syria's desire for a comprehensive solution which 'requires a settlement on all fronts' and calls for 'total Israeli withdrawal from the Golan Heights and the evacuation and dismantling of various settlements from occupied Syrian lands'. These two requirements, which consistently characterize Syrian negotiating positions, were repeated throughout 1993.[31]

Until September 1993, Syria enjoyed a great deal of attention as one of the principal parties setting the tone in the Arab–Israeli peace talks. Recognized as the most likely area of conflagration, the Israel–Syria front is given significant importance in the talks. Although overshadowed by Israeli–Palestinian events in the latter part of 1993, Syria is likely to regain its prominence when negotiations resume in early 1994.

Israel's position *vis-à-vis* Syria shifted when, with the Labour election victory in July 1992, Itamar Rabinovich was appointed to head its delegation to the Israeli–Syrian talks. Although Israel then acknowledged a willingness to discuss an exchange of land for peace on the Golan, it fell short of Syria's requirement for full withdrawal. For its part, Israel insists on a full peace which entails open borders, embassies, diplomatic relations, normal cultural and commercial relations, and mutual security arrangements.[32]

After the Declaration of Principles was signed and passed by a large majority in the Israeli Knesset (Parliament), Rabin reported on the Syrian front that 'there is a draft declaration of principles, but it has not yet passed the problematic clause of the depth of withdrawal and the clause on the substance of peace'.[33] With implementation likely to take some time, Rabin is playing a balancing game, shoring up support for the Israel–PLO deal before forging ahead on another front. Already declaring his intention to put the question of withdrawal from the Golan to a referendum, Rabin is not likely to move too quickly on the Syrian front. Polls in Israel indicate that a great majority do not favour withdrawing from the Golan. In May 1993, 62 per cent (a figure slightly lower than that of January 1993) thought that Israel should not give up any of the Golan. Thirty-six per cent of respondents thought that Israel should withdraw from some of the territory, with the majority of them (19 per cent) agreeing to 'a small part'.[34] It is worth noting that among military officials familiar with the defensibility of Israel a different line of thinking is apparent.

---

[31] The text of the proposed statement of principles is reproduced in appendix 3A.
[32] Migdalovitz (note 4), p. 10.
[33] *Ma'ariv*, as reported in *Mideast Mirror*, 24 Sep. 1993, p. 2.
[34] Results of a Jerusalem Report/Smith Research Center poll conducted while the ninth round of talks was under way, reported in 'Exclusive poll: 62 per cent oppose a land-for-peace deal on the Golan Heights', *Jerusalem Report*, 3 June 1993, p. 4.

Polls of Israeli reserve generals indicate that 71 per cent think that security arrangements are possible if much of the Golan is returned to Syria.[35]

The Israeli–Jordanian track

The Jordanian track has proved to be less contentious than the Israeli–Palestinian or Israeli–Syrian negotiations. However, progress has been tempered by the pace of talks on the other fronts. Early on in the Madrid process, Israel and Jordan had been negotiating a common agenda. They had reached an agreement on the agenda in principle in the October/November 1992 round of bilateral talks, and came to full agreement in the ninth round in June 1993. Jordan, however, would not sign the agenda until progress was made in the other bilateral talks. On 14 September, one day after the signing of the Israeli–Palestinian Declaration of Principles, Israel and Jordan initialled their Common Agenda. While simply stating the intentions of both parties to conclude a peace agreement, the Common Agenda is notable in so far as it delineates the common interests of Israel and Jordan. Both agree to the goal of achieving a 'just, lasting and comprehensive peace', and they commit themselves to address a number of issues including security, water, refugees and displaced persons, borders and territorial matters.[36]

V. The Norway talks

The secret talks held over the course of eight months in Norway were a surprise to the world. Taking place at a time when the official negotiations were all but stalled, they shocked even the Arab and Israeli delegations meeting in Washington when it was revealed that these contacts had been going on without their knowledge and had resulted in a Declaration of Principles which by August 1993 had been initialled by Israel and the PLO.

The Norwegian Institute for Applied Social Science (FAFO) in Oslo was instrumental in facilitating the secret contacts between the Israelis and Palestinians. What began as exploratory discussions between Israeli academic and political activist Yair Hirschfeld and PLO aide Ahmed Krai turned into serious direct negotiations between Israel and the PLO, engaging the attentions of, and in the later stages the direct involvement of, Yitzhak Rabin and Yasser Arafat. The talks took place in secluded villas, private homes and apartments in Norway, Sweden and France under the sponsorship of the then Norwegian Foreign Minister, Johan Jørgen Holst, and key figures in FAFO. Without the involvement of third-party interests of a superpower such as the USA, this small Norwegian group helped set the stage for a successful outcome.

---

[35] Rabin, E., 'A survey: about 70 per cent of the senior reserve officers believe in conceding most of the territories', *Ha'aretz*, 21 June 1992, as translated by Project Nishma, Washington, DC.

[36] Appendix 3A gives the complete text of the Common Agenda.

In the history of Middle East relations, adversaries and mediators have used both public negotiations and private 'back channels' to resolve regional conflicts. Although the fact of such talks is rarely publicized, Arab and Israeli interlocutors have met in private forums over the years. Some such contacts have been official while others were unofficially initated by non-governmental organizations or private citizens. As the Israeli–Palestinian negotiations held in Norway reveal, secret talks offer certain benefits, but also face a number of challenges.

One advantage is that private talks can be more informal and can allow for a free exchange of ideas. At the start of the Norway talks, Hirschfeld and Krai worked together, seeing their conflict as a shared problem, and 'brainstormed' about ways to solve it. Operating beyond public scrutiny, ideas can be presented and discussed without participants losing face or damaging their negotiating stature. This atmosphere allows participants to explore options that official delegations may not even consider on principle. For such discussions to be effective, it is necessary for participants to operate with realistic assessments of the limits of what is acceptable to their respective leaders. In Norway, the first meeting between Hirschfeld and Krai had many of these characteristics. Coming together to find a solution, they were able to explore scenarios without making them negotiating postures.

Another advantage of back-channel talks is the benefit that can come from extended stays in secluded settings. As with the Norway talks and other such forums, the long hours spent in sessions, over meals and during breaks can contribute to creating a congenial atmosphere and to breaking down the personal animosity that often colours public negotiations. In private, talks which necessarily go through a negotiation process can develop at a comfortable pace. They are not driven, as public forums can be, by expectations fuelled in part by an active press eager for a story or a need to demonstrate results or advantage to constituencies back home. Israelis and Palestinians met in the Norway talks in about 14 sessions over more than eight months. Their meetings at times produced results, and at times were deadlocked, but they persisted without interruption until they reached agreement. Meanwhile the focusing of public attention on the official talks caused negotiators at times to walk out, at times to downgrade their delegations and to prevent even the exploration of certain issues.

Despite numerous advantages, there are also disadvantages to secret talks. Being in the public arena can add to the momentum of progress, and their visibility can further encourage participants to achieve results. Public gestures can play a role in breaking a deadlock or shifting perceptions in a way that secret talks cannot. A striking example is former Egyptian President Anwar Sadat's trip to Jerusalem to address the Israeli Knesset in 1977. This single act had a transformational effect on the region, allowing what did not seem possible one day to be seen in a different light the next.

Another challenge of secret negotiations is that negotiators do not have the opportunity to cultivate a base of support among their constituencies. With the discussions in Norway, when they arrived at an agreement, Arafat and Rabin then had to sell the agreement to their home constituencies. The internal discord that resulted among the Palestinian leadership led to the resignation of several members of the official negotiating team, as well as to conflict within the PLO. In Israel, the disclosure served to deepen the rift between Labour and Likud.

The negotiations that resulted in the Declaration of Principles were remarkable, occurring at a time when the official talks were so visibly gaining little ground. Their success has encouraged Israel and its other interlocutors to pursue other opportunities for direct discussions.

The Declaration of Principles

The signing of the Declaration of Principles on 13 September 1993 was the result of more than eight months of secret negotiations. Four days earlier, on 9 September, Arafat and Rabin had exchanged letters of mutual recognition.[37] Arafat recognized Israel's right to exist, reinforced his acceptance of UN Security Council Resolutions 242 and 338[38] and of the peace process, and declared his commitment to the peaceful resolution of conflicts. He declared that articles of the Palestinian Covenant which contradict these commitments were invalid and pledged himself to submit changes to the Palestine National Council. He also called upon the Palestinians of the West Bank and Gaza to reject the use of violence. Rabin, departing from long-standing Israeli policy, recognized the PLO as the representative of the Palestinian people and agreed to conduct direct negotiations.

Committing the signatories to a 'comprehensive peace settlement', the Declaration has the central purpose of establishing a Palestinian Interim Self-Government Authority in the West Bank and Gaza. It allows for a five-year process during which specific details are to be resolved. The issues to be addressed include the type of Palestinian representation, the holding of elections, the breadth of authority of the representation and continued negotiation to settle the outstanding issues of Jerusalem, refugees, Israeli settlements and borders. After entry into force on 13 October, the first phase of the Declaration was supposed to be initiated on 13 December. At the end of 1993, however, high-level delegations of Palestinian and Israeli negotiators had still not resolved the details of the interim phase. Among the points under contention for the first phase are the size of the Jericho area from which Israel will withdraw, control over the border crossings between the West Bank and Jordan and between Gaza and Egypt, and Israel's authority concerning security matters in the territories.

Although the 13 December deadline for initiating the transfer of power passed without any movement of forces, observers are generally confident that

[37] Reproduced in appendix 3A.
[38] See note 29.

the first steps of withdrawal are close at hand. In the first months of 1994, negotiations have yielded agreement on a number of the outstanding issues. Nevertheless, the later stages, during which some of the most contentious issues will be addressed, still pose a formidable challenge to Israel and the PLO.

Implementation of the Declaration of Principles: the challenges

The Declaration allows for a phased process, each stage of which is contingent on negotiation over progressively more difficult issues. It initiates an interim period in which a Palestinian authority gains limited control over a portion of Gaza and the West Bank. Although the PLO has billed it as the first step towards independence, the protocols of the Declaration do not guarantee more than limited autonomy. The signatories have only committed themselves to negotiate with one another on the final status. The issues put off until 'final status' negotiations, scheduled to begin by the beginning of 1996, include some of the most contentious—Jerusalem, refugees and Israeli settlements.

The Declaration calls for steps to be taken by states in the region and by the international community to ensure its successful implementation. The World Bank has taken a leading role in co-ordinating the international development effort by securing from the international community an estimated $2.5 billion for the first five years after the signing of the Declaration and by establishing oversight bodies to help co-ordinate economic and social development of the territories. Jordan and Egypt have been training Palestinian police officers to assume responsibility for internal security in the territories. The delay in the transfer of authority is not only a matter of the inability of Israel and the PLO to reach agreement on the outstanding issues; it also highlights the practical, logistical difficulties the Palestinians face in assuming this responsibility. Three months after the signing of the Declaration a sufficient police force had not yet been trained to take on their duties and the formation of institutions to implement the agreement on the ground was incomplete and had become a divisive issue for the PLO and the Palestinians on the West Bank and in Gaza.

This conflict between 'external' and 'internal' Palestinians resulted in the resignation of several of the principal delegates to the peace negotiations. After her resignation, Hanan Ashrawi, one of the most prominent of the delegates, announced the establishment of an organization to monitor the new Palestinian authority and its respect for Palestinians' human rights.

Within Israel and the Palestinian communities there are elements of both opposition to and support for the Declaration of Principles. In Israel, opposition parties including Likud, the radical Moledet and Tsomet parties and some of the settler movements have long expressed their lack of confidence in Labour's intention to make peace with the Palestinians.[39] Benyamin Netanyahu, the new head of Likud, at first reacted strongly against the Declar-

---

[39] Susser, L., 'Ready to fight', *Jerusalem Report*, 3 June 1993, p. 16.

ation. Members of his party and others vowed that a new Israeli government would not honour the peace, and some called for a referendum on the Declaration. However, after a three-day debate in the Knesset during which most of the 120 members spoke, it was approved with 61 votes for, 50 against and 6 abstentions. Although Labour, with a coalition majority, was destined to win, three Likud members broke party ranks and voted for the Declaration.[40] Polls taken shortly after the signing of the Declaration also showed approval among the general population, with 62 per cent of Israelis 'for' or 'definitely for' the plan.[41]

Arafat is faced with opposition not only from radical elements of the Palestinian community but also from the political leadership within the PLO and the local leadership in the territories. Conflict between the PLO and West Bank and Gaza Palestinians is not new. Originally official PLO representatives were excluded from the official negotiations because Israel refused to meet directly with them. *Ad hoc* arrangements with unofficial PLO advisers, later formalized in a joint negotiating committee, thus characterized the negotiations. Although sometimes at odds with Arafat, local leaders regularly declared their loyalty to the PLO. As the talks concerning the details of the Declaration continued into 1994, however, the conflict became more marked. Questions remain as to who will administer the development funds and local institutions and what degree of democratic participation Arafat will allow. Arafat has been criticized by other members of the PLO for not sharing power[42] and by the leadership in the territories for 'dictating negotiating positions'.[43] A poll taken in July 1993 in the West Bank and Gaza indicated that more than 87 per cent of the Palestinians thought that there was a need for democratic reform in the PLO.[44] As one assessment of these results concludes, it 'implies an overwhelming Palestinian demand that the one-man rule of PLO Chairman Yasser Arafat come to an end'.[45]

Some observers feel that Arafat gave away too much in the Declaration of Principles and the letters of recognition exchanged a few days earlier. In one sober assessment of the accord, it is described as having 'no clear end point, no final ground, no agreement on a two-state solution or self determination . . . also having played all his cards, Arafat no longer has chips with Syria, Egypt, and Jordan'.[46] The disparity between the actual agreement and expectations will continue to present problems to the Palestinian leadership. The transition from revolutionary movement to governing authority presents many chal-

---

[40] 'Arabs and Israel: talk and travel', *The Economist*, 25 Sep. 1993, pp. 53–54.

[41] Poll conducted by the Guttman Institute of Applied Social Research, cited in '62 per cent of Israelis support "Gaza-Jericho first"', *Mideast Mirror*, 13 Sep. 1993.

[42] Perry, M., 'The PLO's civil war: Arafat–Hassan conflict bares internal divisions', *Middle East Insight*, May–June 1993, pp. 22, 24.

[43] Mark (note 21).

[44] The poll was conducted by the Jerusalem Media and Communications Center in association with CNN and Netherlands TV. See *Mideast Mirror*, 4 Aug. 1993, pp. 8–9.

[45] Commentary in the Arabic daily *Asharq al-Awsat*, reported in *Mideast Mirror*, 4 Aug. 1993, p. 10.

[46] 'Deadlines for peace', *Christian Science Monitor*, 14 Dec. 1993, p. 22, editorial.

lenges to the PLO. Since the interim period in many ways will be held up as a test in future negotiations, Palestinians have little time to make the adjustment.

Some 'rejectionist' Palestinian groups based in Lebanon and Syria still pose a potential threat to the PLO and the success of the Declaration. They are now presumably being reined in by Assad, but a change in the political atmosphere could bring about a different reaction from these groups. Hamas and 'rejectionist' groups within Israel similarly pose a challenge to the success of the agreement.

VI. Co-operation

Bilateral peace efforts are strengthened by progress in multilateral and private initiatives. Although political agreements are required before real changes can take place on the ground, developments particularly in the areas of economic co-operation and regional environmental protection have contributed to instituting a culture of Arab–Israeli and international co-operation in the Middle East. Likewise, once political agreements are implemented, the resulting stability is likely to allow considerable economic benefits.

The international commitment to fund the development of the West Bank and Gaza provides a strong motivation for other countries in the peace talks. With the financial commitment also comes access to international markets and a long-term interest in the development of the region. Additionally, according to several analyses, countries in the region stand to benefit considerably from the integration of their own markets and trade into a regional system. As one study prepared by economists at the World Bank for use by the multilateral Working Group on Regional Economic Development shows, the benefits are both financial and political. 'Regional co-operation in the areas of trade, labour, capital and especially multi-country projects will contribute to region-wide prosperity and will help strengthen interaction in political and social spheres', says the study.[47] The authors counsel, however, that co-operation needs to be combined with domestic reforms and with creating a more welcoming environment for private investment.

At present, the region is not highly integrated in the areas of trade, communications, water utilization, environmental management or energy use. These are areas in which co-operation is likely and can be very beneficial. In 1993, only 6 per cent of trade in the region was between countries of the region.[48] In the field of communications, it is impossible to make direct telephone calls between many countries in the region. There are no telephone links between

[47] Diwan, I. and Squire, L., 'Economic Development and Cooperation in the Middle East and North Africa', World Bank Discussion Paper (World Bank: New York, Nov. 1993). Note: 'The findings and conclusions of the paper are entirely those of the author(s) and should not be attributed to the World Bank, its affiliated organizations, or to members of its Board of Directors or the countries they represent.'

[48] Diwan and Squire (note 47).

Israel and any of its neighbouring countries except Egypt, and even telephone lines between some Arab countries are routed through Europe.

In October 1993, Jordan and the PLO initialled an economic agreement which established a framework for co-operation in the fields of banking and finance, trade, labour, investment, tourism, customs and tariffs. (The agreement was subsequently signed with few amendments in January 1994.)[49] Focusing first on banking and trade, Jordan in particular is eager to secure the economic benefits expected to result from the implementation of the Declaration of Principles.

As contentious political questions begin to be resolved, one finds that business people are eager to make contact with one another and are taking advantage of the change in political climate. Jordanian and Israeli business and economic leaders have been meeting formally and informally since the September 1993 agreement.[50] Once the Jordanian–PLO economic agreement was signed, Jordan and Israel came to an understanding on the establishment of Jordanian banks in the territories, Jordan's first priority in the accord. In the field of energy, Egyptian and Israeli engineers and business people are exploring the possibility of linking the electricity grids of Israel and Egypt to improve their own systems and to be able to service Gaza as well.[51] These are examples of the activity and opportunity that a peace agreement can generate.

Such economic activity contributes to the stability of the region by establishing shared interests and, at the same time, can make the region more prosperous and self-sustaining. One study suggests 'a potential after-peace market for US$2.2 billion a year in Israeli goods to Syria, Jordan, Egypt, Saudi Arabia, and the United Arab Emirates'.[52] Another assessment predicts that Jordanian access to West Bank and Gazan markets alone will provide Jordan with an estimated $300 million in annual revenues.[53]

In the environmental field, Arab and Israeli delegations have had cordial meetings about the region's problems. Since the first multilateral meeting on the environment in May 1992 in Tokyo, protection of the Gulf of Aqaba has been emphasized as a major negotiating topic. In the first year of talks numerous proposals were introduced concerning joint projects to tackle environmental problems. However, without agreement on the political front, little progress was made until after the signing of the Declaration. Shortly afterwards, in the 15–17 November meeting of the working group delegates from 40 countries and international as well as regional organizations reached agreement on

---

[49] 'Jordan–PLO Economic Agreement, January 7 1994', reproduced in Near East Economic Progress Report, no. 1 (Harvard University, Institute for Social and Economic Policy in the Middle East: Cambridge, Mass.: Mar. 1994), appendix 4, pp. 26–27; Amr, W., 'Jordan and PLO sign economic agreement', Jordan Times, 8 Jan. 1994.

[50] Ma'ariv, 21 Dec. 1993, translated in 'Economic survey from the Hebrew press', Embassy of Israel Washington, DC, Dec. 1993, p. 3.

[51] Globes, 1 Dec. 1993, translated in 'Economic survey from the Hebrew press' (note 50), p. 4.

[52] Sandler, N., 'Best deal forward', Jerusalem Report, 9 Sep. 1993, p. 39. The article cites a study by the Armand Hammer Fund of Tel Aviv University and discusses the readiness of some businessmen in Israel and the Arab world to meet and do business with one another.

[53] Tal (note 8), p. 53.

approximately 20 environmental projects concerning oil spills and other ecological disasters in the Gulf of Aqaba. The agreements marked the first negotiated settlement between Israel and Jordan in the more than two years of peace talks. Co-operation in the environmental sector and the contact that it entails contribute to the web of interdependent relations and thus to the stability of the region.[54]

VII. Conclusion

The progress that has been made in terms of agreements signed, relationships forged and perceptions transformed is not irreversible, but events have shown the advances to be durable. In March 1994, a serious challenge was presented to the parties engaged in the Arab–Israeli negotiations when a US-born Israeli fanatic opened fire on Palestinians as they prayed at a mosque in Hebron on the West Bank. This act deeply affected both Muslim and Jewish communities in and outside the region. Yasser Arafat received numerous telephone calls from Israeli leaders, as did many of those involved in the official and unofficial negotiations. The personal bonds, political commitments and political investment that have already been made have strengthened the cause of a peaceful settlement in the region and the peace talks have survived the tragedy. Other efforts to sabotage the agreement can be expected and it is impossible to predict whether a future incident will reverse the progress that has been made.

The Arab–Israeli peace talks are premised on the need for a comprehensive settlement of Arab–Israeli conflicts. One dynamic apparent in these negotiations is the cross-fertilization among the various bilateral and multilateral tracks. Progress in one area affects developments in others, contributing to the momentum towards a comprehensive peace. The Declaration of Principles, then the Israeli–Jordanian Common Agenda, then the economic and environmental relationships that emerged attest to this trend. Success in these areas puts pressure on other tracks, and successive agreements could spur further agreement again. In the vocabulary of the Middle East, the cycle of violence that has characterized the region for the past 45 years could, since the steps taken in 1993, begin to be replaced by a cycle of peace.

[54] Eisendorf, R. and Gerstein, M., 'Focus: environmental cooperation in the Middle East', *Bulletin of Regional Cooperation in the Middle East*, vol. 3, no. 1 (spring 1994), p. 12.

Appendix 3A. Documents on the Middle East peace process

LETTERS BETWEEN ISRAELI PRIME MINISTER RABIN, PLO CHAIRMAN ARAFAT AND NORWEGIAN FOREIGN MINISTER HOLST, 9 SEPTEMBER 1993

Letters reprinted from press reports, Washington, DC, 10 September 1993

Mr Chairman,

In response to your letter of Sept. 9, 1993, I wish to confirm to you that in light of the PLO commitments included in your letter the Government of Israel has decided to recognize the PLO as the representative of the Palestinian people and commence negotiations with the PLO within the Middle East peace process.

> Yitzhak Rabin
> Prime Minister of Israel

Mr Prime Minister,

The signing of the Declaration of Principles marks a new era in the history of the Middle East. In firm conviction thereof, I would like to confirm the following PLO commitments:

The PLO recognizes the right of the State of Israel to exist in peace and security.

The PLO accepts United Nations Security Council Resolutions 242 and 338.

The PLO commits itself to the Middle East peace process and to a peaceful resolution of the conflict between the two sides and declares that all outstanding issues relating to permanent status will be resolved through negotiations.

The PLO considers that the signing of the Declaration of Principles constitutes a historic event, inaugurating a new epoch of peaceful coexistence, free from violence and all other acts which endanger peace and stability. Accordingly, the PLO renounces the use of terrorism and other acts of violence and will assume responsibility over all PLO elements and personnel in order to assure their compliance, prevent violations and discipline violators.

In view of the promise of a new era and the signing of the Declaration of Principles and based on Palestinian acceptance of Security Council Resolutions 242 and 338, the PLO affirms that those articles of the Palestinian Covenant which deny Israel's right to exist and the provisions of the Covenant which are inconsistent with the commitments of this letter are now inoperative and are no longer valid. Consequently, the PLO undertakes to submit to the Palestinian National Council for formal approval the necessary changes in regard to the Palestinian Covenant.

Sincerely,

> Yasir Arafat
> Chairman
> Executive Committee
> Palestine Liberation Organization

Dear Minister Holst,

I would like to confirm to you that upon the signing of the Declaration of Principles I will include the following positions in my public statements:

In light of the new era marked by the signing of the Declaration of Principles the PLO encourages and calls upon the Palestinian people in the West Bank and Gaza Strip to take part in the steps leading to the normalization of life, rejecting violence and terrorism, contributing to peace and stability and participating actively in shaping reconstruction, economic development and cooperation.

Sincerely

> Yasir Arafat
> Chairman
> Executive Committee

> Palestine Liberation Organization

Source: US Department of State, *Dispatch Supplement*, vol. 4, no. 4 (Sep. 1993), p. 24.

DECLARATION OF PRINCIPLES ON INTERIM SELF-GOVERNMENT ARRANGEMENTS

Washington, DC, 13 September 1993

The Government of the State of Israel and the PLO team (in the Jordanian–Palestinian delegation to the Middle East Peace Conference) (the 'Palestinian Delegation'), representing the Palestinian people, agree that it is time to put an end to decades of confrontation and conflict, recognize their mutual legitimate and political rights, and strive to live in peaceful coexistence and mutual dignity and security and achieve a just, lasting and comprehensive peace settlement and historic reconciliation through the agreed political process. Accordingly, the two sides agree to the following principles:

Article I. Aim of the negotiations

The aim of the Israeli–Palestinian negotiations within the current Middle East peace process is, among other things, to establish a Palestinian Interim Self-Government Authority, the elected Council (the 'Council'), for the Palestinian people in the West Bank and the Gaza Strip, for a transitional period not exceeding five years, leading to a permanent settlement based on Security Council Resolutions 242 and 338.

It is understood that the interim arrangements are an integral part of the whole peace process and that the negotiations on the permanent status will lead to the implementation of Security Council Resolutions 242 and 338.

Article II. Framework for the interim period

The agreed framework for the interim period is set forth in this Declaration of Principles.

Article III. Elections

1. In order that the Palestinian people in the West Bank and Gaza Strip may govern themselves according to democratic principles, direct, free and general political elections will be held for the Council under agreed supervision and international observation, while the Palestinian police will ensure public order.

2. An agreement will be concluded on the exact mode and conditions of the elections in accordance with the protocol attached as Annex 1, with the goal of holding the elec-

tions not later than nine months after the entry into force of this Declaration of Principles.

3. These elections will constitute a significant interim preparatory step toward the realization of the legitimate rights of the Palestinian people and their just requirements.

Article IV. Jurisdiction

Jurisdiction of the Council will cover West Bank and Gaza Strip territory, except for issues that will be negotiated in the permanent status negotiations. The two sides view the West Bank and the Gaza Strip as a single territorial unit, whose integrity will be preserved during the interim period.

Article V. Transitional period and permanent status negotiations

1. The five-year transitional period will begin upon the withdrawal from the Gaza Strip and Jericho area.

2. Permanent status negotiations will commence as soon as possible, but not later than the beginning of the third year of the interim period, between the Government of Israel and the Palestinian people representatives.

3. It is understood that these negotiations shall cover remaining issues, including: Jerusalem, refugees, settlements, security arrangements, borders, relations and co-operation with other neighbors, and other issues of common interest.

4. The two parties agree that the outcome of the permanent status negotiations should not be prejudiced or pre-empted by agreements reached for the interim period.

Article VI. Preparatory transfer of powers and responsibilities

1. Upon the entry into force of this Declaration of Principles and the withdrawal from the Gaza Strip and the Jericho area, a transfer of authority from the Israeli military government and its Civil Administration to the authorised Palestinians for this task, as detailed herein, will commence. This transfer of authority will be of a preparatory nature until the inauguration of the Council.

2. Immediately after the entry into force of this Declaration of Principles and the withdrawal from the Gaza Strip and Jericho area, with the view to promoting economic development in the West Bank and Gaza Strip, authority will be transferred to the Palestin-

ians on the following spheres: education and culture, health, social welfare, direct taxation, and tourism. The Palestinian side will commence in building the Palestinian police force, as agreed upon. Pending the inauguration of the Council, the two parties may negotiate the transfer of additional powers and responsibilities, as agreed upon.

Article VII. Interim agreement

1. The Israeli and Palestinian delegations will negotiate an agreement on the interim period (the 'Interim Agreement').

2. The Interim Agreement shall specify, among other things, the structure of the Council, the number of its members, and the transfer of powers and responsibilities from the Israeli military government and its Civil Administration to the Council. The Interim Agreement shall also specify the Council's executive authority, legislative authority in accordance with Article IX below, and the independent Palestinian judicial organs.

3. The Interim Agreement shall include arrangements, to be implemented upon the inauguration of the Council, for the assumption by the Council of all of the powers and responsibilities transferred previously in accordance with Article VI above.

4. In order to enable the Council to promote economic growth, upon its inauguration, the Council will establish, among other things, a Palestinian Electricity Authority, a Gaza Sea Port Authority, a Palestinian Development Bank, a Palestinian Export Promotion Board, a Palestinian Environmental Authority, a Palestinian Land Authority and a Palestinian Water Administration Authority, and any other Authorities agreed upon, in accordance with the Interim Agreement that will specify their powers and responsibilities.

5. After the inauguration of the Council, the Civil Administration will be dissolved, and the Israeli military government will be withdrawn.

Article VIII. Public order and security

In order to guarantee public order and internal security for the Palestinians of the West Bank and the Gaza Strip, the Council will establish a strong police force, while Israel will continue to carry the responsibility for defending against external threats, as well as the responsibility for overall security of Israelis for the purpose of safeguarding their internal security and public order.

Article IX. Laws and military orders

1. The Council will be empowered to legislate, in accordance with the Interim Agreement, within all authorities transferred to it.

2. Both parties will review jointly laws and military orders presently in force in remaining spheres.

Article X. Joint Israeli–Palestinian Liaison Committee

In order to provide for a smooth implementation of this Declaration of Principles and any subsequent agreements pertaining to the interim period, upon the entry into force of this Declaration of Principles, a Joint Israeli–Palestinian Liaison Committee will be established in order to deal with issues requiring coordination, other issues of common interest, and disputes.

Article XI. Israeli–Palestinian cooperation in economic fields

Recognizing the mutual benefit of cooperation in promoting the development of the West Bank, the Gaza Strip and Israel, upon the entry into force of this Declaration of Principles, an Israeli–Palestinian Economic Cooperation Committee will be established in order to develop and implement in a cooperative manner the programs identified in the protocols attached as Annex III and Annex IV.

Article XII. Liaison and cooperation with Jordan and Egypt

The two parties will invite the Governments of Jordan and Egypt to participate in establishing further liaison and cooperation arrangements between the Government of Israel and the Palestinian representatives, on the one hand, and the Governments of Jordan and Egypt, on the other hand, to promote cooperation between them. These arrangements will include the constitution of a Continuing Committee that will decide by agreement on the modalities of admission of persons displaced from the West Bank and Gaza Strip in 1967, together with necessary measures to prevent disruption and disorder. Other matters of common concern will be dealt with by this Committee.

Article XIII. Redeployment of Israeli forces

1. After the entry into force of this Declaration of Principles, and not later than the

eve of elections for the Council, a redeployment of Israeli military forces in the West Bank and the Gaza Strip will take place, in addition to withdrawal of Israeli forces carried out in accordance with Article XIV.

2. In redeploying its military forces, Israel will be guided by the principle that its military forces should be redeployed outside populated areas.

3. Further redeployments to specified locations will be gradually implemented commensurate with the assumption of responsibility for public order and internal security by the Palestinian police force pursuant to Article VIII above.

Article XIV. Israeli withdrawal from the Gaza Strip and Jericho area

Israel will withdraw from the Gaza Strip and Jericho area, as detailed in the protocol attached as Annex II.

Article XV. Resolution of disputes

1. Disputes arising out of the application or interpretation of this Declaration of Principles, or any subsequent agreements pertaining to the interim period, shall be resolved by negotiations through the Joint Liaison Committee to be established pursuant to Article X above.

2. Disputes which cannot be settled by negotiations may be resolved by a mechanism of conciliation to be agreed upon by the parties.

3. The parties may agree to submit to arbitration disputes relating to the interim period, which cannot be settled through conciliation. To this end, upon the agreement of both parties, the parties will establish an Arbitration Committee.

Article XVI. Israeli–Palestinian cooperation concerning regional programs

Both parties view the multilateral working groups as an appropriate instrument for promoting a 'Marshall Plan', the regional programs and other programs, including special programs for the West Bank and Gaza Strip, as indicated in the protocol attached as Annex IV.

Article XVII. Miscellaneous provisions

1. This Declaration of Principles will enter into force one month after its signing.

2. All protocols annexed to this Declaration of Principles and Agreed Minutes pertaining thereto shall be regarded as an integral part hereof.

. . . .

For the Government of Israel: (Shimon Peres)

For the PLO: (Mahmoud Abbas)

. . . .

ANNEX I

Protocol on the mode and conditions of elections

1. Palestinians of Jerusalem who live there will have the right to participate in the election process, according to an agreement between the two sides.

2. In addition, the election agreement should cover, among other things, the following issues:

(*a*) the system of elections;

(*b*) the mode of the agreed supervision and international observation and their personal composition; and

(*c*) rules and regulations regarding election campaign, including agreed arrangements for the organizing of mass media, and the possibility of licensing a broadcasting and TV station.

3. The future status of displaced Palestinians who were registered on 4th June 1967 will not be prejudiced because they are unable to participate in the election process due to practical reasons.

ANNEX II

Protocol on withdrawal of Israeli forces from the Gaza Strip and Jericho area

1. The two sides will conclude and sign within two months from the date of entry into force of this Declaration of Principles, an agreement on the withdrawal of Israeli military forces from the Gaza Strip and Jericho area. This agreement will include comprehensive arrangements to apply in the Gaza Strip and the Jericho area subsequent to the Israeli withdrawal.

2. Israel will implement an accelerated and scheduled withdrawal of Israeli military forces from the Gaza Strip and Jericho area, beginning immediately with the signing of the agreement on the Gaza Strip and Jericho area and to be completed within a period not

exceeding four months after the signing of this agreement.

3. The above agreement will include, among other things:

(a) Arrangements for a smooth and peaceful transfer of authority from the Israeli military government and its Civil Administration to the Palestinian representatives.

(b) Structure, powers and responsibilities of the Palestinian authority in these areas, except: external security, settlements, Israelis, foreign relations, and other mutually agreed matters.

(c) Arrangements for the assumption of internal security and public order by the Palestinian police force consisting of police officers recruited locally and from abroad (holding Jordanian passports and Palestinian documents issued by Egypt). Those who will participate in the Palestinian police force coming from abroad should be trained as police and police officers.

(d) A temporary international or foreign presence, as agreed upon.

(e) Establishment of a joint Palestinian–Israeli Coordination and Cooperation Committee for mutual security purposes.

(f) An economic development and stabilization program, including the establishment of an Emergency Fund, to encourage foreign investment, and financial and economic support. Both sides will coordinate and cooperate jointly and unilaterally with regional and international parties to support these aims.

(g) Arrangements for a safe passage for persons and transportation between the Gaza Strip and Jericho area.

4. The above agreement will include arrangements for coordination between both parties regarding passages:

(a) Gaza–Egypt; and

(b) Jericho–Jordan.

5. The offices responsible for carrying out the powers and responsibilities of the Palestinian authority under this Annex II and Article VI of the Declaration of Principles will be located in the Gaza Strip and in the Jericho area pending the inauguration of the Council.

6. Other than these agreed arrangements, the status of the Gaza Strip and Jericho area will continue to be an integral part of the West Bank and Gaza Strip, and will not be changed in the interim period.

ANNEX III

Protocol on Israeli–Palestinian cooperation in economic and development programs

The two sides agree to establish an Israeli–Palestinian Continuing Committee for Economic Cooperation, focusing, among other things, on the following:

1. Cooperation in the field of water, including a Water Development Program prepared by experts from both sides, which will also specify the mode of cooperation in the management of water resources in the West Bank and Gaza Strip, and will include proposals for studies and plans on water rights of each party, as well as on the equitable utilization of joint water resources for implementation in and beyond the interim period.

2. Cooperation in the field of electricity, including an Electricity Development Program, which will also specify the mode of cooperation for the production, maintenance, purchase and sale of electricity resources.

3. Cooperation in the field of energy, including an Energy Development Program, which will provide for the exploitation of oil and gas for industrial purposes, particularly in the Gaza Strip and in the Negev, and will encourage further joint exploitation of other energy resources. This Program may also provide for the construction of a Petrochemical industrial complex in the Gaza Strip and the construction of oil and gas pipelines.

4. Cooperation in the field of finance, including a Financial Development and Action Program for the encouragement of international investment in the West Bank and the Gaza Strip, and in Israel, as well as the establishment of a Palestinian Development Bank.

5. Cooperation in the field of transport and communications, including a Program, which will define guidelines for the establishment of a Gaza Sea Port Area, and will provide for the establishing of transport and communications lines to and from the West Bank and the Gaza Strip to Israel and to other countries. In addition, this Program will provide for carrying out the necessary construction of roads, railways, communications lines, etc.

6. Cooperation in the field of trade, including studies, and Trade Promotion Programs,

which will encourage local, regional and inter-regional trade, as well as a feasibility study of creating free trade zones in the Gaza Strip and in Israel, mutual access to these zones, and cooperation in other areas related to trade and commerce.

7. Cooperation in the field of industry, including Industrial Development Programs, which will provide for the establishment of joint Israeli–Palestinian Industrial Research and Development Centers, will promote Palestinian–Israeli joint ventures, and provide guidelines for cooperation in the textile, food, pharmaceutical, electronics, diamonds, computer and science-based industries.

8. A program for cooperation in, and regulation of, labor relations and cooperation in social welfare issues.

9. A Human Resources Development and Cooperation Plan, providing for joint Israeli–Palestinian workshops and seminars, and for the establishment of joint vocational training centres, research institutes and data banks.

10. An Environmental Protection Plan, providing for joint and/or coordinated measures in this sphere.

11. A program for developing coordination and cooperation in the field of communication and media.

12. Any other programs of mutual interest.

ANNEX IV

Protocol on Israeli–Palestinian cooperation concerning regional development programs

1. The two sides will cooperate in the context of the multilateral peace efforts in promoting a Development Program for the region, including the West Bank and the Gaza Strip, to be initiated by the G-7. The parties will request the G-7 to seek the participation in this program of other interested states, such as members of the Organisation for Economic Cooperation and Development, regional Arab states and institutions, as well as members of the private sector.

2. The Development Program will consist of two elements:

(a) an Economic Development Program for the West Bank and the Gaza Strip.

(b) a Regional Economic Development Program.

A. The Economic Development Program for the West Bank and the Gaza Strip will consist of the following elements:

(1) A Social Rehabilitation Program, including a Housing and Construction Program.

(2) A Small and Medium Business Development Plan.

(3) An Infrastructure Development Program (water, electricity, transportation and communications, etc.).

(4) A Human Resources Plan.

(5) Other programs.

B. The Regional Economic Development Program may consist of the following elements:

(1) The establishment of a Middle East Development Fund, as a first step, and a Middle East Development Bank, as a second step.

(2) The development of a joint Israeli–Palestinian–Jordanian Plan for coordinated exploitation of the Dead Sea area.

(3) The Mediterranean Sea (Gaza)–Dead Sea Canal.

(4) Regional Desalinization and other water development projects.

(5) A regional plan for agricultural development, including a coordinated regional effort for the prevention of desertification.

(6) Interconnection of electricity grids.

(7) Regional cooperation for the transfer, distribution and industrial exploitation of gas, oil and other energy resources.

(8) A Regional Tourism, Transportation and Telecommunications Development Plan.

(9) Regional cooperation in other spheres.

3. The two sides will encourage the multilateral working groups, and will coordinate towards their success. The two parties will encourage inter-sessional activities, as well as pre-feasibility and feasibility studies, within the various multilateral working groups.

AGREED MINUTES TO THE DECLARATION OF PRINCIPLES ON INTERIM SELF-GOVERNMENT ARRANGEMENTS

A. General understandings and agreements

Any powers and responsibilities transferred to the Palestinians pursuant to the Declaration of Principles prior to the inauguration of the Council will be subject to the same principles pertaining to Article IV, as set out in these Agreed Minutes below.

B. Specific understandings and agreements

ARTICLE IV

It is understood that:

1. Jurisdiction of the Council will cover West Bank and Gaza Strip territory, except for issues that will be negotiated in the permanent status negotiations: Jerusalem, settlements, military locations, and Israelis.

2. The Council's jurisdiction will apply with regard to the agreed powers, responsibilities, spheres and authorities transferred to it.

ARTICLE VI(2)

It is agreed that the transfer of authority will be as follows:

1. The Palestinian side will inform the Israeli side of the names of the authorised Palestinians who will assume the powers, authorities and responsibilities that will be transferred to the Palestinians according to the Declaration of Principles in the following fields: education and culture, health, social welfare, direct taxation, tourism, and any other authorities agreed upon.

2. It is understood that the rights and obligations of these offices will not be affected.

3. Each of the spheres described above will continue to enjoy existing budgetary allocations in accordance with arrangements to be mutually agreed upon. These arrangements also will provide for the necessary adjustments required in order to take into account the taxes collected by the direct taxation office.

4. Upon the execution of the Declaration of Principles, the Israeli and Palestinian delegations will immediately commence negotiations on a detailed plan for the transfer of authority on the above offices in accordance with the above understandings.

ARTICLE VII(2)

The Interim Agreement will also include arrangements for coordination and cooperation.

ARTICLE VII(5)

The withdrawal of the military government will not prevent Israel from exercising the powers and responsibilities not transferred to the Council.

ARTICLE VIII

It is understood that the Interim Agreement will include arrangements for cooperation and coordination between the two parties in this regard. It is also agreed that the transfer of powers and responsibilities to the Palestinian police will be accomplished in a phased manner, as agreed in the Interim Agreement.

ARTICLE X

It is agreed that, upon the entry into force of the Declaration of Principles, the Israeli and Palestinian delegations will exchange the names of the individuals designated by them as members of the Joint Israeli-Palestinian Liaison Committee. It is further agreed that each side will have an equal number of members in the Joint Committee. The Joint Committee will reach decisions by agreement. The Joint Committee may add other technicians and experts, as necessary. The Joint Committee will decide on the frequency and place or places of its meetings.

ANNEX II

It is understood that, subsequent to the Israeli withdrawal, Israel will continue to be responsible for external security, and for internal security and public order of settlements and Israelis. Israeli military forces and civilians may continue to use roads freely within the Gaza Strip and the Jericho area.

. . . .

For the Government of Israel: (Shimon Peres)
For the PLO: (Mahmoud Abbas)

. . . .

Source: US Department of State, *Dispatch Supplement*, vol. 4, no. 4 (Sep. 1993), pp. 2–6.

ISRAEL–JORDAN COMMON AGENDA

Washington, DC, 14 September 1993

A. Goal:

The achievement of a just, lasting and comprehensive peace between the Arab States, the Palestinians and Israel as per the Madrid invitation.

B. Components of Israel–Jordan [Jordan–Israel] Peace Negotiations:

1. Searching for steps to arrive at a state of peace based on Security Council Resolutions

242 and 338 in all their aspects.

2. Security:

(a) Refraining from actions or activities by either side that may adversely affect the security of the other or may prejudge the final outcome of negotiations.

(b) Threats to security resulting from all kinds of terrorism.

(c) (i) Mutual commitment not to threaten each other by any use of force and not to use weapons by one side against the other including conventional and non-conventional mass destruction weapons.

(ii) Mutual commitment, as a matter of priority and as soon as possible, to work towards a Middle East free from weapons of mass destruction, conventional and non-conventional weapons; this goal is to be achieved in the context of a comprehensive, lasting and stable peace characterized by the renunciation of the use of force, reconciliation and openness.

Note: The above (item c-ii) may be revised in accordance with relevant agreements to be reached in the Multilateral Working Group on Arms Control and Regional Security.

(d) Mutually agreed upon security arrangements and security confidence building measures.

3. Water:

(a) Securing the rightful water shares of the two sides.

(b) Searching for ways to alleviate water shortage.

4. Refugees and displaced persons:

Achieving an agreed just solution to the bilateral aspects of the problem of refugees and displaced persons in accordance with international law.

5. Borders and territorial matters:

Settlement of territorial matters and agreed definitive delimitation and demarcation of the international boundary between Israel and Jordan [Jordan–Israel] with reference to the boundary definition under the Mandate, without prejudice to the status of any territories that came under Israeli Military Government control in 1967. Both parties will respect and comply with the above international boundary.

6. Exploring the potentials of future bilateral cooperation, within a regional context where appropriate, in the following.

(a) Natural resources:
– Water, energy and environment
– Rift Valley development
(b) Human resources:
– Demography
– Labor
– Health
– Education
– Drug control
(c) Infrastructure:
– Transportation: land and air
– Communication
(d) Economic areas including tourism

7. Phasing the discussion, agreement and implementation of the items above including appropriate mechanisms for negotiations in specific fields.

8. Discussion on matters related to both tracks to be decided upon in common by the two tracks.

C. It is anticipated that the above endeavor will ultimately, following the attainment of mutually satisfactory solutions to the elements of this agenda, culminate in a peace treaty.

Source: US Department of State, *Dispatch Supplement*, vol. 4, no. 4 (Sep. 1993), p. 17.

REPORTED TEXT OF SYRIA'S PROPOSAL FOR A JOINT STATEMENT OF PRINCIPLES WITH ISRAEL

26 October 1992

1. The aim of peace: a just and comprehensive peace based on Security Council Resolutions 242 and 338.

2. A comprehensive solution in the region: The goal is the establishment of a just peace. This requires a settlement on all fronts.

3. Mutual security.

4. Holding continuous and serious negotiations because Syria is interested in peace.

5. The mechanism of implementation:

A. Pursuant to the first clause, the two sides will begin drawing up mechanism for implementing Resolution 242 within a determined timetable that takes into account the two sides' commitments to agreements in accordance with UN resolutions.

B. Total Israeli withdrawal from the Syrian Golan Heights and the evacuation and dismantling of various settlements from occupied Syrian lands, since this contravenes international law and the Geneva Convention.

C. Proclaiming an end to the state of war or the allegation of the existence of such a state.

D. The two sides' acknowledgement of and respect for each other's sovereignty, political independence, and regional peace as well as for their mutual right to live in peace within secure and recognized borders in accordance with the principles of international legitimacy.

6. Formation of executive working groups as well as military and technical committees.

7. Security arrangements and guarantees:

A. Security guarantees will be issued by the UN Security Council and the sponsoring states.

B. As a manifestation of goodwill and in commitment to and as a guarantee of security and political independence, demilitarized areas will be set up, with monitoring posts, to be manned by UN, Russian, or US forces.

8. The two sides pledge to respect international charters and principles.

9. The agreement will be documented at the United Nations.

Source: Al-Manar, Jerusalem, 26 Oct. 1992, quoted in FBIS-NES, 28 Oct. 1992.

4. South-East Asia and the new Asia–Pacific security dialogue

TREVOR FINDLAY*

I. Introduction

For a part of the world that had hitherto lacked formal structures for conduct-ing a dialogue on security issues, Asia–Pacific in 1993 witnessed a momen-tous development—the creation of an ASEAN Regional Forum, designed to eventually encompass all the states of the region. The year also saw the first informal Asia–Pacific summit meeting, held in Seattle, Washington, following a meeting of the Asia–Pacific Economic Cooperation (APEC) forum. This chapter examines the evolution of an Asia–Pacific regional security dialogue and the key role played by South-East Asia, a subregion of growing economic importance, relative peace and largely co-operative international relations. Particular attention is paid to the role of the subregion's most economically and politically buoyant segment, the six states which form the Association of South-East Asian Nations (ASEAN).[1]

For the purposes of this chapter, South-East Asia is taken to comprise Brunei, Cambodia, Indonesia, Laos, Malaysia, Myanmar (formerly Burma), the Philippines, Singapore, Thailand and Viet Nam. The Asia–Pacific region is taken to denote all the states of South-East Asia and those of North-East Asia (China, Hong Kong, Japan, the two Korean states, Macao, Mongolia, Russia and Taiwan) plus Australia, Canada, New Zealand, Papua New Guinea, the USA and the island states of the South Pacific.

II. South-East Asian security

South-East Asia, once a region of chronic instability and economic backward-ness, is emerging not only as an economic powerhouse but also as a locus of efforts to create a broader Asia–Pacific regionalism, in both the economic and security fields. This is partly because, politically and economically, South-East Asia is the most coherent of the Asia–Pacific subregions.

South-East Asia has also been stirred to new regional co-operation by the end of the cold war, an historic sea-change that has brought with it innumer-able security benefits but which has also created strategic uncertainty.

---

[1] ASEAN was founded in the 1967 Bangkok Declaration by Indonesia, Malaysia, the Philippines, Singapore and Thailand. Brunei joined in 1984.

* Olga Hardardóttir of the SIPRI Project on Peacekeeping and Regional Security assisted in researching this chapter.

Benefits of the end of the cold war

Apart from generally easing global tensions and ending the stand-off between the two nuclear superpowers, the end of the cold war and collapse of the Soviet Union have had numerous direct and indirect effects on South-East Asia, some of which have taken time to work themselves through the sub-regional security system.

One early strategic benefit was the retreat of Soviet military power from Asia–Pacific. Most of its military presence at Cam Ranh Bay in Viet Nam had been removed and its naval deployments in the Pacific Ocean dramatically curtailed by the time the Soviet Union itself disappeared in late 1991.[2] Neither is likely to be reinstated by Russia in the near future. Soviet economic and military assistance to the three Indochinese states—Cambodia, Laos and Viet Nam—also ceased, leading to modification of their hard-line domestic and foreign policies.

Other direct results of the end of the cold war—the unilateral withdrawals of British, Russian and US tactical and short-range nuclear weapons from naval platforms and cuts in the number of Russian and US strategic submarine-launched nuclear weapons as part of the Strategic Arms Reduction Talks (START) process—are also of direct benefit to South-East Asian security.[3] These remove the danger of a surface nuclear weapon incident at sea, lessen the chance of an accidental launch of a sea-based nuclear weapon and decrease the possibility of nuclear contamination of the sea.[4] Combined with the closure of US bases in the Philippines at Clark Field and Subic Bay in 1992, these developments have helped to achieve *de facto* one of the long-standing arms control goals of the ASEAN states, a South-East Asian Nuclear Weapon-Free Zone (SEANWFZ). The closure of the US bases has also removed one of the long-standing obstacles to ASEAN's Zone of Peace, Freedom and Neutrality (ZOPFAN), declared in 1971. However, neither of these declaratory measures is likely to be formally implemented by the ASEAN countries—history has passed them by.

Another product of the end of the cold war, the 1993 Chemical Weapons Convention (CWC),[5] which all the South-East Asian states have signed, also

---

[2] See Kelly, R. J. (Admiral), 'Changing superpower maritime roles', eds R. Babbage and S. Bateman, *Maritime Change: Issues for Asia* (Allen & Unwin: Sydney, 1993).

[3] As a result of the 1991 START I Treaty, the 1993 START II Treaty and the demise of the Soviet Union, there have also been cuts in numbers and a geographical contraction of land-based nuclear weapons deployed in the vicinity of South-East Asia. Of particular benefit to the subregion will be the removal of nuclear weapons from the closest former Soviet republic, Kazakhstan (which borders China, Russia and Mongolia), and its assumption of the status of non-nuclear weapon state through accession to the Nuclear Non-Proliferation Treaty. See also chapter 16 in this volume.

[4] Strategic nuclear weapons continue to be deployed on submarines in Asia–Pacific, although their numbers will decline. All US submarines remain nuclear-powered. The USA also retains the right to redeploy nuclear weapons, including bombs and cruise missiles, to the region at short notice as part of a 'nuclear expeditionary force'.

[5] For details of the CWC and its negotiation, see Findlay, T., *Peace Through Chemistry: The New Chemical Weapons Convention*, Monograph no. 14 (Peace Research Centre, Australian National University: Canberra, 1993); and chapters on chemical and biological weapon developments in previous *SIPRI Yearbooks*. See also chapter 17 in this volume.

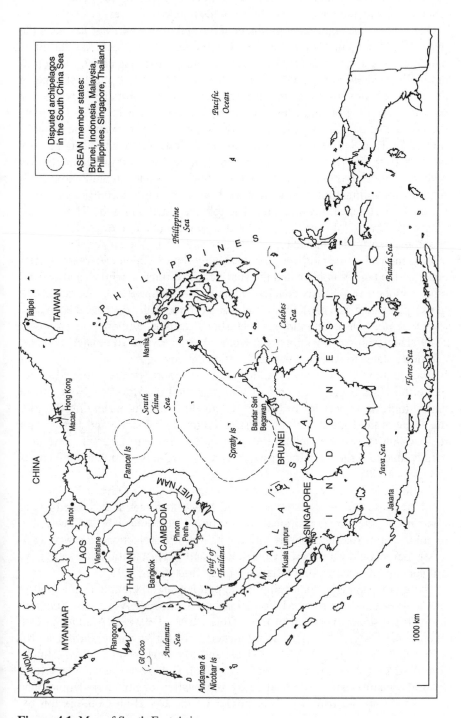

Figure 4.1. Map of South-East Asia

promises security benefits for the region, perhaps leading to greater acceptance of disarmament and arms control in the region in future.

One of the most significant products of the end of the cold war has been the peace settlement in Cambodia, which although not perfect, has de-internationalized and marginalized the civil war and returned the country to democratically elected, constitutional and civil government for the first time in decades. The situation in Cambodia had been a major obstacle to peace and security in the region since the end of the Viet Nam War in 1973. The murderous rule of the Khmer Rouge, its overthrow by Viet Nam and the installation of the Hun Sen regime left the country diplomatically and economically isolated from the rest of the region and delayed Viet Nam's reconciliation with both South-East Asia and the West. Armed resistance to the Phnom Penh regime, including that by the Khmer Rouge, permitted continuing international interference in Cambodia. The refugee situation on the Thai border, extensive laying of mines by all sides, environmental degradation and economic deprivation added to the miseries of the Cambodian people.

With the end of the cold war, the dissolving Soviet Union and Warsaw Pact ended aid to both Viet Nam and the Hun Sen Government, while Thailand and other members of ASEAN concluded that Indo-China was more lucrative as a marketplace than as a battlefield. Viet Nam, economically distressed and eager to pursue *doi moi* (economic 'restructuring') at home, withdrew its troops in 1989. The resulting possibility of a Khmer Rouge revival stimulated Western and other states to seek a negotiated settlement among the battle-weary Cambodian parties. China began winding down support for the Khmer Rouge, while the USA began overtures to Viet Nam and the Hun Sen Government and withdrew support for the anti-government coalition occupying Cambodia's seat at the United Nations. Australia, France, Indonesia and Japan, with the backing of ASEAN and a reinvigorated UN Security Council, were ultimately able to forge the Paris Peace Accords between the Cambodian factions in October 1991.

While the peace process almost came unstuck when the Khmer Rouge violated the cease-fire, refused to disarm and canton its forces and attacked ethnic Vietnamese, the UN Transitional Authority in Cambodia (UNTAC) was able to guide Cambodia successfully through its May 1993 elections, the writing of a new democratic Cambodian Constitution and the installation of a new government and monarch, King Sihanouk, on 24 September 1993.

These developments are leading to the political and economic re-integration of Cambodia and the rest of Indo-China into South-East Asia. Viet Nam and Laos, for instance, acceded to the 1976 ASEAN Treaty of Amity and Co-operation in July 1992. Malaysian Finance Minister Anwar Ibrahim has proposed that the three Indochinese states and Myanmar should all eventually join ASEAN.[6] A direct improvement in South-East Asian security resulting from the Cambodian settlement is the repatriation of 360 000 Cambodians back to Cambodia from the Thai border by the UN High Commission for

---

[6] *Phnom Penh Post*, 22 Oct.–4 Nov. 1993, p. 14.

Refugees (UNHCR). The flow of so-called 'boat people' from Viet Nam has also ended as economic conditions there have improved. These developments have eased tensions with neighbours such as Malaysia and those further afield such as Australia, Hong Kong and Japan.[7]

Economic success and internal stability

Most of the states of South-East Asia have in the past two decades experienced both a marked decline in internal instability and rising economic prosperity.[8] Singapore is already considered one of Asia's economic 'dragons', while Indonesia, Malaysia and Thailand are precocious 'little dragons'. Estimated growth rates for 1993 are: Indonesia 6 per cent, up from 5.5 per cent in 1992; Malaysia 7.6 per cent, down from 8 per cent; Thailand 7.3–8.3 per cent, up from 7.4 per cent; and Singapore 5.5–6.5 per cent, up from 5.6 per cent.[9] Even the 'sick man of ASEAN', the Philippines, is beginning to turn its economy around, its projected growth rate rising in 1993 to 3 per cent from zero in 1992. Oil-rich Brunei, meanwhile, continues to have one of the highest per capita incomes in the world. As Viet Nam, whose economy grew by an estimated 7 per cent in 1993,[10] emerges from economic isolation, its potential is widely judged to be comparable to that of Thailand and Malaysia. This leaves Cambodia, Laos and Myanmar as the 'Third World' of South-East Asia, although none is without economic promise.

The collapse of Soviet communism has reinforced a long-term decline in the fortunes of communist insurgencies in the region dating from the withdrawal of Chinese support following US President Richard Nixon's visit to Beijing in 1972. Today the communist insurgency in the Philippines is the only one of any note and is itself waning. Democracy, however, is still fragile or only partially realized in many parts of South-East Asia—Indonesia and Thailand being cases in point. The transition to a post-Suharto era in Indonesia is fraught with uncertainties. In Indonesia and elsewhere in South-East Asia, human rights are only partially ensured.

Despite the decline or demise of the various communist insurgencies that plagued the region in the 1950s and 1960s, some states remain threatened by armed rebellion on the part of religious, ethnic or ethno-nationalist groups.[11] In Indonesia alone these include the Pemerintahan Revolusioner Republik (in central and West Sumatra), the Permesta revolt (southern Sulawesi), the Organisai Papua Merdeka (Irian Jaya), Aceh Merdeka (Aceh) and Fretilin

---

[7] The UNHCR decided in Feb. 1994 to phase out immediately the special treatment accorded to Vietnamese boat refugees; in future they will not be resettled in third countries but will be encouraged to return home to Viet Nam. *International Herald Tribune*, 15 Feb. 1994, p. 2.

[8] See Hewison, K., Robison, R. and Roden, G. (eds), *Southeast Asia in the 1990s: Authoritarianism, Democracy and Capitalism* (Allen & Unwin: Sydney, 1993).

[9] 'Economic indicators, selected Asian countries', *Far Eastern Economic Review*, 11 Nov. 1993, p. 77.

[10] *Newsweek*, 21 Feb. 1994, p. 24.

[11] The following details are from Acharya, A., International Institute for Strategic Studies, *A New Regional Order in South-East Asia: ASEAN in the Post-Cold War Era*, Adelphi Paper no. 279 (Brassey's: London, 1993), p. 19.

(East Timor). The Philippine Government confronts both a Moro National Liberation Front and a Moro Islamic Liberation Front (in Mindanao), while Thailand has its Pattani United Liberation Organization (in southern Thailand). Cambodia is still not free of the Khmer Rouge, although defections are weakening its strength, and negotiations with the new government may yet lead to political compromise and an end to the conflict.

Myanmar, in contrast, has several ethnic insurgencies (the biggest involving the Karens and Kachins) which have been seeking to secede ever since the country gained independence in 1947. Peace talks in 1993 with several groups[12] resulted in an historic cease-fire agreement with the Kachin rebels, the strongest insurgent force, in October, reportedly after pressure from China on the group.[13] Myanmar's authoritarian State Law and Order Restoration Council (SLORC) government also continued to face pro-democracy rebels dating from its nullification of election results in 1990, its detention of election winner and Nobel Prize laureate Aung San Suu Kyi and its violent crackdown on dissent. In self-imposed isolation for most of its post-independence history under the autarchic policies of General Ne Win's 'Burmese Way to Socialism', Myanmar remained in 1993 the state most removed from mainstream South-East Asian economics and politics. Economically decimated by past government policies, it is the only state in South-East Asia not to have adopted free market reforms, although it tentatively began opening up its economy to outside influences in 1993. Myanmar also continued to have one of the worst human rights records in South-East Asia, although in 1993 it made modest improvements.[14] It also attempted to improve relations with its neighbours by negotiating with Bangladesh over the thousands of Rohingya Muslims it had previously expelled into that impoverished country[15] and moving towards re-establishing diplomatic relations with Cambodia after a 30-year break.[16]

External security problems

South-East Asian states are not of course devoid of external security problems, some of which have their origins in the end of the cold war. Strategic uncertainty characterizes the current security discourse in the subregion, particularly regarding the future roles of China, Japan and the USA.[17] As Malaysian Defence Minister Najib Razak has put it, the end of the cold war has made the security environment in the region 'fluid and unpredictable', and states should therefore 'prepare for the worst scenario'.[18]

---

[12] *The Independent*, 19 Jan. 1994, p. 12.

[13] *Jane's Defence Weekly*, 23 Oct. 1993, p. 16; *Far Eastern Economic Review*, 21 Oct. 1993, p. 32.

[14] Amnesty International, 'Myanmar: Human Rights Developments July to December 1993' (Amnesty International: London, Jan. 1994).

[15] See Lawson, S., 'Sins of the SLORC', *Pacific Research*, May 1992, pp. 13–14.

[16] *The Independent*, 19 Jan. 1994, p. 12; *Phnom Penh Post*, 11–24 Feb. 1994, p. 4.

[17] Ker, P. and Mack, A., 'The evolving security discourse in Asia–Pacific', Paper presented at the Conference on Economic and Security Cooperation in the Asia–Pacific: Agendas for the 1990s, Australian National University, Canberra, 28–30 July 1993, p. 12.

[18] *The Age* (Melbourne), 13 July 1993, p. 9.

A major fear of many states is the emergence of a 'power vacuum' in the region as the result of a US retreat from the Western Pacific—spurred by the declining Russian threat, US domestic problems, the determination of the Clinton Administration to give these problems priority over foreign policy and the reappearance of the isolationism that has been a recurring theme of US politics.

The unexpectedly sudden US withdrawal from Subic Bay and Clark Field in the Philippines, precipitated by a volcanic eruption and completed by 31 December 1992, was, however, tempered by agreements with Indonesia, Malaysia and Singapore for access to air fields and ship berthing and repair facilities. The Philippines, Thailand and even Brunei subsequently also offered the USA increased military co-operation.[19] Other US military installations, in addition to those in the Philippines, have been closed as part of general restructuring and budget cuts (most notably in South Korea and Okinawa), and the US naval presence in the Pacific Ocean is scheduled to decline further. Planned troop cuts in South Korea have, however, been halted and there appears to be no inclination, at least prior to a comprehensive peace settlement in Korea, to withdraw entirely US forces from South Korea and Japan. The USA retains its bilateral defence alliances and agreements with the Philippines and Thailand—and in the broader Asia–Pacific region with Australia, Japan and South Korea. With one of its component states, Hawaii, located in the mid-Pacific and with continuing responsibilities to its territories and former territories in the Western Pacific, the United States will necessarily remain a Pacific power. Whether this would translate into a willingness to intervene militarily in Asia–Pacific is questionable. Since the Viet Nam War, US intervention in mainland South-East Asia has been highly improbable.

South-East Asian fears of a US retreat are compounded by concerns that South-East Asia might now be open to power projection by China, Japan and/or India. China is the most enigmatic and feared of South-East Asia's neighbours. It is perceived as creating 'leaner and meaner' military forces, including a blue-water naval capability.[20] It is beginning to project its military power beyond the South China Sea, its navy making port calls to Myanmar and Pakistan. Although it has ended its support for the Khmer Rouge in Cambodia, China is now a major arms supplier to Myanmar and is helping to upgrade that country's air and naval capacity, including that on the Coco Islands just north of India's Andaman Islands.[21] China continues to repress dissidents, Tibetans and other minority peoples and is involved in a bitter dispute with Britain over the democratization of Hong Kong prior to 1997, when the British colony reverts to Chinese rule.

On the other hand, China has embarked on economic reforms that have created astounding economic growth (estimated to be 12 per cent in 1993), par-

---

[19] *International Defense Review*, Nov. 1993, p. 878.
[20] You Ji and You Xu, 'In search of blue water power: the PLA Navy's Maritime Strategy in the 1990s', *Pacific Review*, vol. 4, no. 2 (1991), pp. 137–49; Yihong Zhang, 'China heads toward blue water', *International Defense Review*, Nov. 1993, pp. 879–80.
[21] *Far East Economic Review*, 16 Dec. 1993, p. 26; Ashton, W., 'The Burmese Navy', *Jane's Intelligence Review*, Jan. 1994, pp. 36–37.

ticularly in its southern and maritime provinces, resulting in increasingly close and complex economic ties with South-East Asia. China has also demonstrated a willingness to assume some of its great-power responsibilities by refraining from exercising its veto in the UN Security Council in order to permit widely supported resolutions to be adopted,[22] participating for the first time in peacekeeping operations, acceding to the Non-Proliferation Treaty (NPT) and signing the Chemical Weapons Convention. All these developments are reassuring to South-East Asia. None the less, China's volatile combination of an ageing communist leadership and a booming quasi-capitalist economy causes South-East Asians justifiable concern about the future stability of China.

For less tangible reasons, Japan is also a security concern to some South-East Asians. Its high net level of military spending, although comparatively low as a percentage of gross national product (GNP), is now the third highest in the world. This is producing an impressive Japanese military force, whose deployment even for peacekeeping duties in Cambodia has revived memories of Japanese aggression and atrocities in South-East Asia in World War II. However, Japan has neither power-projection capabilities, such as aircraft-carriers and long-range strike aircraft, nor weapons of mass destruction. The Japanese polity, by and large anti-militarist and anti-nuclear, is extremely sensitive to the problems that such capabilities would bring. It is also increasingly prepared to acknowledge the historical legacy of World War II—although the thorough rewriting of Japanese school textbooks would be welcomed by South-East Asians. The Japanese Government's willingness to provide increasing amounts of foreign aid to the poorer South-East Asian states and run the political risks of deploying peacekeepers in Cambodia can be viewed as positive symbols of Japan's desire to play a role in world politics that is commensurate with its economic strength. A seat on the UN Security Council and its close involvement in the Asia–Pacific regional security dialogue would provide further reassurance to South-East Asia of Japan's honourable intentions.

India, geographically closer than China or Japan to the heart of South-East Asia—its naval and air facilities on the Andaman and Nicobar islands are closer to Myanmar, Thailand, Malaysia and Indonesia than to India—is occasionally, but without much evidence or conviction, cited as a possible future threat. Although it is a nuclear weapon-capable state and a perennial great-power contender, India is dogged by enormous economic problems and security difficulties on its western and northern flanks, issues that are sufficient to keep it preoccupied for decades. India has not developed a power projection capability (one able to reach beyond Sri Lanka and the Maldives) and is not expected to do so in the near future.[23] India's declining military spending, slowing naval modernization and the initiation of joint naval exer-

---

[22] China, despite its own political or ideological qualms, has permitted or acquiesced in UN Security Council decisions to authorize Desert Storm, dispatch to and extend peacekeeping deployments in Cambodia, Somalia, Yugoslavia and elsewhere, criticize the Khmer Rouge and impose sanctions on Libya.

[23] See chapter 10 in this volume for details.

cises and military exchanges with Indonesia, Malaysia and Singapore have reportedly helped ease ASEAN fears.[24]

In addition to intra-state security problems, South-East Asia also has a multitude of territorial or border disputes, most of them quiescent. Malaysia has territorial disputes with all its ASEAN partners, the most serious being with the Philippines over Sabah.[25] Cambodia has disputes with Thailand and Viet Nam, including a maritime dispute with the latter. Maritime boundary disputes have increasingly arisen as Exclusive Economic Zones (EEZs) and territorial seas deriving from the 1982 UN Law of the Sea Convention have been mapped out and resources within them identified. South-East Asian states, with the exception of land-locked Laos, have acquired comparatively large EEZs which they desire to exploit and feel obliged to defend.[26] South-East Asian waters are troubled by widespread piracy, one factor which has driven the affected states into closer co-operation in maritime matters.[27]

Potentially the most dangerous territorial issues affecting South-East Asia are those centred on the Spratly Islands in the South China Sea.[28] Located between Malaysia, the Philippines and Viet Nam, these comprise scores of poorly delineated, uninhabited, largely barren islets, rocks and coral reefs, some of them permanently under water. China claims all of them, on the basis of its view of the South China Sea as historically Chinese waters (as does Taiwan), while the other claimants—Brunei, Malaysia, the Philippines and Viet Nam—claim only parts of the Spratlys. All claimants except Brunei militarily occupy certain islands. China and Viet Nam clashed militarily over their respective claims in 1973 and 1988. The Paracel Islands north-west of the Spratlys, which were seized from Viet Nam by China in 1974, are also still claimed by Viet Nam and Taiwan.[29]

The situation is exacerbated by the reputed presence of major oil deposits in the area, although the physical evidence for this is slight. Indonesia has organized a series of informal workshops on the Spratlys issue, attended by all claimants, including China, but without any negotiated outcome. In July 1992 ASEAN agreed to a Joint Declaration on the South China Sea, which called on the claimants to establish a code of conduct to resolve all jurisdictional disputes without resort to the use of force. Viet Nam wholeheartedly endorsed

[24] According to Satu P. Limaye, Japan Institute of International Affairs, Tokyo, reported in Richardson M., 'ASEAN nations and India warm up', *International Herald Tribune*, 29–30 Jan. 1994, p. 5.
[25] See Acharya (note 11), pp. 30–31.
[26] According to the Malaysian Maritime Enforcement Co-ordinating Centre, of the 15 maritime boundaries in the South China Sea (excluding the Gulf of Thailand), 12 are disputed, 2 have been agreed (1 partially) and 1 has been resolved through a joint exploration agreement. Cited in Acharya (note 11), p. 32.
[27] The International Maritime Organization has reported that attacks in the Molucca Straits between Indonesia, Malaysia and Singapore have virtually ceased but that attacks in the South China Sea between China and the Philippines are increasing. James, B., 'Paramilitary pirates reported raiding ships in South China Sea', *International Herald Tribune*, 10 Mar. 1994, p. 8.
[28] For details, see Findlay, T., 'Spratlys arise as flashpoint', *Defense News*, vol. 7, no. 48 (30 Nov.–6 Dec. 1992); Thomas, B. L., 'The Spratly Islands imbroglio: a tangled web of conflict', Working Paper no. 74 (Peace Research Centre, Australian National University: Canberra, Apr. 1990).
[29] Hamzah, B.A., *The Spratlies: What Can Be Done to Enhance Confidence*, ISIS Research Note (Institute of Strategic and International Studies (ISIS) Malaysia: Kuala Lumpur, 1990), p. 4.

the document, while China concurred with 'some of its basic principles'.[30] While reiterating its claims, Beijing has repeatedly attempted to reassure South-East Asian states, including Viet Nam, of its peaceful intentions and its willingness to set these aside in the interests of peaceful co-operation. However, tensions are likely to recur as China's naval power and oil exploration by competing claimants expand.

While none of South-East Asia's territorial disputes—including that over the Spratlys—is likely to lead to major armed conflict, their potential for damaging intra-regional relations remains. It is partly as a result of such disputes and potential disputes, and the general air of strategic uncertainty in the region at large, that all the ASEAN states are turning away from their previous preoccupation with internal security and 'nation building' to concentrate more on external security. This has led them to modernize their regular armed forces, *inter alia* through the acquisition of high-technology weaponry. Naval and air capabilities, some of them suitable for power projection, have received particular attention, prompting some observers to fear an incipient arms race.[31] The acquisition of such forces may itself be a source of regional insecurity unless properly managed.[32]

On the other hand, there have been moves by some South-East Asian states, most notably Indonesia, Malaysia and Singapore, towards attenuation of their 'security dilemma' through collective or common security approaches, such as confidence-building measures (CBMs) and security dialogue. Their economic success has, moreover, given these states the confidence and clout to put them in the vanguard of Asia–Pacific regionalism.

The role of ASEAN in South-East Asia

The role of South-East Asia in the advancement of Asia–Pacific regionalism is greatly facilitated by the existence of ASEAN, the most notable subregional organization in the Asia–Pacific region. Although it has not succeeded in achieving its original goals of close-knit economic integration—only recently has it been able to agree on the goal of an ASEAN free trade area by 2007— ASEAN has given a political coherence to the subregion that other parts of Asia–Pacific sorely lack. This has afforded the ASEAN states a springboard, collectively and individually, from which to influence the security architecture of the broader Asia–Pacific region.

ASEAN had traditionally refrained from dealing with security or military issues. While its founding 1967 Bangkok Declaration included as a goal the

[30] Lewis, P., 'Vietnam nears ASEAN pact amid Spratlys claim', *Defense News*, 28 Sep.–4 Oct. 1992, p. 8.

[31] For a discussion of arms acquisitions in the Asia–Pacific region and allegations of an arms race, see appendix 13E in this volume.

[32] As far as is known, no South-East Asian states have acquired weapons of mass destruction. All (except Brunei and Singapore) are party to the 1925 Geneva Protocol, the 1972 Biological Weapons Convention (Myanmar has signed but not ratified), and all have signed the 1993 Chemical Weapons Convention. All are party to the 1968 NPT (in 1992 Myanmar became the last to accede) and have signed safeguards agreements with the IAEA where required (the exceptions being Cambodia, Laos and Myanmar). See annexe A in this volume for parties to all the major multilateral arms control agreements.

promotion of 'peace and stability', its 1976 Concord specifically excluded security issues from ASEAN's purview.[33] Discussion of such issues ran the risk of reviving intra-ASEAN territorial disputes, such as the Philippines–Malaysia conflict over Sabah, and revealing differences in strategic outlook, notably over the presence of US bases in the Philippines. Regional defence co-operation among ASEAN members, such as joint exercises, occurred only on a bilateral basis or, in the case of Malaysia and Singapore, through the 1971 Five Power Defence Arrangement (FPDA) with Australia, New Zealand and the United Kingdom.

Despite such self-imposed limitations, ASEAN dealt with some broader security concepts, notably ZOPFAN and SEANWFZ.[34] It also began to move into more day-to-day security issues with its involvement in the Cambodia question after Viet Nam's invasion in 1989. Subsequently, ASEAN played a key part in the Cambodia peace plan, including the deployment by all of its members of peacekeeping contingents. Individual ASEAN members also began to take regional security initiatives, such as Indonesia's Spratly dispute workshops, Singapore's hosting of bilateral talks between China and Taiwan and talks between the Philippine Government and Muslim insurgency leaders held in Jakarta in 1993.[35]

In 1979 ASEAN established the ASEAN Post Ministerial Conference (ASEAN–PMC) with a number of 'dialogue partners': Australia, Canada, Japan, South Korea, New Zealand, the United States and the European Community (EC). This forum has engaged in a multilateral political and security dialogue—on issues of ASEAN's choosing. ASEAN further enhanced its broader regionalist credentials when China (which has requested dialogue partner status) and Russia were granted guest status by the ASEAN Ministerial Meeting in 1991, meaning that they could have separate consultations during the ASEAN–PMC but not observe the actual PMC meetings. Laos and Viet Nam received ASEAN–PMC observer status when they signed the 1976 Treaty of Amity and Co-operation in 1992.[36] It was this network of dialogue partnerships that provided the foundation for ASEAN to establish the ASEAN Regional Forum in 1993. ASEAN, seemingly more secure than ever in its own South-East Asian subregionalism, had by this time clearly begun to see itself as the centre of gravity of an Asia–Pacific security dialogue.

III. Evolution of an Asia–Pacific security dialogue

The Asia–Pacific region sprawls across the globe from far eastern Russia to the South Island of New Zealand and from Myanmar to Hawaii. The region is also sometimes taken to encompass the west coasts of Canada and the United

---

[33] Wanandi, J., 'Asia–Pacific security forums: rationale and options from an ASEAN perspective', D. Ball, W. L. Grant and J. Wanandi, *Security Cooperation in the Asia–Pacific Region*, Significant Issues Series, vol. 15, no. 5 (Center for Strategic and International Studies: Washington, DC, 1993), p. 17.

[34] See Natalegawa, M., 'De-nuking Southeast Asia', *Pacific Research*, Feb. 1993, pp. 8–10.

[35] *International Herald Tribune*, 8 Nov. 1993, p. 2.

[36] See Wanandi (note 33), p 11.

States and sometimes the micro-states of the South Pacific. When referred to as the Pacific Rim, the region is assumed also to include the Pacific seaboard states of Latin America. The geographical spread and divergent definitions of the Asia–Pacific region in part explain why regionalism—in the political, economic and security fields—has been so slow to develop. Other factors include the great economic and cultural diversity of the region—compare Mongolia with Australia, for instance—and the weakness and self-absorption of many of the region's newly independent states after World War II. The naval superiority of the USA and the presence in the North Pacific of its cold war antagonist, the Soviet Union, an Asia–Pacific power in its own right, also served to dampen regionalist sentiment. Furthermore, an array of wars, conflicts and disputes—the Korean War and the Viet Nam War being the most destructive—prevented the emergence of region-wide co-operative arrangements.

Hence, unlike Europe, Latin America, Africa, South Asia and the Arab world, Asia–Pacific has no regional organization to approximate the Conference on Security and Co-operation in Europe (CSCE), the Organization of American States (OAS), the Organization of African Unity (OAU), the South Asian Association for Regional Co-operation (SAARC) or the Arab League. Until now there has never been a region-wide multilateral security dialogue in Asia–Pacific. Even at a subregional level such dialogue has, until very recently, been rare. Regional security issues have been almost exclusively dealt with bilaterally or in global forums such as the United Nations.

The establishment of a multilateral security dialogue in the Asia–Pacific region has therefore been a painstaking process. General Secretary Mikhail Gorbachev first proposed such an idea as far back as 1986, in a speech in Vladivostok, subsequently in an interview with the Indonesian journal *Merdeka* in 1987 and in further speeches in Krasnoyarsk (1988) and Beijing (1989). Proposals were later made by Australia, Canada and Mongolia, the latter two only in respect of the North Pacific. Australian Foreign Minister Gareth Evans went so far as to coin a name—the Conference on Security and Co-operation in Asia (CSCA)—for his proposed forum.

All these proposals were met with widespread scepticism and suspicion—partly because they came from states located on the fringes of the region. South-East Asians were especially wary of ideas that appeared to suggest the emulation of non-Asian models such as the CSCE.[37] Asia was seen as strategically, politically, economically and culturally different from Europe. Postcolonial sensitivities were also a factor, particularly on the part of Indonesia and Malaysia. Additionally, most Asian states denied that there was a need for a regional security dialogue, arguing that they had other priorities, such as economic development and internal stability, and a different notion of security. Others, notably Japan, felt that regional security initiatives should not

---

[37] See Evans, G. and Grant, B., *Australia's Foreign Relations in the World of the 1990s* (Carlton: Melbourne University Press, 1991), pp. 110–12; Evans, G., 'What Asia needs is a Europe-style CSCA', *International Herald Tribune*, 27 July 1990, p. 5. For analysis of the CSCA proposal, see Findlay, T., *Asia/Pacific CSBMs: A Prospectus*, Working Paper no. 90 (Peace Research Centre, Australian National University: Canberra, 1990), pp. 2–4.

precede the settlement of outstanding issues, namely, Japan's dispute with the Soviet Union over the Northern Territories. China was extremely wary and unresponsive.

Under the Reagan and early Bush Administrations, the US attitude towards Asia–Pacific security was 'if it ain't broke, don't fix it'. The USA suggested that its bilateral connections, including alliances, with key states of the region were sufficient to ensure regional security. It also saw a regional security forum as a potential platform for the USSR to exert greater influence over the region. Finally, as the pre-eminent naval power in Asia–Pacific, the USA feared that such a forum might be tempted to negotiate naval CBMs—seen as a 'slippery slope' towards naval arms control.

APEC paves the way

In the meantime, the economic dynamism of Asia–Pacific was creating a growing economic regionalism which led to the establishment of several economically oriented regional organizations, which in turn paved the way for a regional security dialogue. US cold war strategy in the region (including substantial military and economic support for Japan, South Korea, Taiwan and Thailand) and Japan's burgeoning economic might, increasingly apparent in regional trade, investment and the transfer offshore of Japanese manufacturing capability, were fashioning an increasingly coherent economic region.[38] Added to these trends were the familial ties of the Chinese business community throughout South-East Asia. The result was a rapidly expanding web of economic relationships between the five Asian economic 'dragons' or 'tigers'—Hong Kong, Japan, South Korea, Singapore and Taiwan—and the rapidly growing 'young dragons' or 'tiger cubs'—southern China, Indonesia, Malaysia and Thailand. Trade among these countries now accounts for about half of their total trade.[39] Intra-Asian trade doubled between 1988 and 1992.[40] So-called 'growth triangles' (China–Taiwan–Hong Kong and Malaysia–Indonesia–Singapore) are forging particularly strong economic interdependencies.[41]

Governments entered the trade field relatively late. Non-governmental and mixed co-operative bodies had long been operating, such as the Pacific Basin Economic Council (PBEC) since 1967, the Pacific Trade and Development (PAFTAD) conferences, beginning in 1968, and the Pacific Economic Co-operation Council, formerly Conference (PECC), a tripartite mix of governmental officials, business leaders and academics, since 1980. Finally, in 1989, a governmental-level body, Asia–Pacific Economic Co-operation (APEC), was established at a meeting in Canberra, at the suggestion of

---

[38] Stubbs, R., 'Geo-politics, geo-economics and the foundations of Asia–Pacific Cooperation', Paper presented at the Conference on Economic and Security Cooperation in the Asia–Pacific: Agenda for the 1990s, Australian National University, Canberra, 28–30 July 1993, p. 1.

[39] Manning, R. A., 'The Asian paradox: toward a new architecture', *World Policy Journal*, vol. 10, no. 3 (fall 1993), p. 60.

[40] *Time*, 22 Nov. 1993, p. 48.

[41] *Time* (Australia), 17 Jan. 1994, pp. 24–25.

Australia. An informal group of Asia–Pacific 'economies', APEC aims to promote trade and economic growth in the region.[42] The designation 'economies' rather than states was designed to entice the three Chinese entities—China, Hong Kong and Taiwan—to join.[43] They did so in 1991, in a move described by the *Asian Wall Street Journal* as 'a triumph of pragmatism over politics'.[44]

APEC has to date been a loosely structured forum for discussion of a broad range of economic issues, initially through annual ministerial meetings but more recently through working groups of senior officials on specific economic, educational and environmental issues. In January 1993 APEC took a critical step towards institutionalization by establishing a Secretariat, headed by an Executive Director, in Singapore.[45]

The ASEAN states were initially reluctant to join APEC, seeing it as a potential rival to ASEAN. ASEAN fears have been somewhat assuaged by the location of the Secretariat in Singapore and a realization that ASEAN as a bloc carries considerable weight in APEC decision making (for instance, it provides the Chair for APEC Senior Officials and Ministerial Meetings every other year).[46] However, Malaysia continued to promote its proposed East Asia Economic Grouping (EAEG) as an alternative to APEC.[47] Only in 1993, through intra-ASEAN compromise, was this parlayed into an East Asian Economic Caucus within APEC, although Malaysia undoubtedly continues to harbour more ambitious designs for its brain-child.

At its Seattle Ministerial Meeting in November 1993, APEC admitted Mexico and Papua New Guinea to membership, while Chile was promised membership in 1994.[48] Macao, Mongolia, Peru, Russia, and Viet Nam have also expressed interest in joining. Although it placed a three-year moratorium on new members after 1994, APEC is moving inexorably towards encompassing the entire Pacific Basin—a development unlikely to be emulated in the security field, given the irrelevance of Latin America to Asian security.

Agreement was not reached, however, on changing the name of APEC to 'Community'.[49] Australia, whose Foreign Minister, Gareth Evans, has described APEC as 'four adjectives in search of a noun',[50] remains the most enthusiastic advocate of such a development, followed closely by the United States. The Seattle meeting also rejected a recommendation by APEC's Group of Eminent Persons for a faster track towards an Asia–Pacific free trade zone. The smaller APEC members fear being drawn into a free trade area with three of the world's largest economies—those of China, Japan and the USA—as

[42] Information provided by the APEC Secretariat, Singapore.

[43] The 'participating economies' are: Australia, Brunei, Canada, China, Hong Kong, Indonesia, Japan, South Korea, Malaysia, New Zealand, Philippines, Singapore, 'Chinese Taipei' (Taiwan), Thailand and the USA.

[44] *Asian Wall Street Journal*, 15 July 1993, p. 8.

[45] The first Executive Director is former US Ambassador William Bodde, Jr. He will be succeeded by Professor Hendra Esmara of Indonesia in 1994.

[46] Willliam Bodde describes APEC as giving ASEAN influence a 'multiplier effect'; Bodde, W., Jr, 'APEC: an idea whose time has come', Address to the East–West Centre, Honolulu, 24 Sep. 1993, p. 6.

[47] *Canberra Times*, 25 July 1993.

[48] *New York Times*, 21 Nov. 1993, p. 14.

[49] *Far Eastern Economic Review*, 2 Dec. 1993, p. 12.

[50] *Time*, 29 Nov. 1993, p. 25.

well as the possibility of trade-linked pressure over human rights. This group, which includes Indonesia and Thailand, favours a slower rate of evolution of APEC, especially since ASEAN's own free-trade area will not be established until 2007, even if all goes according to plan. Malaysia, idiosyncratically, opposes any enhancement of APEC's role at this stage.[51]

Despite these intra-APEC differences about its future role in the economic field, APEC is seen by some observers as a framework in which security issues might ultimately be considered. Both Australia and Japan[52] have made such suggestions. Apart from Malaysian opposition, the China–Taiwan question will, however, continue to be a barrier to such a development. It is one thing to have China and Taiwan discuss economic co-operation, in which they are increasingly heavily involved bilaterally, but quite another to expect them, under the polite fiction of being 'economies' rather than states, to discuss sensitive political issues such as the Spratly Islands dispute or missile proliferation.

While it is unlikely that APEC will ever evolve into a multi-faceted CSCE-type forum, its survival and growth in the face of widespread scepticism and opposition have proved that an Asia–Pacific dialogue in at least one field is feasible. Moreover, as Winston Lord, the Clinton Administration's Assistant Secretary of State for East Asia, has admitted, APEC helps 'anchor' the USA in Asia, the implication being that this may have a spillover effect in the security field.[53]

'Second track' diplomacy

In addition to the growth of economic regionalism, so-called 'second track' diplomacy seems to have been critical in stimulating the evolution of a government-level regional security dialogue in Asia–Pacific.[54] Beginning in the late 1980s, this intensive series of informal consultations, research projects and conferences on Asia–Pacific security, involving a mix of academic and governmental representatives, appears to have been seminal in turning regional opinion around. Many of the members of ASEAN–ISIS (the ASEAN Institutes of Strategic and International Studies), an umbrella organization which brings together the international and strategic studies institutes of the ASEAN states, have close links with government. Among the most important examples of 'second track' diplomacy were the annual Kuala Lumpur round-table talks organized by the Institute of Strategic and International Studies Malaysia, the Kathmandu conferences organized by the UN Department (now Centre) for Disarmament Affairs, the North Pacific Co-operative Security

---

[51] Interview with William Bodde, *International Herald Tribune*, 8 Nov. 1993, p. 2.

[52] Johnson, T., 'Japan low-key in regional security debate', *Mainichi Daily News*, 31 Dec. 1992.

[53] Interview with William Bodde, *Asian Wall Street Journal*, 20 May 1993.

[54] A survey by Paul Evans discovered 16 'trans-Pacific' dialogue channels for multilateral discussions on Asia–Pacific security issues. See Evans, P. M., 'The Council for Security Cooperation in Asia Pacific: context and prospects', Paper presented at the Conference on Economic and Security Cooperation in the Asia–Pacific: Agenda for the 1990s, Australian National University, Canberra, 28–30 July 1993, pp. 15–17.

Dialogue (NPCSD) programme run by York University with Canadian Government funding,[55] and the early work of the Australian National University Peace Research Centre on CBMs and regional security in the North Pacific.[56]

Eventually, this second-track movement set an example to governments by establishing, in November 1992 in Seoul, a forum for conducting a non-governmental regional security dialogue, the Council for Security Co-operation in the Asia–Pacific (CSCAP).[57] CSCAP preceded the establishment of the ASEAN Regional Forum by six months. As in the evolution of the government-level regional security dialogue, it was ASEAN players which led the way, with ASEAN–ISIS being instrumental in CSCAP's foundation.

Key policy shifts

In 1992 and 1993 the prospects for an institutionalized regional security dialogue improved markedly as a result of changes in Japanese and US policies and the evolution of ASEAN thinking.

By 1991 Japan was vocally supporting an institutionalized dialogue, its foreign ministry officials having carefully studied the ideas aired in the second-track diplomacy deliberations. Japan's search for a political role in the region commensurate with its economic might was also a factor in its policy change. In July 1991 Japan surprised the ASEAN–PMC in Kuala Lumpur by proposing that political and security issues be added to its agenda,[58] an idea already recommended by ASEAN–ISIS in June and accepted by the Kuala Lumpur Ministerial Meeting which had preceded the PMC.[59] A further proposal that each PMC be preceded by meetings of senior officials to give the forum more depth was not immediately accepted.

In July 1992, Japanese Prime Minister Kiichi Miyazawa told the National Press Club in Washington that he favoured a 'two-track approach' involving a dialogue on specific subregional disputes (undoubtedly a reference to its Northern Territories dispute with Russia) presumably among the parties directly involved and an Asia–Pacific-wide dialogue on broader political/security issues.[60] In the same month Japan and ASEAN agreed to transform their Japan–ASEAN forum, established in 1977 to enhance co-operation

[55] See Henderson, S., 'Canada and Asia Pacific security: the North Pacific cooperative security dialogue—recent trends', Working Paper no. 1 (North Pacific Cooperative Security Dialogue Research Programme, York University: North York, Ont., Nov. 1991).

[56] Mack, A., 'Dialogs for defence', *Asia–Pacific Defence Reporter*, Feb./Mar. 1993, p. 15.

[57] CSCAP was founded by a group of 10 non-governmental research institutes from the region (Australia, Canada, Indonesia, Japan, South Korea, Malaysia, the Philippines, Singapore, Thailand and the USA), meeting under the auspices of the Pacific Forum/Center for Strategic and International Studies (CSIS). It was officially launched on 9 June 1993 at ISIS Malaysia's annual Asia–Pacific round-table talks in Kuala Lumpur. China and Russia are notable absentees. See Jordan, A. A., 'Foreword' in Ball *et al.* (note 33), p. xi.

[58] *International Defense Review*, Nov. 1993, p. 875.

[59] ASEAN–ISIS, 'A time for initiative: proposals for the consideration of the Fourth ASEAN Summit', 4 June 1991.

[60] Findlay, T., 'Dialogue about dialogue continues', *Pacific Research*, Nov. 1992, p. 24.

in non-political fields, into a forum for discussion of political issues, including security.[61]

As for the United States, with the end of the cold war, cuts in its overseas military deployments, the closure of its Philippine bases and the long-term prospect of a further pullback across the Pacific, it began slowly to appreciate the potential value of a regional security dialogue. It was goaded in this direction by Australia, Canada and at a later stage Japan. Towards the end of the Bush Administration, the US bureaucracy had swung around to restrained support. Winston Lord signalled the shift in US policy in April 1993 by calling for the development of 'new mechanisms to manage or prevent' emerging regional problems.[62]

China eventually added its voice to those supporting a regional security dialogue, although seemingly more as a result of not wishing to be left out than from conviction.[63] In his first major foreign policy address, in May 1993, South Korean President Kim Young Sam also called vaguely for 'the promotion of multilateral security dialogue in the Asia–Pacific region'.[64] Russia continued the support for a regional security dialogue that the Soviet Union under Gorbachev had so persistently advocated. Although its preoccupation with European security and with its own grave internal problems left scant political or diplomatic capacity to devote to Asia–Pacific, Russia none the less continued to propose specific measures for enhancing security in the region. For instance, Foreign Minister Andrey Kozyrev proposed the establishment of regional conflict prevention and strategic research centres.[65]

ASEAN takes charge

It was ultimately ASEAN which seized the initiative and brought the regional security dialogue concept to fruition. The dramatic shifts in US and Japanese policy seemed to have coincided with a realization by ASEAN that the USA would not be permanently engaged militarily in the region. A regional security dialogue could at least help retain US political involvement in South-East Asian security. The extensive 'dialogue about a dialogue', at both official and 'second-track' levels, had, moreover, convinced ASEAN policy makers that they were not being asked to copy the European model slavishly and rush into arrangements that did not suit them.[66] With greater exposure to the concept of common security, regional policy makers seemed to see a genuine need for managing their security dilemmas—such as the Spratly Islands dispute—to

[61] Soeya, Y., 'The evolution of Japanese thinking and policies on cooperative security in the 1980s and 1990s', Paper presented at the Conference on Economic and Security Cooperation in the Asia–Pacific: Agendas for the 1990s, Australian National University, Canberra, 28–30 July 1993, p. 8.

[62] Findlay, T., 'Regional dialogue hots up', *Pacific Research*, May 1993, pp. 19–20.

[63] Wu Kesheng, 'Round-up of the Conference of Research Institutes in Asia and the Pacific', *Peace* (Chinese People's Association for Peace and Disarmament, Beijing), no. 26 (June 1992), pp. 6–9.

[64] 'Text of Pacific era and Korea's new diplomacy by President Kim Young Sam', *Korea Annual 1993* (Yonhap News Agency: Seoul, 1993), p. 394.

[65] Ryan, S. L., 'ASEAN's regional security forum: giving Southeast Asia a voice in world affairs', *Asian Defence Journal*, Sep. 1993, p. 58.

[66] For details, see Mack (note 56).

avoid creating misperceptions of intention, instigating a regional arms race or, in the worst case, triggering armed conflict.[67]

Perhaps the most important factor driving ASEAN to seize the initiative, however, was its realization that if such a development was as inevitable as it now seemed, then it would be in ASEAN's interest to be in the vanguard. ASEAN could thereby protect its individual and collective interests, vet membership invitations, and shape the content and form of the dialogue (such contentious items as East Timor and Malaysia's treatment of its Indian and Chinese minorities could, for instance, be excluded).

Moreover, the ASEAN states had come to realize that their organization was beginning to enhance their influence and stature both individually and collectively. The proof lay in ASEAN's role in the Cambodia settlement (especially through the Jakarta Informal Meetings, JIMs), the decision to locate the APEC Secretariat in Singapore, ASEAN's bloc influence on APEC decisions and the growing role of its individual members in wider Asia–Pacific diplomacy. Furthermore, ASEAN already had its PMC, in which most of the key regional players were already represented, on which to base a more thorough-going regional security dialogue.

At the fourth annual ASEAN summit meeting in Singapore in January 1992 there was agreement on an enhanced dialogue on security issues taking place at the ASEAN–PMC.[68] In February 1992, at a meeting in Tokyo, ASEAN agreed to Japan's proposal for a Senior Officials Meeting (SOM) prior to each ASEAN–PMC.[69] The first SOM was held in Singapore in May 1993, with an extensive agenda including preventive diplomacy and conflict management, non-proliferation, UN peacekeeping, the UN Conventional Arms Transfer, exchanges of information among defence planners, prior notification of military exercises and ZOPFAN and SEANWFZ.[70]

Within ASEAN itself, security discussions would also assume a more prominent place. At the annual ASEAN Ministerial Meeting in July 1993 it was agreed that the dialogue on security co-operation involving ASEAN foreign and defence ministers that had begun in Manila in June 1992 (notably

---

[67] A key influence was ASEAN–ISIS, with its close links to government and the policy recommendations contained in its timely June 1991 'A time for initiative' (see note 59). According to Stewart Henderson, 'A collective decision was reached (driven by Indonesia, Malaysia and Thailand) that some serious re-thinking of ASEAN's approaches to regional security was needed and that ASEAN should counter 'out-of-region' security issues with its own proposals. The result was an increase in government-directed research by the major think-tanks, paralleled by policy papers from several foreign ministries.' See Henderson (note 55), p. 12. Amitav Acharya contends that another key factor was the attempt by the Aquino Government in the Philippines—as part of its campaign to avoid the Philippine legislature banning the US bases—to have ASEAN endorse the US military presence as a stabilizing factor in the region. Although this attempt failed, Manila's hosting of a semi-official conference in June 1991, where ASEAN security co-operation was extensively discussed, appears to have been influential in putting forward alternative ideas. Thailand followed with a similar meeting in Nov. 1991. See Acharya (note 11), p. 59.

[68] Quoted in Acharya (note 11), p. 3.

[69] Soeya (note 61), p. 8.

[70] The SOM agreed to undertake further research in 4 areas: non-proliferation regimes and their application at the regional level; conflict prevention and management, including peacekeeping; security co-operation in North-East Asia; and confidence-building measures applicable to the region. See Chairman's Statement, ASEAN Post-Ministerial Conferences, Senior Officials Meeting, Singapore, 20–21 May 1993.

on the Spratlys issue) should continue.[71] These ministers are scheduled to meet next in Bangkok in late January or early February 1994 to discuss a wide range of issues, including arms transfers and procurement, notification of military exercises, refugees and piracy.

The ASEAN Regional Forum

In July 1993 the ASEAN Ministerial Meeting surprised observers by agreeing to establish an ASEAN Regional Forum for the wider Asia–Pacific region. The new Forum will include five new countries in addition to the ASEAN–PMC group: China, Laos, Papua New Guinea, Russia and Viet Nam will join Australia, Canada, the European Union (EU), Japan, South Korea, New Zealand, the United States and the six ASEAN members. The 18-member group will meet for the first time in July 1994. Australian Foreign Minister Gareth Evans, whose own proposal for a CSCA had been rejected several years before, called the establishment of the Forum an 'historic milestone'.[72]

While the agenda for the Regional Forum is at this stage unclear, a pressing requirement in Asia–Pacific is for transparency, a phenomenon still largely alien to the defence culture of the region. It should be possible to begin with relatively basic transparency measures (such as military doctrine seminars) while working gradually towards more sophisticated measures (such as revealing the capabilities of newly acquired equipment) as confidence builds, as has occurred in Europe. A beginning was made in June 1993 when Malaysia hosted a 'defence dialogue', a forum for defence officials from ASEAN, Australia, the USA and other states to discuss such transparency issues as threat assessment, doctrine and acquisitions.[73] Even more significant would be the establishment of an Asian Arms Transfers Register as proposed by the Malaysian Defence Minister.[74] So far there has been a reasonable response by Asia–Pacific states to the new UN Register of Conventional Arms.[75]

A second agenda item would comprise more wide-ranging confidence- and security-building measures (CSBMs). Such measures, widely practised in Europe, are designed to reduce or eliminate mutual misperceptions, suspicions and fears by making military intentions more explicit. Such measures are relatively rare in South-East Asia, although they have been increasingly adopted elsewhere in the Asian region, especially between India and China,[76]

---

[71] International Institute for Strategic Studies (IISS), *The Military Balance 1993–1994* (Brassey's: London, 1993), p. 146.

[72] See Ryan (note 65), p. 60.

[73] See Manning (note 39), p. 59.

[74] Mohamed Najib bin Tun Abdul Razak, 'Towards cooperative security and regional stability: the Malaysian view', ed. D. Horner, *The Army and the Future: Land Forces in Australia and South-East Asia* (Department of Defence, Army Office: Canberra, 1993), p. 137.

[75] Laurance, E. J., Wezeman, S. T. and Wulf, H., SIPRI, *Arms Watch: SIPRI Report on the First Year of the UN Register of Conventional Arms*, SIPRI Research Report no. 6 (Oxford University Press: Oxford, 1993), p. 18. Those which submitted returns in the first year (1993, with data for 1992) were: Australia, Canada, China, Fiji, Japan, Malaysia, Mongolia, New Zealand, Papua New Guinea, Philippines, Russia, Singapore, Solomon Islands, South Korea and the USA. States in the vicinity which replied were India, Pakistan, Sri Lanka and Kazakhstan.

[76] McGirk, T., 'India and China sign pact to ease Himalayan dispute', *The Independent*, 8 Sep. 1993.

India and Pakistan, and China and Russia[77] on their respective frontiers. Such measures include advance notification of military manœuvres, so-called 'hot-lines' between political and military leaders and co-operation in avoiding airspace violations. Given the importance of sea traffic in the region, a multi-lateral incidents at sea agreement[78] is one important possibility for Asia–Pacific. Quasi-military co-operation regimes have also been suggested, including a regional maritime surveillance and safety regime and a regional airspace surveillance and control regime.[79] A concern will be to match specific proposals to the strategic culture of the region.[80]

A third item, a favourite of the USA, is the implementation of regional measures to stem the proliferation of weapons of mass destruction and their delivery systems. The Regional Forum could be used to support the NPT (especially in view of the 1995 NPT Review and Extension Conference[81]) and the CWC (especially in the early days of its implementation). Japan is currently leading moves to establish a uniform Asian dual-use technology control regime. Senior officials from ASEAN, Australia, Hong Kong, South Korea and the USA met in Tokyo in October 1993 for an initial seminar on export controls on such technology.[82] For an Asian regime to work properly, the participation of China, North Korea and Taiwan will be essential.

A fourth role for a regional forum would be the discussion of regional disputes involving a wide range of states, such as the Spratlys issue. Bilateral conflicts (such as the Northern Territories dispute) are likely to be kept out of the Forum by the parties involved. In such cases the Regional Forum could, however, extend a 'good offices' function to the parties. In the longer term a regional conflict prevention centre is a possibility.

A fifth role would be the integration of the states of Indo-China—Cambodia, Laos and Viet Nam—back into the Asia–Pacific security system after a long absence. Their membership of APEC and ASEAN would assist this process. Their involvement in meaningful regional security discussions would—given Indo-China's history—be an extremely positive development.

Sixth, the Regional Forum will have to deal with 'problem' states in Asia–Pacific, at present North Korea and Myanmar. Addressing the North Korean issue in the Forum would be problematic given the presence of China. As for Myanmar, in view of the sensitivity of the South-East Asian states to Western concern about human rights violations in the region—a concern which they regard as interference in their internal affairs—the question of how to engender change in Myanmar and reintegrate it into the region will be a major chal-

[77] *International Herald Tribune*, 6 Dec. 1993, p. 6.

[78] For a discussion of incidents at sea agreements and the text of early agreements, see Fieldhouse, R., SIPRI, *Security at Sea* (Oxford University Press: Oxford, 1990), pp. 203–19, 256–64.

[79] See Ball (note 33), pp. 20–21, for a list of proposed regional confidence- and security-building measures for the Asia–Pacific region.

[80] See Ball (note 33), pp. 23–24.

[81] See also chapter 15 in this volume.

[82] Burgess, L. and Usui, N., 'Japan leads quest for Asian export control', *Defense News*, 1–7 Nov. 1993, pp. 1, 36.

lenge for the Forum and for ASEAN itself. Clearly, Myanmar's admission to ASEAN and the Regional Forum cannot at this stage be countenanced.

Finally, the Forum will provide an opportunity simply for states to exchange views on the concept of security itself. It is likely that vastly different and conflicting notions will be aired. Indeed, neither ASEAN nor any other participant seems at present to have any idea of what the basic conceptual assumptions of Forum discussions are likely to be, whether those of 'common security', 'co-operative security', 'collective security', 'comprehensive security' or some other formulation.[83] None the less such an exchange will be unprecedented and may lead to a greater appreciation of each other's national perspectives.

The ASEAN Regional Forum is likely to be complemented by what may become annual APEC heads of government meetings, the first of which was held in Seattle in November 1993. The idea of an Asia–Pacific summit meeting, bringing together the heads of government of all the APEC members, was first proposed by Australian Prime Minister Paul Keating in July 1991. Supported by Indonesia and Japan, the idea was taken up in July 1993 by President Clinton, who proposed an Asia–Pacific 'informal leadership conference' summit meeting following the fifth APEC Annual Ministerial Meeting.[84] The summit meeting, the largest Asia–Pacific heads of government gathering since 1966,[85] was held in closed-door sessions, without advisers, on Blake Island near Seattle. In addition to the Taiwanese President, who bowed to Chinese sensibilities and stayed away, Malaysian Prime Minister Mahathir bin Mohamad was the only APEC leader not to attend. The only visible result of the summit meeting was an economic 'Vision Statement', directed mostly at the then deadlocked General Agreement on Tariffs and Trade (GATT). Yet, the gathering arguably ushered in the beginnings of an Asia–Pacific 'community' and launched a series of Asia–Pacific gatherings at the highest levels that can only be conducive to the growth of co-operative regionalism.[86] A second summit meeting will be held in Jakarta in 1994, while a third is mooted for Japan in 1995.

Many obstacles to a productive regional security dialogue in Asia–Pacific remain, not least of which is the region's diversity. This includes a 'North–South' dimension, pitting developing (in many cases rapidly developing) states such as China, Indonesia and Malaysia against the region's developed states—Australia, Canada, New Zealand and the USA. Differences are especially acute over trade and human rights. Moreover, there are profound dissimilarities between the security situations of two of Asia–Pacific's sub-regions—North-East Asia and South-East Asia. These differences have been compounded by the location between them of Indo-China—for decades war-

---

[83] For a useful discussion of various concepts of security in the Asia–Pacific context, see Mack, A., *Concepts of Security in the Post-Cold War*, Working Paper 1993/8 (Department of International Relations, Australian National University: Canberra, 1993).
[84] *Asian Wall Street Journal*, 15 July 1993, pp. 1, 8.
[85] In that year President Johnson convened an Asia–Pacific summit meeting in Manila to enlist support for US policy in Viet Nam. *New York Times*, 21 Nov. 1993, p. 14.
[86] Bergsten, C. F., 'Sunrise in Seattle', *International Economic Insights*, vol. 5, no. 1 (Jan./Feb. 1994), pp. 18–20.

torn and today economically backward. Some observers fail to detect any region-wide security problems that might be considered by an Asia–Pacific security dialogue and remain unconvinced that involving all states in the region will necessarily improve the prospects for resolving subregional conflicts.

What this new regional security dialogue will mean for Asia–Pacific's various components is not yet entirely clear. For ASEAN it will probably mean greater influence and a reinforcement of intra-ASEAN efforts to enhance its security environment through co-operative means. Indeed, there is a danger that ASEAN will have too much influence on the agenda and outcome of deliberations in its Regional Forum. For Indo-China, its involvement in the regional dialogue could mean a new beginning in its tortured relationships with its neighbours and great powers further afield. For Australia, Canada, New Zealand and the USA, often regarded as essentially outsiders, the new dialogue will help consolidate their place in the security affairs of the region. For Papua New Guinea, the lone Melanesian member so far, it is an opportunity to inject South Pacific island concerns—for the first time— directly into the broader Asia–Pacific debate.

For North-East Asia, however, the benefits are not so obvious. The Forum may have difficulty focusing on issues specific to North-East Asia since ASEAN's agenda is likely to be focused on its own subregion of Asia–Pacific. In addition, the Forum does not include two key players from North-East Asia—Taiwan and North Korea—a situation which will take some time to resolve. Nor are Hong Kong and Macao represented as separate 'entities', as they are in APEC. Mongolia is also missing from the current list of invitees. Until these membership gaps are resolved, crucial security-related problems such as those facing the Korean peninsula cannot be fully addressed. Even broader topics such as nuclear weapon proliferation and military transparency may meet with resistance if participants, such as China, sense that discussions are directed against them or are contrary to their national security interests.[87] Domestic preoccupations, particularly in China, South Korea and Russia, may preclude the active participation of some North-East Asian powers. Finally, relationships between some of the subregion's key members, such as those between Russia and Japan and Japan and China, are so sensitive that they may only be willing to engage in perfunctory talks in the context of a region-wide security dialogue. Hence, while the ASEAN Regional Forum shows great promise in broadening the regional dialogue generally, its contribution to a multilateral security dialogue relevant to North-East Asia is as yet unclear. It is in North-East Asia that the implantation of habits of dialogue on security issues—and broader regional co-operation—will be most difficult to achieve.[88]

---

[87] Ferguson, G., 'ASEAN broadens base for regional stability: concern over China is focus of new forum', *Defense News*, 2–8 Aug. 1993.
[88] See chapter 5 in this volume.

IV. Conclusions

The nascent regional dialogue that has emerged in Asia–Pacific in the past decade, in both the economic and security areas, is a welcome development for global security. As the fastest growing region of the world in economic and trade terms, it is heartening that Asia–Pacific is moving towards discussion of its region-wide security problems in a co-operative framework rather than towards using the weapons which it is increasingly able to afford.

Although the original ideas on regionalist co-operative structures for Asia–Pacific came from the region's periphery—Australia, Canada and the Soviet Union—it is ASEAN that has provided most of the regionalist momentum of the past few years. In contrast, North-East Asia, lacking subregional structures and plagued by major continuing security challenges, has been largely passive—with the important and relatively recent exception of Japan.

While it remains to be seen how effective the new ASEAN Regional Forum and future APEC summits will be in helping to create true regionalism, in producing practical regional security benefits or in tackling specific security problems, the fact that the states of Asia–Pacific are developing a 'habit of dialogue' is in itself no mean feat.

5. North-East Asia and multilateral security institutions

BATES GILL

I. Introduction

While much of the current optimism regarding the future of multilateral security institutions focuses on the Asia–Pacific region, participation in such institutions by countries in the subregion of North-East Asia remains highly problematic. At a first glance, relations among North-East Asian governments lack certain critical prerequisites for the establishment of such institutions: a modicum of trust and mutual confidence and consensus on what the means of co-operation should be.[1] Moreover, the absence of such institutions is rooted in complex factors of culture, history and geography, upon which must be overlaid the more contemporary complexities of post-World War II animosities, territorial disputes, cold war legacies, domestic political transitions and uncertainties in the strategic climate.

An assessment of North-East Asia which includes a close reading of its history, its contemporary developments and its record thus far in developing multilateral security institutions highlights the difficult challenges which lie ahead for such arrangements. This chapter considers these challenges in three principal sections, beginning with a brief historical summary of security relations in the subregion, followed by an account of current developments influencing multilateral security institutions and concluding with a review of past, current and possible future multilateral security efforts in North-East Asia.

For the purposes of this chapter, North-East Asia includes China (the People's Republic of China), Hong Kong, Japan, North Korea (the Democratic People's Republic of Korea), South Korea (the Republic of Korea), Macao, Mongolia, Russia and Taiwan (the Republic of China).

II. Challenges of history

Strategic culture

Identifiable cultural traits infuse the conduct of foreign relations, influence decision making, help identify and define threats and responses to them, and thus affect the dynamics of international relations in important ways. This notion of 'national character' or 'strategic culture' has been most often

---

[1] In this chapter, 'multilateral security institutions' are defined as formal inter-governmental organizations which serve to prevent or reduce the likelihood of conflict through multilateral efforts of preventive diplomacy, development and co-ordination of confidence-building measures and conflict resolution.

addressed in the literature of international relations in the context of the cold war as a way of understanding the international behaviour of the great powers, particularly the superpowers. Until recently, little work had considered the impact of Asian or Chinese strategic culture upon the conduct of Asian foreign policy.[2]

A number of aspects of strategic culture in North-East Asia have an important influence on the establishment of multilateral security structures in the subregion. These include: a preference for face-to-face, informal, private discussions over many-sided, structured, highly public meetings; a preference for preserving an image of consensus and avoiding the more adversarial approach inherent in the Western practice of majority rule; a proclaimed resistance to interference in the internal affairs of other countries; a more fatalistic rather than progressivist understanding of humanity's place in and impact on history; a preference for hierarchical structures as opposed to the universalist and egalitarian structures which are familiar in the West; and a greater tolerance for involvement of the military in politics as well as in socio-economic decision making.

With the dynamism and economic success of Asia have come a greater confidence and willingness to question Western values and influence. This mood is reflected in Asian strategic culture and views about regional security. One prominent Chinese analyst, in discussing the possibilities of multilateral security co-operation in North-East Asia, rejects what he views as Western notions of the international order and calls for an 'Oriental Renaissance' as the foundation for international relations and regional security.[3] More broadly, there is a growing movement in Asia to reappraise the organizing concepts of Western political life more critically, questioning the role of democratic processes as necessary prerequisites for long-range stability and expressing concern for the threat posed to Asia by Western values of democracy and excessive freedom.[4] As one diplomat from North-East Asia concludes, only 'an

---

[2] See the the the classic discussion of 'national character' as it relates to 'national power' in Morgenthau, H. J., *Politics Among Nations: The Struggle for Power and Peace*, 4th edn (Alfred A. Knopf: New York, 1967), pp. 122–29. See also Snyder, J., *The Soviet Strategic Culture* (Rand Corporation: Santa Monica, Calif., 1977). Historical approaches to understanding Chinese culture and strategic issues include Johnston, A. I., *An Inquiry into Strategic Culture: Chinese Strategic Thought, the Parabellum Paradigm, and Grand Strategic Choice in Ming China*, Ph.D. dissertation (University of Michigan: Ann Arbor, 1993). A very useful initial effort to link culture to current issues of security in the Asia–Pacific region is Ball, D., *Strategic Culture in the Asia–Pacific Region (With Some Implications for Regional Security Cooperation)*, Strategic and Defence Studies Centre Working Paper no. 270 (Australian National University: Canberra, 1993). See also Wang Jisi, *Comparing Chinese and American Conceptions of Security*, North Pacific Cooperative Security Dialogue Research Programme Working Paper no. 17 (York University: North York, Ont., Sep. 1992); Wang Yong, *Chinese Confucian Thought and Post-Cold War Asian Pacific Security Cooperation*, North Pacific Cooperative Security Dialogue Research Programme Working Paper no. 18 (York University: North York, Ont., Oct. 1992).

[3] Lu Zhongwei, 'Security of Northeast Asia and prospects for multilateral consultation', *Contemporary International Relations* (Beijing), Nov. 1992. The 'Oriental Renaissance' calls for adherence to the 'Five Principles of Peaceful Co-Existence' developed by China in the 1950s: mutual respect for territorial integrity and sovereignty, non-aggression, non-interference in other countries' internal affairs, equality and mutual benefit, and peaceful co-existence.

[4] Kishore Mahbubani, 'The dangers of decadence: what the West can learn from the rest', *Foreign Affairs*, Sep.–Oct. 1993, pp. 10–14; Koh, T., 'The 10 values that undergird East Asian strength and success', *International Herald Tribune*, 11–12 Dec. 1993, p. 6.

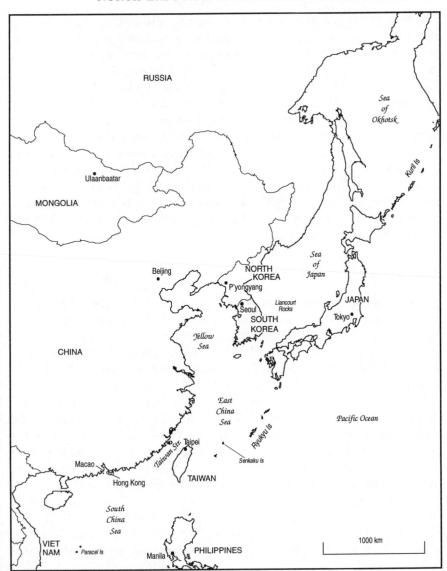

Figure 5.1. Map of North-East Asia

Asiatic approach based on gradualism and patience' will contribute to shaping a new security order for that part of the world.[5]

Historical lack of 'normal' relations

Gerald Segal notes that North-East Asia has had no 'natural' or 'normal' international relations for nearly two centuries.[6] As a result of the historical

---

[5] Hee Kwon Park, 'Multilateral security cooperation', *Pacific Review*, vol. 6, no. 3 (1993), p. 264.
[6] This argument is developed in Segal, G., *Rethinking the Pacific* (Clarendon Press: Oxford, 1990).

traditions and upheavals in the region's security relations, it has only been in the past 10–20 years that all of the countries in the subregion have begun to reach an historical point at which their leaders could more deeply consider the possibility of 'normalized' relationships. The unfolding of history in North-East Asia has thus not included a broad experience with multilateralism for the countries of the subregion. One respected Chinese analyst, James T. H. Tang, argues that the centuries-old Chinese tributary system up until the mid-19th century, followed by 100 years of imperialism, revolution and world war and the subsequent cold war era, has meant that 'historical development in East Asia . . . does not augur well for multilateralism in Northeast Asia'.[7] The complex shifts of power and influence which inevitably attend realignments to a new order will present difficult challenges to the institutionalization of regional order. At the very least, what this 'normal pattern' should reflect will remain unclear for some time.

Post-World War II problems

In the context of forging multilateral security institutions, several aspects of the subregion's post-war history merit closer scrutiny: wartime memories and suspicions, territorial disputes and bilateral alliances.

Nearly 50 years after World War II, bitter memories continue to poison relations between Japan and its neighbours in spite of efforts on all sides to ease these tensions. While in high-level politics there is at least a rhetorical effort to come to grips with remaining hatreds and painful memories, suspicions and animosity persist to a degree not fully appreciated outside the region. One long-time observer of international affairs in the region notes that the mutually felt acrimony between Japan and Korea 'could eventually prove to be a key catalyst in a confrontation between the two countries'.[8] Warfare and confrontation in North-East Asia during the post-war period also recall painful memories. Millions of lives were lost in the Chinese civil war of 1945–50 and in the wars in Korea (1950–53) and Viet Nam (1961–73). The latter two conflicts involved a number of North-East Asian states, including China, North Korea, South Korea and Taiwan, in addition to the United States.

Indeed, today, several countries in the region remain officially at war with one another. In spite of improved bilateral relations across the Taiwan Strait, the two Chinese governments are still officially in a state of civil war. The White Paper on the 'Taiwan question' issued by Beijing in August 1993 states that China is 'entitled to use any means it deems necessary, including military

---

[7] Tang, J. T. H., *Multilateralism in Northeast Asian International Security: An Illusion or a Realistic Hope?*, North Pacific Cooperative Security Dialogue Research Programme Working Paper no. 26 (York University: North York, Ont., Oct. 1992), p. 8.

[8] Hisayoshi Ina, *A New Multilateral Approach for the Pacific: Beyond the Bilateral Security Network*, Foreign Policy Institute Papers (Paul H. Nitze School of Advanced International Studies, Johns Hopkins University: Washington, DC, 1993), p. 10.

ones, to uphold its sovereignty and territorial integrity'.[9] It also stipulates that China opposes the participation of delegates from Taiwan in either inter-governmental or non-governmental organizations in which they would represent Taiwan as a sovereign entity.[10]

Russia and Japan have not officially declared an end to their World War II hostilities, which began with the Soviet declaration of war against Japan in August 1945. The two Korean states, while having formally signed an armistice agreement in 1953, are still technically 'at war' and face one another across the world's most heavily militarized border, both sides forward deployed and constantly prepared for all-out conflict. These disputes not only intensify the substantive problem of reaching agreements under highly strained and sensitive conditions, but in some cases, such as between the two Korean governments and the two Chinese governments, fundamental matters of legitimacy and representation are at stake as well.

Territorial disputes and clashing claims of sovereignty are connected to the continuing 'state of war' among countries in the subregion. A peace treaty between Japan and Russia is unlikely to be concluded before the two countries can resolve their conflicting claims to the Kuril Islands, a process which in itself faces difficult prospects because of political pressures on both sides.[11] Russian President Boris Yeltsin's long-awaited visit to Japan in October 1993 did little to resolve the issue, and Russian and Japanese actions and statements before and after the summit meeting may have hardened positions rather than softened them.[12] While the two Chinese governments do not dispute that the Spratly and Paracel Islands of the South China Sea are Chinese territory, they independently assert themselves through the deployment and stationing of military forces in the region as the legitimate representative for those claims.[13] China, Taiwan and Japan all lay claim to the Senkaku (Chinese name, Diaoyutai) Islands in the East China Sea. Japan and South Korea have disputed claims over the Liancourt Rocks in the Sea of Japan (Japanese name, Takeshima; Korean name, Tak-do). The latter two disputes are currently dormant, but they remain symbolically important to all the claimants.[14]

Finally, the post-war history of bilateral security ties in the subregion raises two important points. First, the endurance of and apparent success in maintaining peace in the region may give pause to those wishing to revamp the

---

[9] *The Taiwan Question and Reunification of China* (Taiwan Affairs Office & Information Office, State Council: Beijing, Aug. 1993), p. 15.

[10] *The Taiwan Question and Reunification of China* (note 9), pp. 21–22.

[11] According to Russian and Japanese polls taken in 1993, 84% of the Japanese support a return of the Kurils while 72.2% of the Russians support retaining the islands in Russia. 'Tokyo', *Asian Defence Journal*, Jan. 1993, p. 154.

[12] See 'Declaration on Japan–Russia relations', in British Broadcasting Corporation, *Summary of World Broadcasts: Asia–Pacific* (hereafter cited as *SWB*), FE/1819, 14 Oct. 1993, pp. D/6–D/8; and Foye, S., 'Russo-Japanese relations: still traveling a rocky road', Radio Free Europe/Radio Liberty, *RFE/FL Research Report*, 5 Nov. 1993, pp. 27–34.

[13] The Paracel Islands are claimed by China, Taiwan and Viet Nam. The Spratly Islands are claimed by Brunei, China, Malaysia, the Philippines, Taiwan and Viet Nam. China and Viet Nam also dispute their boundaries in the Gulf of Tonking. Anderson, E., *An Atlas of World Political Flashpoints* (Pinter Reference: London, 1993), pp. 211–13.

[14] See Anderson (note 13), pp. 116–17, 173–75.

system, although, as the experience of the Conference on Security and Co-operation in Europe (CSCE) has shown, multilateral security relationships can develop side-by-side with pre-existing security commitments. In Japan, a foreign policy rooted in the US–Japanese relationship will for the foreseeable future have the upper hand over a more independent regionalist or multilateral approach to foreign relations.[15] Furthermore, not only is the US presence seen as a guarantee against 'outside' aggression, but it is also viewed as containing 'inside' aggression, that is, containing Japanese and South Korean ambitions.

Second, bilateralism may slow the process of independent, indigenously developed foreign policy. In the past, the policies of the United States and the former Soviet Union often directed or heavily influenced the conduct of the international relations of countries in North-East Asia. Now, with the end of the cold war, these relationships are undergoing significant change. As these countries seek to define their security roles more independently in the region and internationally, they assume a role that is not customary for them to play. Also, under the direction of the former superpowers, leaders in North-East Asia were very clear about the origin and nature of national security threats and this facilitated the development of well-defined alliance structures to address those threats. Today, security threats in the subregion are not so easily identified but rather are diffuse, ill-defined and not readily framed within neat ideological concepts. Multilateralism in security affairs will present new and difficult rules and roles for the states in this region.

III. Current developments influencing multilateral security

This section summarizes some of the most significant recent developments in North-East Asia and their impact on the establishment of multilateral security institutions in the subregion. These developments can be categorized in three principal areas: international uncertainties, domestic transitions and improvements in bilateral relations.

International uncertainties

Recent developments at the international level within the subregion suggest a lack of certainty as to the strategic intentions of countries in North-East Asia. This in turn undermines the development of mutual trust, which is so necessary for the formation of effective security institutions.

The future intentions of Japan are a long-standing concern of the subregion. However, in a speech before the Diet (Japanese Parliament) in August, and again before the UN General Assembly in September, Prime Minister Morihiro Hosokawa assuaged doubts about Japan's nuclear intentions by declaring his country's full support for an indefinite extension of the 1968

---

[15] Levin, N., Lorell, M. and Alexander, A., *The Wary Warriors: Future Directions in Japanese Security Policies* (Rand Corporation: Santa Monica, Calif., 1993), pp. 106–23; Brown, E., 'The debate over Japan's strategic future: bilateralism versus regionalism', *Asian Survey*, vol. 33, no. 6 (June 1993), pp. 543–59.

Non-Proliferation Treaty (NPT).[16] Doubts surrounding Japan's nuclear policy are also balanced by the strong pacifist and anti-nuclear sentiment within Japanese society and the expectation that strong international reaction would follow any Japanese decision to 'go nuclear'.

At the level of conventional power, the suspicions of Japan's neighbours were fuelled in September 1993 when Japan held its largest military manœuvres since World War II.[17] At approximately \$42.5 billion, the Japan Defense Agency's 1994 budget request continued to make the country one of the world's leaders in military expenditure. The Japanese military is a fully modernized and highly sophisticated conventional force, although it is constitutionally restricted to operate only in a defensive role. The decisive defeat of Japan's Socialist Party in the 1993 legislative elections signals the weakening of one of Japan's most powerful advocates of pacifism and a strengthening of conservative political forces, calling for a reappraisal of the country's postwar constitution, particularly with regard to Japan's future international role in political, military and security affairs.[18] The debate over Japan's future international role intensified when Hosokawa's Defence Minister, Keisuke Nakanishi, resigned under pressure after stating in December that the constitution was outdated and required amendment to allow Japan's full participation in UN peacekeeping missions.[19]

The activities of North Korea in 1993 did little to resolve the many questions its neighbours have about its strategic intentions. The enigma of the North Korean nuclear weapon development programme raises the greatest concern and contributed to bringing the Korean peninsula to the highest level of tension since the mid-1970s.[20] Some doubts remained as to exactly how much Pyongyang had achieved in its projects to develop nuclear weapons and the means to deliver them. The Director of the US Central Intelligence Agency, Robert Gates, stated in January 1993 that North Korea could have enough fissile material to build one bomb; his successor, James Woolsey, confirmed this assessment in later statements in 1993.[21] The South Korean

---

[16] Japanese officials, including the Foreign Minister, had suggested publicly in mid-1993 that Japan was reconsidering its endorsement of an indefinite extension of the NPT, scheduled to be settled at the 1995 NPT Review and Extension Conference. 'Non-proliferation treaty: chronology', Institute for Defense and Disarmament Studies, *Arms Control Reporter* (IDDS: Brookline, Mass.), sheet 602.B.251, Oct. 1993; 'Non-Proliferation Treaty: chronology', *Arms Control Reporter*, sheet 602.B.252, Oct. 1993; Smith, C., 'Unclear signals: nuclear weapons' policy shrouded in ambiguities', *Far Eastern Economic Review*, 30 Sep. 1993, p. 24. See also McCarthy, T., 'Tokyo soothes fears over its nuclear aims', *The Independent*, 2 Feb. 1994, p. 11; and chapter 15 in this volume.

[17] 'Tokyo holds massive exercises', *Asian Defence Journal*, Nov. 1993, p. 60; 'Les plus importants manoeuvres militaires de l'après-guerre', *Le Monde*, 3 Sep. 1993, p. 6.

[18] Even before the July 1993 elections in which the Socialists lost nearly half of their seats in the 511-seat lower house of the Diet (from 134 seats to 70), the Party considered revising its platform to give up its claims that the Japanese military is unconstitutional. 'Socialist reversal', *Far Eastern Economic Review*, 13 May 1993, p. 14.

[19] 'La démission du ministre de la défense crée une brèche dans la coalition', *Le Monde*, 4 Dec. 1993, p. 7; Sanger, D. E., 'Hosokawa cuts loose his defense chief', *International Herald Tribune*, 3 Dec. 1993, p. 5.

[20] See also chapter 15 in this volume.

[21] Statements are cited in 'Korean peace zone: chronology', *Arms Control Reporter*, sheet 457.B.127, Feb. 1993; and sheet 457.B.179, Sep. 1993. See also Albright, D., Berkhout, F. and Walker, W.,

Defence Ministry claimed in a report in October 1993 that North Korea had successfully tested detonators and that they would be capable of producing one or two weapons by 1995.[22]

In addition to the nuclear weapon issue, other disturbing developments in North Korea raise strategic concerns. In response to the US–South Korean 'Team Spirit' military exercises in March 1993, North Korean authorities announced a state of high military alert and placed the country on 'semi-war' footing, saying that 'all-out war can break out at any moment', although some questioned the true extent of these 'alerts'.[23] In May, North Korea successfully test-launched its 1000-km range Rodong I ballistic missile, displaying its capability to reach targets in South Korea and in Japan.

China has been especially active in the past several years in building up its military capabilities, as evidenced by steadily increasing military budgets and a stepped-up programme of weapon and weapon technology acquisition from abroad, especially from Russia. Between 1988 and 1993, the official Chinese military budget grew nominally by nearly 100 per cent and by 60 per cent in real terms.[24] However, while the official budget may give some indication as to overall trends of military spending, it reveals nothing about vast 'off-budget' revenues which augment military spending. These include monies dispersed by the government to 'non-military' lines in the budget, such as military-related research and development, construction projects or costs covered at the provincial and local levels. More importantly, no reliable figures account for the earnings generated by arms sales or by increasingly lucrative activities and investments of the People's Liberation Army (PLA) in the commercial civilian sector in China and abroad. These funds allow the PLA to purchase advanced weaponry and weapon technology from abroad to significantly enhance its military capabilities.

The future role of Russia as an important player in North-East Asia remains uncertain and is, in the words of one Russian analyst, 'in search of a concept'.[25] President Yeltsin made three important visits to the region in less than one year: to South Korea in November 1992, to China in December 1992 and to Japan in October 1993. During his visit to South Korea, he set the tone for Russia's Asia policy when he stated that by 'declaring our desire to become a full member of the community of Asia–Pacific countries, we are following—I am not hiding this—our national interests'. He added that Russia's foreign

'Countries of concern: Iraq, North Korea, Iran and Algeria', in SIPRI, *World Inventory of Plutonium and Highly Enriched Uranium 1992* (Oxford University Press: Oxford, 1993), chapter 10.

[22] Report cited in 'U.S. and Seoul give North a warning', *International Herald Tribune*, 14 Oct. 1993, p. 2.

[23] See 'South's white paper outlines North's nuclear and military capability', *SWB*, FE/1810, 15 Oct. 1993, p. D/8; reports cited under 'War at any time', *Asian Recorder*, 2–8 Apr. 1993, p. 23027; and *Asian Defence Journal*, Mar. 1993, p. 84.

[24] Kristof, N. D., 'The rise of China', *Foreign Affairs*, Nov.–Dec. 1993, p. 65; 'Chinese military spending soaring, CIA reports', *International Herald Tribune*, 31 July–1 Aug. 1993, p. 4. See also chapter 12, section V in this volume.

[25] Bogaturov, A. D., 'The Yeltsin Administration policy in the Far East: in search of a concept', *Harriman Institute Forum*, vol. 6, no. 12 (Harriman Institute, Columbia University: New York, Aug. 1993).

policy was 'turning from' the West to the Asia–Pacific region.[26] However, the domestic crises of Russia in 1993 have slowed Russia's activist agenda in North-East Asia. Nevertheless, Russia remains a key player, even if comparatively dormant at present. In particular, Russia's military forces in the subregion continue to cause concern. The 1993 Japanese defence White Paper states that Russia 'still presents a destabilizing factor' in the Asia–Pacific region, with 320 000 troops, 70 major surface combatants, 75 submarines and some 1400 combat aircraft in North-East Asia.[27] The imperatives of Russian economic survival, Russia's continued military presence in the subregion and geopolitical realities suggest that the Russian role in the region will remain critical, although its exact outlines are at present unclear.

Domestic transitions

Countries in North-East Asia are undergoing a period of domestic political transition. For Japan, South Korea and Taiwan, the transition brings a potentially raucous period of political transparency and democratization. For China, Hong Kong and North Korea, it brings an historic and possibly rocky period of succession. For Russia, the economic, social and political turbulence that already prevails in the country will continue for the foreseeable future.

In Taiwan, the reform and democratization process of the past several years has contributed to more open political factionalism, which reveals itself in increasingly influential opposition parties on the one hand and as widening rifts within the ruling Nationalist Party (Kuomintang or KMT) on the other. Significantly, KMT divisions involve not only opposing viewpoints about continued KMT power, party corruption and the pace of domestic political reform but also Taiwan's future role in the world, including sensitive issues of Taiwan's relationship to the mainland, membership in the United Nations and participation in regional security institutions.

Not unlike former Liberal Democratic Party (LDP) Prime Minister Kiichi Miyazawa of Japan, President Lee Teng-hui of Taiwan must face opposition from both sides of the political spectrum, while he tries to hold together the weakening centre. Lee comes to this task as only the third major leader of Taiwan and the KMT since 1928. He heads a party which has been in power longer than any other in the world, which may be its greatest weakness. Taiwan plans to hold its first direct presidential elections in 1996. The strong

---

[26] Quotations drawn from 'Addresses ROK National Assembly', Foreign Broadcast Information Service, *Daily Report–Central Eurasia (FBIS-SOV)*, FBIS-SOV-92-224, 19 Nov. 1992, p. 12.

[27] *Defence of Japan 1993*, the Japanese Defense Agency White Paper, quoted in Naoaki Usui, 'Japanese emphasize readiness in JDA plan', *Defense News*, 2–8 Aug. 1993, p. 1. These figures for Russian military power in the subregion differ markedly from Russian estimates. According to General Gennadiy Dmitrievich Ivanov, director general of the Russian armed forces' construction and reform bureau, Russian troop strength in the Far East has been reduced to 120 000. See Kensuke Ebata, 'Russia announces halving of Far East forces', *International Defense Review*, Apr. 1993, p. 267. Other analyses suggest that Russian military capability in the Pacific is limited by the economic and political chaos in the country. Young, P. L., 'What future for the Russian Pacific Navy?', *Asian Defence Journal*, May 1993, pp. 32–36.

probability that the Nationalist Party will face a stiff and well-organized opposition will keep it focused on domestic politics.

For China, the positive future promised by economic reform is clouded by the combination of post-Deng succession uncertainties and the effects of rapid socio-economic change. The passing of Deng Xiaoping will mark an historic generational transition of the kind China has not known in its 45-year history. Deng, whose 90th birthday is in 1994, was quite ill in 1993 and rarely appeared before the general public.[28] Anticipating the delicate manœuvring that will follow Deng's passing, and wishing to ensure that the transition will be a smooth one, the Chinese officially promote the notion of 'collective leadership'. The long-term domestic political importance of this transition lies in the understanding that the legitimacy of future Chinese leaders will not be judged in the dimming light of revolutionary achievements and ideological struggles, but rather in the harsher light of nation building and progress in the livelihoods of Chinese people.

Within the larger society, a varied set of domestic problems arose in association with economic reform: official corruption, divisive regionalism, scattered uprisings among the peasantry, separatism in the west, renewed dissident movements and difficulties connected with an overheated economy.[29] The Communist Party admits to its own set of related problems: paraphrasing an important speech made by Communist Party head Jiang Zemin in August 1993, the *People's Daily* warned, 'if we are inattentive and allow [corruption] to spread, then it will be the death of our party, the death of the people's regime, and the death of our great task of socialist modernization'.[30] Other reports, largely based on Chinese economic prospects, presented a more optimistic outlook—the so-called 'Hong Kong school'—on China's future stability.[31] Yet, economic reforms and growth call into question the very legitimacy of the Party and undermine the traditional relationship between the communist state and society in China. The Chinese leadership walks a precar-

---

[28] In 1993, Deng made only one appearance before the general public, in Jan. Tyler, P. E., 'Deng, gaunt and frail, appears on TV for the first time in a year', *International Herald Tribune*, 10 Feb. 1994, p. 2; 'Kaye, L., 'Bribery bandwagon', *Far Eastern Economic Review*, 2 Sep. 1993, p. 11.

[29] For example, see Deron, F., 'Le président du Kazakhstan s'est inquiété du déploiement de troupes chinoises en Asie centrale', *Le Monde*, 21 Oct. 1993, p. 5; Kristof, N. D. 'China's Muslims look to break away', *International Herald Tribune*, 16 Aug. 1993, p. 1; 'Muslim rage', *Far Eastern Economic Review*, 28 Oct. 1993, p. 15; Segal, G., 'Cracks in China', *Jane's Intelligence Review*, Sep. 1993, pp. 427–28; 'Beijing keeps pressure on Tibet dissenters', *Asian Defence Review*, July 1993, p. 84; 'Des dissidents coördonnent leurs efforts', *Le Monde*, 29 Nov. 1993, p. 6; 'Peace plea to Peking', *The Independent*, 15 Nov. 1993, p. 12; Tyler, P. E., 'China's economy: out of control or only a mess?', *International Herald Tribune*, 4 Oct. 1993, p. 1; 'Can the centre hold?', *The Economist*, 6 Nov. 1993, p. 78.

[30] *Renmin Ribao* [People's Daily], 23 Aug. 1993, p. 1, translated in *Inside China Mainland*, vol. 15, no. 10 (Oct. 1993), p. 5; see also Kaye, L., 'Bribery Bandwagon', *Far Eastern Economic Review*, 2 Sep. 1993, p. 11; Walker, T., 'Chinese shot in corruption purge', *Financial Times*, 1 Nov. 1993, p. 4.

[31] An excellent example of this optimism is found in Morgan Stanley International Investment Research, *China!: Report on the Morgan Stanley Tour of China* (Morgan Stanley International: New York, autumn 1993). The head of the Morgan Stanley Tour, Barton Biggs, was quoted as saying, 'After eight days in China, I'm tuned in, over-fed and maximum bullish'. *Far Eastern Economic Review*, 14 Oct. 1993, p. 11. See also the comments of the director and chief executive of the Bank of East Asia Ltd in Li, K. P, 'Watch for a prosperous China soon', *International Herald Tribune*, 5 Oct. 1993, p. 4; and Overholt, W. H., *China: The Next Economic Superpower* (Weidenfeld & Nicolson: London, 1993).

ious tightrope, a situation which will require the most nuanced and subtle political balancing act.[32]

In an historic political development for post-war Japan, the LDP in July 1993 suffered its first legislative defeat since 1955 in the lower house of the Diet, thus ushering in a coalition under the leadership of Prime Minister Morihiro Hosokawa. The new Prime Minister was sworn in on 9 August 1993 and, in presentations before the Diet, stressed the importance of domestic reform. His efforts to clean up politics in Japan, to reform the electoral system, and to open up and stimulate the lagging Japanese economy, while at the same time maintaining the solidarity of his diverse coalition, will divert Japan's political energy inward, rendering significant manœuvres at the international level difficult. The reconstitution of the Japanese electoral system will do much to dismantle one-party dominance and will give Japan a more fractious and less cohesive political party system than it has known for the past 40 years.[33]

In South Korea, President Kim Young Sam, who was elected in December 1992 and assumed office in February 1993, wasted little time in launching political and economic reforms. In major addresses to the nation in 1993, Kim continuously stressed the importance of domestic reforms, which formed the principal base of his campaign platform and the principal focus of his first year in office.[34] The reforms exposed politicians, officials and bureaucrats to charges of corruption and misuse of power—by the end of the year, some 1000 senior officials had been sanctioned, fired or imprisoned by the government[35]—and called into question the way in which politics have been handled in South Korea for over 40 years. Some questioned whether Kim's 'New Korea' campaign was in fact a veiled political attack on his political, military and corporate adversaries, those past, present and future.[36] Either way, Kim's bold efforts display a concerted attempt to change the South Korean political system in ways which will crowd the domestic agenda for the foreseeable future.

In North Korea, President Kim Il Sung, 82 years old in 1994, has groomed his son, Kim Jong Il, to take the reins of power in the country's first succession. The younger Kim, 53 years of age in 1994, has for many years served at the uppermost reaches of North Korean circles of power: he is second only to his father in terms of the official positions he holds, including Vice-President of the Republic and Supreme Commander of the Armed Forces. In a move in

[32] Deron, F., 'Le parti communiste entend maintenir son pouvoir dans une économie en march vers le capitalisme', Le Monde, 16 Nov. 1993, p. 3.

[33] 'Transparence électorale au Japon', Le Monde, 18 Nov. 1993, p. 1.

[34] See Kim Young Sam's inaugural address, 'Full text of presidential inauguration address', Korean Journal of International Studies, vol. 24, no. 1 (spring 1993), pp. 120–24; 'President Kim Young-Sam's remarks at the opening of press conference marking his first 100 days in office', Korea Annual 1993 (Yonhap News Agency: Seoul, 1993), pp. 395–96; and Kim's first address as President to the South Korean legislature, 'President addresses National Assembly', SWB, FE/1801, 23 Sep. 1993, pp. D/8–D/11.

[35] 'Role reversal', The Economist, 13 Nov. 1993, p. 63.

[36] Young Il Choi, 'Kim Young Sam's reforms and people's response', Korea Report (Washington, DC), fall 1993, pp. 3–6; Shim Jae Hoon and Paisley, E., 'Whirlwind honeymoon', Far Eastern Economic Review, 24 June 1993, pp. 18–19.

1993 seen as an effort to solidify his ties to the army, he succeeded his father as head of the National Defence Commission.[37] It is extremely difficult, however, to gauge with certainty the extent of Kim Jong Il's popularity and influence inside and outside of the centres of power.

The nature of these domestic political circumstances affects multilateralism in North-East Asia in at least three ways. First, the management of political developments at home diverts energy from participation in international structures. Second, the political fragility described here weakens leaders' abilities to conduct bold initiatives abroad, both because they may not enjoy sturdy political backing domestically and because counterparts on the international stage may question the legitimacy and long-term commitment which certain current leaders in the region can bring to the negotiating table. Third, when new generations of leaders come to power with little experience, they may be less skilled in balancing domestic and international pressures and at the same time may have trouble successfully bringing their country's interests to bear on the difficult negotiation process which will characterize discussions of regional security mechanisms.

Improvements in bilateral relations

In recent years, the most encouraging developments concerning security in North-East Asia have largely resulted from bilateral initiatives.

North and South Korea reached a series of important agreements in early 1992, their first formal agreements in nearly 20 years: the Agreement on Reconciliation, Nonaggression, and Exchanges and Co-operation; the Joint Declaration on the Denuclearization of the Korean Peninsula; and agreements to establish a joint military commission, liaison offices and a commission on exchanges and co-operation.[38] In March 1992 the two sides held the first meetings of the Joint Nuclear Control Commission and the Inter-Korean Military Commission, and liaison offices were set up by the two sides in May, in the truce village of Panmunjom, to facilitate official contacts. However, while these developments may provide the groundwork for future talks, continuing disputes between the two sides—largely related to North Korea's suspected nuclear ambitions and to the continued US–South Korean 'Team Spirit' military exercises—sidetracked substantive progress towards reconciliation.

As noted above, Russian bilateral initiatives in the subregion were quite active in 1992 and 1993. During his visit to South Korea in November 1992, President Yeltsin expressed 'profound regret' for the downing of Korean Air Lines Flight 007 by a Soviet fighter aircraft in 1983, rejected the 'logic of Stalin's policy' which contributed to the Korean War, and promoted an across-the-board improvement in Russian–South Korean political, military, economic and cultural ties. During his visit, Russian–South Korean relations were codified in the Treaty on Basic Relations between the Republic of Korea

---

[37] *Asian Defence Journal*, May 1993, p. 76.

[38] Statements on and texts of these agreements can be found in *Korea Annual 1992* (Yonhap News Agency: Seoul, 1992), pp. 85–90, 392–97, 400–402.

and the Russian Federation, signed to govern the friendly expansion of their relationship.[39] Similarly, Yeltsin's visit to Japan in October 1993 was indicative of improved relations between Moscow and Tokyo, in spite of numerous unpleasant incidents leading up to the visit.[40] Yeltsin apologized to Japan for the inhumane treatment of Japanese prisoners-of-war suffered at the hands of the Soviet Army following World War II and stated that the Kuril Islands issue 'exists and must be resolved someday'. Both statements were seen as significant improvements over previous Soviet intransigence on these issues.[41] In a declaration on Japanese–Russian relations concluded at the end of Yeltsin's visit, the two sides agreed that the Kuril Islands issue 'must be overcome', on the basis of 'principles of law and justice'.[42] However, the two sides were unable to reach agreement on two contentious issues: a peace treaty to formally end World War II hostilities and a resolution to their disputed claims to the Kuril Islands.

Sino-Russian relations also improved markedly, building upon Soviet President Mikhail Gorbachev's ground-breaking visit in May 1989 and the April 1990 decision by the two former antagonists to work towards the reduction of troops along their common border.[43] Since then, the Sino-Russian relationship has achieved a number of bilateral commitments, including efforts to establish a demilitarized zone extending 100 km on either side of their border, closer military-to-military ties, a five-year agreement governing military visits and the exchange of force level and doctrinal information, and the plan to sign an agreement in 1994 intended to reduce the likelihood of military conflict between the two countries.[44] Much of this progress came in the wake of President Yeltsin's visit to China in December 1992. At that time, the two sides solidified friendly relations with the signing of over 20 documents on co-operation, including agreements not to take part in alliances aimed against one another, on military and technological co-operation, on space exploration, on nuclear power generation, and on trade and economic co-operation. They also signed an agreement to govern the reduction of military forces on the Sino-Russian border to strictly defensive levels by 2000.[45] In November 1993, during a visit to Beijing by Russian Defence Minister Pavel Grachev, the two

---

[39] Examples of Yeltsin's statements during his visit to South Korea are found in FBIS-SOV-92-224, 19 Nov. 1992, pp. 9–14; and FBIS-SOV-92-225, 20 Nov. 1992, pp. 9–12.

[40] For details of Russia–Japan relations and the Yeltsin–Hosokawa summit meeting, see Foye, S., 'Russo-Japanese relations: still traveling a rocky road', *RFE/RL Research Report*, 5 Nov. 1993, pp. 27–34.

[41] Smith, C. 'The bear hug', *Far Eastern Economic Review*, 21 Oct. 1993, p. 12.

[42] 'Declaration on Japan–Russia relations', *SWB*, FE/1819, 14 Oct. 1993, pp. D/6–D/8.

[43] In 1993 similar bilateral agreements were signed between China and its two other principal antagonists in Asia, Viet Nam and India. See Agreement between the Government of the Republic of India and the Government of the People's Republic of China on the Maintenance of Peace and Tranquility Along the Line of Actual Control in the India–China Border Areas, signed in Beijing on 7 Sep. 1993; 'China and Vietnam sign border pact', *International Herald Tribune*, 20 Oct. 1993, p. 2.

[44] Tyler, P. E., 'China and Russia act to avoid conflicts', *International Herald Tribune*, 6 Dec. 1993, p. 6; 'Terms trip "very successful"', FBIS-SOV-93-217, 12 Nov. 1993, p. 17; 'China near Russian defense pact', *International Herald Tribune*, 9 Nov. 1993, p. 2; Karniol, R., 'Treaty between China and Russia in sight', *Jane's Defence Weekly*, 18 Sep. 1993, p. 8.

[45] On agreements reached during the Yeltsin visit to China, and on the visit generally, see FBIS-SOV-92-243, 17 Dec. 1992, pp. 16–19; and FBIS-SOV-92-244, 18 Dec. 1992, pp. 6–9.

sides agreed to boost their number and level of military exchanges and communication channels and to inform one another about military doctrine and manœuvres.[46] Following his visit, Grachev said that the two sides had 'agreed [that] security in the Asian–Pacific region will be more durable, if [their] bilateral relations are strong'.[47]

In 1993, China and Taiwan launched a series of historic bilateral discussions, beginning in April with the unprecedented talks held in Singapore between the Association for Relations Across the Straits (ARATS) from the mainland and the Straits Exchange Foundation (SEF) from Taiwan. ARATS and SEF were established by their respective governments as unofficial bodies to generate greater contacts between the two sides and to reach practical resolutions to certain bilateral issues. Both ARATS and SEF agreed that the April 1993 talks would be practical in nature, addressing largely economic questions. The April talks resulted in preliminary agreement regarding mail delivery and notarial matters in cross-Straits activities and on the exchange of youth, media and scientific delegations, and set out practicalities and future plans for continuing dialogue at this level.[48] At the Singapore meeting, the two sides agreed that the agenda for future talks would include: discussions on the repatriation from Taiwan of illegal mainland immigrants; smuggling and piracy in the Taiwan Strait; resolution of fisheries disputes; intellectual property rights; and cross-Straits co-operation between the two sides' judicial systems.

Direct mail delivery across the Taiwan Strait began on 1 June 1993, and the two sides signed an initial agreement regarding copyright protection in August.[49] However, the ARATS–SEF talks stalled during their meetings in late August, with the Taiwan side claiming that its counterparts were unprepared to discuss that which had been agreed upon in April. This temporary suspension also coincided with the publication of China's White Paper on 'the Taiwan question', which, among other things, reiterated the mainland's claims to Taiwan and asserted China's sovereign right to use military means, if necessary, to achieve reunification.[50] Talks resumed on 2–7 November, and the two sides discussed items on a three-part agenda: the return of illegal immigrants from the mainland, fisheries disputes, and procedures governing the exchange of SEF and ARATS delegates. The talks are scheduled to continue in 1994.

China's reports on the progress and future of the talks tended to be much more optimistic and placed high economic and political expectations on the dialogue. On the other hand, Taiwan's response to the talks tended to be more

[46] Tyler, P. E., 'China and Russia act to avoid conflicts', International Herald Tribune, 6 Dec. 1993, p. 6.
[47] Grachev, quoted in 'Terms trip "very successful"' (note 44).
[48] The texts of these initial agreements are found in 'Association for relations across the Straits (ARATS) (Established in the People's Republic of China)—Straits Exchange Foundation (SEF) (Established in the Republic of China): agreements concerning cross-Strait activities', International Legal Materials, vol. 32, no. 5 (Sep. 1993), pp. 1221–27.
[49] 'Direct mail between mainland and Taiwan', Beijing Review, 21–27 June 1993, p. 5; Free China Journal, 3 Sep. 1993, p. 1.
[50] The Taiwan Question and Reunification of China (note 9).

cautious, not wishing to rush toward closer ties on Beijing's terms, a reflection of the more conservative stance taken by the official Taiwan agency which oversees the SEF, the Mainland Affairs Council.[51]

Traditionally wary bilateral relations between China, Japan and South Korea took more positive turns in recent years as well. Sino-Japanese relations were given a great boost in November 1992, when the Japanese Emperor visited China for the first time in history. In May 1993, China and Japan agreed to initiate a bilateral security dialogue; in supporting this move, Chinese Foreign Minister Qian Qichen said that it was premature to begin building regional security institutions.[52] South Korea and China established diplomatic relations in August 1992, and the two countries' relationship has blossomed, particularly in the economic sphere. In 1993, as a result of their improved relationship, China and South Korea held bilateral talks to reach understandings and approaches on the increasingly tense situation on the Korean peninsula.[53] Japanese Prime Minister Hosokawa and South Korean President Kim held a fruitful summit meeting in South Korea in November 1993 in an atmosphere much improved over previous high-ranking meetings between the two countries. In contrast to previous summit meetings, the issues of Japanese wartime atrocities and economic differences were addressed openly and satisfactorily, while the two sides expressed common positions on certain regional problems.[54] Official Japanese apologies in 1993 to the peoples of North-East Asia subjected to cruelties by imperial Japan also helped to defuse tensions and soothe bilateral relations between Japan and its neighbours.

In the absence of multilateral security institutions for North-East Asia, these developments in bilateral ties made significant contributions toward establishing and maintaining greater confidence and stability within the subregion.

IV. The record for North-East Asian multilateralism

In North-East Asia no multilateral security institutions have been established that are comparable to such organizations as the CSCE or collective defence arrangements such as NATO or the now-defunct South-East Asia Treaty Organization (SEATO). North-East Asia is one of the few major subregions that are not organized within some kind of regional multilateral security regime. In fact, multilateralism in general is not as prevalent in North-East Asia as it is elsewhere in Asia–Pacific.

---

[51] Baum, J., 'Strait line', *Far Eastern Economic Review*, 28 Oct. 1993, pp. 18–19. The results of two polls taken in Taiwan, one in the midst of the first ARATS–SEF talks on 28 Apr. and another taken on 1 Sep., revealed a decrease in the number of respondents who viewed the mainland's attitude to Taiwan as 'friendly'; as compared with the first poll, the second poll also showed a decrease in the number of persons who wished to see unification with China, and an increase of those who preferred either independence or a maintenance of the status quo. See *Free China Journal*, 3 Sep. 1993, p. 1.

[52] *Arms Control Reporter*, sheet 850.367, June 1993.

[53] 'Beijing and Seoul hold secret talks over North', *International Herald Tribune*, 17 Nov. 1993, p. 5.

[54] 'Role reversal', *The Economist*, 13 Nov. 1993 p. 63; Smith, C., 'New men, old ghosts', *Far Eastern Economic Review*, 11 Nov. 1993, p. 20; 'Korea, Japan open future-oriented ties', *Newsreview* (Seoul), 13 Nov. 1993, p. 4.

Numerous proposals made during the cold war period attempted to establish such institutions for the region, although most of these proposals came from countries peripheral to North-East Asia and tended to be directed at the entire Asia–Pacific, not just North-East Asia. The Soviet Union was considered to be the most vocal and avid proponent of multilateral security institutions, with declarations of support for such arrangements dating back to proposals put forward by General Secretary Leonid Brezhnev in the late 1960s. Soviet leader Mikhail Gorbachev made several proposals for an Asian security system, but they tended to imply a broader region than just North-East Asia.

In a separate initiative, in early 1990 the Mongolian Deputy Foreign Minister called for the creation of a 'permanent machinery for holding regular consultations and negotiations on pressing international issues' and suggested convening an official gathering to discuss security-related issues with representatives from China, Japan, North Korea, South Korea, Mongolia, the Soviet Union and the United States.[55] Such a meeting has not been convened. Canadian efforts, first put forward by former Foreign Minister Joe Clark in his 1990 speeches in Tokyo, Jakarta and Victoria, focused mainly on the North Pacific region and resulted in the establishment of the semi-official North Pacific Co-operative Security Dialogue (see below).[56]

Current developments

More recently, in September 1992, South Korean President Roh Tae Woo took up before the United Nations a proposal he first made to that body in 1988: a 'Consultative Conference for Peace in North-East Asia'. He called for dialogue aimed at establishing 'mutual understanding and a forum of cooperation' to achieve a peaceful North-East Asia.[57] During President Yeltsin's visit to South Korea in November 1992, he expressed support for Roh's idea of dialogue in North-East Asia to build confidence and mutual understanding in the region and called for 'multilateral consultations by experts on issues of strengthening security' and for the creation in South Korea of a multilateral centre for prevention of conflict on the Korean peninsula.[58] In September 1992, Taiwan leader Lee Teng-hui expressed support for 'a system for protecting the collective security of the region', while Foreign Minister Frederick Chien believes that 'a regional collective security system

[55] Quoted in Findlay, T., *Asia/Pacific CSBMs: A Prospectus*, Peace Research Centre Working Paper no. 90 (Australian National University, Peace Research Centre: Canberra, 1990), p. 13, citing 'Statement by Khumbagyn Olzvoy, Deputy Foreign Minister of Mongolia', United Nations Meeting on Confidence-Building Measures in the Asia/Pacific Region, Kathmandu, Nepal, 29–31 Jan. 1990.

[56] For a discussion of past initiatives aimed at security dialogue for the entire Asia–Pacific region, see chapter 4 in this volume.

[57] 'President Roh Tae Woo's address to the United Nations General Assembly', *Korea Annual 1993* (Yonhap News Agency: Seoul, 1993), pp. 396–401.

[58] 'Addresses ROK National Assembly', FBIS-SOV-92-224, 19 Nov. 1992, p. 13. See also 'Korean–Russian joint statement', *Korea Annual 1993* (Yonhap News Agency: Seoul, 1993), p. 402.

should be considered'.[59] Other regional leaders, such as former Japanese Prime Minister Kiichi Miyazawa and South Korean President Kim Young Sam, have recently voiced their support for multilateral security dialogue for the entire Asia–Pacific region.[60] China has expressed support for 'diversified forms of bilateral or regional dialogue at various levels and through various channels'.[61]

In 1993 both Japan and the United States, traditionally recalcitrant about multilateral security institutions in North-East Asia, gave their clearest indications yet that they favoured the further development of such discussions for the region. For example, the Japanese Defense Agency annual White Paper suggested that Japan should encourage security dialogue with its neighbours in Asia–Pacific[62] and, in its first year in office, the Clinton Administration advocated a more open US policy regarding multilateral approaches to security in the region.[63] However, Japan and the United States continued to emphasize the fundamental importance of upholding and improving US bilateral security ties in the region over formal multilateral security dialogue. In the tradition of his LDP predecessors, Hosokawa emphasized the importance of bilateral security ties with the United States.[64] On the eve of the Asia–Pacific Economic Cooperation (APEC) summit meeting in November 1993, Hosokawa said that 'it is neither necessary nor realistic to have a collective security set-up like NATO in the region', but he added that 'there must be political and security dialogue among countries in the region to further increase a sense of reassurance'.[65] In March 1993, a senior US diplomat denied reports that the United States wanted to create an Asian version of the CSCE, saying that it did not 'see the need for a highly structured body such as the CSCE' in Asia–Pacific.[66] Nevertheless, the USA and Japan exhibited small but significant changes in policy, which may signal a greater willingness on the part of regional players to explore more seriously the possibilities of multilateral security institutions for North-East Asia.

Non-governmental initiatives for security forums—such as the Council for Security and Co-operation in the Asia–Pacific (CSCAP) and the North Pacific Co-operative Security Dialogue (NPCSD)—are principally 'second-track' or quasi-official processes which bring together scholars and regional officials

---

[59] Lee, quoted in *Regional Security and Economic Cooperation: The Case for the Asian–Pacific Region* (Government Information Office: Taipei, Oct. 1992), p. 13; Chien quoted in 'ROC in forefront of Far East development', *Free China Journal*, 10 Dec. 1993, p. 7.

[60] 'Japanese Prime Minister's Asia policy speech in Bangkok', *SWB*, FE/1589, 18 Jan. 1993, p. A/2-1; 'Text of Pacific Era and Korea's new diplomacy by President Kim Young Sam', *Korea Annual 1993* (Yonhap News Agency: Seoul, 1993), p. 394.

[61] See 'Jiang Zemin gives views on foreign and trade policy to Japanese newspaper', *SWB*, FE/1763, 10 Aug. 1993, p. A1/2.

[62] See 'Japan', *Asia–Pacific Defence Reporter*, Oct.–Nov. 1993, p. 21.

[63] See President Bill Clinton's 10 July 1993 speech before the National Assembly of the Republic of Korea, 'Fundamentals of security for a new Pacific community', *US Department of State Dispatch*, 19 July 1993, pp. 509–12; Munro, N., 'U.S. opens scope of Asian accords', *Defense News*, 22–28 Nov. 1993, p. 3.

[64] See the speech by Prime Minister Hosokawa in *SWB*, FE/1801, 23 Sep. 1993, p. D/1.

[65] Prime Minister Hosokawa offered these remarks in a Nov. 1993 interview: 'The view from Japan', *Far Eastern Economic Review*, 2 Dec. 1993, p. 14.

[66] Quoted in *Arms Control Reporter*, sheet 850.363, Mar. 1993.

acting in their private capacities.[67] The NPCSD programme, which was supported by the Canadian Department of External Affairs and International Trade, brought together scholars and officials from seven North Pacific countries—Canada, China, Japan, North Korea, South Korea, Russia and the United States (Mongolia and Taiwan were not included)—for workshops and conferences. This programme has officially ended but claims to have facilitated a 'habit of dialogue' for the region and carries on the work of NPCSD in the form of follow-on studies.[68] A 'first-track' or official element of the NPCSD is a less structured and open-ended process, which serves to explore the possibilities of dialogue on security issues without imposing a predetermined framework on the region. In the words of Canada's Ambassador for Disarmament, the emphasis is on 'consultation, not negotiation'.[69] It remains to be seen how successful second-track efforts will be in developing an official multilateral security institution for North-East Asia.[70]

One of the most promising recent developments regarding security institutions for the countries of North-East Asia has taken place outside the region, in the newly formed Association of South-East Asian Nations (ASEAN) Regional Forum. While the ASEAN Regional Forum offers great promise, its contribution to forming a multilateral security institution for North-East Asia is as yet unclear and remains in its nascent stages.

Future possibilities

The most serious security question in the subregion—the stability of the Korean peninsula and particularly the question of nuclear weapons in North Korea—appears amenable to a multilateral solution. Japan, South Korea and the USA already work closely on security-related questions, talks which intensified over the course of 1992 and 1993, particularly in response to developments on the Korean peninsula.[71] In March 1993, Japan went a step further in expressing the idea that Washington, Seoul and Tokyo consider forming a multilateral security dialogue.[72] At the urging of South Korea and Japan, and with the assistance of China, North Korea and the USA came

[67] See chapter 4 in this volume for more detailed discussion of the ASEAN Regional Forum and the role of North-East Asia within it, as well as the role of APEC and CSCAP in Asia–Pacific regionalism.

[68] *Programmes and Activities, 1992–94* (Centre for International and Strategic Studies, York University: North York, Ont., Oct. 1993); and 'Changing conceptions of conflict and security in a post-Westphalian world order', unpublished research programme (Centre for International and Strategic Studies, York University, Ont., 1993). See also Sa Benwang, 'An analysis of the Canadian initiative for a North Pacific cooperative security dialogue', *Contemporary International Relations* (Beijing), Dec. 1992, pp. 16–19.

[69] Mason, P., 'Asia Pacific security forums—rationale and options—Canadian views', ed. K. Clements, *Peace and Security in the Asia Pacific Region: Post-Cold War Problems and Prospects* (United Nations University Press: Tokyo, 1993), p. 293.

[70] Mack, A., 'Dialogs for defence', *Asia–Pacific Defence Reporter*, Feb.–Mar. 1993, p. 15.

[71] Pons, P., 'La politique nucléaire nord-coréenne inquiète à la fois Toyko, Séoul et Washington', *Le Monde*, 6 Nov. 1993, p. 3; Fic, V., 'Japan and US plan joint defence against threat', *Asian Defence Journal*, Sep. 1993, p. 46; Naoaki Usui, 'U.S., Japan monitor Korean missiles', *Defense News*, 9–15 Aug. 1993, p. 28.

[72] Young Sun Song, 'Prospects for a new Asia–Pacific multilateral security arrangement', *Korean Journal of Defense Analysis*, summer 1993, p. 197.

together in mid-1993 and held high-level talks aimed at resolving their differ-ences.[73] More formally, many prominent observers envision the establishment of a 'two plus four' arrangement in which China, Japan, Russia and the USA work together with the two Korean states to resolve the security dilemmas of the divided peninsula.[74] If a 'two plus four' arrangement were to succeed, it could evolve into a security-oriented forum for the region as a whole.

However, even on the clearly urgent issue of Korean peninsula security, there remain a number of unresolved issues which divide the prospective members of a multilateral forum addressing the problem, even among those which are currently allies. South Korea has reason to fear that such a process will either bog down and delay unification, or, should the process move for-ward, that Seoul would be limited in its ability to fully determine its direction and outcome. In discussions in 1993 held in response to the nuclear and bal-listic missile threat posed by North Korea, the USA and Japan exposed their differences on issues of burden-sharing and technology transfer.[75] In propos-ing a 'two plus four' arrangement, then US Secretary of State James Baker clearly emphasized the primacy of US bilateral security partnerships and sug-gested that the arrangement be '*ad hoc*' rather than formalized in nature. Fur-thermore, extremely delicate diplomacy will be required to convince North Korea that such an arrangement is not simply a collective security pact aimed at Pyongyang.

V. Conclusions

In the face of the challenges presented by the cultural, historical and contem-porary political realities attending this subregion's complex domestic and international relationships, the aims of past efforts to create an effective and functioning regional security institution for North-East Asia remain un-realized. The development of effective regional or subregional multilateral security institutions in Asia–Pacific will be a long and drawn-out process even under the best of conditions. Here, one may take a page or two from the lengthy experience of such organizations as the CSCE or ASEAN, which, after decades of discussions and negotiations, continue to grapple with their roles as multilateral security institutions.

The 1993 successes of the APEC Seattle summit meeting and the establish-ment of the ASEAN Regional Forum were encouraging developments, but they should not bring false hope to the tasks of multilateralism in Asia–Pacific as a whole and in North-East Asia in particular. Level-headed and rational multilateral security initiatives will surely bear fruit over the long term in

---

[73] 'Beijing offers to mediate in Korea', *International Herald Tribune*, 21 Oct. 1993, p. 2; Moffett, G. D. and Grier, P., 'Persuading North Korea not to build the bomb', *Christian Science Monitor*, 29 Apr. 1992, p. 3.
[74] For example, see Geng Huicheng, 'Multi-national co-ordination: feasibility in Asia–Pacific', *Contemporary International Relations* (Beijing), Nov. 1992; Baker, J. A., 'America in Asia: emerging archi-tecture for a Pacific community', *Foreign Affairs*, winter 1991/92, p. 13.
[75] Reid, T. R., 'Aspin calms Tokyo fears on defense', *International Herald Tribune*, 3 Nov. 1993, p. 1.

developing a more secure environment for North-East Asia and should be welcomed and supported. However, such efforts must bear in mind and maintain due respect for the challenging task they seek to address.

6. Conflict developments on the territory of the former Soviet Union

VLADIMIR BARANOVSKY*

I. Introduction

The former Soviet Union remained the scene of domestic instability and inter-state conflict in 1993. These problems stem from the transition from totalitarianism to democracy, from a state-owned economic system to market economies and from a single centralized state to multiple state entities. The establishment of a new, stable balance of forces within the former Soviet Union is a formidable challenge for the newly independent states, which are seeking to consolidate their international position while being increasingly aware of their deep interdependence.

II. Background

The main conflict-related factors affecting overall stability within the former Soviet Union can be summarized as: (*a*) domestic power struggles; (*b*) economic crises; (*c*) separatism; (*d*) the issue of the rights of ethnic minorities; and (*e*) the Soviet military legacy.

Domestic power struggles

Domestic power struggles, sometimes involving armed confrontation, characterized 1993. Civil wars continued in Georgia and Tajikistan. In most of Central Asia the political opposition was severely suppressed. In Russia, the confrontation between President Boris Yeltsin and the predominantly anti-reformist Supreme Soviet resulted in mass riots, the use of regular armed forces and numerous casualties in September–October 1993 in Moscow.[1] The national referendum on 12 December 1993 confirmed Russia's new constitution, but in simultaneous parliamentary elections over 40 per cent of the vote went to populist, nationalist and traditional communist candidates—a clear sign of increasing political polarization.

---

[1] See SIPRI, 'Crisis in Russia: facts and figures, people and data', SIPRI Fact Sheet, Oct. 1993 (available from SIPRI).

* Shannon Kile, Research Assistant on the SIPRI Project on Russia's Security Agenda and Georgi Otyrba of Abkhazian State University, Sukhumi, Visiting Researcher at SIPRI, assisted in researching this chapter.

Figure 6.1. New countries on the territory of the former Soviet Union

Economic crises

The overall economic situation worsened as the breakup of the old economic system continued. While market elements were only slowly introduced, price liberalization measures were attempted without adequate de-monopolization and huge subsidies propped up inefficient producers. High deficit spending, insufficient and inconsistent new legislation and a general disintegration of traditional economic links between the post-Soviet states further contributed to the economic decline. In 1993 the overall drop in productivity of the former Soviet republics combined reached 16 per cent. Even in Russia, with its relative economic advantages compared to other post-Soviet states (diversified production, a highly skilled labour force and abundant natural resources), industrial production decreased by about one-third over two years.[2]

A continued dramatic slide in living standards holds the potential for a social explosion. Some 45–50 million people (about 30 per cent of the total population) in Russia live below the poverty line, and hidden unemployment

---

[2] *Izvestia,* 21 Dec. 1993, p. 1. The government claims that the downward trend has already reached its lowest level and that a number of positive signs were evident in 1993. See *Izvestia,* 31 Dec. 1993, p. 2.

is estimated at 7–9 million people.[3] The future of the reformist course is in danger, as evidenced by the dramatic civil unrest in the autumn of 1993 in Moscow. The price to be paid for inconsistency in carrying out necessary reforms could be high indeed if a failure to adopt significant changes results in an economic standstill, as it has in Ukraine. Coupled with civil or inter-state wars, an economic collapse could quickly lead to political chaos, as it has in Georgia. The consequences of the economic crisis for conflict development are twofold: domestically, extremist and anti-reformist forces could gain increasing public support and the power to influence (either directly or indirectly) official policy; and, internationally, the newly independent states could become more vulnerable to external pressures, on the one hand, and more responsive to the idea of some sort of reintegration, on the other.

Separatism

The most explosive manifestation of separatism in the former Soviet Union continues to be found in the Transcaucasus (Nagorno-Karabakh in Azerbaijan and Abkhazia in Georgia). In Moldova, the so-called Trans-Dniester Republic remains a *de facto* independent entity. In Russia, the trend towards disintegration has been deflected by the constitution of December 1993, which denies sovereignty and the right of secession to autonomous republics and basically equates these entities with Russian territorial–administrative regions. However, the new constitution failed to receive 50 per cent of the vote in 8 republics (out of 21), while one republic—Chechnia—persists in asserting self-proclaimed independence. The potential for separatism also exists in Ukraine (with respect to Crimea), Kazakhstan (in the northern areas) and Estonia (in the north-eastern part of the country). In all three cases, the core issue concerns the rights and the status of the Russian-speaking population.

The rights of ethnic minorities

This issue of protecting the rights of ethnic minorities is either the cause of or one of the major elements involved in most post-Soviet conflicts. Indeed, ethno-nationalism seems to have replaced communism as the quasi-official ideology. Protection of the rights of 25 million Russians in the 'near abroad'[4] has been officially proclaimed as one of the main priorities of Russian foreign policy—to the serious concern of the other post-Soviet states. The flow of refugees also contributes to further tensions both within and between the new

---

[3] See, for example, *Nezavisimaya Gazeta*, 23 Dec. 1993, p. 4. The official figure for unemployment is below 1 million.

[4] In Russian political parlance, the term 'near abroad' refers to the other post-Soviet states. Some prominent Russian experts include them in the 'first circle' of Moscow's security policy interests. See Goodby, J. E. and Morel, B. (eds), SIPRI, *The Limited Partnership: Building a Russian–US Security Community* (Oxford University Press: Oxford, 1993), p. 76.

states.[5] In Russia alone, the influx of refugees increased to about 2 million people in 1993.

The Soviet military heritage

The withdrawal of Russian armed forces proceeded unevenly in 1993. Russian troop levels in the Baltic area have been substantiantially reduced but remain, however, a matter of political tension and diplomatic negotiation. In the conflict zones of Transcaucasus and Central Asia, the direct participants compete both in seeking the involvement of the Russian military and in blaming them for supporting the opposing side. Meanwhile, Russia has been advancing the argument that its military presence is essential for stability. In Ukraine, the dispute with Russia over control of nuclear weapons[6] and ownership of the Black Sea Fleet continues. Both issues—which seem to be deliberately manipulated by Ukraine and dramatized by Russia—remain a source of serious conflict between the two largest former republics of the USSR.

The Commonwealth of Independent States

In 1993 the Commonwealth of Independent States (CIS) continued its ephemeral existence as a structure for minimizing conflict between its members and providing them with a type of legal framework for mutual interaction. During its second year of operation, the CIS expanded its membership[7] and broadened its focus, recognizing the importance of economic factors for the post-Soviet states and the crucial role played by Russia in the search for solutions.

Arguably, Russia won the undeclared economic war against the other post-Soviet states in 1993. The inherent predominance of the Russian sector of the former Soviet economy was reinforced by Russia's more radical reformist course, while the other CIS states have in fact preserved inherited and outdated economic systems. Dependence upon Russia became the most important element of interaction between Russia and the other CIS states in 1993, giving Russia powerful leverage on non-economic issues as well.

At the same time, Russia is reluctant to shoulder the huge financial burden to ensure the survival of the traumatized economies of the CIS.[8] A 'rouble zone of a new type' (agreed in September 1993) was designed according to rigid terms so as to protect Russia from the hyper-inflation experienced by other CIS members.[9] These countries were required to introduce their own

[5] *Argumenty i Fakty*, no. 34 (Aug. 1993), p. 12.

[6] See chapter 16 in this volume.

[7] At the time of writing the CIS consisted of Armenia, Azerbaijan, Belarus, Georgia, Kazakhstan, Kyrgyzstan, Moldova, Russia, Tajikistan, Turkmenistan, Ukraine and Uzbekistan.

[8] In 1992 Russia's *de facto* financial assistance to the other CIS members was estimated at $17.2 billion. See *Nezavisimaya Gazeta*, 19 Nov. 1993, p. 4.

[9] On 6 Sep. 1993, Armenia, Tajikistan and Uzbekistan joined Belarus, Russia and Ukraine in a plan to make the rouble their common currency. The terms of the accord gave strong powers to the Russian Central Bank, which would be the only authority allowed to issue roubles. See 'Five nations plan to join Russia in ruble zone', *International Herald Tribune*, 8 Sep. 1993, p. 5. See also *Le Monde*, 10 Sep.

currencies and to limit their financial interaction within the CIS through a 'payment union' under which Russia will be free from excessive economic constraints while retaining the rouble as by far the strongest currency. This approach made possible the agreement on an 'economic union' on 29 September 1993, which was aimed at re-establishing the links between the goods producers within the former Soviet Union. Still it seems that the economic rationale has not necessarily prevailed over political considerations—as in the entry of Belarus and Tajikistan into the Russian currency zone.[10]

In 1993 the CIS opted for a more realistic military strategy, abandoning the ambitious goal of creating joint armed forces which remained largely an organization on paper. Over 70 decisions concerning the formation of joint armed forces had come to nothing, as national defence authorities were increasingly opposed to even the idea of military integration. In June 1993 the CIS Joint Armed Forces High Command was formally abolished and replaced by the Headquarters for the Co-ordination of Military Co-operation, with clearly much more limited functions.

On 24 September 1993 the CIS participants agreed to establish collective peacekeeping forces which would consist of national units with joint supply and logistical support. The initial size of the forces was set at 25 000, with the immediate task being to perform peacekeeping duties in Tajikistan.[11] Whether the establishment of peacekeeping forces does more than provide Russia with multilateral legal coverage of its military presence in the area remains to be seen.

A possible Russian military role has apparently been the most significant incentive (apart from economic factors) for Georgia to join the CIS (as ratified in March 1994), although Georgia had earlier vigorously rejected membership. The decision to join was dramatic and was perceived as a matter of national survival—to choose between a Russia-led alliance and complete collapse. Azerbaijan also decided to join the CIS in October 1993. Moldova has reconsidered its non-ratification of the CIS documents after parliamentary elections in February 1994. As a result, the CIS has been substantially enlarged to embrace virtually all of the territory of the former USSR, with the exception of the Baltic states.

Moreover, Georgia and Azerbaijan decided to accede to the Treaty on Collective Security, signed on 15 May 1992 in Tashkent, Uzbekistan, by six CIS members.[12] This resulted in Azerbaijan and Armenia—two states at war against each other—becoming members of the same alliance, although it must be noted that in many respects the alliance remains more of a political frame-

1993, p. 1; and the interview with Russian Vice Prime Minister Alexander Shokhin in *Moscow News*, no. 47 (Nov. 1993).

[10] The initial 'price' for Moscow for uniting the currency systems of Russia and Belarus is estimated at $1.4 billion. See *Vek*, no. 16 (85) (29 Apr.–5 May 1994), p. 4.

[11] *Krasnaya Zvezda*, 28 Sep. 1993, p. 1.

[12] The members were Armenia, Kazakhstan, Kyrgyzstan, Russia, Tajikistan and Uzbekistan. See *Izvestia*, 22 Sep. 1993, p. 2.

work than a multilateral military structure. Significantly, Belarus has also opted to accede to the Treaty while continuing to maintain its neutrality.[13]

The above changes within the CIS in 1993 were possible largely because of the renunciation by Russia of formal supranationalism, which is perceived by nearly all of Russia's partners as threatening the restoration of the former Tsarist/Soviet empire. However, these countries also appear to be willing (or pressed) to acknowledge both their interdependence with and the leadership of Russia in many areas. Significantly, the first chairmanship of the CIS, inaugurated at the heads of state meeting in Ashkhabad, Turkmenistan, on 24–25 December 1993, was conferred on Russian President Boris Yeltsin.

III. The Baltic area

Estonia, Latvia and Lithuania in 1993 were quiet compared with zones of more overt instability in the former Soviet Union. However, several conflict-related issues deserve close attention. These concern: (a) the withdrawal of Russian troops;[14] (b) the protection of the civil rights of Russian-speaking populations; (c) territorial issues; (d) the Kaliningrad region; and (e) the changing international status of the area.

The Russian-speaking populations

Russia is seriously concerned about the problem of civil rights for the Russian-speaking populations in Estonia, Latvia and Lithuania, although the situation and its conflict-generating potential are not identical in all three countries.

In Lithuania, citizenship was extended to all residents, including ethnic non-Lithuanians (approximately 20 per cent of the population; 9 per cent are Russians). This served to reduce Russian concern and contributed to a more co-operative approach concerning the issue of troop withdrawals.

The legislation in Estonia and Latvia concerning citizenship is considered by many observers to be discriminatory against non-titular ethnic groups (38 and 48 per cent of the total population in Estonia and Latvia, respectively; Russians comprise 30 and 34 per cent, respectively).[15] According to some overly dramatic assessments, the new norms could open the way to ethnic cleansing,[16] a local variant of apartheid[17] or an ethnic explosion.[18] Both Estonia and Latvia justify their restrictive measures by the necessity of preserving (or rather restoring) their ethno-national identities; at the same time

---

[13] *Nezavisimaya Gazeta*, 1 July 1993, p. 3; 14 July 1993, p. 3.

[14] The debate over and the process of withdrawal of Russian troops are the subject of a detailed presentation in chapter 14 in this volume.

[15] These figures are taken from the 1989 Soviet census.

[16] See, for example, the interview with Russian Foreign Minister Andrey Kozyrev, 'Caging Russia's monsters', *Newsweek*, vol. 73, no. 7 (14 Feb. 1994), p. 56. See also *Krasnaya Zvezda*, 24 June 1993, p. 1.

[17] *Krasnaya Zvezda*, 26 June 1993, p. 1.

[18] *Izvestia*, 3 July 1993, p. 4.

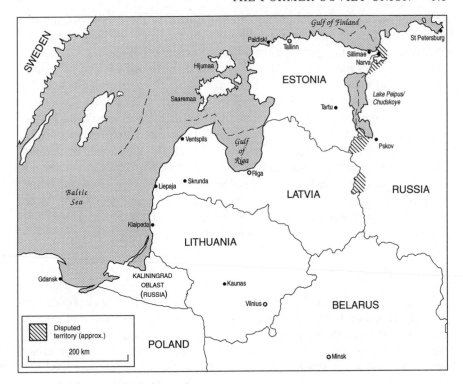

Figure 6.2. Map of the Baltic region

they reject accusations concerning human rights violations and consider their laws to be in accordance with international standards, referring, *inter alia*, to the international expertise they have consulted.

The total number of Russians who have left the Baltic states since independence has been estimated at 10 000–15 000[19]—a relatively low number compared to other post-Soviet states. Still, the implementation of some legal provisions could easily raise tensions as, for example, the decision taken in November 1993 in Latvia to issue 'orders of departure' to persons who do not have permanent registration and citizenship and therefore must depart the country within seven days.[20] In Estonia, a potential source of serious domestic conflict lies in the north-eastern part of the country, specifically the cities of Narva and Sillamae. A predominantly Russian population in this area is increasingly sympathetic to the idea of autonomony for the region. A local referendum held on the issue in July 1993 was condemned by the Estonian Government as being illegal and constituting a threat to stability.[21]

Russia has repeatedly demonstrated its readiness to protect the interests of the Russian-speaking populations in Estonia and Latvia. This has been mani-

[19] *Moscow News*, 10 Aug. 1993, p. 7.
[20] *Krasnaya Zvezda*, 23 Nov. 1993, p. 3.
[21] *Izvestia*, 30 June 1993, p. 1; *Komsomol'skaya Pravda*, 1 July 1993, p. 3; *Nezavisimaya Gazeta*, 1 July 1993, p. 3; 7 July 1993, p. 3; 8 July 1993, p. 3.

fested by stern official statements (up to the level of the President), indirect linkage with troop withdrawal (although this linkage has been denied by Russia) and economic pressure (as with the suspension of natural gas deliveries to Estonia in June 1993).[22] Russia expressed its concerns in various important political bodies in 1993, including the Baltic Co-operation Council, the Conference on Security and Co-operation in Europe (CSCE), the Council of Europe and the UN.[23] This contributed to making these international institutions more responsive to Russian arguments. Special CSCE missions were sent to both Estonia and Latvia, and CSCE High Commissioner on national Minorities Max van der Stoel addressed letters to high officials in Estonia and Latvia containing specific recommendations for improving laws concerning citizenship and alien status.[24] Although almost all recommendations were accepted and resulted in some softening of the legislation,[25] Russia still considers the progress achieved to be insufficient.[26]

Territorial issues

After the collapse of the Soviet Union, the 'internal' borders in the Baltic area were upgraded to the status of inter-state frontiers. However, these borders do not correspond to those which existed when Estonia, Latvia and Lithuania were annexed by the USSR in 1940. Estonia had a large area of borderland territory (2449 km^2) which it had received from Russia under the 1920 Tartu (Yuryev) Treaty and was officially returned to Russian administration in 1994, while Latvia possessed the Pytalovskiy district of Russia's Pskov region (1293.5 km^2).[27] These areas are populated overwhelmingly by Russians (over 90 per cent of the population), and both countries have apparently opted not to raise any territorial claims. In addition, a return to the *status quo ante* in the Baltic area would mean a substantial reduction in the territory of Lithuania (part of its present territory belonged to Poland prior to World War II).

Nevertheless, the conflict potential of the territorial questions should not be ignored. The validity of the Tartu Treaty is confirmed by the 1992 constitution of Estonia, and Estonia has repeatedly protested against the alleged attempts of Russia 'to turn the administrative line into a state frontier'.[28] Not surprisingly, this has been vigorously rejected by Russia. Although the issue could

[22] *Le Monde*, 28 June 1993, p. 3; Lucas, E., 'Troops to stay?', *Baltic Independent*, vol. 4, no. 196 (21–27 Jan. 1994), p. 1.

[23] See the article by Russian Deputy Foreign Minister Vitaliy Churkin in *Nezavisimaya Gazeta*, 3 July 1993, p. 1.

[24] *Moscow News*, 10 Aug. 1993, p. 7; British American Security Information Council, *BASIC Reports*, no. 32 (1993), pp. 3–4; CSCE, Secretary General, *Annual Report 1993 on CSCE Activities* (CSCE: Vienna, 31 Oct. 1993), p. 10.

[25] *Izvestia*, 31 July 1993, p. 8; *Literaturnaya Gazeta*, 1 Dec. 1993, p. 9.

[26] *Izvestia*, 3 Dec. 1993, p. 3.

[27] *Krasnaya Zvezda*, 27 May 1992, p. 1.

[28] *Izvestia*, 22 July 1992, p. 2; *Izvestia*, 24 July 1992, p. 1; *Krasnaya Zvezda*, 19 Jan. 1993, p. 3. The Estonian Government has claimed that under the terms of the Tartu Treaty, in which Soviet Russia recognized Estonia's independence, it has a right to border territories annexed by the USSR in 1994. See 'Estonia may give up territorial claims, opposition asserts', *Baltic Independent*, vol. 4, no. 165 (11–17 June 1993), p. 3.

remain essentially one of a symbolic diplomatic disagreement, it could be instrumental in blocking the negotiation process, thus contributing to increased tension in the Baltic area.

Even more destabilizing is the prospect of a chain reaction with respect to the frontiers which were changed after World War II. Significantly, in Finland the territorial issue (which had long been considered a taboo subject) became a matter of public debate in the 1994 presidential campaign.[29]

Paradoxically, the territorial problem could be turned around—taking into account the success of nationalist candidates in the parliamentary elections in Russia in December 1993. It is not surprising that the declared intention of right-wing political leader Vladimir Zhirinovsky to re-establish Russia within the borders of the former Soviet Union has given rise to serious concern in the Baltic states.[30] Indeed, Zhirinovsky's earlier statements on the restoration of the pre-1917 borders, even if not regarded as realistic, provoked a similar reaction in Finland.

Kaliningrad

The Kaliningrad region, which became an exclave of Russia after the dissolution of the Soviet Union and the independence of the Baltic states, has acquired special strategic value for Russia because most of the other military ports and facilities in the area are 'lost' to Russian use. On the other hand, the concentration of Russian military might in the Kaliningrad region will inevitably generate concern among neighbouring states, especially Lithuania and Poland.[31]

The overall population of the Kaliningrad region is about 1 million. The strength of the armed forces—estimated at about 200 000 (Russian sources give 100 000), with some 600 tanks, 900 armoured combat vehicles and 700 artillery pieces—is considered by many observers to be excessive.[32] The total combat potential is equivalent to eight divisions and corresponds, for example, to about 70 per cent of the entire Polish armed forces.[33] However, the over-concentration is to a great extent the result of the withdrawal of Russian troops from Germany and Poland and numbers will probably be reduced to about 60 000.[34] At the same time, some observers assume that a certain level of Russian military presence in Kaliningrad would be a necessary element in the

---

[29] *Izvestia*, 27 Apr. 1993, p. 3.

[30] Herbert, D., 'Baltic leaders alarmed by Russian elections', *Baltic Independent*, vol. 4, no. 192 (17–23 Dec. 1993), pp. 1–2.

[31] See Boye, R., 'Kaliningrad stirs fear among Poles', *The Times*, 15 May 1992, p. 9. See also *Izvestia*, 20 Apr. 1992, p. 7; and *Izvestia*, 5 May 1993, p. 3.

[32] See Radio Free Europe/Radio Liberty, *RFE/RL Research Report,* vol. 2, no. 36 (10 Sep. 1993), p. 40.

[33] See Kochanowski, F., 'A Polish perspective on the future of the Baltic sea region', Unpublished paper submitted to the Conference on the Future of Kaliningrad and Baltic Security, Centre for Defence Studies, King's College, University of London, 4 June 1993.

[34] *Izvestia*, 9 Apr. 1994, p. 3.

emerging new balance of forces in the Baltic area.[35] Otherwise, according to this logic, excessive militarization of the Gulf of Finland could hardly be avoided, and Russia's security concerns would be focused upon Finland.[36]

Of special importance for Russia is the establishment of reliable communication links between the 'mainland' and Kaliningrad—which in itself is a delicate problem because of the important military component of such links. In 1993 Russia and Lithuania commenced negotiations on an agreement on transit to and from the Kaliningrad region across Lithuanian territory. Another agreement will deal with the transit across Lithuania of Russian troops withdrawing from Germany.[37]

The collapse of the cold war order opens the possibility of considering a number of theoretical (and often highly unrealistic) options with respect to Kaliningrad. Under one option it would become an autonomous republic within the Russian Federation. Another possibility is for it to serve as an entity with special links to a Baltic 'Euroregion' or a 'Hanseatic region'. Other options include partition, the establishment of a condominium by its two neighbouring states, Latvia and Poland, independence or reunification with Germany.[38] Clearly, some of these scenarios could result in an international crisis with the threat of destabilizing more than just the immediate vicinity. In terms of practical policy, however, none of the international actors in the Baltic area (and least of all Germany) seems interested in changing or undermining the *status quo*.

In the economic field, on the contrary, maintaining the *status quo* would mean a disaster for the province, which has been kept for almost half a century in complete isolation as a Soviet military outpost. Kaliningrad's far-reaching demilitarization, the establishment of a special economic zone in the region, its extensive involvement in co-operation among the Baltic littoral states,[39] as well as financial and technical assistance from abroad are the most important elements of a would-be economic renascence. The major challenge consists in opening the region up to the outside world, on the one hand, and preventing it from being transformed into an arena of competing political interests, on the other. An adequate balance between the two remains to be found.

International balance

In 1993 the public debate in the Baltic states has been increasingly focused on the issue of their global orientation in the international arena. The concerns

---

[35] See Borodin, M. and Trenin, D., 'Perspektivy Kaliningrada' ['Perspectives from Kaliningrad'], *Nezavisimaya Gazeta*, 5 Nov. 1993, p. 1.

[36] See *Voennaya Mysl'*, nos 6–7, 1992, p. 12.

[37] See *Nezavisimaya Gazeta*, 16 Dec. 1992, p. 2.

[38] See Hoff, M. and Timmermann, H., 'Kaliningrad: Russia's future gateway to Europe?', *RFE/RL Research Report*, vol. 2, no. 36 (10 Sep. 1993), pp. 37–43; Petersen, P. A. and Petersen, S. C., 'The Kaliningrad garrison state', *Jane's Intelligence Review*, Feb. 1993, pp. 59–62.

[39] In 1992 Russia signed agreements with Poland and Lithuania on co-operation with respect to the Kaliningrad region. See *Diplomaticheskiy Vestnik*, no. 13–14 (15–31 July 1992), p. 78; *Diplomaticheskiy Vestnik*, no. 17–18 (15–30 Sep. 1992), pp. 57–59.

about 'the existential threat' from the East which were predominant during the first year of independence are gradually being supplemented with realistic assessments about the geopolitical situation and the importance of co-operative economic and political relations with Russia. This issue, however, remains a matter of serious domestic controversy as, for example, in Lithuania, where the post-Sajudis political leadership is reproached by the opposition for unwarranted *rapprochement* with Moscow.

Simultaneously, and as a matter of another interpretation of geopolitical realities, the option of getting Western institutions involved in the 'security vacuum' in the region is being given increased attention. This includes raising the question of participation in NATO—this being allegedly the only reliable guarantee against unpredictable developments in and around the post-Soviet Baltic area.[40] Whatever the arguments in favour of such a scenario might be (especially in the light of the December 1993 parliamentary elections in Russia), it seems obvious that the reaction of Russia would not be neutral—which could become the most serious conflict-generating factor in the foreseeable future in this region.

IV. Russia and Ukraine

Russia and Ukraine are the two largest former republics of the USSR, far exceeding the other successor states in terms of population, economic potential and military might. The character of their interaction is of crucial importance for conflict developments in the post-Soviet geopolitical region.

The context

In 1993 the Ukrainian economy deteriorated to the verge of collapse. Meanwhile, Russia—all its hardships of economic transformation notwithstanding—is regarded by the vast majority of Ukrainians as a land of prosperity. Compared with the Ukrainian currency unit (the karbovanets) the rouble is strong and reliable.[41] Ukraine's economic dependence on Russia has become obvious and overwhelming.

In Ukraine the issue of relations with Russia has become a matter of special importance, generating sharp debates and creating a specific background for policy-making with respect to any conflict-related problems. A pragmatically oriented part of the political class is increasingly advocating a more co-operative (and, by extension, a more concessionist) line with respect to Russia— even at the expense of some symbolically important features of sovereignty. The other side of the coin has been the rising sensitivity of the 'nation state'- oriented political forces, anxious that any deals with Russia would inevitably

---

[40] *Izvestia*, 2 Nov. 1993, p. 3; *Krasnaya Zvezda*, 9 Nov. 1993, p. 3. Estonia, Latvia and Lithuania have applied to participate in NATO's Partnership for Peace programme. See *Baltic Independent*, vol. 4, no. 198 (4–10 Feb. 1994), p. 1.
[41] The annual inflation rate in 1993 was 1000% in Russia and 38 000% in Ukraine.

be made 'from a position of weakness', thus damaging the independence of Ukraine, making it a junior partner and even threatening to turn it into a kind of protectorate.

This domestic polarization in Ukraine has been aggravated by regional imbalances with some ethnically related aspects. The record of Kiev's policy with respect to ethnic groups could be seriously damaged by the economic crisis since among the most heavily affected regions are those in the eastern part of Ukraine, populated predominantly by Russian speakers.

As a result, Ukraine's ability to pursue a coherent policy towards Russia seems to have been seriously disturbed. Any compromise *between* Moscow and Kiev has been conditioned (and limited) by compromises *within* Ukraine that had to be reached either before or after the deal. The failure to reach these nullified some of the conflict-minimizing steps agreed to by the two sides in 1993.

Russia, on the contrary, seemed to have become more confident in 1993—in striking contrast with 1992, when the prevailing feeling in Moscow was that of having been deceived by a Ukraine which had 'opted out' instead of making good its expected acceptance of the CIS pattern as a substitute for the Soviet Union. The initial frustration gradually gave place to a rational consideration that the policy of Ukraine would be inevitably constrained by its own self-generated problems. This, however, did not mean that inelegant attempts at direct pressure were completely renounced and replaced by a *laissez-faire* approach.

The Russian Government also had to face its own domestic opposition to the official policy with respect to Ukraine, with critics arguing for a more aggressive approach (in particular on the issue of territorial claims). This has certainly contributed to making Russia more demanding and belligerent. The enforced dissolution of the Supreme Soviet in September–October 1993 permitted Moscow to get rid of the most objectionable political aspects of deliberations on the 'Ukrainian question' without, however, renouncing some elements of rigidity resulting from its perceived ability and declared intention of playing a leading role within the post-Soviet geopolitical area as a whole.

Nuclear weapons

During 1993 Russia continued its energetic efforts to consolidate its position as the only nuclear weapon successor state to the Soviet Union, being extremely vigilant of any perceived attempts to the contrary, especially on the part of Ukraine. The latter was desperately trying to get political, economic and security gains for its *de facto* nuclear weapon status. These overlapping interests of the two countries have created grounds for serious conflict.

Ownership of nuclear weapons

In July 1993, Ukraine proclaimed itself the owner of the strategic nuclear warheads deployed or stored on Ukrainian soil.[42] The move was most obviously
dictated by economic considerations (coupled with demands for compensation
for tactical nuclear weapons removed to Russia in 1992). Moscow saw in
those steps a clear indication that Ukraine intends to delay the weapon transfer
to Russia, in flagrant violation of its earlier commitments;[43] according to
Russian Defence Minister Pavel Grachev, Ukraine had actually proclaimed
itself a nuclear state.[44]

Control over nuclear weapons

The personnel servicing the Ukrainian nuclear weapons had been made
accountable to Kiev in April 1992 when the 43rd Rocket Army and the 46th
Airborne Army were incorporated in the Ukrainian national armed forces; in
May 1992 the flight crews of all strategic bombers were ordered to take an
oath of allegiance to Ukraine.[45] However, the missiles are still under the operational control of Moscow, as confirmed by, among others, Grachev. Russia is
reported to have broken its promise to provide Kiev with technical negative
control. Intelligence sources both in Russia and in the West consider that
Ukraine is working on breaking the codes for the missiles to be able not only
to veto their use but also to activate the flight plans on the missiles and to fire
them.[46] According to some estimates, Ukraine could establish partial control
over nuclear charges in something between a few months and a year and a
half.[47]

Ukraine and the START I Treaty

Under the 1991 US–Soviet Treaty on the Reduction and Limitation of Strategic Offensive Arms (the START I Treaty) and the 1992 Lisbon Protocol,
Ukraine was to transfer all 176 strategic nuclear missiles to Russia for destruction. In 1993 Kiev stated that those agreements cover only one of two missile
types deployed on Ukrainian soil—the SS-19,[48] maintaining that the 46 SS-24
multiple independently targetable re-entry vehicle (MIRVed) warhead missiles should be excluded from the agreement and negotiated separately by
Ukraine, the United States and Russia.[49] Interestingly, this would not directly
affect Russia's security since the SS-24s, whose shortest range in testing was
over 3000 km, would by no means enable Ukraine to threaten European

[42] See chapter 16 in this volume.
[43] 'The Statement of the Government of the Russian Federation, 5 Feb. 1993', *Diplomaticheskiy Vest-nik*, no. 9–10 (May 1993), pp. 9–14. See also chapter 16 in this volume.
[44] *Izvestia*, 23 July 1993, p. 1.
[45] *Krasnaya Zvezda*, 7 Apr. 1993, pp. 1 and 3.
[46] *Financial Times*, 17 Aug. 1993, p. 2
[47] *Moscow News*, no. 45 (5 Nov. 1993), p. 10.
[48] *Izvestia*, 12 Aug. 1993, p. 1.
[49] *International Herald Tribune*, 31 July 1993, p. 2.

Russia; instead, a nuclear deterrent role might be performed by the SS-19s, which were tested at slightly more than 1000 km, but they are scheduled to be dismantled. Moscow, however, insists that all the nuclear warheads be transferred to Russia within two years after Ukrainian ratification of the START I Treaty.[50]

Safety of nuclear devices

Russia has repeatedly expressed serious concerns about the technical state of nuclear weapons on Ukrainian soil—both because of inadequate conditions of storage and because Russian servicing personnel were denied access.[51] The Ukrainian side initially rejected those allegations but later was reported to be applying for the assistance of Russia's nuclear specialists in dealing with dangerously increased temperature and radiation levels in the storage facilities in Pervomaisk.[52] Asserting that nuclear warheads in Ukraine were deteriorating, Russian Foreign Minister Andrey Kozyrev couched his warnings in almost apocalyptic terms, predicting a 'tragedy much worse than Chernobyl'.[53]

On most of those issues of contention, a breakthrough seemed to have been achieved on 3 September 1993 at the Russian–Ukrainian summit meeting in Massandra, Crimea, where the premiers of the two states signed three protocols on guarantees of surveillance over nuclear weapons deployed in Ukraine and on the utilization of nuclear charges. It was envisaged that the nuclear warheads would be transferred to Russia for dismantling in exchange for adequate financial compensation and supply of uranium for power stations in Ukraine.[54] However, upon completion of the official ceremony, the Ukrainian side introduced some hastily hand-written amendments (stipulating their intention to retain the SS-24 missiles) into the signed documents under the pretext that they were not fully consistent with prior understandings.[55]

The conflict between Russia and Ukraine reached its apex with the adoption by the Ukrainian Parliament of 13 conditions within the framework of the long-awaited ratification of the START I Treaty and the Lisbon Protocol (18 November 1993).[56] Moscow's official reaction was one of extreme nervousness;[57] Foreign Minister Kozyrev claimed 'we assist . . . the emergence of a new nuclear state',[58] whereas Russian diplomacy tried to sensitize the international community, pointing to the fact that the nuclear non-proliferation regime would be irreparably damaged if Ukraine were allowed to go nuclear.

However, some prominent experts in Russia consider that Moscow should avoid over-reaction, which could only damage the prospects of resolving the

---

[50] Izvestia, 6 Nov. 1993, p. 3.
[51] Izvestia, 7 Apr. 1993, p. 5; Izvestia, 15 Sep. 1993, p. 1.
[52] Nezavisimaya Gazeta, 15 Sep. 1993, p. 2.
[53] The Independent, 6 Nov. 1993; International Herald Tribune, 7 Nov. 1993, p. 1.
[54] Financial Times, 5 Sep. 1993, p. 1.
[55] Moscow News, no. 45 (5 Nov. 1993), p. 10.
[56] See chapter 8 in this volume.
[57] Nezavisimaya Gazeta, 20 Nov. 1993, p. 1 and 3; Izvestia, 23 Nov. 1993, p. 1.
[58] Krasnaya Zvezda, 23 Nov. 1993, p. 3.

issue. Since missiles are almost the only trump-card of Ukraine in its disastrous economic and explosive political situation, it is natural that Kiev should attempt to use them as a bargaining-chip for keeping Russia at bay and drawing Western political attention and economic aid. There are serious grounds for believing that the nuclear weapon problem depends on the overall context of Russian–Ukrainian relations, rather than vice versa. If so, Moscow should pay more attention to Kiev's demand for effective security guarantees in order to improve the chances for Ukraine's acceptance of non-nuclear weapon status.[59]

Another factor affecting the Ukrainian stand on nuclear weapons in the most direct way was domestic developments in Russia. Significantly, after the departure of the bellicose Vice-President Alexander Rutskoy in September 1993 and the dissolution of the Supreme Soviet (where the most antagonistic voices prevailed), Ukrainian 'intransigence' could no longer refer to 'hostile' and 'neo-imperialist' trends in the Russian Parliament to justify the need to retain nuclear weapons on Ukrainian territory. This contributed to advancing ratification of the START I Treaty by six months: it had been expected to be delayed until at least April 1994. When, two months later, the elections in Russia brought success to nationalists and the USSR-nostalgic forces, the pro-nuclear lobby in Ukraine obtained the most convincing argument in favour of its approach.

Finally, Russia's efforts aimed at denuclearizing Ukraine brought results only because of the catastrophic state of the Ukrainian economy and with the assistance of the USA. In January 1994 Ukraine agreed to sign the Trilateral Statement which reiterated the pledge to get rid of nuclear weapons. The move, reluctantly approved by the Ukrainian Parliament, does not, however, guarantee acceding to the NPT.[60]

The Black Sea Fleet

The dispute over ownership and control of the Black Sea Fleet remained one of the main irritants in Russian–Ukrainian relations in 1993. Both sides have developed a set of strategic, historical, economic and technical arguments to support their claims. The issue of the Fleet has become one of symbolic importance both for Ukraine and for Russia, generating sharp domestic debates and causing the political élites to be extremely sensitive towards possible compromises.[61] A number of approaches have been tried without resulting in a permanent settlement. These included joint command, division of the Fleet and selling the Fleet to Russia.

[59] Arbatov, A., 'Nuclear missile prestige or real security?', *Moscow News*, no. 49 (3 Dec. 1993), pp. 1 and 6.

[60] *Izvestia*, 5 Feb. 1994, p. 3. For the text of the Trilateral Statement, see appendix 16A.

[61] Clarke, D. L., 'Rusting fleet renews debate on navy's mission', *RFE/RL Research Report*, no. 25 (18 June 1993).

Joint command

Joint command of the Black Sea Fleet was decided upon at the Russian–Ukrainian summit meeting held in Yalta on 3 August 1992. It was a transitional measure intended to last until the end of 1995. However, both sides seemed to prefer postponing rather than addressing tough concrete issues; in fact, the only reported case of their successful co-operation was the joint nomination of the new commander—Vice-Admiral Eduard Baltin of Russia. In principle, both sides could see some advantages in keeping the joint command over the long run: for Ukraine, this might be the only way to maintain its claims concerning the Fleet, even if only symbolic, since they could by no means be supported financially;[62] for Russia this would permit preservation of the unity of the Fleet, which is strongly advocated by the military. However, joint command as a definite settlement would be possible only on the basis of the broader military integration of Russia and Ukraine, which has been unacceptable for the latter.

Division of the Fleet

At the summit meeting of 17 June 1993 Presidents Boris Yeltsin and Leonid Kravchuk agreed to split the Fleet evenly.[63] This decision, however, was criticized by nationalists in both countries, but more importantly it met with a stern protest from the Fleet officer corps. Significantly, only 2 per cent of the officers had decided to transfer to the Ukrainian Navy, while the majority refused to subordinate themselves to the decision of the presidents. This latter move was reportedly supported by the military establishment in Russia, including Defence Minister Pavel Grachev.[64] President Kravchuk later conceded that the decision on splitting the Fleet 'no longer corresponds to the real situation'.[65]

Selling the Fleet to Russia

On 3 September 1993, at the summit meeting in Massandra, Crimea, between Presidents Yeltsin and Kravchuk, the latter agreed to exchange Ukraine's share of the prized Black Sea Fleet to Russia in return for debt relief. The deal was dictated by the rapidly worsening economic position of Ukraine, which was unable to cover the soaring cost of gas and oil supplied from Russia, which in turn had refused to continue delivery without being paid.[66]

The agreement reached in Massandra generated strong opposition in Ukraine as being humiliating and damaging the country's sovereignty.[67] The

---

[62] See *Moscow News*, no. 46 (12 Nov. 1993), p. 12.

[63] ITAR–TASS, 17 June 1993. For an analysis of the agreement, see Lepingwell, J. W. R., 'The Black Sea Fleet agreement: progress or empty promises?', *RFE/RL Research Report*, no. 28 (9 July 1993), pp. 48–55.

[64] *Financial Times*, 11 July 1993, p. 24; *Nezavisimaya Gazeta*, 14 Sep. 1993, p. 2.

[65] *Financial Times*, 5 Sep. 1993, p. 1.

[66] *Nezavisimaya Gazeta*, 4 Sep. 1993, p. 1.

[67] *Krasnaya Zvezda*, 7 Sep. 1993, p. 3; *Izvestia*, 8 Sep. 1993, p. 4; 9 Sep. 1993, p. 2.

nationalist-oriented forces considered the concession unjustified, since one-sixteenth of the total former Soviet Navy on which Ukraine allegedly has the right to insist would be at least twice the size of the Black Sea Fleet.[68] Significantly, the very fact of a specific agreement having been reached in Massandra was later denied by the Ukrainian side—just as in the case of earlier agreements on nuclear weapons.[69]

As for the economic parameters of the deal, the concrete figures have never been discussed officially but will be a matter of serious disagreement. According to some estimates, the total value of the Ukrainian part of the Fleet is three times the Ukrainian debt to Russia (equivalent to $15 billion and $5 billion respectively).[70] If so, it remains an open question whether Russia would be ready to pay such a sum of money for military assets of doubtful strategic importance, which might in any event be claimed without paying any compensation.

Another issue left unresolved by the Massandra agreement is that of Sevastopol, the home port of the Black Sea Fleet. The problem is not only more important than the ownership of 300 ships (which would literally 'float around' without a home port) but also more of a conflict-generating one, since the city, which now finds itself in an independent Ukraine, has historically belonged to Russia, is mainly populated by Russians and was officially reclaimed by the Supreme Soviet in July 1993.[71] Yeltsin and Kravchuk discussed the possibility of Russia renting Sevastopol—which is in fact the only realistic option because no other Black Sea port is large enough to support the Fleet. However, the idea reportedly floundered on objections from too many direct and indirect actors—Russian supporters of territorial claims renouncing any acknowledgement of Ukrainian ownership, Ukrainian nationalists rejecting the concept of foreign armed forces on Ukrainian soil and Crimean local authorities seeking a share of any rent.[72]

Meanwhile, throughout 1993 the Ukrainian Ministry of Defence repeatedly issued orders aimed at capturing units and facilities of the Black Sea Fleet, whereas on numerous occasions ship crews hoisted the flag of Saint Andrew (the ensign of the Russian Navy) and addressed ultimatums to both presidents. The tension has reached such a level that an accident or a deliberate action could result in an explosion and prompt both sides to take measures fraught with serious consequences.

Crimea

During the Soviet era the sudden decision of General Secretary Nikita Khrushchev in 1954 to turn over Crimea to Ukraine to mark the 300th

---

[68] *Nezavisimaya Gazeta*, 8 Sep. 1993, p. 2; *Krasnaya Zvezda*, 9 Sep. 1993, p. 3.
[69] *Nezavisimaya Gazeta*, 7 Sep. 1993, p. 1; *Izvestia*, 9 Sep. 1993, p. 2; *Moscow News*, no. 46 (12 Nov. 1993), p. 12.
[70] *Nezavisimaya Gazeta*, 8 Sep. 1993, p. 1.
[71] *Financial Times*, 11 July 1993, p. 24; *The Guardian*, 4 Sep. 1993, p. 1.
[72] *International Herald Tribune*, 4–5 Sep. 1993, p. 1.

anniversary of its 'reunification' with Russia (in 1654 according to a decision of the Pereyaslav Rada) did not have any practical importance. However, after the dissolution of the USSR, the issue has become a source of tension between Ukraine and Russia. The latter seemed to have an understandable psychological reluctance to accept the 'loss' of territory incorporated into Russia over two centuries ago and which had never been connected to Ukraine—either culturally or ethnically.[73] However, Russia finally opted for the principle of inviolability of former Soviet internal borders—thus recognizing the territorial integrity of Ukraine and Crimea as a part of it.

This approach has contributed to minimizing the Russian–Ukrainian conflict over Crimea. It should be noted that the Russian Government has distanced itself from extremist claims initiated by the dissolved Supreme Soviet. This has permitted the Ukrainian side to become more co-operative since its territorial integrity was not officially questioned; significantly, the idea of leasing Sevastopol was first raised at the political level on 11 August 1993 by Prime Minister Leonid Kuchma of Ukraine.[74] Ivan Yemelyanov, the representative of the President of Ukraine in Sevastopol at the time, even mentioned the possibility of establishing in the future a joint Russian–Ukrainian protectorate over Crimea.[75]

Nevertheless, the potential for conflict between Russia and Ukraine over Crimea remains. It is sustained both by active local pro-Russian irredentism and through links with a number of other disputes between the two states.

Increasingly sceptical about the virtues of Ukrainian independence and frustrated by the deteriorating economic situation, voters gave strong support to the representative of the pro-Russian lobby, Yuriy Meshkov, during the Crimean presidential election of 30 January 1994.[76] Meshkov, however, seems since to have opted for a more cautious approach with respect to the idea of reunification with Russia—taking into account both the overwhelming dependence of Crimea on Ukraine for vital supplies (including electricity and fresh water) and Russia's reluctance to allow its relations with Ukraine to become hostage to the peninsula's politics.

For Ukraine, the pro-independence trend in Crimea, even if it is (for the time being) relatively marginal and contained at the local level, is a matter of serious concern. The growing autonomy of Crimea with respect to institutions, laws on ownership of private property, the legislature, and so on is perceived as creating *de facto* a basis for a future independent sovereign state.[77]

In fact, capitalizing on Russian–Ukrainian disagreements is only rational on the part of the local authorities of Crimea. However, keeping those disagreements within certain limits is essential for avoiding an overall destabilization of the peninsula—and even more so for resolving its economic and social

---

[73] Over 70% of the population of the peninsula are Russian.
[74] *Krasnaya Zvezda*, 12 Aug. 1993, p. 1.
[75] *Krasnaya Zvezda*, 17 Sep. 1993, p. 3.
[76] Voter turnout was 75%, of which 73% voted for Yuriy Meshkov. See *Moscow News*, no. 5 (4–10 Feb. 1994), p. 5.
[77] *Izvestia*, 11 Aug. 1993, p. 2.

problems. For example, the establishment of a free economic zone in Crimea will probably require demilitarization of the area—which would be impossible without a consensus between Ukraine and Russia.[78] Sometimes apparent moves towards a more co-operative approach by Ukraine and Russia could be interpreted as blackmail—as, for example, in the case of the statement by a Crimean official that if Ukraine refuses to join the CIS economic union, Crimea should do so separately.[79] Whether this could serve as a factor of *rapprochement* between Russia and Ukraine is an open question; nevertheless, the appeal of Nikolay Bagrov, the former head of the local legislature in Crimea, inviting Ukraine and Russia to act as 'collective guarantor' of Crimea's security, deserves mention.[80] The newly elected Crimean President, Yuriy Meshkov, reportedly intends to suggest to both Ukraine and Russia that they agree upon demilitarization of the peninsula and its defence in the framework of the CIS collective security system.[81]

The situation in Crimea is aggravated by the problem of reintegrating Crimean Tatars who are returning to the area from Soviet-era exile and are insisting on representation in the local legislature.[82] Their total number has increased from about 40 000 in 1989 to 250 000 in 1993, that is, 8 per cent of the population.[83] Significantly, their leaders stress the idea of Crimean statehood within Ukraine and reject any prospect of reunification with Russia (some radicals have even expressed a preference for joining Turkey).[84]

The potential Russian–Ukrainian territorial dispute has from the beginning been connected to the overall context of relations between the two states. Ukraine insists on unambiguous recognition of territorial integrity, suspecting that Russia is looking for leverage in order to impose closer integration at the expense of Ukrainian independence. It is unacceptable to Ukraine that official Russian renunciation of territorial claims, as well as proposed 'security guarantees', should be conditional on the participation of Ukraine in the CIS.[85] Incidentally, influential political forces within Crimea claim that the issue could be resolved only on the basis of establishing confederative links between Russia and Ukraine resulting in 'removal of customs barriers and frontiers, creation of united armed forces, introduction of a joint currency and taxation policy, development of a co-ordinated foreign policy'.[86]

The link between the 'Crimean problem' and the dispute over the Black Sea Fleet is obvious. It is true that the causal relationship, from Russia's perspective, might be interpreted in both ways: access to the Crimean peninsula is vital because of claims over the Fleet, or the Fleet is only an effective instru-

---

[78] *Vek*, no. 42 (20 Oct.–4 Nov. 1993), p. 6.
[79] *Nezavisimaya Gazeta*, 22 Sep. 1993, p. 3.
[80] *Izvestia/Finansovye Izvestia*, 31 Aug. 1993, p. 2; *Nezavisimaya Gazeta*, 1 Sep. 1993, p. 3.
[81] *Krasnaya Zvezda*, 1 Feb. 1994, p. 3.
[82] *Nezavisimaya Gazeta*, 28 July 1993, p. 3; *Nezavisimaya Gazeta*, 6 Oct. 1993, p. 3; *Izvestia*, 5 Aug. 1993, p. 1.
[83] *Le Monde diplomatique,* Jan. 1994, p. 8.
[84] *Nezavisimaya Gazeta*, 25 Aug. 1993, p. 3.
[85] *Izvestia*, 25 July 1993, p. 3.
[86] *Nezavisimaya Gazeta*, 16 July 1993, p. 3.

ment to highlight the territorial ambitions as retroactive compensation for all the 'losses' resulting from the collapse of the USSR. From Ukraine's point of view, the linkage might provide some additional room for manœuvre in the bargaining process.

The issue of Crimea is of primary importance for some other aspects of Russian–Ukrainian relations as well. For example, the Crimean issue is strongly connected with the future of nuclear weapons on Ukrainian territory. Unless other states recognize the territorial integrity of Ukraine and undertake a commitment to defend it in case of aggression, stated a prominent parliamentarian and one of Kiev's foreign policy makers, Dmitro Pavlychko, 'to transfer the nuclear weapons to the country which addresses territorial claims to us would be a betrayal without any justification'.[87]

V. The Trans-Dniester region of Moldova

The area on the left bank of the Dniester River had the status of autonomous republic within Ukraine until 1940, when it was united with Bessarabia, taken by the USSR from Romania. The status of the new entity was upgraded, and Moldova became one of the constituent republics of the USSR. After Moldova (with two-thirds of the population being ethnic Romanians) became independent, its reunification with Romania was put on the political agenda, although not as a matter of immediate priority. This created a strong incentive for separatism in the Trans-Dniester region, which proclaimed independence. During the spring and summer of 1992 armed clashes, reportedly with the active participation of the Russian (formerly Soviet) 14th Army, resulted in numerous casualties and brought about an acute crisis—which ended only after external political involvement, first of Russia and then of the CSCE.[88] In 1993 the conflict remained relatively quiet, and there was modest progress towards a settlement.

International efforts

On the basis of conclusions formulated by the personal representative of the CSCE Chairman-in-Office, the CSCE established a Mission of Long Duration to Moldova.[89] Aimed at initiating consultations with all interested parties and reaching a peaceful solution, it developed a package of documents and decided to send observers to monitor elections in Moldova (27 February 1994).[90] Russia also aspires to play an active role as mediator. Trilateral

---

[87] *Nezavisimaya Gazeta*, 30 July 1993, p. 3. See also his statement quoted in *Financial Times*, 11 July 1993, p. 24.

[88] Russian press reports have claimed that the activities of the 14th Army in Moldova were authorized by the Russian Ministry of Defence. See Socor, V., 'Russian daily says attack on Moldova authorized by Moscow', *RFE/RL News Briefs*, vol. 3, no. 6 (31 Jan.–4 Feb. 1994), p. 20.

[89] See 'Report on the conflict in the Left-Bank Dniester areas of the Republic of Moldova', CSCE Communication no. 43, 2 Feb. 1993, Prague; 'Decision taken by the Committee of Senior Officials', CSCE/19–CSO/*Journal*, no. 3 (4 Feb. 1993), Prague, Annex 3.

[90] *Nezavisimaya Gazeta*, 11 Nov. 1993, p. 3.

peacemaking forces (Moldovan, Russian and Trans-Dniestrian), deployed in the area of conflict in 1992, have remained, although giving rise to controversial assessments of their efficiency.

Status of the region

Several rounds of negotiations have not brought any significant results. The Moldovan Government has expressed its readiness to offer special status to the Trans-Dniester region (up to economic autonomy), but only if based on the principle of territorial integrity (confirmed by the CSCE and the Russian–Moldovan agreement of 21 July 1992).[91] The self-proclaimed 'Trans-Dniester Republic' insists on continuation of the *status quo*, recognition of independence, confederative links to the future Moldova, the right to create its own armed forces and inter-state negotiations.[92]

Russian troop withdrawal[93]

From the 30 000 Soviet troops originally stationed in Moldova, the strength of the 14th Russian Army deployed in the Trans-Dniester region has dropped below the level of a standard mechanized division.[94] In May 1993 President Yeltsin and Moldovan President Mircea Snegur reached an agreement in principle according to which the 14th Army will withdraw from the region. By the end of 1993, seven rounds of negotiations on the practicalities of withdrawal had been conducted. Moldova has reportedly agreed to cover part of the expenses of withdrawal (as demanded by the Russian side) but insists that funds should be provided by selling military equipment and stores, whereas the 14th Army command would like to have the material transferred to the Trans-Dniester region. The 'principle of synchronization' accepted at the negotiations connects withdrawal with a political settlement; Moldova would like to set a time-limit for the withdrawal (1 July 1994) whereas Russian specialists' assessments envisage that the withdrawal will take not less than two or three years.[95]

Although in 1993 the conflict was basically contained, overall stability in the region is tenuous. The Moldovan Government claims that the Trans-Dniester authorities are delaying negotiations and seeking to expand their control over contested areas. Their political unco-operativeness and irreconcilability were also manifested by the severe sentences imposed on some

---

[91] *Diplomaticheskiy Vestnik*, no. 15–16 (15–31 Aug. 1992), pp. 33–36; Socor, V., 'Moldova accepts CSCE conflict settlement plan', *RFE/RL News Briefs*, vol. 3, no. 6 (31 Jan.–4 Feb. 1994), p. 15.

[92] *Izvestia*, 5 Mar. 1993; *Nezavisimaya Gazeta*, 25 June 1993, p. 3; *Nezavisimaya Gazeta*, 8 Dec. 1993, p. 3.

[93] See chapter 14 in this volume.

[94] As of Jan. 1993, the Russian 14th Army's manpower strength, according to the Russian Ministry of Defence, was 6081. See Rotfeld, A. D., Final Report on the Conflict in the Left-Bank Dniester Areas of the Republic of Moldova, 31 Jan. 1993, Prague, pp. 15–16. Another estimate gives 8500. See *International Observer*, no. 7 (21 July 1993), p. 889.

[95] *Krasnaya Zvezda*, 13 Nov. 1993, p. 2.

Moldovan activists by the court in Tiraspol at what was widely regarded as an unfair trial, provoking a strong political reaction in Romania.

In Moldova, Trans-Dniester separatism is widely believed to be politically backed by Russia and organizationally supported by the 14th Army. General Alexander Lebed, the commander of the 14th Army, has repeatedly stated that it would take at least 10–15 years to redeploy all the Russian units because 60 per cent of his troops are from the Trans-Dniester area or have found a home there.[96] The Russian peacekeepers have also been reproached for partiality.[97] Moldova seems to be interested in securing the more active involvement of the CSCE—in particular, in the negotiations with Russia on troop withdrawal. However, the Russian side has insisted on holding bilateral talks, ruling out the presence of CSCE observers at the negotiations, as requested by Moldova and the CSCE mission.[98]

Russia's role as peacekeeper and Moldova's overall relations with Russia have apparently been issues of acute domestic debate in Moldova. Significantly, at the United Nations General Assembly the Moldovan Foreign Minister resolutely objected to Russia's search for a UN peacekeeping mandate on the former Soviet territory—only to be fired immediately afterwards.[99] Non-ratification of the CIS agreement resulted in the interruption of economic links and cost Moldova 40 billion roubles over a three-month period; not surprisingly a co-operative approach towards Moscow has been gradually gaining increasing support,[100] manifested convincingly in the parliamentary elections on 27 February 1994. Economic factors also play an extremely important role in the whole 'Trans-Dniestrian problem' since the rebel area accounts for 57 per cent of industrial production in Moldova.[101]

The 'Trans-Dniester Republic' had active supporters in the Russian Supreme Soviet. Volunteers from the region reportedly participated in the riots in Moscow on the side of the dissolved parliament. Whether the defeat of the latter could reduce the ambitions of the Trans-Dniestrians and make them more conciliatory remains an open question. However, this might be the hidden cause of the reported disagreements between the 14th Army command and Tiraspol's local authorities.[102]

VI. The Caucasus

During 1993 the Caucasus was the scene of the heaviest fighting on the territory of the former Soviet Union. Over 40 current or potential ethnic and terri-

---

[96] *International Observer*, no. 7 (21 July 1993), p. 889.
[97] *Vecherniy Kishinev*, 3 Nov. 1993, p. 1.
[98] *Izvestia*, 28 Oct. 1993, p. 2; Socor, V., 'Moldova: democracy advances, independence at risk', *RFE/RL Research Report*, vol. 3, no. 1 (7 Jan. 1994), p. 47.
[99] *Nezavisimaya Gazeta*, 29 Oct. 1993, p. 3.
[100] *Izvestia*, 30 Oct. 1993, p. 2.
[101] *Izvestia*, 3 Nov. 1993, p. 2.
[102] *Nezavisimaya Gazeta*, 15 Sep. 1993, p. 3; *Krasnaya Zvezda*, 21 Jan. 1994, p. 3.

torial conflicts[103] make the Caucasus extremely unstable, in a period of deep transformation when old political structures have substantially eroded but new ones often lack legitimacy and efficiency.

Most of the ongoing conflicts in the Caucasus fall into three broad categories, being generated by: (a) power struggles between competing political forces; (b) local demands for greater autonomy (up to independence) from the central authorities; or (c) unsettled borders and conflicting territorial claims between different state entities or constituent ethnic groups. In many cases, different types of conflict overlap and reinforce each other. At stake are also broader geostrategic interests of in- and out-of-area international actors and the emerging political orientations of newly independent states in the Caucasus.

Nagorno-Karabakh

Developments in Nagorno-Karabakh in 1993 were characterized by ongoing military activities on the part of the secessionist forces, on the one hand, and by diplomatic efforts to achieve a political settlement, on the other.

The armed forces of Nagorno-Karabakh established control over the so-called Lachin corridor, thus creating a territorial link with and a channel for supply from Armenia. Later on, the offensive started to develop both in eastern and in southern directions, with the aim of establishing a kind of extended security zone in the immediate proximity of the Nagorno-Karabakh territory and resulting in unquestionable military success for the secessionists. The Azerbaijani armed forces failed to organize any serious resistance and were reported to have started a counter-offensive only by the end of 1993[104] when Baku had lost control of about 20–25 per cent of the territory of the country.[105] The number of refugees and 'displaced people' from the occupied territories totalled at least 1 million,[106] that is over 10 per cent of the country's population (some estimates are even higher).[107]

Against the background of mounting battlefield defeats, a coup staged in Baku on 4 June 1993 toppled the year-old Azerbaijani Popular Front Government and President Ebulfez Elcibey, the last former dissident in power in the former Soviet Union, and returned ex-communist leader Geidar Aliev to power. The event marked not only the loss of the democratic option and the establishment of a 'normal' third world-type authoritarian regime,[108] but also a fundamental change of direction in foreign and security policy, to an openly

---

[103] See Kolossov, V., *Ethno-Territorial Conflicts and Boundaries in the Former Soviet Union*, Territory Briefing 2 (International Boundaries Research Unit, University of Durham: Durham, UK, 1992).

[104] *Izvestia*, 31 Dec. 1993, p. 3.

[105] *Le Monde*, 14–15 Nov. 1993, p. 5; *Nezavisimaya Gazeta*, 25 Dec. 1993, p. 1.

[106] *International Herald Tribune*, 17 Sep. 1993, p. 2; *Izvestia*, 4 Nov. 1993, p. 1.

[107] *Moscow News*, no. 48 (26 Nov. 1993), p. 5.

[108] See Furman, D., 'Vozvraschenie v tretiy mir' ['Return to the Third World'], *Svobodnaya Mysl'*, no. 11 (July 1993), pp. 16–28.

pro-Russian orientation. Presumably, this could not help but affect Russia's view of the conflict.

During 1993, the parties directly involved in the Nagorno-Karabakh conflict intensified their diplomatic efforts. Azerbaijan oriented its international activity towards compensating for military defeats; Armenia attempted to play down the threat of UN condemnation and isolation in the region; and the secessionist leadership of Nagorno-Karabakh sought to translate its military achievements into political ones ('land for peace and political status'). The efforts of the CSCE Minsk Group (which had been set up in order to organize a conference on the political status of Nagorno-Karabakh) were aimed at stopping the hostilities and resulted in a peace plan accepted by Armenia and Nagorno-Karabakh.[109] Azerbaijan, however, rejected the plan, insisting on unconditional troop withdrawal from all occupied territories and expressing reluctance to accept the secessionists as a direct party to the conflict.[110]

An important new dimension of the conflict over Nagorno-Karabakh has been the increased involvement of external actors. Turkey has actively helped Azerbaijan in training its military, provided it with diplomatic support and played an important role in maintaining a *de facto* blockade of Armenia.[111] Iran has expressed serious concerns that the Armenian–Karabakh offensive would result in a massive flow of refugees into its northern provinces, resulting in separatist demands by millions of Iranian Azeris. Indeed, uncontrolled passage across the border by refugees (although on a relatively limited scale) took place in September 1993, and limited preventive actions by the Iranian armed forces were reported (provoking official concern in Moscow).[112] Significantly, ideas of a possible intervention aimed at preventing further deterioration of the situation in the area and externalization of the conflict have become a matter of public (although not official) debate, including the most 'exotic' and unrealistic forms of interference—such as joint military action by Iran and Turkey.[113]

Not surprisingly, Russia reacted nervously to the prospect of external intervention, which could explain the increased Russian activism in the area. Russia initiated contacts between the parties in the conflict, pressured for an extension of a temporary cease-fire and expressed a readiness to involve itself

---

[109] The Minsk Group, when set up in Mar. 1992, comprised 9 members—Belarus, Czechoslovakia, France, Germany, Italy, Russia, Sweden, Turkey and the USA—and developed an 'Adjusted Timetable of Urgent Steps to Implement Security Council Resolutions 822 and 853', setting out a comprehensive set of measures to end the conflict, including troop withdrawals and the establishment of a permanent cease-fire. See *Annual Report 1993 on CSCE Activities* (note 24), p. 9.

[110] *Nezavisimaya Gazeta*, 26 Nov. 1993, p. 1. A diplomatic breakthrough may be in sight, however, as the defence ministers of Armenia and Azerbaijan have agreed to a Russian-mediated cease-fire and a withdrawal of the forces of both sides to predetermined positions; a complete withdrawal of Armenian forces will depend on further negotiations. Lloyd, J., 'Nagorno-Karabakh peace plan', *Financial Times*, 21 Feb. 1994, p. 1.

[111] *Nezavisimaya Gazeta*, 16 Sep. 1993, p. 3; *Nezavisimaya Gazeta*, 6 Nov. 1993, p. 3; Lloyd, J., 'Azeris offer peace talks', *Financial Times*, 9 Sep. 1993, p. 3.

[112] *Nezavisimaya Gazeta*, 3 Sep. 1993, pp. 1 and 2; *Nezavisimaya Gazeta*, 8 Sep. 1993, p. 2; *Izvestia*, 4 Sep. 1993, p. 2; *Izvestia*, 10 Sep. 1993, p. 3.

[113] *Izvestia*, 26 Aug 1993, p. 3.

Figure 6.3. Map of the Caucasus

in peacekeeping activities (a proposal which reportedly was not received with great enthusiasm).[114]

A planned conference on the status of Nagorno-Karabakh will be a decisive test of conflict management in the area. Agreeing upon effective autonomous status for the region within Azerbaijan may be the only practical way out of the vicious circle.

Abkhazia

The conflict in Abkhazia, an autonomous territory in Georgia, entered a phase of war-fighting after the local parliament proclaimed on 23 July 1992 a return to the 1925 constitution,[115] prompting the Georgian Government to introduce troops which established control over part of Abkhazia. The situation deteriorated markedly in early July 1993 when the Abkhazian side launched a new offensive to capture the capital of the region, Sukhumi. Russia's mediation efforts resulted in a cease-fire accord (reached in Sochi on 27 July 1993) which was nevertheless violated by the resumption of the Abkhazian offensive on 16 September 1993, culminating in the badly organized Georgian defend-

---

[114] *Nezavisimaya Gazeta*, 11 Nov. 1993, p. 3.

[115] The 1925 constitution proclaimed Abkhazia to be a 'sovereign state exercising state power over its territory independently of any other power'. At the same time, the constitution stipulated that Abkhazia 'enters' Georgia on the basis of a special treaty.

ers being pushed out of the city.[116] Numerous atrocities were committed against the civilian population (several thousand were reportedly killed) and up to 120 000–150 000 Georgians fled the area.[117]

The role of Russia in the developments in and around Abkhazia seems to have been a result of conflicting interests and perceptions within Russia itself. Reports indicate that logistical support from the Russian armed forces was essential for the military success of the Abkhazian side, which was assisted also by numerous volunteers from the autonomous republics in Russian North Caucasus.[118] Georgian President Eduard Shevardnadze repeatedly and fiercely criticized Russia for its lack of neutrality and unwillingness to guarantee the cease-fire agreement to end the fighting. At the same time Russia officially condemned the violation of the agreement by Abkhazia and imposed broad economic sanctions, including a cut-off of electricity supplies from Russian power plants—at the risk of provoking a strong negative reaction in North Caucasus. Moreover, rejecting an option of accepting the Abkhazian conquests as a *fait accompli*, the Russian Foreign Ministry stated unambiguously that settlement was only possible on the basis of returning to the cease-fire agreement.[119]

As a result of these apparently incoherent actions, Georgia was in fact forced to recognize that the key to settlement is in Russian hands. Significantly, after Shevardnadze opted to join the CIS and acknowledged the vital importance of close relations with Russia, the latter started to highlight the idea of preserving the territorial integrity of Georgia as the only possible way to re-establish peace in the republic—provided it accepts a federation-type constitutional order and raises the status of the constituent entities.

The meeting of the conflicting parties in Geneva, initiated by UN decision and mediated by Russia, resulted on 1 December 1993 in the signing of a memorandum of understanding stipulating a cease-fire, an increase in the number of international observers,[120] an exchange of prisoners and the return of refugees. It was agreed that an expert group on the status of Abkhazia with participation of specialists from the UN, the CSCE and Russia would meet in Moscow.[121] However, the return of refugees scheduled to begin on 10 February 1994 was prevented by intensified fighting within the breakaway republic.[122] Later, on 4 April 1994, both sides agreed in Moscow upon a cease-fire, renunciation of the use of force and the repatriation of refugees.[123] How-

---

[116] Fuller, E., 'Russia's diplomatic offensive in the Transcaucasus', *RFE/RL Research Report*, vol. 2, no. 39 (10 Oct. 1993), pp. 30–31.

[117] *Krasnaya Zvezda*, 8 Sep. 1993, p. 2; *Literaturnaya Gazeta*, 20 Oct. 1993, p. 2.

[118] *Nezavisimaya Gazeta*, 24 Nov. 1993, p. 1; Goltz, T., 'Letter from Eurasia: the hidden Russian hand', *Foreign Policy*, no. 92 (fall 1993), pp. 112–13.

[119] *Izvestia*, 25 Nov. 1993, p. 2; 'Russians threaten rebels in Georgia with power cut-off', *International Herald Tribune*, 18–19 Sep. 1993, p. 2.

[120] On 31 Jan. 1994, the Security Council renewed the mandate of the UN observer force currently deployed in Abkhazia until 7 Mar.; no UN peacekeeping force was to be sent to the region until 'substantial progress' on a political settlement was made. See Fuller, E., 'No UN peacekeepers for Georgia', *RFE/RL News Briefs*, vol. 3, no. 6 (31 Jan.–4 Feb. 1994), p. 6.

[121] *Le Monde*, 3 Dec. 1993, p. 6; *Izvestia*, 3 Dec. 1993, p. 1; *Nezavisimaya Gazeta*, 9 Feb. 1994, p. 3.

[122] *Izvestia*, 10 Feb. 1994, p. 2.

[123] *Izvestia*, 5 Apr. 1994, p. 1.

ever, the whole process of settlement seems to be seriously complicated by the absence of both mechanisms for implementing the agreements and effective peacekeeping measures to separate the parties to conflict.

Georgia

Georgia's defeat in Abkhazia was coupled with the renewal of the rebellion staged by the loyalists of former Georgian President Zviad Gamsakhurdia, who had been forced from office in January 1992. Hoping that the power base and popular support which Shevardnadze had enjoyed would collapse after the spectacular loss of Sukhumi, the loyalists started an offensive in Mengrelia, the western area of the country from where Gamsakhurdia had come.

The hostilities, which lasted two months, can be characterized as a civil war, with some qualifications. According to reports, it was a strange war, closer to farce than to large-scale tragedy. The triumphant movement of Gamsa-khurdia's supporters at the first stage and later the no less triumphant counter-offensive of government forces did not meet serious resistance; in both cases opposing forces disappeared just as ephemerally. 'Landing units' arriving in a half dozen or so private Zhiguli automobiles were able to 'conquer' whole towns. Only two towns were actually stormed, with the total number of victims being less than two dozen.[124] The worst estimates of the overall casualties during the civil war do not exceed several hundred.[125]

In fact, Shevardnadze's opponents were contesting control of a system which had almost completely fallen apart and was in a state of virtual paralysis. Shevardnadze managed to keep control mainly because the competing forces were no less anarchic and lacked any meaningful unifying ideas, let alone serious political alternatives. The power struggle is quite revealing when viewed against the overall situation in the country—unprecedented administrative chaos, an explosion of criminality, and marauding and pillaging by armed irregulars.[126] Georgia faces economic collapse, with 80 per cent of industries not functioning; the living standard of 90 per cent of the population has fallen below the poverty level, the average monthly wage by the end of 1993 being equivalent to the market cost of a few eggs.[127]

Against this background, the decisive move of Eduard Shevardnadze to opt for Georgian membership in the CIS and a kind of 'special relationship' with Russia might have been motivated by a quite rational consideration to involve Russia on its side against both political opponents and separatists as the only chance for Georgia's political and economic survival.[128] One of the first actions along this line was the legalization of the Russian military presence

---

[124] *Krasnaya Zvezda*, 25 Nov. 1993, p. 1.

[125] *Nezavisimaya Gazeta*, 29 Oct. 1993, p. 1.

[126] *Nezavisimaya Gazeta*, 12 Nov, 1993, p. 3.

[127] *Izvestia*, 9 Nov. 1993, p. 4; *Moscow News*, no. 49 (3 Dec. 1993), p. 4.

[128] *Nezavisimaya Gazeta*, 11 Nov, 1993, p. 5. Russian military assistance appears to have been crucial in the Shevardnadze Government's sudden reversal of its perilous battlefield situation. See Levine, S., 'Russian aid helped Georgia turn tide of battle', *International Herald Tribune*, 28 Oct. 1993, p. 5.

(estimated at about 20 000): the terms of the military co-operation agreement (9 October 1993) were that Russia would keep its garrisons in Tbilisi and two other cities and rent the naval base at Poti and several airfields.

To re-establish minimal order on the main lines of communications and to restore control over the vital flows of supply, the Russian armed forces were asked in October 1993 to place under protection the ports and the railroads in the western part of the country.[129] Azerbaijan and Armenia, connected to the Black Sea shore by the railroad going via Tbilisi, were also invited to take part in the mission.[130] Russia also used the naval infantry of the Black Sea Fleet, which landed on 4 November 1993 in the port of Poti; significantly, the whole operation required only minimal forces (about 500 personnel) which were withdrawn by the end of the month.[131]

The official visit of President Yeltsin to Georgia in February 1994 resulted in the emerging co-operative status of bilateral relations being legalized.[132] The parties agreed to take measures for ensuring mutual security and defence and to jointly protect the external borders of Georgia; Russia will create three military bases in Georgia and assist it in establishing a national army (including arms transfer). It should be noted that the very fact of military co-operation with Georgia was strongly criticized by the newly elected Russian Parliament, which was concerned that this would give Tbilisi a free hand in Abkhazia.[133]

North Caucasus

Instabilities in the North Caucasus area of the Russian Federation, comprising seven autonomous republics (Adygei, Chechnia, Dagestan, Ingushetia, Kabardino-Balkaria, Karachai-Circassia and North Ossetia), are generated by the cumulative legacy of numerous border changes and ethnic persecutions during the Soviet era and reinforced by territorial grievances and ethno-nationalist extremism of the post-Soviet period. In 1993, the conflict potential in the North Caucasus largely centred around two issues: (a) the relations between the republics of North Ossetia and Ingushetia; and (b) the situation in and status of another republic, Chechnia.

The conflict between North Ossetia and Ingushetia

The first challenge consisted in containing the conflict between North Ossetia and Ingushetia and minimizing the consequences of an outbreak of violence in

---

[129] *Izvestia*, 30 Oct. 1993, p. 1; *Izvestia*, 3 Nov. 1993, p. 1; *Izvestia*, 5 Nov. 1993, p. 1; *Le Monde*, 6 Nov. 1993, p. 4.

[130] *Le Monde*, 22 Oct. 1993, p. 5; *Le Monde*, 27 Oct. 1993, p. 3.

[131] *Krasnaya Zvezda*, 18 Nov. 1993, p. 1; *Krasnaya Zvezda*, 2 Dec. 1993, p. 1.

[132] The Russian–Georgian Treaty of Friendship, Neighbourly Relations and Co-operation was signed on 3 Feb. 1994, together with several military-related agreements. The agreements allow Russia to maintain 3 military bases in Georgia until the end of 1995. See *Nezavisimaya Gazeta*, 2 Feb. 1994, p. 1; *Segodnia*, 10 Feb. 1994, p. 1; *Moscow News*, no. 6 (6–13 Feb. 1994), p. 6; and Hiatt, F., 'Georgia signs military accord and re-enters Russian sphere', *International Herald Tribune*, 4 Feb. 1994, pp. 1 and 4.

[133] *Izvestia*, 4 Feb. 1994, pp. 1 and 4.

November 1992. In that instance, a dispute over territory resulted in numerous casualties and the taking of hostages, pushed thousands of refugees out of the region and compelled Russia to impose a state of emergency and to deploy regular armed forces into the area.

Despite the continuation of the state of emergency, the instability continued in 1993. There were numerous reports of shootings, explosions and illegal arms transfers involving armoured combat vehicles, machine-guns, grenade launchers, and so on.[134] During the first 11 months of 1993, casualties in the emergency zone numbered 75 killed and 88 wounded.[135] The temporary administration established by the central government has been trying to disarm irregulars and to organize the return of refugees, but without any substantial results. In an attempt to achieve a breakthrough, President Yeltsin held talks with North Caucasian leaders on 6 December 1993 in Nal'chik. A compromise of sorts was reached between North Ossetia and Ingushetia—the former accepted that Ingushi refugees which had been forced out of its territory could return, whereas the latter renounced its territorial claims. Whether the deal opens the way out of the standstill remains to be seen.

Chechnia

The autonomous republic of Chechnia declared full independence from Russia in 1991. It did not sign the Federal Treaty (defining the status of Russia's constituent territories) in 1992 and refused to participate in parliamentary elections or in the December 1993 referendum on the new Russian constitution. The initial reaction of the authorities in Moscow to these developments could be described as one of nervousness, but the forces favouring non-interventionism seemingly prevailed—apparently in the hope that the situation would change after the anticipated peaceful or forceful removal of Chechnian President Dzhokhar Dudayev. Meanwhile, numerous reports pointed to increasing economic and political chaos in the republic, which also affected adjacent areas, disturbing lines of transit (especially railroads) and communication and turning Chechnia into a safe haven for criminals inaccessible to Russia's police and judicial systems.

Both of the above-mentioned conflict areas in the North Caucasus are not only adjacent to each other but also closely interrelated as far as Russia's policy is concerned. According to some observers, Russia, either directly or indirectly, gave a 'green light' to violence in North Ossetia in order to have a pretext for a concentration of forces against Chechnia.[136]

By the end of 1993, Moscow seemed to be politically and psychologically ready for tough decisions leading up to sealing the borders and isolating Chechnia—without, however, recognizing its independence.[137] Dudayev, for

---

[134] *Krasnaya Zvezda*, 17 Nov. 1993, p. 1.

[135] *Krasnaya Zvezda*, 24 Nov. 1993, p. 3.

[136] Dementyeva, I., 'Voyna i mir Prigorodnogo Rayona' ['War and peace in "Prigorodniy rayon"'], *Izvestia*, 25 Jan. 1994, p. 6; *Izvestia*, 26 Jan. 1994, p. 10; *Izvestia*, 27 Jan. 1994, p. 6; *Izvestia*, 28 Jan. 1994, p. 7; *Izvestia*, 29 Jan. 1994, p. 10.

[137] *Nezavisimaya Gazeta*, 8 Dec. 1993, p. 1.

his part, declared that sending in troops to protect the railway line that crosses the republic amounted to a declaration of war which would inevitably spread inside Russia.[138]

VII. Tajikistan

In 1993 Tajikistan remained one of the most unstable of the new independent states, suffering the effects of a two-year civil war. With a population of 5.6 million before the war, Tajikistan has suffered over 300 000 casualties. The overall number of refugees is estimated to be over 1.5 million, with half of them having to flee the country.[139]

An unfinished civil war

The claim of the head of parliament and effective head of state, Imomali Rakhmonov, that the civil war in Tajikistan is over[140] could not help but meet with serious scepticism. Despite its declared intention to proceed with national reconciliation, the Tajik Government reportedly persecutes its opponents in the most severe way—from banning opposition parties and suppressing any signs of public political disagreements[141] to assassination of and use of the death penalty against opposition politicians.[142] Significantly, the Tajik Ministry of the Interior reacted to reports by Amnesty International on civil rights violations in Tajikistan by describing the human rights group as a 'terrorist organization'.[143]

The authorities in Dushanbe denounce the opposition as threatening the country with Islamic fundamentalism. Indeed, the extremist part of the anti-government political spectrum does fit into that category. However, the extensive use of the anti-fundamentalist argument seems primarily aimed at getting rid of any opposition to the current political leadership. Fundamentalist trends might indeed be reinforced by the belligerence and atrocities being practised against opponents to the regime.

Another consequence is violence directed against the Government. Resorting extensively to force, the Tajik Government managed to suppress massive armed resistance in the country. Nevertheless, by the end of 1993, over 500 guerrillas reportedly were continuing to fight in the mountains.[144] More importantly, a significant base of armed opposition still exists, since over half of the refugees which had fled to neighbouring Afghanistan are reluctant to return because of political persecution and threats to their lives.[145] Such irre-

---

[138] *The Guardian*, 9 Dec. 1993, p. 6.
[139] *Nezavisimaya Gazeta*, 4 Nov. 1993, p. 2.
[140] *Nezavisimaya Gazeta*, 20 Nov. 1993, p. 1.
[141] *Izvestia*, 23 June 1993, p. 1.
[142] *Nezavisimaya Gazeta*, 28 Aug. 1993, p. 3.
[143] *Nezavisimaya Gazeta*, 8 Dec. 1993, p. 3.
[144] *Nezavisimaya Gazeta*, 11 Nov. 1993, p. 3.
[145] *Le Monde*, 25 Nov. 1993, p. 6.

concilable opposition provides broad opportunities for recruiting militia among the refugees.

The passage of the Mujahideen over the Tajik–Afghan frontier (which is over 1000 km long and often cuts across high mountains) has become routine, generating border conflicts and involving uncontrolled armed groups in fighting. Because of the lack of viable political structures in both countries, border control has become extremely ineffective. However, a number of local cease-fire agreements have reportedly been concluded and observed by lower-level field commanders.[146]

The situation in Tajikistan is complicated by local rivalries between élites from different regions which often tend to develop into armed clashes.[147] Neither is it clear to what extent the Gorno-Badakhshan autonomous region (in the mountainous Pamir area) will remain loyal (or at least neutral) to the central Tajik Government. The aerial bombardments reportedly organized by Dushanbe within the offensive started in August 1993 will hardly serve to increase support for the current regime in this largely inaccessible area in which opposition forces could establish a basis for long-lasting resistance.[148]

Russia's involvement

In 1993, Russia's policy towards Tajikistan changed from one of hesitation to one of active and decisive involvement. The initial reluctance seems to have been caused by, among other factors, the debate within the Russian policy-making community. Finally, Russia opted decisively for active engagement in developments in Tajikistan, which may indicate a change in Russian policy towards its other neighbours in the near abroad.

The current regime is widely believed to have been unable to come to power without support from the Russian military deployed in the republic.[149] The perceived threat of 'Islamic extremism' (or of overall chaos) was apparently viewed as outweighing the risks of a scenario similar to Soviet aggression in Afghanistan (although the latter scenario has been assessed by a number of analysts and politicians as having seriously damaged Russia's security interests).[150] Indeed, the Russian military deployed in Tajikistan has continued to play an active (if not predominant) role in preventing a new outbreak of large-scale civil war and may be the only force able to fulfil this mission.[151] This, however, will only be so if Russia is prepared forcibly to suppress the

---

[146] *Le Monde*, 25 Nov. 1993, p. 6.

[147] *Nezavisimaya Gazeta*, 28 Dec. 1993, p. 3.

[148] *Izvestia*, 5 Aug. 1993, p. 1; *Nezavisimaya Gazeta*, 3 Aug. 1993, p. 1; *Le Monde*, 10 Aug. 1993, p. 4.

[149] See 'Helsinki Watch report addressed to President Yeltsin', *Nezavisimaya Gazeta*, 9 Nov. 1993, p. 5. See also the article by Chairman of the opposition Democratic Party Shodmon Yusupov in *Nezavisimaya Gazeta*, 25 Aug. 1993, p. 1. See also the testimony of the Russian military in *Nezavisimaya Gazeta*, 9 Feb. 1994, pp. 1 and 3.

[150] *Nezavisimaya Gazeta*, 9 July 1993, p. 3; 20 July 1993, p. 2; 21 July 1993, pp. 1, 3.

[151] Orr, M., 'The civil war in Tajikistan', *Jane's Intelligence Review*, Apr. 1993, pp. 181–84.

armed opposition—which makes Moscow increasingly hostage to its political choice, thus risking involving Russia in a new 'alien' war.

It should be noted, however, that Russia, using diplomatic means, has been pressuring the leadership in Dushanbe to resolve the conflict through political rather than military means and to open a dialogue with the opposition. Indeed, such a dialogue was even presented as the main condition of support from Moscow. It is also true that this highly publicized pressure has not borne any discernible results, but this did not prevent Russia from concluding in May 1993 a bilateral Treaty on Friendship, Co-operation and Mutual Assistance with Tajikistan.[152] The first negotiations between the parties finally began in April 1994 in Moscow under the aegis of the UN and with Russian mediation.[153]

The protection of the 'external border' of Tajikistan is perceived as being of vital importance to Russian security. Alternatively, it is argued that Russia— in order to prevent a mass influx of drugs, arms and criminals from the south—would have to 'close' its newly established (and so far unmanned) frontier with Kazakhstan, which is several times longer than the external border of Tajikistan. In July 1993, a Mujahideen attack against one of the border troop posts, manned mainly by Russian military personnel, killed about 24 and wounded 18. This attack provided a decisive incentive for Moscow to take serious measures in order to keep the border under strict control.[154] Moreover, retaliatory and even preventive aerial and artillery strikes against Mujahideen bases in the border areas of Afghanistan have been reported, risking further escalation and internationalization of the conflict.[155]

One of Russia's concerns is the fate of the Russian-speaking population in Tajikistan (since the time of independence their total number has reportedly fallen from 300 000 to 80 000).[156] However, the problem is much broader and affects all of Central Asia, even if no dramatic 'exodus' has so far taken place in other republics. Foreign Minister Kozyrev considers that the situation in Central Asia is better than in the Baltic states since no official discrimination is practised—on the contrary, authorities are allegedly doing their best to keep the Russian specialists.[157] However, other sources (also from the Foreign Ministry) give a quite different assessment: cultural incompatibility and increasing pressure from regional élites create 'absolutely unacceptable conditions' for the everyday life of the Russian-speaking peoples, forcing them out. Paradoxically, migration (according to the same source) from such 'oases of democracy' in Central Asia as Kazakhstan and Kyrgyzstan is even higher than from Tajikistan,[158] whereas the idea of double citizenship strongly advocated

[152] Martin, K., 'Tajikistan: civil war without end?', *RFE/RL Research Report*, vol. 2, no. 33 (20 Aug. 1993), p. 27.

[153] *Izvestia*, 6 Apr. 1994, p. 1.

[154] See Sherr, J., 'Escalation of the Tajikistan conflict', *Jane's Intelligence Review*, Nov. 1993, pp. 514–16; Korolov, M., 'Russians thrown into Tajik breach', *The Guardian*, 6 Sep. 1993, p. 5.

[155] *Izvestia*, 31 July 1993, p. 3; *Nezavisimaya Gazeta*, 16 Nov. 1993, p. 3.

[156] 'Imperfect peace', *The Economist*, 14 Nov. 1992, p. 40.

[157] *Nezavisimaya Gazeta*, 11 Nov. 1993, p. 3.

[158] *Nezavisimaya Gazeta*, 20 Nov. 1993, p. 3; *Izvestia*, 8 Dec. 1993, p. 3.

by Moscow was accepted in December 1993 only by Turkmenistan (which has the lowest percentage of Russians living in the country).

Devastated by a large-scale civil war, Tajikistan has found itself in the worst economic situation of any post-Soviet state. There have hardly been any significant attempts at ensuring economic survival. Not surprisingly, Tajikistan was the only CIS member to accept all the conditions presented by Moscow with respect to financial integration—and the only one to renounce introducing its own currency, with the new Russian roubles being delivered by the Central Bank of Russia. Remaining in the rouble zone would certainly be helpful for preserving the economic links between the two states, the price for Russia being some additional financial burden and for Tajikistan that of a *de facto* status as an economic protectorate. Economic dependence, however, is quite in accordance with the political and military aspects of the situation in a country which has become a loyal, if extremely unstable and thus not very reliable, ally of Russia in Central Asia.[159]

A multilateral pattern

As a signatory to the 1992 Tashkent Treaty on Collective Security, Tajikistan is eligible for military assistance from the other CIS members—provided they assess the situation as a threat from 'external aggression'. The neighbouring states do have reason to be concerned with instabilities in Tajikistan, but even more threatening for most of the Central Asian regimes could have been the example of a challenge addressed to the 'renewed' communist/Soviet élites. Not surprisingly, they have substantially contributed to 'antifundamentalist alarmism' in and beyond Central Asia.

Russia, for its part, is certainly interested in not operating alone. The political (as well as military and financial) support from Tajikistan's neighbours is not only essential, but in fact a *sine qua non* since any Russian actions beyond its borders would be extremely vulnerable if not endorsed by the other CIS members. Those states, in turn, were probably seeking to off-load military costs on to Russia, while at the same time attempting to create a precedent of using Russian forces to suppress internal opponents.

Negotiations on the multilateral CIS efforts continued during much of 1993, the allies of Russia being reluctant to share costs or to send their own troops. Of the 'collective peacekeeping forces' of 25 000 troops (see above) in Tajikistan, the Russian contribution (the 201st Motorized Rifle Division deployed in the area since the Soviet times) is by far the most substantial, and the participation of four other Central Asian states, even if only symbolic, gives the intervention some legitimacy.

This legitimacy is, however, relatively limited. This might change if peacekeeping activities in Tajikistan are allowed to operate under the UN flag and efforts to protect the Tajik borders are secured by the CSCE or North Atlantic Cooperation Council (NACC). Russian diplomatic moves (for example, a

---

[159] See *Moscow News*, no. 49 (3 Dec. 1993), p. 4.

suggestion for a joint CSCE/UN peacemaking and crisis-management mission to be tested in Tajikistan)[160] have so far failed to achieve any substantial results, but they could hardly be criticized for incoherence or inconsistency.

VIII. Conclusions: Russia's role in conflict management

Instability on the territory of the former USSR seems set to become a lasting phenomenon fraught with the danger of serious conflicts. No universally effective means exist to settle the conflicts, but reducing their scope and containing them within certain limits may be a realistic prospect, provided that the parties involved are ready to devote the necessary political, financial and military resources.

During 1993 Russia substantially consolidated its position within the post-Soviet geopolitical area. Russia's economic potential, although severely damaged over the past two years, has become one of the strongest factors affecting most of the post-Soviet states. In fact, they have come to recognize that economic realities make partnership with Russia essential for their survival. This undoubtedly has important implications for conflict management throughout the former USSR, highlighting in particular the CIS pattern of peacekeeping.

Russia's direct and indirect role in the development of armed conflicts has become more prominent. Criticized for taking sides in a number of domestic conflicts (such as in Abkhazia, Tajikistan and the Trans-Dniester region), the Russian armed forces have operated as the most important or only available factor for minimizing chaos and preventing hostilities on a larger scale.

Responding to increasing domestic criticism of its alleged inability to protect the interests of Russians in the near abroad, Russia in 1993 began emphasizing the importance of a special peacemaking mission within the former Soviet Union to head off the development of a scenario resembling that of the former Yugoslavia.[161] Russia's security and other interests in the near abroad have also been highlighted as the reason (or the pretext) for more active involvement and even as a justification for assuming a kind of 'neo-imperial' 'regional superpower' role in its immediate vicinity.

Arguing that 'nobody could replace Russia in making peace' (in the former Soviet Union),[162] Russia attempted to obtain a mandate from the international community for peacekeeping within the post-Soviet area. This might legitimize a Russian military presence in neighbouring states, elicit political and possibly financial support, and provide for the sharing of responsibility in case of failure. Significantly, the Russian approach received a relatively tolerant hearing from the leading Western countries (France, Germany, Italy, the UK and the USA) but was vigorously rejected by a number of other international actors—most importantly by the countries of the near abroad themselves.

[160] *Krasnaya Zvezda*, 24 Nov. 1993, p. 3.
[161] See *Financial Times*, 2 Dec. 1993, p. 2.
[162] *Nezavisimaya Gazeta*, 22 Sep. 1993, p. 1.

Russia's increasing activism in the near abroad could be easily interpreted as a new form of covert or even open colonialism.[163] Russia is also suspected of creating (or re-creating) a sphere of influence in which access to other international actors will be denied; its proclaimed desire to involve the international community (which apparently does not fit a 'new Monroe doctrine' pattern) allegedly testifies that Moscow wants to have the West's blessing rather than letting it in; its impartiality in domestic or inter-state conflicts is also questioned. Not surprisingly, some UN officials reacted negatively as well, pointing out that peacekeepers cannot be taken from adjacent countries suspected of having too keen an interest in the outcome of a particular conflict.

However, because non-engagement in CIS affairs remains the prevailing approach in most Western countries and the UN is by no means in a position to provide peacekeepers for conflicts on the territory of the former Soviet Union, the choice might come down to a Russian-held peace or no peace at all. If so, Moscow can hardly be blamed for the lack of alternatives.

[163] See Eyal, J., 'Russia's covert colonialism', *The Independent*, 16 Nov. 1993, p. 19.

7. Europe: towards a new regional security regime

ADAM DANIEL ROTFELD

I. Introduction

The end of the cold war started the process of a fundamental transformation of the security regime in Europe. These changes were not only desired but also in various ways initiated, promoted and supported by various parties for various reasons. At first, their aim was to overcome the division of Europe[1] and to establish a system of common and co-operative security.[2] However, when the changes took place, they came as a surprise: in the event neither politicians nor experts were prepared to absorb them, so fast and radical were they. Domestically, they were not expected peacefully to change the foundations of the totalitarian system and undermine the legitimacy of one-party government. Externally, the dissolution of the Warsaw Treaty Organization (WTO) and the breakup of the Soviet Union brought a complete change of the environment determining European security. New prerequisites were created for shaping a regional security regime based on a common system of values—respect for the rule of law, democracy, pluralism, human rights and the reintroduction of the market economy. The final document of the Paris summit meeting of the Conference on Security and Co-operation in Europe (CSCE) of November 1990 stated: 'The era of confrontation and division of Europe is ended . . . Ours is a time for fulfilling the hopes and expectations our peoples have cherished for decades: steadfast commitment to democracy based on human rights and fundamental freedoms; prosperity through economic liberty and social justice; and equal security for all our countries'.[3] The signatories of the

---

[1] For example, the Final Act of the CSCE formulated as one of the goals to be pursued by the participating states 'overcoming the confrontation stemming from the character of their past relations'. Conference on Security and Co-operation in Europe, Final Act (Helsinki, 1975), reproduced in Rotfeld, A. D. (ed.), SIPRI, *From Helsinki to Helsinki and Beyond: Analysis and Documents of the Conference on Security and Co-operation in Europe, 1973–93* (Oxford University Press: Oxford, forthcoming 1994).

[2] The objectives and the terminology formulated in the Palme Report (Independent Commission on Disarmament and Security Issues, *Common Security, A Programme for Disarmament* (Pan Books: London, 1982) were taken over in NATO documents. For example, the London Declaration on a Transformed North Atlantic Alliance (6 July 1990) stated: 'We recognize that, in the new Europe, the security of every state is inseparably linked to the security of its neighbours. NATO must become an institution where Europeans, Canadians and Americans work together not only for the common defence, but to build new partnerships with all the nations of Europe. The Atlantic Community must reach out to the countries of the East which were our adversaries in the Cold War, and extend to them the hand of friendship.' The text is reproduced in Rotfeld, A. D. and Stützle, W. (eds), SIPRI, *Germany and Europe in Transition* (Oxford University Press: Oxford, 1991), p. 150.

[3] The Charter of Paris for a New Europe, reproduced in SIPRI, *SIPRI Yearbook 1991: World Armaments and Disarmament* (Oxford University Press: Oxford, 1991), appendix 17B, pp. 603–10.

Charter of Paris also recognized 'the freedom of States to choose their own security arrangements'.[4] These declarations were reaffirmed two years later, in the CSCE Helsinki Summit Declaration of 10 July 1992. In that document the new experience of instability, conflicts and new threats had already found expression: 'Still, the legacy of the past remains strong. We are faced with challenges and opportunities, but also with serious difficulties and disappointments'.[5]

The transformation of the security regime in Europe has encountered fundamental problems. Formulation of the goals and the programme has been found to be much easier than putting the accords into effect, for three reasons.

First, it emerged that, although the WTO has ceased to exist, the division of Europe into two zones has not been overcome. An invisible line separates the European states of greater and assured security, united within the framework of NATO and the European Union (EU), from the Central and East European (CEE) states, which are not anchored in any security structures and are effectively left outside the main current of the integrating world. Moreover, some of these countries have found themselves in conflict with others or involved in national and ethnic tensions and conflicts.

Second, European security is determined in equal measure by international and by domestic circumstances. The main challenges for European security in 1993 are the war in Bosnia and Herzegovina and the crisis developing in Russia and on other former Soviet territories. The economic recession in the West in 1993 has been accompanied by a deep slump in the East, particularly in the Baltic states, Belarus, Russia, Ukraine and other countries which declared their independence after the collapse of the Soviet Union. The situation in this part of Europe, including Albania, Bulgaria and Romania, in many respects bears analogy with that of the Weimar Republic after World War I. This is a conflict-engendering, even explosive state of affairs, the origins of which are not external but internal threats.

Third, the existing multilateral security structures in Europe, however numerous and well-functioning, are not fully adequate to the new requirements and challenges. Even more important, in the ongoing political debate a new strategy or new organization of regional security has not yet emerged to which the main actors would be ready to subordinate or entrust their own national security.

In this context, some basic questions were raised in 1993. How should the European security system be transformed? Could Russia and the CEE states be integrated into the existing West European security structures, and if so how?[6] What kind of relations would develop between NATO and Russia?

[4] See note 3.

[5] CSCE, Helsinki Document 1992: The Challenges of Change, partly reproduced in *SIPRI Yearbook 1993: World Armaments and Disarmament* (Oxford University Press: Oxford, 1993), appendix 5A, pp. 190–209. In this context, it is worth mentioning that the programme adopted at Helsinki has no longer declared the goal of equal security, but promised to intensify co-operation for democracy, prosperity and 'equal rights of security' (para. 4).

[6] Central and Eastern Europe includes Bulgaria, the Czech Republic, Hungary, Poland, Romania and Slovakia.

Should the CEE states be kept out of NATO and be recognized as a zone of special security interest for Russia? What kind of US or transformed NATO involvement in the security of CEE was possible—common defence or a co-operative security organization? What role was to be played by the CSCE in the functioning of a new European security system?

II. The main determinants

The process of shaping a regional security system abounds in internal contradictions. In 1993, tendencies towards integration were dominant in Western Europe, culminating in the entry into force of the Treaty on European Union (the Maastricht Treaty) and the provisions for a 'common foreign and security policy'.[7] Numerous differences notwithstanding, within this group of states the search for a common denominator has been paramount.[8]

In the area described today as the CEE states, disintegration has progressed.[9] Divergencies have been increasing and clashes of interest have reappeared between the former WTO members and Russia, between the participants in the Visegrad Group (the Czech Republic, Hungary, Poland and Slovakia), and between the states formed on the territory of the former Soviet Union. A sort of race began among the CEE states for a better starting position in the run-up to joining the EU and NATO.[10] Russia has counteracted this tendency in various ways, directly and indirectly. The political fragmentation of the CEE states is demonstrated by their attitude to basic security challenges. It was highlighted in their responses to the development of events in Russia, in their complete inaction and helplessness in the face of the war in Bosnia and Herzegovina, and in their inability to formulate a common position on fundamental security issues during the visit of US President Bill Clinton to Europe in January 1994.[11] In their turn, the Western states have pursued a dual-track political strategy towards their eastern neighbours, on the one hand encouraging the states of the subregion to get closer to each other,[12] and on the other

---

[7] European Communities, Treaty on European Union (European Communities, Office for Official Publications: Luxembourg, 1992), Title V: Provisions on a Common Foreign and Security Policy, pp. 123–29. The Provisions on a Common Foreign and Security Policy are partly reproduced in appendix 7A. See also figure 7.1 and section VI in this chapter.

[8] George, B., 'European and transatlantic security in a revolutionary age', North Atlantic Assembly, Political Committee, 1993 Reports, Oct. 1993, p. 6.

[9] For a broader discussion of the causes of this state of affairs, see Cowen Karp, R. (ed.), SIPRI, Central and Eastern Europe: The Challenge of Transition (Oxford University Press: Oxford, 1993), pp. 9–11.

[10] The Prime Minister of the Czech Republic, Vaclav Klaus, openly came out against co-operation within the Visegrad Group, 'for fear of the Czech Republic being held back in its own drive to obtain membership in the EC and NATO. The Czech Republic's shift toward a go-it-alone approach since 1992 has not ended co-operation altogether, but it has cast doubt on how much the Visegrad Group can accomplish.' See Security for Europe Project: Final Report, Dec. 1993 (Center for Foreign Policy Development of the Thomas J. Watson, Jr Institute for International Studies, Brown University: Providence, R.I., 1993), pp. 50–51.

[11] US Information Service, Stockholm, 'Clinton European trip, news background' (Special Edition), 9–14 Jan. 1994.

[12] 'The tendency for the West to handle the region as a bloc strengthened in 1993 . . . A group of six instead of three is being mentioned, so underlining the view that a bloc approach will make the region's

hand under various pretences putting off a decision on the inclusion of those states in the West European political, military and economic structures.[13]

The centrifugal tendencies and a kind of re-nationalization of security policies have not, however, hindered the process of institutionalization initiated four years ago on the pan-European level within the CSCE. This involves both the process of political consultation and the development of new structures and missions. They serve early-warning, conflict-prevention, conflict-management and conflict-resolution functions and are known in the European context as the tools of preventive diplomacy.[14]

It remains to be seen which of the existing institutions is willing and to what extent it is willing to fill the security vacuum left after the dissolution of the WTO and the collapse of the bipolar system. The question is on what foundations the future regional security system in Europe will rest. Will it be a restructured and expanded North Atlantic Alliance, a developed concept of security identity within the EU or a pan-European organization for security as agreed in CSCE negotiations and covering the area from Vancouver in the west to Vladivostok in the east?

III. Towards an expanded NATO

The question of expanding NATO eastward has dominated the political debate on the future of the North Atlantic Alliance. Three principal attitudes have come to the fore: (a) determined opposition to expansion, (b) advocacy of accepting new members into the Alliance, particularly those from the CEE region, and (c) support for a middle-of-the-road course such as postponing the decision, formulating preconditions or providing for associate status or other step-by-step solutions. The attitude of the main NATO powers to the CEE countries' wish to join NATO was differentiated and evolved during 1993. Germany has stood for expanding NATO eastward; the UK has been against this; the USA has oscillated between these two extremes; and France introduced a draft Pact for Stability in Europe (the 'Balladur Plan', described in section IV). The debate which in previous years had been rather theoretical

---

problems easier to handle and help the small countries of the region to enter the institutions of European integration of secondary importance.' See a report published by three Hungarian research institutes—the Center for Security and Defence Studies, the Institute for World Economics and the Hungarian Institute of Foreign Affairs: *The World in 1993, A Hungarian View* (Budapest, Dec. 1993), p. 16.

[13] Latawski, P., 'Droga Polski do NATO—problemy i perspektywy' [Poland's road to NATO—problems and perspectives], *Sprawy Międzynarodowe*, no. 3 (1993), pp. 8ff.; Parzymies, S., 'Unia Europejska a Europa Środkowa [The European Union and Central Europe], *Sprawy Międzynarodowe*, no. 3 (1993), pp. 89–110. For the causes of NATO's reluctance to accept the CEE states, see also Taylor, T., 'NATO and Central Europe', *NATO Review*, Oct. 1991, pp. 18–19.

[14] CSCE, Secretary General, *Annual Report 1993 on CSCE Activities* (CSCE: Vienna, 31 Oct. 1993), reproduced in Rotfeld (note 1). See also the three relevant chapters by A. D. Rotfeld in the *SIPRI Yearbooks 1991–1993*: 'New security structures in Europe: concepts, proposals and decisions', *SIPRI Yearbook 1991* (note 3), pp. 585–600; 'European security structures in transition', *SIPRI Yearbook 1992: World Armaments and Disarmament* (Oxford University Press: Oxford, 1992), pp. 563–82; 'The CSCE: towards a security organization', *SIPRI Yearbook 1993* (note 5), pp. 171–218, and the introductory chapter in this volume.

and concerned rather vague hypothetical situations[15] in 1993 has had to deal with specific operational decisions and political developments.

Different countries' positions concerning a future security system in Europe have been mainly shaped following political events in Russia and the war in Bosnia and Herzegovina.[16] One view is that 'NATO is the true Great Power in Europe today'[17] and should guarantee 'existing frontiers in the Balkans and Eastern Europe, so as to deprive transnational ethnic rivalry of its political and military explosiveness'.[18] Opponents of such a political concept asserted that 'such a course reflects philosophical inertia, an inability or unwillingness to jettison old concepts and models of thought in the face of utterly changed circumstances'.[19] Some US analysts argued that the political West (i.e., NATO) 'is not a natural construct but a highly artificial one . . . It is extremely doubtful whether it can now survive the disappearance of that enemy' (a hostile East).[20] In their opinion the question of expanding NATO is of much less importance than that of its continued existence in the shape in which it has functioned over the past 45 years.

The Western view

The plans to expand NATO membership have provoked contradictory responses both in the East and in the West. The obstacles for new CEE states on the road to NATO membership generally fall into two categories, political and functional.[21]

The political obstacles are mainly consideration for Russia and fears of entangling NATO in national and ethnic conflicts among CEE nations. Moving NATO to the east would—in the view of the opponents of expanding the Atlantic Alliance—hinder democratic changes in security policy inside Russia, separate Russia from Europe and deepen its sense of threat and isolation. In effect, it would facilitate an enhancement of the role and impact of nationalist–conservative forces and in the longer run contribute to a new militarization of Russian foreign policy.

NATO politicians have expressed an opinion that admission of CEE states to the Atlantic Alliance will be interpreted in Russia as an attempt to isolate, encircle and separate it from the West. For the West, for many reasons the

---

[15] Some examples of this are the discussions initiated by articles such as: Snyder, J., 'Averting anarchy in the new Europe', *International Security*, vol. 14, no. 4 (spring 1990), pp. 5–41; Mearsheimer, J. J., 'Back to the future: instability in Europe after the cold war', *International Security*, vol. 15, no. 1 (summer 1990), pp. 5–56; van Evera, S., 'Primed for peace: Europe after the cold war', *International Security*, vol. 15, no. 3 (winter 1990–91), pp. 7–57.

[16] Two essays on NATO's future in *Foreign Affairs,* Sep.–Oct. 1993, presented opposing views. Three analysts from the Rand Corporation (R. D. Asmus, R. L. Kugler and F. S. Larrabee) argued that NATO is the only potentially effective security organization for an enlarged Europe. See Asmus, R. D. *et al.*, 'Building a new NATO', *Foreign Affairs,* Sep.–Oct. 1993, pp. 28–40. Another concept was presented in the same issue by O. Harries: 'The collapse of "the West"', pp. 41–53.

[17] Pfaff, W., 'Invitation to war', *Foreign Affairs* (summer 1993), p. 99.

[18] Pfaff (note 17), p. 107.

[19] Harries (note 16), p. 41.

[20] Harries (note 16), p. 42.

[21] Some of those obstacles were characterized in a systematic way by Latawski (note 13), pp. 67–88.

Russian position on the issue of expanding NATO was essential in making a decision. The Western states' attitude has been contingent upon the transformation taking place in Russia and on caution about anything that could even potentially harm the process of democratic reform or strengthen the conservative camp there. President Clinton addressed the following questions to the North Atlantic summit meeting in Brussels on 10 January 1994: 'Why should we now draw a new line through Europe just a little further east? Why should we now do something which could foreclose the best possible future for Europe?' He went on to answer: 'The best possible future would be a democratic Russia committed to the security of all its European neighbours. The best possible future would be a democratic Ukraine, a democratic government in every one of the newly-independent states of the former Soviet Union, all committed to market co-operation, to common security and to democratic ideals. We should not foreclose that possibility'.[22] It has remained unclear to what extent admission of Central European states to NATO would close or make difficult the road to democratic change and the market economy in the East.

Russia, however, was not the only reason for the Atlantic Alliance's unwillingness to give any security guarantees to Central and Eastern Europe. Among the reasons for Western restraint, caution and sometimes overt reluctance on the part of the West European security structures to embrace the new democracies in Eastern Europe is above all the lack of an overall future-oriented vision or concept of security. In such a situation the only response is the rationalization of the prevailing conservative policy, accompanied by declarations about the need for change, adjustment to new challenges and threats, and so on. Most often the solution to the problems of today is being sought in the concepts which were tried and tested in the past. In effect, the new rhetoric, new institutions and procedures were to revive the old concept of the balance of power. A conservative approach has gained the upper hand, directed at maintaining NATO's functions and mandate in their present shape. The rationale for this was fear that basic reforms can only promote centrifugal tendencies, lead to the Alliance's disintegration, and shift tensions to the western part of the continent.

NATO states have not definitely determined their attitude towards the concept of expanding the Alliance. Various views have been voiced, but doubts and reservations have been predominant and there is widespread awareness that a decision with respect to one of the CEE states or the Visegrad Group would open the question of membership of other states.[23] The admission to NATO of such a large group of former adversaries when the Alliance has no clear enemy would change both the area covered by the guarantees of the

---

[22] See President Clinton's remarks to the North Atlantic Council Summit, Brussels, 10 Jan. 1994: US Information Service, Stockholm, *Wireless File*, 10 Jan. 1994, p. 4.

[23] At various stages such a wish has been expressed by almost all the states of the region—Bulgaria, Romania and the 4 members of the Visegrad Group—and by Albania, Slovenia, Ukraine and Lithuania, which formally applied for membership in Jan. 1994.

1949 North Atlantic Treaty[24] and, more importantly, the character and ways of managing and functioning of the Alliance. The institutions shaped to suit the needs of its 16 members would have to be substantially rebuilt. The Alliance would turn into a system of collective security, a role for which it is not prepared.

The functional obstacles include the necessity of major restructuring—changes in training, command and equipment of the armed forces of the former WTO members—requiring new infrastructure and heavy expenditure both by the states applying for membership and by existing members. The fundamental obstacle, however, is connected with the fact that the majority of Alliance members do not identify their individual and collective security interests with NATO's shift to the east. At the same time the line of division between proponents and opponents of NATO expansion runs not between individual states but inside the states members of the Alliance which have political decisions to take on this matter.

The inclusion of the CEE states in NATO would mean a fundamental change of the Alliance. This is why a definition of criteria for membership of NATO is essential. These criteria would include in particular a commitment on the part of new members to respect the principles of democracy in their internal order, civil political control over the armed forces, renunciation of any territorial claims, respect for human rights and the rights of minorities in these states and full participation in various forms of NATO activity, from peace-keeping to armed defence.

Specific recommendations presented by the proponents of radical transformation of NATO have been confined to the enlargement of Alliance[25] and institutional reforms.[26]

One particular question is that of a new role for the USA and the extent to which it identifies its own national security interests with the security of Europe as a whole. In this context two positions in the ongoing debate deserve attention. The proponents of limited US involvement in European affairs argue that the Clinton Administration 'has an ambitious domestic agenda and little interest in or feel for foreign policy';[27] opponents interpret it as a 'possible US retreat from global leadership in the name of multilateralism'[28] and see a new strategic bargain between Europe and the USA in a quite different way: new strategic challenges emerging throughout Europe 'could directly impact vital American national interests'.[29] From that point of view the debate on military involvement in Bosnia and Herzegovina is a conflict about allied

---

[24] North Atlantic Treaty, Washington, DC, 4 Apr. 1949, reproduced as appendix I in *NATO Handbook* (NATO, Office of Information and Press: Brussels, 1992), pp. 143–46.

[25] See more on this in the report published by the Windsor Group, *NATO: The Case for Enlargement* (Institute for European Defence and Strategic Studies: [London], Dec. 1993), pp. 7–12.

[26] Asmus *et al.* (note 16), p. 39.

[27] Harries (note 16), p. 52.

[28] Lugar, R., 'NATO: out of area or out of business,' Address given by a member of the US Senate Foreign Relations and Intelligence Committees and Co-Chairman of the Senate Arms Control Observers Group before the Overseas Writers Club on 24 June 1993. See US Information Service, Stockholm, *Wireless File,* 7 July 1993, pp. 24–28.

[29] See Lugar (note 28), p. 24.

unity and the willingness of Europeans and Americans to adjust their cold war political and security institutions and missions to the changing geostrategic circumstances in and around Europe.

Senator Richard Lugar has criticized the US Administration concept which classifies Western Europe as a vital interest of the USA, while the CEE countries are not. 'This narrow American definition of American interests is becoming a kind of new conventional wisdom. It is wrong and needs to be corrected.'[30] The present Administration strategy, he argues, mostly amounts to a new rhetoric and some amendments to the existing institutions and procedures; Senator Lugar demands changes in the very nature of NATO. 'The choice is not between an old NATO and a new NATO, but rather between a new NATO and no NATO.'[31] The gist of his proposal and the arguments of other proponents of radical change[32] can be summarized as follows. In the light of new threats, the concept of security cannot be confined to maintaining old structures, the aim of which was the defence of Western Europe, but must be to forge a more balanced alliance capable of dealing with the new instability to the east and the south. Along with the end of the cold war, the strategic distinction between Europe's centre and its periphery has been wiped away.[33] Instability in the East threatens to revive old rivalries between Germany and Russia. The distinction between what were known during the cold war as 'in area' and 'out of area' crises has become ambiguous and artificial. Furthermore, the majority of future conflicts will probably fall into what was in the past considered 'out of area'. In other words, what was formerly on the margin should be seen now and in the future as a central issue.

Russia's view

The Russian position on this matter was until 1993 ambiguous. During his visit to Warsaw on 25 August 1993, President Boris Yeltsin stated that he sympathized with Poland's desire to join NATO. A formula in the Joint Polish–Russian Declaration of 25 August 1993 reflected this.[34] However, having returned to Moscow, Yeltsin revised his position. On 15 September 1993 he wrote a letter to President Clinton and other Western leaders in which he opposed the possible admission of the CEE states to NATO. He pointed out that such a decision would provoke a negative response on the part of Russian society. 'Not only the opposition, but the moderates, too, would no doubt see this as a sort of neo-isolation of the country, as opposed to its natural introduc-

---

[30] See Lugar (note 28), p. 25.

[31] See Lugar (note 28), p. 29. Prof. Michael Mandelbaum also described the choice as that 'between a new NATO and no NATO', *Washington Post*, 6 Sep. 1993. See also Odom, W. E., 'Strategic realignment in Europe: NATO's obligation to the East', in *NATO: The Case for Enlargement* (note 25).

[32] See the view expressed by the group of senior analysts at the RAND Corporation in Asmus *et al.* (note 16).

[33] Asmus *et al.* (note 16), p. 29.

[34] 'ITAR-TASS carries Russian–Polish Joint Declaration', Foreign Broadcast Information Service, *Daily Report—Central Eurasia (FBIS–SOV)*, FBIS-SOV-93-164, 26 Aug. 1993, pp. 13–15. President Yeltsin said: '[s]uch a move would not be counter to Russian interests nor to the pan-European integration process'. See *International Herald Tribune*, 26 Aug. 1993.

tion into the Euro-Atlantic space'.[35] He drew attention to the fact that the Treaty on the Final Settlement with Respect to Germany[36] prohibited the stationing of foreign troops in Germany's eastern *Länder*, thus ruling out any possibility of expansion of the NATO area to the east. Russia, asserted Yeltsin, favoured a situation in which its relations with NATO would be 'by several degrees warmer than those between the Alliance and Eastern Europe'.[37] In other words, Russia did not treat NATO as an enemy—on the contrary, it wished to move closer to the Alliance—but it did not wish CEE states to become NATO members, since that would mean that they could not be seen either as a Russian security zone or as a zone of Russian special interest and rights. At the end of his letter, President Yeltsin expressed Russia's readiness, 'together with NATO, to offer official security guarantees to the East European states with a focus on ensuring sovereignty, territorial integrity, inviolability of frontiers, and maintenance of peace in the region. Such guarantees could be stipulated in a political statement or co-operation agreement between the Russian Federation and NATO'.[38] In this way Russia signalled that it seeks a *droit de regard* over the decision on expanding the Alliance, on the one hand, and pretends to determine the ways and forms of ensuring the security of its close neighbours, on the other.

The will and positions of the CEE states were simply ignored in the letter. It is telling that they had not expressed any interest in guarantees by Russia. The Yeltsin letter clearly referred to the NATO debate on the further evolution of the Atlantic Alliance and its role in new circumstances.[39] The overtly stated goal was to stave off decisions which would prejudge the matter of NATO's eastward expansion. It is worth recalling here that, in accordance with Article 10 of the North Atlantic Treaty of 1949, admission to NATO is decided only by the member states.[40] Furthermore, Principle I of the Final Act of the CSCE (1975) provides that participating states 'have the right to belong or not to belong to international organizations, to be or not to be a party to bilateral or multilateral treaties including the right to be or not be a party to treaties of alliance; they also have the right to neutrality'.[41] Russia's interpretation is that those rights may be exercised under the conditions defined by it as being in accordance with Russia's national security interests.

[35] See the letter of Russian President Boris Yeltsin to US President Bill Clinton, 15 Sep. 1993, reproduced in appendix 7A.
[36] Treaty on the Final Settlement with Respect to Germany (Moscow, 12 Sep. 1990), reproduced in Rotfeld and Stützle (note 2), pp. 183–85.
[37] See note 35.
[38] See note 35.
[39] In his letter, Yeltsin wrote: 'We know that at present preparations are under way for a special NATO summit meeting which will be discussing strategic aspects of the Alliance's evolution and its role in new conditions' (note 35).
[40] 'The Parties may, by unanimous agreement, invite any other European State in a position to further the principles of this Treaty and to contribute to the security of the North Atlantic area to accede to this Treaty.' See *NATO Handbook* (note 24) p. 145.
[41] Conference on Security and Co-operation in Europe, Final Act (note 1), p. 10.

The Central and East European view

In 1993, the choice was made and officially declared by all states of the region. The reasons for this choice were the changes in the domestic system, the will to make themselves permanently independent from Russia, irrespective of whether it is a communist or anti-communist power, and the need for political stability rather than any military threat.[42] The increased interest of the new democracies in joining the Atlantic structures and, even more, the European ones—the EU and the Western European Union (WEU)—results from the fear that in the face of the dramatic development of the situation in Russia they might find themselves in a zone of increased threat or of 'thinned-out' security.[43] Given the vacuum which was left after the dissolution of the Warsaw Pact, they might be treated by Russia as a 'buffer zone' or an area of Russian security interest. In particular, their interest also arises from the possibility of power in Russia being taken by proponents of neo-imperial, militaristic and nationalist policy. Internally, NATO membership would promote stability of system transformation, the strengthening of political pluralism, respect for democratic freedoms and human rights, and the development of a market economy. From this point of view, the setting of criteria—political and economic stability—which would qualify states for membership of NATO was demanded.[44] Externally, the Atlantic Alliance has become a priority in the security policies of the CEE states and is no longer seen as one of the dilemmas.[45]

An open question remains the premises and time-scale of implementation of the new West-oriented policy. For many analysts it was obvious that admission cannot take place immediately. The debate which started and the comments of politicians have rather aimed to usher in a process and outline a timetable for NATO membership. In this context, it has been pointed out that there is a distinction between the status of signatory of the North Atlantic Treaty (France is among the 16) and being part of the integrated military structure (which France is not). A step-by-step process of inclusion of the CEE states in NATO is sought: at first, countries of the region would be given a kind of 'soft' security guarantee, accompanied by increasing direct co-ordination and co-operation with the Alliance.[46] The second phase, after signing the North Atlantic Treaty, would lead to the finalization of adjustment actions initiated earlier, including the adoption of new military doctrines, organizational and logistic changes, rearmament and the development of new defence infrastruc-

---

[42] The opinions of representatives of the Visegrad Group, for instance, were systematically presented in *NATO: The Case for Enlargement* (note 25) in contributions by Svetoslav Bombik (Slovakia), Pavel Bratinka (Czech Republic), Jerzy M. Nowakowski (Poland), W. E. Odom (USA) and Tamas Waschler (Hungary).

[43] Kuźniar, R., 'Jak wyjść ze strefy rozrzedzonego bezpieczeństwa' [How to get out of the zone of thinned-out security], *Rzeczpospolita*, 18 Oct. 1993, p. 19.

[44] Bratinka (note 42).

[45] *Report on the State of National Security: External Aspects* (Polish Institute of International Affairs: Warsaw, 1993), p. 60.

[46] Kuźniar (note 43), p. 19.

tures adequate to NATO standards. The third and last phase would be incorporation into the military organization of the Atlantic Alliance.

In Central Europe, such institutional links with the West have been sought as would make the process of transformation irreversible. 'Since full membership in the EU is realistically not available until the end of this decade, NATO is the only structure able to help us reach this objective rapidly and safely.'[47] These words of the Hungarian Foreign Minister were echoed by numerous politicians of the Visegrad Group and other states of the region.[48] For those states a main threat is uncertainty about the situation and the sense of isolation *vis-à-vis* the reviving neo-imperial ambitions of Russia.

Their calls addressed to NATO, the WEU and the EU were not left unanswered.

IV. Towards a security partnership

The essential transformations and changes in the security landscape in 1993 forced all the relevant Western structures and pan-European institutions painfully to confront their identity crisis. The process of transformation started earlier has been speeded up in the light of the new situation—the developments in Russia, the war in Bosnia and Herzegovina, mounting ethnic conflicts and CEE expectations. After an intense debate, a number of decisions taken by NATO (October 1993–January 1994) and the WEU (November 1993) aimed at an institutional rapprochement with the CEE countries. Considering them together with the relevant decisions and organizational changes which were adopted at the fourth meeting of the Council of the Ministers of the CSCE in Rome in November–December 1993, one can speak of a preliminary outline of a new regional security system in Europe.

The NATO Travemünde meeting

An informal discussion meeting of the defence ministers of the Atlantic Alliance in Travemünde (20–21 October 1993) was a reaction equally to the mounting crisis in NATO[49] and to the demands of Central and Eastern Europe.

---

[47] Jeszensky, G., 'Central Europe: slow return to the West', *Hungarian Observer,* vol. 7, no. 2 (Feb. 1994), p. 2.

[48] See, e.g., the article by the Minister of Foreign Affairs of Poland, Andrzej Olechowski, 'Polska chce zostać członkiem NATO: Jak wyjść z szarej strefy bezpieczeństwa' [Poland wants to be a NATO member. How to get out of the grey zone of security], *Rzeczpospolita,* 29 Dec. 1993: '[US Secretary of State Warren] Christopher called Central Europe "a vacuum in terms of security and stability". Life abhors a vacuum. Therefore a question arises who will fill it and when and how. Indeed, in this context one must see our strivings to consolidate the relations with the USA and other institutions responsible for Western security.' Zbigniew Brzezinski in 'The way forward for an inspired NATO', *International Herald Tribune,* 2 Dec. 1993, answering the question how NATO should respond to the security vacuum in CEE, contended that a NATO-sponsored 'coalition for regional security' could involve tighter coordination and integration by stages of Central European states into NATO's command, logistic, planning and training systems.

[49] Summarized by Scott Sullivan: 'When the Soviet empire collapsed in 1989, the North Atlantic Organization lost the best enemy it ever had. In Western defence circles, cynics suggested that it had also

They focused their two-day discussion on five subjects: (*a*) the situation in the former Yugoslavia; (*b*) wider perspectives of NATO's role in peacekeeping; (*c*) transatlantic solidarity and the development of a European Security and Defence Identity; (*d*) the future of defence-related co-operation with countries of CEE; and (*e*) the danger of proliferation of weapons of mass destruction and ballistic missiles.[50]

It was the first meeting of this kind. Although the subjects for discussion were official US proposals, it was not intended to make any decisions in Travemünde, but to prepare a joint position before the NATO summit meeting in Brussels (10 January 1994). One of the proposals concerned a Partnership for Peace (PFP) with CEE countries, and another aimed at giving US concerns about the proliferation of nuclear and other weapons and missiles a higher priority on the NATO agenda and particularly that for the January 1994 summit meeting.[51] Discussions on extending security co-operation to CEE countries and statements by NATO Secretary General Manfred Wörner, US Secretary of Defense Les Aspin and German Defence Minister Volker Rühe sought to explain that, while the proposed partnership—joint training, exercises and consultation—would exclude immediate membership or NATO security guarantees, they would not rule them out forever.[52] The Travemünde meeting took up 'the broad topic of relations, with a view toward defining a new and closer net of contacts with neighbours and institutions'.[53] Wörner's concept of 'affiliate membership' for the CEE countries in NATO—a link with the Alliance in the form of political consultations but without the security guarantees under Article 5 of the North Atlantic Treaty—was also discussed.[54]

The Aspin plan and statements made by other ministers stressed the need for a 'strategic relationship' with Russia and Ukraine. Other issues of high priority for NATO's long-term future under consideration in Travemünde included the forms of a closer relationship between NATO and the emerging European Security and Defence Identity and ties with the WEU, intended to avoid duplication on the one hand and to improve the climate between the two pillars of the Alliance on the other.[55]

---

lost its reason for being and should be discreetly disbanded. Four years later NATO's future is more of an issue than ever.' 'NATO's identity crisis', *Newsweek*, 1 Nov. 1993, p. 8.

[50] See NATO Press Communiqué M-DM-1(93)64, Brussels, 21 Oct. 1993.

[51] *Atlantic News*, no. 2564, 22 Oct. 1993.

[52] See note 51.

[53] See note 51.

[54] Article 5 of the Washington Treaty of 4 Apr. 1949 defines the security guarantees as follows: 'The Parties agree that an armed attack against one or more of them in Europe or North America shall be considered an attack against them all, and consequently they agree that, if such an armed attack occurs, each of them, in exercise of the right of individual or collective self-defence recognised by Article 51 of the Charter of the United Nations, will assist the Party or Parties so attacked by taking forthwith, individually, and in concert with the other Parties, such action as it deems necessary, including the use of armed force, to restore and maintain the security of the North Atlantic area. Any such armed attack and all measures taken as a result thereof shall immediately be reported to the Security Council. Such measures shall be terminated when the Security Council has taken the measures necessary to restore and maintain international peace and security.' *NATO Handbook* (note 23), p. 144.

[55] See note 51.

The EU and the WEU

The Treaty on European Union entered into force on 1 November 1993.[56] In this document the 12 member states committed themselves to 'define and implement a common foreign and security policy'.[57] The objectives of this policy were defined as follows:

– to safeguard the common values, fundamental interests and independence of the Union;
– to strengthen the security of the Union and its Member States in all ways;
– to preserve peace and strengthen international security, in accordance with the principles of the United Nations Charter as well as the principles of the Helsinki Final Act and the objectives of the Paris Charter;
– to promote international co-operation;
– to develop and consolidate democracy and the rule of law, and respect for human rights and fundamental freedoms.[58]

The Maastricht Treaty obliged the member states to support 'the Union's external and security policy actively and unreservedly in a spirit of loyalty and mutual solidarity'.[59] It determines unambiguously the scope of obligations of the present and future participants of the EU: irrespective of whether those states were formerly neutral, upon ratification of the Treaty on European Union they are bound to accept its provisions 'unreservedly'. The body co-ordinating the common security policy is the Council which 'shall define a common position'. Member states have to ensure that their national policies conform to the common positions;[60] they have to co-ordinate their actions in international organizations and at international conferences, 'including the eventual framing of a common defence policy, which might in time lead to a common defence'.[61]

The WEU is, under the Maastricht Treaty, an integral part of the development of the Union. It is requested to elaborate and implement decisions and actions of the Union which have defence implications. The necessary practical arrangements will be adopted by the Council in agreement with the WEU institutions.[62] The policies of the EU have to respect obligations undertaken by the member states under the North Atlantic Treaty.[63] In other words, EU decisions should be compatible with the common security and defence policy established within the framework of NATO and the WEU. This does not

---

[56] Commonly known as the Maastricht Treaty, it was agreed by the Heads of State or Government of the European Community at Maastricht on 11 Dec. 1991, was signed on 7 Feb. 1992 and entered into force on 1 Nov. 1993 after ratification by all member states.
[57] Treaty on European Union (note 7), Article J.1, p. 123.
[58] Treaty on European Union (note 7), Article J.1.2, pp. 123–24.
[59] A member of the Union, reads Article J.1.4, 'shall refrain from any action which is contrary to the interests of the Union or likely to impair its effectiveness as a cohesive force in international relations'. See Treaty on European Union (note 7), p. 124.
[60] Treaty on European Union (note 7), Article J.2.2, p. 124.
[61] Treaty on European Union (note 7), Article J.4.1, p. 126.
[62] Treaty on European Union (note 7), Article J.4.2, p. 126.
[63] Treaty on European Union (note 7), Article J.4.4, p. 126.

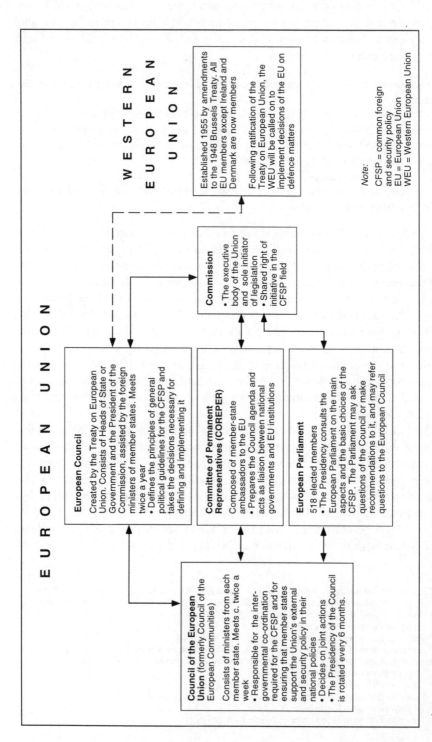

Figure 7.1. European Union institutions in the field of foreign, security and defence policy

exclude or prevent the development of closer co-operation between two or more states on a bilateral level in the WEU and the Atlantic Alliance. An illustration of this type of bilateral co-operation is the agreement governing relations between NATO and the Franco-German corps, signed in Brussels on 21 January 1993 by the Supreme Allied Commander, Europe (SACEUR) and the German and French chiefs of staff.[64] It should be noted that under this agreement the Franco-German corps, decided upon in October 1991 by President François Mitterrand of France and Chancellor Helmut Kohl of Germany, will be under NATO operational command in the event of attack— a sign that French defence and security policy moved closer towards that of the Atlantic Alliance during 1993.[65]

On 29 October 1993, on the eve of the Treaty's entry into force, the European Council confirmed in its conclusions that the Union's common policy will embrace all aspects of security.[66] European security, the adopted document states, will strive to reduce the risks and uncertainties that could impair the territorial integrity and political independence of the Union and its member states, their democratic character and economic stability or the stability of neighbouring states. In this context, the task of the WEU is to put fully into effect the provisions of the Treaty as soon as possible. The WEU Council of Ministers reaffirmed that the WEU was fully prepared to play its new role under the Treaty on European Union and the Maastricht Declaration of the WEU member states.[67] The ministers also stressed their resolve to develop the WEU as a European pillar of the North Atlantic Alliance.

The declared goals have not been restricted to Western Europe. On 12 November 1993, almost two weeks after the Maastricht Treaty came into force, the foreign ministers of France and Germany visiting Warsaw supported Poland and other CEE states in their search for 'a closer association with European and transatlantic security structures'.[68] France and Germany considered it 'a natural extension of the increasingly close co-operation of those states with the European Union' given the prospect of their accession. During the Warsaw meeting, ministers Alain Juppé and Klaus Kinkel informed their Polish counterpart, Andrzej Olechowski, that the NATO summit meeting in January 1994 would neither make a decision regarding the admission of Poland and other CEE states to the North Atlantic Alliance nor set a timetable for their accession.[69] For this reason a specific form of co-operation in defence

---

[64] The agreement itself was not published. During the signing ceremony, NATO Secretary General Manfred Wörner expressed the view that that agreement was 'a cornerstone in the building of a new Euro-Atlantic security order'. *Atlantic News*, no. 2492 (22 Jan. 1993); *Le Monde*, 12 Mar. 1993.

[65] France accepted this provision in Mar. 1993: *Le Monde*, 12 Mar. 1993. Since Apr. 1993, France has participated in the debates in the NATO Military Committee.

[66] Conseil européen de Bruxelles, Conclusions de la Présidence, 29 Oct. 1993.

[67] WEU, Luxembourg Declaration of the WEU Council of Ministers, 22 Nov. 1993 (WEU Press notice). The Maastricht Declaration is the Declaration on Western European Union by Belgium, Germany, Spain, France, Italy, Luxembourg, the Netherlands, Portugal and the UK on the role of the WEU and its relations with the EU and the Atlantic Alliance, published as part of the Final Act of the Treaty on European Union. See Treaty on European Union (note 7), pp. 242–46.

[68] Réunion des Ministres des affaires étrangères d'Allemagne, de Pologne et de France, Déclaration commune, Warsaw, 12 Nov. 1993.

[69] *Stuttgarter Zeitung,* 13 Nov. 1993.

and security matters with Poland and other CEE states could be an association with the WEU; however, this would not give any guarantees of security. France and Germany did not consult the UK or other WEU members about the promises given in Warsaw. In effect, their common position was the lowest common political denominator. Consequently, the WEU Council of Ministers declaration adopted 10 days later in Luxembourg cut back even the Warsaw promise and boiled down to a general statement on the need for closer consultation on security issues between the WEU and Central European partners.[70]

Two German researchers from the International Bertelsmann Forum were right in saying: 'In the present interim period, the foreign policy of many European states tends to make use of well-tried political devices. Balance-of-power policies that aim to preserve or restore an equilibrium have once again become a dominant feature of European politics'.[71] A return to balance-of-power politics would generate a re-nationalization of security policy against all commitments undertaken within the Atlantic Alliance, the EU and the WEU. On the other hand, it would be erroneous to ignore the reality that national interests are still a priority and of decisive importance in decision making. Multilateralism should determine forms and procedures for harmonizing national security policies rather than replace them. 'In fact, integration has become a survival recipe for nation states.'[72] The paradox is that the success of integration will be determined by taking duly into account the differences between states and regions, divergent cultural traditions and varying levels of development. This also applies—and is not seldom the main factor—to allowing for divergent national interests and premises in Europe's common defence and security policy.

Out of the need to overcome the contradiction between respect for national interests and the elaboration of a broad pan-European vision of security, the French concept of a Pact for Stability in Europe was born.

The Pact for Stability in Europe

This French initiative was a follow-up to the ideas of President Mitterrand of December 1989 concerning a European Confederation, developed and elaborated in the proposals of then Foreign Minister Roland Dumas of May 1991.[73] The draft of a confederation was contrived as a surrogate pan-European settlement. Addressed mainly to CEE states which were left outside the structures unifying the rest of Europe, it was too general and superficial to inspire a serious political debate. In fact, it offered a loose mechanism for political consultations but failed to address the new threats and other security problems which also face the CEE states.

---

[70] See Luxembourg Declaration (note 67), para. 5.

[71] Weidenfeld, W. and Janning, J., 'New patterns of balance for Europe', *International Herald Tribune*, 28 Oct. 1993.

[72] Weidenfeld and Janning (note 71).

[73] A detailed draft model of a European Confederation was presented on 10 May 1991 in the form of a French memorandum to the other governments concerned.

The draft Pact for Stability in Europe, known as the Balladur Plan, was submitted for consideration to the European Council in Copenhagen on 22 June 1993.[74] Its significance would be in complementing the economic might of the EU with elements of political and military security and stability covering all the European continent. France proposed to call a special conference for this purpose to carry on the work initiated and partly carried out by the CSCE.[75]

It is worth considering the content, participants and other modalities of the Stability Pact. The content would be (a) to determine and put into effect principles concerning the inviolability of borders and respect for the rights of minorities, and (b) to co-ordinate the activities of numerous institutions and structures which aim at ensuring the effectiveness and the implementation of those principles. In other words, the essence of the Pact would be not to draw up new tenets or call into being new institutions, but to agree on new forms and ways of putting into effect the already binding norms through the existing institutions. It would in practice make admission of the CEE states to the EU conditional on settling such issues as might constitute a potential threat to stability in Europe, and therefore would require the conclusion of new agreements to make possible monitoring of the observation of commitments on borders and national minorities. The conference, as proposed under the Balladur Plan, would consider what kind of associated measures could perform a preventive function in ensuring stability. In this context, such measures as (a) association of the CEE states with the WEU, (b) military co-operation between the CEE states and the members of the EU, NATO and the WEU, and (c) strengthening of the CSCE institutions are taken into account.

Participation in the Pact would be determined by its content. In the first place, this is a project addressed mainly to the CEE states which, in some senses, are considered as future members of the EU. It is also aimed (a) at the existing members of the EU, the USA and Canada, whose importance for maintaining security in Europe is evident, at the very least because of their participation in NATO and the CSCE; (b) at some East European states, such as Belarus, Moldova, Russia and Ukraine, which have problems of frontiers and minorities that affect other states of the region; and (c) at the Baltic states which do not belong to the Commonwealth of Independent States (CIS) and have declared their wish to join the EU.[76] The Balladur Plan also envisages a

---

[74] The text is reproduced in appendix 7A. The Copenhagen meeting of the European Council of 21–22 June 1993 decided to examine the proposal and report back at its meeting in Brussels in Dec. 1993. This meeting adopted a synthetic report on the Pact with a view to convening a preparatory conference. *La politique étrangère de la France, Textes et documents* (published by the French Ministry of Foreign Affairs), Nov./Dec. 1993, pp. 228–29.

[75] The first conference to discuss the draft Pact which France is proposing to its Community partners should convene on 26–27 May 1994 in Paris.

[76] The French memorandum envisages the participation of 40 states in the Pact: (a) members of the EU (12); (b) North America (2); (c) North, Central and Eastern Europe—Albania, Austria, Belarus, Bulgaria, the Czech Republic, Estonia, Finland, Hungary, Iceland, Latvia, Lithuania, Moldova, Norway, Poland, Romania, Russia, Slovakia, Sweden, Switzerland, Turkey and Ukraine (21); and (d) of the following states of the former Yugoslavia which would be eligible to join, depending on the development of the situation at the London Conference and on their territories, Bosnia and Herzegovina, Croatia, Macedonia, former Yugoslavia (Serbia and Montenegro), and Slovenia (5).

list of incentives which the EU might use in favour of states which agreed to observe the principles that the conference would adopt.

Preparation of the special conference could take place with the help of the CSCE framework. At the same time, EU members would provide a draft declaration reaffirming the principles concerning frontiers and national minorities and a list of problems connected with frontiers and minorities in the CEE region. The preparatory conference for the Pact would determine its attitude to the declaration prepared by the members of the EU and establish 'negotiating tables'; a preliminary meeting of the conference would be held after six months to give an incentive to or sanction the results of the individual 'tables'. A concluding conference would approve the individual agreements and present proposals for the strengthening of the CSCE under the Pact for Stability in Europe.

What is new in the French plan is, on the one hand, a considerable promotion of preventive diplomacy for ensuring stability in Europe, and, on the other hand, the taking up of the delicate and sensitive issue of peaceful change of frontiers. The plan also constitutes an attempt to overcome the deadlock in which both the security policy of France and that of the EU have found themselves. Although it pays attention to two key issues—frontiers and minorities—it proceeds from the conviction that they may be solved if the modalities for entering negotiations can be ensured. There are, however, other no less important sources of tension and instability—economic collapse in Central Europe and other phenomena related to system transformation—and the military aspects of security such as arms transfers, proliferation, and so on.

Procedural issues and formal logic in the proposed Pact prevailed over the political implications of the expected solutions. It is an example of model thinking in terms of a Grand Design. Ominously, threats of a revision of European frontiers to which the Plan might throw open the gates would be counterproductive. Instead of stabilization it could lead to serious instability; instead of tensions being reduced, the risk of conflict could increase. From the point of view of some CEE states, it is difficult to accept the assumption that they would be parties at the proposed conference while the Western states played the role of arbiter. Finally, the proposed method of non-discrimination among the states of the region—except for former Yugoslavia (Serbia and Montenegro)—however formally correct, may do more harm than good from the political point of view, since there are still tensions between some states and some minority issues are unresolved (although other states, such as Poland and the Czech Republic, have settled the matter of their borders and respect for the minorities on their own territories). Also unclear are relations between the conference and the Pact for Stability on the one hand and the CSCE on the other. The question can be asked whether it would not be better to make use of the existing CSCE structures, all the more so since they are agreed with a view to the new needs of security after the end of the cold war.

The CSCE and the new Europe

The decisions taken during the Council of Ministers meeting in Rome in November–December 1993 can be assessed as a qualitatively new element in that they impart to the whole process initiated at Helsinki the character of an international security organization.[77] Because of its origins, the CSCE is a unique organization: its functions, forms, structures and procedures are not contained in any single document. They have undergone and will continue to undergo a certain evolution and change, adjusting to the new situation. The qualitatively new element is that, while preserving the flexibility and openness of the CSCE process, decisions were taken during 1993 to enhance the ability of the institutions to accomplish their tasks better and more effectively. This concerns both CSCE decision making and structures.

The decision-making process

In the past, all CSCE decisions were taken by consensus.[78] Changes in this respect were initiated at the First Meeting of the CSCE Council of Ministers in Berlin (19–21 June 1991).[79] In practice, all general norms of a political nature were to be adopted by consensus, while their implementation in specific situations did not require this. The Rome meeting of the Council of Ministers decided to confirm that existing practice should take the form of a new procedural rule—direct action to be undertaken 'through agreed mechanisms activated by a limited number of participating States'.[80] This type of decision making undoubtedly enhanced the operability and efficiency of the CSCE.

New operational structures

Following the mandate from the Stockholm Council meeting of December 1992, an *ad hoc* group on CSCE structures and operations was established to prepare decisions on a single organizational structure.[81] The subject under consideration was the consolidation and development of the CSCE structures. With the aim of making the work more efficient and improving the CSCE's capabilities for day-to-day operational tasks, the Rome meeting created a permanent body for political consultation and strengthening decision making in Vienna, the Permanent Committee of the CSCE.[82] This Committee should review the relevance and operation of existing mechanisms 'with a view to increasing their effectiveness'. In May 1993, the Council decided on the

[77] CSCE, Fourth Meeting of the Council, Rome, 1993, CSCE and the New Europe: Our Security is Indivisible, Decisions of the Rome Council Meeting (Rome, Dec. 1993), reproduced in appendix 7A.
[78] In accordance with the Rules of Procedure (para. 69) defined by the Final Recommendations of the Helsinki Consultations, as adopted in Helsinki, 8 June 1973, reproduced in Rotfeld (note 1), pp. 1–9.
[79] For an analysis of the process in 1990–92, see Rotfeld, 1992 (note 14).
[80] CSCE, Fourth Meeting of the Council, Rome 1993, Decisions of the Rome Council Meeting, CSCE document CSCE/4-C/Dec. 1 (Rome, Dec. 1993), para. VII.2, p. 13, reproduced in appendix 7A.
[81] See figure 7.2.
[82] This new institution replaced the Vienna Group, which had functioned since the Helsinki summit meeting as an informal, permanent operational CSCE organ. See also the diagram of the single organization structure of the CSCE, figure 7.2.

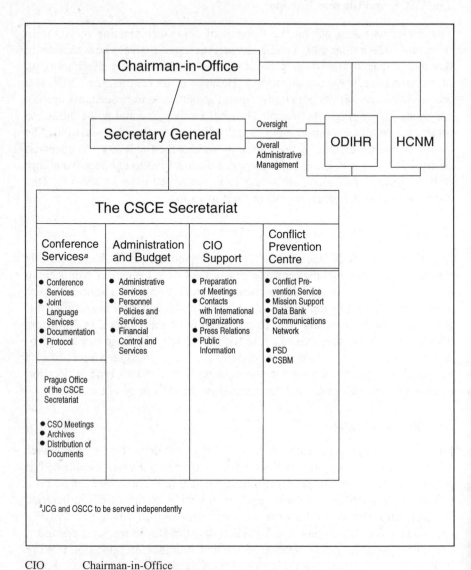

Source: Swedish proposal tabled at the CSCE Forum for Security Co-operation, Vienna, 26 Oct. 1993, Annex 1.

CIO   Chairman-in-Office
CSBM   Confidence- and security-building measure
CSO   Committee of Senior Officials
HCNM   High Commissioner for National Minorities
JCG   Joint Consultative Group
ODIHR   Office for Democratic Institutions and Human Rights
OSCC   Open Skies Consultative Commission
PSD   Peaceful settlement of disputes

Figure 7.2. The CSCE single organization structure

appointment of the first CSCE Secretary General, Wilhelm Höynck (Germany).[83]

Legal capacities

At its Rome meeting (30 November–1 December 1993), the CSCE Council took some decisions based on the report prepared by the CSCE *Ad Hoc* Group of Legal and Other Experts on the relevance of an agreement granting an internationally recognized status to the CSCE institutions.[84] From the very beginning the governments hosting the CSCE institutions (the Secretariat, the Conflict Prevention Centre and the Office for Democratic Institutions and Human Rights, the ODIHR) offered them treatment comparable to that accorded to the UN and its personnel. In Rome, the Ministers agreed on the usefulness of legal capacity being granted to the CSCE institutions and missions in the territories of all participating states. As a result of the Rome Council Meeting the CSCE has 'the capacity to contract, to acquire and dispose of movable and immovable property, and to institute and participate in legal proceedings'.[85]

CSCE activities

At the third meeting of the CSCE Council in Stockholm on 15 December 1992, the ministers of foreign affairs agreed to pursue a strategy of active diplomacy. The Chairman-in-Office (CIO), the Swedish Minister for Foreign Affairs Margaretha af Ugglas, received a clear mandate: (*a*) to make innovative use of the tools of preventive diplomacy and crisis management; (*b*) to strengthen the CSCE as a community of values; (*c*) to improve the co-operation of the CSCE with other international organizations; and (*d*) to review the internal structures of the CSCE. Remarkable progress was achieved in accomplishing all these objectives.[86] The CSCE Secretary General pointed out in his first Annual Report that particular attention was given to the new operational capabilities of the CSCE established by the 1992 Helsinki summit meeting and reconfirmed and specified by the Stockholm Council Meeting, 'focusing on early warning, conflict prevention and crisis management'.[87] The concrete and practical CSCE contributions to these areas are not publicized and therefore often underestimated. The CSCE Forum for Security Co-operation (FSC) in November 1993 adopted four important documents and continued negotiations on the other items of the Programme of Immediate

---

[83] The CSCE Secretary General took up office in Vienna on 15 June 1993.

[84] CSCE, Fourth Meeting of the Council, Rome, 1993, Legal Capacity and Privileges and Immunities, CSCE document CSCE/4-C/Dec. 2, Rome, 1 Dec. 1993, reproduced in appendix 7A.

[85] See note 84.

[86] Statement made at the Fourth CSCE Council Meeting in Rome by the outgoing CIO, the Minister for Foreign Affairs of Sweden, Margaretha af Ugglas, Rome, 30 Nov. 1993.

[87] CSCE, Secretary General, *Annual Report 1993* (note 14).

Action.[88] It is expected that FSC negotiations will bring concrete decisions to be approved by the CSCE Budapest summit meeting in the autumn of 1994.

CSCE missions

Important examples of the CSCE's work in this context are the eight CSCE missions with conflict prevention and crisis management mandates deployed in the Balkan, Baltic and Caucasus areas. For the efficiency of those missions, patience and flexible, discreet and authoritative advice were essential. Three missions of long duration were deployed before the end of 1992: in former Yugoslavia to Kosovo, Sanjak and Vojvodina[89] and a spillover monitor mission to Skopje (Macedonia);[90] and a mission to Georgia with the main task of promoting negotiations between the conflicting parties and seeking a peaceful political settlement. In August 1993, this mission developed a 'CSCE Concept for a Settlement of the Georgian–Ossetian Conflict'.[91]

On the basis of the accumulated experience, the following new CSCE missions of long duration were deployed in 1993: to Moldova 'in order to facilitate the achievement of a lasting, comprehensive political settlement of the conflict in all its aspects';[92] to Estonia with a view to promoting stability, dialogue and understanding between the communities in the country;[93] and to Latvia to advise the Latvian Government and authorities as well as institutions, organizations and individuals, mainly on citizenship issues and related matters.[94] The Rome Council meeting decided to establish a new CSCE

[88] CSCE, Special Committee of the Forum for Security Co-operation, Programme of military contacts and co-operation; Stabilizing measures for localized crisis situations; Principles concerning conventional arms transfers; Defence planning. CSCE, Forum for Security Co-operation, 49th Plenary Meeting of the Special Committee, *Journal*, no. 49 (24 Nov.–1 Dec. 1993), p. 1 and Annexes 1–4. See also chapter 14 in this volume. On the original FSC agenda, see also Rotfeld, A. D., 'The CSCE: towards a security organization', *SIPRI Yearbook 1993* (note 5), pp. 182–84; Walker, J., *Security and Arms Control in Post-confrontation Europe*, SIPRI (Oxford University Press: Oxford, 1994).

[89] The mission, deployed on 8 Sep. 1992, comprised 12, later 20, CSCE monitor-members. For its mandate, see Decision on Missions of Long Duration, Fifteenth Meeting of the Committee of Senior Officials, Prague, 1992, *Journal*, no. 2 (14 Aug. 1992), Annex 1, reproduced in Rotfeld (note 1).

[90] The mission, deployed in Sep. 1992 by decision of the 16th CSO Meeting, comprised 7 CSCE monitor-members (8 were authorized). Two EC Monitor Mission members are under the operational command of the CSCE Head of Mission. It has also established co-ordination between the CSCE and UNPROFOR-Macedonia Command. See CSCE, Secretary General, *Annual Report 1993* (note 14); Sixteenth Meeting of the Committee of Senior Officials, Prague, 1992, *Journal*, no. 3 (18 Sep. 1992), Annex 1.

[91] The mission to Georgia was deployed on 3 Dec. 1992. Its mandate covers both the South Ossetian and the Abkhazian conflicts; in practice, however, this mission has focused its activities on South Ossetia, while the leading role as regards Abkhazia is played by the UN. The size of the mission was 8 members. CSCE, Seventeenth Meeting of the Committee of Senior Officials, Prague, 1992, *Journal*, no. 2 (6 Nov. 1992), Annex 2.

[92] Mandate of the CSCE Mission to Moldova (deployed 25 Apr. 1993) based on the Final Report on the Conflict in the Left Bank Dniester Area of the Republic of Moldova by the Personal Representative of the Chairman-in-Office of the CSCE Council, Adam Daniel Rotfeld, Prague, 31 Jan. 1993; CSCE, Nineteenth Meeting of the Committee of Senior Officials, Prague, 1993, *Journal*, no. 3 (4 Feb. 1993), Annex 3.

[93] This mission was deployed on 15 Feb. 1993 with 6 members. For its mandate, see CSCE, Eighteenth Meeting of the Committee of Senior Officials, Stockholm, 1992, *Journal*, no. 3 (13 Dec. 1992), Annex 2.

[94] The mandate was adopted at the 23rd meeting of the CSO, 23 Sep. 1993. See CSCE, Twenty-third Meeting of the Committee of Senior Officials, Prague, 1993, *Journal*, no. 3 (23 Sep. 1993), Annex 3.

Mission to Tajikistan. Its mandate, in a country where an ugly civil war is going on, seems euphemistic: to maintain contact with and facilitate dialogue and confidence building between regionalist and political forces and actively promote respect for human rights.[95]

Seven Sanctions Assistance Missions were also launched to advise the authorities of the host countries on the implementation of sanctions carried out in accordance with the UN Security Council resolutions[96] and to provide practical assistance to help these authorities to enforce sanctions rigorously. CSCE missions in the field co-operate closely with the EU. On 4 February 1993, the Committee of Senior Officials appointed a Sanctions Co-ordinator who was tasked to ensure the oversight of sanctions, to assess the implementation and to advise both missions and countries in the region how to implement sanctions more effectively.[97]

On 6–14 October 1993 the CIO dispatched to the conflict area of Nagorno-Karabakh her personal representative who, assisted by a team of experts, prepared a detailed report with an analysis of the political and military situation, conclusions and recommendations. This report spoke in favour of establishing permanent representations in the region to demonstrate specific CSCE involvement and to help prepare the ground for a monitor mission. In May 1993 the Initial Operation Group started practical preparations for a permanent CSCE Mission to Nagorno-Karabakh. The Minsk Group,[98] after extensive negotiations, developed an 'Adjusted Timetable of Urgent Steps to Implement Security Council Resolutions 822 and 853' based on a step-by-step approach consisting of a mutually responsive series of measures.[99]

The Head of the Mission and one member started to work in Riga on 19 Nov. 1993. As of 21 Dec. 1993, the number of mission members was increased to 6.

[95] Decisions of the Rome Council Meeting (note 80), p. 6. This Mission was initially composed of 4 persons and was instructed to co-operate and co-ordinate with the UN representation in Dushanbe in the fulfilment of its tasks.

[96] UN Security Council Resolution no. 713 of 25 Sep. 1991 on an arms embargo against all the former Yugoslav republics; Resolution no. 757 of 30 May 1992 on sanctions against Serbia and Montenegro (UN document S/RES/757); Resolution no. 787 of 16 Nov. 1992 interdicting the transshipment of sensitive goods (UN document S/RES/787); and Resolution no. 820 on the further tightening of sanctions, including the services sector.

[97] In 1993, 7 Sanctions Assistance Missions were operating in Albania (established 5 Apr. 1993), Bulgaria (10 Oct. 1992), Croatia (27 Jan. 1993), Hungary (4 Oct. 1992), Macedonia (8 Nov. 1992), Romania (29 Oct. 1992) and Ukraine (17 Feb. 1993). More than 160 experts were working for the missions and the central structure in Brussels (the Sanctions Co-ordinator's Office and the Sanctions Assistance Missions Communications Centre, the latter being financed and partly staffed by the EU). See CSCE, Secretary General, *Annual Report 1993* (note 14), p. 8.

[98] The decision to prepare the Minsk Conference on the situation in Nagorno-Karabakh under the auspices of the CSCE was taken at the first additional meeting of the Council of Foreign Ministers in Helsinki on 24 Mar. 1992.

[99] CSCE, Secretary General, *Annual Report 1993* (note 14). It includes withdrawal of troops from the districts of Kubatli, Agdam, Fizuli, Djebrail, Kolbadjar and Aartakert, the restoration of all communications and transportation, the establishment of a permanent and comprehensive cease-fire with CSCE monitoring and the opening of the Minsk Conference. The cease-fire established at the end of Aug. 1993 was interrupted on 21 Oct. 1993.

The High Commissioner on National Minorities

The creation of the office of the High Commissioner on National Minorities (HNCM) by decision of the Helsinki summit meeting stemmed from the fact that the situation of national and ethnic minorities emerged as the most important conflict-generating factor. The first HCNM[100] has made a 'real success story' of this new CSCE tool.[101] His activities were addressed to Albania, the Baltic states, Hungary, Macedonia, Romania and Slovakia. He discussed the sensitive minority issues in those countries with both the competent authorities and representatives of the minorities. Since January 1993, he has been involved in the search for ways of managing the situation of the Russian populations of Estonia and Latvia; his activities were focused both on seeking acceptable solutions for the conflicting parties and on drafting legislation on citizenship and naturalization in the respective countries. He also offered his support in reducing the tensions between Romania and Hungary: the Council for Ethnic Minorities in Romania was provided with international expertise and experience on specific issues. He recommended that the Romanian Government take action to combat expressions of ethnic hatred and to investigate and prosecute perpetrators of violent attacks on other ethnic groups, particularly against Roma.[102] He consulted the Government of Macedonia and Albanian representatives on a number of conflict-generating issues such as the arrest of a number of Albanians in connection with an arms find.[103] Macedonia accepted his report and recommendations. In Albania, the HCNM's recommendations focused on the plight of the Greek minority, in particular education in the Greek language, the setting up of a minority office within the government and the resolution of the issue of confiscated church property. Similarly the High Commissioner submitted two sets of recommendations, with respect to the Hungarian minority in Slovakia and the Slovak minority in Hungary. All his recommendations were accepted by the governments to which they were addressed. His report on the Roma was also presented to the CSO meeting in Prague (21–23 September 1993).[104]

The human dimension

In the past, this sphere of CSCE activities concerned the adoption of a common system of values, principles and norms. In 1993, CSCE work in this respect focused on implementation. Institutionally, the ODIHR tackles the problems in this field. The first Implementation Meeting on Human Dimension

---

[100] Mr Max van der Stoel, former Foreign Minister of the Netherlands, was appointed to the post of the CSCE High Commissioner on National Minorities on 15 Dec. 1992 by the Council meeting in Stockholm. The Office of the HCNM was set up in The Hague and became operational in Jan. 1993.

[101] As expressed by delegates to the CSO and by the CSCE Secretary General: Address by the Secretary General of the CSCE, Wilhelm Höynck, to the Royal Association for Military Science and the Netherlands Society for International Affairs on the Role of the CSCE in the new European security environment, The Hague, 4 Oct. 1993.

[102] *ODIHR Bulletin*, Warsaw, vol. 2, no. 1 (winter 1994), p. 46.

[103] See note 101.

[104] On the HCNM's activities, see also the *ODIHR Bulletin,* vol. 1, nos. 2–3 (1993).

Issues (27 September–15 October 1993) provided a comprehensive review of the situation in the CSCE area. The new tasks in this regard concern not so much the need to agree new joint documents as the practical and continuous integration of the human dimension into the political consultation process of the CSCE.[105] One of the tasks of the ODIHR is its responsibility for managing the Moscow Human Dimension mechanism. This Mechanism has been successfully activated four times.[106]

The ODIHR has also monitored elections and referenda in various CSCE states: the federal, republican, regional and local elections in the former Yugoslavia (Serbia and Montenegro, December 1992), the nationwide referendum in Russia (25 April 1993), the parliamentary election (June 1993) and referendum (August 1993) in Latvia, the presidential election in Azerbaijan (October 1993) and the parliamentary election in Russia (December 1993).

The CIO, accompanied by a team of experts, visited the newly admitted member states in Central Asia and Transcaucasia. Discussions with the representatives of those countries were focused on explaining the full range of CSCE standards and on ways and forms of activating the role of the new participating states in the Helsinki process.[107] These activities should be seen in the broader context of the efforts of the UN, the EU, the Council of Europe, the WEU and NATO.

The CSCE and other international organizations

The Helsinki summit meeting declared that the CSCE is a regional arrangement in the sense of Chapter VIII of the UN Charter and 'as such provides an important link between European and global security'.[108] The Helsinki Document recommended that the CSCE participating states should improve contacts and practical co-operation with appropriate international organizations. Following these recommendations as well as the decisions of the Stockholm Council (15 December 1992), the CIO took a series of initiatives. The most important one resulted in an exchange of letters between the CIO and the UN Secretary-General in May 1993, which constitutes a framework for co-operation between the UN and the CSCE. Under this arrangement, the CSCE and

---

[105] See also CSCE, Secretary General, *Annual Report 1993* (note 14), pp. 11–13. Specific aspects of the human dimension were discussed at a series of seminars organized by the ODIHR, such as the Seminars on Tolerance (16–20 Nov. 1993), on Migration, Including Refugees and Displaced Persons (20–23 Apr. 1993), on Case Studies on National Minority Issues (24–28 May 1993) and on Free Media (2–5 Nov. 1993).

[106] It was set in motion (1) by the 12 EC countries and the United States on the question of reports of atrocities and attacks on unarmed civilians in Croatia and Bosnia and Herzegovina (Sep.–Oct. 1992); (2) by Estonia in order to study its legislation and compare it and its implementation with universally accepted human rights norms (Dec. 1992); (3) by Moldova to investigate legislation and implementation of minorities rights and inter-ethnic relations on the territory of Moldova (Jan.–Feb. 1993); and (4) by the CSO to investigate reports of human rights violations in Serbia and Montenegro (specifically the beating up and imprisonment of Vuk and Danica Draskoviç and the banning of the Serbian Renewal Party). As the CSCE Secretary General noted, this mission was unable to fulfil its task because of lack of Serbian co-operation. CSCE, Secretary General, *Annual Report 1993* (note 14), p. 13.

[107] The Chairman-in-Office visited Georgia, Azerbaijan and Armenia (24–27 Oct. 1993), seeking to offer a CSCE contribution to end the conflicts in the Transcaucasus.

[108] CSCE, Helsinki Document 1992 (note 5), p. 32.

the UN are committed 'to maintain close contact to ensure co-ordination, complementarity, possible mutual support and to avoid duplication in the planning and carrying out of activities'.[109] This relates in particular to conflict prevention and the political settlement of conflicts. The UN General Assembly on 13 October 1993 also unanimously adopted a resolution inviting the CSCE to participate in the sessions and work of the General Assembly in the capacity of observer.[110] The CIO represented the CSCE at the UN World Conference on Human Rights (Vienna, 14–25 June 1993).

In this context closer contacts and co-operation being developed between the CSCE, the Council of Europe and the UN office on human rights in Geneva should also be noted. Last but not least, mention should be made of contacts established between the CSCE and NATO ensuring mutual exchange of information on their respective activities.[111]

An assessment

The CSCE's activities were developing in 1993 mainly in three fields: (*a*) preventive diplomacy and crisis management; (*b*) integration of the human dimension (democracy, human rights and the state of law) into a broader security and political process; and (*c*) the strengthening and rationalization of CSCE structures, transforming them into a regular international organization and developing mutually reinforcing co-operation between the new CSCE institutions and the UN and other intergovernmental organizations of a regional character—the Council of Europe, NATO and NACC (the North Atlantic Cooperation Council) and the WEU. Undoubtedly, consistent efforts were made in 1993 to achieve these objectives.[112] Remarkable results, although not broadly publicized, were achieved in putting in motion two new instruments of preventive diplomacy—local CSCE missions in potential conflict areas and the activities of the HCNM. Crucial for CSCE efficiency were commitment and devotion, flexibility and discretion as well as authoritative advice based on broad international support. In all cases, the personal qualifications and prestige which the HCNM and the heads of mission enjoy are difficult to overestimate. The CSCE has proved to be instrumental in searching for consensus among the parties involved in various disputes.[113]

Although the list of CSCE accomplishments in 1993 looks impressive, the general assessment is also determined by its shortcomings and failures. It is true that the CSCE, together with the UN and the WEU, deserves the credit for staving off a spillover of the conflict in the Balkans into the Kosovo area and Macedonia as well as enforcing the UN sanctions against former Yugo-

---

[109] Swedish Ministry for Foreign Affairs, Framework for co-operation and co-ordination between the United Nations Secretariat and the Conference on Security and Co-operation in Europe, Press release (New York, 26 May 1993), reproduced in appendix 7A.

[110] UN General Assembly resolution 48/5 (13 Oct. 1993), UN document A/48/L.6 and Add. 1.

[111] CSCE, Secretary General, *Annual Report 1993* (note 14), p. 16.

[112] Statement (note 86).

[113] For instance, an agreement on the speedy and complete withdrawal of Russian troops from all Baltic states was made possible by the active role played by the CSCE. See Statement (note 86).

slavia (Serbia and Montenegro). However, neither the CSCE nor any other multilateral regional and universal organization has managed definitively to end the armed conflicts in Bosnia and Herzegovina, Georgia, Nagorno-Karabakh and other regions of the former Soviet Union. The experience of 1993 confirms the view that CSCE institutions are appropriate to preventive diplomacy but inadequate to enforcing peace. It should be remembered that the CSCE does not possess a military power or any other tools of that ilk[114] but has only its own prestige to persuade the parties involved to end a conflict.

The importance of the fact that the CSCE required the newly admitted countries to adopt the principles and norms determining the common system of values can hardly be overestimated. However, the observation of these norms in practice calls for strenuous efforts in shaping new democratic institutions and procedures. It is much easier to reach agreement on abstract tenets and formulae than to apply them in practice.

The role of the CSCE is determined in remarkable measure by the great powers' attitude to the newly established institutions and participation in their activities. It is in the nature of great powers to take advantage of multilateral organizations as an instrument for their own policies. The CSCE is no exception to that rule. Examples are Russia's demands in 1993 for the 'blessing' of the international community, and the UN and the CSCE in particular, on the operation of its armed forces on the territory of the CIS. On 28 February 1993, President Yeltsin stated: 'I believe the time has come for authoritative international organizations, including the UN, to grant Russia special powers as guarantor of peace and stability in this region'.[115] Russian representatives repeated calls for international legitimization of Russia's peacekeeping and peacemaking operations.

Russia's efforts to obtain an extensive mandate to operate on CIS territories on behalf of international organizations and with appropriate financial support from the international community prompted numerous reservations, chiefly from the Central European delegates. Positive though the Russian representatives' way of referring to UN and CSCE authority was, in that it declared respect for the principles and norms of both organizations, any mandate to act on their behalf should be strictly defined for every case and its implementation subject to provisions for international control and supervision agreed in advance. The right of a great power to ensure its own security cannot be allowed

---

[114] Col Richard M. Connaughton, formerly the British Army's Head of Defence Studies, wrote recently: 'Those who envisage the CSCE emerging as a pan-European security body utilizing collective security mechanism in lieu of NATO's collective defence paradigm are excessively optimistic. The CSCE is at best a forum of states which will never enjoy the strength or power to become an executive body'. See 'The European organizations and intervention', ed. D. J. Quinn, *Peace Support Operations and the US Military* (National Defense University Press: Washington, DC, 1994), p. 190.

[115] Reported by ITAR-TASS, 1 Mar. 1993. See also Crow, S., 'Russia seeks leadership in regional peacekeeping', Radio Free Europe/Radio Liberty, *RFE/RL Research Report*, vol. 2, no. 15 (9 Apr. 1993). On 3 Mar. the Russian Government presented an official document to the UN discussing Russia's role in peacekeeping on the territory of the CIS. In his appeal to the CIS leaders on 17 Mar., Yeltsin said 'the experience of international operations in keeping the peace, especially direct support for our joint efforts by the UN, the CSCE and other organizations, will also be useful'. See *Nezavisimaya Gazeta*, 18 Mar. 1993, p. 1; Crow, S., 'Russia promotes the CIS as an international organization', *RFE/RL Research Report*, vol. 3, no. 11 (18 Mar. 1994).

to give legitimacy to a special role for Russia while ignoring the sovereignty of the states described by it as the 'near abroad'. The outgoing CIO, Minister af Ugglas, said in her last statement on the one hand that key members of the CSCE community should be called upon to play a full and active role, but on the other that '[the] CSCE must use their influence without becoming their instrument . . . The CSCE must not give legitimacy to any action which is not completely in line with its principles'.[116] Truly, the CSCE has neither means nor power nor even intention to take upon itself a role as peacekeeper in the various conflicts springing up across the area from Vancouver to Vladivostok.

The Council of Ministers meeting in Rome agreed to strengthen the CSCE role 'as a pan-European and transatlantic forum for co-operative security as well as for political consultation on the basis of equality'. The Rome Document declared that, irrespective of the histories and backgrounds of the CSCE states, 'their security is truly indivisible'.[117] Developments in 1993 did not bear out this declaration. One of the main weaknesses of the CSCE, like the UN and many other international organizations, is taking programme documents and the institutions and structures called into being on their basis as a new reality in the field of security. Consequently, structural change is becoming an aim in itself. In fact, decisions and institutions seldom lead to desirable changes and solutions, and often create an illusion of transformation. They are there to satisfy the public expectation that governments will not ignore or look idly on at the numerous conflicts taking place. An awesome gap opens wider between declared intentions and the capability to realize them.[118]

The effectiveness of the organization of security is determined by the extent to which its basic documents are convergent with operational activity. The gap between words and deeds, between the broad goals and the very limited means at the disposal of the CSCE, ignores and undermines the importance of credibility.

In the past (1975–89), the CSCE played an important role in changing the character of the relations between the East and the West. It contributed to overcoming the divisions between the power blocs, to emphasizing the great importance of the human dimension, particularly respect for the rights of the individual, and to promoting the 'free flow of people, information and ideas'. After the end of the cold war (1990–91), the CSCE was an irreplaceable and unique forum for the finalization of the unprecedented agreements in arms control and military confidence and security building. At that time the Treaty on Conventional Armed Forces in Europe (CFE Treaty), the documents on the third generation of confidence- and security-building measures (CSBMs), the Treaty on Open Skies and other arrangements were agreed, which turned the

---

[116] Statement (note 86).

[117] CSCE, Fourth Meeting of the Council (note 77).

[118] In his critical analysis of President Clinton's foreign policy, Henry Kissinger addressed the following comments to the US Administration: 'The disparity between avowed purpose and actual policy threatens US foreign policy with growing irrelevance.' See 'The growing irrelevance of US foreign policy', *New York Post*, 1 Mar. 1994.

concept of military-related openness, transparency and predictability into operational policy among the 53 participating states.

A new task, tackled in Helsinki in July 1992 and elaborated at Stockholm and Rome, is to ensure that Europe's security is indivisible not only in declarations but also in reality. Although 1993 has brought about some progress in this respect, the fragmentation of European security still prevails. The new challenge is that of preventing Europe from splitting into various areas with fundamentally different security interests and turning 'into a mosaic of incompatible security arrangements'.[119] Fulfilling this task depends in greater measure on whether the great powers will extend their political and financial support to the CSCE than on new decisions of an organizational and procedural nature; more on collaboration with the multilateral security structures already existing in Europe than on taking over their tasks for which they are not suitable. The fact that the 1993 Rome decisions recommended deepening of CSCE co-operation with the UN as well as with the EU and NATO bears witness to the unique role the CSCE has to play, but the assessment of that role is possible only in a broader context and in correct proportions as part of the regional security system in Europe as a whole.[120] Indeed, critical opinions concerning the limited effectiveness of the CSCE may and should be addressed to the same, or a greater, extent to those multilateral structures which deal with military security aspects in Europe. This is why the preparations for and the decisions made at the NATO Brussels meeting on 10–11 January 1994 were of particular importance.[121]

The Partnership for Peace

In creating a regional security system in Europe, the best hopes have been based on the Partnership for Peace. That programme, opened to all the former WTO countries, along with other non-NATO nations, initiates a new stage in building a new type of co-operative security system in Europe.

The NATO states set off on the journey towards inviting other European states to join the PFP more than three years ago. The documents of the NATO summit meetings in London (July 1990) and Copenhagen (June 1991) reflected its new interest in the security of CEE.[122] In October 1991 US Secretary of State James Baker and German Foreign Minister Hans-Dietrich

---

[119] See Address by the Secretary General of the CSCE (note 101).

[120] Ambassador Wilhelm Höynck noted in this regard: 'The CSCE cannot do it alone. And with regard to most scenarios even not in the first place . . . Asking too much of the CSCE will hurt, and is actually hurting, its real potential'. See Address by the Secretary General of the CSCE (note 101).

[121] NATO Press Communiqué M-1(92)3, Brussels, 11 Jan. 1994, reproduced in appendix 7A.

[122] 'Any form of coercion or intimidation' of the CEE states would be regarded as a matter of 'direct and natural concern' to NATO: NATO, Partnership with the countries of Central and Eastern Europe, Statement issued by the North Atlantic Council meeting in Ministerial Session in Copenhagen, 6 June 1991. Published in *NATO Review*, June 1991, pp. 28–29. See also the document of the London summit meeting: London Declaration on a transformed North Atlantic Alliance, issued by the Heads of State and Government participating in the Meeting of the North Atlantic Council in London, 6 July 1990, published in NATO, *The Transformation of an Alliance: The Decisions of NATO's Heads of State and Government* (NATO: Brussels, [1992]), pp. 5–14.

Genscher jointly proposed the establishment of NACC.[123] The decision to do this was taken by the NATO summit meeting in Rome (November 1991)[124] and implemented by the North Atlantic Council meeting in Brussels (December 1991).[125] The membership of NACC was originally open to the CEE states, including the Baltic states and the Soviet Union; after its dissolution the membership was extended to all the former Soviet republics. In April 1992, the defence ministries of NACC states decided to concentrate on co-operation in the following areas: military strategies, defence management, the legal framework for military forces, harmonization of defence planning and arms control, exercises and training, defence education, reserve forces, environmental protection, air traffic control, search and rescue, the military contribution to humanitarian aid and military medicine.[126]

In December 1992, the NACC meeting decided to supplement this list by adding peacekeeping operations. A special NACC *Ad Hoc* Group on Cooperation in Peacekeeping elaborated in its Report to the Ministers (Athens, June 1993) conceptual guidelines and a programme for future co-operation.[127] This programme involved the CEE countries in NATO peacekeeping activities; on the other hand, some of those countries offered NATO a possibility of using their facilities for peacekeeping training.[128] NACC provided a useful forum for discussion of the current security issues and for acquainting the CEE states with NATO procedures and plans. However, NACC membership fell short of the most important expectations of those states in the sphere of security. An optimal solution for them would be admission to NATO or the offer of security guarantees by the Alliance. Russia perceived such a scenario as tending to isolate it. In turn, the states of the Atlantic Alliance proceeded from the assumption that the fundamental change of circumstances in Europe calls not only for a new vision of security but also for adequate measures to realize it without detriment to NATO's collective interests. A flexible solution was therefore sought which would enable NATO to control the situation or give it a kind of *droit de regard* over the changes taking place in all armies of the former WTO, and particularly the Russian Army, and would open up new perspectives for negotiating the membership of the Alliance in future, while not

[123] Larrabee, F. S., 'East European security after the cold war', RAND National Defense Research Institute, Santa Monica, Calif., 1993, p. 68. See US Department of State, Joint Statement by Secretary of State James A. Baker III and Hans-Dietrich Genscher, Minister of Foreign Affairs of the Federal Republic of Germany, Washington DC, 2 Oct., 1991.

[124] NATO, Rome Declaration on Peace and Cooperation, Press Communiqué (Brussels, 8 Nov. 1991). Published in NATO, *The Transformation of an Alliance* (note 122), pp. 15–28.

[125] NATO, Final Communiqué issued by the North Atlantic Council Meeting in Ministerial Session, Press Communiqué M-NAC-2(91)110, Brussels, 19 Dec. 1991; NATO, North Atlantic Cooperation Council statement on dialogue, partnership and cooperation, Press Communiqué M-NACC-1(91)111, Brussels, 20 Dec. 1991. Both reproduced in *SIPRI Yearbook 1992: World Armaments and Disarmament* (Oxford University Press: Oxford, 1992), pp. 587–92.

[126] NATO Press Communiqué M-DMCP-1(92), Brussels, 1 Apr. 1992.

[127] Report to Ministers by the NACC *Ad Hoc* Group on Co-operation in Peacekeeping. NATO Press release, M-NAC-1(93)40, 11 June 1993, reproduced in appendix 7A and in Rotfeld (note 1).

[128] F. Stephen Larrabee noted that 'Poland, for instance, has extensive peacekeeping experience . . . However, the participation of many East European countries in peacekeeping activities is likely to depend on their ability to overcome current economic difficulties and develop healthy economies.' See note 123.

committing NATO to immediate expansion. Such a solution would not draw new lines of division, although the conditions of co-operation of NATO and the individual new partners would differ. Finally, the essential thing was that the growth of the imperial ambitions of Russia and the unpredictable development of events there made NATO realize that closer and more specific ties than NACC's are necessary for the CEE states.

Given this, the programme of the PFP was launched, which could be termed NACC-2 were it not that: (*a*) it is open for all states outside the Alliance, including the former neutral and non-aligned European states, and not only for the former WTO members as was the case with NACC; (*b*) it goes beyond dialogue and co-operation to forge a real partnership; and (*c*) it initiates an enlargement of NATO 'when other countries are capable of fulfilling their NATO responsibilities'.[129] Like NACC, the programme does not give security guarantees. The *Invitation* offered to non-NATO states contains a promise: 'NATO will consult with any active participant in the Partnership if that partner perceives a direct threat to its territorial integrity, political independence or security'.[130] Within the scope set as the result of individual negotiations with the interested states, NATO will work in concrete ways towards transparency in defence budgeting, promoting democratic control of defence ministries, joint planning, joint military exercises and creating an ability to operate with NATO forces in such fields as peacekeeping, search and rescue and humanitarian operations, and others as may be agreed. The states participating in this programme are invited to send permanent liaison officers to NATO headquarters and a separate Partnership Coordination Cell at Mons in Belgium which would 'under the authority of the North Atlantic Council, carry out the military planning necessary to implement the Partnership programmes'.

The PFP is an answer to two questions: (*a*) how NATO perceives the necessity of adapting to the new challenges to security; and (*b*) how it will expand its relations with the European states remaining out of the Alliance. A number of outstanding issues still remain. For instance, it is not clear whether the initiators intend the main functions of the PFP to be those of a *sui generis* clearing-house or those of a framework for operational collaboration, particularly in solving ethnic conflicts; whether it will contribute to shaping a common security area or will be a new form of institutionalizing a division of Europe into states which have full security guarantees and those that are devoid of such guarantees; or whether for non-NATO members the PFP

---

[129] Statement by US President Bill Clinton at the NATO Council summit meeting, Brussels, 10 Jan. 1994 (note 22).

[130] Reproduced in appendix 7A and in Rotfeld (note 1). The appendix attached to the *Invitation* is the *Partnership for Peace Framework Document* which was adopted by all states interested in acceding to the programme. The formula of acceptance reads: 'In response to the Partnership for Peace Invitation issued and signed by the Heads of State and Government of the member States of the North Atlantic Treaty Organization participating in the meeting of the North Atlantic Council held at NATO Headquarters, Brussels, on 10th and 11th January 1994, I, the undersigned, Head of Government of . . . hereby accept the invitation to the Partnership for Peace and subscribe to the Partnership for Peace Framework Document'. By 9 May 1994, 17 states had signed—Albania, Azerbaijan, Bulgaria, the Czech Republic, Estonia, Finland, Georgia, Hungary, Latvia, Lithuania, Moldova, Poland, Romania, Slovakia, Slovenia, Sweden and Ukraine.

means an initial step on the road to the expansion of the Alliance[131] or a step towards a basic transformation of the regional security system.[132] Lastly, it is not clear whether all states will have an equal status and role to play, or whether, as demanded by Russia, some of them will obtain special status within the PFP.[133]

V. Conclusions

The problems facing Europe after the end of the cold war can only partially be solved with the measures, institutions and procedures relevant to the time of the division of Europe into blocs and confrontation among them. The new threats call not only for new instruments of action but, first of all, for a new philosophy and a new political strategy adequate to the new challenges. The issue is not only to create new institutions or to agree on new political declarations, however necessary and useful both often prove: it is rather the sufficient adjustment of the mandate and functions of the European security institutions to the new requirements.

The multilateral security structures are tools which work of the will of member states, commensurate with their political and military commitment. In other words, the operation of NATO, the EU/WEU and the CSCE cannot be analysed and assessed without an understanding of the policies of the main powers—France, Germany, Russia, the UK and the USA—as well as numerous other small- and medium-sized states. The fact that the members of the EU undertook under the Maastricht Treaty to conduct a common European security and defence policy does not mean that such a common policy has automatically become a reality. The fact that NATO as early as 1990 adopted a declaration on the Alliance's transformation does not mean that a radical change of the organization has followed. The fact that numerous documents were devoted to the programmes of co-operation between the CSCE and NATO, NACC, the PFP, EU/WEU and other organizations does not mean that the system based 'on mutually reinforcing institutions' announced at Helsinki has taken on real political form. Regrettably, international organizations and states which belong to them attached much more weight to their own areas of action and responsibility than to declarations on 'common', 'co-operative' and 'indivisible' security.

---

[131] The NATO leaders confirmed in their *Invitation* addressed to non-members that 'the Alliance, as provided for in Article 10 of the Washington Treaty, remains open to the membership of other European states in a position to further the principles of the treaty and to contribute to the security of the North Atlantic area. We expect and would welcome NATO expansion that would reach to democratic states to our East, as part of an evolutionary process, taking into account political and security developments in the whole of Europe.'

[132] Wörner, M., 'Shaping the alliance of the future', *NATO Review*, Feb. 1994.

[133] See also Mihalka, M., 'NATO's Partnership for Peace, squaring the circle: NATO's offer to the East', *RFE/RL Research Report*, vol. 3, no. 12 (25 Mar. 1994); Lippman, T. W., 'Partnership for Peace's new look: a protective shield against Moscow', *Washington Post*, 8 Feb. 1994; Lynch, A., 'After empire: Russia and its western neighbours', *RFE/RL Research Report*, vol. 3, no. 12 (25 Mar. 1994); van Heuven, M., 'Partnership for Peace: an American view', RAND Corporation, Santa Monica, Calif., 1993.

This does not mean that in 1993 no essential and positive changes have taken place in shaping the regional security system in Europe as laid down in Chapter VIII of the UN Charter. These changes are part and parcel of the process which is evolutionary, and not revolutionary.

The most serious challenge for the system of regional security in Europe is conflicts—ethnic, national and religious. Some of them can be solved through preventive diplomacy and by means of the peaceful settlement of disputes. Others require determined joint action by the international community if the latter wishes to maintain its credibility. In extreme cases this entails armed intervention. However, acting on behalf of and on the mandate of the international community should not mean legitimizing a carve-up into new zones of influence of the great powers or a policy of hegemonism. The main task of the system that emerges after the breakup of the bipolar world is the final overcoming of the existing divisions, not the creation of new ones.

Neither the Partnership for Peace nor NATO expansion nor the strengthening of new CSCE mechanisms will in themselves solve Europe's security problems. Institutional improvements can contribute to the alleviation of tensions and to co-operation between states, but the factors determining security remain the stabilization of the economic and social situation in the region as well as power politics. 1993 brought a foretaste of the opening up of Western structures towards the CEE states. Putting into effect the concept of 'expanded security'[134] would require the adoption of decisions which would cause impotent institutions to become so important that they would be able not only to take new resolutions but even to stave off armed conflicts and aggression.

The rationale of a European security arrangement does not consist in the elimination of conflicts of interests. They are natural and will exist in relations between states. The essence of the system of co-operative security is to have conflicts settled on the basis of agreed norms and procedures, within the framework of common institutions.[135] 1993 did not bring ready-made solutions, but opened up a new beginning.

---

[134] See Klaus Kinkel, Federal Minister of Foreign Affairs of Germany, in his article 'Das Konzept der erweiterten Sicherheit—Baustein einer europäischen Sicherheitsarchitektur' [The concept of expanded security: building blocks for a European security architecture], *Frankfurter Rundschau*, 16 Dec. 1993.

[135] Nolan, J. E., 'The concept of co-operative security in the 21st century' (Brookings Institution: Washington, DC, 1994), p. 5.

Appendix 7A. Documents on European security

Brussels, 18 December 1992

Introduction

The Foreign Ministers and Representatives of the member countries of the North Atlantic Cooperation Council have agreed to the following Work Plan for 1993 building on the foundations of dialogue, partnership and cooperation already established.

Political and security-related matters

Topics:

– Political and security related matters;
– Conceptual approaches to arms control and disarmament;
– Conceptual and operational aspects related to peacekeeping;
– Nuclear disarmament and the security of new non-nuclear weapon states;

Activities:

– Consultations of the Political Committee with cooperation partners, including as appropriate with experts, as a rule every two months;
– Consultations on specific issues in brainstorming format at Ambassadorial level;
– Consultations on peacekeeping and related matters, starting in a brainstorming format at Ambassadorial level followed by ad hoc meetings of political–military experts, as agreed by Ambassadors, leading to cooperation among interested NACC members in preparation for peacekeeping activities, including: joint sessions on planning of peacekeeping missions; joint participation in peacekeeping training; and consideration of possible joint peacekeeping exercises;
– Special consultations with cooperation partners on regional security issues, including enlarged Political Committee meetings focused on such issues;
– Meetings of each Regional Experts Group with experts from partner countries once a year;

Defence planning issues and military matters

Topics:

– Principles and key aspects of strategy including crisis management, defensiveness, sufficiency and flexibility;
– Issues of defence planning;
– Force and command structures;
– Military contribution to conceptual approaches to all arms control and disarmament issues;
– Views on military exercises;
– Democratic control over armed forces;
– Planning, management and analysis of national defence programmes and budgets;
– Concepts and methods of training and education in the defence field;
– Consultations on concepts of modernisation of command and control systems, including communications and information systems;
– Reserve forces including mix of active and reserve forces, force structures, training, categories, operational readiness and mobilisation;
– Conceptual discussion on the potential role of the armed forces in natural and technological disaster clean-up;

Activities:

– Consultations of the Military Committee in a cooperation session at Chief of Staff level, and other MC meetings with the cooperation partners and consultations in other appropriate fora;
– Military contacts including high-level visits, staff talks and other exchanges, such as port visits;
– Exploratory team and expert team visits;
– Participation by cooperation partners in special and/or regular courses at the NATO Defence College and at the NATO School (SHAPE) at Oberammergau;
– Continuation of invitations to MNC Seminars like SHAPEX and to NAC Sea Day;
– Workshop on training and education, early 1993;
– Seminar on Defensive Military Strategy Structures and Posture;

– A special course to be held in Russia, similar to those taking place in NATO institutions in Rome and Oberammergau;

Defence conversion

Topic:

– Defence conversion, including its human dimension.

Activities:

– Definition of pilot projects supported by nations on the basis of a mechanism and procedures established by the Economic Committee;

– Establishment of a data base on technical expertise and studies on examples of defence industry conversion in the NATO countries;

– Exploratory study of the need and feasibility for establishing a data base on defence industry to be converted in cooperation partner countries.

Economic issues

Topic:

– Inter-relationship of defence expenditure and budgets with the economy.

Activities:

– Consultations of the Economic Committee in sessions reinforced by experts with cooperation partners every 3 months;

– Participation of partner countries in the annual NATO colloquium on economic developments.

Science

Topic:

– Participation of cooperation partners' scientists in NATO science programmes giving emphasis to priority areas of interest to NATO and Cooperation Partners.

Activities:

– Meeting of the Science Committee with counterparts from cooperation partner countries once a year;

– Attendance of scientists from cooperation partner countries in the new Advanced Research Perspective Programme activities (ARPP) and in Advanced Study Institutes (ASI) and Advanced Research Workshops (ARW) (approximately 2000 scientists from cooperation partner countries);

– Holding ARPP, ASI and ARW meetings in cooperation partner countries (approximately 25 meetings);

– Participation of scientists from cooperation partner countries in the Collaborative Research Grants Programme (approximately 130 grants);

– Sending proceedings of NATO's scientific meetings to a central library in each cooperation partner country;

– Sponsoring visits of experts to cooperation partners' laboratories (approximately 15 visits);

– Sponsoring linkage grants between NATO and cooperation partners' laboratories (approximately 70 grants);

– Participation of scientists from cooperation partner countries in the Science Fellowships Programme (approximately 150–200 participants);

– Assisting cooperation partners in the assessment of research proposals through the use of the NATO peer review network of referees and experts;

– Disseminating literature on the Science programme to scientists in cooperation partner countries;

– Ways should be sought to involve Cooperation Partners in some Phase III projects of the Science for Stability Programme.

Challenges of modern society (CCMS)

Topics:

– Defence-related environmental issues;
– Pilot studies of interest to cooperation partners.

Activities:

– Meeting of the Committee on the Challenges of Modern Society with counterparts from cooperation partner countries once a year;

– Participation of cooperation partners' experts in pilot study meetings;

– Participation of cooperation partners' experts in workshops, conferences and seminars related to CCMS pilot studies;

– Dissemination of information on CCMS pilot studies, workshops, conferences and seminars, as well as approved reports to cooperation partners;

– Pilot study on defence base cleanups;

– Pilot study on protecting civil populations from toxic material spills during movements of military and other dangerous, defence-related goods;

– Pilot study on existing cross-border environmental problems emanating from defence-related installations and activities.

Dissemination of information

Topic:

– Dissemination of information about NATO in the countries of cooperation partners.

Activities:

– A meeting of the Committee on Information and Cultural Relations (CICR) with cooperation partners;
– Information about NATO will be disseminated as widely as possible in the countries of cooperation partners, in particular to the relevant institutions and organisations, inter alia through embassies of NATO member countries serving as contact points and other diplomatic liaison channels;
– Close cooperation with information centres established by those cooperation partner countries interested and able to provide the necessary facilities, support personnel and services;
– Visits to NATO by groups;[1]
– Sponsorship of a number of cooperation partners' representatives to attend seminars in Allied countries;[1]
– Co-sponsorship with cooperation partners of seminars/workshops;
– NATO speakers' tours to cooperation partner states;[1]
– Expansion of Democratic Institutions Fellowships programme (individual and institutional);[1]
– Increased dissemination of NATO documentation in cooperation partner states, including specialised brochures and video clips.

Policy planning consultations

Topic:

– A mid- and long-term foreign and security policy issue; such an issue might include the formulation of foreign policy in a democratic state.

Activity:

– A meeting of NATO's Atlantic Policy Advisory Group with cooperation partners.

Air traffic management

Topic:

– Civil–military coordination of air traffic management.

Activity:

– Two enlarged CEAC plenary sessions

---

[1] Specific numbers of activities will be decided later.

and, as appropriate, subordinate group meetings to discuss civil–military coordination.

Source: NATO, Press Communiqué M-NACC-2(92) 110 (revised), 18 Dec. 1992.

FRAMEWORK FOR CO-OPERATION AND CO-ORDINATION BETWEEN THE UNITED NATIONS SECRETARIAT AND THE CONFERENCE ON SECURITY AND CO-OPERATION IN EUROPE

New York, 26 May 1993

The Secretary-General of the United Nations and the Chairman of the Council of the Conference on Security and Co-operation in Europe,

Desirous of continuing and further strengthening the co-operation and co-ordination between the United Nations and the Conference on Security and Co-operation in Europe in all fields of mutual interest, in particular those relating to maintaining international peace and security and promoting respect for human rights within the CSCE area, and in accordance with the Charter of the United Nations and relevant United Nations General Assembly and Security Council resolutions as well as decisions by the CSCE Council and the CSCE Committee of Senior Officials,

Have, as part of the continuing development of mutual relations, agreed to the following:

(1) The Secretary-General of the United Nations and the Chairman-in-Office of the CSCE Council and their respective representatives will hold consultations on a regular basis in particular on co-operation and co-ordination of activities of common interest.

(2) The Permanent Mission to the United Nations of the CSCE participating State holding the Office of Chairman will serve as the point of contact of the CSCE and as the representative of the Chairman-in-Office in contacts with the United Nations Secretariat in New York and in Geneva on appropriate activities of common interest. The CSCE delegation of the CSCE participating State holding the Office of Chairman, the CSCE Secretary-General and other CSCE institutions in Vienna will serve as points of contact in Vienna.

(3) Official information on relevant issues, including documents and decisions as well

as specific reports, will be exchanged as appropriate between the United Nations and the CSCE.

(4) The Secretary-General of the United Nations and the Chairman-in-Office of the CSCE, assisted or represented as appropriate by the Secretary-General of the CSCE and other institutions of the CSCE, undertake to maintain close contact to ensure co-ordination, complementarity, possible mutual support and to avoid duplication in the planning and carrying out of activities. This relates in particular to long-term efforts to prevent conflicts and promote political settlement of conflicts.

(5) Such contacts should take the form of
– consultation on the preparation, initiation and implementation of fact finding and other missions e.g. timing, composition, terms of reference
– exchange of information between UN and CSCE representatives in the field on the situation in the area of their responsibility including movements and other activities of missions.

(6) In addition co-operation may cover
– exchange of information in preparing reports of missions
– examination of the possibility of joint reports
– examination of the possibilities of various kinds of mutual assistance in the field
– examination of the possibility of joint missions.

(7) The forms of co-operation referred to above (paras. 5 and 6) may be applicable to peacekeeping operations in the CSCE region.

(8) The CSCE, in planning and carrying out peacekeeping activities, may, as appropriate, draw upon the technical assistance and advice of the United Nations.

(9) In principle the United Nations and the CSCE will bear their respective costs related to joint activities. Whenever necessary a precise division of costs related to a joint activity will be agreed upon.

(10) Letters of Understanding should be concluded as appropriate for each co-ordinated area of activity.

Source: Swedish Ministry for Foreign Affairs, Agreement concerning cooperation and coordination between the UN and the CSCE, Press Release, 26 May 1993.

REPORT TO MINISTERS BY THE NACC AD HOC GROUP ON COOPERATION IN PEACEKEEPING

Athens, 11 June 1993

In accordance with the decision taken at the North Atlantic Cooperation Council meeting on 18th December 1992, an Ad Hoc Group on Cooperation in Peacekeeping was established with the aim of developing a common understanding on the political principles of and the tools for peacekeeping, and to share experience and thereby develop common practical approaches and cooperation in support of peacekeeping under the responsibility of the UN or the CSCE.

PART I: CONCEPTUAL APPROACHES

1. Definitions

There is no single, generally accepted definition of peacekeeping. There is a need to develop a common understanding of peacekeeping, proceeding from the definitions and concepts of peacekeeping contained in the relevant UN and CSCE documents, including the UN Secretary General's Agenda for Peace. Traditionally, peacekeeping has been used to describe operations based on Chapter VI of the UN Charter. Operations similar to those conducted under Chapter VI may be carried out under the authority of the CSCE on the basis of the 1992 Helsinki Document. Operations based on recent extensions of the concept of peacekeeping, aimed at the protection or establishment of peace and based on Chapter VII of the UN Charter, have been carried out under the authority of the UN Security Council.

In considering NACC cooperation in peacekeeping, the following definitions may be useful:

Conflict prevention

Includes different activities, in particular, under Chapter VI of the UN Charter, ranging from diplomatic initiatives to preventive deployment of troops, intended to prevent disputes from escalating into armed conflicts or from spreading. Conflict prevention can include fact-finding missions, consultation, warnings, inspections and monitoring. Preventive deployments normally consist of civilians and/or military forces being deployed to avert a crisis.

Peacemaking

Diplomatic actions conducted after the commencement of conflict, with the aim of establishing a peaceful settlement. They can include the provision of good offices, mediation, conciliation and such actions as diplomatic isolation and sanctions.

Peacekeeping

Peacekeeping, narrowly defined, is the containment, moderation and/or termination of hostilities between or within States, through the medium of an impartial third party intervention, organised and directed internationally; using military forces, and civilians to complement the political process of conflict resolution and to restore and maintain peace.

Peacekeeping operations based on Chapter VI of the UN Charter have traditionally involved the deployment of a peacekeeping force in the field, with the consent of the parties, including supervising demarcation lines, monitoring ceasefires and controlling buffer zones, disarming and demobilising warring factions and supervising borders. Over the past few years, the UN has significantly expanded the type of military operations carried out under 'peacekeeping', to include for example protection of humanitarian relief and refugee operations. Peacekeeping operations may also contain substantial civilian elements, usually under the command of a civilian head of mission, such as civilian police, electoral or human rights monitors.

Peace-enforcement

Action under Chapter VII of the UN Charter using military means to restore peace in an area of conflict. This can include dealing with an inter-State conflict or with internal conflict to meet a humanitarian need or where state institutions have largely collapsed.

Peace-building

Post-conflict action to identify and support structures which will tend to strengthen and solidify a political settlement in order to avoid a return to conflict. It includes mechanisms to identify and support structures which will tend to consolidate peace, advance a sense of confidence and well-being and support economic reconstruction, and may require military as well as civilian involvement.

2. General principles[1]

The following general principles served as guidelines for the preparation of the more

detailed criteria and operational principles outlined further in Section 3.

Peacekeeping can be carried out only under the authority of the UN Security Council, or of the CSCE in accordance with the CSCE Document agreed in Helsinki in July 1992 and other relevant CSCE documents.

Peacekeeping will be carried out on a case-by-case basis and at all times in conformity with the purposes and principles of the Charter of the United Nations.

Decisions of concerned States or organisations on participation in peacekeeping activities are taken in each specific case in response to a request by the UN or the CSCE.

It is for the UN or CSCE, through consultations with contributing States and organisations, to define in each case the arrangements for the conduct of a peacekeeping operation, including command relationships.[2]

Peacekeeping is undertaken in cases of conflict within or among States in support of ongoing efforts to restore peace and stability by a political solution.[3]

Peacekeeping is intended to complement the political process of dispute resolution and is not a substitute for a negotiated settlement.

Peacekeeping requires a clear political objective and a precise mandate, as decided by the UN or the CSCE.

3. Criteria and operational principles

The following are intended to apply equally to preventive deployment, peacekeeping and peace-enforcement, unless otherwise indicated.

a. Criteria

Clear and precise mandate

The basis for any mission is a clear and precise mandate of the UN or the CSCE, developed through consultations with contributing States and organisations and/or interested parties, covering all of the essential elements of the operation to be performed.

---

[1] These principles were agreed on 15th March by Ambassadors in the meeting of the North Atlantic Council with Cooperation Partners.

[2] In developing Section 3, the Ad Hoc Group has taken the view that this should not be interpreted as giving the mandating body the power to make unilateral decisions on command relationships. Contributing States and organisations will themselves remain responsible for deciding whether command arrangements are appropriate before contributing forces.

[3] It is the common understanding that these efforts can also be undertaken in order to maintain peace or address potential conflicts.

Consent of the parties to the conflict

Consent and cooperation of the parties to the conflict are essential prerequisites for a UN peacekeeping operation based on Chapter VI of the UN Charter or for a CSCE peacekeeping operation. Exceptions are possible only if an operation has been based on Chapter VII of the Charter by the UN Security Council.

Transparency

The goals and means of implementation of an operation and the relationship between them need to be as transparent as possible, compatible with operational requirements.

An active information policy should be conducted to improve the awareness and understanding of international public opinion.

Impartiality

All aspects of an operation need to be conducted impartially, in a manner compatible with the nature of the operation, as defined by its mandate.

Credibility

The contributors to the mission should have, and be seen to have, the political will and capability to accomplish the objectives of the mandate.

Credibility is essential for the success of an operation, and depends, inter alia, on the political determination demonstrated by the international organisations and States concerned and on clear and achievable military and/or other aims, on the availability of sufficient material resources and on the quality and training of the personnel involved.

The planning and execution of a mission need to be at all times consistent with the aims and objectives to be achieved.

It will ultimately be up to the mandating body (UN or the CSCE), together with those implementing the operation, to assess respect for the two latter criteria.

b. Operational principles

Command and coordination

Unity of command of military forces is essential.

In its organisation, the command structure of a peacekeeping operation should take account of the specificity of each operation and of the assets, including command structures, which are made available to carry it out by the contributing States or organisations, keeping in mind the key requirement for military efficiency.

To be fully effective and efficient, there should be close coordination of all aspects of an operation, including political, civilian, administrative, legal, humanitarian and military.

Use of force

In all types of operations, the extent to which force can be used needs to be clearly defined either in the mandate or in the terms of reference.

If authorised, use of force must be carefully controlled, flexible and, at the lowest level consistent with the execution of the mandate.

Forces involved in any operation retain the inherent right of self-defence at all times.

Safety of personnel

A commitment to the protection of personnel involved in an operation should be inherent in the decision to conduct an operation.

Participation

All member states of the mandating body (UN or CSCE) are eligible to volunteer.

The mandating body (UN or CSCE) may invite states or organisations to provide forces or resources.

The mandating body (UN or CSCE) is not obliged to accept all offers but may choose which offers to accept.

The choice of contributors should take account of cultural, historical and political sensitivities and provide for multinationality of an operation.

When States or organisations have been invited to provide forces or resources, the nature or composition of them should be determined in consultation with the mandating body (UN or CSCE).

Financial considerations

Missions should have adequate financing. In general, costs are the collective responsibility of the member States of the mandating body (UN or CSCE) and will be shared on the basis of the rules applied by that body.

PART II: GUIDELINES FOR NACC COOPERATION IN PEACEKEEPING

4. Principles of cooperation

NACC cooperation in peacekeeping, as defined in the annual NACC Work Plans, may include recent extensions of this concept.

Conceptual and practical aspects of NACC cooperation in peacekeeping are based primarily on the relevant documents and practices of the UN and the CSCE.

Participation of NACC members in co-operation activities is voluntary. All NACC members are eligible to take part in all co-operation activities.

As a general rule, participation in activities on cooperation in peacekeeping should be open to interested non-NACC CSCE members who could, on the basis of specific experience and expertise in this area, make important contributions in:

(a) meetings of the Ad Hoc Group as observers; and

(b) information sessions of the Groups and in cooperative activities decided by it.

5. NACC cooperation with other international institutions and fora, in particular the UN and the CSCE

The following guidelines apply to programmes and activities of the Ad Hoc Group.

– Maximum transparency and cooperation with the UN and CSCE.

– Coordination of specific activities to avoid duplication of work and to encourage complementarity.

– Invitation, as appropriate, to a representative of the CSCE Chairman-in-Office to attend meetings of the Ad Hoc Group.

– Tasking of the Chairman of the Ad Hoc Group or his representative to inform the CSCE regularly and to address relevant CSCE fora, as appropriate.

6. Financial considerations

Cooperative activities in peacekeeping cannot be conducted if they are not properly funded. The initial measures set out in Part III below, as far as they concern courses, seminars or workshops organised by member countries of the North Atlantic Co-operation Council, are based on the following pattern: unless otherwise agreed, the organising country bears the cost for the local expenses, including board and lodging, while the travelling expenses will be borne by the participants. The Ad Hoc Group will, as the need arises, develop financial considerations as appropriate.

PART III: MEASURES FOR PRACTICAL COOPERATION IN PEACEKEEPING

7. Development of a common understanding of operational concepts and requirements for peacekeeping

a. Objectives:

To develop a common understanding of operational concepts and requirements for peacekeeping by exchanging experiences, ideas, and doctrines; to examine concepts and doctrine with a view to the development of common guidelines in support of peacekeeping.

b. Actions:

(1) To exchange national concepts and doctrine on peacekeeping within the Ad Hoc Group.

(2) To consider jointly conceptual aspects of peacekeeping, to exchange experiences in peacekeeping operations and to compare peacekeeping doctrines at a conference of high level political and military representatives, which is now scheduled for the period 30th June to 2nd July 1993 and will be hosted by the Czech Republic. A detailed report on the seminar will be prepared by the NATO Secretariat and the NATO Military Authorities and will be submitted to the Ad Hoc Group in September 1993. Lessons drawn from this conference and future action will be considered by the Group.

(3) To exchange experiences in peacekeeping, taking into account experiences in operations related to the former Yugoslavia, making use, inter alia, of all available opportunities of meetings of high level military representatives. A first such exchange took place during the meeting of Chiefs of Defence Staff in Cooperation Session, on 28th April 1993. The Ad Hoc Group welcomed the written report provided by the Chairman of the Military Committee in Chiefs of Staff Session with Cooperation Partners.

c. Element for further development:

Continuation of an organised exchange of experiences within the Ad Hoc Group building on the results of the Prague seminar, with a view to the further development of common guidelines in support of peacekeeping, set out in paragraphs 1 to 6 of this report.

8. Cooperation in planning for peacekeeping activities

a. Objectives:

To identify and examine principal planning issues, commencing initially with key issues such as command and control; to compare and harmonise planning methods and procedures, so as to facilitate the ability of Partners to cooperate practically in peacekeeping and to develop an understanding of assets required and resources available for contributions both to preparations for peacekeeping and to peacekeeping operations themselves.

b. Actions:

To facilitate cooperative peacekeeping planning activity, starting with a discussion in the Ad Hoc Group. Discussions should cover initially:

(1) assets and capabilities required for peacekeeping.

(2) the possibility and utility of developing a data base of available resources (e.g. personnel, equipment, forces, infrastructure, and supplies), perhaps using an appropriate questionnaire.

(3) the requirements for forces, procedures and equipment to facilitate cooperation in peacekeeping.

c. Elements for further development:

Each of the areas set out at b. above should be the subject of reports to the Ad Hoc Group by the Military Authorities. There were valuable results in this respect at the meeting of the MCCS with Cooperation Partners on 28th April. Further reports should cover:

(1) Identification of capabilities which could be made available to the UN or CSCE, subject to consideration on a case-by-case basis

(2) developing a common understanding on planning areas (command, control, communication and information systems, support, logistic military information, rules of engagement, education, etc.) on the basis of the general principles, criteria and guidelines set out in Parts I and II.

9. Development of a common technical basis in peacekeeping

a. Objectives:

To identify technical aspects of peacekeeping in order to develop a common basis and understanding. These might include, inter alia, terminology, interoperability issues, and procedural matters.

b. Actions:

(1) To create an Ad Hoc Technical Sub-Group reporting to the Ad Hoc Group and with the participation of the Military Authorities, under the chairmanship of ASG DDP, to identify issues and methods of cooperation on the basis of national contributions and a report by the NATO Military Authorities building on their own contacts with Cooperation Partners.

(2) One action that has already been completed was a workshop, held in, and organised by, the Netherlands, on 'Communications for Peacekeeping Operations'. A summary of the report of that workshop is attached as Annex A [not reproduced here].

(3) As further steps,

(*a*) To hold a workshop to cover additional technical aspects, such as infrastructure in support of peacekeeping and equipment interoperability, and

(*b*) to conduct research into technical aspects of peacekeeping, inter alia, peacekeeping terminology, interoperability issues and procedural matters, based on proposals to be developed further by the United States and other delegations.

c. Elements for further development:

The following are areas on which the group might focus initially in considering interoperability issues

(1) Equipment

– Communications

– Transportation

– Petrol, Oil and Lubricants

– Ammunition

(2) Organisation and Procedures

– Command and Control

– Communications

– Transportation

– Materials Handling

– Medical Support

Further details on a number of these areas are dealt with in paragraphs 10 and 11. Proposals for development of these elements will be considered by the Ad Hoc Technical Sub-Group.

10. Peacekeeping training, education and exercises

a. Objectives:

To share experiences and to develop practical cooperation in the fields of training, education and exercises, in order to develop common training standards, enhance interoperability and improve operational effectiveness.

b. Actions:

(1) As a first step, information will be exchanged in the Ad Hoc Technical Sub-Group on national training programmes for peacekeeping. The exchange will include, inter alia, information on the structure of training, training facilities and the subjects covered in the training programmes. On this basis, the Ad Hoc Group will consider the scope for

common training programmes and standards for national individuals and forces involved in peacekeeping, and the feasibility of peacekeeping exercises, including objectives, character and financial and other resources implications.

(2) To conduct a pilot course for unit commanders on peacekeeping, with an initial course to be organised by the Czech Republic at Cesky Krumlov from the 17th May until the 11th June.

(3) The seminar on training, scheduled to take place in Bucharest, 18th–21st October 1993, as part of the Military Cooperation Programme, may also focus on Peacekeeping.

(4) To conduct a workshop of civil and military experts to explore the feasibility of joint exercises in peacekeeping, concentrating initially on humanitarian missions, including the management of refugee movements, the distribution of essential supplies, and the organisation of medical assistance.

(5) To conduct a course on peacekeeping at the SHAPE school in Oberammergau, Germany from 8th to 11th November 1993.

(6) To conduct a seminar in Copenhagen, 17th–19th November 1993, on 'Peacekeeping Experiences: Generation, Training and Education, and Planning—the Applicability of the Nordic Approach to Cooperation in Peacekeeping'.

(7) To make places available to NACC members, whenever practicable, on national specialised peacekeeping courses.

(8) To expand the national logistics peacekeeping training course in Norway to include additional places for officers from NACC members.

c. Elements for further development:

It is proposed that discussions and exchanges on peacekeeping training use the following framework. For Units, Commanders and Staff Personnel:

(1) Basic Military Training

(2) Specialised Training (specific training for any peacekeeping mission)

(3) Orientation Training/Education (for a particular mission).

Further detail on (1) to (3) is attached as Annex B [not reproduced here].

The Ad Hoc Technical Sub-Group should examine these issues further in the light of the seminars and courses which have now been arranged.

11. Logistics aspects of peacekeeping

a. Objectives:

To identify specific logistics issues within peacekeeping operations and to consider possibilities for cooperation in the logistics area.

b. Actions:

(1) The International Secretariat will present proposals for a specific programme in this area to the Ad Hoc Group, taking into account national contributions and the work of the NATO Military Authorities.

(2) To organise a seminar on logistics in Norway. This seminar has been scheduled for 1st–5th November 1993 and a detailed programme has been presented to the Ad Hoc Group.

c. Elements for further development:

(1) Canada is considering organising a workshop on logistics support for peacekeeping which would be conducted after completion of its current work on a new UN Logistics Peacekeeping Manual. The Ad Hoc Group may consider the follow-on requirement for a training course for logisticians incorporating elements of this and other similar endeavours.

(2) Logistics experts will contribute actively to all endeavours under paragraphs 7 to 10, which have logistical implications.

(3) Possible approaches to increased effectiveness of logistic support in cooperative peacekeeping to be discussed by Ad Hoc Group building on common logistic planning principles:

– UN field service
– National responsibility
– Multinational pools
– Mutual assistance, role specialisation
– Lead nation
– Host nation.

The International Staff will submit detailed proposals to the Ad Hoc Group for taking these issues further, on the basis of contributions by NACC member states and NATO's military authorities, taking into account the results of the logistics seminar to be held in Norway. In this context consideration might be given to the need to establish an Ad Hoc Logistics Sub-Group.

Source: NATO, Press Release M-NACC-1(93) 40, 11 June 1993.

FRENCH PROPOSAL FOR A PACT ON STABILITY IN EUROPE

Submitted to the summit meeting of the European Council, Copenhagen, 22 June 1993[1]

1. Why a European initiative for a Pact on stability?

The end of the division of Europe has made it possible for all countries on the continent (notably in the CSCE) to adopt common principles concerning borders or minority rights. The many institutions existing in the political, economic or military arenas have developed their action and have endeavoured to support implementation of these principles.

The break-up of Yugoslavia into several states and the war which has torn Bosnia-Herzegovina apart have revealed the acuteness of the problem of minorities and the powerlessness of the international community, including the Europe of the Twelve, to apply the principles to which they have adhered.

It is urgent today to learn lessons from this experience. It is incumbent upon the European Community to do so with all interested partners in order to address the most serious problems facing the European continent. Should it fail to carry out this exercise or should it fail to do so successfully, it is clear that the Community's international authority would be at stake. On the contrary, restoring peace on the European continent would contribute to the success of the difficult transition being experienced by the Central and Eastern European countries and those of the former Soviet Union; it could have a decisive effect on growth.

The Twelve have a *major interest* in the stability and security of a continent in which they are the most solid element. They have the *economic weight* to encourage this stability and, if they have the political will, the means to consolidate it with their allies. Actively seeking this result should be the first task of the Common Foreign and Security Policy provided in the Maastricht Treaty. Such is the object of the conference France

is proposing to its Community partners and which it places within the continuity of work already carried out in the framework of the CSCE. This conference should result in the signature of a European Pact, made up of several agreements between the countries concerned which would create with each other a process of entente and cooperation likely to encourage European stability.

2. What content shall be given to the Pact?

The principal objective of the Pact would be, pragmatically speaking:

– to set out in detail and implement, in the countries whose relations are not yet stabilized by membership in one of the main European political bodies, the principles already defined in regard to borders and minorities;

– to organize and coordinate the action of the many existing institutions to provide the best possible guarantee for these principles.

A. Consolidation of borders

The preparatory conference should not limit its action to solemnly reaffirming the inviolability of borders in Europe. It must lead to the conclusion of friendship agreements founded on respect for the rights of minorities, since the violation of these rights risks causing international complications.

Without taking sides a priori, the possibility cannot be ruled out that these agreements may lead to minor rectifications of borders, the intangibility of which would then be established by the conference. The states participating in the conference would thus collectively serve as guarantors of these bilateral agreements.

B. Minorities

With respect to principles, existing texts have gradually evolved from a purely individual conception of the rights of persons belonging to minorities towards a conception taking account of their collective aspect and the very close tie linking them to security problems.

At the present time, nationals of Council of Europe member countries have the *right of individual appeal* in regard to the European Convention on Human Rights. The 'Court of Conciliation and Arbitration', ratification of which by the interested countries must be hastened, can deal with *disputes between states*. Finally, the High Commissioner [on] National Minorities existing within the CSCE can examine the *collective rights of a minority*.

Pursuing this evolution, the conference

---

[1] [The European Council examined the French proposal at the Copenhagen meeting and adopted a synthetic report on the issue at its next meeting in Brussels, 11 Dec. 1993. *La politique étrangère de la France, Textes et documents,* Nov./Dec. 1993, pp. 228–29.]

preparing the Pact would examine a report requested by the Twelve of the High Commissioner [on] National Minorities and would set as an objective to be attained within a given period (eight months):

– *leading the Eastern and Central European countries to set out among themselves agreements of a nature to provide practical solutions on a case-by-case basis to their minority problems.* This examination would take place by regional sub-units, the states directly concerned associating other members of the conference whose presence would be accepted as moderators.

– *setting out preventive procedures* capable of keeping violations of rights of minorities from leading to security problems. The role and powers of the *High Commissioner [on] National Minorities* should be reappraised. Should the High Commissioner play a role of adviser for minorities so as to make better known *all the institutional mechanisms capable of ensuring their satisfactory presentation* (means of election, presence in the administrative hierarchy, arrangements for coexistence between religions, etc.)? How can preventive action be more effective? Should the Commissioner also have a right of appeal and before what body? (Would the Summit of the Heads of State of the Twelve agree to hear the Commissioner once a year?)

C. Incentives and flanking measures

The preparatory conference should examine the best way to lead European countries to respect the principles to which they adhere and propose flanking measures that could be taken to encourage peace and stability in Europe. The *incentives* and flanking measures depending essentially on the will of the Twelve are:

– political: to respond to the expectations of Central European countries and certain Eastern European countries, the Community would contemplate *eventual new memberships, on the express condition that, within the framework of the conference,* the problems likely to threaten European stability are resolved. This condition would, of course, be necessary but not sufficient. The Community would have to determine whether these countries are in a position to become members.

– economic: can the Community decide to provide *specific assistance to countries taking particular care to solve their problems relating to minorities* (for accompanying projects in specific regions), *immigration* or *refugees* (setting up resettlement programmes)? In the opposite case, can it also decide to *cut off all cooperation ties with a country flagrantly violating the rights of minorities or calling existing borders into question?* The Yugoslav experience shows that such incentives have their limits when they are not implemented in timely fashion.

The preparatory conference should examine the *flanking measures* that could be taken to encourage this stability in a preventive way.

More precisely, it could:

– study the possibility for the WEU to admit as associate members the countries adhering to a European agreement whose membership in the European Union is an eventual possibility and to develop military cooperation with them, notably in the area of peacekeeping. Could units available rapidly for this type of operation be designated in advance?

– foster military cooperation among Central and Eastern European countries, the Twelve, NATO and the WEU.

– propose practical measures to strengthen the CSCE institutions.

3. What participants, what procedure, what timetable?

Participation in preparation of the Pact

The list of countries invited is naturally linked to the objective of the conference, which is to stabilize the Central and Eastern European countries which may eventually be associated to varying degrees with the European Union. The *United States and Canada*, which have an interest in European balance, on the one hand, *Russia, Belarus, Ukraine and Moldova*, which have problems relating to borders or minorities with the Central European or Balkan countries, on the other, and the *Baltic countries*, which do not belong to the CIS and are not excluded from the perspective of *European Union,* should logically be invited.

The definition of the objective of the preparatory conference would make it possible *not to exclude the CIS countries closest to us,* without encroaching upon debate within this body which is not within the competence of the Twelve. It would also explain how this initiative does not duplicate the CSCE.

The draft Pact could be prepared as follows:

(a) The Twelve, based on the work of

senior officials of the CSCE and the preparatory conference for the definition of a 'code of conduct', would prepare:
– a *draft declaration* reaffirming the principles concerning borders and minorities;
– a list of problems relating to borders and minorities in the Central and Western European countries which would justify the creation of a *negotiating table*. If such a group already exists in the CSCE, it would be reactivated by the conference;
– a *list of incentives* the Community could implement in favour of countries agreeing to respect the principles approved by the conference.

(*b*) The Pact preparatory conference would then meet for several days in plenary session. It would issue its position on the text prepared by the Twelve and would set up negotiating tables which would be given six months to depose their conclusions.

The preparatory conference is clearly an exercise in *preventive diplomacy* very different in nature from the curative measures required in ex-Yugoslavia. In these conditions, the possible links between the London Conference on ex-Yugoslavia and the Conference on Stability will be dependent on developments on location.

(*c*) *An interim meeting would be held at the end of a six-month period to sanction the achievements* of certain negotiating tables or to give new impetus to those progressing more slowly.

(*d*) *A final conference, two months later:*
– would establish, in a 'European Pact', the particular agreements concluded in the regional negotiations, including those setting out possible rectifications of borders;
– would agree on flanking measures;
– would make proposals designed to increase the authority of the CSCE (role of the Secretary General, the High Commissioner [on] National Minorities, etc.);
– would agree to support the activity of the Court of Arbitration.

A *summary version of the timetable for the preparation and unfolding of the preparatory conference could be as follows*:
– 21–22 June: presentation of the memorandum to the Copenhagen European Summit, which is expected to give a mandate to the competent bodies under the authority of the Council of Ministers to prepare the documents necessary for the convening of the conference;
– within four months: convening of the preparatory conference by the Twelve and

the start of work (around six months);
– second half of 1994: interim meeting reviewing the progress of work;
– two months later: final conference.

Possible participants

1. The Twelve	12
2. Countries interested in stability in Europe:	
– United States	
– Canada	2
3. The countries of Northern, Central and Eastern Europe concerned:	
– Russian Federation	
– Austria	
– Norway	
– Sweden	
– Iceland	
– Switzerland	
– Finland	
– Poland	
– Hungary	
– Czech Republic	
– Slovakia	
– Bulgaria	
– Romania	
– Albania	
– Estonia	
– Latvia	
– Lithuania	
– Ukraine	
– Belarus	
– Moldova	
– Turkey	21
4. The countries of ex-Yugoslavia will be associated in terms of developments of the London Conference and of the situation on location:	
– Croatia	
– Slovenia	
– Bosnia-Herzegovina	
– Serbia Montenegro	
– Ex-Yugoslav Republic of Macedonia	5

Source: Agence Europe, *Europe Documents,* no. 1846 (26 June 1993), pp. 1, 5. Reproduced by kind permission of Agence Europe, Brussels.

RUSSIAN PRESIDENT BORIS YELTSIN'S LETTER TO US PRESIDENT BILL CLINTON

15 September 1993

Dear Bill:

By way of continuing our frank exchanges on pressing international issues I would like to share with you some of my thoughts prompted, in particular, by my recent conversations with the leaders of Poland, Czechia, and Slovakia.

The present attitudes of these countries, as well as some other states of Central and Eastern Europe, are indicative of their rather clearly expressed desire to get closer to NATO, to achieve a certain form of integration with the alliance. Of course, we expressed understanding for the sovereign right of each state to choose ways of ensuring its own security, including through participation in politico-military alliances. We are sympathetic to the less-than-nostalgic sentiments of the East Europeans about the past 'cooperation' within the framework of the Warsaw Pact. Our general impression is that they do have grounds for certain apprehensions about their security.

At the same time I cannot fail to express our concern over the fact that the debate about possible evolution of NATO increasingly dwells on the option of quantitative build-up of the Alliance by adding East European countries to it.

Frankly, we support a different approach, one which would lead to a truly pan-European security system, which envisions collective actions (but not under the bloc membership criterion) for the purpose of preventing and resolving crises and conflicts raging presently in Europe. Security must be indivisible and must rest on pan-European structures.

The main threat to Europe now is posed not by the East–West confrontation, but by inter-ethnic conflicts of a new generation. A quantitative increase of NATO will hardly resolve the task of countering them effectively. What we need to do is build up the anti-crisis, peace-making potential encompassing the whole continent.

We understand, of course, that a possible integration of East European countries with NATO will not automatically produce a situation where the Alliance would somehow turn against Russia. We do not see NATO as a bloc opposing us. But it is important to take into account how our public opinion may react to such a step. Not only the opposition, but the moderates, too, would no doubt see this as a sort of neo-isolation of the country as opposed to its natural introduction into the Euro-Atlantic space.

I would also like to call your attention to the fact that the Treaty on the Final Settlement with Respect to Germany signed in September 1990, particularly those of its provisions that prohibit stationing of foreign troops within the FRG's eastern lands, excludes, by its meaning, the possibility of expansion of the NATO zone to the East.

We know that at present preparations are under way for a special NATO summit meeting which will be discussing strategic aspects of the Alliance's evolution and its role in new conditions. We in Russia have an interest in constructive decisions by this summit adequate to the radical changes which have occurred in Europe and in the world. We hope that it is this prudent, unhurried approach that will prevail in making the choice of new parameters of the 'East politics'.

And generally, we favor a situation where the relations between our country and NATO would be by several degrees warmer than those between the Alliance and Eastern Europe. NATO–Russia rapprochement, including through their interaction in the peace-making area, should proceed on a faster track. The East Europeans, too, could be involved in this process.

Over [the] longer term one should not, perhaps, rule out our joining NATO. But for the time being, this is a theoretical proposition.

Today, I would like to suggest to you and our other NATO partners to jointly reflect about the possibilities to meet security needs of the East Europeans.

For example, we would be prepared, together with NATO, to offer official security guarantees to the East European states with a focus on ensuring sovereignty, territorial integrity, inviolability of frontiers, and maintenance of peace in the region. Such guarantees could be stipulated in a political statement or cooperation agreement between the Russian Federation and NATO.

Naturally, we are open to discussion of other proposals and would welcome intensification of the Russian–American dialogue in this respect during the period prior to the upcoming NATO summit.

Sincerely,
Boris Yeltsin

Source: SIPRI archive.

TREATY ON EUROPEAN UNION (MAASTRICHT TREATY): PROVISIONS ON EUROPEAN SECURITY

Signed in Maastricht, The Netherlands, on 11 December1991. Entered into force on 1 November 1993

Excerpts

TITLE I. COMMON PROVISIONS

Article A

By this Treaty, the High Contracting Parties establish among themselves a European Union, hereinafter called 'the Union'.

This Treaty marks a new stage in the process of creating an ever closer union among the peoples of Europe, in which decisions are taken as closely as possible to the citizen.

The Union shall be founded on the European Communities, supplemented by the policies and forms of cooperation established by this Treaty. Its task shall be to organize, in a manner demonstrating consistency and solidarity, relations between the Member States and between their peoples.

Article B

The Union shall set itself the following objectives:

- to promote economic and social progress which is balanced and sustainable, in particular through the creation of an area without internal frontiers, through the strengthening of economic and social cohesion and through the establishment of economic and monetary union, ultimately including a single currency in accordance with the provisions of this Treaty;

- to assert its identity on the international scene, in particular through the implementation of a common foreign and security policy including the eventual framing of a common defence policy, which might in time lead to a common defence;

- to strengthen the protection of the rights and interests of the nationals of its Member States through the introduction of a citizenship of the Union;

- to develop close cooperation on justice and home affairs;

- to maintain in full the *acquis communautaire* and build on it with a view to considering, through the procedure referred to in Article N (2), to what extent the policies and forms of cooperation introduced by this Treaty may need to be revised with the aim of ensuring the effectiveness of the mechan-

isms and the institutions of the Community.

The objectives of the Union shall be achieved as provided in this Treaty and in accordance with the conditions and the timetable set out therein while respecting the principle of subsidiarity as defined in Article 3b of the Treaty establishing the European Community.

. . .

Article D

The European Council shall provide the Union with the necessary impetus for its development and shall define the general political guidelines thereof.

The European Council shall bring together the Heads of State or Government of the Member States and the President of the Commission. They shall be assisted by the Ministers for Foreign Affairs of the Member States and by a Member of the Commission. The European Council shall meet at least twice a year, under the chairmanship of the Head of State or Government of the Member State which holds the Presidency of the Council.

The European Council shall submit to the European Parliament a report after each of its meetings and a yearly written report on the progress achieved by the Union.

. . .

Article F

1. The Union shall respect the national identities of its Member States, whose systems of government are founded on the principles of democracy.

2. The Union shall respect fundamental rights, as guaranteed by the European Convention for the Protection of Human Rights and Fundamental Freedoms signed in Rome on 4 November 1950 and as they result from the constitutional traditions common to the Member States, as general principles of Community law.

3. The Union shall provide itself with the means necessary to attain its objectives and carry through its policies.

. . .

TITLE V. PROVISIONS ON A COMMON FOREIGN AND SECURITY POLICY

Article J

A common foreign and security policy is hereby established which shall be governed by the following provisions.

Article J.1

1. The Union and its Member States shall define and implement a common foreign and security policy, governed by the provisions of this Title and covering all areas of foreign and security policy.

2. The objectives of the common foreign and security policy shall be:
– to safeguard the common values, fundamental interests and independence of the Union;
– to strengthen the security of the Union and its Member States in all ways;
– to preserve peace and strengthen international security, in accordance with the principles of the United Nations Charter as well as the principles of the Helsinki Final Act and the objectives of the Paris Charter;
– to promote international cooperation;
– to develop and consolidate democracy and the rule of law, and respect for human rights and fundamental freedoms.

3. The Union shall pursue these objectives:
– by establishing systematic cooperation between Member States in the conduct of policy, in accordance with Article J.2;
– by gradually implementing, in accordance with Article J.3, joint action in the areas in which the Member States have important interests in common.

4. The Member States shall support the Union's external and security policy actively and unreservedly in a spirit of loyalty and mutual solidarity. They shall refrain from any action which is contrary to the interests of the Union or likely to impair its effectiveness as a cohesive force in international relations. The Council shall ensure that these principles are complied with.

Article J.2

1. Member States shall inform and consult one another within the Council on any matter of foreign and security policy of general interest in order to ensure that their combined influence is exerted as effectively as possible by means of concerted and convergent action.

2. Whenever it deems it necessary, the Council shall define a common position.
Member States shall ensure that their national policies conform to the common positions.

3. Member States shall coordinate their action in international organizations and at international conferences. They shall uphold the common positions in such forums.

In international organizations and at international conferences where not all the Member States participate, those which do take part shall uphold the common positions.

Article J.3

The procedure for adopting joint action in matters covered by the foreign and security policy shall be the following:

1. The Council shall decide, on the basis of general guidelines from the European Council, that a matter should be the subject of joint action.
Whenever the Council decides on the principle of joint action, it shall lay down the specific scope, the Union's general and specific objectives in carrying out such action, if necessary its duration, and the means, procedures and conditions for its implementation.

2. The Council shall, when adopting joint action and at any stage during its development, define those matters on which decisions are to be taken by a qualified majority.
Where the Council is required to act by a qualified majority pursuant to the preceding subparagraph, the votes of its members shall be weighted in accordance with Article 148(2) of the Treaty establishing the European Community, and for their adoption, acts of the Council shall require at least 54 votes in favour, cast by at least eight members.

3. If there is a change in circumstances having a substantial effect on a question subject to joint action, the Council shall review the principles and objectives of that action and take the necessary decisions. As long as the Council has not acted, the joint action shall stand.

4. Joint actions shall commit the Member States in the positions they adopt and in the conduct of their activity.

5. Whenever there is any plan to adopt a national position or take national action pursuant to a joint action, information shall be provided in time to allow, if necessary, for prior consultations within the Council. The obligation to provide prior information shall not apply to measures which are merely a national transposition of Council decisions.

6. In cases of imperative need arising from changes in the situation and failing a Council decision, Member States may take the necessary measures as a matter of urgency having regard to the general objectives of the joint action. The Member State concerned shall inform the Council immediately of any such measures.

7. Should there be any major difficulties in implementing a joint action, a Member State shall refer them to the Council which shall discuss them and seek appropriate solutions. Such solutions shall not run counter to the objectives of the joint action or impair its effectiveness.

Article J.4

1. The common foreign and security policy shall include all questions related to the security of the Union, including the eventual framing of a common defence policy, which might in time lead to a common defence.

2. The Union requests the Western European Union (WEU), which is an integral part of the development of the Union, to elaborate and implement decisions and actions of the Union which have defence implications. The Council shall, in agreement with the institutions of the WEU, adopt the necessary practical arrangements.

3. Issues having defence implications dealt with under this Article shall not be subject to the procedures set out in Article J.3.

4. The policy of the Union in accordance with this Article shall not prejudice the specific character of the security and defence policy of certain Member States and shall respect the obligations of certain Member States under the North Atlantic Treaty and be compatible with the common security and defence policy established within that framework.

5. The provisions of this Article shall not prevent the development of closer cooperation between two or more Member States on a bilateral level, in the framework of the WEU and the Atlantic Alliance, provided such cooperation does not run counter to or impede that provided for in this Title.

6. With a view to furthering the objective of this Treaty, and having in view the date of 1998 in the context of Article XII of the Brussels Treaty, the provisions of this Article may be revised as provided for in Article N(2) on the basis of a report to be presented in 1996 by the Council to the European Council, which shall include an evaluation of the progress made and the experience gained until then.

Article J.5

1. The Presidency shall represent the Union in matters coming within the common foreign and security policy.

2. The Presidency shall be responsible for the implementation of common measures; in

that capacity it shall in principle express the position of the Union in international organizations and international conferences.

3. In the tasks referred to in paragraphs 1 and 2, the Presidency shall be assisted if need be by the previous and next Member States to hold the Presidency. The Commission shall be fully associated in these tasks.

4. Without prejudice to Article J.2(3) and Article J.3(4), Member States represented in international organizations or international conferences where not all the Member States participate shall keep the latter informed of any matter of common interest.

Member States which are also members of the United Nations Security Council will concert and keep the other Member States fully informed. Member States which are permanent members of the Security Council will, in the execution of their functions, ensure the defence of the positions and the interests of the Union, without prejudice to their responsibilities under the provisions of the United Nations Charter.

Article J.6

The diplomatic and consular missions of the Member States and the Commission Delegations in third countries and international conferences, and their representations to international organizations, shall cooperate in ensuring that the common positions and common measures adopted by the Council are complied with and implemented.

They shall step up cooperation by exchanging information, carrying out joint assessments and contributing to the implementation of the provisions referred to in Article 8c of the Treaty establishing the European Community.

Article J.7

The Presidency shall consult the European Parliament on the main aspects and the basic choices of the common foreign and security policy and shall ensure that the views of the European Parliament are duly taken into consideration. The European Parliament shall be kept regularly informed by the Presidency and the Commission of the development of the Union's foreign and security policy.

The European Parliament may ask questions of the Council or make recommendations to it. It shall hold an annual debate on progress in implementing the common foreign and security policy.

Article J.8

1. The European Council shall define the

principles of and general guidelines for the common foreign and security policy.

2. The Council shall take the decisions necessary for defining and implementing the common foreign and security policy on the basis of the general guidelines adopted by the European Council. It shall ensure the unity, consistency and effectiveness of action by the Union.

The Council shall act unanimously, except for procedural questions and in the case referred to in Article J.3(2).

3. Any Member State or the Commission may refer to the Council any question relating to the common foreign and security policy and may submit proposals to the Council.

4. In cases requiring a rapid decision, the Presidency, of its own motion, or at the request of the Commission or a Member State, shall convene an extraordinary Council meeting within 48 hours or, in an emergency, within a shorter period.

5. Without prejudice to Article 151 of the Treaty establishing the European Community, a Political Committee consisting of Political Directors shall monitor the international situation in the areas covered by common foreign and security policy and contribute to the definition of policies by delivering opinions to the Council at the request of the Council or on its own initiative. It shall also monitor the implementation of agreed policies, without prejudice to the responsibility of the Presidency and the Commission.

Article J.9

The Commission shall be fully associated with the work carried out in the common foreign and security policy field.

Article J.10

On the occasion of any review of the security provisions under Article J.4, the Conference which is convened to that effect shall also examine whether any other amendments need to be made to provisions relating to the common foreign and security policy.

Article J.11

1. The provisions referred to in Articles 137, 138, 139 to 142, 146, 147, 150 to 153, 157 to 163 and 217 of the Treaty establishing the European Community shall apply to the provisions relating to the areas referred to in this Title.

2. Administrative expenditure which the provisions relating to the areas referred to in this Title entail for the institutions shall be charged to the budget of the European Communities.

The Council may also:

– either decide unanimously that operational expenditure to which the implementation of those provisions gives rise is to be charged to the budget of the European Communities; in that event, the budgetary procedure laid down in the Treaty establishing the European Community shall be applicable;

– or determine that such expenditure shall be charged to the Member States, where appropriate in accordance with a scale to be decided.

. . .

FINAL ACT

. . .

DECLARATIONS

. . .

27. Declaration on Voting in the Field of the Common Foreign and Security Policy

The Conference agrees that, with regard to Council decisions requiring unanimity, Member States will, to the extent possible, avoid preventing a unanimous decision where a qualified majority exists in favour of that decision.

28. Declaration on Practical Arrangements in the Field of the Common Foreign and Security Policy

The Conference agrees that the division of work between the Political Committee and the Committee of Permanent Representatives will be examined at a later stage, as will the practical arrangements for merging the Political Cooperation Secretariat with the General Secretariat of the Council and for cooperation between the latter and the Commission.

29. Declaration on the Use of Languages in the Field of the Common Foreign and Security Policy

The Conference agrees that the use of languages shall be in accordance with the rules of the European Communities.

For Coreu communications, the current practice of European political cooperation will serve as a guide for the time being.

All common foreign and security policy texts which are submitted to or adopted at meetings of the European Council and of the Council as well as all texts which are to be published are immediately and simultaneously translated into all the official Community languages.

30. Declaration on Western European Union

The Conference notes the following declarations:

I. Declaration by Belgium, Germany, Spain, France, Italy, Luxembourg, the Netherlands, Portugal and the United Kingdom of Great Britain and Northern Ireland, which are members of the Western European Union and also members of the European Union on

The Role of the Western European Union and its Relations with the European Union and with the Atlantic Alliance

Introduction

1. WEU Member States agree on the need to develop a genuine European security and defence identity and a greater European responsibility on defence matters. This identity will be pursued through a gradual process involving successive phases. WEU will form an integral part of the process of the development of the European Union and will enhance its contribution to solidarity within the Atlantic Alliance. WEU Member States agree to strengthen the role of WEU, in the longer term perspective of a common defence policy within the European Union which might in time lead to a common defence, compatible with that of the Atlantic Alliance.

2. WEU will be developed as the defence component of the European Union and as a means to strengthen the European pillar of the Atlantic Alliance. To this end, it will formulate common European defence policy and carry forward its concrete implementation through the further development of its own operational role.

WEU Member States take note of Article J.4 relating to the common foreign and security policy of the Treaty on European Union which reads as follows:

'*1. The common foreign and security policy shall include all questions related to the security of the Union, including the eventual framing of a common defence policy, which might in time lead to a common defence.*

2. The Union requests the Western European Union (WEU), which is an integral part of the development of the Union, to elaborate and implement decisions and

actions of the Union which have defence implications. The Council shall, in agreement with the institutions of the WEU, adopt the necessary practical arrangements.

3. Issues having defence implications dealt with under this Article shall not be subject to the procedures set out in Article J.3.

4. The policy of the Union in accordance with this Article shall not prejudice the specific character of the security and defence policy of certain Member States and shall respect the obligations of certain Member States under the North Atlantic Treaty and be compatible with the common security and defence policy established within the framework.

5. The provisions of this Article shall not prevent the development of closer cooperation between two or more Member States on a bilateral level, in the framework of the WEU and the Atlantic Alliance, provided such cooperation does not run counter to or impede that provided for in this Title.

6. With a view to furthering the objective of this Treaty, and having in view the date of 1998 in the context of Article XII of the Brussels Treaty, the provisions of this Article may be revised as provided for in Article N(2) on the basis of a report to be presented in 1996 by the Council to the European Council, which shall include an evaluation of the progress made and the experience gained until then.'

A—WEU's relations with European Union

3. The objective is to build up WEU in stages as the defence component of the European Union. To this end, WEU is prepared, at the request of the European Union, to elaborate and implement decisions and actions of the Union which have defence implications.

To this end, WEU will take the following measures to develop a close working relationship with the Union:
– as appropriate, synchronization of the dates and venues of meetings and harmonization of working methods;
– establishment of close cooperation between the Council and Secretariat-General of WEU on the one hand, and the Council of the Union and General Secretariat of the Council on the other;
– consideration of the harmonization of the sequence and duration of the respective Presidencies;

– arranging for appropriate modalities so as to ensure that the Commission of the European Communities is regularly informed and, as appropriate, consulted on WEU activities in accordance with the role of the Commission in the common foreign and security policy as defined in the Treaty on European Union;

– encouragement of closer cooperation between the Parliamentary Assembly of WEU and the European Parliament.

The WEU Council shall, in agreement with the competent bodies of the European Union, adopt the necessary practical arrangements.

B—WEU's relations with the Atlantic Alliance

4. The objective is to develop WEU as a means to strengthen the European pillar of the Atlantic Alliance. Accordingly WEU is prepared to develop further the close working links between WEU and the Alliance and to strengthen the role, responsibilities and contributions of WEU Member States in the Alliance. This will be undertaken on the basis of the necessary transparency and complementarity between the emerging European security and defence identity and the Alliance. WEU will act in conformity with the positions adopted in the Atlantic Alliance.

– WEU Member States will intensify their coordination on Alliance issues which represent an important common interest with the aim of introducing joint positions agreed in WEU into the process of consultation in the Alliance which will remain the essential forum for consultation among its members and the venue for agreement on policies bearing on the security and defence commitments of Allies under the North Atlantic Treaty.

– Where necessary, dates and venues of meetings will be synchronized and working methods harmonized.

– Close cooperation will be established between the Secretariats-General of WEU and NATO.

C—Operational role of WEU

5. WEU's operational role will be strengthened by examining and defining appropriate missions, structures and means, covering in particular:

– WEU planning cell;

– closer military cooperation complementary to the Alliance in particular in the fields of logistics, transport, training and strategic surveillance;

– meetings of WEU Chiefs of Defence Staff;

– military units answerable to WEU.

Other proposals will be examined further, including:

– enhanced cooperation in the field of armaments with the aim of creating a European armaments agency;

– development of the WEU Institute into a European Security and Defence Academy.

Arrangements aimed at giving WEU a stronger operational role will be fully compatible with the military dispositions necessary to ensure the collective defence of all Allies.

D—Other measures

6. As a consequence of the measures set out above, and in order to facilitate the strengthening of WEU's role, the seat of the WEU Council and Secretariat will be transferred to Brussels.

7. Representation on the WEU Council must be such that the Council is able to exercise its functions continuously in accordance with Article VIII of the modified Brussels Treaty. Member States may draw on a double-hatting formula, to be worked out, consisting of their representatives to the Alliance and to the European Union.

8. WEU notes that, in accordance with the provisions of Article J.4(6) concerning the common foreign and security policy of the Treaty on European Union, the Union will decide to review the provisions of this Article with a view to furthering the objective to be set by it in accordance with procedure defined. The WEU will re-examine the present provisions in 1996. This re-examination will take account of the progress and experience acquired and will extend to relations between WEU and the Atlantic Alliance.

II. Declaration by Belgium, Germany, Spain, France, Italy, Luxembourg, the Netherlands, Portugal, and the United Kingdom of Great Britain and Northern Ireland which are members of the Western European Union

'The Member States of WEU welcome the development of the European security and defence identity. They are determined, taking into account the role of WEU as the defence component of the European Union and as the means to strengthen the European pillar *of the Atlantic Alliance, to put the relationship between WEU and the other European States on a new basis for the sake of stability and security in Europe. In this spirit, they propose the following:*

States which are members of the European Union are invited to accede to WEU on conditions to be agreed in accordance with Article XI of the modified Brussels Treaty, or to become observers if they so wish. Simultaneously, other European Member States of NATO are invited to become associate members of WEU in a way which will give them the possibility of participating fully in the activities of WEU.

The Member States of WEU assume that treaties and agreements corresponding with the above proposals will be concluded before 31 December 1992.'

. . .

Source: European Communities, *Treaty on European Union* (Office for Official Publications of the European Communities: Luxembourg, 1992).

DECISIONS OF THE ROME CSCE COUNCIL MEETING

Fourth Meeting of the CSCE Council, Rome, 1 December 1993

I. Regional issues

1. Bosnia-Herzegovina, Croatia, Yugoslavia (Serbia and Montenegro) and the situation in the region.

1.1. War motivated by aggressive nationalism and territorial gains is still raging in Bosnia-Herzegovina causing further immense suffering to the civilian population. At the same time danger of war persists in Croatia.

Violations of basic human rights continue unabated and the policy and practice of ethnic cleansing is being pursued unhindered. All hostilities must stop immediately. Efforts of the international community to stop the war must be continued in order that a durable, fair and just political solution could urgently be found along the principles agreed by all parties at the ICFY.

The Ministers reaffirmed their commitment to a comprehensive solution of all issues dealt with by the ICFY.

The Ministers welcomed the resumption of the peace talks in Geneva, which resulted from presentation of an Action Plan by the European Union. They urged the parties to take advantage of the initiative represented by the European Union Action Plan to reach a political solution to the conflict.

The Ministers reconfirmed their support for the sovereignty, territorial integrity and independence of the Republic of Bosnia-Herzegovina and of all countries in the region, and refuse to recognize any territorial acquisition by force.

They reaffirmed their earlier decisions which have yet to be implemented, especially, in the light of the onslaught of winter conditions, those concerning the need to re-open airports and establish humanitarian corridors and safe areas.

The current situation in UNPA zones jeopardizes the territorial integrity of Croatia. These territories should be peacefully reintegrated into the political and legal system of Croatia. Tension and armed incidents continue there, threatening the renewal of hostilities. An agreed *modus vivendi* in UNPA zones should be achieved. Mutual recognition of Yugoslavia (Serbia and Montenegro) and Croatia would be an essential element for stability in their relations and in the region as a whole.

Those responsible for brutal violations of human rights must be held accountable. The Ministers in this context welcome that the International War Crimes Tribunal has begun its work. They expressed particular concern over violations of human rights committed by paramilitary troops.

1.2. The Ministers underlined the importance of continued CSCE focus on Yugoslavia (Serbia and Montenegro) and mandated continued monitoring of compliance with CSCE norms and principles, promotion of respect for human rights and protection of national minorities in the whole of Yugoslavia (Serbia and Montenegro).

They continued to believe that an international presence in Kosovo, Sandjak and Vojvodina would help to prevent the spillover of the conflict to these regions. They called for the early and unconditional return of the Missions of Long Duration to Kosovo, Sandjak and Vojvodina as part of the overall CSCE efforts to ease local tensions, guard against violations of human rights, encourage dialogue and reconciliation between the communities. They called for the establishment and promotion of democratic rights, processes and institutions as well as for the renewal of talks on the future status of Kosovo.

1.3. They stressed that a decisive condition for participation in the CSCE is the full compliance by Yugoslavia (Serbia and Montenegro) with all CSCE principles, commitments and decisions.

1.4. Concerned about the risks for a spill-over of the conflict to the former Yugoslav Republic of Macedonia the Ministers instructed the CSCE Spillover Monitor Mission to Skopje to continue its activities unabated.

1.5. The Ministers agreed that the important work of the Sanctions Assistance Missions (SAMs), set up to monitor the implementation of United Nations Security Council resolutions on sanctions, will continue undiminished.

The Ministers recognized that States in the region bear a major economic burden of the implementation of the sanctions. In order to help ease the unintended negative consequences of the sanctions for States in the region, the Ministers decided to hold a special ad hoc meeting of senior officials which will focus on identifying priorities for various international projects to assist affected States in the region to better cope with the effects of the sanctions. The EU/CSCE Sanctions Co-ordinator will invite relevant international organizations to participate and contribute to this meeting. It will be held before the end of January 1994.

1.6. Looking to the future, the Ministers affirmed their intention to participate actively in efforts to build a just and lasting peace in the region. They stressed that the CSCE stands ready, in co-operation with others, to contribute to a future process of reconciliation, rehabilitation and rebuilding of democratic institutions and processes and the rule of law.

The Ministers requested the Permanent Committee of the CSCE to examine how the CSCE institutions, CSCE missions and other instruments, expertise and regional experience could best be utilized in future concerted international efforts to this end, in co-ordination with the United Nations and ICFY.

1.7. The Ministers affirmed that military security and stability in South Eastern Europe is important for peace and stability in the CSCE area as a whole.

The Ministers agreed that, as a complement to the continuing efforts towards achieving a comprehensive settlement to the conflict and issues dealt with by the ICFY, a CSCE contribution to regional security

through arms control and disarmament as well as confidence- and security-building should be examined by the CSCE Forum for Security Co-operation.

2. Georgia

2.1. Faced with the alarming situation in Georgia the Ministers stressed that the territorial integrity and sovereignty of the Republic of Georgia must be preserved. They pledged to respond with generosity to the appeals for humanitarian assistance, in particular by the United Nations, and to intensify the efforts of the CSCE to help stabilize the situation in the country.

2.2. The Ministers welcomed the beginning of talks with the parties to the Abkhasian conflict in Geneva under the United Nations auspices and with the participation of the CSCE. The CSCE stands ready to contribute to the negotiations of a stable ceasefire and a political solution to the conflict, as well as to co-operate with the United Nations efforts in Abkhazia, for example by dispatching observers or providing liaison officers.

2.3. The Ministers strongly urged the parties to the Georgian–Ossetian conflict to break the present stalemate and begin, without preconditions, a political dialogue that would lead to the convening of an international conference under CSCE auspices and with United Nations participation, to negotiate a solution to the conflict. They also requested the Personal Representative of the Chairman-in-Office and the CSCE mission on the basis of the report by the Chairman-in-Office of the Council on her visit to the Transcaucasian States to elaborate a proposal, for the consideration by the CSO, for possible arrangements for liaison with the Joint Peacekeeping Forces established under the Sochi Agreement of 24 June 1992. The existing mandate and rules of engagement of these forces would be examined by the Personal Representative and the CSCE Mission with a view to establishing more comprehensive monitoring and oversight of the activities of the Joint Peacekeeping Forces.

2.4. The Ministers decided that the responsibilities of the CSCE Mission should be widened to include also the promotion of respect for human rights in the whole of Georgia and the rendering of assistance for the development of legal and democratic institutions and processes, including the elaboration of a new constitution for Georgia. Administrative and financial implications of these additional tasks should be decided by the Permanent Committee of the CSCE on the basis of a proposal by the Personal Representative of the Chairman-in-Office.

The Ministers also requested the ODIHR to identify, where possible in co-operation with the Council of Europe, specific projects to develop the legal and democratic foundations of the Republic of Georgia.

2.5. The Ministers asked the Chairman-in-Office to pursue with the United Nations, as a matter of urgency, the recommendation by the Chairman-in-Office of the Council that a joint CSCE/United Nations Special Representative at high level be appointed with a mandate to address the whole range of problems facing the country and to co-ordinate the efforts of the CSCE and United Nations in Georgia. They requested the Chairman-in-Office to inform the CSO or the Permanent Committee of the CSCE on the results of his efforts.

3. Moldova

3.1. While welcoming that there had been no fighting over the past year, the Ministers expressed concern that the lack of progress in finding a political solution to the problems related to the Trans-Dniester region impeded the development of stability and democracy in the Republic of Moldova. The Ministers also stressed that the use of military forces to stabilize the situation cannot be a substitute for a political solution of the problems.

3.2. The Ministers called on all parties involved urgently to speed up negotiations on a special status for the Trans-Dniester region within the context of independence, sovereignty and territorial integrity of the Republic of Moldova and bring them to a mutually acceptable solution. They urged the parties to address the language problems and to make full use of the confidence-building and other proposals made by the CSCE mission to facilitate the negotiating process. They instructed the CSCE Mission to seek to play an even more active role in maintaining contact with the parties and promoting an early political settlement.

The Ministers also called for early progress in negotiations on the early, orderly and complete withdrawal of the Russian 14th Army from Moldova. They stressed that progress on the withdrawal of these troops cannot be linked to any other question, with due regard to existing agreements. They called on the parties concerned to facilitate the work of the CSCE Mission by allowing it to follow closely the negotiations, to participate

in the meetings of the Joint Control Commission and to move freely in the security zone. The Ministers expressed their own full support for the achievement of these objectives.

3.3. The Ministers agreed that long-term peace and stability in Moldova also required the development of democratic structures and processes and the implementation of commitments to human rights for the whole of Moldova. They therefore welcomed the decision of the government to hold elections for a new parliament and its intention to draft a new constitution. They also instructed the CSCE Mission to continue to promote the full respect for human rights and the rule of law, including in individual cases such as the trial of the so-called 'Ilascu group'.

The Ministers requested the ODIHR to continue and expand its co-operation with the Government of Moldova on legal and human rights issues and to prepare for a central role in monitoring the forthcoming electoral process in all parts of the Republic of Moldova.

4. Tajikistan

4.1. The Ministers reiterated their concern over the situation in Tajikistan. They expressed their determination to help stabilize the situation within Tajikistan in close co-operation with the United Nations and to create favourable conditions for progress towards democracy. They noted collective efforts in this regard by a group of member countries in the CIS.

4.2. The Ministers decided to establish a CSCE Mission to Tajikistan. The Mission will maintain contact with and facilitate dialogue and confidence-building between regionalist and political forces in the country; actively promote respect for human rights; promote and monitor the adherence to CSCE norms and principles; promote ways and means for the CSCE to assist in the development of legal and democratic political institutions and processes; keep the CSCE informed about further developments.

4.3. The CSCE Mission will initially be composed of four persons. It will co-operate and co-ordinate with the United Nations representation in Dushanbe in the fulfilment of its tasks. The Chairman-in-Office will remain in contact with the United Nations on these matters. The Head of Mission will explore practical ways and means to co-ordinate the efforts in the field, including the possibility of joint office facilities. He/She will submit a proposal for administrative and financial modalities for the mission to the Permanent Committee of the CSCE for decision not later than 15 January 1994.

5. Baltic States

The Ministers recalled the commitments undertaken under paragraph 15 of the Helsinki Summit Declaration 1992 and in the Stockholm Summary of Conclusions.

They stressed the political significance of the speedy withdrawal of the remaining Russian troops from the territories of the Baltic States. They welcomed the completion of the withdrawal of Russian troops from Lithuania by 31 August 1993.

They concluded that it is necessary to further intensify the ongoing pullout of troops and called upon the participating States concerned promptly to conclude appropriate agreements, including timetables, which will allow to complete the orderly withdrawal of troops, including settlement on the military installation in Skrunda.

II. Further development of the capabilities of the CSCE in conflict prevention and crisis management

1. The Ministers stressed the importance of actively pursuing the deliberations which have been initiated by the CSO on the further development of the capabilities of the CSCE in conflict prevention and crisis management.

2. The Ministers agreed that the CSCE could consider, on a case-by-case basis and under specific conditions, the setting up of CSCE co-operative arrangements in order inter alia to ensure that the role and functions of a third party military force in a conflict area are consistent with CSCE principles and objectives.

3. The Ministers mandated the CSO and the Permanent Committee to further elaborate conditions and necessary provisions for possible CSCE arrangements of this nature. In carrying out this task they will bear in mind the proposals examined by the CSO and be guided inter alia by the following principles and considerations essential to the CSCE arrangements as well as to the activities of a third party military force: Respect for sovereignty and territorial integrity; consent of the parties; impartiality; multinational character; clear mandate; transparency; integral link to a political process for conflict resolution; plan for orderly withdrawal.

4. The Ministers requested the CSO to take a decision on this matter if possible at

its 25th meeting.

III. High Commissioner on National Minorities

Bearing in mind the close interrelationship between questions relating to national minorities and conflict prevention, the Ministers encouraged the High Commissioner on National Minorities (HCNM) to pursue his activities under his Mandate. They recognized the HCNM as an innovative and effective asset in early warning and preventive diplomacy. The Ministers stressed the importance of participating States co-operating fully with the High Commissioner and supporting follow-up and implementation of his recommendations. They welcomed the decision by the CSO to increase the resources available to the HCNM.

IV. The human dimension

1. The Ministers reiterated that human dimension issues are fundamental to the comprehensive security concept of the CSCE. They noted that adherence to human dimension commitments remains to be consolidated in large parts of the CSCE area, and expressed particular concern that civilians continue to be the victims of atrocities in ongoing conflicts in the CSCE area. Concerned by the root causes of tension stemming from historical prejudices, the Ministers called for efforts, inter alia, through education, to promote tolerance and consciousness of belonging to a system of common values. The Ministers stressed that implementation of human dimension commitments must be a focus of attention in the CSCE's conflict prevention efforts.

2. To this end the Ministers decided to strengthen the instruments of conflict prevention and early warning which are available within the human dimension of CSCE. They emphasized the need in this context for enhanced co-operation and co-ordination with relevant international organizations such as the Council of Europe, as well as with non-governmental organizations.

The following decisions were taken:

3. The political consultation process and CSCE missions

– In order to further political consideration and action under the human dimension, the decision-making bodies of the CSCE will consider human dimension issues on a regular basis as an integral part of deliberations relating to European security. Resources and information will be made available by the ODIHR in support of such consideration.

– Further emphasis will be given to human dimension issues in mandates of CSCE missions as well as in the follow-up of mission reports. To this end the ODIHR will be given an enhanced role in the preparation of CSCE missions, *inter alia*, in providing information and advice to missions in accordance with its expertise.

– In the context of conflict prevention and crisis management, the issue of mass migration, namely displaced persons and refugees, will be addressed, as appropriate, by the CSO and the Permanent Committee of the CSCE, taking into account the role of other relevant international bodies.

4. Office for Democratic Institutions and Human Rights

The Ministers decided to strengthen the ODIHR's functions and operations. *Inter alia*, the ODIHR will enhance its activities under its mandate in the following areas:

– the building of an expanded database of experts in fields relevant to the human dimension. Participating States and non-governmental organizations are requested to inform the ODIHR of experts available in fields relevant to the human dimension;

– enhancement of its role in comprehensive election monitoring;

– strengthened co-operation with relevant international organizations in order to co-ordinate activities and identify possible areas of joint endeavour;

– receiving information provided by NGOs having relevant experience in the human dimension field;

– serving as a point of contact for information provided by participating States in accordance with CSCE commitments;

– disseminating general information on the human dimension, and international humanitarian law.

The Ministers determined that in order to fulfil its new tasks, the ODIHR should be granted additional resources. They requested the CSO to consider the financial and administrative implications of strengthening the ODIHR as outlined above.

5. Streamlining the Moscow Mechanism

Recognizing the Moscow Mechanism as a significant inter-governmental instrument for follow-up within the human dimension, the Ministers agreed to develop its effectiveness and promote its use, by expanding the resource list and shortening time-frames under the mechanism. Also the Permanent Committee of the CSCE will be empowered to trigger the mechanism as well as to take follow-up action based on rapporteur's reports. To this end it was decided to modify the mechanism in accordance with annex A.

6. Building on the work of the Implementation Meeting on Human Dimension Issues and the Human Dimension Seminars

– The Ministers attached significance to the outcome of the first Implementation Meeting on Human Dimension Issues, as well as the human dimension seminars conducted. The results of the Implementation Meeting on Human Dimension Issues were welcomed and the CSO and the Permanent Committee of the CSCE were tasked to consider relevant follow-up to them.

– Enhanced follow-up by the political bodies of the CSCE based on summaries of meetings and seminars in the human dimension will be sought. The ODIHR, in consultation with interested participating States, is invited to present further proposals for appropriate follow-up action resulting from human dimension seminars to forthcoming CSO or Permanent Committee meetings.

– The Ministers expressed their appreciation of the work carried out at the Seminar on Free Media to stimulate editorially independent broadcast media and a free press. They reiterated their commitment to safeguard freedom of expression, a basic human right, and stressed the necessity of independent media for a free and open society. To this end the Ministers decided that better use should be made of the CSCE human dimension instruments to promote open and diverse media, including exploring the possibility of utilizing CSCE missions.

– Human dimension seminars will be held before the Budapest Review Conference on the subjects of migrant workers, local democracy and, if time and the resources of the ODIHR permit, on Roma in the CSCE region. Other topics proposed in the course of the Implementation Meeting on Human Dimension Issues should be considered for inclusion in the programme of seminars for 1995 and thereafter.

V. The economic dimension

1. The Ministers recalled the basic importance of economic transformation, development and co-operation to the realization of

the CSCE's comprehensive concept of security. This concept emphasizes the interrelation between developing democratic institutions and market economics. Economic co-operation is essential to strengthening security and stability in the CSCE area. The Ministers agreed that the CSCE, with its broad participation, should play an active role in promoting co-operation in the economic dimension, which should be developed, *inter alia*, by working closely with relevant economic, financial and developmental organizations. They requested the Permanent Committee of the CSCE to integrate more fully the economic dimension into its consideration of tasks facing the CSCE.

2. To ensure that the CSCE complements efforts by other international and non-governmental organizations, the Ministers requested the Permanent Committee to identify practical means of deepening dialogue and expanding co-operative projects with such organizations.

3. They agreed that the CSCE should contribute to contacts and dialogue which help expand mutual understanding of the requirements for sustainable economic development. They also considered practical pursuit of the economic dimension to be an important aspect of the Programme of Co-ordinated Support for newly admitted States.

4. The Ministers expressed satisfaction with the first session of the CSCE Economic Forum, held in Prague 15–17 March 1993 and welcomed the prospect of the second annual Economic Forum in March 1994. To ensure continuity of the work on the economic dimension, the Ministers agreed to provide permanent support for the Economic Forum and its follow-on activities through the CSCE Secretariat operating within existing resources. In this connection, the Ministers decided to designate an existing position for an economic expert to pursue such tasks.

5. They welcomed the Government of Kyrgyzstan's decision to host the first follow-up seminar to the Forum in February 1994. They called upon participating States, the Chairman-in-Office and the CSCE Secretariat to co-operate in organizing this and future such meetings.

VI. Co-operation and contacts with the United Nations as well as with European and transatlantic organizations and institutions

1. The Ministers agreed that to pursue the CSCE objective of a stronger commitment to short and long term conflict prevention and crisis management requires improved consultations and co-ordination with international organizations.

2. They agreed that, to achieve this, CSCE efforts to further improve relations with the United Nations should be continued. The basis will be the 'Framework for co-operation and co-ordination between the United Nations Secretariat and the Conference on Security and Co-operation in Europe', and CSCE's recently obtained observer status to the United Nations General Assembly. Furthermore, the Ministers agreed that establishing organized forms for consultations and co-operation with other European and Transatlantic institutions and organizations is essential to encourage a sense of wider community, as referred to in the Helsinki Summit Declaration. They also encouraged subregional organizations and arrangements to explore ways of supporting the CSCE.

3. The Ministers requested the Chairman-in-Office, assisted by the CSCE Troika and the Secretary General, as appropriate, to pursue talks with these institutions and organizations with a view to establishing improved arrangements for consultations and for co-ordination of activities. The Ministers requested the Chairman-in-Office to report to the Committee of Senior Officials on the evolution of these talks and to submit as appropriate proposals for co-operation arrangements.

VII. CSCE structures and operations

1. The Ministers reaffirmed that significant enhancement of the political effectiveness and operational capability of the CSCE is critical to achieving the goals they have defined for it.

2. They recalled the two mutually supporting forms of action by the CSCE: those joint political decisions taken in accordance with consensus rules and direct action through agreed mechanisms activated by a limited number of participating States.

3. To ensure improved capabilities for day-to-day operational tasks of the CSCE, the Ministers created a permanent body for political consultations and decision-making in Vienna, the Permanent Committee of the CSCE.

4. The Ministers decided that the Permanent Committee should review the relevance and operation of existing mechanisms with a view to increasing their effectiveness.

5. The Ministers also endorsed the decision to establish a CSCE Secretariat in Vienna as an important step towards further efficiency in administrative and secretariat support services. Further evolution of CSCE's operational capabilities will be based on the overriding objective of a non-bureaucratic, cost-efficient and flexible administrative structure which can be adapted to changing tasks.

6. The Ministers considered also problems which have arisen because of a shortage of economic and human resources for CSCE operations, especially preventive diplomacy missions. They decided that the question of providing adequate resources, in the form of expertise as well as of finance, for the CSCE to fulfil its promise will be vigorously pursued.

7. Institutional arrangements for political consultation and decision-making

7.1. In order to enhance the capacity of the CSCE to respond to challenges in the CSCE area, the Ministers decided to create a permanent body consisting of representatives of the participating States for political consultations and decision-making in Vienna. The new body will be responsible for the day-to-day operational tasks of the CSCE under the chairmanship of the Chairman-in-Office and will meet under the name of the Permanent Committee of the CSCE. The Permanent Committee will conduct comprehensive and regular consultations and, when the CSO is not in session, take decisions on all issues pertinent to the CSCE. The Permanent Committee will be responsible to the CSO, and undertake preliminary discussion of items suggested for the agenda of the CSO. The CSO will continue to lay down political guidelines and take key decisions between Council meetings.

7.2. With a view to strengthening the interrelation and complementarity of the CSCE decision-making process in the fields of arms control, disarmament and confidence and security-building, security co-operation and conflict prevention, the Ministers decided to dissolve the Consultative Committee of the Conflict Prevention Centre as set up by the Paris supplementary document and transfer its competence to the Permanent Committee and the Forum for Security Co-operation in the following way:

7.3. The Permanent Committee will, in addition to the mandate as above, hold the meetings of the participating States which

may be convened under the mechanism on unusual military activities.

7.4. The Forum for Security Co-operation will, in addition to current tasks

– assume responsibility for the implementation of CSBMs,

– prepare seminars on military doctrine and such other seminars as may be agreed by the participating States,

– hold the annual implementation assessment meetings,

– provide the forum for discussion and clarification, as necessary, of information exchanged under agreed CSBMs.

8. CSCE Secretariat

The Ministers endorsed the decision by the CSO to establish a CSCE Secretariat in Vienna with an office in Prague. The Secretariat will include departments for conference services, administration and budget, Chairman-in-Office support and the Conflict Prevention Centre.

9. Ensuring necessary resources and expertise for the CSCE

. . .

11. The Ministers have taken note with appreciation of the report of the ad hoc Group of Legal and Other Experts. The Ministers adopted a decision on legal capacity and privileges and immunities that recommends implementation of the following three basic elements (CSCE/4-C/Dec.2):

– The CSCE participating States will, subject to their constitutional, legislative and related requirements, confer legal capacity on CSCE institutions in accordance with the provisions adopted by the Ministers;

– The CSCE participating States will, subject to their constitutional, legislative and related requirements, confer privileges and immunities on CSCE institutions, permanent missions of the participating States, representatives of participating States, CSCE officials and members of CSCE missions in accordance with the provisions adopted by the Ministers;

– The CSCE may issue CSCE Identity Cards in accordance with the form adopted by the Ministers.

VIII. Integration of recently admitted participating States

1. The Ministers commended the steps that had been taken to improve the integration of the recently admitted participating States. They expressed appreciation for the

visits to several of these States undertaken by the Chairman-in-Office and recommended that the programme of visits be continued. In this task, the Chairman-in-Office will be assisted by members of the Troika. They requested the Secretary General to ensure continued effective follow up of the visits of the Chairman-in-Office to the Central Asian and Transcaucasian participating States. In this connection, they welcomed the establishment, since they last met in Stockholm, of permanent representations in Vienna by Armenia, Georgia, Kyrgyzstan, Lithuania and Tajikistan and commended the financial support that is being rendered by the Government of Austria to some of these representations. They also emphasized the importance of having all recently admitted participating States represented in Vienna at the earliest possible date.

2. The Ministers underlined the importance of the Human Dimension in the further integration of the recently admitted participating States. While many of these States are in a difficult period of political and economic transition, the Ministers expressed their expectation that the recently admitted participating States would do their utmost to ensure the implementation in their countries of all CSCE principles and commitments, also in times of crisis. They commended the role played by the ODIHR in helping to build democratic institutions in the recently admitted participating States. They requested ODIHR to intensify its efforts to identify and implement co-operation projects with these States within the framework of the Programe of Co-ordinated Support. They noted also the important contribution made by the Human Dimension seminars organized by the ODIHR to increased understanding of the problems arising from the process of integration. They agreed on the importance of making full use of the experience gained at these seminars.

IX. Relations between non-participating Mediterranean States and the CSCE

The Ministers, welcoming the further development of contacts between the CSCE and non-participating Mediterranean States which share the principles and objectives of the CSCE, called on the Chairman-in-Office and, as appropriate, the Secretary General to promote the full use of the exchange of information and views recently agreed upon by participating States.

X. Declaration on aggressive nationalism, racism, chauvinism, xenophobia and anti-semitism

1. Recalling their decisions taken at the Stockholm Council Meeting, the Ministers noted with deep concern the growing manifestations of aggressive nationalism, such as territorial expansionism, as well as racism, chauvinism, xenophobia and anti-semitism. These run directly counter to the principles and commitments of the CSCE.

2. The Ministers also noted that these phenomena can lead to violence, secessionism by the use of force and ethnic strife, and in their worst instances to the barbaric practices of mass deportation, ethnic cleansing and violence against innocent civilians.

3. Aggressive nationalism, racism, chauvinism, xenophobia and anti-semitism create ethnic, political and social tensions within and between States. They also undermine international stability and worldwide efforts to place universal human rights on a firm foundation.

4. The Ministers focused attention on the need for urgent action to enforce the strict observance of the norms of international humanitarian law, including the prosecution and punishment of those guilty of war crimes and other crimes against humanity.

5. The Ministers agreed that the CSCE must play an important role in these efforts. The clear standards of behaviour reflected in CSCE commitments include active support for the equal rights of all individuals in accordance with international law and for the protection of national minorities.

6. The Ministers decided to keep this issue high on the agenda of the CSCE and therefore decided:

– to task the Permanent Committee to study possible follow-up actions;

– to invite the High Commissioner on National Minorities, in light of his mandate, to pay particular attention to all aspects of aggressive nationalism, racism, chauvinism, xenophobia and anti-semitism;

– to request the ODIHR to pay special attention to these phenomena and to apply resources as necessary . . .

. . .

Source: CSCE, Fourth Meeting of the Council, Rome, 1993, Decisions of the Rome Council Meeting, CSCE document CSCE/4-C/Dec.1, 1 Dec. 1993.

LEGAL CAPACITY AND PRIVILEGES AND IMMUNITIES

Fourth Meeting of the CSCE Council, Rome, 1 December 1993

1. At its Rome Meeting from 30 November to 1 December 1993, the CSCE Council considered the report submitted to the 24th CSO Meeting by the CSCE ad hoc Group of Legal and Other Experts on the relevance of an agreement granting internationally recognized status to the CSCE institutions.

2. The Ministers reaffirmed the importance of enhancing the ability of the institutions to better accomplish their functions, while preserving the flexibility and openness of the CSCE process. They agreed that, in order to help achieve a firmer basis for security and co-operation among all CSCE participating States, the CSCE would benefit from clearer administrative structures and a well defined operational framework.

3. The Ministers were encouraged by the fact that the Governments hosting the CSCE Secretariat, the Conflict Prevention Centre (CPC) and the Office for Democratic Institutions and Human Rights (ODIHR) have taken steps under their laws to confer upon these institutions and CSCE personnel as well as representatives of the CSCE participating States treatment comparable to that accorded to the United Nations and its personnel and to the representatives to it.

4. The Ministers noted the expanded operations within CSCE participating States of CSCE institutions and their personnel and of CSCE missions and the importance that all participating States provide for those institutions and individuals appropriate treatment.

5. The Ministers agreed on the usefulness of legal capacity being granted to the CSCE institutions in the territories of all the CSCE participating States, in particular the capacity to contract, to acquire and dispose of movable and immovable property, and to institute and participate in legal proceedings.

6. The Ministers further agreed that it was appropriate that certain privileges and immunities be granted to the CSCE institutions and their officers and staffs, as well as to the Secretary General of the CSCE and the High Commissioner on National Minorities and their staffs, members of CSCE missions and the representatives of the participating States to the extent necessary to the exercise of their duties.

7. In most participating States, however, the competence to make rules concerning the legal status of the CSCE institutions and privileges and immunities rests with the legislature.

8. In view of these considerations and in order to assist in harmonizing the rules to be applied, the Ministers adopted the provisions set out in Annex 1. They recommend that participating States implement these provisions, subject to their constitutional and related requirements.

The participating States will inform the Secretary General of the CSCE of the steps taken in this respect no later than 31 December 1994.

9. The Ministers agreed that the present decision supersedes paragraph I.1 (Legal Basis) of Recommendations of the ad hoc Group of Experts of the participating States on administrative, financial and personnel arrangements for the CSCE institutional structures created by the Paris Summit, adopted by the Committee of Senior Officials on 29 January 1991 (document CSCE/HB/Dec. 1), and that it does not apply to other undertakings with respect to privileges and immunities made within the framework of the CSCE.

It is understood, however, that this decision does not affect the treatment conferred upon the CSCE institutions referred to in paragraph 3 above, to the CSCE personnel as well as to the representatives of the CSCE participating States by legislation or administrative measures taken by the host States in accordance with the above decision adopted by the Committee of Senior Officials (document CSCE/HB/Dec.1).

ANNEX 1

Provisions concerning the Legal Capacity of the CSCE Institutions and Privileges and Immunities

Legal capacity of the CSCE institutions

1. The CSCE participating States will, subject to their constitutional, legislative and related requirements, confer such legal capacity as is necessary for the exercise of their functions, and in particular the capacity to contract, to acquire and dispose of movable and immovable property, and to institute and participate in legal proceedings, on the following CSCE institutions:

– The CSCE Secretariat,

– The Office for Democratic Institutions and Human Rights (ODIHR),

– Any other CSCE institution determined by the CSCE Council.

Privileges and immunities

GENERAL

2. The CSCE participating States will, subject to their constitutional, legislative and related requirements, confer the privileges and immunities as set out in paragraphs 4–16 below.

3. Privileges and immunities will be accorded to the CSCE institutions in the interests of those institutions. Immunity may be waived by the Secretary General of the CSCE in consultation with the Chairman-in-Office.

Privileges and immunities will be accorded to individuals not for the personal benefit of the individuals concerned, but in order to safeguard the independent exercise of their functions. Immunity will be waived in any case where the immunity would impede the course of justice and can be waived without prejudice to the purpose for which the immunity is accorded. Decision to waive immunity will be taken:

– with respect to officers and staff of the CSCE institutions and to members of CSCE missions, by the Secretary General of the CSCE in consultation with the Chairman-in-Office;

– with respect to the Secretary General and the High Commissioner on National Minorities, by the Chairman-in-Office.

The Government concerned may waive immunity with respect to its representatives.

CSCE INSTITUTIONS

. . .

10. The CSCE institutions will enjoy for their official communications the same treatment as that accorded to diplomatic missions.

PERMANENT MISSIONS OF THE PARTICIPATING STATES

. . .

REPRESENTATIVES OF PARTICIPATING STATES

. . .

CSCE OFFICIALS

. . .

MEMBERS OF CSCE MISSIONS

. . .

CSCE identity card

17. The CSCE may issue a CSCE Identity Card to persons on official duty travel for the CSCE. The document, which will not substitute for ordinary travel documents, will be issued in accordance with the form set out in Annex A [not reproduced here] and will entitle the bearer to the treatment specified therein.

18. Applications for visas (where required) from the holders of CSCE Identity Cards will be dealt with as speedily as possible.

. . .

Source: CSCE, Fourth Meeting of the Council, Rome, 1993, Legal capacity and privileges and immunities, CSCE document CSCE/4-C/Dec.2, 1 Dec. 1993.

CSCE AND THE NEW EUROPE—OUR SECURITY IS INDIVISIBLE

DECISIONS OF THE ROME CSCE COUNCIL MEETING

Fourth Meeting of the CSCE Council, Rome, 1 December 1993

The CSCE Council held its Fourth Meeting in Rome from 30 November to 1 December 1993.

The Ministers expressed deep concern that threats to peace and stability proliferate and that crises, widespread violence and open confrontations persist. They strongly condemned the increasing violations of human rights and humanitarian law and the attempt of countries to acquire territories by the use of force. The increasing flow of refugees and appalling human suffering caused by armed conflicts must be urgently alleviated. The Ministers reiterated the personal accountability of those responsible for crimes against humanity.

Despite these events, there is encouraging progress in human rights, democracy and the rule of law in several parts of the CSCE area. The Ministers expressed satisfaction with the spread of free elections and development of democratic institutions registered in many participating States. The Ministers intended to ensure that the CSCE provides appropriate support for these efforts.

To promote the process of democratic change, the Ministers reiterated their determination to base their common action on solidarity, the comprehensive concept of security and freedom of choice of security relations. By utilizing the CSCE agreed set of standards and principles, participating States can demonstrate their unity of purpose and action and thus help to make security indivisible.

The Ministers agreed to strengthen the CSCE role as a pan-European and transatlantic forum for co-operative security as well as for political consultation on the basis of equality. The CSCE can be especially valuable as the first line of joint action on the underlying causes of conflict. At the heart of the CSCE efforts is the struggle to protect human rights and fundamental freedoms in the CSCE area.

The Ministers stressed the need to make wider use of CSCE capabilities in early warning and preventive diplomacy and to further integrate the human dimension in this endeavour. They commended the contribution of the High Commissioner on National Minorities to the development of these capabilities. They furthermore welcomed an increased role of the Office for Democratic Institutions and Human Rights in the human dimension, as well as the contributions of the CSCE missions in the field of conflict prevention and crisis management. The goal of further efforts should be to improve abilities to address potential crises at an early stage.

The Ministers also welcomed proposals to undertake jointly specific action to enhance stability.

In this respect the Ministers expressed appreciation for the presentation of the initiative for a Pact for Stability made by the European Union.

They also welcomed the proposed Partnership for Peace initiative being worked out among participants in the North Atlantic Co-operation Council.

The Ministers agreed to pursue the possibility of enhancing capabilities to apply CSCE crisis management arrangements on a case-by-case basis to situations involving third party forces when such arrangements are determined to be supportive of CSCE objectives.

The Ministers agreed to commit the necessary political, human and financial resources to the expanding operational tasks of the CSCE. They pledged to utilize the innovative means which the CSCE can bring to bear in dealing with the day-to-day challenges of change.

The Ministers also agreed to deepen the CSCE co-operation with the United Nations, as well as with European and transatlantic organizations. They welcomed all co-operative efforts by such organizations to make contributions toward stability.

The Ministers underlined the importance of the work of the Forum for Security Co-operation. They encouraged completion of the Programme for Immediate Action, including the proposal to establish a Code of Conduct.

Looking towards the Budapest Summit in December 1994, the Ministers determined to make their co-operation more concrete and effective through the action programme below. In so doing, the CSCE participating States will demonstrate that however varied their histories and backgrounds, their security is truly indivisible.

To give substance and direction to their commitments, the Ministers have agreed on an action programme to be implemented through the decisions which they have adopted today.

These decisions, *inter alia,* address the following issues:

(*a*) The situation in Bosnia-Herzegovina, Croatia and Yugoslavia (Serbia and Montenegro). Examination, as a complement to the efforts of the ICFY, of a CSCE contribution to regional security.

The responsibilities of the CSCE Mission in Georgia will be widened to include the promotion of human rights and the development of democratic institutions. A proposal will be elaborated on possible arrangements for CSCE liaison with and monitoring of the Joint Peacekeeping Forces established under the Sochi Agreement of 24 June 1992.

In Moldova, the work of the CSCE Mission will be intensified.

A new CSCE Mission will be sent to Tajikistan, to help build democratic institutions and processes there.

The remaining Russian troops will shortly complete their orderly withdrawal from the territories of the Baltic States as agreed.

(*b*) CSCE crisis management capabilities regarding situations involving third party military forces will be further considered.

(*c*) The role of the High Commissioner on National Minorities will be enhanced.

(*d*) The human dimension will be further integrated into the CSCE political consultation process; the ODIHR will be reinforced.

(*e*) The CSCE will play a more active role in promoting co-operation in the economic dimension.

(f) Co-operation and contacts with the United Nations and European and trans-atlantic organizations shall be improved.

(g) A Permanent Committee of the CSCE for political consultations and decision making will be created in Vienna, where also a new CSCE Secretariat with comprehensive tasks will be established. A decision on CSCE legal capacity was taken.

(h) Integration of recently admitted participating States will receive new impetus.

(i) Relations between the CSCE and non-participating Mediterranean States will be further developed.

(j) The role of the CSCE in combating aggressive nationalism, racism, chauvinism, xenophobia and anti-semitism will be strengthened.

Source: CSCE, Fourth Meeting of the Council, Rome, 1993, CSCE and the New Europe—Our Security is Indivisible, Decisions of the Rome Council Meeting, CSCE document, Rome, 1993.

DECLARATION OF THE HEADS OF STATE AND GOVERNMENT PARTICIPATING IN THE MEETING OF THE NORTH ATLANTIC COUNCIL, 11 JANUARY 1994

Brussels, 11 January 1994

1. We, the Heads of State and Government of the member countries of the North Atlantic Alliance, have gathered in Brussels to renew our Alliance in light of the historic transformations affecting the entire continent of Europe. We welcome the new climate of cooperation that has emerged in Europe with the end of the period of global confrontation embodied in the Cold War. However, we must also note that other causes of instability, tension and conflict have emerged. We therefore confirm the enduring validity and indispensability of our Alliance. It is based on a strong transatlantic link, the expression of a shared destiny. It reflects a European Security and Defence Identity gradually emerging as the expression of a mature Europe. It is reaching out to establish new patterns of cooperation throughout Europe. It rests, as also reflected in Article 2 of the Washington Treaty, upon close collaboration in all fields.

Building on our decisions in London and Rome and on our new Strategic Concept, we are undertaking initiatives designed to con-tribute to lasting peace, stability, and well-being in the whole of Europe, which has always been our Alliance's fundamental goal. We have agreed:

– to adapt further the Alliance's political and military structures to reflect both the full spectrum of its roles and the development of the emerging European Security and Defence Identity, and endorse the concept of Combined Joint Task Forces;

– to reaffirm that the Alliance remains open to the membership of other European countries;

– to launch a major initiative through a Partnership for Peace, in which we invite Partners to join us in new political and military efforts to work alongside the Alliance;

– to intensify our efforts against the proliferation of weapons of mass destruction and their means of delivery.

2. We reaffirm our strong commitment to the transatlantic link, which is the bedrock of NATO. The continued substantial presence of United States forces in Europe is a fundamentally important aspect of that link. All our countries wish to continue the direct involvement of the United States and Canada in the security of Europe. We note that this is also the expressed wish of the new democracies of the East, which see in the transatlantic link an irreplaceable pledge of security and stability for Europe as a whole. The fuller integration of the countries of Central and Eastern Europe and of the former Soviet Union into a Europe whole and free cannot be successful without the strong and active participation of all Allies on both sides of the Atlantic.

3. Today, we confirm and renew this link between North America and a Europe developing a Common Foreign and Security Policy and taking on greater responsibility on defence matters. We welcome the entry into force of the Treaty of Maastricht and the launching of the European Union, which will strengthen the European pillar of the Alliance and allow it to make a more coherent contribution to the security of all the Allies. We reaffirm that the Alliance is the essential forum for consultation among its members and the venue for agreement on policies bearing on the security and defence commitments of Allies under the Washington Treaty.

4. We give our full support to the development of a European Security and Defence Identity which, as called for in the Maastricht Treaty, in the longer term

perspective of a common defence policy within the European Union, might in time lead to a common defence compatible with that of the Atlantic Alliance. The emergence of a European Security and Defence Identity will strengthen the European pillar of the Alliance while reinforcing the transatlantic link and will enable European Allies to take greater responsibility for their common security and defence. The Alliance and the European Union share common strategic interests.

5. We support strengthening the European pillar of the Alliance through the Western European Union, which is being developed as the defence component of the European Union. The Alliance's organisation and resources will be adjusted so as to facilitate this. We welcome the close and growing co-operation between NATO and the WEU that has been achieved on the basis of agreed principles of complementarity and transparency. In future contingencies, NATO and the WEU will consult, including as necessary through joint Council meetings, on how to address such contingencies.

6. We therefore stand ready to make collective assets of the Alliance available, on the basis of consultations in the North Atlantic Council, for WEU operations undertaken by the European Allies in pursuit of their Common Foreign and Security Policy. We support the development of separable but not separate capabilities which could respond to European requirements and contribute to Alliance security. Better European co-ordination and planning will also strengthen the European pillar and the Alliance itself. Integrated and multinational European structures, as they are further developed in the context of an emerging European Security and Defence Identity, will also increasingly have a similarly important role to play in enhancing the Allies' ability to work together in the common defence and other tasks.

7. In pursuit of our common transatlantic security requirements, NATO increasingly will be called upon to undertake missions in addition to the traditional and fundamental task of collective defence of its members, which remains a core function. We reaffirm our offer to support, on a case by case basis in accordance with our own procedures, peacekeeping and other operations under the authority of the UN Security Council or the responsibility of the CSCE, including by making available Alliance resources and ex-

pertise. Participation in any such operation or mission will remain subject to decisions of member states in accordance with national constitutions.

8. Against this background, NATO must continue the adaptation of its command and force structure in line with requirements for flexible and timely responses contained in the Alliance's Strategic Concept. We also will need to strengthen the European pillar of the Alliance by facilitating the use of our military capabilities for NATO and European/WEU operations, and assist participation of non-NATO partners in joint peacekeeping operations and other contingencies as envisaged under the Partnership for Peace.

9. Therefore, we direct the North Atlantic Council in Permanent Session, with the advice of the NATO Military Authorities, to examine how the Alliance's political and military structures and procedures might be developed and adapted to conduct more efficiently and flexibly the Alliance's missions, including peacekeeping, as well as to improve cooperation with the WEU and to reflect the emerging European Security and Defence Identity. As part of this process, we endorse the concept of Combined Joint Task Forces as a means to facilitate contingency operations, including operations with participating nations outside the Alliance. We have directed the North Atlantic Council, with the advice of the NATO Military Authorities, to develop this concept and establish the necessary capabilities. The Council, with the advice of the NATO Military Authorities, and in coordination with the WEU, will work on implementation in a manner that provides separable but not separate military capabilities that could be employed by NATO or the WEU. The North Atlantic Council in Permanent Session will report on the implementation of these decisions to Ministers at their next regular meeting in June 1994.

10. Our own security is inseparably linked to that of all other states in Europe. The consolidation and preservation throughout the continent of democratic societies and their freedom from any form of coercion or intimidation are therefore of direct and material concern to us, as they are to all other CSCE states under the commitments of the Helsinki Final Act and the Charter of Paris. We remain deeply committed to further strengthening the CSCE, which is the only organisation comprising all European

and North American countries, as an instrument of preventive diplomacy, conflict prevention, cooperative security, and the advancement of democracy and human rights. We actively support the efforts to enhance the operational capabilities of the CSCE for early warning, conflict prevention, and crisis management.

11. As part of our overall effort to promote preventive diplomacy, we welcome the European Union proposal for a Pact on Stability in Europe, will contribute to its elaboration, and look forward to the opening conference which will take place in Paris in the Spring.

12. Building on the close and long-standing partnership among the North American and European Allies, we are committed to enhancing security and stability in the whole of Europe. We therefore wish to strengthen ties with the democratic states to our East. We reaffirm that the Alliance, as provided for in Article 10 of the Washington Treaty, remains open to membership of other European states in a position to further the principles of the Treaty and to contribute to the security of the North Atlantic area. We expect and would welcome NATO expansion that would reach to democratic states to our East, as part of an evolutionary process, taking into account political and security developments in the whole of Europe.

13. We have decided to launch an immediate and practical programme that will transform the relationship between NATO and participating states. This new programme goes beyond dialogue and co-operation to forge a real partnership—a Partnership for Peace. We invite the other states participating in the NACC, and other CSCE countries able and willing to contribute to this programme, to join with us in this Partnership. Active participation in the Partnership for Peace will play an important role in the evolutionary process of the expansion of NATO.

14. The Partnership for Peace, which will operate under the authority of the North Atlantic Council, will forge new security relationships between the North Atlantic Alliance and its Partners for Peace. Partner states will be invited by the North Atlantic Council to participate in political and military bodies at NATO Headquarters with respect to Partnership activities. The Partnership will expand and intensify political and military cooperation throughout Europe,

increase stability, diminish threats to peace, and build strengthened relationships by promoting the spirit of practical cooperation and commitment to democratic principles that underpin our Alliance. NATO will consult with any active participant in the Partnership if that partner perceives a direct threat to its territorial integrity, political independence, or security. At a pace and scope determined by the capacity and desire of the individual participating states, we will work in concrete ways towards transparency in defence budgeting, promoting democratic control of defence ministries, joint planning, joint military exercises, and creating an ability to operate with NATO forces in such fields as peacekeeping, search and rescue and humanitarian operations, and others as may be agreed.

15. To promote closer military co-operation and interoperability, we will propose, within the Partnership framework, peacekeeping field exercises beginning in 1994. To coordinate joint military activities within the Partnership, we will invite states participating in the Partnership to send permanent liaison officers to NATO Headquarters and a separate Partnership Coordination Cell at Mons (Belgium) that would, under the authority of the North Atlantic Council, carry out the military planning necessary to implement the Partnership programmes.

16. Since its inception two years ago, the North Atlantic Cooperation Council has greatly expanded the depth and scope of its activities. We will continue to work with all our NACC partners to build cooperative relationships across the entire spectrum of the Alliance's activities. With the expansion of NACC activities and the establishment of the Partnership for Peace, we have decided to offer permanent facilities at NATO Headquarters for personnel from NACC countries and other Partnership for Peace participants in order to improve our working relationships and facilitate closer cooperation.

17. Proliferation of weapons of mass destruction and their delivery means constitutes a threat to international security and is a matter of concern to NATO. We have decided to intensify and expand NATO's political and defence efforts against proliferation, taking into account the work already under way in other international fora and institutions. In this regard, we direct that work begin immediately in appropriate fora

of the Alliance to develop an overall policy framework to consider how to reinforce ongoing prevention efforts and how to reduce the proliferation threat and protect against it.

18. We attach crucial importance to the full and timely implementation of existing arms control and disarmament agreements as well as to achieving further progress on key issues of arms control and disarmament, such as:

– the indefinite and unconditional extension of the Treaty on Non-Proliferation of Nuclear Weapons, and work towards an enhanced verification regime;

– the early entry into force of the Convention on Chemical Weapons and new measures to strengthen the Biological Weapons Convention;

– the negotiation of a universal and verifiable Comprehensive Test Ban Treaty;

– issues on the agenda of the CSCE Forum for Security Cooperation;

– ensuring the integrity of the CFE Treaty and full compliance with all its provisions.

19. We condemn all acts of international terrorism. They constitute flagrant violations of human dignity and rights and are a threat to the conduct of normal international relations. In accordance with our national legislation, we stress the need for the most effective cooperation possible to prevent and suppress this scourge.

20. We reaffirm our support for political and economic reform in Russia and welcome the adoption of a new constitution and the holding of democratic parliamentary elections by the people of the Russian Federation. This is a major step forward in the establishment of a framework for the development of durable democratic institutions. We further welcome the Russian government's firm commitment to democratic and market reform and to a reformist foreign policy. These are important for security and stability in Europe. We believe that an independent, democratic, stable and nuclear-weapons-free Ukraine would likewise contribute to security and stability. We will continue to encourage and support the reform processes in both countries and to develop cooperation with them, as with other countries in Central and Eastern Europe.

21. The situation in Southern Caucasus continues to be of special concern. We condemn the use of force for territorial gains. Respect for the territorial integrity, independence and sovereignty of Armenia, Azerbaijan and Georgia is essential to the establishment of peace, stability and cooperation in the region. We call upon all states to join international efforts under the aegis of the United Nations and the CSCE aimed at solving existing problems.

22. We reiterate our conviction that security in Europe is greatly affected by security in the Mediterranean. We strongly welcome the agreements recently concluded in the Middle East peace process which offer an historic opportunity for a peaceful and lasting settlement in the area. This much-awaited breakthrough has had a positive impact on the overall situation in the Mediterranean, thus opening the way to consider measures to promote dialogue, understanding and confidence-building between the countries in the region. We direct the Council in Permanent Session to continue to review the overall situation, and we encourage all efforts conducive to strengthening regional stability.

23. As members of the Alliance, we deplore the continuing conflict in the former Yugoslavia. We continue to believe that the conflict in Bosnia must be settled at the negotiating table and not on the battlefield. Only the parties can bring peace to the former Yugoslavia. Only they can agree to lay down their arms and end the violence which for these many months has only served to demonstrate that no side can prevail in its pursuit of military victory.

24. We are united in supporting the efforts of the United Nations and the European Union to secure a negotiated settlement of the conflict in Bosnia, agreeable to all parties, and we commend the European Union Action Plan of 22 November 1993 to secure such a negotiated settlement. We reaffirm our determination to contribute to the implementation of a viable settlement reached in good faith. We commend the front-line states for their key role in enforcing sanctions against those who continue to promote violence and aggression. We welcome the cooperation between NATO and the WEU in maintaining sanctions enforcement in the Adriatic.

25. We denounce the violations by the parties of the agreements they have already signed to implement a ceasefire and to permit the unimpeded delivery of humanitarian assistance to the victims of this terrible conflict. This situation cannot be tolerated. We urge all the parties to respect their agree-

ments. We are determined to eliminate obstacles to the accomplishment of the UNPROFOR mandate. We will continue operations to enforce the No-Fly Zone over Bosnia. We call for the full implementation of the UNSC Resolutions regarding the reinforcement of UNPROFOR. We reaffirm our readiness, under the authority of the United Nations Security Council and in accordance with the Alliance decisions of 2 and 9 August 1993, to carry out air strikes in order to prevent the strangulation of Sarajevo, the safe areas and other threatened areas in Bosnia-Herzegovina. In this context, we urge the UNPROFOR authorities to draw up urgently plans to ensure that the blocked rotation of the UNPROFOR contingent in Srebrenica can take place and to examine how the airport at Tuzla can be opened for humanitarian relief purposes.

26. The past five years have brought historic opportunities as well as new uncertainties and instabilities to Europe. Our Alliance has moved to adapt itself to the new circumstances, and today we have taken decisions in key areas. We have given our full support to the development of a European Security and Defence Identity. We have endorsed the concept of Combined Joint Task Forces as a means to adapt the Alliance to its future tasks. We have opened a new perspective of progressively closer relationships with the countries of Central and Eastern Europe and of the former Soviet Union. In doing all this we have renewed our Alliance as a joint endeavour of North America and Europe permanently committed to their common and indivisible security. The challenges we face are many and serious. The decisions we have taken today will better enable us to meet them.

Source: NATO, Press Communiqué M-1 (94) 3, 11 Jan. 1994.

PARTNERSHIP FOR PEACE: INVITATION

Issued by the Heads of State and Government participating in the meeting of the North Atlantic Council

Brussels, 10 January 1994

We, the Heads of State and Government of the member countries of the North Atlantic Alliance, building on the close and long-standing partnership among the North American and European Allies, are committed to enhancing security and stability in the whole of Europe. We therefore wish to strengthen ties with the democratic states to our East. We reaffirm that the Alliance, as provided for in Article 10 of the Washington Treaty, remains open to the membership of other European states in a position to further the principles of the Treaty and to contribute to the security of the North Atlantic area. We expect and would welcome NATO expansion that would reach to democratic states to our East, as part of an evolutionary process, taking into account political and security developments in the whole of Europe.

We have today launched an immediate and practical programme that will transform the relationship between NATO and participating states. This new programme goes beyond dialogue and cooperation to forge a real partnership—a Partnership for Peace. We therefore invite the other states participating in the NACC and other CSCE countries able and willing to contribute to this programme, to join with us in this partnership. Active participation in the Partnership for Peace will play an important role in the evolutionary process of the expansion of NATO.

The Partnership for Peace, which will operate under the authority of the North Atlantic Council, will forge new security relationships between the North Atlantic Alliance and its Partners for Peace. Partner states will be invited by the North Atlantic Council to participate in political and military bodies at NATO Headquarters with respect to Partnership activities. The Partnership will expand and intensify political and military cooperation throughout Europe, increase stability, diminish threats to peace, and build strengthened relationships by promoting the spirit of practical cooperation and commitment to democratic principles that underpin our Alliance. NATO will consult with any active participant in the Partnership if that partner perceives a direct threat to its territorial integrity, political independence, or security. At a pace and scope determined by the capacity and desire of the individual participating states, we will work in concrete ways towards transparency in defence budgeting, promoting democratic control of defence ministries, joint planning, joint military exercises, and creating an ability to operate with NATO forces in such fields as peacekeeping, search and rescue and humanitarian operations, and others as may be agreed.

To promote closer military cooperation and interoperability, we will propose, within the Partnership framework, peacekeeping field exercises beginning in 1994. To co-ordinate joint military activities within the Partnership, we will invite states participating in the Partnership to send permanent liaison officers to NATO Headquarters and a separate Partnership Coordination Cell at Mons (Belgium) that would, under the authority of the North Atlantic Council, carry out the military planning necessary to implement the Partnership programmes.

Since its inception two years ago, the North Atlantic Cooperation Council has greatly expanded the depth and scope of its activities. We will continue to work with all our NACC partners to build cooperative relationships across the entire spectrum of the Alliance's activities. With the expansion of NACC activities and the establishment of the Partnership for Peace, we have decided to offer permanent facilities at NATO Headquarters for personnel from NACC countries and other Partnership for Peace participants in order to improve our working relationships and facilitate closer cooperation.

ANNEX

Partnership for Peace: Framework Document

1. Further to the invitation extended by the NATO Heads of State and Government at their meeting on 10th/11th January, 1994, the member states of the North Atlantic Alliance and the other states subscribing to this document, resolved to deepen their political and military ties and to contribute further to the strengthening of security within the Euro-Atlantic area, hereby establish, within the framework of the North Atlantic Cooperation Council, this Partnership for Peace.

2. This Partnership is established as an expression of a joint conviction that stability and security in the Euro-Atlantic area can be achieved only through cooperation and common action. Protection and promotion of fundamental freedoms and human rights, and safeguarding of freedom, justice, and peace through democracy are shared values fundamental to the Partnership. In joining the Partnership, the member States of the North Atlantic Alliance and the other States sub-

scribing to this document recall that they are committed to the preservation of democratic societies, their freedom from coercion and intimidation, and the maintenance of the principles of international law. They reaffirm their commitment to fulfil in good faith the obligations of the Charter of the United Nations and the principles of the Universal Declaration on Human Rights; specifically, to refrain from the threat or use of force against the territorial integrity or political independence of any State, to respect existing borders and to settle disputes by peaceful means. They also reaffirm their commitment to the Helsinki Final Act and all subsequent CSCE documents and to the fulfilment of the commitments and obligations they have undertaken in the field of disarmament and arms control.

3. The other states subscribing to this document will cooperate with the North Atlantic Treaty Organization in pursuing the following objectives:

(*a*) facilitation of transparency in national defence planning and budgeting processes;

(*b*) ensuring democratic control of defence forces;

(*c*) maintenance of the capability and readiness to contribute, subject to constitutional considerations, to operations under the authority of the UN and/or the responsibility of the CSCE;

(*d*) the development of cooperative military relations with NATO, for the purpose of joint planning, training, and exercises in order to strengthen their ability to undertake missions in the fields of peacekeeping, search and rescue, humanitarian operations, and others as may subsequently be agreed;

(*e*) the development, over the longer term, of forces that are better able to operate with those of the members of the North Atlantic Alliance.

4. The other subscribing states will provide to the NATO Authorities Presentation Documents identifying the steps they will take to achieve the political goals of the Partnership and the military and other assets that might be used for Partnership activities. NATO will propose a programme of Partnership exercises and other activities consistent with the Partnership's objectives. Based on this programme and its Presentation Document, each subscribing state will develop with NATO an individual Partnership Programme.

5. In preparing and implementing their individual Partnership Programmes, other sub-

scribing states may, at their own expense and in agreement with the Alliance and, as necessary, relevant Belgian authorities, establish their own liaison office with NATO Headquarters in Brussels. This will facilitate their participation in NACC/Partnership meetings and activities, as well as certain others by invitation. They will also make available personnel, assets, facilities and capabilities necessary and appropriate for carrying out the agreed Partnership Programme. NATO will assist them, as appropriate, in formulating and executing their individual Partnership Programmes.

6. The other subscribing states accept the following understandings:

– those who envisage participation in missions referred to in paragraph 3(d) will, where appropriate, take part in related NATO exercises;

– they will fund their own participation in Partnership activities, and will endeavour otherwise to share the burdens of mounting exercises in which they take part;

– they may send, after appropriate agreement, permanent liaison officers to a separate Partnership Coordination Cell at Mons (Belgium) that would, under the authority of the North Atlantic Council, carry out the military planning necessary to implement the Partnership Programmes;

– those participating in planning and military exercises will have access to certain NATO technical data relevant to interoperability;

– building upon the CSCE measures on defence planning, the other subscribing states and NATO countries will exchange information on the steps that have been taken or are being taken to promote transparency in defence planning and budgeting and to ensure the democratic control of armed forces;

– they may participate in a reciprocal exchange of information on defence planning and budgeting which will be developed within the framework of the NACC/Partnership for Peace.

7. In keeping with their commitment to the objectives of this Partnership for Peace, the members of the North Atlantic Alliance will:

– develop with the other subscribing states a planning and review process to provide a basis for identifying and evaluating forces and capabilities that might be made available by them for multinational training, exercises, and operations in conjunction with Alliance forces;

– promote military and political coordination at NATO Headquarters in order to provide direction and guidance relevant to Partnership activities with the other subscribing states, including planning, training, exercises and the development of doctrine.

8. NATO will consult with any active participant in the Partnership if that Partner perceives a direct threat to its territorial integrity, political independence, or security.

_____

Source: NATO, Press Communiqué M-1(94)2, 10 Jan. 1994.

Part II. Weapons and technology proliferation, 1993

8. Nuclear weapon developments

DUNBAR LOCKWOOD

I. Introduction

All of the five declared nuclear weapon states continued to deploy, or at least develop, new nuclear weapon systems in 1993. With the possible exception of China, they also continued to retire older nuclear weapons, scale back earlier modernization plans or cancel weapons that were under development. Confronted with weak economies and the difficulty of defining a clear and present security threat, the British, French, Russian and US governments found that they could not justify allocating scarce resources to their respective nuclear weapon programmes at the levels maintained in the recent past.

The end of the confrontational relationship with the USSR, progressively declining defence budgets and the negotiation of the two Strategic Arms Reduction Treaties (START) have compelled the United States to continue reducing the size of its nuclear weapon arsenal. The number of US strategic nuclear weapons accordingly declined by about 440 in 1993. In drawing down its strategic nuclear forces, the USA has generally retained the most modern strategic weapon systems in its inventory, retired the oldest systems and continued to build only the new systems for which Congress has already appropriated funding, for example, B-2 bombers and Trident submarines. In addition, the 1991 START I and 1993 START II treaties have provided clear guidelines for the composition of future US strategic forces, encouraging some force structure options while limiting or foreclosing others.

With respect to its remaining tactical nuclear weapons, almost all of which were withdrawn between September 1991 and June 1992, the USA plans to dismantle all ground-launched warheads, retain some relatively small number of the naval warheads in storage in the USA while dismantling the remainder, and keep several hundred gravity bombs for delivery by aircraft, stored in the USA and deployed in Western Europe.

Neither the Russian nor the US government provided much new information in 1993 on nuclear weapons on the territory of the former USSR. The data that were available suggested that the size and composition of Russian nuclear forces did not change much in 1993. The development and production of new nuclear weapon systems in Russia have ground to a virtual halt, and the retirement of older, existing weapons has been carried out at a relatively slow pace. As for the non-Russian former Soviet republics, Belarus and Kazakhstan gave clear signs that they are willing to eliminate the nuclear weapons now located on their respective territories, but as of early 1994 the Ukrainian Parliament

(Rada) had not yet approved the government's earlier commitment to become a non-nuclear weapon state.[1]

As in 1992, the United Kingdom decided in 1993 to scale back some of its non-strategic nuclear weapon programmes and has cut its overall nuclear weapon stockpile to the lowest level since the early 1960s. The planned introduction of Trident submarines during the rest of the 1990s, however, will actually increase the total number of British nuclear weapons as well as vastly improve the accuracy and range of the British submarine-launched ballistic missile (SLBM) force.

France, unlike Russia, the UK and the USA, has several new nuclear weapon programmes under development, including a new class of submarine, two types of SLBM—one of which could also be deployed as an intercontinental ballistic missile (ICBM)—a nuclear-capable fighter aircraft and an air-to-surface missile (ASM). However, some of these French programmes may be scaled back or scrapped altogether because of budget constraints.

China's nuclear weapon programme remains shrouded in secrecy, but it appears that China is continuing slowly to upgrade and expand its forces with the development of new types of ballistic missile and the acquisition of nuclear-capable aircraft from Russia. China, unlike the other nuclear weapon powers, has steadily increased its defence budget since the end of the cold war. According to US Central Intelligence Agency (CIA) estimates, China's defence expenditures in 1992 increased by nearly 14 per cent, for the fourth consecutive year of nominal double-digit increases.[2] Furthermore, the US intelligence community estimates that the Chinese military 'can expect significant budget increases by the end of this decade'.[3] Presumably, these increases will make more resources available for the development of new nuclear weapons. According to some analysts, China's ultimate goal is to build up its nuclear capabilities to the extent that it can settle regional security issues on its own terms without concern that it could be politically coerced by Russia or the United States.[4]

---

[1] For details, see chapter 16 in this volume.

[2] US Central Intelligence Agency, 'China's economy in 1992 and 1993: grappling with the risks of rapid growth', a research paper submitted to the Subcommittee on Technology and National Security of the Joint Economic Committee, 30 July 1993, p. 10; see also International Institute for Strategic Studies (IISS), *The Military Balance 1992–1993* (Brassey's: London, 1992), p. 144; IISS, *The Military Balance 1993–1994* (Brassey's: London, 1993), p. 152; Oxnam, R., 'China in transition: military might', MacNeil Lehrer News Hour, WNET, New York, N.Y., show #4800, 17 Nov. 1993; Senator Larry Pressler, *Congressional Record*, 20 Nov. 1993, p. S16655. See also chapter 12, section V, in this volume.

[3] Lt-General James R. Clapper, Jr, Director, US Defense Intelligence Agency (DIA), Written statement submitted to the Senate Select Intelligence Committee, 25 Jan. 1994, p. 7.

[4] Godwin, P. and Shulz, J. J., 'Arming the dragon for the 21st century: China's defense modernization program', *Arms Control Today*, Dec. 1993, pp. 6–7; Ball, D., MacNeil Lehrer News Hour (note 2). For a detailed discussion of China's nuclear strategy, see Xue, L., 'Evolution of China's nuclear strategy', eds J. C. Hopkins and W. Hu, *Strategic Views from the Second Tier: The Nuclear Weapons Policies of France, Britain, and China* (University of California Institute on Global Conflict and Cooperation: San Diego, Calif., 1994), pp. 167–92.

II. US nuclear weapon programmes

The Nuclear Posture Review

At a 29 October 1993 press conference, then US Defense Secretary Les Aspin announced that the US Department of Defense (DOD) planned to conduct 'the first nuclear [weapon] policy review in 15 years and . . . the first Defense Department review ever to incorporate revisions of policy doctrine, force structure, operations, safety, and security and arms control all in one look'.[5] The review, which is scheduled for completion in the late spring or early summer of 1994, will address six issues related to US nuclear weapons: (*a*) the role of nuclear weapons in security; (*b*) the nuclear force structure needed to carry out required missions; (*c*) nuclear force operations and alert levels; (*d*) security and safety of nuclear weapons; (*e*) the relationship between the nuclear posture and counter-proliferation policy; and (*f*) the nuclear posture and its relationship to 'threat reduction policy with the former Soviet Union'.

Two of the most controversial and important issues which the new study will grapple with are whether the USA should maintain its policy of providing 'negative security assurances' to non-nuclear weapon states and whether to adopt a new 'no-first-use' policy.[6]

ICBMs

As of late 1993, the USA had removed some 250 of its 450 Minuteman II missiles from their silos,[7] a process started in late 1991.[8] The remaining missiles, which have been off alert since September 1991, are scheduled for withdrawal by 1995, irrespective of the status of the two START treaties.[9] Consistent with the START I Treaty rules for removing an ICBM from accountability, the first Minuteman II missile silo was blown up at Whiteman Air Force Base (AFB), Missouri, on 8 December 1993.[10]

The Minuteman III missile, which was first deployed in 1970, remains on alert,[11] and the USA intends to extend its service lifetime until at least the year

---

[5] Les Aspin, US Secretary of Defense, Press Conference, 29 Oct. 1993, Federal News Service (FNS) Transcript; see also Les Aspin, US Secretary of Defense, *Annual Report to the President and the Congress* (US Government Printing Office: Washington, DC, Jan. 1994), p. 147.

[6] For a discussion of the implications of these issues for nuclear arms control and nuclear weapon non-proliferation, see chapters 15 and 16 in this volume.

[7] Public Affairs offices for Malmstrom AFB, Montana, Ellsworth AFB, South Dakota, and Whiteman AFB, Missouri, private communications with the author, Dec. 1993.

[8] *Fiscal Year 1994 Arms Control Impact Statements* (US Government Printing Office: Washington, DC, 1993), p. 4.

[9] Dr William Perry, Deputy Secretary of Defense, Testimony before the Senate Committee on Governmental Affairs, 10 June 1993, p. 3; US Department of Defense, *Report of the Secretary of Defense Dick Cheney to the President and the Congress* (US Government Printing Office: Washington, DC, 1993), pp. 67, 149.

[10] Associated Press, 'US destroys missile silo; 499 to go', *New York Times*, 10 Dec. 1993, p. A23; Levins, H., 'Goodbye to old cold warriors', *St. Louis Post Dispatch*, 9 Dec. 1993, p. 1.

[11] *Fiscal Year 1994 Arms Control Impact Statements* (note 8), p. 4.

2010.[12] As part of the Minuteman III service lifetime extension programme, the Air Force would like to improve its capability to quickly re-target these missiles and to upgrade their guidance systems in the next decade to give them an accuracy similar to that of the MX (Peacekeeper) missile.[13] Assuming that the START II Treaty is ratified, the USA will download all of its Minuteman IIIs from three warheads each to one each. Once the Treaty is fully implemented, the US ICBM force would consist of a total of 500 single-warhead Minuteman III missiles deployed at three bases. Under current plans, if the START II Treaty enters into force, the 50 MX ICBMs will remain on alert status until the beginning of their scheduled draw-down, which would begin in the year 2000 and should be completed by 1 January 2003. The US Air Force plans to keep flight-testing the MX missile through the mid-1990s.[14]

SSBNs

The United States withdrew seven Poseidon submarines from service in calendar year 1993 and will retire the remaining three by the end of fiscal year (FY) 1994.[15] These submarines, which were built in the 1960s, were retired to save money, to comply with the START I Treaty (whose entry into force is anticipated in 1994) and to provide W-76 warheads for the Trident II missiles deployed on Trident SSBNs (strategic, ballistic-missile, nuclear-powered submarines) based at King's Bay, Georgia.

The 14th Trident submarine, the *USS Nebraska*, was commissioned in July 1993 and became the sixth Trident submarine to be armed with the Trident II missile; all six submarines are based at King's Bay. (The other eight operational Trident submarines, which are armed with the Trident I missile, are based at Bangor, Washington.) The remaining four Trident submarines are under various stages of construction at the Electric Boat Company in Groton, Connecticut, which plans to deliver one new submarine to the US Navy each year until 1997. At that point, the USA would have a total of 18 SSBNs—10 in the Atlantic Ocean carrying 24 Trident II missiles each and 8 in the Pacific Ocean carrying 24 Trident I missiles each. (However, some Pentagon analysts have advocated that some of the older Trident submarines in the Pacific Fleet, which were initially deployed in the early 1980s, be retired early rather than undergo an expensive replacement of their nuclear reactor cores.[16]) To get

---

[12] US Department of Defense, Report of the Secretary of Defense Dick Cheney (note 9), pp. 69–70.

[13] Department of Defense Appropriations, Fiscal Year 1994, Hearing before the Subcommittee on the Department of Defense of the Committee on Appropriations, US House of Representatives, 103rd Congress (US Government Printing Office: Washington, DC, 1993), Part 5, pp. 313–14.

[14] Department of Defense Appropriations (note 13), Part 5, p. 254; see also *Fiscal Year 1994 Arms Control Impact Statements* (note 8), p. 4.

[15] Department of Defense Appropriations (note 13), Part 4, p. 186; 'Ships' status changes: 1 Jan. 1992–31 Dec. 1992', *US Naval Institute Proceedings*, Sep. 1993, pp. 107–109; 'Notebook', *US Naval Institute Proceedings*, Dec. 1993, p. 111; 'Bidding farewell to the fleet', *Navy Times*, 15–19 Nov. 1993, pp. 42, 44.

[16] Hitchens, T. and Munro, N., 'Pentagon review might terminate nuclear, spy plans', *Defense News*, 18–24 Oct. 1993, p. 3; see also Mosher, D., *Rethinking the Trident Force* (Congressional Budget Office: Washington, DC, July 1993), pp. xv–xvi.

below the START II Treaty limit of 1750 SLBM warheads, the Navy plans to download its 432 Trident SLBMs from 8 warheads each to 4, for a total of 1728 warheads.[17]

Through FY 1994, Congress has appropriated funding for a total of 319 Trident II missiles. In order to outfit all 10 submarines in the Atlantic Fleet and maintain its flight-test programme, as of 1993 the Navy planned to purchase an additional 109 missiles through FY 1999, making a total purchase of 428.[18] The decision on whether to retrofit the eight Trident submarines based in the Pacific Ocean with the Trident II missile will not be made until early 1995,[19] and even if the USA does decide to go forward with the retrofit, it would not be carried out until the first decade of the next century. If the retrofit is carried out, the Navy would require approximately 200 additional Trident II missiles.[20]

Bombers

The US Air Force plans to retire the remaining B-52G bomber aircraft, all of which are dedicated to a conventional mission, in 1994.[21] It has also decided to give 47 of the existing 95 B-52H bombers enhanced conventional capabilities. In explaining its decision to retire all of the B-52Gs and upgrade some of the B-52Hs, the Air Force pointed out that the latter aircraft is newer, more fuel-efficient and significantly less expensive to maintain.[22] The other half of the B-52Hs are slated for retirement in 1995, pending the outcome of the Nuclear Posture Review.[23]

The Air Force has decided that all the B-1Bs will be 'reoriented to a purely conventional role' by 1998.[24] This decision to make the B-1B the 'backbone' of the US conventional heavy bomber force was based on the fact that the B-1B has more modern capabilities than the B-52 (e.g., it can fly faster and lower and is more difficult to detect by radar) and that the number of B-1Bs will vastly exceed the number of B-2s.[25]

In their new role, the B-1B bombers would still be accountable under the START I Treaty but would be exempted from the START II Treaty limit of 3500 deployed strategic warheads. The START II Treaty does not require that

---

[17] Mosher (note 16), p. xii.

[18] Department of Defense Authorization for Appropriations, Fiscal Year 1994, Hearing before the Committee on Armed Services Subcommittee on Nuclear Deterrence, Arms Control and Defense Intelligence, US Senate, 103rd Congress (US Government Printing Office: Washington, DC, 1993), Part 7, p. 8.

[19] Department of Defense Appropriations (note 13) Part 4, p. 179; Aspin, *Annual Report to the President and the Congress* (note 5), p. 149.

[20] Mosher (note 16), p. xii.

[21] Department of Defense Appropriations (note 13), Part 5, p. 268.

[22] Department of Defense Appropriations (note 13), Part 5, p. 268; Department of the Air Force, *The Bomber Road Map*, June 1992, p. 8.

[23] Aspin, *Annual Report to the President and the Congress* (note 5), pp. 27, 147.

[24] General Lee Butler, Commander-in-Chief of the US Strategic Command, Testimony before the Senate Armed Services Committee, 22 Apr. 1993, Federal News Service transcript, p. 5; Aspin, *Annual Report to the President and the Congress* (note 5), p. 27.

[25] Department of the Air Force, *The Bomber Road Map* (note 22), p. 9.

Table 8.1. US strategic nuclear forces, January 1994

Type	Designation	No. deployed	Year first deployed	Range (km)[a]	Warheads x yield	Warheads in stockpile
Bombers						
B-52-H[b]	Stratofortress	95	1961	16 000 ⎫	ALCM 5–150 kt	1 200
B-1B[c]	Lancer	95	1986	19 000 ⎬	ACM 5–150 kt	460
B-2[d]	Spirit	1	1993	11 000 ⎭	Bombs, various	1 400
Total		**191**				**3 060**
ICBMs[e]						
LGM-30F[f]	Minuteman II	200	1966	11 300	1 x 1.2 Mt	200
LGM-30G[g]	Minuteman III					
	Mk 12	200	1970	13 000	3 x 170 kt	600
	Mk 12A	300	1979	13 000	3 x 335 kt	900
LGM-118	MX/Peacekeeper	50	1986	11 000	10 x 300 kt	500
Total		**750**				**2 200**
SLBMs						
UGM-96A[h]	Trident I C-4	240	1979	7 400	8 x 100 kt	1 920
UGM-133A[i]	Trident II D-5	144	1990	7 400	8 x 100–475 kt	1 152
Total		**384**				**3 072**

[a] Range for aircraft indicates combat radius, without in-flight refuelling.

[b] B-52Hs can carry up to 20 ALCMs/ACMs each, but only about 1000 nuclear ALCMs and 460 ACMs are available for deployment; the 95 B-52Hs listed above include 2 test planes at Edwards AFB, California. The DOD now plans to reduce the B-52H fleet to 48 in FY 1995, but the ongoing Nuclear Posture Review could lead to a decision to retain a higher number.

[c] The B-1B can carry the B53/B62/B83 bombs. Rockwell built 100 B-1Bs. Four have crashed, and 1 is used as a trainer at Ellsworth AFB, South Dakota, and is not considered 'operational'. The USA plans to 'reorient' all of its B-1Bs to conventional missions. These aircraft will count towards START I Treaty limits, but not towards START II Treaty limits.

[d] The B-2 can carry the B61/B83 bombs. The first operational B-2 was delivered to White-man AFB, Missouri, on 17 Dec. 1993. Four additional B-2s are scheduled for delivery in FY 1994, and the Air Force plans to field a total of 20 operational B-2s by the late 1990s.

[e] The criterion for whether an ICBM is included in this table (e.g., Minuteman IIs) is whether the missile is still in the silo; that is, once a missile has been removed from its silo, it is considered, for the purposes of this table, to be retired. This is not the same as being START-accountable. The START I Treaty requires that the silos are blown up; for example, if the strict START Treaty counting rules were applied, nearly 450 Minuteman IIs are still accountable.

[f] Approximately 250 Minuteman II missiles had been removed from their silos by Jan. 1994. The remaining 200 missiles (90 at Malmstrom AFB, Montana; 90 at Whiteman AFB, Missouri; and 20 at Ellsworth AFB, South Dakota) are scheduled to be removed from their silos by 1995. The first Minuteman II silo was destroyed in Dec. 1993 at Whiteman AFB.

[g] During this decade, the Air Force plans to consolidate its Minuteman III missiles at 3 bases. To this end, it has begun to deploy Minuteman III missiles in empty Minuteman II silos at Malmstrom AFB, Montana. (Consequently, the current number of Minuteman III missiles now exceeds 500 but will decline again to 500 when 1 of the 3 other existing Minuteman III bases is closed.) Eventually, Malmstrom AFB will have 200 Minuteman IIIs and the other 300 Minuteman IIIs will be divided between the 2 remaining bases.

h In calendar year 1993, 7 Poseidon submarines were deactivated. The remaining 3 Poseidon SSBNs will be removed from service in FY 1994. The 240 Trident I C-4 missiles are deployed on 3 16-missile Poseidon submarines and on the 8 24-missile Ohio Class submarines in the Pacific Fleet. (The 3 remaining Poseidon submarines—the USS *Simon Bolivar*, the USS *Stonewall Jackson* and the USS *Vallejo*—based in Charleston, South Carolina, are scheduled to be decommissioned in FY 1994.)

i The 144 Trident II D-5 missiles are deployed on 6 Ohio Class submarines stationed at King's Bay, Georgia, the newest of which, the USS *Nebraska*, is scheduled to begin patrols in 1994. By 1997, 4 more Ohio Class submarines are scheduled to be delivered to King's Bay, providing the Navy with a total of 10 SSBNs in the Atlantic Fleet carrying 240 Trident II D-5 missiles and 8 SSBNs in the Pacific Fleet carrying 192 Trident I C-4 missiles.

Sources: Les Aspin, Secretary of Defense, *Annual Report to the President and the Congress*, Jan. 1994, p. 7; Dick Cheney, Secretary of Defense, *Annual Report to the President and the Congress*, Jan. 1993, p. 68; US Air Force Public Affairs, personal communications; US Navy Public Affairs, personal communications; Department of Defense, 'The Bottom–Up Review: forces for a new era', 1 Sep. 1993, p. 17; Mosher, D., *Rethinking the Trident Force* (Congressional Budget Office (CBO): Washington, DC, July 1993), p. 11; Natural Resources Defense Council (NRDC); Department of Appropriations, Fiscal Year 1994, Hearing before the Subcommittee on the Department of Defense of the Committee on Appropriations (US Government Printing Office: Washington, DC, 1993), Part 4, p. 186; *US Naval Institute Proceedings*, Dec. 1993, p. 111; *US Naval Institute Proceedings*, Sep. 1993, pp. 107–109; author's estimates.

aircraft that have been reoriented to a conventional role be physically altered, but it does prohibit the storage of nuclear bomber weapons at bases for such aircraft. In addition, their crews may not train or conduct exercises for nuclear missions. The DOD now plans to put 24 of the 96 B-1Bs in 'attrition reserve', starting in 1995.[26] Although these aircraft would still fly on a regular basis, they would require fewer personnel and less maintenance to support them.

Currently, six B-2s are being flight-tested at Edwards AFB, California.[27] In October 1993, Secretary of Defense Les Aspin asked Congress to release $2.2 billion in procurement funds that had been placed in escrow for the B-2, submitting documentation that the bomber was meeting performance requirements specified by Congress. (At that time, about one-third of the 4000-hour flight-test programme had been completed.)[28] Subsequently, Congress voted to release the money for building the last five aircraft. In addition, Congress, which has complained about the cost of the B-2 for many years, limited the number of B-2s that may be built to 20 operational aircraft and one test aircraft and capped the total amount that may be spent on research, development, testing, evaluation and procurement at $44.4 billion.[29]

The first operational B-2 bomber was delivered to Whiteman AFB, Missouri, in December 1993.[30] Four additional B-2s will be delivered in

---

[26] Aspin (note 5), p. 27.

[27] Five of the six B-2 test aircraft will eventually be converted to operational status.

[28] 'Aspin seeks release of delayed B-2 funds', *Aviation Week & Space Technology*, 25 Oct. 1993, p. 28.

[29] *Congressional Record*, 10 Nov. 1993, p. H9191. (The figure $44.4 billion is in current US dollars.)

[30] Sia, R. H. P., 'Air Force accepts first B-2 bomber', *Baltimore Sun*, 18 Dec. 1993, p. 1; 'Air Force prepares to operate B-2 bomber', *Aviation Week & Space Technology*, 13–20 Dec. 1993, pp. 29–30.

1994,[31] and by the late 1990s the USA will have deployed all 20 operational B-2 bombers.

In accordance with a 28 January 1992 unilateral initiative taken by then President George Bush, the USA terminated the production of the Advanced Cruise Missile (ACM) in the summer of 1993.[32] A total of 460 of these missiles are now stored at K. I. Sawyer AFB, Michigan, and Minot AFB, North Dakota,[33] where they are available for deployment on B-52Hs, which can carry up to 12 ACMs each.[34] Bush's 1992 decision to cancel the ACM programme was based on several factors. The programme was plagued with technical problems and cost overruns, the Air Force already had approximately 1000 relatively new nuclear-armed air-launched cruise missiles (ALCMs), the former Soviet air defence network had basically collapsed, and US force structure plans and START I and START II bomber counting rules effectively preclude the deployment of ACMs on the B-1B bomber.

III. Former Soviet and CIS nuclear weapon programmes

Russia

ICBMs

In anticipation of the implementation of the START I Treaty, Russia has begun retiring some older ICBMs.[35] During the course of 1993, there were sporadic reports on the status of these ICBM deactivations. In October 1993, the International Institute for Strategic Studies (IISS) reported that 'during the last 12 months, 100 SS-11s have been withdrawn' from their silos.[36] In the summer of 1993, Russia began the process of blowing up the 60 SS-11 ICBM silos at Bershet; all the SS-11 ICBMs are scheduled for dismantlement by 1995.[37] Colonel-General Igor Sergeyev, Commander-in-Chief of the Strategic Rocket Forces (SRF), reported in May 1993 that 10 SS-13s had been removed from 'combat status' at Yoshkar-Ola.[38] A '60 Minutes' television report

---

[31] Department of Defense Appropriations (note 13), Part 4, p. 324.

[32] Douglas, E., 'San Diego assembly line rolls out its final advanced cruise missile', *San Diego Union Tribune*, 5 Aug. 1993, p. C-1; Department of Defense Appropriations (note 13), Part 5, p. 268. For the text of the Bush initiative, see SIPRI, *SIPRI Yearbook 1992: World Armaments and Disarmament* (Oxford University Press: Oxford, 1992), appendix 2A, pp. 88–89. The ACM is designed to be 'stealthier' (i.e., harder to detect by air defence radars) than older cruise missiles.

[33] Opall, B., 'New cruise missile is ready, US Air Force is not', *Defense News*, 26 July–1 Aug. 1993, p. 1.

[34] B-52Hs can also carry 8 ALCMs internally in a rotary launcher, making a total of 20 cruise missiles.

[35] *Current Developments in the Former Soviet Union*, Hearing before the Committee on Armed Services, US Senate, 103rd Congress, Senate hearing 103-242 (US Government Printing Office: Washington, DC, 1993), p. 38.

[36] IISS, *The Military Balance 1993–1994* (note 2), p. 96.

[37] 'Destruction of Kama region ICBM silos under way', *Pravda*, 12 Aug. 1993, p. 1, in Foreign Broadcast Information Service, *Daily Report–Central Eurasia* (hereafter FBIS-SOV), FBIS-SOV-93-155, 13 Aug. 1993, p. 40.

[38] 'Interview with Colonel-General I. Sergeyev, Commander-in-Chief, Strategic Rocket Forces', *Izvestia*, 14 May 1993, pp. 1–2. (The *Izvestia* article indicated that the phrase 'removed from combat status' meant that the 10 SS-13 missiles had been removed from their silos.)

broadcast on CBS on 31 October 1993, which included video footage and interviews at the Vypolozovo base, indicated that Moscow has not yet retired any of the remaining 47 SS-17 ICBMs it declared in the START I Treaty Memorandum of Understanding. Russia also retired six SS-18s in 1993, according to the IISS.[39]

Russian ICBM production continues to decline. The US Defense Intelligence Agency (DIA) estimated that Russia produced 45–75 strategic ballistic missiles in 1992—down by at least 60 per cent from the 190–205 that the USSR produced in 1990.[40] In February 1993 the CIA National Intelligence Officer for Strategic Programs, Dr Lawrence Gershwin, said: 'today the only strategic missile in production at all is the SS-25 road mobile ICBM, and that production is down from what it historically has been. We are really at a rather low point in missile production'.[41]

New ICBMs

The US intelligence community now expects Russia, over the next 10 years, to develop and deploy two new types of ICBM—a silo-based single-warhead SS-25 type missile and a road-mobile single-warhead SS-25 type missile.[42] Gershwin testified in early 1993 that neither of these missiles had been flight-tested[43] and, as of the end of the year, there were no new reports to the contrary.

SSBNs

Admiral Felix Gromov, Commander-in-Chief of the Russian Navy, said in 1993 that 'the construction of new strategic submarines is not planned for the near future, although designers continue to work in this field'.[44] Admiral Gromov added that, by the year 2000, Russia would reduce the number of its SSBNs to 24:[45] presumably 6 Typhoon, 7 Delta IV and 11 Delta III Class submarines. US intelligence officials echoed Gromov in their public statements to the US Congress in 1993. In February CIA analyst Gershwin stated that, for the first time since the 1960s, Russia has stopped producing ballistic missile submarines and that the US intelligence community does not 'anticipate a resumption of the production of ballistic missile submarines until

[39] IISS, *The Military Balance 1993–1994* (note 2), p. 96.

[40] William Grundmann, Director for Combat Support, Defense Intelligence Agency, Testimony before the Joint Economic Committee, 11 June 1993, p. 18; see also Shaposhnikov, Y., 'The armed forces: to a new quality', eds T. P. Johnson and S. E. Miller, *Russian Security After the Cold War* (Brassey's: McLean, Va., 1994), p. 192.

[41] *Current Developments in the Former Soviet Union* (note 35), p. 30.

[42] *Current Developments in the Former Soviet Union* (note 35), p. 8; *Proliferation Threats of the 1990s*, Hearing before the Committee on Governmental Affairs, US Senate, 103rd Congress, Senate hearing 103-208 (US Government Printing Office: Washington, DC, 1993), p. 41; 'CIA expects Russia to deploy three new ballistic missiles by 2000', *Aerospace Daily*, 4 Feb. 1993, p. 195.

[43] *Current Developments in the Former Soviet Union* (note 35), p. 30; *Proliferation Threats of the 1990s* (note 42), pp. 40–41.

[44] Admiral Felix Gromov, Commander-in-Chief of the Russian Navy, 'Reforming the Russian Navy', *Naval Forces*, vol. 14, no. 4 (1993), p. 7.

[45] Gromov (note 44), p. 10.

. . . sometime after the year 2000'.[46] Three months later, Rear Admiral Edward Sheafer, Director of US Naval Intelligence, said that 'the Russians will still retain nearly two dozen SSBNs . . . after the year 2000'.[47] According to the IISS, Russia has begun dismantling Delta I and Yankee Class submarines.[48]

Russian SSBN alert rates have dropped significantly in the past few years. In May 1993, Admiral Sheafer told Congress that in 1992 'the average number of Russian SSBNs at sea on patrol at any given time declined to approximately one third of 1991 levels'.[49] Unclassified sources suggest that Sheafer was estimating six SSBNs at sea at any given time in 1991 and two in 1992.[50]

SLBMs

Russia is developing a new SLBM for deployment on Typhoon Class submarines.[51] This follow-on to the SS-N-20 missile had not been flight-tested as of early May 1993, but US naval intelligence projects that 'the missile should begin flight testing soon'.[52] According to an April 1993 Russian press report, the SS-N-20 follow-on development is scheduled to be completed by 1996.[53] US Naval intelligence expects that all six of the Typhoon SSBNs will be retrofitted with the follow-on to the SS-N-20 by the late 1990s.[54]

Bombers

Moscow's strategic bomber production has steadily declined in recent years. The US DIA estimated that Russia produced 20 bombers in 1992—down by more than 40 per cent from the 35 bombers that the USSR produced in 1990.[55] Furthermore, statements from Russian President Boris Yeltsin,[56] former Commander-in-Chief of Commonwealth of Independent States (CIS) military forces Yevgeny Shaposhnikov,[57] US intelligence projections[58] and press

---

[46] *Current Developments in the Former Soviet Union* (note 35), p. 31.

[47] Rear Admiral Edward Sheafer, Director, US Naval Intelligence, Posture Statement, 3 May 1993, p. 40.

[48] IISS, *The Military Balance 1993–1994* (note 2), p. 96; Handler, J., Private communications with the author, Jan. 1994. (Handler's observations, while touring the Severodvinsk and Pavlovskoye shipyards in Oct. 1991, also seem to confirm that Delta I dismantlement is under way.)

[49] Sheafer (note 47), p. 46.

[50] Cushman, J. H., Jr, 'US Navy's periscopes still follow Soviet fleet', *New York Times*, 23 Feb. 1992, p. A14; Blair, B. G., *The Logic of Accidental Nuclear War* (Brookings Institution: Washington, DC, 1993), p. 103; see also 'No new subs', *Aviation Week & Space Technology*, 23 Nov. 1992, p. 25.

[51] *Current Developments in the Former Soviet Union* (note 35), p. 8; Sheafer (note 47), p. 44.

[52] Sheafer (note 47), p. 44.

[53] Sheafer (note 47), p. 44.

[54] Sheafer (note 47), p. 44.

[55] Grundmann (note 40), p. 18.

[56] 'Yeltsin delivers statement on disarmament', Moscow Teleradiokompaniya Ostankino Television First Program Network, FBIS-SOV-92-019, 29 Jan. 1992, p. 1; *SIPRI Yearbook 1992* (note 32), p. 90.

[57] Shaposhnikov (note 40), p. 191.

[58] Lt-General James Clapper, Jr, Director, Defense Intelligence Agency, Statement before the Senate Armed Services Committee, 22 Jan. 1992, in *Threat Assessment, Military Strategy, and Defense Planning,* Hearing 102-755 (US Government Printing Office: Washington, DC, 1992), p. 33.

reports[59] all suggest that Russia has not produced any new strategic bombers since the summer of 1992.

In addition to the cessation of strategic bomber production, it has been reported that Russian strategic bomber crews have now cut back their training from 100–110 flight hours per year to 70. (By comparison, US bomber crews log approximately 300 hours per year.)[60]

Despite the cutbacks in resources allocated to bombers, Russia continued to maintain at least half a dozen Tu-160 Blackjack bombers in 1993. The continued maintenance of these aircraft is presumably relatively costly, given the long list of technical problems that need to be addressed to make the Blackjacks a viable fleet.[61] It appears that these six aircraft divide their time between the Zhukovsky Flight Research Centre just south of Moscow[62] and Engels AFB on the Volga River near Saratov.[63]

Reportedly, the Russian strategic bomber force has recently been restructured in order to conform with the new military doctrine which stresses preparation for tactical missions around Russia's periphery. Blackjack, Bear and Backfire bomber crews have begun training as a 'composite force' to deliver conventional weapons to targets near Russia's borders.[64]

Tactical nuclear weapons

Russia has begun dismantling some of the tactical nuclear warheads that were withdrawn from Ukraine in 1992, according to both Russian and Ukrainian officials. Reportedly, half of these warheads (1000–1500) had been dismantled as of the spring of 1993.[65]

Consistent with commitments made by then Soviet President Mikhail Gorbachev in October 1991 and Russian President Yeltsin in January 1992, the Russian Ministry of Defence announced in February 1993 that all tactical nuclear weapons had been withdrawn from its ships and submarines.[66]

[59] Velovich, A., 'Kazan produces final batch of Blackjacks', *Flight International*, 12–18 Aug. 1992, p. 22; Covault, C., 'Russia debates doctrine, bomber, fighter decisions', *Aviation Week & Space Technology*, 31 May 1993, p. 23.

[60] Covault, C., 'Russian bomber force seeks tactical role', *Aviation Week & Space Technology*, 15 Nov. 1993, p. 44.

[61] See, for example, 'Nuclear notebook', *Bulletin of the Atomic Scientists*, July/Aug. 1990, p. 48.

[62] Covault, C., 'Russian Zhukovsky facility shows flight test diversity', *Aviation Week & Space Technology*, 14 June 1993, p. 67.

[63] Covault (note 60), p. 49; Covault, C., 'Russia launches exercise of composite strike force', *Aviation Week & Space Technology*, 15 Nov. 1993, p. 51; Velovich (note 59), p. 22; 'New long-range cruise missile launched from Tu-160', Moscow Russian Television Network, 31 Oct. 1992, in FBIS-SOV-92-216, 6 Nov. 1992, p. 2.

[64] Covault (note 60), p. 44.

[65] *Management and Disposition of Excess Weapons Plutonium* (National Academy Press: Washington, DC, 1994), p. 105; see also *Current Developments in the Former Soviet Union* (note 35), p. 38.

[66] Shapiro, M., 'Russian Navy rids itself of tactical nuclear arms', *Washington Post*, 5 Feb. 1993, p. A31; 'Tactical nuclear arms removed from vessels', ITAR-TASS, 4 Feb. 1993, in FBIS-SOV-93-022, 4 Feb. 1993, p. 1.

Table 8.2. CIS strategic nuclear forces, January 1994

Type	NATO designation	No. deployed	Year first deployed	Range (km)[a]	Warheads x yield	Warheads in stockpile
Bombers						
Tu-95M[b]	Bear-H6	27	1984	12 800	6 x AS-15A ALCMs, bombs	162
Tu-95M[b]	Bear-H16	57	1984	12 800	16 x AS-15A ALCMs, bombs	912
Tu-160[c]	Blackjack	25	1987	11 000	12 x AS-15B ALCMs or AS-16 SRAMs, bombs	300
Total		**109**				**1 374**
ICBMs[d]						
SS-17[e]	Spanker	40	1979	10 000	4 x 750 kt	160
SS-18[f]	Satan	290	1979	11 000	10 x 550-750 kt	2 900
SS-19[g]	Stiletto	280	1979	10 000	6 x 550 kt	1 680
SS-24 M1/M2[h]	Scalpel	36/56	1987	10 000	10 x 550 kt	920
SS-25[i]	Sickle	405	1985	10 500	1 x 550 kt	405
Total		**1 051/1 071**				**6 065**
SLBMs[j]						
SS-N-8 M2	Sawfly	64	1973	9 100	1 x 1.5 Mt	64
SS-N-18 M1	Stingray	224	1978	6 500	3 x 500 kt	672
SS-N-20[k]	Sturgeon	120	1983	8 300	10 x 200 kt	1 200
SS-N-23	Skiff	112	1986	9 000	4 x 100 kt	448
Total		**520**				**2 384**

[a] Range for aircraft indicates combat radius, without in-flight refuelling.

[b] All 40 Bear-H bombers (27 Bear-H6s and 13 Bear-H16s) that were based in Kazakhstan have now been withdrawn to Russia; there are still 21 Bear-H16s in Ukraine, at Uzin.

[c] 19 Blackjacks are based in Ukraine at Priluki; 6 Blackjacks in Russia appear to divide their time between the Zhukovsky Flight Research Centre just south of Moscow and Engels AFB near Saratov. The Blackjacks at Priluki are not 'fully operational', according to US intelligence.

[d] The criterion for whether an ICBM is included in this table (e.g., SS-19s in Ukraine and SS-18s in Russia and Kazakhstan) is whether the missile is still in the silo; that is, once a missile has been removed from its silo, it is considered, for the purposes of this table, to be retired. This is not the same as being START-accountable. The START Treaty requires that the silos are blown up; for example, if the strict START Treaty counting rules were applied, 308 SS-18s and 300 SS-19s would still be accountable.

[e] All of the remaining SS-17s are based at Vypolozovo in Russia and are scheduled for retirement in the near future.

[f] In the START I Treaty MOU, the Soviet Union declared 104 SS-18s in Kazakhstan and 204 in Russia. Based on unofficial but reliable resources, this table assumes that 12 SS-18s in Kazakhstan and 6 in Russia had been removed from their silos as of early 1994. Under the START I Treaty, Russia would be permitted to retain 154 SS-18s. If the START II Treaty is fully implemented, all SS-18 missiles will be destroyed, but Russia may convert up to 90 SS-18 silos for deployment of single-warhead ICBMs.

g In the START I Treaty MOU, the Soviet Union declared 130 SS-19s in Ukraine and 170 in Russia. During 1993, Ukraine removed 20 SS-19s from their silos at Pervomaysk.

h Of the 56 silo-based SS-24 M2s, 46 are in Ukraine at Pervomaysk and 10 are in Russia at Tatishchevo. During 1993, Ukraine removed the warheads from 20 of the 46 SS-24s and pledged to remove the warheads from the remaining 26 by mid-Nov. 1994. All 36 rail-based SS-24 M1s are in Russia—12 each at Bershet, Kostroma and Krasnoyarsk.

i SS-25s are deployed in both Russia and Belarus. SS-25 deployment in Belarus peaked in Dec. 1991 at 81 missiles. In Dec. 1993, the Belarussian Defence Ministry announced that 27 SS-25s had been withdrawn to Russia, where they will become part of Russia's ICBM forces. It is expected that the remaining 54 SS-25s in Belarus will be transferred to Russia in the next year or two. The SS-25, which is assembled at Votkinsk in Russia, is the only CIS strategic weapon system still under production. US intelligence estimates that Russia will flight-test and deploy a follow-on to the SS-25 during the next decade.

j Although there is little information available on the status of Yankee and Delta I Class SSBNs, it is assumed here that they are in the process of being withdrawn from operational service because of budgetary pressures and in anticipation of START I Treaty implementation. The 64 SS-N-8s are deployed on 4 Delta II Class SSBNs; the 224 S-N-18s are deployed on 14 Delta IIIs; the 120 SS-N-20s are deployed on 6 Typhoons; and the 112 SS-N-23s are deployed on 7 Delta IVs. All of these SSBNs are based on the Kola Peninsula except for 9 Delta IIIs which are based at Petropavlosk on the Kamchatka Peninsula. No additional SSBN production is expected before the year 2000.

k US intelligence estimates that Russia will flight-test and deploy a follow-on to the SS-N-20 during this decade.

Sources: START I Treaty Memorandum of Understanding, 1 Sep. 1990; US Department of Defense, *Military Forces in Transition*, Washington, DC, Sep. 1991; Congressional testimony by Dr Lawrence Gershwin, National Intelligence Officer for Strategic Programs, US Central Intelligence Agency (CIA); Natural Resources Defense Council (NRDC); 'Nuclear notebook', *Bulletin of the Atomic Scientists*, Mar./Apr. 1994, p. 63; International Institute for Strategic Studies (IISS), *The Military Balance 1993–1994* (Brassey's: London, 1993), pp. 96, 99; Starr, B., *Jane's Defence Weekly*, 27 Mar. 1993, p. 7; author's estimates.

Command and control

The continued political and economic turmoil in Russia intensified international concerns in 1993 about: (*a*) the possible breakdown of central control over strategic nuclear weapons; (*b*) the potential for the 'leakage' of warheads or fissile material to terrorists or potential proliferators outside Russia; and (*c*) the prospect for a 'brain drain' in which former nuclear weapon scientists sell their expertise to the highest bidder.

CIA Director James Woolsey told the US Congress on 28 July 1993: 'The Russians continue to maintain strong centralized control of their nuclear forces, and we think that under current circumstances, there is little prospect of a failure of control. But we are concerned about the future'.[67] DIA Director Lt-General James Clapper added on 25 January 1994 that 'all strategic nuclear weapons [in the former Soviet Union] remain under control of President Yeltsin and the [Russian] General Staff'.[68] Regarding 'leakage', Woolsey said

---

[67] *US Security Policy Toward Rogue Regimes,* Hearing before the Foreign Affairs Committee, Subcommittee on International Security, International Organizations and Human Rights, US House of Representatives, 103rd Congress (US Government Printing Office: Washington, DC, 1994), p. 83.

[68] Clapper (note 3), p. 4.

on 25 January 1994 that 'to date, reports of illegal transfers of [nuclear] weapons do not appear credible. As for weapons-grade material, we are not aware of any illegal transfers in quantities sufficient to produce a nuclear weapon'.[69] Viktor Mikhailov, head of the Russian Federation's Ministry of Atomic Energy (MINATOM), told *NUKEM Market Report* on 9 September 1993: 'As far as Russia is concerned, atomic weapons have never disappeared and controls are strong . . . As far as nuclear materials are concerned, three cases of theft were reported to our Ministry. Two cases involved low enriched uranium and one involved high enriched uranium that was stolen from our fuel fabrication facilities'.[70] Mikhailov did not say how much highly enriched uranium (HEU) was stolen or whether it was ever recovered.

On the 'brain drain' issue, Woolsey said in his July 1993 testimony that 'delays in pay, deteriorating working conditions, and uncertain futures are apparently spurring Russian specialists to seek emigration despite official restrictions on such travel'.[71] However, he tempered that statement by noting that most of the scientists emigrating from the former Soviet Union had not been involved in the actual design of weapons of mass destruction and that most of them were emigrating to the West. He added that China has been 'aggressively recruiting' weapon scientists from the CIS and that India, Iraq, North Korea and Pakistan have all expressed interest in hiring them as well.[72] Amplifying this in his January 1994 testimony, Woolsey said that the 'combination of declining morale in the military, increased organized crime, and efforts by states like Iran seeking to purchase nuclear material or expertise will make these matters a major concern . . . through this decade and beyond'.[73]

Belarus

The number of SS-25 ICBMs in Belarus—missile systems which have been and remain under Russian control—peaked at 81 in 1991.[74] By September 1993 the Strategic Rocket Forces had begun withdrawing SS-25 ICBMs from Belarussian territory to Russia,[75] where they are expected to be incorporated

---

[69] James Woolsey, Director, US Central Intelligence, Written statement submitted to the Senate Select Intelligence Committee, 25 Jan. 1994, p. 12; see also *US Security Policy Toward Rogue Regimes* (note 67), p. 79; Aspin (note 5), p. 60; Office of Technology Assessment, *Technologies Underlying Weapons of Mass Destruction* (US Government Printing Office: Washington, DC, Dec. 1993), pp. 4, 128.

[70] Martin, E., 'A conversation with Viktor Mikhailov', *NUKEM Market Report*, Oct. 1993.

[71] *US Security Policy Toward Rogue Regimes* (note 67), p. 79. In Jan. 1992, then CIA Director Robert Gates said that 'of about 1 million people involved in the Soviet nuclear weapons program overall, we [US intelligence] calculate only about 1,000 or 2,000 of those really have the critical skills necessary to design nuclear weapons'; *Threat Assessment . . .* (note 58), p. 37.

[72] *US Security Policy Toward Rogue Regimes* (note 67), p. 33.

[73] Woolsey (note 69), p. 12.

[74] 'Belarus approves schedule for withdrawal of nuclear missiles', INTERFAX, 26 Oct. 1992, in FBIS-SOV-92-208, 27 Oct. 1992, p. 3; Robert Gates, Director, US Central Intelligence, Statement before the House Foreign Affairs Committee, 25 Feb. 1992, p. 4 (Gates said that the USSR was still deploying SS-25s in Belarus as late as Dec. 1991).

[75] Ashton Carter, Assistant Secretary of Defense for Nuclear Security and Counterproliferation, Testimony before the House Foreign Affairs Committee, 21 Sep. 1993, p. 3.

into Russia's ICBM forces rather than dismantled.[76] (In November 1992 it was reported that some or all of these SS-25 missiles will be based at Vypolozovo in Russia, where SS-17 ICBMs are currently based.[77]) In December 1993 the Belarussian Defence Ministry announced that three regiments (27 missiles) had been withdrawn.[78] Reportedly, all the remaining 54 SS-25s will be transferred to Russia by 1995.[79]

Kazakhstan

All of the approximately 1400 warheads based in Kazakhstan remain under Russian control. By the end of 1993, the SRF had removed a dozen of the 104 SS-18 ICBMs located in Kazakhstan from their silos and transferred them to Russia.[80] It was reported in late February 1994 that the last 4 of the 40 Bear-H bombers based at Semipalatinsk had been withdrawn to Russia.[81]

Kazakhstan appears to be firmly committed to eliminating all of the nuclear weapons on its territory. It ratified the START I Treaty on 2 July 1992[82] and deposited the instruments of accession to the 1968 Non-Proliferation Treaty (NPT) with the United States on 14 February 1993.[83]

Ukraine

In the START I Treaty Memorandum of Understanding, the USSR declared that it had 176 ICBMs based in Ukraine—46 10-warhead SS-24s and 130 SS-19s. The liquid-fuel SS-19s, which were first deployed in the 1970s, are now nearing the end of their service lifetime and are considered to be a potential safety hazard. Since July 1993, Ukraine has removed at least two regiments of SS-19s (20 missiles with 120 warheads) from their silos at Pervo-

[76] *Current Developments in the Former Soviet Union* (note 35), p. 20.

[77] 'Russian Deputy Defense Minister on nuclear missile forces', *Izvestia*, 13 Nov. 1992, p. 1, in FBIS-SOV-92-220, 13 Nov. 1992, p. 2; 'Defense official assesses missile forces future', *Krasnaya Zvezda*, 14 Nov. 1992, p. 1, in FBIS-SOV-92-221, 16 Nov. 1992, pp. 2–3; 'Deputy Defense Minister views future missile forces', *Nezavisimaya Gazeta*, 19 Nov. 1992, pp. 1–2, in FBIS-SOV-92-235, 7 Dec. 1992, p. 11.

[78] Markus, U., 'Strategic missiles withdrawn from Belarus', Radio Free Europe/Radio Liberty Research Institute, *Military Notes*, no. 245 (23 Dec. 1993).

[79] Markus, U., 'Belarussian disarmament', Radio Free Europe/Radio Liberty (hereafter RFE/RL), *RFE/RL Daily Report*, no. 54 (18 Mar. 1994).

[80] Morrison, D. C., 'Uke nukes', *National Journal*, 18 Dec. 1993, p. 3026; Hiatt, F., 'US reward sought for ceding A-arms', *Washington Post*, 14 Feb. 1994, p. A17; Sieff, M., 'US arms-control official notes progress with former foes', *Washington Times*, 15 Oct. 1993, p. A15; Ashton Carter, Assistant Secretary of Defense for Nuclear Security and Counterproliferation, Written statement submitted to the House Appropriations Committee, Subcommittee on Defense, 9 Mar. 1994, p. 5.

[81] Foye, S., 'All strategic bombers out of Kazakhstan', *RFE/RL Military Notes*, no. 37 (23 Feb. 1994); 'Strategic bombers leave Kazakhstan', *Washington Times*, 1 Mar. 1994, p. A13; Radio Moscow, 'Last strategic bombers leave Kazakhstan', 1 Mar. 1994, in FBIS-SOV-94-041, 2 Mar. 1994, p. 49.

[82] 'Lisbon Protocol: START I and the Nuclear Non-Proliferation Treaty', Arms Control and Disarmament Agency (ACDA), Office of Public Information, Fact Sheet, 11 Jan. 1994, p. 1.

[83] President Bill Clinton, Press Conference, 14 Feb. 1994, Federal News Service Transcript, p. 2; see also Ifill, G., 'US will triple its foreign aid to Kazakhstan', *New York Times*, 15 Feb. 1994, p. A3. (The Kazakh Parliament voted to accede to the NPT on 13 Dec. 1993. See Smith, R. J., 'Kazakhstan ratifies nuclear control pact, will get US aid', *Washington Post*, 14 Dec. 1993, p. A20; Berke, R. L., 'Prodded by Gore, Kazakhstan signs arms accord', *New York Times*, 14 Dec. 1993, p. A15.)

maysk and appears to be committed to retiring all of the remaining SS-19s.[84] In November 1993 Ukrainian President Leonid Kravchuk announced that Ukraine would deactivate at least 50 missiles, including some SS-24s, by March 1994.[85]

On 20 December 1993, Ukrainian Deputy Prime Minister Valery Shmarov announced that Ukraine had deactivated 17 of the more modern solid-fuel SS-24 ICBMs by removing the warheads from the missiles[86] and would deactivate a total of 20 SS-24s by the end of 1993.[87] On 14 January 1994, the presidents of Russia, Ukraine and the USA signed a Trilateral Statement in Moscow, committing Ukraine to deactivate all 46 SS-24s within 10 months (i.e., by 14 November 1994). In addition, the Statement committed Ukraine to withdraw a combined total of at least 200 SS-19 and SS-24 warheads to Russia within 10 months. Finally, all warheads on Ukrainian territory would be transferred to Russia 'during the seven-year period as provided by the START I treaty',[88] but press reports said that Kravchuk agreed in a confidential letter to Yeltsin that all the warheads would be withdrawn within three years.[89] In the first week of March 1994, Ukraine transported a total of 60 SS-19 and SS-24 warheads to Russia by railway.[90]

The CIA has told Congress that it estimates that there are 42 strategic bombers in Ukraine.[91] These apparently include 19 Blackjacks at Priluki, 21 Bear-Hs at Uzin and two older Bear aircraft in storage at Uzin.[92] However, these bombers are not considered to be fully operational.[93] CIA analyst Gershwin, for example, told the US Congress in February 1993 that the Blackjack bombers at Priluki do not fly. He added, 'we don't think that there is much chance at all today that Ukraine could, in fact, use the bombers that it has with nuclear warheads on board'.[94] A December 1993 *New York Times*

---

[84] See, for example, Mann, P., 'Ukrainian SS-24s slated for prompt deactivation', *Aviation Week & Space Technology*, 24 Jan. 1994, p. 39.

[85] Reuter, Paris, 'Kravchuk proposes defusing Ukraine nuclear arsenal', 29 Nov. 1993; Smith, R. J., 'Ukraine to deactivate 50 missiles by spring', *Washington Post*, 10 Dec. 1993, p. A52; Morrison (note 80), p. 3026.

[86] The SS-24 missiles, whose warheads were removed in late 1993, were apparently left in their silos.

[87] Gordon, M., 'Kiev acts quickly on pledge to remove warheads', *New York Times*, 21 Dec. 1993, p. A14.

[88] The text of the 14 Jan. 1994 Trilateral Statement and its annex is printed in *Arms Control Today*, vol. 24, no. 1 (Jan./Feb. 1994), pp. 21–22; see also appendix 16A in this volume.

[89] Smith, R. J., 'US, Ukraine, Russia near deal on arms', *Washington Post*, 9 Jan. 1994, p. A33; Smith, R. J. and Belliveau, J., 'Dismantling Ukraine's warheads', *Washington Post*, 15 Jan. 1994, p. A15. For details on the Trilateral Statement, see chapter 16 in this volume.

[90] Carter (note 80), p. 5.

[91] *Proliferation Threats of the 1990s* (note 42), p. 144; *Current Developments in the Former Soviet Union* (note 35), p. 20.

[92] An Apr. 1993 'trip report' from a congressional delegation led by Representatives Gephardt and Michel said that there were 19 Blackjacks and 21 Bear-Hs in Ukraine. The START I Memorandum of Understanding also lists a Bear-A and a Bear-B in storage at Uzin. Another breakdown that is sometimes given for the 42 bombers in Ukraine is: 20 Blackjacks and 22 Bear-Hs; see, for example, International Institute for Strategic Studies, *The Military Balance 1993–1994* (note 2), p. 99; and Starr, B., *Jane's Defence Weekly*, 27 Mar. 1993, p. 7.

[93] *Proliferation Threats of the 1990s* (note 42), p. 144.

[94] *Proliferation Threats of the 1990s* (note 42), p. 38.

account reported that the Bear-Hs at Uzin 'have only rarely been able to leave the ground'.[95]

Command and control

Although a number of press reports have suggested that Ukraine could (and may be trying to) gain operational control over the nuclear weapons on its territory, the obstacles to gaining control over and maintaining these forces have generally been understated.[96] With respect to ICBMs, it is widely believed that missile crew officers who are loyal to Russia still operate the launch control centres.[97] Personnel loyal to Ukraine would therefore probably have to gain access to these facilities by force. They would then have to break or circumvent the codes for the permissive action links (PALs), electronic locks intended to prevent unauthorized launch. According to Bruce Blair, a senior fellow at the Brookings Institution:

any attempt to pick the lock would be automatically reported to Moscow (the General Staff war room as well as the Strategic Rocket Force headquarters). The General Staff can then send special commands that isolate the deviant launch centres and transfer launch control to other loyal command posts. If the lock is somehow picked, the General Staff can transmit a command . . . that negates the local action and restores the blocking function. The General Staff has the technical ability to instruct all the unmanned missiles to disregard any commands from any command post in Ukraine.[98]

In addition, a Ukrainian move to break or circumvent the codes could risk precipitating a Russian military attack against Ukraine. Even if Ukraine could gain access and defeat the PALs, it would still have to re-target the ICBMs from the USA to Russia. This would be difficult for several reasons. First, without satellite imagery, Ukraine probably lacks the precise geographical data necessary to re-target the systems. Second, the guidance systems for the more modern solid-fuel SS-24s are built in Russia.[99]

Even if Ukraine could obtain the geographical data and build its own guidance system, there would be other hurdles to clear. Since the SS-24 is currently designed to have intercontinental range (5500 km or more) and has a minimum range of 3000 km, it would have to be completely redesigned to strike any targets west of the Ural mountains, such as Moscow or St Petersburg.[100] The liquid-fuel SS-19s, for their part, are seen as nearly obsolete and

---

[95] Jehl, D., 'Ukraine: a nuclear power, but untested loyalties', *New York Times*, 2 Dec. 1993, p. A16.
[96] See, for example, Coll, S. and Smith, J., 'In fight over warheads, Kiev seeks upper hand', *International Herald Tribune*, 4 June 1993, pp. 1, 4.
[97] Bruce Blair, Brookings Institution, Written statement submitted to the Senate Foreign Relations Committee subcommittee on Europe, 24 June 1993, p. 3; Blair (note 50), p. 87.
[98] Blair (note 97), p. 5; see also Morrison (note 80), p. 3026.
[99] Blair (note 97), p. 4, 6.
[100] Blair (note 97), p. 6; Blair (note 50), p. 89; Kincade, W. H., 'Nuclear weapons in Ukraine: hollow threat, wasting asset', *Arms Control Today*, July/Aug. 1993, p. 15.

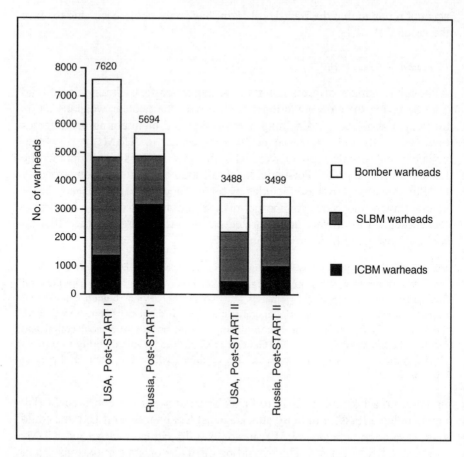

Figure 8.1. Projected US and Russian strategic nuclear forces after implementation of the START I and START II treaties

Note: ICBM and SLBM warhead attributions are based on the START I Treaty Memorandum of Understanding. Bomber loadings are based on the START II Memorandum of Understanding. The numbers of bombers are different from those in table 8.1 because these figures include only START-accountable bombers.

Post-START I strategic nuclear forces, projected

US delivery vehicles

   ICBMs: 300 Minuteman IIIs downloaded to one warhead each; 200 Minuteman IIIs with three warheads each; 50 Peacekeepers (MX).

   SLBMs: 192 Trident Is (C-4); 240 Trident IIs (D-5).

   Bombers: 47 B-52Hs; 94 B-1Bs; 20 B-2s. (Under the terms of START I, all dual-capable heavy bombers, including the B-1B, will be counted as carrying strategic nuclear weapons unless they are physically altered so as to be unable to do so.)

Russian delivery vehicles

   ICBMs: 154 SS-18s; 105 SS-19s; 10 SS-24s (silo-based); 33 SS-24s (rail-mobile); 500 SS-25s (road-mobile); 50 SS-25s, mod. 2 (road-mobile); 50 SS-25s, mod. 2 (silo-based).

   SLBMs: 176 SS-N-18s; 120 SS-N-20s downloaded to six warheads each; 112 SS-N-23s.

Bombers: 36 Tu-95 Bear-Hs (equipped to carry 16 nuclear cruise missiles each); 27 Tu-95 Bear-Hs (equipped to carry six nuclear cruise missiles each); 5 Tu-160 Blackjacks.

Post-START II strategic nuclear forces, projected*

US delivery vehicles

ICBMs: 500 Minuteman IIIs downloaded to one warhead each.
SLBMs: 192 Trident Is (C-4) downloaded to four warheads each; 240 Trident IIs (D-5) downloaded to four warheads each.
Bombers: 47 B-52-Hs (equipped to carry 20 ALCMs/ACMs each); 20 B-2s.

Russian delivery vehicles

ICBMs: 500 SS-25s (road-mobile); 100 SS-25s, mod. 2 (road-mobile); 300 SS-25s, mod. 2 (silo-based, including 90 based in converted SS-18 silos); 105 SS-19s downloaded to one warhead each.
SLBMs: 176 SS-N-18s; 120 SS-N-20s downloaded to six warheads each; 112 SS-N-23s.
Bomber aircraft: 36 Tu-95 Bear-Hs (equipped to carry 16 nuclear cruise missiles each); 27 Tu-95 Bear-Hs (equipped to carry six nuclear cruise missiles each); 5 Tu-160 Blackjacks.

*Assumptions for Russian strategic forces under START I and START II.

ICBMs: It is assumed that Russia will give its Strategic Rocket Forces enough priority to find sufficient economic resources eventually to build and deploy 400 SS-25s, mod. 2 (100 road-mobile and 300 silo-based). Alternatively, Russia could deploy a modified version of its SS-N-20 follow-on SLBM (downloaded to one warhead each) in existing ICBM silos or simply deploy a significantly smaller number of ICBMs than estimated in this figure.

SLBMs: Although Russia could retain 192 SS-N-18 SLBMs on 12 Delta III ballistic missile submarines under the provisions of both START I and START II, Admiral Felix Gromov, Commander-in-Chief of the Russian Navy, indicated in 1993 that Russia now plans to retain 176 SS-N-18 SLBMs on 11 Delta III submarines.

Bombers: It is assumed that all 40 Tu-95 Bear-H bombers based in Kazakhstan have been withdrawn to Russia, but that Ukraine will not return to Russia any of the approximately 19 Tu-160 Blackjack or 21 Tu-95 Bear-H bombers currently based on its territory.

It is also assumed that Russia will maintain 5 Tu-160 Blackjack bombers and one Blackjack test aircraft.

Sources: For US forces: START I Treaty Memorandum of Understanding, Sep. 1990; Department of Defense Fact Sheet, 'US strategic nuclear forces', June 1992; Arms Control and Disarmament (ACDA) Fact Sheet, 'The Joint Understanding on the Elimination of MIRVed ICBMs and Further Reduction in Strategic Offensive Arms', 2 July 1992, p. 2; Senate Foreign Relations Committee, *Report on the START Treaty,* Executive Report 102-53, pp. 18–19; Dick Cheney, *Report of the Secretary of Defense to the President and the Congress,* Feb. 1992, p. 60; Dick Cheney, *Report of the Secretary of Defense to the President and the Congress,* Jan. 1993, p. 68; Les Aspin, *Report of the Secretary of Defense to the President and the Congress,* Jan. 1994, p. 147; US Air Force Public Affairs; US Navy Public Affairs; author's estimates.

For Russian forces: Arbatov, A. (ed.), *Implications of the START II Treaty for US–Russian Relations* (Henry L. Stimson Center: Washington, DC, 1993), p. 6; Statement of Ted Warner, Senior Defense Analyst, RAND Corporation, before the Senate Foreign Relations Committee, 3 Mar. 1992, as cited in *The START Treaty,* Senate Hearing 102-607, Part 1 (US Government Printing Office: Washington, DC, 1992), pp. 228–29; Department of Defense, *Military Forces in Transition,* Sep. 1991; START I Treaty Memorandum of Understanding, Sep. 1990; Gromov, F., 'Reforming the Russian Navy', *Naval Forces,* vol. 14, no. 4 (1993), p. 10; author's estimates.

potentially a safety hazard. In addition to all of the above, Ukraine has no flight-test facility to test these ICBMs.[101]

It is not entirely clear who controls the nuclear warheads associated with the Bear-H and Blackjack aircraft located on Ukrainian territory,[102] and developing a nuclear force with aircraft-delivered weapons might actually be a more feasible option for Ukraine than an ICBM force. Nevertheless, it would not be easy for Ukraine to field an operational nuclear bomber force. For example, Blair maintains that, while Ukrainian conscripts patrol the perimeter of the two bomber bases where nuclear weapons are stored, the officers that have actual custodianship of the storage areas probably report to the Russian General Staff.[103] In any case, it has been widely reported that Russian troops removed the cassette tapes with the guidance software from the AS-15 cruise missiles stored in Ukraine.[104] The PALs on the cruise missile warheads, albeit relatively primitive, are believed to remain intact.[105] In addition, as noted above, the bomber force, which suffers from a shortage of fuel, spare parts and air crew training, is less than fully operational.

In addition to these difficulties, Ukraine lacks a nuclear weapon infrastructure[106] and appears to lack the money to build one. For example, Ukraine does not have any facilities to produce tritium. Since tritium decays rapidly, the yield of the nuclear warheads on Ukrainian territory would fall (and may have already fallen) precipitously without tritium replenishment from Russia. Ukraine also lacks uranium enrichment, plutonium reprocessing, and missile and warhead test facilities. Finally, Ukraine's nuclear forces, concentrated at four bases and lacking an early-warning network, would be extremely vulnerable to a pre-emptive Russian attack.[107]

IV. British nuclear weapon programmes

SSBNs

The UK's three remaining Polaris submarines are scheduled to be replaced by four new Trident submarines by the turn of the century. The first Trident

---

[101] See the START I Treaty Memorandum of Understanding in 'Treaty between the United States of America and the Union of Soviet Socialist Republics on the Reduction and Limitation of Strategic Offensive Arms', *Dispatch* (US Department of State, Bureau of Public Affairs), vol. 2, supplement no. 5 (Oct. 1991), pp. 120–45.

[102] *Proliferation Threats of the 1990s* (note 42), p. 38.

[103] Blair, B., private conversation with the author, Feb. 1994; see also Morrison (note 80), p. 3026.

[104] Blair (note 97), p. 5; Kincade (note 100), p. 15.

[105] Blair (note 97), p. 6.

[106] For a detailed discussion of the infrastructure that Ukraine lacks to sustain a credible nuclear force, see Kincade (note 100), pp. 13–18; Arbatov, A. (ed.), *Implications of the START II Treaty for US–Russian Relations,* Report no. 9 (Henry L. Stimson Center: Washington, DC, 1993), pp. 30–32. See also 'Radetsky addresses Supreme Council on START', Radio Ukraine, 3 Feb. 1994, in FBIS-SOV-94-025, 7 Feb. 1994, p. 41.

[107] For a comprehensive discussion of the dangers attending the creation of an independent Ukrainian nuclear force, see Miller, S. E., 'The case against a Ukrainian nuclear deterrent', *Foreign Affairs,* vol. 72, no. 3 (summer 1993), pp. 67–80.

submarine, the *HMS Vanguard*, completed sea trials in January 1993.[108] It was accepted into Royal Navy service on 14 September 1993,[109] and according to British Defence Minister Malcolm Rifkind 'remains on course for entering into operational service on schedule around the end of 1994 or the beginning of 1995'.[110] The second Trident submarine, the *HMS Victorious*, was rolled out of the Devonshire Dock Hall at Barrow-in-Furness on 29 September 1993.[111] Rifkind said in October 1993 that construction on the other two submarines, the *HMS Vigilant* and the *HMS Venerable*, 'is proceeding well'.[112] The keel of the *Venerable* was laid down in February 1993.[113]

As late as October 1993, British officials had said that each Trident submarine would carry no more than 128 warheads. (Since British Trident submarines carry 16 missiles each, a Trident missile could carry an average of up to 8 warheads under this plan.) However, in a significant policy change, Rifkind announced in November that each Trident submarine will carry 'no more than 96 warheads, and may carry significantly fewer'[114]—an average of no more than 6 warheads per missile. He added that, based on current British plans, 'the total explosive power carried on each Trident submarine will not be much changed from [that of the] Polaris'. Therefore, he argued, the decision to reduce the maximum number of warheads per submarine 'should lay to rest comments and speculation about Trident representing a major growth in the size of the United Kingdom's nuclear armoury'.[115]

Rifkind's statement is misleading because the deployment of the Trident II will constitute a significant increase in capability over the Polaris missile, both in quantitative and qualitative terms. The Polaris missiles carried multiple re-entry vehicles (MRVs) while the Trident II missiles will carry multiple independently targetable re-entry vehicles (MIRVs). Therefore, even under the new plan, a Trident submarine could, at least theoretically, launch missiles against up to as many as six times more targets than a Polaris submarine. Furthermore, the yield of the warheads on the Trident II missile will be more than twice the yield of the warheads on the current SLBM. Since 1982, under the Chevaline programme, the UK has armed its Polaris missiles with two A-3TK warheads, each with an estimated yield of 40 kt, plus devices to assist warhead penetration of the Russian anti-ballistic missile (ABM) system. However, the Trident II is expected to carry warheads with yields of 100 kt.[116]

---

[108] *Statement on the Defence Estimates 1993* (Her Majesty's Stationery Office: London, July 1993), p. 63.
[109] Parliamentary Debates, House of Commons, *Official Report* (Her Majesty's Stationery Office: London, 1993), 18 Oct. 1993, column 33.
[110] Malcolm Rifkind, UK Defence Minister, Address before the Centre for Defence Studies, London, 16 Nov. 1993.
[111] *Official Report* (note 109), column 33.
[112] *Official Report* (note 109), column 33.
[113] IISS, *The Military Balance 1993–1994* (note 2), p. 32.
[114] Rifkind (note 110); Miller, C., 'Britain to cut nuclear firepower 25 percent', *Defense News*, 22–28 Nov. 1993, p. 32.
[115] Rifkind (note 110).
[116] Howard, S. and Ionno, S., 'The U.K. Trident programme: secrecy and dependence in the 1990s', BASIC Report 93-5 (British American Security Information Council (BASIC): London, Sep. 1993), p. 5; 'Nuclear notebook', *Bulletin of the American Scientists,* Sep. 1993, p. 57; Mosher (note 16), p. 4.

Table 8.3. British nuclear forces, January 1994[a]

Type	Designation	No. deployed	Date deployed	Range (km)[b]	Warheads x yield	Warheads in stockpile
Aircraft[c]						
GR.1	Tornado	72	1982	1 300	1–2 x 200–400 kt ⎫	100[e]
S2B	Buccaneer	27	1971	1 700	1 x 200–400 kt[d] ⎭	
SLBMs						
A3-TK	Polaris	48	1982[f]	4 700	2 x 40 kt	100[g]

[a] The US nuclear weapons for certified British systems have been removed from Europe and returned to the USA, specifically for the 11 Nimrod ASW aircraft based at RAF St Magwan, Cornwall, UK, the 1 Army regiment with 12 Lance launchers and the 4 Army artillery regiments with 120 M109 howitzers in Germany. Squadron No. 42, the Nimrod maritime patrol squadron, disbanded in Oct. 1992, but St Magwan will remain a forward base for Nimrods and will have other roles. The 50 Missile Regiment (Lance) and the 56 Special Weapons Battery Royal Artillery were disbanded in 1993.

[b] Range for aircraft indicates combat radius, without in-flight refuelling.

[c] The Royal Air Force will eventually operate 8 squadrons of dual-capable strike/attack Tornados. The 3 squadrons at Laarbruch, Germany (Nos 15, 16, 20) were disbanded between Sep. 1991 and May 1992. A fourth squadron there (No. 2) was equipped with the Tornado reconnaissance variant and went to RAF Marham to join a reconnaissance squadron already there (No. 13). The 2 squadrons previously at Marham (Nos 27 and 617) will redeploy to Lossiemouth, Scotland, in 1993–94, replacing Buccaneer squadrons Nos 12 and 208 in the maritime/strike role. The Tornado squadrons will be redesignated Nos 12 and 617. The 4 squadrons at RAF Bruggen, Germany (Nos 9, 14, 17, 31) will remain. All 8 squadrons, including the 2 reconnaissance squadrons, will be nuclear-capable, down from 11.

[d] The US Defense Intelligence Agency has confirmed that the RAF Tornados 'use two types of nuclear weapons, however exact types are unknown'. The DIA further concludes that each RAF Tornado is capable of carrying 2 nuclear bombs, 1 on each of the 2 outboard fuselage stations.

[e] The total stockpile of WE-177 tactical nuclear gravity bombs was estimated to have been about 200, of which 175 were versions A and B. The C version of the WE-177 was assigned to selected Royal Navy (RN) Sea Harrier FRS.1 aircraft and ASW helicopters. The WE-177C existed in both a free-fall and depth-bomb modification. There were an estimated 25 WE-177Cs, each with a yield of approximately 10 kt. Following the Bush–Gorbachev initiatives of 27 Sep. and 5 Oct. 1991, British Secretary of State for Defence Tom King said that 'we will no longer routinely carry nuclear weapons on our ships'. On 15 June 1992 the Defence Minister announced that all naval tactical nuclear weapons had been removed from surface ships and aircraft, that the nuclear mission would be eliminated and that the 'weapons previously earmarked for this role will be destroyed'. The 1992 White Paper stated that 'As part of the cut in NATO's stockpile we will also reduce the number of British free-fall nuclear bombs by more than half'. A number of British nuclear bombs were returned to the UK. In table 8.4, a total inventory of strike variants of approximately 100 is assumed, including those for training and for spares. The 1993 White Paper stated that the WE-177 'is currently expected to remain in service until well into the next century'.

[f] The 2-warhead Polaris A3-TK (Chevaline) was first deployed in 1982 and has now completely replaced the original 3-warhead Polaris A-3 missile, first deployed in 1968.

[g] It is now thought that the UK produced only enough warheads for 3 full boatloads of missiles, or 48 missiles, with a total of 96 warheads. In Mar. 1987 French President Mitterrand stated that Britain had '90 to 100 [strategic] warheads'.

Source: Norris, R. S., Burrows, A. S. and Fieldhouse, R. W., *Nuclear Weapons Databook Vol. V: British, French and Chinese Nuclear Weapons* (Westview: Boulder, Colo., 1994), p. 9; 'Nuclear notebook', *Bulletin of the Atomic Scientists*, Sep. 1993, p. 57.

Therefore, in addition to the ability to target warheads independently and the dramatic improvements in missile range and accuracy, Trident II missiles will also carry far more explosive power than the current British Polaris force, contrary to Rifkind's contention. The decision to reduce the number of warheads on Trident submarines was based on several factors. First, with the evaporation of the Soviet threat, fewer warheads are required. Second, with US and Russian nuclear cutbacks, there is significant international and domestic political pressure on the UK to scale down its planned deployment. Third, Britain's problems with its nuclear warhead production complex may preclude it from producing a sufficient amount of fissile material for more Trident warheads. Finally, there are no signs that Russia is planning to upgrade its ABM system to an extent that would justify more British Trident warheads.

SLBMs

As of 1993, the UK had purchased 44 Trident II missiles from the USA.[117] Reportedly, the Royal Navy intends to purchase more than two dozen additional missiles, making a total of about 70.[118] The UK has already begun production of warheads for these missiles.[119]

Bombers

The Royal Air Force has reduced the number of squadrons of dual-capable Tornado strike/attack aircraft from 11 to 8: four Tornado squadrons will remain at their base in Bruggen, Germany; two more squadrons are now based at Marham, UK, in a reconnaissance role; and two more squadrons will be used in a maritime anti-ship role at Lossiemouth, Scotland.[120] The remaining 27 Buccaneers, an aircraft that was initially deployed in 1971, will be retired in 1994.[121] In a major policy shift, the UK announced in October 1993 that it had decided to cancel the nuclear tactical air-to-surface missile (TASM) programme.[122] Since the WE-177 gravity bomb, which the TASM was intended to replace, is scheduled for retirement sometime after 'the first few years of the next century',[123] the decision to scrap the TASM will, in effect, take the

---

[117] Department of Defense Appropriations (note 13), Part 4, p. 192.
[118] Miller (note 114), p. 32; 'Britain's Trident cuts won't affect Lockheed's D-5 totals, Rifkind says', *Aerospace Daily*, 18 Nov. 1993, p. 289
[119] 'Nuclear notebook', *Bulletin of the Atomic Scientists*, Sep. 1993, p. 57.
[120] 'Nuclear notebook', *Bulletin of the Atomic Scientists*, Sep. 1993, p. 57.
[121] Rifkind (note 110).
[122] *Official Report* (note 109), column 34.
[123] *Official Report* (note 109), column 35.

Royal Air Force out of the nuclear weapon business in the next decade, leaving the Trident forces as the UK's sole nuclear deterrent.

The British Government offered several reasons to explain its decision to cancel the TASM programme. The TASM, which entered development in the mid- to late 1980s, was intended to counter 'increasingly effective' Warsaw Pact air defence systems. With the dissolution of the USSR and the Warsaw Pact, the British Ministry of Defence, which is now under pressure to cut its budget, concluded that the requirement for a nuclear stand-off weapon was not a sufficiently high priority to justify the expense of procuring a new nuclear delivery system.[124] Estimates for the savings resulting from termination of the TASM programme range from £750 million to £2 billion ($1–3 billion).[125] In addition, the Defence Ministry said that its Trident submarines will have the flexibility to provide a sub-strategic deterrent—currently provided by Tornado aircraft—'at little additional cost'.[126] According to press reports, some Trident missiles would be armed with a single warhead for this 'sub-strategic' deterrent role.[127] In a 16 November 1993 speech to the Centre for Defence Studies in London, Rifkind made his case for a 'sub-strategic deterrent' as follows:

. . . the ability to undertake a massive strike with strategic systems is not enough to ensure deterrence. An aggressor might, in certain circumstances, gamble on a lack of will ultimately to resort to such dire action. It is therefore important for the credibility of our deterrent that the United Kingdom also possesses the capability to undertake a more limited nuclear strike in order to induce a political decision to halt aggression by delivering an unmistakable message of our willingness to defend our vital interests to the utmost.[128]

In addition to the above reasons, US President Clinton's 3 July 1993 decision to extend the moratorium on nuclear testing at the Nevada Test Site—where the UK conducts its tests—combined with the limits imposed on British testing by a US law enacted in October 1992,[129] may have precluded Britain from developing a new warhead for the TASM.

---

[124] *Official Report* (note 109), column 34; Rifkind (note 110).

[125] 'Cost doubts linger as tactical Trident terminates TASM', *Jane's Defence Weekly*, 30 Oct. 1993, p. 21; Miller, C. and Witt, M. J., 'Britain's budget war intensifies', *Defense News*, 25–31 Oct. 1993, p. 16.

[126] *Official Report* (note 109), column 34; Rifkind's address (note 110).

[127] Miller and Witt (note 125); Cook, N., '"Tactical" Trident set to kill RAF's TASM', *Jane's Defence Weekly*, 3 July 1993, p. 5; Brown C., 'Scaled-down Trident to replace new missile', *The Independent*, 15 Apr. 1993, p. 8.

[128] Rifkind (note 110).

[129] The text of the 'Hatfield Amendment', which limits the UK to one test in Nevada per fiscal year through 1996, is printed in the *Congressional Record*, 24 Sep. 1992, p. H9424. See appendix 8A for the yield, date and location of the nuclear explosion conducted in 1993; see also chapter 16 in this volume.

V. French nuclear weapon programmes

Ssbns

In May 1992 France announced that it would reduce the number of new SSBNs it plans to build from six to four. The first of these submarines, *Le Triomphant*, was rolled out of the construction facility in Cherbourg on 13 July 1993. It was scheduled to begin sea trials by the end of 1993 and to go on its first operational patrol in March 1996. The second Triomphant Class submarine, *Le Téméraire*, is under construction; the third, *Le Vigilant*, was authorized by the French Defence Minister in May 1993 and is scheduled to enter into service in 2001.[130] The fourth and final Triomphant Class submarine is expected to enter service in the year 2005.[131]

Slbms

Le Foudroyant, the last of the Inflexible Class submarines to be equipped with the six-warhead M-4 SLBM, returned to service in February 1993.[132] Previously, *Le Foudroyant* had carried the single-warhead M20 SLBM. Now all five of France's operational submarines are armed with the MIRVed M-4 SLBM.

The new Triomphant Class SSBNs will carry the M-45 SLBMs, missiles that are expected to carry six warheads each, until the M-5 missile, currently under development, becomes operational in about 2005. However, the introduction of the M-5 could be postponed because of budgetary constraints. US Naval Intelligence Director Sheafer told the US Congress in May 1993 that France may 'delay development of the new longer-ranged M-5 SLBM until well into the next century'.[133] Subsequently, some press accounts suggested that France may decide to scrap the M-5 SLBM programme altogether in order to save money.[134] The fate of the M-5 will have implications for France's land-based ballistic missile forces, since some French officials have advocated using a modified version of the M-5 to replace the 18 ageing land-based S-3 intermediate-range ballistic missiles (IRBMs). Among others,

---

[130] Jannsen Lok, J., 'New SSBN "walks out" amid cuts protest', *Jane's Defence Weekly*, 24 July 1993, p. 6; 'Nuclear notebook', *Bulletin of the Atomic Scientists*, Oct. 1993, p. 56; de Briganti, G., 'France plans sub buy amid cuts in budget', *Defense News*, 31 May–6 June, 1993, p. 6.

[131] 'Nuclear notebook' (note 130), p. 56.

[132] Lewis, J.A.C., 'M4 now carried on all French SSBNs', *Jane's Defence Weekly*, 27 Feb. 1993, p. 18. French President Mitterrand, however, has not yet ruled out the deployment of a land-based version of the M-5; see 'Mitterrand does not rule out M-5 missile deployment', *Le Monde*, 11 Jan. 1994, p. 3, in FBIS–West Europe (FBIS-WE), 31 Jan. 1994, p. 36. For a detailed discussion of French force structure and strategy issues, see Yost, D. S., 'Nuclear weapons issues in France', eds Hopkins and Hu (note 4), pp. 18–104.

[133] Sheafer (note 47), p. 23.

[134] See, for example, 'Key projects threatened as France weighs up its options', *Jane's Defence Weekly*, 24 July 1993, p. 19.

Table 8.4. French nuclear forces, January 1994

Type	No. deployed	Year first deployed	Range (km)^a	Warheads x yield	Warheads in stockpile
Land-based aircraft					
Mirage IVP	18	1986	1 570	1 x 300 kt ASMP	18
Mirage 2000N	45^b	1988	27 500	1 x 300 kt ASMP	42
Carrier-based aircraft					
Super Etendard	24	1978	650	1 x 300 kt ASMP	20^c
Land-based missiles					
S3D	18	1980	3 500	1 x 1 Mt	18
Hadès^d	(30)	1992	480	1 x 80 kt	30
SLBMs^e					
M-4A/B	64	1985	6 000	6 x 150 kt	384

^{a} Range for aircraft indicates combat radius, without in-flight refuelling, and does not include the 90- to 350-km range of the ASMP air-to-surface missile (where applicable).

^{b} Only 45 of the 75 Mirage 2000Ns have nuclear missions. On 11 Sep. 1991 President Mitterrand announced that as of 1 Sep. the AN-52 gravity bomb, which had been carried by Jaguar As and Super Etendards, had been withdrawn from service. Forty-two ASMPs are allocated to the 3 squadrons of Mirage 2000Ns.

^{c} The Super Etendard used to carry 1 AN 52 bomb. At full strength, the AN 52 equipped 3 squadrons of Super Etendards (24 of the 36 nuclear-capable aircraft): Flottilles 11F, 14F and 17F based at Landivisiau and Hyères, respectively. From mid-1989 these squadrons began receiving the ASMP missile. By mid-1990, all 24 aircraft (to be configured to carry the ASMP) were operational. Although originally about 50–55 Super Etendard aircraft were intended to carry the ASMP, because of budgetary constraints the number fell to 24.

^{d} France has decided to store 15 Hadès launchers and 30 Hadès missiles at Suippes.

^{e} Upon returning from its 58th and final patrol on 5 Feb. 1991, *Le Redoutable* was retired along with the last M-20 SLBMs. The 5 remaining SSBNs are all deployed with the M-4A/B missile. Although there are 80 launch tubes on the 5 SSBNs, only 4 sets of SLBMs were bought and thus the number of TN 70/71 warheads in the stockpile is assumed to be 384, probably with a small number of spares.

Source: Norris, R. S., Burrows, A. S. and Fieldhouse, R. W., *Nuclear Weapons Databook Vol. V: British, French and Chinese Nuclear Weapons* (Westview: Boulder, Co., 1994), p. 10; 'Nuclear notebook', *Bulletin of the Atomic Scientists*, Oct. 1993, p. 56.

General Vincent Lanata, the French Air Force Chief of Staff, has argued that France can only afford to maintain bombers along with its SSBNs.[135]

---

[135] Lewis, J. A. C., 'France "should keep airborne option"', *Jane's Defence Weekly*, 14 Aug. 1993, p. 6.

Bombers

France now plans to retire its 18 Mirage IV aircraft in 1996 or 1997.[136] The Mirage IV's 300-km range Air-Sol Moyenne Portée (ASMP) nuclear ASMs will eventually be deployed on the Rafale D, which is scheduled to become operational in 2005.[137] France currently maintains 45 Mirage 2000Ns in three squadrons with the ASMP as well as 30 more in two squadrons equipped with conventional weapons. In the interim period between the retirement of the Mirage IV and the introduction of the Rafale D, some of the ASMP missiles may be deployed on a fourth squadron of Mirage 2000 aircraft. A production decision on the 1300-km range Air-Sol-Longue Portée (ASLP) is not expected for several years.[138] The British October 1993 announcement terminating the TASM programme may damage prospects for procurement of the ASLP. France had hoped to defray its costs by developing the new nuclear-armed ASM jointly with the UK. A spokesman for the French company Aérospatiale said on 16 October: 'It is unlikely that the French government will continue with the project alone'.[139]

Reportedly, French officials were disappointed by the British decision, and some said that it may have dealt a severe blow to plans for greater co-ordination of French and British nuclear forces.[140] Less than a month before the UK announced its decision to cancel the TASM, British and French defence officials met in Paris in a forum called the Anglo-French Joint Commission on Nuclear Policy and Doctrine to discuss, *inter alia*, co-ordination of SSBN patrols, monitoring nuclear forces in the former Soviet Union and developing new nuclear delivery vehicles.[141]

Short-range tactical nuclear weapons

The remaining Pluton missiles, which have a range of only 120 km, were retired by the end of 1993.[142] In June, the French Government publicly confirmed for the first time that France has retained 30 short-range Hadès missiles and 15 mobile launchers in storage at Suippes.[143]

VI. Chinese nuclear weapon programmes

Relatively little new information surfaced in 1993 about Chinese nuclear weapon programmes, but most of the available data suggest that China contin-

---

[136] 'Nuclear notebook' (note 130), p. 56; *Le Monde,* 24 June 1993, in FBIS-WE, 30 June 1993, cited in *Arms Control Reporter* 7/93, sheet 611.E-4.4, July 1993.
[137] 'Nuclear notebook' (note 130), p. 56. The Rafale M is slated to be deployed with conventional weapons on the new Charles de Gaulle aircraft-carrier in 1998.
[138] 'Nuclear notebook' (note 130), p. 56.
[139] MacLeod, A., 'With deficit looming, Britain aims for leaner armed force', *Christian Science Monitor,* 20 Oct. 1993, p. 3.
[140] Drodziak, W., 'Britain scraps missile project', *Washington Post,* 23 Oct. 1993, p. 20A.
[141] de Briganti, G. and Witt, M. J., 'France, Britain pursue nuclear ties', *Defense News,* 27 Sep.– 3 Oct. 1993, p. 1.
[142] IISS, *The Military Balance 1993–1994* (note 2), p. 32; 'Nuclear notebook' (note 130), p. 56.
[143] *Le Monde,* 24 June 1993 (note 136).

ued to modernize and augment its forces slowly during the year. A number of systems appear to be under development, including two new mobile ICBMs— a single-warhead system and a MIRVed system which could also be used as an SLBM.

ICBMs

China currently deploys only a handful of land-based missiles with inter-continental range, all of which are liquid-fuelled and based in fixed silos.[144] In order to improve the reliability and survivability of its land-based forces, China is now trying to develop solid-fuel, mobile ICBMs.[145]

Many US analysts believe that China is also trying to develop new land-based missiles with increased range and with the capability to carry MIRVed warheads. In order to accomplish these goals, it appears that China would have to decrease the size and weight of its current warheads. According to US Government officials and private analysts, China's 5 October 1993 underground nuclear test at Lop Nor was probably part of a series of tests to develop more compact warheads for its new mobile ICBMs,[146] possibly for the single-warhead DF-31 ICBM or for the DF-41, which is expected to carry MIRVs.[147] (Some have compared the DF-31 and DF-41 to the Russian single-warhead SS-25 and 10-warhead SS-24 ICBMs, respectively.[148]) China's commitment to negotiate a comprehensive test ban (CTB) only by 1996—a commitment undertaken in 1993—may represent its estimate of how long it will take the country to complete the test programme for the development of new warheads for these ICBMs. (Chinese officials, however, claim that the purpose of planned tests is to incorporate safety features into their nuclear warheads, such as insensitive high explosives.[149])

It appears that, as part of its effort to develop solid-fuel, mobile ICBMs, China has actively recruited former Soviet weapon scientists and engineers to work in China. James Woolsey, CIA Director, told Congress on 28 July 1993 that China is 'the country that is probably most aggressively recruiting CIS scientists to help with a wide number of weapons programs'.[150] Woolsey added that 'there is substantial movement along those lines'.[151] Subsequent to

[144] Lewis, J. W. and Hua, D., 'China's ballistic missile programs: technologies, strategies, goals', *International Security*, vol. 17, no. 2 (fall 1992), p. 19.

[145] Lewis and Hua (note 144), pp. 28–29; Yan, K. and McCarthy T., 'China's missile bureaucracy', *Jane's Intelligence Review*, Jan. 1993, p. 41; Mann, J., 'China upgrading nuclear arms, experts say', *Los Angeles Times*, 9 Nov. 1993, p. 2C; Godwin and Schulz (note 4), p. 7.

[146] Mann (note 145), p. 2C; Taylor, R. A., 'Test ban flouted by China', *Washington Times*, 6 Nov. 1993, p. A1; Sun, L. H., 'China resumes nuclear tests; US prepares to follow suit', *Washington Post*, 6 Oct. 1993, p. A23; Gupta, V., 'Assessment of the Chinese nuclear test site near Lop Nor', *Jane's Intelligence Review*, Aug. 1993, p. 380; Lewis and Hua (note 144), p. 30; Godwin and Schulz (note 4), p. 7.

[147] Lewis and Hua (note 144), p. 11; 'Nuclear notebook', *Bulletin of the Atomic Scientists*, Nov. 1993, p. 57.

[148] Pressler (note 2), p. S16655.

[149] *The Comprehensive Test Ban: Views from the Chinese Nuclear Weapons Laboratories* (Natural Resources Defense Council: Washington, DC, 1993), pp. ii, 26; see also Shen, D., 'Toward a nuclear-weapon-free world: a Chinese perspective', *Bulletin of the Atomic Scientists*, Mar./Apr. 1994, pp. 52–53.

[150] Woolsey (note 67), p. 33.

[151] Woolsey (note 67), p. 33.

Table 8.5. Chinese nuclear forces, January 1994

Type	NATO designation	No. deployed	Year first deployed	Range (km)	Warheads x yield	Warheads in stockpile
Bombers[a]						
H-5	B-5	30	1968	1 200	1 x bomb	
H-6	B-6	120	1965	3 100	1 x bomb	150
Q-5	A-5	30	1970	400	1 x bomb	
H-7	?	0	1994?	?	1 x bomb	
Land-based missiles[b]						
DF-3A	CSS-2	50	1971	2 800	1 x 1–3 Mt	50
DF-4	CSS-3	20	1980	4 750	1 x 1–3 Mt	20
DF-5A	CSS-4	4	1981	13 000	1 x 3–5 Mt	4
DF-21	CSS-6	36	1985–86	1 800	1 x 200–300 kt	36
DF-31	–	0	Late 1990s?	8 000	1 x 200–300 kt	?
DF-41	–	0	2010?	12 000	MIRV	?
SLBMs[c]						
JL-1	CSS-N-3	24	1986	1 700	1 x 200–300 kt	24
JL-2	CSS-N-4	0	Late 1990s	8 000	1 x 200–300 kt	?

[a] All figures for bomber aircraft are for nuclear-configured versions only. 150 bombs are assumed for the force. Hundreds of aircraft are deployed in non-nuclear versions. The aircraft bombs are estimated to have yields between 10 kt and 3 Mt.

[b] The Chinese define missile ranges as follows: short-range, < 1000 km; medium-range, 1000–3000 km; long-range, 3000–8000 km; intercontinental-range, > 8000 km.

[c] Two SLBMs are presumed to be available for rapid deployment on the Golf Class submarine (SSB). The nuclear capability of the M-9 is unconfirmed and thus not included.

Source: Norris, R. S., Burrows, A. S. and Fieldhouse, R. W., *Nuclear Weapons Databook Vol. V: British, French and Chinese Nuclear Weapons* (Westview: Boulder, Colo., 1994), p. 11; 'Nuclear notebook', *Bulletin of the Atomic Scientists*, Nov. 1993, p. 57; Lewis, J. W. and Hua D., 'China's ballistic missile programs: technologies, strategies, goals', *International Security*, vol. 17, no. 2 (fall 1992), pp. 5–40.

Woolsey's statements, a spate of press reports indicated that the flow of CIS weapon designers to China continued on a large scale in late 1993.[152]

China is interested in acquiring technology from the CIS, particularly from Russia, to improve the range and accuracy of its ballistic missiles, especially technology that would help China build a missile similar in design to Russia's SS-25 mobile, solid-fuel ICBM.[153] China has also approached Ukraine, seeking help to improve Chinese ballistic missile technology.[154] (The former Soviet Union's SS-18 and SS-24 ICBMs were both built in Ukraine.)

[152] See, for example, Fialka, J. J., 'US fears China's success in skimming cream of weapons experts from Russia', *Wall Street Journal*, 14 Oct. 1993, p. 12; Atlas, T., 'Russia's brain drain has fallout', *Chicago Tribune*, 24 Oct. 1993, p. 7; Tyler, P., 'Russia and China sign a military agreement', *New York Times*, 10 Nov. 1993, p. A15.

[153] Fialka (note 152), p. 12; Sieff, M., 'Missile buildup in China could threaten US', *Washington Times*, 12 Nov. 1993, p. A16; Atlas (note 152), Section 1, p. 7; Mann (note 145), p. 2C; Tyler (note 152), p. A13.

[154] de Selding, P. B., 'China seeks Ukraine's expertise', *Space News*, 29 Nov.–5 Dec. 1993, p. 1.

Ssbns and SLBMs

The US intelligence community now believes that China has halted or slowed SSBN production, at least for the near future. In May 1993 Admiral Sheafer told Congress that China's 'nuclear-powered submarine construction program effort has probably at least temporarily ended at the current half dozen ballistic missile and attack units, although designs for new units in both categories are undoubtedly in preparation'.[155] China currently has one Xia Class SSBN and five Han Class SSNs, according to the IISS.[156] The slow pace of SSBN production may be due, *inter alia*, to the technical difficulties China has experienced in developing nuclear reactors for its submarines and solid fuel for its SLBMs.[157]

The JL-2 SLBM, which is currently under development and expected to be operational as early as the mid-1990s, is a variant of the DF-31 ICBM.[158]

Bombers

China may have decided to purchase nuclear-capable aircraft from Russia and other foreign countries rather than continuing indigenous development of new aircraft. Reportedly, the Hong-7 bomber, which was first flight-tested in 1988, still remains under development, but China has purchased a number of Su-27 'Flanker' fighter aircraft from Russia. *Jane's Defence Weekly* reported in early 1994 that China was operating a squadron of 26 Su-27s at Wuhu, a base near Shanghai.[159] According to press accounts, China has ordered a total of 50–75 Su-27s (including those that have already been delivered) plus four or more Tu-22M 'Backfire' bombers.[160] China has also demonstrated interest in purchasing Soviet-built Su-24 'Fencers' and MiG-29 'Fulcrums' from Iran.[161]

Land-based tactical nuclear weapons

Although there is no official confirmation that Chinese tactical nuclear war-heads exist, Robert S. Norris, a Senior Staff Analyst at the Natural Resources Defense Council (NRDC), estimated in 1993 that the Chinese nuclear arsenal includes up to 150 tactical nuclear weapons, composed of artillery shells, short-range rockets and atomic demolition munitions. Given the deterioration of relations between China and the USSR in the 1960s and 1970s and the fact that tactical nuclear weapons would have sufficient range to strike Soviet forces crossing the Sino-Soviet border, China may well have had an incentive to develop such weapons. In addition, Norris pointed out that China reportedly

---

[155] Sheafer (note 47), p. 30.
[156] IISS, *The Military Balance 1993–1994* (note 2), p. 152.
[157] 'Nuclear notebook' (note 147), p. 57; Lewis and Hua (note 144), pp. 26–27.
[158] Lewis and Hua (note 144), pp. 28–29.
[159] 'First picture of Chinese "Flanker"', *Jane's Defence Weekly*, 12 Feb. 1994, p. 6.
[160] Ackerman, J. A. and Dunn, M. C., 'Chinese airpower revs up', *Air Force Magazine*, July 1993, p. 59; see also 'Chasing the 20th century', *Jane's Defence Weekly*, 19 Feb. 1994, p. 26.
[161] 'Nuclear notebook' (note 147), p. 57.

conducted a large military exercise in June 1982, simulating the use of tactical nuclear weapons by both the Soviet Union and China.[162]

VII. Conclusions

With the demise of the Soviet Union and the disbandment of the Warsaw Pact, the most likely scenario for the use of nuclear weapons by the major powers—the escalation of an East–West conflict in Central Europe—has disappeared. In the wake of this transformation of the strategic environment, the arms control community has redoubled its efforts to stigmatize and delegitimize nuclear weapons, arguing that their political and military utility are extremely limited. These efforts include a push for a CTB, a ban on the production of fissile material for weapons and deeper reductions in strategic warheads than those required by the START II Treaty. Despite these efforts, one central fact remains: nuclear weapons are not going to disappear soon. Although there appears to be a consensus among the five declared nuclear powers that the role of nuclear weapons in international relations has diminished to a large degree, there is no indication that the USA, Russia, China, France or the UK plan to abandon modernization plans for their nuclear weapons in the foreseeable future. In general, these governments continue to make four broad arguments for maintaining nuclear weapons: (a) to deter existing nuclear threats (even though these threats are sometimes difficult to identify); (b) to provide a 'hedge' against the re-emergence of an old nuclear threat (e.g., an imperialistic Russia); (c) to deter new nuclear threats (e.g., nuclear proliferation in the developing world); and (d) to maintain or increase international status, prestige and influence. In 1993, the USA and the UK began to consider adding a fifth broad argument to this list: nuclear weapons may be needed to deter or respond to the threat of chemical or biological weapons.[163] This new rationale—subsumed in the phrase 'deterring weapons of mass destruction'—could prove highly controversial because all five of the declared nuclear weapon powers currently have a long-standing policy of not using or threatening to use nuclear weapons against non-nuclear parties to the NPT. In any event, if the arms control community wishes to build an international consensus that continued development and testing of nuclear weapons are unacceptable, it must be prepared to respond to all five of these arguments.

---

[162] 'Nuclear notebook' (note 147), p. 57.

[163] For sources for the USA, see Aspin, *Annual Report to the President and the Congress* (note 5), p. 61; 'Targeting rethink may lead to non-nuclear STRATCOM role', *Jane's Defence Weekly*, 22 May 1993, p. 19; Schmitt, E., 'Head of nuclear forces plans for a new world', *New York Times*, 25 Feb. 1993, p. B7. For sources for the UK, see Rifkind (note 110). See also chapter 16 in this volume.

Appendix 8A. Nuclear explosions, 1945–93

RAGNHILD FERM

I. Introduction

After the first nuclear weapons were developed and tested, nuclear tests were conducted primarily to validate refinements in the design of weapons, to develop new
warhead designs, to achieve efficiency and economy in the use of fissionable materials and to make the weapon assembly compatible with the means of delivery. Designs
which have not been fully tested through explosions have not been considered to be
reliable.

Many weapon designers, at least in the United States, claim that explosive testing
is necessary to have confidence in a new design. Security and safety tests are claimed
to be necessary when protective devices for nuclear weapons change the nuclear
assembly or its components significantly enough to modify the design of the weapon.
Finally, many assert that tests are needed to retain a core of experienced weapon
designers, whose accumulated knowledge is indispensable for maintaining confidence in the nuclear weapon stockpile.

While simulation tests can be conducted in laboratories, most experts agree that for
developing new weapon designs simulation tests cannot completely replace nuclear
explosions.[1]

The only nuclear explosion carried out in 1993 was that conducted by China.
France, Russia and the USA abided by their unilaterally announced test moratoria
throughout the year.

II. The United States and the United Kingdom

On 3 July 1993, President Bill Clinton announced that he had decided to extend the
US moratorium on nuclear tests which was introduced nine months earlier. The
extended moratorium would last at least through September 1994, as long as no other
state conducted a nuclear test. President Clinton also called on the other nuclear
weapon states to do the same. If another state did conduct a test during the US moratorium, the President would 'direct the Department of Energy (DOE) to prepare to
conduct additional tests while seeking approval to do so from Congress'.[2] The DOE
is expected to maintain a capability to resume testing. On 14 March 1994, Clinton
extended the US moratorium through September 1995.[3]

The US Congress had decided in 1992 that the US testing programme should be
terminated by 30 September 1996 'unless a foreign state conducts a nuclear test after
this date' but after a limited number of safety tests had been conducted. Three of

---

[1] For a discussion of the progress in negotiations at the Conference on Disarmament on a comprehensive test ban, see chapter 16 in this volume.
[2] 'Moratorium extended on US nuclear testing', *US Department of State Dispatch,* vol. 4, no. 28
(12 July 1993), p. 501.
[3] 'US extends moratorium on nuclear testing', *Wireless File* (United States Information Service, US
Embassy: Stockholm, 15 Mar. 1994), p. 7.

these tests were probably earmarked for the UK. President Clinton stated in July 1993 that his Administration had now determined that the US nuclear weapons are safe and reliable.[4]

As the UK has since 1962 conducted its nuclear tests jointly with the USA, at the Nevada Test Site, the US moratorium also prevents the UK from carrying out tests. The UK has over the years held the view that, since it needs to carry out limited testing to maintain the safety of its nuclear arsenal, it supports a nuclear comprehensive test ban treaty (CTBT) only as a long-term goal. However, in August 1993 the British delegate to the Conference on Disarmament (CD) stated that the UK is now fully committed to negotiations on a comprehensive test ban.[5]

In December 1993, when releasing classified information on the US nuclear weapon programme of the preceding 50 years, the US DOE disclosed that the USA had conducted 204 more nuclear weapon tests than had been reported officially.[6] All these tests were carried out underground, at the Nevada Test Site, after the signing of the 1963 Partial Test Ban Treaty (PTBT). According to DOE officials, all data on nuclear tests carried out at the Nevada Test Site have now been declassified. The reason given for not previously having announced all the tests was that the USA wanted to inhibit Soviet monitoring of US testing activities.

The DOE reported that all these tests were weapon-related and conducted in shafts. One of them, carried out in 1964, was a joint US–British test. The DOE did not give exact yields, 'in order to protect nuclear weapon design capabilities'.[7] Accidental on-site release of radioactivity from the explosions was reported. No information on off-site radiation was provided, since all such releases of radiation, it was claimed, were announced when the releases occurred. Additional information regarding the depth of burial and exact time of the tests was also made available.[8]

Of these previously unannounced tests, 111 were already known to both US and Soviet/Russian seismologists who have studied data and seismic records on tests for many years.[9] The clandestine, unannounced tests reported by these experts have over the years been entered in the SIPRI tables on nuclear explosions. Tables 8A.2–8A.4 below include all the 204 declassified tests.

Together with the US Department of Defense, the DOE also released classified information on the yields of the tests conducted in the Pacific Ocean—all atmospheric, or in four cases carried out under water—prior to the US–Soviet test moratorium of 1958–61.

III. Russia

The Soviet Union/Russia has not conducted a nuclear explosion since October 1990. President Boris Yeltsin extended earlier Soviet/Russian test moratoria, and on 21 October 1993, as a reaction to the Chinese test, the Russian Government made a statement that it did not plan to resume its nuclear testing programme but reserved the

---

[4] *US Department of State Dispatch* (note 2).
[5] Conference on Disarmament document CD/PV.658, 5 Aug. 1993, pp. 12–14.
[6] *Openness Press Conference, Fact Sheets* (US Department of Energy: Washington, DC, 7 Dec. 1993).
[7] *Openness Press Conference, Fact Sheets* (note 5).
[8] *Openness Press Conference, Fact Sheets* (note 5).
[9] The original research was carried out by Riley R. Geary, Seismological Laboratory of the California Institute of Technology.

right to reconsider its decision 'if the situation in this sphere continues to develop unfavourably'.[10]

IV. France

In a speech held at the Chemical Weapons Convention signing ceremony in Paris in January 1993, President François Mitterrand stated that France would maintain the test moratorium announced in April 1992, as long as other states refrained from testing. He repeated this statement in early July, after President Clinton's announcement of the extended US moratorium. However, the French Prime Minister as well as the National Assembly (Parliament) is not in favour of a test ban, and the Atomic Energy and Defence Departments are pushing for a resumption of the French testing programme, arguing that an extended moratorium would delay the new M-45 submarine-launched ballistic missile (SLBM) warhead and development of the warhead for the M-5 SLBM and the ASLP (Air-Sol-Longue Portée) missile. In December 1993, a parliamentary group established by the Defence Committee of the National Assembly to study the implications of a permanent cessation of testing on the French nuclear force presented a report stating that, since the French simulation technique is not yet sufficiently developed to replace ordinary testing, France cannot guarantee the function of its nuclear force if its nuclear testing programme is cancelled. The group envisages approximately 20 more French nuclear tests.[11]

V. China

According to intelligence reports, China had been preparing for a nuclear explosion for over a year when it conducted an explosion on 5 October 1993. Reconnaissance satellite pictures had shown that construction work for an underground nuclear explosion was going on at the Chinese test site in the Lop Nor area, in north-western China.[12] The 1993 Chinese test was the 39th nuclear explosion conducted by China since its nuclear testing programme started in 1964. The blast was detected by over 70 seismic stations throughout the world. According to the Swedish National Defence Research Establishment (FOA), the body wave magnitude was 6.4, which in this environment would be equivalent to a yield of approximately 80–160 kt.

The Chinese explosion raised strong criticism from all over the world, especially from the other acknowledged nuclear weapon states. However, none of them terminated its moratorium.

---

[10] 'Government statement on China's nuclear test, Text of Statement', FBIS-SOV-93-203, 22 Oct. 1993.

[11] *Le Monde*, 17 Dec. 1993.

[12] *Trust and Verify*, Bulletin of the Verification Technology Information Centre (VERTIC), Oct. 1993.

Table 8A.1. Registered nuclear explosion in 1993

Date	Origin time (GMT)	Latitude (deg)	Longitude (deg)	Region	Body wave magnitude[a]
China					
5 Oct.	020000.0	41. N	89. E	Lop Nor	6.4

[a] Body wave magnitude (m_b) indicates the size of the event. In order to be able to give a reasonably correct estimate of the yield it is necessary to have detailed information, for example, on the geological conditions of the area where the test is conducted. Giving the m_b figure is therefore an unambiguous way of listing the size of an explosion. m_b data were provided by the Swedish National Defence Research Establishment (FOA).

Table 8A.2. Estimated number of nuclear explosions 16 July 1945–5 August 1963 (the signing of the Partial Test Ban Treaty)

a = atmospheric; u = underground

Year	USA a	USA u	USSR a	USSR u	UK a	UK u	France a	France u	Total
1945	3	0							**3**
1946	2[a]	0							**2**
1947	0	0							**0**
1948	3	0							**3**
1949	0	0	1	0					**1**
1950	0	0	0	0					**0**
1951	15	1	2	0					**18**
1952	10	0	0	0	1	0			**11**
1953	11	0	5	0	2	0			**18**
1954	6	0	9	0	0	0			**15**
1955	17[a]	1	6[a]	0	0	0			**24**
1956	18	0	8	0	6	0			**32**
1957	27	5	18[a]	0	7	0			**57**
1958	62[b]	15	35	0	5	0			**117**
1959	0	0	0	0	0	0			**0**[c]
1960	0	0	0	0	0	0	3	0	**3**[c]
1961	0	10	52[a]	1	0	0	1	1	**65**[c]
1962	39[a]	57	71	1	0	2[d]	0	1	**171**
1 Jan.–5 Aug. 1963	4	25	0	0	0	0	0	2	**31**
Total	**217**	**114**	**207**[f]	**2**[c]	**21**	**2**	**4**	**4**	**571**

[a] One of these tests was carried out under water.

[b] Two of these tests were carried out under water.

[c] The UK, the USA and the USSR observed a moratorium on testing in the period Nov. 1958–Sep. 1961.

[d] These two tests were conducted jointly with the USA at the Nevada Test Site. They are not included in the column for the USA.

Table 8A.3. Estimated number of nuclear explosions 6 August 1963–31 December 1993

a = atmospheric; u = underground

Year	USA[a] a	USA[a] u	USSR/Russia a	USSR/Russia u	UK[a] a	UK[a] u	France a	France u	China a	China u	India a	India u	Total
6 Aug.–31 Dec.													
1963	0	18	0	0	0	0	0	1					19
1964	0	45	0	10	0	2	0	3	1	0			61
1965	0	38	0	14	0	1	0	4	1	0			58
1966	0	48	0	18	0	0	5	1	3	0			75
1967	0	42	0	17	0	0	3	0	2	0			64
1968	0	55[b]	0	18	0	0	5	0	1	0			79
1969	0	46	0	18	0	0	0	0	1	1			66
1970	0	38	0	14	0	0	8	0	1	0			61
1971	0	24	0	23	0	0	5	0	1	0			53
1972	0	26	0	25	0	0	3	0	2	0			56
1973	0	24[c]	0	17	0	0	5	0	1	0			47
1974	0	22	0	21	0	1	8	0	1	0	0	1	54
1975	0	22	0	19	0	0	0	2	0	1	0	0	44
1976	0	20	0	21	0	1	0	4	3	1	0	0	50
1977	0	20	0	23	0	0	0	8	1	0	0	0	52
1978	0	19	0	29	0	2	0	8	2	1	0	0	61
1979	0	15	0	32	0	1	0	9	1	0	0	0	58
1980	0	14	0	25	0	3	0	11	1	0	0	0	54
1981	0	16	0	21	0	1	0	12	0	0	0	0	50
1982	0	18	0	21	0	1	0	9	0	1	0	0	50
1983	0	18	0	28	0	1	0	9	0	2	0	0	58
1984	0	18	0	29	0	2	0	8	0	2	0	0	59
1985	0	17	0	12[d]	0	1	0	8	0	0	0	0	38
1986	0	14	0	0[d]	0	1	0	8	0	0	0	0	23
1987	0	14	0	26	0	1	0	8	0	1	0	0	50
1988	0	15	0	16	0	0	0	8	0	1	0	0	40
1989	0	11	0	8	0	1	0	8	0	0	0	0	28
1990	0	8	0	1	0	1	0	6	0	2	0	0	18
1991	0	7	0	0	0	1	0	6	0	0	0	0	14
1992	0	6	0	0	0	0	0	0	0	2	0	0	8
1993	0	0	0	0	0	0	0	0	0	1	0	0	1
Total	**0**	**698**	**0**	**506**	**0**	**22**	**42**	**141**	**23**	**16**	**0**	**1**	**1 449**

[a] See note a, table 8A.4.

[b] Five devices used simultaneously in the same explosion (a peaceful nuclear explosion, PNE, to develop peaceful uses for atomic energy) are counted here as one explosion.

[c] Three devices used simultaneously in the same explosion (a peaceful nuclear explosion, PNE, to develop peaceful uses for atomic energy) are counted here as one explosion.

[d] The USSR observed a unilateral moratorium on testing in the period Aug. 1985–Feb. 1987.

Table 8A.4. Estimated number of nuclear explosions 16 July 1945–31 December 1993

USA[a]	USSR/Russia	UK[a]	France[b]	China	India	Total
1 029	715	45	191	39	1	2 020

[a] All British tests from 1962 have been conducted jointly with the United States at the Nevada Test Site. Therefore, the number of US tests is actually higher than indicated here. This total includes tests for safety purposes, irrespective of the yields and irrespective of whether they have caused a nuclear explosion or not.

[b] This total, unlike that for the USA, does not include tests for safety purposes (of which there were 12, not yet identified by date).

Sources for tables 8A.1–8A.4

Swedish National Defence Research Establishment (FOA), various estimates; Reports from the Australian Seismological Centre, Bureau of Mineral Resources, Geology and Geophysics, Canberra; New Zealand Department of Scientific and Industrial Research (DSIR), Geology and Geophysics, Wellington; *Krasnaya Zvezda*, 13 Sep. 1990; *Pravda*, 24 Oct. 1990; US Department of Energy (DOE), *Summary List of Previously Unannounced Tests* (DOE: Washington, DC, 1993); Norris, R. S., Burrows, A. S. and Fieldhouse, R. W., 'British, French and Chinese nuclear weapons', *Nuclear Weapons Databook*, Vol. V (Natural Resources Defense Council (NRDC): Washington, DC, 1994); Assemblée Nationale, *Rapport d'information*, 15 Dec. 1993; Norris, R. S. and Cochran, T. B., 'United States nuclear tests July 1945 to 31 December 1992', *Nuclear Weapons Databook*, Working Paper NWD 94-1 (Natural Resources Defense Council (NRDC): Washington, DC, 1 Feb. 1994).

9. Chemical weapon developments

THOMAS STOCK and ANNA DE GEER*

I. Introduction

The Chemical Weapons Convention (CWC) was opened for signature in Paris in January 1993, and the broad support for it is manifested by the 154 signatories as of 10 December 1993. There is optimism that the CWC will enter into force in 1995, after at least 65 nations have ratified it. The current challenge is to transform the provisions of the Convention into operational procedures.[1]

The CWC bans all activities related to possession, acquisition, development, transfer and use of chemical weapons (CW); the 1925 Geneva Protocol earlier established the prohibition on CW use.

The crucial questions for 1993 were: Has the overwhelming support for the CWC begun to affect the behaviour of states in the CW area? Are there signs of decreasing CW proliferation?

This chapter focuses on events and developments related to CW such as: proliferation and non-proliferation, accusations of alleged use, allegations of acquisition of CW capability, destruction programmes, new discoveries of old and abandoned chemical weapons, and new developments in protection and detection.[2] It also presents information on relevant disarmament undertakings in 1993.

II. Proliferation

Chemical weapon proliferation is seen by many as one of the major security concerns of the 1990s. However, the number of countries alleged to have CW programmes has not changed significantly in recent years.[3] In May 1993 the Deputy Assistant to the US Secretary of Defense claimed that at least 24 countries have a CW capability.[4] It is very difficult to prove such allegations owing

---

[1] Institutionalization of the CWC, including national and international implementation measures, is discussed in chapter 17 in this volume.

[2] Biological weapon (BW) disarmament is discussed in chapter 18 in this volume. The activities of the United Nations Special Commission on Iraq (UNSCOM) in 1993 are reported in chapter 19 in this volume.

[3] See Stock, T., 'Chemical and biological weapons: developments and proliferation', SIPRI, *SIPRI Yearbook 1993: World Armaments and Disarmament* (Oxford University Press: Oxford, 1993), p. 268.

[4] *Statement by Dr B. Richardson*, Deputy Assistant to the Secretary of Defense (Chemical Matters), before the Subcommittee on Defense Committee on Appropriations, US House of Representatives,

* References were gathered from the SIPRI CBW Programme Data Base and were also kindly provided by J. P. Perry Robinson, Science Policy Research Unit, University of Sussex, UK, from the Sussex–Harvard Information Bank.

to the manner in which the information on which such claims are based is acquired and analysed.[5] CW capability may be determined on the basis of whether a country: (a) has chemical weapons; (b) is seeking to build up a CW programme; (c) has the necessary technology, know-how and material to start CW production (even if it has not yet done so); or (d) has access to CW delivery systems. A country's decision to obtain chemical weapons is first and foremost a political one that is influenced by various factors.[6] To some extent the CWC will improve the ability to verify allegations of such activity, but a perfect arms control regime in the CW field is an impossibility. It may be more important to change the political behaviour of states by delegitimizing CW acquisition.

In 1993 two major reports were published which assess the CW proliferation risk. The first, a Russian Foreign Intelligence Service report on the proliferation of weapons of mass destruction, mentions 9 countries that are alleged to have CW or a CW capability.[7] The report is the first such study published by Russia. The second, *Proliferation of Weapons of Mass Destruction: Assessing the Risk*,[8] by the US Office of Technology Assessment (OTA) makes similar claims about 11 countries. Only 6 of the 9 countries mentioned in the Russian report correspond with the OTA report.[9] Although the reports should not be viewed uncritically, they indicate countries that deserve particular attention as regards CW proliferation.[10]

The control of exports of CW precursors and dual-use chemical technology and equipment as well as their re-export is a serious proliferation problem. An example of this is the new information which appeared in 1993 in the UK that indicated that 26 tons of hydrogen fluoride were permitted to be shipped to Egypt in May 1986 despite accusations that Egypt was helping Iraq to build up its CW arsenal.[11] The British company involved had previously shipped 60 tons of hydrogen fluoride to Egypt.

In early 1993 the proposed sale of a chemical plant by British Petroleum (BP) America to Iran caused debate in the *United States*. The plant was intended to produce acrylonitrile for subsequent use in the production of syn-

---

5 May 1993, Department of Defense Appropriations for 1994 (US Government Printing Office: Washington, DC, 1993), p. 609. According to Richardson, 24 countries have 'some kind of chemical warfare program' where 'chemicals' are defined as lethal agents (mustard gas, nerve agents, etc.) He estimates that 9 nations have a biological warfare capability.

[5] See Lundin, S. J., Stock, T. and Geissler, E., 'Chemical and biological warfare and arms control developments in 1991', SIPRI, *SIPRI Yearbook 1992: World Armaments and Disarmament* (Oxford University Press: Oxford, 1992), p. 161.

[6] See Lundin, Stock and Geissler (note 5); Stock, T., 'Chemical weapons proliferation: some lessons', *asien afrika latinamerika*, vol. 20 (1992), pp. 1–8.

[7] Russian Federation Foreign Intelligence Service Report, *A New Challenge After the Cold War: Proliferation of Weapons of Mass Destruction*, JPRS-TND-93-007.

[8] US Congress, Office of Technology Assessment (OTA), *Proliferation of Weapons of Mass Destruction: Assessing the Risks*, OTA-ISC-559 (US Government Printing Office: Washington, DC, Aug. 1993).

[9] The six countries are Iran, Iraq, Israel, North Korea, Libya and Syria.

[10] The countries mentioned in the Russian report as having CW programmes are: Chile, India, Iran, Iraq, Israel, Libya, North Korea, Pakistan and Syria. The US report lists the following countries: China, Egypt, Iran, Iraq, Israel, Libya, Myanmar, North Korea, Syria, Taiwan and Viet Nam.

[11] Connett, D., 'Ministers permitted export of nerve gas', *The Independent*, 21 Sep. 1993, p. 4.

thetic fibres. However, there was great concern about the large quantity of hydrogen cyanide that the plant would inevitably produce as a by-product.[12] The BP director of patents and licensing indicated that the proposed export had been approved by the US Department of Defense (DOD) on condition that the plant be modified to prevent diversion of hydrogen cyanide,[13] and that Iran allow BP to monitor the plant.[14] The sale was not permitted.[15]

The construction of an alleged CW plant in Tarhuna, Libya created controversy in *Germany*. German companies had previously been implicated in the construction of Pharma-150, a CW facility in Rabta, Libya,[16] and it was acknowledged that German firms had also supplied equipment to the Tarhuna plant. However, the equipment supplied was of ambiguous nature (primarily drilling equipment and cables) and had been used to build a tunnel at the alleged CW factory.[17] Two companies immediately ceased delivery and will not face prosecution, but charges may be brought against a third company.[18] Germany has since modified its export laws to prevent any future such deliveries.[19] Trials continued involving the companies which had earlier assisted Libya and Iraq to construct CW plants.[20] Legal proceedings at Darmstadt had to be suspended after an expert witness was relieved of his duties by the court. A new trial will have to be held.[21]

Thailand was also alleged to be involved in the construction of the Tarhuna plant. Three private Thai companies had supplied workers and equipment to Libya. The same companies had been involved in supplying technology and workers for construction of the Rabta Pharma-150 plant.[22] The Secretary-General of the Thai National Security Council stated that it was impossible to impose a ban on the companies as Thailand is a 'free democratic country'.[23] In September 1993 the USA, Thailand's largest export market, increased pres-

---

[12] Smith, J. R., 'A chemical plant for Iran? Poison gas at issue as U.S. weighs sale', *International Herald Tribune*, 6 Jan. 1993, p. 1.

[13] Hydrogen cyanide is listed on Schedule 3 of the CWC. The CWC schedules list chemicals regulated by it.

[14] Smith, J. and Behr, P., 'Administration bars chemical plant sale to Iran, two other controversial export proposals are left unresolved by meeting', *Washington Post*, 6 Jan. 1993, p. A23.

[15] 'Proposed sales of equipment to Iran under study', *Wireless* File, no. 2 (United States Information Service, US Embassy: Stockholm, 5 Jan. 1993), p. 1.

[16] See Lundin, S. J., 'Chemical and biological warfare: developments in 1988', SIPRI, *SIPRI Yearbook 1989: World Armaments and Disarmament* (Oxford University Press: Oxford, 1989), p. 111; Lundin, S. J., 'Chemical and biological warfare: developments in 1989', SIPRI, *SIPRI Yearbook 1990: World Armaments and Disarmament* (Oxford University Press: Oxford, 1990), pp. 119–22; Lundin, S. J. and Stock, T., 'Chemical and biological warfare: developments in 1990', SIPRI, *SIPRI Yearbook 1991: World Armaments and Disarmament* (Oxford University Press: Oxford, 1991), pp. 91–93.

[17] 'German firm tied to Libya gas plant', *International Herald Tribune*, 17 Mar. 1993, p. 2.

[18] Associated Press, 'Germany says firms aid Libya on gas plant', *Washington Post*, 17 Feb. 1993, p. A22.

[19] Smith, J. R., 'Libya's new poison gas effort assailed, foreign assistance to plant violates U.N. embargo, U.S. says', *Washington Post*, 19 Feb. 1993, p. A27.

[20] Feuck, J., 'Darmstädter Irak-Giftgas-Prozeß ist nach 15 Monaten geplatzt' ['Darmstadt Iraq poison gas trial collapses after 15 months'], *Frankfurter Rundschau*, 13 July 1993, p. 2.

[21] 'German executive admits selling rocket technology to Iraq', *Aerospace Daily*, 13 Sep. 1993, p. 424.

[22] 'Thai participation in chemical weapons projects noted', in Foreign Broadcast Information Service, *Daily Report–Near East and South Asia (FBIS-NES)*, FBIS-NES-93-059, 30 Mar. 1993, p. 29.

[23] 'Security chief, minister view situation', in Foreign Broadcast Information Service, *Daily Report–East Asia (FBIS-EAS)*, FBIS-EAS-93-059, 30 Mar. 1993, p. 49.

sure on Thailand to force it to withdraw the 200 workers involved in construction of the plant.[24] Under US pressure the Thai Government arrested one
of the owners of a company involved in construction of the plant on charges
of contracting Thai workers abroad without government consent.[25] Two job-
placement firms which were involved were also closed.[26] In retaliation, Libya
threatened to expel several thousand of the 25 000 Thais working in the construction business in Libya.[27] The threat was later revoked and attributed to a
misunderstanding between the two countries.[28]

In August 1993 relations between *China* and the USA were strained by US
allegations that a Chinese cargo vessel bound for Iran was carrying thiodigly-
col and thionyl chloride, chemical precursors that can be used for the production of mustard and nerve gas.[29] The USA, which based its information on
intelligence sources, demanded that the ship, the *Yin He,* be inspected.[30] China
refused to allow such an inspection, denied that the ship was carrying chemicals and accused the USA of interfering. For almost three weeks the *Yin He*
was not allowed to dock at any port until Saudi Arabia allowed it to dock in
Dammam for inspection.[31] Representatives from China, Saudi Arabia and the
USA inspected the vessel and found nothing, confirming China's repeated
denials to be true. China subsequently demanded an official apology and compensation from the USA.[32] The USA refused but praised China for its co-
operation.[33] The incident caused debate about the right of the USA to demand
inspection. The CWC allows such 'challenge inspections', but since the CWC
has not yet entered into force and neither the USA nor China are states parties,
the US demand for inspection had no basis in international law.[34]

---

[24] Tasker, R., 'The Libyan connection, US puts pressure on Thais building chemical plant', *Far East-ern Economic Review,* 16 Sep. 1993, p. 27.

[25] Shenon, P., 'US tries to stop Thai work on Libyan chemical arms plants', *The Guardian,* 27 Oct. 1993, p. 4.

[26] 'Thailand targets 3 firms over Libya', *International Herald Tribune,* 28 Oct. 1993, p. 2.

[27] Shenon, P., 'Libya expels Thais in chemical weapons dispute', *New York Times,* 10 Nov. 1993, p. A14.

[28] 'Thais won't be expelled Libyan says', *International Herald Tribune,* 24 Nov. 1993, p. 5.

[29] Kristof, N. D., 'China says U.S. is harassing ship suspected of taking arms to Iran', *New York Times,* 9 Aug. 1993, p. A6.

[30] Carlson, B. K., 'Illegala kemikalier jagas, kinesiskt containerfartyg genomsöks i saudisk hamn' ['Illegal chemicals are hunted: Chinese container ship is searched in Saudi harbour'], *Svenska Dagbladet* (Stockholm, Sweden), 27 Aug. 1993, p. 4

[31] Duke, L., 'China seeks apology in ship search, poison gas material not found by U.S.', *Washington Post,* 5 Sep. 1993, p. A43.

[32] Tyler, P. E., 'China wants U.S. apology over ship', *International Herald Tribune,* 6 Sep. 1993, p. 1; 'Statement by the Ministry of Foreign Affairs of the People's Republic of China on the "Yin He" Incident, dated 4 September 1993', PrepCom document PC-IV/12, 27 Sep. 1993.

[33] Ember, L., 'Search of Chinese ship fails to find chemicals', *Chemical & Engineering News,* vol. 71, no. 37 (13 Sep. 1993), p. 8; 'Statement by the Delegation of the United States of America to the Preparatory Commission for the Organisation for the Prohibition of Chemical Weapons, dated 29 September 1993', PrepCom document PC-IV/16, 29 Sep. 1993.

[34] Ember, L., 'U.S. alleges China ships chemical agents to Iran', *Chemical & Engineering News,* vol. 71, no. 33 (16 Aug. 1993), p. 6.

III. Non-proliferation measures

The possible entry into force in 1995 of the CWC combined with the new security environment that developed after the end of the cold war has created a changed climate for international control regimes. Export control regimes either have had to change their policies or, in some cases, have ceased to exist. The two groups most relevant to CW are the Australia Group[35] and the Coordinating Committee on Multilateral Export Controls (COCOM). States which are CWC signatories have voiced concern about the restrictions of the Australia Group on the trade of chemicals. The perception that COCOM's policies have discriminated against certain countries coupled with the desire of COCOM member countries to promote international trade forced COCOM to reconsider its agenda. In November 1993 the decision was taken to dissolve COCOM and replace it with a new body that would not discriminate against Eastern Europe or Russia.[36]

The Australia Group

The Australia Group must also reconsider its future under the CWC. Three main approaches have been suggested: (a) to dissolve the group, (b) to continue work on export control until states parties to the CWC are confident that the CWC functions properly, and (c) to formalize the group, thereby creating a legal mandate.[37] Option b may be the best solution.[38] The Australia Group is most likely to make a difference to CW proliferation in the areas of national implementation and export control. The experience gained by the Australia Group in co-ordinating export controls between its member countries and providing export control measures with effective procedures cannot readily be found elsewhere. The states parties and the Organisation for the Prohibition of Chemical Weapons (OPCW) can both benefit from the experience of the Australia Group.[39]

The Australia Group met in Paris on 7–10 June 1993; working group meetings were held starting 2 June to discuss export lists controlling biological weapons (BW), CW dual-use equipment, CW precursors and more effective export controls.[40] A final version of the Group's Control List of Dual-Use

---

[35] The Australia Group is a group of states which meets twice a year to monitor the proliferation of chemical and biological products. For its activities in 1993, see chapter 17 in this volume.

[36] 'Obsolete COCOM to be dissolved', *Jane's Defence Weekly*, vol. 20, no. 22 (27 Nov. 1993), p. 8. COCOM was completely dissolved in Mar. 1994.

[37] *Ad Hoc* Working Group on Non-Proliferation and Arms Control, *Non-Proliferation and Arms Control: Issues and Options for the Clinton Administration*, Jan. 1993, as outlined by the *ad hoc* group which was established during Clinton's election campaign to advise Clinton on non-proliferation and arms control issues.

[38] Although option b was recommended by the *Ad Hoc* Working Group on Non-Proliferation and Arms Control, the future of the Australia Group will be decided and agreed by all members of the Australia Group.

[39] 'The Australia Group and the Chemical Weapons Convention', editorial comment, *Chemical Weapons Convention Bulletin*, no. 21 (Sep. 1993), p. 5.

[40] Institute for Defense and Disarmament Studies, *Arms Control Reporter* (IDDS: Brookline, Mass., 1993), sheet 704.B.552, Oct. 1993.

Chemical Manufacturing Facilities and Equipment, and Related Technology to control the transfer of equipment was presented.[41] A second meeting, held on 6–9 December 1993, addressed *inter alia* the problem of streamlining licensing procedures in order to facilitate international trade under the CWC without contributing to the proliferation of weapons of mass destruction.[42]

The Australia Group expanded its membership in 1993 with the addition of Argentina, Hungary and Iceland as permanent members.[43] Hungary, with its large chemical equipment industry,[44] is an important addition. The Australia Group retained 54 chemicals on its export control list as agreed at its June 1992 meeting.[45]

The European Union

In 1993 there was intense debate on export controls, including those relevant to CW, in the *European Union* (EU). Debate centred on issues related to the will to move towards integration while simultaneously retaining national sovereignty. In Germany, for example, recession and structural change led to debate about the possibility of less stringent export controls at the end of 1993.[46] If CW-related export controls between member states are removed— as is allowed for by the Australia Group—one country might be able to export goods through another country with weaker controls, since external export control systems vary widely among EU member states. Article 223 of the Treaty of Rome contributes to the problem; it states that 'defense-related goods are exempted from Common Market regulations'.[47] Dual-use goods can be seen as defence-related products and are thus excluded from control.[48] The list under Article 223 also explicitly includes CW and BW materials.[49]

[41] Australia Group, *Press Release*, Australian Embassy, Paris, 2–10 June 1993. The Proposed List of Plant Pathogens for Export Controls and a revised version of the Proposed List of Biological Agents for Export Control were also presented.

[42] Australia Group, *Press Release*, Australia Group Meeting, Australian Embassy, Paris, 6–9 Dec. 1993, Australia Group document AG/Dec93/Press/Chair/12. The importance of early ratification of the CWC was stressed.

[43] Current members are: Argentina, Australia, Austria, Belgium, Canada, Denmark, Finland, France, Germany, Greece, Hungary, Iceland, Ireland, Italy, Japan, Luxembourg, the Netherlands, New Zealand, Norway, Portugal, Spain, Sweden, Switzerland, the UK and the USA. The European Union (EU) is an observer.

[44] Odessey, B., 'Biological export controls list agreed', *Wireless File*, no. 111 (United States Information Service, US Embassy: Stockholm, 11 June 1993), p. 20.

[45] See Stock (note 3), p. 269.

[46] 'Kanzleramt befürwortet einfachere Waffenexportrichtlinien' ['Chancellor's office favouring simpler guidelines for arms exports'], *Frankfurter Allgemeine Zeitung*, 10 Jan. 1994, p. 1; 'Euro-Exportkontrollen in der Sackgasse' ['Euro export controls in a dead end street'], *Frankfurter Allgemeine Zeitung*, 12 Nov. 1993, p. 15.

[47] Müller, H., 'The export control debate in the "new" European Community', *Arms Control Today*, vol. 23, no. 2 (Mar. 1993), pp. 10–14.

[48] See Müller (note 47).

[49] Brzoska, M. and Lock, P. (eds), SIPRI, *Restructuring of Arms Production in Western Europe* (Oxford University Press: Oxford, 1992), appendix E, p. 219.

Export controls under the CWC

The CWC provisions for the transfer of chemicals suggest that each state party will have to revise trade regulations and export controls as regards declarations of quantities exported, end-user statements, control of re-exports, and the like.[50] The existing control policies of some countries may be sufficient; others will have to be improved or adjusted. The chemical industry will carry most of the burden of reporting and requesting licences for the export and transfer of Schedule 2 and 3 chemicals to countries which are not parties to the CWC.[51] Other industries such as those which produce textiles, leather and plastic could also be affected.[52] Surveys of the chemical industry in Japan and the USA have, for example, made clear that a wide range of facilities will be covered by CWC regulations.

In January 1993 *Japan* announced that up to 1000 factories would be affected by international inspections when the CWC enters into force.[53] Later estimates suggest that only 100 chemical factories would be subject to international inspections, although the assessment of the Japanese Trade Ministry is that 2000–3000 chemical plants would need to submit regular reports to the government.[54] The Ministry of International Trade and Industry (MITI) has asked Japanese corporations to conduct a review of their export systems.[55]

The *United States* also has a large chemical industry. An August 1993 OTA study estimated that 200–300 US facilities 'produce, process, or consume more than the threshold quantity' of Schedule 2 chemicals.[56] For Schedule 3 chemicals the number is about 1000; approximately 10 000 plants produce discrete organic chemicals.[57] The OTA also noted that a few biotechnology–pharmaceutical companies produce Schedule 1 chemicals.

The Clinton Administration is aware of the importance of maintaining and strengthening export controls on CW precursors and technology as the USA is a member of the Australia Group. However, there are conflicting pressures within the US Government both to strengthen export controls in order to enhance non-proliferation measures and to relax these same controls to

[50] See Stock (note 1); Robinson, J. P. P., Stock, T. and Sutherland, R. G., 'The Chemical Weapons Convention: the success of chemical disarmament negotiations', *SIPRI Yearbook 1993* (note 3), pp. 705–34; 'The Convention on the Prohibition of the Development, Production, Stockpiling and Use of Chemical Weapons and on their Destruction', *SIPRI Yearbook 1993* (note 3), pp. 735–56.

[51] Three years after entry into force of the CWC only states parties will be allowed to transfer and export Schedule 2 chemicals. See Annex 2, Part VII.C of the CWC . The transfer of Schedule 1 chemicals is allowed only between states parties. The provisions for Schedule 3 chemicals will be revised five years after entry into force of the CWC. See Annex 2, Part VIII.C of the CWC.

[52] Sutherland, R. G., *Chemical Weapons Convention Verification: Handbook on Scheduled Chemicals*, Ottawa, Aug. 1993, mimeo.

[53] 'Law on international checks of chemical plants', in FBIS-EAS-93-008, 13 Jan. 1993, p. 4.

[54] 'About 100 Japanese chemical factories would be subject to international inspections', *Arms Control Reporter,* sheet 704.E-2.87, May 1993.

[55] 'MITI to tighten weapons-related exports', in FBIS-EAS-93-069, 13 Apr. 1993, p. 9.

[56] OTA, *The Chemical Weapons Convention; Effects on the U.S. Chemical Industry*, OTA-BP-ISC-106 (US Government Printing Office: Washington, DC, Aug. 1993), p. 15.

[57] Ember, L., 'Chemical arms treaty's effect on industry noted', *Chemical & Engineering News*, vol. 71, no. 33 (16 Aug. 1993), p. 17. The CWC defines a discrete organic chemical as 'any chemical belonging to the class of chemical compounds consisting of all compounds of carbon except for its oxides, sulfides and metal carbonates'; discrete organic chemicals will be limited under the PSF.

promote US exports. This creates confusion about the implementation of export control policies. The 1993 Military Critical Technologies List stipulates that 'export controls should cover and be limited to militarily critical goods and technologies'; it aims to achieve 'protection of critical technologies and products while removing restrictions on technologies and products that are not critical'.[58] However, the proper application of US export control regulations is suffering owing to budget restrictions and strategies designed to increase US exports. Then Deputy Secretary of Defense William J. Perry noted that 'technological developments are widely dispersed and that there are no effective means of controlling them. Therefore it serves no purpose to continue impeding American industrial exports'.[59] Close advisers to former US Secretary of Defense Les Aspin favoured lifting 98 per cent of the existing controls, and the DOD is studying the creation of a $1 billion fund to encourage arms exports.[60] The scheme would streamline export controls by 'requiring clearer identification of controlled items and firm guidelines for licensing' while easing other controls that impede US exports.[61]

In the USA and throughout the world substances and materials which can be used in the production of CW are under tighter export control than ever before. However, the effect of an easing of export control policies must be monitored for its potential effect on proliferation of CW-related materials and technology.[62]

In 1993 much concern about CW proliferation related to the unstable situation in the successor states to the *former Soviet Union*. Although no reports surfaced to prove that chemicals or CW-related material had been transferred from the territory of the former Soviet Union, the threat of such an occurrence appears realistic.[63] According to the Director of the US Central Intelligence Agency (CIA), 'the lure of large illegal profits' combined with 'legal, personnel and funding problems' could tend to slow the Russian Government's attempts to hinder proliferation of Russian arms and military know-how.[64] On 31 May 1993 in Almaty (Alma-Ata), the heads of the Foreign Economic Relations Ministries of the Commonwealth of Independent States (CIS) approved an agreement setting up the CIS Export Control Council under the Russian Export Control Commission.[65] The CIS states agreed:

[58] Ropelewski, R., 'Export control shifts aim to convert, diversify', *SIGNAL*, June 1993, pp. 69–70.

[59] 'Sensitive exports: an era of "decontrol"', *Intelligence Newsletter*, no. 228 (11 Nov. 1993), pp. 1, 6.

[60] See 'Sensitive exports: an era of "decontrol"' (note 59).

[61] Le Sueur, S. C., 'Lawmakers press to ease U.S. export controls', *Defense News*, vol. 8, no. 43 (1–7 Nov. 1993), pp. 3, 36.

[62] The International Seminar Against the Proliferation of Chemical and Biological Weapons in Oslo, Norway, on 13–14 Dec. 1993 is illustrative of attempts to contribute to the control of exports.

[63] *Countering the Chemical and Biological Weapons Threat in the Post-Soviet World*, Report of the Special Inquiry into the Chemical and Biological Threat of the Committee on Armed Services, US House of Representatives, 102nd Congress, 2nd session, 23 Feb. 1993 (US Government Printing Office: Washington, DC, 1993), p. 18.

[64] Smith, J. R., 'Nuclear-export control in Russia called weak', *International Herald Tribune*, 26 Feb. 1993, p. 2.

[65] 'CIS to control exports of "dangerous technologies"', in Foreign Broadcast Information Service, *Daily Report–Central Eurasia (FBIS-SOV)*, FBIS-SOV-93-107, 7 June 1993, p. 1.

To bring national export control systems in line with existing international regimes;

To complete the work on creating operating national export control systems in CIS countries;

To hold at least twice a year regular conferences of CIS countries' representatives on matters related to control over the export of raw and other materials, export, technologies, and services, which may be used for the creation of the weapons of mass destruction;

In the period leading up to the next conference, scheduled for the end of the year in Minsk, representatives of the Republic of Belarus will act as coordinators of the organization of national export control systems within the CIS.[66]

On 30 August 1993, *Russia* took measures to improve its own export control system with the signing of an agreement to organize the exchange of information between the Ministry of Foreign Economic Relations and the Economy Ministry.[67] The data bases of the ministries, which register quotas and licences for controlled products, will be pooled to enable Russia to better detect potential violators.

Armenia is also setting up an export control commission to cover *inter alia* dual-use products, including those used in the production of CW.[68]

IV. Allegations of the use and possession of chemical weapons

Alleged use of CW

Any discussion of the alleged use of chemical weapons must consider the specific circumstances of the situation in question and of the parties involved. An allegation of CW use could be used to attempt to gain international political support or to create sympathy. The threat of CW use, as in the former Yugoslavia, might serve as a political tool to deter military action by enemy forces. Evaluation of claims of alleged CW use and threats of CW use must therefore take into account the country's domestic and international political situation and its CW capability.

In 1993 *Iraq* was again accused of using CW. In May 1993 reports alleged that Iraq had dumped 'tens of tonnes' of chemical substances in its marshlands, in an attempt to hide them from United Nations inspectors, thereby poisoning the inhabitants in that area.[69] By September 1993 the allegations had escalated to accusing Iraq of killing 'hundreds of Marsh Arabs using chemical weapons'.[70] Emma Nicholson, a member of the British Parliament who has been active in bringing the fate of the Marsh Arabs to public attention,

---

[66] See 'CIS to control exports of "dangerous technologies"' (note 65).

[67] 'New export control system created', in FBIS-SOV-93-168, 1 Sep. 1993, p. 27. The agreement's official name is On Organizing the Exchange of Information Between the Russian Federation Ministry of Foreign Economic Relations and the Russian Ministry of the Economy Within the Framework of the Creation of a Single Automated System of Control (SASC) Over the Export of Strategic Goods.

[68] 'Commission to oversee export control of weapons materials', in FBIS-SOV-93-085, 5 May 1993, p. 62.

[69] 'Chemicals dumped in marshes, many poisoned', in FBIS-NES-93-087, 7 May, 1993, p. 28.

[70] 'Iraq use of chemicals in doubt', *The Independent*, 23 Oct. 1993, p. 14.

obtained information about a CW attack in the marshlands on 28 and 29 September 1993. She gave this information to the United Nations Special Commission on Iraq (UNSCOM),[71] which assembled a team to investigate the situation.[72] According to Nicholson, 'it appears that the gas was phosgene'.[73] The UNSCOM investigating team took samples of the soil, water and fauna, but by the end of 1993 analysis of these samples had not yet determined whether or not CW agents were used.[74] A period of two months had passed between the alleged use and the investigation, and traces of chemicals could thus have disappeared. In early 1994 information was presented which did not confirm the alleged CW use.[75]

There have been numerous allegations that *Iraq* used CW in the 1980–88 Iraq–Iran War, but only a few of these allegations have been proved.[76] In June 1992 US scientists from Physicians for Human Rights had collected soil samples from craters in the Kurdish village Birjinni in Iraq, where a CW attack was said to have taken place in 1988.[77] In May 1993 it was reported that the samples which had been sent to the British Chemical & Biological Defence Establishment at Porton Down had been analysed using gas chromatography–mass spectrometry with selected ion monitoring.[78] The samples were found to contain traces of mustard gas, the nerve agent sarin and various degradation products.[79] Proof of CW use is generally regarded as difficult to establish unless the site can be checked within hours or at least days after a CW attack. Detection in 1993 of traces of CW use in 1988 is thus remarkable. This example of detection long after use may facilitate CWC verification procedures for detecting or confirming alleged CW use.[80] CW proliferation may also be discouraged if the use of CW can be detected years afterwards.[81]

In 1993 there were many claims of the alleged use or threat of use of CW in the *former Yugoslavia*. In February 1993 Muslim forces in Tuzla announced their decision to use CW. Official government sources stated that 'By preventing us from obtaining the necessary weapons to defend ourselves, the international community is breaching the main principles of international law, leaving us no other alternative but to use all available means to save the lives

[71] See chapter 19 in this volume.

[72] *Hansard* (Commons), Foreign Affairs and Defence, 19 Nov. 1993, p. 168; see also chapter 19 in this volume.

[73] See *Hansard* (note 72).

[74] UNSCOM, *Press Release*, 22 Nov. 1993.

[75] See chapter 19 in this volume.

[76] See Robinson, J. P. P., 'Chemical and biological warfare: developments in 1986', SIPRI, *SIPRI Yearbook 1987: World Armaments and Disarmament* (Oxford University Press: Oxford, 1987), p. 106; Urquhart, B., 'The United Nations and the Iraq–Iran War', *SIPRI Yearbook 1988* (note 16), pp. 509–10; Lundin (note 16), pp. 102–3.

[77] Webb, J., 'Iraq caught out over nerve gas attack', *New Scientist*, vol. 138, no. 1871 (1 May 1993), p. 4.

[78] Ember, L., 'Chemical weapons residues verify Iraqi use on Kurds', *Chemical & Engineering News*, vol. 71, no. 18 (3 May 1993), pp. 8–9.

[79] See Ember (note 78).

[80] 'Chemical analysis, assured access and open publication', editorial comment, *Chemical Weapons Convention Bulletin*, no. 20 (June 1993), p. 7.

[81] Macilwain, C., 'Study proves Iraq used nerve gas', *Nature*, vol. 363, no. 6424 (6 May 1993), p. 3.

of more than 1 million people facing the threat of destruction by the Serbian and Montenegrin aggressor. . . . Our decision to use chemical resources is final'.[82] There continues to be uncertainty about who is in possession of the CW arsenal of the former Yugoslav National Army.[83]

Reports appeared in both February and March 1993 of alleged use by Serbs of 'toxic gases' in Brcko, Bosnia.[84] In June 1993 reports began to appear of alleged use by Croats of CW against the Republic of Serb Krajina.[85] In Bosnia, Muslim forces again threatened to use CW if the Serb attack on Gorazde was not stopped.[86] In July 1993 media reports emerged of Muslim forces using what was called a 'riot control gas with some other noxious agent mixed in'[87] against Bosnian Croats. Following several reports of Muslim use of CW against Croats, Bosnians and Serbs the UN launched an investigation of a Serb military position in Boskovici, where the Bosnian Serb Army claimed that three attacks had occurred. The CW agents were suspected to be chlorine gas and in some instances tear-gas.[88] In October Muslims were again accused of using chlorine gas against Serb forces.[89] In the United Nations Protection Force (UNPROFOR) report submitted to the UN Security Council in October 1993[90] it was reported that Bosnian Muslims have admitted using CW—primarily chlorine gas and in some instances tear-gas.[91] Although there is no definite proof of chemical warfare agent use in the former Yugoslavia, it appears likely that at least chlorine gas was used.[92] However, the UNPROFOR report did not provide evidence of the use of chlorine gas or any other agent.[93] Again the time which elapsed between the alleged use and the investigation may be significant.

New allegations of CW use by various factions in *Angola* were reported in 1993. In January 1993 the Popular Movement for the Liberation of Angola

[82] 'Tuzla fighters to use "chemicals" against Serbs', in Foreign Broadcast Information Service, *Daily Report–East Europe (FBIS-EEU)*, FBIS-EEU-93-024, 8 Feb. 1993, p. 51.

[83] Allegations of CW possession by the former Yugoslav National Army is discussed below in the subsection on 'possession and alleged possession of CW'.

[84] 'Serbs reportedly using chemical agents in Brcko', in FBIS-EEU-93-027, 11 Feb. 1993, p. 33; 'Commander accuses Serbs of using chemical weapons', in FBIS-EEU-93-028, 12 Feb. 1993, p. 30; Ottaway, D. B., 'Serbs batter Sarajevo with artillery fire, fiercest barrage in months rains down as blockade of Eastern Muslim enclaves continues', *Washington Post*, 19 Mar. 1993, p. A47.

[85] 'Croats reportedly shelling RSK with chemical weapons', in FBIS-EEU-93-093, 17 May 1993, p. 37.

[86] TT-Reuter, 'Hot om kemisk krigsföring' ['Threat of chemical warfare'], *Dagens Nyheter* (Stockholm, Sweden), 20 June 1993, p. 10.

[87] Bellamy, C., 'Muslim forces hurl improvised gas grenades at Croats', *The Independent*, 12 July 1993, p. 10.

[88] 'Chemical weapons claims probed', *Jane's Defence Weekly*, vol. 20, no. 8 (21 Aug. 1993), p. 5. The use of tear-gas is prohibited under the CWC if it is used as a means of warfare.

[89] 'Muslims reportedly use poisonous gases on Serbs', in FBIS-EEU-93-203, 22 Oct. 1993, p. 21; 'Muslims accused again of using CW rounds', *Jane's Defence Weekly*, 23 Oct. 1993, p. 8.

[90] 'Muslims admit use', in FBIS-EEU-93-204, 25 Oct. 1993, p. 34; United Nations Security Council, 'Letter dated 27 October 1993 from the Chargé d'Affaires A. D. of the Permanent Mission of the Federal Republic of Yugoslavia to the United Nations addressed to the President of the Security Council', United Nations Security Council document S/26672, 31 Oct., 1993.

[91] See TT-Reuter (note 86); 'Chemical weapons claims probed' (note 88).

[92] 'Chemical weapons used by Bosnian Army', *Croatian Voice*, 29 Oct. 1993, p. 15.

[93] See UN Security Council document S/26672 (note 90).

(MPLA) was accused of dropping CW bombs on the city of Ndalatando,[94] while the União Nacional Para a Independência Total de Angola (National Union for the Total Independence of Angola, UNITA) accused the Angolan Government of using CW against civilians in the city of Huambo.[95]

In 1993 attention focused on the cases of so-called 'steppage-gait' syndrome (in which partial paralysis of the lower limbs occurs) that had been reported by UNITA forces between 1986 and 1990.[96] Although no samples had been collected from the immediate area where the syndrome manifested itself, a number of hypotheses, including CW use, were put forward to explain the symptoms of those affected.[97] A satisfactory scientific investigation has not been able to be conducted, and no apparent link between CW and the syndrome can be established. Nevertheless, it is apparent that once symptoms occur which are perceived as CW-related, it is difficult to assuage fears of CW use.

Possession and alleged possession of CW

Allegations of possession of CW by *North Korea* continued to be made in 1993. In May 1993 the US DOD announced its strong belief that North Korea has a CW capability.[98] Eight production sites[99] and six storage sites[100] were alleged to be located in North Korea. According to the CIA, North Korea is capable of producing nerve gas, blood agents and mustard gas.[101]

There have been allegations of a large CW industry in *Iran* since the Iraq–Iran War. The Director of the CIA also testified in early 1993 that there is evidence of an Iranian CW programme which includes choking, blister and blood agents, some of which were purchased from Hungarian firms.[102] Estimates of the size of the Iranian CW stockpile range from several hundred tons to 2000 tons.[103] These allegations are disputed by the President of Iran, who has stated that they are 'baseless and incorrect'.[104] The USA demonstrated its cautious

[94] 'Use of chemical weapons charged', in Foreign Broadcast Information Service, *Daily Report–Sub-Saharan Africa (FBIS-AFR)*, FBIS-AFR-93-001, 4 Jan. 1993, p. 15.

[95] 'Government said using chemical weapons', in FBIS-AFR-93-010, 15 Jan. 1993, p. 32.

[96] Davey, B. J., 'The "steppage-gait" patients in Angola: chemical warfare?', *ASA Newsletter*, no. 36 (10 June, 1993), p. 14.

[97] Davey, B. J., 'Chemical warfare in Angola?' *Jane's Intelligence Review*, vol. 5, no. 6 (June 1993), pp. 280–83.

[98] *Proliferation Threats of the 1990's*, Hearing before the Committee on Governmental Affairs, US Senate, 103rd Congress, 1st session (US Government Printing Office: Washington, DC, 24 Feb. 1993).

[99] The production sites are said to be: Anju, Aoji-ri, Ch'ongjin, Hamhung-Hungnam, Manpo, Sinhung, Sinuiju and Sunch'on. Bermudez, J. S., Jr, 'North Korea's chemical and biological warfare arsenal', *Jane's Intelligence Review*, vol. 5, no. 5 (May 1993), p. 228; 'Germany: BND analyses DPRK chemical warfare capability', *West Europe Intelligence Report: Focus*, 30 April 1993.

[100] Two storage sites are said to be located in Sanumni; the others in Hwangchon, Samsandong, Sariwon and Wangjabong. See Bermudez (note 99).

[101] See *Proliferation Threats of the 1990's* (note 98).

[102] White, D., 'Iran may soon have N-weapons', *Financial Times*, 9 Mar. 1993; Spector, L., 'Iranian N-program featured on US documentary', *Nuclear Non-Proliferation Network Bulletin Board*, 4 Apr. 1993, item 42.

[103] See White (note 102).

[104] BBC Monitoring Service, 'President Rafsanjani gives Islamic Republic Day interview', *Summary of World Broadcasts (SWB)*, 2 Apr. 1993. In addition, Iran is a signatory to the CWC.

approach to Iran when it stopped a Chinese cargo vessel bound for a port in Iran and opposed the sale of a US BP chemical plant.[105] There were numerous threats of CW use in the war in the *former Yugoslavia* in 1993, but whether or not chemical weapons actually exist in the former Yugoslavia continues to be disputed. CW production is reported to have occurred primarily at Potoci, north of Mostar, in what is now Bosnia and Herzegovina.[106] It is also claimed that the facility produced several different chemical agents. Before the Yugoslav National Army withdrew from Bosnia, it is alleged that all equipment from the plant was relocated to Serbia. Another report mentions a plant in Baric, Serbia, which supposedly produces phosgene.[107] The same report lists CS, BZ, sarin and mustard gas as domestically produced CW agents in the former Yugoslavia.[108] Another source of concern is the large chemical complex in Tuzla and the threat by Muslims to blow up the complex.[109] In addition to the reports that the former Yugoslav National Army conducted a CW programme, there is also evidence that ammunition was filled with CW.[110]

Libya is alleged to be attempting to acquire or add to a CW arsenal. Allegations in 1993 claimed that a CW plant is located near the town of Tarhuna, 64 km south-east of Tripoli.[111] The plant—a copy of the Pharma-150 plant in Rabta, which was apparently destroyed by fire in 1990—is alleged to be a subterranean facility capable of producing and storing 'poison gas'.[112] Libya claims that the plant is part of 'the Great Man-Made River' project which is designed to provide water to the desert nation's North Africa coast.[113] It is claimed that Libya has produced at least 100 tons of CW agent, mostly mustard gas[114] as well as some sarin.[115]

In *Russia* the case of the scientist Vil Mirzayanov, who is accused of disclosing state secrets, continued to make headlines,[116] and his trial began on

---

[105] See the discussion of proliferation in section II above.

[106] *Production of Chemical Weapons at the Military Technical Institute-Mostar Plant by the former Yugoslav National Army (JNA)*, Report submitted by Croatia at the Regional Seminar on National Authority and National Implementation Measures for the Chemical Weapons Convention, Warsaw, 7–8 Dec. 1993.

[107] Vego, M., 'The new Yugoslav defence industry: part 2', *Jane's Intelligence Review*, vol. 5, no. 12 (Dec. 1993), p. 546.

[108] According to Croatia, 100 tons of CS were produced between 1978 and 1989. See Vego (note 107); Production of Chemical Weapons at the Military Technical Institute-Mostar Plant by the former Yugoslav National Army (JNA) (note 106).

[109] See 'Muslims reportedly use poisonous gases on Serbs' (note 89); TT-Reuter (note 86); Stock (note 3), p. 263.

[110] Kati´c, H., 'Proizvodnja Kemijskog Oruzja Bivse ja u Vojnotehnickom Institutu: Pogon Mostar', *Hrvatski Vojnik [Croatian Soldier]*, 17 Prosinca 1993['Production of chemical weapons at the Military Technical Institute: Mostar plant'], pp. 39–40; see also *Production of Chemical Weapons at the Military Technical Institute-Mostar Plant by the former Yugoslav National Army (JNA)* (note 106).

[111] Jehl, D., 'U.S. says Libya is building a 2d poison-gas plant', *New York Times*, 18 Feb. 1993, p. A7.

[112] Mitchener, B., 'German firms linked to Libyan mustard gas factory', *International Herald Tribune*, 18 Feb. 1993, p. 2.

[113] 'Libyan denunciation', *Washington Post*, 21 Feb. 1993, p. A30.

[114] The estimate does not include the Tarhuna site as this plant is not in operation.

[115] See *Chemical Weapons Convention Bulletin*, no. 22 (Dec. 1993), p. 12.

[116] See Stock (note 3), p. 266.

24 January 1994.[117] Mirzayanov's colleagues voiced support by giving interviews about their work at the national Organic Chemistry and Technology Institute (GSNIIOKhT). One of them, Vladimir Uglev, claimed that he took part in the testing of a new Russian nerve agent, Novichok-8, at Shikhany.[118] According to Uglev, an undetermined quantity of the agent was produced and is currently stored somewhere in the Bryansk region.[119] While there has been international support for the scientists,[120] the Director of GSNIIOKhT has officially stated that his institute is a pharmacology complex.[121] Several Russian officials have expressed concern that Mirzayanov has caused Russia political, moral and economic damage.[122]

V. The 'Gulf War syndrome'

More than two years after the end of the 1991 Persian Gulf War new allegations of the possible release of CW agents were made in the USA. In June 1993 testimony was given to the Veterans Affairs Subcommittee of the House of Representatives on the so-called 'Gulf War syndrome' in response to the health complaints of veterans of the Gulf War.[123] These veterans suffer a variety of symptoms including fatigue, loss of memory, body sores, hair loss, and intestinal and heart problems and believe that these symptoms were caused by contact with war-related contaminants.[124] There were also reports in the UK that some British soldiers who served in the Coalition forces suffer similar symptoms.[125]

In September US Senator Donald W. Riegle, Jr, reported on a staff investigation of the Gulf War syndrome,[126] which states 'Despite the Department of Defense's position that no evidence exists for exposure to chemical warfare agents during the Gulf War, this investigation indicates that there is substantial evidence supporting claims that US servicemen and women were exposed to low level chemical warfare agents and possibly biological toxins from a variety of possible sources'.[127] The report describes two episodes in which US forces may have come under Iraqi chemical and biological warfare (CBW)

---

[117] Seltzer, R. 'U.S. scientists protest Russian chemist's trial', *Chemical & Engineering News*, vol. 72, no. 4 (24 Jan. 1994), pp. 8–9.

[118] Vishnyakov, O., 'An interview with a noose around the neck', *New Times International*, vol. 10 (Mar. 1993), pp. 22–23.

[119] See Vishnyakov (note 118).

[120] Colby, G., 'Fabricating guilt', *Bulletin of the Atomic Scientists*, vol. 8 (Oct. 1993), pp. 12–13.

[121] 'Moscow institute defended against CW charge', in FBIS-SOV-93-118, 22 June 1993, p. 32.

[122] 'The security consequences of Mirzayanov's disclosures on Russian binary research', *Arms Control Reporter*, sheet 704.E-2. 97, Oct. 1993.

[123] 'Gulf War GIs fight mystery illnesses', *International Herald Tribune*, 11 June 1993; Cockburn, P., 'Gulf War "guinea-pigs" tell Senate of mystery illness', *The Independent*, 2 July 1993, p. 13.

[124] 'Gulf War GIs fight mystery illnesses' (note 123); 'Golfkriegsveteranen sprechen von irakischem Chemiewaffeneinsatz' ['Gulf War veterans report Iraqi use of chemical weapons'], *Frankfurter Allgemeine Zeitung*, 2 July 1993, p. 3.

[125] Pilkington, E., 'Doctor claims she caught "Gulf syndrome" at UK base', *The Guardian*, 24 Dec. 1993.

[126] *Gulf War Syndrome: The Case for Multiple Origin Mixed Chemical/Biotoxin Warfare Related Disorders*, Staff report to US Senator Donald W. Riegle, Jr, 9 Sep. 1993, US Senate, mimeo.

[127] See *Gulf War Syndrome* (note 126).

attack and mentions a July 1993 Czechoslovak Government report on the detection of traces of sarin in the air in an area near the Saudi–Iraqi border.[128] The report suggests the need for further investigation to clarify the issue.

As of November 1993 the DOD continued to maintain that US forces had not found evidence of Iraqi use of CW during the Gulf War; nevertheless the Army is reviewing the Czechoslovak report.[129] On 10 November 1993 the US Secretary of Defense stated that after preliminary review no link had been found between the small amounts of CW agents reported and the health problems suffered by some veterans.[130] He pointed out that reports of the detection of chemical warfare agents by a Czechoslovak military unit appear reliable, but that the USA could not confirm the validity of the three incidents of detection (sarin, twice and mustard gas, once). This statement can be interpreted as contradicting earlier ones that no chemical warfare agents were detected at all during the Gulf War.[131] In October 1993 a US team visited Prague and concluded that the training of the former Czechoslovak unit was adequate and the detection equipment satisfactory.[132] The Secretary of Defense announced the formation of an independent panel of scientific experts to conduct further examinations and to review the Pentagon's preliminary report. The US Coalition allies, particularly Saudi Arabia, which had troops in the area where the agents were detected, are to be questioned as to whether they had CW or related materials in the region.[133] In December 1993 a French officer revealed that during the war nerve agents and mustard gas had been detected in the area in question.[134] A US Marine Corps chemical warfare officer said that his unit twice detected blister agent during the ground war.[135]

In December 1993 it was suggested that Gulf War syndrome may be a side-effect of anti-nerve gas pills containing pyridostigmine bromide that soldiers were required to take.[136] If the US Government refuses to accept the syndrome as war-related, compensation will be denied to veterans who suffer from it. There are some similarities to the denial of claims by veterans who were exposed to Agent Orange in the Viet Nam War.[137] Nevertheless, the 1994 Defence Bill includes $1.2 million to study the possible health effects on Gulf

---

[128] McAllister, B., 'Riegle suggests Iraq conducted chemical warfare', *Washington Post*, 10 Sep. 1993, p. A18.

[129] 'Defense Department Report, Tuesday, November 2: DOD reviews reports of Gulf War chemical use', *Wireless File* (United States Information Service, US Embassy: Stockholm, 2 Nov. 1993), pp. 2–3.

[130] Office of the Assistant Secretary of Defense, 'No health linkage found in chemical agent detection', *News Release*, Washington, DC, 10 Nov. 1993.

[131] McAllister, B., 'Chemical agent exposure in Gulf War acknowledged', *Washington Post*, 11 Nov. 1993, p. A33; 'U.S. is unsure of toxic agent use in Gulf War', *International Herald Tribune*, 11 Nov. 1993, p. 1.

[132] Porth, J. S., 'Pentagon finds Gulf War chemical agent report valid', *Wireless File* (United States Information Service, US Embassy: Stockholm, 10 Nov. 1993), pp. 3–4.

[133] Starr, B., 'USA to quiz Saudis on Gulf War CW traces', *Jane's Defence Weekly*, vol. 20, no. 21 (20 Nov. 1993), p. 7.

[134] 'France says Gulf troops detected chemicals', *Washington Post*, 5 Dec. 1993, p. A24.

[135] 'Marines detected gas in Gulf War', *International Herald Tribune*, 17 Nov. 1993.

[136] Tisdall, S., 'Gulf syndrome victims point to nerve gas pills', *The Guardian*, 24 Dec. 1993.

[137] Hilts, P. J., 'In medical dispute, it's Gulf War veterans vs. the Pentagon', *International Herald Tribune*, 24 Nov. 1993, p. 3.

War veterans 'of exposure to low levels of oil smoke and other chemicals'.[138] The Gulf War syndrome is likely to continue to receive attention owing to its political implications.

VI. CW destruction

The destruction of CW stockpiles is required of all states parties to the CWC. In 1993 the focus was on the US and Russian destruction programmes. Owing to the possible entry into force of the CWC in 1995, the disarmament community is greatly concerned about the possibility that the two major CW possessor states may be unable to meet the CWC time-schedule and conclude destruction within 10 years despite the fact that destruction of the US stockpile has already begun. Under the detailed CWC destruction schedule a possessor state must destroy at least 1 per cent of its stock within 3 years after entry into force, 20 per cent within 5 years, 45 per cent within 7 years, and the remaining stock within 10 years.[139]

The situations of the USA and Russia differ. In the USA, with just over 30 000 tons of chemical agent at eight continental locations, a destruction programme is currently being implemented. However, environmental problems and budgetary constraints could slow the process.[140] Russia has some 40 000 agent tons to destroy. It is still in the process of setting up its destruction programme and has major problems associated with funding and carrying out the programme.

There may be other nations with smaller CW stockpiles which must also be destroyed under the CWC.

The 1990 US–Soviet agreement

The 1989 Wyoming Memorandum of Understanding (MOU)[141] and the 1990 Agreement between the United States of America and the Union of Soviet Socialist Republics on Destruction and Non-Production of Chemical Weapons and on Measures to Facilitate the Multilateral Convention on Banning Chemical Weapons[142] include two phases of data exchange, reciprocal visits and inspections which were to have been implemented before the CWC was signed.[143] Phase I was successfully completed; however, the details of Phase II remain unresolved and are still under discussion. The US Interagency has approved the wording of the 1990 Agreement, while the Russian Government

---

[138] Towell, P., 'Hill follows Clinton's lead but worries about pace', *Congressional Quarterly*, vol. 51, no. 48 (4 Dec. 1993), pp. 3312–15.

[139] CWC, Article IV and Annex on Verification, part IV (A), para. 17, Conference on Disarmament document CD/1170, 26 Aug. 1992, p. 93.

[140] Smithson, A. E., 'Chemical destruction: the work begins', *Bulletin of the Atomic Scientists*, vol. 49, no. 4 (1993), pp. 38–42.

[141] Lundin, S. J., 'Multilateral and bilateral talks on chemical and biological weapons', *SIPRI Yearbook 1990* (note 16), pp. 531–32.

[142] The text of the Agreement is reproduced in *SIPRI Yearbook 1991* (note 16), pp. 536–39.

[143] '26 March 1993', *Arms Control Reporter*, sheet 704.B.549, July 1993.

has not yet approved it.[144] In January 1993 Russia and the USA resumed bilateral talks in Geneva which continued until the end of March 1993.[145] In February 1993 a US delegation visited a Russian facility in Volgograd.[146] Progress was made in solving questions related to Phase II of the MOU, and the inspection schedule under the 1990 Agreement was adjusted as a result of the signing of the CWC by Russia and the USA.[147] The time-schedule for destruction under the 1990 Agreement was also adjusted to conform with the CWC.[148] In November 1993 unresolved issues were discussed, including a possible change of the Agreement which would allow Russia to convert CW component chemicals to civilian use.[149] At a January 1994 summit meeting in Moscow both Russia and the USA stated that the 'implementing documents for the Wyoming Memorandum of Understanding' were concluded and that both sides have agreed to work on 'implementing documents for the bilateral agreement' as soon as possible.[150]

The US destruction programme

A revised schedule for the US destruction programme contained in the fiscal year (FY) 1993 defence authorization bill pushed the completion date to December 2004.[151] The destruction operation at the Newport Army Ammunition Plant (the facility where destruction is to start latest) is planned to be finished in April 2003.[152] It continues to receive criticism with questions being raised about so-called 'baseline technology'.[153]

Official figures for the US CW stockpile given in the FY 1994 Arms Control Impact Statements in 1993 list 28 000 agent tons of mustard gas and nerve agents in munitions which have lost their utility, and 3200 tons of usable

---

[144] See *Statement by Dr B. Richardson* (note 4), p. 641.

[145] See *Arms Control Reporter* (note 143).

[146] '22 March 1993', *Arms Control Reporter*, sheet 704.B.548, Mar. 1993.

[147] '8 June 1993', *Arms Control Reporter*, sheet 704.B.553, Oct. 1993. Russia and the USA had previously agreed to conduct 5 challenge inspections prior to signature of the CWC. These were now eliminated. The 5 initial inspections to be conducted after CWC signature were rescheduled with 1 practice challenge inspection at a site selected by the host, and 4 challenge inspections at both declared and undeclared sites.

[148] Destruction is now scheduled to begin by 30 June 1997 (the previous date was 31 Dec. 1992), and to finish by 30 June 2004 (previously 31 Dec. 2002).

[149] '22–29 November 1993', *Arms Control Reporter*, sheet 704.B.560–61, Jan. 1994.

[150] 'Joint Statement by the President of the Russian Federation and the President of the United States on Non-Proliferation of Weapons of Mass Destruction and Means of Their Delivery', in FBIS-SOV-94-010, 14 Jan. 1994, pp. 16–17.

[151] See Stock (note 3), pp. 273–77.

[152] In the authorization bill for FY1993 the US Congress extended the programme completion date to 31 Dec. 2004. The new revised schedule for the destruction programme is based on plans to build one plant per year with the exception of FY 1995, when two facilities (at Umatilla and Pine Bluff Arsenal) are scheduled to be built. Construction of the last facility (Newport) will start in 1999; the disposal operation at Newport will be completed in Apr. 2003.

[153] 'Baseline technology' involves the use of robots for disassembling the weapons and incineration for burning the liquid agent, waste, explosives, propellant and contaminated metal components.

agents in artillery projectiles, spray tanks and bombs.[154] The amount of usable agents is 200 tons less than the figure reported in the FY 1993 statement.[155]

The US destruction programme costs increased in 1993. A January 1993 General Accounting Office (GAO) report describes the various delays and operational difficulties which the Johnston Atoll Chemical Agent Disposal System (JACADS) in the Pacific, south-west of Hawaii has experienced; it also outlines the problems the Army is having in obtaining environmental permits for the construction and future operation of other planned destruction facilities in the continental United States.[156] The report raises doubts that the Army will be able to meet the CW destruction timetable owing to opposition to incineration by local citizens and environmental groups and problems in obtaining temporary permit authorizations. The report estimates the cost of the destruction programme through December 2000 at $7.9 billion but does not estimate the cost of extending programme completion to December 2004. In April 1993 a new figure of $8.6 billion was presented for the overall cost of the US destruction programme.[157] The cost increased because of delays caused by a congressional requirement that a study of alternative technologies be conducted,[158] and because of programme stretch-out. (Table 9.1 presents the revised planning schedule for the US destruction programme but does not take into account the impact of the results of the evaluation of alternative technologies or system failures.)

The national defense authorization bill for FY 1994, signed by President Bill Clinton in November 1993, allocated $379.6 million[159] for the Chemical Demilitarization Program.[160]

At JACADS the fourth and final phase of its Operational Verification Test (OVT) began on 23 September 1992 and ended on 6 March 1993. During the four OVT phases the following items were destroyed: approximately 35 000 kg of the nerve agent GB, approximately 61 000 kg of the nerve agent VX, approximately 79 000 kg of mustard gas, 21 454 M55 rockets, 68 ton-containers and 35 873 projectiles.[161] The facility will continue to destroy 105-mm mustard gas-filled projectiles, thereafter 105-mm GB-filled bombs,

[154] FY 1994 Arms Control Impact Statements, 103rd Congress, 1st session, Joint Committee Print (US Government Printing Office: Washington, DC, Sep. 1993), p. 14.

[155] '3 June', Arms Control Reporter, sheet 704.E-1.19, Apr. 1993.

[156] US General Accounting Office (GAO), Chemical Weapons Destruction: Issues Affecting Program Cost, Schedule, and Performance, Report to the Chairman, Subcommittee on Environment, Energy and Natural Resources, Committee on Government Operations, US House of Representatives, GAO/NSIAD-93-50, Jan. 1993, p. 20.

[157] Weinschenk, A., 'Chemical weapons destruction program costs $700 million more', Defense Week, vol. 14, no. 16 (19 Apr. 1993), p. 2.

[158] See Stock (note 3), p. 274.

[159] Congressional Quarterly, vol. 51, no. 45 (13 Nov. 1993), p. 3136, gives a figure of $389.9 million.

[160] Congress deleted the requested amount for construction at the Anniston chemical agent disposal facility ($108.9 million) in FY 1993. See statement by M. W. Owen, Acting Assistant Secretary of the Army, Department of Defense Appropriations for 1994, Hearings before a Subcommittee of the Committee on Appropriations, US House of Representatives, 103rd Congress, 1st session (US Government Printing Office: Washington, DC, 1993), pp. 600–1.

[161] 'OVT completed', Chemical Demilitarization Update, vol. 2, no. 3 (July 1993), p. 3.

Table 9.1. Revised US chemical disposal planning schedule

Location	Start of prove-out	Start of operation	End of operation
Johnston Atoll Chemical Agent Disposal Facility Pacific Ocean	Aug. 1988	July 1990	Feb. 1996
Aberdeen Proving Ground Chemical Disposal Training Facility Edgewood, Maryland	..	Oct. 1991	Apr. 2002
Tooele Army Depot Tooele, Utah	Aug. 1993	Feb. 1995	Apr. 2000
Anniston Army Depot Anniston, Alabama	Jan. 1997	July 1998	Aug. 2001
Umatilla Army Depot Hermiston, Oregon	Nov. 1997	May 1999	Dec. 2001
Pine Bluff Arsenal Pine Bluff, Arkansas	Sep. 1997	Mar. 1999	Nov. 2001
Pueblo Army Depot Pueblo, Colorado	Nov. 1998	May 2000	Jan. 2002
Lexington-Blue Grass Depot Richmond, Kentucky	Nov. 1999	May 2001	Oct. 2002
Aberdeen Proving Ground Edgewood, Maryland	June 2000	June 2001	June 2002
Newport Army Ammunition Plant Newport, Indiana	June 2001	June 2002	Apr. 2003

Source: Department of Defense Appropriations for 1994, Hearings before a Subcommittee of the Committee on Appropriations, US House of Representatives, 103rd Congress (US Government Printing Office: Washington, DC, 1993), p. 598.

155-mm GB shells and ton containers, and installation material. As with all previous OVTs, the MITRE Corporation (a non-profit company affiliated with the Massachusetts Institute of Technology) evaluated the operation. In an April 1993 preliminary draft of its final report, it concluded that JACADS has demonstrated its ability to destroy munition types such as rockets, ton containers and projectiles. The plant met short-term through-put goals; however, the long-term average process rate was not achieved.[162] The design of the plant, according to the MITRE corporation, has no apparent fundamental problems and achieves safety and environmental goals; nevertheless there is a need to continue to make improvements in order to ensure that safety and environmental requirements continue to be met.[163]

---

[162] In OVT Phase I, 11 VX rockets were destroyed (the goal was 8); in Phase II, 7 rockets were destroyed (the goal was 12) and in Phase III, 17 rockets were destroyed (the goal was 24). See *Chemical Weapons Destruction* (note 156).

[163] 'Correction', *Chemical Demilitarization Update*, vol. 2, no. 3 (July 1993), p. 3.

In May 1993 Greenpeace issued a report on the difficulties and failures at JACADS, especially in its programme for the destruction of GB and VX.[164] The report lists all occasions of the release of various agents and malfunctions. In August 1993 the US Army opened the Tooele Chemical Disposal Facility (TOCDF) at Tooele, Utah,[165] where 42 per cent of the US CW stockpile is stored, containing the CW agents mustard gas, VX and GB in bulk and various types of ammunition. The overall cost of this plant is estimated at $347 million.[166] Laboratory training, which began in 1991, will be completed in April 1994. Systemization will be finished in January 1995, and the destruction operation will start in February 1995. It is planned to continue until April 2000.[167]

At Umatilla, Oregon, where 12 per cent of the US CW stockpile is located, the construction of two incinerators was scheduled to begin in February 1993 but did not start.[168] A new date of January 1995 has been set for the start of construction at both the Umatilla and Pine Bluff, Arkansas, facilities.

The Russian destruction programme

In February 1993 a representative from Russia's Committee on Conventional Problems of Chemical and Biological Weapons made the optimistic statement that the Russian CW destruction programme would be completed by 2005 at a cost of 3 billion roubles ($543 million).[169] The rouble figure was low, and in May a new figure of 500 billion roubles was presented.[170] The then Head of the Russian Federation President's Committee on Matters Pertaining to Chemical and Biological Weapons, Academician Anatoly Kuntsevich, later estimated the cost of the 10-year destruction programme at 600 billion roubles.[171] By the end of 1993 Kuntsevich pointed out that Russia would be unable to destroy its stocks by the date required under the CWC unless $1 billion of foreign technological aid is provided.[172]

In April 1993, President Boris Yeltsin issued a presidential statement on CW destruction outlining the principles on which the programme is based. The programme aims to guarantee 'complete safety as regards human life and the environment'. CW destruction is to start 'only upon positive findings by state expert examination on the program as a whole and on each installa-

[164] Costner, P., *Chemical Weapons Demilitarization and Disposal: Johnston Atoll Chemical Disposal System, GB and VX Campaigns* (Greenpeace: Washington, DC, 12 May 1993).
[165] 'What about TOCDF?', *Chemical Demilitarization Update*, vol. 2, no. 3 (July 1993), p. 4.
[166] 'What about TOCDF?' (note 165).
[167] 'Tooele systemization effort only 4 months away', *Chemical Demilitarization Update*, vol. 2, no. 2 (Apr. 1993), p. 1.
[168] 'Update on existing and planned facilities, 1 April', *Arms Control Reporter*, sheet 704.E-1.23–25, Apr. 1993.
[169] 'Russia to completely destroy chemical weapons by 2005', Moscow Radio Rossii Network (in Russian), in FBIS-SOV-93-030, 17 Feb. 1993, p. 5.
[170] 'Experts discuss chemical weapons disposal problems, solutions', in FBIS-SOV-93-100, 26 May 1993, p. 1.
[171] 'Panel head on implementing CW treaty', in FBIS-SOV-93-118, 22 June 1993, pp. 29–30.
[172] Gordon, M. R., 'Safety and money stymie plans to rid Russia of chemical weapons', *International Herald Tribune*, 2 Dec. 1993, p. 8.

tion'.[173] Scientists, specialists and the public are to be involved. The statement appeals to the executive bodies of the Udmurtia, Chuvashia and Saratov oblasts, where destruction facilities are planned, to support the draft state programme.

At January 1993 hearings in the Russian Parliament information was presented that the Parliament of Chuvashia (Novocheboksarsk in Chuvashia is a planned destruction site) had decided to ban the transportation of CW to its territory for destruction. Tatarstan and other Volga oblasts indicated that they will respond in a similar fashion.[174]

The Russian CW stockpile is located at seven places: one each in the Kurgan, Penza, Kirov, Saratov and Bryansk oblasts and two in the Udmurtia oblast (in Kizner and Kambarka).[175] The overall figure of 40 000 agent tonnes equals approximately 32 300 agent tonnes of nerve agents (sarin, soman and V agent), 7700 agent tonnes of blister agents (mustard gas, lewisite and mustard gas/lewisite mixture)[176]—of the 7700 tonnes only 700 tonnes are estimated to be mustard gas[177]—and 5 agent tonnes of phosgene.[178] In February 1993 for the first time foreign journalists visited the CW storage facility at Kambarka in Udmurtia, where 6300 tonnes of lewisite[179] have been stored in 80 storage tanks since the early 1950s.[180]

The First Moscow International Conference on Chemical and Biological Disarmament, Demilitarization and Conversion (jointly arranged by the Russian Federation President's Committee on Matters Pertaining to the Chemical and Biological Weapons Conventions, the Russian Academy of Science and several US institutes) was held in May 1993.[181] Experts from more than 20 countries discussed problems related to destruction technology, the environment and verification.[182] The meeting focused on the planned destruction of

---

[173] 'Presidential statement on chemical arms destruction', in FBIS-SOV-93-079, 27 Apr. 1993, pp. 35–36.

[174] 'Parliament discusses Chemical Weapons Convention', in FBIS-SOV-93-013, 22 Jan. 1993, pp. 45–46.

[175] 'Scientist questions chemical weapons stockpile figures', Radio Free Europe/Radio Liberty, *RFE/RL News Briefs*: 19–22 Jan. 1993, supplement to the *RFE/RL Research Report*, vol. 2, no. 5 (1993), p. 4; 'Parliament discusses Chemical Weapons Convention', in FBIS-SOV-93-013, 22 Jan. 1993, pp. 45–46.

[176] The 1992 draft of the Comprehensive Programme for the Phased Destruction of Chemical Weapons in the Russian Federation lists 6400 agent tonnes of lewisite stored at Kambarka, and 225 agent tonnes of lewisite, 690 agent tonnes of mustard gas and 210 agent tonnes of a mustard gas/lewisite mixture at Gorny.

[177] Umiarov, I. A. et al., 'Methods of mustard and lewisite disposal and waste recovery', *Journal of the Mendeleev Russian Chemical Society*, vol. 37, no. 3 (1993), pp. 25–29. The exact figure may be 690 agent tonnes for mustard gas based upon the Russian draft programme for CW destruction.

[178] Garrett, B., C., *Commentary on Russian Reaction to Chemical Weapons Stockpile Destruction, I. Russian Press Reports, 1992–March 1993*, CBACI Special Report no. 93-01 (Chemical & Biological Arms Control Institute: Alexandria, Va., Apr. 1993), p. 1.

[179] Russian sources name a figure of 6400 tonnes for Kambarka.

[180] House, E. K., and Revzin, P., 'Toxic dump: arsenal of poison gas languishes as Russia is unable to destroy it', *Wall Street Journal*, 25 Feb. 1993.

[181] 'Funds needed to destroy arms', in FBIS-SOV-93-096, 20 May 1993, p. 1; 'Chemical weapons disarmament conference open', in FBIS-SOV-93-096, 20 May 1993, p. 1.

[182] Olson, K. and Flakne, N. (eds), *MOSCON 93*, Proceedings of the First Moscow Conference on Chemical and Biological Disarmament, Demilitarization and Conversion (Chemical and Biological Arms Control Institute: Alexandria, Va., May, 1993).

the Russian CW stockpile. In his closing remarks, Kuntsevich reiterated the Russian plan to begin destruction of its CW stocks in 1997 despite the financial and technical challenges posed by such an undertaking. The first phase, which is to destroy 43 per cent of the stockpile, is to be finished by 2004.[183] The draft programme plans for the destruction of 9800 agent tonnes of nerve agents, 6600 agent tonnes of lewisite, 690 agent tonnes of mustard gas and 210 agent tonnes of mustard gas/lewisite mixture by 2004.[184]

In August 1993 it was announced that President Yeltsin had ordered the establishment of a governmental commission to assume responsibility for the selection of destruction sites.[185] However, by October 1993 the commission had yet to begin its work.[186]

International co-operation with Russia

Several states are co-operating with Russia to destroy its CW stockpile. By May 1993 the USA had committed itself to provide up to $55 million to assist Russian CW destruction of which $2 million has been spent to set up and begin operating a Moscow office. Approximately $30 million will be spent to establish an analytical laboratory for CW destruction which will be equipped with modern analytical technology.[187]

In September 1993 the US Army Chemical Material Destruction Agency started the Russian Intern Familiarization Programme, a six-month course to train Russian interns about the US CW destruction programme.[188] The interns will be familiarized with the technical and operational aspects of the US demilitarization programme, receive training and visit JACADS and TOCDF.

A December 1992 agreement between Russia and Germany[189] led to the signing of a contract with the German company L.U.B. for the 1994 construction of a pilot plant which will destroy approximately 700 tonnes of lewis-

---

[183] 'Panel head on implementing CW treaty', in FBIS-SOV-93-118, 22 June 1993, pp. 29–30.

[184] *Comprehensive Programme for the Phased Destruction of Chemical Weapons in the Russian Federation*, Moscow, 1992, draft (in Russian).

[185] 'Yeltsin orders establishment of chemical arms commission', in FBIS-SOV-93-152, 10 Aug. 1993, p. 23.

[186] 'Chemical weapons: are they easy to eliminate?', *Krasnaya Zvezda* (Moscow), 22 Oct. 1993, pp. 1–2.

[187] Hearings before a Subcommittee on the Department of Defense of the Committee on Appropriations, US House of Representatives, 103rd Congress, 1st session, 5 May 1993 (United States Government Printing Office: Washington, DC, 1993), p. 642; *ASA Newsletter*, no. 37 (12 Aug., 1993), p. 9. 'Pentagon provides assistance to former Soviet Union', DOD 11/24/93 News Release, *Wireless File* (United States Information Service, US Embassy: Stockholm, 2 Dec. 1993), pp. 6–9.

[188] 'Russian intern program underway this fall', *Chemical Demilitarization Update*, vol. 2, issue no. 3 (July 1993), pp. 1, 4; 'Russian interns start training at USACMDA', *Chemical Demilitarization Update*, vol. 2, no. 4 (Nov. 1993), p. 3. The programme was one of five elements of the 1992 Memorandum of Agreement between the Department of Defense and Russian Presidential Committee on Conventional Problems of Chemical and Biological Weapons.

[189] The agreement, Abkommen zwischen der Regierung der Bundesrepublik Deutschland und der Regierung der Russischen Föderation über Hifeleistung für die Russische Föderation bei der Eliminierung der von ihr zu reduzierenden nuklearen und chemischen Waffen [Agreement between the Government of the Federal Republic of Germany and the Russian Federation on Support for the Russian Federation in Their Elimination of Their Nuclear and Chemical Weapons Which They are Obliged to Reduce], was signed on 16 Dec. 1992; see also 'Lurgi entsorgt Kampfstoffe in Rußland' ['Lurgi is also destroying CW in Russia'], *Frankfurter Allgemeine Zeitung*, 28 Oct. 1993, p. 23.

ite.[190] The plant will be located in Saratov in the Gorny oblast and will cost 60 million DM.[191] Negotiations about construction of a second plant at Kambarka are under way.

After a visit to Stockholm by Kuntsevich, Sweden agreed to assist Russia by examining the risks associated with the storage and destruction of the Russian CW stockpile.[192] Other countries such as France, Italy and the Netherlands have been asked to support the Russian destruction programme or already do so.[193]

Destruction technologies and alternative technologies

In 1992 the US Congress authorized a study of alternative destruction technologies, and in June 1993 the US National Research Council (NRC) released a report prepared by the Committee on Alternative Technologies.[194] It concluded, after studying 28 different processes or technologies, that 'a number of alternative technologies exist that can supplement or replace the current controversial baseline disassembly high-temperature incineration system for destroying the US stockpile of chemical weapons'.[195] The report lists five categories of technologies and processes.[196] However, these technologies will require development and demonstration time, in some cases up to 12 years. The report will be considered by the NRC's Committee on Review & Evaluation of the Army Chemical Stockpile Disposal Programme, and recommendations on disposal will be made to the Army. The Army is bound by the 1993 Defense Authorization Act to submit a report to Congress by 31 December 1993 commenting on the NRC study.

One goal was the finding of alternative technical processes which function at temperatures below that needed for incineration. One such technique is super-critical water oxidation in which water is heated to 374°C under high pressure (221 bars) until it becomes a super-critical fluid with totally different physical and chemical properties. The highly reactive fluid is able to reduce even very large and complex organic molecules to carbon dioxide and

---

[190] 'German–Russian agreement on chemical weapons', *Atlantic News*, vol. 27, no. 2565 (27 Oct. 1993), p. 3.

[191] 'Lurgi soll chemische Kampfstoffe im Gebiet Saratow vernichten' ['Lurgi to destroy CW in the Saratow region'], *Frankfurter Allgemeine Zeitung*, 12 Nov. 1993, p. 9; 'C-Waffen-Entsorgung soll nächstes Jahr anlaufen' ['CW destruction to start next year'], *Süddeutsche Zeitung*. 12 Nov. 1993, p. 8.

[192] 'Projekt om kemvapen får miljon' ['Chemical weapon project gets a million'], *Svenska Dagbladet* (Stockholm, Sweden), 10 May 1993, p. 5.

[193] See Olson and Flakne (note 182).

[194] Committee on Alternative Chemical Demilitarization Technologies, Board on Army Science and Technology, Commission on Engineering and Technical Systems, *Alternative Technologies for the Destruction of Chemical Agents & Munitions* (National Research Council: Washington, DC, 1993).

[195] Ember, L., 'Options exist for destroying U.S. chemical arms', *Chemical & Engineering News*, vol. 71, no. 25 (21 June 1993), p. 30.

[196] The 5 groups are: (*a*) low-temperature, low-pressure, liquid-phase detoxification (converting the agent to less toxic compounds); (*b*) low-temperature, low-pressure, liquid-phase oxidation processes, including biological oxidation (agent reacts with oxygen to form carbon dioxide, water and salts, in the event of complete oxidation, or mineralization); (*c*) moderate-temperature, high-pressure oxidation; (*d*) high-temperature, low-pressure pyrolysis (heat is used to destroy molecular bonds); and (*e*) high-temperature, low-pressure oxidation.

inorganic acids and salts.[197] Research and development (R&D) on super-critical water oxidation is being conducted in several countries. In the USA the DOD is funding a General Atomics project to investigate the possibility of using this technology to destroy warfare agents and missile propellants.[198] Another alternative technique was originally used for waste treatment in the nuclear industry. It is based on an electrochemical process using nitric acid and silver and a temperature of less than 100°C.[199]

In the USA work on cryofracture destruction technology continues, and design verification tests have been completed. If the Army opts for this technology, after review by the Army Systems Acquisition Review Council, a cryofracture plant may be built at Pueblo, Colorado.[200] Cryofracture has yet to be tested on a complete munition in a totally integrated cryofracture line.

In Russia R&D continues on suitable techniques for destruction of the Russian CW stockpile. A two-stage process for the destruction of lewisite is under consideration. The first step is chemical hydrolysis, while the second step is chemical electrolysis. The process will recover arsenic with a yield of 99 per cent.[201]

VII. Old CW ammunition

In 1993 the issue of old ammunition and old chemical ammunition[202] received increased attention.[203] In January 1993 unexploded and unearthed World War I chemical motor and artillery shells were found at Spring Valley, Washington, DC, close to American University.[204] Records show that from 1917 to 1919 the US Army conducted CW research and training at the university's Ward Circle campus. By February 1993 the Army had removed 141 pieces.[205]

In October 1992 the US Army Chemical Materiel Destruction Agency was formed with two programme managers: one for Chemical Demilitarization and one for Non-Stockpile Chemical Materiel (NSCM); the latter administers the Non-Stockpile Chemical Destruction Programme. In November 1993 the Army submitted to Congress its final survey and analysis report on NSCM, as called for in the FY 1993 Defense Authorization Act. The survey indicated

---

[197] Coyle, A., 'Just add water and, look, no more toxic waste', *The Independent*, 12 Apr. 1993, p. 13; Beard, J., 'Destroying toxic wastes in a pressure cooker', *New Scientist*, vol. 131, no. 1883 (24 July 1993), p. 19; 'Pressure cooker for arms destruction', *Intelligence Newsletter*, 2 Sep. 1993, p. 2.

[198] See Beard (note 197).

[199] Brown, P., 'Dounreay patents poisons destroyer', *The Guardian*, 30 Dec. 1992, p. 8.

[200] See Statement by M. W. Owen (note 159), p. 626.

[201] Arefiev, S. V. et al., 'Preparation for disposal of bulk stored lewisite', *Journal of the Mendeleev Russian Chemical Society*, vol. 37, no. 3 (1993), pp. 37–39.

[202] Article II of the CWC defines old CW as: '(a) Chemical weapons which were produced before 1925; or (b) Chemical weapons produced in the period between 1925 and 1946 that have deteriorated to such extent that they can no longer be used as chemical weapons'.

[203] SIPRI is conducting research on the challenge of old chemical weapons and toxic armament wastes. A conference on the topic was held at the NBC Defence Research Establishment, Munster, Germany, in Oct. 1993. SIPRI Chemical & Biological Warfare Studies no. 16 will report on the project.

[204] Thomas-Lester, A. and Masters, B. A., '25 houses evacuated as WWI shells examined', *Washington Post*, 7 Jan. 1993, pp. B1, B3.

[205] Rhodes, J. and Tracy, M. F., 'Operation safe removal is an Army success', *CBIAC Newsletter*, vol. 7, no. 2 (spring 1993), pp. 1–2.

that there may be CW remains at 215 sites in 33 US states. These sites are locations where munitions have been disposed of, or where they may have been buried.[206] The costs of destroying all NSCM is estimated at $17.7 billion over the next 40 years.

Old CW were left in China by the former Japanese Army.[207] In January 1993 the Japanese Government announced just prior to the Paris CWC signing conference that a team will be sent to China to make an inventory of the abandoned weapons.[208]

There was new information in 1993 about past CW dumping at sea. In May 1993 the Japanese newspaper *Asahi Shimbun* reported that in the late 1940s the former USSR dumped approximately 30 000 tonnes of mustard gas in artillery shells and metal containers in the Sea of Japan and in the sea north of Siberia.[209] The Japanese Government requested information about the incident. It was also revealed that the Japanese Army had sunk mustard gas containers in Tokyo Bay, Beppu Bay and elsewhere after World War II.[210] In August 1993 two former officials of a Japanese Imperial Army factory stated in a Japanese broadcast that in November 1945 bombs filled with mustard gas, lewisite and hydrogen cyanide were dumped in the sea under US Army supervision some 18 kilometres south-east of Ube at a depth of 30 metres.[211]

In April 1993 the first meeting of the newly established *Ad Hoc* Working Group on Dumped Chemical Munition of the Baltic Marine Environment Protection Commission of the Helsinki Commission (HELCOM CHEMU) was held in St Petersburg.[212] The meeting discussed various aspects of the problem, including: (*a*) definition of the scope of the work of the working group; (*b*) review of the status of national reports concerning dumped CW munitions; (*c*) assessment of possible relocation of the dumped material by various means; and (*d*) preliminary conclusions concerning the assessment of the effects and hazards to the marine environment. Denmark, Latvia and Sweden presented national reports, and the other participants briefed the meeting about available and forthcoming reports. The meeting agreed on the agenda for future work.

---

[206] Program Manager for Non-stockpile Chemical Materiel, *Non-Stockpile Chemical Materiel Program: Survey and Analysis Report* (US Army Chemical Materiel Destruction Agency: Aberdeen Proving Ground, Edgewood, Md., Nov. 1993).

[207] Stock (note 3), pp. 283–84.

[208] 'Tokyo to assess chemical weapons left in PRC', in FBIS-EAS-93-006, 11 Jan. 1993, pp. 7–8.

[209] 'Soviet CW dumping', *Trust & Verify*, 1993; 'Sowjetarmee versenkte 30 000 Tonnen Giftgas' ['Soviet Army sank 30 000 tonnes of poison gas'], *Süddeutsche Zeitung*, 12 May 1993, p. 7.

[210] 'USSR, Japan allegedly dumped mustard gas at sea', in FBIS-SOV-93-091, 13 May 1993, p. 2.

[211] 'Army dumped poison gas bombs in inland sea in 1945', in FBIS-EAS-93-162, 24 Aug. 1993, pp. 5–6.

[212] Baltic Marine Environment Protection Commission, Helsinki Commission, *Ad Hoc* Working Group on Dumped Chemical Munition (HELCOM CHEMU), Report of the 1st Meeting, St Petersburg, Russia, 19–21 Apr. 1993, HELCOM CHEMU 1/8. The meeting was attended by delegations from Denmark, Finland, Germany, Lithuania, Poland, Russia and Sweden and by observers from Latvia, Norway, the UK and the USA as well as from the Coalition Clean Baltic (CCB) and Greenpeace International.

In May 1993 Germany presented a national report on a survey of dumped CW munitions in the south and west Baltic Sea.[213] The report stated that of the approximately 300 000 tonnes of chemical ammunition produced by Germany in the period prior to 1945, 42 000–65 000 tonnes were dumped in the Baltic Sea prior to 1948. The report also addressed the potential danger of various chemical warfare agents to the marine environment and their probable long-term behaviour. Recommendations were made with respect to future action, and more detailed investigations were recommended.

In September 1993 the second HELCOM CHEMU meeting took place in Vilnius with the addition of a delegation from Estonia.[214] Russia submitted a national report for the first time, but it contained information on dumping only until 1947.[215] The meeting requested that Russia provide further information on dumping activities after 1947 as soon as possible. Poland also presented its national report.[216] The UK and the USA, present as observers, gave detailed information about the dumping of captured German CW munitions and stated that the UK and the USA did not dump munitions in the Baltic Sea after World War II.[217] On the basis of national reports it was determined that approximately 40 000 tonnes of CW munitions, containing about 12 000 tonnes of agents, had been dumped in the Baltic Sea prior to 1948. It was noted that neither mustard gas nor other chemical warfare agents have ever been detected in edible fish or their food in the Baltic Sea. In January 1994 Denmark hosted a HELCOM CHEMU meeting, and proposals for further studies, conclusions and recommendations for further action were submitted to a March 1994 ministerial meeting of the Helsinki Commission.

VIII. New developments in chemical detection techniques

In January 1993 the US GAO released a review of the DOD's programme to design, develop and field CW and BW agent detection equipment, especially taking into consideration the detection capability which was available during Operation Desert Storm in 1991.[218] It noted that Coalition forces were able to detect all known Iraqi CW agents but had limited ability to detect BW agents.

---

[213] *ChemischeKampfstoffmunition in der südlichen und westlichen Ostsee: Bestandsaufnahme, Bewertung und Empfehlung*, Bericht der Bund/Länder-Arbeitsgruppe Chemische Kampfstoffe in der Ostsee [*Chemical Munitions in the Southern and Western Baltic Sea: Compilation, Assessment and Recommendations*] (Federal Maritime and Hydrographic Agency: Hamburg, 1993).

[214] Baltic Marine Environment Protection Commission, Helsinki Commission, *Ad Hoc* Working Group on Dumped Chemical Munition (HELCOM CHEMU), Report of the 2nd Meeting, Vilnius, Lithuania, 28–30 Oct. 1993, HELCOM CHEMU 2/8; Helsinki Commission, *Press Release*, Vilnius, 30 Sep. 1993.

[215] Russia, 'Complex analysis of the hazard related to the captured German chemical weapon dumped in the Baltic Sea', HELCOM CHEMU 2/2/1/Rev.1, 27 Sep. 1993.

[216] Poland, 'National report on war gases and ammunition dumped in the Polish economic zone of the Baltic Sea', HELCOM CHEMU 2/2/4, 17 Sep. 1993.

[217] USA, 'Study of the sea disposal of chemical munitions', HELCOM CHEMU 2/2, 8 Sep. 1993; UK, 'Report on sea dumping of chemical weapons by the United Kingdom in the Skagerrak waters post World War II' HELCOM CHEMU 2/2/5, 28 Sep. 1993.

[218] US General Accounting Office, *Chemical and Biological Defense: US Forces are not Adequately Equipped to Detect All Threats*, Report to the Chairman, Committee on Governmental Affairs, US Senate, GAO/NSIAD-93-2, Jan. 1993.

The US Army has traditionally focused on developing technologies to detect CW rather than BW agents. After Desert Storm the Army accelerated its efforts to develop BW agent detectors.

In 1993 experts were still trying to draw lessons from Desert Storm for future nuclear, biological and chemical (NBC) defence and detection.[219] A need was perceived to have a central unit in the armed forces to oversee all CW and BW questions. Detection equipment must be designed which is more flexible and which takes into account various environmental and climatic combat conditions. The wearing of personal NBC protective equipment has a major impact on combat efficiency; awareness of this must be reflected in troop training.[220]

The entry into force of the CWC might affect R&D on detection instrumentation as they are required for the CWC verification system. A November 1993 International Workshop on Doctrine and Instruments for Detection and Monitoring of Chemical Warfare Agents focused *inter alia* on future requirements for detecting and monitoring CW agents.[221]

IX. Conclusions

The large number of states which signed the CWC in 1993 demonstrated a will to prepare for its entry into force. However, some negative trends in CW armament and proliferation continued in 1993. The alleged attempt by Libya to construct a second CW production plant caused great concern, especially claims that several countries had aided Libya. Such assistance could be seen as a violation of the UN weapons embargo against Libya.

Growing political tension in the former Soviet republics, combined with market shortages, recession in industrialized countries and continuing proliferation, raised new questions about the efficiency of export control policies. Existing and well-functioning export controls, such as those of the Australia Group, must be reconsidered in light of the demands by some countries that they be abolished under the CWC. The dissolution of COCOM was not unexpected, but a common export control policy which includes the new republics on the territory of the former Soviet Union has yet to emerge.

Application of international procedures to verify allegations of use remains difficult, a situation which will improve under the CWC. In 1993 there was intense debate about allegations that Iraq had used CW against the Marsh Arabs in southern Iraq, which could not be confirmed by UNSCOM. Allegations of CW use in the former Yugoslavia multiplied but were not confirmed. New evidence surfaced in 1993 about an alleged CW programme in the former Yugoslavia.

---

[219] Otter, T., 'Chemical warfare defence: putting the lessons of the Gulf War in context', *Military Technology*, , vol. 16, no. 12 (1992), pp. 44–52; Fowler, W., 'Defence against the NBC threat', *Defence*, vol. 24, no. 4 (Apr. 1993), pp. 13–17.

[220] See *Statement by Dr B. Richardson* (note 4), p. 613.

[221] Approximately 70 experts from 15 nations participated in the workshop, which was hosted by Sweden. See Garrett, B, 'The IDM workshop', *ASA Newsletter*, 93-6, no. 39 (9 Dec. 1993), p. 3.

There was no change in the number of countries alleged to have or alleged to be attempting to acquire a CW capability or arsenal. Suspicions about possible North Korean CW and BW programmes were fuelled to some extent by its suspected activities as regards nuclear weapons.

In 1993 it was estimated that destruction of the US CW stockpile will be completed by 2004 at a total cost of over $8.6 billion. The JACADS facility finished its operation verification tests and proved that incineration technology can destroy CW with a relative degree of efficiency and in an environmentally safe manner. An NRC report on alternative technologies evaluated 28 destruction technologies. However, many of these alternatives will require years of development and testing. The US Army must soon complete its review of possible alternative destruction methods; a final decision on the methods to be used in the future is expected in 1994.

Russia continues to face the challenge of completing its draft CW destruction programme. Protests from communities where destruction is planned to take place and major financial difficulties seem likely to delay the process. International financial and technical support has increased, but more is needed.

The number of states experiencing problems with old and abandoned CW is increasing. Their removal and destruction will be very expensive. Increased public attention was given to past dumping of CW at sea, particularly that which occurred in the Baltic Sea. National and international surveys attempted to quantify what was dumped.

The Persian Gulf War experience and the continuing evaluation of protection against CW and BW have led to re-evaluation of training, detection, and command and control options. The design of hardware, such as protective masks and suits, will be affected by these new findings. Greater emphasis is likely to be given to BW protection and to early warning.

In 1993 questions were raised in the USA about whether health problems suffered by veterans of the Gulf War could be linked to the possible release of CW agents during the war. Early reports of illness were consistently denied by the US Government. To some extent, the political response is reminiscent of the Agent Orange debate.

Further allegations of proliferation or of CW use could have a negative impact on the future chemical disarmament environment, or they could strengthen the will to do everything possible so that the CWC can enter into force in 1995.

10. Military technology: the case of India

ERIC ARNETT

I. Introduction

The Indian military technology base crossed new thresholds in 1993, as the first indigenously designed tanks and battlefield-support missiles were delivered to the armed services for field trials. At the same time, however, a closer examination of these and other projects suggests that Indian research and development (R&D) is not progressing as rapidly or as far as its leaders had hoped and observers had predicted. The obstacles preventing India from developing a more advanced military technology base are primarily technical and economic, stemming from chronic problems with project management rather than any lack of scientific resources.[1] This conclusion is especially important, because 1993 marked a decade since the management reforms in the Defence R&D Organization (DRDO) under the Indira Gandhi Administration were promulgated.

Indian military R&D programmes have arrived at some immediate goals, but have not created the anticipated technological momentum that would allow them to move from limited import substitution to indigenous innovation. Consequently, reports to the effect that sophisticated conventional or nuclear weapons are easily or inevitably within the grasp of India or other countries that do not share India's scientific resources should be viewed with scepticism. India's strategic space, long-range strike and power-projection programmes show every sign of having been frozen or set back. This chapter concludes that the talents of Indian scientists and engineers would be best applied by strengthening their demonstrated abilities in component design and building on this expertise with limited foreign partnerships in design and production of selected major systems with an emphasis on identifying and exploiting competitive niches. Such an approach, which is increasingly popular elsewhere, would pay greater dividends if the resources devoted to indigenous design of complete major systems were released.

This analysis of Indian military R&D examines the DRDO's three biggest projects, the Prithvi missile, the Arjun tank and the Light Combat Aircraft (LCA), in the context of India's effort to become self-reliant in design and

---

[1] This chapter considers only Indian R&D, but it should be remembered that production, maintenance, doctrine and operation of advanced technologies also present important challenges to any state's military. These and related questions are being examined more completely in the cases of China, Iran and Pakistan as well as India in the SIPRI study on military technology in the context of national goals and development. For a similar analysis of US military R&D, see Arnett, E. H. and Kokoski, R., 'Military technology and international security: the case of the USA', SIPRI, *SIPRI Yearbook 1993: World Armaments and Disarmament* (Oxford University Press: Oxford, 1993), p. 308.

production of defence technology (section II). Self-reliance is important not only because it has been a guiding principle of Indian military R&D, but also because the ability of states to overcome technological obstacles in developing military technology bases has been a contentious issue among researchers and policy makers interested in proliferation. Developments in these three programmes are then used to evaluate competing hypotheses regarding obstacles to proliferation (section III), and to assess the prospects for India's longer-term projects of a more strategic nature: the space programme and research on intermediate-range ballistic missiles, aircraft-carriers and nuclear submarines (section IV).

II. The DRDO and India's quest for self-sufficiency

India has the largest, oldest and most diverse modern military industry in the developing world.[2] Its scientific establishment is not only the largest in the developing world, but is also larger than those of most industrialized countries.[3] By the mid-1980s, India's military industry seemed to be learning some lessons from the failures of its first designs, and observers expected it to continue smoothly up the learning curve to the point at which advanced designs would be produced by the mid-1990s.[4] Yet, despite an energetic drive for technological independence, India imports major systems in greater volume than any other country, developing or industrialized.[5] It is probably the largest importer of components as well, despite having an overall military budget less than one-fifth the size of those of France, Germany or the United Kingdom.

Indian leaders and technology managers distinguish between self-*sufficiency*, which they have come to define as autarky and see as unattainable,[6] and self-*reliance*, which implies more modest goals. From the military planner's perspective, the two most important aspects of self-reliance have been hedging against any disruption in the supply of spare parts caused by changes in the international political system,[7] and fielding systems that are

[2] This includes capacity built by the British beginning in 1872 and inherited at independence. Additional capacity was added beginning in 1962 in response to the war with China. Anthony, I., 'The "third tier" countries', ed. H. Wulf, SIPRI, *Arms Industry Limited* (Oxford University Press: Oxford, 1993), p. 368; Balachandran, G., 'Development directions', *Strategic Digest*, Jan. 1984, p. 17; Smith, C., SIPRI, *India's Ad Hoc Arsenal: Direction or Drift in Defence Policy?* (Oxford University Press: Oxford, 1994), pp. 146–47.

[3] Chellaney, B., *Technology and Security: Implications of the Expanding Web of Technology Controls* (Centre for Policy Research: New Delhi, 1993), p. 24. Uncertainties about China's military industry and scientific base make direct comparison with it difficult.

[4] Graham, T. W., 'India', ed. J. E. Katz, *Arms Production in Developing Countries* (Lexington Books: Lexington, Mass., 1984), p. 172.

[5] Volume of arms imports is measured by SIPRI's value data. See chapter 13 in this volume.

[6] As recently as 1988, however, some Indians still held out this goal. Anthony, I., *The Arms Trade and Medium Powers: Case Studies of India and Pakistan 1947–1990* (Harvester Wheatsheaf: Hemel Hempstead, 1992), p. 118.

[7] Guarding against disruption can mean producing parts domestically or receiving them reliably from foreign suppliers. The second approach can be pursued through a close relationship with one supplier (although there is still some risk that the relationship will sour) or, preferably for an outspokenly non-aligned state like India, cordial relationships with several suppliers so that the loss of any one would not

appropriate for the special conditions of the sub-continent, especially the high altitudes of the Himalayan mountains, the heat and dust of the Rajasthan desert and the high ambient temperature of the Indian Ocean. Indian military and industrial leaders have sought the state of the art, not only to ensure technological advantage, but also to demonstrate that India's capabilities compare favourably with those of industrialized countries. Local production from indigenous designs is also intended to help the balance of payments[8] and provide employment for those with scientific and technical skills who might otherwise seek opportunities abroad.[9]

The sceptical observer might question whether these attributes, taken together, constitute a workable definition of self-reliance that can be operationalized to clarify policy choices, or simply a rubric under which continued investments in big military science projects can be justified politically. Nevertheless, they offer standards by which India's major programmes can be measured, as is done for the Prithvi, the Arjun and the LCA in this section. This focus on self-reliance not only allows an evaluation of Indian military R&D on its own terms, it also illuminates a contentious issue in the scholarly discussion of military technology and non-proliferation: whether there remain technological barriers to proliferation.

The DRDO

Most Indian military research and development is undertaken by the DRDO through its 47 laboratories and establishments. In addition, each of eight state-owned production firms operates its own R&D programme, much as Western defence firms do. Of a projected Rs 192 billion ($6.2 billion)[10] defence budget for 1993–94, Rs 9.52 billion ($310 million or 5 per cent) are earmarked for the DRDO[11] and Rs 4.70 billion ($150 million) for the Defence Ordnance Fac-

be catastrophic (although the probability of at least one individual relationship souring increases, as does the burden of supporting several different examples of the same technology). Thomas, R. G. C., 'Strategies of recipient autonomy: the case of India', eds Kwang-Il Baek, R. D. McLaurin and Chung-in Moon, *The Dilemma of Third World Defense Industries: Supplier Control or Recipient Autonomy?* (Westview Press: Boulder, Colo., 1989), pp. 186–87, 195–200.

[8] India has long produced major weapon systems under licence, including propeller-driven and jet aircraft, warships, tanks, artillery and radar.

[9] This last motivation is often reiterated by Indian managers, but local employment of technical labour can only be considered a benefit to society if the products are of value in their own right, a judgement that must be made on other grounds. The controversial argument that military R&D and production can contribute to national economic development does not appear to be as popular in India at present as it has been at times elsewhere. Balachandran (note 2), p. 34.

[10] Actual outlays came to Rs 215 b. ($6.9 b.). The defence budget declined in real terms from Rs 168 b ($8.1 b.) in 1991 to Rs 180 b. ($6.8 b.) in 1992; military expenditure fell from Rs 154 b. ($9.6 b.) in 1990 to Rs 165 b. ($9.0 b.) in 1991. Indian military expenditure is roughly 3% of GDP and has been declining since its historical peak, $9.8 b., in 1987. SIPRI, *SIPRI Yearbook 1992: World Armaments and Disarmament* (Oxford University Press: Oxford, 1992), appendix 7A, pp. 255, 260. Figures are in current rupees, and 1988 dollars.

[11] Ministry of Defence, *Annual Report 1992–93* (Government of India Photolitho Press: Faridabad, 1993), p. 13. This represents a real increase of 21% from the 1992–93 R&D budget of Rs 7.21 b. ($250 m.) and 3.7% from the 1991–92 budget of Rs 6.82 b. ($300 m.). Figures are in current rupees and

tories, of which Rs 28.4 million ($920 000) were for R&D.[12] This section reviews the R&D activities of the DRDO in 1993.[13]

The year 1993 was the first full one in office for the DRDO's new Director General, A. P. J. Abdul Kalam, previously Director of the Defence R&D Laboratory (DRDL) and of the Integrated Guided Missile Development Programme (IGMDP). The DRDO employs about 25 000 people (about 6000 scientists and engineers and 10 000 technicians) and supports research at several universities.

Since its creation in 1958, the DRDO has produced a broad range of weapon systems, components, munitions and supplies for domestic production, including everything from warships to firearms. In 1983, then Director General V. S. Arunachalam[14] took advantage of the government's willingness to increase the DRDO budget in order to mobilize more resources in support of three major projects: the IGMDP, the Arjun tank and the LCA.[15] These three projects were intended not only to promulgate more effective management practices and overcome India's problems with indigenously designed major weapon systems, but also to go beyond the previous emphasis on import substitution to develop an innovative military industry that could compete on the international market.

The Prithvi missile

Of the DRDO's two major accomplishments in 1993, the delivery of the first Prithvi (Earth) battlefield support missiles to the Army[16] as its five-year development testing programme was completed, marks the greater achievement from the perspective of self-reliance. The Prithvi is the first of four missiles designed without foreign assistance under the IGMDP to be delivered to the armed forces.[17] The culmination of a two-decade R&D effort,[18] the Prithvi missile comes in three variants, depending on the trade-off between range and

1993 dollars. For comparison, patterns in military R&D spending in the industrialized countries were summarized in Arnett and Kokoski (note 1), p. 308. See also chapter 13 in this volume.

[12] Government of India, *Defence Services Estimates 1993–94* (Government of India Press: New Delhi, 1993), pp. 5, 6, 82.

[13] In the 1994/95 budget, the DRDO budget has remained constant while the defence budget as a whole increased by 7% to Rs 215 b. ($7.4 b.). Bedi, R., 'India stems the fall in its defence spending', *Jane's Defence Weekly*, 12 Mar. 1994, p. 3.

[14] Arunachalam, Director General of the DRDO for more than 10 years, began a two-year leave on 10 July 1992 and took up residence at Carnegie Mellon University. Whether he will return to the DRDO is uncertain. Kalam is expected to retire before Arunachalam's leave ends in July 1994.

[15] The import substitution effort was also reinvigorated, and the 1980s saw the development of new electronic warfare systems (Ajantha), radars (the Indra series), sonars (Apsoh) and target drones (PTA, or Pilotless Target Aircraft), as well as a new radio network (AREN).

[16] Some reports claim an initial delivery of missiles in May 1993 to a depot on the Pakistani border not far from Lahore. *Hindustan Times*, 22 May 1993 (cited in Pande, S., 'MTCR and the Third World: impact assessment', *Strategic Analysis*, Oct. 1993, p. 845). The Prithvi will become operational in June 1994; see Joshi, M., 'Missile program on hold', *Asia–Pacific Defence Reporter*, Apr.–May 1994, p. 20.

[17] Three other missiles are expected to reach production within a year or two: the Nag (Snake) top-attack anti-tank missile, and the Trishul (Trident) and Akash (Sky) air-defence missiles.

[18] Although the IGMDP began in 1983, Indian scientists had been working on short-range missiles for a decade by then, reverse engineering a liquid-fuel rocket motor from a Soviet anti-aircraft missile. This motor was adapted for the Prithvi.

payload: the first can carry 500 kg over a distance of 250 km; the second, 1000 kg over 150 km; and the third, 250 kg over 350 km. Software permits target updating and in-flight manœuvring to avoid defences. The Prithvi's unitary and cluster payloads can be changed in the field.

Its role can be expected to be similar to that of the US Army Tactical Missile System (ATACMS),[19] but it is somewhat less flexible, being limited in particular by the decision to use liquid fuel and the Indian Army's limited battlefield surveillance capabilities at the missile's full range.[20] Strictly speaking, the Prithvi system should include an integrated surveillance and mission planning support capability and is incomplete without one.[21] Although the Army has accepted the first delivery of the Prithvi and is beginning field testing, it is reportedly reluctant to buy more in quantity, given a procurement budget that has fallen by 17 per cent in three years.[22] Bharat Dynamics, the government-owned manufacturer, expects to produce 40–50 missiles per year at a cost of Rs 16 million ($520 000) apiece.

The first delivery of the Prithvi demonstrates a level of technological competence not previously evident but leaves several questions unanswered. Because it uses some foreign components and alloys,[23] the Prithvi does not meet the first requirement of self-reliance (as outlined above), at least during initial production. Even if the simplicity of the Prithvi missile's design makes its indigenization possible, other programmes will not necessarily progress as smoothly if more complex technologies are involved. While its role may be similar to that of the ATACMS, the Prithvi missile is more closely comparable to the Soviet Scud-B or the German V-2.

The Arjun tank

Any judgement about the DRDO's second major accomplishment of 1993, the delivery of 6 Arjun (Archer) tanks to the Army for trials, must be more equi-

[19] Use of the 150-km range ATACMS in the Persian Gulf War is discussed in US Department of Defense, *Conduct of the Persian Gulf War* (Department of Defense: Washington, DC, 1992), Appendix T: Performance of Selected Weapons Systems, p. T-149.

[20] Sidhu, W. P. S., 'Prithvi missile—tactical gap: Army has yet to find a role for the weapon', *India Today*, 15 Sep. 1992, pp. 84–85.

[21] The complete system into which a missile fits is both much more complex and expensive than the missile itself, and much more difficult to assess. An especially useful discussion in the context of the US Tomahawk cruise missile is Standoff Weapons Panel, Offense-Defense Working Group, *Extended-Range Conventional Weapon Systems*, an appendix to the *Discriminate Deterrence* report (US Department of Defense: Washington, DC, 1988).

[22] Gupta, S., Sidhu, W. P. S. and Sandhu, K., 'A middle-aged military machine', *India Today*, 30 Apr. 1993, p. 76. The Indian Air Force, which is responsible for close air support and interdiction, has also expressed an interest in the Prithvi.

[23] Banerji, I., 'The Integrated Guided Missile Development Program', *Indian Defence Review*, July 1990, p. 101. Officials give the 'foreign content' of the first Prithvis as 15% or 20%, but express the hope that the figure will drop to 5% over time. Such estimates are a staple of DRDO publicity, but are not really meaningful in the context of self-reliance unless their vulnerability to disruption is stipulated, nor is the methodology by which they are derived transparent. Self-reliance could allow 100% foreign content if there were reasonable assurances of supply, but cannot allow even 1% foreign supply of vital components that are liable to be cut off. Foreign content has been calculated as the fraction of cost or value, or the fraction of weight, number of parts or (in the case of the advanced light helicopter) skin area. Often it is not explained at all.

vocal. Sanctioned by the government in 1974, the Arjun programme was originally to have produced a prototype in 1980 for deployment in 1985. The two prototypes field-tested in March 1993 were found to be acceptable, but concerns about the integration of the imported fire-control system remain. The main gun, an indigenous design, is of the older, rifled type, rather than the smooth bore that is the current standard elsewhere.[24] The domestically developed Kanchan composite armour is so heavy that the tank cannot use many of India's tank transporters and assault bridges.[25] The Arjun is also much wider than required in order to accommodate its troublesome domestically designed suspension, limiting its flexibility on the narrow bridges and mountain passes characteristic of India's contested northern regions.[26]

Changes in service requirements have touched off a vicious cycle of programme delays.[27] Early delays postponed full-scale production until the end of the decade, and led the Indian Army to plan the upgrade of 1100 older Vijayanta tanks of British design.[28] A separate decision to transfer Rs 2 billion ($60 million) from the Arjun programme may set back full-scale production another decade, until 2008,[29] necessitating additional interim measures. Israel has approached the Indian Army, offering to upgrade India's T-72M1 tanks, which are being produced under licence from Russia at the rate of 65 tanks per year. Russia, in turn, has offered the army its T-72S and T-80U tanks.[30]

From the perspective of self-reliance, the Arjun programme has yet to show the promise hoped for. Although the DRDO estimates that 55 per cent of the tank is Indian-made (75 per cent if it enters production with an Indian engine and fire-control system),[31] several military sources put the portion lower: 'Nearly 50 percent of the "indigenous" Arjun tank components are from Germany alone, involving massive foreign exchange.'[32] The design is both vulnerable to disruption and not especially sensitive to India's special requirements. In addition to the Arjun's problems with weight and width, its German

---

[24] Shankar Jha, P., 'A scam worse than Bofors?', *The Hindu*, 10 Aug. 1993. The DRDO asserts that the gun of older design is more appropriate for attacking bunkers, despite its weaknesses as an anti-tank weapon. Among other manufacturers, only the UK still designs tanks around a 120-mm rifled cannon.

[25] 'Arjun tank in serious trouble', *World Weapons Review*, 12 Aug. 1992, p. 1.

[26] See note 25.

[27] Sengupta, P., 'Indian armoured doctrine and modernisation', *Military Technology*, May 1992, p. 35.

[28] Bedi, R., 'Arjun delays bring Vijayanta upgrade back on track', *Jane's Defence Weekly*, 3 July 1993, p. 19.

[29] Raghuvanshi, V., 'Upgrade may stall new Indian tank production', *Defense News*, 13–17 Sep. 1993, p. 1.

[30] Bedi (note 28), p. 19.

[31] Ministry of Defence estimates provided by G. Balachandran, personal correspondence, 1 Mar. 1994, p. 6. The Arjun was originally to be equipped with both, but the engine design in particular has been troubled.

[32] Sawhney, P., 'Limited production of Arjun tank on the cards', *Indian Express*, 25 Feb. 1993. Service estimates of the Arjun's domestic content have been consistently lower than those of the DRDO, although the discrepancy can probably be traced to different methods of calculating foreign content rather than misrepresentation. Another source estimates 55% of the Arjun's unit cost will be foreign exchange. Smith (note 2), p. 150.

engine overheats in desert conditions.[33] None the less, some of the Arjun's domestically designed components demonstrate India's ability to apply its technical talents on subsystems and save foreign-exchange funds. In hopes of a further improvement in the balance of payments, the DRDO has entered the Arjun in the crowded international tank market, displaying it at military exhibitions with an asking unit price of Rs 70 million ($2 million).[34] This compares with $4 million for Western tanks and $0.25–2.5 million for the Chinese and Russian tanks with which the Arjun is roughly comparable.

The LCA

The LCA programme continued to stumble along in 1993, highlighting a number of difficulties with domestic design. Begun in 1983, the LCA was originally intended to replace the licence-built Ajeet and MiG-21 fighters by 1991, but the prototype is still incomplete. Rs 20 billion ($600 million) have been spent thus far,[35] the eventual total development cost is expected to be at least Rs 50 billion ($2 billion),[36] and the first flight is not expected before 1996. At present, DRDO spokesmen still express the hope that the LCA will begin production by 1995 and enter service in 2001, but industry observers suggest 2005 is a more likely date for initial production.[37] As a result, the Air Force has increased its order for MiG-29 aircraft and will overhaul its MiG-21 fleet, a decision that may leave little capital or need to procure the LCA later. These considerations and the effects of delays on the design's competitiveness were such that a 1990 commission chaired by the former chief designer recommended that the programme be halted after the prototypes were completed.[38]

Even as the LCA struggles with the problems of domestic design, it remains heavily dependent on imported technology without addressing specifically Indian requirements. At present, 70 per cent of the LCA's components are to be imported, in part because indigenous components of domestic design—

---

[33] This problem is the result of the Indian project managers' engine specifications and the tank's weight, rather than any shortcoming or insensitivity of the German technology. Abu Dhabi will re-engine its French LeClerc tanks with a more powerful German engine from the same manufacturer.

[34] 'Indigenous tank launched', *Asian Recorder*, 19–25 Mar. 1993, p. 22997. The export market has often been an express goal of Indian programmes, and indigenous production is seen as a way of avoiding end-user restrictions on foreign components that would have to be re-exported. For the period 1989–93, India was not among the top 15 exporters of major systems. See chapter 13 of this volume. India's only exports in 1992 declared to the UN Arms Register consisted of 4 armoured vehicles (2 British, 2 Soviet) transferred to the Maldives.

[35] Gupta, Sidhu and Sandhu (note 22), p. 76.

[36] 'India', *Milavnews*, vol. 30, no. 632 (Dec. 1991).

[37] 'Indian LCA may be ready by 2005', *The Telegraph*, 23 Feb. 1993; 'India', *Asia–Pacific Defence Reporter*, Feb.–Mar. 1992, p. 30; and *Milavnews* (note 36). Wing design will not be complete until 1995, according to the programme director, so production would have to be concurrent with design (a practice that has fallen from favour elsewhere). 'A project with promise', *The Hindu*, 28 Jan. 1993. Fly-by-wire software has proved difficult for most producers to debug adequately before flight testing, as demonstrated by the crashes of the US F-22 prototype and the first two examples of the Swedish JAS-39, as well as the delayed first flight of the European Fighter Aircraft.

[38] 'India's LCA project severely reduced', *Defense and Foreign Affairs Weekly*, 3–9 June 1990, p. 1.

most notably the engine—have not made it off the test stand.[39] Electronics will be supplied by Martin Marietta (USA), Ericsson (Sweden), Dassault (France) and Allied Signal (USA), engines by General Electric (USA), and composite parts by Northrop (USA) and British Aerospace (UK),[40] making construction dependent on the good will of at least four foreign governments. Even so, the DRDO expects the LCA to save both general expenditure and foreign exchange. Unit costs are expected to be in the range of $17–22 million.[41]

III. Implications for the Indian military technology base

A recent SIPRI study concludes that India's 'chances of developing and sustaining an arms industry are receding further into the distance for economic and technological reasons.'[42] A prominent observer of Indian military affairs has drawn the opposite conclusion: 'New Delhi's sheer military and technical capabilities are growing at a rate that would make a decision to increase arms technically easy and economically manageable. The barriers to a fully-fledged Indian programme . . . are political, not technical or economic.'[43] Other observers have gone further to argue that technology does not present a significant barrier to proliferation.[44] In his 'counter-proliferation speech', then US Defense Secretary Les Aspin told the US National Academy of Sciences that developing countries 'no longer have to import all the sophisticated technology they need. They are "growing" it at home. The growth of indigenous technology can completely change the nonproliferation equation.'[45] Aspin's successor, William J. Perry, agrees that 'technological developments are widely dispersed and that there are no effective means of controlling them.'[46] Indian observers would like to think this is true. G. Balachandran, a journalist with contacts in the Defence Ministry has written, 'Nations will be able to

---

[39] *Milavnews* (note 36).

[40] 'Force modernisation in the Asia-Pacific', *Asian Defence Journal*, Apr. 1991, p. 7; 'US flight control for India's LCA', *Jane's Defence Weekly*, 4 Dec. 1993, p. 14.

[41] Raghuvanshi, V., 'India reverses, seeks Light Combat Aircraft partner abroad', *Defense News*, 10–16 Jan. 1994, p. 4. The lower figure can only be achieved with a foreign partnership.

[42] Anthony, I., 'The "third tier" countries', ed. Wulf (note 2), p. 362.

[43] Cohen, S. P., 'The regional impact of a reforming India', *Asia's International Role in the Post-Cold War Era*, IISS Adelphi Paper 276 (Brassey's: London, 1993), pp. 87–88. The political barrier Cohen identifies is 'access to advanced technology'. In recent correspondence (Mar. 1994), Cohen recently returned from a year's sabbatical in the Ford Foundation's New Delhi office) revised his assessment: '[The SIPRI study is] probably more right than I was when I wrote so positively. A year in India changed my mind.'

[44] See, for example, Nolan, J. E., *Trappings of Power: Ballistic Missiles in the Third World* (Brookings Institution: Washington, DC, 1991) and discussion of her conclusion that US military supremacy is at risk as a result in Arnett and Kokoski (note 1), p. 309.

[45] Aspin, L., Remarks to the NAS Committee on International Security and Arms Control, Dec. 1993. Aspin had previously identified the states of concern to the USA as Iran, Iraq and North Korea, all of which have fewer scientific resources than India.

[46] 'Sensitive exports: an era of "decontrol"', *Intelligence Newsletter*, 11 Nov. 1993, pp. 1, 6. Perry made this argument in the context of the Clinton Administration's preference to lift 98% of existing export controls.

embark on strategic programmes on their own with little assistance from western firms for supply of critical items.'[47]

Developments in 1993 tended to confirm the first conclusion, that India has yet to solve a number of problems in developing its military technology base.[48] Are the obstacles preventing India from developing a more advanced military technology base more properly ascribed to technical and economic reasons, or to other reasons? The answers to these questions have implications for India's long-term strategic programmes to develop systems able to reach beyond southern Asia and the Indian Ocean, which are discussed in section IV.

To recapitulate the weaknesses identified in the Prithvi, Arjun and LCA programmes from the point of view of self-reliance, none of these systems can be built by India alone, the primary goal of the self-reliance campaign (and a major issue in the scholarly debate over proliferation). In fact, the difficulty of assessing vulnerability to foreign suppliers and the necessity of teaming up with more experienced firms suggest that India's attention should be redirected away from eliminating foreign content, in favour of adding value in niches where Indian science and engineering are strong, for example, electronics and software.[49] This has been more true than ever since procurement budgets have been shrinking almost everywhere and the performance of US technology was demonstrated in the war against Iraq, damping both domestic and international demand for less advanced designs.

The second major goal of the self-reliance campaign has been producing systems that can function effectively in especially harsh areas of the subcontinent. The pattern of Indian procurement shows that this goal can be met with imports, licensed production and indigenous designs developed in close co-operation with foreign partners using imported components and materials when necessary. In fact, relatively few requirements involve special designs, judging from the performance of imported systems in past Indian wars. Further, special requirements have made indigenous designs unnecessarily complicated in cases where they have been changed during the R&D process, and may not be met in any case, as is the case with the Arjun.

Indigenous designs have not given India a technological advantage over Pakistan, which until recently received complete systems, spare components and training from the USA. India continues to rely on its strategic depth and sheer numbers for successful defence on its western border. India's local conventional advantage over China can be ascribed to receiving Russian systems

---

[47] Balachandran, G., 'Technology futures: how the cookie crumbles', *Economic Times*, 21 May 1992.

[48] This discussion addresses only military R&D and the technology base, not production, maintenance and operation, which can be expected to present additional obstacles for India.

[49] A full assessment of any major weapon system can only be complete with access to information about its electronics suite, which now consumes more than half the expense of most Western offerings. While India's non-military electronics industry is one of its most promising, the global trend has been towards diverging innovation paths for military and civilian electronics. Friedman, N., 'Smart weapons, smart platforms: The new economics of defense', ed. E. H. Arnett, *Science and International Security: New Perspectives for a Changing World Order* (American Association for the Advancement of Science [AAAS hereafter]: Washington, DC, 1991).

before China does (an advantage that it is losing as China's ability to pay in hard currency increases and India's decreases) and China's preference for focusing its military attention elsewhere, while an advantage over the smaller states of the Indian Ocean can be taken as a given by Indian planners.

Indigenous designs were also intended to foster India's international prestige, save on foreign exchange and slow the exodus of science and technology graduates. The failure of the New Delhi 'Group of 15' summit meeting in April 1994 indicates that India's prestige is lower than it once was among developing countries.[50] Savings on foreign exchange have not yet been realized. Science and technology graduates continue to leave the country, and the problems with DRDO programmes suggest that those who remain are not able to apply their talents as productively as might be wished.

Technological and economic obstacles

If the Prithvi, Arjun and LCA share a common problem, it is that of systems integration. Indian scientists and engineers have demonstrated that they can conduct high-quality theoretical research, develop modern components and produce working prototypes of simple systems. Yet when it comes to making a large number of components work together in concert, the record of Indian applied science, engineering and project management is less impressive. Clearly scientific expertise alone cannot ensure smooth progress in the stages before production, since the DRDO has had so much trouble producing working prototypes in every recent major R&D programme. This mixed record can best be explained by phenomena that are most appropriately termed technological obstacles, defined to include not only access to expertise, which India obviously has, but also the ability to apply that expertise through project management to produce a working model.

Changing requirements

The first requirement of effective project management for systems integration is to establish firmly fixed design requirements that component designers can work to. In the case of the DRDO, design requirements have not remained fixed, and changes have imposed a burden on engineers and project managers. Difficult relations between the DRDO and the services hamper the setting of requirements and keeping them in place.[51] While the DRDO sees changing service requirements undoing its design work, the services complain that the DRDO is insufficiently responsive to their requirements.[52] In fact, the root of this conflict is perhaps the most important aspect of the culture of the Indian military technology base: indigenous military R&D may boost the prestige of

[50] Burns, J. F., 'Delhi summit vies with G-7 in cost and empty pomposity', *International Herald Tribune*, 1 Apr. 1994, p. 15.
[51] Sengupta (note 27), p. 35.
[52] Balachandran (note 2), p. 16, 36.

the DRDO and arguably the country, but indigenously designed major weapon systems are seen as low-status goods by the armed services, who would rather have the highest technology available. Imports usually involve side payments to procurement personnel, an additional incentive to those making crucial decisions. As a result, the services have an incentive not only to change requirements in order to justify foreign purchases, but also actively to sabotage indigenous projects.[53]

Resources and decision making

A second requirement of effective project management is that adequate resources be provided and choices made between competing projects or approaches if resources are limited. As then Director General of the DRDO, V. S. Arunachalam, acknowledged: 'It is funding and decision-making that are delaying the [LCA] programme. . . . The maturing of technology takes years. You need staying power.'[54] The failure of earlier Indian efforts to design major weapon systems stemmed in part from a technology base that was spread too thinly, a consideration that led to the expansion of the DRDO in 1983 and the launch of the IGMDP and the LCA programme. That these projects were meant to demonstrate more competent management practices makes it that much more important to explain their difficulties.

Ironically, the decline in the services' procurement budgets will make it difficult for them to buy the fruits of the DRDO's labours until the costly commitment to more R&D—staying power—is relaxed, a problem that was foreseen a decade ago.[55] The 1994–95 defence budget provides Rs 68.3 billion ($2.2 billion) of Rs 230 billion ($7.4 billion), or about 30 per cent, for procurement. Although the R&D budget only consumes 5 per cent of the Defence Ministry's budget, it is one of the only discretionary portions from which relief for the procurement budget can come. Even if the DRDO budget were cut, the capital committed to imported interim systems will make additional expenditures on indigenous systems difficult for the services to afford. Further, funds that are spent on platforms—whether imported, produced domestically under licence, or indigenous—will not be available for advanced munitions that could make even elderly platforms more effective in some circumstances. Military planners in other countries see technological developments allowing them to make do with older platforms, but only if they are supported by advanced command and control capabilities, appropriate electronic warfare equipment and smart weapons. Thus, the weaknesses of India's indigenously designed platforms might be overcome, but only if they

---

[53] Smith (note 2), pp. 177, 223.
[54] Silverberg, D., 'One on one: V.S. Arunachalam', *Defense News*, 24 Feb. 1992, p. 86. The Air Chief Marshal has made the same point, saying that 'budgetary and technical reasons' have delayed the LCA by a decade. Bedi, R., 'The Jane's interview, Air Chief Marshal Swaroop Krishna Kaul', *Jane's Defence Weekly*, 6 Nov. 1993, p. 56.
[55] Balachandran (note 2), p. 40.

do not absorb all of its procurement budget and the Defence Ministry's prefer-ence for acquiring platforms rather than weapons is reconsidered.[56]

Military R&D and the national technology base

Government-sponsored industrial or non-military research does not fertilize military R&D in India as it increasingly does in the industrialized economies and some other developing countries, because military, nuclear and space R&D crowd out both of these areas of endeavour,[57] and are isolated from them.[58] Government R&D is not complemented by robust private-sector R&D, as it is in Western countries where government science is typically one-third of the national effort. As a result, despite its plentiful scientific resources, India ranks 31 among 131 countries in patents awarded over the past 30 years and 84 in inventiveness (patents earned per capita).[59]

Advanced technology and culture

In 1990, then Defence Minister K. C. Pant observed: 'We are yet to develop a truly indigenous capability to design and develop weapons and equipment of higher levels of sophistication. A truly national ethos and culture must emerge and only then can it be said that the country is self-reliant in a technological sense.'[60] As Pant implicitly recognizes, economic and technological choices are embedded in culture, and at some point it becomes unnecessarily abstract and complex to distinguish among these three causes.[61] A number of argu-ments have been made about the cultures of organizations and their effects on innovation. This scholarship suggests both that some types of innovation are beyond the capabilities of certain types of organization,[62] and that national cultures strongly influence organizations' culture, even among the industrial

---

[56] At present, there is already a shortage of munitions for existing platforms, the remedy of which will also strain the procurement budget. Gupta, Sidhu and Sandhu (note 22), p. 75. The necessity of increas-ing spending for readiness if the risk of war is taken seriously is illustrated by the operational availability of newly imported MiG-29s falling to 'as low as 30%' because of shortages of imported maintenance items seen as too expensive: 'Disbanding 4 MiG-21 squadrons', *Asian Recorder*, 18–24 June 1993, p. 23207.

[57] In 1991, defence, space and atomic energy together accounted for about 60% of Indian R&D, com-pared with 10% for industrial R&D and even less for other applications. Sharma, D., 'India's lopsided science', *Bulletin of the Atomic Scientists*, May 1991, p. 35. In the 1993–94 budget, the ratio went from 6 : 1 to greater than 9 : 1. Ministry of Finance, *1993–4 Budget: Demand for Grants* (Government of India: New Delhi, 1993).

[58] US Congress, Office of Technology Assessment, *Global Arms Trade: Commerce in Advanced Military Technology and Weapons* (US Government Printing Office: Washington, DC, 1991), p. 154.

[59] Demarest, G. B. 'Patent earnings and military power', *Arms Control*, vol. 14, no. 3 (Dec. 1993), p. 445.

[60] 'Country survey: India—Industry builds up strength', *Jane's Defence Weekly*, 26 May 1990, p. 1038.

[61] The USA's relative decline in commercial technology, to take another example, stems not from a lack of scientific and technical talent, but from risk-averse management (a product of compensation and reporting practices) and under-capitalization, which in turn can be traced to deregulating the savings and loan industry, the leveraged buy-out craze, and a national reluctance to save.

[62] In the specific context of military innovation, see Evangelista, M., *Innovation and the Arms Race* (Cornell University Press: Ithaca, N.Y., 1987).

democracies.[63] In India, there is some debate as to whether the DRDO's difficulties with systems integration stem from the organization's bureaucratic culture and are therefore amenable to a new round of reform, or from aspects of the national culture that might be more difficult to overcome.[64]

The culture of the DRDO. Some critics of the DRDO have traced its mixed record to the personality of the Director General during its expansion in the 1980s, V. S. Arunachalam.[65] They say that he was free to make choices among projects given foreseeable limits on resources, but instead escalated the existing DRDO across-the-board import substitution effort in hopes of duplicating a complete Western military technology base at precisely the time that Western states were moving away from comprehensive national approaches in favour of niche specializations. Arunachalam inspired a loyal following within the DRDO, but that loyalty has been likened to a cult of personality that inhibited free discussion of alternatives. In addition, changing requirements, test failures, other programme delays, criticism in the popular press and a widening gap between Indian projects and the Western state of the art are demoralizing for DRDO personnel.[66] Lack of informed independent oversight and corruption are also frequently mentioned constraints on effective choices.[67] While DRDO projects are often audited by the government's Comptroller and Auditor General, the extent of matters subject to this review is strictly circumscribed.[68] Internal oversight is weakened by the short tenures and limited expertise of politically appointed defence ministers.[69]

The effect of India's culture on science and technology projects. Some aspects of the DRDO bureaucratic culture are typical of organizations anywhere, especially in cases where fiscal resources are increased quickly and substantially, as were the DRDO's and those of another major enterprise of the mid- and late 1980s, the US Strategic Defense Initiative. Others stem from aspects of Indian national culture, both as a post-colonial secular democracy and as the inheritor of Hindu values. For example, the Indian Parliament is free to inquire into the DRDO's affairs more carefully, but chooses not to do

[63] The most carefully examined comparison in management cultures has been between Japan and the USA. Roots of these differences range from firms' recruiting practices and the influence of business schools to child-rearing traditions and socialization in the home and schoolroom.
[64] This chapter only characterizes the Indian military technology base, but not Indian science, more broadly except as it is applicable to military projects, nor cultural obstacles that might be imposed on effective manufacturing, operation and maintenance of advanced systems.
[65] For example, Karp, A., SIPRI, *Ballistic Missile Proliferation* (Oxford University Press: Oxford, forthcoming). For similar arguments about specific programme managers, see Smith (note 2), pp. 161–62. Smith also faults Nehru's original organization of the Defence Ministry and the armed forces (p. 222).
[66] The DRDO has been hit hard by criticism in the Indian press, and this criticism has not always been fair or well-founded. G. Balachandran, personal communication, Mar. 1994; and R. P. Singh, personal communication, Dec. 1993.
[67] Balachandran (note 2), p. 14; Smith (note 2), pp. 217–19.
[68] There is no Indian equivalent of the US Congressional Budget Office or General Accounting Office. Balachandran (note 2), p. 15.
[69] Arunachalam 'served under five prime ministers and nearly a dozen defence ministers' during the 10 years before his leave. G. Balachandran, personal communication, 1 Mar. 1994, p. 3.

so.[70] This lack of oversight practically institutionalizes the role of unfettered personality, a characteristic of Indian science since independence.[71]

India's scientific ethos has been characterized as 'including elements of bureaucratization and inflexibility in government planning, a strong policy emphasis on import substitution rather than international competitiveness, [and] political control over the research agenda' with poor performance on implementation of basic science and co-operation between government and industry.[72] While bureaucracy and corruption have been hallmarks of post-colonial Indian administration, the distaste for applied science among those with access to scientific education and career prospects can be seen as an heritage of the caste system.[73] The fact that Indian engineers have made careers in project management and applied research in Western organizations suggests that difficulties in the Indian military industrial base derive from institutional factors or the norms of Indian management and relevant education rather than any pervasive effect of Hinduism on the individual.

Political obstacles

Ironically, one of the greatest political obstacles to Indian technological self-reliance may have been the choice to pursue self-sufficiency and then self-reliance in themselves, foreclosing more effective options for innovation and development. The failed attempt at across-the-board import substitution derived from an ideological conception of technology transfer that now appears to have been incorrect. Few countries continue to believe that the route to an innovative technology sector and national economic development leads through autonomous design and production of most goods. Most countries explicitly accept this reality, including the USA, the only state that might have achieved it. India, however, despite its reliance on imported materials, components, expertise and finished goods, still uses the rhetoric of self-reliance as a staple of public debate and continues to devote scarce capital and scientific resources to projects that needlessly duplicate technology that could be purchased abroad.

Given the number of more convincing explanations, it is difficult to accept the conclusion that outside political pressure is the main factor preventing India from modernizing through domestic production. It is true that Indians fear the possibility that they will be singled out in US legislation, as Pakistan has been, and have their access to all US technology and aid cut off, but

[70] Balachandran (note 2), p. 14.

[71] B. Wariavwalla, personal communication, 24 Feb. 1994.

[72] Hill, S. and Liyanage, S., UNESCO, *The Status of Indian Science and Technology Capabilities* (University of Wollongong Centre for Research Policy: Wollongong, Australia, 1990), p. i. See also the discussion of reform in Chellaney (note 3), pp. 29–35.

[73] R. P. Singh, personal communication, Dec. 1993. Affirmative action programmes increasing access to higher education for castes that traditionally have been denied it might ameliorate this concern in the long run if the beneficiaries chose appropriate careers and were able to advance. P. Chopra, personal communication, 25 Feb. 1994, p. 2.

Indian commentary suggests that political pressure creates a countervailing determination to demonstrate that Indians will not be cowed by forces they see as arrogant, hypocritical and bent on denying India its rightful place in the hierarchy of nations.

IV. Prospects for longer-term programmes

The Indian Government continues to pursue several ambitious projects which are further from completion than the IGMDP, the Arjun and the LCA, but garner more critical attention from abroad. These projects are of a strategic nature, that is, upon completion, they would contribute to a capability to affect events beyond the immediate region. The probability of their succeeding can be extrapolated from the above analysis. They can be divided between the space programme and those suitable for long-range strike (the Agni intermediate-range ballistic missile) or power-projection (the aircraft-carrier and nuclear submarine projects).

Space

In 1993, a year when the US National Aeronautical and Space Administration (NASA)'s troubles served as a reminder that access to space is still not simple or cheap for anyone, a newly developed Indian rocket failed, losing the earth-observation satellite it was carrying.[74] India has a fairly advanced space programme administered by the Indian Space Research Organization (ISRO).[75] The main emphases of the ISRO are communications and earth observation, for which it builds its own satellites and ground stations.[76] These applications are of some use for military purposes, but a more ambitious military space programme is not an immediate prospect. The first Insat 2, a domestically developed and produced communications and observation satellite, was launched in 1992. It replaced a similar satellite, Insat 1, bought from Ford Aerospace. There is enough foreign content in the Insat 2 series that completion of the third and fourth examples has been delayed by a US embargo on co-operation between US firms and the ISRO.

The ISRO began working with sounding rockets in the early 1970s, and built its first indigenously designed solid-fuel booster in 1979. In 1980, the ISRO placed a 35-kg satellite into a low orbit with a four-stage booster, the SLV-3 (SLV stands for space-launch vehicle), a project managed by A. P. J.

---

[74] Agence France-Presse, 'India rocket fails after launching', *International Herald Tribune*, 21 Sep. 1993, p. 7. The satellite was an Indian-designed IRS-1 carrying German imaging equipment.

[75] In 1962, the National Committee for Space Research was established within the Department of Atomic Energy. ISRO was founded as a separate organization in 1969, and in 1972 the cabinet-level Department of Space was created. The IGMDP was spun off from ISRO in 1983 as part of the DRDO's reinvigoration, but co-operation and technology transfer between the two have been spotty.

[76] Marcus, D. J., 'Embargo threatens India's space program schedule', *Space News*, 20–26 July 1992, p. 9. India built its first two satellites in the late 1970s, but both failed in orbit. Both relied on the Soviet Union for key components and were launched into space on Soviet boosters.

Abdul Kalam, now acting Director General of the DRDO. Since then, ISRO has developed two somewhat more powerful boosters, the two-stage augmented SLV (ASLV) and the four-stage polar SLV (PSLV), but continues to rely on foreign launch services for higher orbits. The first two ASLV launches, in 1987 and 1988, suffered failures later traced to flaws in the solid fuel, the uniform casting of which is a difficult manufacturing problem. A third ASLV launch in 1992 placed a 150-kg satellite in a low orbit which could not be maintained.[77] On 20 September 1993, the first launch of the PSLV failed after faulty separation between the first and second stages.[78] These developments suggest that the ISRO, which is often seen as more effectively managed than the DRDO, also has trouble with systems integration.

Despite the problems with the ASLV and the PSLV, the ISRO is developing a much more powerful booster designated the geostationary SLV, which is intended to lift payloads as massive as 2500 kg to geostationary orbit.[79] The GSLV project requires a high-altitude cryogenic liquid-fuel booster, and may have been set back beyond the end of the century by the official cancellation of a technology transfer deal with Glavkosmos, a Russian firm. The conflict between India and Russia on one side and the USA on the other reached a climax in 1993 when Russia hosted intense but secret bilateral negotiations to alleviate US concerns about the deal. Originally, Glavkosmos was to provide two cryogenic rocket motors and supporting technologies—high-speed, low-temperature pumps, materials and precision manufacture[80]—to the ISRO. US legislation, the 1991 Missile Technology Control Act (MTCA),[81] forces the Clinton Administration to penalize both Glavkosmos and the ISRO for a period of two years (May 1992–94), despite the apparent reluctance of some US officials to risk relations with Russia (and India, to a lesser extent) over a technology of slight military utility.

---

[77] Lenorovitz, J. M., 'India seeks larger role in commercial satellite market', *Aviation Week & Space Technology*, 27 July 1992.

[78] The PSLV uses solid fuel for the first and third stage, including 6 SLV-3 boosters strapped on to the first, and liquid fuel for the second and fourth stages. It is designed to place payloads of mass approaching 1000 kg in low orbits. Lawler, A. and V. Raghuvanshi, 'India's rocket effort fails', *Space News*, 27 Sep.–3 Oct. 1993, p. 1.

[79] On the military applications of the different orbits, see Arnett, E., *Antisatellite Weapons* (AAAS: Washington, DC, 1991), p. 2.

[80] 'Russian decision spurs scientists', *Asian Recorder*, 6–12 Aug. 1993, p. 23316.

[81] The MTCA—which should not be confused with the Reagan Administration's Missile Technology Control Regime, a voluntary network for co-ordinating export control policy—mandates sanctions against organizations participating in specified types of missile technology transfer. Sanctions may be waived by the President, as has been done in the cases of China and Israel on other occasions. The MTCA is one of 20 pieces of legislation that force the executive branch of the US Government to take stronger action against proliferation than it might otherwise choose. Nine have been passed since 1990. Davis, Z. S., *Nonproliferation Regimes: Policies to Control the Spread of Nuclear, Chemical, and Biological Weapons and Missiles* (Congressional Research Service: Washington, DC, 1993). In general, the Clinton Administration has sought to take a more co-operative approach to non-proliferation and regional security more generally, as described in a significant document associated with the campaign: Carter, A. B., Perry, W. J. and Steinbruner, J. D., *A New Concept of Cooperative Security* (Brookings Institution: Washington, DC, 1992), especially pp. 39–40. (Perry is now President Clinton's Secretary of Defense and Carter is Assistant Secretary of Defense for Nuclear Security and Counter-proliferation.)

Reports of the eventual compromise and its implications conflict. The motors are being provided to the ISRO, but the technology transfer package has officially been cancelled.[82] The USA sought assurances from Russia that supporting technology to facilitate Indian production of more motors would not be transferred, but such an agreement would be difficult to verify, especially since India is determined to develop the technology anyway.[83] Despite outrage in India and Russia, some observers saw the arrangement, announced on 4 August 1993, as a way of allowing the deal to go through while permitting Clinton to save face before 'non-proliferation hawks' in the US Congress. Fifteen Indian scientists are still being trained at Glavkosmos and plans reportedly have been transferred to them.[84] Nevertheless, the incident is likely to deter foreign firms that might otherwise have provided technology to the ISRO for the GSLV and other aspects of the space programme, hobbling it for the foreseeable future.

Systems for long-range strike and power projection

The DRDO has long sought to develop a range of platforms and systems that could be used to deliver payloads over considerable distances. Although the immediate rationale is to strengthen and multiply the measures that could be taken to deter or counter-attack China, these projects have drawn attention primarily as potential nuclear delivery systems.

While there is considerable disagreement about the destiny of the Indian nuclear weapon programme and the best ways of affecting Indian attitudes and policies towards it,[85] most observers agree that it is sitting at present on a plateau. According to a recent SIPRI study, India has the materials and technical wherewithal to produce 45–75 nuclear weapons 'in a matter of weeks'.[86] On 24 February 1993, the Clinton Administration's Director of Central Intelligence, James Woolsey, told a Senate committee that India appeared to be pursuing the capability to make fusion weapons, reiterating a long-standing

---

[82] P. V. Narasimha Rao, Statement in the Rajya Sabha (the upper house of the Parliament), 18 Aug. 1993, reproduced in 'Cryogenic deal with Russia', *Strategic Digest*, Nov. 1993, p. 1844.

[83] Manchanda, R., 'Shedding illusions about Indo-US defence co-operation', *Economic and Political Weekly*, 7–14 Aug. 1993, p. 1637.

[84] Lepingwell, J., 'Indian official asserts rocket deal still on', Radio Free Europe/Radio Liberty, *RFE/RL News Briefs*, 13–17 Sep. 1993, p. 5; 'Washington outlook: export saga', *Aviation Week & Space Technology*, 25 Oct. 1993, p. 19.

[85] The breadth of the debate—from Gandhian and leftist pacifists through potential arms controllers and incrementalists to realist deployment advocates and reactive 'weaponize now' hawks—is discussed in Graham, T. W., 'Nuclear deterrence, arms control, and confidence building in South Asia', ed. Arnett (note 49), pp. 123–34.

[86] Albright, D., Berkhout, F. and Walker, W., SIPRI, *World Inventory of Plutonium and Highly Enriched Uranium, 1992* (Oxford University Press: Oxford, 1993), p. 161. Earlier estimates were higher, but the Madras I, Madras II and Dhruva reactors and reprocessing facilities have operated at less than half of the expected capacity because of technical problems. Spector, L. S., and Smith, J. R., *Nuclear Ambitions: The Spread of Nuclear Weapons 1989–1990* (Westview Press: Boulder, Colo., 1990), p. 72. Indian reviewers of this chapter all expressed doubts that even the smaller amount had been produced.

Central Intelligence Agency (CIA) concern.[87] One school of thought sees India as uninterested in deploying a nuclear arsenal, but another claims that the deployment decision awaits completion of appropriate delivery systems, particularly intermediate- or long-range missiles. India already deploys a wide range of piloted aircraft that could be used for nuclear delivery, and its declared policy is that it seeks only to preserve an option to deploy weapons should international developments warrant. Many foreign fears of the nuclear option are centred on the possibility that the Hindu-nationalist Indian People's Party (Bharatiya Janata, or BJP) might come to power and change this policy.[88]

The Agni missile

In 1989, 1992 and again in 1994, India tested the Agni (Fire), which is designed to carry a 1-tonne payload 2500 km. Few observers expect it to enter production for several years,[89] and the Indian Government has told Parliament that there are no plans to induct it for military use.[90] Officials refer to the Agni as a technology demonstrator, meaning a test-bed for a number of components which might be included in an operational missile if a military requirement for one is established.[91] It is not clear that the ability to build and fire a test missile implies the ability to manufacture and maintain an alert force of several missiles. At a minimum, the decision to deploy the Agni would require a complete series of tests.[92]

Many observers are sceptical of the Agni's utility as a non-nuclear delivery system, because ballistic missiles in its class are inevitably less accurate than other methods of delivery.[93] They deduce that it will be deployed with a nuc-

[87] US Congress, Senate Committee on Governmental Affairs, *Proliferation Threats of the 1990's* (US Government Printing Office: Washington, DC, 1993), p. 31.

[88] The BJP moderated its stance on nuclear weapons in 1993 to attract centrist voters in the November regional elections, but was dealt a set-back anyway. BJP politicians have served in coalition governments and did not press for any change in the policy of preserving an option, but the policy of a hypothetical BJP national government is difficult to predict.

[89] Kalam has speculated that, if adequate resources were provided, Agnis could be mass-produced beginning within 5 years at a unit cost of Rs 30 m. ($1 m.). Menon, A. K., 'We can design any missile', *India Today*, 15 June 1989, p. 12.

[90] 'India: another Prithvi test', *Milavnews*, vol. 30, no. 353 (Mar. 1991), p. 11.

[91] Some Western commentators have asserted that the 'technology demonstrator' designation is an example of dissembling double-speak, meant to allow India to develop an intermediate-range ballistic missile (IRBM) without taking the political heat for it. A closer examination of the evolution of the Agni design over the course of its testing programme and the pace of testing itself suggests this interpretation is unwarranted. Joshi, M., 'Agni's launch raises questions', *Times of India*, 22 Feb. 1994, p. 28.

[92] The Prithvi, for example, was tested 12 times before being released to the Army and Air Force, both of which will conduct additional tests before declaring it fully operational.

[93] Kalam's claim (in *Milavnews*, Mar. 1991, p. 11) that the Agni's expected CEP (circular error probable, that is, the mean miss distance) is only 60 m is hard to accept. The US Pershing 2 IRBM, which relied on satellite imagery for terminal guidance, was the culmination of a long development programme and had a CEP of 40 m over 1800 km. Soviet IRBMs never achieved comparable accuracy. China is reportedly re-configuring its nuclear-armed DF-21 IRBM for non-nuclear missions. The DF-21 can carry 600 kg 1700 km. 'China switches IRBMs to conventional role', *Jane's Defence Weekly*, vol. 21, no. 5 (1994), p. 4. The limitations of IRBMs for conventional military applications are reviewed in Postol, T. and Morel, B., 'A technical assessment of the Soviet TBM threat', eds D. L. Hafner and J. Roper, *ATBMs and Western Security: Missile Defenses for Europe* (Ballinger: New York, 1988), p. 95.

lear warhead as a signal to China, although most major targets in China would remain outside the Agni's range. Some go so far as to claim that the Agni programme is the technological bottleneck from which an operational Indian nuclear capability will emerge.[94] Arunachalam has suggested that deployment of the Agni might wait until a terminal-guidance system was developed that permitted accurate delivery of a conventional payload.[95] If a manœuvring warhead and terminal guidance system are included in order to make a conventionally armed missile accurate, a complex mission-planning support system will have to be developed and deployed. A finned re-entry vehicle was included in the third Agni test, but there is no sign that appropriate software or support have been developed.[96]

The Agni design blends liquid-fuel rocket motors[97] with indigenously developed components, including the re-entry heat shield, guidance system and staging mechanisms. The recent literature suggests that designing these may present insuperable barriers for some developing countries, and that India's particular problems with project management may prevent them from fielding missiles of range greater than 1500–2000 km.[98] In the first two tests, staging and launch failures prevented any assessment of the other two systems.[99] The third test, postponed for a month, featured a new stage-separation system, which performed well according to initial reports.[100]

The Agni is a completely indigenous design,[101] like the Prithvi but considerably more complex. India's chronic problem of systems integration in programmes of this level of complexity has only been overcome in cases where

[94] The most complete (if not strained) example of this argument is presented in Spector and Smith (note 86), pp. 74–76.

[95] Copley, G., 'Unrestrained ambition', *Defense and Foreign Affairs*, Apr. 1990, p. 32. Conventionally armed ballistic missiles might be attractive to Indian planners because of their concerns about losing their edge with piloted aircraft. Recent US exports to Pakistan may prevent India from achieving air superiority and leave Indian airfields open to attack in a hypothetical future war. Mobile IRBMs are a counter to both difficulties, although the variety of targets they can attack effectively is limited by their inaccuracy. Arnett, E. H., 'Technology and military doctrine: criteria for evaluation', ed. W. T. Wander, *Advanced Weaponry in the Developing World* (AAAS: Washington, DC, 1994).

[96] Joshi (note 91).

[97] The first stage comes from the SLV-3, the second from the Prithvi. Despite this example of technology transfer from the ISRO to the DRDO, the ISRO has been reluctant to share its expertise in producing solid-fuel rocket motors, which are preferable in many military applications, especially if missiles are to be transportable. Joshi (note 91).

[98] Karp (note 65) and Wander, W. T., 'The proliferation of ballistic missiles: motives, technologies, and threats', eds W. T. Wander and E. H. Arnett, *The Proliferation of Advanced Weaponry: Technology, Motivations, and Responses* (AAAS: Washington, DC, 1992). The first and third Agni tests were at ranges of 750 km and 1000 km, respectively; see Joshi (note 16).

[99] Banerji, I., 'The Integrated Guided Missile development program', *Indian Defence Review*, July 1990, p. 106; Ministry of Defence (note 11), p. 69; and Joshi (note 91).

[100] Joshi (note 91). As seen above, the ISRO has not completely solved the staging problem. Staging of liquid-fuel boosters like those of the Agni and the PSLV is more complex than that of solid-fuel boosters.

[101] The inertial guidance system and material for the heat shield may have been designed with German advice, although the extent of assistance is the subject of disagreement. Fialka, J. J., 'Space research fuels arms proliferation: Indian missile suggests US, West German parenthood', *Wall Street Journal*, 6 July 1989, p. 8; Milhollin, G., 'India's missiles: with a little help from our friends', *Bulletin of the Atomic Scientists*, Nov. 1989, pp. 34–35; and in particular Chellaney, B., *Nuclear Proliferation: The US–Indian Conflict* (Sangam Books: London, 1993), pp. 283–89.

there is foreign management assistance.[102] Another characteristic the Agni shares with the Prithvi is that its design is unlikely to be revised drastically or completely reconsidered in response to changing service requirements. However, this is largely because of the lack of any service requirement whatsoever for the Agni, a significant barrier to its deployment in the procurement budget crisis. The Indian Air Force has not been given a strategic or nuclear bombardment mission for which it might use the Agni, nor does the army require a missile with the Agni's range.

The same fundamental advantages and obstacles would be associated with the more demanding development of an Indian long-range or intercontinental ballistic missile, although there is no public evidence that such a programme exists. On 24 February 1993, US Director of Central Intelligence James Woolsey, echoing Bush Administration Defense Secretary Richard Cheney's testimony of the previous month to the word, told the Senate Governmental Affairs Committee, 'Over the next ten years we are likely to see several Third World countries at least establish the infrastructure and develop the technical knowledge that is necessary to undertake ICBM [intercontinental ballistic missile] and space launch vehicle development.' In response to a Senate inquiry, the CIA said India has 'the technical capability to develop [ICBMs] by the year 2000', but that they would not.[103] Ten months later, the US National Intelligence Estimate concluded, 'Analysis of all available information shows a low probability that [India or] any other country will acquire this [ICBM] capability during the next 15 years.'[104]

Nuclear-propelled submarines

The Indian Navy having returned a leased Soviet nuclear-powered submarine (SSN) after safety problems and the expiration of its lease, the DRDO continues work on an indigenous design. Earlier speculation that as many as eight SSNs would be bought or leased has petered out. Although SSNs have several uses, some observers speculate that the Indian programme is intended to provide an invulnerable launching platform for nuclear weapons.[105] Delays are thought to make completion of the first indigenously designed SSN, an ambition of Indian naval planners for more than two and a half decades,

---

[102] The cause of failure in the second Agni test—vibration-induced software failure two seconds after ignition—was discovered by a Russian consultant. Joshi (note 91).

[103] US Congress (note 87), p. 133.

[104] 'CIA says threat of missile strike on US is slight', *International Herald Tribune*, 27 Dec. 1993, p. 3.

[105] Although the popular imagination usually associates nuclear-propelled submarines with the long-range nuclear-strike mission, naval planners more often see SSNs as invulnerable 'sea-denial assets', that is, they can complicate or prevent a superior force's exploiting control of the sea. Both US and Soviet planners expected to use their SSNs this way. The history and implications of SSNs for Indian maritime strategy suggest that the US presence in the Indian Ocean was a stronger motivation for the SSN programme. Further, even in the 1950s, SSNs were seen by Indian naval planners as a way of establishing presence as far away as Indonesian and Chinese waters. Anthony (note 6), pp. 70, 94; Arnett, E. H., *Attack Submarines: Modernization, Proliferation, and Arms Control* (AAAS: Washington, DC, 1991); Thomas, R. G. C., 'The politics of Indian naval rearmament, 1962–74', *Pacific Community*, Apr. 1975, p. 457.

impossible before the turn of the century.[106] In the meantime, all Indian submarine construction halted in 1991 with the completion of the second of two licence-built German diesel attack submarines.[107]

An SSN presents very demanding problems of systems design and integration which Indian engineers are attacking with little outside assistance or operational experience, aside from those associated with similar aspects of diesel-submarine construction and operation. The nature of SSN operations, usually independent of other forces, will probably prevent the navy from changing its requirements significantly during the R&D cycle, but the service's procurement budget, smaller and harder hit than those of the air force and the army, is unlikely to accommodate a sustained commitment to a programme with so small an internal constituency and little institutional support or public visibility. Construction of the elaborate support facilities would also be fiscally daunting.

Aircraft-carriers

The Indian Navy operates two elderly British-built aircraft-carriers and has commissioned a feasibility study to examine the prospects of designing and building replacements with French assistance. Early expectations were ambitious, but by 1992 budget pressure had pushed the earliest prospective deployment 'well past the turn of the century.'[108] Initial preferences for a ship capable of handling high-performance aircraft gave way after delivery of a French consultants' report to a smaller, more affordable size capable of carrying only 12 vertical takeoff and landing (VTOL) aircraft.

The aircraft-carrier project combines two challenges with which Indian design teams have had problems. An aircraft-carrier is a very complex system of systems and is especially vulnerable to changing service requirements.[109] French design and systems integration assistance would no doubt be invaluable, as would the Indian Navy's operational experience with VTOL aircraft based at sea, but doubts about the sustainability and vulnerability of carriers will force the Indian Navy to choose between this major commitment with an additional investment in supporting craft, and a more modest approach based on land-based aircraft.

V. Conclusions

Events in 1993 reconfirmed India's dependence on foreign suppliers of technology and project management expertise, but also underlined the risks for its freedom of action inherent in that dependence. The nature of the resulting

---

[106] Chellaney, B., 'The challenge of nuclear arms control in South Asia', *Survival*, vol. 35, no. 3 (autumn 1993), p. 133; 'Force modernisation in the Asia–Pacific', *Asian Defence Journal*, Apr. 1991, p. 8.

[107] 'India', *Asia-Pacific Defence Reporter*, Oct.–Nov. 1992, p. 23.

[108] 'India', *US NAval Institute Proceedings*, Mar. 1992, p. 129.

[109] Lehman, J. F., *Aircraft Carriers: The Real Choices* (Praeger Publishers: New York, 1979).

dilemma suggests that the managers of India's nascent military technology base were right to abandon their quixotic quest for an unattainable autarky in favour of a more co-operative approach, but that they have not gone far enough in the right direction. The DRDO's three showpiece projects still constitute a costly detour. Big technology projects with too many foreign partners leave the DRDO open to manipulation or sabotage from both the Indian armed services and political developments in the supplier states. Smaller projects, like the DRDO's component programmes, in niches where India can be competitive and partnerships with one or a few foreign entities are more likely to weather the DRDO's unreliable domestic and international relationships. Such an approach offers incremental improvements in the technology base that can be managed, rather than great leaps forward, which may appear brave at first blush but hold strong prospects for disappointment in the longer term.

Not only are big projects extravagant to the point of being counter-productive, they (and, to a lesser extent, major weapon systems generally) are becoming less relevant to India's security for political and technical reasons. Politically, India appears less likely to fight a major war than ever before in its post-colonial history. Relations with Pakistan, while not good, are improving. More importantly, both sides apparently see the costs of future wars drastically outweighing the benefits, with or without nuclear weapons. The result of this understanding has not been a diminution of conflict, however, but the redirection of conflict into provocation and violence short of war. Additional increments of Indian military capability may strengthen the no-war understanding marginally, but are less likely to have an effect on these lower levels of violence while providing an additional incentive for Pakistan to continue its nuclear programme.

In a more clearly positive development, September 1993 saw India and China sign an agreement recognizing the line of actual control and reducing the number of troops deployed along their shared border. Although the agreement culminates a five-year thaw begun by Rajiv Gandhi's 1988 visit to Beijing, neither side completely renounced its claim to the contested territory, which totals 119 000 km^2. The agreement commits them to negotiate a peaceful solution to the dispute, and withdrawals have begun.[110]

In the domain of military technology, major weapon systems are declining in significance as their electronics suites and the weapon systems they carry assume much greater importance, and political and doctrinal changes are now recognized to have much greater effects on regional stability than technology in itself. The Indian military technology base's more important role for the foreseeable future will be providing electronics and munitions to keep systems already in the force structure operational and combat-worthy.

---

[110] *Agreement between the Government of the Republic of India and the Government of the People's Republic of China on the Maintenance of Peace and Tranquillity Along the Line of Actual Control in the India–China Border Areas* (7 Sep. 1993). As many as 35 000 Indian troops had already been transferred to Kashmir for counter-insurgency operations. Sawhney, P., 'Massive troop pullout from China border', *Indian Express*, 24 Dec. 1992.

Realizing that India could not hope to vault directly to the vanguard of military technology, the architects of India's indigenous technology programmes saw them as a way to invest in long-term ascendancy to technological independence and international competitiveness, acknowledging a brief period during which Indian systems would not be as effective as alternatives available on the international market. Programmes like the Arjun and the LCA were seen as stepping-stones to a mature, innovative military technology base of world class. It now appears that either the period for catching up is much longer than was expected, or that the strategy itself was misconceived. There is no sign that Indian designs are or will be competitive on the dwindling international market, nor that the completion of initial indigenous designs will lead to the innovative momentum that will allow Indian engineers to build new models on the shoulders of their predecessors. In fact, tensions between funding more R&D and procuring hardware may keep even the stepping-stone systems from being fielded. Further, the strategic programmes show every sign of having been frozen or set back. Nevertheless, it is likely that India's achievements will allow it to continue to equip the Indian armed forces well enough to complete their assigned tasks.

Although some of India's problems are highly idiosyncratic, the year's developments offered equally clear lessons for students of the proliferation issue. Most importantly, access to technology continues to be a consequential obstacle to the spread of military capabilities, even for a country that enjoys the rich scientific resources that India does. Many of the weaknesses of India's scientific organizations are present in other countries of proliferation concern. As a result, these countries are unlikely to develop vigorous military technology bases without the co-operation of outside actors. On the other hand, political pressure alone intended to reduce demand for military technology is at least as likely to act as a goad to states and organizations that do not accept condescension lightly.

11. Non-lethal weapons: a case study of new technology developments

RICHARD KOKOSKI

I. Introduction

Military forces have traditionally invested in such proven disabling or non-lethal measures as electronic warfare; camouflage, concealment and deception (CC&D); and psychological warfare. New technologies are making it increasingly possible to develop weapons which fall into the disabling or non-lethal category, and new international situations and obligations are making them seem more and more attractive in some quarters as instruments which could prove useful in cases where less than lethal force is required or desirable.

With dramatic cuts in nuclear forces under way, budget cut-backs forcing 'down-sizing' in most other military areas as well and reassessment of traditional military procurement patterns, renewed efforts are also being made within defence establishments, particularly in the USA, to investigate new types of technology and weapon. One result of this has been a renewed effort to develop capabilities in non-lethal weapon technology, and 1993 saw the launch of new efforts to give a coherent structure to the non-lethal research effort in the USA.

Among the important concerns raised by the development of these weapons is not only whether they are truly non-lethal but also whether the perception of them as such will be destabilizing and make war more likely in some situations. Proponents of non-lethal weapons predict that the next conflict in which the USA is involved will serve to demonstrate the new capabilities of these weapons just as the 1991 Persian Gulf War showcased precision-guided munitions.[1] It is therefore particularly important to investigate these programmes at the present time. Their acceleration, made possible in part by new technological opportunities, raises a number of vital questions which prudence dictates be considered as the further development of these weapons proceeds.

An important first question is that of definition. Although many definitions have been put forward[2] they all share certain important elements, as discussed in section II. The extent and importance of the new initiatives, especially regarding renewed emphasis on non-lethal technologies in the USA and new

---

[1] Pine, A., 'Pentagon pursuing nonlethal weapons', *The Virginian-Pilot and the Ledger-Star*, 19 Dec. 1993, p. A1.
[2] In the *SIPRI Yearbook 1993* non-lethal warfare was defined briefly as being 'designed to avoid casualties and long-term damage and to immobilize people rapidly for a short time'. See Stock, T., 'Chemical and biological weapons: development and proliferation', SIPRI, *SIPRI Yearbook 1993: World Armaments and Disarmament* (Oxford University Press: Oxford, 1993), p. 267.

NATO investigations into the roles which they might play in enforcing no-fly zones in particular, are discussed in section III. In an exposition of specific non-lethal technologies and weapons now being investigated, which follows in section IV, a clear distinction is made where possible between more recent innovations and those weapons which have already been developed or have been under consideration for some time.

The operational aspects of the potential introduction of and any meaningful reliance on non-lethal technologies are examined in section V. The various applications that the military has proposed for these new weapons are also described, including their application for counter-terrorist and peacekeeping actions. Possible uses in the area of law enforcement are also discussed. An overall assessment of the current state of developments is given in section VI, which examines possible consequences of the development or refinement of non-lethal weapon technologies in the uses for which they have been suggested. As far as the classified nature of most of the programmes permits, the geographical distribution of the research and development (R&D) efforts as well as the budgetary allocations are elaborated upon. Finally the arms control implications of this type of weaponry are discussed with reference in particular to the 1972 Biological Weapons Convention (BWC), the 1993 Chemical Weapons Convention (CWC) and the dangers associated with their potential proliferation.

II. Definition

A senior advisory group was to begin meeting in early 1994 to give an overarching coherency to the non-lethal weapon effort in the USA. Developments to date, however, have not taken place under any central authority and as a result a number of specific operative definitions have been put forward. Disabling or non-lethal weapons in the current context can generally be said to include both old measures and new technological initiatives aimed at producing disabling effects without necessarily causing significant harm to persons.

While referring to the same classification of weapons there is also some discussion of the proper term that should be used to describe them. Preferences include 'non-lethal', 'disabling', 'less-than-lethal' and that adopted for the above-mentioned US advisory panel: 'low-collateral, less-than-lethal'. Disabling might be considered the better term since non-lethal or less-than-lethal would tend to imply that the result of use would not lead to death—and as one expert has aptly noted, 'enough marshmallows will kill you if properly placed'.[3] According to one official of the US Department of Defense (DOD) the term non-lethal warfare is 'an almost obscene oxymoron'.[4] Of course, weapons designed to disable may in fact cause much more harm than the term might at first imply. Disabling a soldier in a conflict situation could easily lead

---

[3] 'Nonlethal weapons give peacekeepers flexibility', *Aviation Week & Space Technology*, 7 Dec. 1992, p. 51.
[4] Morrison, D. C., 'Bang! Bang! You've been inhibited', *National Journal*, 28 Mar. 1992, p. 759.

to his death by the more lethal weapons already being employed. For clarity and brevity the term most often quoted in the current literature—non-lethal—is used throughout this chapter except where explicit programmes or references under discussion make use of other terminology.

Definitive ideas of the concept of non-lethal weapons as they are currently being investigated can be found in statements released by some of the defence establishments engaged in the research. The US Army's Armament Research, Development and Engineering Center (ARDEC) has stated that work is under way on many technologies and weapons to 'effectively disable, dazzle or incapacitate aircraft, missiles, armoured vehicles, personnel and other equipment while minimising collateral damage'.[5] A concept paper prepared by the Army's Training and Doctrine Command (TRADOC) points to the opportunities presented by non-lethal technologies, 'with potential for development into weaponry that can disable or destroy an enemy's capability without causing significant injury, excessive property destruction or widespread environmental damage'.[6] The TRADOC paper goes on to define disabling measures as those which:

are directed against system components or human abilities or senses to prevent normal operation of equipment or personnel. These measures cause human impairment such as temporary loss of eyesight, loss of equilibrium, and nausea. They can also inhibit use of equipment such as air intakes, optical ports, optical sighting devices, laser and radar range finders, automatic weapons acquisition systems and electromagnetic devices.[7]

The findings of an influential report by the Washington Center for Strategic and International Studies (CSIS) on the 'Military Technical Revolution' not only indicate how the weapons can be categorized but also point towards some of the possible repercussions of their development and employment. 'If U.S. forces were able, through electronic, electromagnetic, directed energy, or other means to incapacitate or render ineffective enemy forces without destroying or killing them, the U.S. conduct of war would be revolutionised. The whole calculus of costs, benefits, and risks would change for both the United States and its potential adversaries.'[8]

Thus an appropriate operative definition of disabling or non-lethal weapons may be taken to be those the *purpose* of which is detrimentally to affect either personnel or equipment with the result that they are less than able to perform adequately the tasks to which they are assigned while at the same time minimizing unintended collateral effects. 'Purpose' is italicized to emphasize that

---

[5] Quoted in Tapscott, M., 'The non-lethal weapons battle', *Defence*, Apr. 1993, p. 37; see also Starr, B., 'USA tries to make war less lethal', *Jane's Defence Weekly*, 31 Oct. 1992, p. 10.
[6] Quoted in Morrison (note 4), p. 758.
[7] Starr, B., 'Non-lethal weapon puzzle for US Army', *International Defense Review*, Apr. 1993, p. 319.
[8] Mazarr, M. J., *The Military Technical Revolution: A Structural Framework*, Final Report of the CSIS study group on the MTR (Center for Strategic and International Studies: Washington, DC, Mar. 1993), p. 43.

the resultant effect may sometimes be more lethal than intended under some circumstances.

III. New initiatives

US efforts

While non-lethal weapons are by no means new,[9] the Persian Gulf War led to a markedly increased interest within the US military in investing in the development of non-lethal technologies. In discussing such technologies, a 1991 draft policy planning paper entitled 'Non-lethal Weapons' stated that the Gulf War had shown that 'this emerging class of weapons and systems is a more civilised means to achieve political ends when lethal or less discriminate force would traditionally be the only option'.[10]

The use of non-lethal weaponry was demonstrated during the Gulf War: some Tomahawk cruise missiles (the accuracy of which in any case minimizes unintended damage) were specially equipped with warheads filled with thousands of spools of carbon fibres. The spools were dropped over Iraqi power stations and unrolled fine carbon fibres which short-circuited various elements of the outdoor switching and transformer segments of the stations, causing them to shut down. Many of the Tomahawk missiles employed during the first night of the War contained these warheads. While the damage caused was minimal the plants were put out of commission for a time, affecting air defences and facilitating further coalition air operations. The intention was to avoid destroying generators that would have taken a long time to repair and the absence of which would have caused needless suffering for the civilian population. Most power stations were hit with conventional bombs, however, so there is some doubt regarding the main intent of using the carbon-fibre warheads in this instance.[11]

In March 1991 development of non-lethal technologies in the context of a broadly based strategy for national security was endorsed by the Under-Secretary of Defense for Policy, Paul Wolfowitz, and a Non-Lethal Warfare Study Group was set up by the then Defense Secretary Dick Cheney. By 1992 the Army alone had planned to invest approximately $100 million to accelerate development of non-lethal technologies over the next five years.[12] Because of disagreement over technology issues and about the autonomy and prominence that should be afforded the initiative, as well as political infighting, the group

---

[9] In the Viet Nam War, for example, riot control agents including tear gas were used, rain clouds were seeded and emulsifiers were dispersed over the Ho Chi Minh Trail in attempts to reduce its usefulness as a supply route. These techniques, with some limited exceptions, did not prove to offer any substantial military advantage. A more recent example of what could be considered as use of a very simple type of non-lethal means was the loud music which was employed to help induce Manuel Noriega to emerge from the Vatican Embassy in 1990. Morrison (note 4), p. 758.

[10] Opall, B., 'Pentagon forges strategy on non-lethal warfare', *Defense News*, 17 Feb. 1992, p. 1.

[11] Fulghum, D. A., 'Secret carbon-fiber warheads blinded Iraqi air defenses', *Aviation Week & Space Technology*, 27 Apr. 1992, p. 18.

[12] Munro, N. and Opall, B., 'Military studies unusual arsenal', *Defense News*, 19–25 Oct. 1992, p. 3; Morrison (note 4), p. 758.

was disbanded before issuing its final report. With the departure of those appointed during the Bush Administration, however, there was a renewed effort to launch a 'Nonlethality Strategy Initiative' overseeing development, policy, strategy and doctrine related to non-lethal weapons.[13]

The Pentagon decided to intensify efforts in the non-lethal area but to increase the level of secrecy as well.[14] Comments from the Pentagon signalled the potential for an effort compared with the Strategic Defense Initiative in the size and scope of the prospective programmes.[15]

It was announced in October 1993 by then Defense Secretary Les Aspin that the Pentagon would initiate a series of studies on non-lethal technologies focusing on equipment, training and force mix. A first progress report was expected by February or March 1994.[16] In addition, one of the areas to be reviewed by a high-level working group set up by US Defense Secretary William Perry to assess possible changes in forces organization and deployment required for the next two decades are new requirements for low-intensity conflict and possible advantages of less-than-lethal technologies.[17]

By the end of 1993 plans were in place by the US Army to appoint a senior advisory group in March 1994 to develop a master plan focusing on doctrine, training and *matériel* issues surrounding non-lethal weapons. The majority of the 'Senior Advisory Group for Low-Collateral, Less-Than-Lethal Weapons' had been selected and a preliminary report drafted by the Battelle Memorial Institute. The final results of the group's effort, due by May 1994, are expected to provide new coherence and direction for further technological development in the field, thus eliminating the duplication which currently exists in R&D, and to address a wide range of legal and policy questions.[18]

At the present time the development of non-lethal weapons in the USA remains distributed among the various armed services, particularly the Army and also the Air Force, and in the weapons laboratories too. The Army's main effort is being made at ARDEC in Picatinny Arsenal in New Jersey under the Low Collateral Damage Munitions (LCDM) programme. The LCDM programme is focused on providing 'increased flexibility in future conflicts, dramatic performance enhancements beyond those obtainable from conventional bullets and bursting munitions, low collateral damage capability [and] minimization of loss of life'.[19] ARDEC is currently carrying out research on more than a dozen different types of disabling technology.[20]

---

[13] Weinschenk, A., 'Boosters again are pushing for "Office of Non-Lethality"', *Defense Week*, 16 Feb. 1993, p. 2; Morrison (note 4), p. 759.

[14] Ricks, T. E., 'Nonlethal arms: new class of weapons could incapacitate foe yet limit casualties', *Wall Street Journal*, 4 Jan. 1993, p. 1.

[15] Opall, B., 'Pentagon units jostle over non-lethal initiative', *Defense News*, 2 Mar. 1992, p. 6.

[16] 'Policymakers to take back seat to users in non-lethal defense', *Aerospace Daily*, vol. 188, no. 32 (17 Nov. 1993), p. 281.

[17] 'US Group to assess military "revolution"', *Jane's Defence Weekly*, 16 Apr. 1994, p. 20.

[18] Weinschenk, A., 'Non-lethal weapons group set to form in March', *Defense Week*, vol. 14, no. 46 (24 Nov. 1993) p. 1.

[19] Tapscott, M. and Atwal, K., 'New weapons that win without killing on DOD's horizon', *Defense Electronics*, Feb. 1993, pp. 42–43.

[20] Starr, B., 'USA tries to make war less lethal', *Jane's Defence Weekly*, 31 Oct. 1992, p. 10.

Substantial work on these weapons is also being carried out by the Advanced Research Projects Agency (ARPA) and at the Lawrence Livermore and Los Alamos national laboratories.[21] Among the seven priorities which have been developed by the US Special Operations Command (USSOCOM) for Army Special Operations Forces (SOF) R&D are less-than-lethal/non-destructive capabilities.[22]

According to a document circulated within the military by the Army's Training and Doctrine Command in 1992 there is now in existence 'a wide range of disabling measures . . . [a situation which was] . . . not true 10 years ago'.[23] The TRADOC document 'Operations Concept for Disabling Measures' outlines in positive terms at the strategic doctrine and training policy level the new spectrum of options which non-lethal weapons could offer in containing crisis situations before lethal force is unavoidable.[24]

NATO initiatives

In January 1994 a new NATO study group began holding meetings that will focus on non-lethal technologies that could be employed to help enforce no-fly zones. Aircraft and helicopters are routinely detected, intercepted and identified violating the UN-mandated no-fly zones in the former Yugoslavia, for example. While jamming and other electronics countermeasures have long been in existence, new non-lethal technologies are being explored which would make it possible to force an aircraft to withdraw and prevent its return without sustaining permanent injury.

The study is based on three guiding principles—compatibility of the non-lethal technology with present air-defence assets, making maximum use of existing sensors and command and control networks, and conforming with the Geneva conventions on rules of warfare. Promising approaches already identified include destroying weapon-guidance systems; disabling the aircraft's engines; degrading fuel, computers or flight characteristics; temporarily blinding the pilot or preventing take-off by coating the runway with chemicals which make it too slippery, or gluing the tyres in place or degrading them. The NATO agency charged with the task is the Advisory Group for Aerospace Research and Development (AGARD). Also addressed by the study, the results of which are due in December 1994, are ways to evaluate the psychological effect of these weapons and an appropriate means of damage assessment.[25]

[21] Opall (note 15), p. 6.

[22] Goodman, G. W., Jr, 'Army Special Operations Command pushes the technology envelope', *Armed Forces Journal International*, Nov. 1993, p. 28.

[23] Quoted in Ricks (note 14), p. 1.

[24] Tapscott and Atwal (note 19), p. 44.

[25] de Briganti, G., 'Lasers, viruses, may rule no-fly zone sky', *Defense News*, 7–13 Feb. 1994, p. 1; *Aviation Week & Space Technology*, 24 Jan. 1994, p. 33.

Other efforts

Countries other than the USA are also investigating the potential of non-lethal technologies. It is known, for instance, that many of these types of technology were under development in the former Soviet Union[26] and research continues in Russia today. Russia is also apparently already close to fielding a microwave weapon. An electromagnetic pulse weapon which can reportedly be fitted into a relatively small warhead was developed at the Arzamas 16 nuclear weapons laboratory.[27]

The British Ministry of Defence has confirmed the existence of a programme for the development of non-lethal weapons, including a microwave weapon. While there is as yet no formal operational requirement for the weapon, renewed emphasis has been placed on the programme as a result of the British defence policy shift to mid-intensity operations including humanitarian convoy escort duty in Bosnia.[28]

IV. Specific technologies and prospective uses

Many technologies are being explored which could be considered to fall into the disabling or non-lethal category. Owing to the classified nature of much of the work it is difficult to assess the full extent to which the various options are being pursued,[29] but some information has come to light on many of the major technologies and programmes currently being conducted. There are also indications of the most likely scenarios for the employment of many of the specific weapons in question, as expressed either by the developers in the military or by independent analysts. The categories that are presented here are by no means definitive but serve only as a preliminary guide to the technologies involved.[30] It should also be noted that much of the information is of

[26] Powerful and compact directed-energy weapons are being developed as part of a long-held Soviet intention to obtain advanced non-nuclear weapons which they believe could make nuclear weapons 'almost obsolete'. Intensive work on lasers began in the 1970s—in the 1980s the crews of US aircraft were dazzled by lasers deployed on Soviet ships. For over 10 years Royal Navy warships have deployed lasers designed to dazzle pilots of attacking aircraft and they were used during the 1982 Falklands campaign. (Zaloga, S., 'Soviets close to deploying battlefield beam weapons', *Armed Forces Journal International*, May 1990; Gallego, F. and Daly, M., 'Laser weapon in Royal Navy service', *Jane's Defence Weekly*, 13 Jan. 1990; Nguyen, H. P., 'Russia's continuing work on space forces', *Orbis*, summer 1993, pp. 417–18; Munro, N., 'Services to link forces, missile-detection satellites', *Defense News*, 19–25 July 1993, p. 36).
[27] Cook, N., 'Russia leads in "pulse" weapons', *Jane's Defence Weekly*, 10 Oct. 1992, p. 5; Fulghum (note 11), p. 18.
[28] Campbell, C., 'The lethal bomb that does not kill', *Sunday Telegraph*, 27 Sep. 1992, p. 6.
[29] As an illustration of the type and focus of classified discussion a recent (16–17 Nov. 1993) classified conference on non-lethal weapons at the Johns Hopkins University Applied Physics Laboratory had as its purpose 'to bring together industry, government, and academia to explore the potential of non-lethal defense and identify requirements so that the defense community can work together in leveraging the non-lethal concept'. *Chemical Warfare/Chemical and Biological Defense Information Analysis Center Newsletter*, vol. 7, no. 2 (spring 1993), p. 7.
[30] One broad categorization that has been used—based on attempting to distinguish between those weapons which would be used against soldiers and those used to disable equipment (see, for example, Kiernan, V., 'War over weapons that can't kill', *New Scientist*, 11 Dec. 1993, p. 14)—has the problem of substantial overlap in that many of the non-lethal technologies affect both equipment and personnel. This is illustrated below.

necessity based on reports originating with weapons laboratories or other military sources who are strong supporters of non-lethal technologies and who may be prone to overstate certain aspects of their effectiveness.

High-power microwaves

With such missions in mind as the enforcement of embargoes and blockades, high-power microwave (HPM) sources are being designed that would disable various electronic systems. The non-nuclear electromagnetic pulse (EMP) created by these weapons generates power surges in electrical equipment which could disable unprotected electronic systems including those on aircraft, tanks and other vehicles as well as communications, radar and computers.[31] Vehicles could be disabled by interfering with the operation of various electronic components. While the EMP effect associated with nuclear weapons has been well appreciated for decades, increasingly sophisticated technology in advanced industrialized nations, notably the USA, the UK and Russia, is now enabling an EMP to be produced from conventional explosives in a relatively small warhead.

HPM warheads have been under development in classified programmes in the USA for a number of years. They can operate by converting the energy released from a conventional explosive into radio-frequency energy, which then causes disruption of electronic systems which are not hardened against them. It is reportedly planned that the technology will be employed in Tomahawk cruise missiles, their most promising potential targets being air defence sites.[32] In addition some Air Force AGM-86 air-launched cruise missiles (ALCMs) are being removed from their nuclear-attack role and are reportedly to be fitted with EMP-generating warheads.[33] Warheads being developed would concentrate their output within a 30-degree swath with a range of several hundred metres.[34] Because the vulnerability of various targets depends on the frequency employed, much HPM research has focused particularly on ultra-wide band sources.[35]

These weapons can also cause unconsciousness without permanent maiming by upsetting the neural pathways in the brain.[36] Defensive microwave research programmes are also under way against the threat of others acquiring or developing this technology. Since electrical equipment can be hardened

---

[31] US Global Strategy Council, *Nonlethality: A Global Strategy White Paper* (US Global Strategy Council: Washington, DC, 1992), p. 1-A; 'Army prepares for non-lethal combat', *Aviation Week & Space Technology*, 24 May 1993, p. 62.

[32] Holzer, R. and Munro, N. 'Microwave weapon stuns Iraqis', *Defense News*, 13–19 Apr. 1992, p. 1.

[33] Fulghum, D. A., 'ALCMs given nonlethal role', *Aviation Week & Space Technology*, 22 Feb. 1993, p. 20.

[34] Fulghum, D. A., 'EMP weapons lead non-lethal technology', *Aviation Week & Space Technology*, 24 May 1993, p. 61.

[35] *Special Technologies for National Security*, Los Alamos National Laboratory, Los Alamos, N.M., p. 8.

[36] Campbell (note 28), p. 6.

against the effects of these weapons optimal advantage would be gained by secrecy about their development or deployment.[37]

Lasers and other directed-energy weapons

Directed-energy munitions, 'Demons', are being developed to blind the sensors on vehicles or aircraft so that they may then be more readily destroyed by more lethal weapons. Light from an explosion-induced shock-wave is used to pump an inexpensive plastic compact laser (CL) 'bullet' or 'optical flash' device which can be loaded in a gun breech, or it is used to heat an inert gas in multi-directional broad-band visible light sources (isotropic radiators, IR) or unidirectional sources (directed radiators, DR). The latter two weapons, also referred to as Optical Munitions, are being developed by ARDEC in conjunction with the Lawrence Livermore National Laboratory (LLNL).[38] DR weapons are also being developed as 'non-lethal, temporary performance degrading, anti-personnel optical munitions'. Being either broad-band or wavelength-agile, these weapons are difficult to counter using single, simple measures.[39]

Lasers have in fact already been established in combat for such tasks as range finding and target designation. Like many types of non-lethal technology various types of laser which could be used to incapacitate sensors and/or personnel by causing temporary or permanent blindness have been explored for years. A great deal has been written not only on the technological aspects but also on the legal, moral and ethical issues surrounding the use of this type of weapon.[40] Laser weapons designed to dazzle[41] enemy pilots have already been deployed on British Royal Navy warships for 10 years.[42] During the Persian Gulf War the US Army deployed to the Gulf but did not use two test versions of the AN/VLO-7 Stingray Electro-Optical Countermeasures System laser, which was designed to blind enemy sensors.[43] There is an additional report that a laser system with a backpack-sized power source designed

---

[37] Cook (note 27), p. 5. It should be noted however that the EMP produced by conventional explosives is quite different (the voltage spike having a much slower rise time) from that produced by a nuclear explosion. Methods of hardening electronics against nuclear EMP have in fact been found to be ineffective against EMP produced by conventional explosives, and new methods of protection are being developed. See Fulghum (note 33), p. 22.

[38] Optical Munitions are described as the non-lethal weapons in the most completely developed stage at ARDEC—see Weinschenk (note 18), p. 14.

[39] *Special Technologies for National Security* (note 35), p. 5; Tapscott and Atwal (note 19), pp. 44, 46. (quote from p. 44).

[40] See in particular Doswald-Beck, L. (ed.), *Blinding Weapons: Reports of the Meetings of Experts Convened by the International Committee of the Red Cross on Battlefield Laser Weapons 1989–91* (International Committee of the Red Cross: Geneva, 1993) and references therein.

[41] Dazzle has been defined as 'a state where an intense beam of light enters the eye and degrades vision by overloading retinal circuits at the site of the retinal image and by flooding the retina with scattered light, thus severely decreasing contrast sensitivity and visual acuity . . . [with the result that] . . . for a period of time . . . visual function is severely depressed'. Doswald-Beck (note 40), p. 121.

[42] Campbell (note 28), p. 6.

[43] Munro, N. and Opall, B., 'Military studies unusual arsenal', *Defense News*, 19–25 Oct. 1992, p. 3; Starr (note 7), p. 319.

for use against oil storage tanks was deployed during the Gulf War, although whether or not it was used has been debated.[44]

Among the newer research efforts a US Army research programme called COBRA is aimed at developing a laser capable of blinding electronic and optical sensors, and had been partially unclassified until several years ago when an outgrowth of the programme allowed development of a laser rifle for use against personnel. At that point the entire programme was reclassified by the DOD. Capable of blinding soldiers without inflicting long-term harm under normal circumstances, the devices become much more destructive, however, under certain conditions—if the soldier targeted is using a telescopic viewing device, for example. This factor is especially important given the possibility of fratricide unless countermeasures are developed for the rifles, 1100 of which have reportedly been obtained by the Army for field tests.[45]

The COBRA is a prototype of the AN/PLQ-5 Laser Countermeasures System—a 30-pound hand-held laser weapon for use in damaging enemy sensors and human eyes. A contract for its production was signed in February 1992 and it is planned that approximately $80 million will be spent on an upgraded version to be produced by 1998.[46] The technological leap that made this type of lightweight, more powerful and more reliable laser weapon possible is the development of newly developed solid-state lasers.[47]

Among the newer technologies being explored, pulsed chemical lasers that could project a high-temperature, high-pressure plasma in front of a target, which would then create a controllable blast wave, are being investigated at ARDEC and the Los Alamos National Laboratory (LANL). Trials were conducted on a compact deuterium fluoride[48] prototype laser in mid-1993.[49]

Very low-frequency sound (infrasound) acoustic beams are proposed, the effects of which may vary, 'causing disorientation, nausea, vomiting, or bowel spasms'.[50] They can, however, inflict serious damage on internal organs at short range. They are being considered to protect fixed installations because of their large size and heavy fuel consumption, but smaller weapons which could be air-dropped for defence of airfields or important transportation routes are planned. The programme manager of disabling technologies at Los Alamos has pointed to situations such as the 1979 siege of the US Embassy in Tehran as an appropriate use for acoustic weapons.[51] Another acoustic weapon, a high-frequency 'acoustic bullet', creates an impact wave which causes an effect similar to being hit with a blunt object by creating a plasma in front of

[44] Tillman, A. C., 'Weapons for the 21st century soldier', International Defense Review, no. 1 (1994), pp. 37–38.

[45] Tapscott and Atwal (note 19), p. 41.

[46] Munro, N., 'Services to link forces, missile-detection satellites', Defense News, 19–25 July 1993, p. 36.

[47] Munro, N., 'Army tests hand-held laser rifles', Defense News, 5 Mar. 1990.

[48] An important reason for the use of deuterium fluoride is that the frequencies at which it lases overlap with the atmospheric propagation window.

[49] Tapscott and Atwal (note 19), p. 46; Tillman (note 44), p. 38.

[50] US Global Strategy Council (note 31), p. 1-A.

[51] Aviation Week & Space Technology (note 3), p. 50.

the target—blunt object trauma is created rather than the more severe damage that would usually be caused by a conventional bullet.[52]

Chemical and biological agents[53]

Chemical and biological agents could be used in a non-lethal context either to incapacitate humans or to hinder the operation of equipment. Liquid metal embrittlement (LME) agents operate by altering the molecular structure of base metals or alloys and could significantly interfere with the operation of aircraft, vehicles, metal treads and bridge supports to which they were applied. Advertised by proponents as millions of times more caustic than hydrofluoric acid, supercaustics could be shell delivered, for example, and used to 'destroy the optics of heavily armoured vehicles, penetrate vision blocks or glass, or be employed to silently destroy key weapons systems or components'.[54] These would probably be deployed as binary weapons—mixed only during delivery—because of the dangers involved in handling them.[55]

Anti-traction technology employs Teflon-type lubricants which could be used to make surfaces slippery and thus deny or complicate the use of railway tracks, roads or runways. On the other side of the coin, polymer adhesives could be used to glue equipment in place and interfere with its proper operation. These two types of agent are sometimes referred to as 'slick'ems' and 'stick'ems', respectively. Chemicals spread on runways or roads could make rubber tyres brittle.[56] Various types of fast-foaming agents have already been designed—to stop terrorists from successfully raiding nuclear installations.[57]

It is proposed that polymer agents used in burst munitions could be used to foul air-breathing engines. Combustion alteration would interfere with the functioning of an engine by changing the viscosity of or otherwise contaminating its fuel.[58] Research is underway on biological agents which would have the effect of turning stored fuel into jelly or contaminate high explosives.[59]

Quickly delivered into the bloodstream through the skin using dimethyl sulfoxide (DMSO), calmative or sleep agents could be used to incapacitate humans in 'antiterrorist actions, counterinsurgency, ethnic violence, riot control, or even selected hostage situations'.[60]

---

[52] Tapscott and Atwal (note 19), p. 45.
[53] See in addition Stock (note 2), pp. 267–68.
[54] US Global Strategy Council (note 31), pp. 2-A, 4-A.
[55] Rothstein, L., 'The "soft kill" solution', *Bulletin of the Atomic Scientists* (Mar.–Apr. 1994), p. 4.
[56] *Aviation Week & Space Technology* (note 3), p. 51; US Global Strategy Council (note 32), p. 4-A; Barry, J. and Morganthau, T., 'Soon, "phasers on stun"', *Newsweek*, 7 Feb. 1994, p. 27.
[57] Barry and Morganthau (note 56), p. 27; Weinschenk (note 18), p. 14.
[58] US Global Strategy Council (note 31), p. 4-A.
[59] *Aviation Week & Space Technology* (note 3), p. 51; Morrison (note 4), p. 759.
[60] US Global Strategy Council (note 31), p. 4-A.

Other technologies

It is proposed that stun technology, which could be used to render people unconscious or incapable of action for a short time, be refined. Current examples of this technology include the flash/bang grenade, the 'taser'—a hand-held electric stunner—and a battery-operated 20 000 candlepower flash-light—the 'dazzler'.[61] It has been proposed that ceramic shards be fired into the air for use against aircraft to damage their engines or to degrade their stealth capabilities to make them more visible.[62] Relatively simple means include entanglements that could be used to foul propellers on aircraft or ships and nets, either metallic shrouds for entrapping vehicles or filament nets for personnel.[63]

Multi-spectral smoke generators would allow visibility to be controlled by providing specifically tailored spectral windows through which only specially designed optical systems of the user could peer.[64]

Introducing computer viruses into the defence networks of an enemy is also being considered.[65] It has been recommended that means be developed to feed deceptive or false information into communications channels and data bases and computer viruses into enemy computer systems. Defensive capabilities must also be developed in this area, especially as the USA itself relies on highly complex command, control, communications and intelligence (C³I) systems.[66]

Edward Teller has proposed non-lethal weapon concepts including, some-what surprisingly, the use of many small, low-yield nuclear bombs (each of about 100 t of TNT equivalent) which could be spread across an entire country in appropriate places to destroy its infrastructure 'without a single casualty'—civilians having been warned in advance of the specific target areas. His esti-mates are that they could be ready for use in just three years at a cost of a few hundred million dollars.[67] He has also let it be known that the Lawrence Livermore National Laboratory is researching the feasibility of a small rocket capable of being 'guided so accurately that it will fly down the muzzle of a gun, make a little pop, destroy the gun, not the gunner'.[68]

V. Operational uses

Some specific uses for the non-lethal weapons being developed are mentioned above in connection with the individual technologies. As with many issues surrounding non-lethal technologies and weapons, either military thought has

[61] US Global Strategy Council (note 31), p. 5-A.

[62] *Aviation Week & Space Technology* (note 3), p. 51.

[63] US Global Strategy Council (note 31), p. 5-A; Barry and Morganthau (note 56), p. 27.

[64] Alexander, J. B., 'Nonlethal weapons and limited force options', Seminar presented to the Council on Foreign Relations, New York, 27 Oct. 1993.

[65] Peterson, A. P., 'Tactical computers vulnerable to malicious software attacks', *Signal*, Nov. 1993, p. 74; Morrison (note 4), p. 759.

[66] *Aviation Week & Space Technology*, 18 Oct. 1993, p. 29.

[67] Kiernan, V., 'War over weapons that can't kill', *New Scientist*, 11 Dec. 1993, p. 16.

[68] 'Bang! You're alive', *Scientific American*, Apr. 1994, p. 12.

not advanced sufficiently in the area or the details are so classified that it is often difficult to elaborate on the manner in which they could be put into operational use. In fact, as many of the technologies reach higher states of development it may not so much be the capability which will be lacking but rather the doctrine and the mandate for implementation.[69]

In general terms, however, as put forward by John Alexander, head of a non-lethal weapon programme at the Los Alamos National Laboratory in the USA, these technologies can be applied 'across the entire spectrum of conflict from operations-short-of-war to high intensity conflict' and ranging from peacekeeping operations to 'strategic paralysis of an adversarial nation-state' and also potentially including the extension of diplomatic options into areas referred to as coercive diplomacy.[70] Included in documents released by the LANL, which is conducting extensive research into non-lethal weapon options, they are envisioned as filling 'the gap between conventional, lethal military weaponry and diplomatic measures, allowing the US to take measured action against hostile forces while minimising risks for civilian bystanders'.[71]

As seen by the US DOD-sponsored CSIS Study Group on the Military Technical Revolution,[72] the main operational environment for deployment of non-lethal weapons, especially in their initial and near-term use, would most likely be in operations associated with peacekeeping and peace-enforcement, possibly in concert with economic sanctions. Here, it is proposed, the main concerns—to limit casualties on all sides, to disarm combatants pre-emptively if possible and to protect civilians—could be met by the use of non-lethal technology. These weapons could enable peacekeeping forces to defend themselves while at the same time maintaining their authority without having to resort to the use of deadly force. At the same time, however, it must be realized that there remains the possibility of unforeseen high casualty rates as well as the potential for permanent side effects and unexpected collateral or environmental damage. In order to facilitate the important goals of avoiding casualties and hostage-taking in peacekeeping operations during which UN or other forces must be protected while avoiding outright hostilities the US military is developing plans to deliver non-lethal weapons by means of unmanned aerial vehicles.[73]

Another important potential area for the application of non-lethal weapons is in dealing with evolving transnational threats—various forms of terrorist activity as well as threats posed by drug cartels, for example, create contingencies in which the additional force options provided by non-lethal weapons could be useful, especially when the safety of hostages or civilians is involved. The fact that citizens of a state that wishes to take action may be

[69] 'DOD urged to adopt nonlethal warfare strategy', *Defense Electronics*, Mar. 1992, p. 22.
[70] Alexander (note 64).
[71] *Special Technologies for National Security* (note 35), p. 3.
[72] Mazarr (note 8), pp. 53–54.
[73] *Aviation Week & Space Technology* (note 3), p. 50.

involved in the activity provides additional complications which may be avoided by the employment of less than lethal force in certain circumstances.[74]

More specifically, referring to the existence of 'extensive capabilities' in the non-lethal weapon area, the possibility of their use against Serbia under UN auspices to protect Bosnia and Herzegovina was raised by Senator Sam Nunn. It was estimated that attacks similar to those using carbon-fibre warheads in the Gulf War could shut down most of the electrical network of Serbia for several days at a time.[75] The Deputy Director of Planning for the US Air Force stated that any intervention in the former Yugoslavia would 'absolutely' include non-lethal weapons.[76] Non-lethal weapons may also blend the sophisticated with the primitive. In the context of the Bosnian conflict, where high priority would be given to avoiding collateral damage and civilian casualties, the possibility of fitting a laser guidance system on a 1000 lb bomb made simply of concrete has been explored by the US military.[77]

Tear gas was used by the Federal Bureau of Investigation (FBI) during the Branch Davidian stand-off in Waco, Texas in 1993, but the use of exotic non-lethal technology, the exact type of which is unsure, was reportedly also considered. Although their use was rejected, the resultant heavy loss of life and the role that non-lethal means might have been able to play in this or similar situations in the future led to further inter-agency debate concerning disabling weapons. A decision was taken to maintain secrecy on the state of their advancement in order to avoid making potential targets aware of the current state of capabilities in this area. As a result of the incident the US Department of Justice also requested the Central Intelligence Agency (CIA) and the Pentagon to join in an effort to find non-lethal technologies which could be employed for civilian law enforcement as well as in military situations.[78]

Former Defense Secretary Les Aspin noted the important potential role of non-lethal weapons in future peace operations, particularly in the areas of crowd control and demilitarized zone monitoring.[79] He stated that 'If we're going to do these new missions, new inventions may be necessary. We want to examine our experience in Somalia, and the experience of others elsewhere, to see what might be necessary in the future.'[80]

Non-lethal weapons that generate an EMP are seen by the military as being of especially significant interest for Special Forces operations for which 'long-range, lightweight, low/no-signature, precision strike capabilities are essential'.[81] EMP combined with optical munitions in particular are seen as having important applications as precursors to or in conjunction with lethal conflict. The resulting degradation of communications, other electronics, and sensor

[74] Starr (note 5), p. 10; Alexander (note 64).
[75] Quoted in Fulghum, D. A., 'U.S. weighs use of nonlethal weapons in Serbia if U.N. decides to fight', *Aviation Week & Space Technology*, 17 Aug. 1992, p. 62.
[76] Ricks, T. E., 'A kinder, gentler war may be in order', *Globe and Mail* (Toronto), 5 Jan. 1993, p. 1.
[77] Covault, C., 'Carrier-based recon vital', *Aviation Week & Space Technology*, 30 Aug. 1993, p. 51.
[78] Barry and Morganthau (note 56), p. 35.
[79] Weinschenk (note 18), p. 14.
[80] Kiernan, V., 'War over weapons that can't kill', *New Scientist*, 11 Dec. 1993, p. 15.
[81] 'Army prepares for non-lethal combat', *Aviation Week & Space Technology*, 24 May 1993, p. 62.

capabilities coupled with temporary blinding of personnel brought about by the use of non-lethal weapons is seen by some in the military as potentially capable of providing a major adjunct to conventional assault.[82]

VI. Assessment

A major potential problem associated with the development and use of non-lethal weapons lies in the possibility of their leading to destabilization. Designed to avoid the heavy damage and casualties usually associated with conflict, non-lethal weapons could in fact make conflict more likely in certain circumstances by appearing to make it more palatable. Current military thinking would have the USA, for example, involved in a military situation only when decisive and overwhelming force can be applied. This threshold for military involvement could be lowered if it is believed that non-lethal weapons could play a significant role in assuring military success quickly and precisely or keeping loss of life low.[83] Public support for certain military operations might be enhanced if it is perceived that the use of non-lethal weapons would avoid substantial casualties on both sides.

The possible spread of non-lethal technologies is closely linked with the question of stability. At the present time the most substantial effort into the development of non-lethal weapons is occurring in the USA and as long as these weapons remain in the hands of a relatively small number of countries there are good prospects that they can be kept under control. However, a major concern is that these technologies will in fact spread. This concern is particularly felt by the USA, whose military forces are dependent on the 'high-tech' weaponry that many of the non-lethal weapons, especially EMP weapons, are intended to be used against.[84] While weapons generating an EMP may currently be under development in only a few highly technologically advanced nations, the fact that they can have such a highly disruptive effect on the electronics on which most military and civilian functions depend makes them attractive to many other countries. More compact and powerful lasers are increasingly available on a commercial basis and many of the countries becoming able to acquire such systems may not be concerned about whether the blinding effects of laser weapons would be temporary or permanent.

Detailed assessment of individual non-lethal technologies or weapons is complicated in many cases by the absence of a detailed knowledge of their specific capabilities and state of advancement. Probably the most potent of the non-lethal technologies under investigation are those which generate an electromagnetic pulse which can affect all kinds of unprotected electronics. Specific missions range from the enforcement of no-fly zones by disabling aircraft on the ground, through the delivery of an initial incapacitating strike

---

[82] Tapscott and Atwal (note 19), p. 45.
[83] Ricks (note 14), p. 1.
[84] Ricks (note 76), p. 1.

as a prelude to full-fledged air assault[85] to the disabling of a good portion of a society that is increasingly reliant on electronics for its functioning. The delivery method most commonly discussed at least in the USA is via cruise missiles, but bombing would also be a possibility. While protection is possible, it can be quite costly and EMP weapons could therefore conceivably prove highly effective.

Just as in the case of EMP weapons, keeping much of the information about the development or specifics of other non-lethal weapons classified, as is current practice, will certainly make it less likely that an adversary will develop or put into effect appropriate countermeasures. However, the absence of widespread knowledge of the potential of the systems could mean the loss of any deterrent effect[86] which they might have had. It must also be possible to protect one's own forces from the effects of these weapons and if this is easily done it may prove only too simple for the opposing force to effect countermeasures. Excessive secrecy can also become counter-productive by encouraging duplication of effort and preventing the free exchange of ideas among specialists—and this has apparently led to much wasted effort in non-lethal technologies.[87]

There are also bound to be problems associated with the actual use of non-lethal weapons. Many non-lethal weapons including lasers, for example, are weather-dependent, which raises logistical difficulties. Non-lethal weapons might be seen as especially useful in low-intensity conflict and here in particular the possibility and consequences of escalation would be an ever-present problem.

While the intent of using non-lethal weapons is to limit the amount of harm done, in some instances the types of technology involved could lead to results more grotesque than many other conventional weapons, raising serious moral questions. Lasers designed to blind sensors, for example, have the potential to explode the eyeballs of a soldier, and microwave beams intended to incapacitate electronics could have a permanent detrimental effect on a soldier's internal organs.[88] It could prove difficult to avoid such occurrences as the magnitude of the effects may be heavily dependent on the range at which they are employed. In addition, effects may depend on the age and state of health of those against whom a non-lethal technology is used. For some agents designed to produce specific physical and psychological effects avoiding lethal doses may prove difficult. As the Chief of the US Special Operations Command has noted, 'We can design a projectile that will not hurt a grown man but that will kill a child, or someone who is old, infirm or sick. I am very interested but I have not found the Holy Grail yet.'[89]

---

[85] Cook (note 27), p. 5; Campbell (note 28), p. 6.

[86] According to Janet Morris of the US Global Strategy Council, in augmenting current lethal strategies, non-lethal weapons would provide a new level of deterrent below both nuclear and conventional weapons ('DOD urged to adopt nonlethal warfare strategy', *Defense Electronics*, Mar. 1992, p. 22).

[87] Kiernan (note 80), p. 14.

[88] Ricks (note 14), p. 1.

[89] Interview with General Wayne Downing, *Defense News*, 11–17 Apr. 1994, p. 30; Pengelley, R., 'Wanted: a watch on non-lethal weapons', *International Defense Review*, Apr. 1994, p. 1.

The inhumanity of many types of laser weapon is self-evident and their international regulation was discussed in a 1991 Round Table Meeting by the Red Cross. The difficulties of classifying and regulating such weapons were apparent, however—for example, the problems of distinguishing between lasers targeted at sensors and those for use against soldiers. The favoured approach was to work towards banning the use of all weapons primarily designed to damage eyesight.[90]

In this context it has been pointed out that the argument that lasers should be considered more humane than other weapons, the primary purpose of which is to kill, is too simplistic—international human rights agreements and national constitutions, for example, may often prohibit inhumane forms of punishment or torture while at the same time allowing capital punishment. This makes it apparent that death itself is not always considered to be the worst form of injury or suffering.[91] It is clear that this argument could also be applied to other types of non-lethal weapon depending on whether their effects could be considered by some to be 'a fate worse than death'. Consideration of these factors should be a prime concern in future attempts to control the use or deployment of non-lethal technologies in general.

Also, while some of these weapons may not be immediately lethal, their use could in fact have lethal consequences. For example, a flash-blinded pilot may be unable to keep or regain control of an aircraft, and a soldier immobilized by a superglue or rendered unconscious by some other agent may be killed by other weapons being employed at the same time.[92]

Another important question which needs to be raised is what are the options once a non-lethal weapon has been used.[93] In some specific instances when the objective of using a non-lethal weapon—sensor-blinding and EMP, for example—is simply to soften up an enemy position as a precursor to more conventional (and deadly) force,[94] the next move is already decided. In cases in which lethal force is to be avoided it may not be readily apparent how to proceed after an enemy tank column has been immobilized, for example, by 'stick'ems' or 'slick'ems' spread in their path. As even advocates point out, therefore, there is the need to have in place a carefully designed and coherent policy, with careful consideration of long-term goals and objectives, before any force—including non-lethal—is applied.[95] These issues are only now beginning to be explored.

There are as yet no arms control measures which deal specifically with non-lethal weapons. However, the CWC, which is expected to enter into force in

---

[90] Beach, H., *Qualitative Arms Control* (The Council for Arms Control: Washington, DC, Feb. 1993), p. 8.

[91] Doswald-Beck (note 40), p. 80.

[92] Garrett, B. C., 'Nonlethal weapons: an oxymoron', unpublished paper, 1993.

[93] Pine (note 1), p. A1.

[94] In many quarters non-lethal weapons were in fact first considered as adjuncts to more conventional systems, designed to immobilize a target temporarily in order to increase the probability of destruction by other means. See Alexander (note 64).

[95] Alexander (note 64).

1995, as well as the BWC already contain provisions which may have a bearing on aspects of their development or use in certain circumstances.

The development of superacids, superglues and many other chemical means which are now being considered under the non-lethal warfare heading could be incompatible with the goals of the CWC.[96] While not yet in force, the CWC *inter alia* would prohibit states parties from developing, producing or otherwise acquiring, stockpiling or retaining or transferring, directly or indirectly chemical weapons. Included in the definition of chemical weapons are those toxic chemicals which 'can cause death, temporary incapacitation or permanent harm to humans or animals'.[97] Supercaustics which, as discussed above, may be meant to disable sensors or other parts of weapon systems could have the potential to cause death or permanent harm to personnel if they come in contact with them.

Another politically sensitive area concerns work on micro-organisms for use as non-lethal weapons. The 1972 BW Convention prohibits the development, production, stockpiling, acquisition or retention of microbial or biological agents for use as weapons. However, biological agents are seen as very attractive as far as many of the prospective non-lethal missions including fuel degradation, for example, are concerned and there is substantial interest in their potential impact in the non-lethal area. An extensive study of biological agents which could pose threats to fuels and materials was recently completed at the Los Alamos National Laboratory[98] and, as has been remarked by John Alexander, head of a programme in non-lethal weaponry there, 'There is almost nothing that some microbe won't eat, so the potential [non-lethal] applications are extensive.'[99] From the arms control perspective, it is important to bear in mind that the development of such agents for offensive warfare purposes would be prohibited by the BWC.

Logistical requirements for the employment of non-lethal weapons could hinder their effectiveness in many circumstances. For example, most of the chemical agents such as superacids and superglues discussed here would need to be employed at relatively short range and the intelligence requirements for targeting them may well be very substantial. It may also prove very difficult to verify which equipment has actually been affected by non-lethal technology and it would therefore be wise to develop the necessary specific damage-assessment techniques in parallel with newly proposed non-lethal weapon systems.[100]

Large and relatively powerful acoustic weapons could prove highly effective in protecting fixed installations such as embassy compounds or other large installations where they could be permanently deployed without their

[96] Garrett (note 92).

[97] The Convention on the Prohibition of the Development, Production, Stockpiling and Use of Chemical Weapons and on their Destruction, Articles I.1, II.1, 2. The CWC is reprinted in SIPRI (note 2), pp. 735–56. For a detailed discussion of new chemical agents and technologies as they relate to the CWC see *Chemical Weapons Convention Bulletin*, no. 23 (Mar. 1994), p. 1.

[98] *Special Technologies for National Security* (note 35), p. 7.

[99] Alexander (note 64).

[100] Ricks (note 14), p. 1; Alexander (note 64).

dimensions presenting a problem. The smaller versions which are now being planned could also serve effective point defence purposes for a limited period of time. Less clear is the advantage that an 'acoustic bullet' would have over, say, a rubber bullet which can be fired from a relatively small weapon.

Superlubricants are believed to be somewhat impractical at the present time because of the large quantities needed for effectiveness and the added need that they be tailored to specific weather conditions.[101] Superglues and super-slippery substances, even if they function as advertised, may be used to make roads or railways impassable to an enemy—but they will then be equally impassable when those using these non-lethal technologies might need to make subsequent use of the same transport routes. If counteracting substances were available then unless their existence or composition remained a closely guarded secret they could as well be used by a prospective enemy or other target.

It has been pointed out that the monetary costs associated with non-lethal weapons may be moderate. In general, new delivery platforms will not be required and many non-lethal weapons will take the form of new munitions or sub-systems which make use of modifications or upgrades of existing weapon systems.[102] However, although the size of the classified effort is difficult to estimate, the 1996 Pentagon budget request could reportedly contain tens of millions of dollars with the programme cost growing to in excess of $1 billion in the next several years.[103]

In spite of the potential difficulties involved in their use as discussed above, there is a concerted effort to promote non-lethal weapons, in the USA in particular. A White Paper on non-lethality released by the Global Strategy Council in Washington—an organization that is lobbying heavily for increased reliance on non-lethal options and which reflects a substantial body of opinion within the military establishment—has gone so far as to state that 'regional and low intensity conflict (adventurism, insurgency, ethnic violence, terrorism, narco-trafficking, domestic crime) can *only* be countered decisively with low lethality operations, tactics and weapons'. It goes on to point out that the consequences of massive force in these circumstances will result in the death of innocents, destruction of property, loss of the media war and the creation of generations of enemies for the USA.[104] As this chapter shows, the development and use of non-lethal weapons pose many problems. Any planned substantial reliance on such weapons will necessitate a serious reassessment of military doctrine as well as a rethinking of overall military planning and strategy.

---

[101] Rothstein (note 55), p. 5.
[102] Alexander (note 64).
[103] Opall, B., 'DoD to boost nonlethal options', *Defense News*, 28 Mar.–3 Apr. 1994, p. 46.
[104] US Global Strategy Council (note 31), p. 1 (emphasis added).

VII. Conclusions

The post cold-war geopolitical situation and new technological developments are enabling new force options involving non-lethal weapons to be envisaged. This chapter explores some key questions related to new developments of these weapons, their prospective uses and the possible repercussions. For the time being, even in the area of the specific technologies involved, the answers have to remain incomplete owing to the classified nature of the research. The new technologies are being explored for use in a variety of military contingencies, including peacekeeping and counter-terrorist activities, as well as for use as a possible precursor to and in concert with more conventional military actions. Interest is also being expressed in their use for civil law enforcement.

All indications point to an increase in funding levels for these weapon programmes (although this is difficult to demonstrate conclusively since most funding is probably buried in classified portions of the budgets). It is also apparent that a consensus is beginning to build, especially in the United States, and that a coherent integrated policy architecture is well on the way to being constructed, although the results of this make-over remain unclear at the present time. However, with the military seeking and being asked to perform a host of new missions and facing new obligations and responsibilities, and with weapon laboratories actively seeking new tasks for their under-employed staffs, the push for new non-lethal weapon technologies is likely to continue.

From the information which is openly available it is amply clear that careful consideration should be given before any further large-scale investment is made in development of the technologies involved. The potential consequences of deploying and actually using these weapons should be continually reassessed and thoroughly understood.

Part III. Military expenditure, arms production and trade, 1993

Chapter 12. World military expenditure

Chapter 13. Arms production and arms trade

12. World military expenditure

NICOLE BALL, BENGT-GÖRAN BERGSTRAND,
STEVEN M. KOSIAK, EVAMARIA LOOSE-WEINTRAUB,
DAVID SHAMBAUGH and ERIK WHITLOCK*

I. Introduction

Data on and estimates of military expenditure developments both in individual countries and in the world at large are not as precise as the figures at first might indicate. Given this word of caution, there is, however, general agreement among most observers of military spending—including certain international organizations, such as the United Nations and the International Monetary Fund (IMF)—on two points: (a) that world military spending peaked around 1986–87, when it reached a level of at least $1000 billion; and (b) that world military spending has continuously declined since then. Developments in 1993 have not shown any break but have been very much in line with this general trend of decreasing military spending.

One way to appraise global military spending trends is to monitor developments among the major military spenders. In the peak years 1986–87, the United States and the Soviet Union each accounted for roughly 30 per cent of global military spending, the whole of NATO about 45 per cent and the Warsaw Treaty Organization (WTO) about 35 per cent, indicating that the two 'superpower alliances' were responsible for at least 80 per cent of the world's military outlays. Accordingly, developments among these major spenders have a very big impact on the aggregated world total.[1]

Section II deals with NATO developments in the United States as well as in the three major European NATO countries—the United Kingdom, France and Germany.[2]

Sections III and IV analyse developments in Russia and in Central and Eastern Europe, respectively. During the cold war, the WTO countries released very little information on their military spending, and there was an occasionally intense debate in the West on the real size of military spending in those countries. In spite of greater openness, the assessment of military spending in

---

[1] Because the SIPRI data base on world military expenditure is in the process of being reconstructed, the world tables are not published in this *Yearbook*. A number of experts on individual countries have contributed to this chapter.
[2] In section II of this chapter, France and Germany are dealt with more extensively than the UK; for more detailed information on British military spending, see Deger, S., 'World military expenditure', SIPRI, *SIPRI Yearbook 1993: World Armaments and Disarmament* (Oxford University Press: Oxford, 1993), chapter 9, section IV.

* N. Ball (section VI), B.-G. Bergstrand (section I and the sections on the UK, France and Germany in section II), S. M. Kosiak (the section on the USA in section II), E. Loose-Weintraub (section IV), D. Shambaugh (section V) and E. Whitlock (section III).

the former East is still difficult, not least because high inflation in many of these countries compels them to continuously revise their budgets and spending plans, making data on annual spending rather uncertain.[3]

Section V analyses military spending in China.[4] The increased economic and strategic significance of China makes it imperative to monitor Chinese developments. It is also one of the few major powers to show an increase and not a decline in military spending. However, China still surrounds its military expenditures with the same kind of secrecy that the Soviet Union previously accorded its military spending, and it is therefore necessary also to examine some of the methodological problems involved.

Finally, section VI deals with the problems of 'conditionality'. Until recently, the questions of Third World military spending and development aid were treated as two different topics, but in the early 1990s it was increasingly argued that the two issues could no longer be separated.

II. NATO

In the early 1990s, both the member states of NATO and the NATO Alliance as such have moved away from the kind of security policies and force postures upheld during the cold war. At the important NATO summit meeting in Rome in November 1991, several far-reaching decisions on NATO's future military posture were made which have already influenced both the level and the distribution of defence spending within NATO. Of particular importance were the agreements to abolish most of the nuclear weapons belonging to NATO; to cut the forces deployed in the NATO Central Europe theatre—the number of soldiers in this region will be reduced from about 2.8 million in 1991 to 2.1 million in 1994; and to reorganize the remaining standing forces into three different types: (*a*) Reaction Forces, consisting of the Immediate Reaction Force, the Rapid Reaction Force and other units; (*b*) the Main Defence Force; and (*c*) the Augmentation Force.[5]

In line with these general policy themes, the NATO nuclear-weapon powers now devote much less attention, and fewer resources, to nuclear weapons, while the size of the armed forces, expressed in numbers of units and in manpower, is continuously decreasing. As shown in table 12.1, the number of people in the armed forces is declining—except in Greece, Luxembourg and Turkey—in all the NATO countries. Between 1989 and 1993, NATO military manpower declined from close to 5.9 million to less than 5.1 million, or by about 13 per cent. (If Greece and Turkey are excluded—and it might be argued that these two countries belong to another geostrategic theatre than the other NATO countries, less affected by so-called East–West relations— NATO forces dropped from about 4.9 million to 4.1 million, representing a 17

---

[3] See *SIPRI Yearbook 1993* (note 2), pp. 351–67, 398–414.
[4] See also appendix 13E in this volume for military expenditure data for the countries of East Asia.
[5] For overall NATO developments, see various issues of the official NATO journal, *NATO Review*, as well as *NATO's Sixteen Nations*.

Table 12.1. NATO armed forces, total military personnel, 1980–93

Figures are in thousands.

Country	1980	1981	1982	1983	1984	1985	1986	1987	1988	1989	1990	1991	1992	1993
North America														
Canada	82	81	82	81	82	83	85	86	88	88	87	86	82	80
USA	2 050	2 168	2 201	2 201	2 222	2 244	2 269	2 279	2 246	2 241	2 181	2 115	1 919	1 837
Europe														
Belgium	108	109	110	109	107	107	107	109	110	110	106	101	79	72
Denmark	33	33	30	30	31	29	28	28	30	31	31	30	28	28
France	575	575	578	578	571	563	558	559	558	554	550	542	522	506
Germany[a]	490	493	491	496	487	495	495	495	495	503	545	457	442	398
Greece	186	188	188	177	197	201	202	199	199	201	201	205	208	213
Italy[b]	474	(479)	(490)	(472)	(482)	504	(482)	504	506	506	493	473	471	450
Luxembourg	1	1	1	1	1	1	1	1	1	1	1	1	1	1
Netherlands	107	108	106	104	103	103	106	106	107	106	104	104	90	86
Norway	40	39	41	41	39	36	38	38	40	43	51	41	42	..
Portugal	88	88	89	93	100	102	101	105	104	104	87	86	80	80
Spain[c]	356	(366)	(372)	(355)	342	314	314	314	304	277	263	246	198	199
Turkey[d]	717	741	769	824	815	814	860	879	847	780	769	804	(804)	811
UK	330	341	334	333	336	334	331	328	324	318	308	301	293	273
NATO total	**5 637**	**5 810**	**5 882**	**5 895**	**5 915**	**5 930**	**5 977**	**6 030**	**5 959**	**5 863**	**5 777**	**5 592**	**5 259**	**(5 076)**

[a] Figures on German manpower refer to West Germany through 1990 and to the united Germany from 1991.

[b] From 1992, NATO has reported lower manpower figures for Italy than before. Consequently no new figures have been given for the years 1981–84 or for 1986. Figures for these years are SIPRI estimates.

[c] NATO has not published figures for Spain for the years 1981–83; figures for these years are SIPRI estimates.

[d] In its Dec. 1993 press release, NATO reported a 1992 manpower figure for Turkey of 704 000, a surprisingly low figure compared to the figures reported for 1991 and 1993. It was therefore assumed that this figure is a misprint and should read 804 000.

( ) SIPRI estimates.

Sources: Various issues of the official journal *NATO Review* and NATO press release 'Financial and economic data relating to NATO defence', 8 Dec. 1993.

per cent decline.) Even if there are no automatic links between the manpower size of the armed forces and defence budgets (monies might be spent on equipment instead of personnel, and a reduction in gross numbers might be offset by higher wages for the remaining manpower, etc.), the decline in NATO military manpower nevertheless gives some rough volume indications of where defence budgets are going.

During the cold war, NATO stressed the importance of heavy mechanized forces, to be used in the perceived NATO–WTO showdown in Central Europe. With the disappearance of this Eastern threat, there is much less need for such forces, and it is in this context that the new distinction between the three new kinds of forces should be understood. The emphasis on highly mobile, less mechanized and élite-like Reaction Forces is here of particular importance, as it signifies a new attitude, both among many NATO member states and on the part of the Alliance at large, of developing new kinds of crisis-management capabilities and forces that could also be used for both peacekeeping and peace-enforcement missions.

These strategic developments have in most NATO countries resulted in either reduced or frozen military budgets. Tables 12.2–12.4 give figures on NATO military spending. NATO aggregated military spending peaked in 1986–87 and has gradually declined ever since, for the entire period by about 15 per cent. For the time being, all NATO countries except Luxembourg and Turkey show stagnating or declining military expenditures.

Within NATO, US military spending currently—based on 1993 spending and exchange-rates—constitutes about 60 per cent of the NATO total; British, French and German spending each constitutes about 8 per cent; and all the other 11 members account for the remaining 15 per cent. Hence, all the figures on NATO aggregate military spending are very much influenced by US developments. In fact, the annual *change* in US military spending is often bigger than the total defence budgets of many other NATO countries. The increase that was noticeable in NATO military spending from 1991 to 1992 could consequently be attributed to the increase in US spending that was seen in 1992, to a large degree a result of the US participation in the 1991 Persian Gulf War.

A careful examination of NATO spending over a longer period of time reveals several different patterns. In some countries, military expenditures increase fairly rapidly, then reach a clear peaking-point and then decline. Belgium, Spain, the UK and the USA are typical examples of such a pattern, where military spending peaked in 1987, 1987, 1984 and 1986, respectively. In Belgium, Spain and the UK, decreases in military spending have resulted in a spending level that in real terms is equivalent to the sums spent on defence during the mid-1970s; however, US military spending is, in real terms, still higher than it was before the 'Reagan buildup'.

As noted above and in table 12.2, Luxembourg and Turkey show a pattern of increased spending. In most other NATO countries—such as Canada, Denmark, France, Greece, Italy, Norway and Portugal—after a period of

Table 12.2. NATO military expenditure, in current figures, 1980–93

Figures are in local currency, current prices.

Country	Currency	1980	1981	1982	1983	1984	1985	1986	1987	1988	1989	1990	1991	1992	1993
North America															
Canada	m. dollars	5 788	6 289	7 802	8 815	9 753	10 332	10 970	11 715	12 336	12 854	13 473	12 830	13 111	13 244
USA	m. dollars	138 191	165 099	189 971	213 626	231 459	258 165	281 105	288 157	293 093	304 085	306 170	280 292	305 141	297 325
Europe															
Belgium	m. francs	115 754	125 689	132 127	136 615	139 113	144 183	152 079	155 422	150 647	152 917	155 205	157 919	132 819	130 028
Denmark	m. kroner	9 117	10 301	11 669	12 574	13 045	13 344	13 333	14 647	15 620	15 963	16 399	17 091	17 129	17 514
France	m. francs	111 672	129 708	148 021	165 029	176 638	186 715	197 080	209 525	215 073	225 331	232 801	240 936	240 874	242 798
Germany[a]	m. D. Marks	48 518	52 193	54 234	56 496	57 274	58 650	60 130	61 354	61 638	63 178	68 376	65 579	65 536	63 854
Greece	m. drachmas	96 975	142 865	176 270	193 340	271 922	321 981	338 465	393 052	471 820	503 032	612 344	693 846	835 458	934 040
Italy	b. lire	7 643	9 548	11 896	13 933	15 901	17 767	19 421	22 872	25 539	27 342	28 007	30 191	30 813	..
Luxembourg	m. francs	1 534	1 715	1 893	2 104	2 234	2 265	2 390	2 730	3 163	2 995	3 233	3 681	3 963	4 025
Netherlands	m. guilders	10 476	11 296	11 921	12 149	12 762	12 901	13 110	13 254	13 300	13 571	13 513	13 548	13 900	13 072
Norway	m. kroner	8 242	9 468	10 956	12 395	12 688	15 446	16 033	18 551	18 865	20 248	21 251	21 313	22 871	22 998
Portugal	m. escudos	43 440	51 917	63 817	76 765	92 009	111 375	139 972	159 288	194 036	229 344	267 299	305 643	341 904	360 088
Spain[b]	m. pesetas	350 423	(379 181)	(435 584)	(500 177)	594 932	674 883	715 306	852 767	835 353	923 375	922 808	947 173	927 852	917 530
Turkey	b. lira	203	313	448	557	803	1 235	1 868	2 477	3 789	7 158	13 866	23 657	42 320	68 733
UK	m. pounds	11 593	12 648	14 870	15 830	17 511	18 301	18 639	19 269	19 290	20 868	22 413	24 518	23 776	23 353

[a] Figures on German military expenditure refer to West Germany through 1990 and to the united Germany from 1991.

[b] NATO has not published figures for Spain for the years 1981–83; figures for these years are SIPRI estimates.

Sources: Various issues of the official NATO journal *NATO Review* and NATO press release 'Financial and economic data relating to NATO defence', 8 Dec. 1993.

Table 12.3. NATO military expenditure, in constant price figures, 1980–93

Figures are expressed in US $m., at 1985 prices and exchange-rates; figures in italics are percentages and show the change from the previous year.

Country	1980	1981[a]	1982	1983	1984	1985	1986	1987	1988	1989	1990	1991	1992	1993
North America														
Canada	5 662	(5 778)	6 125	6 616	7 094	7 566	7 760	8 003	8 044	8 004	8 145	7 589	7 618	7 552
		2.0	*6.0*	*8.0*	*7.2*	*6.7*	*2.6*	*3.1*	*0.5*	*-0.5*	*1.8*	*-6.8*	*0.4*	*-0.9*
USA	192 288	(204 541)	215 868	232 153	243 025	258 165	278 519	273 661	269 654	268 622	262 024	227 292	242 414	229 065
		6.4	*5.5*	*7.5*	*4.7*	*6.2*	*7.9*	*-1.7*	*-1.5*	*-0.4*	*-2.5*	*-13.3*	*6.7*	*-5.5*
Europe														
Belgium	2 449	(2 460)	2 468	2 457	2 425	2 428	2 549	2 594	2 484	2 424	2 393	2 356	1 934	1 856
		0.5	*0.3*	*-0.4*	*-1.3*	*0.1*	*5.0*	*1.8*	*-4.2*	*-2.4*	*-1.2*	*-1.5*	*-17.9*	*-4.0*
Denmark	1 248	(1 250)	1 252	1 262	1 248	1 259	1 255	1 283	1 320	1 307	1 310	1 332	1 297	1 300
		0.1	*0.1*	*0.8*	*-1.1*	*0.9*	*-0.3*	*2.3*	*2.9*	*-1.0*	*0.3*	*1.6*	*-2.6*	*0.3*
France	19 294	(19 797)	20 307	20 889	20 837	20 780	20 848	21 497	21 415	21 732	21 777	21 860	21 363	21 050
		2.6	*2.6*	*2.9*	*-0.2*	*-0.3*	*0.3*	*3.1*	*-0.4*	*1.5*	*0.2*	*0.4*	*-2.3*	*-1.5*
Germany[b]	19 340	(19 709)	19 914	20 174	20 043	19 922	19 922	19 838	19 576	19 558	20 465	18 892	17 929	16 765
		1.9	*1.0*	*1.3*	*-0.7*	*-0.6*	*0.0*	*-0.4*	*-1.3*	*-0.1*	*4.6*	*-7.7*	*-5.1*	*-6.5*
Greece	1 773	(1 993)	2 154	1 982	2 317	2 331	2 090	2 129	2 202	2 083	2 104	1 995	2 082	2 084
		12.4	*8.1*	*-8.0*	*16.9*	*0.6*	*-10.3*	*1.9*	*3.4*	*-5.4*	*1.0*	*-5.2*	*4.4*	*0.1*
Italy	8 144	(8 329)	8 556	8 767	9 014	9 305	9 379	10 005	10 440	10 342	9 794	9 609	9 736	..
		2.3	*2.7*	*2.5*	*2.8*	*3.2*	*0.8*	*6.7*	*4.4*	*-0.9*	*-5.3*	*-1.9*	*1.3*	
Luxembourg	34	(36)	37	39	39	38	40	45	52	47	50	54	57	56
		5.1	*3.5*	*3.5*	*0.5*	*-1.6*	*3.6*	*13.4*	*15.2*	*-8.1*	*4.5*	*9.2*	*4.7*	*-1.8*
Netherlands	3 507	(3 634)	3 731	3 750	3 870	3 884	4 032	4 070	4 082	4 132	4 026	3 919	3 907	3 638
		3.6	*2.7*	*0.5*	*3.2*	*0.4*	*3.8*	*0.9*	*0.3*	*1.2*	*-2.6*	*-2.7*	*-0.3*	*-6.9*
Norway	1 471	(1 517)	1 572	1 635	1 560	1 797	1 764	1 935	1 865	1 921	1 937	1 872	1 972	1 953
		3.2	*3.7*	*4.0*	*-4.6*	*15.2*	*-1.8*	*9.7*	*-3.6*	*3.0*	*0.8*	*-3.3*	*5.3*	*-1.0*

Portugal	684	(689)	695	674	643	654	681	698	762	797	812	814	809	793
	..	*0.7*	*0.9*	*-3.1*	*-4.6*	*1.6*	*4.2*	*2.5*	*9.1*	*4.6*	*2.0*	*0.2*	*-0.7*	*-2.0*
Spain[c]	3 530	(3 564)	(3 625)	(3 694)	3 798	3 969	3 793	4 267	3 955	4 085	3 804	3 654	3 358	3 178
	..	*1.0*	*1.7*	*1.9*	*2.8*	*4.5*	*-4.4*	*12.5*	*-7.3*	*3.3*	*-6.9*	*-3.9*	*-8.1*	*-5.4*
Turkey	2 170	(2 233)	2 311	2 208	2 180	2 365	2 673	2 639	2 727	3 055	3 513	3 611	3 789	3 877
	..	*2.9*	*3.5*	*-4.4*	*-1.3*	*8.5*	*13.0*	*-1.3*	*3.4*	*12.0*	*15.0*	*2.8*	*4.9*	*2.3*
UK	21 347	(21 861)	22 944	23 042	23 955	23 724	23 173	22 549	21 358	21 666	21 635	21 744	20 059	19 082
	..	*2.4*	*5.0*	*0.4*	*4.0*	*-1.0*	*-2.3*	*-2.7*	*-5.3*	*1.4*	*-0.1*	*0.5*	*-7.8*	*-4.9*
NATO Europe	84 993	(87 072)	89 565	90 572	91 929	92 456	92 197	93 549	92 239	93 150	93 621	91 713	88 290	(85 367)
	..	*2.4*	*2.9*	*1.1*	*1.5*	*0.6*	*-0.3*	*1.5*	*-1.4*	*1.0*	*0.5*	*-2.0*	*-3.7*	*-3.3*
NATO total	282 943	(297 391)	311 558	329 342	342 048	358 188	378 476	375 213	369 937	369 776	363 790	326 594	338 323	(321 984)
	..	*5.1*	*4.8*	*5.7*	*3.9*	*4.7*	*5.7*	*-0.9*	*-1.4*	*0.0*	*-1.6*	*-10.2*	*3.6*	*-4.8*

[a] NATO has not published constant price figures for 1981; hence, all 1981 figures are SIPRI estimates.

[b] Figures on German military expenditure refer to West Germany through 1990 and to the united Germany from 1991.

[c] NATO has not published figures for Spain for the years 1981–83; figures for these years are SIPRI estimates.

Sources: Various issues of the official journal *NATO Review* and NATO press release 'Financial and economic data relating to NATO defence', 8 Dec. 1993.

Table 12.4. NATO military expenditure, as a share of GDP, 1980–93

Figures are percentages.

	1980	1981	1982	1983	1984	1985	1986	1987	1988	1989	1990	1991	1992	1993
North America														
Canada	1.9	1.8	2.1	2.2	2.2	2.2	2.2	2.1	2.0	2.0	2.0	1.9	1.9	1.9
USA	5.1	5.4	6.0	6.3	6.1	6.4	6.6	6.3	6.0	5.8	5.5	4.9	5.1	4.8
Europe														
Belgium	3.3	3.4	3.3	3.2	3.1	3.0	3.0	2.9	2.6	2.5	2.4	2.3	1.9	1.8
Denmark	2.4	2.5	2.5	2.5	2.3	2.2	2.0	2.1	2.1	2.1	2.0	2.1	2.0	2.0
France	4.0	4.1	4.1	4.1	4.0	4.0	3.9	3.9	3.8	3.7	3.6	3.6	3.4	3.4
Germany[a]	3.3	3.4	3.4	3.4	3.3	3.2	3.1	3.1	2.9	2.8	2.8	2.2–2.5	2.0–2.7	2.0–2.6
Greece	5.7	7.0	6.8	6.3	7.1	7.0	6.1	6.3	6.3	5.7	5.8	5.4	5.5	5.4
Italy	2.0	2.1	2.2	2.2	2.2	2.2	2.2	2.3	2.3	2.3	2.1	2.1	2.0	2.0
Luxembourg	1.2	1.2	1.2	1.2	1.2	1.1	1.1	1.2	1.3	1.1	1.1	1.2	1.2	1.2
Netherlands	3.1	3.2	3.2	3.2	3.2	3.1	3.1	3.0	2.9	2.8	2.6	2.5	2.5	2.3
Norway	2.9	2.9	3.0	3.1	2.8	3.1	3.1	3.3	3.2	3.3	3.2	3.1	3.3	3.2
Portugal	3.5	3.5	3.4	3.3	3.3	3.2	3.2	3.1	3.2	3.2	3.1	3.1	3.0	2.9
Spain	2.3	2.3	2.3	2.4	2.4	2.4	2.2	2.4	2.1	2.1	1.8	1.7	1.6	1.5
Turkey	4.7	4.9	5.2	4.8	4.4	4.5	4.8	4.2	3.8	4.3	4.9	5.1	4.7	4.8
UK	5.0	5.0	5.3	5.2	5.4	5.1	4.8	4.5	4.1	4.0	4.1	4.3	4.0	3.8

[a] For Germany, figures in the columns for 1991–93: the first figure is for German military spending related only to West German GDP, and the second figure to total German GDP, including the eastern *Länder*.

Sources: In this table, the figures in table 12.2 on military spending are related to figures on gross domestic product (GDP), usually taken from the International Monetary Fund publication *International Financial Statistics*. In the various issues of the official journal *NATO Review* and NATO press release 'Financial and economic data relating to NATO defence', 8 Dec. 1993, figures on the share of military spending related to GDP have also been reported. For some countries and years, these NATO figures differ from those given in this table.

Table 12.5. NATO distribution of military expenditures, by category, 1980–93

All figures are percentages.

Country	Category	1980–84	1985	1986	1987	1988	1989	1990	1991	1992	1993
North America											
Canada	Personnel	50.7	45.1	46.7	46.1	45.4	47.9	50.0	49.4	49.9	48.1
	Equipment	17.8	18.5	20.2	21.4	20.1	18.4	17.0	18.1	18.6	19.1
	Infrastructure	2.3	1.8	2.6	2.6	2.9	3.7	3.9	3.4	3.1	2.4
	Other operating expenditures	29.0	34.0	30.5	29.9	31.6	30.0	29.2	29.2	28.3	30.4
USA	Personnel	41.9	37.5	35.8	35.9	37.6	38.2	36.6	43.2	39.3	38.6
	Equipment	21.9	25.7	25.8	26.5	24.8	25.3	24.8	27.3	22.9	21.5
	Infrastructure	1.6	1.6	1.8	2.0	2.0	1.7	1.7	1.2	1.4	1.8
	Other operating expenditures	34.5	35.1	36.6	35.5	35.6	34.9	36.9	28.2	36.4	38.1
Europe											
Belgium	Personnel	61.8	63.0	61.2	62.1	63.7	67.1	68.4	68.9	65.3	68.0
	Equipment	13.8	12.7	12.9	13.1	12.0	9.9	7.9	8.2	8.2	8.5
	Infrastructure	5.5	3.5	4.4	4.6	3.9	3.0	3.8	2.8	5.2	3.7
	Other operating expenditures	18.8	19.9	21.5	20.3	20.4	20.0	19.9	20.1	21.2	19.7
Denmark	Personnel	54.6	53.8	56.1	55.2	58.0	59.8	58.4	57.2	56.2	57.5
	Equipment	16.9	13.8	14.0	14.9	14.4	13.1	14.9	15.8	17.8	17.8
	Infrastructure	2.8	3.8	3.3	2.8	3.4	4.0	3.4	4.3	3.7	2.5
	Other operating expenditures	25.7	28.5	26.5	27.1	24.2	23.1	23.4	22.7	21.8	22.3
Germany[a]	Personnel	46.6	46.1	48.5	49.2	49.7	51.1	52.1	56.6	58.6	59.2
	Equipment	20.0	14.8	20.4	20.1	19.3	19.0	17.7	15.6	13.3	12.0
	Infrastructure	5.4	6.0	6.1	5.8	5.6	5.8	5.9	4.9	4.5	5.2
	Other operating expenditures	28.0	33.1	25.0	24.9	25.5	24.0	24.3	22.9	23.6	23.6

Country	Category	1980–84	1985	1986	1987	1988	1989	1990	1991	1992	1993
Greece	Personnel	54.6	59.6	61.8	61.7	58.2	61.5	64.1	64.4	61.4	60.8
	Equipment	17.4	14.5	15.8	17.2	23.3	21.9	21.4	20.3	23.4	24.1
	Infrastructure	2.8	3.1	1.9	1.9	2.3	2.6	2.1	1.7	2.4	2.5
	Other operating expenditures	24.9	23.3	20.5	19.2	16.1	14.0	12.3	13.6	12.8	12.6
Italy	Personnel	59.1	55.6	57.7	59.0	57.8	58.7	61.6	64.1	63.7	..
	Equipment	17.4	18.8	18.4	20.6	20.5	20.5	17.5	16.3	15.0	..
	Infrastructure	2.3	2.5	3.3	2.4	2.5	2.3	2.8	2.3	2.7	..
	Other operating expenditures	21.0	23.2	20.6	18.0	19.2	18.5	18.1	17.2	18.5	..
Luxembourg	Personnel	77.5	78.6	77.6	76.8	74.7	77.1	79.6	70.6	75.8	75.4
	Equipment	1.8	4.0	3.1	3.9	2.8	3.8	3.2	5.4	4.6	4.4
	Infrastructure	10.3	3.3	8.1	8.9	5.5	7.1	7.0	14.8	10.6	10.6
	Other operating expenditures	10.2	10.4	11.1	10.3	16.9	11.9	10.2	9.2	9.0	9.6
Netherlands	Personnel	55.3	51.2	51.3	53.6	54.3	53.7	53.9	55.2	57.5	58.1
	Equipment	20.5	23.4	20.3	17.8	20.4	17.6	17.9	15.6	14.2	10.4
	Infrastructure	3.7	4.2	4.6	4.7	5.2	6.6	5.9	6.2	5.8	5.5
	Other operating expenditures	20.3	20.5	23.8	23.9	20.1	22.2	22.3	22.9	22.6	26.0
Norway	Personnel	48.8	42.7	45.6	43.3	45.6	42.6	43.3	46.3	43.8	45.1
	Equipment	19.4	24.9	20.2	20.4	18.8	24.8	22.6	22.0	24.4	24.2
	Infrastructure	5.0	9.1	7.5	9.7	8.2	8.7	9.8	9.5	9.8	8.2
	Other operating expenditures	26.7	25.4	26.6	26.5	27.4	24.0	24.3	22.3	22.1	22.5
Portugal	Personnel	66.6	69.3	66.2	65.7	66.3	71.4	73.1	74.9	80.5	79.9
	Equipment	5.5	3.3	6.3	10.1	10.5	11.9	10.3	8.5	2.2	6.2
	Infrastructure	5.9	5.7	3.7	3.7	4.1	2.8	3.4	3.4	5.3	3.5
	Other operating expenditures	21.9	23.2	23.9	20.6	19.0	14.0	13.3	13.2	12.0	10.5

Spain									
Personnel	..	..	49.7	54.5	57.3	62.0	64.7	69.5	69.4
Equipment	..	23.6	24.7	20.7	18.3	12.7	12.9	10.9	11.4
Infrastructure	..	..	4.0	3.2	3.1	2.3	1.6	1.0	0.9
Other operating expenditures	..	..	21.6	21.6	21.3	23.0	20.8	18.7	18.4
Turkey									
Personnel	36.9	33.3	34.7	35.6	46.1	48.3	48.5	48.7	49.6
Equipment	13.6	17.9	21.1	22.5	17.2	20.0	22.7	24.8	25.6
Infrastructure	7.3	6.1	5.9	4.5	3.8	3.2	2.8	3.5	3.2
Other operating expenditures	41.8	42.6	38.3	37.5	32.9	28.5	26.0	23.0	21.6
UK									
Personnel	37.4	39.0	39.0	40.7	39.5	40.6	41.7	43.8	42.1
Equipment	26.2	25.2	24.7	25.4	22.0	17.9	19.4	18.1	15.7
Infrastructure	2.7	3.9	3.7	4.1	4.1	5.1	4.4	2.9	3.8
Other operating expenditures	33.5	31.8	32.6	29.7	34.4	36.4	34.5	35.2	38.4

[a] Figures on German military expenditure refer to West Germany through 1990 and to the united Germany from 1991.

Sources: Various issues of the official NATO journal *NATO Review* and NATO press release 'Financial and economic data relating to NATO defence', 8 Dec. 1993.

Table 12.6. NATO military equipment expenditure, in constant price figures, 1980–93

Figures are expressed in US $m., at 1985 prices and exchange-rates; figures in italics are percentages and show the change from the previous year.

Country	1980–84	1985	1986	1987	1988	1989	1990	1991	1992	1993
North America										
Canada	1 113	1 400	1 568	1 713	1 617	1 473	1 385	1 374	1 417	1 442
	. .	*. .*	*12.0*	*9.3*	*–5.6*	*–8.9*	*–6.0*	*–0.8*	*3.2*	*1.8*
USA	47 649	66 348	71 858	72 520	66 874	67 961	64 982	62 051	55 513	49 249
	. .	*. .*	*8.3*	*0.9*	*–7.8*	*1.6*	*–4.4*	*–4.5*	*–10.5*	*–11.3*
Europe										
Belgium	338	308	329	340	298	240	189	193	159	158
	. .	*. .*	*6.6*	*3.4*	*–12.3*	*–19.5*	*–21.2*	*2.2*	*–17.9*	*–0.5*
Denmark	212	174	176	191	190	171	195	210	231	231
	. .	*. .*	*1.1*	*8.8*	*–0.6*	*–10.0*	*14.0*	*7.8*	*9.7*	*0.3*
Germany[a]	3 967	2 948	4 064	3 987	3 778	3 716	3 622	2 947	2 385	2 012
	. .	*. .*	*37.8*	*–1.9*	*–5.2*	*–1.6*	*–2.5*	*–18.6*	*–19.1*	*–15.6*
Greece	356	338	330	366	513	456	450	405	487	502
	. .	*. .*	*–2.3*	*10.9*	*40.1*	*–11.1*	*–1.3*	*–10.1*	*20.3*	*3.1*
Italy	1 490	1 749	1 726	2 061	2 140	2 120	1 714	1 566	1 460	. .
	. .	*. .*	*–1.3*	*19.4*	*3.8*	*–0.9*	*–19.2*	*–8.6*	*–6.8*	
Luxembourg	1	2	1	2	1	2	2	3	3	2
	. .	*. .*	*–19.7*	*42.6*	*–17.3*	*24.7*	*–12.0*	*84.3*	*–10.8*	*–6.1*
Netherlands	758	909	818	724	833	727	721	611	555	378
	. .	*. .*	*–10.0*	*–11.5*	*15.0*	*–12.7*	*–0.9*	*–15.2*	*–9.2*	*–31.8*
Norway	301	447	356	395	351	476	438	412	481	473
	. .	*. .*	*–20.3*	*10.8*	*–11.2*	*35.9*	*–8.1*	*–5.9*	*16.8*	*–1.8*

Portugal	37	22	43	70	80	95	84	69	18	49
		..	*98.9*	*64.3*	*13.5*	*18.6*	*-11.8*	*-17.3*	*-74.3*	*176.3*
Spain	..	..	895	1 054	819	748	483	471	366	362
			..	*17.8*	*-22.3*	*-8.7*	*-35.4*	*-2.4*	*-22.3*	*-1.0*
Turkey	202	322	478	557	614	525	703	820	940	992
		..	*48.7*	*16.4*	*10.2*	*-14.4*	*33.7*	*16.7*	*14.6*	*5.6*
UK	5 929	6 405	5 840	5 570	5 425	4 767	3 873	4 218	3 631	2 996
		..	*-8.8*	*-4.6*	*-2.6*	*-12.1*	*-18.8*	*8.9*	*-13.9*	*-17.5*
NATO total	**(63 172)**	**(82 266)**	**88 482**	**89 550**	**83 533**	**83 478**	**78 840**	**75 351**	**67 644**	**(60 298)**
	..	*..*	*7.6*	*1.2*	*-6.7*	*-0.1*	*-5.6*	*-4.4*	*-10.2*	*-10.9*

[a] Figures on German military expenditure refer to West Germany through 1990 and to the united Germany from 1991.

( ) SIPRI estimate.

Sources: The figures in this table were calculated on the basis of the figures in tables 12.3 and 12.5. The results of this calculation should not be taken as being very exact but rather as an indication of general trends.

more or less rapidly increasing spending, military expenditures have been frozen at their current level. Until recently, such a long-term pattern of increased and then stagnating spending also applied to Germany and the Netherlands, but in the early 1990s military expenditures have decreased in both countries.

Since the late 1980s, NATO has published figures for both military spending totals and—except for the case of France—the distribution among four kinds of expenditure: 'personnel', 'equipment', 'infrastructure' and 'other operating expenditures'. By a process of elimination, it could probably be assumed that the latter category primarily includes expenditure for operations and maintenance (O&M). These data are reproduced and elaborated in tables 12.5 and 12.6.

A closer look at the data shows, first, that the NATO countries represent rather different spending structures, particularly regarding the ratio between personnel and equipment expenditures. Second, in most countries that previously increased military spending, a significant share of the new allocations for defence was spent on new equipment. When defence budgets have been cut or frozen, this has often meant less procurement. Hence, both because defence budgets decrease and because equipment takes a lesser share of a smaller cake than before, procurement has declined in most NATO countries—again, the exceptions are Greece and Turkey, and to some degree Luxembourg, as well as the two Scandinavian members, Denmark and Norway—and NATO aggregated equipment spending has declined by a third during the period 1986/87–1993, signifying a decline for defence procurement budgets twice as rapid as the general 15 per cent decline in total military spending. As noted in the *SIPRI Yearbook 1993*, such a decline 'will have significant implications for the defence industrial base'.[6]

The United States

In November 1993, the US Congress passed and President Bill Clinton signed a fiscal year (FY) 1994 budget for National Defense which provided a total of $261 billion in budget authority (BA).[7] The budget marks the ninth straight year in which the US defence budget has declined in real (inflation-adjusted) terms.[8] Altogether, the US defence budget has fallen 33 per cent since FY 1985. Although Congress cut the Administration's overall defence budget request by $2.6 billion and made a few significant programmatic changes, the

---

[6] *SIPRI Yearbook 1993* (note 2), p. 371; see also chapter 13 in this volume.

[7] The figures in this section refer to domestic US data on manpower and military spending, which differ from the data in tables 12.1–12.6, for which the common NATO definitions are used. In the USA, the National Defense budget function (050) includes Department of Defense funding (051), defence activities of the Department of Energy and other defence-related programmes. Budget authority (BA) represents the amount of funding the Department of Defense may obligate though hiring personnel or signing contracts for goods and services. Outlays, by contrast, represent the actual cash expenditures made to liquidate these obligations. Unless otherwise stated, all funding levels cited in this section refer to BA.

[8] All funding increases and decreases noted in this section are expressed in real terms.

Table 12.7. The March 1993 Clinton National Defense Funding Plan[a]

Figures are in US $b. Figures in italics are percentages.

	FY 1993	1994	1995	1996	1997	1998	1993–98
Budget Authority							
Current dollars	273.0	260.9	261.1	253.7	246.0	253.9	1 548.6
FY 1994 dollars	278.4	260.9	256.0	243.7	231.7	234.0	1 504.7
Real change	..	*– 6.3*	*– 1.9*	*– 4.8*	*– 4.9*	*1.0*	*– 15.9*
Outlays							
Current dollars	283.5	274.1	269.9	264.2	246.8	252.5	1 591.0
FY 1994 dollars	289.3	274.1	264.5	253.6	232.4	232.6	1 546.5
Real change	..	*– 5.3*	*– 3.5*	*– 4.1*	*– 8.4*	*0.1*	*– 19.6*

[a] FY 1994 budget authority estimates are from the FY 1994 National Defense Authorization Act passed by Congress and signed by the President in Nov. 1993. All other figures are from the Administration's Mar. 1993 budget request. Estimates exclude costs and allied contributions associated with Operation Desert Shield/Storm.

Source: Defense Budget Project. See also *Budget of the United States Government, Fiscal Year 1994* (US Government Printing Office: Washington, DC, 1993), appendix 'Federal Programs by Function and Subfunction'.

Administration's proposal emerged from the congressional budget process generally intact. The most noteworthy changes were Congress's $3.9 billion reduction in the Administration's request for research and development (R&D) funding, including a deep cut in funding for ballistic missile defence (BMD) programmes, a $2.1 billion cut in O&M funding and the inclusion of an unrequested 2.2 per cent military pay rise.

When the Administration submitted its budget to Congress in March 1993, it announced a significant cut in planned funding for national defence and a major reduction in the size of the US force posture (see table 12.7). Roughly consistent with presidential candidate Clinton's pledges during the 1992 presidential campaign, the new Administration proposed cutting some $127 billion from the Bush Administration's FY 1994–98 adjusted baseline[9]— resulting in a 16 per cent reduction in funding over this period—and reducing the active-duty military to 1.4 million personnel. By comparison, the Bush Administration had projected an 8 per cent cut in funding through FY 1998 and an active-duty end-strength target of 1.6 million.

While the Administration's March 1993 budget submission projected 'top-line' totals for the defence budget through FY 1998, it provided a detailed budgetary breakdown only for the FY 1994 request. The Administration announced that its plans beyond FY 1994 would be shaped by the results of a

[9] See DOD News Release, 'FY 1994 Defense Budget Begins New Era', 27 Mar. 1993, p. 1. According to the Office of Management and Budget (OMB), the Bush Jan. 1993 defence budget plan—adjusted to reflect updated (lower) pay rate and inflation assumptions, changes in locality pay and $18 billion in presumed under-funding—would have totalled $1.41 trillion between FY 1994 and FY 1998. The Administration estimated total savings through FY 1997 to be about $88 billion. During the campaign, Clinton pledged to cut roughly $60 billion from the Bush plan through FY 1997. For a discussion of different baselines, see Defense Budget Project, 'Issue Brief: Clinton defense budget compared to various baselines: how big is the cut?', 9 Mar. 1993.

major review of US defence requirements and programmes—the so-called 'Bottom–Up Review' (BUR). The Administration intended to use the BUR as the basis for setting its long-term plans concerning such diverse issues as the size and shape of the military's force structure and how to proceed with the development of next-generation weapon systems.

The FY 1994 budget request

The Administration's FY 1994 defence budget request included $250.7 billion for the Department of Defense (DOD), $11.5 billion for Department of Energy (DOE) defence activities and $1.2 billion for other defence-related programmes (see table 12.8). The Administration's proposal intentionally deferred decisions on major weapon programmes pending the results of the BUR; the budget request included large savings in the procurement account, but these were to be achieved by 'nibbling at the edges' of a wide variety of existing programmes rather than through the outright cancellation of any major new systems. In other areas, the Administration's budget request reflected a desire to keep readiness levels high, reduce military manpower at a relatively moderate pace and increase reliance on reserve forces.

The Administration proposed reorienting BMD efforts and holding funding for the programme to its FY 1993 level, $2.5 billion below the FY 1994 level proposed by Bush. But the proposed budget continued to fund the development of all of the other major next-generation weapon systems included in the Bush plan pending the results of the BUR, most of them at or near the levels proposed by the Bush Administration. Reflecting this 'place-holder' approach, under the proposed budget total R&D funding was to be cut by only 1 per cent from the FY 1993 level. This approach was also reflected in the Administration's proposal for procurement funding. The budget request made deeper cuts in procurement than in any other account—$5.8 billion below the level proposed by Bush and 17 per cent below the FY 1993 procurement funding level—but these savings were to be achieved through essentially across-the-board reductions in a wide variety of programmes rather than through programme terminations.

In presenting its FY 1994 budget proposal, the Administration claimed to place a high priority on maintaining US forces at high levels of readiness. It is certainly true that the proposed FY 1994 budget protected O&M funding relative to some other accounts (especially procurement). However, the Administration's submission—which showed a 1.2 per cent real *increase* in O&M funding—provided a somewhat exaggerated sense of just how much protection this account was afforded. This is because the Administration's $89.5 billion FY 1994 O&M budget request included funding for several new initiatives that were unrelated to combat readiness, including $888 million for aid to the former Soviet Union and other 'Global Cooperative Initiatives', and because it included transfers of some funds, previously included in other accounts, to the O&M budget. In reality, the request—adjusted to include only those elements found in the FY 1993 O&M budget—reflected a real decline in

O&M funding. According to the US Air Force, for example, the changed O&M counting rules masked what would otherwise have been a proposed reduction of 2.6 percent in the service's O&M budget between FY 1993 and FY 1994. Nevertheless, the rate of decline projected in the proposed budget was still substantially lower than the rate of decline experienced over the previous three years, during which time US Air Force O&M funding fell by a total of 20.1 per cent. The Pentagon claimed that this slowing of the rate of decline in O&M funding was needed to allow reductions in overhead and infrastructure to catch up with cuts to programmes directly related to combat readiness (e.g., aircraft flying hours and ship steaming days).

The new Administration proposed only a modest acceleration of the pace of reductions in active-duty military personnel in FY 1993 and FY 1994. The request included cuts in active-duty end-strength of 80 000 in FY 1993 and 108 000 in FY 1994. By comparison, the Bush budget would have cut 62 000 active-duty personnel in FY 1993 and 83 000 in FY 1994. In terms of budgetary savings, however, the most significant personnel-related measure included in the Administration's budget request was a proposal to freeze military pay in FY 1994 and reduce, by 1 per cent, projected pay increases over the FY 1995–97 period. This was to be part of a government-wide pay freeze and limit on pay raises affecting civilian DOD personnel as well. In addition, the Administration proposed deferring until FY 1995 the locality pay increase projected for federal civilian employees. Altogether, the Administration estimated that these pay-related actions would generate $18 billion in defence savings over the period FY 1994–97.

Consistent with presidential candidate Clinton's campaign rhetoric, the Administration's FY 1994 request projected a smaller reduction in National Guard and Reserve personnel than the Bush plan. Under the Administration plan, reserve personnel end-strength was to be cut to 1.02 million in FY 1994, a cut of 60 400 from the FY 1993 level, but 89 500 above the FY 1994 level proposed by Bush.

Congressional action

The National Defense Authorization Act passed by Congress cut $2.6 billion from the Administration's overall FY 1994 funding request.[10] In making this reduction, Congress was motivated primarily by the need to reduce FY 1994 outlays—which the Congressional Budget Office (CBO) estimated would exceed the Administration's original projection—sufficient to keep below the

---

[10] The Defense Authorization Act provides the legislative authority to appropriate funding for DOD, defence-related DOE and other defence-related programmes. The actual appropriation of funding, however, is provided in the Defense Appropriations Act (which covers about 90% of the programmes included in the Authorization Act) and several smaller appropriation acts (especially the Military Construction and the Energy and Water Appropriations Acts).

Table 12.8. US National Defense Budget Authority by title, selected years, FY 1985–94
Figures are in US $b. Figures in italics are percentages; change adjusted for inflation.

	FY 1985	FY 1993[a]	FY 1994 Request[b]	FY 1994 Enacted[b]	FY 1985–94 Change
Military personnel					
Current prices	67.8	76.3	70.1	70.2	..
1994 prices	88.9	77.2	70.1	70.2	..
Real change	*..*	*– 13.1*	*– 9.2*	*– 9.1*	*– 21.0*
O&M					
Current prices	77.8	86.4	89.5	87.4	..
1994 prices	103.6	88.4	89.5	87.4	..
Real change	*..*	*– 14.7*	*1.2*	*– 1.1*	*– 15.6*
Procurement					
Current prices	96.8	53.6	45.5	46.3	..
1994 prices	126.6	54.9	45.5	46.3	..
Real change	*..*	*– 56.6*	*– 17.1*	*– 15.6*	*– 63.4*
R&D					
Current prices	31.3	38.2	38.6	34.7	..
1994 prices	41.5	39.1	38.6	34.7	..
Real change	*..*	*– 5.8*	*– 1.2*	*– 11.3*	*– 16.4*
Military construction					
Current prices	5.5	4.5	5.8	6.4	..
1994 prices	7.3	4.6	5.8	6.4	..
Real change	*..*	*– 37.0*	*26.0*	*39.1*	*– 12.3*
Family housing					
Current prices	2.9	3.9	3.8	3.6	..
1994 prices	3.8	4.0	3.8	3.6	..
Real change	*..*	*5.3*	*– 5.0*	*– 10.0*	*– 5.3*
Other					
Current prices	4.7	– 3.8	– 2.8	0.3	..
1994 prices	6.2	– 3.9	– 2.8	0.3	..
Real change	*..*	*..*	*..*	*..*	*..*
DOD total					
Current prices	**286.8**	**259.1**	**250.7**	**248.9**	..
1994 prices	**378.0**	**264.2**	**250.7**	**248.9**	..
Real change	*..*	*– 30.1*	*– 5.1*	*– 5.8*	*– 34.2*
DOE defence activities					
Current prices	7.3	12.1	11.5	10.9	..
1994 prices	9.6	12.2	11.5	10.9	..
Real change	*..*	*27.1*	*– 5.7*	*– 10.7*	*13.5*
Other defence-related					
Current prices	0.5	1.8	1.2	1.1	..
1994 prices	0.7	1.8	1.2	1.1	..
Real change	*..*	*177*	*– 35*	*– 40*	*66*
National defence total					
Current prices	**294.7**	**273.0**	**263.4**	**260.9**	..
1994 prices	**388.3**	**278.2**	**263.4**	**260.9**	..
Real change	*..*	*– 28.4*	*– 5.3*	*– 6.2*	*– 32.8*

Deflators—FY 1994 (used to calculate changes in real terms)

Military personnel	0.7623	0.9888	1.0000	1.0000
O&M	0.7510	0.9770	1.0000	1.0000
Procurement	0.7648	0.9760	1.0000	1.0000
R&D	0.7539	0.9770	1.0000	1.0000
Military construction	0.7550	0.9788	1.0000	1.0000
Family housing	0.7623	0.9763	1.0000	1.0000
Other	0.7588	0.9807	1.0000	1.0000
DOD	0.7588	0.9807	1.0000	1.0000

[a] The percentage change in the FY 1993 column refers to the cumulative change from the budget authority peak in FY 1985.

[b] The change in the two columns for FY 1994 refers to the change from FY 1993.

Source: Defense Budget Project, based on US Department of Defense data.

congressional budget resolution's outlay cap.[11] With the exception of ballistic missile defences, the Authorization Act approved funding for all the major acquisition programmes included in the Administration's request—as modified by the BUR (which was released at the beginning of September). In addition to the cut in BMD funding, the major differences between the Administration's FY 1994 request and the final Authorization Act approved by Congress include significant cuts in the overall R&D and O&M budgets and the inclusion of an unrequested 2.2 per cent pay rise for military personnel. The total level of funding provided in the Authorization Act is about $3.2 billion below the level approved in the House of Representatives' version of the Authorization Bill and some $1.3 billion below the level approved in the Senate Defense Authorization Bill. The following section details how the Administration's request for various programmes and budgetary accounts fared during congressional deliberations over the FY 1994 National Defense Authorization Act. In addition, the funding levels included in the FY 1994 Defense Appropriations Act are noted, where those levels differ significantly from the levels in the Authorization Act.[12]

Although accounting for an ever smaller share of the defence budget, strategic weapon acquisition was once again the focus of a good deal of debate in Congress. The Authorization Act fully funded the Administration's $1.7 billion request for the B-2 bomber, while reaffirming the earlier decision to cap the programme at 20 aircraft. In addition, in response to the DOD certification that the bomber had passed a number of performance tests stipulated by Congress, the passage of the Act served to release $2.2 billion in previously

---

[11] In its annual budget resolution, Congress sets BA and outlay ceilings for the defence budget and the 17 other discretionary domestic and international budget functions. The differences between the Administration's original estimate of FY 1994 outlays and CBO re-estimates were due not only to technical differences in 'scoring' but also to certain congressional actions, including the inclusion of a military pay rise.

[12] The overall budget levels included in the various appropriations acts are generally consistent with the levels included in the Defense Authorization Act, but the Authorization and Appropriations Acts often contain differences in funding levels for specific accounts and programmes within that total. The DOD typically tries to resolve these differences by, for example, requesting authorization (for funding that has been appropriated but not authorized) in subsequent budgets and informal discussions with the leadership and staffs of the Armed Services Committees and Defense Appropriations Subcommittees.

frozen B-2 bomber funds. The Authorization Act fully funded the $1.2 billion request for the Trident II (D-5) missile programme as well. However, the Appropriations Act requires that before the money can be spent, the President must certify that the other signatories of the 1993 START II Treaty have rejected a proposal that 'detubing' be accepted as a treaty-compliant option for eliminating submarine-launched ballistic missile (SLBM) launchers. The Authorization Act provided a total of $3.015 billion for BMD programmes, about $750 million less than requested—including $253 million for the 'Brilliant Eyes' space-based sensor,[13] which the Act transfers into a separate space surveillance account. In addition, the Act limits spending on certain systems, pending an analysis of their consistency with the traditional interpretation of the 1972 Anti-Ballistic Missile (ABM) Treaty, and modifies the Missile Defense Act of 1991 by replacing the requirement that a single-site defence be *deployed* in the USA, with language supporting the *development* of such a system. By comparison, the Appropriations Act provides $2.9 billion for BMD programmes.

Congress essentially approved the deep cuts in overall procurement funding proposed by the Administration and made only a few modest changes in specific procurement programmes. Consistent with the BUR, the final Authorization Act fully funded the Administration's $2.3 billion request for development of the new F-22 fighter aircraft and $1.4 billion request for development of the new E/F version of the F/A-18 fighter, while cancelling the A/FX fighter and the Multi-Role Fighter (MRF) programmes.[14] The Appropriations Act likewise fully funded the F/A-18E/F and cancelled the A/FX and MRF programmes. Unlike the Authorization Act, however, it cut funding for the F-22 fighter by $163 million. Reflecting the BUR decision to end procurement of the current-generation F-16 fighter, the Authorization Act funded the last 12 aircraft in FY 1994 (half the number requested). Conversely, reflecting the BUR decision to continue production of the F/A-18C/D fighter, the Authorization Act fully funded the Administration's $1.4 billion request for 36 F/A-18C/D aircraft in FY 1994.

The problem-plagued C-17 cargo aircraft was again closely scrutinized by Congress. The Authorization Act created a new $2.3 billion inter-theatre airlift account, which includes $1.7 billion for the procurement of four C-17s in FY 1994 and $188 million in advance procurement funding for six aircraft in FY 1995. It also includes $100 million for the procurement of non-developmental airlift alternatives (e.g., commercial wide-body aircraft) and $300 million to be used either to buy two additional C-17s or other alternative airlift aircraft in FY 1994. By comparison, the Appropriations Act provided $1.9

[13] See Pike, J., 'Military use of outer space', SIPRI, *SIPRI Yearbook 1991: World Armaments and Disarmament* (Oxford University Press: Oxford, 1991), chapter 3, section II, pp. 50, 53–54.

[14] In addition, the Pentagon's Bottom–Up Review calls for the future establishment of a Joint Advanced Strike Technology Program for the development of next-generation aircraft.

billion for six C-17 aircraft in FY 1994 and fully funded the Administration's $246 million request for C-17 advance procurement funding.[15]

The other major acquisition programmes approved in the FY 1994 Authorization Act include: $10 million for continued development of the Marine Corps' V-22 Osprey 'tilt-rotor' transport aircraft, which presidential candidate Clinton supported during the campaign and which emerged a winner from the BUR; $367 million, as requested, for continued prototype development of the Army's planned Comanche scout/attack helicopter; $2.9 billion, as requested, for three DDG-51 destroyers; and $449 million, as requested, for development of the new Centurion attack submarine.

Congress' deepest cuts to the Administration's FY 1994 defence budget request came from the R&D account. Between FY 1985 and FY 1993, DOD R&D funding was reduced by only 6 per cent. The Administration's FY 1994 request, which included a 1 per cent reduction from FY 1993, similarly sought to protect R&D funding. However, Congress cut the FY 1994 R&D budget relatively deeply. The final Authorization Act provided $34.7 billion for R&D in FY 1994, $3.9 billion less than requested. These cuts were motivated mainly by the need to stay below the budget resolution's FY 1994 outlay caps and were obtained largely through cuts in BMD funding.

The next largest budget reduction came from O&M. Both the House and Senate authorization reports raised concerns about early signs that the readiness of US military forces to fight effectively at short notice might be eroding. Nevertheless, the final Authorization Act provided $87.4 billion for O&M in FY 1994, $2.1 billion less than requested. The conferees cut some $3 billion from overhead and infrastructure elements of the O&M budget and increased funding for programmes more directly related to the combat readiness of US forces by some $900 million. The Appropriations Act cut the Administration's O&M request by some $650 million. It is unclear whether these O&M funding reductions will have a significant negative impact on the readiness of US forces in FY 1994.

Congress only slightly modified the Administration's FY 1994 active-duty end-strength target. The Authorization Act provides for 2900 more active-duty personnel than requested, bringing the FY 1994 end-strength target to 1 623 500. As in previous years, Congress favoured the reserves more than did the Administration. The Authorization Act included a reserve end-strength target of 1 039 400 for FY 1994, 11 900 more personnel than requested. In addition, the Authorization Act provided $990 million in unrequested procurement funding for the reserves. By comparison, the Appropriations Act increased the FY 1994 reserve end-strength level by 5300 above the Administration's request and provided $1.2 billion in unrequested procurement funding for the reserves.

---

[15] On 15 Dec. 1993, the DOD announced that it would procure a total of at least 40 C-17s, but that production would be halted if the McDonnell-Douglas Corporation could not make sufficient improvements in the programme. In that case, rather than building the 120 C-17s currently planned, the Air Force would acquire additional C-5 transports or some other alternative.

By far the most important change to the Administration's personnel-related budget request was Congress's decision to approve an unrequested 2.2 per cent pay raise for active-duty personnel.

In other action, Congress reduced the Administration's request for DOE defence activities by $675 million to $10.9 billion, including $3.6 billion for weapon activities and $5.2 billion for environmental clean-up. The Authorization Act also added about $300 million to the Administration's $1.6 billion request for worker, community and industry defence transition assistance pro-'grammes. The Appropriations Act provided some $1.8 billion for these programmes.

Future budgets

In March 1993, when the new Administration submitted its FY 1994 defence budget request, it projected a $261 billion request for FY 1995 and projected that funding for defence would fall to $254 billion by FY 1998. The Administration is likely to make some modest adjustments to these funding estimates when it submits its FY 1995 defence budget request in February 1994. What the overall effect of these adjustments is likely to be, however, is unclear. On the plus side, in May 1993, on the advice of a special panel of experts, the Administration said it would add a total of $2–5 billion to defence budgets through FY 1997 to cover some areas of suspected under-funding—related mainly to overstated management-reform savings. In addition, in December 1994, the Administration said that it would add some $10 billion to the budget through FY 1999 to cover the costs of the military pay rise passed by Congress. On the downside, however, the Administration also indicated in December that it might not provide the $20 billion which the Pentagon would need to offset the effects of higher (than previously estimated) inflation over the period FY 1995–99.[16] Worse yet, this $20 billion shortfall would hit a defence plan that is already $13 billion short of reaching the BUR $104 billion five-year savings target.

No matter how the Administration adjusts its FY 1995 defence budget request and FY 1996–99 defence budget projections, its plan is likely to disappoint a large number of members of Congress. Republicans and a significant number of conservative and moderate Democrats in Congress have expressed deep concern about what they see as the too rapid decline in US defence spending and will strongly oppose any Administration move to accelerate those reductions further. On the other hand, an even more potent group may be those members of Congress pushing for still deeper cuts in defence. At the close of the FY 1994 budget debate, Congress only narrowly defeated a deficit reduction proposal offered by Timothy Penny (Democrat, from Minnesota) and John Kasich (Republican, from Ohio) that would have cut an additional $90 billion in federal spending over the next five years, including as

---

[16] See Clymer, A., '95 budget projects drop in deficit to $190 billion', *Washington Post*, 23 Dec. 1993, p. A16.

much as $16 billion from the defence budget. Another deficit reduction effort is likely in 1994, as is a renewed effort to pass a balanced budget amendment. If passed by Congress, ratified by enough states and effectively enforced, such a balanced budget amendment could force a drastic reduction in future defence budgets—perhaps doubling or even tripling the rate of decline envisioned in the March 1993 Clinton plan.

Much of the debate over the FY 1995 defence budget is likely to focus on the affordability of the Administration's plans over the next five years. The Administration has stated its determination to maintain high levels of combat readiness and to embrace the 1.4 million-person force structure detailed in the BUR. Unfortunately, meeting these objectives within the topline budgets included in the five-year plan will leave relatively little money for investing in future capability—for procurement and R&D. Procurement funding has already been cut dramatically, having declined 63 per cent since 1985. R&D funding was cut relatively deeply for the first time in FY 1994, falling 11 per cent in just one year. It remains to be seen to what extent Congress will also focus on the affordability of the Administration's defence plan *beyond* the next five years. That the BUR is affordable over the long term is likely to be even a more difficult case for the Administration to make effectively. While investment funding can be cut back disproportionately in the short term, it cannot be put off indefinitely without having a substantial effect on capability. Over the long term, perhaps the most critical question to be faced by the Administration and Congress will be whether the relatively large BUR force structure should be retained, or whether a smaller force structure—which could be more affordably modernized—should be adopted.

The United Kingdom

As shown in table 12.3, British military spending peaked in 1984, and since then has declined by over 20 per cent. The sudden increase in 1991 can to a large degree, as in the US case, be attributed to British participation in the 1991 Persian Gulf War, and it did not reverse the general trend of declining British military spending.

In 1990, some general policy guidelines were outlined in the 'Options for Change' statement, suggesting a smaller—the armed forces were to be reduced by about 30 per cent—but more potent, better trained and equipped force.[17] In accordance with these guidelines, the British armed forces have been subject to both a rather thorough reorganization and manpower cuts.[18] In the autumn 1992 *Statement on Government Expenditures*, the FY 1993/94 (1 April to 31 March) defence budget was cut from £24.52 billion to £23.52 billion; for FY 1994/95, the defence allocation was £23.75 billion, and for FY 1995/96, £23.22 billion (figures refer to the national definition). In real

[17] See *SIPRI Yearbook 1993* (note 2), footnote 44, p. 378.
[18] See *SIPRI Yearbook 1993* (note 2), pp. 378–80.

terms, military expenditure is supposed to decline by 12 per cent during the six-year period FY 1990/91–1995/96.[19]

In July 1993, the *Statement on the Defence Estimates 1993*, called 'Defending Our Future', was announced. This Statement suggested further cuts, in addition to those announced in 'Options for Change'. According to various policy documents and 'Defending Our Future', the British armed forces have three major tasks: (*a*) to ensure the security of the UK and its dependent territories; (*b*) to ensure against any major threat to the UK and its allies; and (*c*) to promote the UK's wider security interests through the maintenance of international peace and stability.[20]

Accordingly, British military capability in areas that were related to a cold war threat could be decreased, in favour of certain new roles. For example, as there no longer exists any Soviet submarine threat to counter in the North Atlantic, the British anti-submarine warfare (ASW) capability and level of operations could be reduced. Consequently, the number of attack submarines will be cut, as well as the numbers of destroyers and frigates; it was also the Navy that was most affected by the announced cuts. With a reduced air threat against the British Isles, the Royal Air Force was to cut the number of air defence fighters, and a planned procurement of a medium surface-to-air missile was cancelled. However, the number of strike aircraft was not reduced, and there were no new additional cuts in the British Army.

During the autumn of 1993, some Members of Parliament in the ruling Conservative Party vowed to vote against any additional reduction in British defence spending. When the future spending figures were announced in November 1993, it was believed that less drastic cuts were suggested than originally intended. For FY 1993/94, military spending was further reduced from £23.52 billion by £110 million to £23.41 billion; for FY 1994/95, the previously stated figure of £23.75 billion was cut by £260 million to £23.49 billion, and for FY 1995/96, the previous figure was cut from £23.22 billion by £520 million to £22.7 billion. For the period as a whole, these figures thus suggest a nominal cut of more than 3 per cent, representing a real decline in military spending of about 7 per cent. The projected military budget for FY 1996/97 is £22.79 billion.[21]

Despite these cuts, the Defence Minister has also revealed rather ambitious plans for new procurement, including an order of 259 new Challenger 2 main battle tanks (MBTs), up to seven new Sandown mine-hunters and new support

[19] Witt, M. J., 'UK report warns of still more cuts', *Defense News*, vol. 7, no. 8 (16 Nov. 1992), p. 3; *Statement on the Defence Estimates 1993*, 'Defending Our Future' (Her Majesty's Stationery Office: London, July 1993), Cm 2270, pp. 75–76; Kemp, I., 'Navy takes the brunt of latest UK cutbacks', *Jane's Defence Weekly*, vol. 20, no. 3 (17 July 1993), p. 8.

[20] 'Defending Our Future' (note 19), e.g., p. 7.

[21] Witt, M. J., 'Parliamentarians threaten UK budget plan', *Defense News*, vol. 8, no. 43 (1–7 Nov. 1993), p. 6; Kemp, I., 'Cuts could "gravely damage" UK forces', *Jane's Defence Weekly*, vol. 20, no. 18 (30 Oct. 1993), p. 8; Bellamy, C., 'Defence: housing sell-off to save cut in new arms', *The Independent*, 1 Dec. 1993, p. 10; Tusa, F., 'Scrambled modernization: the dust settles on latest UK budget cuts', *Armed Forces Journal International*, Jan. 1994, p. 4.

helicopters for the Royal Air Force; the British Army would also be increased by 3000 soldiers.[22]

France

Even though French military spending shows a steady increase for the previous few decades, the rate of increase started to decline and level off in the early 1990s. This decline in the increase of the rate of spending has raised questions concerning whether current expenditures really suffice to pay for the present defence posture.[23]

There have also been several statements made on the need for increased defence budgets, in particular to cover the increasing costs of France's major weapon programmes, but such statements have not, at least not yet, resulted in any significant rise in military spending. Similarly, no overall priority seems to have been made between the different programmes, in the sense that not one of the development programmes—including the new fighter aircraft, Rafale; the construction of a new aircraft-carrier, the *Charles de Gaulle*; the Leclerc tank programme, and the French–German Tiger helicopter project—has been cancelled. Instead, to make ends meet, the French Government has decided either to stretch out the programmes over a longer period of time or to reduce them in volume.[24]

The absence of clear priorities between these weapon programmes has not meant that the French armed forces have been saved from major changes. When the 1992 budget was discussed, it was also revealed that the French Army would be reduced from about 285 000 men to about 225 000 in 1997, and that the French Army would more distinctively be divided into one mechanized force, primarily aimed for the European operations, and the Force d'Action Rapide, to be used for out-of-area operations. French Air Force bases were to be reorganized and reduced in number, and the overall number of French fighter aircraft was to be cut from its then level of 450 to 400. The French Navy is also to be reorganized, with an Atlantic Fleet containing an anti-mine force and submarine force, based in Brest, and a Mediterranean Fleet containing mostly surface vessels, based in Toulon.[25]

[22] Miller, C., 'Arms-buy plan fails to silence UK budget critics', *Defense News*, vol. 8, no. 48 (6–12 Dec. 1993), p. 3; Kemp, I., 'UK orders confirmed despite defence cuts', *Jane's Defence Weekly*, vol. 20, no. 24 (11 Dec. 1993), p. 8; Bellamy, C., 'Extra front-line soldiers and tanks promised', *The Independent*, 2 Dec. 1993, p. 13; Fairhall, D., 'Army to get new tanks and troops', *The Guardian*, 2 Dec. 1993, p. 13.
[23] For an overview of the current issues facing French defence, see several articles in *Defense News*, vol. 8, no. 28 (27 Sep.–3 Oct. 1993).
[24] For an overview of French defence and military spending in the early 1990s, see, for instance, several articles in *Defense News*, vol. 7, no. 42 (19–25 Oct. 1992); Lewis, J. A. C., 'Joxe preserves major French programmes', *Jane's Defence Weekly*, vol. 17, no. 21 (23 Nov. 1991), p. 987; Lewis, J. A. C., 'Joxe bridges gap rather than mapping the future', *Jane's Defence Weekly*, vol. 18, no. 3 (18 July 1992), p. 15; Tusa, F., 'Increased program, personnel costs threaten French and British budgets', *Armed Forces Journal International*, Jan. 1993, p. 8.
[25] Lewis, J. A. C., 'More cuts, naval shake-up planned', *Jane's Defence Weekly*, vol. 17, no. 18 (2 May 1992), p. 754. See also de Briganti, G., 'Government review aims to pare military forces', *Defense News*, vol. 8, no. 38 (27 Sep.–3 Oct. 1993), p. 12.

Two prevalent trends in French military allocations and force posture developments during the early 1990s concern the downgrading of nuclear weapons and what one might call an upgrading of France's crisis-management capability. Even though nuclear weapons still play an important role in French defence, they nevertheless receive much less emphasis than previously. Army units equipped with the nuclear missile Pluton are about to be, or have already been, disbanded. In 1992 the number of nuclear-powered ballistic-missile submarines (SSBNs) to be procured for the next 15 years was reduced from six to four.[26] In March 1993, it was revealed that while French nuclear weapons and systems previously had taken about 30 per cent of the defence budget, they would in future be allocated only a 20 per cent share.[27]

Efforts to improve the French crisis-management capability relate to several programmes. French spending on new intelligence and information systems—which include French military space activities, such as the Syracuse II and Helios project—has increased rapidly.[28] In line with the increased role for intelligence activities, the French intelligence service has also been reorganized.[29] The increased weight given to the Force d'Action Rapide signifies the growing importance of mobility.

Defence policy after the 1993 change of government

In the elections to the National Assembly in March 1993, the Socialist government lost power to a centre–right coalition between the neo-Gaullist Rally for the Republic (RPR) and the centre–right Union for French Democracy (UDF), headed by Edouard Balladur as Prime Minister and with François Léotard as Defence Minister. One of the first decisions of the new government was to appoint a new commission, under Marceau Long, to prepare a White Paper on French security and defence policy. The last time a French White Paper was presented was in 1972, and a new White Paper must presumably address both strategic issues like international system changes, international co-operation, nuclear weapons and conscription as well as long-term defence spending levels.[30]

---

[26] 'France to build fewer SSBNs', *Jane's Defence Weekly*, vol. 17, no. 19 (9 May 1992), p. 789.

[27] Valmy, M., 'Frankreichs Wehrbudget: Weiterhin Vorrang für die Kernwaffen' [France's defence budget: still a preference for nuclear weapons], *Europäische Wehrkunde*, vol. 39, no. 4 (1990), p. 225; 'French quietly cut arsenal by 100', *Jane's Defence Weekly*, vol. 19, no. 13 (27 Mar. 1993), p. 5; 'According to Joxe Report, France has cut spending on nuclear weapons by 17% over four years', *Atlantic News*, no. 2510 (24 Mar. 1993), p. 4.

[28] 'Priorités: espace et renseignement, Le projet du budget de la défense pour 1993' [Priorities: space and intelligence, the defence budget project for 1993], *Armées d'aujourd'hui*, no. 175 (Nov. 1992), p. 16; Lewis, J. A. C., 'France to increase military space work', *Jane's Defence Weekly*, vol. 19, no. 2 (9 Jan. 1993), p. 7.

[29] 'New DRA agency begins operations', *Jane's Defence Weekly*, vol. 17, no. 18 (2 May 1992), p. 752.

[30] Lewis, J. A. C., 'French Government looks ahead to long-term change', *Jane's Defence Weekly*, vol. 19, no. 16 (17 Apr. 1993), p. 14; Reed, C., 'France is forced to rethink policy in climate of change', *Jane's Defence Weekly*, vol. 19, no. 19 (8 May 1993), p. 18; 'Le Livre Blanc: question de choix' [The White Paper: a matter of choice], *Armées d'aujourd'hui*, no. 183 (Sep. 1993), p. 12.

During the first months of 1993, there was some confusion regarding the impact that the change of government would have on French defence spending. When assuming power, the new Prime Minister argued for cuts in all kinds of government expenditures to reduce the deficit, and it was not clear whether defence was going to be exempted from these cuts. As the former Socialist government had started to freeze or reduce several kinds of defence spending, particularly in procurement, it was argued, for instance by the arms industry, that defence ought to be exempted from the general policy of government expenditure cut-backs.[31]

The manner in which French military spending has been handled regarding FY 1993 is actually somewhat complicated; in brief, the following has happened. In November 1992 the French Parliament approved a defence budget for 1993 of 197.9 billion francs ($37.5 billion)—excluding pensions—of which 'procurement' ('title V') constituted 102.9 billion francs. In February 1993, the previous Socialist government decided to freeze 3 billion francs of the defence budget until the end of the year and to cut procurement spending by 2.5 billion francs, to cover increased social spending. (Under French regulations, the Finance Ministry may freeze the budgets of other departments, thereby preventing appropriated funds from being utilized.) In addition, a further 3.5 billion franc cut was also going to be made, but these monies were to be returned later in 1993 to the defence sector, when the French armed forces would be compensated for various outlays, most notably their participation in UN peacekeeping operations. In May, the new government presented a new and revised defence spending plan, signifying a further decline in French military spending, and roughly 100 items were to be cut.[32]

Despite this decline in military spending, the new Defence Minister François Léotard also made statements in favour of increased defence spending and the acquisition of new material. In May he revealed that France would acquire another SSBN in the year 2001.[33] Defence Minister Léotard also proclaimed that the French defence budget in 1994, and in the following years, was to increase from its present 2.8 per cent share of French gross domestic product (GDP) (using the French national definition of military spending) to its 1990 level of a 3.4 per cent share.[34] To raise military expenditure from one year to another by at least 20 per cent, as the proposition to increase the military spending share implies, is of course not impossible during exceptional

[31] de Briganti, G., 'Industry says France's new government may be boon', *Defense News*, vol. 8, no. 13 (5 Apr. 1993), p. 1; 'French firms braced for more defence cuts', *Jane's Defence Weekly*, 1 May 1993, p. 16.

[32] Several articles in *Armées d'aujourd'hui*; no. 177 (Feb. 1993); de Briganti, G., 'France cuts, freezes arms procurement funds', *Defense News*, vol. 8, no. 5 (8–14 Feb. 1993), p. 1; de Galard, J., 'Le budget de la défense amputé de 5.5 milliards de francs' [The defence budget is cut by 5.5 billion francs], *Air & Cosmos/ Aviation Magazine*, no. 1427 (24 May 1993), p. 35; 'French Army takes brunt of forces cut', *Jane's Defence Weekly*, vol. 19, no. 23 (5 June 1993), p. 5; Lewis, J. A. C., 'Léotard pledges aid as defence cuts hit', *Jane's Defence Weekly*, vol. 19, no. 24 (12 June 1993), p. 8.

[33] de Briganti, G., 'France plans sub buy amid cuts in budget', *Defense News*, vol. 8, no. 21 (31 May–6 June 1993), p. 6.

[34] de Briganti, G., 'France may renew spending', *Defence News*, vol. 8, no. 17 (3–9 May 1993), p. 3; 'Léotard aims to raise defence spending in '94', *Jane's Defence Weekly*, vol. 19, no.22 (29 May 1993), p. 8.

circumstances, but hardly likely under normal conditions. When the budget was later revealed, French military expenditure was, at best, to remain at its previous level.

The 1994 defence budget was presented in October 1993. Excluding pensions of 48.7 billion francs, the defence budget was to increase in nominal terms by 1.3 per cent to 193.82 billion francs. However, as the French defence forces under-spent in 1993 and did not use a 5.5 billion-franc compensation which they were supposed to receive in late 1993, in an unusual carry-over, these extra monies were included in the 1994 budget, increasing the budget to 199.3 billion francs ($35.3 billion), representing a 3.6 per cent nominal increase over actual 1993 spending.[35]

Defence Minister Léotard called this increase 'an enormous effort', and it is therefore worth noting that the proposed increase still represents, in real terms, at best frozen French defence spending.[36] Also, economic and industrial factors seem to have been just as important for the budget presented as any strategic considerations.[37]

The 1994 budget also gives procurement a clear priority, and procurement spending is to rise by 5.7 per cent, to 103 billion francs, compared to a 1.4 per cent increase, to 96.3 billion francs, for the personnel and operations budget, and the 1994 budget supported all major ongoing equipment projects. Some of the most important cuts concerned spending on nuclear programmes, which are to be reduced by 8.8 per cent. Despite the procurement priority, some programmes were nevertheless reduced and/or further stretched out. The increase in procurement will make it possible for the French Army to order 44 new Leclerc tanks, multiple-launcher rocket system (MLRS) launchers, support vehicles, and so on, and the Navy a new amphibious transport ship, new naval fighters and patrol aircraft. The Air Force will order its first series of Rafale fighter aircraft as well as new Mirage 2000-5 fighters.

Spending on space programmes will continue to rise, by 13.8 per cent, and in late 1994 the first Helios observation satellite will be launched. In fact, France's military space procurement budget has increased rapidly: in 1987, about 758 million francs were allocated to space, an amount that has nominally increased fivefold to 4.2 billion francs. Despite this increase, in early 1994 the French Parliament Defence Committee criticized the government for not allocating enough resources to military space programmes and called for

[35] Several articles in *Armées d'aujourd'hui*, no. 187 (Feb. 1994); de Briganti, G., 'French spending jumps, as West cuts back, France boosts defense budget', *Defense News*, vol. 8, no. 40 (11–17 Oct. 1993), p.1; 'France's acquisition budget set at $17b', *Jane's Defence Weekly*, vol. 20, no. 11 (11 Sep. 1993), p. 24; 'French budget backs major projects', *Jane's Defence Weekly*, vol. 20, no. 14 (2 Oct. 1993), p. 5; Lewis, J. A. C., 'French spending rise secures major items', *Jane's Defence Weekly*, vol. 20, no. 16 (16 Oct. 1993), p. 15; Sparaco, P., 'France stretches defense programs', *Aviation Week & Space Technology*, 18 Oct. 1993, p. 98; de Galard, J., 'Budget de la défense: 103 mdf pour l'équipement' [The defence budget: 103 billion francs for equipment], *Air & Cosmos/Aviation International*, no. 1443 (18–24 Oct. 1993), p. 23; de Galard, J., 'Le budget défense 94 à la loupe' [The defence budget 94 under the magnifying glass], *Air & Cosmos/Aviation International*, no. 1448 (22–28 Nov. 1993), p. 43.

[36] Tusa, F., 'France and Germany face tough budget decisions', *Armed Forces Journal International*, Jan. 1994, p. 7.

[37] Lewis, J. A. C., 'Why France decided to buck the defence spending trend', *Jane's Defence Weekly*, vol. 20, no. 17 (23 Oct. 1993), p. 20.

an annual increase in the military space budget by 2 billion francs, to meet the goals France has stated concerning its military space policy.[38]

Germany

In the early 1990s, German security policy and defence spending were influenced by three different circumstances that will probably continue to determine German developments and decisions for some years to come. The first of these is the impact of reductions required by the 1990 Treaty on Conventional Armed Forces in Europe (CFE Treaty). During the autumn of 1990, when Germany was unified, several agreements were made on the size of the German forces, and in the CFE Treaty it was agreed that on 31 December 1994 the German armed forces would be reduced to 370 000 men, which would signify a substantial decrease in manpower. Similar reductions are also to be implemented regarding the number of tanks, armoured personnel carriers (APCs), artillery, fighter aircraft, and so on, where the new ceiling often points to a lower level than the old FRG inventory, and much lower than the amalgamated all-German holdings at the time of unification.[39]

The second factor is the need to develop a viable defence posture. During the cold war, the FRG faced a very clear threat, but after unification and the withdrawal of all Soviet/Russian troops, expected to be completed in August 1994, some 'existential' questions about threat perceptions and force postures must be addressed. It is against this background that the German debate on, for example, participation in peacekeeping operations should be seen, since the decisions taken could create precedents and have wide-ranging implications for the future.

The third factor is the importance of economic and budgetary constraints. In the absence of both clear threats and viable defence guidelines, German military spending has been more influenced by economic considerations, in an *ad hoc* manner, than by any strategic grand design. As the cost of unification has increased, most other kinds of spending have been cut to release fresh monies for programmes related to the economic and social situation in the eastern *Länder*. Thus, although both German defence and budgetary developments

---

[38] de Selding, P. B., 'French Committee: find more francs for military space', *Space News*, vol. 5, no. 4 (24–30 Jan. 1994), p. 14. See also 'Le budget des services communs, des enjeux majeurs' [The budget for common services, major stakes], *Armées d'aujourd'hui*, no. 187 (Feb. 1994), p. 52.

[39] For an overview of German defence, see, e.g., 'The Bundeswehr—special issue', *NATO's Sixteen Nations*, vol. 36, no. 6 (1991); Kemp, I. (ed.), 'JDW country survey–Germany', *Jane's Defence Weekly*, vol. 16, no. 14 (5 Oct. 1991); Heckman, E., 'The Bundeswehr's new orientation, a new stucture—consequences in materiel', *Military Technology*, vol. 17, no. 2 (1993), p. 34. The unification of the two German armed forces is treated in e.g. 'Die Bundeswehr in beigetretenen Teil Deutschlands' [The Bundeswehr in the unified parts of Germany], *Soldat und Technik*, vol. 33, no. 11 (Nov. 1990), p. 773; Steinseifer, F., 'Streitkräfte im Vereinten Deutschland—Integration der NVA' [Armed forces in united Germany: the integration of the NVA], *Wehrtechnik*, vol. 22, no. 11 (Nov. 1990), p. 73; Wilz, B., 'The unification of the two German armed forces', *Military Technology*, vol. 15, no. 2 (1991), p. 14. Some figures on the ceilings allowed under the CFE Treaty are discussed in Plügge, M., 'Bundeswehr wrestles with reductions', *International Defence Review*, vol. 24, no. 1 (1991), p. 12; and Brückner, G. E., 'Personalbegrenzungen für die Streitkräfte in Europa' [Manpower cuts for armed forces in Europe], *Soldat und Technik*, vol. 35, no. 11 (Nov. 1992), p. 704.

have been subject to occasionally intense debate, relatively little attention—somewhat paradoxically, and with the exception of the European Fighter Aircraft (EFA) issue—has been paid to what could have been the overlap between these two separate debates, the question of military spending.

Declining defence spending and the problems of plan revision

After a period of steady increase during the 1970s, the growth of German defence spending came to a halt around 1979–80, and during the 1980s spending remained at a constant level. In the early 1990s, German military spending decreased rather rapidly; in real terms, in 1993 it was nearly 20 per cent lower than in 1990.

In January 1992 a long-term defence plan, the *Bundeswehrplan 1993*, was presented. While the document was not published, many of the details were released to the press. Among the points made, defence spending during the next 12 years, 1993–2005, should be kept at a constant level of DM 50 billion ($32 billion), indicating a 5 per cent lower spending level than the then prevailing level. The proposed cuts primarily affected the German Army and primarily procurement. Plans for a new MBT (the Leopard 3) and for new APCs were among the scrapped programmes. It was explicitly stated that the new security environment in Europe had reduced the danger of a sudden attack from the East, and, consequently, there was less need than before for systems to counter such a threat. Instead, there was a new need for new mobile light systems and units.[40]

In the *Bundeswehrplan 1993* proposal, there is also a clear tendency to concentrate defence research allocations to fewer projects of higher priority. It is interesting to note that hardly any cuts were made in the allocation to the command, control, communications and intelligence (C^3I) programmes, nor were there any cuts in the programmes for acquiring a new radar surveillance system for eastern Germany nor in the acquisition of various kinds of simulator.

In 1992 the question of German participation in the multinational EFA programme emerged as one of the biggest issues in German military spending—and the issue is still far from being resolved. According to the German view, the proposed aircraft was far too heavy and expensive. Germany needs a new aircraft, as a replacement for its aged Phantom fighters, but such a replacement should be a lighter and cheaper aircraft than the planned EFA. Over the years, German participation in the EFA programme has been gradually reduced.

---

[40] Parker, C., 'Germany plans sharp cuts in spending on military', *Financial Times*, 13 Jan. 1992; Hitchens, T., 'German cuts hit army the hardest', *Defense News*, vol. 7, no. 3 (20 Jan. 1992), p. 4; 'Army takes brunt of cuts', *Jane's Defence Weekly*, vol. 17, no. 3 (18 Jan. 1992), p. 69; Burroughs, D., 'Germany slashes defense procurement plans by 27%', *Armed Forces Journal International*, Feb. 1992, p. 20; Fauth, H., 'Neuer Rüstungsplan für die Bundeswehr—Minus 43,7 Milliarden in zwölf Haushaltsjahren' [A new armaments plan for the Bundeswehr: 43.7 billion less in twelve fiscal years], *Europäische Sicherheit*, vol. 41, no. 2 (Feb. 1992), p. 71; 'Entscheidungen zur Rüstungsplanung' [Decisions on armaments planning], *Soldat und Technik*, no. 2 (1992), p. 102.

In July 1992 it was revealed that defence spending would be cut from DM 52.1 billion ($33.4 billion) in 1992 to DM 50.8 billion ($32.5 billion) in 1993, signifying a reduction in real terms of 6.5 per cent. The defence budget was also to include some salary increases of DM 1.4 billion that previously had been paid from other accounts.[41] At the same time, Defence Minister Volker Rühe also indicated that the *Bundeswehrplan 1993* was no longer valid and that defence spending must be reduced further, particularly spending on procurement. Consequently, it was no longer possible to plan for a defence budget level around DM 50 billion ($32 billion); instead, a level of around DM 45 billion ($28.8 billion) was more appropriate.[42]

In November 1992 a proposal was made to further reduce the 1993 budget by DM 540 million, signifying a real decline of over 8 per cent in 1993.[43] Soon after this proposal, the German Parliament approved a budget of DM 50.1 billion ($32.1 billion).

In December 1992 a new long-term policy document, *Bundeswehrplan 1994*, was presented, covering the 10-year period 1996–2005. The 1993 *Bundeswehrplan*, supposed to fix spending levels for 12 years, had thus not officially survived even for 12 months. The *Bundeswehrplan 1994* was, however, very much in line with the principles revealed by Defence Minister Rühe during the summer. In the *Bundeswehrplan 1993*, a general spending level of about DM 50 billion had been proposed, but during the summer it was suggested that a level of only DM 45 billion was more probable. In the *Bundeswehrplan 1994* it was stated that military expenditures would gradually be reduced to DM 46 billion in 1996, and that this level would be preserved until 2005. The greatest difference between the two 'Bundeswehr plans' is that procurement is further reduced, by about DM 24 billion for the period 1996–2005.[44]

When the new 'Bundeswehr plan' was presented, some of the strategic priorities and assumptions underlying the plan were also revealed. As the Eastern threat receded, fewer anti-tank systems were needed and anti-tank systems were therefore greatly reduced. For the same reasons, there was less need for an ASW capability, and the plans to acquire new additional ASW helicopters were abolished. Decisions on the possible acquisition of the EFA would be postponed until 1995.

Greater emphasis was, however, put on mobile reaction units. Defence Minister Rühe has been a rather outspoken advocate of increased German partici-

---

[41] 'German defense budget set to shrink by 2.5 per cent', *International Defense Review*, vol. 25, no. 8 (1992), p. 724; 'Verteidigungshaushalt 1993 setzt Eckdaten' [Defence budget 1993 is finalized], *Soldat und Technik*, vol. 35, no. 8 (Aug. 1992), p. 510; Hitchens, T., 'German unification spells trouble for defense budget', *Defense News*, vol. 7, no. 36 (7–13 Sep. 1992), p. 28.

[42] Burroughs, D., 'Germany's pullout from EFA program signals freefall in defense spending', *Armed Forces Journal International*, Aug. 1992, p. 29.

[43] de Briganti, G., 'Germany carves into budget: European Fighter Aircraft might lose one-third of development funding', *Defense News*, vol. 7, no. 45 (9–15 Nov. 1992), p. 1.

[44] de Briganti, G., 'Germany to reduce, freeze budget: Ruehe's long-range plan includes crisis-reaction force for overseas action', *Defense News*, vol. 7, no. 51 (21–27 Dec. 1992), p. 3; Schulte, H., 'Germany plans new $15 b spending cuts', *Jane's Defence Weekly*, vol. 19, no. 1 (2 Jan. 1993), p. 4; 'Tightening the belt', *Flight International*, vol. 142, no. 4350 (23 Dec. 1992–5 Jan. 1993), p. 19.

pation in various international operations. When the plan was presented, it was also revealed which military units would be earmarked for certain rapid reaction missions, either to NATO, the Eurocorps or UN assignments.[45]

In early February 1993 further cuts were announced, and the 1993 budget was cut by DM 863 million; thereafter, future defence budgets would be cut by DM 700 million per year during 1994–96. Thus, from July 1992 to February 1993, the 1993 defence budget had on three occasions been both cut and modified—using a comparable definition—from initially DM 50.8 billion to the equivalent of DM 47.9 billion, signifying a reduction in real terms of close to 10 per cent. This third cut also indicates that, for the second time in less than a year, what was thought of as a long-term policy and spending guidelines document had been toppled within a few months by a general need to reduce government spending, primarily to release new spending for the eastern *Länder*. At the same time, Defence Minister Rühe also announced that he had cancelled a DM 3 billion project for German acquisition of a high-altitude electronic surveillance aircraft ('spy-plane') called Lapas.[46]

An annual parliamentary report on the state of the German armed forces in March 1993 aroused some concern. The report concluded that for certain psychological and material reasons the German armed forces were hardly in a position to fight.[47]

The main points in the 1994 general budget were disclosed in July 1993. Various cuts in social spending were introduced, particularly in unemployment benefits, in order to reduce government outlays and the deficit. At the same time, some figures on the 1994 defence budget were also announced, indicating a defence budget (apparently of a revised making, including more expenditure categories than before) of some DM 48.6 billion.[48]

On 18 January 1994, further German defence cuts were announced, and, as part of a general budget cut, the current German defence budget for 1994 was reduced from the earlier DM 48.6 billion level by 1.25 billion to DM 47.3 billion. As defence spending is estimated to have reached DM 49.85 billion

[45] Schulte, H., 'Germans emphasize rapid reaction', *Jane's Defence Weekly*, vol. 19, no. 2 (9 Jan. 1993), p. 6; 'German Bundeswehr: emphasis on rapid reaction forces', *International Defence Review*, vol. 26, no. 1 (1993), p. 9.

[46] Peel, Q., 'Bonn prepares a new round of defence cuts', *Financial Times*, 9 Feb. 1993; Genillard, A., 'Germans press on with defence cuts', *Financial Times*, 13 Feb. 1993; 'Germany topples *Bundeswehrplan 94*', *International Defence Review*, vol. 26, no. 3 (1993), p. 188; de Briganti, G. and Leopold, G., 'Ruehe remains resilient, downplays row with Kohl', *Defense News*, vol. 8, no. 7 (22–28 Feb. 1993), p. 4; de Briganti, G. 'German cutbacks kill Lapas project: legislative foes still urge fraud probe', *Defense News*, vol. 8, no. 5 (8–14 Feb. 1993), p. 4.

[47] 'FRG: critical and alarming report on the Bundeswehr', *Atlantic News*, no. 2511 (26 Mar. 1993), p. 4; Peel, Q., 'German forces unable to take part in any foreign operations', *Financial Times*, 24 Mar. 1993.

[48] Peel, Q., 'Bonn acts to curb deficit with $12 bn spending cut', *Financial Times*, 14 July 1993; 'Defence budget to be cut 2.5% next year', *Jane's Defence Weekly*, vol. 20, no. 3 (17 July 1993), p. 5; 'Im Blickpunkt: Finanzplan bis 1997' [In focus: fiscal plans until 1997], *Soldat und Technik*, vol. 36, no. 9 (Sep. 1993), p. 553.

for 1993, a cut to DM 47.3 billion for 1994 would represent a real decline of about 8.5 per cent.[49]

III. Russia

The level of defence spending in Russia during 1993, as in 1992, was primarily a function of the government's struggle to control overall state expenditure in order to reduce the rampant inflation characteristic of the nation's economic transition; military manpower and weapon policies were secondary or tertiary considerations. Despite dismay at the chaos produced in the armed forces and defence industry by the massive reduction of defence spending by at least one-third in 1992,[50] and in spite of pressure from the defence lobby and a free-spending parliament, the government managed to hold military expenditures as a percentage of GDP to about the same level in 1993 as in 1992. Holding the line on spending, however, was achieved at the cost of the continued disintegration of the armed forces and the defence industry. Only towards the end of 1993 did the government show signs of effectively reorienting its policy focus towards formulating objectives for the defence sector which better match its drastically diminished resources in the changed political and economic environment of the post-cold war period.

Any effort to describe the level, structure and major implications of 1993 military expenditure in Russia is hampered by a number of general features of the Russian transitional economy that make it difficult to interpret the data relevant to such an analysis. One of these features is the high rate of inflation unleashed by the price liberalization in January 1992, which has made tracing real economic magnitudes in any detail at best a time-consuming endeavour. From September 1992 to September 1993, price indices for the output of the machine-building industry increased by 797 per cent, for construction materials by 982 per cent, and for consumer prices by over 1100 per cent, according to the Russian State Committee for Statistics.[51] More disaggregated, up-to-date price indices that would make deflating the various components of military expenditure worthwhile generally did not exist at the time of writing. Moreover, state authorities and the press have often been remiss about reporting which prices were used in the calculation of the expenditures which they were making public. Finally, the scale of the price rises, combined with an inability to account for much economic activity in Russia (particularly in the private sector), make even a comparison of military expenditure with broader economic aggregates, such as GDP, tenuous.

[49] de Briganti, G., 'Germany to slash defense further', *Defense News*, vol. 9, no. 3 (24–30 Jan. 1994), p. 1; 'Military budgets: Germany', *Atlantic News*, no. 2590 (22 Jan. 1994), p. 3; 'German budget falls', *Jane's Defence Weekly*, vol. 21, no. 6 (12 Feb. 1994), p. 1.

[50] *SIPRI Yearbook 1993* (note 2), p. 357. See also Schröder, H., *The Russian Military Budget in the Years 1992 and 1993*, Current Analysis no. 35 (16 Aug. 1993), Bundesinstitut für Ostwissenschaftliche und Internationale Studien, Cologne (in German).

[51] Russian Federation, State Committee for Statistics, *Social Economic Situation of the Russian Federation in January–September 1993*, Economic Survey no. 10 (Republikanskii informatsion-noizdatel'skii tsentr: Moscow, 1993), pp. 82–84 (in Russian).

Inflation also exacerbates another feature of the Russian economy relevant to measuring military expenditure—relative price distortion. This distortion, which obscures accurate valuation of the flow of resources within the economy, arises fundamentally from the extensive subsidies, non-market credits and administered prices still found in Russia's initial stage of radical economic reform. A third and perhaps the most troublesome general feature of the Russian economic environment for analysis of state spending was the increased politicization of the budget process in the new Russian state. 'Politicization' here refers not only to the struggle between the parliament and the government that produced multiple revisions in the budget over 1993. More broadly, it also refers to the fact that the budget numbers were often used for political purposes and thus truly reflected neither the ability nor the intention of budget planners to meet spending targets.

The 1993 budgetary process

The budgetary process in Russia in 1993 was more conflictual and arduous than it was in 1992. The clash of diverse philosophies about the role of state spending and perceived trade-offs between price and output stabilization intensified against a background of vigorous lobbying efforts by economic interest groups. It was characteristic that, until the suspension of the parliament by Russian President Boris Yeltsin's decree on 21 September 1993, the government and parliament together had managed to approve a new budget for 1993 nearly every month. First submitted by the government for parliamentary approval on 16 December 1992, the draft budget law 'On the Budget System of the Russian Federation for 1993' (hereafter referred to as the 1993 Budget Law) went back and forth between the two bodies several times over the course of the next six months, each time undergoing significant revision in its projected revenues, expenditures and prices.[52] The tense process seemed to be on its way to resolution in May, when the president and the parliament had a draft which they were both able to sign. Total expenditures were set at 18.725 trillion roubles ($23.4 billion) against estimated revenues of 10.202 trillion roubles ($12.8 billion), thus producing a deficit of about 8.5 trillion roubles ($10.6 billion).[53]

There were complications, however. For one thing, the government and the parliament were becoming increasingly polarized in their commitment to stabilizing inflation. The parliament, determined to slow the deterioration of the economy through financial infusions from the state, attached some modifications to the budget law that stipulated substantial additional expenditures. Within the government, on the other hand, the argument was gaining strength that the structure of the current budget implied a dangerously high level of

---

[52] Reuter, 29 Jan. 1993; Supreme Soviet of the Russian Federation, *Vedomosti Verkhovnogo Soveta Rossiyskoi Federatsii*, no. 7 (18 Feb. 1993), pp. 436–37, and no. 10 (11 Mar. 1993), pp. 620–21 (in Russian); 'Information, not telepropaganda, is what is needed', *Rossiyskaya Gazeta*, 26 Mar. 1993, p. 1 (in Russian).

[53] Here, all calculations of dollar figures are based on the assumed exchange-rate of $1 = 800 roubles.

spending by the end of the year. As a result, pursuant to the presidential decree 'On Several Measures to Restrain Inflation' of 3 June 1993, on 1 July the government submitted to the parliament a set of modifications to the 1993 Budget Law that would have cut overall federal expenditures by 20 per cent with the intention of holding the deficit to about 10 per cent of GDP.[54]

The budgetary process had now reached a stalemate. When the parliament finally approved a set of modifications to the Budget Law on 22 July 1993, the implied deficit was calculated at an enormous 20–25 per cent of GDP.[55] After two vetoes, Yeltsin chose to deal in a more decisive fashion with the unrepentant legislature, which had so long blocked his efforts at economic and political reform. On 21 September 1993 he suspended the parliament and called for new elections.

However, as became obvious after its routing, the parliament was not the only obstacle to achieving the government's overriding budgetary objective of keeping the deficit within 10 per cent of GDP. There remained greater political and financial realities that exerted upward pressure on federal spending which had little to do with the parliament's free-spending inclinations. According to an analysis by the Ministry of Finance, a combination of explicit or implicit indexation of expenditures to inflation and subsequent promises made by the government itself could be expected to push the deficit foreseen in its July 1993 budget to 22.2 trillion roubles ($27.8 billion), or 14 per cent of GDP, by the end of the year.[56]

The Ministry of Finance therefore set about devising yet another set of modifications to the budget that involved across-the-board expenditure cuts. What emerged in November 1993 was a Ministry of Finance budget that proved to be the last comprehensive version of the year.[57] It envisaged expenditures of 43.91 trillion roubles ($54.9 billion), which, against expected revenues of 26.68 trillion, implied a deficit of about 17 trillion roubles. Unfortunately, these estimates were not long-lived either. In early December 1993 the Ministry of Finance was forced to issue some 1.6 trillion roubles in new expenditures to pay for prior spending commitments.[58] More fundamentally, however, it appeared that revenues would be nowhere near enough to enable achievement of the planned year-end deficit of only 10 per cent of GDP. First Deputy Prime Minister Oleg Soskovets had said in late November 1993 that the 5.5 trillion roubles in deficit spending projected for the fourth quarter of

---

[54] Reuter, 22 July 1993; 'Parliament once again recalculates appropriations for the year', *Kommersant-Daily*, 25 July 1993, p. 3 (in Russian).

[55] 'The budget is modified under the grave-like silence of MinFin', *Rossiyskaya Gazeta*, 23 July 1993, p. 1 (in Russian).

[56] Russian Federation, Ministry of Finance, Note no. 1-10/2-204, 28 Oct. 1993 (in Russian).

[57] 'MinFin warns: the country is on the verge of hyperinflation', *Izvestia*, 12 Nov. 1993, p. 1 (in Russian).

[58] 'The budget has holes and Finance officials have a headache', *Rossiyskaya Gazeta*, 7 Dec. 1993, p. 1; and 'Generosity a week before the elections', *Rabochaya tribuna*, 7 Dec. 1993, p. 1 (in Russian). On 23 Dec. Yeltsin issued a decree and the government a resolution modifying the expenditure and deficit targets accordingly. See 'Russian authorities go to meet Western creditors', *Kommersant-Daily*, 23 Dec. 1993, p. 2; 'The budget of the Russian Federation for the fourth quarter is modified', *Segodnya*, 23 Dec. 1993, p. 3; and 'The government of the Russian Federation accepts the modifications of budget expenditures', *Segodnya*, 28 Dec. 1993, p. 1.

1993 under the Ministry of Finance budget would rise to at least 10 trillion roubles.[59] It is not exactly clear at the time of writing how the Ministry will paper over this reality, but one source has reported that 6 trillion roubles of 1993 deficit spending is being sequestered for release in 1994.[60]

Planned military expenditures

By the end of 1993, two different sets of figures on defence spending were available (see table 12.9). One set emerged from the 1993 Budget Law passed in May, and the other was the over-optimistic Ministry of Finance projection from November. Beyond the general problems associated with tracing state spending mentioned above, there are a number of obstacles to interpreting these defence figures, in particular. First, there is the problem of separating military and non-military expenditures from aggregated budget allocations.

Table 12.9 lists, in addition to the official budget defence allocation (OBDA), several other defence-related expenditures. These are civil defence, expenditures on mobilization capacity, payments to dependants and children of the military, additional military housing construction not covered in the OBDA, the maintenance of so-called special objects, the clean-up of nuclear accidents, disarmament and arms industry conversion. It can reasonably be argued that some of these items should be left out of the calculation of defence spending since they do not contribute to national security.[61] On the other hand, the military expenditure figures in table 12.9 are not complete and leave out some state spending associated with national defence. Perhaps most conspicuously absent are defence-related expenditures for internal security forces. Still more defence-related expenditures may be hidden under more general budget items such as foreign economic activities, science and technology, and government investments.[62] Financing of conversion programmes provided in the form of negative-interest loans[63] has also been excluded, as have nuclear and space programmes.

The figures in table 12.9 are drawn from the federal budget of the Russian Federation. Although military housing construction costs which were channelled through regional budgets in previous years[64] were listed explicitly under

---

[59] 'Russia restores import tariffs on some foods', *Financial Times,* 30 Nov. 1993, p. 2.

[60] 'Yeltsin sets opposing courses', *Financial Times,* 24 Dec. 1993, p. 2.

[61] Cost separation is even a problem in the superficially straightforward OBDA. For example, First Deputy Minister of Defense Andrey Kokoshin said recently that *two-thirds* of state financing on orders for defence industry output (within the 'procurement' sub-category of the OBDA) go to cover social expenses such as the building and maintenance of kindergartens, schools, hospitals and apartments as well as keeping excess labour employed. See 'Presidential decree supports the defense order', *Rossiyskie Vesti,* 24 Nov. 1993, pp. 1, 2.

[62] See Tedstrom, J., '"Glasnost" and the Soviet defense budget', *Report on the USSR,* 19 July 1991, pp. 6–14.

[63] A World Bank report suggests that, at least in 1992, conversion credits were actually listed as subsidies in the state budget; see *1993 Economic Review: Russian Federation* (International Monetary Fund: Washington, DC, June 1993), p. 139, footnote 7. However, in the Ministry of Finance budget of Nov. 1993, budget credits and subsidies for conversion appear to be distinguished from one another.

[64] See Wallich, C. I., 'Fiscal decentralization: intergovernmental relations in Russia', *Studies of Economies in Transformation,* no. 6 (World Bank: Washington, DC, 1993), p. 38.

Table 12.9. Planned Russian military expenditure, 1993

Figures are in b. current roubles; figures in italics are percentages.

	Mid-year 1993 Budget Law	Share of total expenditure	Ministry of Finance Plan	Share of total expenditure
OBDA	3 115.51	*16.64*	7 241.20	*16.49*
OBDA/GDP	*7.23*	..	*4.26*	..
Defence-related	729.64	..	1 689.18	..
Civil defence	28.40	*0.15*	66.80	..
Mobilization	16.10	*0.09*	47.70	*0.11*
Payments to dependants and children of military	8.30	*0.04*	23.50	*0.05*
Housing construction	213.10	*1.14*	500.58	*1.14*
Maintenance of 'special objects'	47.70	*0.25*	109.20	*0.25*
Clean-up of nuclear accidents	275.10	*1.47*	542.20	*1.23*
Disarming	28.14	*0.15*	52.80	*0.12*
Conversion	112.80	*0.60*	346.40	*0.79*
Total defence	**3 845.15**	**20.53**	**8 930.38**	**20.34**
Total expenditure	18 725.10	..	43 910.20	..
Total defence/GDP	**8.92**	..	**5.25**	..

Sources: *Rossiyskaya Gazeta*, 1 June 1993, p. 6 (in Russian); Russian Federation, Ministry of Finance, Note no. 1-10/2-204, 28 Oct. 1993 (in Russian), appendix.

the investment funds transferred to regional budgets in the 1993 Budget Law,[65] the possibility cannot be excluded that local and regional budgets may have been a source of other financing, but these expenditures are almost impossible to trace and are almost certainly marginal. It may also be assumed that extra-budgetary funds played a marginal role in financing defence and defence-related activities.[66] Erring on the side of over-estimation, it can be supposed that these omissions from table 12.9 would account for an additional 5–10 per cent of total military expenditure.

Finally, as discussed in the section above, at the end of December there was an increase in state expenditure that was unforeseen in the November Ministry of Finance plan. Among the modifications was an increase in the OBDA to 4476 billion roubles for the fourth quarter, implying a year-end total of 8177 billion roubles.[67] If one assumes that all defence-related expenditures were similarly boosted by 13 per cent, the items in table 12.9 would total something on the order of 10 090 billion roubles.

On the basis of these assumptions, two broad conclusions can be drawn about planned Russian military expenditures in 1993. First, these expenditures

[65] In the Ministry of Finance budget of Nov. 1993, these construction costs were not disaggregated from the total transfers to sub-national budgets. It is here assumed that the same share of total federal budgetary expenditures (1.14%) went to military housing construction as provided for under the 1993 Budget Law.

[66] Of course, a fund exists for conversion itself, but it may be excluded from consideration as its receipts appear to come from enterprises within the defence sector.

[67] Interfax, 23 Dec. 1993.

Table 12.10. The structure of OBDA for the Soviet Union, 1989–91, and for Russia, 1992–93

Figures are percentages of the total.

Spending category	1989	1990	1991	1992[a]	1993
Personnel, O&M	26.13	27.18	33.40	54.70	49.95
Procurement	42.17	43.66	37.30	16.11	18.28
R&D	19.79	18.59	16.70	10.58	7.21
Construction	5.95	5.35	6.33[b]	12.78	16.50
Pensions	2.98	3.38	4.12[b]	3.02	5.50
Nuclear energy industry	2.98	1.83	1.93[b]	2.83	1.58
Miscellaneous	–	–	–	–	0.97

[a] The structure of the OBDA for 1992 is taken from the budget law dated 17 July 1992 rather than from the more aggregated final budget modifications.

[b] Denotes an estimate, based on the structure of spending foreseen in the Law on the Union Budget for 1991, a planned 2 billion rouble overall reduction. See *Nezavisimaya Gazeta*, 12 Jan. 1991.

Sources: *Ekonomicheskaya Gazeta*, no. 35 (1992); 'The army doesn't need any more money', *Krasnaya Zvezda*, 24 Sep. 1992, p. 2; *Izvestia*, 12 Jan. 1991, p. 4; Russian Federation, Ministry of Finance, Note no. 1-10/2-204, 28 Oct. 1993 (in Russian), appendix.

dropped slightly in terms of their share of GDP and overall government expenditures in comparison with 1992. The 1992 OBDA planned expenditure item of 847.82 billion roubles was just under 5 per cent of Russia's 17 trillion rouble GDP and 21.9 per cent of total federal outlays in 1992. According to the Ministry of Finance plan of November 1993, OBDA expenditures would have been somewhat over 4 per cent of GDP and 16 per cent of total outlays. Even allowing for the additional 936 billion roubles approved by Yeltsin in mid-December 1993, OBDA outlays would fall short of 5 per cent of GDP. Beyond the OBDA, it is noted that the size of other related military expenditures relative to GDP and overall federal expenditures probably did not change significantly between 1992 and 1993.[68] Hence, these observations on the size of the OBDA are generalizable to total defence spending.

The lack of up-to-date and disaggregated price indices rules out an unequivocal assertion that planned military expenditures in 1993 were lower in real terms than in 1992. If cost structures in the defence sector were analogous to those in the Russian economy as a whole, it could be assumed that real military expenditures shrank with real GDP.[69] However, since nominal wages in the defence sector and the armed forces and price indices for the machine-

[68] The sum for cleaning up nuclear accidents, disarmament and conversion remained at 0.8–0.9% of GDP and 2–4% of total federal outlays in the 1992 and 1993 budgets. Other defence-related expenditures were not disaggregated in the published 1992 federal budget.

[69] Goskomstat, the State Committee for Statistics, reports that GDP declined by 12% in 1993, according to a Russian Television broadcast on 10 Jan. 1994.

building (a proxy for procurement) and construction sectors seem to have grown less than the GDP price deflator, this assumption cannot be made.[70]

A second set of observations concerns the structure of defence spending. It would appear from table 12.9 that the shares of OBDA spending (16.5 per cent) and other spending categories in total expenditures stayed relatively stable over the course of the year. More interesting, of course, is the structure of spending in 1993 as compared with that in previous years. The change in structure is indicated in table 12.10. The 1993 state budget includes some changes in the reporting of defence spending, in particular with regard to the appearance of new entries in defence-related expenditure. Moreover, other defence-related expenditures have been inconsistently reported in the past. The sub-categories of expenditure found in OBDA, in contrast, have been consistent over time, and this is why only the OBDA structure is presented in table 12.10.

Table 12.10 suggests that there might have been some effort to reallocate resources among categories of defence spending in 1993. After years of a steady increase, the share of expenditures on personnel and O&M seems to have been reduced somewhat to allow for increases elsewhere in the overall allocation. Perhaps reflecting an attempt to offset some of the damage caused to industry after the accelerated massive drop in arms orders in 1992, the share of planned spending on procurement increased notably. Indeed, although official procurement expenditures remained roughly the same relative to GDP from 1992 to 1993 (at about 0.8 per cent of GDP), given the slower growth in machine-building prices than in the GDP deflator, it may be assumed that real procurement spending rose in 1993. Construction also seemed to be a beneficiary of the shift in spending shares. The increases in construction (presumably a significant amount of housing) and pensions may be evidence of the desire to offset some of the deterioration in the standard of living of current and former members of the armed forces and their families.

Implications of stagnant spending

The level and structure of planned defence spending as well as the combative budgetary process in 1993 created severe financial problems for the armed forces and defence industry. Low wages and the deterioration of other personnel benefits, more or less stagnant arms procurement and chronic delays in budgetary transfers to pay off all sorts of state contracts sustained the chaotic character dominating the process of down-sizing the Russian military establishment.

For the armed forces, low pay and housing shortages ensured that the manpower problems persisted in 1993.[71] Conscripts saw the quadrupling of their

---

[70] The only major cost component of the defence sector that seems to have increased faster than the GDP price deflator was energy, rising some 1856% from Sep. 1992 to Sep. 1993, according to Goskomstat. See note 51.

[71] The manpower problems in the Russian armed forces in 1993 have been well documented in the following articles of the Radio Free Europe/Radio Liberty *RFE/RL Research Report:* Lepingwell, J., 'Is

nominal earnings from January to September undercut by an increase in consumer prices of roughly 650 per cent.[72] Moreover, in the first part of the year, the Ministry of Defence debt to the Army and Navy rose to 1.25 trillion roubles, most of which was associated with personnel costs.[73] The size of this financial shortfall meant, for example, that entire units operated for several weeks on end without pay. Although the backlog of debt seemed to have been considerably reduced by the fourth quarter of the year, payment delays plagued the armed forces throughout 1993. As for military housing, the increased share of total defence appropriations for construction did not reduce the overall shortage accentuated by the continuing withdrawal of Russian forces from Eastern Europe and the countries of the former Soviet Union. Minister of Defence Pavel Grachev has claimed that the number of officers without proper housing would rise from 120 000 in early 1993 to 400 000 in 1994.[74]

Since May 1992 the size of the Russian Army has dropped by just under a half million, according to Grachev,[75] and there are suspicions that the real figure is a good deal higher than that. Of course, much of the decline can be attributed to intended reductions or to the higher number of exemptions allowed by the February 1993 Law on Military Service.[76] However, there is no disputing that the erosion of material benefits offered to members of the armed forces is contributing to shrinkage in personnel.

The impact of constrained finances had a detrimental effect on the structure of the armed forces as well. Widespread draft dodging will further reduce the ratio of soldiers to officers, which was expected to drop to less than 1 : 1 after the double demobilization in the autumn of 1993.[77] Moreover, although the leadership had hoped that many of the planned reductions of the officer corps (40 000–90 000 individuals on average annually by 1995[78]) would be from among the older officers, it appears that it is the younger officers who are being lost in greater numbers. The Defence Ministry has reported that the rate

---

the military disintegrating from within?', vol. 2, no. 25 (18 June 1993), p. 16; Foye, S., 'Rebuilding the Russian armed forces', vol. 2, no. 30 (23 July 1993), pp. 49–57; Foye, S., 'Russia's defense establishment in disarray', vol. 2, no. 36 (10 Sep. 1993), pp. 49–54; and Foye S., 'The armed forces of the CIS: legacies and strategies', vol. 3, no. 1 (7 Jan. 1994), pp. 18–21.

[72] 'Social status of the Russian serviceman should not decrease', *Krasnaya Zvezda*, 30 Jan. 1993, p. 1; and 'Finally, military pay is increased', *Krasnaya Zvezda*, 18 Sep. 1993, p. 1. Anecdotal evidence suggests that by the end of 1993 the real incomes of military servicemen may have crept up to their 1992 levels. However, they were still significantly lower than the 1990 and 1991 levels.

[73] What lay behind this accumulation of non-payments, according to Vasiliy Borobev, head of the Main Administration of the Defense Budget and Financing of the Ministry of Defense, was that the Ministry of Finance continued to transfer funds to the Ministry of Defence on the basis of indicators of the budget modifications of July, which were calculated in May–June prices. See 'There are no simple decisions in the financial sphere', *Krasnaya Zvezda*, 17 Dec. 1993, p. 1 (in Russian).

[74] See Lepingwell (note 71), p. 15, where it is suggested that this total probably includes some enlisted personnel as well.

[75] ITAR-TASS, 29 Dec. 1994 (in Russian).

[76] In Sep. 1993, Yeltsin signed a decree modifying this law by revoking deferments previously granted to students of Russian and technical schools.

[77] This tendency is expected to worsen in 1994. See 'Next year there will be more officers than soldiers in the Russian Army', *Nezavisimaya Gazeta*, 2 July 1993, pp. 1, 3 (in Russian).

[78] Lepingwell (note 71), p. 15.

at which officers under the age of 30 years are resigning their commissions was on the rise in 1993.[79]

Decline reigns in the arms industry as well. After years of gradual reduction in procurement orders, struggle over which direction weapon acquisition policy should take and the breakdown of the centralized supply system, the industry was dealt a new shock in 1992 when the state reduced its defence orders by 65–68 per cent. In 1993, as noted above, planned real procurement spending might have increased slightly, but this has had little noticeable positive effect on the industry. Indeed, as was the case with the armed forces, budgetary allocations to the defence industry were chronically delayed in 1993. The outstanding bills owed to the defence sector grew from around 400 billion roubles in mid-1993 to 800–900 billion roubles in December.[80] Towards the end of 1993, President Yeltsin did take some formal action to restore order in the procurement system and prevent payments delays,[81] but the Ministry of Defence continued to report that these problems were not resolved and that, by the beginning of 1994, 70 per cent of the production lines in the defence sector had been idled.[82]

The stagnant planned budgetary allocations and delinquent payments to the sector preserved the most common type of shrinkage in the military defence complex in Russia observed since the start of *perestroika*: 'spontaneous' conversion. Unable to pay competitive wages,[83] the sector continued to lose highly qualified workers; management cast about for whatever means they could find to increase the utilization of capital, in many cases transferring resources to quasi-private ventures outside the state defence industry. The severity of this disintegration has stood in sharp contrast to the state-directed conversion programme of military industry output, which, despite continued major federal funding,[84] has been widely regarded as a failure. Indeed, while it is true that the value of civilian output now exceeds that of military output in a greater share of defence sector enterprises than ever before,[85] there were signs that the conversion of the output mix of military enterprises was slowing down in 1993. The share of total production of converting enterprises that was of civilian output dropped slightly from mid-1992 (73.2 per cent) to mid-1993

---

[79] 'Service by contract: the forces receive not only professionals, but problems too', *Krasnaya Zvezda*, 18 Aug. 1993, p. 1 (in Russian).

[80] These bills appear to be for state orders for both equipment and R&D work. See ITAR-TASS, 6 July 1993 (in Russian); Interfax, 25 Nov. 1993; and 'Debt on the defense order must be returned', *Krasnaya Zvezda*, 24 Dec. 1993, p. 1 (in Russian).

[81] Presidential Decree no. 1850 'On the stabilization of the economic situation of enterprises and organizations of the defense industry and measures for securing the state defense order', dated 6 Nov. 1993, in, for example, *Dokumenty*, no. 232 (30 Nov. 1993), insert in *Rossiyskie vesti* (in Russian).

[82] ITAR-TASS, 17 Jan. 1993 (in Russian).

[83] In 1993 wages remained about 60% of the average in Russian industry. 'Why wages are low', *Krasnaya Zvezda*, 13 Mar. 1993, p. 5 (in Russian); 'Oboronka' seizes a monopoly in the refrigerator sphere, but dreams of arms exports above all else', *Izvestia*, 30 Dec. 1993, p. 4.

[84] In addition to the nearly 350 billion roubles allocated to conversion under the final 1993 draft budget for the year (shown in table 12.9) in grants, there was more than 700 billion roubles in loans.

[85] Russian Federation, State Committee for Statistics, The development of economic reforms in the regions of the Russian Federation no. 10 (Moscow: Republikanskii informatsionno-izdatel'skii tsentr, 1993), pp. 138–39 (in Russian).

(73.1 per cent).[86] Defence industry enterprises in St Petersburg, Khalmg Tangch, the Kaluzhskaya, Kostromskaya, Orlovskaya, Tul'skaya, Krasnodarskaya, Kurganskaya, Amurskaya and Rostovskaya oblasts, and the Krasnodarskii and Stavropolskii krais all experienced drops of 15 per cent or more in their relative share of civilian output.

This is not to say that the state did not seek more effective policies to deal with the economic trauma of the arms industry, however. The Russian Government became much more serious in 1993 about finding new markets for the excess capacity of the arms industry rather than switching it to civilian production. The government had already announced in 1992 that it intended to help revive arms exports, which had suffered a continuous decline since 1987. Soviet arms exports, the overwhelming majority of which had been produced by Russian firms, fell in value from over $17 billion in 1987 to less than $4 billion in 1991.[87] According to Russian sources, the nation's arms exports for 1992 were in the neighbourhood of $2.5 billion to under $1.9 billion.[88] Throughout 1993, many observers suggested that export earnings were falling further, a suggestion confirmed by Minister of External Economic Relations Oleg Davydov, who said in late December that Russia had exported a mere $1.2 billion in weapons over the course of the year.[89] The focus of the government's efforts to boost arms exports was to reorganize the arms export system (developed in 1992 and existing throughout 1993) that allowed four specialized associations—Oboronexport, Spetsvneshtekhnika, Promexport, and the Main Directorate for Collaboration and Cooperation—and a number of independent arms producers to sell weapons abroad.[90] Aside from the disappearance of East European, Afghan and some African customers, the competition among these exporters reportedly had a serious negative impact on sales revenues. After much debate throughout 1993 on an approach to reforming the system, in mid-November Yeltsin signed a decree establishing a state-owned company, Rosvooruzhenie, which will co-ordinate much of the arms export activity by absorbing most of the associations and enterprises with the right to export arms.[91]

There was also growing evidence that the arms industry's deep and protracted decline was finally forcing policy makers to gather the heretofore fragmented policies of conversion, export promotion and selective support of industry into a general industrial strategy. The vision of creating a core of

[86] Note that comments made by Viktor Glukhikh, Chairman of the State Committee of the Russian Federation on the Defense Branches of Industry, later in the year suggested that a higher share—nearly 80% of production of defence enterprises—was civilian. ITAR-TASS, 7 Dec. 1993 (in Russian).

[87] Sachse, T., 'Russian Arms Export Policy', Report no. 4, Bundesinstitut fü Ostwissenschaftliche und Internationale Studien, Cologne, 1993, p. 7 (in German). The dollar figures listed refer to estimated values of arms transfers, not of sales receipts. Soviet arms were often given away or sold on credit which will never be repaid.

[88] Reuter, 1 Dec. 1993, 'Russia fights for a place on the world markets for weapons', Kommersant, no. 48 (1993), pp. 10–11; 'Russia boosts arms exports', Financial Times, 1 Dec. 1993, p. 2.

[89] ITAR-TASS, 28 Dec. 1993; and Reuter, 28 Dec. 1993.

[90] Reuter (note 88), pp. 10–11; and Foye, S., 'Russian arms exports after the cold war', Radio Free Europe/Radio Liberty, RFE/RL Research Report, vol. 2, no. 13 (26 Mar. 1993), pp. 58–66.

[91] 'Weapons producers propose to reverse the presidential decree', Kommersant-Daily, 22 Dec. 1993, p. 4 (in Russian).

enterprises supported by the state and focusing their resources on the development and production of advanced military equipment seems to have found its way into the government's general approach to industrial policy.[92] This effort was reflected in the government's conversion programme for 1993–95, which targeted specific advanced technologies, and in its draft industrial programme.[93] The adoption in late 1993 of a new military doctrine, which promised to assist in the development of a rational procurement policy, may facilitate the effort.

Summary

The following major observations may be drawn from this survey of available information on the level, structure and impact of Russian military expenditure in 1993.

1. Despite broadly expressed alarm among Russian state authorities at the chaos in the defence sector caused by the drastic cuts in spending in 1992, military expenditures in 1993 remained on the same level as 1992 as a percentage of GDP. It is also worth noting that there is no evidence of a widely expected pay-off to the military for its support in the attack on the parliament on 3–4 October 1993.

2. The efforts to achieve the stabilization of prices through fiscal and monetary austerity remain the chief preoccupation of the Russian state; the fate of the military establishment remained a second- or third-order concern. This general statement must be slightly qualified by the fact that some adjustment in the structure of planned spending seems to have been made to offset the particularly acute manpower problems (e.g., the housing shortage) and curtailment in arms production.

3. The dissolution of parliament did not stabilize the budgetary process. The Defence Ministry continues to work on a very unsure financial basis.

4. Although a reduction in the resources devoted to the defence sector is an expressed goal of the state and only appropriate in the post-cold war era, the process continues to be largely unmanaged. This is evident in the implementation of enormous financial constriction before effective planning of downsizing the sector. The result has been the disproportionate loss of some of the sector's best labour and capital resources in the armed forces and the defence industry.

5. New efforts were initiated in 1993 to facilitate the rational down-sizing of the military–industrial complex, through utilizing excess capacities for meeting non-domestic military needs and selective support to enterprises within a broader programme of industrial policy. However, these efforts, by their nature, will take some time to show results.

---

[92] The relationship between the military and broader industrial policy, a relatively new phenomenon in civil–military relations, is explored in Cooper, J., 'Transforming Russia's defense industrial base', *Survival,* vol. 34, no. 4 (winter 1993), pp. 147–62.

[93] ITAR-TASS and Interfax, 3 June 1993; the government's draft programme on industrial policy was published in *Promyshlennaya Gazeta, no. 3* (insert to *Rossiyskie Vesti),* 11 Dec. 1993, p. 2 (in Russian).

IV. Central and Eastern Europe

This section discusses military expenditure in the six Central and East European countries—Bulgaria, the Czech Republic, Hungary, Poland, Romania and the Slovak Republic. It evaluates the region's official defence budgets and presents estimates of military expenditures at current values. The expenditure estimates probably represent minimum levels, because they only account for the obvious defence activities. However, although published official defence budgets are lacking in sufficient detail to serve as measures of defence costs, these official statistics are useful for identifying trends.[94]

In the Central and East European region, processes of systemic transformation have been accompanied by exceptionally radical measures aimed at a remodelling of the economies along civilian lines. The methods of transformation have not been the same in all the countries of Central and Eastern Europe. While Bulgaria and Poland have opted for a radical approach involving overnight replacement of central planning by a free market, the Czech Republic, Hungary, Romania and Slovakia have opted for a more gradual, evolutionary approach. The inescapable process of reconstruction has turned out to be far more costly than was expected, and a growing disparity in levels of development as between Western and Eastern Europe is evident.

While European unity in the *political* sphere is making progress, the *economic* gap between the two regions is widening. All the post-communist economies are struggling with the problems of macroeconomic stabilization, the slow pace of privatization of state enterprises and property, the pathologies of post-communist banking and financial systems, and the unresolved questions of the desirability of, and mechanism for, regional economic (re)integration.

Although the process of change in national military expenditure began in the mid-1980s under the influence of the changing situation in East–West relations, the breakthrough came with the launching of reforms of the politico-military and economic system and with the change of direction in each of the countries in the region. Difficulties of a political kind are created by the fact that redefinition of the concept of national security and the debate on defence doctrine and the prospective structure of the armed forces are still in progress in Central and Eastern Europe. This means that the future equipment needs of the armed services and the possibilities of meeting these needs by means of domestic or external procurement have not yet been defined. Financial factors have, of course, a significant impact on military spending—poor growth performance has contributed to the decline in military spending. As can be seen from tables 12.11–12.16, budgets have been cut in nominal terms in all the countries up to 1992, when they started to increase slightly. Procurement spending has been drastically reduced and there is almost no acquisition of

---

[94] For a more detailed review of these countries' military expenditure, see Loose-Weintraub, E., 'Military expenditure in Central and East European countries', *SIPRI Yearbook 1993* (note 2), appendix 9A, pp. 398–414.

new weapons. This has serious consequences for the arms industry because of the slump in production and exports, with attendant unemployment, company debt and social hardship. Restructuring defence enterprises requires large financial inputs which these enterprises do not have.[95]

The Czech Republic

Reduction of the numbers of military personnel and items of armament, relocation, gradual professionalization and modernization are continuing tasks.

The restructuring of the Czech Republic's armed forces is scheduled to be completed by 1997, by which time, under the CFE Treaty, the armed forces will be limited to no more than 93 300 troops—a reduction from the present holding of 106 500.[96]

Table 12.11. The Czech Republic's military expenditure allocation, 1993

Figures are in current m. korunas. Figures in italics are percentage shares.

	1993	Share of total expenditure
Personnel	10 038	*46.5*
O&M[a]	7 814	*36.2*
Procurement	1 878	*8.7*
Construction	1 610	*7.5*
R&D	243	*1.1*
Total	**21 583**	*100*

[a] O&M includes civilian personnel cost.

Source: The Czech submission to the CSCE Instrument for Standardized International Reporting of Military Expenditure, provided by the Embassy of the Czech Republic in Stockholm, 15 Jan. 1994.

According to the 1993 budget estimates submitted to parliament, total military expenditure will be 21.6 billion korunas ($794.1 million), which corresponds to 6 per cent of total government expenditure.[97] Procurement expenditure will be only 8.7 per cent of the total defence allocation. In the light of the heavy reductions taking place in the production of military goods in the Czech Republic, as in the other Central and East European countries, military enterprises (with the possible exception of Aero Vodochody and Tatra) are either on the verge of or in a state of bankruptcy and are forced to resort to simple

[95] For a description of the overall size and structure of the defence industries in Central and Eastern Europe, readers are referred to Anthony, I. (ed.), SIPRI, *The Future of the Defence Industries in Central and Eastern Europe,* SIPRI Research Report No. 7 (Oxford University Press: Oxford, forthcoming in 1994).

[96] International Institute for Strategic Studies (IISS), *The Military Balance 1993–1994* (Brassey's: London, 1994), p. 79.

[97] Czech Republic, Ministry of Defence, *Law of Military Budgets,* C 10/1993, provided by the Embassy of the Czech Republic in Stockholm, 15 Jan. 1994.

survival techniques or to engage in renewed political lobbying in order to rescue their positions.[98]

Military expenditure has been shifted away from procurement towards O&M. Of the O&M share of 36.2 per cent reported for 1993, most was spent on materials, spare parts, repairs and training aids which were of a civilian nature. Personnel cost, at 46.5 per cent, accounts for the greatest share of the budget. All the military forces of Central and Eastern Europe, including those of the Czech Republic, carried out a considerable amount of work for the civilian economy. Apart from working in agriculture, soldiers were for example assigned to help construct the Temelin and Mochovce nuclear power plants, reconstruct Prague Castle and help build the Prague subway system.[99] In the transition to market reforms and given the accompanying increased unemployment, military labour will in the future probably not be needed in the civilian sector.

The Slovak Republic

Since the break-up on 1 January 1993 of the 74-year old Czechoslovakia into two separate states, foreign policy and security interests and priorities are still being formed. The economic consequences of the split are in many ways unpredictable. As of early 1994, Slovakia did not have the infrastructure needed for its future armed forces, especially not for its air force. The CFE Treaty will leave the armed forces with approximately 47 000 men, 478 tanks and 115 military aircraft.[100] Even such vital assets as airfields, accommodation facilities for military personnel and depots for ammunition are needed, and Slovakia is not expected to have the necessary resources to build them for years to come. Some military supplies and hardware will be left in storage in the Czech Republic for transfer to Slovakia by the end of 1994.

The Slovak defence budget for 1993 was 8.6 billion Slovak korunas ($283.3 million), equivalent to 5.4 per cent of total government expenditure.[101] The budget was described by the Defence Ministry as hardly covering the armed forces' maintenance costs, which absorb 92 per cent of the entire budget, while only about 8 per cent was to be spent on procurement, construction and R&D. This trend will continue since the 1994 military budget allocation will increase by only 2 billion Slovak korunas.[102] In an effort to improve the military hardware situation, a Slovak–Russian intergovernmental commission for trade and technical co-operation signed an agreement for the delivery to the Slovak armed forces of special technical equipment worth $180 million.[103] A protocol was signed in November 1993 whereby Russia

[98] McNally, B., 'Slovaks follow Czech industry lead', *Defense News,* vol. 8, no. 45 (15–21 Nov. 1993), p. 25.

[99] Foreign Broadcast Information Service (FBIS), FBIS-CEEC-89-196, 12 Oct. 1992, pp. 16–17.

[100] International Institute for Strategic Studies (note 96), p. 252.

[101] *Eyes on the East,* 5 Jan. 1993, pp. 4–5.

[102] Radio Free Europe/Radio Liberty, *RFE/RL Research Report,* supplement, vol. 2, no. 49 (29 Nov.– 3 Dec. 1993), p. 13.

[103] Radio Free Europe/Radio Liberty, *RFE/RL Research Report* (note 102), p. 14.

Table 12.12. The Slovak Republic's military expenditure, 1993

Figures are in current m. Slovak korunas. Figures in italics are percentage shares.

	1993	Share of total expenditure
Operating cost[a]	7 945	*92.0*
Investment cost[b]	684	*7.9*
Total	**8 629**	*100*

[a] Includes O&M, personnel (military and civilian), pensions and other social expenditure.
[b] Investment cost includes procurement, construction and R&D.
Source: Adapted from the Slovak Ministry of Defence budget, information provided by the Embassy of the Slovak Republic in Stockholm, 28 Jan. 1994.

will reduce its debt to Slovakia through the delivery of military hardware in a deal similar to the one concluded with Hungary in 1992.[104] One attempt the government has made to revive its heavy armaments industrial base is its initiative to organize state-owned defence industries into a production and sales consortium. The government will initially fund the consortium with 10 million Slovak korunas ($304 000).[105] Although many of the member companies are scheduled for privatization, their membership in the consortium will probably ensure that the government will remain the main shareholder. At the same time the Slovak Government is expected to begin writing off as much as 5 billion Slovak korunas ($152 million) of inter-enterprise debt among the 20 largest defence manufacturers.[106]

Neither of the two successor states has the means to undertake the needed modernization of its armed forces, nor has either so far presented a sound long-term financial plan for the transition from the former Soviet-standard equipment. Not only has the break-up been very costly but it may yet cause further political disputes since certain military installations (such as air defence) and R&D programmes are in principle impossible to divide.[107]

Hungary

Hungary has published fairly detailed figures on military spending in previous years. These figures reflect the changing composition of Hungarian military expenditure. The reduction in military spending began in the mid-1980s and is still continuing. While military expenditure constituted 2.5 per cent of GDP in

---

[104] McNally (note 98).
[105] McNally (note 98).
[106] McNally (note 98).
[107] Urban, J., 'The Czech and Slovak Republics: security consequences of the breakup of the CSFR', ed. R. Cowen Karp, SIPRI, *Central and Eastern Europe: The Challenge of Transition* (Oxford University Press: Oxford, 1993), pp. 120–21.

Table 12.13. Hungarian military expenditure allocation: official figures, 1989–93

Figures are in current b. forint. Figures in italics are percentages.

	1989	1990	1991	1992	1993
Operating cost[a]	36.2	41.5	47.6	53.9	61.1
Share of total	*75.8*	*79.3*	*88.1*	*88.8*	*94.7*
Investment cost[b]	11.5	10.8	6.4	6.8	3.4
Share of total	*24.1*	*20.7*	*11.9*	*11.2*	*5.3*
Total	**47.7**	**52.3**	**54.0**	**60.7**	**64.5**
	100	*100*	*100*	*100*	*100*

[a] Includes O&M, personnel (military and civilian), pensions and other social expenditure.

[b] Investment cost includes procurement, construction and R&D.

Source: Compiled from the Hungarian Federal Ministry of Defence budgets for 1989–93, information provided by the Hungarian Library of Parliament, 11 Jan. 1994.

1989, it amounted to only 1.88 per cent in 1993.[108] In real terms, this corresponds to a fall of more than 40 per cent for the same period.[109]

The parliament approved the 1993 defence budget of 64.5 billion forint ($1.16 billion), which corresponds to 1.9 per cent of GDP and represents an increase of about 4 billion forint over the allocation for 1992. The Hungarian Parliament did not approve a 700 million forint ($77.3 million) defence spending increase because the long-term defence plan has not been approved by parliament.[110] Nearly half of the defence budget, or 31 billion forint, will be spent on personnel costs and social security allowances. Officers' wages will be raised by 15 per cent (or 5000 forint per year) and by 26 per cent for conscripts and military school students; 8 billion forint are to be spent on military construction. Support for the armed forces has been increased as a result of the continuing war in the former Yugoslavia, and both the government coalition and the opposition members of the parliamentary Defence Committee have agreed that no further cuts are possible without endangering the army's combat effectiveness.[111] From the 94.7 per cent earmarked for operating cost, about 3.7 per cent can be used for renewal and general overhaul of fixed assets and 21 per cent for the replacement of stocks used, that is, for purchases of new equipment. In 1993 the share of the budget spent on operating costs will rise by about 20 per cent compared to 1989, while R&D will drop further from 11 per cent in 1989 to 8.9 per cent.

On the basis of the figures mentioned above it cannot be expected in the short term that the Hungarian armed forces will be in a position to purchase

[108] Gyarmati, I., 'Hungarian security policy for the 1990s', *Defence and Disarmament Alternatives,* vol. 3, no. 4 (Apr. 1991), p. 3.

[109] 'Pointer', *Jane's Intelligence Review,* Jan. 1994, p. 7; and Janza, K., 'The price of reform in the armed forces', *Tárdsadalmi Szeml,* vol. 4, no. 8–9 (Aug.–Sep. 1992), p. 74.

[110] 'Hungarian Parliament rebuffs military funding request', *Defense News,* vol. 8, no. 27 (12–18 July 1993), p. 20.

[111] Reisch, A., 'The Hungarian Army in transition', Radio Free Europe/Radio Liberty, *RFE/RL Research Report,* vol. 2, no. 5 (5 Mar. 1993), pp. 38–52.

any new military equipment. Restructuring of the armed forces certainly requires additional financial resources, with special emphasis on the development of air defence, which has practically collapsed following the dissolution of the old security structure in Hungary and in the region as a whole.

Poland

The Polish Government began to reduce the size of its armed forces as early as 1987. Military expenditure also began to fall in real terms after 1987, although it increased in nominal terms because of high inflation. From 1987 to 1991 military spending at constant prices dropped by one-third, and the trend is continuing.[112] As in Hungary and the former Czechoslovakia, the new regime in Poland has released substantially more information about the composition of military expenditure. However, since 1993 the information has been less disaggregated in both Hungary and Poland and is therefore a poorer reflection of the composition of military expenditure.

The new Polish Government, elected in September 1993, had to ask the parliament to postpone until the end of 1993 the deadline for submission of the draft budget for 1994. Relatively little information is therefore available at the time of writing. The Polish Ministry of Defence budget was set to increase substantially to about 38.4 trillion zlotys ($2.25 billion). This was an increase of more than 50 per cent over the 1992 budget and exceeded the 1993 rate of inflation of about 37 per cent.[113] One explanation for the increase in the official defence budget is the transfer of accounts whereby some indirect government subsidies to the military sector are now included in the defence budget. Another explanation is the extra increase in personnel cost by 6.4 trillion zlotys (16.7 per cent of the total) for pensions and other social expenditures. O&M costs have also increased slightly. The armed forces are being modernized and were reduced from 400 000 in 1988 to about 287 500 men by the beginning of 1993,[114] a reduction resulting not only from international agreements such as the CFE Treaty but also from changes in military doctrine and the dramatic deterioration in the Polish economy during the 1980s and early 1990s.[115]

Part of the increase in the 1992 military expenditure of 24.4 billion zlotys ($1.83 billion) has probably been set aside to purchase new military equipment, since the Polish armed forces have systematically reduced procurement both from domestic suppliers and from abroad. The first priority for new equipment is air defence, including air control systems, anti-tank weapons and artillery which the Polish forces plan to change from largely Russian-made equipment to more advanced Western models. Some of the equipment will

---

[112] Poland, Ministry of National Defence, *Polish Army, Facts and Figures (In the Transition Period)*, (Ministry of National Defence: Warsaw, 1991), p. 36.
[113] *Trends in Developing Economies, Extracts*, vol. 1, *Eastern Europe and Central Asia* (World Bank: Washington, DC, 1993), p. 58.
[114] International Institute for Strategic Studies (note 96), p. 85.
[115] 'Poland sees steep cut in defense spending', *Defense News*, vol. 8, no. 9 (8–14 Mar. 1993), p. 2.

Table 12.14. Polish military expenditure allocation: official figures, 1989–93

Figures are in current b. zlotys. Figures in italics are percentages.

	1989	1990	1991	1992	1993
Operating cost[a]	1 550	9 947	13 487	19 726	32 053
Share of total	*70.0*	*66.6*	*73.7*	*80.9*	*83.6*
Investment cost[b]	664	4 998	4 813	4 648	6 290
Share of total	*30.0*	*33.4*	*26.3*	*19.1*	*16.4*
Total	**2 214**	**14 945**	**18 300**	**24 374**	**38 343**
	100	*100*	*100*	*100*	*100*

[a] Includes O&M, personnel (military and civilian), pensions and other social expenditure.

[b] Investment cost includes procurement, construction and R&D.

Sources: Poland, Ministry of Defence, Strategic Studies Department, *UN Definition of Military Budgets*, provided by the Polish Embassy in Stockholm, 15 Jan. 1994; CSBM/Vienna Document 1992, *Military Budgets, Information for the Fiscal Year 1993*, CSBM/PL/93/014.

probably be acquired from domestic arms producers.[116] The Polish arms industry is still waiting for the government to present a plan to restructure the entire sector; no money is allocated in the state budget for the first phase of arms industry restructuring. While the legal and financial context of the arms industry needs to be determined, the enterprises' debts have continued to grow, reaching over 14 trillion zlotys in the first quarter of 1993.[117]

Bulgaria

Until 1989, Bulgaria had not published information on its military budgets since 1970.[118] With a new government installed in January 1993, the Bulgarian armed forces are making progress in becoming depoliticized, and the reduction in the number of personnel to 99 400—lower than the 104 000 permitted under the CFE Treaty—was completed in 1993.[119] National service has been cut to 12 months from 18.

At 54.5 per cent of the total, personnel cost takes the largest proportion of the budget, probably because of an attempt partially to fund the restructuring of the Bulgarian armed forces. Aside from reductions in personnel numbers, Bulgaria also has plans to reorganize its military formations. Formerly, the army was organized in motorized infantry divisions and tank brigades. Currently, the Bulgarians are discussing the idea of converting all divisions into brigades.[120] This move would not only make Bulgarian armed forces more

[116] *RFE/RL Research Report,* supplement, vol. 2, no. 45 (1–5 Nov. 1993), p. 12.

[117] *Warsaw Voice,* 5 Sep. 1993, p. B3.

[118] Alton, T., *et al., Military Expenditure in Eastern Europe, Post World War II to 1979* (L.W. International: New York, 1980), p. 2.

[119] International Institute for Strategic Studies (note 96), pp. 75 and 225.

[120] 'Defense Minister queried on military reductions', *Danas,* 27 June 1989, pp. 56–58, as translated in FBIS-EEU-89-128 (6 July 1989), p. 7.

Table 12.15. Bulgarian military expenditure allocation: official figures, 1989–93

Figures are in current m. levas. Figures in italics are percentages.

	1989	1990	1991	1992	1993
Operating cost[a]	481.1	980.1	3 298.0	5 103.4	8 000.1
Share of total	*28.6*	*59.1*	*83.5*	*88.4*	*92.4*
Investment cost[b]	1 201.2	678.3	650.1	667.5	654.4
Share of total	*71.4*	*41.0*	*16.3*	*12.0*	*7.6*
Total	**1 682.2**	**1 658.4**	**3 948.1**	**5 771.0**	**8 654.5**
	100	*100*	*100*	*100*	*100*

[a] Includes O&M, personnel (military and civilian), pensions and other social expenditure.
[b] Includes procurement, construction and R&D.
Source: CSBM/Vienna Document 1992, *Military Budgets, Information for the Fiscal Year 1993*, CSBM/BG/93/014; Bulgarian Ministry of Defence, Finance Department, *UN Definition of Military Budgets*, provided by the Bulgarian Embassy in Stockholm, 19 Jan. 1994.

manœuvrable but could also reduce costs through a further reduction in personnel.

While operating costs (personnel and O&M) account for about 92.4 per cent, capital costs (procurement, R&D and construction) account for the remaining 7.6 per cent. There have been substantial cuts in procurement to 5.4 per cent of the total 1993 defence budget of 8.7 billion levas ($1.18 billion). Reduced orders in the defence industries and the presence of substantial excess capacity (80–85 per cent)[121] clearly demonstrate that weapon purchases have fallen. Apart from the lack of procurement orders, the arms producers are burdened with enterprise indebtedness which has been estimated at more than 3 billion levas in 1992, half of which is in the form of credits taken to fulfil previous state orders.[122] While the former republics of the then USSR still owe Bulgaria some $50 million for weapons that have been delivered,[123] Bulgaria's chances of collecting $1 billion in outstanding debts from Iraq, following the introduction of the UN arms embargo in late 1990, have also deteriorated significantly.[124] Due to Bulgaria's lack of foreign currency and the precarious financial situation in the arms industry and in the country as a whole, a re-equipment programme is not expected to begin until the late 1990s. A number of former GDR weapon systems have been transferred and some spare parts will be supplied by Russia under an agreement reached during Bulgarian Defence Minister Valentin Alexandrov's visit to Moscow at the end of 1993.[125]

---

[121] *Eye on the East*, 6 Mar. 1993, pp. 7–8.
[122] Engelbrekt, K., 'Bulgaria and the arms trade', in *RFE/RL Research Report*, vol. 2, no. 7 (12 Feb. 1993), p. 45.
[123] Engelbrekt (note 122), p. 46.
[124] Engelbrekt (note 122), p. 44.
[125] 'Bulgaria poised for reform', *Jane's Defence Weekly*, 2 Oct. 1993, p. 21.

Romania

Although Romania has had the poorest record of all the Central and Eastern European countries in providing statistical data on its economy, it was the first to release relatively extensive information on military spending. Table 12.16 provides a breakdown of expenditures from 1990.

Romania has devoted the bulk of its military expenditure to the army, which has been reduced to 203 100, of which 125 000 are conscripts. The CFE Treaty limits military manpower to 230 248. However, Romania made a slow start in eliminating military equipment in excess of the CFE Treaty limits.[126]

Table 12.16. Romanian military expenditure allocation: official figures, 1990–93

Figures are in current m. lei. Figures in italics are percentages.

	1990	1991	1992	1993
Personnel	5 917	10 764	42 000	97 763
Share of total	*17.5*	*33.2*	*26.5*	*37.4*
O&M[a]	5 749	7 704	61 068	101 437
Share of total	*17.0*	*23.8*	*38.5*	*38.8*
Procurement	21 151	12 807	52 901	57 570
Share of total	*62.6*	*39.5*	*33.4*	*22.0*
Construction	527	653	959	2 800
Share of total	*1.6*	*2.0*	*0.6*	*1.1*
R&D	448	450	1 590	2 060
Share of total	*1.3*	*1.4*	*1.0*	*0.8*
Total	**33 792**	**32 378**	**158 518**[b]	**261 630**
	100	*100*	*100*	*100*

[a] Includes civilian personnel cost.

[b] The 1992 submission to the United Nations gives the total figure of 138 558 billion lei; however, this does not include an additional 20 billion lei that was approved by the parliament in July 1992, of which 5 billion lei was for O&M and 15 billion lei for capital expenditure, according to an Economic Committee Meeting with Co-operating Partners, Brussels, 30 Sep.– 2 Oct. 1992.

Source: Romania, Ministry of National Defence, *Laws of Military Budgets 1982–92,* provided by the Romanian Embassy, Stockholm, 30 Nov. 1992. For 1993: CSCE, Instrument for Standardized International Reporting of Military Expenditure, provided by the Romanian Embassy in Stockholm, 15 Jan. 1994.

Of the 261.6 billion lei ($851 million), operating cost (personnel and O&M) accounts for about 76 per cent, with capital cost (procurement, R&D and construction) accounting for the remaining 24 per cent. The share of procurement at 22 per cent is still the highest for all the countries in Central and East European countries, although it has fallen by about 40 per cent compared to 1990. Romania seems to have spent roughly one-quarter of its entire budget on investment, including procurement and R&D.

---

[126] International Institute for Strategic Studies (note 96), pp. 84, 252.

V. China[127]

In his annual budget presentation to the National People's Congress, on 16 March 1993 Chinese Finance Minister Liu Zhongli announced that China's (official) defence budget would increase to 42.5 billion yuan ($7.3 billion).[128] This allocation signifies an increase over the 1992 defence budget by 13.5 per cent and represents approximately 8.3 per cent of total budgeted expenditure of 512 billion yuan; the official defence budget amounts to about 1.6 per cent of estimated gross national product (GNP).[129] According to official Chinese sources, national inflation in 1993 was 13 per cent, signifying a real increase of 0.5 per cent in official Chinese defence spending in 1993.

This slight rise in the official budget is, however, only a small fraction of China's total military expenditure, as much military spending is financed through other sources. Seen in a longer perspective, post-1988 official budgets have also increased more rapidly than inflation. After a decade of declining defence budgets, official Chinese military budgets started to grow in 1988, and the increase in 1993 was the fourth consecutive rise. Since 1988 Chinese budgets have nearly doubled in current prices, from 21.5 billion yuan to 42.5 billion yuan. Chinese officials maintain that this increase was more than offset

---

[127] Numerous interviews with active and retired Chinese military personnel helped to provide data and estimates for this section. In addition, the following Chinese sources were used: Lin Yichang and Wu Xizhi, *Guofang Jingjixue jichu* [Basic Defence Economics], (Beijing Academy of Military Sciences Press: Beijing, 1991); Editorial Board (eds), 'Contemporary China series', *Dangdai Zhongguo jundui de houqin gongzuo* [Military Logistical Work in Contemporary China], (China Academy of Social Sciences Press: Beijing, 1990); Editorial Board (eds), 'Contemporary China series', *Dangdai Zhongguo caizheng* [Finance in Contemporary China], (China Academy of Social Sciences Press: Beijing, 1988); People's University Reprint Series, *Junshi* [Military Affairs], various years and issues; People's Liberation Army Logistics College Technology Research Section (ed.), *Junshi houqin cidian* [Dictionary on Military Logistics], (Liberation Army Press: Beijing, 1991); Chinese Military Encyclopedia Editing Group (eds), *Jundui houqin fence* [Section on Military Logistics], (Academy of Military Sciences Press: Beijing, 1985); Zhang Zhenlong (ed.), *Junshi jingjixue* [Military Economics], (Liaoning People's Press: Shenyang, 1988); Jin Songde *et al.*, *Guofang jingjilun* [National Defence Economic Theory], (Liberation Army Press: Beijing, 1987); Jiang Baoqi (ed.), *Zhongguo guofang jingji fazhan zhanlue yanjiu* [Research on the Strategy of China's Military Industrial Development], (National Defence University Press: Beijing, 1990); Gao Dianzhi, *Zhongguo guofang jingji guanli yanjiu* [Research on the Management of China's National Defence Economy], (Academy of Military Sciences Press: Beijing, 1991); Sun Zhenyuan, *Zhongguo guofang jingji jianshi* [The Construction of China's National Defence Economy], (Academy of Military Sciences Press: Beijing, 1991); Qiao Guanglie (ed.), *Zhongguo renmin jiefangjun houqin jianshi* [History of PLA Logistics Building], (National Defence University Press: Beijing, 1989); Wang Dangying *et al.*, *Guofang fazhan zhanlue yanjiu* [Research on National Defence Strategy], (National Defence University Press: Beijing, 1988).

[128] 'China. NPC Session. Budget Report', *Keesing's Record of World Events*, vol. 39, no. 3 (Mar. 1993), p. 39364. The dollar figures in this section are at the 1993 exchange-rate of $1 = 5.25 yuan. With the devaluation of the yuan on 1 Jan. 1994, the conversion rate soared to $1 = 8.7 yuan. This will, in turn, dramatically affect (downwards) estimates of future Chinese defence spending as expressed in US dollar values.

[129] This section shows that the official figure for military expenditure should be revised substantially upwards. There is also some uncertainty concerning the size of China's GNP. The figure 1.6 per cent is derived from dividing the official defence budget by GNP figures announced by the International Monetary Fund, which for 1992 reported a Chinese GNP of 2404 billion yuan. Calculations based on higher military spending and/or lower GNP figures would naturally increase the share of GNP allocated to defence. As an illustration of the range of estimates that exists, it could, e.g., be mentioned that the Japanese Defence White Paper has stated that Chinese military spending was 3.2% of GNP; see Kiernan, T. and Usui, N., 'Chinese buildup of forces stirs regional concern', *Defense News*, vol. 8, no. 35 (6–12 Sep. 1993), p. 8.

by inflation, but the aggregated official inflation rate (as measured in retail prices) for the period 1988–93 was only about 45 per cent (because of the 1989–91 austerity programme). Thus, about one-third of the rise in the defence budget was in real terms (considering the impact of compounded growth over the period).

Accounting for the defence budget increases

The Chinese defence budget increase comes at a time when, for the first time since the Communist Party came to power in 1949 and reaching back 150 years, China faces no identifiable or pressing national security threat. China's borders are presently peaceful, although continued disagreements over demarcations still exist with India (over the Aksai Chin region), Japan (over the Diaoyutai Islands), and Russia and several South-East Asian states (over the Spratly and Paracel Islands). China has stated that it seeks to resolve its disputes through negotiation, and in 1993 diplomatic progress was made in each case.[130]

Why has the Chinese defence budget increased so sharply? In addition to China's longer-term desire to be the dominant power in the region, there are five other possible reasons.

1. Chinese defence planners view the East Asian security environment as highly fluid and potentially threatening. They have apparently adopted the philosophy that the best defence in uncertain times is a strong offence. Various publications by the People's Liberation Army (PLA) National Defence University, the Academy of Military Sciences and other military institutions reveal this uncertainty, and active planning for a wide range of contingencies exists—from an assault on or blockade of Taiwan to renewed border conflicts with Viet Nam or India to possible war over the Spratly Islands. Thus, the end of the cold war has brought China added security but has not reduced the uncertainty over its future regional security environment.

2. This uncertainty has dovetailed with changes in the PLA military doctrine, evident since the late 1980s but accentuated by the 1991 Persian Gulf War. In 1986 Chinese security specialists and national leaders began to revise their previous view that global war was inevitable and that it would involve nuclear weapons. Instead, they began to express the view that, for the foreseeable future, international conflict would be characterized by limited and regional wars (*youxian zhubu zhanzheng*). In such low-intensity conflicts Chinese analysts saw several attributes as crucial to victory: high-technology 'smart' weapons; electronic warfare; ground and air mobility; naval projection; and rapid deployment units. The Gulf War confirmed these conclusions of Chinese defence planners, and at the same time caused deep consternation as the PLA contemplated its comparable order of battle. As a result, the PLA embarked on a systematic attempt to improve its force readiness and projec-

---

[130] See also chapters 4 and 5 in this volume.

tion capability (particularly air and naval). This doctrinal shift has required increased allocations for the Air Force, Navy and R&D sectors.

3. The third reason for increased military expenditure is that allocations during the 1980s fell far short of costs needed to maintain and garrison more than 3 million service personnel, pensions and other costs associated with demobilization of an estimated 600 000 troops, weapon procurement and various other operating costs. A relatively low level of military expenditure was justified during the 1980s on the basis that developing the overall national economy took priority. Although the armed forces expressed reservations, defence was ranked as the last priority among the 'four modernizations'.

Under these conditions, PLA units were instructed to earn revenue wherever and however possible in order to compensate for inadequate central allocations. Military industries began the process of conversion in earnest, and today, according to official sources, 65 per cent of defence factories produce civilian goods.

4. As the national economy expanded dramatically during the late 1980s, senior PLA generals began questioning the rationale for low and inadequate defence budgets. Their assessments of modern warfare and the PLA's backwardness gave further force to their arguments for budget increases. With a spectacular growth in GNP (13 per cent in 1992 and 1993), the PLA has argued for an expanded piece of the pie.

5. Since 1989 the military has been playing an increased role in internal Chinese politics. Increased budget outlays are one way in which the PLA exacts its price for supporting and sustaining the Communist Party in power. Increased military membership on the 14th Central Committee reflects the PLA's raised profile in national politics, and their role in the coming succession to the post-Deng Xiaoping era will be central.

Taken together, these five factors help to explain the reversal in defence budget allocations at the outset of the 1990s. It is not sufficient to conclude that the shift was merely a reward for the military's suppression of pro-democracy demonstrators in 1989. The costs associated with down-sizing the PLA force structure while upgrading its order-of-battle in order to pursue multiple missions and contingencies are substantial and have required investment.

Calculating Chinese military expenditure

The official figure for the Chinese defence budget is a fraction of the revenue available to the People's Liberation Army and falls far short of estimated expenditure. PLA net spending was probably in the neighbourhood of $35.6 billion in 1993. This estimate is derived from proceeds to the PLA revenue base which are detailed below and plausibly included: $7.3 billion in the official defence budget; $14.3 billion in possible direct allocations to defence industries; $5 billion in additional R&D investment; $3 billion for maintenance of the People's Armed Police (PAP); $2.5 billion in local contributions for regional force maintenance; $1.5 billion for militia maintenance; and $2 billion for pensions and demobilization costs. In addition, the PLA brought in an estimated income during 1993 of $1.5 billion in arms sales; $5 billion in commercial earnings; and $2.5 billion in regional unit agricultural and sideline production. Thus, its total revenue base is an estimated $44.6 billion—more than six times larger than the official budget.

Difficulties in calculating the Chinese defence budget abound. To compound uncertainties, in his 1993 annual budget speech Finance Minister Liu announced the defence allocation as part of the 91.28 billion yuan 'expenses for building up the national strength', of which 44.454 billion yuan were earmarked for 'administrative expenses'.[131] Liu did not elaborate the differences between 'administrative' and 'national defence' expenditure, but it may signal a more transparent calculation on the government's part, whereby salaries and other administrative overheads are separated from arms procurement, R&D and training costs. If this is the case, a 91 billion yuan figure is closer to reality—although still considerably short of the mark.

All defence budgets contain hidden costs, and the Chinese defence budget is no exception. However, in the Chinese case, the important points are that (a) the military receives a large amount of revenue through extra-budgetary earnings generated by a wide variety of commercial activities, and (b) a considerable amount of defence-related expenditure is passed through other budgets. It therefore makes much more sense for analysts to think in terms of the overall *revenue base* rather than central budgetary allocations when estimating the financial resources at the disposal of the PLA.

The PLA's considerable extra-budgetary earnings have become an important supplement to its overall revenue base and operating expenses. These come not only from converted industries (many of which are struggling or failing) but also from a wide range of commercial schemes. The PLA owns some of China's prime real estate and has leased it out at high rents. Many local airlines are owned and managed by PLA front companies. PLA ships and other modes of transport are put to good commercial use (and are heavily involved in smuggling rings). The PLA's once élite hospitals will now admit those who can afford the price of admission. Virtually every military unit has set up one form or another of cottage industry, and many are involved in joint ventures with foreign entities. The General Staff Department has invested in several 'five-star' hotels in China, including Beijing's luxurious Palace Hotel. Even the vaunted Second Artillery, which is responsible for the PLA strategic nuclear forces, is a partner in the Baskin & Robbins ice cream outlet in Beijing.

Such off-budget revenue now brings into PLA coffers an estimated $5 billion per year, according to an internal study conducted by the Chinese National Defence University (coincidentally, this is also the figure estimated by the US Central Intelligence Agency in its 1993 annual survey of the

---

[131] 'Finance Minister reports on state budgets', Foreign Broadcast Information Service (FBIS), *China Daily Report*, 16 Mar. 1993, p. 36.

Chinese economy[132]). The majority of these earnings remain with the unit which generated them and do not make their way into the General Logistics Department's budget stream. There exist, in fact, explicit PLA financial regulations that permit the generating unit to keep its own revenue. They help to defray local operating costs and compensate for the inadequate allocations from Beijing.

The official defence budget primarily pays for O&M costs, plus ordnance procurement and R&D. This does not mean that the defence budget pays for *all* O&M or R&D costs, as this is certainly not the case. Individual units now generate approximately half (in some cases more) of daily O&M costs through their commercial activities. This includes, importantly, food production. Salaries and a variety of daily maintenance costs are also topped up through proceeds from units' extra-curricular activities. Similarly, procurement and R&D costs are also supplemented from off-budget revenue.

It appears that the official defence budget does *not* include funds for: (*a*) equipment production (as distinct from procurement); (*b*) some research, development, testing, and evaluation (RDT&E) costs; (*c*) the paramilitary PAP; (*d*) a percentage of troop maintenance costs for regional force units; (*e*) militia maintenance; and (*f*) pensions and demobilization costs. How are these costs paid for?

1. Arms production costs are allocated directly by the State Council to the relevant defence industry/ministry (Electronics, Ordnance, Nuclear, Aeronautics & Astronautics and Shipbuilding) rather than being carried in the defence budget. These ministerial budgets are not made public in the Finance Minister's annual budget speech, nor are they available in the *Tongji Nianjian* (*Annual Statistical Yearbook*). These line-item expenditures to the defence industries could easily amount to 15 billion yuan apiece or 75 billion yuan ($14.3 billion) total, not to mention the extracurricular earnings by the ministries themselves.

When the ground, air or naval forces seek to *procure* a given weapon system, these procurement costs are apparently borne by the given service arm, as allocated through their annual appropriation as part of the defence budget. The revenue available for procurement, however, is fixed in the defence budget and calculated during the annual budget bidding process overseen jointly by the Finance and Equipment Bureaus of the PLA General Logistics Department. In recent years the Air Force has received the largest allocations, followed by the Navy and ground forces. When a service seeks to procure a given system, it contracts with the relevant ministry, which sub-contracts to the factories concerned. However, the price paid for the hardware is fixed by the Commission of Science, Technology and Industry for National Defense (COSTIND or *Guofang ke-gongwei*). These prices are fixed at an arbitrarily low level, although COSTIND is currently considering proposals to establish

[132] Directorate of Intelligence (CIA), *China's Economy in 1992 and 1993: Grappling with the Risks of Rapid Growth* (US Central Intelligence Agency: Washington, DC, 1993), p. 9.

prices at market value (which will increase procurement prices dramatically and, *ceteris paribus,* drive up military expenditure accordingly). Once prices are set and contracts signed, payment is made, apparently for finished items upon delivery. Thus procurement prices do not meet production costs, which must be borne by the defence industries concerned. Therefore, under the current system the defence industries are largely responsible for their production costs while sharing R&D costs with COSTIND.

Another source of production revenue, in addition to the defence budget, is the state allocations for military conversion. Nearly 70 per cent of military factories now produce civilian goods, and during the Seventh Five-Year Plan (1991–95) the State Council earmarked 6 billion yuan ($1.14 billion, at 1991 exchange-rates) for facilitating conversion.

2. Estimating the channels and amounts of funding for R&D is a real conundrum. They appear to be derived from three sources—COSTIND, the State Science and Technology Commission (CAST) and the defence industries themselves—although the division of labour and investment between them is unclear.[133] Of the three, COSTIND is clearly the principal source of R&D funds. A certain amount of expenditure is also paid through the separate line-item defence industry budgets, although presumably this pertains to upgrading production technology (applied research) rather than basic research on system design and performance. The latter is undertaken in a number of military research institutes. In some cases these institutes are affiliated with the ministerial defence industries and in others they are independent entities. In either case their R&D costs are apparently contributed directly by COSTIND.

The COSTIND budget, in turn, is divided between the official defence budget and a specific line-item allocation from the State Council, as administratively COSTIND has dual lines of control to both the Ministry of Defence and the State Council. Again, like all other military units, COSTIND has numerous additional sources of income that are used to supplement these allocations; thus, R&D costs do not take up as much of the defence budget as might be assumed. A third source of R&D funds is those allocated through CAST. Although the percentage is unclear, CAST expenditures on military-related R&D could total $5 billion.

3. The People's Armed Police (*Wu-Jing*) is undoubtedly funded via the Ministry of Public Security budget, although some sources indicate that it is partially paid for out of Ministry of State Security funds. The *Wu-Jing* is now a 1 million-strong force, comprised largely of demobilized soldiers from the PLA. It is the state's first line of defence against internal civil unrest. In 1989 the *Wu-Jing* proved totally incapable of handling the 1989 Tiananmen demonstrations but it has subsequently been retrained and rearmed. Since 1989 the *Wu-Jing* has been used to suppress both ethnic and peasant uprisings (which

---

[133] See also Frankenstein, J., 'The People's Republic of China: arms production, industrial strategy and problems of history', ed. H. Wulf, SIPRI, *Arms Industry Limited* (Oxford University Press: Oxford, 1993), chapter 14.

resulted in deaths) as well as urban demonstrations. Maintenance of PAP forces cost an estimated $3 billion in 1993.

4. Allocations for garrisoning and maintaining regional force units (as distinct from main force units, which are maintained primarily through central funding) are paid partially through the civilian provincial budgets, although a large percentage (perhaps 50 per cent) is now generated by individual units. Salaries are apparently paid from the central defence budget but are topped up with extra earnings and bonuses from sideline production and commercial ventures. Most regional force units maintain cultivated land from which they produce the majority of their foodstuffs and earned units an estimated $2.5 billion in 1993.

5. The costs of maintaining the militia and reserves are also borne jointly, where the 'three-thirds' policy is in effect. According to the 1990 'Regulations on Militia Work' issued by the Central Military Commission and State Council, there is a special allocation in the annual state budget for militia maintenance (one-third). Another third is supported by local governments, while the militia units themselves are required to contribute the final third of their maintenance costs. Evidently, however, with an increasing central budget deficit and other more pressing costs, militia units have increasingly had to rely on their own resources in recent years. This revenue plausibly totalled $1.5 billion in 1993.

Reserve units also operate on the 'three-thirds' principle, but in their case maintenance costs are split between Military Districts, provincial governments, and the units themselves.

6. Since 1987 the PLA has demobilized approximately 650 000 troops. It is estimated that approximately 10 per cent have been officers. The costs of demobilization have been substantial, particularly for the officer corps who have required/demanded large pensions and perquisites. They are permitted to maintain their salaries, plus retirement bonuses and pensions, housing, travel funds, free health and hospital care, and often a car and driver for higher-ranking officers. These costs are not covered in the official defence budget either, but are paid for through the Ministry of Civil Affairs, which is responsible for civilian cadre retirements as well. Once they are demobilized, the local Civil Affairs Bureau attempts to share maintenance costs with the relevant municipal government—which, in many cases, ends up footing 50 per cent of the bill. Central Military Commission Chairman and Communist Party General Secretary Jiang Zemin, as well as senior military officials, have frequently commented on the need to give 'high priority' to these demobilizations. A conservative estimate for pensions and related costs in 1993 is the equivalent of $2 billion, but it could easily total $5 billion or more *per annum* in recent years.

Prospects

The trend for increased defence outlays can be expected to continue in coming years. While such increases are a reversal of the pattern seen during the 1980s, they must be kept in perspective. The PLA's operating revenue base is substantial but remains a fraction of the defence budgets of most developed countries and hardly enough to maintain a force structure of 3 million, much less acquire state-of-the-art weaponry. Moreover, as the Chinese economy continues to grow at double-digit rates, so too will inflation rise rapidly.

Substantial problems remain in calculating Chinese military expenditure and the PLA overall revenue base. No doubt, the PLA itself does not know how much money it generates or spends. Currency conversion and establishing equivalent costs have always been difficult but will be made more so by the sharp devaluation of the yuan on 1 January 1994. (For example, the official defence budget for 1994 rose to 52 billion yuan, but this is only equivalent to approximately $6 billion at 1994 exchange-rates, while the 42.5 billion yuan in 1993 equalled $7.3 billion.) Some members of the Chinese defence community indicated in late 1993 that a Defence White Paper was being contemplated for 1994, in order to answer critics and clarify uncertainties about Chinese defence spending, doctrine and force deployments. Given the analytical problems noted above, needless to say, such increased transparency would be welcome.

VI. Development co-operation and military reform

During the cold war, the foreign policy concerns of the major powers fostered high military budgets, the growth of domestic defence industrial sectors, preparations for war as a means of resolving disputes and politically active armed forces. The costs of these policies were extremely high, particularly in the developing world and the former Soviet Union. The large sums of money devoted to housing, feeding, paying and arming unnecessarily large security forces in the poor parts of the world produced serious imbalances between military budgets and other public-sector expenditures vital for sustained economic growth and development. The high priority accorded the military sector contributed to preventing the emergence of accountable government, without which neither economic development nor political stability can be sustained. Internal and regional conflicts caused an estimated 40 million deaths and led to bloated military budgets, further undermining opportunities for development.

None the less, development assistance was frequently delivered to developing countries prior to the end of the cold war, without regard to the economic, social or political consequences of the buildup of their military capacity. Even when military budgets clearly diverted resources from economic and socio-political development, aid-giving agencies shied away from examining these expenditures. Rather, major bilateral donors such as the USA and the USSR tended to provide economic assistance specifically to enable governments to maintain military capabilities at levels that could not have been sustained by domestic resources alone. More generally, the donor community ignored the fact that financing provided for non-military purposes, particularly budget support and balance-of-payment funding, enables governments to increase their military budgets if they are so inclined.

Putting the military on the development agenda

Before the Berlin Wall was breached in 1989, there was virtually no constituency within the international development community for integrating military spending and related factors into aid and official lending decisions. By December 1993 all that had changed, as evidenced by the Organisation for Economic Co-operation and Development (OECD) Development Assistance Committee's (DAC) approval of the *Orientations on Participatory Development and Good Governance* (PDGG).[134] Among other things, this document underscores the links between excessive military spending, politically active armed forces and conflict, and outlines specific actions that bilateral aid donors can take to strengthen civilian control over the military and reduce military spending in recipient countries. Not only is reducing the economic and political burden of the security sector now firmly entrenched on the donor community's development agenda, but many aid recipients have also acknowledged this to be a legitimate topic in aid dialogues.

This shift was due in no small measure to the decision by International Monetary Fund (IMF) Managing Director Michel Camdessus and World Bank President Barber Conable, Jr, to begin speaking out about the imbalances between security spending and resources available for economic and social development in 1989, even before the fall of communist regimes in Eastern Europe signalled the beginning of the end of the cold war.

At first glance, the World Bank and the IMF might seem unlikely leaders of an effort to introduce security-related considerations into the development dialogue. Their mandates are economic, prohibiting them from basing lending decisions on political criteria. The World Bank and the IMF have, however, established convincing economic arguments for examining military budgets. Camdessus, for example, has argued that the IMF's concern with identifying 'unproductive or wasteful spending', including military spending, is 'just an extension and intensification of our traditional work to help countries improve their macroeconomic policies'.[135]

World Bank and IMF concern was important in making military budgets a legitimate topic of discussion among the bilateral donors, but the end of the cold war and the 1991 Persian Gulf War were crucial in providing the necessary political motivation. Canada, Germany, Japan, the Netherlands and the

---

[134] Organisation for Economic Co-operation and Development, *DAC Orientations on Participatory Development and Good Governance*, OCDE/GD (93)191 (OECD: Paris, 1993).

[135] International Monetary Fund Board of Governors, '1991 Annual Meetings', Press Release no. 64, Bangkok, Thailand, 17 Oct. 1991, p. 2.

Nordic countries have been particularly active in this regard. Under the Bush Administration, the USA joined the UK and France in seeking to avoid incorporating military considerations into aid dialogues, in large part because it sought to curtail criticism of its arms transfer policies. The Clinton Administration, which did not alter US arms transfer policies during its first year in office, has placed democratization at the centre of US aid policies, including support for the military-reform objectives laid out in the DAC PDGG document.[136]

The DAC consensus

The recognition that common approaches among donors are not only desirable but also feasible emerged with surprising rapidity. In 1991 the few individuals within the development community who were thinking about the role of development assistance in supporting military reform agreed that a common approach to the military sector was not likely to emerge in the near future. In the spring of 1992, the DAC held the first in a series of discussions that ultimately resulted in the December 1993 endorsement of the PDGG paper. By late 1992 the outlines of the DAC consensus were evident.

1. *Policy dialogue and positive incentives are the preferred tools in linking development co-operation with military reform.* There is widespread agreement that sanctions and conditions are to be imposed only when other, more collaborative efforts clearly fail. Lenders have expressed particular interest in 'positive measures' that will assist recipient governments in reducing the size, cost and political clout of their military sectors or that will support conflict resolution and post-conflict reconstruction and reconciliation. Some of the most frequently mentioned programmes include demobilization, veteran retraining schemes, defence industry conversion, improved fiscal management of the security sector, enhanced civilian expertise in military affairs and dialogues on the role of the military in democratic societies.

Donors increasingly recognize that military reform programmes formulated in collaboration with recipients have a much greater chance of success than those imposed from outside. For their part, aid recipients are increasingly seeking lender assistance for these purposes. Countries such as Cambodia, El Salvador, Mozambique, Namibia, Nicaragua, Rwanda and Uganda have sought donor assistance in developing and implementing programmes to down-size the military sector, promote political reconciliation and repair the ravages of protracted civil wars.

2. *Improving transparency in the military budgeting process is vital.* Transparency has two distinct elements: (*a*) obtaining information on the level of

---

[136] The evolution of donor policies is traced in Ball, N., *Pressing for Peace: Can Aid Induce Reform?* (Overseas Development Council (ODC): Washington, DC, 1992); Ball, N., 'Development aid for military reform: a pathway to peace', *Policy Focus*, no. 6 (ODC: Washington, DC, 1993); and Kan, S., *Military Expenditures by Developing Countries: Foreign Aid Policy Issues*, 93-999F (Congressional Research Service: Washington, DC, 3 Nov. 1993).

security expenditure, and (b) opening up the military budgeting and planning process. Fostering openness and accountability in the public sector is the best recipe for long-term control over security budgets. The development community has thus far focused its efforts primarily on collecting more accurate data with which to evaluate the economic costs associated with recipients' security sectors. Only a few projects have been undertaken to strengthen institutional capacity in the security sector.

Both strands are in evidence in the PDGG document. DAC members pledge themselves to support efforts by organizations such as the IMF to develop 'transparent, reliable, and comparable data on military expenditure patterns, uses, and trends'.[137] They also propose to identify the ways in which civilian expertise in defence budgeting and appropriations can be strengthened.

3. *Greater co-ordination among lenders and within individual bilateral donor governments will facilitate military reform.* The PDGG document places considerable emphasis on co-ordinating donor actions. Multilateral policy co-ordination is desirable because different members of the international development community have different strengths and mandates. By identifying what each member can do best, the development community can respond quickly and efficiently to recipients' needs in the area of security reform. The Uganda demobilization programme, co-ordinated by the World Bank and supported by some 10 bilateral and multilateral donors, offers a model for donor–donor and donor–government collaboration in this area.[138]

Co-ordination has other benefits as well. It reduces the likelihood that the recipient governments will face conflicting demands from the international community. This in turn increases the likelihood that the desired reform will be undertaken or, in the case of conflict resolution, that the parties involved will take serious steps to resolve the conflict. In the USA, recognition of the value of co-ordinated action has led the Agency for International Development (AID) to establish the Office of Crisis and Transition Management, among other reasons, to co-ordinate US aid to countries undergoing the transition from war to peace. In the Netherlands, the ministers for development co-operation and defence jointly released a policy memorandum on humanitarian assistance in November 1993. Swedish aid officials meet on an *ad hoc* basis with their counterparts from the military to discuss issues of mutual concern, for example, Sweden's contribution to UN peacekeeping operations in the former Yugoslavia.[139] Efforts such as these should be continued and expanded.

Co-ordination also contributes to distributing the financial burdens among the donor countries. Given the current economic climate in many OECD countries, this is an important consideration. Additionally, collaboration among bilateral donors and the multilateral development agencies might make

[137] Organisation for Economic Co-operation and Development (note 134), p. 25.
[138] Colletta, N. J. and Ball, N., 'War to peace transition in Uganda', *Finance & Development*, June 1993, pp. 36–39.
[139] The Netherlands policy memorandum is *Humanitarian Aid Between Conflict and Development* (Ministry of Foreign Affairs: The Hague, Nov. 1993). Information on Sweden is from a private communication with Carin Norberg, Assistant Director-General, Swedish International Development Agency (SIDA).

it easier for the international financial institutions to participate in reform efforts despite the prohibition in their articles of agreement on basing lending decisions on political criteria and the reluctance of many staff members of international financial institutions to address this complex and politically sensitive issue.[140]

4. *In order to create the conditions under which military expenditures can safely decrease, it may be necessary to create or strengthen regional and global collective security arrangements and promote domestic political liberalization.* While local, regional and international political institutions must play the leading role in these areas, the international development community can also support peace-building efforts, such as civilianizing police forces and promoting regional security dialogues. The peace accords in Cambodia, El Salvador and Mozambique were all negotiated on this premise. The international development community must now decide how commitments of this nature can be met in a period of widespread reluctance to expand aid budgets. DAC members began to explore how best to address these issues in November 1993 at an in-house seminar organized by the Development Cooperation Directorate on 'Peace Operations and Aid', and the PDGG document notes the value of strengthening mutual security arrangements and regional defence agreements.

5. *To build credibility and to avoid charges of discrimination and unwarranted interference in borrowers' affairs, lenders should be willing to accept the same norms for themselves that they apply to the developing countries.* The two points most frequently raised in this context in discussions among donors are, first, the need to restrain the conventional arms trade and, second, the bilateral donors' responsibility to control the proliferation of arms-production capabilities, particularly for weapons of mass destruction.

The discrepancy between pressing aid recipients to reduce military spending while using exports to resolve the problem of excess capacity in donors' domestic defence industries was stressed in the PDGG paper. The USA, which emerged as the pre-eminent supplier of arms to developing countries in 1991 following the end of the Gulf War and the collapse of the Soviet Union, argues that its transfers—the vast bulk of which are now to oil-rich countries such as Saudi Arabia and East Asian newly industrializing economies (NIEs) such as South Korea and Taiwan—are not economically destabilizing. Leaving aside Saudi Arabia's recent request to stretch out payments for the $30 billion in US weapons and related services ordered since 1989 and the

---

[140] Section 10 ('Political Activity Prohibited') of Article IV of the World Bank's *Articles of Agreement* states, 'The Bank and its officers shall not interfere in the political affairs of any member; nor shall they be influenced in their decisions by the political character of the member concerned. Only economic considerations shall be relevant to their decisions, and these considerations shall be weighed impartially in order to achieve the purposes stated in Article I'. International Bank for Reconstruction and Development (IBRD), *Articles of Agreement (as amended effective February 16, 1989)* (World Bank: Washington, DC, 1989), p. 13. Article I of the IMF *Articles of Agreement* states that 'The Fund shall be guided in all of its policies and decisions by the purposes set forth in this Article', all of which are strictly economic in nature. *Articles of Agreement of the International Monetary Fund (Amended effective July 28, 1969)* (IMF: Washington, DC, 1969), p. 3.

politico-military implications of arms transfers to this wealthier group of countries, a significant volume of US weapons continues to be provided to poorer countries through the Excess Defense Articles Programme and traditional military assistance.[141] These transfers clearly run the risk of undermining the United States' credibility as it moves into the mainstream of policy making on aid and military reform.

Prospects

The international development community has recognized that the security sector can no longer retain its highly privileged status, immune from domestic and international scrutiny, if sustainable development is to become a reality for the 1.3 billion people estimated by the United Nations Development Programme (UNDP) to be living in poverty at the beginning of the 1990s. It has also concluded that policy dialogue, aid for reforming governments and pressure that falls short of explicit conditionality are the preferred modes of influencing recipients' behaviour in the military sector. The specific areas for action identified in the PDGG document represent a significant step forward by bilateral donors and will ultimately influence the course adopted by the IMF, the World Bank and the regional development banks.

Yet many challenges remain. Despite the valuable insights gained over the past few years into the types of programme that will help aid recipients reduce the economic and political burden of their military sectors and the apparent success of efforts such as the Uganda veterans' assistance programme, much more needs to be learned about programme design and implementation. The international development community also needs to take concrete steps to enhance co-ordination.

Perhaps the greatest challenge of all, however, is determining the priority donors will accord military reform programmes. Activities such as reintegrating ex-combatants, creating civilian police forces and engendering dialogue on the role of the military in democratic societies are often viewed as competing with 'traditional' development programmes rather than one of the basic building-blocks of sustainable development. Yet, it is increasingly clear that, without a strong commitment on the part of the development community to helping create an environment of domestic and regional peace and an appropriate balance of power between civilians and the military, the prospects for achieving sustainable development will be severely compromised.

---

[141] Lancaster, J. and Mintz, J., 'Strapped Saudis seek to stretch out payments for US arms', *Washington Post*, 7 Jan. 1994, pp. A1, A15.

13. Arms production and arms trade

IAN ANTHONY, PAUL CLAESSON, AGNÈS COURADES
ALLEBECK, ELISABETH SKÖNS and SIEMON T. WEZEMAN

I. Introduction

The downward trend in military expenditure in the major centres of arms production reported in recent years continued in 1993.[1] Moreover, within these
overall reductions arms procurement budgets were perhaps more severely
affected than other forms of military expenditure. Under these conditions the
global arms industry has continued to experience difficulties.

The reductions in government allocations to domestic defence industries
have been most marked in Central and Eastern Europe—including the countries which have emerged on the territory of the former Soviet Union. In Central Europe there is a demand for military equipment to re-equip armed forces
whose inventories are dominated by Soviet weapon systems. Sustained economic growth among the countries of Central and Eastern Europe would
almost certainly translate into significant orders for the local military industries. However, there seems little prospect that governments will implement
new equipment programmes quickly enough to avoid having to shut down a
large part of the existing military industry.

In these circumstances arms industries across Central and Eastern Europe
depend on government subsidy and foreign sales for their survival. Government subsidies have been forthcoming and there is little evidence of major
cuts in production capacity—although much capacity is idle—or large-scale
redundancies—although many workers with marketable skills seem to have
left the defence sector voluntarily. It is sometimes suggested that military
industries exert disproportionate political influence in Central and Eastern
Europe and that they use this influence to their economic advantage. However,
there is no evidence that military industrialists were informed (let alone consulted) before major reductions in procurement expenditure were made in
1991 and 1992. Neither were these industries able to win significantly greater
allocations in 1993. It is therefore unlikely that subsidies can be relied upon
into the indefinite future. It seems more likely that a rationalization of the
defence industry in Central and Eastern Europe remains inevitable.

The 100 leading arms-producing companies in the Organisation for Economic Co-operation and Development (OECD) area (94 of the 100) and the
developing world (the remaining 6) experienced a decline of about $8 billion
(in current prices) in their combined arms sales in 1991–92. Since 1992 was a
year of continued concentration of production in the arms industry, this

---

[1] See chapter 12 in this volume.

decline in sales among the top 100 companies (see table 13.4) was probably smaller than for the rest of the industry. The overall decline in arms sales in OECD and developing countries can be expected to have been even sharper.

The global value of foreign deliveries of major conventional weapons in 1993 is estimated by SIPRI to have been $21 975 million in 1990 US dollars. The figure recorded for 1993 in this Yearbook is roughly the same as that recorded for 1992. It is normally the case that the value of deliveries recorded for the previous year is revised upwards as new and better information becomes available. For example, in the *SIPRI Yearbook 1993* the value of deliveries for the year 1992 was recorded as $18.4 billion. If the pattern of upward revision is repeated next year, it may be shown that a slight upturn in the volume of international arms transfers occurred in 1993. This figure still includes significant deliveries of second-hand equipment, a consequence of the de-militarization of Germany and the implementation of the 1990 Treaty on Conventional Armed Forces in Europe (CFE). It also includes deliveries of major conventional weapons from US inventories to countries which participated in the coalition against Iraq in the 1991 Persian Gulf War. The inclusion of this equipment tends to mask the depressed volume of deliveries of new major conventional weapon platforms.

The global trade in major conventional weapons remains a highly concentrated activity dominated by a small number of suppliers and recipients. The five major suppliers in 1993 accounted for 86 per cent of total deliveries while the 25 major recipients accounted for about 90 per cent of total deliveries.

The USA remained the dominant supplier of major conventional weapons, accounting for 48 per cent of all deliveries—compared with over 51 per cent in 1992. However, Russia accounted for 21 per cent of deliveries recorded for 1993—a significant increase over its share in 1992. This partly reflected the transfers of major platforms built by the Soviet arms industry against orders from the Soviet armed forces which were never delivered to or paid for by Russia. The deliveries of MiG-29 fighter aircraft to Hungary and Slovakia were examples of such transfers. In reality no currency was exchanged for these systems, which were offset against Soviet debts inherited by Russia.

The countries of the European Union collectively supplied 20 per cent of major conventional weapons in 1993. Three countries—Germany, France and the UK—accounted for around 85 per cent of this figure.

Arms imports also remained concentrated among a relatively small number of countries. In 1993 Asia and Europe remained the primary recipients of transfers of major conventional weapons. Among Asian countries India was still the largest recipient of major conventional weapon systems with modernization programmes based on major foreign systems continuing in the Army, Navy, Air Force and Coast Guard. In Europe, Turkey received the largest share of major conventional weapons, partly reflecting the continuing 'cascade' of weapon systems associated with the CFE Treaty. However, Turkey is also modernizing its Army, Navy, Air Force and paramilitary forces with major conventional weapon systems of foreign origin.

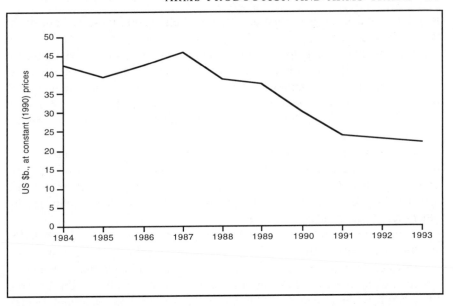

Figure 13.1. The downward trend in the aggregate value of deliveries of major conventional weapon systems, 1984–93

Note: Data are SIPRI trend-indicator values in US $b. (1990). SIPRI arms transfer value data are a volume index which indicates the average trend in physical deliveries of major conventional weapons. Since the SIPRI arms trade statistics do not reflect purchase prices, they are not comparable with economic statistics such as national accounts or foreign trade statistics, nor with the arms sales data reported below in the sections on arms production. The methods used for the valuation of SIPRI arms trade statistics are described in appendix 13D.

Source: SIPRI arms trade data base.

The share of major conventional weapons received by countries in the Middle East has increased since 1991 as equipment programmes agreed in the wake of the Persian Gulf War have been implemented. The primary recipients of this equipment have been Israel and countries located on the Arabian peninsula. In addition Egypt has begun to take delivery of systems such as the F-16 fighter aircraft and the M-1 Abrams main battle tank acquired under programmes which pre-date the war.

II. Defence industries in Central and Eastern Europe

Each of the major centres of global defence industrial production is being forced to adjust to the consequences of the downward trend in military expenditure and arms supplies. Nowhere is this more true than in Central and Eastern Europe.[2] Since the overall size and structure of the defence industries

[2] This section focuses on the Czech Republic, Hungary, Poland, Romania, Russia, Slovakia and Ukraine.

in Central and Eastern Europe are described elsewhere, these are not dealt with in this chapter.[3]

Russia plainly intends to preserve a significant defence industrial base to support an ambitious foreign and security policy. While most of Russia's existing production capacities are under-utilized it is not clear that any have been shed. Much plant and machinery has been mothballed and many employees have been kept on, but without work, paid through direct or indirect government subsidy.

Ukraine and—to a lesser extent—other newly independent countries formerly part of the USSR are host to industries conceived as part of a single entity, the Soviet defence industry. The adjustment process here is also affected by the residual economic inter-dependency of these countries in other, non-defence industrial activities.

Elsewhere in Central and Eastern Europe no defence industries approach the size or complexity of those in Russia and it seems unlikely that any of these countries can retain their current capacities for system integration or the construction of complex weapon platforms. The possible exception to this general trend could be the Czech Republic, where Aero Vodochody is a military aircraft manufacturer with a competitive product—the L-39/59 series jet trainer.

The smaller Central European countries have no aspirations to autarkic defence industries. Rather, their policies reflect the desire to preserve employment and industrial production during the transition to what they hope will be incorporation into the global civilian economy. However, one or two producers may successfully find a market niche for their defence equipment—for example, Czech jet trainer aircraft or Polish light-utility aircraft. Central European countries are more likely to concentrate limited resources on the repair and maintenance of equipment in service together with the production of the necessary consumable items (spare parts and ordnance) required to give the armed forces a modest independent military capability.

Levels of military expenditure have shrunk faster in Central and Eastern Europe than elsewhere in Europe.[4] Moreover, within these shrinking budgets the allocations to equipment procurement have been reduced more than other forms of defence spending. Government orders to industry represent a shrinking percentage of a shrinking budget.

To illustrate with the case of Russia, the Ministry of Defence scaled back procurement dramatically in 1992 (see table 13.1). Procurement did not

---

[3] For background information readers are referred to *SIPRI Yearbooks* 1990, 1991 and 1992; Wulf, H. (ed.), SIPRI, *Arms Industry Limited* (Oxford University Press: Oxford, 1993); Proceedings of the Seminar on Defence Conversion co-sponsored by the Danish Folketing and the North Atlantic Assembly, Copenhagen 6–9 Jan. 1992; Proceedings of the NATO Co-operation Council Defence Conversion Seminar, Brussels, 20–22 May 1992; *The Former Soviet Union in Transition*, Vol. 2, Study Papers submitted to the Joint Economic Committee, Congress of the United States (US Government Printing Office: Washington, DC, May 1993); *Defense Conversion and Arms Transfers: The Legacy of the Soviet Era Arms Industry* (Institute for Foreign Policy Analysis: Washington, DC, July 1993). This section is based on Anthony, I. (ed.), *The Future of Defence Industries in Central and Eastern Europe*, SIPRI Research Report no. 7 (Oxford University Press: Oxford, 1994).

[4] See chapter 12 in this volume.

Table 13.1. Reductions in procurement by the Russian Ministry of Defence in 1992 compared with those by the Soviet Ministry of Defence in 1991

System type	Reduction in value of procurement (%)
Inter-continental ballistic missiles	55
Submarine-launched ballistic missiles	39
Tactical missiles	81
Surface-to-air missiles	80
Air-to-air missiles	80
Aircraft	80
Tanks	97
Field artillery	97
Multiple Rocket Launchers	76
Space satellites with space launch vehicles	34

Source: Ministry of Defence, Russian Federation

increase in 1993. The Air Force stopped orders entirely for the MiG-29, Il-76, An-124 and An-72 aircraft. Orders for the following aircraft and helicopters were reduced to nominal numbers: Tu-160, Su-27, Su-27UB, MiG-29M, MiG-29UB, Mi-26 and Mi-8. New construction of warships has almost stopped while the average time for completion of ships and submarines has increased to five years for smaller designs and nine years for more complex vessels.[5]

The defence industry has undoubtedly received off-budget payments across the whole of Central and Eastern Europe. However, there is little evidence that these subsidies are being used to continue production. Instead they have been used in large part to pay salaries to employees without a task.

By 1993 out of a sample of 1500 enterprises in St Petersburg 300 were idle, 400 were working short hours and 140 enterprises were on the verge of closing production. Moreover, St Petersburg is not yet believed to have reached the bottom of the recession.[6] Up to 30 per cent of the scientific and technically trained personnel in St Petersburg have chosen to leave the defence sector.

In stable conditions the allocation of resources is a central issue in understanding policy. In the circumstances prevailing in Central and Eastern Europe the absence of functioning legal, administrative and industrial structures makes it impossible to implement fiscal and budget policies.

For all of 1991 and at least the first half of 1992 many of the industries of Central and Eastern Europe continued production at roughly the previous level without either orders or payment. This has generated significant unsold inven-

---

[5] Comments of Vadim I. Vlasov, Assistant to the First Deputy Minister of Defence, Russian Federation, at the SIPRI Workshop on The Future of the Defence Industries of Central and Eastern Europe, 29–30 Apr. 1993.

[6] Comments of Nina Oding, Head of Research, Leontief Centre, St Petersburg at the SIPRI Workshop (note 5). Similar disruption is revealed in other regional case studies. See, for example, Kachalin, V. V., 'Defense industry conversion: A case study of the Kaluga region', *Harriman Institute Forum*, vol. 6, no. 10 (June 1993), pp. 1–12.

tories held by the producers and also inter-enterprise debts. Debts were compounded by the failure of governments to pay for items on order.

Questions such as 'how much money went to the defence industry and how did this amount change compared with the previous year?' or 'how many people are employed in the defence industry and how has this number changed?' are, for Central and Eastern Europe, impossible to answer. Therefore, the primary focus of this section is the process of restructuring which has taken place within the defence industries of Central and Eastern Europe. The emphasis is on both government measures and those taken by industry itself.

Defining the defence industry in Central and Eastern Europe

Across Central and Eastern Europe tasks which in a market economy would usually be the responsibility of an integrated company or industrial group are still often performed by government agencies.

The Russian law 'On conversion' identifies design or scientific research organizations, science and production associations, production associations and plants as business units engaged in the defence industry.

Design or scientific research organizations with production capacity for prototyping and advanced development, but without serial production capacities, seem to have been largely confined to Russia, but there are isolated examples elsewhere in Central and Eastern Europe (such as Antonov in Ukraine).

Science and production associations have the capacity to perform a wide spectrum of operations within the overall production cycle. Some of them are significant industrial assets with tens of thousands of workers distributed across five or more locations. While few if any such associations undertake all basic research and technical development themselves, they have significant in-house capabilities in this regard. However, most of these capacities would presumably be directed at developing processing technologies. These also seem to be largely confined to Russia although there are isolated examples of such organizations in Central European countries—PZL in Poland, for example, or ZTS in Slovakia.

Production associations group together a number of factories performing serial production or closely interdependent manufacturing tasks.

Plants or single factories are engaged only in one limited manufacturing task. These entities are widely dispersed across the territory of the former Soviet Union.[7] Moreover, individual plants which contributed to Soviet military production are also to be found in Central Europe.

In some cases the technologies provided by these plants were critical to the performance of military systems. Often the technologies were dual-use—for example, military electronics, telecommunications components and optronics

---

[7] Cooper, J., 'The Soviet Union and the successor republics: defence industries coming to terms with disunion', ed. Wulf (note 3).

Table 13.2. Employment structure of Russian defence industry enterprises, 1993

Number of employees	<1000	1 001–5 000	5 001–10 000	>10 000
Percentage of defence enterprises	5.8	49.8	28.3	16.1

Source: Presentation of Alexander Ozhegov at the FOA (Swedish National Defence Research Establishment) symposium on the Russian Defence Industry, Stockholm, 20–22 Oct. 1993.

were produced in countries such as Bulgaria, the former German Democratic Republic and Hungary as well as in the Baltic states and other newly independent countries. Russia, in order to avoid dependence on any of these independent countries for critical technologies, is engaged in a process of import substitution. Under these conditions there is a fear that without a change in the structure of defence decision-making in Russia the interest in dual-use technology development may lead to a militarization of civil industry rather than a re-orientation of military research and development (R&D).[8]

One recent estimate suggests that the total number of facilities engaged in defence production in the former Soviet Union was 3000–5000. Of these no more than 150 were major final assembly plants. Around 1500 were engaged in research, development or testing while the rest comprised a wide range of activities,[9] including raw material processing and the production of semi-finished goods, as well as a host of services aimed at meeting the general needs of employees.

As more and more plant-level and local studies are carried out it becomes clear that data for each business unit typically include activities that have little or nothing to do with the production of defence equipment and which in a market economy would be contracted out to other companies.[10] Functions undertaken by what was nominally the defence sector included health care, child care and the provision of sports and recreation facilities, all of which are commonly organized at the enterprise level.

The collocation of business units combining many different activities was prevalent across Central and Eastern Europe. This phenomenon of collocation has made the available data on the structure of enterprises in the defence industry difficult to interpret. Table 13.2 suggests that in Russia—with by far the largest defence industry in the former Eastern bloc—production is undertaken by very large units.

Collocation reflected the widespread lack of faith in the system of distribution and the risk of local shortages of materials and goods, in spite of the preferential treatment the defence industry enjoyed. Jacques Sapir has des-

---

[8] Cooper, J., 'Transforming Russia's defence industrial base', *Survival*, vol. 35 no. 4 (winter 1993–94).

[9] US Central Intelligence Agency Directorate of Intelligence, *The Defense Industries of the Newly Independent States of Eurasia* (CIA: Washington, DC, Jan. 1993).

[10] See, for example, the appendices of Deutsche Industrie Consult, *Profile of the Region Nizhniy Novgorod*, Westdeutsche Landesbank, Mar. 1993.

cribed this process of reducing reliance on supplies from distant locations as 'the production equivalent to hoarding stocks'.[11]

Industrial restructuring in Central and Eastern Europe

In the *Russian* defence sector the most radical current proposal for re-organizing business units is the creation of Financial–Industrial Groups.

Financial–Industrial Groups would bring together in a joint venture Russian units with design and production capabilities. A group would include at least one financial unit—such as a bank or an investment fund—as well as a trading organization to handle offset transactions. Its preferred structure would include both military and non-military industrial units with non-military production accounting for 50 per cent of sales or more. One of the first groups—the Russian Armament Corporation—was formed in 1993 bringing together the Almaz science and production association; the Fakel machine-building design bureaux; serial production plants in Moscow, St Petersburg, Nizhniy Novgorod and Novosibirsk; the Spetsvneshtekhnika State Foreign Economic Commission; the Oboronexport trading association; the Inkombank; and the Central Industrial Investment Check Fund.[12] It is hoped that viable companies able to operate in a market economy will emerge from these groups.

The number of entities within Russia that will be organized in this way is not clear. In preparing privatization legislation Chairman of the State Committee for State Property Anatoly Chubais has said that 20 per cent of the defence industry will not be available for private investment but will remain in full government ownership. The State Committee on the Defence Industry has suggested a figure of 25 per cent. In both cases the percentage is applied to the entities listed as being essential for the fulfilment of the State Defence Order. This would mean that in the region of 400–500 entities will remain in full government ownership.[13] It seems likely that this group of industrial units would include those engaged mainly in military production whose survival in the market would be unlikely under present conditions.

In the *Czech Republic* the process of industrial restructuring has begun in the aircraft industry as well as other sectors. After Aero-holding established 11 subsidiaries in 1991, vouchers which gave limited ownership rights were distributed to employees who subsequently had the right to retain or sell them. After the first wave of voucher distribution 36 per cent of shares are held by individual shareholders and investment funds. However, the government-owned National Property Fund intends to retain its share holding of 64 per cent.[14]

[11] Sapir, J., *The Russian Defence Related Industries Conversion Process*, mimeo, Centre d'Études des Modes d'Industrialisation, Paris, Oct. 1993, p. 12.

[12] *Daily Report—Central Eurasia (FBIS-SOV)* FBIS-SOV-93-173, 9 Sep. 1993, pp. 43–45.

[13] *Radio Free Europe/Radio Liberty (RFE/RL) News Briefs*, 6 Dec. 1993; Cooper (note 8), p. 157. Note that these are plans for privatization—if and when they are implemented remain open questions.

[14] Presentation of Adam Stranak, Vice-President Engineering, Aero Vodochody, at the SIPRI Workshop (note 5).

Aero Vodochody's core business is the development, production and maintenance of military jet trainer aircraft. It is a world leader within this field, having sold nearly 6500 jet trainers to 25 countries world-wide. However, a dramatic decrease in sales after the dissolution of the Warsaw Treaty Organization (WTO) and the general recession in the aircraft market has led to a proposal intended to save core businesses and design capacities. Its strategy is based on achieving diversified activities in (a) military jet trainers and lightweight fighter aircraft; (b) design and development of small utility passenger aircraft; and (c) sub-contracting work in the civil aviation area.

The programme is financed by income from sales and through commercial loans taken out in Western Europe. In the period 1989–92 military aircraft have been developed with foreign companies in Europe, Israel and the USA. International participation in civil aviation projects is still being negotiated.

Military production in *Slovakia* represented 60 per cent of total Czechoslovakian military production in the 1980s—and accounts for more than 20 per cent of the total engineering production of Slovakia. Czechoslovak army consumption was approximately 20 per cent of production while the rest was for foreign recipients. The countries of the former WTO were recipients of approximately 60 per cent of total production.[15]

In present circumstances there is no prospect for maintaining this level of industrial capacity in Slovakia. According to Peter Magvasi, Financial Director of the largest Slovakian defence producer ZTS TEES Martin:

The requirements of the Slovak army in peace conditions, as well as in alert situations, occupy between 5 and 20 per cent of manufacturing capacities in Slovakia for tracked vehicles, artillery and rocket means and ammunition of large calibre. The Slovak Army will utilize only 2–6 per cent of these capacities over the next 3 to 5 years which cannot guarantee their survival. Saving these capacities is only possible via export sales which are clearly related to the world political situation and the foreign policy of the Slovak Republic.

As indicated in table 13.3, the reduction in demand for military goods is reflected in reduced employment in specific Slovak enterprises.

In 1991 military equipment sales accounted for 50.6 per cent of total sales. The reduction in military sales is a major crisis. ZTS TEES Martin is not only a defence producer but also an industrial group which is being restructured to prepare for operations in the civil market economy. In common with many Central European arms producers it was highly export-dependent. However, the defence division was no more export-dependent than other parts of ZTS. In 1991 over 90 per cent of its total production was for export. The strategy of ZTS TEES Martin is to re-organize as a group consisting of three sections: a headquarters, a manufacturing section consisting of eight divisions each specializing in one form of industrial production and a service and support section. Within this group military equipment is produced along with heavy earth moving and construction equipment in one of the eight manufacturing

[15] Comments of Peter Magvasi, Financial Director of the largest Slovakian defence producer ZTS TEES Martin, at the SIPRI Workshop (note 5).

Table 13.3. Employment in Slovak enterprises engaged in military production

Enterprise	No. of employees in the year		
	1990	1991	1992
ZTS Dubnica	13 935	11 842	9 834
ZTS TEES Martin	13 188	9 100	6 717
PS Povazká Bystrica	11 347	9 157	7 651
PPS Detva	6 078	4 793	4 100
Vihorlat Snina	5 626	4 953	3 787
Totals for these enterprises	**50 174**	**39 845**	**32 089**

Source: Weichhardt, R. (ed.), *Economic Developments in Cooperation Partner Countries from a Sectoral Perspective: Colloquium, 30 June, 1 and 2 July 1993* (NATO, Economics Directorate and Office of Information and Press: Brussels, 1993), p. 122.

divisions. The other divisions produce diesel engines, tractor engines, tractors, machine tools of various kinds, metal castings and forestry equipment.

The goal of ZTS TEES Martin is to establish each of its manufacturing divisions as independent companies. It is hoped that several can become independent as parts of foreign joint ventures.[16] Even though reductions in employment are inevitable the intention is to reduce dependence on defence sales.

In *Hungary* the defence industry—among the smallest in Central and Eastern Europe—was highly export dependent. The Hungarian industry was primarily active as a manufacturer of components and dual-use items which were subsequently incorporated into equipment assembled elsewhere in the WTO. However, given that the defence industry represented a small share— around 2 per cent—of industrial production in Hungary, the government has not been particularly influenced by the difficulties of the defence industry. As a result, 'the number of companies concerned with defence industrial activities is continuously decreasing as they face bankruptcy and liquidation procedures, privatization or, in more hopeful cases, division into more product-oriented units'.[17] By the beginning of 1993 'most defense industry enterprises had gone through multiple stages of transformation of legal form and internal organization. As a consequence most of them were divided to smaller, quasi-independent enterprises which, although still mostly state-owned, were prepared for future privatization.'[18] Although thus far the privatization process has been most far-reaching in Hungary, the government has ensured that a core defence industry remains. Legislation states that production considered vital to the Hungarian armed forces will remain in state ownership. The government will retain a 25 per cent stake in two companies and full ownership of five companies specialized in arms production.

[16] Presentation of Juraj Kovacik, ZTS Engine Division, at the SIPRI Workshop (note 5).
[17] Presentation of Laslo Kocsis, Director for Arms Trade, Hungarian Ministry of Foreign Economic Relations, at the SIPRI Workshop (note 5).
[18] Presentation of Yudit Kiss, an independent analyst specializing in the Central European defence industry, at the SIPRI Workshop (note 5).

III. The 'SIPRI 100'

The combined arms sales of the top 100 arms-producing companies in the OECD and developing countries amounted to $167.7 billion in 1992.[19] In 1991 the sales of these same companies added up to $175.4 billion. Their sales have thus declined by $8 billion over one year, in current prices.

Within the reduced total, US companies accounted for a smaller share in 1992 than in 1991, while the share of other OECD countries (Western Europe, Canada and Japan) increased. The share in the top 100 total of the six companies in the developing world remained constant (table 13.4).

The process of structural adjustment to lower sales volumes continued in 1992 and 1993. In Italy the restructuring of the arms industry has become part of a more general transformation of the state-owned industrial sector. Some countries seek to limit the full impact of the market on their military industrial bases, such as France (see section IV) and Israel (see below) which try to sustain these through government subsidies. Few arms-producing companies in developing countries are able to face the more aggressive conditions on the global market.

The changes in arms sales in individual countries were more accentuated during 1992 than in previous years reported by SIPRI (table 13.5). This has resulted in significant shifts in the ranking of companies (see appendix 13A, table 13A). The largest changes in arms sales are in the majority of cases associated with major structural measures in response to lower sales levels and changed market conditions which were pronounced during 1992. This is especially true for the USA, where seven major acquisitions took place in the arms industry during 1992.[20] Two US companies previously on the SIPRI 100 list ceased their arms production activities in 1992: LTV and Morrison.

All three French companies listed in table 13.5 have been involved in major restructuring of their production and/or ownership arrangements. DCN is undergoing an extensive restructuring process along the same lines as GIAT Industries underwent earlier. It has cut employment sharply and is making great efforts to expand in the international market for conventional submarines and frigates.[21] Matra Hachette, a large media conglomerate, is a newcomer on the arms market, in 1992 acquiring Matra Défense, one of the four major missile producers in Western Europe. The decline in British Aerospace sales is the result of plant closures and cuts rather than planned restructuring.[22]

---

[19] These data are derived from the SIPRI data base on the arms industry in OECD and developing countries excluding China. It is not possible to include comparable data on the arms industry in other areas, the more important exclusions being companies in China and in Central and Eastern Europe.

[20] Described in Anthony, I., et al., 'Arms production and arms trade', SIPRI, *SIPRI Yearbook 1993: World Armaments and Disarmament* (Oxford University Press: Oxford, 1993), pp. 433–35.

[21] *La crise de l'industrie de défense*, Rapport d'information N°552, déposé par la Commission de la défense nationale et des forces armées par M. René Galy-Dejean, Assemblée Nationale, 5 Oct. 1993, p. 14; 'Selling French naval know-how', *Jane's Defence Weekly*, 16 Oct 1993, pp. 52–53; and 'DCN— a leading European naval shipyard', *Asian Defence Journal*, Dec. 1993, pp. 71–79.

[22] Differences in company strategy used by the major arms producers in the European Union are analysed in a study for the European Parliament, *European Armaments Industry: Research, Technological Development and Conversion, Final Report*, Scientific and Technological Options Assessment, Directorate General for Research, European Parliament, Nov. 1993, chapter III.

Table 13.4. Regional/national shares of arms sales for the top 100 arms-producing companies in OECD and developing countries, 1992 compared to 1991

Number of companies 1992	Region/ country	Share of total arms sales (%) 1991	Share of total arms sales (%) 1992	Arms sales 1992 ($b.)
46	USA	61.3	59.6	99.9
40	West European OECD	32.3	33.7	56.6
14	France	12.0	13.1	22.0
11	UK	9.9	9.8	16.5
7	FRG	4.8	5.0	8.4
3	Italy	3.0	3.2	5.3
2	Sweden	0.8	1.0	1.7
2	Switzerland	1.1	1.0	1.6
1	Spain	0.8	0.7	1.1
8	Other OECD	4.0	4.3	7.1
6	Japan	3.4	3.8	6.3
2	Canada	0.7	0.5	0.8
6	Developing countries	2.4	2.4	4.1
3	Israel	1.2	1.3	2.2
2	India	0.7	0.7	1.2
1	South Africa	0.4	0.4	0.7
100	**Total**	**100.0**	**100.0**	**167.7**

Source: Appendix 13A.

Table 13.5. Companies whose arms sales changed the most in absolute terms, 1992 Figures are in US $m.

Company	Country	Arms sales 1992	Change 1991–92
Companies with decreased arms sales of US $400 m. or more:			
General Dynamics	USA	3 200	– 4 420
General Motors	USA	5 400	– 2 100
McDonnell Douglas	USA	9 290	– 910
General Electric	USA	5 300	– 820
DCN	France	2 980	– 730
British Aerospace	UK	7 070	– 480
Boeing	USA	4 700	– 400
Companies with increased arms sales of US $400 m. or more:			
Matra Hachette	France	1 030	+ 1 030
Carlyle	USA	1 530	> + 1 000
IBM	USA	2 000	+ 700
Loral	USA	3 050	+ 450
GIAT Industries	France	1 660	+ 440

Source: Appendix 13A.

National restructuring in 1993

Few new large-scale restructuring measures were announced during 1993 compared to the previous three years, although the implementation of earlier decisions involved major actual restructuring activities during the year. The process of restructuring is likely to continue over the next few years, however, since down-sizing has not yet resulted in an adjustment of production capacity to demand.[23]

In the USA, the more important acquisitions announced in 1993 were that by the Carlyle Group of Magnavox Electronics Systems from Philips' US subsidiary and the purchase by Loral of Federal Systems, the defence division of IBM. Other major restructuring measures include Grumman's decision to give up its role as a military airframe contractor and instead focus on systems integration, a decision which will involve a one-third reduction in its overall production capacity.[24] Several companies announced a separation between military and commercial activities.[25]

In Europe talks continued but were not completed during 1993 on mergers in the over-sized missile industry, in which production to date has to a large extent taken the form of European co-operation projects. The two merger combinations under negotiation concerned the missile units of British Aerospace (UK) with Matra (France) and of Aérospatiale (France) with DASA (Germany), but other combinations are possible as well.[26]

Italy

The turbulence that marked Italy's economic and political circumstances in 1993 also found expression in the ongoing restructuring of the country's arms industry. Part of a greater scheme to reform the bloated state-run industrial sector, characterized by a discredited system of political patronage, unbridled state financial intervention and low productivity, this effort involves, *inter alia*: (*a*) the liquidation of the heavily indebted EFIM state-owned industry group; (*b*) the 'partial privatization'[27] of four other state holdings, notably the widely diversified IRI group;[28] (*c*) the transfer of EFIM's eight arms com-

---

[23] This is also expected by industry. In a 1993 study of North American aerospace industry attitudes, almost all companies expected significantly more consolidation and about 60% expected a large number of sub-contractors to leave the business; see 'Merger wave to continue', *Financial Times,* 8 June 1993, p. 10. Similar industrial attitudes prevail in Europe; see, e.g., Feuchtmeyer, E., 'The European armaments market—an industrialist's concern', *Military Technology,* Oct. 1993, pp. 40–45; and 'European companies find strength in mergers', *Defense News,* 19–25 July 1993, pp. 1 and 18.

[24] *Jane's Defence Weekly,* 13 Nov. 1993, p. 7 and *Aviation Week & Space Technology,* 24 Jan. 1994.

[25] Rockwell announced a reorganization of its defence activities into a separate Defence Systems group and Litton announced a spin-off of its commercial activities into a separate company.

[26] See, e.g., 'Marriage of minds', *Jane's Defence Weekly,* 15 Jan. 1994, pp. 29–30.

[27] '[T]he Italian government merely wishes to strengthen the state-owned corporations and collect new risk capital through partial privatisation, without selling companies to private industrial investors or liberalising monopolistic services. . . . In Italy, partial privatisation mostly means that a shareholder, e.g. Iri or Eni, sells a minority holding in its subsidiaries to private investors who have no interest in company administration or management.' Gallo, R., 'Italy fudges privatisation', *Financial Times,* 12 Jan. 1993, p. 14. Professor Riccardo Gallo is a former Vice-Chairman of IRI.

[28] The other three holdings are (with predominant activity): ENI (oil refineries and distribution), ENEL (electrical energy) and INA (insurance).

panies to Finmeccanica, the main subholding for IRI's arms interests;[29] and (*d*) the reincorporation of Finmeccanica as a production company, involving the amalgamation of its subsidiary manufacturing companies into three production divisions.[30] As a result of these transformations, Finmeccanica emerges as the dominant 'national champion' of the Italian arms industry, consolidating (with Fincantieri on the naval construction side) all state-controlled arms interests under IRI's banner.[31] In addition, Finmeccanica has significant minority interests in many of the remaining producers in the private sector, including those in companies within the second-placed FIAT group.[32]

Initiated in July 1992 and brought towards completion in late 1993,[33] this restructuring served three quite different agendas. First, it addressed EFIM's acute debt crisis. Second, in the context of the ongoing political and economic reform process, it provided an opportune vehicle for an assault on post-war Italy's rampant system of political patronage in its public utilities.[34] Third, by consolidating the state's arms interests in Finmeccanica, in effect exempting the sector from deregulation, it provided the means for continued state subsidy and support for the national arms industry. Specifically, it enabled the state to salvage the heavily indebted EFIM subsidiaries, notably Agusta, from default or sale abroad.[35] More generally, as a response to shrinking defence orders and drastically declining foreign sales,[36] the new structure allows for greater coordination of production and procurement planning, in keeping with suggestions made by Defence Minister Salvo Andò as part of a 1992 defence

[29] The 8 companies are: Agusta, Agusta Omi, Agusta Sistemi, Breda Meccanica Bresciana, Elicotteri Meridionali, Officine Galileo, OTO Melara and SMA. See Tamburello, S., 'Agusta e il "militare" Efim passeranno in affitto all'Iri, Nasce la nuova Finmeccanica', *Corriere della Sera*, 21 Oct. 1992; de Briganti, G. and Politi, A., 'Italy's Finmeccanica to take over failed EFIM', *Defense News*, 21 Dec. 1992, p. 8.

[30] The 3 new divisions are: Alenia (aerospace), Ansaldo (machinery, transportation and construction) and Elsag (electronics). The new company structure became effective on 18 Feb. 1993. See Tamburello, S., 'Finmeccanica ad alta fusione', *Corriere della Sera*, 23 Dec. 1992; Simonian, H., 'Finmeccanica details terms of incorporation', *Financial Times*, 24 Dec. 1992, p. 10; Tamburello, S., 'Ecco la nuova Finmeccanica, Fuse Alenia, Elsag e Ansaldo con maxi-aumento di capitale', *Corriere della Sera*, 19 Feb. 1993; 'Ecco Finmeccanica SpA', *JP4*, vol. 22, no. 4 (Apr. 1993), p. 8.

[31] See Sparraco, P., 'Italian-owned firms to merge defense sectors', *Aviation Week & Space Technology*, 16 Aug. 1993, p. 46; Sutton, O., 'Italy's "polo unico" moves closer to reality', *Interavia*, vol. 49, no. 575 (Feb. 1994), pp. 22–27.

[32] For a breakdown of Finmeccanica's minority arms holdings, see de Briganti, G. and Politi, A., 'Italy continues to reshape defense industry', *Defense News*, 22–28 Feb. 1992, p. 6.

[33] The 'partial privatization' of IRI is to be completed by the end of 1996.

[34] 'As part of a political deal, Efim was allowed to be a Socialist fief, while IRI . . . was in the hands of the Christian Democrats . . . Breaking the political hold on Efim and reshaping the entire role of the public sector was [Prime Minister Giuliano] Amato's prime objective in liquidating the holding. Indeed, as a Socialist linked to the then leader, Mr Bettino Craxi, he saw getting rid of Efim as a demonstration of his own impartiality and concrete proof that the state was set to reduce its interventionist role in industry and would no longer underwrite lossmaking businesses.' See Graham, R., 'Liquidation exposes Italian economic fault lines', *Financial Times*, 19 July 1993, p. 2.

[35] Graham, R., 'Efim defence transfer agreed', *Financial Times*, 15 July 1993, p, 14; Graham, R., 'Rome plots survival course for defence industry', *Financial Times*, 19 July 1993, p. 2.

[36] See 'Italy: future products a puzzle', *Financial Times*, 8 June 1993, p. XIII; 'Le chiffre d'affaires de l'industrie aerospatiale italienne a chute de 2,8% en 92', *Air & Cosmos*, no. 1431 (21–27 June 1993), p. 18.

review,[37] and for a stronger international position of the Italian industry, in particular with regard to future production alliances.[38]

The transfer to Finmeccanica of the eight EFIM companies was marked by controversy and delays. The liquidation itself was messy, the result of a series of complicating factors—a severe currency crisis, an enormous public sector deficit and the collapse of the parties of the ruling coalition following revelations of widespread corruption (in which also officials high up in the EFIM hierarchy were implicated[39]). A dispute between the Government and the European Commission over state subsidies blocked the transfer for several months, and caused further embarrassment to the Amato Government as it tried to iron out a settlement with EFIM's foreign creditors.[40] To top it all, a disagreement between the Government and Finmeccanica over the terms of the transfer led to yet further delays. Against protests by EFIM's state-appointed liquidator, Finmeccanica insisted that the Government recapitalize the eight companies and commit itself to sufficient orders to make them financially viable.[41]

The developing countries

Apart from China (which is not included in the SIPRI arms industry data base), Israel, India and South Africa are the only developing countries (outside Central and Eastern Europe) in the SIPRI 100 list.

Arms industries in the so-called developing world consist of a very heterogeneous group of companies from a similarly heterogeneous group of countries. A generalization with some qualification about these industries is that the downturn and recent stabilization of the international market for military equipment has had a particularly strong impact on them. This is the result of several factors: (a) many of these companies were strongly export-dependent owing to small domestic arms procurement budgets; (b) in an environment of stiffening competition on the global market, they were at a disadvantage in

---

[37] See Valpolini, P., 'Il modello "rivisitato"', *Panorama Difesa*, vol. 12, no. 95 (Jan. 1993), p. 33. For a discussion of the procurement implications of Andò's 'New Defence Model', see 'One on one', interview with Gastone Savio, Italy's Parliamentary Defence Committee Chairman, *Defense News*, 8–14 Mar. 1993, p. 30.

[38] 'Overview: Italy's defense industry', *World Aerospace & Defense Intelligence*, 4 June 1993, p. 10.

[39] Among the many public officials implicated in the ongoing kickback investigations are 41 managers of five EFIM arms companies (Agusta, Agusta Omi, Agusta Sistemi and the Finbreda and Sistemi e Spazio subholdings). 'Crac Efim, Predieri denuncia 41 manager', *Corriere della Sera*, 20 Oct. 1993. In Jan. 1994, EFIM's last chairman, Gaetano Mancini, was arrested on charges of false accounting and fraud in connection with the restructuring of the group's aluminium sector. Lane, D., 'Ex-chief of Efim arrested', *Financial Times*, 25 Jan. 1994, p. 2.

[40] Sormani, P., 'La Cee denuncia Roma: aiuti all'Efim illegittimi', *Corriere della Sera*, 28 Jan. 1993; 'Conto più pesante per l'Efim in affitto', *Il Sole–24 Ore*, 31 Mar. 1993; Graham, R. and Simonian, H., 'Efim liquidation blocked by EC dispute', *Financial Times*, 19 July 1993, p. 1; Cavalli, M., 'Dalla Cee luce verde all'Efim', *Il Sole–24 Ore*, 9 Sep. 1993.

[41] 'Le condizioni di Fabiani all'Efim', *Il Sole–24 Ore*, 15 June 1993; Bufacchi, I., 'Finmeccanica: "Sì ai debiti Efim ma solo con lo sconto sul prezzo"', *Il Sole–24 Ore*, 2 Sep. 1993; 'Disagreement on price delays EFIM transfer', *Defense News*, 27 Sep.–3 Oct. 1993, p. 2; Bufacchi, I., 'Efim, la difesa a Fabiani, I debiti restano a Predieri', *Il Sole–24 Ore*, 9 Jan. 1994; 'Finmeccanica akquiriert Efim-Rüstungsunternehmen', *Neue Zürcher Zeitung*, 21 Jan. 1994, p. 11.

terms of export financing and other sales-support instruments available to companies in many wealthier countries; and (c) in addition to the impact of the general market decline, some of these companies were also particularly strongly affected by the termination of highly arms-consuming conflicts, such as the 1980–88 Iraq–Iran War. Their efforts to diversify into increased civilian production have in general been a very difficult process.[42]

Industries with a low or zero dependence on exports and thus not subject to these generalizations include China, India,[43] North Korea and South Africa. All of these are, however, instead confronted by lower domestic demand. In *South Africa*, the arms industry has been subject to significant downsizing, but is none the less still sizeable.[44] There is a debate on the future defence industrial policy under a new democratic government from May 1994. Three basic elements included in the current policy developed in the early 1990s are: measures to increase exports of military equipment; commercial application of military technology; and counter-trade requirements on all arms import contracts, part of which must involve the domestic arms industry.[45] In the current debate there are demands for a policy with a stronger focus on diversification and government assistance in the restructuring of the arms industry, built on the assumption that arms exports will not increase to the extent expected by industry.[46]

In several semi-industrialized countries, such as Indonesia, Singapore, South Korea, Taiwan and Turkey, arms production has become part of the general industrialization process, and takes place in co-operation with major arms-producing companies in the industrialized countries. These industries have not run into the short-term difficulties referred to above, mainly because of government budgetary support to major weapon programmes. Their permanent challenge to build more sophisticated systems will, however, most likely push them into a situation in which they are more vulnerable to success or failure on the export market.[47]

Israel has a relatively large and technologically advanced arms industry composed of three major state-owned producers (all on the SIPRI 100 list)— Israel Aircraft Industries, Rafael Armaments Development Authority and TAAS (formerly Israel Military Industries)—and several smaller firms. It has a strong dependence on exports—70 per cent on average during the past 15

---

[42] The problems involved in this process are described and the need for co-operation from industrial aid donor countries in these efforts is developed in Huck, B. J., 'Arms industry and conversion in developing countries', *Peace and the Sciences*, Sep. 1993, pp. 32–38.

[43] The arms production programme in India is described in chapter 10 in this volume.

[44] Employing a total of 70 000 people according to the General Manager of Armscor, the national procurement agency; see de Waal, T., 'Commercialisation of the defence industry—issues faced in the procurement of arms', *South African Defence Review* (Institute for Defence Policy, South Africa), no. 11 (1993), p. 10.

[45] Buys, A., 'The future of the South African armaments industry', *South African Defence Review*, no. 7 (1992), pp. 5–9.

[46] Fanaroff, B., 'The arms industry—industrial relations and industrial policy', *South African Defence Review*, no. 11 (1993), pp. 11–15. Dr Fanaroff is the National Secretary of the National Union of Metalworkers of South Africa.

[47] Bitencourt, L. A., 'The problems of defense industrialization for developing states', Paper presented at the UNIDIR/IFPA Conference on Arms and Technology Transfers, Geneva, 14–15 Feb. 1994.

years[48]—and has developed close ties with the US market through defence industrial co-operation.[49] In addition to the US export market, the Israeli arms industry is increasing exports and industrial co-operation with the countries in Central and Eastern Europe, and more recently also in Asia.[50] Many of these deals are in electronics, especially retrofits in military aerospace, a field in which Israel became involved early.

The decline in international arms sales has had a strong impact on the state-owned arms producers in Israel, for which diversification strategies in general have not been successful.[51] Government policy aims at significant production cuts, a process that has resulted in massive lay-offs of personnel in 1993 and will continue in 1994.[52] In a difficult labour market environment, strong trade unions have resisted this development, including measures such as sharp employment cuts, reduced working hours and reduced wages. The government has pursued an active policy including considerable subsidies in support of restructuring and for laid-off personnel.[53]

IV. Policies for the defence industrial base: France and the USA

The defence industrial bases in the leading arms-producing countries face major challenges as a result of reduced volumes of arms procurement, both domestically and in foreign markets, following the end of the cold war and the budgetary constraints facing the defence ministries in many countries. Lower levels of arms production contain the promise of a redistribution in resource allocations from the military to the civilian sector: relatively more technological innovation in the commercial field; release of productive resources for the civilian economy; and a shift in government expenditures from military to social requirements. Whether and to what extent these potentials will be realized is largely a matter of government policy. While the industry can go far in adjusting itself to changing market conditions, a coherent policy on the development of the defence industrial base can be pursued only by governments.

France and the USA are two countries with over-sized arms-production capacities, with a historical reliance on domestic arms production for national arms procurement and with changing force requirements. This section describes the policies of their governments towards the restructuring of their arms industries.

---

[48] Prime and Defence Minister Yitzhak Rabin, in an interview for *Defense News*, 31 May–6 June 1993, p. 30.

[49] This relationship is concisely and in detail described in Gold, D., *Israel as an American Non-NATO Ally: Parameters of Defense-Industrial Co-operation,* Jaffee Center for Strategic Studies, Tel Aviv University, Study No. 19 (Jerusalem Post: Jerusalem, 1991 and Westview Press: Boulder, Colo., 1993).

[50] 'Israel industries targets new territories', *International Defense Review*, July 1993, pp. 577–78.

[51] 'State-run sector fights for a future', *Jane's Defence Weekly*, 6 Feb. 1993, pp. 29–30.

[52] David Ivry, Director General of the Israeli Defence Ministry, interview in 'Sweeping changes in Israel's defence structure', *International Defense Review*, Mar. 1993, pp. 27–28.

[53] See, e.g., 'Shake-up in Israel's defense industry', *International Defense Review,* Apr. 1993, pp. 302–304.

Policy issues

The two main objectives of policy makers in the down-sizing of defence industrial bases are, first, the maintenance of a technologically competitive defence industrial base capable of fulfilling lower and changed requirements for military equipment, and second, the strengthening of commercial production and the civilian economy in exchange for reductions in the defence industrial base. These objectives require a set of long-term plans and policies, the most important of which are: a long-term plan for the military force structure, a vigorous R&D policy and a policy for the transfer of resources from military to civil product development and manufacture.

The strategy of civil–military integration is an option in the intersection between these two objectives. By integrating as much as possible the production of military equipment with the production of commercial, or civilian, products it would be possible, it is believed, to reach two goals simultaneously: to produce military equipment at lower rates, more flexibly and at lower costs, and, on the other hand, to contribute to a growing and more competitive national economy. The first goal would be achieved by introducing more commercial business practices into the procurement process, and by increased use of commercial products and dual-use technologies for military purposes, which would decrease reliance on products, production lines and technologies exclusively for arms procurement, the second through the inherent shift of resources from the military to the civilian sector.

The potential for civil-military integration has emerged as a result of technological developments. It is mainly three types of technological change during the past 10 years which have created this potential: (a) the change from mass production to flexible manufacturing as the most competitive method of production; (b) the shift in technological superiority from military to civilian production in many fields; and (c) the increased commonality in the key technologies used for military and commercial products. All these developments work in the same direction: to the benefit of those arms producers which can better exploit civilian products, technologies and production methods.[54]

Two additional relevant policy issues are policies for transition and arms exports. Short-term measures to facilitate the adjustment process during the transition period can help to avoid excessive economic and social costs. These include labour market policies and regionally targeted measures to stimulate new small-scale firms and relocation of existing enterprises. The option of exports is an explicit part of company strategy to meet the current crisis in many of the major arms-producing companies. Although exports are not a solution to the decline of the defence industrial base, individual companies hope to capture a sufficient slice of the market to carry it through a tough restructuring period. Governments are faced with the dilemma of balancing the fate of individual production lines or firms with the possible political and security repercussions following increased export volumes.

[54] For an interesting description of this strategy in relation to US policy, see Gansler, J. S., 'Transforming the US defence industrial base', *Survival*, vol. 35, no. 4 (winter 1993), pp. 130–46.

Governments can rely more or less on two types of approach in the scale-down of their defence industrial base: the *laissez-faire* approach, leaving the decisions entirely with the individual companies, and, on the other hand, government intervention to try to influence the size and structure of the future scaled-down industry. While the *laissez-faire* approach may have the advantage of pressing prices downwards, although competition is rather restricted in most arms markets, it may also lead to an undesired industrial structure, through the close-down of units which may have a critical role in the future. Government intervention, on the other hand, is not easy and often takes the form of financial subsidies with consequent high budgetary costs, and distorting effects on competition, prices and quality, but allows control over the direction of the process and often also includes a softening of the social consequences of the adjustment process. A third alternative, of temporary government support to its main contractors to help them pass through a difficult period, is currently not seen as a feasible option, since the demand for military equipment is reduced not only temporarily but is expected to stay low in a long-term perspective.

France

As a vital part of French security policy, France has maintained a defence industrial base capable of producing the full range of armaments, including nuclear weapons.[55] Successive governments have implemented a coherent policy to maintain a broad defence industrial base. Its procurement policy has been to purchase almost all its weapons from national producers or at least from firms with some French ownership. During the past two decades international co-operation has been an important part of French arms procurement policy.[56] Its arms export policy has facilitated the use of arms export incomes to reduce unit costs of French weapon systems. Budgeting policy for military R&D and procurement in a five-year military programming law has allowed the companies to plan their coming orders.

The French industrial policy in response to the current crisis has been described as a two-pronged one: to preserve and promote technological competences of the arms industry, and to rely on collaboration within the West European arms industry, with French companies in a dominant role.[57]

---

[55] For a comprehensive analysis of the French arms industry, see Chesnais, F. and Serfati, C., *L'armement en France: genèse, ampleur et coût d'une industrie* (Nathan: Paris, 1992); Hébert, J-P., *Stratégie française et industrie d'armement*, Fondation des Etudes de Défense Nationale, Paris, 1991.

[56] French armaments co-operation is described in Serfati, C., 'Reorientation of French companies', eds M. Brzoska and P. Lock, SIPRI, *Restructuring of Arms Production in Western Europe* (Oxford University Press: Oxford, 1992), chapter 8.

[57] US Congress, Office of Technology Assessment, *Lessons in Restructuring Defense Industry: The French Experience—Background Paper*, OTA-BP-ISC-96 (US Government Printing Office: Washington, DC, June 1992).

Table 13.6. The French arms industry: domestic sales and exports, 1983–92

1983	1984	1985	1986	1987	1988	1989	1990	1991	1992
1. Total sales of the arms industry (FF b., constant 1992 prices):									
124.2	132.3	132.3	130.3	124.7	131.1	131.5	132.1	119.0	113.1
2. Domestic sales (FF b., constant 1992 prices):									
76.6	75.9	76.7	78.5	85.0	88.0	90.7	91.2	89.0	84.1
3. Arms exports (Export deliveries of military equipment, FF b., constant 1992 prices):									
47.6	56.4	55.6	51.8	39.7	43.1	40.8	41.0	29.9	29.0
4. Export share of arms industry sales (3 as a share of 1, per cent):									
38.3	*42.6*	*42.0*	*39.8*	*31.9*	*32.9*	*31.0*	*31.0*	*25.2*	*25.6*

Source: Commissariat du Plan, *L'avenir des industries liées à la défense* (Documentation Française: Paris, Dec. 1993), p. 75.

The centralized agency known as the General Delegation for Armament (DGA)[58] which reports directly to the Minister of Defence has been the main tool of French defence industrial policy. The DGA is responsible for the definition, development and production of military equipment for the French armed forces and for export.

Background

The French arms industry has relied significantly on exports, accounting for around 40 per cent of total French arms sales in the early 1980s (table 13.6). Between 1985 and 1992 the volume of French arms exports was almost halved. Until 1990 this was compensated for by rising domestic procurement, but since 1990 total arms industry sales have dropped by 14 per cent.

This simultaneous decline in French arms procurement and arms exports has resulted in a substantial draw-down of France's defence industrial base, although not as much as in some other Western major arms-producing countries, such as Germany and the USA. In 1992 French arms industry employment was cut by around 18 000 jobs—one-quarter of all jobs lost in the entire industrial sector that year. The industry has forecasted a further reduction of 40 000 jobs (in defence and aerospace) between January 1993 and December 1995.[59]

Arms industry output corresponds to 2 per cent of gross national product (GNP). Employment in direct arms production is 230 000, accounting for about 5 per cent of total industrial employment. An additional 100 000 jobs depend on arms production on the sub-contractor level. Nearly four-fifths of the French arms industry is state-owned. The arms industry has a high degree

---

[58] DGA (Délégation Générale de l'Armement).
[59] *La crise de l'industrie de défense,* Rapport d'information N°552, déposé par la Commission de la défense nationale et des forces armées par M. René Galy-Dejean, Assemblée Nationale, 5 Oct. 1993, pp. 20 and 23.

of concentration, with 13 companies accounting for 80 per cent of arms sales, although an estimated 5000 companies have production in this sector.[60]

Procurement policy

A new five-year military programming law for the period 1995–2000 will be debated and adopted in the spring of 1994. It will be based on a new White Paper on Defence, expected in early 1994, in which French security policy in the post-communist period will be defined, oriented towards the role it wants to play as the major European defence industrial power.

It became clear in 1993 that the new (centre-right) government of Edouard Balladur, which came into power in May 1993, did not accept the possible weakening of the French defence industrial base. Blaming the previous (Socialist) government for the past two years of delays and cancellations of military equipment programmes, Defence Minister François Léotard decided to reallocate all the funding for military equipment which had been cancelled in 1993 (a total of FF 9 billion over the two years 1993–94).[61] This resulted in a military equipment budget 5.7 per cent higher than the revised 1993 budget, an increase 5–6 times higher than for 1994 equipment budgets in other sectors.[62] The level of future military procurement should be at least the same as in the 1994 budget.[63]

R&D policy

The shift to an R&D-intensive procurement policy, which started early in France, is continuing. This is not only the result of cut-backs in expenditures on military equipment, but also a strategy to preserve French technological competitiveness.

The government plans to increase government expenditures on military R&D, which at its current level of FF 30 billion accounts for about one-third of total government expenditures on R&D, in order to maintain the technological level of industry in special areas of competence and of strategic importance, such as in the space and communications sectors.[64]

Restructuring policy

Intense public concern in reaction to planned employment cuts in both military and civilian production led to a change in government policy during 1993. The planned employment cuts in state-owned arms-producing companies were

[60] Note 59, pp. 8–9.

[61] Avis présenté au nom de la Commission des affaires étrangères sur le projet de loi de finances pour 1994, par M. Roland Nungesser, Assemblée National, N° 582, 7 Oct. 1993, p.12.

[62] Response in Parliament of Defence Minister François Léotard on the defence budget 1994. Débats parlementaires, Assemblée Nationale, compte rendu intégral, 1ère séance du mercredi 10 novembre 1993, *Journal Officiel de la République Française*, N°81 [1] A.N. (C.R.), 11 Nov. 1993, p. 5718.

[63] Defence Minister Léotard, *Dossier de présentation à la presse du projet de budget de la défense 1994*, Service de l'Information et des Relations Publiques des Armées, Ministère de la Défense (Oct. 1993), p. 1.

[64] *Dossier 1994* (note 63), p. 1.

cancelled and new restructuring plans were negotiated, which took into consideration the increases in the 1994 military budget.[65] No more employment cuts in the arms industry were planned for 1994.[66]

The mid-1993 decision by the new government to include three major arms-producing companies—Aérospatiale, Snecma and Thomson-CSF—among 21 state-owned companies to be privatized, appeared as a major watershed in French defence industrial policy.[67] However, by the end of the year the implementation of this decision seemed limited and not imminent, especially since it did not include a time limit. In addition, privatization will most likely be only partial, because of the decision by President Mitterrand in 1991 allowing a maximum of 49 per cent privatization of defence contractors.[68]

The large French budget deficit was the prime motivation behind the decision: the government needed the revenue and the companies needed access to capital markets because of insufficient government funding. The main obstacle to the process was low interest among investors, because of the possible need for recapitalization and the uncertain future of the sector. In November, following the recommendations of the parliamentary defence committee, the Government presented a plan to inject new capital into major arms-producing companies, including Aérospatiale, GIAT Industries and Snecma.[69] Snecma was the first beneficiary, with a FF 750 million subsidy,[70] and Aérospatiale was next with a FF 2 billion capital allocation.[71]

International co-operation

Although French companies have benefited from a sole-source contract system in national procurement, they face hard competition on foreign markets. Therefore, it is French policy to promote a strong European arms industry through collaboration. This involves the difficult dilemma for the French Government of having to choose between maintaining the independence of France's defence industrial base or engaging in European collaboration, at the cost of losing its current tight control over arms production and protection of its technological know-how. The latter alternative is seen as unavoidable by some French observers. A recent study by the Commissariat Géneral du Plan, a special advisory body to the Prime Minister, recommends that France's

---

[65] *Le Monde*, 17 Sep. 1993, p. 17; and Response in Parliament of Defence Minister François Léotard (note 62), p. 5718.

[66] Rapport fait au nom de la commission des finances, de l'économie générale et du plan sur le projet de loi de finances pour 1994 par M. Philippe Auberger, Assemblée Nationale, N° 580, 7 Oct. 1993, p. 61.

[67] *Le Monde*, 28 June 1993, p. 17. These three are among 21 state-owned companies to be sold.

[68] OTA (note 57), p. 20.

[69] Response in Parliament of Defence Minister François Léotard (note 62), p. 57. See also 'EC must probe $136 m hand-out for SNECMA', *Jane's Defence Weekly*, 10 July 1993, p. 6; and 'Paris moves to boost defence industry', *Interavia Air Letter*, 18 Nov. 1993, p. 4.

[70] *Aviation Week & Space Technology*, 4 Oct. 1993, p. 19.

[71] *Le Monde*, 4 Feb. 1994, p. 15.

policy of 'independence in armaments' should be reconsidered and arms procurement be opened to its European partners.[72] The new government has declared its commitment to industrial co-operation, ventures and mergers with European partners for next generation programmes, which are expected to be too expensive for individual national budgets. The privatization plan announced in 1993 allows for a greater share of foreign ownership from European Community (EC) countries than the previous limit of 20 per cent of company shares.[73] This may facilitate cross-ownership with foreign companies, but it is unlikely that foreign interests will be allowed to obtain control of a French arms-producing firm. It is the position of the defence committee that French national interests must be protected and that the risk of foreign financial control of defence-related companies cannot be accepted.[74]

Support to affected areas

France has several, although small, programmes to support areas and workers affected by cuts in arms production. In 1991 the Ministry of Defence created the Delegation for Restructuring (DAR),[75] with the task of supporting affected areas.[76] Together with regional authorities, the DAR manages the Fund for Defence Restructuring (FRED).[77] The FRED supplies investment aid both for the strengthening of existing small- and medium-sized firms and industries, and for the establishment of new enterprises in these areas. Although this special government effort to promote conversion was generally received positively, its potential effect on employment has been questioned, not least because of its financial limitations.[78]

In 1993 a new fund called *Accompagnement structurel des industries de défense* (ASTRID) was created by the DGA to help small and medium-sized sub-contractors in the defence sector. The almost 5000 companies on the sub-contractor level, where competition is hard in contrast to prime contractor conditions, have suffered severely during recent years.[79] ASTRID is a venture-capital fund with a capital of about FF700 million. Unlike FRED it is disconnected from the traditional military budget.[80] DGA exerts influence on the allocation of ASTRID funds in providing the technical and financial evaluation of the applicant firm's creation, development or restructuring.

---

[72] Commissariat du Plan, *L'avenir des industries liées à la défense* (Documentation Française: Paris, Dec. 1993); see e.g. pp. 59–63. The need for international integration and collaboration of the French arms industry is described in Serfati (note 56).

[73] 'France to privatize aerospace firms', *Aviation Week & Space Technology*, 31 May 1993, p. 17; 'French privatization may open industry's doors', *Defense News*, 31 May–6 June, 1993 p. 3; 'French privatization gives lift to aerospace industry', *World Aerospace & Defense Intelligence*, 18 June 1993, pp. 3–4.

[74] 'Privatization plan faces criticism', *Aviation Week & Space Technology*, 26 July 1993, p. 28.

[75] DAR stands for Délégation aux restructurations.

[76] Commissariat Général du Plan (note 72), p. 213.

[77] FRED stands for Fonds pour les restructurations de la défense. *L'avenir* (note 76), p. 213.

[78] The FRED received an original allocation of FF 100 m., increased to FF 240 m. in 1993.

[79] Response in Parliament of Defence Minister François Léotard (note 62), pp. 5723–24.

[80] *La Tribune Desfossés*, 22 June 1993.

The United States

US policy towards its defence industrial base has undergone a strong reorientation during the Clinton Administration. From a previous strong reliance on market forces, government intervention has become perceived as crucial for the adjustment of the arms industry to significantly lower levels of production.

The challenges to the US arms industry and policy makers were identified in a series of studies by the Office of Technology Assessment in the early 1990s.[81] The Bush Administration responded to these challenges with a new weapon acquisition policy that emphasized two basic elements: (a) the upgrading of existing systems rather than the initiation of new ones, and (b) a shift in expenditures from production towards military R&D.

The Clinton Administration defence industrial policy consists mainly of three proposed initiatives: first to help create high-skill jobs in non-military and dual-use technology areas; second to promote economic growth while preserving a strong defence technology and industrial base; and third to implement procurement reforms and to reduce the cost to arms-producing companies of government contracts.[82] Measures to ease the transition and to support especially affected regions, communities, firms and labour have been decided on the basis of the recommendations of a comprehensive study by the Defense Conversion Commission appointed by the Department of Defense (DOD) in 1992.[83]

The basic task is to shift US national priorities from a focus on national security to a focus on competitiveness of industry.[84] The strategy for achieving this (sustaining an industrial base with greatly reduced arms production and limited R&D financing) is based on integration of the military and commercial sectors. Three important measures of this strategy are: (a) greater freedom for defence companies to use their independent R&D work for dual-use purposes; (b) changes in the DOD approach to militarily unique specifications, contract procedures and security requirements; and (c) a focus of DOD R&D efforts on dual-use technologies (for both military and commercial use).[85]

---

[81] US Congress, Office of Technology Assessment, *Adjusting to a New Security Environment: The Defense Technology and Industrial Base Challenge*, Background Paper, OTA-BP-ISC-79 (US Government Printing Office: Washington, DC, Feb. 1991).

[82] Described by Pagliano, G. J., 'Defense industrial base issues', *Defense Policy: Major Issues in 1993*, Congressional Research Service, Washington, DC, 25 May 1993, pp. 51–53.

[83] *Adjusting to the Drawdown*, Report of the Defence Conversion Commission, Department of Defence, Washington, DC, 31 Dec. 1992.

[84] Prabhakar, A., Director, National Institute of Standards and Technology (NIST), Statement in hearings before the US House of Representatives, Subcommitte on Technology, Environment and Aviation, Committee on Science, Space and Technology, *Defense Conversion Initiatives: Progress and Plans*, 20 July 1993, p. 9.

[85] Denman, G. L., Director, Advanced Research Projects Agency (ARPA, previously DARPA), Statement in *Defense Conversion Initiatives: Progress and Plans* (note 84), pp. 19–20.

Table 13.7. The US arms industry: expenditures, deliveries and employment, 1983–92

1983	1984	1985	1986	1987	1988	1989	1990	1991	1992
1. DOD procurement expenditures (Outlays, FY, US $b., current prices):									
53.6	61.9	70.4	76.5	80.7	77.2	81.6	81.0	82.0	74.9
2. Foreign Military Sales (FMS) deliveries (US $b., current prices):									
10.6	8.2	7.5	7.2	10.9	8.8	6.9	7.4	8.8	9.7
2a. FMS and commercial deliveries (US $b., current prices):									
11.6	10.6	11.1	9.2	14.3	14.8	11.2	10.1	9.7	..
3. Employment in the arms industry (thousands):									
2 530	2 785	3 100	3 315	3 365	3 310	3 295	3 150	2 900	..

Note: Procurement expenditures do not include all domestic purchases of military equipment, some are financed through the account for operations and maintenance; the US definitions of FMS and Commercial Sales of military equipment cover more than the equipment, in particular, a significant share of exports are services.

Sources: 1. Budget of the US Government Fiscal Year 1994 and Supplement for Fiscal Year 1993 (Office of Management and Budget: Washington, DC, 1993); *2. Foreign Military Sales, Foreign Military Construction Sales and Military Assistance Facts as of 30 Sep. 1992*, DOD, Security Assistance Agency; 2a. Center for Defense Information, 'International arms sales: Race to disaster', *The Defense Monitor*, vol. 22, no. 9 (1993), p. 2; 3. OTA, *After the Cold War: Living with Lower Defense Spending* (US Government Printing Office: Washington, DC, Feb. 1992), p. 61.

Background

The US budget for arms procurement has decreased from $97 billion in fiscal year (FY) 1985 to $46 billion for FY1994 (approved budget authority, in current prices).[86] The planned reductions for the next five-year period are even greater: a reduction of 16 per cent (in real terms) in total military expenditures for the period FY1994–98, a large part of which is likely to fall on procurement.[87]

The impact of these reductions in US arms production on defence-related industrial employment are significant. Cuts decided already in 1991 were estimated to result in a loss of 1.3–1.4 million jobs in the industry over the period 1991–2001, including about 350 000 in 1993.[88]

Defence exports account for 10–15 per cent of DOD procurement[89]—and arms exports probably considerably less of total US arms sales (see note to table 13.7).

[86] See chapter 12 in this volume, table 12.8; see also 'Hill follows Clinton's lead but worries about pace', *Congressional Quarterly*, 4 Dec. 1993, p. 3314.
[87] See chapter 12 in this volume, tables 12.7 and 12.8.
[88] US Congress, Office of Technology Assessment, *After the Cold War: Living with Lower Defense Spending* (US Government Printing Office: Washington, DC, Feb. 1992), p. 19.
[89] *Adjusting to the Drawdown*, 1992 (note 83), p. 35.

Research and development policy (The New Technology Plan)

In February 1993 President Clinton presented a technology investment plan, *Technology for America's Economic Growth: A New Direction to Build Economic Strength*, with the objective of strengthening US competitiveness in global civil markets through accelerated development of key technologies, and including nearly $12.5 billion for targeted technology projects through 1998. The report formulates a national technology policy with a new approach to industrial technology development. The previous policy to rely on federal investments in basic science and military and space R&D to disseminate into civilian industry, is to be replaced by a policy emphasizing commercially relevant R&D and co-operative strategies for federal and industry technology requirements with the purpose of stimulating strategic R&D and economic growth.[90]

The new policy involves a significant shift in the ratio between civil and military R&D—from the 40 : 60 ratio existing up to 1993 to a civilian share exceeding 50 per cent by 1998, although expenditures on military R&D are also increasing. The FY1994 budget proposal included a total of $72 billion for federal R&D expenditures (excluding R&D facilities), an increase of 3 per cent. The civilian share was $30 billion, a 5 per cent increase over FY1993, while military R&D increased by 1 per cent to $42 billion.[91]

Two important mechanisms to implement the plan are, first, to promote dual-use of DOD-financed science and technology,[92] and, second, to promote domestic technology transfer: to ease restrictions on inter-firm co-operation in production, and to encourage joint ventures between DOD laboratories and private companies.[93] Common manufacturing processes and production lines are a critical part of the strategy to integrate the defence industrial base with the civilian base.

The Technology Reinvestment Programme (TRP) is one of the main vehicles for the implementation of this dual-use investment strategy (see below).

Procurement planning

Defence industrial concerns also play a role in decisions on the weapon procurement programme. In the September 1993 Bottom-Up Review, the DOD blueprint for the future force structure required to win 'two nearly simultaneous major regional conflicts' and have spare capacity elsewhere, was pre-

---

[90] US policy issues and options in the field of military R&D are described in Arnett, E. and Kokoski, R., 'Military technology and international security: the case of the USA', SIPRI 1993 (note 20), chapter 8. For a description of Clinton's R&D policy, see also Shapley, D., 'Clintonizing science policy', *Bulletin of the Atomic Scientists*, vol. 49, no. 10 (Dec. 1993), pp. 39–43.

[91] 'Federal R&D expenditures', *Budget of the United States Government Fiscal Year 1994* (OMB: Washington, DC, Apr. 1993), pp. 43–44. The R&D budget approved by Congress for the DOD only was $35 b., an 11% decrease over FY 1993 (see table 12.8 in this volume).

[92] Denman (note 85), p. 16.

[93] 'Clinton Administration signals strong scientific thrusts for industrial vigor', *Signal*, Mar. 1993, p. 11; and 'Clinton offers US technology plan', *Aviation Week & Space Technology*, 1 Mar. 1993, p. 18.

sented by Defense Secretary Les Aspin. He explained that this review gave much greater weight to industrial base issues than previous reviews of US force modernization requirements. Thus, in addition to issues of force structure and modernization needs, one of the procurement policy objectives of the DOD is to sustain the defence industrial base in critical and defence-unique areas. Decisions to preserve the industrial bases for submarines, aircraft-carriers and armoured vehicles, for example, may therefore lead to a higher number of these systems than warranted by modernization requirements for the planning period.[94]

Weapons acquisition reform

The need to introduce commercial business practices in DOD acquisitions has long been recognized through a series of studies with recommendations on the acquisition problems, but few firm decisions have been made over the years. Many of the acquisition reforms decided in 1986 as a result of the recommendations by the Packard Commission were never implemented. In 1993 Congress and the DOD came far along the way towards streamlining the system for DOD acquisitions.[95] Both DOD proposals and congressional initiatives on this issue were based on a series of proposals presented in January 1993 by the Advisory Panel on Streamlining Acquisition Laws, the so-called Section 800 Commission.[96] The purpose of these proposals was to encourage the integration of the military and commercial industrial sectors. Another objective was to reduce overhead costs, which currently account for 30–40 per cent of military programmes, compared to an average of 10 per cent in commercial projects.[97] Any substantial progress in implementing radical acquisition reform is likely to take time, because of the widespread resistance to this type of measure.[98]

International co-operation policy

In late 1993 the Department of Defense proposed an expansion in US participation in co-operative research and development projects with NATO countries and Japan. This would mean a revitalization of the so-called Nunn programme for armaments R&D co-operation established by Congress in 1985, which never became as extensive as expected. Congress has been unwilling to

[94] 'Saving industrial base key in bottom-up review', *Aviation Week & Space Technology*, 6 Sep. 1993, p. 24. See also 'Aspin sets stage for defence switch', *Financial Times*, 2 Sep. 1993, p. 5.
[95] See, for example, 'US acts to streamline defense acquisition', *Aviation Week & Space Technology*, 1 Nov. 1993, pp. 28–29.
[96] Section 800 is that part of the Defense Authorization Act for FY1991 that created this nine-member panel.
[97] According to the then Deputy Defense Secretary William Perry, in 'Pentagon begins the latest acquisition reform battle', *Jane's Defence Weekly*, 10 July 1993, p. 19.
[98] At least four years according to then Deputy Defense Secretary William Perry; see 'Once again, reformers tilt at acquisition dragon', *Defense News*, 22–28 Nov. 1993, p. 44.

appropriate funds for this programme, and in 1993 cut the proposed FY1994 budget for this co-operation programme from $58 million to $42 million.[99]

Support to affected areas (Defence Conversion and Reinvestment)

In March 1993 President Clinton announced a plan for Defence Conversion and Reinvestment. It is a five-year plan (for the period FY1993–97) involving federal expenditures of about $20 billion (including $1.8 billion for FY 1993) to ease the difficulties of military expenditure cuts on communities, workers and servicemen. It is a mixed programme covering worker training and adjustment assistance, aid to hard-hit communities, assistance for industries to develop technologies with dual military and commercial applications, and assistance to arms-producing firms to convert to the production of civilian technologies. By the year FY 1997 the mix in allocations will be about 22 per cent of the total to assistance to displaced workers and hard-hit communities and 78 per cent to technology and conversion funding.[100]

The TRP is a funding programme, managed by the DOD Advanced Research Projects Agency (ARPA),[101] from which companies can seek awards for dual-use technology development and application. The 1994 programme of $474 million received a total of 2850 applications for awards amounting to a total sum of $8.5 billion from 12 000 companies, universities, state and local governments, and federal research laboratories.[102]

V. The trade in major conventional weapons

As noted in the introduction, the downward trend in deliveries of major conventional weapons reported in recent *SIPRI Yearbooks* appears to have stabilized.

The data recorded in this *Yearbook* are the first to take advantage of the information available in the United Nations Register of Conventional Arms. The UN Register has permitted some improvements in the quality of SIPRI data.[103] One of the difficulties faced in compiling SIPRI data is the problem of establishing an accurate delivery schedule in cases where the overall scale of a given programme is known. The availability of the UN Register has made it possible to establish with greater accuracy delivery schedules for many systems in the years 1991, 1992 and 1993.

The leading suppliers and recipients of major conventional weapons in the period 1989–93 are listed in tables 13.8 and 13.9, respectively. The United

---

[99] 'Pentagon to revitalize the NATO-Nunn programme', *Jane's Defence Weekly*, 4 Dec. 1993, pp. 19–20.

[100] Knight, E., 'Defense Economic Adjustment and Conversion programs', *Defense Policy: Major Issues in 1993* (Congressional Research Service: Washington, DC, 25 May 1993), p. 56.

[101] Formerly DARPA.

[102] 'Clinton funds 55 more proposals under TRP', *Defense News*, 29 Nov.–5 Dec. 1993, p. 26.

[103] Serious problems in making use of the data in the UN Register stem from the lack of comparability between export and import returns submitted by governments and the failure of many returns to disaggregate equipment within the seven Register categories.

States remained the dominant supplier of major conventional weapons although the total volume of US supplies decreased from the level recorded for 1992. The USA increased the volume of deliveries to Turkey, Taiwan, Australia, Spain and Saudi Arabia. This was outweighed by the lower volume of deliveries to Greece, the United Kingdom, Israel and Japan.

The other country for which a significant reduction in the volume of foreign deliveries has been recorded over the past two years is China as programmes with Bangladesh and Thailand have come to an end. Towards the end of 1993 there were reports of an agreement between China and Myanmar including naval patrol craft and up to 250 armoured vehicles. China seems likely to continue to find customers for certain types of equipment and to be a factor in the international arms market.

Several countries have recorded significant recent increases in the volume of supplies. The largest increases were recorded for Russia, which reflects the implementation of programmes with India. Some of these are long-standing naval programmes. However, during the visit of President Yeltsin to New Delhi in January 1993 Russia and India reached agreement on financing arrangements which cleared the way for further transfers of military equipment including MiG-29 fighter aircraft and other air defence systems. In 1993 Russia also delivered MiG-29 fighter aircraft to Hungary and Slovakia. These aircraft were built for the Soviet Air Force but never paid for.

Recipients which recorded the largest increases in the volume of equipment deliveries were Hungary, India and Indonesia. Hungary and India are mentioned above. Indonesia began to take delivery of the first of 39 naval vessels of various kinds from the inventory of the former German Democratic Republic. Indonesia has paid very little for these vessels, though significant costs will be associated with the construction in Indonesia of facilities needed to operate, repair and maintain the ships.

One recipient country which has shown a consistent fall in the volume of deliveries across the past five years is Japan—although it remains a significant consumer of major conventional weapons. Some high-profile programmes—notably the production of F-15 fighter aircraft by Mitsubishi Heavy Industries—are ending. Other programmes, usually involving the production of systems of US origin in Japan, have recently been slowed down.[104]

In each of the past several years SIPRI has presented the most recent data available for those countries which regularly publish arms export values. All of the data in table 13.10 are taken from official national documents. As a result there is no commonality in the definitions used to compile the data. Public statements by government officials—for France, Russia, the United Kingdom and the United States—were excluded since the basis for the statements was impossible to determine. The export values in these public statements were typically much higher than the official national data.

---

[104] Arms procurement in East Asia is discussed further in appendix 13E.

Table 13.8. The leading suppliers of major conventional weapons, 1989–93

The countries are ranked according to 1989–93 aggregate exports. Figures are trend-indicator values expressed in US $m., at constant (1990) prices. Totals are rounded.

Suppliers		1989	1990	1991	1992	1993	1989–93
To the industrialized world							
1	USA	7 817	6 291	7 554	7 182	5 727	34 570
2	USSR/Russia	4 033	3 108	461	223	1 201	9 026
3	Germany, FR	643	776	1 981	1 671	867	5 937
4	France	788	380	97	665	578	2 508
5	UK	687	261	71	191	390	1 600
6	Czechoslovakia[a]	499	583	0	0	0	1 082
7	Switzerland	113	157	341	307	72	990
8	Netherlands	69	120	268	284	227	967
9	Italy	70	47	191	256	327	891
10	German DR	367	245	0	0	0	612
11	Sweden	142	101	65	120	46	473
12	Spain	312	6	31	43	30	422
13	Poland	116	152	36	0	0	303
14	Israel	100	54	61	27	0	242
15	Norway	92	6	43	75	0	217
	Others	371	119	42	92	85	710
	Total	**16 218**	**12 407**	**11 242**	**11 135**	**9 550**	**60 552**
To the developing world							
1	USSR/Russia	10 496	6 798	2 728	3 042	3 331	26 396
2	USA	3 549	4 530	4 568	4 607	4 799	22 054
3	China	945	1 351	1 882	1 074	427	5 678
4	France	2 000	1 784	728	376	367	5 256
5	UK	1 853	1 181	623	719	580	4 956
6	Germany, FR	310	852	430	197	966	2 755
7	Czechoslovakia[a]	225	85	74	270	482	1 137
8	Netherlands	420	173	204	110	72	978
9	Israel	241	149	151	117	232	891
10	Korea, North	0	0	138	86	420	644
11	Yugoslavia	0	60	533	21	0	615
12	Italy	139	171	107	103	42	563
13	Ukraine	0	0	0	400	46	446
14	Sweden	233	117	42	2	38	432
15	Spain	254	81	30	26	12	403
	Others	731	594	411	520	611	2 867
	Total	**21 397**	**17 925**	**12 650**	**11 671**	**12 425**	**76 068**
To all countries							
1	USA	11 366	10 821	12 122	11 789	10 526	56 624
2	USSR/Russia	14 529	9 907	3 189	3 265	4 532	35 422
3	Germany, FR	953	1 627	2 410	1 868	1 833	8 692
4	France	2 788	2 164	825	1 041	945	7 763
5	UK	2 541	1 442	694	910	969	6 556
6	China	1 009	1 351	1 882	1 074	427	5 742
7	Czechoslovakia[a]	724	669	74	270	482	2 219
8	Netherlands	489	293	471	393	299	1 945
9	Italy	208	218	299	359	369	1 454
10	Israel	341	203	212	144	232	1 133
11	Switzerland	137	192	369	335	72	1 105
12	Sweden	375	219	107	122	83	905
13	Spain	566	87	61	68	43	825
14	German DR	510	245	0	0	0	755
15	Korea, North	0	0	138	86	420	644
	Others	1 079	896	1 037	1 082	742	4 836
	Total	**37 616**	**30 332**	**23 891**	**22 806**	**21 975**	**136 620**

Source: SIPRI arms trade data base.

[a] For the years 1989–92 the data refer to the former Czechoslovakia; for 1993 the data refer to the Czech Republic only.

Table 13.9. The leading recipients of major conventional weapons, 1989–93

The countries are ranked according to 1989–93 aggregate imports. Figures are trend-indicator values expressed in US $m., at constant (1990) prices. Totals are rounded.

Recipients		1989	1990	1991	1992	1993	1989–93
1	India	4 368	1 488	1 325	1 151	2 146	10 478
2	Japan	2 637	1 734	1 496	1 384	1 006	8 256
3	Saudi Arabia	1 974	2 607	1 002	1 131	1 324	8 039
4	Turkey	1 183	889	887	2 245	2 525	7 729
5	Greece	1 470	1 174	890	2 309	414	6 257
6	Afghanistan	2 622	2 414	1 215	0	0	6 251
7	Germany, FR	1 190	1 361	1 283	566	583	4 983
8	Egypt	214	1 168	775	976	1 481	4 614
9	Pakistan	753	1 038	1 080	210	491	3 571
10	China	70	237	246	2 073	802	3 427
11	Israel	209	28	1 359	1 062	474	3 132
12	Korea, South	1 113	546	304	395	513	2 870
13	Thailand	504	419	794	790	268	2 775
14	Taiwan	247	503	828	400	754	2 732
15	Iran	371	853	260	230	867	2 582
16	Australia	713	437	253	401	700	2 505
17	United Arab Emirates	774	936	127	155	499	2 491
18	Spain	805	780	111	243	462	2 400
19	UK	117	103	901	1 112	148	2 380
20	Czechoslovakia[a]	1 492	835	47	4	0	2 378
21	Kuwait	61	273	608	793	573	2 308
22	Canada	159	203	989	501	324	2 176
23	USA	547	119	332	572	415	1 986
24	Iraq	1 438	507	0	0	0	1 945
25	USSR/Russia	1 016	891	36	0	0	1 942
26	Poland	1 263	334	143	0	2	1 742
27	Korea, North	1 066	636	15	24	0	1 742
28	France	169	45	981	384	149	1 726
29	Indonesia	206	187	236	71	858	1 558
30	Portugal	38	101	1 103	3	292	1 537
31	Netherlands	616	191	321	123	200	1 451
32	German DR	683	649	0	0	0	1 332
33	Norway	347	313	239	182	111	1 193
34	Hungary	36	36	29	0	1 071	1 171
35	Syria	395	28	138	341	243	1 145
36	Bulgaria	87	624	398	12	0	1 121
37	Switzerland	191	317	236	286	84	1 113
38	Finland	83	100	59	298	528	1 069
39	Singapore	72	389	319	66	172	1 017
40	Bangladesh	401	161	126	258	0	945
41	Chile	167	214	92	242	179	894
42	Romania	105	659	38	46	43	891
43	Angola	92	748	0	0	4	844
44	Brazil	588	157	25	27	41	839
45	Algeria	637	40	81	37	20	815
46	Belgium	198	206	208	70	93	776
47	Italy	194	108	134	82	120	637
48	Bahrain	82	394	44	64	32	616
49	Libya	589	0	0	0	0	589
50	Myanmar	20	96	336	48	70	569
	Others	3 243	2 057	1 444	1 439	894	9 077
	Total	**37 616**	**30 332**	**23 891**	**22 806**	**21 975**	**136 620**

Source: SIPRI arms trade data base.

[a] For the years 1989–92 the data refer to the former Czechoslovakia; for 1993 the data refer to the Czech Republic only

Table 13.10. Official arms export data, 1991–92

Country	Year	Value	Comments
Canada	1992	C$361.9 m.	Value of export permits for military goods
France	1992	FF 29 b.	Value of deliveries of defence materiel
Germany	1991	DM 4.13 b.	Export of Weapons of War
	1992	DM 2.64 b.	Export of Weapons of War
Poland	1992	$67.3 m.	Value of exports of arms equipment, spare parts and ammunition
Sweden	1992	SEK 3360 m.	Value of export licenses for war materiel
	1992	SEK 2753 m.	Value of exports of military equipment
Switzerland	1992	SF 259 m.	Value of exports of military materiel
United Kingdom	1992	£1.5 b.	Value of defence equipment which passed the UK customs barrier
United States	1992	$14.9 b.	Value of Foreign Military Sales accepted in Fiscal Year 1992
	1992	$9.7 b.	Value of FMS deliveries in Fiscal Year 1992
	1992	$2.3 b.	Value of commercial exports licensed in Fiscal Year 1992

Notes: Comments in the table are worded as closely as possible to the details given in the source documents.

VI. The first year of the UN Register of Conventional Arms

In 1993 government reports for calendar year 1992 on the transfer of major conventional weapons, in seven categories, were submitted to the United Nations in compliance with General Assembly Resolution 46/36 L (1991) and the report of the UN Secretary-General (1992).[105]

Of the UN member states and observer states invited,[106] 83 governments responded to the Secretary-General's request. Most of the countries which failed to respond probably did not conduct any trade in the seven categories identified by the UN as subject to reporting. However, key groups of arms importers did not report—particularly governments in the Middle East and Asia, although some significant importers—notably Egypt and Israel—did report.

The results of the UN Register confirmed the findings about the trade in major conventional weapons reported in the *SIPRI Yearbook 1993*. Partly as a result of the NATO 'cascade' of arms transfers following the 1990 CFE

---

[105] The background to the establishment of the UN Register was reported in Anthony, I., *et al.*, 'The trade in major conventional weapons', SIPRI, *SIPRI Yearbook 1992: World Armaments and Disarmament* (Oxford University Press: Oxford, 1992), chapter 8 and in SIPRI 1993 (note 20), appendix 10F. The first year of reports to the Register are analysed in Laurance, E. J., Wezeman, S. T. and Wulf, H., *Arms Watch: SIPRI Report on the First Year of the UN Register of Conventional Arms*, SIPRI Research Report no. 6 (Oxford University Press: Oxford, 1993).

[106] The Secretary-General's request was sent to 186 countries: all the UN member states (184 as of Aug. 1993) and two observer states (the Holy See [Vatican City] and Switzerland). Taiwan, a major arms-importing country but not a UN member state, was not asked to report to the UN Register.

Treaty,[107] Greece and Turkey emerged as the major importers of major conventional weapons. The USA held the dominant position as a supplier of conventional weapons and was the major exporter in several of the seven weapon categories. Germany was the second most important supplier, with deliveries in each of the seven weapon categories.

Some information on arms transfers that had not previously been publicly known was contained in the returns to the Register—most of it referring to land systems. Examples include the transfer of artillery by Italy to Nigeria; of armour and artillery by Romania to Moldova; of artillery by China to Iran; and of artillery by France to Saudi Arabia.

Some publicly known arms transfers were *not* reported by countries participating in the UN Register. A 'grey area' of systems has been created by broad definitions for attack helicopters and combat aircraft used in the Register. As a result, some countries chose not to report systems that, according to public information, do meet the UN Register definitions. Examples include: the transfer of trainer aircraft to Thailand from Switzerland; of trainer aircraft to Colombia from Brazil; of trainer aircraft to Egypt from Czechoslovakia; and of US helicopters to the Philippines.

Some transfers of major conventional weapons which clearly meet the parameters of the Register and which were widely discussed in public sources in 1992 were not reported to the UN. There is no way of verifying these public reports. The most prominent cases were deliveries of surface-to-surface missiles from China to Pakistan and deliveries of Russian combat aircraft to Iran. China, Pakistan and Russia all responded to the request of the Secretary-General but Iran did not.

In most cases, suppliers and recipients did not co-ordinate their returns to the Register. Only 51 of the 192 entries submitted by suppliers and recipients applying to the same transfer matched. In a cross-check of the UN Register (a comparison of the entries of exporters and importers), 126 entries (or 66 per cent) could not be verified since one of the parties did not participate in the UN Register or did not report the particular transfers; 17 entries gave conflicting information on the number of items reported; and 51 entries matched.

Making a cross-check on the items transferred rather than the entries, of the reported items 90 per cent of the tanks, 32 per cent of the armoured combat vehicles, 48 per cent of the large-calibre artillery, 67 per cent of the combat aircraft, 43 per cent of the attack helicopters, 15 per cent of the warships and 13 per cent of the missiles and missile launchers could be verified. The lack of confirmed information on arms transfers is partly the result of non-reporting. However, differences also occur because of different procedural approaches taken by the various governments in defining precise weapon categories, delivery dates or ownership.

---

[107] The CFE Treaty ceiling on certain weapon categories has led to a 'cascade' within NATO: weapons that exceed the numerical ceilings for Germany, the Netherlands and the United States are being transferred to other NATO countries which in turn have agreed to destroy older equipment. The cascade has been described in successive SIPRI *Yearbooks*.

VII. Arms transfer control discussions in 1993

The discussion of arms transfer controls continued in 1993 in several multilateral forums. In NATO a draft code of conduct on weapons acquisition procedures has been in preparation for more than a year. However, while final agreement seemed close in December 1993, in the end no document could be signed before the end of the year. Similarly, within the European Union the Commission has been working on a draft regulation on dual-use export controls for a considerable period. For more than a year the document in circulation has been referred to as a final draft. However, no formal agreement had been reached by the end of 1993.

National decisions that altered export regulations were made in 1993 by a range of countries including Belgium, Bulgaria, Canada, the Czech Republic, Japan, Poland, Russia, Sweden, the UK and the USA.[108]

Multilateral discussions

In multilateral discussions the most important developments in 1993 took place in the Conference on Security and Co-operation in Europe (CSCE), the Co-ordinating Committee on Multilateral Export Controls (COCOM) and the Missile Technology Control Regime (MTCR). In November 1993 the members of the MTCR met in Switzerland and decided to take a more active approach to preventing missile transfers by states not members of the regime.[109] The most far-reaching changes in 1993 came with the dissolution of COCOM.

COCOM

Following the significant revisions made in the COCOM Industrial List beginning in 1990 it had been widely predicted that the embargo on transfers to countries in Central and Eastern Europe would be lifted by the participating governments. However, the general assumption was that the process would be gradual. Target countries would be removed from embargo on a 'case-by-case' basis as they demonstrated their capacity to operate effective national export regulations.[110] The COCOM Co-operation Forum was the mechanism by which this phased transition would occur. Hungary was removed from the list of countries under embargo in 1992 while the Baltic states, Poland, the Czech Republic and Slovakia were candidates for such a decision in 1993.

---

[108] Section VII discusses identified changes in national export regulations. It is not necessarily comprehensive.

[109] Recent developments in the MTCR are discussed in the *SIPRI Yearbook 1993* (note 20) and developments in the CSCE are discussed in chapter 14 of this volume.

[110] See, for example, Cupitt, R. T., 'The future of COCOM', eds G. K. Bertsch and S. Elliott Gower, *Export Controls in Transition: Perspectives, Problems and Prospects* (Duke University Press: Durham, N.C., 1992). However, by 1993 several key states of the former Soviet Union had not demonstrated any such national capacities; see Bertsch, G. K. and Cupitt, R. T., 'Nonproliferation in the 1990s: Enhancing international co-operation on export controls', *Washington Quarterly*, vol. 16, no. 4 (autumn 1993), pp. 53–70.

More preliminary discussions were underway with Bulgaria and Romania, both of which are in the process of revising their export control systems.[111] Similar treatment for other states of the former USSR, including Belarus, Russia and Ukraine, was believed to be further in the future.

Consequently it came as something of a surprise when, at a high-level meeting in the Netherlands on 16 November 1993 the representatives of the participating governments agreed that COCOM should be terminated in its existing form as quickly as possible but no later than 31 March 1994.[112] The issue of the future of multilateral export controls was discussed by COCOM members at a follow-on high-level meeting in the Netherlands in January 1994. With this in mind three working groups were established to examine the modalities of a follow-on regime. The working groups were made up of COCOM members and no observer status was accorded to other states.

The primary motivation for the change came from the United States. At the January meeting the USA intended to propose a new multi-national arrangement to replace COCOM. According to Lynn Davis, US Under-secretary of State for International Security Affairs, a group of countries including the existing members, China, Russia, Sweden and Switzerland will be invited to discuss a new body formed to control the transfer of arms and technology with military applications to a new target grouping. According to Davis 'Iran, Iraq, North Korea and Libya are on our minds as we put together a new regime'.[113] However, at the time of writing no public information was available about the outcome of the January meeting.

National discussions

In *Belgium* the regulations governing arms exports were revised in 1993 when, on 6 April 1993, regulations based on a new Royal decree came into force.[114] The new regulations deal with controlled items detailed in two categories in an annexe to the decree. These are category A, chemical and biological agents, and category B, conventional military equipment and munitions. The regulations do not apply to nuclear materials which are regulated in separate legislation. The new regulation includes a detailed description of the licensing process.

In *Bulgaria* the government announced a new export-licensing policy on 3 February 1994. Four state-trading firms—Arminex, Elmed Engineering, Kintex and Teraton—were previously the only agencies permitted to establish contact with foreign customers. Individual producers may now sell their products direct to overseas customers subject to an export licence granted by the inter-departmental Commission on Arms Production and Trade.[115]

[111] *US Department of State Dispatch Supplement*, vol. 4, no. 3 (Aug. 1993).
[112] *Atlantic News*, 19 Nov. 1993, p. 4; *Defence Industry Digest*, Dec. 1993, p. 17.
[113] *Jane's Defence Weekly*, 27 Nov. 1993, p. 8.
[114] Arrêté royal réglementant l'importation, l'exportation et transit d'armes, de munitions et de matériel devant servir spécialement à un usage militaire et de la technologie y afférente, signed 8 Mar. 1993.
[115] *Balkan News & East European Report*, 13 Feb. 1994, p. 9.

In *Canada* the government responded in 1993 to the 1992 Bosley/McCreath report which recommended modifications in Canada's export law and practice.[116] Several of these modifications would have given parliament a role in decision making and reduced the discretion of the government in granting export licences. This would have been achieved by creating a Munitions Country Control List and giving Parliament the right to approve amendments to that list. The government refused all 20 recommendations presented in the report.[117]

In the *Czech Republic* the basic structure of export regulations was inherited from the former Czechoslovakia. However, the licensing authority is now an office within the Ministry of Industry and Trade (previously it was within the Federal Ministry of Foreign Trade).

In 1992 a Decree issued by the Czechoslovakian Ministry of Foreign Trade expanded the range of controlled goods and technologies by introducing a list based on the COCOM industrial core list, a list of nuclear dual-use items and a list of chemical weapon precursors. These lists are still in use in the Czech Republic. However, in 1993 the control lists were amended further to incorporate items on the MTCR Equipment and Technology Annex.[118]

In *Japan* 1993 saw the publication of the first report of the Security Export Control Committee. This body was established in September 1992 under the Industrial Structure Council of the Ministry of International Trade and Industry. The intention in founding the Committee was to enhance the Japanese export control system. On a national basis Japan is currently reviewing controlled destinations, controlled items and licensing procedures designed with the intention of introducing a new export control system in the near term.[119] Japanese regulations already incorporate control lists associated with multilateral groupings of which Japan is a member. However, the Committee will consider whether Japan should go beyond these lists on a national basis and incorporate some of the lists and practices currently in use in the United States, Germany and the United Kingdom in new regulations.

The Security Export Control Committee was also tasked to look for contributions which Japan could make to strengthening international export control systems. In this context Japan sponsored regional discussions aimed at raising the profile of the issue of security export controls among Asian countries, particularly those which have developed significant electronic and telecommunication industries.[120]

In *Poland* as part of the wider discussion about restructuring the defence industry it was decided to try to introduce the more widespread use of com-

---

[116] *The Future of Canadian Military Goods, Production and Export*, Report of the Standing Committee on External Affairs and International Trade, House of Commons, Ottawa, Sep. 1992.

[117] Government response to the Bosley/McCreath report provided by the Canadian Embassy in Stockholm.

[118] *The Worldwide Guide to Export Controls, 1992–93* (Export Control Publications: Chertsey, Surrey, Nov. 1993).

[119] *The Future of Security Export Controls* (unofficial translation), Security Export Control Committee, Ministry of International Trade and Industry, Tokyo, 25 Mar. 1993.

[120] Burgess, L. and Usui, N., 'Japan leads quest for Asian export control', *Defense News*, 1–7 Nov. 1993, pp. 1, 36.

mercial practices in the defence industry. Producers were given greater freedom to establish independent contact with prospective foreign suppliers. Under Polish export regulations foreign transfers of controlled items must be licensed by an office of the Ministry of Foreign Economic Relations before deliveries can take place legally. However, the question arose whether all contacts and preliminary discussions with potential customers should also be reported to the licensing authority. Amendments to the export regulations to clarify which entities could legally enter into discussions with foreign customers and at what point such contacts need be reported were being discussed in 1993. Government regulation was exercised through the requirement to obtain a licence before delivering any goods. This system led to a series of scandals related to export control which caused political embarrassment both within Poland and between Poland and other countries—most notably Germany and the United States.[121]

In *Russia* an Export Control Commission was created by Presidential decrees in early 1992. On 4 March 1993 the Export Control Commission held its first meeting.[122] At the end of 1993 export regulations were still based on Presidential decrees rather than a law. In 1993 an inter-agency group led by representatives of the Ministry of Foreign Affairs was drawing up a draft basic law on import and export regulation.[123] In parallel, a parliamentary group drawn from four permanent committees—on Industry and Energy; International Affairs; Defence and Security; and Budget, Taxation and Pricing—has been drafting an export control law for more than 18 months but it had not been presented to Parliament before the dissolution of the legislature on 21 September 1993.

In 1993 it was necessary to modify the export control procedures to limit the number of Russian business entities licensed to carry out foreign sales of controlled goods. In the original apparatus established in May 1992 foreign trade corporations (including the producers themselves) were permitted to initiate independent contacts with prospective foreign customers. However, this led to a series of cases in which the foreign contacts established by some producers and dealers were politically embarrassing for the Russian Government. In other cases several producers and dealers were trying to manage the same transaction simultaneously and without co-ordination.[124] As a result the government limited the number of business entities licensed to initiate foreign contacts to three government-owned agencies—Oboronexport, Spetsvneshtekhnika and the GUSK—and Promexport, an organ of the State Committee on Defence Industries.

---

[121] The background to several of these scandals is outlined in Sabbat-Swidlicka, A., 'Poland's arms trade faces new conditions', *RFE/RL Research Report*, vol. 2, no. 6 (5 Feb. 1993), pp. 49–53.

[122] Khripunov, I., 'Non-proliferation export controls in the Former Soviet Union', ed. K. C. Bailey, *The Director's Series on Proliferation* (Lawrence Livermore National Laboratory: University of California, 7 June 1993), p. 13.

[123] Kortunov, S., 'The Russian perspective', eds K. Peabody O'Brien and H. Cato, *The Arms Trade in a Transitional Economy*, a Global Outlook Conference Report (Global Outlook: Palo Alto, Calif., Oct. 1993).

[124] 'Russian defence sales: The insider's view', *Military Technology*, Dec. 1993, pp. 40–57.

Although they increasingly market their activities in the commercial press each of these agencies was initially subordinate to the Main Directorate for Military-Technical Co-operation within the Ministry for Foreign Economic Relations and each has a direct line of descent from the bureaucratic structure of the former USSR. Oboronexport was formerly the General Engineering Department in the Soviet Ministry of Foreign Economic Relations; Spetsvneshtekhnika was formerly the General Technical Department and GUSK was the General Co-operation Department.[125] In November President Yeltsin further modified the management of arms exports by placing all three bodies under the overall control of a single body, the Rosvooruzhenie.[126]

In 1993 the Russian Government added two new lists of controlled items to the licensing procedure: dual-use equipment and appropriate technologies applied for nuclear purposes and a list of equipment, materials and technologies used for missile production.[127]

In *Sweden* several decisions were taken on new recipient countries for Swedish military equipment during the first year of implementation of new arms export regulations.[128] In most cases the decisions related to exports of 'other military equipment'—military equipment without a direct destructive impact. There is a presumption to approve export licences unless a recipient country is (a) involved in armed conflict with another state; (b) internal armed disturbances are taking place in the recipient country; (c) widespread and serious violations of human rights are taking place.[129] The determination of whether or not these conditions are met is ultimately made by the Minister for Foreign Trade. However, the guidance of the Inspectorate General for Military Equipment plays a key role in determining the decision outcome. Further legislation relating to export regulations is possible in the near term. In 1993 a government commission proposed a new law to regulate exports of strategically sensitive goods.[130] It expands restrictions for dual-use high technology goods from re-exports only to all exports, including domestically produced goods.

In the *United Kingdom* an independent judicial enquiry established after the collapse of a prosecution against British businessmen accused of making illegal sales to Iraq continued its deliberations. A final report was expected in

---

[125] 'Russian arms export policy detailed', *Military Technology*, Oct. 1992.

[126] FBIS-SOV-93-248, 29 Dec. 1993, p. 27; FBIS-SOV-94-018, 27 Jan. 1994, pp. 22–23; *Moscow News*, no. 5, 4–10 Feb. 1994, p. 3.

[127] Russia now operates five control lists. In addition to the two mentioned there is a munitions list; a list of raw and other materials, equipment, technologies and scientific research used for producing conventional arms; military equipment; and a list of chemicals and technologies designed for peaceful purposes but which can be used for chemical weapons production. Correspondence with Nikolai Revenko, Counsellor for Disarmament and Military Technology Control, Ministry of Foreign Affairs; 9 Nov. 1993.

[128] *Regeringens proposition med förslag till lag om krigsmateriel* [Swedish Government Bill proposal for the Military Equipment Act], Bill 1991/92:174 (Government Printer: Stockholm, 1992). The new legislation took effect from 1 Jan. 1993.

[129] *Sweden's Policy on Arms Exports*, Ministry for Foreign Affairs Information 1993:1, pp. 24–25.

[130] *Kontrollen över export av strategiskt känsliga varor* [Control of the export of strategically sensitive goods], SOU 1993:56 (Ministry for Foreign Affairs: Stockholm, 1993).

1994 although it is not clear whether changes in British national export regulations will result from its publication.

In 1993 the *United States* Administration initiated a review of arms export policy. However, recent changes in the declaratory policy and regulatory initiatives can be seen as part of a wider effort to reduce the obstacles to international sales by US companies. The US-led changes in the COCOM embargo are discussed above. The Clinton Administration has also initiated a process of 'streamlining' national export controls which is intended to reduce or eliminate overlapping competence between the Department of State and Department of Commerce in export licensing and to reduce or eliminate the duplication of equipment categories on export control lists. In particular, there is a clear intention to de-regulate exports of dual-use technology and equipment, focusing export controls more on military equipment and especially on technologies and materials considered critical to the development and production of weapons of mass destruction.[131]

The US Congress is a central actor in this process as it is required to reauthorize the Export Administration Act, the legislation which gives the Department of Commerce jurisdiction over licensing of certain types of security-sensitive exports. It is the view of several congressmen that the entire export control apparatus needs to be re-structured broadly along the lines also proposed by the President. In hearings on the problems of US export controls Representative Sam Gejdenson underlined the view that present export controls damage US economic interests while 'advances in technology have outstripped the ability to control dual use equipment. Much of what we are making is too small, too good and too commonly available for us to have any realistic expectation of keeping it out of the hands of dangerous countries.'[132]

VIII. United Nations arms embargoes

While governments have always regarded sanctions of various kinds as a useful political tool the cold war limited the occasions when mandatory UN arms embargoes could be used before Iraq invaded Kuwait in August 1990. An arms embargo is one form of sanction which can be adopted either in conjunction with broader measures or independently. This section deals only with arms embargoes.[133]

---

[131] 'White House Fact Sheet on Non-Proliferation Policy and Export Control Policy', 27 Sep. 1993, reproduced in *Arms Control Today*, Nov. 1993, pp. 27–28.

[132] *Problems of US Export Controls*, Hearings before the House of Representatives Committee on Foreign Affairs, Subcommittee on Economic Policy, Trade and Environment, 9 and 23 June 1993 (US Government Printing Office: Washington, DC, 1993).

[133] The issue of economic sanctions is discussed in chapter 1 of this volume. Recent discussions of economic sanctions also include *Serbia-Montenegro: Implementation of UN Economic Sanctions*, GAO/NSIAD-93-174 (US General Accounting Office: Washington, DC, Apr. 1993); Ngobi, J., 'Economic sanctions: limitations and improvements', *Peace Research*, vol. 25, no. 3 (Aug. 1993); Clawson, P., *How has Saddam Hussein Survived? Economic Sanctions 1990–93*, McNair Paper 22, Institute for National Strategic Studies (National Defense University, Washington, DC, Aug. 1993); *Bulletin of the Atomic Scientists*, Nov. 1993, pp. 14–49.

Table 13.11. UN Security Council resolutions mandating arms embargoes, 1977–93

Country/grouping	Security Council resolution	Date passed
South Africa	Resolution 418	4 Nov. 1977
Iraq	Resolution 661	6 Aug. 1990
	Resolution 687	3 Apr. 1991
Former Yugoslavia	Resolution 713	25 Sep. 1991
Somalia	Resolution 733	23 Jan. 1992
Libya	Resolution 748	31 Mar. 1992
Liberia	Resolution 788	19 Nov. 1992
Haiti	Resolution 841	16 June 1993
UNITA	Resolution 864	15 Sep. 1993

Note: In addition there were mandatory embargoes on Korea (1951) and Southern Rhodesia (1966).

In the new security environment arms embargoes have emerged as a diplomatic 'weapon of choice'. Since 1990 the Security Council has imposed mandatory arms embargoes on six UN member states—Iraq, the former Yugoslavia, Somalia, Libya, Liberia and Haiti—as well as one non-state grouping (the National Union for the Total Independence of Angola, UNITA). During the cold war civil wars and military coups similar to those that have occurred in Liberia and Haiti did not trigger mandatory UN sanctions. Threats to international peace and security—such as the Iraqi invasion of Iran in 1980—failed to elicit a mandatory arms embargo.

Arms embargoes are seen as a measure short of the use of force which can send a political signal and exert some coercive pressure on a target country or group. As such, they are increasingly seen as a form of peacemaking.[134] In time it is possible that specific criteria that would lead to the imposition of an arms embargo could be developed—for example, the overthrow of a democratically elected government or the movement of armed forces across a recognized international border. With a near certainty of punitive sanctions such criteria might have a preventive or deterrent function. However, 'hard' criteria might simply reduce the probability of issues being raised at the UN.

Multilateral co-operation in harmonizing and enforcing export regulations is a process in its infancy and, not surprisingly, there has been a great deal of 'learning by doing'. It will be important for the UN, all four European regional bodies and national governments to evaluate and absorb the lessons learned from the process. There are political and economic costs in interrupting international trade in pursuit of political objectives. If the use of sanctions, including arms embargoes, is to be supported by the international community then both their probable effectiveness and their probable success need to be considered before they are imposed. Six questions should be addressed:

---

[134] The developing roles of peacekeeping, peacemaking and peace enforcement are discussed in chapter 1.

1. What is the purpose of the embargo?

2. What enforcement mechanisms exist or can realistically be created to ensure its effectiveness?

3. What is the level of willingness within the international community to support the embargo?

4. How is the embargo viewed by other countries located in the same region as the target country?

5. Are governments prepared to take action when violations are revealed?

6. Is the military impact the embargo is likely to have consistent with the political objectives the embargo seeks to achieve?

Without addressing these questions in evaluating arms embargoes there is a danger that the use of arms embargoes may be discredited because they are occasionally applied under circumstances which are inappropriate.

Against this background it is useful to review the implementation of embargoes with special attention to the two which have attracted the most widespread attention—on Iraq and the former Yugoslavia. This section reviews current arms embargoes with two issues in mind. First, are they effective—that is, to what extent do they prevent the transfer of arms to the target country or group? Second, are they successful—that is, do they help achieve the political goal that they set themselves?

The implementation of the embargoes

The administration of each embargo is the responsibility of a separate Sanctions Committee directly subordinate to the Security Council. However, the work of all these committees is supported by a single secretariat located in the UN Department of Political and Security Council Affairs.

Embargo implementation is not a UN responsibility but rests with the member states. Following the imposition of each embargo the UN secretariat requests information from members about the steps that they are taking to implement the embargo. All UN members have pledged in Article 2.5 of the Charter to 'refrain from giving assistance against which the United Nations is taking preventive or enforcement action'. This creates a legal obligation on member states to establish administrative controls on the export of goods subject to one or more UN embargo. As noted above, establishing such controls was a major focus of government activity in 1993 in both the CSCE and the COCOM grouping.

Beyond the border controls operated by exporting countries there are few cases where the physical movement of goods into a country under embargo is systematically monitored or impeded.

In the case of Iraq customs officials inspect the documents accompanying all shipments of goods into Iraq at recognized border crossings. A 3-metre high sand berm has been constructed along the Iraqi–Jordanian border to reduce the incidence of smuggling across one long and porous land border and to channel the movement of goods to monitored crossing points. The construction of defensive fortifications along the border with Kuwait begun in 1993 will also act as a physical barrier to smuggling. There are no such man-made physical obstacles along Iraq's borders with Iran or Turkey.[135]

In the case of the former Yugoslavia the UN Secretariat has established links with European regional organizations in an effort to enforce trade sanctions against Serbia and Montenegro.[136] The UN has direct electronic contact with the NATO/Western European Union (WEU) monitoring teams in the Adriatic and with the EC/CSCE Sanctions Assistance Missions located in Bulgaria, Croatia, Hungary and Romania as well as with the UN Protection Forces (UNPROFOR). In this way it is possible for monitors on the ground to verify whether or not goods entering Serbia and Montenegro have been exempted from sanctions. One of the problems in monitoring sanctions noted in 1992—the continued movement of ships on the River Danube—was partly alleviated by the stationing of a WEU sanctions assistance mission along the river.[137] These actions related to economic sanctions have an impact on the implementation of the UN arms embargo in that monitors examine cargo entering Serbia and Montenegro. Monitors are not concerned with the flow of goods into and out of Bosnia and Herzegovina, Croatia, Slovenia or Macedonia.

Embargo effectiveness

Flawless embargo enforcement is unlikely to be possible even in cases where geography is helpful. Examples can be provided which indicate that embargo enforcement is imperfect in the former Yugoslavia—where the international community has committed substantial human and technical resources to assist with implementation.

For non-government observers (including parliamentarians) there is no satisfactory means of measuring the degree to which present embargoes leak. In 1992 the WEU Assembly recommended that the WEU Council of Ministers publish evidence of any known breach of sanctions but in particular 'cases where arms or other military equipment were exported to the Serbs and other warring factions'. In its reply to this recommendation the Council confirmed that all such evidence remained classified.[138] The UN Security Council is similarly reluctant. The secretariat responsible for co-ordinating the implementation of the embargo only releases information to governments.

Some of the alleged violations of the arms embargoes against Iraq and the former Yugoslavia would, if proved, represent serious breaches.

One report draws attention to a visit to Iraq by the then Chief of General Staff of the armed forces of the Federal Republic of Yugoslavia (Serbia and

---

[135] *Asian Recorder*, 16–22 Sep. 1992, p. 22584; *Financial Times*, 17 Sep. 1993, p. 8.
[136] This linkage is described in chapter 10 of *SIPRI Yearbook 1993* (note 20).
[137] *WEU Initiatives on the Danube and in the Adriatic*, Report on behalf of the Defence Committee submitted by Mr Marten and Sir Keith Speed, Proceedings of the 39th Ordinary Session, Assembly of the Western European Union, Part I: Assembly Documents (Paris, June 1993).
[138] Note 137, para. 43.

Montenegro), Zivota Panic, in March 1993.[139] Quoting Croatian and Slovenian sources the report suggests that Panic offered military assistance to Iraq in exchange for oil and spare parts for aircraft of Soviet design from Iraq's inventory. Co-operation allegedly includes transfers of M-84 tanks, artillery rockets, assault rifles and ammunition all from Serbian production.[140]

There is no evidence that this co-operation has yet begun and the evidence with regard to Iraq is generally ambiguous. Iraq retained its conventional defence industrial potential despite the magnitude of its defeat in 1991 and could, in the absence of sanctions, restore production of munitions and some major conventional weapons at significant levels.

In mid-1993 a report by a Subcommittee of the US House of Representatives claimed that Iraq had already 'resumed production of a very wide range of conventional weaponry'.[141] Iraqi production of tanks, artillery rockets, ammunition and spare parts was said to have resumed by 1993. Some production could have been achieved by cannibalizing equipment that was not destroyed or captured during operation Desert Storm and by using in-country stockpiles of materials. However, other accounts underline that the production of rockets and ammunition cannot continue at any significant level under the comprehensive trade embargo in place against Iraq.[142] No such violations have been acknowledged by UN sanctions monitors or reported to the United Nations by governments. While border inspections have revealed cases of goods travelling with false documentation, there are no acknowledged cases where this involved defence-related equipment.

In the former Yugoslavia a number of clear-cut cases of arms embargo violations have been documented while many allegations have been neither proved nor disproved. Alleged violations of the embargo against the former Yugoslavia have usually involved limited (compared with the inventories already in the hands of warring parties) consignments of small arms and infantry equipment. In the course of the war units have regularly exchanged territory and equipment stocks have been captured. In one operation north of Tuzla Bosnian forces captured 100 Serbian vehicles containing 15 000 weapons together with ammunition.[143] Operations of this kind appear to be a more important source of re-supply than the international black market.

---

[139] Bata, J., 'Serbia's secret contacts abroad', *Aussenpolitik*, no. 4 (1993), pp. 373–82. Panic was one of 42 senior officers replaced by President Milosevic in Aug. 1993.

[140] Before sanctions were imposed the Federal Republic of Yugoslavia (Serbia and Montenegro) consolidated arms production in Serbia, consolidated foreign exchange reserves in overseas accounts and developed a strategic stockpile of materials needed to continue production. Palairet, M., 'How long can the Milosevic regime withstand sanctions?', *RFE/RL Research Report*, vol. 2, no. 34 (Aug. 27 1993).

[141] Timmerman, K. R., *Iraq Rebuilds its Military Industries*, Staff Report of the Subcommittee on International Security, International Organizations and Human Rights, Committee on Foreign Affairs, House of Representatives, Washington, DC, 29 June 1993; Timmerman, K. R., 'The Remilitarization of Iraq', *The Nonproliferation Review*, vol. 1, no. 1 (fall 1993), pp. 32–34.

[142] Eisenstadt, M., *Like a Phoenix from the Ashes: The Future of Iraqi Military Power*, Washington Institute for Near East Studies Policy Paper no. 36, Washington, DC, 1993, pp. 62–63.

[143] *RFE/RL Research Report*, vol. 2, no. 23 (4 June 1993), p. 9. See also Karp, A., 'Arming ethnic conflict', *Arms Control Today*, Sep. 1993, pp. 8–13.

In its second report to the Security Council the Sanctions Committee noted 46 reported violations of the sanctions of which two were confirmed. Of these two confirmed violations one was the delivery of weapons and military equipment to Zagreb airport, Croatia, by an Iranian transport aircraft. The shipment was destroyed under UNPROFOR supervision.[144]

In July 1993 Slovenian authorities seized a consignment of assault rifles and mortars together with ammunition at an airport near Maribor, Slovenia. The Serbian press suggested that the consignment was part of an agreement between Slovenian officials and the Bosnian government. This agreement might even have been known to and approved of by the two Presidents.[145]

In September 1993 unnamed diplomats in Croatia and representatives of UNPROFOR reported that six or perhaps more MiG-21 fighters had been obtained by Croatia from foreign sources.[146] However, these aircraft were almost certainly obtained through the defection of Croatian pilots serving in the air force of the former Yugoslavia.[147]

British, Croatian and German newspaper reports in 1993 made mention of sales by Russian arms dealers to Serb irregular forces in the Krajina region of Croatia. This equipment, which was alleged to include land-based anti-aircraft missiles and T-55 tanks, was apparently taken illegally from the stockpiles kept by the KGB and transferred via Romania.[148] These reports were denied by Russian authorities and seem implausible given the size of the equipment concerned and the presence of sanctions monitors in Romania.

Several cases in which individuals attempted to violate the arms embargo highlighted the activities of multi-national networks of private arms dealers. In July 1993 it was alleged that on two occasions Panamanian officials—including the vice-consul in Barcelona—had provided false documentation to assist illegal transfers of small arms. In one case a consignment of sub-machine guns and handguns of Czech origin was to have been sent to Bosnia in a deal organized by an Italian businessman.[149] In another case small arms of Austrian origin would have been supplied to Bosnia.[150] The Panama Government acknowledged that a 'disgraceful scandal' had occurred but the specific details were not confirmed in the public report issued about the affair.[151]

In mid-1993 six Bolivian Foreign Ministry officials were implicated in an effort to supply eight Russian T-72 tanks to Croatian forces.[152] In a somewhat similar deal two Bolivian officials were put on trial in October 1993 charged

---

[144] UN document S/25027, 30 Dec. 1992.

[145] *RFE/RL News Briefs*, vol. 2, no. 33 (9–13 Aug. 1993), p. 14; *International Herald Tribune*, 15 Oct. 1993, p. 2.

[146] *New York Times*, 23 Sep. 1993, p. A9; *World Aerospace & Defense Intelligence*, 1 Oct. 1993, p. 10.

[147] Vego, M., 'The new Yugoslav defence industry', *Jane's Intelligence Review*, Nov. 1993, pp. 502–505.

[148] The reports are highlighted in Bata, J., 'Serbia's secret contacts abroad', *Aussenpolitik*, no. 4 (1993), p. 379.

[149] *Latin American Weekly Report*, 12 Aug. 1993, p. 363.

[150] Note 149, p. 384.

[151] *International Herald Tribune*, 18 Aug. 1993, p. 8; *Latin American Weekly Report*, 9 Sep. 1993, p. 420.

[152] *Latin American Weekly Report*, 8 July 1993, p. 311.

with providing forged documents to assist an international arms trafficking operation that included one Portuguese, two Israeli, one Iranian, two Austrian and two Chilean nationals.[153] It was not clear which of the warring parties in the former Yugoslavia would have received these weapons.

In each case the effort to supply arms to warring parties in the former Yugoslavia was detected by European export control authorities, monitored by intelligence agencies and interdicted by police or customs officers. In each case the government within which corruption was alleged to have taken place moved to establish a judicial enquiry or a criminal prosecution of the individuals identified. From this point of view they underline the steps taken by governments to enforce the arms embargo.

Evaluating the success of UN arms embargoes

Perfect effectiveness need not be required for an embargo to be judged a success. An arms embargo—like any sanction—is intended to signal the disapproval of the international community for a particular event or events. At this level of evaluation the passage of a resolution is in itself a success. A recent study of the war in the former Yugoslavia concluded that 'much of the European and wider world community has certainly observed the agreed economic sanctions and arms embargo'.[154] Without a UN directive the combatants in the former Yugoslavia would have been able to find suppliers prepared to meet their requirements for commercial or political reasons.

Different governments have different definitions of what constitutes success or failure in any given case. This reflects their different levels of interest and policy goals in relation to the target of the embargo. At a national level these levels of interest and policy goals are not fixed and arms embargoes are only one of a range of measures employed in pursuit of these shifting objectives. The willingness to commit the human and material resources needed to establish an embargo (and accept the financial losses associated with the reduction in trade) is also related to the importance of the issues at stake and also changes across time. A comprehensive evaluation of success would have to be made on a country-by-country basis taking all these factors into account. Nevertheless, since the Security Council resolution establishing the embargo indicates some international agreement, it is reasonable to judge embargoes against the goals defined in the resolutions which established them.

Judged in these terms none of the embargoes had succeeded fully by the end of December 1993. Libya had not surrendered for trial the individuals accused of terrorist offences; President Aristide had not been returned to office in Haiti and in each case of armed conflict other than the former Yugoslavia at least one warring party remained outside the political process.

---

[153] *New York Times*, 2 Sep. 1993, p. A12; *InterPress Service*, 22 Oct. 1993.
[154] Griffiths, S. I., *Nationalism and Ethnic Conflict: Threats to European Security*, SIPRI Research Report no. 5 (Oxford University Press: Oxford, 1993), p. 52.

Table 13.12. Stated objectives of the UN Security Council resolutions mandating arms embargoes

Resolution	Minimum objective as stated in resolution
687	Settlement of the Iraq–Kuwait border; ratify existing nuclear, biological, and chemical arms control and disarmament agreements; give a binding undertaking never to develop nuclear, biological or chemical weapons; ratify international conventions on hostages and terrorism; return Kuwaiti citizens and property or compensate Kuwait for them; take steps to repay outstanding foreign debt.
713	All parties to the conflict in former Yugoslavia urged to settle disputes peacefully in the framework of the process established by the European Community with the support of the CSCE; respect for the cease-fire agreements reached on 17 and 22 September 1991.
733	Somali factions must participate in a political process organized by the Organization for African Unity and the League of Arab States under the co-ordination of the UN Secretary-General.
748	Libya must 'cease all forms of terrorist action and all assistance to terrorist groups' and 'promptly, by concrete actions, demonstrate its renunciation of terrorism'.
788	All Liberian warring parties must adhere to the Yamoussoukro IV Accord of 30 October 1991.
841	All Haitian parties must accept the outcome of the negotiations conducted by the Special Envoy for Haiti representing the United Nations and the Organization of American States, Mr Dante Caputo.
864	UNITA must accept the results of the 1992 Angolan national elections and the peace settlement known as the Paz Accords.

Resolution 713 was an effort to lend UN support to political initiatives then underway in the EC and CSCE which had the objective of establishing a peaceful dialogue between the parties to resolve the future political and constitutional arrangements for Yugoslavia. The framework for the dialogue was the Declaration of 3 September 1991 by the CSCE that 'no territorial gains or changes within Yugoslavia brought about by violence are acceptable'. Therefore, it was intended to have a political function (signalling to the parties that the United Nations would not accept a military solution to the future political arrangements in Yugoslavia) and, to a lesser extent, a preventive function (denying any potential warring parties access to foreign supplies).

Resolution 713 was a response to the war which began in Croatia in mid-1991. In September 1991 the Yugoslav political crisis was two years old—if dated from the decision of Slovenia to initiate its secession. However, no foreign country had recognized Slovenia and Croatia as independent. A brief 10-day war in Slovenia was over. Fighting was taking place between Croatian and Serb forces in Croatia but not in Bosnia and Herzegovina. There were no foreign (i.e. non-Yugoslav) military forces in the former Yugoslavia.

As events unfolded in Yugoslavia the political background to the embargo changed radically. First, important countries—the most important being Germany—decided that it was better to recognize the declarations of independence by new countries wishing to secede from Yugoslavia than to seek a new political arrangement in the framework of a single state. Second, the international community decided not to enforce the territorial settlement implied by the recognition of newly independent states. Third, fighting moved from Croatia to Bosnia and Herzegovina and escalated in intensity.

As the political background changed, so the objectives of the embargo changed too. The embargo was seen less as a diplomatic tool and increasingly as a measure that might help reduce the scale and duration of the fighting.

Improving the effectiveness of embargo implementation

Some issues benefit from *global approaches*. One is the issue of defining more precisely which goods should be subject to a UN arms embargo. Another is the issue of the public release of information.

At present there is no single form of wording used within the resolutions which impose mandatory embargoes. The phrases 'weapons and military equipment'; 'weapons and ammunition, military vehicles and equipment, paramilitary police equipment and spare parts for the aforementioned' and 'arms and related *matériel* of all types' are all used in one or more of the resolutions. While the meaning of the words arms and weapons is clearly linked to the lethality of an item, the precise definition of 'military equipment' and 'related *matériel*' is left to national discretion and is open to wide differences of interpretation. As a result, two countries faced with a decision about whether or not to permit the export of a given item may quite legally reach different conclusions. This creates scope for suspicion that export controls are in practice being manipulated to gain commercial advantages.

The UN might usefully consider whether at least a core list of military equipment can be agreed universally. While many countries would wish to go much further in defining military equipment for the purposes of their national export controls, the establishment of such a list would be an important step forward for others.

The refusal of one government to publish information about suspected or real violations by others reflects the reluctance of governments to embarrass (let alone punish) one another. However, the implementation of UN decisions rests on the national political processes of the members. Therefore, this refusal also makes it less likely that governments will come under domestic pressure to establish the administrative procedures needed to implement UN decisions or be held accountable for their failure to do so.

The EC/CSCE implementation mechanisms and NATO/WEU monitoring mechanisms established for the former Yugoslavia represent an important phase in the development of *regional approaches* to embargo implementation. These efforts will test the feasibility of using regional organizations to implement decisions taken by the United Nations. In the case of the former Yugoslavia it is difficult to persuade non-Europeans that the suffering of that group of countries or the political issues at stake are more important than those elsewhere. Moreover, the effectiveness of an embargo is likely to be low where one or more country in the region is not committed to monitoring and enforcing it. It is therefore logical and inevitable that regional organizations assume the primary burden of managing local developments.

Where a consensus that an embargo is desirable can be established it is not always easy to maintain. The long discussions in 1993 about whether to sustain the arms embargo against the successor states to former Yugoslavia other than Serbia and Montenegro underlines this. The governments of Slovenia, Croatia or Bosnia make no secret of their desire to secure access to military equipment. In fact, this is one primary focus of their current diplomacy. Conversely, a primary focus of Serbian diplomacy is to ensure the fullest possible enforcement of the arms embargo since they are the best armed and supplied of the local states and in a position to support the logistical needs of Bosnian Serb forces.[155]

In their efforts to circumvent the embargo or, ideally, have it lifted altogether, the governments of Bosnia and Slovenia have widespread sympathy from governments.[156] The primary beneficiary of a lifting of the embargo would be Croatia—since there is no access to Bosnian Muslim forces except through enemy-held territory. Unless a major power was to enter the war on the side of the Bosnian Government, arms would have to be smuggled through Croatian or Serb-held territory (which would be difficult to achieve with militarily-significant quantities of equipment). Equally, it would be difficult to persuade all countries to respect an arms embargo on the Federal Republic of Yugoslavia (Serbia and Montenegro) alone. Under these conditions a lifting of the arms embargo could quickly lead to the re-opening of large-scale arms production in Serbia and an unravelling of the wider trade sanctions currently in place against the FR Yugoslavia.

Finally, *national approaches* are currently of primary importance in embargo implementation. Even if governments released information on the number or nature of successful preventive actions the success-rate of export regulations cannot be measured. It cannot be known how many transfers would have taken place in the absence of national regulations or how many would-be exporters were deterred from seeking business in the former Yugoslavia because of national prohibitions. However, the vast majority of arms producers and dealers respect national export regulations voluntarily. Moreover, there is evidence of some progress in the development of national control systems in several important countries. Two of the successes in enforcing the embargo against the former Yugoslavia stemmed from the export control authorities of the Czech Republic and Russia.

---

[155] Of the first 45 cases of alleged violations reported to the UN Sanctions Committee 31 were made by the government of the Federal Republic of Yugoslavia (Serbia and Montenegro). For this reason it might be argued that maintaining the embargo but allowing occasional leaks is a useful lever for the major powers to hold against Serbia.

[156] This feeling is not confined to governments. At least two aid workers have been expelled from Bosnia for smuggling arms in vehicles belonging to the charity Feed the Children. The aid workers commented 'the only regret we've got is that we couldn't do more', see *The Guardian*, 4 Sep. 1993, p. 3.

Appendix 13A. The 100 largest arms-producing companies, 1992

IAN ANTHONY, PAUL CLAESSON, GERD HAGMEYER-GAVERUS, ELISABETH SKÖNS and SIEMON T. WEZEMAN

Table 13A contains information on the 100 largest arms-producing companies in the OECD and the developing countries ranked by their arms sales in 1992.[1] Companies with the designation *S* in the column for rank in 1992 are subsidiaries; their arms sales are included in the figure in column 6 for the holding company. Subsidiaries are listed in the position where they would appear if they were independent companies. In order to facilitate comparison with data for the previous year, the rank order and arms sales figures for 1991 are also given. Where new data for 1991 have become available, this information is included in the table; thus the 1991 rank order and the arms sales figures for some companies which appeared in table 10A in the *SIPRI Yearbook 1993* have been revised.

Sources and methods

Sources of data. The data in the table are based on the following sources: company reports, a questionnaire sent to over 400 companies, and corporation news published in the business sections of newspapers and military journals. Company archives, marketing reports, government publication of prime contracts and country surveys were also consulted. In many cases exact figures on arms sales were not available, mainly because companies often do not report their arms sales or lump them together with other activities. Estimates were therefore made.

Definitions. Data on total sales, profits and employment are for the entire company, not for the arms-producing sector alone. Profit data are after taxes in all cases when the company provides such data. Employment data are either a year-end or a yearly average figure as reported by the company. Data are reported cn the fiscal year basis reported by the company in its annual report.

Exchange-rates. To convert local currency figures into US dollars, the period-average of market exchange-rates of the International Monetary Fund, *International Financial Statistics,* was used.

Key to abbreviations in column 5. A = artillery, Ac = aircraft, El = electronics, Eng = engines, Mi = missiles, MV = military vehicles, SA/O = small arms/ordnance, Sh = ships, and Oth = other.

---

[1] The 24 member countries of the Organization for Economic Co-operation and Development are: Australia, Austria, Belgium, Canada, Denmark, Germany, Finland, France, Greece, Iceland, Ireland, Italy, Japan, Luxembourg, the Netherlands, New Zealand, Norway, Portugal, Spain, Sweden, Switzerland, Turkey, the UK and the USA (Yugoslavia participates with special status). For the countries in the developing world, see appendix 13B.

Table 13A. The 100 largest arms-producing companies in the OECD and developing countries, 1992

Figures in columns 6, 7, 8 and 10 are in US $m.

1	2	3	4	5	6	7	8	9	10	11
Rank[a]		Company[b]	Country	Industry	Arms sales		Total sales	Col. 6 as	Profit	Employment
1992	1991				1992	1991[c]	1992	% of col. 8	1992	1992
1	1	McDonnell Douglas	USA	Ac El Mi	9 290	10 200	17 384	53	-781	87 377
2	3	British Aerospace	UK	Ac A El Mi SA/O	7 070	7 550	17 615	40	-1 640	102 500
3	5	Lockheed	USA	Ac	6 700	6 900	10 138	66	-283	71 700
4	4	General Motors, GM	USA	Ac Eng El Mi	5 400	7 500	132 775	4	-23 498	750 000
S	S	Hughes Electronics (GM)	USA	Ac El	5 400	6 600	12 300	44	-92	90 000
5	6	General Electric	USA	Ac Eng	5 300	6 120	62 202	9	4 725	268 000
6	10	Thomson S.A.	France	El Mi	4 980	4 800	13 409	37	-4	100 768
S	S	Thomson-CSF (Thomson S.A.)	France	El Mi	4 980	4 800	6 460	77	287	42 350
7	8	Northrop	USA	Ac	4 960	5 100	5 550	89	121	33 600
8	9	Raytheon	USA	El Mi	4 800	5 100	9 058	53	635	63 900
9	7	Boeing	USA	Ac El Mi	4 700	5 100	30 184	16	1 635	143 000
10	11	Martin Marietta	USA	Mi	4 400	4 560	5 954	74	345	56 000
11	13	United Technologies, UTC	USA	Ac El Mi	4 300	4 000	21 641	20	-287	178 000
12	15	Daimler Benz	FRG	Ac Eng MV El	4 120	3 920	63 104	7	929	376 467
S	S	DASA New (Daimler Benz)[d]	FRG	Ac Eng El Mi	4 060	:	11 062	37	-218	81 872
13	14	GEC	UK	El	3 750	3 960	16 614	23	946	93 228
14	12	Rockwell International	USA	Ac El Mi	3 750	4 000	10 910	34	483	78 685
15	19	Litton Industries	USA	El Sh	3 380	3 150	5 693	59	174	49 500
16	17	Aérospatiale Groupe	France	Ac Mi	3 290	3 450	9 871	33	-450	46 110
17	2	General Dynamics	USA	MV Sh	3 200	7 620	3 472	92	248	56 800
18	23	Loral	USA	El	3 050	2 600	3 335	91	-92	24 500
19	22	Mitsubishi Heavy Industries	Japan	Ac MV Mi Sh	3 000	2 630	22 304	13	640	66 000

		Company	Country							
20	16	DCN	France	Sh	2 980	3 710	3 117	*96*	:	26 200
21	20	Grumman	USA	Ac El	2 980	2 900	3 504	*85*	−123	21 200
22	18	IRI	Italy	Ac Eng El Mi Sh	2 930	3 190	61 597	*5*	−3 450	345 485
S	S	Finmeccanica (IRI)	Italy	Ac Eng El Mi	2 730	2 710	8 988	*30*	152	51 503
23	21	TRW	USA	MV Oth	2 600	2 800	8 311	*31*	−156	64 100
24	25	Tenneco	USA	Sh	2 270	2 220	13 139	*17*	−1 323	79 000
S	S	Newport News (Tenneco)	USA	Sh	2 270	2 220	2 265	*100*	249	24 500
25	27	Dassault Aviation	France	Ac	2 160	1 870	2 732	*79*	33	10 661
S	S	Alenia (Finmeccanica)	Italy	Ac Eng El Mi	2 110	2 140	3 066	*69*	:	18 433
S	S	Westinghouse Electric	USA	El	2 100	2 300	8 447	*25*	−1 291	109 050
26	24	IBM	USA	El Oth	2 000	1 300	65 096	*3*	−4 965	308 010
27	37	Pratt & Whitney (UTC)	USA	Eng	2 000	1 830	6 940	*29*	−235	40 644
S	S	Texas Instruments	USA	El	2 000	1 950	7 440	*27*	247	60 577
28	26	Federal Systems (IBM)	USA	Oth	2 000	:	3 000	*67*	71	11 750
S	S	Aérospatiale (Aérosp. Groupe)	France	Ac Mi	1 910	:	5 950	*32*	:	:
29	29	Textron	USA	Ac Eng MV	1 800	1 800	8 348	*22*	−355	54 000
30	31	CEA Industrie	France	Oth	1 780	1 750	7 405	*24*	181	39 800
31	33	Rolls Royce	UK	Eng	1 760	1 680	6 289	*28*	−369	55 000
32	32	Unisys	USA	El	1 700	1 750	8 422	*20*	361	54 300
33	39	GIAT Industries	France	A MV SA/O	1 660	1 220	2 059	*81*	:	:
34	34	E-Systems	USA	El	1 650	1 550	2 094	*79*	−69	18 590
35	30	Allied Signal	USA	Ac El Oth	1 580	1 790	12 042	*13*	−712	89 300
36	−	Carlyle	USA	Ac El Oth	1 530	:	4 500	*34*	:	40
37	38	EFIM^e	Italy	Ac MV El	1 430	1 270	:	:	:	:
38	36	SNECMA Groupe	France	Eng Oth	1 340	1 320	4 314	*31*	−150	25 307
S	S	Eurocopter SA (Aérospatiale/DASA, FRG)	France	Ac	1 290	:	2 191	*59*	5	11 950
39	40	Israel Aircraft Industries	Israel	Ac El Mi	1 270	1 200	1 571	*81*	−85	16 412
40	42	ITT	USA	El	1 200	1 200	21 651	*6*	−260	106 000
41	53	Celsius	Sweden	Sh	1 170	870	1 800	*65*	79	13 894
42	35	INI	Spain	Ac A MV El Sh	1 140	1 330	22 272	*5*	−704	140 736

1	2	3	4	5	6	7	8	9	10	11
Rank[a]					Arms sales					
1992	1991	Company[b]	Country	Industry	1992	1991[c]	Total sales 1992	Col. 6 as % of col. 8	Profit 1992	Employment 1992
43	45	Gencorp	USA	Ac Eng El Mi SA/O Oth	1 120	1 110	1 937	58	22	13 900
S	S	Aerojet (Gencorp)	USA	Ac Eng El Mi SA/O Oth	1 120	1 090	1 140	98	22	6 000
44	43	FMC	USA	MV Sh Oth	1 110	1 170	3 974	28	−76	22 097
45	41	GTE	USA	El	1 050	1 200	20 000	5	−754	131 000
46	–	Matra Hachette[f]	France	El Oth	1 030	0	10 409	10	−67	44 394
47	46	Alliant Tech Systems	USA	SA/O	1 010	1 100	1 005	100	−114	4 500
48	49	Kawasaki Heavy Industries	Japan	Ac Eng Sh	1 000	1 050	8 611	12	114	22 222
49	54	FIAT	Italy	Eng MV	950	850	44 458	2	523	285 482
S	–	Loral Vought Systems (Loral)	USA	Mi	950	0	950	100	..	..
50	52	Siemens	FRG	El	930	900	50 272	2	1 252	413 000
51	50	Ordnance Factories	India	A SA/O Oth	870	930	965	90	..	173 000[g]
52	64	Mitsubishi Electric	Japan	El Mi	850	710	25 743	3	225	107 589
53	55	Diehl	FRG	El SA/O	840	800	1 945	43	..	15 517
54	44	Oerlikon-Bührle	Switzerl.	Ac A El SA/O	830	1 170	2 537	33	26	16 359
S	S	SNECMA (SNECMA Groupe)	France	Eng	810	850	2 557	32	−112	13 405
S	–	Vought Aircraft (Carlyle/ Northrop)	USA	Ac	800	0	1 000	80	..	7 300
55	58	Rheinmetall	FRG	A MV El SA/O	780	770	2 006	39	13	13 304
56	60	Harris	USA	El	780	760	3 004	26	75	28 300
57	59	Thyssen	FRG	MV Sh	770	770	5 575	14	295	47 073
S	S	Matra Défense (Matra Hachette)	France	Mi	770	840	769	100	52	3 200

		Company	Country	Sector						
58	66	Eidgenössische Rüstungsbetriebe	Switzerl.	Ac Eng A SA/O	770	690	821	94	1	4 286
59	47	Harsco	USA	MV	770	1 060	1 625	47	84	9 600
60	51	VSEL Consortium	UK	MV Sh	760	920	780	97	62	9 820
61	65	Denel[h]	S. Africa	A Ac El Mi MV SA/O	740	710	989	75	82	14 500
62	63	Bath Iron Works	USA	Sh	720	720	800	90	..	9 000
S	S	MTU (DASA)	FRG	Eng	690	690	2 313	30	−95	16 338
S	S	EFIM Finbreda (EFIM)[e]	Italy	A MV El	680	560	748	91	−437	3 530
S	S	Bofors (Celsius)[j]	Sweden	A MV SA/O	680	740	703	97	38	5 356
63	67	Thiokol	USA	Eng Mi SA/O Oth	650	690	1 312	50	63	11 200
64	61	Ishikawajima-Harima	Japan	Eng Sh	640	740	8 195	8	140	27 614
S	S	Dornier (DASA)	FRG	Ac El Mi	640	410	1 718	37	−34	9 071
65	73	Motorola	USA	El	640	600	11 303	6	453	107 000
S	S	EFIM Aviofer (EFIM)[e]	Italy	Ac	620	410	..	..	..	:
S	S	Oto Melara (EFIM Finbreda)	Italy	A MV Mi	610	480	607	100	−136	1 917
66	74	SAGEM Groupe	France	El	600	590	2 315	26	88	14 576
67	72	Hercules	USA	Ac Mi	600	600	2 865	21	168	15 420
68	70	Sequa	USA	Eng El Oth	600	610	1 868	32	..	13 800
69	56	Bremer Vulkan	FRG	Eng El Sh	590	780	2 630	22	48	20 346
S	S	Oerlikon-Contraves AG (Oerlikon-Bührle)	Switzerl.	A El Mi SA/O	590	..	868	68	..	2 548
S	S	Agusta (EFIM Aviofer)	Italy	Ac	560	410	686	82	−696	6 990
70	71	Smiths Industries	UK	El	550	600	1 122	49	121	11 200
S	S	Dynamit Nobel (Metallgesellschaft)	FRG	SA/O Oth	530	190	1 665	32	..	12 300
71	80	Dassault Electronique	France	El	530	490	732	72	−43	3 196
72	77	Avondale Industries	USA	Sh	530	530	592	90	−11	6 500
73	78	Saab-Scania	Sweden	Ac Eng El Mi	520	520	4 635	11	65	28 800
74	76	Westland Group	UK	Ac	510	530	745	68	37	8 766
75	62	CAE Industries	Canada	El	500	730	827	60	26	10 000g
76	79	Teledyne	USA	Eng El Mi	500	500	2 888	17	33	23 800

1	2	3	4	5	6	7	8	9	10	11
Rank^a					Arms sales					
1992	1991	Company^b	Country	Industry	1992	1991^c	Total sales 1992	Col. 6 as % of col. 8	Profit 1992	Employment 1992
77	81	TAAS^j	Israel	A MV SA/O	480	490	516	93	-209	9 000
78	86	Racal Electronics	UK	El	480	440	2 248	21	91	23 144
79	57	Alcatel-Alsthom	France	El	470	780	30 541	2	1 597	203 000
80	–	NEC	Japan	El	460	360	27 753	2	-357	140 969
S	S	CASA (INI)	Spain	Ac	460	670	897	51	-35	8 999
81	–	Oshkosh Truck	USA	MV	460	270	641	72	9	2 474
82	75	Lucas Industries	UK	Ac	440	570	4 184	11	-16	50 569
83	89	Labinal	France	El	430	420	1 728	25	29	16 300
S	S	EN Bazan (INI)	Spain	Eng Sh	430	350	504	85	-78	8 560
84	97	Dyncorp	USA	Ac El	430	390	1 000	43	..	22 000
85	–	Vickers	UK	Eng MV SA/O	420	360	1 269	33	-48	10 422
S	S	BDM Holdings (Carlyle)	USA	Oth	420	..	424	99	..	..
86	84	Rafael	Israel	SA/O Oth	410	450	460	89	-10	5 100
87	88	Devonport Management	UK	Sh	410	430	461	89	16	5 276
S	S	AVCO (Textron)	USA	Ac	410	450	..	..	..	..
88	98	Mitre	USA	El	410	390	..	..	..	..
89	69	AT&T	USA	El	400	650	64 904	1	3 807	312 700
S	S	CFM International (General Electric/SNECMA, France)	USA	Ac Eng	400	400	..	..	..	..
90	95	Penn Central	USA	Oth	400	400	..	..	..	12 100^g
S	S	SAGEM (SAGEM Groupe)	France	El	390	400	1 024	38	37	5 679
S	S	Krauss-Maffei (Mannesmann)	FRG	MV	370	400	1 025	36	6	5 395
91	92	Mannesmann	FRG	MV	370	400	17 941	2	40	136 747
92	–	SNPE	France	A SA/O	370	340	796	46	-13	6 483

93	87	Esco Electronics	USA	El	370	440	406	91	1	5 000
S	S	Sextant Avionique (Thomson-CSF/Aérospatiale)	France	El	360	330	1 033	35	..	7 525
S		FIAT Aviazione (FIAT)	Italy	Eng	360	370	729	49	..	4 656
94	90	Toshiba	Japan	El Mi	360	420	36 538	1	162	173 000
S		Hollandse Signaalapparaten (Thomson-CSF, France)	Netherl.	El	360	410	376	96	–49	3 280
95	–	Sundstrand	USA	Ac	360	370	1 673	22	–122	12 300
S	S	Thyssen Henschel (Thyssen)	FRG	MV	350	180	539	65	..	3 115
96	99	Olin	USA	Ac El SA/O Oth	350	380	22 376	2	9	13 500
97	–	Renault[g]	France	Eng MV	340	320	33 889	1	1 077	146 604
98	85	Bombardier	Canada	Ac	330	440	3 680	9	110	34 300
99	100	Hindustan Aeronautics[g]	India	Ac Mi	330	370	378	87	21	40 336
100	93	Hunting	UK	SA/O	330	400	1 430	23	..	7 665

.. Data not available.

[a] Companies with the designation S in the column for rank are subsidiaries. The rank designation in the column for 1991 may not correspond to that given in table 10A in the SIPRI Yearbook 1993. A dash (–) in this column indicates either that the company did not produce arms in 1991, in which case there is a zero (0) in column 7, or that it did not rank among the 100 largest companies in table 10A in the SIPRI Yearbook 1993, in which case figures for arms sales in 1991 do appear in column 7.

[b] Names in parentheses after the name of the ranked company are the names of the holding companies.

[c] A zero (0) in this column indicates that the company did not produce arms in 1991, but began arms production in 1992, or that in 1991 the company did not exist as it was structured in 1992.

[d] 1992 data for DASA are not comparable to 1991 data, owing to major structural changes.

[e] EFIM was under liquidation in 1992, but EFIM Aviofer, Finbreda and Sistemi e Spazio were maintained as sub-holdings to EFIM throughout the year, pending transfer of their subsidiary production companies to Finmeccanica (IRI) in January 1994 (see section III, chapter 13).

[f] Matra Hachette merged with Matra Groupe in 1992. The 1991 arms sales of Matra Groupe were $1050 m.

[g] Data are for 1991.

[h] Data for 1991 (col. 7) are for Armscor, the predecessor of Denel.

[i] Formerly Swedish Ordnance.

[j] Formerly Israel Military Industries.

Note: The authors acknowledge financial assistance to operate the SIPRI arms production data bank from The John D. and Catherine T. MacArthur Foundation and assistance in the data collection provided by Anthony Bartzokas (Athens), Centre d'Estudis sobre la Pau i el Desarmament (Barcelona), Agnès Courades Allebeck (Paris), Defence Research & Analysis (London), Ken Epps (Ontario), Ernst Gülcher (Antwerp), Peter Hug (Bern), Masako Ikegami (Uppsala), Keidanren (Tokyo), Rudi Leo (Vienna), Rita Manchandi (New Delhi), Reuven Pedatzur (Tel Aviv), Giulio Perani (Rome), Gülay Günlük-Senesen (Istanbul) and Werner Voß (Bremen).

Appendix 13B. Tables of the volume of the trade in major conventional weapons, 1984–93

IAN ANTHONY, PAUL CLAESSON, GERD HAGMEYER-GAVERUS, ELISABETH SKÖNS and SIEMON T. WEZEMAN

Table 13B.1. Volume of imports of major conventional weapons

Figures are SIPRI trend-indicator values, as expressed in US $m., at constant (1990) prices.

	1984	1985	1986	1987	1988	1989	1990	1991	1992	1993
World total	42 416	39 510	42 412	45 896	38937	37 615	30 332	23 892	22 806	21 975
Developing world	28 912	26 381	27 963	30 991	23 086	21 397	17 925	12 650	11 671	12 354
LDCs	1 077	1 042	1 708	1351	2 221	3 328	2 971	1 745	309	70
Industrialized world	13 504	13 129	14 449	14 905	15 851	16 218	12 407	11 242	11 135	9 621
Europe	10 336	9 562	10 892	11 286	12 017	12 236	9 998	8 191	8 265	7 128
EU	3 770	2 373	3 216	2 991	4 104	5 140	4 093	5 979	4 981	2 557
Other Europe	6 566	7 189	7 676	8 294	7 913	7 096	5 905	2 213	3 284	4 571
Americas	5 703	3 762	2 937	3 494	1 827	2 414	1 635	2 131	1 666	1 145
North	1 140	1 425	1 081	1 335	800	769	344	1 323	1 091	762
Central	756	816	694	338	243	385	443	145	0	0
South	3 806	1 521	1 162	1 821	785	1260	848	662	574	383
Africa	4 254	4 153	3 645	3 161	2 412	1977	1 348	413	638	135
Sub-Saharan	2 494	2 396	2 317	2 524	1 888	493	1 206	233	586	115
Asia	7 458	9 701	11 975	11 771	12 252	14 378	9 986	8 480	6 978	7 304
Middle East	14 156	11 956	12 101	15 555	9 620	5 867	6 909	4 350	4 790	5 515
Oceania	510	377	862	629	809	743	457	326	470	748
ASEAN	1 441	1 166	1 080	1 428	1 368	864	1 038	1 405	1 013	1 501
CSCE	11 472	10 981	11 918	12 524	12 676	12 942	10 320	9 512	9 338	7 796
NATO	5 936	4 593	4 926	5 843	6 447	7 377	5 617	8 398	8 469	5 932
OECD	8 500	7 741	8 101	8 768	10 261	11 152	8 275	10 551	10 927	8 385
OPEC	10 944	9 815	9 193	9 949	7 185	6 236	5 673	2 911	2 684	4 289

The following countries are included in each region:[a]

Developing world: Algeria, Angola, Argentina, Bahamas, Bahrain, Bangladesh, Barbados, Belize, Benin, Bolivia, Botswana, Brazil, Brunei, Burkina Faso, Burundi, Cambodia, Cameroon, Cape Verde, Central African Republic, Chad, Chile, China, Colombia, Comoros, Congo, Costa Rica, Cote d'Ivoire, Cuba, Cyprus, Afghanistan, Djibouti, Dominica, Dominican Republic, Ecuador, Egypt, El Salvador, Equatorial Guinea, Ethiopia, Fiji, Gabon, Gambia, Ghana, Guatemala, Guinea, Guinea Bissau, Guyana, Haiti, Honduras, India, Indonesia, Iran, Iraq, Israel, Jamaica, Jordan, Kenya, Kiribati, North Korea, South Korea, Kuwait, Laos, Lebanon, Lesotho, Liberia, Libya, Madagascar, Malawi, Malaysia, Mali, Marshall Islands, Mauritania, Mauritius, Mexico, Fed. States of Micronesia, Mongolia, Morocco, Mozambique, Myanmar, Namibia, Nepal, Nicaragua, Niger, Nigeria, Oman, Pakistan, Panama, Papua New Guinea, Paraguay, Peru, Philippines, Qatar, Rwanda, Samoa, Saudi Arabia, Senegal, Seychelles, Sierra Leone, Singapore, Solomon Islands, Somalia, South Africa, Sri Lanka, St Vincent & the Grenadines, Sudan, Suriname, Swaziland, Syria, Tahiti, Taiwan, Tanzania, Thailand, Togo, Tonga, Trinidad & Tobago, Tunisia, Tuvalu, Uganda, United Arab Emirates, Uruguay, Vanuatu, Venezuela, Viet Nam, Yemen, North Yemen, South Yemen, Zaire, Zambia, Zimbabwe.

Less developed countries (LDCs):[b] Afghanistan, Bangladesh, Benin, Botswana, Burkina Faso, Burundi, Cape Verde, Central African Republic, Chad, Comoros, Djibouti, Equatorial Guinea, Ethiopia,

Table 13B.2. Volume of exports of major conventional weapons

Figures are SIPRI trend-indicator values, as expressed in US $m., at constant (1990) prices.

	1984	1985	1986	1987	1988	1989	1990	1991	1992	1993
World total	42 416	39 510	42 412	45 896	38937	37 615	30 332	23 892	22 806	21 975
Developing world	3 115	2 530	2 818	4 679	3493	1 828	1 826	2 522	1 554	1 321
LDCs	27	2	31	96	3	0	0	0	0	0
Industrialized world	39 301	36 980	39 594	41 217	35444	35 787	28 506	21 370	21 252	20 654
Europe	26 988	26 836	27 765	27 533	23308	24 346	17 506	9 174	9 291	9 943
EU	11 186	9 014	8 001	7 366	6678	7 632	5 964	4 769	4 665	4 492
Other Europe	15 802	17 822	19 765	20 167	16630	16 714	11 541	4 405	4 626	5 451
Americas	12 618	10 326	12 003	14 253	12543	11 604	10 963	12 187	12 083	10 796
North	12 235	10 091	11 815	13 666	12127	11 436	10 888	12 137	11 937	10 671
Central	0	0	0	1	0	1	4	2	99	54
South	383	236	188	586	416	167	71	48	47	72
Africa	98	109	85	259	125	0	37	33	76	23
Sub-Saharan	52	78	48	177	69	0	7	33	76	23
Asia	1 993	1 801	1 868	3 201	2377	1 152	1 471	2 206	1 188	951
Middle East	659	402	687	631	575	507	243	230	168	252
Oceania	59	35	5	18	10	6	112	62	1	10
ASEAN	58	65	26	68	33	8	1	1	4	20
CSCE	39 223	36 926	39 580	41 199	35435	35 782	28 394	21 311	21 227	20 614
NATO	23 435	19 147	19 826	21 083	18825	19 160	16 862	16 949	16 677	15 163
OECD	23 795	19 770	20 304	21 593	19495	19 698	17 405	17 509	17 202	15 384
OPEC	97	66	98	237	247	26	33	18	0	8

Gambia, Guinea, Guinea Bissau, Haiti, Laos, Lesotho, Liberia, Malawi, Mali, Mauritania, Mozambique, Myanmar, Nepal, Niger, Rwanda, Samoa, Sierra Leone, Somalia, Sudan, Tanzania, Togo, Uganda, Vanuatu, North Yemen, South Yemen.

Industrialized world: Albania, Armenia, Australia, Austria, Azerbaijan, Belarus, Belgium, Bosnia and Herzegovina, Bulgaria, Canada, Croatia, Czechoslovakia, Czech Republic, Denmark, Estonia, Finland, France, Georgia, FR Germany, German DR, Germany, Greece, Hungary, Iceland, Ireland, Italy, Japan, Kazakhstan, Kyrgyzstan, Latvia, Liechtenstein, Lithuania, Luxembourg, Malta, Moldova, Monaco, Netherlands, New Zealand, Norway, Poland, Portugal, Romania, Russia, Slovakia, Slovenia, Spain, Sweden, Switzerland, Tajikistan, Turkey, Turkmenistan, Ukraine, UK, USA, USSR, Uzbekistan, Yugoslavia.

Europe: Albania, Armenia, Austria, Azerbaijan, Belarus, Belgium, Bosnia and Herzegovina, Bulgaria, Croatia, Cyprus, Czechoslovakia, Czech Republic, Denmark, Estonia, Finland, France, Georgia, FR Germany, German DR, Germany, Greece, Hungary, Iceland, Ireland, Italy, Latvia, Liechtenstein, Lithuania, Luxembourg, Malta, Moldova, Monaco, Netherlands, Norway, Poland, Portugal, Romania, Russia, Slovakia, Slovenia, Spain, Sweden, Switzerland, Turkey, Ukraine, UK, USSR, Yugoslavia.

European Union (EU): Belgium, Denmark, France, FR Germany, Germany, Greece, Ireland, Italy, Luxembourg, Netherlands, Portugal (1986), Spain (1986), UK.

Other Europe: Albania, Armenia, Austria, Azerbaijan, Belarus, Bosnia and Herzegovina, Bulgaria, Croatia, Cyprus, Czechoslovakia, Estonia, Finland, Georgia, German DR, Hungary, Iceland, Kazakhstan, Kyrgyzstan, Latvia, Liechtenstein, Lithuania, Malta, Moldova, Monaco, Norway, Poland, Romania, Russia, Slovakia, Slovenia, Sweden, Switzerland, Tajikistan, Turkey, Turkmenistan, Ukraine, USSR, Uzbekistan, Yugoslavia.

Americas: Argentina, Bahamas, Barbados, Belize, Bolivia, Brazil, Canada, Chile, Colombia, Costa Rica, Cuba, Dominica, Dominican Republic, Ecuador, El Salvador, Guatemala, Guyana, Haiti, Honduras, Jamaica, Mexico, Nicaragua, Panama, Paraguay, Peru, St Vincent & the Grenadines, Suriname, Trinidad & Tobago, Uruguay, USA, Venezuela.

North America: Canada, Mexico, USA.

Central America: Barbados, Bahamas, Belize, Costa Rica, Cuba, Dominica, Dominican Republic, Guatemala, Haiti, Honduras, Jamaica, Nicaragua, Panama, El Salvador, St Vincent & the Grenadines, Trinidad & Tobago.

South America: Argentina, Bolivia, Brazil, Chile, Colombia, Ecuador, Guyana, Paraguay, Peru, Suriname, Uruguay, Venezuela.

Africa: Algeria, Angola, Benin, Botswana, Burkina Faso, Burundi, Cameroon, Cape Verde, Central African Republic, Chad, Comoros, Congo, Cote d'Ivoire, Djibouti, Equatorial Guinea, Ethiopia, Gabon, Gambia, Ghana, Guinea, Guinea Bissau, Kenya, Lesotho, Liberia, Libya, Madagascar, Malawi, Mali, Mauritania, Mauritius, Morocco, Mozambique, Namibia, Niger, Nigeria, Rwanda, Senegal, Seychelles, Sierra Leone, Somalia, South Africa, Sudan, Swaziland, Tanzania, Togo, Tunisia, Uganda, Zaire, Zambia, Zimbabwe.

Sub-Saharan Africa: Angola, Benin, Botswana, Burkina Faso, Burundi, Cameroon, Cape Verde, Central African Republic, Chad, Comoros, Congo, Cote d'Ivoire, Djibouti, Equatorial Guinea, Ethiopia, Gabon, Gambia, Ghana, Guinea, Guinea Bissau, Kenya, Lesotho, Liberia, Madagascar, Malawi, Mali, Mauritania, Mauritius, Mozambique, Namibia, Niger, Nigeria, Rwanda, Senegal, Seychelles, Sierra Leone, Somalia, South Africa, Sudan, Swaziland, Tanzania, Togo, Uganda, Zaire, Zambia, Zimbabwe.

Middle East: Bahrain, Egypt, Iran, Iraq, Israel, Jordan, Kuwait, Lebanon, Oman, Qatar, Saudi Arabia, Syria, United Arab Emirates, Yemen, North Yemen, South Yemen.

Asia: Afghanistan, Bangladesh, Brunei, Cambodia, China, India, Indonesia, Japan, Kazakhstan, North Korea, South Korea, Kyrgyzstan, Laos, Malaysia, Mongolia, Myanmar, Nepal, Pakistan, Philippines, Singapore, Sri Lanka, Taiwan, Tajikistan, Thailand, Turkmenistan, Uzbekistan, Viet Nam.

Oceania: Australia, Fiji, Kiribati, Marshall Islands, Fed. States of Micronesia, New Zealand, Papua New Guinea, Samoa, Solomon Islands, Tahiti, Tonga, Tuvalu, Vanuatu.

Association of South-East Asian Nations (ASEAN): Brunei, Indonesia, Malaysia, Philippines, Singapore, Thailand.

Conference on Security and Co-operation in Europe (CSCE):[c] Albania (1991), Armenia (1992), Austria, Azerbaijan (1992), Belarus (1992), Belgium, Bosnia and Herzegovina (1992), Bulgaria, Canada, Croatia (1992), Cyprus, Czechoslovakia, Czech Republic (1993), Denmark, Estonia (1991), Finland, France, Georgia (1992), FR Germany, German DR, Germany, Greece, Hungary, Iceland, Ireland, Italy, Kazakhstan (1992), Kyrgyzstan (1992), Latvia (1991), Liechtenstein, Lithuania (1991), Luxembourg, Malta, Moldova (1992), Monaco, Netherlands, Norway, Poland, Portugal, Romania, Russia (1992), Slovakia (1993), Slovenia (1992), Spain, Sweden, Switzerland, Tajikistan (1992), Turkey, Turkmenistan (1992), Ukraine (1992), UK, USA, USSR, Uzbekistan (1992), Yugoslavia.

NATO: Belgium, Canada, Denmark, France, FR Germany, Germany, Greece, Iceland, Italy, Luxembourg, Netherlands, Norway, Portugal, Spain, Turkey, UK, USA.

Organization for Economic Co-operation and Development (OECD): Austria, Australia, Belgium, Canada, Denmark, Finland, France, Germany, FR, Germany, Greece, Iceland, Ireland, Italy, Japan, Luxembourg, Netherlands, Norway, New Zealand, Portugal, Spain, Sweden, Switzerland, Turkey, UK, USA.

Organization of Petroleum Exporting Countries (OPEC): Algeria, Ecuador, Gabon, Indonesia, Iran, Iraq, Kuwait, Libya, Nigeria, Qatar, Saudi Arabia, United Arab Emirates, Venezuela.

[a] Only countries for which there is an entry in the SIPRI arms trade data base are included.

[b] As defined by the International Monetary Fund

[c] For a current list of CSCE participating states see the table at the end of the glossary

Source: SIPRI arms trade data base

Appendix 13C. Register of the trade in and licensed production of major conventional weapons in industrialized and developing countries, 1993

IAN ANTHONY, PAUL CLAESSON, GERD HAGMEYER-GAVERUS, ELISABETH SKÖNS and SIEMON T. WEZEMAN

This register lists major weapons on order or under delivery, or for which the licence was bought and production was under way or completed during 1993. 'Year(s)' of deliveries' includes aggregates of all deliveries and licensed production since the beginning of the contract. Entries are alphabetical, by recipient, supplier and licenser. Abbreviations, acronyms and conventions are explained at the end of the register. Sources and methods are explained in appendix 13D.

Recipient/ supplier (S) or licenser (L)	No. ordered	Weapon designation	Weapon description	Year of order/ licence	Year(s) of deliveries	No. delivered/ produced	Comments
Algeria							
S: Egypt	(200)	Fahd	APC	1992	1992–93	(103)	
L: UK	3	Kebir Class	Patrol craft	(1990)			
Angola							
S: Spain	2	C-212-300MPA	Maritime patrol	(1990)			
	4	Mandume Class	Patrol craft	1991	1993	4	
Switzerland	8	PC-7 Turbo Trainer	Trainer aircraft	(1989)	1990	6	
Argentina							
S: Canada	150	Model 212	Helicopter	1990	1992–93	(8)	Limited local assembly
Netherlands	6	DA-05	Surveillance radar	(1979)	1985–90	(4)	For 6 Meko-140 Type frigates; status of last 2 uncertain
	6	WM-28	Fire control radar	(1979)	1985–90	(4)	For 6 Meko-140 Type frigates; status of last 2 uncertain

Recipient/ supplier (S) or licenser (L)	No. ordered	Weapon designation	Weapon description	Year of order/ licence	Year(s) of deliveries	No. delivered/ produced	Comments
USA	36	A-4M Skyhawk II	Fighter/ground attack	1993			Ex-US Marine Corps; deal worth $125 m incl 8 spare engines, maintenance and support; sale of additional 16 possible
	2	C-130E Hercules	Transport aircraft	1992			Ex-US Air Force
	20	OV-1 Mohawk	Reconnaissance plane	1993	1993	(10)	Ex-US Army
	1	Maumee Class	Tanker	1993	1993	1	Ex-US Navy
L: Canada	..	Model 412	Helicopter	1991			Licence authorizes sales to Latin American countries
Germany, FR	6	Meko-140 Type	Frigate	1980	1985–90	4	Last 2 available for export, but completion delayed owing to lack of funds
	3	TR-1700 Type	Submarine	1977			In addition to 2 delivered direct; original order for 4 cut to 3
Italy	..	A-109 Hirundo	Helicopter	1988			Deal worth $120 m
Australia							
S: Canada	97	LAV-25	AIFV	1992			Deal worth $200 m incl spares and training; several versions
Sweden	8	9LV	Fire control radar	(1991)			For 8 Meko-200 Type frigates
	8	Sea Giraffe 150	Surveillance radar	1991			For 8 Meko-200 Type frigates
USA	4	CH-47D Chinook	Helicopter	1992			Exchanged for 11 ex-Australian Air Force CH-47Cs
	15	F-111G	Fighter/bomber	1993	1993	15	Ex-US Air Force; deal worth $146 m incl spares and support
	3	P-3C Orion	ASW/maritime patrol	1993			
	2	AN/SPG-60	Fire control radar	1985	1992–93	2	For 2 FFG-7 Class frigates
	2	AN/SPS-49	Surveillance radar	1985	1992–93	2	For 2 FFG-7 Class frigates
	2	Phalanx	CIWS	1985	1992–93	2	For 2 FFG-7 Class frigates
	2	RIM-66A Launcher	ShAM system	1985	1992–93	2	For 2 FFG-7 Class frigates
	8	Seasparrow VLS	ShAM system	(1991)			For 8 Meko-200 Type frigates
	2	WM-28	Fire control radar	1985	1992–93	2	For 2 FFG-7 Class frigates

No.	Designation	Description	Year of order	Year(s) of deliveries	No. delivered	Comments
L: Germany, FR						
(128)	NATO Seasparrow	ShAM	(1991)			For 8 Meko-200 Type frigates
(48)	RGM-84A Harpoon	ShShM	1987	1992–93	(48)	For 2 FFG-7 Class frigates
(64)	RIM-66A Standard-1	ShAM	(1987)	1992–93	(64)	Deal worth $50 m; for 2 FFG-7 Class frigates
1	Adams Class	Destroyer	1993			Ex-US Navy; deal worth $2.2 m; for spares
10	Meko-200 Type	Frigate	1989			Incl 8 for Australia and 2 for New Zealand; option on 2 more for New Zealand; Australian designation Anzac Class
Sweden						
6	Type 471	Submarine	1987			Deal worth $2.8 b; Australian designation Collins Class
USA						
2	FFG-7 Class	Frigate	1983	1992–93	2	
Austria						
S: France						
500	Mistral	Portable SAM	1993	1993	(72)	Deal worth $129 m incl launchers (offsets $344 m)
Sweden						
500	RBS-56 Bill	Anti-tank missile	1989	1989–93	(500)	Deal worth $80 m
UK						
2	BAe-146	Transport aircraft	1991			For Austrian UN relief activities
USA						
24	M-109A2 155mm	Self-propelled gun	1988	1989–91	(18)	Deal worth $36 m
54	M-109A5 155mm	Self-propelled gun	(1993)			
Bahrain						
S: Netherlands						
13	M-110A2 203mm	Self-propelled gun	1993			Ex-Dutch Army
3	M-577A2	APC/command post	1993			Ex-Dutch Army
2	M-578	ARV	1993			Ex-Dutch Army
USA						
8	AH-64A Apache	Helicopter	1991			
115	M-113A2	APC	1991	1992–93	(115)	Ex-US Army
25	M-60A3 Patton	Main battle tank	1991	1993	(25)	For 8 AH-64A helicopters
450	AGM-114A Hellfire	Anti-tank missile	1990			
Bangladesh						
S: China						
(21)	F-7M Airguard	Fighter	1992			Replacing aircraft lost in cyclone

Recipient/ supplier (S) or licenser (L)	No. ordered	Weapon designation	Weapon description	Year of order/ licence	Year(s) of deliveries	No. delivered/ produced	Comments
Belgium							
S: France	714	Mistral	Portable SAM	1988	1991–93	(400)	Deal worth $93 m incl 118 launchers (offsets 75%)
	290	Mistral	Portable SAM	1991			Second order; deal incl 24 launchers
USA	545	AIM-9M Sidewinder	Air-to-air missile	1988			Deal worth $49 m
	940	AIM-9M Sidewinder	Air-to-air missile	1989			Deal worth $80 m
L: Italy	45	A-109BA Hirundo	Helicopter	1988	1992–93	45	Incl 28 armed with TOW anti-tank missiles
Bolivia							
S: USA	1	C-130B Hercules	Transport aircraft	1993			Ex-US Air Force; deal worth $1 m
Brazil							
S: France	20	AS-550 Fennec	Helicopter	1992	1992–93	(15)	Deal worth $25 m
Italy	..	FILA	Fire control radar	(1987)	1989–93	(15)	
Netherlands	3	M-101A1 105mm	Towed gun	1993	1993	3	Ex-Dutch Army; refurbished before delivery
UK	9	Super Lynx	Helicopter	1993			For Navy; deal worth $221 m incl refurbishment of 5 Brazilian Navy Lynx to Super Lynx
USA	2	Knox Class	Frigate	1993			Ex-US Navy; lease worth $6 m; follow-on lease of 2 likely
L: Germany, FR	2	Type 209/3	Submarine	1984			In addition to 1 delivered direct
Singapore	6	Grauna Class	Patrol craft	1987	1993	2	Option on 2 more
UK	..	L-118 105mm	Towed gun	1991			
Brunei							
S: Germany, FR	(96)	AIM-9L Sidewinder	Air-to-air missile	1989			For 16 Hawk 100 fighter/trainers
Indonesia	1	CN-235M	Transport	1989			Status uncertain
	3	CN-235MPA	Maritime patrol	1989			
UK	16	Hawk 100	Fighter/trainer	1989			Deal worth $260 m

Supplier	No.	Weapon designation	Weapon description				Comments
Bulgaria							
L: USSR	..	MT-LB	APC	(1970)	1972–92	1200	
Canada							
S: France	4 500	Eryx	Anti-tank missile	1992	1993	(500)	Deal incl 425 launchers (offsets 100%)
Netherlands	4	DA-08	Surveillance radar	1986	1991	2	For 4 re-fitted Tribal Class destroyers
	4	LW-08	Surveillance radar	1986	1991	2	For 4 re-fitted Tribal Class destroyers
	8	STIR	Fire control radar	1986	1991	4	For 4 re-fitted Tribal Class destroyers
	24	STIR	Fire control radar	(1985)	1991–93	(10)	For 12 Halifax (City) Class frigates
Sweden	12	Sea Giraffe 150	Surveillance radar	(1985)	1988–93	(5)	For 12 Halifax (City) Class frigates
Switzerland	36	ADATS	AAV(M)	1986	1988–93	(36)	Deal worth $1 b incl SAMs, AA guns and radars
	(288)	ADATS LOS-FH	SAM	1986	1988–93	(288)	
UK	12	T-67C Firefly	Trainer aircraft	1991	1993	(12)	
	1	Oberon Class	Submarine	1992	1993	1	Ex-UK Navy; for spares
USA	12	AN/SPS-49	Surveillance radar	1985	1990–93	(5)	For 12 Halifax (City) Class frigates
	2	AN/TPS-70	Surveillance radar	1990	1992–93	(2)	Deal worth $23 m
	4	Phalanx	CIWS	1987	1991–92	(2)	For 4 re-fitted Tribal Class destroyers
	6	Phalanx	CIWS	1986	1991–93	(2)	For 6 Halifax (City) Class frigates
	6	Phalanx	CIWS	1990		(5)	Deal worth $32 m; for second batch of 6 Halifax (City) Class frigates
	12	RGM-84A Launcher	ShShM system	1983	1991–93	(5)	For 12 Halifax (City) Class frigates
	12	Seasparrow VLS	ShAM system	1983	1991–93	(5)	For 12 Halifax (City) Class frigates; part of deal worth $75 m
	4	Standard VLS	Fire control radar	1986	1991–92	2	For 4 re-fitted Tribal Class destroyers
	..	RGM-84A Harpoon	ShShM	1988	1991–93	(80)	For 12 Halifax (City) Class frigates
	116	RIM-66M Standard-2	ShAM	1986	1991	(58)	For 4 re-fitted Tribal Class destroyers
	336	Seasparrow	ShAM	1984	1991–93	(130)	For 12 Halifax (City) Class frigates; part of deal worth $75 m
L: USA	100	Model 412	Helicopter	1992	1993	1	Deal worth $844 m
Chile							
S: Canada	1	Bell 230	Helicopter	(1993)	1993	1	Leased for evaluation by Navy for SAR

Recipient/ supplier (S) or licenser (L)	No. ordered	Weapon designation	Weapon description	Year of order/ licence	Year(s) of deliveries	No. delivered/ produced	Comments
France	6	AS-332 Super Puma	Helicopter	1988	1988–93	6	Part of deal worth $77 m
	2	AS-532 Mk-2 Cougar	Helicopter	1992			For Navy; replacing 1988 order for 4 AS-565
	..	AM-39 Exocet	Anti-ship missile	1992			For 2 AS-532 helicopters
	(1 400)	Mistral	Portable SAM	(1990)	1990–93	(800)	
Germany, FR	(30)	Bo-105CB	Helicopter	1985	1986–92	(18)	
Israel	2	Phalcon	AEW&C aircraft	(1989)	1993	1	Deal worth $500 m incl 4 Boeing 707 transports
	(8)	Barak Launcher	ShAM system	1989	1993	1	For re-fit of 4 Prat and 4 Condell Class frigates
	(256)	Barak 1	ShAM	1989	1993	(32)	For re-fit of 4 Prat and 4 Condell Class frigates
USA	8	P-3A Orion	ASW/maritime patrol	(1993)	1993	(3)	Ex-US Navy; delivered unarmed
L: South Africa							
UK	..	G-5 155 mm	Towed gun	1989	1990	(6)	
	..	Rayo	MRL	1986			
China							
S: Italy	85	Aspide	SAM/ShAM	1989	1990–91	(55)	
USA	6	CH-47D Chinook	Helicopter	1989			Deliveries suspended in June 1989
	2	AN/TPQ-37	Tracking radar	(1987)	1993	2	
USSR/Russia	1	Il-28 Beagle	Bomber	1992	1993	1	Ex-Russian Air Force; exchanged for canned fruit
	4	Il-76 Candid	Transport aircraft	1993	1993	4	
	40	MiG-29 Fulcrum	Fighter	1991			
	24	MiG-31 Foxhound	Fighter	1992			Status uncertain
	12	Su-24 Fencer	Fighter/bomber	(1990)			
	(288)	AA-8 Aphid	Air-to-air missile	1992			
	(1)	SA-10b SAMS	SAM system	1992	1993	(1)	
	(100)	SA-10b Grumble	SAM	(1992)	1993	(100)	For 1 SA-10b SAM system
L: France	(30)	AS-365N Dauphin 2	Helicopter	1988	1992–93	2	Chinese designation Z-9A Haitun
Israel	..	Python III	SAM/ShAM	(1989)	1990–93	1 996	Chinese designation PL-8H
	..	Python III	Air-to-air missile	1990	1990–93	(3 227)	Chinese designation PL-9

Colombia

S:	No.	Weapon designation	Weapon description	Year of order	Year of delivery	No. delivered	Comments
Brazil	14	EMB-312 Tucano	Trainer aircraft			14	

Cyprus

S:	No.	Weapon designation	Weapon description	Year of order	Year of delivery	No. delivered	Comments
France	..	MM-40 CDS	Coast defence system	1989			For MM-40 CDS coast defence system
	..	MM-40 Exocet	Coast defence missile	1989			

Denmark

S:	No.	Weapon designation	Weapon description	Year of order	Year of delivery	No. delivered	Comments
France	(9)	TRS-2620	Surveillance radar	1991			
Germany, FR	140	Leopard 1A3	Main battle tank	(1991)	1993	(70)	CFE cascade; ex-FRG Army
	6	TRS-3D	Surveillance radar	1990	1992–93	4	For 6 Standardflex 300 patrol craft/MCM ships
	3	TRS-3D	Surveillance radar	1993	1993	(1)	For re-fit of 3 Niels Juel Class corvettes
Netherlands	14	Leopard ARV	ARV	1993			Ex-Dutch Army
	8	Leopard BL	Bridge layer	1993			Ex-Dutch Army
Sweden	13	9LV	Fire control radar	(1988)	1989–93	(11)	For 13 Standardflex 300 patrol craft/MCM ships
USA	50	M-113A2	APC	(1991)	1992–93	50	To be modified in Denmark to AIFV
	1	RGM-84A CDS	Coast defence system	1991			
	162	AGM-65D Maverick	ASM	1989			For F-16 fighters; deal worth $24 m
	840	FIM-92A Stinger	Portable SAM	1991			
	(24)	RGM-84A Harpoon	ShShM	1991			For RGM-84A CDS coast defence system

Egypt

S:	No.	Weapon designation	Weapon description	Year of order	Year of delivery	No. delivered	Comments
Czechoslovakia	48	L-59	Jet trainer aircraft	1991	1993	(48)	Deal worth $204 m
USA	24	AH-64A Apache	Helicopter	1990			Deal worth $488 m incl 492 AGM-114A missiles
	2	E-2C Hawkeye	AEW&C aircraft	1989	1990–93	2	Deal worth $84 m
	42	F-16C Fighting Falcon	Fighter	1987	1991–93	(42)	Incl F-16D trainer version; from Turkish production line; deal worth $1.6 b incl spare engines and armament
	46	F-16C Fighting Falcon	Fighter	1991			
	1	F-4E Phantom II	Fighter	1993	1993	1	Ex-US Air Force
	25	M-48 Chaparral	AAV(M)	1990	1992–93	(20)	Deal worth $220 m incl 432 MIM-72H missiles and radar

Recipient/ supplier (S) or licenser (L)	No. ordered	Weapon designation	Weapon description	Year of order/ licence	Year(s) of deliveries	No. delivered/ produced	Comments
	(7)	M-577A2	APC/command post	1990	1992–93	(6)	To be fitted with Trackstar radar for use with Chaparral SAM system
	340	M-60A3 Patton	Main battle tank	1993			Ex-US Army; deal worth $84 m
	(7)	Trackstar	Surveillance radar	1990	1992–93	(6)	To be fitted on M-577A2 APCs; part of Chaparral SAM system
	492	AGM-114A Hellfire	Anti-tank missile	1990			For 24 AH-64A helicopters
	7 511	BGM-71D TOW-2	Anti-tank missile	1988	1989–93	(2 500)	Deal worth $180 m incl 180 launchers, 504 night vision sights and spares
	432	MIM-72H	SAM	1990	1992–93	(400)	For Chaparral SAM system
	29	UGM-84A Harpoon	SuShM	1990			For 4 re-fitted Romeo Class submarines; deal worth $69 m
	2	Knox Class	Frigate	1993			Ex-US Navy; lease worth $6 m
	3	Swiftships MCM	MCM ship	1991			Order number may be up to 6
L: Germany, FR	..	Fahd	APC	1978	1986–93	566	Developed for Egyptian production; incl production for export
UK	..	Swingfire	Anti-tank missile	1977	1979–93	8 956	
USA	(499)	M-1A1 Abrams	Main battle tank	1988	1993	140	Deal worth $2 b incl 25 delivered direct
	..	AIM-9P Sidewinder	Air-to-air missile	(1988)	1990–93	1 621	In addition to 37 assembled from kits
Estonia							
S: Germany, FR	2	L-410UVP Turbolet	Transport aircraft	(1992)	1993	2	Former GDR equipment; gift
Fiji							
S: Australia	3	ASI-315	Patrol craft	1992			Pacific Forum aid programme

Recipient / Supplier (S) or Licenser (L)	Weapon designation	Weapon description	No. ordered	Year of order	Year(s) of deliveries	No. delivered	Comments
Finland							
S: France	Crotale NG SAMS	SAM system	20	1990	1993	20	Deal worth $230 m incl VT-1 SAMs
	TRS-2230/15	Surveillance radar	10	1990	1993	10	Deal worth $200 m
	VT-1	SAM	(480)	1988	1993	(480)	For 20 Crotale NG SAM systems
Germany, FR	Do-228-200MP	Maritime patrol	2	1992	1993	1	For Border Guard
Sweden	Giraffe 100	Surveillance radar	4	1992	1993		
UK	Hawk	Jet trainer aircraft	7	1990	1993	7	
	Marksman	AAA system	..	1992			Second order; to be fitted in Finland on T-55 main battle tank chassis
USA	F/A-18C/D Hornet	Fighter	64	1992	1992	(3)	Incl 7 F/A-18D trainer version; limited assembly in Finland
	AIM-120A AMRAAM	Air-to-air missile	(128)	1992	1992		For 64 F/A-18 fighters
	AIM-9M Sidewinder	Air-to-air missile	(384)	1992	1992		For 64 F/A-18 fighters
France							
S: Brazil	EMB-312 Tucano	Trainer aircraft	80	1991	1993	9	Deal worth $170 m
Germany, FR	Alpha Jet	Jet trainer aircraft	(40)	1992			Ex-FRG Air Force
Italy	Argos 45	Surveillance radar	28	(1990)	1991–93	(28)	
USA	VT-1	SAM	1 000	1988	1990–93	(1 000)	Incl 700 for re-export
L: USA	MLRS 227mm	MRL	55	1985	1985–93	(50)	
	VT-1	SAM	..	1991			
Gabon							
S: France	Mygale	SAM system	(5)	(1990)	1992–93	(4)	
Georgia							
S: Russia	T-72	Main battle tank	5	1993	1993	5	Ex-Russian Army; transferred by Russian forces in Georgia

Recipient/ supplier (S) or licenser (L)	No. ordered	Weapon designation	Weapon description	Year of order/ licence	Year(s) of deliveries	No. delivered/ produced	Comments
Germany, FR							
S: France	200	Apache	ASM	1992			For Tornado fighter/bombers;FRG designation MAW
Italy	..	Argos 73	Surveillance radar	1991			For 4 Brandenburg Class (Type 123) frigates
Netherlands	4	LW-08	Surveillance radar	(1989)			For 4 Brandenburg Class (Type 123) frigates
	5	Smart	Surveillance radar	1989			For 4 Brandenburg Class (Type 123) frigates and a training centre
USA	8	STIR	Fire control radar	1989			For 4 Brandenburg Class (Type 123) frigates
	5	AN/FPS-117	Surveillance radar	1992	1993	(2)	Deal worth $94 m incl 2 simulators and spares (offsets 100%)
	4	Seasparrow VLS	ShAM system	1989			For 4 Brandenburg Class (Type 123) frigates
	(1 182)	AGM-88 HARM	Anti-radar missile	1987	1988–93	(1 080)	For Tornado ECR fighter/bombers
	175	AIM-120A AMRAAM	Air-to-air missile	1991			For upgraded F-4F fighters
	1644	MIM-104 Patriot	SAM	1984	1989–93	(1 504)	
	(64)	Seasparrow	ShAM	1989			For 4 Brandenburg Class (Type 123) frigates
L: USA	150	MLRS 227mm	MRL	1985	1989–93	150	
	..	AIM-120A AMRAAM	Air-to-air missile	1989			
	4500	FIM-92A Stinger	Portable SAM	1987	1992–93	1 250	Deal worth $81 m
	(1 500)	RIM-116A RAM	ShAM	1985	1989–93	567	
Greece							
S: Germany, FR	(27)	RF-4E Phantom II	Reconnaissance plane	1991	1992–93	(10)	Ex-FRG Air Force
	150	RM-70 122mm	MRL	1991	1993	(50)	Former GDR equipment
	..	BMP-1	AIFV	1991	1992	(2)	Former GDR equipment; part of aid worth $605 m for unspecified mix of 500 BMP-1 and MT-LB
	..	MT-LB	APC	1991	1992	(1)	Former GDR equipment; part of aid worth $605 m for unspecified mix of 500 BMP-1 and MT-LB
	75	Leopard 1A3	Main battle tank	(1991)	1993	(75)	CFE cascade; ex-FRG Army; refurbished to A5GR standard before delivery
	200	M-113A1	APC	(1991)			CFE cascade; ex-FRG Army
	(64)	NATO Seasparrow	ShAM	(1988)	1992	(16)	For 4 Meko-200 Type frigates

Supplier	No.	Weapon designation	Weapon description	Year of order	Year(s) of deliveries	No. delivered	Comments
Netherlands	177	M-113A1	APC	1991		1	Ex-Dutch Army
	4	DA-08	Surveillance radar	1988	1992	1	For 4 Meko-200 Type frigates
	4	MW-08	Surveillance radar	(1989)	1992	1	For 4 Meko-200 Type frigates
	3	RGM-84A Launcher	ShShM system	1992	1993	1	On 3 Kortenaer Class frigates
	3	Seasparrow Launcher	ShAM system	1992	1993	1	On 3 Kortenaer Class frigates
	8	STIR	Fire control radar	1989	1992	2	For 4 Meko-200 Type frigates
	3	Kortenaer Class	Frigate	1992	1993	1	Ex-Dutch Navy; deal worth $211 m
Norway	..	Penguin-2-7	Anti-ship missile	1993			For SH-60B helicopters; deal worth $21 m
UK	32	F-4K Phantom II	Fighter	1992			Ex-UK Air Force
USA	12	AH-64A Apache	Helicopter	(1991)			Deal worth $505 m incl 3 spare engines, EW systems, support and spares; option on 8 more
	40	F-16C Fighting Falcon	Fighter	1993			Deal worth $1.8 b incl 10 spare engines and 40 LANTIRN pods
	5	SH-60B Seahawk	Helicopter	1991			Deal worth $161 m; option on 7 more; for Meko-200 Type frigates
	100	M-30 107mm	Mortar	1991	1993	(35)	CFE cascade; ex-US Army
	312	M-60A3 Patton	Main battle tank	(1990)	1990–93	(312)	CFE cascade; ex-US Army
	8	Phalanx	CIWS	(1987)	1992	2	For 4 Meko-200 Type frigates
	3	Phalanx	CIWS	1992	1992	3	On 3 Knox Class frigates
	4	RGM-84A Launcher	ShShM system	1989	1992	1	For 4 Meko-200 Type frigates
	4	Seasparrow VLS	ShAM system	1988	1992	1	For 4 Meko-200 Type frigates
	446	AGM-114A Hellfire	ASM	1991			For 12 AH-64A helicopters
	1 500	FIM-92A Stinger	Portable SAM	1988	1989–93	(1 250)	Deal worth $124 m incl 500 launchers
	32	RGM-84A Harpoon	ShShM	1993	1993	(16)	For Knox Class frigates; part of deal worth $170 m incl torpedoes, ASROC and ammunition
	114	RIM-66A Standard-1	ShAM	1991	1992–93	(114)	For Adams Class destroyers; deal worth $19 m
L: Austria	192	Steyr 4K-7FA	APC	1987	1991–93	(192)	Greek designation Leonidas 2; incl production for export
Denmark	2	Osprey 55 Type	Patrol craft	1990	1993	(1)	
Germany, FR	3	Meko-200 Type	Frigate	1988			Deal worth $1.2 b incl 1 delivered direct (offsets $250 m); partly financed by FRG and USA

Recipient/ supplier (S) or licenser (L)	No. ordered	Weapon designation	Weapon description	Year of order/ licence	Year(s) of deliveries	No. delivered/ produced	Comments
Hungary							
S: Germany, FR	20	L-39Z Albatros	Jet trainer aircraft	1993	1993	20	Former GDR equipment; deal worth $45 m incl spare parts and support
Russia	28	MiG-29C Fulcrum	Fighter	1993	1993	28	Incl MiG-29UB trainer version
	(56)	AA-10 Alamo	Air-to-air missile	1993	1993	(56)	For 28 MiG-29 fighters
	(112)	AA-8 Aphid	Air-to-air missile	1993	1993	(112)	For 28 MiG-29 fighters
India							
S: France	..	PSM-33	Surveillance radar	1988	1990–93	(4)	
Germany, FR	–1	Aditya Class	Support ship	1987	1992	1	Option on 1 more
USSR/Russia	10	Mi-26 Halo	Helicopter	1988	1993	(10)	
	(20)	MiG-29C Fulcrum	Fighter	1993	1993		Deal worth $500 m; incl 6 MiG-29UB trainer version
	..	2S6	AAV(G/M)	1992	1993	(50)	Part of larger deal incl aircraft and tanks; $830 m extended in credits for total deal
	..	SA-19	SAM	1992	1993	(400)	For 2S6 AAV(G/M)s
	8	Bass Tilt	Fire control radar	1983	1989–91	4	For 8 Khukri Class corvettes
	..	SA-11 SAMS	SAM system	1992	1993	(1)	Part of larger deal incl aircraft and tanks
	..	SA-11 Gadfly	SAM	1992	1993	(28)	For SA-11 SAM system
	8	SS-N-2 Styx Launcher	ShShM system	1983	1989–91	4	For 8 Khukri Class corvettes
	7	SS-N-2 Styx Launcher	ShShM system	1987	1991–93	3	For 7 Vibhuti (Tarantul I) Class fast attack craft
	3	SS-N-2 Styx Launcher	ShShM system	1993			For 3 Project 16A Improved Godavari Class frigates
	..	SA-N-5 Grail	ShAM	(1983)	1989–91	(160)	For 8 Khukri Class corvettes
	..	SA-N-5 Grail	ShAM	1987	1991–93	(120)	For 7 Vibhuti (Tarantul I) Class fast attack craft
	..	SS-N-2C Styx	ShShM	1983	1989–91	(48)	For 8 Khukri Class corvettes
	(36)	SS-N-2C Styx	ShShM	1987	1991–93	(36)	For 7 Vibhuti (Tarantul I) Class fast attack craft
	..	SS-N-2E Styx	ShShM	1993			For 3 Project 16A Improved Godavari Class frigates
	..	SS-N-22 Sunburn	ShShM	1992			For Delhi Class destroyers

Recipient/supplier	No.	Weapon designation	Weapon description	Year of order	Year(s) of deliveries	No. delivered	Comments
L: France	..	SA-316B Alouette III	Helicopter	(1962)	1964–93	(212)	Indian designation Chetak; also produced for civil use
Germany, FR	(15 000)	Milan 2	Anti-tank missile	1992	1993	(3 019)	
	43	Do-228	Transport aircraft	1983	1987–93	(37)	Incl 33 for Coast Guard and 27 for Navy
	60	Do-228MP	Maritime patrol	1983	1987–93	(19)	In addition to 2 delivered direct
	2	Type 1500	Submarine	1981	1992	(1)	In addition to 3 delivered direct
Korea, South	7	Sukanya Class	OPV	1987	1990–93	(5)	In addition to direct deliveries
Netherlands	212	Flycatcher	Fire control radar	(1987)	1988–93	(102)	Indian designation MuFAR
UK	..	Cymbeline Mk-1	Tracking radar	(1988)	1989–93	(20)	Indian designation Bahadur
USSR/Russia	200	MiG-27 Flogger D	Fighter/ground attack	1983	1984–93	(117)	Indian designation Sarath
	..	BMP-2	AIFV	1983	1987–93	(775)	In addition to 500 delivered direct
	500	T-72	Main battle tank	(1980)	1987–93	(406)	Indian designation Astra
	..	AA-8 Aphid	Air-to-air missile	(1986)			
	..	AT-4 Spigot	Anti-tank missile	1983	1990–93	(900)	For BMP-2 AIFVs
	7	Tarantul I Class	Fast attack craft	1987	1991–93	(3)	Indian designation Vibhuti Class; order may reach 15
Indonesia							
S: Germany, FR	12	Frosch Class	Landing ship	1992	1993	(3)	Part of deal for 39 former GDR ships; refurbished before delivery
	2	Frosch II Class	Supply ship	1992			Part of deal for 39 former GDR ships; refurbished before delivery
	9	Kondor Class	Minesweeper	1992			Part of deal for 39 former GDR ships; refurbished before delivery
	16	Parchim Class	Corvette	1992	1993	(9)	Part of deal for 39 former GDR ships; refurbished before delivery
UK	12	Hawk 100	Fighter/trainer	1993			Option on 16 more likely to be used
	12	Hawk 200	Fighter/ground attack	1993			Option on more
	(14)	AR-325	Surveillance radar	1989	1991–93	(6)	
L: France	..	AS-332 Super Puma	Helicopter	1983	1985–93	(9)	Incl production for civil use
Germany, FR	(100)	Bo-105CB	Helicopter	1987	1988–93	(60)	
Spain	..	CN-212-200 Aviocar	Transport aircraft	1976	1978–92	(40)	Incl maritime patrol and civil versions

Recipient/ supplier (S) or licenser (L)	No. ordered	Weapon designation	Weapon description	Year of order/ licence	Year(s) of deliveries	No. delivered/ produced	Comments
Iran							
S: China							
	(75)	F-7M Airguard	Fighter	(1991)			Second order
	(8)	HQ-2B SAMS	SAM system	(1989)	1990–93	(8)	
	(96)	HQ-2B	SAM	1989	1990–93	(96)	For 8 HQ-2B SAM systems
	(10)	Hegu Class	Fast attack craft	(1993)			Number may be 12
Korea, North							
	..	Scud C launcher	Mobile SSM system	(1991)	1993	(5)	Agreement apparently includes production equipment; number may be up to 200
	(170)	Scud C	SSM	(1991)	1993	(170)	
USSR/Russia							
	2	A-50 Mainstay	AEW&C aircraft	1992			Part of deal worth $2.5 b signed in July 1992
	(48)	MiG-29C Fulcrum	Fighter	1992			Part of deal worth $2.5 b signed in July 1992
	24	MiG-31 Foxhound	Fighter	1992			Part of deal worth $2.5 b signed in July 1992
	..	Su-24 Fencer	Fighter/bomber	(1991)			Could be up to 24
	12	Tu-22M Backfire	Bomber	1992			Status uncertain
	(500)	T-72	Main battle tank	1989	1990–93	(200)	
	(72)	AS-16 Kickback	ASM	1992			For Tu-22 Backfire bombers; could be AS-6 Kingfish
	2	Kilo Class	Submarine	1991	1992–93	2	Deal worth $750 m; option on 1 more
	1	Kilo Class	Submarine	1993			In addition to 2 ordered earlier; status uncertain
	..	SA-5 Gammon	SAM	1992	1993	(12)	Part of deal worth $2.5 b signed in July 1992
	(16)	SS-N-22 Sunburn	Coast defence missile	(1993)	1993	(16)	For coast defence system
Israel							
S: Germany, FR							
	2	Dolphin	Submarine	1991			Deal worth $570 m; partly financed by FRG
USA							
	7	AH-64A Apache	Helicopter	(1992)			Deal worth $140 m
	17	AH-64A Apache	Helicopter	1992			Ex-US Army
	30	F-16C Fighting Falcon	Fighter	1988	1991–93	(30)	
	30	F-16D Fighting Falcon	Fighter/trainer	1988	1991–93	(30)	
	6	CH-53D Stallion	Helicopter	1992			Ex-US Air Force; deal worth $13.2 m
	(10)	UH-60 Blackhawk	Helicopter	(1992)			
	9	MLRS 227/mm	MRL	1993			Deal worth $100 m incl rockets and support

No.	Weapon designation	Weapon description	Year of order	Year(s) of deliveries	No. delivered/ produced	Comments
6	M-577A2	APC/command post	1993			For 3 Saar 5 Class corvettes
3	RGM-84A Launcher	ShShM system	(1988)			Deal worth $32 m incl support
300	AIM-9S Sidewinder	Air-to-air missile	1990	1993	(100)	
..	FIM-92A Stinger	Portable SAM	1990	1993	(100)	
(48)	RGM-84A Harpoon	ShShM	(1988)			For 3 Saar 5 Class corvettes
3	Saar 5 Class	Corvette	1988			Built in USA to Israeli design
Italy						
S: Germany, FR						
8	Do-228-200	Transport aircraft	1990	1991–93	(6)	10-year lease worth $454 m
UK						
24	Tornado F-3 ADV	Fighter	1993	1993		Deal worth $521.7 m
USA						
13	AV-8B Harrier II Plus	Fighter/ground attack	1990			
3	AV-8B Harrier II Plus	Fighter/ground attack	1991	1993	10	Ex-US Marine Corps; lease; for Italian UN forces in Somalia
10	M-60A1 Patton	Main battle tank	1993			
4	AN/FPS-117	Surveillance radar	1990	1993	(1)	For 2 Animoso Class destroyers
2	RIM-66A Launcher	ShAM system	(1987)	1992–93	2	
446	AGM-88 HARM	Anti-radar missile	1992	1993	(30)	For Tornado fighters; deal worth $145 m
..	BGM-71D TOW-2	Anti-tank missile	1987	1990–93	(840)	For A-129 Mangusta helicopters
(80)	RIM-66A Standard-1	ShAM	1987	1992–93	(80)	For 2 Animoso Class destroyers
L: France						
..	Aster 15/30	SAM	1988			Part of deal incl co-development of Aster ShAM system
USA						
..	AB-206B	Helicopter	1972	1978–93	(674)	Incl production for export and civil use
..	AB-212	Helicopter	1970	1971–93	(184)	Incl production for export
..	AB-212ASW	Helicopter	1975	1975–91	(105)	Incl production for export
..	AB-412 Griffon	Helicopter	1980	1982–93	(88)	Incl production for export
50	Model 500E	Helicopter	1987	1987–93	(38)	
13	S-61R Pelican	Helicopter	1990	1991–93	(10)	
22	MLRS 227mm	MRL	1985	1990–93	(22)	
Japan						
S: UK						
3	BAe-125-800	Transport aircraft	1991			Second order
USA						
2	B-767 AWACS	AEW&C aircraft	1993			Deal worth $840 m; follow-on order for 2 expected

Recipient/ supplier (S) or licenser (L)	No. ordered	Weapon designation	Weapon description	Year of order/ licence	Year(s) of deliveries	No. delivered/ produced	Comments
	6	Beechjet 400T	Transport aircraft	1992	1993	3	Deal worth $170 m
	2	E-2C Hawkeye	AEW&C aircraft	1990	1993	2	For SAR
	2	Model 412HP	Helicopter	(1991)	1993	2	For Maritime Safety Agency
	..	S-76C	Helicopter	1993	1993	(1)	Deal worth $362 m; status of Japanese production uncertain
	36	MLRS 227mm	MRL	1993			
	2	AN/SPY-1D	Surveillance radar	1992			Part of Aegis system for 2 Kongo Class destroyers
	6	Phalanx	CIWS	1988	1993	(2)	For 3 Kongo Class destroyers; deal worth $66 m
	1	RGM-84A Launcher	ShShM system	1993	1993	1	For first of 3 Kongo Class destroyers
	1	Standard VLS	Fire control radar	(1988)	1993	1	Part of Aegis system for first of 3 Kongo Class destroyers
	75	AGM-84A Harpoon	Anti-ship missile	1990	1991–93	(53)	Deal worth $125 m
	14	RGM-84A Harpoon	ShShM	1993	1993	(14)	For first of 3 Kongo Class destroyers; deal worth $35 m incl spares
	46	RIM-66C/ Standard-2	ShAM	1993	1993	46	For first of 3 Kongo Class destroyers; deal worth $48 m
	..	Seasparrow	ShAM	1993			Deal worth $13.4 m
L: France							
Germany, FR	..	TB-120mm	Mortar	1992	1993	47	Incl 20 delivered direct
Italy	176	FH-70 155mm	Towed gun	1984	1989–93	151	Deal worth $170 m; option on 3 more
USA	3	Sparviero Class	Fast attack craft	1990	1993	2	
	49	CH-47D Chinook	Helicopter	(1984)	1986–93	46	
	2	EP-3C Orion	Elint aircraft	1992	1993	1	Second order
	55	F-15J Eagle	Fighter	1985	1988–93	52	
	(130)	FS-X	Fighter	1988			Based on F-16C; US firms guaranteed 42% of work
	52	Model 205 Kai	Helicopter	1991	1992–93	26	
	83	Model 209 AH-1S	Helicopter	1982	1984–93	67	
	..	OH-6J	Helicopter	1977	1978–93	157	
	70	P-3C Orion	ASW/maritime patrol	1985	1987–93	51	
	52	SH-60J Seahawk	Helicopter	1988	1991–93	26	Incl 31 ASW and 21 SAR versions

	No.	Weapon designation	Weapon description	Year of order	Year(s) of deliveries	No. delivered/ produced	Comments
	46	UH-60J Blackhawk	Helicopter	1988	1990–93	16	For F-15 fighters; deal worth $477 m
	1 330	AIM-7M Sparrow	Air-to-air missile	1990	1990–93	583	
	..	BGM-71C 1-TOW	Anti-tank missile	(1983)	1985–93	5 874	
	980	MIM-104 Patriot	SAM	1984	1989–93	834	
	..	MIM-23B HAWK	SAM	1978	1978–93	3 204	
Kiribati							
S: Australia	1	ASI-315	Patrol craft	1992			Pacific Forum aid programme
Korea, North							
L: China	..	Romeo Class	Submarine	1973	1975–92	19	
Korea, South							
S: France	1000	Mistral	Portable SAM	1992	1993	(200)	Deal worth $180 m (offsets 25%)
Germany, FR	1	Type 209/3	Submarine	1987	1993	1	Deal worth $600 m
Netherlands	..	Goalkeeper	CIWS	1991			For KDX-2000 Type frigates
	1	STIR	Fire control radar	(1992)			For first of KDX-2000 Type frigates
Spain	12	CN-235M	Transport aircraft	1992	1993	2	Deal worth $164 m
Switzerland	20	PC-9	Trainer aircraft	1993			Deal worth $66 m
UK	20	Hawk	Jet trainer aircraft	1990	1992–93	20	Deal worth $140 m
USA	37	AH-64A Apache	Helicopter	1992			Deal worth $997 m incl 775 Hellfire missiles and 8 spare engines
	48	F-16C Fighting Falcon	Fighter	1991			Deal worth $2.52 b incl 72 licensed production, 12 spare engines and 20 LANTIRN pods
	8	P-3C Orion Update-3	ASW/maritime patrol	1990			Deal worth $840 m incl spare engines, training and spares
	77	UH-60 Blackhawk	Helicopter	1990	1991–93	(27)	Deal worth $500 m incl 3 delivered direct
	3	AN/FPS-117	Surveillance radar	1990	1992–93	(2)	
	1	RGM-84A Launcher	ShShM system	(1992)			For first of KDX-2000 Type frigates
	..	Seasparrow VLS	ShAM system	1990			For KDX-2000 Type frigates
	775	AGM-114A Hellfire	ASM	1992			For 37 AH-64A helicopters
	127	AGM-65D Maverick	ASM	1993			For 37 AH-64A helicopters

Recipient/ supplier (S) or licenser (L)	No. ordered	Weapon designation	Weapon description	Year of order/ licence	Year(s) of deliveries	No. delivered/ produced	Comments
	28	AGM-84A Harpoon	Anti-ship missile	1992			For P-3C Orion aircraft; deal worth $58 m incl technical assistance
	40	AGM-88 HARM	Anti-radar missile	1992			
	190	AIM-120A AMRAAM	Air-to-air missile	1993			
	179	AIM-7M Sparrow	Air-to-air missile	1991	1992–93	(179)	Deal worth $31 m
	300	AIM-9S Sidewinder	Air-to-air missile	1993			Part of deal worth $34 m incl spares and support
	(24)	RGM-84A Harpoon	ShShM	(1992)			For first of 9 KDX-2000 Type frigates
	21	Seasparrow	ShAM	1990			For KDX-2000 Type frigates; deal worth $33 m incl training rounds and support
L: Germany, FR	2	Type 209/3	Submarine	1987			
	3	Type 209/3	Submarine	1989			In addition to 1 delivered direct
	3	Type 209/3	Submarine	1992			
Japan	30	BK-117	Helicopter	1990	1992–93	20	
USA	72	F-16C Fighting Falcon	Fighter	1991			Part of deal worth $2.52 b
	242	M-109A2 155mm	Self-propelled gun	1989	1991–93	150	Deal worth $260 m
	(743)	K-1 ROKIT	Main battle tank	1980	1985–93	660	
	..	M-167 Vulcan	AAA system	(1986)	1986–93	76	
Kuwait							
S: Australia	2	OPV-310 Type	Patrol craft	1992	1993	2	
	2	OPV-310 Type	Patrol craft	1992	1993	2	Second order
UK	254	MCV-80 Warrior	AIFV	1993			Deal worth $740 m
USA	40	F/A-18C/D Hornet	Fighter	1988	1991–93	40	Deal worth $1.9 b incl 8 F/A-18D trainer version and armament
	218	M-1A2 Abrams	Main battle tank	1992			Part of deal worth $4.5 b
	16	M-113A3	APC	1992			Part of deal worth $4.5 b; option on 109
	30	M-577A2	APC/command post	1992			Part of deal worth $4.5 b, option on 22
	46	M-88A1	ARV	1992			Part of deal worth $4.5 b

No.	Designation	Description	Year of order	Year of delivery	No. delivered	Comments
1	AN/FPS-117	Surveillance radar	1992	1993	1	Deal worth $92 m
6	I-HAWK SAMS	SAM system	1992			Part of deal worth $2.5 b
1	Patriot SAMS	SAM system	1992			Part of deal worth $2.5 b
5	Patriot SAMS	SAM system	(1993)			Deal worth $327 m incl 210 missiles (offsets 30%)
300	AGM-65G Maverick	Anti-ship missile	1988	1991–93	(300)	For F/A-18 fighters
40	AGM-84A Harpoon	Anti-ship missile	1988			For F/A-18 fighters
200	AIM-7F Sparrow	Air-to-air missile	1988	1992–93	(200)	For F/A-18 fighters
120	AIM-9L Sidewinder	Air-to-air missile	1988	1992–93	(120)	For F/A-18 fighters
210	MIM-104 PAC-2	SAM	1992			Part of deal worth $2.5 b
342	MIM-23B HAWK	SAM	1992			Part of deal worth $2.5 b incl Patriot missile systems, training and support
Latvia						
S: Germany, FR						
2	L-410UVP Turbolet	Transport aircraft	(1992)	1993	2	Former GDR equipment; gift
2	Kondor Class	Minesweeper	1992			Former GDR equipment
3	Osa II Class	Fast attack craft	1992			Former GDR equipment
Lithuania						
S: Germany, FR						
2	L-410UVP Turbolet	Transport aircraft	1992	1993	2	Former GDR equipment; gift
Russia						
8	L-39C Albatros	Jet trainer aircraft	1993	1993	4	Ex-Russian Air Force; deal worth $0.08 m; incl 4 from Russian stocks in Kyrgyzstan
2	Stenka Class	Fast attack craft	1992			Ex-Russian Navy
2	Turya Class	Fast attack craft	1992	1993	2	Ex-Russian Navy
Malaysia						
S: France						
2	MM-40 Launcher	ShShM system	1992			For 2 Frigate 2000 Type frigates; deal worth $181 m
(48)	MM-40 Exocet	ShShM	1992			For 2 Frigate 2000 Type frigates
Netherlands						
2	DA-08	Surveillance radar	1992			For 2 Frigate 2000 Type frigates
Russia						
6	Mi-24 Hind E	Helicopter	1993			Part of deal incl MiG-29; Mi-35 export version
18	MiG-29C Fulcrum	Fighter	1993			Incl 6 MiG-29UB trainer version; status uncertain
Sweden						
2	Sea Giraffe 150	Surveillance radar	1992			For 2 Frigate 2000 Type frigates

Recipient/ supplier (S) or licenser (L)	No. ordered	Weapon designation	Weapon description	Year of order/ licence	Year(s) of deliveries	No. delivered/ produced	Comments
UK	10	Hawk 100	Fighter/trainer	1990			Part of a deal worth $740 m incl 18 Hawk 200 aircraft, weapons, training and services
	18	Hawk 200	Fighter/ground attack	1990			
	3	Martello 743-D	Surveillance radar	1990	1992–93	(3)	Part of deal worth $190 m
	12	Rapier SAMS	SAM system	1988			
	2	Seawolf VLS	ShAM system	1992			For 2 Frigate 2000 Type frigates
	(576)	Improved Rapier	SAM	1988			
	(96)	Seawolf 2	ShAM	1992			For 2 Frigate 2000 Type frigates
	..	Starburst	Portable SAM	1993			
	2	Frigate 2000 Type	Corvette	1992			Deal worth $600 m incl spares, training and support
USA	4	B-200T Maritime	Maritime patrol	1992	1993	1	
	8	F/A-18D Hornet	Fighter	1993			Offsets $250 m
	50	AGM-84A Harpoon	Anti-ship missile	1993			For F/A-18 fighters
	51	AIM-7M Sparrow	Air-to-air missile	1993			For F/A-18 fighters
	110	AIM-9S Sidewinder	Air-to-air missile	1993			For F/A-18 fighters
Mauritius S: UK	1	BN-2T Maritime	Maritime patrol	1992	1993	1	
Mexico S: USA	10	Model 530MG	Helicopter	1992	1993	(10)	
Morocco S: Denmark	2	Osprey 55 Type	OPV	1990			
Italy	2	Aspide/Albatros	ShAM system	1992			For 2 Assad Class corvettes
	2	Otomat 2 Launcher	ShShM system	1992			For 2 Assad Class corvettes
	2	RAN-12L/X	Surveillance radar	1992			For 2 Assad Class corvettes
	4	RTN-10X	Fire control radar	1992			For 2 Assad Class corvettes

No.	Designation	Type	Order date	Delivery	Delivered	Comments
Spain						
14	Aspide	ShAM	1992			For 2 Assad Class corvettes
(36)	Otomat 2	ShShM	1992			For 2 Assad Class corvettes
2	Assad Class	Corvette	1992			Deal worth $250 m; option on 2 more; originally built for Iraq, but embargoed
6	C-212-300MPA	Maritime patrol	1989			Part of deal worth $350 m
1	Super F-30 Class	Frigate	1991			Part of deal worth $350 m incl 6 C-212 aircraft and electronic equipment; status uncertain
USA						
1	Knox Class	Frigate	1993			Ex-US Navy; lease worth $3 m
Myanmar						
S: China						
(2)	Y-8	Transport aircraft	(1991)	1992–93	(2)	
10	Hainan Class	Patrol craft	1990	1991–93	10	
Namibia						
S: Denmark						
1	Osprey Type	Patrol craft	1993	1993	1	Ex-Danish Ministry of Fisheries; refurbished before delivery; aid
USA						
6	O-2A	Utility plane	1992			Ex-US Army: aid
Netherlands						
S: Canada						
7	CH-47C Chinook	Helicopter	(1993)			Ex-Canadian Air Force; to be upgraded to CH-47D in USA
France						
17	AS-532 Cougar	Helicopter	1993			Deal worth $245 m (offsets 120%)
Germany, FR						
25	Buffel	ARV	1990	1992–93	(16)	Option on 10–15 more
Italy						
3	AB-412 Griffon	Helicopter	1992	1993	(1)	Deal worth $22.8 m; for SAR
USA						
2	C-130H-30 Hercules	Transport aircraft	1993			Deal worth $127 m
6	CH-47D Chinook	Helicopter	1993			In addition to 7 from Canada being upgraded in USA
8	RGM-84A Launcher	ShShM system	1988	1991–93	5	For 8 Karel Doorman Class frigates
8	Seasparrow VLS	ShAM system	1985	1991–93	5	For 8 Karel Doorman Class frigates
(40)	AGM-84A Harpoon	Anti-ship missile	1988			Status uncertain
290	AIM-9M Sidewinder	Air-to-air missile	1993			For F-16 fighters; deal worth $27 m
(192)	RGM-84A Harpoon	ShShM	1988	1991–93	(120)	For 8 Karel Doorman Class frigates
(128)	Seasparrow	ShAM	1985	1991–93	(80)	For 8 Karel Doorman Class frigates

Recipient/ supplier (S) or licenser (L)	No. ordered	Weapon designation	Weapon description	Year of order/ licence	Year(s) of deliveries	No. delivered/ produced	Comments
New Zealand							
S: Australia	2	Meko-200 Type	Frigate	1989			Option on 2 more; deal worth $554.7 m
Italy	18	MB-339C	Jet trainer aircraft	1990	1991–93	18	Deal worth $157 m incl spares and support
Sweden	2	9LV	Fire control radar	1991			For 2 Meko-200 Type frigates
	2	Sea Giraffe 150	Surveillance radar	1991			For 2 Meko-200 Type frigates
	2	Seasparrow VLS	ShAM system	1992			For 2 Meko-200 Type frigates
USA	..	NATO Seasparrow	ShAM	(1991)			For 2 Meko-200 Type frigates
Nigeria							
S: Brazil	..	EE-9 Cascavel	Armoured car	(1992)	1993	(75)	
France	..	VBL	Scout car	(1992)	1993	(10)	
UK	80	MBT Mk-3	Main battle tank	1990	1991–93	(75)	Deal worth $282 m, order may reach 150
L: USA	..	Air Beetle	Trainer	1988	1988–92	(3)	
Norway							
S: France	7200	Eryx	Anti-tank missile	1993			Deal worth $115 m incl 424 launchers
	400	Mistral	Portable SAM	1990	1992–93	(200)	Deal worth $60 m (offsets 75%)
Germany, FR	92	Leopard 1A1	Main battle tank	1991	1992–93	(60)	CFE cascade; ex-FRG Army
Sweden	(9)	Giraffe 50AT	Surveillance radar	1989	1992–93	(6)	Deal worth $90 m
	(360)	RBS-70	Portable SAM	1989	1991–93	(270)	Deal worth $80 m (offsets 45%); sixth order
UK	2	Sea King HAR-3	Helicopter	1993			Deal worth $22.5 m
USA	136	M-113A1	APC	1991	1993	134	CFE cascade; ex-US Army
	100	AIM-120A AMRAAM	Air-to-air missile	1989			Deal worth $75 m, for F-16 fighters
	7 612	BGM-71D TOW-2	Anti-tank missile	1985	1987–93	(6 000)	Deal worth $126 m incl 300 launchers and spares
Oman							
S: France	2	Crotale NG Naval	ShAM system	1992			For 2 Muheet Class corvettes
	2	MM-40 Launcher	ShShM system	1992			For 2 Muheet Class corvettes

Supplier	No.	Weapon designation	Weapon description	Year of order	Year of delivery	No. delivered	Comments
	(48)	MM-40 Exocet	ShShM	1992			For 2 Muheet Class corvettes
	(48)	VT-1	SAM	1992			For Crotale NG Naval ShAM system for 2 Muheet Class corvettes
Netherlands	3	P-400 Class	Patrol craft	1993			For 2 Muheet Class corvettes
UK	2	MW-08	Surveillance radar	1992	1992		Deal worth $225 m incl 12 Hawk 200 version
	4	Hawk 100	Fighter/trainer	1989			Deal worth $225 m incl 4 Hawk 100 version
	12	Hawk 200	Fighter/ground attack	1990			
	18	Challenger 2	Main battle tank	1993	1993		Deal worth $225 m incl 4 ARV version, 4 Stormer APCs and 2 training tanks; option on 18 more
	4	Challenger ARV	ARV	1993			
	4	FV-4333 Stormer	APC/command post	1993			
	..	Improved Rapier	SAM	1992	1993	(20)	Deal worth $60 m
	..	Starstreak	SAM	1993			
	2	Muheet Class	Corvette	1992			Deal worth $225 m
USA	..	M-88A1	ARV	1992	1992		Unknown quantity ordered
	(96)	AIM-9L Sidewinder	Air-to-air missile	1990	1990		For 16 Hawk 100/200 aircraft
	1	Knox Class	Frigate	1993	1993	(1)	Ex-US Navy; lease worth $3 m
Pakistan							
S: China	98	A-5 Fantan A	Fighter/ground attack	(1991)	1993		Second order
	40	F-7M Airguard	Fighter	(1991)	1993	(20)	Includes 20 trainer versions
	25	Karakorum-8	Jet trainer aircraft	1987			
France	12	SA-315B Lama	Helicopter	1992	1992–93	(12)	Deal worth $17.7 m
	1	Eridan Class	MCM ship	1992			In addition to one ex-French Navy and one built locally
UK	1	BN-2A Defender	Transport aircraft	(1992)	1993	1	
	(6)	Lynx	Helicopter	(1993)			For 6 Amazon Class frigates
	..	MM-38 Launcher	ShShM system	1993	1993	2	May be up to 6; on Amazon Class frigates
	6	Seacat Launcher	ShAM system	1993	1993	2	On 6 Amazon Class frigates
	..	Seacat	ShAM	1993	1993	(24)	For 6 Amazon Class frigates
	6	Amazon Class	Frigate	1993	1993	(2)	Ex-UK Navy; deal worth $90 m

Recipient/ supplier (S) or licenser (L)	No. ordered	Weapon designation	Weapon description	Year of order/ licence	Year(s) of deliveries	No. delivered/ produced	Comments
USA	(20)	M-109A2 155mm	Self-propelled gun	1988			Deal worth $40 m incl M-198 guns and support equipment
	..	AN/TPQ-36	Tracking radar	(1990)			Deal worth $65 m
	4	AN/TPQ-37	Tracking radar	(1985)	1987–89	(3)	
	2 386	BGM-71D TOW-2	Anti-tank missile	1987			Deal incl 144 launchers
L: China	..	Karakorum-8	Jet trainer aircraft	1993			Following direct delivery/local assembly of 25
	(450)	T-69-II	Main battle tank	(1989)	1991–93	222	Deal worth $1.2 b
	..	T-85	Main battle tank	1990	1993	12	
	..	Anza	Portable SAM	(1988)	1989–93	450	
	..	Red Arrow 8	Anti-tank missile	1989	1990–93	200	
France	1	Eridan Class	MCM ship	1992			In addition to 2 built in France
Sweden	..	Shahbaz	Trainer aircraft	1987	1992–93	16	Derived from Mushakh (Saab Supporter)
USA	..	LAADS	Surveillance radar	(1989)			Lead items delivered from 1989
Peru							
S: Nicaragua	14	Mi-17 Hip H	Helicopter	1992	1992–93	14	Ex-Nicaraguan Air Force; part of deal worth $25 m
	2	Mi-8 Hip E	Helicopter	1992	1993	2	Ex-Nicaraguan Air Force; part of deal worth $25 m
	12	BTR-60P	APC	1992	1993	12	Ex-Nicaraguan Army; part of deal worth $25 m
	216	SA-16 Gimlet	Portable SAM	1992	1992–93	(216)	Ex-Nicaraguan Army, part of deal worth $25 m; deal also incl 72 launchers
USA	18	Model 280FX	Helicopter	1991	1993	10	For Army
Philippines							
S: Australia	3	PC-57M Type	Fast attack craft	1990			Status uncertain
China	2	LSV Type	Landing ship	1991			
France	3	MM-40 Launcher	ShShM system	1991			For 3 Cormoran Class fast attack craft
	..	MM-40 Exocet	ShShM	1992			For 3 Cormoran Class fast attack craft
Italy	36	S-211	Jet trainer aircraft	1988	1989–93	24	

Supplier	No.	Weapon designation	Weapon description	Year of order	Year of deliveries	No. delivered	Comments
Netherlands	16	SF-260TP	Trainer aircraft	1992	1993	6	Deal worth $52 m; for local assembly
Russia	3	WM-22	Fire control radar	(1991)			For 3 PC-57M Type fast attack craft
	1	Yak-18T	Light plane	(1993)			
Spain	3	Cormoran Class	Fast attack craft	1991			Deal worth $100 m
UK	150	FS-100 Simba	APC	1992	1993		Deal worth $46 m
USA	10	Model 205 UH-1H	Helicopter	(1990)	1992–93	(7)	Ex-US Army
	8	Model 530MG	Helicopter	1992	1992–93	(10)	Deal worth $11 m
	12	V-300 Commando	APC	1993		8	Deal worth $18.2 m incl 12 FSV version
	12	V-300 FSV Commando	AIFV	1993			Deal worth $18.2 m incl 12 APC version
	2	Besson class	Landing ship	1992	1993	2	Deal worth $32.2 m; option on 1 more

Poland

Supplier	No.	Weapon designation	Weapon description	Year of order	Year of deliveries	No. delivered	Comments
S: USSR	(8)	An-28	Transport aircraft	(1992)	1993	1	Version with Polish electronics used for SAR

Portugal

Supplier	No.	Weapon designation	Weapon description	Year of order	Year of deliveries	No. delivered	Comments
S: Germany, FR	50	Alpha Jet	Jet trainer aircraft	1993	1993	(50)	Ex-FRG Air Force
	..	LARS 110mm	MRL	(1991)	(1991)		CFE cascade; ex-FRG Army
	50	M-113A1	APC	1993	1993		Ex-FRG Army
Netherlands	104	M-113A1	APC	1991	1993	(103)	CFE cascade; ex-Dutch Army
Spain	2	C-212-300MPA	Maritime patrol	1993	1993		Deal worth $19.6 m; half of cost paid by EC
UK	5	Super Lynx	Helicopter	1990	1993	5	Incl 3 re-built ex-UK Navy Lynx; for 3 Meko-200 Type frigates; deal worth $81 m (offsets 25%)
	1	Watchman	Surveillance radar	1993	1993		NATO aid
	1	Rover Class	Support ship	1993	1993	1	Ex-UK Navy
USA	17	F-16A Fighting Falcon	Fighter	1990			Ex-US Air Force; in exchange for US base rights in the Azores
	3	F-16B Fighting Falcon	Fighter/trainer	1990			Ex-US Air Force; in exchange for US base rights in the Azores
	(40)	Model 205 UH-1H	Helicopter	1989			
	(12)	Model 209 AH-1G	Helicopter	1989			Ex-US Air Force; in exchange for US base rights in the Azores

Qatar

Supplier	No.	Weapon designation	Weapon description	Year of order	Year of deliveries	No. delivered	Comments
S: Brazil	..	Astros II	MRL	(1991)	1992	(4)	

Recipient/ supplier (S) or licenser (L)	No. ordered	Weapon designation	Weapon description	Year of order/ licence	Year(s) of deliveries	No. delivered/ produced	Comments
France	..	VBL	Scout car	(1992)	1993	(10)	
	4	Crotale NG Naval	ShAM system	1992			For 4 Vita Class fast attack craft
	4	MM-40 Launcher	ShShM system	1992			For 4 Vita Class fast attack craft
	500	Mistral	Portable SAM	1990	1992–93	(200)	
	(96)	MM-40 Exocet	ShShM	1992			For 4 Vita Class fast attack craft
Netherlands	4	Goalkeeper	CIWS	1992			For 4 Vita Class fast attack craft
UK	4	Vita Class	Fast attack craft	1992			Deal worth $200 m
Romania							
L: France	..	SA-330 Puma	Helicopter	1977	1978–93	180	Incl production for export and civil use
UK	..	BN-2A Islander	Transport aircraft	1968	1969–93	460	Most for export in civilian version
USSR	..	Yak-52	Trainer aircraft	1976	1979–93	1 625	Most for export to USSR
	..	SA-7 Grail	Portable SAM	(1978)	1978–93	400	Most for export to USSR
Saudi Arabia							
S: Canada	1 117	LAV-25	AIFV	1990	1992–93	(512)	Deal worth $700 m; 384 LAV-25 and 733 other LAV versions
UK	20	Hawk 100	Fighter/trainer	1993			
	40	Hawk 200	Fighter/ground attack	1993			
	48	Tornado IDS	Fighter/bomber	1993			
	88	WS-70 Blackhawk	Helicopter	1993			
	461	Piranha 8x8	APC	1990	1992–93	(89)	Deal worth $400 m; several versions
	200	ALARM	ARM	1986	1991–93	(180)	For Tornado IDS fighter/bombers
	(480)	Sea Eagle	Anti-ship missile	1985			For Tornado IDS fighter/bombers
USA	3	Sandown Class	MCM ship	1988	1991–93	2	Option on 3 more; Saudi designation Al Jawf Class
	12	AH-64A Apache	Helicopter	1990	1993	12	Deal worth $300 m
	72	F-15S Strike Eagle	Fighter/bomber	1992			Deal worth $9 b incl 24 spare engines, 48 navigation pods and armament
	7	KC-130H Hercules	Tanker/transport	1990			Part of deal worth $750 m incl C-130H transport aircraft

No.	Weapon designation	Weapon description	Year of order	Year of deliveries	No. delivered	Comments
8	UH-60 Blackhawk	Helicopter	1992			Medevac version; deal worth $225 m
315	M-1A2 Abrams	Main battle tank	1990	1993	(100)	Deal worth $1.5 b
150	M-1A2 Abrams	Main battle tank	1990			
400	M-2A1 Bradley	AIFV	1990	1992–93	(202)	
8	Patriot SAMS	SAM system	1990	1993	(4)	Deal worth $984 m incl 384 missiles, 6 radars and support
13	Patriot SAMS	SAM system	1992			Deal worth $1.03 b incl 761 missiles
362	AGM-114A Hellfire	Anti-tank missile	1993	1993	(150)	For 12 AH-64A helicopters; deal worth $606 m incl 3500 rockets, 40 trucks and a simulator
900	AGM-65D/G Maverick	ASM	1992			For 48 F-15 fighters; mix of D and G versions
770	AIM-7M Sparrow	Air-to-air missile	1991	1992–93	(500)	Part of deal worth $365 m incl laser-guided bombs
300	AIM-7M Sparrow	Air-to-air missile	1992			For 72 F-15S fighter/bombers
300	AIM-9S Sidewinder	Air-to-air missile	1992			For 72 F-15S fighter/bombers
4 460	BGM-71D TOW-2	Anti-tank missile	1988	1989–93	(2 500)	
2 000	BGM-71D TOW-2	Anti-tank missile	1990			
384	MIM-104 PAC-2	SAM	1990	1993	(192)	Deal worth $55 m incl 116 launchers
761	MIM-104 PAC-2	SAM	1992			Deal worth $1.03 b incl 13 Patriot SAMS

Singapore

S: France

No.	Weapon designation	Weapon description	Year of order	Year of deliveries	No. delivered	Comments
36	LG-1 105mm	Towed gun	1990	1991–93	(36)	Supplied with 30 launchers; follow-on order for Navy probable
150	Mistral	Portable SAM	1992			

Israel

| 6 | Barak Launcher | ShAM system | (1992) | 1993 | (3) | For 6 Victory Class corvettes |
| (700) | Barak 1 | ShAM | (1992) | 1993 | (50) | For 6 Victory Class corvettes |

Netherlands

| 4 | F-50 Maritime Enforcer | ASW/maritime patrol | 1991 | | | Option on 2 more |

South Africa

| 1 | Lancelot Class | Landing ship | 1992 | 1992 | 1 | Second-hand; acquired from private company |

Sweden

| 4 | Landsort Class | MCM ship | 1991 | 1993 | 1 | |

USA

11	F-16C Fighting Falcon	Fighter	1992	1993	(9)	Deal worth $330 m incl 9 leased and based in USA
9	F-16C Fighting Falcon	Fighter	1993			In addition to 9 leased and 2 bought as attrition replacements
20	AGM-84A Harpoon	Anti-ship missile	1991			
50	AIM-7M Sparrow	Air-to-air missile	1993			For F-16 fighters
36	AIM-9S Sidewinder	Air-to-air missile	1993			For F-16 fighters

Recipient/ supplier (S) or licenser (L)	No. ordered	Weapon designation	Weapon description	Year of order/ licence	Year(s) of deliveries	No. delivered/ produced	Comments
Slovakia							
S: Russia	5	MiG-29C Fulcrum	Fighter	1993	1993	(2)	Part of deal worth $180 m; payment for Russian debts with Slovak Republic
South Africa							
S: Switzerland	60	PC-7 Turbo Trainer	Trainer aircraft	1993			Deal worth $130 m (offsets 55%)
Spain							
S: France	840	Mistral	Portable SAM	1991	1992–93	(300)	Deal worth $154 m incl 200 launchers (offsets 50%)
Germany, FR	1	Darss Class	Support ship	1993	1993	1	Former GDR ship; re-fitted in Spain for Elint duties
USA	8	AV-8B Harrier II Plus	Fighter/ground attack	1992	1992–93		Deal worth $257 m; final assembly in Spain
	2	Citation II	Transport aircraft	(1992)	1992–93	2	For aerial survey/photo-reconnaissance
	1	F/A-18L Hornet	Fighter	1990			Attrition replacement
	8	S-76C	Helicopter	1991	1991–93	8	
	6	SH-60B Seahawk	Helicopter	1991	1992	2	Deal worth $251 m, for FFG-7 Class frigates
	1	TAV-8B Harrier II	Fighter/trainer	1992			Deal worth $25 m
	83	M-110A2 203mm	Self-propelled gun	1991	1993	(41)	CFE cascade; ex-US Army
	100	M-113A1	APC	1991	1993	(100)	CFE cascade; ex-US Army
	260	M-60A3 Patton	Main battle tank	1991	1992–93	(260)	CFE cascade; ex-US Army
	4	RGM-84A CDS	Coast defence system	1988	1993	(4)	
	200	AIM-120A AMRAAM	Air-to-air missile	1990	1993	(100)	Deal worth $132 m; for F/A-18L fighters
	2 000	BGM-71D TOW-2	Anti-tank missile	1987			Deal worth $1 b incl 200 launchers
	16	RGM-84A Harpoon	Coast defence missile	1989	1993	(16)	For 4 RGM-84A coast defence systems
	(16)	RGM-84A Harpoon	ShShM	1989			For 2 FFG-7 Class frigates
	150	RIM-66A Standard-1	ShAM	(1989)	1992–93	(34)	Deal worth $88 m; for FFG-7 and Baleares Class frigates
L: UK	4	Sandown Class	MCM ship	1993			
USA	2	FFG-7 Class	Frigate	1990			Spanish designation Santa Maria Class

Supplier	No. ordered	Weapon designation	Weapon description	1992	1993	No. delivered	Comments
Sri Lanka							
S: Russia	3	Mi-17 Hip H	Helicopter	1992	1993	3	
Sweden							
S: France	...	TRS-2620	Surveillance radar	1990	1991	(1)	Former GDR equipment; deal worth $10.3 m
Germany, FR	800	MT-LB	APC	1993	1993	(400)	Deal worth $23.8 m
Italy	5	AB-412 Griffon	Helicopter	1993	1993	(1)	Ex-US Air Force; part of deal worth $60 m
USA	1	Gulfstream IV	Transport aircraft	1992	1993	1	Part of deal worth $60 m
USA	2	Gulfstream IV	Transport aircraft	1992			
Switzerland							
S: France	12	AS-332 Super Puma	Helicopter	1989	1991–93	(12)	Deal worth $190 m (offsets 100%)
UK	3	Watchman	Surveillance radar	1990	1992–93	(2)	
USA	34	F/A-18C/D Hornet	Fighter	1993			Deal worth $2.3 b; incl 8 F/A-18D trainer version
USA	(500)	AGM-65B Maverick	ASM	1991			For F-5 fighters
USA	...	AIM-120A AMRAAM	Air-to-air missile	1988			For F/A-18 Hornet fighters
USA	(204)	AIM-9L Sidewinder	Air-to-air missile	(1988)			For F/A-18 Hornet fighters
USA	12 000	BGM-71D TOW-2	Anti-tank missile	(1985)	1988–93	(4 712)	Deal worth $209 m incl 400 launchers and night-vision sights
USA	3 500	FIM-92A Stinger	Portable SAM	1988	1993	(250)	Deal worth $315 m; licensed production under discussion
L: Germany, FR	345	Leopard 2	Main battle tank	1983	1987–93	(345)	Deal worth $1400 m incl 35 delivered direct
Syria							
S: Czechoslovakia	(252)	T-72	Main battle tank	1991	1992–93	161	Order may be up to 300 and may include 90 T-55s
Korea, North	(150)	Scud C	SSM	1989	1991–93	(100)	At least 20 delivered via Iran
Taiwan							
S: France	60	Mirage-2000-5	Fighter	1992			Deal worth $2.6 b; option on 40 more (offsets 10%)
France	(1 500)	Mica	Air-to-air missile	(1992)			Deal worth $1.2 b incl R-550; for 60 Mirage-2000-5 fighters
France	(500)	R-550 Magic II	Air-to-air missile	1992			Deal worth $1.2 b incl Mica; for 60 Mirage-2000-5 fighters

Recipient/ supplier (S) or licenser (L)	No. ordered	Weapon designation	Weapon description	Year of order/ licence	Year(s) of deliveries	No. delivered/ produced	Comments
USA	6	La Fayette Class	Frigate	1991			Deal worth $4.7 b
	12	C-130H Hercules	Transport aircraft	1993			Deal worth $620 m incl spares and support
	4	E-2C Hawkeye	AEW&C aircraft	1993			Deal worth $700 m
	150	F-16A Fighting Falcon	Fighter	1992			Deal worth $5.8 b incl spare engines and missiles
	18	Model 209 AH-1W	Helicopter	1991	1993	8	Option on 24 more
	26	OH-58D Kiowa	Helicopter	1992	1993	4	Deal worth $367 m
	12	SH-2F Seasprite	Helicopter	1992	1993	(6)	Deal worth $161 m incl spare engines; ex-US Navy
	200	M-60A3 Patton	Main battle tank	1991	1993		Deal worth $185 m; ex-US Army
	..	AN/MPQ-53	Fire control radar	(1991)	1992	(1)	
	7	Patriot SAMS	SAM system	1993			Deal worth $1.3 b incl missiles
	3	Phalanx	CIWS	1992	1992–93	3	On 3 Knox Class frigates
	6	Phalanx	CIWS	1991	1993	1	For 6 Cheng Kung FFG-7 Class frigates
	3	RGM-84A Launcher	ShShM system	1992	1992–93	3	On 3 Knox Class frigates
	6	RIM-66A Launcher	ShAM system	1989	1993	1	For 6 licence-built Cheng Kung (FFG-7) Class frigates
	1	Standard VLS	Fire control radar	1993			Deal worth $103 m incl spares and support; for Tien Tan (FFG-7) Class
	684	AGM-114A Hellfire	ASM	(1991)	1993	(200)	Deal worth $11.7 m; for OH-58D and AH-1W helicopters
	600	AIM-7M Sparrow	Air-to-air missile	1992			For 150 F-16 fighters
	900	AIM-9S Sidewinder	Air-to-air missile	1992			For 150 F-16 fighters
	..	MIM-104 PAC-2	SAM	1993			Deal worth $1.2 b incl 7 Patriot SAM systems
	..	RIM-116A RAM	ShAM	1993			For 6 Cheng Kung (FFG-7) Class frigates
	38	RGM-84A Harpoon	ShShM	1992	1993	38	Deal worth $68 m; for 3 Knox Class frigates
	97	RIM-66A Standard-1	ShAM	1991	1993	(40)	Deal worth $55 m incl spares and support; for Cheng Kung (FFG-7) Class frigates
	3	Knox Class	Frigate	1992	1992–93	3	Ex-US Navy; 5-year lease worth $236 m incl training and logistics
	3	Knox Class	Frigate	1993			Ex-US Navy; lease

L: USA	6	FFG-7	Frigate	1989	1993	1	Taiwanese designation Cheng Kung (PFG-2) Class
Thailand							
S: Canada	20	Model 212	Helicopter	1993			Deal worth $120 m
China	(900)	HN-5A	Portable SAM	1991			Deal worth $46 m incl 90 launchers
	2	Naresuan Class	Frigate	1989			Weapons and electronics to be fitted in Thailand
Czechoslovakia	36	L-39Z Albatros	Jet trainer aircraft	1992	1993	(10)	Deal worth $200 m; version with Israeli avionics
France	20	Crotale NG SAMS	SAM system	1991	1993	(5)	
	(480)	VT-1	SAM	1991	1993	(120)	For Crotale NG SAM system
Italy	6	G-222	Transport aircraft	1993			Deal worth $120 m; option on 4-6 more
Netherlands	2	LW-08	Surveillance radar	(1989)			For 2 Naresuan Class frigates
	4	STIR	Fire control radar	1992			For 2 Naresuan Class frigates
Spain	1	Chakri Naruebet	AALS	1992			Deal worth $228 m for unarmed vessel
USA	38	A-7E Corsair II	Fighter/ground attack	1993			Ex-US Navy; deal worth $30 m; incl 6 TA-7 trainer version and 8 for spares
	4	C-130H-30 Hercules	Transport aircraft	1991			Deal worth $382 m incl support
	3	E-2C Hawkeye	AEW&C aircraft	1991	1993	(2)	
	18	F-16A Fighting Falcon	Fighter	1991			Incl 4 F-16B trainer version; deal worth $547 m incl 4 spare engines, 6 LANTIRN pods, spares and support
	3	P-3B Orion	ASW/maritime patrol	1989			Deal worth $140 m incl Harpoon anti-ship missiles; ex-US Navy
	6	SH-60B Seahawk	Helicopter	1993	1993		Deal worth $186 m incl spare engines, support and spares; for Navy
	20	M-109A5 155mm	Self-propelled gun	(1991)	1993	(10)	Deal worth $63 m
	350	M-48A5 Patton	Main battle tank	1990			Ex-US Army
	(300)	M-60A1 Patton	Main battle tank	1990	1993	(53)	Ex-US Army
	2	Seasparrow VLS	ShAM system	(1991)			For 2 Naresuan Class frigates
	16	AGM-84A Harpoon	Anti-ship missile	1990			For 3 P-3B ASW/maritime patrol aircraft
	(48)	Seasparrow	ShAM	(1991)			For 2 Naresuan Class frigates
	4	Knox Class	Frigate	1992			Ex-US Navy; 2-year lease worth $12 m

Recipient/ supplier (S) or licenser (L)	No. ordered	Weapon designation	Weapon description	Year of order/ licence	Year(s) of deliveries	No. delivered/ produced	Comments
Turkey							
S: Canada	10	Model 206L	Helicopter	1993			Deal worth $25 m incl licensed production of 14
France	20	AS-532 Cougar	Helicopter	1993			Deal worth $253 m (offsets $162 m)
	14	TRS-22XX	Surveillance radar	1987	1993	(1)	Deal worth $150 m
Germany, FR	46	RF-4E Phantom II	Reconnaissance plane	1991	1992–93	22	Ex-FRG Air Force; part of 'Materialhilfe 3' aid programme worth $907 m
	131	LARS 110mm	MRL	(1991)	1993	(50)	CFE cascade; ex-FRG Army
	131	M-110A2 203mm	Self-propelled gun	(1991)	1993	(25)	CFE cascade; ex-FRG Army
	100	Leopard 1A1	Main battle tank	(1991)	1992–93	(22)	CFE cascade; ex-FRG Army
	20	M-48 ARV	ARV	(1991)	1993	20	Ex-FRG Army
	10	M-48 AVLB	Bridge layer	(1991)	1993	(10)	Ex-FRG Army
	197	Ratac-S	Battlefield radar	1992			Most for local assembly
	1	Meko-200 Type	Frigate	1990			Deal worth $465 m incl 1 built in Turkey
	1	Meko-200 Type	Frigate	1992			Deal worth $525 m incl 1 built in Turkey
	1	Rhein Class	Support ship	1991	1993	1	Ex-FRG Navy
Italy	100	M-113A1	APC	(1991)			Ex-Italian Army
	4	Seaguard/Sea Zenith	CIWS	1990			For 2 Meko-200 Type frigates
	4	Seaguard/Sea Zenith	CIWS	1992			For 2 Meko-200 Type frigates
	(48)	Aspide	ShAM	1990			For 2 Meko-200 Type frigates
Russia	20	Mi-17 Hip H	Helicopter	1992	1993	17	Part of deal worth $75 m incl armoured vehicles and other equipment
	(25)	BTR-60P	APC	1993	1993	(25)	Ex-Russian Army; part of deal worth $75 m; incl unspecified number of BTR-80
UK	1	BN-2T MSSA	AEW aircraft	1993	1993	1	Option on 3 more
USA	50	A-10A Thunderbolt II	Close support plane	1993	1993	(15)	Ex-US Air Force; deal worth $160 m incl training, spares and support; status uncertain
	40	F-4E Phantom II	Fighter	1991	1991–93	(40)	Ex-US Air Force
	16	Model 209 AH-1S	Helicopter	1990	1993	16	Ex-US Army
	5	Model 209 AH-1W	Helicopter	(1992)	1993	5	Deal worth $110 m incl spares and support
	6	Model 337	Utility plane	1992	1993	(6)	Ex-US Army

No.	Weapon designation	Weapon description	Year of order	Year(s) of deliveries	No. delivered	Comments
10	P-3A Orion	ASW/maritime patrol	1991			Ex-US Navy
3	T-38 Talon	Jet trainer aircraft	1991	1993	3	Ex-US Air Force; deal worth $0.8 m
40	T-38 Talon	Jet trainer aircraft	1992	1993	40	Ex-US Air Force; deal worth $11 m
45	UH-60 Blackhawk	Helicopter	1992	1993	45	Deal worth $1.1 b incl 50 licensed production
24	MLRS 227mm	MRL	1993			Deal worth $289 m incl 1772 rockets, spares and support
300	M-113A1	APC	1990	1992–93	(300)	Ex-US Army
(250)	M-113A1	APC	(1991)			CFE cascade; ex-US Army
164	M-60A1 Patton	Main battle tank	(1991)	1992–93	(109)	CFE cascade; ex-US Army
600	M-60A3 Patton	Main battle tank	(1990)	1992–93	(600)	Southern Region amendment aid programme; ex-US Army
658	M-60A3 Patton	Main battle tank	(1991)	1992–93	(500)	CFE cascade; ex-US Army
124	V-150 Commando	APC	1992	1992–93	(84)	For Police and Gendarmerie
1	AN/FPS-117	Surveillance radar	1991	1993	1	Deal worth $15 m; options on 2 more
5	AN/TPQ-36	Tracking radar	1992			Deal worth $28 m
4	Phalanx	CIWS	1993	1993	4	On 4 Knox Class frigates
4	RGM-84A Launcher	ShShM system	1992	1993	4	On 4 Knox Class frigates
2	RGM-84A Launcher	ShShM system	1990			For 2 Meko-200 Type frigates
2	RGM-84A Launcher	ShShM system	1992			For 2 Meko-200 Type frigates
2	Seasparrow Launcher	ShAM system	1990			For 2 Meko-200 Type frigates
2	Seasparrow Launcher	ShAM system	1992			For 2 Meko-200 Type frigates
274	AGM-65G Maverick	ASM	1991			For 2 Meko-200 Type frigates
100	AGM-88 HARM	Anti-radar missile	1993	1993	(100)	For F-16 fighters
96	AIM-120A AMRAAM	Air-to-air missile	1993			Deal worth $17 m; for F-16 fighters
310	AIM-9S Sidewinder	Air-to-air missile	1990	1993	(100)	Deal worth $30 m incl training missiles
32	RGM-84A Harpoon	ShShM	1993	1993	(32)	For 4 Knox Class frigates
(48)	RGM-84A Harpoon	ShShM	(1990)			For 2 Meko-200 Type frigates
(48)	RGM-84A Harpoon	ShShM	1992			For 2 Meko-200 Type frigates
4	Knox Class	Frigate	1993	1993	4	Ex-US Navy; lease
L: Canada						
14	Model-206L	Helicopter	1993			Part of deal worth $25 m incl 10 delivered direct
Germany, FR						
2	FPB-57 Type	Fast attack craft	1991			Deal worth $143 m
3	FPB-57 Type	Fast attack craft	1993			Deal worth $250 m
1	Meko-200 Type	Frigate	1990			Deal worth $465 m incl 1 delivered direct

Recipient/ supplier (S) or licenser (L)	No. ordered	Weapon designation	Weapon description	Year of order/ licence	Year(s) of deliveries	No. delivered/ produced	Comments
	1	Meko-200 Type	Frigate	1992			Deal worth $525 m incl 1 delivered direct
	2	Type 209/3	Submarine	1987			Deal worth $263 m; option on 4 more
Italy	24	SF-260D	Trainer aircraft	1990	1992–93	10	Deal worth $550 m incl 2 delivered direct
Spain	50	CN-235M	Transport aircraft	1991	1992–93	9	Part of deal worth $4 b incl 8 delivered direct
USA	152	F-16C Fighting Falcon	Fighter	1984	1987–93	142	Deal worth $2.8 b incl 12 spare engines
	40	F-16C Fighting Falcon	Fighter	1992			In addition to 45 delivered direct; option on 55 more
	50	UH-60 Blackhawk	Helicopter	1992			Deal worth $1 b (offsets $700 m); incl APC and
	1 698	AIFV	AIFV	1988	1990–93	497	other versions

Tuvalu

S: Australia	1	ASI-315	Patrol craft	1992			Pacific Forum aid programme

United Arab Emirates

S: France	390	Leclerc	Main battle tank	1993			Deal worth $4.6 b, incl 46 ARVs (offsets 60%)
	46	Leclerc ARV	ARV	1993			
	500	Mistral	Portable SAM	1988	1993	(250)	Used with twin launchers on HMMV light vehicles
Indonesia	7	CN-235M	Transport	1992	1993	2	Deal worth $108 m
Italy	(6)	AB-412 Griffon	Helicopter	1991	1992–93	2	For Dubai; deal worth $30 m incl spares and support
Romania	10	SA-330 Puma	Helicopter	1993	1993	(2)	For Abu Dhabi
Russia	250	BMP-3	AIFV	1992	1992–93	250	For Abu Dhabi
South Africa	78	G-6 155mm	Self-propelled gun	1990	1991–93	(54)	For Abu Dhabi; part of deal worth $340 m
UK	18	Hawk 100	Fighter/trainer	1989	1993	10	Deal worth $680 m incl AGM-114A missiles
USA	20	AH-64A Apache	Helicopter	1991	1993	6	Deal worth $54.9 m
	2	C-130H Hercules	Transport	1991			Part of deal worth $300 m
	1	AN/TPS-70	Surveillance radar	1993			For 20 AH-64A helicopters
	620	AGM-114A Hellfire	Anti-tank missile	1991	1993	(186)	

United Kingdom

	No.	Weapon designation	Weapon description	Year of order	Year(s) of deliveries	No. delivered	Comments
S: Australia	6	ASI-315	Patrol craft	1991	1992–93	6	For Hong Kong Police
USA	3	CH-47D Chinook	Helicopter	1993			
	210	AIM-120A AMRAAM	Air-to-air missile	1992	1993	(100)	
	220	AIM-9S Sidewinder	Air-to-air missile	1990	1991–93	(220)	Deal worth $23 m, incl spares and support
L: Brazil	128	EMB-312H Tucano	Trainer aircraft	1985	1987–93	(128)	Deal worth $145–150 m; option on 15 more
Switzerland	(1 000)	Piranha 8x8	APC	1991	1992–93	(90)	Production for export; incl several versions
USA	89	WS-70 Blackhawk	Helicopter	1987	1987	(1)	Production for export
	57	MLRS 227mm	MRL	1985	1989–93	(48)	In addition to 4 delivered direct
	..	BGM-71A TOW	Anti-tank missile	1980	1982–93	(28 726)	

USA

	No.	Weapon designation	Weapon description	Year of order	Year(s) of deliveries	No. delivered	Comments
S: Australia	11	CH-47C Chinook	Helicopter	1991	1991		Ex-Australian Air Force; part of payment for 4 CH-47D helicopters for Australia
Germany, FR	48	Tpz-1 Fuchs	APC	(1991)	1991–93	48	NBC reconnaissance version; US designation M-93 Fox
Norway	82	Penguin-2-7	Anti-ship missile	1992	1992	(24)	For SH-60B helicopters
Russia	20	SS-N-22 Sunburn	ShShM	1993			For use as target drones; status uncertain
Spain	(6)	C-212-300 Aviocar	Transport aircraft	1989	1990–92	(5)	Test bed for tactical reconnaissance radar
UK	38	T-67M260 Firefly	Trainer aircraft	1992	1993	2	Deal worth $12 m; option on 75
L: Germany, FR	210	Tpz-1 Fuchs	APC	1990			NBC reconnaissance version; US designation M-93 Fox
Italy	12	Osprey Class	MCM ship	1986	1993	2	
Japan	(113)	Beechjet 400T	Transport aircraft	1990	1992–93	58	Deal worth $489 m; for use as trainer; US designation T-1A Jayhawk
Netherlands	(115)	WM-28	Fire control radar	(1973)	1977–93	108	
UK	302	T-45 Goshawk	Jet trainer aircraft	1986	1988–93	22	Incl 31 for export; US designation Mk-92
	436	M-119 105mm	Towed gun	1987	1990–93	136	Deal worth $512 m incl 32 simulators; for Navy
	13	Cyclone Class	Patrol craft	1990	1992–93	8	

Recipient/ supplier (S) or licenser (L)	No. ordered	Weapon designation	Weapon description	Year of order/ licence	Year(s) of deliveries	No. delivered/ produced	Comments
Venezuela							
S: France	18	Mirage 50EV	Fighter	1988	1991–93	(18)	Incl several rebuilt Mirage 5 fighters
	(50)	AM-39 Exocet	Anti-ship missile	(1988)			For Mirage 50 fighters
	(100)	R-550 Magic-2	Air-to-air missile	1988	1991–93	(100)	For Mirage 50 fighters; deal worth $30 m
Italy	(14)	Otomat-2	ShShM	1992	1992–93	14	Deal worth $16.8 m
USA	6	RGM-84A Launcher	ShShM system	1989			For 6 Constitucion Class fast attack craft; part of deal worth $50 m
	18	RGM-84A Harpoon	ShShM	1989			For 6 Constitucion Class fast attack craft; part of deal worth $50 m
	2	Knox Class	Frigate	1993			Ex-US Navy; 2-year lease worth $6 m

Abbreviations and acronyms:

AA	Anti-aircraft	CIWS	Close-in weapon system
AAA	Anti-aircraft artillery	Elint	Electronic intelligence
AALS	Amphibious assault landing ship	EW	Electronic warfare
AAV(G)	Anti-aircraft vehicle (gun-armed)	incl	Including/includes
AAV(M)	Anti-aircraft vehicle (missile–armed)	MCM	Mine countermeasures (ship)
AAV(G/M)	Anti-aicarft vehicle (gun and missile armed)	MRL	Multiple rocket launcher
		OPV	Offshore patrol vessel
AEW	Airborne early-warning	SAM	Surface-to-air missile
AEW&C	Airborne early-warning and control	SAMS	Surface-to-air missile system
AIFV	Armoured infantry fighting vehicle	SAR	Search and rescue
APC	Armoured personnel carrier	ShAM	Ship-to-air missile
ARM	Anti-radar missile	ShShM	Ship-to-ship missile
ARV	Armoured recovery vehicle	SuShM	Submarine-to-ship missile
ASM	Air-to-surface missile	VIP	Very important person
ASW	Anti-submarine warfare	VLS	Vertical launch system
CDS	Coast defence system		

Conventions:

. .		Data not available or not applicable
–		Negligible figure (< 0.5) or none
( )		Uncertain data or SIPRI estimate

Appendix 13D. Sources and methods

I. The SIPRI sources

The sources of the data presented in the arms trade registers are of five general types: newspapers; periodicals and journals; books, monographs and annual reference works; official national documents; and documents issued by international and inter-governmental organizations. The registers are largely compiled from information contained in around 200 publications searched regularly.

Published information cannot provide a comprehensive picture because the arms trade is not fully reported in the open literature. Published reports provide partial information, and substantial disagreement among reports is common. Therefore, the exercise of judgement and the making of estimates are important elements in compiling the SIPRI arms trade data base. Order dates and the delivery dates for arms transactions are continuously revised in the light of new information, but where they are not disclosed the dates are estimated. Exact numbers of weapons ordered and delivered may not always be known and are sometimes estimated—particularly with respect to missiles. It is common for reports of arms deals involving large platforms—ships, aircraft and armoured vehicles—to ignore missile armaments classified as major weapons by SIPRI. Unless there is explicit evidence that platforms were disarmed or altered before delivery, it is assumed that a weapons fit specified in one of the major reference works such as the *Jane's* or *Interavia* series is carried.

II. Selection criteria

SIPRI arms trade data cover five categories of major weapons or systems: aircraft, armour and artillery, guidance and radar systems, missiles, and warships. Statistics presented refer to the value of the trade in these five categories only. The registers and statistics do not include trade in small arms, artillery under 100-mm calibre, ammunition, support items, services and components or component technology, except for specific items. Publicly available information is inadequate to track these items satisfactorily.

There are two criteria for the selection of major weapon transfers for the registers. The first is that of military application. The aircraft category excludes aerobatic aeroplanes and gliders. Transport aircraft and VIP transports are included only if they bear military insignia or are otherwise confirmed as military registered. Micro-light aircraft, remotely piloted vehicles and drones are not included although these systems are increasingly finding military applications.

The armour and artillery category includes all types of tanks, tank destroyers, armoured cars, armoured personnel carriers, armoured support vehicles, infantry combat vehicles as well as multiple rocket launchers, self-propelled and towed guns and howitzers with a calibre equal to or above 100 mm. Military lorries, jeeps and other unarmoured support vehicles are not included.

The category of guidance and radar systems is a residual category for electronic-tracking, target-acquisition, fire-control, launch and guidance systems that are either (*a*) deployed independently of a weapon system listed under another weapon category (e.g., certain ground-based SAM launch systems) or (*b*) shipborne missile-launch or point-defence (CIWS) systems. The values of acquisition, fire-control, launch and guidance systems on aircraft and armoured vehicles are included in the value of the respective aircraft or armoured vehicle. The reason for treating shipborne systems separately is that a given type of ship is often equipped with numerous combinations of different surveillance, acquisition, launch and guidance systems.

The missile category includes only guided missiles. Unguided artillery rockets, man-portable anti-armour rockets and free-fall aerial munitions (e.g., 'iron bombs') are excluded. In the naval sphere, anti-submarine rockets and torpedoes are excluded.

The ship category excludes small patrol craft (with a displacement of less than 100 t), unless they carry cannon with a calibre equal to or above 100 mm; missiles or torpedoes; research vessels; tugs and ice-breakers. Combat support vessels such as fleet replenishment ships are included.

The second criterion for selection of items is the identity of the buyer. Items must be destined for the armed forces, paramilitary forces, intelligence agencies or police of another country. Arms supplied to guerrilla forces pose a problem. For example, if weapons are delivered to the Contra rebels they are listed as imports to Nicaragua with a comment in the arms trade register indicating the local recipient. The entry of any arms transfer is made corresponding to the five weapon categories listed above. This means that missiles and their guidance/launch vehicles are often entered separately under their respective category in the arms trade register.

III. The value of the arms trade

The SIPRI system for arms trade evaluation is designed as a *trend-measuring device*, to permit measurement of changes in the total flow of major weapons and its geographic pattern. Expressing the evaluation in monetary terms reflects both the quantity and quality of the weapons transferred. Aggregate values and shares are based only on *actual deliveries* during the year/years covered in the relevant tables and figures.

The SIPRI valuation system is not comparable to official economic statistics such as gross domestic product, public expenditure and export/import figures. The monetary values chosen do not correspond to the actual prices paid, which vary considerably depending on different pricing methods, the length of production runs and the terms involved in individual transactions. For instance, a deal may or may not cover spare parts, training, support equipment, compensation, offset arrangements for the local industries in the buying country, and so on. Furthermore, to use only actual sales prices—even assuming that the information were available for all deals, which it is not—military aid and grants would be excluded, and the total flow of arms would therefore not be measured.

Production under licence is included in the arms trade statistics in such a way as to reflect the import share embodied in the weapon. In reality, this share is normally high in the beginning, gradually decreasing over time. However, as SIPRI makes a single estimate of the import share for each weapon produced under licence, the value of arms produced under licence agreements may be slightly overstated.

IV. Conventions

The following conventions are used in appendices 13B and 13C:

. .	Data not available or not applicable
–	Negligible figure (<0.5) or none
( )	Uncertain data or SIPRI estimate

Appendix 13E. Arms acquisitions in East Asia

BATES GILL*

I. Data on arms acquisitions in East Asia

At a time in the post-cold war era when the international arms trade is in decline,[1] numerous reports have pointed with concern to an arms buildup or arms race in East Asia.[2] As a contribution to these discussions, this appendix provides data on East Asian arms acquisitions, focusing on the period 1984–93.[3] To determine trends regarding East Asian arms acquisitions, data on three selected indicators are presented in this section. These indicators are: (*a*) past and current arms production and acquisitions; (*b*) expected future acquisitions; and (*c*) military expenditure in East Asia.

The data presented here are drawn from the currently available open sources, but unfortunately, because of a lack of complete information, especially with regard to domestic production in several countries, they fall short of the ideal and fully comprehensive presentation of data on the three sources of acquisitions: imports, licensed production and indigenous production. Reliance on available information, especially data on arms trade, licensed production and military expenditure does provide indicators to make an informed assessment on arms acquisitions in East Asia.

Past and current arms production and acquisitions

Arms imports and licensed production

Table 13E.1 indicates the volume of arms delivered to and licensed production in East Asia between 1984 and 1993. The table also indicates the volume of East Asian arms imports and licensed production as a percentage of the total global volume of arms imports and licensed production.

Arms imports and licensed production may also be measured by the number of weapon systems transferred. The figures in table 13E.2 show the number of weapon systems imported by East Asia or produced under licence between 1984 and 1993, broken down by weapon categories and sub-categories.

* This work has been generously supported by the American–Scandinavian Foundation.

[1] See appendix 13B in this volume.

[2] See, e.g., Klare, M. T., 'The next great arms race', *Foreign Affairs* (summer 1993), p. 136; Ball, D., *Trends in Military Acquisitions in the Asia–Pacific Region: Implications for Security and Prospects for Constraints and Controls*, Strategic and Defence Studies Centre Working Paper no. 273 (Australian National University: Canberra, 1993); Le Corre, P., 'La fièvre des armes', *Bilan*, July–Aug. 1993, p. 42; Mack, A., *Arms Proliferation in the Asia–Pacific: Causes and Prospects for Control*, Research School of Pacific Studies Department of International Relations Working Paper no. 1992/10 (Australian National University: Canberra, Dec. 1992); Segal, G., 'Managing new arms races in the Asia/Pacific', *Washington Quarterly* (summer 1992), p. 83; Segal, G., 'New arms races in Asia', *Jane's Intelligence Review* (June 1992), p. 269; Mack, A. and Ball, D., 'The military build-up in Asia–Pacific', *Pacific Review*, vol. 5, no. 3 (1992), p. 197.

[3] For this study, East Asia includes: Brunei, Cambodia, China, Indonesia, Japan, North Korea, South Korea, Laos, Malaysia, Myanmar, Philippines, Singapore, Taiwan, Thailand and Viet Nam.

Table 13E.1. Trends in the import and licensed production of major conventional weapons in East Asia, 1984–93

Data in row A are SIPRI trend-indicator values in US $m. (1990); row B indicates the East Asian percentage share of the total global volume of arms imports and licensed production.

	1984	1985	1986	1987	1988	1989	1990	1991	1992	1993
A	5 258	6 274	5 829	5 281	6 900	6 221	4 874	4 630	5336	4 646
B	*12.4*	*15.9*	*13.7*	*11.5*	*17.7*	*16.5*	*16.1*	*19.4*	*23.4*	*21.1*

Note: SIPRI arms transfer data are an index which indicates trends in deliveries of major conventional weapons. SIPRI arms trade statistics do not reflect purchase prices and are not comparable with economic statistics such as national accounts or foreign trade statistics. The methods used for the valuation of SIPRI arms trade statistics are described in appendix 13D.
Source: SIPRI arms trade data base.

Tables 13E.1 and 13E.2 indicate a downward trend in deliveries of major conventional weapons to the region during 1984–93. The decline has been particularly precipitous since 1988. In 1988, the volume of arms deliveries to East Asia reached nearly $7 billion, as expressed in SIPRI trend-indicator values. Since then, the volume of arms imports to the region has shown a general downward trend. The increase shown for 1992 can be largely attributed to the Chinese acquisition of aircraft from Russia in that year, which accounted for more than 36 per cent of the arms imported by the region in 1992 when calculated in SIPRI trend-indicator values.[4]

Similarly, for almost all of the systems categorized in table 13E.2, the number of weapons imported or produced under licence declined, in some cases by 50 per cent or more. Despite this overall decline, however, East Asia's share of the total world arms imports and licensed production has shown an increase over the period 1984–93, reaching 23.4 per cent in 1992 and 21.1 per cent in 1993. This trend indicates that the decline in global arms imports is more rapid than that in East Asian imports .

Over time certain countries consistently lead the region in arms imports, while deliveries to certain other countries remain consistently low. For example, Japan has consistently been one of the major weapon importers in the world, not only in East Asia, and accounted for one-third of the major weapons imported by and produced under licence in East Asia during 1984–93 when measured in SIPRI trend-indicator values. On the other hand, the volume of arms imports for other countries in East Asia is relatively small: the total volume of arms imports to Brunei, Cambodia, Laos, Myanmar and the Philippines combined for the entire 10-year period 1984–93 is less than the volume of arms imports to Japan in 1989 alone.[5]

The data on arms trade and licensed production also indicate a heavier concentration of activity among the countries of North-East Asia—China, Japan, North Korea, South Korea and Taiwan. These five importers accounted for nearly three-quarters— 73 per cent—of the volume of the region's total imports between 1984 and 1993 as measured by SIPRI trend-indicator values. Recently, during 1991–93, even as North Korean imports have fallen drastically, the North-East Asia sub-region remained a significant arms import market within East Asia, accounting for 85 per cent of aircraft imports and 89 per cent of missile imports.[6]

---

[4] Derived from the SIPRI arms trade data base.
[5] Derived from the SIPRI arms trade data base
[6] Figures are derived from the SIPRI arms trade data base.

Table 13E.2. Number of major conventional weapon systems imported by or produced under licence in East Asia, 1984–93

Weapon category	1984	1985	1986	1987	1988	1989	1990	1991	1992	1993
Aircraft	316	424	425	314	355	351	255	242	209	163
Helicopter	151	229	245	137	147	145	135	127	105	92
Combat jet[a]	73	126	84	134	151	164	52	54	51	17
Trainer	51	26	57	12	22	12	21	28	31	30
Transport	21	25	26	15	19	23	21	11	12	12
MP/ASW	18	16	8	9	8	7	7	10	7	8
Other[b]	2	2	5	7	8	0	19	12	3	4
Missiles	1 838	3 380	4 246	3 485	3 578	3 393	4 175	4 237	3 244	3 382
SAM/ShAM	368	1 287	1 387	1 161	620	671	1 049	1 048	886	1 221
Portable SAM	201	111	111	461	449	144	116	216	0	200
Anti-ship	245	261	249	254	309	207	239	174	106	70
ATM/ASM	109	753	1 553	753	1 057	1 049	1 303	1 175	1 073	851
Air-to-Air	915	933	911	775	1 063	1 277	1 468	1 624	1 179	1 040
SSM	0	35	35	81	80	45	0	0	0	0
Naval vessels	24	25	24	15	11	6	9	13	15	23
Frigates	2	2	3	1	1	2	0	2	4	2
Corvettes	1	0	0	2	0	0	4	2	0	9
MCM	0	0	5	3	3	1	3	2	0	1
Patrol craft	6	4	3	1	2	1	1	5	4	3
FAC	11	13	8	2	0	0	0	0	4	2
Submarines	4	4	4	5	5	1	1	1	1	1
Other[c]	0	2	1	1	0	1	0	1	2	5
Armour	748	653	498	757	338	581	809	552	236	133
Tanks	147	243	205	275	244	489	470	324	185	126
APC/AIFV	552	349	261	458	82	92	318	208	51	0
Other[d]	49	61	32	24	12	0	21	20	0	7
Artillery	287	224	141	159	216	165	97	101	119	158
TG	180	121	53	71	83	80	40	42	60	42
SPG	82	78	78	77	77	45	45	50	50	60
MRL	25	25	0	1	46	30	0	0	0	0
Other[e]	0	0	10	10	10	10	12	9	9	56
Guidance & radar	16	23	33	29	14	16	19	33	34	11
Surveillance	9	18	20	13	4	3	8	9	10	6
Fire control	7	5	13	16	10	13	11	24	24	5

[a] Includes fighters, ground-attack and close-support aircraft.

[b] Includes airborne early-warning (AEW) aircraft, electronic-intelligence (ELINT) aircraft, bombers, reconnaissance and surveillance aircraft, and light aircraft.

[c] Includes landing craft, survey ships and other support ships.

[d] Includes scout cars, armoured recovery vehicles, armoured artillery vehicles and bridge layers.

[e] Includes mortars and anti-aircraft artillery systems.

Source: Derived from SIPRI arms trade data base. A description of the sources and methods used to develop this table is given in appendix 13D.

Table 13E.3. Production of major conventional weapons in East Asia, 1993

Country	Weapon systems/comments
China	*Full range of major conventional weapons:* licensed production of submarines, helicopters and ShAMs; most indigenously produced weapons based on Soviet designs from 1950s and 1960s: J-5 and K-8 trainers, J-6, J-7, J-8II fighters, Q-5 attack aircraft and variants, Y-8 transport aircraft, Z-8 helicopters and SH-5 flying boats; Type 85II, Type 80 and T-90 prototype and other heavy armour and artillery, radars; AS-365N helicopter produced under licence; indigenous XJ-10 jet fighter under development; extensive indigenous production of SAMs, ASMs, ATMs, SSMs and anti-ship missiles, as well as naval vessels; negotiations underway to produce aircraft jointly with Russia; Chinese weapon production has slowed in recent years, and the qualitative levels of Chinese weapons remain significantly behind those produced by Western, Russian and Japanese defence industries
Indonesia	*Helicopters; patrol craft; transport aircraft:* helicopters and patrol craft are produced under licence; transport aircraft produced under licence and co-produced; Indonesian arms industries manufacture high-quality products, but they remain dependent on foreign inputs
Japan	*Full range of major conventional weapons:* F-15J fighter aircraft and P-3C ASW/ maritime patrol and electronic intelligence aircraft produced under licence; wide range of helicopters (CH-47D, AH-1S, OH-6J, SH-60J, UH-60J), missile systems (including SAMs, anti-tank missiles and air-to-air missiles) and heavy artillery produced under licence; indigenous production includes T-4 jet trainer, AAM-1, SSM-1 and ASM-1 missiles, Type 90 MBT and a wide range of other artillery, armoured vehicles, and anti-tank and anti-ship missiles; world's second-largest military shipbuilding industry produces wide range of naval vessels including submarines, destroyers, frigates, MCMs, FACs, patrol craft, amphibious forces; Japanese defence industries produce highly sophisticated weaponry with the assistance of foreign suppliers, particularly the USA
North Korea	*Wide range of major conventional weapons:* Romeo class submarines, missile systems (including Scud-B SSMs) and armoured vehicles produced under licence; T-62 MBTs, light tanks, other armoured vehicles, MRLs, artillery, mini-submarines, frigates, FACs, patrol craft and MCMs mostly based on Soviet or Chinese models; the sophistication of weapons produced by North Korea is low in comparison to those produced by its neighbours in the region, a problem exacerbated by the reduction in technological and economic assistance provided by China and the former USSR
South Korea	*Wide range of major conventional weapons:* 72 F-16Cs to be produced under licence; Type 209/3 submarines, BK-117 helicopters, SAMs, K-1 MBTs, and armoured vehicles and artillery produced under licence; extensive indigenous production of naval vessels (including frigates, corvettes, FACs and amphibious vessels) and armour and artillery (including infantry fighting vehicles, anti-aircraft guns and MRLs); the relatively high level of sophistication of weaponry produced by South Korea is dependent on foreign assistance and inputs, especially from the United States
Singapore	*Helicopters; naval vessels; artillery:* helicopters, corvettes, MCMs and FACs produced under licence; indigenous production of 155-mm gun; production of small amphibious vessels and patrol craft since 1970s
Taiwan	*Wide range of major conventional weapons:* licensed production of frigates; limited indigenous production of light tank has stopped; indigenous production of SSMs, ASMs, SAMs; indigenous production of FACs, patrol craft and small amphibious vessels; indigenously developed A-1 Ching-kuo fighter to be produced and deployed 1994–99; indigenous production of AIFVs, MRLs and heavy artillery; arms production in Taiwan, particularly in more advanced weaponry, e.g., aircraft and missiles, is reliant on foreign inputs

Sources: *Jane's All the World's Aircraft* (Jane's Information Group: Coulsdon, Surrey, several editions); *Jane's Fighting Ships* (Jane's Information Group: Coulsdon, Surrey, several editions); *Jane's Armour and Artillery* (Jane's Information Group: Coulsdon, Surrey, several editions); *Jane's Weapons Systems* (Jane's Information Group: Coulsdon, Surrey, several editions); Wulf, H., ed., SIPRI, *Arms Industry Limited* (Oxford University Press: Oxford, 1993); SIPRI arms trade data base.

Domestic production and procurement

Seven countries in East Asia produce significant quantities of major conventional weapons. These countries may be classified as 'second-tier' producers—Japan and China—and 'third-tier' producers—Indonesia, North Korea, South Korea, Singapore, and Taiwan.[7] Table 13E.3 shows the types of major weapon produced domestically by these seven countries.

Studies on third-tier defence industries indicate that growth in indigenous production and licensed production of weapons has stabilized and even declined, and that the defence industries of these countries will be hard pressed in the future for technological and economic reasons to establish full-fledged indigenous production of all types of major weapon system.[8] As table 13E.3 indicates, most weapons produced by third-tier countries have been produced under licence. Of these producers, at present only South Korea and Taiwan are in a position to manufacture large amounts of indigenously produced advanced weaponry, and they typically require close continued co-operation with outside suppliers of technology to do so.[9]

China and Japan are capable of producing all types of major conventional weapon. However, the future of Chinese and Japanese defence production is uncertain. Much of China's sprawling defence production infrastructure lies idle. Estimates suggest that China currently may utilize as little as 10 per cent of its defence production capacity; 70 per cent of defence industries have diversified into production of civilian goods.[10] Whether China can make significant strides forward in developing a modernized defence industry—even as its neighbours advance their military capabilities through indigenous and foreign procurement—remains an open question.

For Japan, declining domestic demand threatens many of its defence industries, but the option of export sales is currently circumscribed by government policies. Japan steadily reduced its spending on weapons procurement from 1990 to 1992, with a reduction of 9.7 per cent between 1990 and 1991 and a further reduction of 2.4 per cent in 1992. Japan's 1993 procurement budget revealed an increase up to $8.23 billion, a result of the purchase of two airborne warning and control system (AWACS) aircraft in that year.[11] Japan's Mid-Term Defence Plan Review of fiscal years 1991–95 called for a reduction in defence procurement spending of 9.8 per cent over the three years 1993–95.[12] Of the cuts in overall defence spending foreseen over

---

[7] See the four-tier classification system developed in Ross, A. L., 'Full circle: conventional proliferation, the international arms trade and Third World arms exports', eds Kwang-il Baek, R. D. McLaurin and Chung-in Moon, *The Dilemma of Third World Defense Industries* (Westview Press: Boulder, Colo., 1989). Another study lists Indonesia, Singapore, South Korea and Taiwan as 'developing defense industrial nations'. See US Congress, Office of Technology Assessment, *Global Arms Trade*, OTA-ISC-460 (US Government Printing Office: Washington, DC, 1991), chapter 7.

[8] See Anthony, I., 'The "third tier" countries: production of major weapons', ed. H. Wulf, SIPRI, *Arms Industry Limited* (Oxford University Press: Oxford, 1993); OTA (note 7), p. 124.

[9] Reed, C., Karniol, R. and Matthews, R., 'Diversity for survival', *Jane's Defence Weekly*, 31 July 1993, p. 15.

[10] 'Making a modern industry', *Jane's Defence Weekly*, 19 Feb. 1994, p. 28.

[11] Naoaki Usui, 'Japanese emphasize readiness in JDA plan', *Defense News*, 2–8 Aug. 1993, p. 1; 'Japanese weapons spending continues to decrease', *Aviation Week & Space Technology*, 26 Apr. 1993, p. 64.

[12] 'Firms plan scale-backs in advance of JDA cuts', *Jane's Defence Weekly*, 1 May 1993, p. 8; 'China updates its military, but business comes first', *Aviation Week & Space Technology*, 15 Mar. 1993, p. 57; Usui, N., 'Japanese workers face upheavals', *Defense News*, 8–14 Feb. 1993, p. 52; Sekigawa, E. and Morrocco, J. D., 'Japan cuts $4.7 billion from defense budget', *Aviation Week & Space Technology*, 4 Jan. 1993, p. 22; Naoaki Usui, 'Spending cut will hit home for Japanese manufacturers', *Defense News*, 21–27 Dec. 1992, p. 9.

these three years, three-quarters will come from weapon procurement.[13] A RAND study concludes that 'the extraordinarily rapid growth of Japanese defense procurement is over' and that 'the distinct possibility is of a leveling off of procurement spending' by Japan.[14]

Future procurement

Table 13E.4 provides an overview of the expected future procurement of major weapons by a number of East Asian countries up to the end of the 1990s. Data on future indigenously produced procurement are particularly difficult to determine, however, the available data on arms imports, licensed production and indigenous production indicate that much of the upcoming weapon procurement for the region will focus on air- and sea-surveillance and defence capabilities. China, Japan, South Korea, Malaysia, Taiwan and Thailand will take delivery of new major surface combatants over the next few years, while China, Japan and South Korea will augment their submarine fleets. Most of the countries listed in table 13E.4 will procure new fighter aircraft before the end of the decade, and several of the countries in the region—Japan, South Korea, Singapore and Taiwan—will expand their fleets of airborne-surveillance and patrol aircraft. Missiles figure prominently as well in the region's future arms procurement schemes, mostly to equip the new aircraft and naval vessels.

East Asia, a region with long coastlines, numerous offshore islands and several island states, will be naturally attracted to purchases related to air and sea surveillance and coastal defence. An overall reduction in the region's domestic insurgencies results in a greater concern for external security problems, including piracy, the protection of offshore resources and territorial claims, and the maintenance of open and safe shipping lanes.

The region-wide need to modernize military forces also helps explain the future procurement trend towards air and sea capabilities. As of 1992, approximately 84 per cent of the region's combat aircraft were based on pre-1966 designs. For Cambodia, China, South Korea, Laos, Myanmar, the Philippines and Taiwan, approximately 90 per cent or more of their combat aircraft were of pre-1966 design.[15] As of 1992, the Philippines' largest naval vessels—2 frigates, 10 corvettes and 8 landing ships—were of World War II vintage; Myanmar's four largest ships were World War II corvettes; most of Thailand's frigates were built in the 1970s and some date back to the 1950s; Indonesia's frigate fleet dates to the 1970s and before; and the bulk of China's destroyer and frigate fleets are between 20 and 30 years old. All of Taiwan's destroyers, frigates and corvettes were of World War II vintage in 1992, and South Korea's fleet of destroyers will be 49 years old in 1994; however, these older ships in the Taiwanese and South Korean fleets have been extensively modernized.[16]

---

[13] Sekigawa and Morrocco (note 12), p. 22.

[14] Levin, N., Lorell, M., and Alexander, A., *The Wary Warriors: Future Directions in Japanese Security Policies* (RAND Corporation: Santa Monica, Calif., 1993), p. 77.

[15] The above data on combat aircraft were calculated from Forsberg, R. and Cohen, J., *The Global Arms Market: Prospects for the Coming Decade* (Institute for Defense and Disarmament Studies: Boston, Mass., Jan. 1994), appendix 1.

[16] *Jane's Fighting Ships, 1992–1993* (Jane's Information Group: Coulsdon, Surrey, 1992).

Military expenditure

Table 13E.5 shows military expenditure data for countries in East Asia since 1985, and the percentage of gross national product (GNP) or gross domestic product (GDP) devoted to military expenditure.

Research on Association of South-East Asian Nations (ASEAN) countries shows that increases in the 'availability of resources'—rapid GNP growth, increases in public revenues, strong balance-of-payments positions—facilitate higher military spending,[17] although increases in military spending do not necessarily lead to increases in weapon procurement. The data in table 13E.5 tend to support this finding: for most countries, military expenditure increases as GNP or GDP increases. However, for most countries, military expenditure as a percentage of GNP or GDP remained relatively stable or declined over the period 1985–93, indicating that military spending lagged behind or grew at approximately the same rate as GNP or GDP. For China, Indonesia, Japan, South Korea, Malaysia, Taiwan and Thailand, military spending as a percentage of GNP or GDP tended to decline or remain relatively steady. North Korea and the Philippines have tended to show an increase in military spending relative to GNP or GDP; Singapore and Myanmar show a more erratic pattern over time.

One report citing Western diplomats and Asian experts states that average growth rates for military spending in the region will increase by about 3 per cent per year, and that growth of defence spending as a percentage of GDP, while expected to remain steady in the near term, could increase significantly in the next 10–20 years.[18] On the other hand, while economic factors may suggest great growth in the East Asian arms market, it will be limited by the fact that most countries in the region are relatively small and have relatively modest defence requirements. In 1992, only four countries in the region had defence procurement budgets exceeding $1 billion, and all of them were in North-East Asia: China, Japan, South Korea and Taiwan.[19] For economic reasons, some countries in the region—including Cambodia, Indonesia, Laos, Myanmar, the Philippines and Viet Nam—are unable or unwilling to give military spending priority over economic development.[20] In addition, some countries have reduced or slowed the growth of funds slated for arms procurement, despite increased economic growth. For 1992, Japan, South Korea, Singapore, Indonesia and Malaysia showed a flat or downward trend in money budgeted for weapon procurement.[21]

Other economic factors would suggest a moderate or even declining arms market for some parts of East Asia. Even in countries with fast-paced economies, it is not at all clear that this growth necessarily translates into increased arms purchases. More important, it remains unclear whether the burgeoning economies of East Asian countries could be hampered by the diversion of economic and financial resources towards military procurement; while some economic benefits can be derived from arms procurement, the negative effects of such policies may temper a significant

---

[17] Denoon, D. B. H., 'Defence spending in ASEAN: an overview', ed. Chin Kin Wah, *Defence Spending in Southeast Asia* (Institute of Southeast Asian Studies: Singapore, 1987), p. 65.

[18] Opall, B., 'Nations eye neighbors, upgrade armed forces', *Defence News*, 6–12 Sep. 1993, p. 8.

[19] Chang, G., 'Selling to the Pacific rim', *International Defense Review* (Nov. 1993), p. 885.

[20] McBeth, J., 'Broken toys', *Far Eastern Economic Review*, 9 Sep. 1993, p. 30; Opall, B., 'Indonesia wields clout amid slowdown', *Defense News*, 6–12 Sep. 1993, p. 16; See also Young, P. L., 'Malaysia's economic development takes priority over defence', *Armed Forces Journal* (July 1993), pp. 37–38.

[21] Leopold, G., 'Asia-Pacific arms rivalry soars', *Defense News*, 26 Oct.–1 Nov. 1992, p. 28.

Table 13E.4. Future procurement of major conventional weapons by selected countries in East Asia through the 1990s

Country	Weapon systems/comments
Brunei	Future procurement is relatively limited to significant upgrade of air defence capabilities with the procurement of 16 Hawk 100 fighter trainers ordered in 1989, and 96 AIM-9L air-to-air missiles to equip these aircraft
China	China's procurement of indigenously produced weaponry in serial production will continue, although probably at reduced levels. Such equipment would include continuing future procurement of T-85II, T-80 and T-90 MBTs, APCs, other armoured vehicles and artillery, radars, missiles, and extensive upgrading of T-59 tanks already in stock. Future procurement of indigenously produced aircraft will be limited to around 24 J-8II fighters and perhaps 12 F-7 fighters per year through the end of the decade; it is possible that China will produce and procure a domestic version of the Russian MiG-31 fighter toward the end of the decade, and/or purchase Russian MiG-29s and Su-24s, but the status of these programmes is uncertain. There is also speculation that China seeks to produce and procure its own indigenously developed next-generation fighter, referred to as the XJ-10. Luhu destroyers, Jiangwei frigates and Ming patrol submarines are in production with deliveries beginning after 1995. Most current and future procurement is likely to be in naval- and aircraft-related systems. Off-the-shelf procurement of complete systems as imports is likely to remain relatively limited.
Indonesia	Future procurement includes refurbished Kondor Class MCMs, Parchim Class corvettes, and Frosch Class landing and supply ships from the former GDR Navy (plans for indigenous production of naval vessels have apparently been delayed). Indonesia will take delivery of 12 Hawk 100 fighter trainers and 12 Hawk 200 fighter/ground attack aircraft in 1995, and will likely place orders for CN-212 transport aircraft produced under licence from Spain, and Bo-105 helicopters produced under licence from Germany. Future procurement may also include continued delivery of AR-325 surveillance radar.
Japan	Future Japanese aircraft procurement includes 2 to 4 B-767 AWACS aircraft, 19 P-3 maritime patrol/ASW aircraft (delivered over next 5 to 6 years), 35 to 40 F-15J fighters (delivered over rest of the decade), 130 FS-X fighters (programme delayed; first deliveries expected in late 1990s) and helicopters. Naval procurement includes 3 Kongo Class destroyers (in service by late 1998), 2 Asagiri Class destroyers (in service by 1996–97), and 2 Harushio class submarines (in service by 1994–95). Japan will procure licenced-produced missiles including the BGM-71C I-TOW ATM, the MIM-104 SAM, the AIM-7M air-to-air missile, and will import Seasparrow ShAMs. Future procurement of indigenously produced land systems will continue, including Type 89 APCs, with as many as 500 Type 90 MBTs procured in the 1990s.
South Korea	Aircraft procurement will include 120 F-16C/D fighters, 72 of which are to be built in South Korea under licence from the United States. In addition, 37 AH-64 helicopters and P-3C Orion maritime patrol/ASW aircraft, and 20 PC-9 trainers from Switzerland will be imported. Naval procurement includes as many as 18 Type 209/3 submarines and perhaps 10 KDX-2000 frigates (first deliveries in 1997-98). Expected future procurement of land-based systems includes M-109 A2 155mm SPGs and the K-1 MBT, both of which are produced under licence from the USA. Missile procurement includes licensed production of Crotale SAMs, and imports of 800 Mistral portable SAMs, Seasparrow and Harpoon missiles for KDX-2000 frigates, AIM-120 and AIM-9S air-to-air missiles, AGM-114A and AGM-65D ASMs, and AGM-88 anti-radar missiles. KTX-2 jet trainer/light attack aircraft in early development stages.
Malaysia	Malaysia will import 10 Hawk 100 fighter/trainers, 18 Hawk 200 fighter/ground attack aircraft, 8 F/A-18 fighters (to be delivered in 1995), and has ordered 18 MiG-29 fighters. Malaysia's expected naval procurement will include 2 F-2000 light corvettes (to be commissioned in 1996–97) and 27 offshore patrol vessels (to be delivered over 10–15

Country	Weapon systems/comments
	years). The F-2000 corvettes will be equipped by imported Seawolf ShAMs and MM-40 Exocet anti-ship missiles, and DA-08 and Sea Giraffe-150 surveillance radar systems, all of which are on order. Also on order are AIM-7M and AIM-9S air-to-air missiles and AGM-84A Harpoon anti-ship missiles which will equip the F/A-18 fighters. Future imports of APCs are also expected.
Philippines	The Philippines will continue to take delivery of Italian S-211 and SF-260TP trainer aircraft assembled from kits. Deliveries of 3 Cormoran Class FACs ordered in 1991 will be equipped with MM-40 Exocet anti-ship missiles imported from France. In addition, the Philippines are expected to launch a naval modernization effort with the future procurement of 30 to 40 coastal vessels and patrol craft over the next decade. Future procurement of land-based systems includes 24 V-300 APCs and 140+ FS-100 Simba scout cars. Possible future procurement of second-hand fighter aircraft.
Singapore	Future Singaporean aircraft procurement will include 4 F-50 Enforcer 2 ASW aircraft, and 9 F-16C fighters which will be bought in 1996. The F-16C fighters will be equipped with AIM-7M, AIM-9P and AIM-9S air-to-air missiles. Singapore will also import 150 or more Mistral SAMs, and 2 to 3 more Landsort minesweepers. Singapore can also be expected to place future orders for its indigenously produced FH-88 howitzer.
Taiwan	Future Taiwan aircraft procurement focuses on 130 A-1 Ching-kuo fighter (deliveries between 1994–99), 150 F-16 fighters (deliveries begin in 1996), 60 Mirage 2000-5 fighters (deliveries to begin in 1995), 12 C-130H transport aircraft, 4 E-2C AEW aircraft, and Model 209, OH-58D and SH-2F helicopters. The F-16 fighters will be equipped with AIM-7M and AIM-9S air-to-air missiles, and the Mirage 2000-5 fighters with Mica and R-550 air-to-air missiles. Other missile procurement includes MIM-104 PAC-2 Patriot SAMs ordered in 1993. In addition, procurement can be expected to continue for locally produced Hsiung Feng anti-ship missiles. Naval procurement includes 6 La Fayette Class frigates, 5 FFG-7 frigates (equipped with RIM-67ASM-1 ShAMs and Phalanx CIWS), 2 PFG-2 frigates (equipped with RIM-116A RAM ShAM missiles) and 3 ex-Knox Class frigates (equipped with RGM-84A Harpoon anti-ship missiles and Phalanx CIWS). These naval vessels are expected to come into service between 1994 and 1999. Procurement of land-based systems includes about 200 ex-US Army M-60A3 MBTs and indigenous production of APCs and artillery systems.
Thailand	Upcoming aircraft procurement for Thailand includes 14 F-16A and 4 F-16B fighters (to be delivered in 1994–99), 26 L-39Z jet trainers (deliveries began in 1993), 38 ex-US Navy A-7E fighter/ground-attack aircraft, 3 E-2C AEW aircraft, 3 P-3B ASW aircraft (armed with RGM-84A Harpoon anti-ship missiles), 1 to 2 C-130H-30 transports, and 6 or more G-222 transports. Future helicopter procurement includes 20 to 40 Model 212 helicopters and 6 SH-60B helicopters. Missile procurement includes several hundred VT-1 SAMs. Thai naval procurement is centered upon the delivery in 1996–97 of the Chakri Nareubet helicopter/STOVL carrier and 2 Naresuan Class frigates (in service in 1995; to be equipped with Seasparrow ShAms), and 4 leased Knox Class frigates. The frigates and carrier will be outfitted with imported weapons and electronics systems. Land systems include continued imports of M-109 155mm SPGs, perhaps up to 350 ex-US Army M-48A5 MBTs and some 250 ex-US Army M-60A1 MBTs are to be delivered; procurement of indigenously produced systems includes MRLs.

Sources: Jane's All the World's Aircraft (Jane's Information Group: Coulsdon, Surrey, several editions); *Jane's Fighting Ships* (Jane's Information Group: Coulsdon, Surrey, several editions); *Jane's Armour and Artillery* (Jane's Information Group: Coulsdon, Surrey, several editions); *Jane's Weapons Systems* (Jane's Information Group: Coulsdon, Surrey, several editions); SIPRI arms trade data base.

Table 13E.5. Military expenditure in East Asia, 1985–93[a]

Figures are in US $m., at constant 1985 prices and exchange-rates.

Country	1985	1986	1987	1988	1989	1990	1991	1992[b]	1993[b]
China[c]	5 965	5 867	5 634	4 846	4 816	5 472	5 783	6 229	6 387
% of GNP	2.2	2.1	1.9	1.5	1.6	1.6	1.6	1.5	1.6
Indonesia	2 341	1 938	1 723	1 694	1 751	1 959	1 724	1 913	1 949
% of GDP	2.7	2.1	1.7	1.6	1.5	1.6	1.5	1.2	1.5
Japan	14 189	15 122	15 830	16 522	17 020	17 506	17 975	18 333	18 412
% of GNP	1.0	1.0	1.0	1.0	1.0	1.0	1.0	1.0	1.0
North Korea[d]	4 575	4 674	4 884	4 517	5 000	5 012	5 075	5 376	5 406
% of GNP	21.0	21.0	21.3	19.1	22.3	21.5	22.9	25.5	26.9
South Korea	4 548	4 888	4 995	5 398	5 733	5 835	6 234	6 762	6 896
% of GDP	4.9	4.7	4.3	4.1	4.1	3.9	3.6	3.8	3.6
Malaysia	1 007	1 040	857	1 640	1 418	1 559	1 670	1 685	1 650
% of GDP	3.2	3.6	2.7	4.6	3.7	3.7	3.7	3.4	3.2
Myanmar	208	181	113	129	256	264	263	237	210
% of GDP	3.0	2.9	1.9	2.5	3.9	3.9	3.8	3.2	3.5
Philippines	409	617	644	794	867	860	808	828	840
% of GDP	1.3	1.9	1.8	2.1	2.2	2.6	2.1	2.2	2.2
Singapore	1 093	1 013	1 029	1 132	1 252	1 454	1 532	1 672	1 838
% of GDP	6.1	5.5	5.0	4.8	4.9	5.2	5.3	5.5	5.8
Taiwan	4 048	3 995	4 362	4 686	4 987	5 253	5 443	5 453	5 212
% of GDP	6.5	5.6	5.5	5.5	5.5	5.5	5.3	5.0	4.6
Thailand	1 626	1 525	1 509	1 508	1 551	1 647	1 813	1 925	2 060
% of GDP	4.4	3.9	3.5	3.0	2.8	2.7	2.6	2.9	3.0

[a] Owing to different methods of accounting and availability of data, the definition of 'military spending' will vary in different countries. Caution should be exercised in comparing data across countries or in calculating aggregate figures for the region. Owing to scarcity of data, information on Brunei, Cambodia, Laos and Viet Nam is not included in the table.

[b] Some figures for 1992 and 1993 are estimates.

[c] Derived from official defence budget figures. Some estimates suggest military-related spending is 2 to 3 times the official defence budget figure. See chapter 12 in this volume..

[d] Figures are based upon estimates that North Korea spends approximately 2.5 times the officially announced defence budget on military-related expenditures, and 20–25% of GNP on military expenditure. Because of scarcity of accurate data on North Korean military spending, these data should be considered as rough estimates.

Principal sources: International Monetary Fund (IMF), *Government Finance Statistics Yearbook 1992* (IMF: Washington, DC, 1992); IMF, *International Financial Statistics* (IMF: Washington, DC, several editions); International Bank for Reconstruction and Development/ The World Bank, *World Tables 1991* (IBRD/The World Bank: Washington, DC, 1991); UN Department of Economic and Social Information and Policy Analysis, *Monthly Bulletin of Statistics* (UN: New York, several editions); UN Economic and Social Commission for Asia and the Pacific (ESCAP), *Statistical Yearbook for Asia and the Pacific, 1992* (ESCAP: Bangkok, 1992); *Europa Yearbook* (Europa Publications Limited: London, several editions); Institute of Southeast Asian Studies, *Regional Outlook: Southeast Asia 1993–94* (Institute of Southeast Asian Studies: Singapore, 1993); Research Institute for Peace and Security, *Asian Security* (Brassey's: London, several editions); Central Bank of China, *Financial Statistics: Taiwan District, The Republic of China* (Central Bank of China: Taipei, several editions); SIPRI, *SIPRI Yearbook* (Oxford University Press: Oxford, several editions); International Institute for Strategic Studies, *The Military Balance* (Brassey's: London, several editions); *Vantage Point* (Seoul), Nov. 1993.

arms buildup.[22] In assessing the future potential of the East Asian arms market, Gareth C.C. Chang, Senior Corporate Vice-President for marketing of GM Hughes Electronics, cautions that the region's 'focus is not on building military might, but commercial growth'.[23]

II. Interpreting the trends

The trends in East Asian arms acquisitions are complex, and their causes and effects cannot be reduced to one single phenomenon. A multitude of factors at the international, regional and domestic levels—including economic, technological, doctrinal, political and military factors—need to be considered to comprehend more fully the ongoing and likely future trends in arms acquisitions in East Asia. Economically, consideration should be given to forces of supply and demand which currently contribute to a buyers' market in East Asia. For recipients, the conditions of such a market can often result in significant economic, financial and technological benefits negotiated as part of an arms transfer package, aspects of arms transfers which may act as powerful incentives to purchase weapons.

Similarly, political factors may also contribute to arms acquisition decisions. At the bilateral level, arms transfers may reflect the political ties—both good and bad—between suppliers and recipients. For example, South Korean arms exports to the Philippines, Australian arms production deals with Malaysia, and US arms exports to Taiwan and to South Korea are in part symbolic of solidifying friendly political ties.[24] On the other hand, declining political relations will constrain or cut off the arms trade between two countries, as was the case with Russian arms exports to North Korea after Moscow and Seoul normalized relations in 1992, and with US military transfers to China, such as the ill-fated 'Peace Pearl' project to upgrade Chinese aircraft, following the Tiananmen Square crisis of 1989. Other politically based decisions which may have a significant impact upon arms exports to the region include the policies adopted by certain European suppliers to curtail and stop arms deals with Taiwan in deference to China.[25] Such political factors can have a significant impact on the region's arms trade: for example, the dramatic decline in North Korean arms imports between 1988 and 1991 accounted for 60 per cent of the region's decline in arms imports for those years.

The arms trade in the region may also partially reflect domestic political considerations for suppliers and recipients. For example, the US–Taiwan F-16 deal was widely viewed as an arrangement made with an eye to US electoral politics in the

---

[22] On reported recent cut-backs or slow-downs in defence spending in the region, see, for example, Yu, S., 'ROC proposes lower budget for next year', *Free China Journal*, 18 Mar. 1994, p. 1; Dawkins, W., 'Japan reviews defence policy', *Financial Times*, 3 Mar. 1994, p. 6; Naoaki Usui, 'Financial woes limit Chinese arms buys', *Defense News*, 28 Feb.–6 Mar. 1994, p. 1; Kiernan, T., 'S. Korean defense spending falls short of previous years', *Defense News*, 21–27 Sep. 1992, p. 25; Naoaki Usui, 'Japan's services worry budget hike will not be enough', *Defense News*, 13–19 Sep. 1994, p. 14; Opall, B., 'Indonesia wields clout amid slowdown', *Defense News*, 6–12 Sep. 1993, p. 16; Naoaki Usui, 'Japanese battle over further defense cuts', *Defense News*, 6–12 Sep. 1994, p. 30.

[23] Chang (note 19), p. 885.

[24] Kiernan, T., 'Boat transfers strengthen Seoul–Manila ties', *Defense News*, 31 May–6 June 1993, p. 12; Ferguson, G., 'Australia, Malaysia examine program to build patrol boats', *Defense News*, 26 July–1 Aug. 1993, p. 12; Segal, G., *The East Asian Balance after the F-16 Sale to Taiwan*, CAPS Papers no. 3 (Chinese Council for Advanced Policy Studies: Taipei, Dec. 1992); 'Patriot missiles could sink talks, North Korea warns', *International Herald Tribune*, 29–30 Jan. 1994, p. 1.

[25] Lewis, P., 'Deal rules out Taiwan as French market', *Jane's Defence Weekly*, 29 Jan. 1994.

presidential campaign of 1992. On the demand side, among several recipient countries in East Asia, the military establishment maintains significant political clout, enough to divert resources towards the purchase of weaponry, both for the purposes of improving the armed forces and to gain personally from the deals through graft.[26]

As noted above, military modernization and doctrinal adjustments will also help explain trends in military acquisitions for East Asia. In addition, arms acquisitions may also be explained as a means to counter a sense of unease in East Asia which results from the shifts of regional power attending the transition from the cold war to the post-cold war order. The perception that Russia and the USA will exercise diminished regional influence leads to the belief that other large powers in the region will become more assertive, or that smaller local powers will exert themselves more forcefully. For some regional rivalries—such as between Taiwan and China, between Japan and North Korea, between North and South Korea, or among the claimants to islands in the South China Sea—tensions may rise when there is a perceived loss of a reliable 'balancer', or if the guarantees of a powerful patron lose their conviction. Sensing such uncertainty, countries will upgrade their defence capabilities. As Mohamed Jawhar, Deputy Director General of Malaysia's Institute of Strategic and International Studies, notes, 'One cannot discount the fact that we do look at our neighbors as we plan our military modernization. So in that sense, one could label it an arms race, but the term is tremendously misleading.'[27]

Finally, in interpreting arms acquisitions trends, it is perhaps most critical to consider the twin factors of context and capability, which remain largely unexplored in the literature. The significance of arms acquisitions cannot be fully understood without an appreciation for the kaleidoscopic assortment of security environments and perceptions which motivate arms acquisitions in East Asia, and the effects of weapon capabilities on the environments and perceptions into which they are introduced. Future efforts to analyse arms acquisitions in the region need to take these numerous factors into account.

While the data presented here do not suggest a rapid arms buildup or arms race in East Asia, a continuing improvement in military capabilities within the region merits ongoing scrutiny. In this regard, regional arms control and security dialogue efforts are welcome complements to continued economic dynamism and prosperity for East Asia.

---

[26] 'Asia's arms race', *The Economist*, 20 Feb. 1993, pp. 19–20.
[27] Quoted in Opall, B., 'Nations eye neighbors, upgrade armed forces', *Defence News*, 6–12 Sep. 1993, p. 8.

Part IV. Arms control and disarmament, 1993

Chapter 14. Conventional arms control and security co-operation in Europe

Chapter 15. Nuclear arms control and an extended non-proliferation regime

Chapter 16. Nuclear arms control

Chapter 17. The Chemical Weapons Convention: institutionalization and preparation for entry into force

Chapter 18. Biological weapon and arms control developments

Chapter 19. UNSCOM: activities in 1993

14. Conventional arms control and security co-operation in Europe

ZDZISLAW LACHOWSKI

I. Introduction

Conventional arms control in Europe reached a peak in the early 1990s with the conclusion of several 'grand accords': the 1990 Treaty on Conventional Armed Forces in Europe (the CFE Treaty, entered into force in 1992), the 1992 Treaty on Open Skies (not yet entered into force) and the 1992 Concluding Act of the Negotiation on Personnel Strength of Conventional Armed Forces in Europe (the CFE-1A Agreement, entered into force with the CFE Treaty). The Vienna Documents 1990 and 1992 on confidence- and security-building measures (CSBMs) were also adopted within the framework of the Conference on Security and Co-operation in Europe (CSCE), developing the traditional CSBMs and adding new ones.[1] Although successful, the agreements served more to close the cold war era than to open a new avenue by strengthening and consolidating the arms control regime on the continent. For example, the CFE regime limits major conventional weapons relevant to the era of East–West confrontation but does not cover the categories of smaller weapon used in waging limited wars and conflicts in Europe today.

Nevertheless, these agreements play a useful role in maintaining a minimum of security co-operation among CSCE states. In the new environment the CFE Treaty enables states to hold the expansion of each other's arsenals in check, thus providing a basis for shared security interests (between, say, Russia and Ukraine, NATO and Russia, Hungary and Romania, Greece and Turkey, etc.). The continuing withdrawal of foreign troops from European states has been subject to various vicissitudes, but is generally contributing to an enhanced sense of security, especially in Central Europe.

New threats and challenges face the international community, notably the flare-up of localized inter-ethnic conflicts within states or across borders. The CSCE Forum for Security Co-operation (FSC) strives, on the one hand, to harmonize the arms control and disarmament commitments and forge a code of conduct in the new environment and, on the other hand, to address other topical issues such as stabilizing measures for local conflicts, non-proliferation and arms transfers.

---

[1] The CFE Treaty is reprinted in SIPRI, *SIPRI Yearbook 1991: World Armaments and Disarmament* (Oxford University Press: Oxford, 1991), pp. 461–74; the Treaty on Open Skies in SIPRI, *SIPRI Yearbook 1993: World Armaments and Disarmament* (Oxford University Press: Oxford, 1993), pp. 653–71; the CFE-1A Agreement in *SIPRI Yearbook 1993*, pp. 683–89; the Vienna Document 1990 in *SIPRI Yearbook 1991*, pp. 475–88; and the Vienna Document 1992 in *SIPRI Yearbook 1993*, pp. 635–53.

This chapter covers the major issues of the European arms control and security agenda in 1993: the implementation of the CFE Treaty, CFE-1A developments, progress in the process of troop withdrawals from Central and Eastern Europe, and the work of the FSC.

II. Implementation of the CFE Treaty

The CFE Treaty set equal ceilings within its Atlantic-to-the-Urals (ATTU) application zone on the treaty-limited equipment (TLE) of the groups of states parties—originally the NATO and the former Warsaw Treaty Organization (WTO) states—essential for launching surprise attack and initiating large-scale offensive operations. Originally there were 22 states parties to the Treaty, increasing to 29 after the dissolution of the Soviet Union. After the split of Czechoslovakia on 1 January 1993, the Czech Republic and Slovakia negotiated and agreed with other states parties a 2:1 division of the limits accepted by Czechoslovakia in 1990. In February 1993, at an Extraordinary Conference of the States Parties, the two new states became CFE signatory states, increasing the number of parties to 30.

The major questions on the agenda of or related to CFE Treaty implementation in 1993 were: *(a)* the developments and issues of the first phase of the TLE reduction period; *(b)* the reduction process; *(c)* flank limits; and *(d)* force cascading.

Inspections

The CFE Treaty includes unprecedented provisions for information exchange, on-site inspection, challenge inspection and on-site monitoring of weapon destruction. A 120-day base-line validation period began on 17 July 1992, starting a flurry of intensive inspection activities among states parties to verify the data provided under the CFE information exchange.[2] All NATO inspections were of former WTO states, which in turn mostly inspected NATO states' TLE holdings, with a few exceptions in which ex-WTO states inspected former allies.

The large number of inspections (mostly of declared military sites) called for a high level of co-ordination and preparatory work.[3] Germany, Russia and the USA used the largest inspection corps of the CFE states parties, each with about 200 personnel. This first implementation stage was generally welcomed as a success. Some minor discrepancies were reported, but no breaches or major differences between declared information and the findings of inspectors were found or reported to the Joint Consultative Group (JCG). Disagreements

---

[2] See Sharp, J. M. O., 'Conventional arms control in Europe', *SIPRI Yearbook 1993* (note 1), pp. 591–617.

[3] In May 1990 the NATO states established a special Verification Co-ordinating Committee in the Alliance headquarters in Brussels in order, *inter alia*, to avert situations in which inspections from different states would converge on one site at the same time.

Table 14.1. CFE and CFE-1A holdings of the Czech Republic and Slovakia as agreed after the division, 1993

	Tanks	Armoured combat vehicles (ACVs)	Artillery	Aircraft	Heli-copters	Personnel
Czech Republic	957	1 367	767	230	50	93 330
Slovakia	478	683	383	115	25	46 670

were resolved bilaterally. Problems of information arose in several former Soviet republics where the status of the armed forces is vague or where the existence of an army has not been declared. Other states parties have generally taken the difficult and complex situation in those states into consideration while expressing concern over areas of conflict such as those in Georgia and Moldova.

The three-year reduction period, which started on 15 November 1992 and is due to last until 16 November 1995, will be equally hectic with about 30 inspections per month, and additional efforts will be needed to streamline the costly process. In January 1993, at its second seminar on CFE-related matters, the NATO Verification Co-ordinating Committee launched a programme of enhanced co-operation to increase the effectiveness of the CFE Treaty Inspection Protocol. Under this programme the West has encouraged participation of the former WTO states in NATO's declared site and reduction inspections (20 per cent and 25 per cent, respectively, of the Alliance's inspections) and thus cut back on the number of 'East-on-East' inspections. This enabled the number of 'West-on-East' inspections to be increased. As a result, more than 40 multinational reduction inspection teams were formed and 25 joint teams conducted inspections to verify TLE holdings.[4] Eastern participants were reported to have offered a similar solution in Eastern-led inspections, but NATO declined, fearing that this would curtail the Allied inspection activities.[5]

In accordance with the NATO invitation to its North Atlantic Cooperation Council (NACC) partners to carry out joint inspections, in mid-March 1993 the first multinational CFE Treaty inspection was conducted in Romania. Its results as well as the organization of joint training programmes for CFE inspectors were welcomed by NACC ministers and representatives.[6]

No central data base or depository exists to record CFE inspections. In the initial stages states parties sent their inspection reports to the JCG but, finding itself flooded with documentation, the Group soon requested that inspection

---

[4] Although the reason frequently given by NATO for conducting joint inspections with NACC partners is to save money, the cost of transporting a NACC inspector by air to join a NATO team often exceeded the cost of transporting an entire 9-member inspection team by land to inspect a neighbouring co-operation partner. *Disarmament Bulletin,* no. 23 (winter 1993/94), p. 3.

[5] Institute for Defense and Disarmament Studies, *Arms Control Reporter* (IDDS: Brookline, Mass.), sheet 407.B.490, 1993.

[6] Statement issued at the meeting of defence ministers at NATO Headquarters, Brussels, on 29 Mar. 1993. See *Atlantic News,* no. 2512 (Annex), (1 Apr. 1993).

reports be furnished only on demand. NATO created its own data base (VERITY) to keep track of the number of inspections but kept no full CFE records. In November 1993, NATO countries decided to open up their verification data base on CFE disarmament to the co-operation partners.[7]

In the first phase of the reduction period (15 November 1992–16 November 1993), over 1000 inspections were made, 700 by Western states and more than 300 by the Eastern group.

Reduction of excess treaty-limited equipment

To comply with the CFE Treaty ceilings TLE items must be destroyed or, in some cases, converted to non-military purposes. Article VIII, paragraph 4(A), requires each state party to destroy 25 per cent of its total reduction liability in each of the five categories of conventional armaments and equipment limited by the Treaty during the first 12 months of phase I.[8] A total of 48 610 TLE items (18 051 tanks, 8766 artillery pieces, 19 251 ACVs, 225 helicopters and 2317 aircraft) must be reduced by 16 November 1995.[9] On 15 December 1992 the states parties provided data within the annual CFE information exchange. Although there were some complaints about violations of parts of the CFE Treaty, those problems were satisfactorily resolved in the JCG.[10]

In January 1993, the JCG resumed weekly plenary meetings in Vienna with informal groups dealing with special issues. At the insistence of East European parties—Romania, Russia and Ukraine in particular—modification of TLE destruction rules to cut costs was discussed in the spring. It was claimed that in the last stages of the CFE Negotiation there had not been sufficient time or experience to calculate the costs involved. Many states agreed that some required procedures were redundant, costly or excessive. Russia indicated that disabling one side of a tank's drive system is as effective as disabling both sides, and that cutting partially through major components such as gun barrels and the turret ring disabled a tank as efficiently as and more economically than cutting completely through those parts.[11] In July the JCG agreed to Russian and German proposals for modifying destruction methods. The German method entailed using a large compactor to crush lightly armoured vehicles (which, although fast, was also criticized as being too costly).

---

[7] The NACC work programme for 1994, issued in Dec. 1993, has been further extended, *inter alia*, to CFE Treaty implementation, including a seminar with co-operation partners and a course for verification teams' inspectors to be held in Komorni Hradek, Czech Republic. See *Work Plan for Dialogue, Partnership and Cooperation 1994*, issued at the NACC meeting, NATO Headquarters, Brussels, on 3 Dec. 1993; Press Communique M-NACC-2 2(93)72, 3 Dec. 1993, p. 2.

[8] CFE Treaty (note 1), Article VIII. By the end of phase II, the parties will destroy at least 60% of their total reduction liabilities, reaching the 100% target by the end of phase III.

[9] International Institute for Strategic Studies (IISS), *The Military Balance 1993–1994* (Brassey's: London, 1993), p. 246.

[10] *Arms Control Reporter*, sheet 407.B.485, 1993; Sharp, J. M. O., 'Conventional arms control in Europe', SIPRI 1993 (note 1), pp. 612–13.

[11] Russia conducted a demonstration in St Petersburg; similarly, Romania suggested modifying destruction methods for ACVs. *Arms Control Reporter*, sheet 407.B.487, 1993.

Although the former Soviet republics had agreed to TLE allocations under the terms of the CFE Treaty (in the Oslo Document of 5 June 1992[12]), they were unable to agree on how to share out the former Soviet responsibility for weapon destruction (the combined notified reduction liabilities of these states were 3469 pieces fewer than those of the Soviet Union[13]). This is difficult for several reasons: some of the former Soviet equipment turned over by Russia to the newly independent states is unusable; other equipment has been lost (i.e., seized or stolen) to non-governmental rebel groups; and some has been destroyed in the wars and conflicts under way in the Caucasus region. Two former republics—Armenia and Azerbaijan—failed to declare their equipment holdings and accept any formal destruction liability. At the same time, the national armies of these two countries have gained considerable strength. Azerbaijan is reported to possess 286 tanks, 480 armoured infantry fighting vehicles (AIFVs) and 372 armoured personnel carriers (APCs), 330 artillery pieces, 50 combat aircraft plus 50 trainers and 8 helicopters; Armenia has 160 tanks, about 200 AIFVs and some 240 APCs, and 257 pieces of artillery.[14] In effect, at the end of the first reduction phase both governments have come under growing criticism for failing to resolve their reduction liabilities. In addition, the dispute between Russia and Ukraine over responsibility for reductions required by the Soviet pledge of 14 June 1991 on coastal defence and naval infantry units[15] is still not settled. Regarding the Soviet pledge on TLE east of the Urals, on 2 September 1993 the defence ministers of Kazakhstan, Russia and Uzbekistan met at a session of the Commonwealth of Independent States (CIS) Joint Consultative Commission in Minsk to discuss their shares in the reduction of weapons withdrawn from the European part of the former USSR. The ministers initialled a joint statement on the quotas (not released) of weapons each state should eliminate by the end of 1995. As Russian Defence Minister Pavel Grachev commented, the only difficulty that remained was that of funding the operation.[16]

As the 16 November deadline drew nearer, numerous CFE officials expressed concern about the difficulties that might hinder other parties, such as Armenia, Azerbaijan, Belarus, Georgia and Russia, from meeting the 25 per cent reduction requirements in time. Reduction activities intensified signifi-

---

[12] The Final Document of the Extraordinary Conference of the States Parties to the CFE Treaty (the Oslo Document), Oslo, 5 June 1992, is reprinted in *SIPRI Yearbook 1993* (note 1), pp. 677–82.

[13] 1072 tanks, 1776 ACVs and 621 artillery pieces. See US General Accounting Office (GAO), *Conventional Arms Control: Former Warsaw Pact Nations' Treaty Compliance and US Cost Control*, GAO Report to Congressional Requesters (GAO: Washington, DC, Dec. 1993), p. 22.

[14] IISS (note 9), pp. 71–73. See also the Russian estimates of May 1993 claiming that Azerbaijan should scrap or convert up to 939 ACVs; Armenia, 159 ACVs; and Georgia, 72. They also implied that Azerbaijan should reduce up to 195 tanks and 68 artillery pieces. GAO (note 13), p. 21.

[15] Sharp, J. M. O., 'Conventional arms control in Europe', SIPRI, *SIPRI Yearbook 1992: World Armaments and Disarmament* (Oxford University Press: Oxford, 1992), pp. 461–62.

[16] Foreign Broadcast Information Service, *Daily Report–Central Eurasia (FBIS-SOV)*, FBIS-SOV-93-170, 3 Sep. 1993; *Arms Control Reporter*, sheet 407.B.492, 1993. Uzbekistan and most of Kazakhstan lie outside the CFE zone of application. By signing the agreement those states thus assumed some of the destruction commitments of the former Soviet Union.

cantly in the autumn of 1993, however.[17] In October Belarus stated that it would be able to meet its TLE destruction requirement for the first reduction phase, but indicated that this would require great effort (Belarus is destroying the armaments of the most heavily armed military district, MD[18]), and recommended that a fund be established for the dismantling of weapons or that the JCG allow some equipment to be sold instead of destroyed. Moreover, the head of the Belorussian delegation indicated that his country would have trouble meeting the target for the second phase.[19] Russia promised to fulfil its first-phase reduction obligations in time, and in mid-November it had to destroy only 20–35 more battle tanks to meet the 25 per cent requirement.[20]

At the third seminar of the NATO Verification Co-ordinating Committee, held on 15–17 November 1993, the implementation of the first CFE Treaty reduction phase was claimed a success by the Western states.[21] Almost all states parties had completed the required weapon cuts, and some had even exceeded their reduction goals. Nevertheless, about 2000 TLE items, of which 600 were battle tanks, were reported to be still missing from the calculations (largely because of the failure of Armenia and Azerbaijan to report). Aside from the failure of former Soviet republics to account for all their TLE, some former WTO nations were reported not always to have followed proper CFE procedures, an omission which resulted in hundreds of their claimed destructions being questioned by Western states.[22]

The November 1993 deadline was successfully met. By 16 November 1993 about 17 450 TLE items—roughly 32 per cent of the total reduction liability—had been destroyed or converted to non-military purposes. The NATO group had reduced its conventional arsenals by over 5700 TLE items. The USA had eliminated all of its excess equipment by November 1993. The former WTO group had reduced its arsenals by over 11 500 items, including 6700 in the former Soviet republics.[23] Russia had cut back 804 tanks, 2368 ACVs, 173 artillery systems, 324 fighter aircraft and 25 strike helicopters,[24] and Ukraine had destroyed 603 tanks, 630 ACVs and 175 combat aircraft.[25]

Targets of 60 per cent and 100 per cent reductions for the next two one-year phases face CFE states parties in the run-up to 16 November 1995. These targets will be particularly difficult for the former WTO states, which have already encountered numerous technical and financial hurdles in reducing

---

[17] While in the first 6 months of the reduction phase the former WTO states cut back 3217 TLE items, in the third quarter (Aug. 15) they reported a reduction of 3106 items; see GAO (note 13), p. 20.

[18] For example, Belarus has an excess of 1400 tanks re-deployed from the Soviet Groups of Forces in Eastern Europe before the collapse of the USSR. See IISS (note 9), p. 69.

[19] *Arms Control Reporter*, sheet 407.B.497, 1993.

[20] *Izvestia*, 19 Nov. 1993.

[21] *Atlantic News*, no. 2572 (19 Nov. 1993).

[22] GAO (note 13), pp. 21–22.

[23] Note 21. The ex-WTO group was collectively to reduce some 900 items in phase I.

[24] Data given by V. Kulyebyakin, head of the Russian delegation to the JCG, to an ITAR-TASS correspondent. Aside from liabilities under the Treaty, an additional 446 tanks, 439 AFVs and 219 artillery systems have been scrapped or converted to non-military use outside the CFE Treaty obligations. See FBIS-SOV-93-221, 18 Nov. 1993, p. 3.

[25] FBIS-SOV-94-018, 27 Jan. 1994. During phase II more than 600 tanks and over 300 ACVs are to be destroyed.

their TLE during phase I. These states must reduce some 70 per cent of their excess holdings over the remaining two years, which will require an even greater effort on their part.

The flank issue

Despite adherence to and compliance with the CFE Treaty, a controversy arose in 1993 about the holdings permitted in the flank zones of Russia.[26] The role of the flank zones has essentially changed since they were negotiated. Previously a rear, peripheral area, the southern flank has become Russia's forward line of defence, facing the volatile and conflict-ridden Caucasus region and growing Islamic fundamentalism further south. These reasons are cited in Russian claims that the relevant Treaty provisions should be modified as they are no longer adequate for Russian security requirements. Throughout the CFE Negotiation Soviet delegates voiced their concern about NATO's attempts to limit Soviet military capabilities on the flanks, and various suggestions were made.[27] After the breakup of the USSR, most of the best Soviet forces and armaments were on foreign soil. Russia attempted to devise various solutions, eventually agreeing to divide the CFE quota of weapons as shown in table 14.2.

The Russian military have never been satisfied with the CFE Treaty. Senior Soviet/Russian officers blamed the outcome on Foreign Ministry diplomats having been too subservient to their Western partners.[28] The first signals of a substantial change in the Russian attitude appeared in early March 1993 with Defence Minister Grachev's complaints about Russia being at a disadvantage vis-à-vis growing violence on its southern borders,[29] and Russian delegates in the JCG began informally sounding out CFE states parties about the possibility of revision. Grachev renewed his suggestions in talks with US Defense Secretary Les Aspin in June without, however, going into details. From the spring through the autumn of 1993, informal, low-key but persistent signals were sent from the Russian Defence Ministry and Government as well as JCG officials, indicating Russia's concerns over the issue. However, it was not until the autumn that Russia made a formal proposal to the JCG on flank limits.

In the midst of a gathering political storm in Russia, President Boris Yeltsin presented a rationale for modifying the flank limits in letters of 17 September

---

[26] For more discussion on the issue of the flank limits, see Clarke, D. L., 'The Russian military and the CFE Treaty', Radio Free Europe/Radio Liberty, *RFE/RL Research Report,* vol. 2, no. 42 (22 Oct. 1993), pp. 38–43.

[27] Sharp, J. M. O., 'Conventional arms control in Europe', SIPRI, *SIPRI Yearbook 1990: World Armaments and Disarmament* (Oxford University Press: Oxford, 1990), pp. 481–84; Sharp, J. M. O., 'Conventional arms control in Europe', *SIPRI Yearbook 1991* (note 1), pp. 418–19; Clarke (note 26), pp. 39–41.

[28] *Segodnya* (Moscow), 7 May 1993, in FBIS-SOV-93-088, 10 May 1993. However, *Segodnya* defence analyst Pavel Felgengauer pointed out that blame should also be laid on the Defence Ministry and the General Staff of the Russian Army.

[29] *Segodnya* (note 28).

Table 14.2. Flank holdings for the former Soviet republics (as agreed in the Tashkent Document of 15 May 1992) and Turkey

	Tanks	Artillery	ACVs	Total
Russia	700	1 280	580	2 560
(Leningrad and North Caucasus MDs)				
In storage	600	400	800	1 800
Ukraine	280	500	350	1 020
(Odessa MD)				
In storage	400	500	–	900
Moldova	210	250	210	670
Georgia	220	285	220	725
Armenia	220	285	220	725
Azerbaijan	220	285	220	725
Turkey	2 795	3 523	3 120	9 438
In ATTU zone				

Source: Based on: Crawford, D., 'Conventional Armed Forces in Europe (CFE): A reprise of the key Treaty elements,' ACDA, 1993 (*Arms Control Reporter,* sheet 407.B.493, 1993).

1993 to France, Denmark (at that time holding the Presidency of the European Community, EC), Norway, the UK, the USA and Turkey.[30] A *démarche* of 28 September which followed Yeltsin's letter, while confirming Russia's commitment to the Treaty, set out four reasons for changing the limits set out in Article V.

1. The Treaty was agreed and adopted under conditions which no longer exist, in which the USSR had a single powerful armed force and a sufficiently stable situation prevailed in the region. Thus the flank limitations now take on a 'unilateral and discriminatory character for Russia'.

2. The existing and potential hotbeds of unrest and conflict in the Trans-caucasus, as well as spreading separatism and fundamentalism, would require a 'substantial military presence' to ensure the Russian security interests, and Russia might need more armaments than permitted by the Treaty.

3. Preservation of the flank limits would hamper an even distribution of forces, most of which would be deployed in the rear areas and the densely populated areas along Russia's western borders and in the Kaliningrad region.[31] Thus it would petrify the East–West orientation of deployments instead of the North–South one suited to the present circumstances. More-over—a veiled warning has been sent—such a configuration could meet the strongest resistance from the military and other political forces.

[30] *Arms Control Reporter,* sheet 407.B.492, 1993.
[31] The Leningrad and North Caucasus MDs cover more than half the European territory of Russia. The Kaliningrad *oblast* is the only remnant of the former Soviet part of the CFE Expanded Central Zone (a small portion of the Baltic MD) which belongs to Russia. Under the CFE Treaty, Russia can and does deploy in the *oblast* considerable conventional forces withdrawn from eastern Germany, the Baltic states and Poland. For more on the problems of the Kaliningrad region, see chapter 6 in this volume.

4. There were strong socio-economic reasons for settling troops withdrawn from abroad in the south: the infrastructure for relocation already exists in the south; and harsh climate and living conditions elsewhere could give rise to social tension and unrest among the troops. This also would imply higher costs and delays in the withdrawal timetable.[32]

Officially, this demand was met with strong criticism and resistance from most CFE states parties. However, Ukraine formally supported the Russian stand in late October 1993[33] (the flank rule puts considerable restrictions on Ukraine in deploying and basing its forces on its own territory[34]), as did Armenia and Belarus.

From the start, Russian suggestions prompted opposition from the USA and other NATO states (particularly Norway and Turkey as the flank states) to any revisions. The most adamant position was taken by Turkey, which voiced concern that Russia was seeking to re-establish a strong military presence in and maintain domination over the strategic area.[35] For the USA and other NATO states the flank issue is at present a minor one; it is feared, however, that it could lead to further demands from other parties and set in motion an irresistible process of dismantling the whole Treaty. Some East European states have already unofficially indicated that, if another party has changes made in the Treaty, they would introduce modifications of their own.[36] Moreover, US officials viewed the CFE Treaty as linked with other international arms control agreements; responding to a congressional plan to amend procedures for the implementation of the START treaties, President Clinton warned that such a move would open the floodgates to changes in the CFE Treaty, too.[37] In June a senior State Department official pointed out that the USA does not want to 'start unraveling a very complicated, somewhat delicately balanced treaty with revisions'.[38] Later, in response to the 28 September *démarche*, a US official stated that he found some Russian arguments unclear or unconvincing: Russia had not claimed that its security was endangered by fighting in Azerbaijan and Georgia; the allusions to Islamic militancy were vague; Russia did not have to cram its forces in the Kaliningrad region— nothing in the Treaty compelled it to do so; and actual troops may be housed

[32] *Arms Control Reporter,* sheets 407.D.85-86 (text of the *démarche*) and 407.B.493-494, 1993. See also the article by the First Deputy Chief of the Russian General Staff, Lt-Gen. Vladimir Zhurbenko, in *Krasnaya Zvezda,* 16 Nov. 1993, FBIS-SOV-220, 17 Nov. 1993.
[33] FBIS-SOV-93-206, 27 Oct. 1993, p. 52.
[34] Ukraine argues that it would prefer to deploy more forces in the Odessa Operational Command (the former MD) bordering on Russia rather than have the bulk of them along the frontier with Romania. However, any revision of the CFE flank limits would be a mixed blessing for Ukraine, since it would also allow Russia to redeploy its forces in the North Caucasus MD, which borders on Ukraine. See Markus, U.,'Recent defense developments in Ukraine', *RFE/RL Research Report,* vol. 3, no. 4 (28 Jan. 1994), pp. 29–31.
[35] In turn, Russian military sources claimed that in Feb. 1993, during the Armenian offensive against Azerbaijan, Turkey's 2nd Army mobilized 39 000 troops and 200 tanks along the Armenian border. *Defense News,* 2–8 Aug. 1993. It is also worth noting that under the CFE Treaty a south-eastern region of Turkey is excluded from the application zone, and arms there are not included in Turkey's allowance.
[36] *Arms Control Reporter,* sheet 407.B.494, 1993.
[37] *Defense News,* 4–10 Oct. 1993, pp.1 and 36.
[38] *Wireless File,* US Information Service, Stockholm, no. 111 (11 June 1993).

in the flank zone while their equipment could be stored outside and brought into the zone temporarily for training and exercises.[39]

Other voices suggest that the West should devote more attention to Russian concerns over its 'front-line' area in the North Caucasus MD. As early as the spring of 1992, some US officials saw difficulties in the sub-zonal solutions that Russia might be confronted with after the dissolution of the USSR.[40] There have already been some suggestions for ways of meeting the Russian concern short of renegotiation of the Treaty. One analyst has indicated the possibility of extending the implementation date for the flank zone ceilings that will not enter into effect until November 1995.[41] Russia can also temporarily deploy an additional 153 battle tanks, 241 ACVs and 140 artillery pieces to the flanks.[42] Moreover, Russia could recategorize some of its forces in the flanks as 'internal security forces' (Article XII of the Treaty allows Russia to locate up to 600 AIFVs on the flanks under this category).[43]

The flank problem, which in the post-cold war era lost most of its East–West security-related acuteness, is bound sooner or later to be solved. Of the 30 parties to the Treaty only Russia and Ukraine are subject to this kind of territorial restriction on their deployments. They are not likely to drop their claims on the CFE flank issue easily. The provisions of Russia's new military doctrine announced in November seem to confirm this. The development of the international situation in the southern states also appears to reinforce Russia's position—despite UN reluctance and the refusal of the CSCE Council Meeting in Rome to recognize Russia's leading role in peacekeeping within the former USSR,[44] only Russia has the will and capabilities to carry out effective peace enforcement in the Transcaucasian region. It is quite possible that the issue will be solved indirectly through a peace-enforcement arrangement or regional security agreements (such as those proposed by Moscow to Armenia, Azerbaijan and Georgia in early 1994)[45] that will allow Russia and other CFE states parties to circumvent the relevant provisions of the Treaty.

Cascading

Cascading—exporting TLE from well-off NATO countries to their poorer partners—has become a source of considerable concern in the wake of the

---

[39] *Arms Control Reporter*, sheet 407.B.493, 1993.

[40] *Arms Control Reporter*, sheet 407.B.469, 1992. A *Defense News* commentary in mid-Aug. 1993 urged Western leaders not to dismiss Russia's request without consideration, arguing that a temporary movement of limited numbers of Russian conventional forces into the region might be in 'the best long-term interest of the West'. *Defense News*, 16–22 Aug. 1993.

[41] *Arms Control Today*, Nov. 1993, p. 25. These suggestions are, however, disputed as requiring major treaty revisions. *Arms Control Reporter*, sheet 407.B.494, 1993.

[42] CFE Treaty (note 1), Article V, para. 1(C).

[43] CFE Treaty (note 1), Article XII. There are three and one-half motorized rifle divisions assigned to the Russian Ministry of Internal Affairs in the North Caucasus MD; see Clarke (note 26).

[44] CSCE, Fourth Meeting of the Council, *CSCE and the New Europe—Our Security is Indivisible*, Rome, 1 Dec. 1993 (reproduced in appendix 7A in this volume).

[45] *International Herald Tribune*, 3 Feb. 1994.

CFE Treaty. The North Atlantic Alliance's cascading policy has constituted a military enterprise in a region where a political solution is necessary. On the one hand, the policy of cascading was for NATO a handy way of transferring large quantities of modern armaments and equipment to less-equipped partners instead of carrying on with the costly process of destruction. This would also allegedly serve the purpose of enhancing regional stability. Thus the USA itself transferred 1993 tanks, 636 ACVs and 180 artillery pieces to five other NATO nations (Greece, Norway, Portugal, Spain and Turkey).[46] On the other hand, cascading was said to be a way of balancing Russia's large-scale shifting of weapons from the CFE Treaty zone of application eastwards beyond the Urals.[47] Consequently Greece and Turkey have emerged as the greatest beneficiaries and two of the world's major arms importers, having been able to acquire enormous quantities of CFE-related heavy armaments free of charge from the USA and other NATO states (Germany and the Netherlands).[48] The equipment holdings of Greece and Turkey have increased so dramatically that NATO strategists soon started to worry about whether the powerful arsenals being built up by the two countries really would enhance regional stability. In 1995, once the CFE Treaty is implemented, Turkey is expected to have a modern arsenal up to 25 per cent larger than that it had in 1992; this growth in Turkish military power has made NATO provide Greece with a comparable amount of weaponry to sustain parity and political stability within the Alliance.[49] Given the tensions between the two rival states and their conflicting interests in the volatile Balkan region, such an influx and buildup of weaponry means there is an increasing risk that they might be used in a future conflict that might easily escalate into a wider and more devastating war. It was rightly observed: 'On a more general level, the weapons exported under the name of cascading result in their being shifted from areas and countries in Europe where they are least likely to be used to those parts of the NATO alliance where their use is most likely.'[50]

III. Implementation of the CFE-1A Agreement

The 1992 CFE-1A Agreement set ceilings on various categories of military personnel in the territories of the then 29 (now 30) participating states in the ATTU zone. Unlike the CFE Treaty, the Agreement is politically binding and not subject to ratification by parliaments. In July 1992 Armenia, Azerbaijan, Georgia and Moldova had still not reported on their manpower. By 1993

[46] GAO (note 13), p. 16.

[47] Feinstein, L., 'CFE: off the endangered list?', *Arms Control Today*, Oct. 1993, p. 6.

[48] For a broader discussion see Goldstein, L., Kokkinides, T. and Plesch, D., 'Fuelling Balkan fires: the West's arming of Greece and Turkey', British American Security Information Council (BASIC) Report 93.3 (Sep. 1993). In 1992 Greece purchased about $2 billion and Turkey nearly $1.5 billion worth of weaponry. Anthony, I., Claesson, P., Sköns, E. and Wezeman, S. T., 'Arms production and arms trade', *SIPRI Yearbook 1993* (note 1), p. 445, table 10.11.

[49] *International Herald Tribune*, 1 Oct. 1993.

[50] Feinstein (note 47), p. 6.

Azerbaijan had declared a personnel strength of 70 000; Georgia 40 000; and Moldova 20 000.

In 1993 CFE-1A participating states continued to reduce and restructure their forces. In the propitious international climate, a number of governments have declared or approved plans for considerable reductions. For instance, in January Belgium approved a five-year reduction plan to cut back its forces from 76 000 to 40 000 personnel.[51]

At the special February 1993 JCG conference at which the Czech Republic and Slovakia were formally confirmed as CFE states parties, both states formally declared their wish to have their CFE and CFE-1A allocations divided in a 2:1 ratio. In June 1993, the Czech Government approved a plan to trim its armed forces to 65 000 by 1996.[52] In line with this, the period of military service for conscripts was shortened to 12 months.

In addition, Germany hinted in early February that along with its procurement freeze it could reduce its manpower ceilings from the declared 370 000 to about 300 000 (or even 250 000, as proposed by the Social Democrat Party, SPD) by 1996. However, facing mounting opposition from the NATO allies, and especially from the USA, Chancellor Helmut Kohl quickly offered assurances that Germany will not cut back the German Army without consulting the Alliance.[53] Pressed by the problems of manpower shortages and money, Germany declared in its Defence Ministry's 'White Book' in early April 1994 that the armed forces ceiling will be lowered to 345 000 in 1994.[54]

At the end of the year, Defence Minister Grachev announced that the Russian military would be reduced to 2.1 million by 1995. This clearly contravenes the September 1992 Russian Law on Defence, which provides for a military force not exceeding 1 per cent of a state's total population, in this case 1.5 million. During 1993, the rate of demobilization was slow (bringing the force down to an estimated 2.3 million personnel at the end of the year); at the same time the Russian military have had to cope with financial constraints on the military budget on the one hand, and growing draft evasion on the other. Given the nationalist–conservative mould of the Parliament after the December 1993 election, it seems that any amendments to the law to handle the military budget and draft problems should not encounter serious opposition; however, the implementation of such a plan would certainly create considerable problems.[55]

[51] *Atlantic News*, no. 2495 (3 Feb. 1993), p. 4.

[52] *Facts about the Army of the Czech Republic*, Prague, 1993, p. 2.

[53] *Financial Times*, 4 Feb. 1993; *Frankfurter Allgemeine Zeitung*, 8 Feb. 1993.

[54] Weissbuch zur Sicherheit der Bundesrepublik Deutschland und zur Lage und Zukunft der Bundeswehr [White Book on the Security of the Federal Republic of Germany and on the State and Future of the Federal Armed Forces], 5 Apr. 1994.

[55] *RFE/RL News Briefs*, vol. 3, no. 3 (27 Dec. 1993–4 Jan. 1994), p. 3. For a discussion of Russian military problems, see Allison, R., 'Russian defence planning: military doctrine and force structures', *Lectures and Contributions to East European Studies at FOA* (Swedish National Defence Research Establishment, Stockholm, 30 June 1993), pp. 11–14.

IV. Troop withdrawals

Withdrawal of Russian troops

The withdrawal of Russian troops from Central and East European states continued steadily during 1993, although its pace was exposed to the vicissitudes of Russian politics and Russia's relations with its neighbours.

Germany

The withdrawal of Russian troops from Germany continued according to the agreed schedule. Russia complained repeatedly about the difficulties of housing returning officers and in July 1993, while assuring visiting German Chancellor Helmut Kohl of Russia's intention to keep to the schedule, President Yeltsin asked Germany for additional financial support to build housing for servicemen.[56] Russia planned to pull back most of the 190 000 troops (including 109 000 soldiers) in 1993, leaving some 37 000 to be withdrawn by 31 August 1994.[57] The pull-out was hampered in the middle of the year by the failing Russian–Lithuanian talks on transferring troops through Lithuanian territory, but later in the year it was reported to be on schedule.[58] At the beginning of 1994 there were still 31 400 Russian soldiers on German soil.[59]

Poland

After the last Russian combat unit left Polish territory in October 1992, about 4000 servicemen remained to assist the pull-out of Russian troops and equipment from Germany. On 17 September 1993, the last Russian troops departed, thus completing the withdrawal of the some 60 000 Soviet troops which had been stationed in Poland since World War II.

The Baltic states

The Russian military presence in Estonia, Latvia and Lithuania also decreased over the year, but the process of withdrawal was not always smooth. The Baltic republics continued to demand that Russia either stick to its withdrawal obligations (Lithuania) or set completion dates and timetables for the pull-out (Estonia and Latvia). Russia attempted to postpone the withdrawals, citing various excuses and pointing mainly to its own domestic problems and concerns over the plight of Russian-speaking minorities in those countries. In spite of Yeltsin's directive of 29 October 1992, suspending the withdrawal of

---

[56] *International Herald Tribune*, 12 July 1993. According to Col.-Gen. M. P. Burlakov, Commander-in-Chief of the Western Group of Forces in Germany, the ratio of withdrawal to resettlement was 9:1. See *Arms Control Reporter*, sheet 407.E-1.132, 1993.

[57] *Frankfurter Allgemeine Zeitung*, 30 Mar. 1993; *Arms Control Reporter*, sheet 407.E-1.125-126, 1993.

[58] *Arms Control Reporter*, sheet 407.E-1.132, 1993; FBIS-SOV-93-198, 15 Oct. 1993, p. 11.

[59] *Atlantic News*, no. 2590 (22 Jan. 1994), p. 3.

Table 14.3. Withdrawal of Russian troops from Central and Eastern Europe, 1993

State	Number of troops in:			Date of completion
	Spring 1993	Autumn 1993	End 1993	
Germany	190 000	58 000	31 400	31 Aug. 1994
Estonia	7 600	4 000	2 600	31 Aug. 1994
Latvia	24 600	16 000	13 000	31 Aug. 1994
Lithuania	10 000	0	0	31 Aug. 1993
Total in Baltic states	**42 200**	**20 000**	**15 600**	..

Note: In both Belarus and Ukraine, the bulk of the armed forces are Russian, and the strategic rocket forces in both countries are guarded by Russian/CIS units. In Belarus, there are 40 000 Russian troops, but so far there are no plans to send them home. The removal from power of President Stanislav Shushkevich in Jan. 1994 seems to have further weakened the Belarussian search for neutrality. Compare Markus, U., 'Belarus a "weak link" in Eastern Europe?', *RFE/RL Research Report*, vol. 2, no. 49 (10 Dec. 1993).

Source: Author's estimates based on: Bungs, D., 'Progress on withdrawal from the Baltic states', *RFE/RL Research Report*, no. 25 (18 June 1993), pp. 50–59; Foreign Broadcast Information Service, *Daily Report–Central Eurasia*, 1993; *Arms Control Reporter*, sheet 407.E-1, 1993; *Atlantic News*, 1993, 1994.

troops from all three Baltic states, which linked that decision to human rights abuses in the region and was confirmed on 29 March 1993 by Pavel Grachev, the pull-out of servicemen and *matériel* continued at a slow rate. In 1993 Russia pursued a differentiated policy towards the three states using a variety of instruments (suspension of talks, forms of military demonstration, low-rank representation at the talks, etc.) which resulted in differently paced troop withdrawals and uneven progress in handling the withdrawal problem. Pulling out Russian troops from the Baltic republics has caused some anxiety among the Scandinavian states over the increase of those troops near Finland's southern border with Russia.[60] The increase in numbers of troops being withdrawn to and amassed in the Kaliningrad area has also given rise to concern in the adjacent states.

Lithuania. Lithuania was seeking to make Russia keep to its September 1992 commitments to withdraw the troops by 31 August 1993. Lithuania was treated differently by Russia in its game to play it off against the other Baltic partners, and the pace of withdrawal from Lithuania was relatively smooth. On 18 May 1993 Lithuanian–Russian talks resumed after an eight-month break. Grachev's visit to Vilnius on 18–19 May, where he confirmed Russia's willingness to meet the August deadline, demonstrated Russia's flexibility. He did not insist strongly on the prior signing of a political treaty on the basic principles of the withdrawal.[61] Lithuanian pragmatism and their 'co-operative'

---

[60] *RFE/RL News Briefs*, vol. 2, no. 43 (18–22 Oct. 1993), p. 12.
[61] However, the lack of a formal agreement on withdrawal with Lithuania was later raised by the Russian delegation as an obstacle in negotiations. *RFE/RL News Briefs*, vol. 2, no. 32 (26 July–6 Aug. 1993), p. 16.

attitude to dealings with Russia (on problems of environmental damage, citizenship, housing, property, social provisions for the departing troops, etc.) on the one hand, and policy considerations in Russian relations with Lithuania's Baltic partners on the other, cleared the way to the solution of Russian military presence in that country.[62]

On 5–6 August Lithuanian–Russian talks continued on other unsettled questions. The Lithuanian negotiators also raised for the first time formally the matter of Russian compensation for damages inflicted on Lithuanian territory. The talks were deadlocked and Russian officials threatened to suspend them. On 17 August Russia 'temporarily' suspended the troop pull-out, which was explained officially three days later: the Russian Defence Ministry accused Lithuania of changing the terms of the draft agreement in an unacceptable way.[63] At the same time, Russia announced that it did not feel bound by the September 1992 withdrawal agreement. A meeting on 21 August between Russian and Lithuanian negotiators led nowhere, and tensions rose. A quiet, unofficial US reminder (in the press) that US aid was linked to a complete Russian pull-out, or agreement on it, from all the Baltic states seems to have exerted effective pressure. The crisis was resolved on 30 August, when Lithuanian President Algirdas Brazauskas stated that he and President Yeltsin had reached agreement on withdrawing the troops the next day. On 31 August, the last Russian combat troops left Lithuania.

Estonia and Latvia. Estonia and Latvia continued to insist on complete withdrawal by the end of 1993. Russia adopted an evasive, temporizing position, raising various related problems, particularly the sizeable Russian-speaking minorities in both countries, accusing the two states of indifference to Russian problems and persisting with the argument that the pull-out should be put off until the end of 1994. Russia's linking of the schedule with its domestic housing problems and with human rights issues in Latvia and Estonia, and repeated accusations from Russian officials during the year, prompted reaction from Western[64] and Scandinavian states,[65] as well as international organizations,[66] calling for immediate withdrawal of the Russian military.

---

[62] *Frankfurter Allgemeine Zeitung,* 25 May 1993. See also Bungs, D., 'Progress on withdrawal from the Baltic states', *RFE/RL Research Report,* no. 25 (18 June 1993), pp. 50–59.

[63] Lithuania reportedly demanded $140 billion compensation for damage caused by Soviet troops over the past 50 years. *International Herald Tribune,* 23 Aug. 1993.

[64] See, e.g., the successive NATO ministerial meeting communiqués in Dec. 1992 and June and Dec. 1993, calling for the 'expeditious' withdrawal of foreign troops from the Baltic states.

[65] *Atlantic News,* no. 2523 (7 May 1993), and no. 2543 (14 July 1993).

[66] In his report to the UN General Assembly, Secretary-General Boutros Boutros-Ghali stated that he and his special envoy Tommy Koh, who headed a UN delegation to the Baltic states in Aug./Sep. 1993, were available as mediators in the negotiations on troop pull-out from the two states. *RFE/RL News Briefs,* vol. 2, no. 36 (23–27 Aug. 1993), and no. 45 (1–5 Nov. 1993), p. 17. In the CSCE the Baltic states have repeatedly raised their security concerns and submitted proposals in the FSC regarding problems of regional security (CSCE document CSCE/FSC/SC.19, Vienna, 16 June 1993) and creating a risk-reduction mechanism regarding the stationing or deployment of foreign troops (CSCE/FSC/SC.18, Vienna, 19 May 1993). The Rome CSCE Council reaffirmed the position that the Russian troops should complete the orderly withdrawal. See *CSCE and the New Europe* (note 44).

In its talks with Latvia, Russia insisted particularly on retaining three strategic installations under its jurisdiction for 5–10 years—the intelligence-gathering installation near Ventspils, the phased-array radar system at Skrunda and the naval base in Liepaja. These were stressed by Russia as being essential to its strategic interests. The outstanding questions including those of human rights for the Russian-speaking inhabitants, financial compensation for damages, social welfare guarantees for servicemen, the housing shortage in Russia and the border (between Russia and Estonia) were raised time and again over the year. Their solution was seen by Moscow as a precondition for completing the Russian withdrawal from the region. In the meantime, some minor accords related to the pull-out were signed, but not those regarding the completion date or the future of Russian strategic facilities in Latvia.[67]

Russia's pull-out talks with its two neighbours were hampered in mid-1993 by the issue of the Estonian Law on Aliens and the Latvian citizenship draft law (dubbed 'ethnic cleansing' and 'deportation politics', respectively, by Russia), which discriminated against the human, political, civil and property rights of the Russian-speaking population. Another issue was that of chemical and nuclear pollution from former Soviet military bases and depots (e.g., the port of Paldiski and the Sillamae waste dump) which Estonia wants Russia to clean up, while the latter demands compensation for its military 'investments' in the country over the past 50 years.[68]

The case of the two Baltic states was strengthened internationally through a 15 November 1993 UN resolution calling for 'the early, orderly and complete withdrawal of foreign military forces'.[69] Shortly afterwards Russian officials pointed out that the problem of withdrawal was technical, not political, and an exact date would be fixed once the issues of material aid (including housing construction) to the troops being withdrawn and of Russia retaining the Skrunda anti-missile system for six more years were resolved.[70] On 1 December the CSCE foreign ministers in Rome urged Russia to speed up its troop withdrawal from the Baltic states and present specific timetables for the process.[71] Russia reportedly changed its tone and offered to return the nuclear submarine base at Paldiski as well as the Ventspils satellite listening post and the Liepaja naval base by 31 August 1994, or soon thereafter.[72] However, after the December election in Russia, the position of the Russian Government hardened again, and a suspension of the withdrawal was suggested.[73]

Successive rounds of talks between Estonia and Russia in the second half of the year made some progress on related questions (e.g., Estonia relaxed earlier

[67] *RFE/RL News Briefs*, vol. 2, no. 24 (1–4 June 193), p. 16.

[68] *Defense News*, 25–31 Oct. 1993, p. 24.

[69] UN document A/48/18, 15 Nov. 1993

[70] Russia is planning to build a similar facility in Baranovichi in Belarus. See also Grachev's statement in FBIS-SOV-93-220, 17 Nov. 1993; *Izvestia*, 18 Nov. 1993.

[71] *CSCE and the New Europe* (note 44).

[72] *Financial Times*, 2 Dec. 1993.

[73] See Kozyrev statement in Murmansk in *Izvestia*, 15 Dec. 1993. On 18 Jan. 1994, ITAR-TASS reported Kozyrev stating that Russian troops should not leave 'those regions that have been the sphere of Russian interest for centuries', and that their leaving would create a 'security vacuum'. *Nezavisimaya Gazeta*, 19 Jan. 1994.

decisions on retired Soviet servicemen[74]). On 28 December the Estonian Government agreed in principle to Russia's proposed August deadline, provided that Russia furnish the timetable for the process and that most of the 2400 Russian troops leave the country at the earliest possible date, preferably at the beginning of 1994, and especially the 144th Motorized Rifle Division quartered in and around Tallinn.[75] However, in early April 1994, Russia officially announced to Estonia that it was definitely abandoning its commitment to withdraw its troops by 31 August 1994.[76]

In October 1993, US Secretary of State Warren Christopher reaffirmed that the USA wanted an early and complete pull-out of Russian troops from Latvia; Congress has authorized $160 million to construct housing units in Russia. He called on Riga to assure full citizenship rights for Latvia's Russian-speaking population.[77] In early January 1994 the Russian–Latvian troop withdrawal negotiations which were reported to be drawing to their conclusion were briefly but dramatically stalled after an incident involving the arrest of two Russian generals in Latvia.[78] On 15 March 1994, Latvia and Russia reached an agreement that the withdrawal be completed by 31 August, and another agreement regarding the Skrunda radar station (to remain under Russian control for another five and a half years, with 500 Russian troops).[79] The withdrawal agreement was eventually signed on 30 April 1994,[80] after an interim deadlock in Russian–Latvian relations caused by President Yeltsin's decree of 5 April on permanent military bases in the former Soviet republics which erroneously included the Skrunda radar station.

The Transcaucasus and Moldova[81]

The Caucasus has witnessed almost constant inter-ethnic conflicts since the collapse of the USSR. Withdrawal of the Russian troops has proceeded in the midst of heavy fighting, which inevitably affected the schedule of the pull-out, to be completed in 1995. In May 1992 Russia and the three Transcaucasian states agreed on the partition and transfer of military equipment from the former Transcaucasus MD to Armenia, Azerbaijan and Georgia 'on the basis of parity'. It began the withdrawal of the 7th Army from Armenia (soon suspended) and the 4th Army from Azerbaijan (started February 1992 and completed May 1993).[82]

[74] FBIS-SOV-93-225, 24 Nov. 1993, p. 73.
[75] FBIS-SOV-93-248, 29 Dec. 1993, p. 55.
[76] Atlantic News, no. 2613, 13 Apr. 1994.
[77] RFE/RL News Briefs, vol. 2, no. 44 (1993), p. 15.
[78] International Herald Tribune, 11 Jan. 1994.
[79] Atlantic News, no. 2607 (18 Mar. 1994).
[80] Atlantic News, no. 2620 (6 May 1994).
[81] According to Russian Foreign Minister Andrey Kozyrev there are about 20 000 troops and military advisers in Trans-Dniester, South Ossetia, western Georgia, Abkhazia, Nagorno-Karabakh and Tajikistan. This figure is contested by NATO, which believes the number of troops is much higher. See Frankfurter Allgemeine Zeitung, 4 Dec. 1993.
[82] See Fuller, E., 'Paramilitary forces dominate fighting in Transcaucasus', RFE/RL Research Report, vol. 2, no. 25 (18 June 1993), pp. 74–82. In Oct. a return of Russian troops was reported to be requested

Table 14.4. Russian troops in the Transcaucasus, 1992–93

State	Mid-1992	Mid-1993	End 1993
Armenia	23 000	5 000	9 000
Azerbaijan	62 000	–	–
Georgia	20 000	5 000	14 000

Source: Estimates based on Foreign Broadcast Information Service, *Daily Report–Central Eurasia,* 1993 and 1994; IISS, *Military Balance 1992–1993* and *1993–1994* (Brassey's: London, 1992 and 1993).

Under the terms of the Russian–Georgian military co-operation agreement of 9 October 1993, 20 000-strong Russian garrisons will be stationed in several strategic places; Russia also rents the Poti naval base and several air-fields.[83] In November it was reported that Russia will provide Georgia with an unspecified amount of weapons and armoured equipment.[84]

At the beginning of 1994, Russia declared that it would like to maintain three bases in Georgia, one in Armenia and one in Azerbaijan with the agreement of the host states, in order to provide regional security in the area.[85]

It is estimated that at present there are about 23 000 Russian troops in the Transcaucasus[86] (see table 14.4).

The present strength of the Russian 14th Army in Moldova is between 5000 and 6000 troops, well below the level of a motor rifle division.[87] Withdrawal from the Left-Bank Dniester area is the most controversial part of Russian–Moldovan relations. Moldova insists on Russian troops leaving by 1 July 1994. The May 1993 withdrawal agreement between Presidents Boris Yeltsin and Mircea Snegur[88] did not decide on the details—schedule, procedure, costs, and so on. The link between the pull-out and the political settlement of the conflict is a daunting obstacle. It is also unclear how an army predominantly composed of local inhabitants can be withdrawn. Military specialists and diplomats believe that the pull-out will take at least two to three years.[89]

Withdrawals of US troops from Europe

In January 1993 a contingent of US troops stationed in Europe left Germany (the 3rd armoured division in Frankfurt). The plan was to reduce US troops in

by Baku; however, it was later firmly denied by Azerbaijani President Geidar Aliev. FBIS-SOV-93-204, 25 Oct. 1993, p. 71.

[83] FBIS-SOV-93-195, 12 Oct. 1993, p. 15–16; FBIS-SOV-93-196, 13 Oct. 1993, p. 13.

[84] FBIS-SOV-93-224, 23 Nov. 1993, p. 17.

[85] *International Herald Tribune,* 3 Feb. 1994.

[86] FBIS-SOV-94-023, 3 Feb. 1994, p. 65.

[87] According to a CSCE permanent representative the figure was 6081 at the beginning of 1993. *Final Report on the Conflict in the Left Bank Dniester Areas of the Republic of Moldova by the Personal Representative of the Chairman-in-Office of the CSCE Council, Adam Daniel Rotfeld (Poland),* Prague, 31 Jan. 1993, p. 15.

[88] FBIS-SOV-93-095, 19 May 1993, p. 62.

[89] FBIS-SOV-93-219, 16 Nov. 1993, p. 19.

Europe by 60 000, reaching a ceiling of 185 000 by October 1993 in accordance with the Bush Administration plan to reduce the US military presence in Europe to 150 000 by 1995. In February Defense Secretary Les Aspin directed the Pentagon to develop a plan to reduce US troops in Europe to 100 000 by the end of fiscal year 1997. This was confirmed at the March NACC meeting, when about 150 000 military personnel were said to be still in Europe.[90]

On 1 July, the Defense Secretary announced the shutdown or reduction of operations at 92 overseas installations, mainly in Europe, including 13 bases with over 1000 personnel and another 13 staffed by 200–1000.[91] This would mean a further reduction of 23 400 US military jobs. In August it was announced that the USA would cut its troop levels to about 100 000, including about 65 000 Army personnel in Germany, about 30 000 Air Force personnel, and about 10 000 Naval forces. By the end of 1995 the Army aims to have left 557 installations in Europe, keeping 301, and the Air Force plans to retain 18 of 35 air bases.[92]

V. The CSCE Forum for Security Co-operation

With the establishment of the Forum for Security Co-operation in September 1992, the security scope of the CSCE expanded considerably. Work in the FSC is guided by the Programme of Immediate Action adopted by the Helsinki Decisions and covering 14 priority areas for arms control and CSBMs.[93] The Forum is the only multilateral arms control negotiating body now in operation. It also serves as a platform for security consultations and exchange of information among CSCE participating states. An important aspect of the work of the Forum is the holding of seminars on some issues of interest, such as those on defence planning and the code of conduct held in 1993, the outcome of which has contributed considerably to the progress in the talks in the working groups.[94]

In 1993 the Forum continued to work on new measures for arms control and for enhancing security and confidence. It was expected that some new agreements would be completed for the CSCE ministerial meeting in Rome in November/December, and others for the Budapest review meeting (scheduled for 10 October–9 December 1994). In the run-up to the Rome Council meeting the FSC and its working groups A and B focused on the following items: (a) harmonization of arms control obligations; (b) a code of conduct for security; (c) stabilizing measures; (d) non-proliferation and arms transfers;

---

[90] Arms Control Reporter, sheets 407.E-1.114 and 127, 1993. In early Jan. 1994, the new US Chairman of the Joint Chiefs of Staff, Gen. John Shalikashvili, confirmed the goal of 100 000, and gave the number of about 158 000 US troops in Europe. Atlantic News, no. 2584 (6 Jan. 1994).

[91] Frankfurter Allgemeine Zeitung, 2 July 1993; International Herald Tribune, 2 July 1993.

[92] International Herald Tribune, 4 Aug. 1993; Arms Control Reporter, sheet 407.E-1.146, 1993.

[93] Published as part of CSCE, Helsinki Document 1992: The Challenges of Change, reprinted in SIPRI Yearbook 1993 (note 1), pp. 205–206.

[94] For broader reporting on FSC (and other CSCE) activities in 1993, see Palmisano, S., 'Das KSZE-Forum für Sicherheitskooperation—Tätigkeitsbericht' [The CSCE Forum for Security Co-operation—Progress Report], Österreichische Militärische Zeitschrift, nos 2–6 (1993) and nos 1–2 (1994).

(*e*) military contacts and co-operation; (*f*) defence planning information exchange; and (*g*) global exchange of military information.[95]

During the year some concern was expressed about the work of the Forum slowing down as the CSCE agenda grew dramatically while the size of the national delegations remained unchanged.[96] In spite of the loaded agenda, in late November the Special Committee of the FSC in Vienna successfully prepared and adopted four texts in accordance with the Programme for Immediate Action on: (*a*) stabilizing measures; (*b*) conventional arms transfers; (*c*) military contacts; and (*d*) defence planning.[97] Since the participating states did not reach consensus on the contents of the principles governing non-proliferation, the four accords could not be endorsed by the Rome meeting.[98] It has not yet been decided by the FSC what form its adopted decisions will take (a separate general document or a set of decisions to be built into a new 'Vienna Document 1994').

Harmonization of arms control obligations

Harmonization of arms control, disarmament and the confidence- and security-building commitments and rights of all CSCE states remains a prime item on the FSC agenda. It involves such elements as information exchange, verification, limitations and institutional arrangements. Proposals made during the FSC negotiations continue to be discussed very actively, but much indicates that harmonization will be a slow process and probably will be reached in stages. Harmonized provisions for information exchange will require all CSCE states to provide more detailed information than is now required under the Vienna Document 1992.

A number of proposals and working papers have been submitted on harmonization. The first proposal, the so-called Visegrad Group 'position paper' submitted in October 1992 by Czechoslovakia, Hungary and Poland, proposed harmonization to extend basic CFE Treaty commitments to non-CFE states and cover five main areas: national levels; information exchange and notifications; verification; review mechanism; and area of application.[99] A NATO proposal, very close to that of the Visegrad Group, suggested extending Vienna Document provisions under the headings of information exchange and notification, verification, limitations and institutions with a special emphasis on priority of provision of information in line with CFE Treaty standards (e.g., lower and more detailed parameters on numbers, types and changes in

[95] *Focus on Vienna*, no. 29 and 30 (Apr. and Aug. 1993).

[96] *Arms Control Reporter*, sheet 407.B.318, 1993.

[97] CSCE Forum for Security Co-operation, 49th Plenary Meeting of the Special Committee, *Journal*, no. 49, Vienna, 24 Nov. 1993; texts reproduced in Rotfeld, A. D. (ed.), SIPRI, *From Helsinki to Helsinki and Beyond: Analysis and Documents of the Conference on Security and Co-operation in Europe, 1973–93* (Oxford University Press: Oxford, forthcoming 1994).

[98] *Disarmament Bulletin*, no. 23 (winter 1993/94), p. 5.

[99] CSCE/FSC/SC.1, Vienna, 7 Oct. 1992.

forces).[100] The NATO and Visegrad concepts generally aim at the maintenance of two regimes, the CFE Treaty regime and a harmonized regime (the 'CFE-down' approach).

The Austrian position paper calls for information exchange measures as in the CFE regime but without automatic alignment of the CSBM and CFE regimes, and for a balance between rights and duties to be granted to states not parties to the CFE Treaty.[101] Generally, such an approach is supported by other states from the former neutral and non-aligned (NNA) group (the 'Vienna Document-up' position).[102]

The Russian position, presented in a working paper of March 1993, is by far the strongest in stressing the importance for all CSCE participating states of establishing a unified information and verification regime based on (and in fact replacing) the CFE and CFE-1A accords and the Vienna Document 1992.[103]

While devoting a significant amount of their work to harmonization, delegations encountered a series of issues and sticking-points regarding the scope of the document (as mentioned above); the form of the harmonization process—a multi-stage process or a one-step comprehensive document; expansion of CFE Treaty restrictions to states not party to the Treaty; solving the question of the CFE 'group of states' category; changing the CFE inspection process and allocations. A very difficult point is that of weapons in storage: some neutral and small non-parties see no benefit in joining the CFE regime since they believe that detailed information on their armed forces (primarily or exclusively defensive and non-active) would weaken the effectiveness of their defence deployments and put them at a disadvantage *vis-à-vis* larger neighbours with more forces at their disposal (e.g., the security interests of Finland, Sweden and Switzerland should not be disregarded).[104] Debates in working group A on harmonization are therefore a long way from from conclusion and there are serious doubts whether the target date of the Budapest review and summit meetings in 1994 will be met.

A code of conduct in the field of security

The discussion on the new code of conduct is expected to lead to a document that might be adopted by the time of the 1994 review meeting. Its status would be politically binding. Proposals and working suggestions by CSCE participat-

---

[100] CSCE/FSC/SC.2, Vienna, 14 Oct. 1992. The NATO document was elaborated in greater detail and illustrated with charts to visualize practical application by a British 'concept paper' proposed in Mar. 1993. CSCE/FSC/SC/A.1, Vienna, 24 Mar. 1993.

[101] CSCE/FSC/SC.4, Vienna, 28 Oct. 1992.

[102] See also the Swedish proposal in CSCE document CSCE/FSC/SC/A.2, Vienna, 7 July 1993.

[103] CSCE/FSC/SC.12, Vienna, 24 Mar. 1993.

[104] *Focus on Vienna*, no. 30, Aug. 1993, p. 4; *Arms Control Reporter*, sheet 407.B.319-320, 1993. At the CSCE Council meeting in Rome on 30 Nov. 1993, Swiss Foreign Minister Flavio Cotti stated that his state would accept CFE-type limits on its armed forces as part of the harmonization. See *Arms Control Reporter*, sheet 402.E-2.4, 1994.

ing states, individually and/or collectively,[105] have provided a basis for substantial discussion among the participants.

The first proposal to be put forward, that of Poland, deals with a broad range of security matters and lays down such elements as: *(a)* norms guiding defence policies and postures (defensive postures for armed forces, sufficiency and restraint in military matters, democratic control of armed forces, internal organization and functioning of armed forces in accordance with international law and humanitarian principles, peaceful domestic use of armed forces); *(b)* norms for the co-operative approach to international security (indivisibility of security, promotion of arms control, security dialogue and co-operation, freedom to choose security arrangements); *(c)* principles guiding conduct in the prevention of conflicts and use of force (conflict prevention and peaceful settlement of disputes, refraining from hostile action or any other action which might aggravate the situation); and *(d)* norms guiding conduct in the event of a conflict (condemnation of acts in violation of the principle of the non-use of force, solidarity with victims of the violation of the non-use of force principle, co-operation in restoring international peace and stability). The Polish proposal has reportedly been found controversial on several counts, for example, the inclusion of elements of future security guarantees in the code (recognition of the right to assistance of CSCE participating states that fall victim to armed aggression), the principle of non-use of force or coercion against peoples peacefully pursuing self-determination, and alleged encroachment on sovereign internal affairs.[106]

The EC–NATO proposals (made without the participation of the USA and Turkey), initially advanced by France, stress and elaborate on an equally impressive range of topics: *(a)* the principle of the non-use of force and the question of borders; *(b)* indivisibility of security and legitimate security interests; *(c)* arms control and disarmament (full implementation of existing agreements, pursuing security-enhancing and stabilizing measures, non-proliferation, restraint in and transparency about arms transfers and the transfer of sensitive military know-how, compliance with the UN Register of Conventional Arms, effective licensing for manufacture, transport and sale of arms, statutory control of export of arms); *(d)* early warning, conflict prevention, crisis management and peaceful settlement of disputes (commitment to consult and co-operate in situations of potential crisis and to use the existing CSCE mechanisms); *(e)* peacekeeping and other CSCE missions (within the CSCE and within the context of co-operation with UN missions); *(f)* democratic political control of armed forces (e.g., subordination of armed forces to the

[105] See the following CSCE documents, all submitted in Vienna: CSCE/FSC/SC.5/Rev. 1, 18 Nov. 1992 (Poland); CSCE/FSC/SC.7, 16 Dec. 1992 (UK/EC plus Canada, Iceland and Norway—'elements' for a code of conduct); CSCE/FSC/SC.8, 16 Dec. 1992 (Turkey); CSCE/FSC/SC.17, 5 May 1993 (Austria, Hungary and Poland); CSCE/FSC/SC/B.2, 3 June 1993 (France's working paper); CSCE/FSC/SC.21, 30 June 1993 (Denmark/EC and Iceland and Norway); CSCE/FSC/SC.22, 15 Sep. 1993 (Austria and Hungary).

[106] Ghebali, V.-Y., 'The CSCE Forum for Security Cooperation: the opening gambits', *NATO Review*, June 1993, p. 27; Borawski, J. and Bruce, G., 'The CSCE Forum for Security Cooperation', *Arms Control Today*, Oct. 1993, p. 15.

constitutional authorities, legal accountability of armed forces for their actions, laying down of rights and obligations with regard to military service); (g) use of armed forces (compatibility with the code of doctrines governing their use, conformity with international humanitarian law, principles and commitments regarding the use of armed forces, including their use internally within states); and (h) observation and monitoring (procedures for publicizing the code and the spelling out of the responsibility of states and individuals in the event of non-observance of the principles and commitments it sets out).

The Austro-Hungarian proposal[107] puts the strongest emphasis on the comprehensive concept of security, including non-military aspects such as human rights, ethnic rights and environment, and consists of such elements as: (a) general concepts guiding security relations among CSCE states (comprehensive concept of security, co-operative security, indivisibility of security, solidarity, sufficiency, regional and trans-frontier co-operation); (b) general principles and commitments guiding security relations among states (stressing such principles as sovereignty and territorial integrity, self-determination, refraining from the threat or use of force, peaceful settlement of disputes, right to self-defence, inadmissibility of territorial acquisition by the threat or use of force, opposition to terrorism and subversion, inviolability of borders, peaceful evolution of states, stationing of forces, fulfilment in good faith of obligations); and (c) commitments with respect to the different aspects of security (human dimension, arms control, CSBMs and disarmament, economic co-operation and the environment) and principles and commitments relating to internal aspects of security (rights of national minorities, democratic political control of armed forces, use of armed forces, early warning, conflict prevention and crisis management and the peaceful settlement of disputes).

These three positions (Turkey's proposal is similar in scope to the Austro-Hungarian one) generally determine the future framework and scope of the code of conduct.

The sticking-point is enforcement of the code of conduct; this was discussed at an FSC seminar in Vienna on 5–6 May 1993. Some delegations want to retain CSCE mechanisms and procedures and at most consider the extension of fact-finding missions to explore apparent breaches (e.g., the EC). Others (e.g., Austria, Poland and Hungary in their 'implementation provisions' proposal) would like to have an amended 'Berlin emergency situation mechanism' applied if need be. A meeting of the Permanent Committee of the CSCE might be called to recommend a course of action to remedy a situation resulting from a violation of the provisions of the code, if necessary by consensus-minus-one. In case of non-compliance with the recommendations of the Committee of Senior Officials (CSO) or the Council of Ministers it might be decided, if necessary by consensus-minus-state(s) concerned, to ask the UN Security Council to take 'appropriate action'.[108] Other states would like to see a new mechanism or procedures to ensure more effective implementation of

[107] Originally elaborated by Hungary.
[108] CSCE/FSC/SC.17, Vienna, 5 May 1993.

the code. In their proposal to develop the Vienna Document 1992,[109] the Visegrad states and Ukraine suggested a mechanism for clarifying the application of CSBMs, and 'creation of possibilities for concerted action in cases of non-compliance', including the 'extension of the "consensus-minus-one" rule in cases of clear, gross and uncorrected violations of CSCE commitments concerning military aspects of security'. The problem of enforcement is crucial in this context and needs further elaboration and negotiation if the code of conduct is to be effective.

Stabilizing measures

The 1992 Helsinki Decisions envisaged 'negotiation of new stabilizing measures and confidence-building measures related to conventional armed forces, including, with due regard to the specific characteristics of the armed forces of individual participating States, measures to address force generation capabilities of active and non-active forces'.[110] These measures might be of a constraining kind and applicable to areas adjacent to the CSCE zone. So far, work in this field has sought to prepare a list of measures that could be applied in regional crises. The NATO proposal submitted on 21 April 1993 set forth an inventory of temporary measures 'to reduce tension and to prevent the outbreak of fighting in crisis situations at [a] regional level'.[111] The measures are seen as options for crisis management and peaceful prevention and settlement of conflicts (a 'golf-bag' of measures). They would not enjoy automatic application or priority use. Nor are they seen as comprehensive or exhaustive, and any other measures may be elaborated in particular cases. CSCE bodies (the Council of Ministers or the CSO) would identify the parties involved and, as necessary, any third parties (if a good offices or a mediating function is required), choose measures and determine which of them should be applied, over what geographical area and for how long, what role CSCE institutions and structures should play, and other modalities of application and implementation. They would also need to be co-ordinated with peacekeeping operations and monitoring/fact-finding missions. The measures would require the prior consent and support of the parties involved in a crisis. Military measures would be applicable to the armed forces involved in a given crisis and applied either before an armed conflict has broken out or after a cease-fire has been established.

The FSC document on stabilizing measures for localized crisis situations,[112] based on the NATO proposal, contains the following catalogue of measures for crisis situations:

---

[109] CSCE/FSC/SC.13, Vienna, 31 Mar. 1993.
[110] CSCE *Helsinki Document 1992: The Challenges of Change*, Helsinki summit meeting, Helsinki, 10 July 1992, Helsinki Decisions, Annex on the Programme for Immediate Action, reprinted in *SIPRI Yearbook 1993* (note 1), p. 205.
[111] CSCE/FSC/SC.15, Vienna, 21 Apr. 1993.
[112] CSCE Forum for Security Co-operation, *Journal* (note 97), Annex 2.

1. Measures of *transparency*, including: extraordinary information exchange (in addition to that provided under the Vienna Document 1992), notification of certain military activities in the crisis area, notification of plans for acquisition and deployment of major weapon and equipment systems;

2. Measures of *constraint* (possibly monitored by third parties), including: the introduction and support of a cease-fire, establishment of demilitarized zones, cessation of military flights over specified areas or border zones, deactivation of certain weapon systems (particularly heavy ones), treatment of irregular forces (subordination, disbandment, disarmament), and constraints on certain military activities;

3. Measures to *reinforce confidence*, including: public statements on matters relevant to a particular crisis situation, observation of certain military activities, liaison teams (possibly multinational), establishment of direct lines of communication ('hot lines'), joint expert teams in support of crisis management (to help clarify situations), and joint co-ordination commissions or teams;

4. Measures for *monitoring of compliance and evaluation* (possibly by CSCE and/or third-party representatives) including: evaluation of data provided under extraordinary information exchange (Group A), inspections, observation of compliance with demilitarized zones, verification of heavy weapons, challenge inspections, and an aerial observation regime.

Non-proliferation and arms transfers

In accordance with the January 1992 CSCE Council Declaration on Non-Proliferation and Arms Transfers[113] and the recommendations contained in the NATO–Central European proposal submitted in the FSC in November 1992,[114] at the Stockholm CSCE Council meeting in December 1992 the CSCE ministers of foreign affairs pledged that their states would become original signatories to the 1993 Chemical Weapons Convention and would seek to ratify it as soon as possible, and that all CSCE participating states not yet parties to the 1972 Biological Weapons Convention and the 1968 Non-Proliferation Treaty (NPT) would become parties to those agreements in the shortest possible time and work for the indefinite extension of the NPT.[115] The proposal submitted at the FSC also called all CSCE participants to commit themselves to full operationalization of the UN Register of Conventional Arms, with regard to which the FSC took an appropriate decision in the spring of 1993. However, as a result of some states' objections regarding the scope of the document, agreement on the non-proliferation principles was not reached by the time of the Rome CSCE Council meeting.

[113] CSCE, Second Meeting of the CSCE Council, Prague, 30–31 Jan. 1992, Declaration on Non-Proliferation and Arms Transfers, CSCE document CSCE/2-C/Dec.1, 31 Jan. 1992; reproduced in Rotfeld (note 97).

[114] CSCE/FSC/SC.6, Vienna, 18 Nov. 1992.

[115] CSCE, Third Meeting of the Council, Summary of Conclusions of the Stockholm Council Meeting, *Shaping a New Europe—the Role of the CSCE*, CSCE/3-C/Dec. 2, Stockholm, 15 Dec. 1992; reprinted in SIPRI 1993 (note 1), see Decision 5, pp. 214–15.

A Document on Principles Governing Conventional Arms Transfers was prepared on the basis of a proposal submitted to the Forum by Denmark on behalf of the EC, NATO and several north and Central European states (Bulgaria, the Czech Republic, Finland, Hungary, Romania and Slovakia).[116] The document contains many principles already laid down in other international documents such as the Guidelines for Conventional Arms Transfers (1991)[117] of the five permanent members of the UN Security Council and the Common Criteria for Arms Exports of the EC States (1991, 1992).[118] However, it did not go beyond a declaration of principles as suggested by some CSCE participants; the complexity of problems involved makes it hardly possible to set up any effective international control of conventional arms transfers. The adoption of common principles by CSCE states is believed to improve national mechanisms which might entail cuts in arms transfers. It is hoped that states that do not yet have regulations for arms export licensing will be prompted to set up such a system.[119]

The Document on Principles Governing Conventional Arms Transfers [120] consists of three sections. Section I is devoted to reaffirming important political positions and commitments of states, such as: (a) the promotion of international peace and security with the least diversion of human and economic resources for armaments; (b) ensuring that arms are not transferred in violation of the purposes and principles of the UN Charter, adherence to the principles of transparency and restraint; (c) acknowledgement of the threat arms buildups pose to international peace and security; and (d) stressing the need for effective national mechanisms for controlling the transfer of conventional arms and related technology. Section II deals with exercising due restraint in arms transfers. Subsection II(a) lists aspects, principles and needs of the internal and international situation and security to be taken into account. Subsection II(b) identifies circumstances in which states should avoid transfers. In Section III states commit themselves to reflect the principles of arms transfer in their national policy documents, mutually assist in establishing effective national mechanisms of controlling the transfer of conventional arms and related technology and exchange information, within the context of their co-operation in the Forum, about legislation and practices in this field.

Military contacts and co-operation

Contacts among the military were foreseen in the Vienna Document 1992. Moreover, in recent years military exchanges have greatly intensified, particularly between NATO and former WTO states, and NACC has a programme for education in defence planning issues and military matters.[121] Given this

---

[116] CSCE/FSC/SC.16, Vienna, 28 Apr. 1993.

[117] Reproduced in *SIPRI Yearbook 1992* (note 15), pp. 304–305.

[118] Anthony, I., *et al.*, 'The trade in major conventional weapons', SIPRI 1992 (note 15), pp. 295–96; and Anthony, I., *et al.*, 'Arms production and arms trade', *SIPRI Yearbook 1993* (note 1), p. 461.

[119] *Focus on Vienna*, no. 30, Aug. 1993, p. 3.

[120] Reproduced in CSCE, Forum for Security Co-operation, *Journal* (note 97), Annex 3.

[121] See, e.g., *Work Plan for Dialogue, Partnership and Cooperation 1994* (note 7).

broad network of co-operation, the main purpose of codifying military contacts seems to be to strengthen this type of co-operative arrangement, with smaller and newer participants gaining experience by listing forms of military exchange and contact which could serve as a guideline for further developing such activities. This non-controversial catalogue[122] builds on the appropriate provisions of the Vienna Document and was prepared on the basis of the NATO proposal[123] and the Russian working documents.[124] It comprises a list of voluntary military exchanges, contacts and visits as well as a catalogue of forms of military co-operation (joint exercises and training, visits to military facilities and formations, observation visits, provision of experts, seminars on co-operation in the military field, and exchange of information on agreements on military contacts and co-operation). The programme has no compulsory provisions and is a politically binding document.

Defence planning information exchange

The Document on Defence Planning[125] was prepared on the basis of the NATO proposal[126] and a Polish–Hungarian paper as well as the Netherlands working document[127] which merged the two former positions and took into account the outcome of a seminar on defence planning held in the spring of 1993. In March 1993 a trial exchange of information took place among Hungary, the Netherlands, Sweden and the USA. The submitted reports were discussed at an FSC seminar on 31 March–2 April 1993 by representatives of the four states, with Poland and the UK participating as 'umpires', and were found to be very helpful for the further process of drafting.[128] The agreed document consists of three parts. Section I is on exchange of information 'to provide transparency about each CSCE participating State's intentions in the medium to long term as regards size, structure, training and equipment of its armed forces, as well as defence policy, doctrines and budgets related thereto, based on their national practice and providing the background for a dialogue among the participating States.' Accordingly, it deals with defence policy and doctrine; force planning (size, structure, personnel, major weapon and equipment systems and deployment of armed forces and the changes thereto); and information on previous expenditures and budgets (coming year, two subsequent fiscal years, and the last two of the coming five years). Section II deals with clarification matters, review and dialogue. It envisages requests for clarification of the information provided, annual discussion meetings (Vienna Document annual implementation assessment meetings may be used for that purpose), and study visits to increase and improve knowledge of national planning procedures and promote dialogue. Section III also calls on states to

---

[122] CSCE, Forum for Security Co-operation, *Journal* (note 97), Annex 1.
[123] CSCE/FSC/SC.9, Vienna, 27 Jan. 1993.
[124] CSCE/FSC/SC.14, Vienna, 13 Mar. 1993; and CSCE/FSC/SC.B.1, Vienna, 20 May 1993.
[125] CSCE, Forum for Security Co-operation, *Journal* (note 97), Annex 4.
[126] CSCE/FSC/SC.3, Vienna, 21 Oct. 1992.
[127] CSCE/FSC/SC.B.3, Vienna, 17 June 1993.
[128] *Focus on Vienna*, no. 30 (Aug. 1993), p. 3.

provide other information reflecting defence policy, military strategies and doctrines and related materials.

Global exchange of military information

The aim of the exchange is to provide all other CSCE participating states with annual information on the military forces of participants located outside the present zone of application of CSBMs (notably Canada, France, Russia, Turkey, the UK and the USA). The global military information exchange will be separate from other information-exchange regimes (the CFE Treaty, the CFE-1A Agreement and the Vienna Document 1992) and not subject to verification or limitation. With US agreement it will cover naval forces and their bases for the first time. Proposals by Russia[129] and NATO[130] are being discussed. They are fairly similar, but a number of provisions remain to be negotiated, including those of figures and parameters. For example, Russia proposes exchanging data on naval vessels of 5000-ton displacement and above, while the USA prefers a 100-ton threshold. The level of information disaggregation for services also differs, the Russian proposal being more intrusive.

Other FSC topics

Other topics addressed so far at the Forum include the development of the Vienna Document 1992 and regional issues. The proposal by the Visegrad countries (by 1993 comprising the Czech Republic, Hungary, Poland and Slovakia) and Ukraine[131] presented a list of amendments and suggestions aimed at strengthening compliance with and effectiveness of CSBMs in crisis situations and at improving the operation of existing measures.[132] Another proposal was made by Estonia regarding foreign military presence on other participating states' territories and information that might be requested by a state on whose territory those troops are stationed or deployed.[133]

As far as regional security issues are concerned, there are two proposals. The first, submitted by the three Baltic states, is for an informal, open-ended group to initiate work on the conceptual definition of regional issues and measures as well as the identification of possible regions subject to discussion and negotiation in the framework of *ad hoc* working groups.[134] The other proposal, submitted by Cyprus, puts forth the criteria for defining regional issues and steps in dealing with an issue.[135] More and more attention is being drawn in the Forum to suggestions submitted by the so-called 'Friends of Bosnia' (Albania, Austria, Bulgaria, Hungary, the USA, Turkey, Bosnia and

---

[129] CSCE/FSC/SC.10, Vienna, 17 Feb. 1993.
[130] CSCE/FSC/SC.11, Vienna, 10 Mar. 1993.
[131] CSCE/FSC/SC.13, Vienna, 31 Mar. 1993
[132] For a broader discussion see appendix 14A in this volume.
[133] CSCE/FSC/SC.18, Vienna, 19 May 1993.
[134] CSCE/FSC/SC.19, Vienna, 16 June 1993.
[135] CSCE/FSC/SC.20, Vienna, 23 June 1993.

Herzegovina, Croatia and Slovenia), in a 'Conceptual Outline' for an 'Arms Control Arrangement for the South-Eastern European Region', which calls for the establishment of limitations and reductions of conventional arms and equipment as well as of military and paramilitary personnel 'in the space of the former SFRY [Socialist Federative Republic of Yugoslavia]'.[136]

VI. Conclusions

The evidence that European conventional arms control is at a crossroads was reinforced in 1993. Its former role as an instrument of East–West relations, a 'stabilizer' of international relations or even a factor substituting for international politics is no longer valid. This became rather irrelevant with the end of the cold war and bipolar division, and there are many doubts about the effectiveness of European arms control today.

The premises of traditional conventional arms control no longer exist. The CFE agreements and the Vienna Documents are considered a success, and their implementation is proceeding smoothly despite minor obstacles. The withdrawal of foreign troops is making headway despite political vicissitudes. These arrangements certainly provide normative reference points in the new situation, where new instruments and institutions have not yet taken root. However, they are far from sufficient. One of the paradoxical aspects of the accomplishments of conventional arms control is that the accords reached are not very relevant to the new circumstances and, consequently, less controversial. While CSCE participating states duly report on compliance with CFE Treaty reduction targets, wars and conflicts in the Caucasus and the former Yugoslavia continue to take a heavy toll of lives and destruction. In other words, new types of challenge, threat and conflict are facing Europe—the fragmentation of the international system and numerous incidents of armed hostilities, chiefly those in Eastern and South-Eastern Europe tinted with ethnic, religious and other colours and developing along geographical lines other than the East–West direction. The functions of arms control are changing from confrontational to co-operative, and the arms control process is becoming more political in character, shifting from a global to a regional perspective.

The mutually reinforcing institutions dealing with the new challenges and menaces are for the most part helpless—their goals and mechanisms were largely shaped in another epoch. Efforts to use new instruments, such as crisis management, conflict resolution and peacekeeping, have failed to contain violence in conflict-ridden areas. Paradoxically, the accruing panoply of arms control instruments, mechanisms, commitments and obligations is growing in

---

[136] These measures would be accompanied by other measures such as redeployment proviions, stabilizing measures and operational constraints for specific border or other areas. It would include categories of weapon covered by the CFE Treaty and also expand that roster to include artillery below 100 mm (a limit sought by NATO) and surface-to-surface missiles. Bouvard, L. and George, B. (co-rapporteurs), Working Group on the New European Security Order. Draft Interim Report, International Secretariat, *The CSCE Forum for Security Cooperation: From Rome to Budapest*, May 1994. See also Kokkinides, T., 'Reducing military tensions in south-eastern Europe', British American Security Information Council (BASIC) Report no. 37 (11 Apr. 1994), pp. 1–2.

reverse proportion to its effectiveness. What is lacking at present is a comprehensive strategy for arms control in Europe. So far there has been no comprehensive conceptual framework of the extent to which arms control can play a role in Europe's future security, the areas in which it can play that role most effectively and the goals to which it should be applied.[137] Instead, Europe is facing considerable confusion as to the future place, tasks and forms of arms control in coping with the qualitatively new situation.

For conventional arms control to play a significant role in European security, a political settlement and a regime in which it could act are required. It is also important to stave off the growing tendency to renationalize defence policies, particularly in Eastern Europe. The concept of interlocking institutions for European security has so far been anything but a success. NATO, let alone the European Union or the Western European Union, continues to be hamstrung by political disagreements and different interests and perceptions among its members. NACC is a framework with an ambitious agenda but one which is operationally ineffective. The CSCE is an institution which can only score some achievements in preventive diplomacy but not in the field of new military policies, where achievements are most essential. Efforts to build a new arms control regime in Europe lack an appropriate legal and political framework within which to become effective. The Partnership for Peace programme gives some new perspectives on co-operation between NATO and other European countries, including some elements of arms control, but it is too early to see what final shape it will take.[138]

Work in the FSC in Vienna is a continued attempt to inject stability into a remarkably destabilized environment. Whether this will be successful remains to be seen. It depends more on the participating states than on the Forum itself, despite its remarkable progress during its first 16 months. By harmonizing conventional arms control and disarmament obligations as well as elaborating a code of conduct it is creating a normative basis and providing a framework for security in Europe. The FSC is addressing a wide range of paramount issues in the new situation, including a variety of arms control matters. The outcome of the Vienna negotiations will need to be strengthened and enforced, perhaps institutionally with a kind of CSCE arms control and disarmament agency. However, the object should be not to advocate new institutions but to make the search for a stable arms control and security regime an adequate and effective one.

Some progress along the road to the 1994 Budapest CSCE review meeting has already been made. When the goals of the Programme for Immediate Action are reached and put into effect, the CSCE stands a chance of becoming a leading institution in the field of European arms control.

---

[137] See Davis, E. L. et al., 'An arms control strategy for the new Europe', RAND Project on Arms Control report, RAND Corporation, Santa Monica, Calif., 1993, p. 17.
[138] See chapter 7 and appendix 7A in this volume.

Appendix 14A. The Vienna confidence- and security-building measures

ZDZISLAW LACHOWSKI

I. Introduction

During 1993, the main problem faced by Conference on Security and Co-operation in Europe (CSCE) participating states was the same as in previous years: lack of compatibility between European confidence- and security-building measures (CSBMs) and arms control regimes, as agreed in the Vienna Documents 1990 and 1992 and other agreements, and the politico-military situation prevailing in the southern and eastern parts of the continent. The war in the former Yugoslavia and armed conflicts and fighting on former Soviet territory have demonstrated that the newly agreed arrangements to enhance confidence and security are still out of step with the fast-developing crisis situations. CSBMs, tailored to 'fair-weather' circumstances, have failed when it comes to dealing with conflicts and hostilities.[1]

In order to streamline the decision-making process in the fields of arms control, disarmament and CSBMs, the CSCE Council meeting in Rome decided in early December 1993 to dissolve the Consultative Committee of the Conflict Prevention Centre (CPC) and hand over its competence to the newly established Permanent Committee of the CSCE for political consultations and decision making, based in Vienna, and the Forum for Security Co-operation (FSC). The Permanent Committee will, *inter alia*, hold meetings under the unusual military activities mechanism, as envisaged in the Vienna Documents. The FSC took over responsibility for the implementation of CSBMs, preparing military doctrine seminars, holding Annual Implementation Assessment Meetings (AIAMs) and providing the venue for discussion and clarification, as necessary, of information exchanged under agreed CSBMs.[2]

II. Implementation

The problems related to the implementation of CSBMs were discussed at the AIAM in Vienna in early May 1993. They included proposals for amending and adjusting the Vienna Document provisions for large-scale military exercises, inspections and evaluation visits; ensuring full implementation of CSBM agreements; and public access to CSBM information.[3]

Generally, delegations assessed the experience of the CSBM regime favourably, stressing that its comprehensive fulfilment by all participants promotes the continua-

---

[1] See Lachowski, Z., 'The Vienna confidence- and security-building measures in 1992', SIPRI, *SIPRI Yearbook 1993: World Armaments and Disarmament* (Oxford University Press: Oxford, 1993), pp. 618–31.

[2] CSCE, Fourth Meeting of the Council, *CSCE and the New Europe—Our Security is Indivisible*, Rome, 1 Dec. 1993 (reproduced in appendix 7A in this volume).

[3] Little has changed since SIPRI reported on public access to CSBM data. See note 1, pp. 629–30.

tion of the CSCE process and constitutes an essential element of strengthening confidence and trust among CSCE states. Implementation of the Vienna Document 1992 provides the participants with valuable experience; problems of interpreting the information received are being solved both multi- and bilaterally. Military contacts foster more understanding and *rapprochement* among participants, and even go beyond the framework set out in the Vienna Documents. Similarly, readiness on the part of some participating states to furnish updated information immediately, not only at the next annual exchange, on major changes in force structure or deployment were welcomed. A suggestion was also made that the CPC Secretariat should prepare reports on the application (or non-application) of the agreed CSBMs.[4]

Military activities

Of five manœuvres notified for 1993, four were conducted. The field training exercise (FTX) 'Dragon Hammer 93' was cancelled because of NATO's involvement in enforcing the no-fly zone over Bosnia and Herzegovina, thus reducing the number of military activities to four.[5] Despite the cancellation of 'Dragon Hammer', the Alliance's 'Reforger-93' exercise went ahead as planned, relying heavily on the use of computer simulations to model the movement of troops and equipment from Italy to Germany. The 'Ardente-93' exercise (not reported in *SIPRI Yearbook 1993* because of lack of information) took place in November: about 15 000 troops from the French, Italian and Spanish rapid deployment forces participated; British, Greek, Netherlands and Turkish units also joined the manœuvre as well as 27 warships, and 40 fighter aircraft and helicopters, for an evacuation operation. The scenario required the rescue of a population of 800 men and women trapped by civil war. During the exercise, the chiefs of staff of the three armies, that is, from France, Italy and Spain, were invited by their defence ministers to develop a project for a common 'pre-planned and non-permanent European air-sea force' ('a Eurocorps of the South') which would have a capacity for the projection of land and air forces to meet Western European Union (WEU) needs alongside an eventual capacity for engagement within the framework of NATO.[6]

Other military activities involving CSCE states did not require notification to the CSCEunder the terms of the Vienna Document 1992. The most outstanding of them were the first Russian–US exercise since World War II (April 1993), rescuing survivors from a simulated plane crash, and a NATO-led naval exercise in June in the Baltic Sea, joined by Lithuania, Poland, Russia and Sweden.[7] NATO conducted its first crisis-management procedural exercise 'NATO CMX 93' (February–March 1993), which, assisted by computers and communication networks, was to put to the test the military and political decision-making process in the event of crises breaking out in the new strategic circumstances.[8]

SIPRI has been informed of five notifiable military activities planned for 1994 (see table 14A). As in preceding years, all but one are to be carried out by NATO. The biggest manœuvre will employ 15 000 troops. Russia and the Central and East

[4] *Focus on Vienna*, no. 30 (Aug. 1993), pp. 7–9.
[5] See Lachowski (note 1), table 12A.3, p. 623.
[6] *Atlantic News*, no. 2569 (10 Nov. 1993), p. 4; *Le Monde*, 11 Nov. 1993.
[7] It was reported in Nov. 1993 that a military exercise had been planned between US and Russian units in Germany. However, Bonn's opposition to such an activity made the USA drop the idea. *International Herald Tribune*, 5 Nov. 1993.
[8] *Atlantic News*, no. 2501 (24 Feb. 1993), p. 3.

European states do not intend to conduct large-scale exercises, a trend that has continued since 1990 when the Warsaw Treaty Organization (WTO) held its last joint manœuvres. Sweden will conduct its next consecutive field training activity, one year after the last one.

Annual exchange of military information

The exchange of military information in the form of the annual calendar provided in December 1993 was a further step in building confidence and strengthening the sense of security among CSCE participating states. The quality of information and its accuracy are steadily improving. However, some of the states did not fulfil their obligations, in particular concerning notifications. For example, as in the case of CFE Treaty exchanges, some of the Transcaucasian states (former Soviet republics) failed to furnish information about their military forces.

Notification and verification

As reported in past *SIPRI Yearbooks*, the post-cold war changes have seen a considerable reduction in large-scale notifiable activities while smaller manœuvres have increased in number and frequency. It is repeatedly suggested therefore that an experts' meeting devoted to these issues be held and the notification and observation thresholds be further lowered to make it possible to fill the 'transparency gap'.

As far as inspections are concerned, efforts are being made to define anew and with more precision the area to be visited in any single inspection as well as to increase the number of inspections and the size of the teams allowed on any single inspection. Similarly, for evaluation visits, it is proposed that the duration of visits and the size of evaluation teams as well as the minimum number of visits any country has to receive be increased. Steps towards evolving an international community of verification experts with a common understanding of the goals and the work of CSBMs are also proposed. An increased use of international inspection and evaluation teams is urged. To these ends, it is suggested that international courses on inspection and other verification mechanisms be organized.[9]

During 1993, 12 inspections were requested. NATO states were the most frequent inspectors, making 11 requests including four from Germany, and former Soviet republics, including Russia, were the most frequently inspected, hosting seven inspections. All but one of the requests were accepted: Armenia declined to accept a Turkish inspection team during the Armenian–Azerbaijani conflict in September.

According to SIPRI estimates, there were 60 evaluation-visit requests in 1993, including one under both the Vienna Document 1992 and the Bulgarian–Turkish 'Edirne Document' provisions.[10] Two of the visits were cancelled and three of them were denied. Altogether, 54 evaluation teams were sent to other participating states.

Communications

The CSCE communications network has existed for over two years, linking 35 end-user stations (three CSCE institutions and the foreign ministries of 32 participating

[9] See note 4, p. 8.
[10] For details of these provisions see Lachowski (note 1), p. 626, footnote 17.

states) by November 1993.[11] All stations, with readily available personal computers, transfer and receive messages which are routed to a central computer switch in the Foreign Ministry of the Netherlands, which automatically relays them to all intended recipients. The network has already proved to be very useful in sending notifications concerning inspection and evaluation documents; however, it also facilitates other exchanges. Information on annual military calendars, budgets, military forces and armaments as well as CSCE meetings is also exchanged. It is hoped that, along with handling CSBM and CFE Treaty information, it may play a key role for the Open Skies Treaty. For the sake of providing rapid information, users are increasingly sending most of their messages using formats that reduce the need for translation.[12]

Towards the 1994 Budapest summit meeting

In addition to the above-mentioned May 1993 AIAM discussion on amending and streamlining various CSBMs, the FSC addressed, among other things, the agenda items 'Development of the Vienna Document 1992' and 'Stabilizing measures for localized crisis situations'.[13] The discussion in the Forum followed two main lines: (a) improving the operation of the existing CSBMs; and (b) the application of CSBMs in crisis situations.

The discussion on the improvement of the CSBM regime was generally aimed at lowering the parameters of various measures and expanding the flow of information on various military activities. Some of the suggestions, as they were raised in the AIAMs in November 1992 and May 1993, are mentioned above.

The Visegrad countries and Ukraine presented a joint proposal.[14] As well as proposing steps to enhance the effectiveness of the Vienna Document provisions, they put forward the following suggestions: to establish a mechanism for clarifying the application of CSBMs; to create possibilities for concerted action in cases of non-compliance (CSBMs for all-weather circumstances, including crises, consultation and consideration of possible actions in cases of non-compliance, extension of the 'consensus-minus-one' rule in cases of grave violations of CSCE commitments concerning military aspects of security, including Vienna Document commitments); to further develop the risk-reduction provisions, including making hosting of visits to dispel concerns about military activities obligatory (in this context Estonia also proposed the increase of information on foreign military forces stationed or deployed on the territory of other states[15]); and to create a mechanism to encourage the application of other CSBMs, particularly those in border areas.

Work on CSBMs in the Forum is still in its initial stages and emphasis so far is on other items. In the run-up to the 1994 Budapest summit meeting the negotiators will face the difficult twofold task of (a) harmonizing measures related to confidence building and strengthening security, including a new set of stabilizing measures already agreed in principle, and (b) enhancing the Vienna Document operability and giving the measures a modicum of enforcement to ensure their efficiency in the new, mostly 'bad-weather' situation.

---

[11] NATO, especially the USA and the UK, plan to provide communications equipment and training to former Soviet republics. Russia is already on the communications network.

[12] *Disarmament Bulletin*, no. 23 (winter 1993/94), p. 7.

[13] For a discussion and the list of new stabilizing measures including those of the confidence-building type, see chapter 14.

[14] CSCE document CSE/FSC/SC.13, Vienna, 31 Mar. 1993.

[15] CSCE document CSE/FSC/SC.18, Vienna, 19 May 1993.

Table 14A. Calendar of planned notifiable military activities in 1994

States/ Location	Dates/ Start window	Type/Name of activity	Area	Level of command	No. of troops	Type of forces or equipment	No. and type of divisions	Comments
1. France, Germany, Greece, Italy, Netherlands, Portugal, Spain, Turkey, UK and USA	4–18 May	FTX 'Dynamic Impact 94'	Cape Teulada, Sardinia, centred on 38°58'N 89°E	NATO AFSOUTH (Major Subordinate Command)	1200 British in multinational amph. force and 500 in btn group (–)	Ground, naval and air forces	1 Commando Group of approx. 1200 men with a battery of six 105-mm light guns. 1 Btn Group (–)	Incorporating crisis management for the joint and combined training of maritime, land, amph. forces and HQ staffs to improve operational effectiveness. Linked with exercises 'Resolute Response' (amph. exercise) and 'Damsel Fair 94'
2. Belgium, Canada, Denmark, France, Germany, Italy, Netherlands, UK and USA	25 Oct.– 22 Nov.	FTX/CAX 'Reforger 94'	Germany and Northern Italy	NATO AFCENT (Major Subordinate Command)	15 000	Army ground forces and aviation and air forces	1 US arm. div., 1 US inf. div.	Show ability to reinforce European theatre. Involves reception of US forces into theatre, deployment of V Corps elements in Germany and to Italy and use of prepositioned equipment. 'Shadow Canyon', 'Counter Guard', and 'Chinese Eye' exercises are components
3. Belgium, Canada, Germany, Italy, Netherlands, Norway, UK and USA	7 days, 5–25 Mar.	FTX 'Arctic Express'	Rossfjord– Selnes–N. Indre Tomasfjord– S. Blomli– Bjørnstad– N. Sildvik	Div. level	14 960	Ground and air forces	1 light div. (reduced), 2 brig. equivalents	Exercise forces in deployment operations and practice co-operation and interoperability between Norway and allied formations

States/ Location	Dates/ Start window	Type/Name of activity	Area	Level of command	No. of troops	Type of forces or equipment	No. and type of divisions	Comments
4. Sweden	2–8 and 9–14 May	FTX 'Sydväst 94'	S Halland, Skåne and Småland. 5 training grounds: Hovdala Skillingaryd Rinkaby Ravlunda Revinge	Exercise in framework of brigs. Each to train on separate training ground	12 500	HQ 13th Div., 46th Inf. Brig., 7th Mech. Brig. and 9th Arm. Brig., and a no. of div. unit brigs are reduced with 1–2 btns. The Air Force will conduct a small no. of sorties		Final basic and refresher training of defence against minor airborne assaults. Consists of a no. of phases, in dislocations, where brig. commanders train their own and attached btns in separate exercises. A communication exercise on div. level to be held
5. Germany, Denmark, Italy, Netherlands and UK	22 Oct.– 8 Nov.	CFX/Livex 'Chinese Eye 94'	Lower Saxony (Germany), Schleswig-Holstein	OSE: CINCENT; OCE: COMBALTAP; OCE: COMLAND JUT	10 500	Army and air force	Jutland Div. (Denmark) (Mech. div.), 6th Arm. Inf. Div. (Germany). HQ ARRC incl. 4 div. response cells	Demonstrate and improve readiness and effectiveness of participating HQ and forces by conducting joint and combined operations, incl. the reception, deployment and employment of reinforcement forces in defence of BALTAP AOR

Note: (−) means that the division is below full strength or not comprised of all its component parts; abbreviations: ARRC = Allied Command Europe Rapid Reaction Corps; AFCENT = Allied Forces Central Europe; AFSOUTH = Allied Forces Southern Europe; amph. = amphibious; AOR = Area of responsibility; arm. = armoured; brig. = brigade; btn = battalion; CAX = Computer-assisted exercise; COMBALTAP = Commander, Allied Forces, Baltic Approaches; CFX = command field exercise; CINCENT = Commander-in-Chief, Central Europe; COMLANDJUT = Commander, Allied Forces, Schleswig-Holstein & Jutland; div. = division; FTX = field training exercise; inf = infantry; mech = mechanized; OCE = Officer conducting the exercise; OSE = Officer scheduling the exercise.

Appendix 14B. The Treaty on Open Skies

ZDZISLAW LACHOWSKI

I. The ratification process

The Treaty on Open Skies was signed at Helsinki on 24 March 1992 with 25 states initialling the agreement. After the signing of the Treaty by Kyrgyzstan in December 1992 and the split of Czechoslovakia on 1 January 1993, the number of signatories rose to 27. By establishing a multilateral regime for the conduct of observation flights by unarmed reconnaissance aircraft over the territories of states parties in the area from Vancouver to Vladivostok, it is becoming the most extensive confidence-building and stability-enhancing venture to promote openness and transparency about military forces and activities.

Table 14B. States that have signed and ratified the Treaty on Open Skies, as of 31 December 1993

State	Deposition of the instrument of ratification	State	Deposition of the instrument of ratification
Belarus		Luxembourg	
Belgium		Norway[b]	
Bulgaria		The Netherlands	
Canada	21 July 1992	Poland	
Czech Republic	21 Dec. 1992	Portugal	
Denmark	21 Jan. 1993	Romania	
France	30 July 1993	Russia	
Germany[a]		Slovakia	21 Dec. 1992
Georgia		Spain	18 Nov. 1993
Greece	9 Sep. 1993	Turkey	
Hungary	11 Aug. 1993	Ukraine	
Iceland	24 June 1993	UK	8 Dec. 1993
Italy		USA	2 Dec. 1993
Kyrgyzstan			

[a] Germany deposited its instrument of ratification on 27 Jan. 1994.
[b] Norway ratified the Treaty on 18 May 1993 but has not deposited its instrument of ratification.
Source: Arms Control Reporter, sheet 409.B.42, 1993.

The ratification of the Treaty proceeded slowly in 1993. There were a number of reasons for this, including the fact that many of the political objectives of the Treaty have become outdated. The fact that the original, mainly US/NATO, intention of making the military sector of the Soviet Union/Russia more transparent had already been achieved in other ways reduced the political urgency of the Treaty. Another important reason is the cost of implementing the provisions of the Open Skies Treaty; many CSCE states simply cannot afford to observe other states on their own because the financial burden is too high. With military budget squeezes across the CSCE area, the Treaty seems to have been de-emphasized.

By the end of January 1993, only Canada, the former Czechoslovakia and Denmark had deposited their instruments of ratification. It was hoped that the Treaty might enter into force for those nations that have deposited instruments during 1993 (at least 20 ratifications are required). However, by the end of the year only 11 states had deposited their documents of ratification with the two co-depositaries—Canada and Hungary.[1]

II. The Consultative Commission

The Open Skies Consultative Commission (OSCC) held regular weekly meetings in Vienna, chiefly dealing with the technical issues of implementing the Treaty, particularly those of sensor resolution and infra-red and video equipment. The issues focused on developing rules for sensor operation and flights, to prevent higher levels of sensor resolution than those allowed by the Treaty. The work also entailed the elaboration of standards for calibrating image-processing equipment, certifying observation equipment and agreeing on methods to format sensor data to be transferred among the parties.[2] The OSCC also resolved the matter of Czech and Slovak flight quotas and considered the establishment of a new scale for the distribution of administrative costs. Working groups met to discuss issues such as sensors, flight rules and procedures, notifications and formats as well as communications and data. The agreed texts will become effective with the Treaty.

The slow progress at the Commission's sessions and the delays in ratification gave the OSCC a lower priority in Vienna in the middle of the year.[3] Because of the slow pace of the work and the ratification process, Canada suggested that the Treaty enter into force provisionally, as the CFE Treaty did in 1992. However, because of a number of differences between the agreements and other divergencies among the signatories, this does not seem possible.

Since the work of the OSCC has increasingly been slowing down, plenary meetings are now planned on a monthly, instead of a weekly, basis for 1994.

III. Trial overflights in 1993

Open Skies signatories continued to conduct trial overflights for training purposes during 1993 pending the entry into force of the Treaty.

In April, the USA and Canada carried out a training flight over Alaska and western Canada to test procedures and operational activities. Both countries have agreed to share future overflights of Ukraine. The US Air Force had already started converting a former WC-135B weather reconnaissance aircraft to carry Open Skies sensors. In June, the aircraft, then designated OC-135B and operated under the command of the On-Site Inspection Agency (OSIA), completed testing and was ready to conduct

---

[1] Norway ratified the Treaty but did not deposit its ratification instrument; *Arms Control Reporter*, sheet 409.B.42, 1993.
[2] *Focus on Vienna*, no. 29 (Apr. 1993); *Arms Control Reporter*, sheet 409.B.41, 1993.
[3] *Arms Control Reporter*, sheet 409.B.39, 1993.

overflights. It was fitted with one KA-91B panoramic camera, two KS-87B oblique-mounted framing cameras and a single KS-87B vertical-mounted framing camera. Over the next four years the USA plans to deploy two additional aircraft with full sensor packages.[4]

On 16–19 June Russia carried out its first trial overflight in the UK using an AN-30 aircraft. A team of 18 Russian and 2 Belarussian personnel flew over several military installations and facilities with the aim of testing and evaluating the draft operating procedures. The visiting crew was accompanied by personnel from the Joint Arms Control Implementation Group (JACIG) which monitored the Russian–Belarussian team's activities and provided onboard expertise on British flying procedures. The trial had two main components: management of the air traffic control problems presented by Treaty flights, and the translation of Open Skies technical limits on camera capabilities into an operable procedure for the use of cameras and the processing of film.[5]

On 10–12 July, the USA and Hungary conducted two overflights of Hungarian military sites, collecting both optical and SAR (synthetic-aperture radar) images.[6] Other overflights in 1993 included those over Russia (by Germany) and Germany (by Russia).[7]

While Open Skies observation aircraft, equipment and flight operation will be costly, further agreements on pooling equipment and operations are expected. Belgium, Luxembourg and the Netherlands concluded a co-operation agreement under which they will operate jointly from the Belgian Air Force base at Melsbroek. The first operations will use a Belgian Hercules C-130, and later operations will be conducted from a similar Netherlands aircraft.[8] In October, it was reported that, in order to cut back on the anticipated costs of implementing the Treaty, 11 nations, including Canada and the Benelux countries, were considering sharing a single Open Skies aircraft with a limited sensor package consisting of video and panoramic cameras.[9] As an additional co-operative venture, the Western European Union is considering the formation of a pool of aircraft for the same purpose.[10]

The idea of using Open Skies for environmental monitoring has also gained currency among signatories, and an experts' meeting was held in December 1992 to discuss the use of sensors and operational procedures for environmental purposes. However, some concern was expressed that environmental preoccupation might detract from the original purpose of the flights allowed under the Treaty.

[4] *Trust and Verify*, no. 42 (Nov. 93); *ACDA Fact Sheet*, 6 July 1993, in *Arms Control Reporter*, sheet 409.B.39, 1993.
[5] *Trust and Verify*, no. 39 (July–Aug. 1993).
[6] *Arms Control Reporter*, sheet 409.B.40, 1993.
[7] *Disarmament Bulletin*, no. 23 (winter 1993/94), p. 7.
[8] *Trust and Verify*, no. 42 (Nov. 1993).
[9] *Arms Control Reporter*, sheet 409.B.41, 1993.
[10] Note 7.

15. Nuclear arms control and an extended non-proliferation regime

JOHN SIMPSON*

I. Introduction

The global environment within which policies of nuclear proliferation and non-proliferation have been pursued was relatively static from the early 1960s, when nuclear non-dissemination and non-proliferation first emerged as serious policy goals, until 1991. One major characteristic of that environment was an understanding between the USA and the USSR that, whatever their differences on other issues, they had a strong mutual interest in preventing more nuclear weapon states (NWS) from emerging. In the late 1960s, they laid the foundations for a global non-proliferation regime, based on the twin foundations of a treaty through which those states without nuclear weapons renounced their acquisition and a mandatory system of accountancy covering all nuclear materials under their jurisdiction. The treaty was the 1968 Non-Proliferation Treaty (NPT); the system of accounting was the INFCIRC/153 safeguards arrangements of the International Atomic Energy Agency (IAEA).[1] In parallel, the security motivations for proliferation were addressed through the nuclear 'umbrellas' extended over their allies by the USA and the USSR.

The nuclear non-proliferation regime has gradually expanded in both scope and membership since the NPT entered into force in 1970. In parallel, there has been questioning of the utility of nuclear weapons in specific military roles and a significant reduction in projections of the global growth in nuclear power capacity. To make it more difficult for a would-be proliferator to import the materials and technology to make nuclear weapons, the advanced industrialized states have implemented restrictive guidelines for their nuclear and missile exports.

From the perspective of a political realist, the end of the confrontational global structures associated with the East–West conflict has changed the foundations of the global non-proliferation regime. As the USSR collapsed, to be replaced by the Russian Federation and several other new states, so too did the ability of the USSR to exercise intrusive control over nuclear proliferation pressures in its former republics and allies. From this perspective, unless some

[1] See Howlett, D. and Simpson, J. (eds), *Nuclear Non-Proliferation: A Reference Handbook* (Longman: Harlow, 1992), p. 175. The Structure and Content of Agreements Between the Agency and States Required in Connection with the Treaty on the Non-Proliferation of Nuclear Weapons, IAEA document INFCIRC/153 (corrected), (IAEA: Vienna, 1983), is reprinted in Howlett and Simpson, pp. 175–92; and in Fischer, D. and Szasz, P., (ed.) J. Goldblat, SIPRI, *Safeguarding the Atom: A Critical Re-Appraisal* (Taylor & Francis: London, 1985), pp. 197–211.

* The author acknowledges the assistance of Ben Cole in the preparation of this chapter.

mechanism arises or is created to replace these foundations, further nuclear proliferation may be inevitable.[2] In North-East Asia, the nuclear situation on the Korean Peninsula during 1993 has highlighted the possible adverse proliferation consequences of the removal of the influence of the former USSR over its allies. These developments have led observers to two differing conclusions: that a need exists to develop new methods and instruments, including military ones, for the dominant global powers to impose non-proliferation on aspirant nuclear proliferators; or alternatively that much more responsibility has been thrust upon the only acceptable mechanism for dealing with existing and emerging nuclear proliferation problems, the voluntarist global regime.

The collapse of the USSR created two new types of proliferation problem: who owns and controls its nuclear weapons and their manufacturing complex; and how to prevent materials and knowledge being disseminated outside its former borders. It also produced significant unilateral nuclear disarmament by the NWS.[3] This has reinforced perceptions of the reduced military and political utility of nuclear weapons, and gone some way towards implementing that part of the NPT 'bargain' which involved nuclear disarmament by the existing NWS. It has also assisted those states to downgrade the significance of their nuclear explosive testing programmes. These developments seem likely to reduce pressures hostile to a lengthy extension of the NPT in 1995.

A series of apparently autonomous events has also had an impact upon the existing nuclear non-proliferation regime. The most visible of these was the revelation of Iraq's nuclear weapon programme. Others have included changes in the situation of the old 'threshold states',[4] and the emergence of a new class of 'NPT renegade states'. Argentina, Brazil, India, Israel, Pakistan and South Africa had been placed in the 'threshold state' category, but since 1992 only India, Israel and Pakistan remain. The effect of these changes and of China and France acceding to the NPT in 1992 has been to strengthen the Treaty by making it near-universal in its membership. It has also reinforced pressures upon the three remaining 'threshold states' to clarify their situation and led to debates about whether the international community should continue to press them to abandon their ambiguous position and accede to the NPT as non-nuclear weapon states (NNWS) or should seek to bring them within the regime by creating a special status for them.

The 'NPT renegade states' are states which are NPT parties but have attempted to acquire nuclear weapons. Iraq initiated this category in 1991, when it became clear that it had been engaged in an extensive nuclear weapon programme. The Democratic People's Republic of Korea (North Korea) has subsequently teetered on the brink of joining (see below), while both Iran and

---

[2] For an example of the argument that changes in the structure of the international system may increase the perceived incentives for states to acquire nuclear weapons, see Mearsheimer, J., 'Back to the future: instability in Europe after the cold war', *International Security*, vol. 15, no. 1 (summer 1990), pp. 5–56.
[3] For its effects to date, see 'Estimated nuclear stockpiles 1945–1993', Nuclear Notebook, *Bulletin of the Atomic Scientists*, vol. 49, no. 10 (Dec. 1993), p. 57.
[4] For example, see Goldblat, J. (ed.), SIPRI, *Non-proliferation: The Why and the Wherefore* (Taylor & Francis: London, 1985), p. 4.

Algeria have been mooted as potential members.[5] The emergence of such states has led to doubts being voiced about the value of the non-proliferation regime based upon the NPT and the effectiveness of its linked IAEA safeguards system. This has led to three types of response being proposed: the strengthening of the existing global regime; the creation of new nuclear weapon-free zones and other regional arms control regimes; and a complete reconceptualization and restructuring of the global regime.

II. The established nuclear non-proliferation regime

Demand and supply side controls

The nuclear non-proliferation regime created after 1968 consisted of a series of linked arrangements and mechanisms to influence the demand for, and control the ability to procure, nuclear explosive devices. Its cornerstone on the demand side has been the NPT, through which NNWS pledged to refrain from acquiring nuclear weapons and to accept IAEA safeguards on all nuclear materials under their jurisdiction.[6] They were, however, to be free to take all steps necessary to develop nuclear energy for peaceful purposes. Nuclear weapon states parties agreed not to transfer nuclear weapons to other states; not to assist NNWS in acquiring nuclear explosive devices; and to negotiate in good faith on nuclear disarmament.[7]

The purpose of IAEA/NPT safeguards is to detect whether materials under the jurisdiction of a NNWS are being diverted to undeclared purposes. The operational aim is to provide timely warning of such diversion, and thus deter it, but not physically to prevent it.[8] The system is intended to reassure states that their neighbours are not seeking to evade their commitments and to persuade them that they need not seek nuclear weapons to insure against others doing so.

Two other sets of arrangement emerged after 1968 to persuade states that nuclear weapons were unnecessary for their security or that of their neighbours: security assurances and nuclear weapon-free zones. Security assurances were a means of providing states with a surrogate for the perceived security advantages of nuclear weapons. Nuclear weapon-free zones were similarly intended to ban nuclear weapons from discrete regions of the world and thus give regional neighbours no incentive for acquiring them. The effect of these demand side arrangements, in addition to other developments, has been to stop

---

[5] For material on Iran, see Programme for Promoting Nuclear Non-Proliferation (PPNN), *Newsbrief*, no. 21 (first quarter, 1993), p. 14; PPNN, *Newsbrief*, no. 22 (second quarter, 1993), p. 14; and PPNN, *Newsbrief*, no. 24 (fourth quarter, 1993), p. 17. For material on Algeria, see 'A chronology of Algerian nuclear developments', *ENSP Bulletin*, 16 Apr. 1991 (Monterey Institute of International Studies); and Gupta, V., 'Algeria's nuclear ambitions', *International Defence Review*, vol. 25, no. 4 (1992), pp. 329–31.

[6] See NPT Articles II and III, reprinted in Howlett and Simpson (note 1), p. 90; and in Goldblat, J., SIPRI, *Agreements for Arms Control: A Critical Survey* (Taylor & Francis: London, 1982), pp. 172–73.

[7] See NPT Articles I and VI, reprinted in Howlett and Simpson (note 1), pp. 89 and 91; and in Goldblat (note 6), pp. 172 and 173.

[8] See Fischer and Szasz (note 1), p. 15.

the process of competitive and imitative nuclear arming which it was assumed in the early 1960s would lead to over 20 NWS being in existence by the 1980s.[9] Instead, a standard has now been established, demonstrated by the reluctance of the 'threshold states' to declare openly their possession of such devices, that no additional states should posses them.

In 1974, India exploded a nuclear device.[10] This served to crystallize concerns which had arisen in the United States and other developed countries that the NPT/IAEA regime alone would not prevent nuclear proliferation from taking place in states outside of the regime. It focused attention on the need to hinder development of nuclear devices and to slow down rates of proliferation. One method of achieving this was preventing imports of appropriate facilities, materials and technology. Although the main targets of these arrangements were states outside the NPT/IAEA regime, one consequence was to imply that IAEA safeguards in themselves might not be sufficient to prevent an NPT state using its nuclear technology for military purposes and that certain nuclear technologies should not be placed in the hands of some states, thus subtly altering part of the basis for the regime. In the 1980s, a similar concern arose over the export of missiles originally developed as delivery systems for nuclear weapons, and agreement was reached in 1987 among a group of Western supplier states on a set of guidelines for the licensing of exports of missiles and missile components.

One final, but usually unacknowledged, component of supply-side controls has been constraints on nuclear explosive testing. The NPT constrains all its NNWS parties from conducting any type of test. In addition, almost all states with the exception of China, France and North Korea are parties to the Treaty Banning Nuclear Weapon Tests in the Atmosphere, in Outer Space and Under Water (the Partial Test Ban Treaty, PTBT) of 1963.[11] However, de facto, a norm appears to have arisen since 1974 that only the five nuclear powers may conduct such explosions. In part, this has resulted from technical confidence in the reliability of first-generation fission devices being achievable without such testing. However, it does mean that states may be deterred from moving on to produce advanced thermonuclear warheads if these cannot be confidently stockpiled without testing.[12]

Supply-side controls may slow down a proliferator and channel its activities into specific directions, as was illustrated in the case of Iraq.[13] However, they will not prevent a determined proliferator with a relevant industrial base from achieving its goal. Only the removal of all motivation to obtain nuclear

[9] The world's leading non-proliferation experts believed in 1966 that: 'the biggest gap in the chain reaction of proliferation may be from the fifth to the sixth nuclear power. From the sixth to the sixteenth the progression might be rapid'. See Buchan, A. (ed.), *A World of Nuclear Powers?* (Prentice Hall: Englewood Cliffs, N.J., 1966), p. 9.

[10] For details, see Spector, L., *Nuclear Proliferation Today* (Carnegie Endowment: Washington, DC, 1984), p. 23, and Alam, M. B., *India's Nuclear Policy* (Mittal: New Delhi, 1988), p. 1.

[11] Text re-printed in Howlett and Simpson (note 1), p. 95; and in Goldblat (note 6), pp. 157–58.

[12] Carson, M., 'The purpose of nuclear test explosions', eds J. Goldblat and D. Cox, SIPRI, *Nuclear Weapon Tests: Prohibition or Limitation?* (Taylor & Francis: London, 1988), p. 37.

[13] Albright, D. and Hibbs, M., 'Iraq's nuclear hide and seek', *Bulletin of the Atomic Scientists*, vol. 47, no. 7 (Sep. 1991), p. 14.

weapons will do that. This is why the nuclear non-proliferation regime rests so heavily on measures affecting the demand side of the proliferation equation and, particularly, on the NPT and the IAEA.

The NPT and the IAEA safeguards system

Significant differences exist between the perceptions of NPT parties on the Treaty's objectives. The most extreme are between those who view it as a tool to prevent nuclear proliferation, and those who regard it as a comprehensive nuclear disarmament treaty. Yet despite these differences, and many states' perceptions that it is not ideal, the number of states which are parties has slowly increased. Five states acceded in 1991, 11 in 1992 and six in 1993, leaving the Treaty with 163 parties at the end of 1993.[14]

The NPT consists of a series of standards of state behaviour, one of which is that its NNWS parties will not seek to acquire nuclear weapons. In practice, the Treaty cannot be amended,[15] but the subsidiary arrangements through which it is implemented can be changed. Since 1991, IAEA safeguards practices have been modified in light of Iraq's attempts to acquire nuclear weapons. In 1992 the Agency's Board of Governors reaffirmed its right to undertake special inspections of suspect facilities and sites in any location within an NPT party. IAEA practices on the supply of information about new or modified facilities were amended to requiring its provision at the design stage, while IAEA inspectors now have a right of access to such facilities when under construction.[16] Finally, the Board reconfirmed the ability of the Agency actively to seek information about nuclear facilities and materials not declared to them by NPT parties and to receive and utilize intelligence or other information supplied by third parties.[17]

The accession of South Africa to the NPT in 1992 provided an occasion to clarify IAEA procedures in another area. South Africa was anxious to demonstrate that all the material it had produced had been placed under safeguards and that all traces of its nuclear weapon programme had been removed, including its weapon test site. It therefore provided detailed records of all fissile material production activities to the IAEA and also allowed Agency inspectors access to all locations they deemed necessary. This was a valuable precedent for the procedures to be followed if additional 'threshold' states accede to the Treaty.

[14] For a comprehensive list of NPT parties and dates of accession, see annex A to this volume. See also PPNN, *Newsbrief*, no. 24 (fourth quarter, 1993), pp. 22–24.

[15] This is because any NPT amendment must obtain the votes of a majority of the parties; all the nuclear weapon states parties; and all parties which at the time the amendment is circulated are members of the Board of Governors of the IAEA before it can be adopted. Its entry into force, *but only for those states which deposit instruments of ratification*, then depends on ratification by the same range of parties. One consequence is that two treaties may result from an amendment process, the amended and the unamended one, each of which will have a different set of parties.

[16] Fischer, D., Sanders, B., Scheinmann, L. and Bunn, G., 'A new nuclear triad: the non-proliferation of nuclear weapons, international verification and the International Atomic Energy Agency', *PPNN Study No. 3* (Mountbatten Centre for International Studies: Southampton, UK, Sep. 1992), pp. 21–22.

[17] PPNN, *Newsbrief*, no. 16 (winter 1991/92), p. 5.

Some of these changed practices were implemented for the first, and so far only, time in the case of North Korea in 1993.[18] The safeguards agreement between North Korea and the IAEA entered into force on 10 April 1992. On 4 May North Korea submitted an Initial Report listing the nuclear material that was subject to safeguards. *Ad hoc* IAEA inspections began in May 1992 to verify the accuracy of this report. Analysis of plutonium samples taken from North Korean stocks indicated that they were derived from reprocessing operations over a period of years, rather than a single campaign as indicated by the Initial Report. In parallel, North Korea protested violently over the restarting of US–South Korean joint military manœuvres, and talks on implementing the bilateral South Korean–North Korean nuclear inspection and control agreement became stalemated. Intelligence information from a third party, the USA, suggested that there existed two sites where waste from this undeclared plutonium reprocessing was stored. On 9 February 1993 the Director General of the IAEA requested that North Korea allow a Special Inspection to give access to specific additional information and to the two alleged storage sites. North Korea refused to allow such access and on 12 March sent a statement to the Agency notifying it of its intention to withdraw from the NPT. On 1 April the IAEA Board of Governors found North Korea in non-compliance with its obligations and decided to report its non-compliance to the UN Security Council. After intensive interchanges between representatives of the IAEA and North Korea, an IAEA inspection team visited North Korea between 10 and 14 May and performed work at the sole operating reactor and at the reprocessing plant. In July, US–North Korean bilateral discussions started, and on 11 July North Korea decided to 'suspend' its withdrawal from the NPT. IAEA inspectors visited North Korea during 3–10 August, but were permitted to carry out only part of their required inspection activities. An Agency team visited Pyongyang during 1–3 September, but no progress was made on resolving outstanding issues. On 8 September, Pyongyang was informed of the need to perform regular inspections over the period 25 September–9 October.

By the end of 1993, it had not proved possible to perform these inspections and the batteries powering the Agency's remote monitoring equipment were in urgent need of renewal. The main issues that remained unresolved were: (*a*) the ability of the IAEA to clarify the reprocessing anomalies; and (*b*) thus whether it possessed undetected plutonium that could be used in weapons; and (*c*) the attempt by North Korea to dictate to the Agency how it should conduct its regular inspection activities in that country. Detection of the alleged anomalies and the subsequent attempts to clarify them were a successful test of the Agency's revised safeguards procedures. However, the resulting impasse did call into question the ability of the international community, and in particular the UN Security Council, to enforce compliance with the procedures of the Agency.[19]

---

[18] For a full account of the North Korean issue, see PPNN, *Newsbrief*, nos 21, 22, 23 and 24 (1993).
[19] PPNN, *Newsbrief*, no. 24 (fourth quarter, 1993), pp. 1–4.

Among the main challenges to the IAEA safeguards system in the coming years will be the increase in the scope of its work and the likelihood that the resources allocated to it will not increase at a commensurate rate. The increases in the scope of its work seem likely to come from three sources: an increase in the nuclear facilities and materials under safeguards; a fissile material cut-off agreement; and a comprehensive test ban treaty (CTBT) which contained provisions for the IAEA to co-ordinate and implement its verification activities. The IAEA has been confronted with new tasks since 1992, such as implementing comprehensive safeguards in Argentina, Brazil, North Korea and South Africa. There is also the prospect of expanding such activities to include materials and facilities in the republics of the former USSR. The need to reduce safeguards expenditure on existing tasks to release resources for new ones precipitated discussions between the IAEA and the European Atomic Energy Community (Euratom) and led to a new partnership approach to safeguards in Euratom being agreed between the two organizations on 28 April 1992.[20] One complicating factor in providing resources for an expansion of Agency tasks is the existence of an informal understanding that the resources allocated to technical assistance in developing states should be roughly equal to expenditure on safeguards.

On a conceptual level, a major issue for the future will be how to move IAEA safeguards from their current narrow materials accounting base to the much wider foundation of safeguards transparency. To implement such a change, the Agency would need to acquire the right to conduct 'any place, any time' inspections. It would also require information on all exports, imports and production of nuclear materials and equipment and relevant non-nuclear materials in states covered by 'comprehensive' (i.e., NPT or full-scope) safeguards agreements. By 1994, about 20 states had agreed to supply such information on a voluntary basis, but mandatory reporting was still being resisted. In addition, Iran had invited IAEA officials to visit facilities in that country, as part of a voluntary policy of enhanced transparency concerning its nuclear activities—or lack of them. Another innovation would be to make use of environmental monitoring systems designed to detect production of enriched uranium and plutonium. Prototypes of such systems are currently being installed in Iraq. The objective of making these changes would be to provide the IAEA with a comprehensive and detailed picture of all nuclear activities within a state, rather than just an accountancy record of the dispositions and flows of fissile materials. The Agency would also be able to acquire information to verify the inventories reported by a state,[21] without the need to resort to the politically difficult special inspection provisions of INFCIRC/153.[22]

---

[20] *IAEA Newsbriefs*, vol. 7, no. 2 (Apr./May 1992); and *IAEA Press Release*, PR 92/23, 29 Apr. 1992.
[21] *IAEA Newsbriefs*, vol. 7, no. 1 (53) (Jan./Feb. 1992); *IAEA Press Release* PR 92/12, 26 Feb. 1992; *Nucleonics Week*, 27 Feb. and 5 Mar. 1992.
[22] Paragraphs 73 and 77 of the standard NPT/IAEA safeguards agreement with a state, usually known as INFCIRC 153, provides the basis for such Special Inspections, reprinted in Howlett and Simpson (note 1), pp. 186–87; and in Fischer and Szasz (note 1), p. 206.

Security assurances

Nuclear proliferation and non-proliferation are issues which strike at the heart of the security concerns of states. The nuclear non-proliferation regime that was created in the late 1960s rested upon two types of security commitments: alliance security guarantees and multilateral security assurances.[23] The first were provided by the 'nuclear umbrellas' and associated stationing of ground forces furnished by the USA and the USSR, which were perceived to make an attack upon allies the equivalent to an attack upon the NWS itself and thus make independent nuclear forces unnecessary. The decision of the Carter Administration to leave US forces in South Korea in the late 1970s in order to prevent development of an independent nuclear weapon programme is a case in point.

Such guarantees were not available to those states which chose not to join a cold war alliance. As a consequence, the non-aligned states demanded from the NWS assurances that their security would not be disadvantaged by retaining their non-nuclear weapon status. These assurances were provided in two forms: positive and negative. The UK, the USA and the USSR made a non-specific positive commitment, through UN Security Council Resolution 255 of 1968, to come to the assistance of any NNWS against which nuclear weapons were used or threatened. Negative assurances were provided through unilateral statements made by all five NWS in the period 1978–82. These statements differed in their nature. The Chinese one was a simple commitment never to use nuclear weapons against a NNWS. Those of France, the UK and USA were qualified by not being operative in the case of a state allied to an existing nuclear weapon power.[24]

The non-aligned states were never fully satisfied with these commitments. Throughout the 1980s Egypt, which was concerned about Israeli nuclear capabilities, argued for more specific positive security assurances, while Nigeria spearheaded a campaign to replace the unilateral negative assurances with a multilateral convention.[25] Some progress in both directions was contained in the draft Final Document of the 1990 NPT Review Conference.[26]

The end of the cold war created a radically changed situation with regard to security guarantees and assurances. The USSR ceased to provide nuclear security guarantees to its allies, while those provided to NATO allies appeared much less necessary than in the past. Demands by Ukraine for security guarantees have included economic as well as military guarantees from both Russia and the USA.[27] It seems highly unlikely that the existing NATO

---

[23] See chapter 16 in this volume.

[24] Reproduced in Howlett and Simpson (note 1), p. 281.

[25] Fischer, D. and Müller, H., 'The Fourth Review of the Non-Proliferation Treaty', *SIPRI Yearbook 1991: World Armaments and Disarmament* (Oxford University Press: Oxford, 1991), pp. 555–84; and Simpson, J., 'The 1990 Review Conference of the NPT, pointer to the future or diplomatic accident', *The Round Table*, no. 318 (1991), pp. 139–54.

[26] For details of the draft document, see IAEA document GC(XXXIV)/INF/290, 12 Sep. 1990.

[27] See chapter 16 in this volume. See also British American Security Information Council, *BASIC Reports*, no. 35 (29 Nov. 1993).

guarantees will be extended to other states. Such states will have to seek additional security commitments through multinational means.[28] Furthermore, one motivation for North Korean intransigence over IAEA inspections appeared to be the loss of the security guarantees previously provided by the USSR.

Although considerable good will exists towards the idea of strengthening existing assurances, it remains unclear how this might be done. The reluctance of the NWS to strengthen the language in the existing positive security assurances arises in part because one of the most obvious states against which the assurance might be implemented, Israel, is a US ally. However, all five NWS may be prepared subscribe to a resolution reaffirming UN Security Council Resolution 255.

Much more room for manœuvre appears to exist with negative security assurances. However, the existing caveat concerning actions in alliance with a NWS still appears to be regarded as a prudent insurance policy by some states, and at least three new concerns have been added in the post-cold war world. One is that until the 1993 Chemical Weapons Convention comes fully into force and a verification protocol is added to the 1972 Biological Weapons Convention, the threat of use of nuclear weapons is seen by some observers as a necessary means to deter states in possession of these weapons.[29] A second is that some qualification needs to be added to the assurance to indicate the point at which NWS will be released from it if, and when, a NNWS proliferates. This makes the solution advocated by some of an agreement not to use nuclear weapons except in response to a nuclear attack difficult for some of the NWS to accept.[30] A third issue is the form that any new security assurance would take. Some have suggested it should be a UN Security Council resolution, others in the form of an international agreement or treaty.[31] One problem with the latter proposal is that it remains unclear what function would be served by states other than the NWS being parties to it.

Security assurances have great symbolic value as a means of offering some substitute for the possession of nuclear weapons until a totally disarmed world is achieved and, in their negative form, as a method of reducing the utility of these weapons. However, the practical problems of reformulating them, together with the end of the bilateral structures of the cold war which were their original stimulus and the crowded agenda of the Conference on Disarmament (CD), suggest that progress may be slow.

---

[28] 'NATO summit produces mix of compromise and coercion', *Jane's Defence Weekly* (Jan. 1994), p. 13.

[29] Wheeler, M. O., 'Positive and negative security assurances', *Arms Control Brief*, vol. 2, no. 2 (Oct. 1993), p. 2.

[30] Such a no-first-use agreement would involve all NWS refraining from initiating their use unless they were attacked with nuclear weapons.

[31] Bunn, G. and Timerbaev, R., 'Security assurances to non-nuclear-weapon states', *The Non-Proliferation Review* (Monterey Institute for International Studies: Monterey, Calif., autumn 1993).

Nuclear weapon-free zones and other regional agreements

Prior to 1968, nuclear weapon-free zones (NWFZs) were originally seen as an alternative to a global nuclear non-proliferation agreement, but they are now regarded as a reinforcement for it and an insurance against its collapse. Three multilateral treaties have created such zones: the 1959 Antarctic Treaty covering the Antarctic region; the 1967 Tlatelolco Treaty covering South and Central America and the Caribbean; and the 1985 Rarotonga Treaty covering the South Pacific.[32] The Antarctic Treaty created a NWFZ on the continent as part of the package of measures which suspended all claims to national sovereignty over it. The Treaty of Tlatelolco, signed in 1967 in advance of the NPT, is only now coming fully into force as a consequence of the decisions of Argentina and Brazil to become full parties, following amendments to bring it into line with their bilateral nuclear safeguarding arrangements involving the IAEA.[33] One interesting aspect of this Treaty, however, is that under Article 28 its operation is suspended if any new NWS emerges anywhere in the world, unless a party waives this provision. Finally, the Rarotonga Treaty, signed in 1985, bars both nuclear weapons and nuclear explosive devices from the territories of those South Pacific states parties to the Treaty, as well as the dumping of nuclear waste.

Although some discussion has taken place on the creation of a nuclear weapon-free zone in Central Europe, expanding upon the zone created in the former German Democratic Republic following the agreements on German unification,[34] no formal proposal has yet emerged. In contrast, considerable progress has been made in negotiating a NWFZ in Africa following the movement to end white rule in South Africa and the accession of South Africa to the NPT. There were expectations that such a treaty would be finalized in March 1994 and signed before the end of the year.[35]

Nuclear export controls

The purpose of these controls has been to make it more difficult for a potential proliferator to acquire nuclear weapons by limiting the ability to import relevant technology and materials. Initially, such controls operated on an East–West basis through the Coordinating Committee on Multilateral Export Con-

---

[32] Reproduced in Howlett and Simpson (note 1), pp. 115–42.

[33] For an informed account of these developments see Redick, J., 'Argentina–Brazil nuclear non-proliferation initiatives', *PPNN Issue Review No. 3* (Mountbatten Centre for International Studies: Southampton, UK, Jan. 1994).

[34] Article V of the Treaty on the final settlement with respect to Germany, 12 Sep. 1990, states: 'Until the completion of the withdrawal of the Soviet armed forces . . . units of German armed forces assigned to military alliance structures in the same way as those in the rest of German territory may also be stationed in that part of Germany, but without nuclear weapon carriers . . . Foreign armed forces and nuclear weapons or their carriers will not be stationed in that part of Germany or deployed there'. The text to the Treaty is reprinted in Rotfeld, A. D. and Stützle, W., *Germany and Europe in Transition* (Oxford University Press: Oxford, 1991), pp. 183–86.

[35] 'Implementation of the Declaration on the Denuclearization of Africa', UN document A/48/371, 18 Oct. 1993.

trols (COCOM) and other similar arrangements, but in 1974 the 'London Club' of nuclear technology and materials supplier nations, including France as a non-party to the NPT, was convened and drew up guidelines, published in 1978. Their key elements were that they were to apply to nuclear facilities and their components, and that 'restraint' was to operate in the export of 'sensitive' technologies.[36] This meant, in effect, that no transfers of reprocessing and enrichment technologies were to take place to states regarded as potential proliferators.

Although the number of states adhering to the guidelines increased slowly during the 1980s, no further meetings of the Nuclear Suppliers Group (NSG) took place until May 1991. In April 1992, in Warsaw, two further measures were agreed to extend the scope of nuclear supplier controls. One was a list of dual-use technologies which would be subject to export controls through national legislation. The second was that exports would only be made to states which were NPT parties or which accepted comprehensive IAEA safeguards. In addition, a system for consultation on export licence applications was created, operated from the Japanese permanent mission to the IAEA in Vienna, to try to prevent a company or state applying consecutively for a licence to import a similar product from a number of supplier states.[37]

The existing nuclear export regime is not a consensual one: rather it is one imposed upon importing states by a small number of supplier nations. As such, it appears to breach the spirit of NPT Article IV, which gives NNWS parties unrestricted access to all forms of peaceful nuclear technology, even though its implementation through the domestic legislation of individual states does not breach the NPT itself. Indeed, such legislation may be mandatory for a supplier state to fulfil its obligations under the Treaty to prevent technology and materials for a nuclear weapon programme being transferred to an aspiring proliferator. The problem, however, is to identify aspiring proliferators in advance with any certainty.

Several emerging nuclear suppliers have been assimilated into this supply regime, and have accepted its guidelines. There still remains a desire on the part of many developing countries, however, to universalize it through both suppliers and recipients agreeing on a common set of rules for supply. However, it appears unlikely that the suppliers would accept guidelines any less rigorous than their own, and thus universalization is unlikely to occur unless developing states are prepared to accept the existing supplier guidelines.

Nuclear testing constraints

A NWS is defined in the NPT as one which exploded a nuclear device prior to 1 January 1967. Nuclear testing is thus the criterion for moving a state from non-nuclear to nuclear weapon status, although any state which has tested

---

[36] Müller, H. and Dunn, L. A., 'Nuclear export controls and supply side restraints: options for reform', *PPNN Study No. 4* (Mountbatten Centre for International Studies: Southampton, UK, 1993), pp. 2–3.
[37] Müller and Dunn (note 36), pp. 5–10.

after that date would logically not be able to accede to the Treaty as either a nuclear weapon or a NNWS. The main constraint on nuclear testing since 1963 has been the PTBT, under which almost all states other than China, France and North Korea have committed themselves not to test in any other medium but underground.[38] Negotiations on a CTBT took place between 1978 and 1980[39] but were then suspended indefinitely. However, after 1975 negotiations on a CTBT became the key criterion for many NNWS to evaluate fulfilment of the NWS NPT Article VI pledge to engage in negotiations on nuclear disarmament, and this was the issue which prevented agreement on a final document at the 1990 Fourth Review Conference on the NPT.[40]

The end of the cold war has led to considerable changes in this situation. Throughout 1993, three of the NWS—France, Russia and the USA—operated voluntary moratoria on nuclear testing, while the UK operated an involuntary one, since it tests in the USA.[41] Only China continued to test.[42] At the same time, it was agreed by all the NWS that they would start negotiations on a CTBT in early 1994 in the CD, with US legislation mandating the US Administration to complete such a Treaty before early 1996.[43]

The negotiation of a CTBT will have two major effects: to buttress the restraints contained in the NPT and to remove the major item of unfinished diplomatic business surrounding that Treaty. NNWS parties to the NPT are already subject to an implicit ban on testing, and thus a CTBT would affect mainly the nuclear weapon parties to the NPT and states which remain outside it. Three significant elements in the drafting of the CTBT, however, will determine its further non-proliferation impact.

One of these elements is the question whether it will contain a definition of what is to be banned. If a definition is attempted, it may have two specific consequences. One would be to prevent the construction of further nuclear explosive testing sites, and thus preclude the type of strategy apparently pursued by South Africa of using the threat to test to gain diplomatic leverage.[44] A second would be to reinforce the ban on activities connected with the development of nuclear weapons, such as the testing of non-nuclear explosive assemblies, that is already implicit in the NPT.[45] However, the problems of agreeing on such definitions, and concerns that activities not covered by the definition would be automatically legitimized, seem likely to deter such attempts to clarify precisely what the ban covers. A third element would be the question whether the entry into force of the Treaty will be made

---

[38] Reproduced in Howlett and Simpson (note 1), p. 95.

[39] Greb, A., 'Survey of past nuclear test ban negotiations', in Goldblat and Cox (note 12), pp. 105–109.

[40] See Fischer and Müller (note 25) and Simpson (note 25).

[41] See chapter 16 in this volume.

[42] See chapter 16 in this volume. See also PPNN, *Newsbrief*, no. 24 (fourth quarter, 1993), p. 8.

[43] See chapter 16 in this volume. See also PPNN, *Newsbrief*, no. 23 (third quarter, 1993), p. 8.

[44] Howlett, D. and Simpson, J., 'Nuclearisation and denuclearisation in South Africa', *Survival*, vol. 35, no. 3 (autumn 1993), p. 158.

[45] Bunn, G. and Timerbaev, R., 'Nuclear "weaponization" under the NPT: what is prohibited, what can be inspected, who should do it?', *PPNN Study 5* (Mountbatten Centre for International Studies: Southampton, UK, Apr. 1994).

conditional upon India, Israel and Pakistan, and possibly other proliferation 'suspects', becoming parties to the Treaty.

While the actual non-proliferation impact of a CTBT may be merely to legalize the ban on testing by NNWS that has existed *de facto* since the Indian explosion in 1974, its diplomatic impact will be considerable. Since its impact will be felt more by NWS than NNWS, it will be seen to balance off some of the discrimination against the latter inherent in the NPT. Above all, it will undoubtedly facilitate a more harmonious review of the NPT in 1995.

III. Options for fundamentally revising the regime

Dealing with fissile materials

The existing NPT/IAEA regime places no formal constraints on the production and stockpiling of fissile or other nuclear materials that could be used in weapons, other than the existence of a legal and political commitment not to do so. However, concern has been expressed at the quantities of fissile material in military stockpiles in the USA and Russia, at the possibilities that some of this material could fall into the hands of proliferators or non-state groups, and at the amount of such material planned for production in civil facilities.[46] These concerns are now the subject of a major conceptual and practical debate, partly because of reduced expectations about the size of future nuclear power generation capacity and the general downgrading of nuclear power as a future source of electricity supply. This debate centres on whether the underlying principles of the nuclear non-proliferation regime, and in particular Article IV of the NPT, should be revised to ban, or at least constrain, the production and/or use of plutonium and highly enriched uranium (HEU) in peaceful applications.

Two distinct practical issues are emerging in this context: how to handle fissile material currently committed to military applications and how to manage safeguarded material that could be used for explosive purposes. In the military context three concerns are being addressed: stopping further military production; eliminating HEU released by nuclear disarmament; and disposing of military plutonium.[47] President Clinton has proposed stopping military production through a multilateral cut-off of the unsafeguarded production of fissile materials. The effect of this would be to terminate production in those reactors and enrichment plants that operate solely for military purposes; to place all other such facilities in NWS under mandatory IAEA safeguards; and to provide the opportunity for placing unsafeguarded fissile material under Agency safeguards.[48] Similar arrangements are also sought in those states

---

[46] For estimated inventories of these materials, see Albright, D., Berkhout, F. and Walker, W., SIPRI, *World Inventory of Plutonium and Highly Enriched Uranium 1992* (Oxford University Press: Oxford, 1993).

[47] For a discussion of the disposal of plutonium from dismantled warheads, see chapter 16 in this volume.

[48] See White House Fact Sheet on President Clinton's Non-Proliferation and Export Control Policy, reproduced in PPNN, *Newsbrief*, no. 23 (third quarter, 1993), p. 23.

which have significant nuclear facilities, but have not yet accepted comprehensive IAEA safeguards (i.e., India, Israel and Pakistan). Under this proposal, however, it would not be mandatory to place existing stockpiles, or ancillary weapon plants such as assembly and dismantling facilities, plutonium recycling/americium separation plants or tritium production and separation facilities under Agency safeguards, thus advantaging states with large stocks of unsafeguarded nuclear materials.

Commitments have been made to place significant quantities of fissile material currently assigned to military uses under IAEA safeguards, and thus to remove them from future use in weapons, as part of these arrangements. If current plans are implemented to 'blend down' former Soviet HEU to low enriched uranium (LEU) and incorporate it in fuel for power reactors, this HEU will cease to exist.[49] Such arrangements would not preclude the use of HEU in military submarine reactors, as this is provided for in Article 14 of the standard IAEA/NPT safeguards agreement.[50]

Disposing of weapon-grade plutonium will be more difficult. Methods proposed include burning it as a fuel in thermal and fast breeder reactors (FBRs); mixing it with highly active waste; and storing it indefinitely.[51] None of these methods has the finality and simplicity of the blending down of HEU. In the short term it seems likely that it will be stored in separated, metallic form, and perhaps even in the form of shaped bomb components. Although it may appear to have no peaceful purposes, it would still be desirable for it to be subject to IAEA safeguards.

Fissile material arising from civil activities has become a challenge to the existing regime, partly because of the changes in the economic context in which nuclear power plants are operated. Uranium has been in relatively plentiful supply for some years, and prices are very low. This depressed market is reinforced by expectations that supplies of LEU will be forthcoming from blending down military HEU, and that little new power reactor capacity will be ordered before the end of the decade, when reactors built in the 1960s will reach the end of their economic life. As a consequence, the short-term economic case for substituting plutonium for enriched uranium as a fuel in existing designs of thermal reactors, or developing FBRs as a complement to them, is very weak, if not non-existent.[52]

In the late 1970s the outlook was very different. Expectations of high uranium prices and shortages of the material in a rapidly expanding reactor market led several states to embark on plans for large-scale separation of plu-

---

[49] PPNN, Newsbrief, no. 19 (autumn 1992), p. 20.

[50] Sanders, B. and Simpson, J., 'Nuclear submarines and non-proliferation: cause for concern', PPNN Occasional Paper No. 2 (Mountbatten Centre for International Studies: Southampton, UK, 1988); and Rauf, T. and Desjardins, M.-F., 'Opening Pandora's Box? Nuclear powered submarines and the spread of nuclear weapons', Aurora Paper, no. 8 (Canadian Centre for Arms Control and Disarmament: Ottawa, 1988).

[51] Berkhout, F. et al., 'Disposition of separated plutonium', Science and Global Security, vol. 3 (1993).

[52] For statistics on this situation, see Uranium in the New World Market: A Statistical Update of Supply and Demand 1991–2010 (Uranium Institute: London, Oct. 1992).

tonium for use as fuel in reactors. Large investments were made in irradiated fuel reprocessing plants, mixed-oxide (MOX) fuel fabrication facilities and FBR development. The former are now being commissioned at a time when there is little, if any, immediate need for their output, although in the medium to long term they may become more relevant if economic conditions change. Moreover, the disposal of separated military plutonium is now on the global agenda, and this material poses fewer technical problems when used for MOX and FBR fuel than plutonium arising from civil power plants. Thus a major question mark now hangs over the utility and rationality of separating plutonium from used fuel, and whether it has a negative or positive economic value. Indeed some observers have proposed that in the case of Japan it would be cheaper for it to stockpile large quantities of uranium ore or LEU at current prices than to engage in plutonium recycling.[53]

Concerns over the creation of large national stockpiles of separated plutonium in both nuclear and NNWS led to proposals for an IAEA international plutonium storage (IPS) system. Lack of agreement over the conditions, if any, to be imposed on national rights to withdraw this material from international storage prevented the proposal progressing, but the idea has now been resurrected in the form of an international plutonium management (IPM) system, encompassing both separated civil material and material transferred from military uses.[54] In parallel, it has become clear that with the possible exception of a very small number of isotope production reactors, all non-power reactors could follow power reactors and be operated on LEU rather than the HEU which was previously used. The United States has been pursuing a programme of expediting such substitution. Thus the technical option now appears to exist for dispensing altogether with the use of HEU for non-military purposes.

This has led to proposals for a radical amendment to the conceptual basis of the NPT non-proliferation regime by having *all* states agree to constrain their nuclear activities by: (*a*) not engaging in reprocessing of reactor fuel or the separation of plutonium from it; (*b*) using only separated plutonium in current stockpiles for MOX fuel and FBR development work; and (*c*) not engaging in any production of HEU, or using it in civil reactors.

One variant on such proposals would be to have stocks of both military and civil origin plutonium transferred to IAEA ownership, and have them control its future use for development and other purposes. This would also facilitate the IAEA operating as a supplier of last resort for states and companies seeking fissile material for peaceful purposes.[55]

Under current political conditions, it seems highly unlikely that the governments and nuclear enterprises in France, Japan, Russia and the United Kingdom would agree to the first two of these constraints, given their heavy

[53] See Leventhal, P. and Dolley, S., *A Japanese strategic uranium reserve: a safe and economic alternative to plutonium* (Nuclear Control Institute: Washington, DC, 16 Nov. 1993).
[54] PPNN, *Newsbrief*, no. 20 (winter 1992), p. 3; and Beranek, J., 'The use of international fuel storage schemes and international fuel cycle activities in a regional context', eds D. Howlett and J. Simpson, *East Asia and Nuclear Non-Proliferation* (Mountbatten Centre for International Studies: Southampton, UK, 1993), p. 72.
[55] The IAEA already has powers to do this in Article IX of its Statute.

investment in facilities for plutonium recycling. Indeed, an indefinite ban may not be desirable, given the uncertainties in the energy market, though one for a finite period of years would appear to be a rational move under current circumstances. Politically, however, a ban on HEU production might be easier to achieve especially if it were phased in over a number of years.

Constraints such as these were initially written into one recent NWFZ agreement, but later removed. They would clearly strengthen the technical basis of the regime, and make IAEA safeguards easier to implement. Yet ultimately the regime is a political one, and the trade-off between the technical advantages of such a change and the political disunity that it would produce among the major supplier states is very difficult to judge. One clear signal from the US Clinton Administration is that, unlike its Carter predecessor in the late 1970s,[56] at the moment it judges that the political disadvantages of such a change outweigh its potential proliferation advantages in reducing the scale of the technical problems facing the IAEA safeguards system.[57]

The START treaties as a non-proliferation measure

One radically new aspect of the post-cold war non-proliferation environment is proliferation arising from the fragmentation of a NWS. The example of the USSR, and the subsequent process of attempting to transfer all its nuclear weapons to the new Russian Federation, has alerted the international community to the fact that NWS may now constitute part of the overall proliferation threat and problem, rather than just acting as an obstacle to universalization of the regime and smoothly conducted reviews of the NPT. One consequence has been that the US–Russian–Commonwealth of Independent States (CIS) nuclear arms control process has become an integral part of the nuclear non-proliferation regime. More specifically, the implementation of START I and the Lisbon protocols should ensure that no more than one NWS emerges from the remains of the former USSR.[58]

Reinforcing compliance mechanisms: counter-proliferation and the UN Security Council

The existing nuclear non-proliferation system, based upon the NPT, operates on voluntarist principles, in so far as states choose not to acquire nuclear weapons following a calculation of the gains and losses that would result from

---

[56] For an account of this policy and the reactions it created, see Brenner, M. J., *Nuclear Power and Non-Proliferation: The Re-Making of US Policy* (Cambridge University Press: Cambridge, 1981); and Wilmshurst, M. J., 'The development of current non-proliferation policies', eds J. Simpson and A. G. McGrew, *The International Nuclear Non-Proliferation System: Challenges and Choices* (Macmillan: London, 1984), pp. 19–54.

[57] PPNN, *Newsbrief*, no. 23 (third quarter, 1993), p. 23.

[58] See chapter 16 in this volume. For text of the Protocol to the Treaty between the United States of America and the Union of Soviet Socialist Republics on the Reduction and Limitation of Strategic Offensive Systems (Lisbon Protocol), 23 May 1992, see SIPRI, *SIPRI Yearbook 1993: World Armaments and Disarmament* (Oxford University Press: Oxford, 1993), pp. 574–75.

such a move. However, as the cases of Iraq and North Korea have demonstrated, there is always a danger of renegade states emerging which may not comply with non-proliferation standards. A significant issue now facing the international community is how to deal with them.

There are two distinct elements to this matter. One is that although the IAEA is now tasked with detecting possible clandestine nuclear weapon programmes, if necessary through Special Inspections, it possesses little ability to impose compliance upon renegade states.[59] Realistically, all it can do is to hand the matter over to the UN Security Council for action. The Council asserted in early 1992 that it regarded proliferation as a threat to the peace,[60] but its ability to act depends on the willingness of its five permanent members to do so, and to agree on an effective course of action. As the case of North Korea has demonstrated, there may be genuine differences between those permanent members over whether persuasion or sanctions, including military ones, are the most appropriate response to concerns over non-compliance.

The second element is the question how permanent members of the Security Council might act to prevent proliferation, and in particular whether they should be prepared to take military action, including ultimately the use of their own nuclear weapons, to achieve this objective. Although a government minister in the United Kingdom has publicly argued that this is not an appropriate role for its nuclear capabilities,[61] considerable discussion has taken place in the United States on the need to possess counter-proliferation options, including some of a military nature.[62] Since the targets of such policies would presumably be fissile material production facilities, it places on the international agenda the circumstances under which it would be legitimate to attack nuclear facilities, and the more practical question of whether the environmental damage and deaths, to both the proliferating state and its neighbours, resulting from such an attack would be an acceptable price to pay for preventing proliferation.[63] It also implies that the nuclear non-proliferation

---

[59] The sanctions the IAEA can impose in the event of non-compliance are very limited, and contained in Article XIX of its Statute, which states that: 'A member which has persistently violated the provisions of this Statute or of any agreement entered by it pursuant to this Statute may be suspended from the exercise of the privileges and rights of membership by the General Conference acting by a two thirds majority of the members present and voting upon recommendation by the Board of Governors'.

[60] UN Security Council, Declaration on Disarmament, Arms Control and Weapons of Mass Destruction, UN document, S/PV.3046, 31 Mar. 1992. Reprinted in PPNN, *Newsbrief*, no. 17 (spring 1992), p. 15.

[61] Memorandum from the Secretary of Defence, 'The defence counterproliferation initiative', Washington, DC, 9 Dec. 1993; and text of speech to Centre for Defence Studies, King's College, London by Rt. Hon. Malcolm Rifkind, UK Minister of Defence, 16 Nov. 1993.

[62] For example, Rodman, P., 'A grown-up's guide to non-proliferation', *National Review*, 5 July 1993, pp. 34–37; Roberts, B., 'From non-proliferation to antiproliferation', *International Security*, vol. 18, no. 1 (summer 1993), pp. 140–71; and *The Counter-Proliferation Debate: Are Military Measures or Other New Initiatives Needed to Supplement the Non-Proliferation Regime?*, Panel Discussion from the Conference on Nuclear Non-Proliferation: The Challenges of a New Era, 17–18 Nov. 1993 (Carnegie Endowment for International Peace: Washington, DC, 1994).

[63] The effect of attacks on reactors and other nuclear installations is discussed in Ramberg, B., *Nuclear Weapons Plants as Weapons for the Enemy: An Unrecognized Military Peril* (University of California Press: Berkeley, Calif., 1984).

regime should move from a voluntarist to an enforced one, with unknown consequences for the inter-state consensus which currently underpins it.

IV. The 1995 NPT Review and Extension Conference

The tasks of the Conference

All of the current issues and debates concerning the nuclear non-proliferation regime in the post-cold war era will play a role to a greater or lesser extent in the next key event in the non-proliferation calendar, the NPT Review and Extension Conference to be held from 17 April to 12 May 1995 at the UN in New York. The negotiators of the NPT agreed to disagree over its duration, and put off a decision on this for 25 years. This period ends on 5 March 1995, and the conference that will start six weeks later has to decide, according to Article X.2 of the NPT, 'whether the Treaty shall continue in force indefinitely, or shall be extended for an additional fixed period or periods. This decision shall be taken by a majority of the Parties to the Treaty.'

In addition, the conference will have the task of reviewing the operation of the NPT. This involves examining its implementation, not its substance. Review conferences have in the past sought to express the results of their deliberations through a consensual final document.

Procedural complications

The actual extension decision will be taken either through a resolution of the conference or as part of its final document. The latter may be politically preferable, as it would be regarded as expressing strong and widespread support for the Treaty. However, the extension decision might then risk becoming a hostage to disputes over the wording of the treaty review document. A vote would result in an unambiguous and absolute decision, but the voting process itself might produce a significant minority opposed to the extension option. This in turn might be interpreted as indicative of a split in the consensual base of the NPT and the NPT non-proliferation regime, and lead to perceptions that adherence to the standards contained in the Treaty had weakened.

Only three options are specified for extending the Treaty: extension for a single fixed period; for additional fixed periods; or indefinitely. The first and last options are unambiguous: a decision to terminate the Treaty at the end of the fixed period, with no mechanism for any extension; or an extension for an indefinite period. By contrast, the middle option is full of ambiguity.[64] It has to be assumed that this option is not identical to an indefinite extension, and thus

---

[64] For a detailed analysis of these issues see Bunn, G., van Doren, C. and Fischer, D., *Options and Opportunities: The NPT Extension Conference of 1995* (Mountbatten Centre for International Studies: Southampton, UK, 1991); and the chapters by George Bunn and Ben Sanders in Simpson, J. and Howlett, D. (eds), *The Future of the Non-Proliferation Treaty*, Southampton Series in International Policy (Macmillan: Basingstoke, 1994, forthcoming).

that some mechanism will be created to decide on the move from one fixed period to another. As the Treaty text offers no guide to this mechanism, any decision to adopt this option would mean that its modalities would need to be spelled out in the extension resolution or, if the decision were a consensual one, in the conference document. Finally, the treaty text could be interpreted as linking the 25-year period before the duration decision to the period or periods specified in the extension options. On this basis, it could be argued that the options available are a single period of 25 years, an indefinite number of 25-year periods or an indefinite extension. However, the possibility that the conference would give itself the power to choose an option different again from those discussed above cannot be excluded, since in the end the decision will be based on political bargaining and interests, rather than legal rules.

In past review conferences, the target has been to obtain unanimous agreement to the text of the review/final document. It must be assumed that this will remain the objective in 1995, although a document which included the extension decision and was not supported by one or two parties might be regarded as acceptable. At the 1995 NPT conference, the Group of Seven leading industrialized states and their allies will probably be able to vote through an indefinite extension of the treaty.[65] If a consensus decision was sought, however, as is mandated by the rules of procedure agreed at the second meeting of the Preparatory Committee of the conference in January 1994, this would necessitate parallel agreement on the wording of the conference final document in at least six substantive areas: allegations that some state parties have assisted nuclear proliferators and that others have attempted to proliferate; security assurances to NNWS; IAEA safeguards; export controls and access by the developing world to nuclear energy; the nuclear disarmament provisions of Article VI; and regional nuclear proliferation situations.

Substantive issues

Controversy over NPT Articles I and II, under which NWS pledge not to transfer weapons and NNWS pledge not to acquire them, has previously focused on allegations that Western NWS provided assistance to Israeli and South African nuclear weapon programmes. Unless a significant breakthrough is made in the Middle East peace process, the Israeli issue will probably continue to be a source of controversy. In addition, if the Ukrainian Parliament continues to argue that former Soviet nuclear weapons on its territory are its own property, Russia may be held responsible for transferring them to Ukraine.[66] No review of the NPT would be complete without some discussion of Iraq's clandestine programme, and a condemnation of this breach of Article II. Whether a similar accusation will be levelled at North Korea remains to be

---

[65] Their commitment to an indefinite extension was made at their meeting in Munich in July 1992. See *The Times*, 9 July 1992.

[66] For details on the Ukrainian Parliament's position regarding nuclear weapons, see chapter 16 in this volume.

seen. Any condemnation of individual states for breaches of these articles is likely to be actively opposed by those states, and thus it is difficult to see how consensus wording in this area can be achieved.

Although security assurances for NNWS are contained in the NPT text, commitments to new proposals in this area are being sought by many such states. The difficulty is to provide them in the form desired by NPT NNWS parties, namely that they should be: (a) in a multilateral legal form; (b) offered collectively by all five NWS; and (c) in the case of positive security assurances, should contain much more detailed and specific statements of the actions to be taken. Existing requests for security assurances from many CIS, Central European and developing states suggest that such new commitments could be a very significant element in securing support for a long extension of the NPT in 1995. However, it remains unlikely that the NWS will be prepared to provide them in a form which in some cases comes close to a nuclear deterrent guarantee, and moreover the work of the CD appears likely to be dominated by negotiations on a CTBT through to 1995, making any early agreement on new security assurances in that body unlikely.

Iraq's clandestine nuclear programme illuminated several of the known limitations of the IAEA safeguards system linked to Article III of the NPT. This may lead to some friction over the degree to which new concepts should underpin it, particularly greater transparency, and over other issues where the IAEA secretariat is seeking to obtain legitimization from the conference for reform in the safeguards system. The debate over safeguards could also encompass the efficacy of further regionalization of safeguards systems, especially the new Euratom partnership agreement,[67] and whether it would be appropriate to institute an IPM system. In addition, measures to expand IAEA safeguards activities in NPT NWS are also likely to be discussed, as part of a strategy of isolating the military nuclear energy activities in these states. This in turn may have a positive impact upon both the debate over Article VI and the extension decision.

Any contradiction between the unrestricted right of access of NPT parties under Article IV to all nuclear energy capabilities and the restrictions placed upon that right by supplier states has to date been more an issue of principle than practice. Nuclear energy's image as an economical and safe source of electricity has been badly dented in both the industrialized and the developing worlds, with the exception of the states on the northern Pacific Rim and Indonesia. However, agreements to constrain dual-use technologies may enhance sensitivities among developing states to the wider technology transfer and development issues involved. More significantly, this could be exacerbated if Iraq attempted to gain support for some relaxation of the constraints placed upon its nuclear energy activities by the UN Security Council Resolutions, and Iran and North Korea were to complain about the de facto restrictions on their ability to obtain nuclear power technology.

---

[67] PPNN, *Newsbrief*, no. 23 (third quarter, 1993), p. 12; and Fischer, Sanders, Scheinmann and Bunn (note 16), pp. 33–37.

A further issue that may be raised in connection with this Article is attacks on nuclear facilities. This was a controversial issue in the review conferences of 1985 and 1990 and could be so again in 1995, especially if Iraq seeks to condemn the attacks on its reactors by the United States in 1991, and if by then the United States Pentagon has articulated more fully a doctrine for using military force against the nuclear facilities of proliferators.

The debates over nuclear disarmament in 1995 will differ significantly from those of the past, if only because of the presence of all the NWS as parties for the first time. The nuclear arms race, interpreted prior to 1991 by the non-aligned movement as the nuclear armament competition between the USA and the USSR, appears to have ceased, given the demise of the Soviet Union. France, Russia, the United Kingdom and the United States will be able to produce evidence that they have been reducing their nuclear weapon stockpiles. The perennial controversy over a ban on nuclear testing and the NPT will undoubtedly recur in 1995, however, unless by the date of the conference a CTBT has been signed or, at the very least, the principles underlying the treaty have been agreed.

Negotiations on a CTBT will start in early 1994 in the CD, but the political pressure for sustaining the current moratorium on testing by France, Russia and the United States (and involuntarily by the UK) through to the 1995 conference may not be strong enough to overcome the pressures within some of these states to test prior to the signature of a CTBT, particularly if an indefinite duration CTBT is to be linked to an NPT of similar term. Any testing by these countries, especially if it occurs in late 1994–early 1995, would be likely to re-ignite the controversy over the links between a CTBT and the NPT, in the absence of a nearly completed treaty.

Past debates over a CTBT have masked, and served as a surrogate for, a more profound debate on the future of nuclear weapons and demands for a 'treaty on general and complete disarmament'. While European states will doubtless point to a reduction in nuclear and conventional disarmament levels in Europe, and demand similar reductions in other regions, friction may result from demands by many parties for a clear commitment by the NWS to a timetable for their nuclear disarmament, given current programmes to replace their nuclear delivery systems. If Ukraine has acceded to the NPT by 1995 it, and possibly other CIS and Baltic states parties, may be expected to press Russia to commit itself to such a timetable. Japan and Germany may also take a much more active and positive stance over nuclear disarmament than they did at the 1990 conference. The totally new set of 'post-cold war' political alignments on the nuclear disarmament issue that could then be generated may have very unpredictable consequences for the debate over the implementation of the disarmament provisions of Article VI, and thus the outcome of the conference.

Regional issues have often proved a major barrier to the achievement of consensus language on a final document at past NPT conferences. It seems likely that the Middle East situation will continue to generate such difficulties for the 1995 conference. All the states in the region are parties to the NPT except Israel, which is believed by many observers to have had an undeclared nuclear weapon stockpile for at least two decades.[68] Unless Israel accedes to the NPT, many Arab states will continue to refuse to sign the Chemical Weapons Convention, and may also resist any proposal for indefinite extension of the Treaty.[69] A second regional problem is likely to be found on the Korean Peninsula, where uncertainty over North Korea's nuclear weapon intentions is already generating some concerns in neighbouring states over the desirability of an indefinite and unconditional commitment to non-nuclear weapon status.[70]

The prognosis for the Conference

Objectively, the 1995 NPT conference offers a more positive prospect for a harmonious review of the Treaty than its four predecessors. The Treaty now has a nearly universal membership, significant movement has taken place since 1990 in the area of nuclear disarmament, and considerable adaptation of the regime, and especially of the implementation of IAEA safeguards, has taken place. But analysis of the potential internal dynamics of the conference suggests it will be no easy task to construct an extension decision and a treaty review document that all, or almost all, of the parties can subscribe to.

It remains probable that holding the conference in New York, where all parties have diplomatic delegations, will make it relatively easy for the Group of Seven to assemble the required majority of states[71] to vote through an indefinite extension to the Treaty. However, the certainty that this will happen, and that irrespective of the vote of any individual state the Treaty will remain in force, may also have the effect of increasing the numbers that might vote against this option as a gesture of defiance and protest on specific issues; to give themselves a justification for withdrawing from the Treaty at a later date; and for a variety of other reasons. How large a minority this might be is uncertain, but if it was sizeable, this would be certain to wound the future authority of the Treaty and the non-proliferation regime.

The alternative to voting is to include the extension decision in a consensus treaty review document. The difficulty with this is that the extension decision can then be directly linked with the other elements of that document, and individual parties or regional groupings may seek to trade their support for indefinite extension for the achievement of language on specific issues acceptable to them. It can be anticipated that in this context Iraq and North Korea would refuse to join a consensus on a final document unless condemnations of their alleged nuclear weapon activity were removed from it, while other states

---

[68] Spector, L., *Going Nuclear* (Ballinger: Cambridge, Mass., 1987), p. 130.

[69] PPNN, *Newsbrief*, no. 21 (first quarter, 1993), p. 2.

[70] See for example, 'NPT after 1995—steps towards elimination of nuclear weapons', *Plutonium*, no. 3 (Oct. 1993), pp. 7–15.

[71] At the end of 1993, the NPT has 162 members, thus 82 states would constitute a simple majority of the parties. See PPNN, *Newsbrief*, no. 24 (fourth quarter, 1993), pp. 22–24, for a comprehensive list.

may have similar demands in other areas, such as nuclear trade and export controls or regional proliferation concerns. There is also an obvious linkage between attempts to obtain an indefinite NPT and a CTBT of indefinite duration. Yet a package deal which allowed support for indefinite extension to be traded off against desired wording in the review part of the final document, even if the package was adopted with a very small number of states outside the consensus, would almost certainly generate more visible support for that extension than a vote, and may thus be the most preferable outcome.

V. The non-proliferation regime in 1993

The first half of 1995 will be a crucial period for the nuclear non-proliferation regime. The outcome of the NPT Conference will determine how long the Treaty will continue to provide the foundations for the regime, as well as affording an authoritative commentary on the changes that have occurred to the regime since the 1990 NPT Review Conference, and the challenges that now face it. For the slow evolution of the regime following its inception in 1968 has been overtaken during the past three years by a succession of revolutionary, rather than evolutionary, changes. Greater international collaboration to prevent nuclear proliferation is visible now that the cold war has ended, as is a merging of the strategic nuclear arms control and the non-proliferation enterprises. The prospect has opened up of a greatly enlarged role for the IAEA, not only in terms of the existing regime but also in verifying nuclear dismantling and a CTBT.

These changes, together with the failure of new declared NWS to emerge since 1964, suggest considerable grounds for optimism about the future of the regime. Yet events which occurred at the end of 1991 have also created a new category of proliferation problem, namely, the consequences of the fragmentation of NWS. No current NWS can be automatically excluded from a place in this category at some point in the future.

The inability of supplier export controls and/or international safeguards on nuclear capabilities to prevent nuclear proliferation has been vividly illustrated by new knowledge on the activities of Iraq, North Korea and South Africa. Yet it remains important to develop such measures further to make the proliferation process more difficult, costly and lengthy, and thus to deter states from embarking upon it. Such technical denial also gives time for political change to occur both within and between states.[72] For the main pillar of the nuclear non-proliferation regime remains the political commitments of the states participating in it, rather than measures to deny materials and technology.

The global development of the non-proliferation standard through adherence to the NPT has been one of the most remarkable developments over the past 30 years, as has the reluctance of 'ambiguous' NWS to violate it publicly.

---

[72] This point has been made frequently in the writing of Lewis Dunn, for example in Müller and Dunn (note 36), p. 20.

This, in turn, is a reflection of changing international perspectives upon the military utility of nuclear weapons and their political status. In the coming decade, the behaviour of the declared NWS is likely to play an increasingly significant role in the evolution of the nuclear non-proliferation regime. De-emphasizing the role of nuclear weapons in their security policies will in itself serve to reinforce the non-proliferation standard, by removing proof of the utility of proliferation, either as a means of obtaining military or political power or as a counter to nuclear threats from the existing NWS.

One of the most remarkable features of the post-cold war situation is the strength of the international political consensus underpinning the nuclear non-proliferation regime. Yet many observers see this strength as illusory, and argue that major changes are necessary if the regime is to meet the challenges of the future. Areas where this applies include the technical concepts under-pinning the regime and the need to bring military ideas and concepts to bear upon the non-proliferation problem. The changes advocated in the technical rules include banning all reprocessing of nuclear fuel, phasing out all use of HEU in research and isotope production reactors, and banning all enrichment of uranium above a level of, perhaps, 20 per cent.[73] Given current economic and commercial circumstances, and the need to dispose of large quantities of weapon-grade plutonium arising from the cold war nuclear arms race, these appear to be eminently rational proposals. Yet the political price of attempting to implement them is almost certainly in conflict with a group of states highly supportive of the existing regime, France, Japan, the Russian Federation and the United Kingdom. The experience of the Carter Administration during the late 1970s suggests that this political price is not worth paying, and the Clinton Administration has given clear signals that it thinks so, too.

An important stimulus producing the second challenge is the perceived inability of the existing regime to address the possibility that more than five NWS exist. One response has been to propose that a new category of 'ambiguous' NWS should be created. If these states have nuclear weapons, the first priority is argued to be to safeguard against accidental, inadvertent or ill-thought-out use.[74] However, this would undermine the rigid division between NWS and NNWS written into the NPT, and would lessen the inducements for 'ambiguous' NWS to follow South Africa and accede to the Treaty as a NNWS.

The development of a much more aggressive policy of physically prevent-ing proliferation, by turning the IAEA Inspectorate into an international nuc-lear police force and by using force to destroy nuclear facilities, is also an important element of the second challenge.[75] Again, this seeks to generate a technical solution to a political problem. It implies moving the cutting edge of

[73] A leading advocate of such changes has been Paul L. Leventhal. See his contribution 'Nuclear export controls: can we plug the leaks', ed. J.-F. Roux, *Limiting the Proliferation of Weapons* (Carleton University Press: Ottawa, 1992), pp. 50–51.
[74] For a detailed discussion of these issues, see Frankel, B. (ed.), *Opaque Nuclear Proliferation: Methodological and Policy Implications* (Cass: London, 1991).
[75] Roberts (note 62), p. 140.

the non-proliferation regime to the UN Security Council, as in the case of Iraq. But it also highlights the fact that some potential proliferators are economically and physically insulated from the wide range of non-violent sticks and carrots that might be used to persuade them to conform to the non-proliferation norm. While the use of force may be the only option that appears available in such circumstances, there is no guarantee that it will be completely successful, and every possibility that it may precipitate ecological disasters and nuclear war. As a bargaining tool, the capability to act in this way may be useful, but any implementation of such a threat may provide only an incomplete answer to the problem, and at the same time have incalculable consequences for the global consensus upon which the current non-proliferation regime rests.

All of these challenges will be present in the background of debates at the 1995 NPT conference, but its outcome is likely to rest on other substantive issues, as well as the management skills displayed during the conference. The growth of the non-proliferation norm since the 1960s offers the prospect of considerable support for a long extension of the NPT. Indeed, the main danger to this probably lies in the procedural and management context of the extension decision. Further initiatives to reinforce the regime through collateral international agreements between NPT parties, however, will clearly assist in the creation of the positive atmosphere necessary to overcome the problems inherent in this context.

Appendix 15A. Documents on nuclear weapon non-proliferation

STATEMENT OF THE DEMOCRATIC PEOPLE'S REPUBLIC OF KOREA ON WITHDRAWAL FROM THE NON-PROLIFERATION TREATY

Pyongyang, 12 March 1993

A grave situation has been created today in our country, which threatens its national sovereignty and the security of our state.

. . .

The accession to the NPT by the DPRK Government was intended to remove the nuclear threats of the United States against the DPRK, never to sacrifice its sovereignty and security for someone's benefit. Because of the imprudent machinations on the part of the United States and its adherent forces, each time we undergo an inspection of the IAEA the nuclear threats against the DPRK increase, and the peace and security on the Korean peninsula is not ensured but disturbed.

All these facts evidently show that the United States, those forces hostile to the DPRK and some officials of the IAEA Secretariat are misapplying the NPT to jeopardize the sovereignty and security of our country, a non-nuclear-weapon state, and stifle our socialist system.

Under such abnormal situation prevailing at present, we are no longer able to fulfil our obligations under the NPT.

The Government of the Democratic People's Republic of Korea declares its decision to withdraw unavoidably from the Nuclear Non-Proliferation Treaty as a measure to defend its supreme interests.

The withdrawal from the NPT is a well-justified self-defensive measure against the nuclear war manoeuvres of the United States and the unjust act of some officials of the IAEA Secretariat against the DPRK. The DPRK's principled stand will remain unchanged until the United States stops its nuclear threats against the DPRK and IAEA Secretariat returns to its principle of independence and impartiality.

Source: Embassy of the Democratic People's Republic of Korea, Stockholm.

NON-PROLIFERATION TREATY: DEMOCRATIC PEOPLE'S REPUBLIC OF KOREA

Letter dated 2 April 1993 addressed to the Secretary-General of the Conference on Disarmament by the Representatives of the Depositary Governments of the Treaty on the Non-Proliferation of Nuclear Weapons transmitting a statement issued by the three Governments on 1 April 1993

Geneva, 2 April 1993

As the representatives in the Conference on Disarmament of the Depositary Governments of the Treaty on the Non-Proliferation of Nuclear Weapons, signed at Washington, London and Moscow on 1 July 1968, we wish to draw your attention to a statement issued by our three Governments on 1 April 1993 with regard to the announcement by the Democratic People's Republic of Korea of its intention to withdraw from the Treaty. The English and Russian language texts of this statement are enclosed.

We should be grateful if you would arrange for this letter and its enclosure to be circulated as an official document of the Conference. It is the hope of our Governments that members of the Conference and non-member participants will wish formally to associate themselves with the statement of the Depositary Governments.

. . .

The Governments of the Russian Federation, United Kingdom, and the United States, which are the Depositary Governments of the Treaty of the Non-Proliferation of Nuclear Weapons (NPT), wish to issue the following statement:

'– We express regret and concern at the announcement by the Democratic People's Republic of Korea (DPRK) of its intention to withdraw from the Treaty on the Non-Proliferation of Nuclear Weapons (NPT).

– Since the NPT is an essential element of international peace and security, DPRK withdrawal from the NPT would constitute a serious threat to regional and international stability.

– We question whether the DPRK's stated reasons for withdrawing from the Treaty constitute extraordinary events relating to the subject matter of the Treaty. In this regard, we recall that we have provided nuclear related security assurances to the DPRK as a non-nuclear weapon state party to the NPT.

– Remaining a party to the Treaty and complying fully with its terms would be in the DPRK's interests. It would help to re-assure the international community about the nature of the DPRK's nuclear programme and the DPRK's desire for positive inter-national relations, including peaceful nuclear cooperation.

– Moreover, DPRK withdrawal from the NPT would jeopardise stability on the Korean peninsula, which has improved in recent years, and undermine efforts to imple-ment the North-South Joint Declaration on Denuclearisation of the Korean Peninsula.

– We urge the DPRK to retract its announcement and to comply fully with its Treaty commitments and its safeguards obli-gations, which remain in force. In this re-spect, we strongly support the efforts of the International Atomic Energy Agency to im-plement its safeguards agreement with the DPRK.'

The three Governments call upon all NPT parties to associate themselves with this statement and to urge the DPRK to recon-sider its position and to fulfil its commit-ments under the Treaty.

Source: Conference on Disarmament document CD/1195, 2 Apr. 1993.

SPEECH BY STATE PRESIDENT F. W. DE KLERK TO PARLIAMENT, 24 MARCH 1993, REGARDING THE NUCLEAR NON-PROLIFERATION TREATY

Pretoria, 24 March 1993

Mr Speaker, when I decided last week to call a joint session, it was my intention to con-centrate on the announcement to Parliament of important information with regard to the Nuclear Non-proliferation Treaty and related matters. Since then certain developments have compelled me to cover a much wider area. I am, however, still commencing with announcements relating to South Africa's nuclear capability.

THE NUCLEAR NON-PROLIFERATION TREATY AND RELATED MATTERS

Honourable Members will recall that when I

delivered my first opening address on 2 February 1990, I emphasised, among other things, the normalisation of South Africa's international relations. An important aspect of this was, and is, the significant contribu-tion that South Africa can and will have to make towards peace, stability and progress in Southern Africa.

With this objective in mind the Govern-ment has—in addition to many other initia-tives in a variety of other spheres—taken far-reaching and drastic decisions with regard to the non-proliferation of all weapons of mass destruction. This includes nuclear, as well as chemical and biological weapons.

The Government acceded to the Nuclear Non-proliferation Treaty (NPT) on 10 July 1991. We became a founder signatory of the United Nations Convention on the Prohibi-tion of the Development, Production, Stock-piling and Use of Chemical Weapons and on their Destruction on 14 January 1993. It is also participating in the current review of the Convention on Biological and Toxin Weapons.

I wish to concentrate today on the Nuclear Non-proliferation Treaty and would like to convey important information to Parliament, the public and the international community. It is important that the integrity of the Republic of South Africa with regard to its commitments to the Nuclear Non-prolifera-tion Treaty should be placed above any doubt.

When a country accedes to the NPT, it undertakes, as from the date of accession, not to manufacture or otherwise acquire nuclear weapons. It also undertakes to enter into a Safeguards Agreement, in terms of which a comprehensive inventory of all the nuclear material and nuclear facilities as they exist for the country as a whole at the time that agreement enters into force, be sub-mitted to the International Atomic Energy Agency. Such facilities and material are then subject to international inspection and verifi-cation. The IAEA also conducts regular inspections to verify the inventory and to ensure that these materials and facilities are used for peaceful purposes only.

Since its accession to the NPT, South Africa has strictly adhered to the conditions of the NPT and has maintained a policy of transparency and professional co-operation with the IAEA. This positive approach has led to South Africa's resuming its seat at the IAEA General Conference, since September 1991, without opposition, after an absence of

12 years.

The process of verifying the completeness of South Africa's declaration of nuclear materials and facilities has proceeded so successfully that the IAEA was in the position to report to the Board of Governors in September 1992, after a large number of IAEA inspections, that nothing had been found to suggest that South Africa's inventory of nuclear materials and facilities was not complete, nor was there anything to suggest that the list of facilities and materials submitted for controls were incomplete.

However, mainly because of the events in Iraq, which violated the conditions of the NPT by launching a clandestine nuclear weapons programme, certain countries have called the effectiveness of the IAEA verification regime into question. Some countries have also alleged that South Africa still has covert aspirations in this regard and that it has not fully disclosed its stockpile of enriched uranium.

Such allegations are regularly taken up by both the local and the international press, and are beginning to take on the dimensions of a campaign. South Africa's present nuclear programme which is directed towards commercialisation including the export of high technology products is in the process placed under suspicion and is harmed. Our country cannot afford this. Accordingly, I wish today to confirm unequivocally that South Africa is adhering strictly to the requirements of the NPT and that it will continue to do so.

I would, however, like to go further. Any doubt about the Government's intentions with regard to nuclear matters, must, for once and all, be removed. For this reason, the Government has decided to provide full information on South Africa's past nuclear programme despite the fact that the NPT does not require this.

At one stage, South Africa did, indeed, develop a limited nuclear deterrent capability.

The decision to develop this limited capability was taken as early as 1974, against the background of a Soviet expansionist threat in Southern Africa, as well as prevailing uncertainty concerning the designs of the Warsaw Pact members.

The build up of the Cuban forces in Angola from 1975 onwards reinforced the perception that a deterrent was necessary—as did South Africa's relative international isolation and the fact that it could not rely on outside assistance, should it be attacked.

Details relating to the limited deterrent capability, and the strategy in this regard, which were at that time developed, are as follows:

– The objective was the provision of 7 nuclear fission devices, which was considered the minimum for testing purposes and for the maintenance thereafter of credible deterrent capability.

– When the decision was taken to terminate the programme, only 6 devices had been completed.

– No advanced nuclear explosives, such as thermo-nuclear explosives, were manufactured.

– The programme was under the direct control of the Head of Government, who decided that it should be managed and implemented by Armscor.

– Knowledge of the existence of the programme was limited to a number of Ministers on a 'need-to-know' basis.

– The strategy was that, if the situation in Southern Africa were to deteriorate seriously, a confidential indication of the deterrent capability would be given to one or more of the major powers, for example the United States, in an attempt to persuade them to intervene.

– It was never the intention to use the devices and from the outset the emphasis was on the deterrence.

This was the situation when I became State President in 1989. As a former Minister of the AEC I was also informed about this.

On my assumption of office as State President it was already evident to me, and also to my colleagues who were also informed, that it was in our national interest that a total reverse—also in respect of our nuclear policy—was called for.

During 1989, the global political situation changed dramatically:

– A cease-fire in Angola was agreed.

– On 22 December 1988, a tripartite agreement was signed at the United Nations with Cuba and Angola which provided for the independence of Namibia and the withdrawal of 50 000 Cuban troops from Angola.

– The Cold War had come to an end and developments leading to the destruction of the Berlin Wall and the break-up of the Soviet-bloc had become the order of the day.

– The prospects of moving away from a confrontational relationship with the international community in general and with our neighbours in Africa, in particular, to one of co-operation and development were good.

In these circumstances a nuclear deterrent had become, not only superfluous, but in fact an obstacle to the development of South Africa's international relations.

World opinion had also become increasingly opposed to nuclear weapons, and significant advantages for South Africa could be forthcoming should it accede to the NPT. Although it already had an advanced nuclear technology base and nuclear industry, accession would facilitate the international exchanges of the new technology for its future development. It could also be of benefit to our neighbouring states and in due course to Africa as a whole.

Within this factual framework, and with consideration to all of the other innovative policy objectives which by then had already began to take on form, it was decided towards the end of 1989 that the pilot enrichment plant at Pelindaba should be closed and decommissioned.

Early in 1990, final effect was given to decisions that:

– all the nuclear devices should be dismantled and destroyed;

– all the nuclear material in Armscor's possession be recast and returned to the AEC where it should be stored according to internationally accepted measures;

– Armscor's facilities should be decontaminated and be used only for non-nuclear commercial purposes;

– after which South Africa should accede to the Non-Proliferation Treaty, thereby submitting all its nuclear materials and facilities to international safeguards.

The implementation of these decisions and instructions proceeded according to plan. The process of dismantling took place under the strict, joint control of the AEC and ARMSCOR. As a further control measure, an eminent professor of nuclear physics, Prof. W. L. Mouton, was appointed as independent auditor to oversee the process. It was his task to satisfy himself that every gram of nuclear material had been accounted for and all the hardware and design information was destroyed. This has been done.

South Africa acceded to the Non-Proliferation Treaty on 10 July 1991 and signed, according to the requirement of the Treaty, a Safeguards Agreement with the IAEA on 16 September 1991 with immediate force and effect.

On 30 October 1991, in accordance with the Safeguards Agreement with the IAEA, South Africa submitted a complete inventory of all nuclear materials and facilities under its jurisdiction which contained such materials on 30 September 1991, since which date all such materials and facilities are subject to international safeguards. South Africa's hands are clean and we are concealing nothing. Permission has now been granted by the Government, with a view to international inspection, for full access to facilities and records of facilities, which in the past were used for the preparation of a nuclear deterrent capability.

I sincerely trust that this unprecedented act, namely the voluntary dismantling of a nuclear deterrent capability, and the voluntary revelation of all relevant information will confirm this Government's effort to assure transparency. I trust also that South Africa's initiative will inspire other countries to take the same steps.

In conclusion, I wish to emphasize that at no time did South Africa acquire nuclear weapons technology or materials from another country, nor has it provided any to any other country, or co-operated with another country in this regard. Our expertise, technology and nuclear materials were fully protected and dealt with strictly according to international standards and agreements. South Africa has never conducted a clandestine nuclear test.

There may be a perception that the decision to abandon the programme means that the investment in the whole enterprise had been wasted. This is not the case.

The enrichment technology developed by the AEC as well as the nuclear materials which were produced, constitute an important asset for South Africa. They will contribute significantly to the ultimate success of the AEC's peaceful commercialisation programme.

The operation of the pilot enrichment plant allowed South Africa to continue operation of the AEC's research reactor, which is also used for the production of radioactive isotopes for medical purposes, during a period when the international community refused to provide nuclear fuel for its operation.

The nuclear material that was used for the devices has been recovered and will be used to enlarge the production of these and other isotopes. SAFARI-I is amongst the very few reactors which can meet this need.

Furthermore, the application of the enrichment technology to the establishment of the semi-commercial enrichment plant provided South Africa with the ability to provide all the nuclear fuel requirements of the Koeberg nuclear power station, and to guarantee this supply at a time when the delivery of nuclear fuel for Koeberg from overseas was denied.

In addition to this, South Africa's accession to the NPT has already led to the lifting of nuclear sanctions by the United States of America. Exchanges of visits with states in Africa have also taken place with a view to agreements on the use of medical isotopes and training programmes. We have become a member of the African Regional Co-operative Agreement (AFRA), an organisation within the IAEA which co-ordinates peaceful, nuclear projects and co-operation between African states in the nuclear field.

The prospects for further co-operation will be enhanced by the establishment of a nuclear weapons free zone in Africa. The Government has already publicly committed itself to this, and believes that it can make a significant contribution to the establishment of peace and security in Southern Africa.

South Africa will soon be taking an active part in the trans-continental discussions on this all-important issue. We will be supported by the fact that South Africa acquired a nuclear capability, and, in recognition of its new relationship with Africa and the broader international community, abandoned it.

Without accession to the NPT none of this would have been possible. I trust that the book on this chapter of the past can now be closed, and that a new one of international co-operation and trust can now be opened.

_____

Source: Newsletter, 10/1993, South African Trade Mission, Harare, Zimbabwe, 25 Mar. 1993.

JOINT STATEMENT BY THE PRESIDENT OF THE RUSSIAN FEDERATION AND THE PRESIDENT OF THE UNITED STATES OF AMERICA ON NON-PROLIFERATION OF WEAPONS OF MASS DESTRUCTION AND THE MEANS OF THEIR DELIVERY

Moscow, 14 January 1994

President Clinton and President Yeltsin, during their meeting in Moscow on January 14, 1994, agreed that the proliferation of weapons of mass destruction and their missile delivery systems represents an acute threat to international security in the period following the end of the Cold War. They declared the resolve of their countries to cooperate actively, and closely with each other, and also with other interested states, for the purpose of preventing and reducing this threat.

The Presidents noted that the proliferation of nuclear weapons creates a serious threat to the security of all states, and expressed their intention to take energetic measures aimed at prevention of such proliferation.

– Considering the Treaty on the Non-Proliferation of Nuclear Weapons as the basis for efforts to ensure the non-proliferation of nuclear weapons, they called for its indefinite and unconditional extension at conference of its participants in 1993, and they urged that all states that have not yet done so accede to this treaty.

– They expressed their resolve to implement effective measures to limit and reduce nuclear weapons. In this connection, they advocated the most rapid possible entry into force of the START I and START II treaties.

– They agreed to review jointly appropriate ways to strengthen security assurances for the states which have renounced the possession of nuclear weapons and that comply strictly with their non-proliferation obligations.

– They expressed their support for the International Atomic Energy Agency in its efforts to carry out its safeguards responsibilities. They also expressed their intention to provide assistance to the agency in the safeguards field, including through joint efforts of their relevant laboratories to improve safeguards.

– They supported the Nuclear Suppliers Group and agreed with the need for effective implementation of the principle of full-scope IAEA safeguards as a condition for nuclear exports with the need for export controls on dual-use materials and technology in the nuclear field.

– They reaffirmed their countries' commitment to the conclusion as soon as possible of an international treaty to achieve a comprehensive ban on nuclear test explosions and welcomed the decision to begin negotiations at the conference on disarmament. They declared their firm intention to provide political support for the negotiating process, and appealed to other states to refrain from carrying out nuclear explosions while these talks are being held.

– They noted that an important contribution to the goal of non-proliferation of nuclear weapons would be made by a verifiable ban on the production of fissile materials for nuclear weapons and by the most rapid conclusion of an international convention to this effect with the widest possible participation of states and on a non-discriminatory basis.

– They agreed to cooperate with each other and also with other states to elaborate measures designed to prevent the accumulation of excessive stocks of fissile materials and over time to reduce such stocks.

– They agreed to establish a joint work group to consider:

(a) including in their voluntary IAEA safeguards offers all source and special fissionable materials, excluding only those facilities associated with activities having direct national security significance;

(b) steps to ensure the transparency and irreversibility of the process of reduction of nuclear weapons, including the possibility of putting a portion of fissionable material under IAEA safeguards. Particular attention would be given to materials released in the process of nuclear disarmament and steps to ensure that these materials would not be used again for nuclear weapons.

– The Presidents also tasked their experts to study options for the long-term disposition of fissile materials, particularly of plutonium, taking into account the issues of non-proliferation, environmental protection, safety, and technical and economic factors.

– They reaffirmed the intention of interested organizations of the two countries to complete within a short time a joint study of the possibilities of terminating the production of weapon-grade plutonium.

– The Presidents agreed that reduction of the risk of theft or diversion of nuclear materials is a high priority, and in this context they noted the usefulness of the September 1993 Agreement to cooperate in improving the system of controls, accounting, and physical protection for nuclear materials. They attached great significance to further joint work on the separate but mutually connected problems of accounting for nuclear materials used in the civilian and military fields.

Both Presidents favoured a further increase in the efforts to prevent the proliferation of chemical and biological weapons.

– As the heads of the countries that have the world's largest stockpiles of chemical weapons, they acknowledged particular responsibility for eliminating the threat posed by these weapons. In this context, they declare their resolute support for the Convention on the Prohibition of Chemical Weapons, and their intention to promote ratification as rapidly as possible and entry into force of the convention not later than 1995.

– To promote implementation of a comprehensive ban on chemical weapons, they welcomed the conclusion of the implementing documents for the Wyoming Memorandum of Understanding and agreed to conclude work in as short a time as possible on the implementing documents for the Bilateral Agreement on the Destruction of Chemical Weapons.

– The Presidents reaffirmed their desire to facilitate the safe, secure, timely, and ecologically sound destruction of chemical weapons in the Russian Federation and the United States. They applauded the joint Chemical Weapons Destruction Work Plan recently concluded between the two countries which leads the way for the United States to provide an additional $30 million in assistance to support an analytical chemical laboratory in Russia to facilitate chemical weapons destruction. The United States also agreed to consider appropriate additional measures to support Russia's chemical weapons destruction program.

– They reiterated the importance of strict compliance with the convention on the Prohibition of Biological and Toxin Weapons and of continued implementation of measures in accordance with the Russia–America–British Statement of September 1992, which provided inter alia for the reciprocal visits of facilities and meetings between experts in order to ensure confidence in the compliance with the convention.

– They supported convening a special conference of the states parties to the Convention on the Prohibition of Biological and Toxin Weapons in order to consider measures that would contribute to transparency and thereby confidence in compliance with the convention and its effectiveness.

The Presidents expressed the determination of their countries to cooperate with each other in preventing the proliferation of missiles capable of carrying weapons of mass destruction.

– They welcomed the conclusion of the Bilateral Memorandum of Understanding between the government of the Russian Federation and the government of the United States of America concerning the Export of Missile Equipment and Technologies, signed in September 1993, noted the importance of this agreement for ensuring mutually beneficial cooperation between the United States and Russia in the field of space exploration, and agreed to collaborate closely in order to ensure its full and timely implementation.

– The United States welcomed Russia's intention to join the Missile Technology Control Regime and undertook to cooperate with Russia in facilitation of its membership at an early date. The Russian Federation and the United States of America are certain that further improving the MTCR, including the prudent expansion of membership, will help reduce the threat of proliferation of missiles and missile technologies in the regional context as well.

The Presidents of the two countries agreed that, in addition to strengthening global norms of non-proliferation and working out agreements to this effect, close cooperation is essential in order to develop policies on non-proliferation applicable to specific regions posing the greatest risk of proliferation of weapons of mass destruction and their means of delivery.

– They agreed that nuclear weapons on the Korean Peninsula would represent a grave threat to regional and international security, and decided that their countries would consult with each other on ways to eliminate this danger. They call upon the DPRK to honour fully its obligation under the Treaty on the Non-Proliferation of Nuclear Weapons and its safeguards agreement with the IAEA in connection with the treaty, and to resolve the problems of safeguards implementation, inter alia, through dialogue between IAEA and DPRK. They also urged full and speedy implementation of the Joint Declaration of the ROK and DPRK on Denuclearization of the Korean Peninsula.

– They support efforts to reach agreement on the establishment of a multilateral forum to consider measures in the field of arms control in non-proliferation that could strengthen security in South Asia. They call on India and Pakistan to join in the negotiation of and become original signatories to the Treaty Banning Nuclear Weapons Test Explosions and the proposed Convention to Ban Production of Fissile Materials for Nuclear Explosives and to refrain from deploying ballistic missiles capable of delivering weapons of mass destruction to each other's territories.

– They agreed that the United States and Russia, as co-chairs in the Middle East peace process, would actively promote progress in the activity of the working group for Arms Control and Regional Security in the Middle East, striving for speedy implementation of confidence-building measures and working toward turning the Middle East into a region free of weapons of mass destruction, where conventional forces would not exceed reasonable defense needs.

– They firmly supported the efforts of the UN Special Commission and the IAEA to put into operation a long-term monitoring system of the military potential of Iraq, and called upon Iraq to comply with all UN Security Council resolutions.

Source: PPNN, *Newsbrief*, no. 25 (first quarter 1994), pp. 16–17.

IAEA BOARD OF GOVERNORS REVIEWS AGENCY'S INSPECTIONS IN THE DEMOCRATIC PEOPLE'S REPUBLIC OF KOREA (DPRK)

Vienna, 22–25 February 1994

In the framework of its meeting in Vienna, February 22–25, the Board of Governors of the International Atomic Energy Agency (IAEA), consisting of representatives from 35 Members States, reviewed the status of the Agency's inspections in the DPRK. The review was conducted on the basis of a report presented by the Director General of the IAEA, Dr. Hans Blix. Representatives from the DPRK participated in the discussions.

The IAEA has so far conducted six inspection missions to the DPRK in performing its responsibilities to verify the correctness and assess the completeness of the DPRK's nuclear inventory as declared in the IAEA last year.

The Director General recently requested special access to additional information and two sites in the DPRK under the articles of the safeguards agreement relating to special inspections in an attempt to clarify the reasons for inconsistencies that have emerged from the IAEA's analyses of samples and measurements. DPRK representatives have indicated willingness to provide more information.

At the conclusion of its discussion on this matter, the Board of Governors adopted the text of a resolution which is attached for information:

The Board of Governors

(a) *Having considered* the Report of the Director General and the statements by the Representative of the Democratic People's Republic of Korea on the Implementation of the Safeguards Agreement between the Democratic People's Republic of Korea and the International Atomic Energy Agency.

(b) *Taking account* of the rights and obligations under the Safeguards Agreement between the Democratic People's Republic of Korea and the International Atomic Energy Agency (INFCIRC/403).

(c) *Taking serious note* of the significant inconsistencies between the Democratic People's Republic of Korea's declaration and the Secretariat's findings resulting from ad hoc inspections and sample analysis which remain unresolved despite extensive discussions.

(d) *Noting* that on February 9, 1993 the Director General, acting on the basis of Articles 73(b) and 77 concerning special inspections, has formally requested the Democratic People's Republic of Korea to grant access to specific additional information and to two locations.

(e) *Recalling* that at its December 1992 session, the Board reiterated the need for full and effective implementation of the Safeguards Agreement voluntarily entered into by the Democratic People's Republic of Korea and had called for full cooperation on the part of the Democratic People's Republic of Korea's authorities.

1. *Calls* for full and prompt implementation of the Safeguards Agreement between the Democratic Peoples Republic of Korea and the International Atomic Energy Agency;

2. *Stresses* that it is essential to verify the correctness and assess the completeness of the Democratic People's Republic of Korea's Initial Report;

3. *Supports* the actions already taken by the Director General in this regard;

4. *Calls upon* the Government of the Democratic People's Republic of Korea urgently to extend full cooperation to the International Atomic Energy Agency to enable the Agency fully to discharge its responsibilities under the Safeguards Agreement and to respond positively and without delay to the Director General's request of February 9, 1993 for access to additional information and two additional sites;

5. *Decides* that access to additional information and two additional sites, referred to in paragraph 4, is essential and urgent in order to resolve differences and to ensure verification of compliance with INFCIRC/403;

6. *Requests* the Director General to transmit this Resolution to the Democratic People's Republic of Korea, to continue dialogue with the Democratic People's Republic of Korea with a view toward urgent resolution of the issues above, and to report again to the Board of Governors on the matter not later than one month from the date of adoption of this resolution at a further meeting of the Board of Governors to be convened for this purpose;

7. *Decides* to remain seized of the matter, and to consider further measures as provided for in the Safeguards Agreement between the International Atomic Energy Agency and the Democratic People's Republic of Korea and Statute of the International Atomic Energy Agency.

Source: PPNN, *Newsbrief*, no 25 (first quarter 1994), pp. 17–18.

16. Nuclear arms control

DUNBAR LOCKWOOD

I. Introduction

A number of positive developments in nuclear arms control highlighted 1993: the United States and Russia signed the START II Treaty; Belarus and Kazakhstan acceded to the 1968 Non-Proliferation Treaty (NPT) as non-nuclear weapon states; fewer nuclear explosions were conducted than in any year since 1959; and the international community reached a consensus for the first time that a multilateral comprehensive test ban treaty (CTBT) should be negotiated. In addition, international support for a ban on the production of fissile material for weapon purposes appeared to become universal as the world's governments became increasingly aware of the need to focus on controlling and disposing of nuclear materials as well as nuclear weapons themselves.

Despite these accomplishments, the 'unfinished business' of the cold war remained unfinished in 1993 since neither the START I nor the START II Treaty entered into force.[1] As the year ended, there were no binding international agreements in force which limited strategic offensive nuclear weapons. In addition, the US and Russian governments declined to adopt several important initiatives that have been advocated by a number of experts, including reciprocal monitoring of nuclear warhead dismantlement, comprehensive declarations of stockpiles of nuclear weapons and all fissile material with reciprocal measures to verify those declarations, and the separation of warheads from their deployed intercontinental ballistic missile (ICBM) launchers.

Finally, a trend that began in 1992 continued in 1993 as much of the nuclear arms control negotiations shifted, in a sense, from a quid pro quo in which Soviet weapons were traded for US weapons to a quid pro quo in which former Soviet weapons were traded for US dollars.

II. The START I Treaty

Although the START I Treaty was signed by the United States and the Soviet Union on 31 July 1991, the accord had still not entered into force by early 1994. The dissolution of the USSR in December 1991 complicated the for-

---

[1] For excerpts of the START I Treaty, see SIPRI, *SIPRI Yearbook 1992: World Armaments and Disarmament* (Oxford University Press: Oxford, 1992), appendix 1A; for the START II Treaty, see SIPRI, *SIPRI Yearbook 1993: World Armaments and Disarmament* (Oxford University Press: Oxford, 1993), appendix 11A.

tunes of the Treaty by creating four new independent states with strategic weapons based on their territories—Belarus, Kazakhstan, Russia and Ukraine.

On 23 May 1992, these four states assumed the USSR's obligations under the START I Treaty by signing the Lisbon Protocol.[2] In addition to making the three non-Russian states signatories to the Treaty (Russia was already effectively a signatory, having assumed the international treaty obligations of the USSR), the Protocol required these states to accede to the NPT as non-nuclear weapon states 'in the shortest possible time'. Earlier that month, the heads of Belarus, Kazakhstan and Ukraine gave letters to the USA committing their respective countries to eliminate all of the strategic nuclear weapons on their territory within seven years of the entry into force of the START I Treaty.[3] Later in 1992, the legislatures of Kazakhstan, Russia and the USA approved the START I Treaty. The US Senate voted in favour of the Treaty on 1 October 1992 with the condition that the Lisbon Protocol and the accompanying three letters carry the same legal obligations as the Treaty itself.[4] The Russian Parliament stipulated that it would not exchange the instruments of ratification for the START I Treaty until after Belarus, Kazakhstan and Ukraine had acceded to the NPT and worked out implementation measures with Russia.

Belarus ratified the START I Treaty on 4 February 1993 and deposited its instruments of accession to the NPT as a non-nuclear weapon state on 22 July. The Kazakh Parliament, which had ratified the START I Treaty on 2 July 1992, voted to accede to the NPT as a non-nuclear weapon state on 13 December 1993,[5] and President Nursultan Nazarbayev deposited the instruments of accession on 14 February 1994.[6] Ukraine ratified the START I Treaty on 18 November 1993 but attached 13 conditions that were tantamount to an official repudiation of its earlier commitment to eliminate all of the nuclear weapons on its territory.[7] Among the conditions, the Parliament (Rada) reiterated Ukraine's claim to ownership and 'administrative control' of the nuclear weapons on its territory and, more importantly, stipulated that Ukraine did not consider itself bound by Article V of the Lisbon Protocol,

---

[2] For the text of the Lisbon Protocol, see *SIPRI Yearbook 1993* (note 1), appendix 11A.

[3] It is worth noting that Ukraine made a commitment at the CIS summit meeting in Minsk on 30 Dec. 1991 to have all of its strategic weapons dismantled by the end of 1994. Thus, the May 1992 commitment to eliminate all of the strategic weapons on its territory within 7 years of the entry into force of the START I Treaty was something of a step backward in terms of Ukraine's commitment to denuclearize quickly.

[4] The USA shall regard actions inconsistent with the commitments assumed under the Lisbon Protocol or the May 1992 letters from the heads of state as 'equivalent under international law to actions inconsistent with the START I treaty'. *Congressional Record*, 1 Oct. 1992, p. S15956; see also *The START Treaty*, Report of the Committee on Foreign Relations, US Senate, 102nd Congress, Executive Report 102-53 (US Government Printing Office: Washngton, DC, 1992), p. 82.

[5] US Arms Control and Disarmament Agency (ACDA), Office of Public Information, Fact Sheet, 11 Jan. 1994, p. 1.

[6] Joint Press Conference with US President Bill Clinton and Kazakh President Nursultan Nazarbayev, Washington, DC, 14 Feb. 1994, Federal News Service (hereafter FNS) Transcript.

[7] ACDA (note 5), p. 1; Lockwood, D., 'Ukrainian Rada ratifies START I, but adds 13 conditions for approval', *Arms Control Today*, vol. 23, no. 10 (Dec. 1993), pp. 17, 26. See also the 1993 Resolution of the Ukrainian Parliament on Ratification of the START I Treaty and the Lisbon Protocol, in appendix 16A.

which requires Ukraine to accede to the NPT as a non-nuclear weapon state 'in the shortest possible time'.

The Ukrainian Rada also stated that only 36 per cent of the launchers and 42 per cent of the nuclear warheads on Ukrainian territory would be subject to elimination. (These percentages are based on the cuts that the USSR was projected to make from the levels of forces it deployed when the Treaty was signed, i.e., from 2500 launchers to 1600, and from 10 345 warheads to 6000.)[8] It also insisted on sweeping security guarantees: that the nuclear powers will 'never use nuclear weapons against Ukraine, never use conventional forces against it, refrain from threat of force . . . respect the territory of the borders of Ukraine, and refrain from economic pressure as a means of resolving any disputes'.

In other key conditions, the Rada stated that it would not exchange the instruments of ratification until after Ukraine had been assured the right to monitor the dismantlement of any warheads transferred from Ukraine; had received adequate compensation for the warheads' fissile material, including the material in tactical warheads withdrawn to Russia in 1992; and had received 'sufficient international financial and technical assistance'.[9]

The Russian–US–Ukrainian Trilateral Statement

On 14 January 1994, the presidents of Russia, the USA and Ukraine signed a nuclear weapon statement.[10] In the Trilateral Statement, Presidents Bill Clinton and Boris Yeltsin informed President Leonid Kravchuk that, once the START I Treaty enters into force and Ukraine accedes to the NPT as a non-nuclear weapon state, the USA and Russia will 'reaffirm their commitment to Ukraine, in accordance with the principles of the CSCE [Conference on Security and Co-operation in Europe] Final Act [of 1975], to respect the independence and sovereignty and the existing borders of the CSCE member states and recognize that border changes can be made only by peaceful and consensual means'. Also in accordance with the CSCE Final Act, they reaffirmed their commit to refrain from 'economic coercion'. In addition, the USA and Russia reiterated the standard 'positive' and 'negative' security assurances they make to all non-nuclear weapon parties to the NPT. The Trilateral Statement noted that the UK, the third NPT depositary state, is 'prepared to offer the same security assurances to Ukraine once it becomes a non-nuclear weapon state party to the NPT'. The Statement also commits the USA to

---

[8] Although the Rada did not provide any breakdown on which of the weapons on Ukrainian territory would be eliminated, one can assume that all or at least most of the reductions would come from the older, liquid-fuel SS-19 ICBM forces.

[9] In 1993 Ukrainian officials usually said that they needed $2.8 billion in assistance for weapon dismantlement—a sum that apparently includes money for environmental clean-up and assistance for any local economic problems caused by the elimination of the weapons, e.g., job training and housing for the former Strategic Rocket Forces. It should be noted that this figure has varied a great deal among Ukrainian officials and rose continuously in 1992 and 1993.

[10] For the text of the Trilateral Statement and Annex, see appendix 16A; and *Arms Control Today*, Jan./Feb. 1994, pp. 21–23.

'work intensively . . . to expand' its 'Nunn–Lugar assistance' to the four former Soviet republics with nuclear weapons on their territories.[11]

The Annex to the Trilateral Statement states that within 10 months of signature (by 14 November 1994) all 46 of the SS-24 ICBMs on Ukrainian territory will be deactivated 'by having their warheads removed'. The Trilateral Statement differs significantly from previous accords in that it requires near-term action. While the Annex makes no mention of the deactivation schedule for Ukraine's 130 SS-19s, Ukraine has already removed at least 20 of these missiles from their silos and is committed to continue deactivating all those systems as well.[12] During the 10-month period, at least 200 of Ukraine's 1240 SS-24 and SS-19 warheads are to be transferred to Russia, where Ukrainian representatives will monitor their dismantlement.[13] The Annex states that all warheads on Ukrainian territory would be transferred to Russia 'during the seven-year period as provided by the START I treaty', but press reports said that President Kravchuk agreed in a letter to Yeltsin that all the warheads would be withdrawn within three years.[14] In a letter from President Yeltsin to President Kravchuk, Russia agreed to write off some of Ukraine's debt for past deliveries of oil and natural gas in compensation for the 2000–3000 tactical warheads that were withdrawn from Ukraine to Russia in 1992. (In the weeks following the January 1994 Moscow summit meeting, Russian and Ukrainian experts, along with US experts who played the role of 'honest brokers', assessed the value of the highly enriched uranium [HEU] in those weapons.) Both these letters were kept confidential in deference to domestic political sensitivities in Ukraine and Russia.

Ukraine's compensation for the HEU contained in the strategic warheads withdrawn from its territory, worth about $1 billion—a sum which represents Ukraine's share of the HEU Agreement signed by the USA and Russia in February 1993 (see section VI below)—will come in the form of low-enriched uranium (LEU) to fuel its civilian power reactors. Under the terms of the Agreement, the US Enrichment Corporation will over 20 years purchase from Russia approximately $11.9 billion worth of reactor-grade uranium derived from 500 tonnes of HEU extracted from dismantled nuclear warheads. The USA stipulated that the HEU Agreement could not be executed until Russia has worked out bilateral agreements with Belarus, Kazakhstan and Ukraine on sharing the proceeds.

---

[11] This refers to assistance under the US 1991 Soviet Nuclear Threat Reduction Act, sponsored by Senators Sam Nunn and Richard Lugar; for background, see *SIPRI Yearbook 1993* (note 1), chapter 11, p. 566; and section VI below.

[12] See, for example, Mann, P., 'Ukrainian SS-24s slated for prompt deactivation', *Aviation Week & Space Technology*, 24 Jan. 1994, p. 39.

[13] Prior to the signing of the Trilateral Statement, Ukraine had already been monitoring the dismantlement of tactical nuclear warheads withdrawn to Russia. See National Academy of Sciences (NAS), *Management and Disposition of Excess Weapons Plutonium* (National Academy Press: Washington, DC, 1994), p. 105.

[14] Smith, R. J., 'US, Ukraine, Russia near deal on arms', *Washington Post*, 9 Jan. 1994, p. A33; Smith, R. J. and Belliveau, J., 'Dismantling Ukraine's warheads', *Washington Post*, 15 Jan. 1994, p. A15.

In response to Ukraine's insistence that it receive compensation simultaneously with the initiation of warhead withdrawal, the Trilateral Statement Annex states that within 10 months—the same amount of time as for the withdrawal of the first 200 ICBMs from Ukraine—Russia will provide Ukraine with 100 t of LEU fuel for nuclear power stations. The Annex specifies that the USA 'will provide $60 million as an advance payment to Russia to be deducted from payments due to Russia under the highly enriched uranium contract. These funds would be available to help cover expenses for the transportation and dismantling of strategic warheads and the production of fuel assemblies'. Subsequent Russian deliveries of LEU to Ukraine are also intended to correspond to the pace of warhead withdrawals.

After the signing of the Trilateral Statement, President Kravchuk argued that the terms—the security assurances, assistance, compensation and Russia's continued maintenance of nuclear missile systems—fulfilled the conditions established by the Rada in its 18 November 1993 resolution regarding ratification of the START I Treaty.[15]

In tacit approval of this position, the Rada overwhelmingly approved a resolution on 3 February 1994 instructing Kravchuk to exchange the instruments of ratification for the START I Treaty. In addition, the resolution acknowledged that the Lisbon Protocol obligation to accede to the NPT does apply to Ukraine—rescinding the Rada's earlier position.[16]

The Rada also held a separate vote on the same day on immediate accession to the NPT in which 193 deputies voted to join the Treaty, 27 voted against and 11 abstained. However, the measure failed by a few dozen votes to achieve the number required by the Ukrainian Constitution to pass legislation, apparently because a large number of the 450 members were absent, campaigning for the 27 March elections.[17] The Rada then deferred another vote on NPT accession, referring the issue to committee for consideration and probably postponing a vote until after the new parliament convenes.

The Rada's failure to vote to accede to the NPT complicates a number of issues. The key security assurances that Ukraine has sought from the USA and Russia are contingent upon Ukraine's accession to the NPT as a non-nuclear weapon state. Ironically, the failure to accede to the NPT will deny Ukraine the security assurances that appeared to be a key factor in its 3 February 1994 decision to effectively drop its conditions for ratifying the START I Treaty. Another problem is that the Russian Parliament stipulated in its resolution of ratification of the START I Treaty in November 1992 that Russia would not exchange the instruments of ratification for START I until after Ukraine

[15] Ukrainian President Leonid Kravchuk, Press Conference, Moscow, 14 Jan. 1994, FNS Transcript, p. 6. For the text of the 1993 Rada resolution, see appendix 16A.
[16] For the text of the 1994 Rada resolution, see appendix 16A. The Rada vote appeared to be influenced by a number of factors: the election of a pro-secessionist president in Crimea; recent indications that Ukraine might divide along ethnic and geographic lines; the free fall of Ukraine's economy; and Ukraine's continued near-total dependence on Russia for energy.
[17] 'Supreme Council passes resolution', Moscow INTERFAX, 3 Feb. 1994, in Foreign Broadcast Information Service, *Daily Report–Central Eurasia* (hereafter FBIS-SOV), FBIS-SOV-94-024, 4 Feb. 1994, p. 46; see also Seely, R., 'A-Arms pacts approved in Ukraine', *Washington Post*, 4 Feb. 1994, p. A1; Lippman, T. W., 'Clinton increases aid, support to Ukraine', *Washington Post*, 5 Mar. 1994, p. A15.

acceded to the NPT. Thus, unless Russia changes its current position, START I cannot enter into force until after Ukraine accedes to the NPT.

Arguments used to persuade the Rada to ratify the START I Treaty

During the debate prior to the Rada's vote on the 3 February 1994 resolution, President Kravchuk and his foreign and defence ministers presented several arguments in favour of unconditional START I Treaty ratification and NPT accession. They argued that approval of these treaties would lead to increased economic aid and security assurances, while failure to do so would lead to Ukraine's international isolation.[18] In a relatively new argument—used more frequently by Russia than Ukraine in the past—Ukrainian leaders asserted that the nuclear warheads on Ukrainian territory were becoming unsafe and could pose a serious hazard to Ukraine's environment if not withdrawn soon to Russia. Borrowing a line from Russian Foreign Minister Andrey Kozyrev, Ukrainian Defence Minister Vitaly Radetsky told the Rada that if the warheads were not transferred to Russia in the near future, this could 'lead to a catastrophe potentially bigger than Chernobyl'.[19]

Although the unpredictable political situation in Ukraine raised questions about whether Ukraine's new parliament would ultimately honour Kiev's obligations to denuclearize, there was some reason to be optimistic in early 1994, as Ukraine and Russia began to implement the Trilateral Statement with transfers of ICBM warheads and fuel rods.[20]

III. The START II Treaty[21]

The landmark START II Treaty was signed by US President George Bush and Russian President Boris Yeltsin in Moscow on 3 January 1993. The Treaty requires the USA and Russia to reduce the number of their deployed strategic nuclear warheads to 3000–3500 each by 1 January 2003. (However, the parties agreed that the reductions could be implemented by 31 December 2000 if the USA provides Russia with sufficient assistance in dismantling its strategic offensive arms.) It also mandates the elimination of all MIRVed (equipped with multiple independently targetable re-entry vehicles) and heavy

---

[18] 'Zlenko on nuclear weapons', Kiev Radio, 3 Feb. 1994, in FBIS-SOV-94-025, 7 Feb. 1994, p. 43; 'Defence Minister warns on danger of old warheads', *Moscow SEGODNYA*, 4 Feb. 1994, p. 1, in FBIS-SOV-94-025, 7 Feb. 1994, p. 45.

[19] Poletz, L., 'Ukraine moves on 1 nuclear pact, delays on another', *Washington Times*, 4 Feb. 1994, p. A14; 'Radetsky addresses Supreme Council on START', Kiev Radio, 3 Feb. 1994, in FBIS-SOV-94-025, 7 Feb. 1994, pp. 41–42; 'Defence Minister warns on danger of old warheads' (note 18), p. 45; see also 'Kravchuk urges Supreme Council to ratify START I, 3 Feb. 1994', in FBIS-SOV-94-024, 4 Feb. 1994, pp. 42, 44.

[20] Lepingwell, J., 'Ukraine receives nuclear fuel', Radio Free Europe/Radio Liberty (hereafter RFE/RL), *RFE/RL Daily Report*, no. 65 (6 Apr. 1994); 'Moscow Trilateral Statement implementation begins', *Arms Control Today*, May 1994, p. 24.

[21] A summary and detailed analysis of the provisions, as well as the Treaty text, are provided in *SIPRI Yearbook 1993* (note 1), pp. 554–59, 576–89.

ICBMs and caps the number of warheads that may be deployed on submarine-launched ballistic missiles (SLBMs) at 1750.

Ratification and implementation

Three steps must be taken before the START II Treaty can enter into force: the START I Treaty must enter into force; the US Senate must provide its advice and consent; and the Russian Parliament must ratify the Treaty.

As stated above, the START I Treaty cannot enter into force until Ukraine agrees to accede to the NPT as a non-nuclear weapon state. With respect to US approval of the START II Treaty, it is clear the Treaty enjoys overwhelming support in the Senate and is expected to pass by more than the two-thirds margin required. (START I was approved by a vote of 93–6.) The Bush Administration submitted the START II Treaty to the Senate in January 1993, and the Senate Foreign Relations Committee (SFRC) conducted four hearings with Clinton (and former Bush) Administration officials in 1993, starting with Secretary of State Warren Christopher on 11 May. Subsequently, however, because the START I Treaty had not entered into force and the political instability and uncertainty in Russia had increased, the Clinton Administration and the SFRC decided that it was not the appropriate time to continue the START II Treaty ratification process. Consequently, as of early 1994 the SFRC had not yet heard planned testimony from the Secretary of Defense, the Joint Chiefs of Staff, the On-Site Inspection Agency (OSIA) or non-governmental witnesses and is not expected to prepare its report on the START II Treaty for the full Senate until at least late 1994.

Russia[22]

The Russian Parliament began consideration of the START II Treaty in early 1993 but gave it a relatively low priority in the wake of the political confrontation between President Yeltsin and the Parliament. During the course of the year, however, it became clear that there was substantial opposition to the Treaty. A number of members of parliament, newspaper editorial writers and think-tank analysts publicly criticized the agreement in harsh terms.

Some of the criticism was based on general opposition to the perceived pro-Western direction of Russian foreign policy under President Yeltsin and Foreign Minister Andrey Kozyrev. In an example of opposition to the general policy rather than the merits of the Treaty itself, then Speaker of the Parliament Ruslan Khasbulatov said on 13 April 1993 that as long as Kozyrev is Foreign Minister, 'it is absurd to even talk about' START II ratification.[23]

---

[22] This section draws largely on Arbatov, A. (ed.), *Implications of the START II Treaty for US–Russian Relations*, Report No. 9 (Henry L. Stimson Center: Washington, DC, 1993), pp. 69–75; Sorokin, K. E., 'Russia after the crisis: the nuclear strategy debate', *Orbis*, vol. 38, no. 1 (winter 1994), pp. 19–40.

[23] *Washington Times*, 14 Apr. 1993, p. 2; Lockwood, D., 'Russian turmoil, Ukrainian action delay START I implementation', *Arms Control Today*, May 1993, p. 23.

Some of the critics charged that the START II Treaty was totally unacceptable to Russia and should be jettisoned altogether, while others argued that the Treaty's perceived inequities could be redressed through the negotiation of amendments or new, supplemental agreements prior to entry into force.

One of the major arguments against the START II Treaty put forward by Russian critics is that the accord would require Russia to eliminate the principal component of its deterrent force—its MIRVed ICBMs—while the accord would allow the USA to retain the principal component of its deterrent force—the Trident SLBMs.[24] Consequently, Russia would have to go through the costly and time-consuming process of completely restructuring the composition of its strategic triad, while the USA could keep its triad intact, including the forces in which it enjoys technological advantages. In a related argument, opponents of the Treaty claim that the cost of dismantling Russian strategic weapons would be prohibitive. Russian critics also argued that the USA would be in a far better position than Russia to break out of the Treaty by quickly 'uploading' its Trident missiles to eight warheads each and deploying its B-1B bombers with nuclear rather than conventional weapons.[25]

It is not clear that the Russian Parliament elected in December 1993 will be any more likely to ratify the START II Treaty than the previous one, elected when the USSR still existed. Thus, Russian ratification of the START II Treaty, unlike US ratification, is far from a foregone conclusion.

IV. No-first-use and negative security assurances

The United States

In October 1993, then US Defense Secretary Les Aspin announced that the Department of Defense (DOD) planned to conduct a Nuclear Posture Review,[26] scheduled for completion in 1994. Among other things, the Review will address the issue of whether the USA should maintain its policy of providing 'negative security assurances' to non-nuclear weapon states and whether to adopt a new 'no-first-use' policy.[27] The conclusions on these two issues could have a profound effect on US non-proliferation policy if they reverse long-standing US positions. The USA has never committed itself to saying that it would not use nuclear weapons first under any circumstances. In fact, US policy in Europe during the cold war was based on retaining the option to use nuclear weapons first, and NATO still maintains this option as a 'last resort'. However, in 1978 the Carter Administration stated that the USA

---

[24] In Jan. 1994, some 55% of Russia's strategic warheads were deployed on ICBMs; approximately 35% of the US strategic warheads were deployed on SLBMs.

[25] For a discussion of START II Treaty rules governing the 'downloading' of strategic ballistic missiles and the reorienting of heavy bombers to conventional missions, see *SIPRI Yearbook 1993* (note 1), pp. 554–55.

[26] See chapter 8, section IV, in this volume.

[27] See, for example, Les Aspin, Secretary of Defense, *Annual Report to the President and the Congress*, Jan. 1994, pp. 7–8; Lockwood, D., 'Pentagon begins policy review of post-cold war nuclear strategy', *Arms Control Today*, vol. 23, no. 10 (Dec. 1993), pp. 23, 27.

'will not use nuclear weapons against any non-nuclear weapon state party to the NPT or any comparable internationally binding commitment not to acquire nuclear explosive devices, except in the case of an attack on the United States, or its territories or armed forces, or its allies, by such a state allied to a nuclear-weapon state or associated with a nuclear-weapon state in carrying out or sustaining the attack'.[28] Subsequent US administrations, including the Clinton Administration, have reaffirmed this policy.[29]

The negative security assurances policy is designed to provide an incentive to encourage countries to adhere to the NPT as non-nuclear weapon states. However, in the wake of the collapse of the strategic East–West confrontation and the increased concerns about North–South regional conflicts, there is now a movement afoot to alter this policy. For example, General Lee Butler, then head of the Strategic Command (STRATCOM), said in 1993 that the USA should be prepared to use nuclear weapons, as well as conventional weapons, against countries that possess or are seeking to possess chemical or biological weapons.[30] Butler and other senior US military officials have argued that the USA needs to improve its ability to retarget nuclear forces quickly so that it could carry out such missions.[31] In January 1994, then Secretary of Defense Les Aspin said, 'Since the United States has forsworn chemical and biological weapons, the role of US nuclear forces in deterring or responding to such non-nuclear threats must be considered'.[32]

Russia

In a 3 November 1993 press conference, Defence Minister Pavel Grachev made it clear that Russia's newly adopted military doctrine does not reaffirm the pledge made in 1982 by Leonid Brezhnev that the USSR would not be the first to use nuclear weapons under any circumstances.[33] Russia announced its new policy on 'negative security assurances', which was first announced at the

---

[28] US Arms Control and Disarmament Agency, *Documents on Disarmament 1978* (US Government Printing Office: Washington, DC, 1980), p. 384. (The qualifying clauses in this statement were intended to preserve the option of using nuclear weapons against North Korea or non-Soviet Warsaw Pact countries.)

[29] For the latest reaffirmation of the US policy on 'negative security' assurances, see John Holum, Director, US Arms Control and Disarmament Agency (ACDA), speech to the Conference on Disarmament, Geneva, Switzerland, 25 Jan. 1994, p. 6.

[30] 'Targeting rethink may lead to non-nuclear STRATCOM role', *Jane's Defence Weekly*, 22 May 1993, p. 19; Schmitt, E., 'Head of nuclear forces plans for a new world', *New York Times*, 25 Feb. 1993, p. B7.

[31] General Lee Butler, Commander-in-Chief, US Strategic Command, Statement before the Senate Armed Services Committee, 22 Apr. 1993, FNS Transcript, p. 3; Department of Defense Authorization for Appropriations, Fiscal Year 1994, Rear Admiral John Mitchell, UN Navy, Director, Strategic Systems Program Office, Prepared statement submitted to the Committee on Armed Services, US Senate, 103rd Congress, Senate hearing 103-303 (US Government Printing Office: Washington, DC, 1993), Part 7, p. 17.

[32] Aspin (note 27), p. 61.

[33] Hiatt, F., 'Russia shifts doctrine on military use', *Washington Post*, 4 Nov. 1993, p. A33. See also Lockwood, D., 'Russia revises nuclear policy, ends Soviet "no-first-use" pledge', *Arms Control Today*, vol. 23, no. 10 (Dec. 1993), p. 19.

Conference on Disarmament (CD) in Geneva on 17 August 1993.[34] Russia's latest iteration of its negative security assurances policy is contained in the Trilateral Statement (see section II above), only slightly changing its previous statements.

Consequently, at the declaratory level, the new Russian policies on 'first-use' and negative security assurances are now very similar to long-standing British, French and US policies. (US Secretary of State Warren Christopher has said that 'the United States and its allies never took the old Soviet doctrine [of first-use] as a serious indication of what the USSR might actually do with its massive arsenal of nuclear weapons'.[35]) The changes in Russia's positions appear to be intended to send a clear message to Ukraine that it should accede to the NPT and transfer all the nuclear warheads on its territory to Russia. (The message may also be meant for China's consumption.) In addition, the new doctrine may be intended to discourage former Soviet republics and former Warsaw Pact states from joining NATO. Finally, the changes in declaratory policy may reflect a sense in Moscow that Russia must now rely more on nuclear weapons both for deterrence and for its status as a major world power.[36] In this context, US intelligence believes that programmes to maintain and modernize Russian strategic forces will continue to be 'relatively well financed'.[37]

China

In the wake of international criticism of its continued nuclear testing, China has stepped up its advocacy for the universal adoption of a no-first-use policy. On 5 October 1993, the day China conducted the only nuclear test of the year, the Chinese Foreign Ministry issued the following statement:

China believes that a pledge by all nuclear-weapon states not to use nuclear weapons at all is of even greater significance [than a CTBT] as it is a more effective step towards the non-proliferation goal underscored by the Treaty on the Non-Proliferation of Nuclear Weapons. To this end, China strongly calls for a parallel negotiation [to the CTB negotiation] by all nuclear-weapon states aimed at concluding an international convention on unconditional non-first-use of nuclear weapons and non-use and non-threat of use of nuclear weapons against non-nuclear states and nuclear-free zones.[38]

---

[34] See Conference on Disarmament, Final Record of the Six Hundred and Sixty-First Plenary Meeting, Geneva, CD document CD/PV.661, 17 Aug. 1993, pp. 4–5; and Bunn, G. and Timerbaev, R., 'Security assurances to non-nuclear weapons states', *Nonproliferation Review,* vol. 1, no. 1 (fall 1993), p. 15.
[35] Warren Christopher, US Secretary of State, Spoken statement before the Senate Foreign Relations Committee, 4 Nov. 1993, FNS Transcript, p. 17.
[36] Lt-General James. R. Clapper, Jr, Director, US Defense Intelligence Agency (DIA), Spoken statement before the Senate Select Intelligence Committee, 25 Jan. 1994, FNS Transcript, pp. 40–41; see also Hiatt, F., 'Russians favoring retention of nuclear deterrent', *Washington Post,* 25 Nov. 1992, p. A1.
[37] Clapper, Written statement to the Senate Select Intelligence Committee (note 36), p. 4.
[38] 'Statement of the Government of the People's Republic of China on the question of nuclear testing, 5 Oct. 1993', in Institute for Defense and Disarmament Studies (IDDS), *Arms Control Reporter* (IDDS: Brookline, Mass.), sheet 608.D.9, Nov. 1993; see also Li, D., 'Foreign policy and arms control, the view

The United Kingdom

Defence Minister Malcolm Rifkind has also recently contributed to the debate on no-first-use and negative security assurances. On 16 November 1993, Rifkind said that he was 'deeply sceptical of suggestions that NATO, or the United Kingdom, should make a declaration of no-first-use of nuclear weapons. The clear implication of any such declaration would be that conventional aggression could be undertaken without fear of crossing the nuclear threshold'. Rifkind also suggested that he might support amending the long-standing British policy of providing negative security assurances to non-nuclear weapon states by saying that these assurances 'were given in the context of the Cold War, when there was no appreciable risk of our facing a chemical or biological attack from any country outside the Warsaw Pact',[39] but the situation has changed today with the proliferation of such weapons of mass destruction.

V. The nuclear testing moratoria and CTB negotiations

Nuclear testing moratoria

In 1993 all of the nuclear powers, except for China, observed unilaterally declared moratoria on nuclear testing. This manifestation of a commitment to end nuclear testing provided an important impetus for new multilateral negotiations for a comprehensive test ban treaty which began in the Conference on Disarmament in January 1994. In addition, moratoria are concrete steps that the nuclear powers can point to as good-faith efforts to fulfil their NPT obligations to seek an end to the nuclear arms race if a CTBT is not achieved by April 1995, when the parties to the NPT convene to consider the extension of that treaty.[40]

The United States

In October 1992, then President Bush signed congressional legislation, referred to as the Hatfield Amendment, into law.[41] This law required an immediate moratorium on all US testing until at least 1 July 1993 and called on the USA to negotiate a CTB by 1996. On 3 July 1993, President Clinton announced that the USA would extend that moratorium 'at least through September of next year [1994], as long as no other nation tests' and called on

---

from China', *Arms Control Today*, Dec. 1993, p. 9; Shen, D., 'Toward a nuclear-weapon-free world: a Chinese perspective', *Bulletin of the Atomic Scientists*, Mar./Apr. 1994, pp. 51–54.

[39] Malcolm Rifkind, British Defence Minister, Address before the Centre for Defence Studies, London, 16 Nov. 1993.

[40] See chapter 15 in this volume for an account of the issues related to the 1995 NPT Review and Extension Conference; see appendix 8A for the nuclear explosions conducted since 1945.

[41] The Hatfield Amendment was one section in the FY 1993 Energy and Water Development Appropriations Act, which included $517 million for the Superconducting Super Collider, an $8 billion project located in Texas, a key state in Bush's re-election effort. For the text of the Hatfield Amendment, see *Congressional Record*, 24 Sep. 1992, p. H9424.

'the other nuclear powers to do the same'. Clinton said that his decision to extend the US moratorium was based on his Administration's assessment that although 'additional nuclear tests could provide for some additional improvements in safety and reliability . . . the price we would pay in conducting those tests now, by undercutting our own non-proliferation goals and ensuring that other nations would resume testing, outweighs these benefits'. However, he added an important caveat: 'if . . . this moratorium is broken by another nation' he would direct the Department of Energy (DOE) 'to prepare to conduct additional tests, while seeking approval to do so from Congress'[42]—a policy that came to be known as 'no-first-test'.

After China conducted a test on 5 October 1993 at Lop Nor, the White House expressed its regrets and urged Beijing to refrain from further tests and join 'a global moratorium'. The White House statement said that Clinton's decision on whether to resume testing would be based on:

fundamental US national security interests, taking into account: the contribution further tests would make to improving the safety and reliability of the US arsenal in preparation for a Comprehensive Test Ban (CTB); the extent to which China and others have responded to the US appeal for a global moratorium on testing; progress in the CTB negotiations; the implications of further US nuclear tests on our broader non-proliferation objectives.[43]

This White House statement, combined with press reports citing anonymous Administration officials, suggested that the USA had backed away from a commitment to an automatic resumption of testing which was implicit in the president's 'no-first-test' policy announced on 3 July.[44]

On 14 March 1994, President Clinton notified Congress that he would extend the US moratorium through September 1995—well beyond the NPT Review and Extension Conference which convenes in April 1995. Clinton based his decision on the criteria he had laid out in October 1993, citing progress in the CTB negotiations and the importance of extending the NPT indefinitely.[45] It now seems very unlikely that the Clinton Administration would push for a resumption of US nuclear testing after September 1995, but if the USA were to make such a decision—under the terms of the Hatfield Amendment—it may conduct a total of five more tests until 30 September

[42] President Clinton's weekly radio address, 3 July 1993, FNS Transcript. During the Administration's internal debate prior to the 3 July announcement, the executive branch considered exempting tests below 1 kt from the Hatfield Amendment restrictions and conducting up to 9 safety and reliability tests before halting testing in 1996; see Lockwood, D., 'Clinton moving away from one-kiloton testing proposal', Arms Control Today, June 1993, p. 23; Lockwood, D., 'Clinton Administration considers plan for nuclear tests', Arms Control Today, July/Aug. 1993, p. 20.

[43] White House Statement, 5 Oct. 1993; see also Lockwood, D., 'China's nuclear test prompts US, others to review test policies', Arms Control Today, Nov. 1993, p. 20.

[44] See, for example, Zamora-Collina, T., 'China bucks ban with bang', Bulletin of the Atomic Scientists, Dec. 1993, p. 3.

[45] The President's Annual Report to the Congress on Nuclear Weapons Testing submitted pursuant to Section 507 of the Energy and Water Development Appropriations Act, 1993, Public Law 102-377 (the Hatfield Amendment), 14 Mar. 1994, pp. 1–3; Statement by the Press Secretary, The White House, 15 Mar. 1994, p. 1; Lippman, T. W. and Marcus, R., 'Moratorium on testing nuclear weapons to extend to 1995', Washington Post, 16 Mar. 1994, p. A14. See also chapter 15 in this volume.

1996 and then cease testing 'unless a foreign state conducts a nuclear test after this date'. (In addition, the Hatfield Amendment stipulates that only one of the five remaining tests could be conducted by the UK if the US President 'determines that it is in the national interests of the United States to do so'.)

Russia

Russia, which has not conducted a nuclear test since becoming the successor state to the former USSR (which conducted its last test on 24 October 1990), indicated after the Chinese test that it did not intend to resuming testing.[46] Although his ministers of atomic energy and defence have suggested in the past that they would like to resume testing at Novaya Zemlya,[47] President Yeltsin has consistently supported an extension of the moratorium and the negotiation of a CTB. In addition to its publicly stated objective of curbing nuclear proliferation, Russia has both environmental and economic reasons for not testing. The US Central Intelligence Agency (CIA) said in 1993 that 'domestic and Scandinavian environmental organizations have publicized concerns about radioactive pollution in the Russian Arctic area' partially due to testing, and added that 'Russia would be hard pressed to devote the resources necessary for a full-fledged nuclear testing program given its current economic crisis'.[48] Nuclear testing at the Semipalatinsk site in Kazakhstan is not an option for Russia because the Kazakh President closed that site in August 1991.[49]

France

France officially announced in April 1992 that it would suspend its testing programme for the rest of that year. In January 1993, at the Paris signing ceremony for the Chemical Weapons Convention, French President François Mitterrand extended the moratorium, contingent on the restraint of other nuclear weapon powers.[50] On 4 July, one day after Clinton announced his decision to extend the US moratorium, the French Government issued a statement saying that 'France confirms that she is in favour of a comprehensive test ban treaty, on the condition that is universal and verifiable'.[51] After

[46] 'Russia to continue testing moratorium', *RFE/RL Daily Report,* no. 204 (22 Oct. 1993); 'Russia to observe test ban despite Chinese blast', Reuter (Moscow), 21 Oct. 1993.
[47] See, for example, Hiatt, F., 'Russia extends test ban', *Washington Post,* 14 Oct. 1992, pp. 1, 24; Burbyga, N. 'Inspection in Novaya Zemlya', *Izvestia,* 25 Sep. 1992, p. 2, in FBIS-SOV-92-190, 30 Sep. 1992, p. 3; 'G-7 talks on nuclear moratorium may meet resistance', *Kommersant Daily,* 9 July 1993, p. 4, in FBIS-SOV-93-131, 12 July 1993, p. 16.
[48] *Proliferation Threats of the 1990s,* Hearing before the Committee on Governmental Affairs, US Senate, 103rd Congress, Senate hearing 103-208 (US Government Printing Office: Washington, DC, 1993), p. 147.
[49] 'President's decree closing Semipalatinsk reported', Alma-Ata Kazakh radio network, 29 Aug. 1991, in FBIS-SOV-91-169, 30 Aug. 1991, p. 126.
[50] Drodziak, W., 'Historic pact bans chemical weapons', *Washington Post,* 14 Jan. 1993, p. A24.
[51] 'Nuclear tests', Communique Issued by the Presidency of the Republic in Paris, 4 July 1993, provided by the French Embassy Press and Information Service in Washington, DC, 9 July 1993.

China's test, Mitterrand made a number of statements suggesting that he would oppose a resumption of testing.[52]

While there is ample evidence that Mitterrand favours an extension of France's moratorium through the negotiation of a CTBT, there seems to be strong support in the French Parliament and especially in the Ministry of Defence for a resumption of testing. In July 1993, President Mitterrand and Prime Minister Edouard Balladur appointed a seven-member committee to determine whether France needs to resume testing. The committee's study, submitted to Balladur on 6 October, concluded that France could refrain from testing until at least mid-1995 (the date by which Mitterrand's term as president will have expired) but might have to resume testing at that point.[53] Defence Minister François Léotard took a similar tack, saying on 7 October 1993 that additional tests are needed to certify the nuclear warhead for the M-45 SLBM (additional tests may also be necessary for France to develop new warheads for the M-5 SLBM and the ASLP air-to-surface missile) and to develop a programme enabling France to simulate nuclear tests.[54] In a July 1993 report, the French Parliament's Finance Committee said that about 20 additional tests would be needed by 1996, in a programme known as 'PALEN', to fully develop the simulation techniques.[55] The French Government submitted a new defence White Paper to the Parliament on 23 February 1994 that said nothing about nuclear testing,[56] thereby indicating that the Defence Ministry would prefer to defer the fight on this issue until after Mitterrand leaves office in the spring of 1995.

The United Kingdom

During the Clinton Administration's internal debate in the spring of 1993 on whether to resume testing after the moratorium mandated by the Hatfield Amendment expired, the UK, which conducts its tests at the US Nevada Test Site, lobbied the State Department to oppose a moratorium extension. In fact, it has been reported that the next test scheduled at the Nevada Test Site before President Bush signed the legislation containing the Hatfield Amendment on

---

[52] Butcher, M., 'France will not test before May 1995', NATO Alerts Network, Briefing Notes, Oct. 1993; Buchanan, D., 'Mitterrand risks Paris split on N-weapons tests', *Financial Times*, 7 Oct. 1993, p. 2; *Wall Street Journal*, 7 Oct. 1993, p. 1.

[53] de Briganti, G., 'French right pushes for nuclear tests', *Defense News*, 11–17 Oct. 1993, p. 3; 'The price of independence', *The Economist*, 16 Oct. 1993, p. 58.

[54] de Briganti (note 53), p. 29; see also Butcher, M., 'Notes on NATO and European testing developments', NATO Alerts Network, Feb. 1994, p. 2.

[55] de Briganti (note 53), p. 29; Cue, E., 'France will not resume testing for now', UPI (Paris), 6 Oct. 1993; 'Une mission parlementaire estime que la France a encore besoin d'une vingtaine d'essais nucléaires', *Le Monde*, 17 Dec. 1993, p. 20.

[56] Butcher (note 54); de Briganti, G., 'French review evades nuclear issues', *Defense News*, 28 Feb.–6 Mar. 1994, p. 4; 'French defence: no change yet', *The Economist*, 19 Feb. 1994, p. 58.

2 October 1992 was for the UK.[57] Since the July 1993 US announcement, however, Britain has publicly accepted the US decision, albeit grudgingly.[58]

Britain had completed its tests on a warhead for the Trident II SLBM, but was interested in developing a version of that warhead with new safety features as well as a warhead for a new air-launched weapon for its Tornado aircraft.[59] In October 1993, however, the UK decided to cancel its nuclear tactical air-to-surface missile programme, primarily for budget reasons.

China

China, which conducted the only nuclear test in 1993, did not declare a testing moratorium and was therefore under no legal or political obligation not to test. It argued that the criticism levelled against it for conducting a test in 1993 was unjustified for several reasons. In an official statement issued by its Foreign Ministry on 5 October 1993, China said that it would never be the first to use nuclear weapons; that it has 'all along stood for the complete prohibition and thorough destruction of nuclear weapons'; and that history has shown that nuclear testing moratoria are 'designed [by the USA and Russia] to maintain nuclear superiority'.[60] China also pointed out that of the five declared nuclear weapon states, it has conducted the smallest number of tests.

In recent years, China has suggested that its support for a CTBT might be contingent upon the USA and Russia taking the lead in halting the testing and production of nuclear weapons and reducing their nuclear arsenals to a level close to China's.[61] It now appears that China is willing to negotiate a CTBT without any preconditions. In fact, China said in its 5 October 1993 statement that it would 'take an active part in the negotiating process and work together with other countries to conclude' a CTBT.[62] It added, however, that it would seek to negotiate a CTBT 'no later than 1996', implying that it intends to test until then.

A comprehensive test ban treaty

In 1993, international support for a CTBT became virtually universal. On 16 December the UN General Assembly adopted by consensus a resolution calling for the negotiation of a multilateral CTBT.[63] This was the first time

---

[57] *Trust and Verify*, Bulletin of the Verification Technology Information Centre (VERTIC), no. 32 (Oct. 1992), p. 1.

[58] For a compilation of quotations from the British Government on nuclear testing, see British American Security Information Council (BASIC), 'UK response to US testing moratorium—cautious but supportive' (BASIC: London, 16 July 1993).

[59] See, for example, Congressman John Spratt, *Congressional Record*, 29 Sep. 1993, p. E2279.

[60] *Arms Control Reporter* (note 38), sheet 608.D.9.

[61] 'First Supplementary List of Ratifications, Accessions, Withdrawals, Etc. for 1992', presented to the British Parliament by the Secretary of State for Foreign and Commonwealth Affairs by Command of Her Majesty, Oct. 1992 (Her Majesty's Stationery Office: London, Oct. 1992), p. 5; *Beijing Zhongguo Xinwen She*, 30 Jan. 1992, in *FBIS–China*, 30 Jan. 1992, in IDDS, *Arms Control Reporter*, sheet 408.B.137, Feb. 1992.

[62] *Arms Control Reporter* (note 61), sheet 608.D.9.

[63] UN General Assembly Resolution 48/70, UN document A/48/671, 16 Dec. 1993.

that the resolution had not been opposed by at least one of the declared nuclear weapon states since such resolutions were first offered at the UN in the 1950s.[64]

During consultations conducted in the second half of 1993, the declared nuclear weapon powers decided that multilateral CTB negotiations would be held in the CD. Before adjourning in September, the CD authorized the chairman of the *Ad Hoc* Committee on a Nuclear Test Ban, Yoshitomo Tanaka from Japan, to hold consultations on the organization and mandate for the CTB negotiations.

On 25 January 1994, the CD began its 1994 session and promptly passed the mandate for CTB negotiations that had been drafted in December 1993.[65] The mandate re-established the *Ad Hoc* Committee on a Nuclear Test Ban, directed that Committee to 'negotiate a universal and multilaterally and effectively verifiable comprehensive nuclear test ban treaty', and established working groups on verification and on legal and institutional issues. (The latter group is responsible for drafting all CTBT provisions except those related to verification.) In addition, the CD appointed Mexican Ambassador Miguel Marin Bosch to chair the *Ad Hoc* Committee, German Ambassador Wolfgang Hoffman to chair the verification working group, and Polish Ambassador Ludwik Dembinsi to chair the legal and institutional working group. The CD completed the first session at the end of March 1994, having produced a number of proposals on a CTBT from different countries but no official draft treaty text.

As the CD representatives prepare for the task of drafting a text for the CTBT in the second session, they will not be starting from scratch. A number of documents are available to provide a foundation from which to build the treaty. The CD has the language from the 1993 Chemical Weapons Convention (CWC) and the 1963 Partial Test Ban Treaty (PTBT), both of which have relevant sections (e.g., on verification, sanctions and definitions) to draw upon as a model for a number of provisions. Just before the CD adjourned, Australia formally submitted a draft treaty that draws heavily from the CWC.[66] In addition, Sweden formally tabled a new draft treaty at the CD on 6 December 1993, revising its earlier submissions.[67] As of the end of the first session, a number of substantive issues had emerged. Marin Bosch indicated that he expects to submit a chairman's draft treaty, based largely on the Australian draft and the text produced by the two working groups, during the second part of the 1994 session, scheduled to start on 16 May 1994.[68]

---

[64] See The President's Annual Report to the Congress on Nuclear Weapons Testing (note 45), pp. 2–3.

[65] See CD document CD/1238, 25 Jan. 1994.

[66] See the letter of 4 Jan. 1994 from Australia to the CD transmitting the text of a working paper entitled 'Comprehensive nuclear test ban treaty: a draft structural outline', in CD document CD/1235, 5 Jan. 1994; and 'Comprehensive test ban treaty: Australian resource paper on draft treaty elements, explanatory notes', CD document CD/NTB/WP.50, 30 Mar. 1994.

[67] Sweden's previous draft treaty was submitted in June 1993; see CD document CD/1202, CD/NTB/WP.19, 3 June 1993.

[68] Herby, P., 'Test ban and fissile material cutoff treaties still in "pre-negotiating mode" in the Conference on Disarmament', Conference on Disarmament Monitoring Project, Geneva, Report no. 3,

Positions on substantive CTB issues as of early 1994[69]

Duration

The Group of 21 (G-21)[70] submitted a list of proposals to the CD on 1 December 1993 calling for a CTB of 'unlimited' duration. The UK called for a treaty of 'indefinite duration', but would not 'rule out any provision for a review of the Treaty after a certain period'. Sweden's December 1993 draft treaty proposed duration of a 'permanent nature' with a review five years after entry into force and at intervals of five years thereafter if called for by a majority of the parties.

As of early 1994, the USA had not put forward a formal proposal on this issue. It has been reported, however, that the USA had floated a proposal at one point during a series of bilateral consultations with other countries in 1993, calling for a duration of 10 years, to be followed by a conference of the parties and the continuation of the treaty unless it was explicitly repudiated.

Definition

Most of the key countries seem to agree that it would not be productive to try to negotiate a precise definition of what constitutes a nuclear explosion. For example, the G-21 has suggested that 'the treaty should define in general terms the prohibition of nuclear tests in all environments and forever. It should avoid a detailed definition of what is a nuclear test'. This general approach, which is supported by a number of countries, including the USA[71] and the UK, has a precedent in both the PTBT and the NPT.

In a related development, some states have proposed that a CTBT should ban not only nuclear explosions but also other related activities. Sweden's draft treaty—but not that of Australia—advocates a ban on *preparations* for a nuclear test, such as drilling and excavating. The USA has said that it has 'strong doubts regarding pre-test verification', contending that such verifica-

11 Mar. 1994, p. 2; Nebehay, S. (Reuter), 'Global nuclear test ban seen by early 1995', 30 Mar. 1994; Lockwood, D., 'Conference on Disarmament sees progress toward a CTB treaty', *Arms Control Today*, May 1994, p. 17.

[69] Unless stated otherwise, the positions listed in this section come from the following documents: Group of 21 working paper, 'Conclusion of a comprehensive nuclear-test-ban treaty', CD document CD/1231, 1 Dec. 1993; Draft treaty submitted to the CD by Swedish Ambassador Lars Norberg, CD document CD/1232, CD/NTB/WP.33, 6 Dec. 1993; Statement to the CD presented by British Ambassador Michael Weston on 25 Jan. 1994; Statement to the CD presented by US Ambassador Stephen Ledogar, CD document CD/PV.669, 3 Feb. 1994; and Hou Zhitong, Head of the Delegation of the People's Republic of China, Statement at the Conference on Disarmament, CD document CD/PV.676, 24 Mar. 1994.

[70] The G-21 (formerly the group of non-aligned countries) now consists of 19 countries: Algeria, Argentina, Brazil, Cuba, Egypt, Ethiopia, India, Indonesia, Iran, Kenya, Mexico, Morocco, Myanmar, Nigeria, Pakistan, Peru, Sri Lanka, Venezuela and Zaire. Sweden has declared itself independent, and Yugoslavia is banned from participation in the CD.

[71] Although the USA opposes the exclusion of threshold and peaceful nuclear explosions, it has made it clear that it believes that 'hydronuclear events' and inertial confinement fusion experiments should not be prohibited in a CTBT. See also Schaper, A., 'The problem of definition', in Arnett, E. (ed.), *Implementing a Comprehensive Test Ban*, SIPRI Research Report No. 8 (Oxford University Press: Oxford, forthcoming in 1994); and Bunn, G. and Timerbaev, R., 'Avoiding the "definition" pitfall to a comprehensive test ban', *Arms Control Today*, May 1993, pp. 15–18.

tion could not be achieved 'without considerable technical and political difficulty and enormous increase in cost'. In a proposal that goes much further than banning preparations for underground tests, Indonesia has proposed that computer simulations for nuclear warhead development be prohibited as well—a position that most observers consider unenforceable.

One potentially contentious issue that has arisen is whether so-called peaceful nuclear explosions (PNEs) should be permitted under a CTBT. On 24 March 1994, Chinese Ambassador Hou Zhitong proposed an alternative definition that would implicitly permit PNEs, saying that a CTBT 'should prohibit at any place and in any environment, any nuclear *weapon* test explosion of any form which releases nuclear energy'.[72] Ambassador Hou also appeared to revive an earlier Chinese position when he said that the CTBT 'should contain provisions' committing nuclear weapon states to a no-first-use policy. A senior US official, however, has emphasized that China is seeking a separate no-first-use pledge in the CD *Ad Hoc* Committee on Negative Security Assurances and has not pressed for any formal linkage with the CTBT.[73]

France and Britain have floated proposals reserving the right to conduct 'safety tests' after the CTBT enters into force. As a senior Clinton Administration official put it, France has 'put down a marker' indicating that under a CTBT it would like to conduct a nuclear test for safety purposes 'every fifth or tenth year'. In response to the French proposal, the official said, 'we've told them, and many other participants [at the CD] have told them that that's a non-starter . . . it is just not going to be in the cards'. He reported that Britain is also calling for 'periodic safety tests' but noted that British safety tests would be precluded by the fact that the British tests are conducted in the USA, which is opposed to allowing any nuclear tests under a CTBT.[74]

Entry into force

During the first part of the 1994 session, the CD produced a number of different positions on entry into force, including the following. Sweden proposed that 'The treaty shall enter into force upon the deposit of instruments of ratification by forty states, including the [five declared] nuclear weapon states'. The USA said that although 'the US does not as yet have a fixed view on entry into force (EIF) . . . it is . . . essential that all nuclear weapons states be party to the treaty at EIF'.[75] The UK proposed that 'at a minimum, all members of the CD should ratify the Treaty before it enters into force'.[76] (The UK also supported expanding the CD's membership by adding 23 new states,

---

[72] Hou Zhitong (note 69), emphasis added.

[73] Senior Clinton Administration officials, Background briefing on a Comprehensive Test Ban Treaty, Department of State, Washington, DC, 14 Apr. 1994, FNS Transcript.

[74] See note 73; see also Lippman, T. W., '"An uphill slog" toward a nuclear test ban', *Washington Post*, 17 Apr. 1994, p. A31; and Johnson, R., *CD's First Session: Fissile Material Cut-off and Nuclear Test Ban Negotiations,* British American Security Information Council (BASIC) Report no. 37 (11 Apr. 1994), pp. 3–4.

[75] Ledogar (note 69).

[76] Weston (note 69).

including Iraq and North Korea.[77]) Russia proposed that the treaty enter into force after it has been ratified by 65 countries, provided that these include 'all states that on the date of the treaty's signature possess nuclear [power] stations and research reactors'.[78] (By comparison, the Chemical Weapons Convention enters into force two years after its opening for signature, or 180 days after it has been ratified by 65 countries, whichever is later.)

Sanctions

Both the USA and the UK have said that the CWC provides a good starting-point for determining what measures should be taken against states that violate the CTBT. The CWC stipulates that in the case of violation of 'particular gravity', the parties shall bring the issue to the UN Security Council to consider sanctions. In addition, the Australian draft treaty includes a similar article for 'non-compliance'.

Verification

Although it is widely agreed that the CTBT verification regime should include a global seismological network supplemented by atmospheric sampling for radio-nuclides and gaseous debris, and on-site inspections, there are still a number of contentious points. Sweden has proposed giving the International Atomic Energy Agency (IAEA) the responsibility for verifying a CTBT. (In February 1994, the IAEA deputy director for external affairs told the CD that CTBT verification would not be inconsistent with the IAEA Charter and the Agency would be interested in this new responsibility if given sufficient resources.) In contrast, the Australian draft calls for the establishment of a new implementing body, modelled after the verification provisions in the CWC. In addition, the USA has expressed serious 'reservations' about assigning CTBT verification responsibilities to the IAEA, arguing that the Agency, which has not had its budget increased in real terms since 1984, already has as much as it can handle with its current NPT responsibilities and likely future tasks related to the proposed treaty on a fissile material production cut-off. The G-21, for its part, has proposed that the decision on an appropriate verification regime should not complicate the entry into force of the CTBT.

---

[77] A total of 38 states participate in the CD, and 50 additional states have applied for membership. It is recommended that membership be 'reviewed' in 1994. The 23 states to be considered for admission include Austria, Bangladesh, Belarus, Cameroon, Chile, Colombia, Finland, Iraq, Israel, North Korea, South Korea, New Zealand, Norway, Senegal, Slovakia, South Africa, Spain, Switzerland, Syria, Turkey, Ukraine, Viet Nam and Zimbabwe. Iraq, Israel, North Korea, South Korea, Libya and Ukraine are already observers. See 'Conference on Disarmament', in *1993 United Nations Handbook* (Wright and Carman, for the New Zealand Ministry of Foreign Affairs and Trade: Wellington, 1993), pp. 44–45. Certain key countries oppose the membership of others: e.g., Iran opposes membership of Israel and the USA opposes participation of any state subject to Chapter 7 of the UN Charter, a condition which applies only to Iraq (the USA is prepared to allow Iraq to join with suspended membership). See also Arnett (note 71).

[78] Herby, P., Conference on Disarmament Monitoring Project, Geneva, *Report no. 1*, 27 Jan. 1994, p. 3.

Another issue that the CD must come to grips with is the extent to which the institution or organization responsible for verification will depend on data from the 'national technical means' of participating states (including reconnaissance satellites as well as seismic systems) and to what extent it will operate some of its own facilities. Related to this issue are important questions about how much verification and inspection is required and who is going to pay for it.[79]

In a related development, the *Ad Hoc* Group of Scientific Experts (established in 1976), which reports to the CD, plans to conduct an experiment starting in January 1995 designed to help co-ordinate and analyse data in near 'real time' from 53 seismological stations around the world. The Group, which is headed by Ola Dahlman of Sweden, met in February 1994 and was scheduled to meet again in late March to prepare a report for the test ban committee on how the findings of the experiment can help to shape the CTBT verification regime. It was reported in early March 1994, however, that Dahlman has voiced concern that only 19 of the 53 seismological stations chosen for use in the 1995 experiment have been made available for this purpose by their host states.[80]

Deadline and linkage to NPT extension[81]

For many years, a number of parties to the Non-Proliferation Treaty have said that their support for the indefinite or long-term extension of the Treaty at the 1995 NPT Review and Extension Conference is contingent upon the completion of or real progress towards a CTBT. In this context, the G-21 group of states proposed in December 1993 that the CD should try to achieve a 'final [treaty] text during 1994'. In 1993 Australia said, 'We think it quite reasonable to aim for a completed or largely completed treaty by the time of the NPT review and extension conference in April 1995'.[82] US Arms Control and Disarmament Agency (ACDA) Director John Holum said in a speech to the CD on 25 January 1994 that it is US policy to conclude a CTBT 'at the earliest possible time'.[83] Russia stated on 14 January 1994 that it 'strongly supported completion of negotiations on a comprehensive test ban at the earliest possible time'.[84] The UK, however, has not advocated a target date. In fact, the British Ambassador to the CD, Michael Weston, made it clear that the UK does not favour the completion of a CTBT before the 1995 NPT Review and Extension Conference when he said that 'the prospect of indefinite extension of the NPT

---

[79] Lippman (note 74).

[80] Herby (note 68), p. 2.

[81] See also chapter 15 in this volume.

[82] IDDS, *Arms Control Reporter,* sheet 608.B.290, Mar. 1994.

[83] Although the Clinton Administration has not accepted direct linkage between the CTBT and NPT extension, Holum acknowledged in Dec. 1993 that 'the CTB is also important to our efforts on NPT' extension. See John Holum, Director, US Arms Control and Disarmament Agency (ACDA), speech to the Arms Control Association, Washington, DC, 13 Dec. 1993, in *Arms Control Today,* Jan./Feb. 1994, p. 5.

[84] Moscow Declaration, Office of the Press Secretary, The White House, 14 Jan. 1994, p. 1.

will be an important factor in convincing us that we can confidently move towards the conclusion of a CTBT'.[85]

On 5 October 1993, the Chinese Foreign Ministry issued a statement saying that China will help work so that a CTBT can be concluded 'no later than 1996',[86] a commitment that the Chinese Foreign Minister had made earlier in the year.[87]

France, for its part, has not taken a position on when a CTB should be concluded. French Ambassador Gerard Errera, however, indicated in a speech on the CD opening day that French support for the conclusion of a CTBT (like that of the UK) would depend in large part on long-term extension of the NPT at the April 1995 Conference.[88] This is significant, because President Mitterrand's term will expire by May 1995 and his successor may well oppose a test ban.

VI. A ban on fissile material production

During 1993 international support for a ban on the production of fissile material for nuclear weapons gathered momentum. President Yeltsin had proposed a ban in 1992,[89] and Russia reiterated that position at the CD on 17 August 1993.[90]

In an address to the UN General Assembly on 27 September 1993, President Clinton proposed the negotiation of a multilateral convention to achieve such a ban.[91] In addition to a fissile material production cut-off, the USA is pushing for greater constraints on the Middle East and South Asia so that countries in these regions would be prohibited from maintaining enrichment or reprocessing facilities—similar to an unimplemented 1991 agreement between North and South Korea. Instead, those states could purchase nuclear fuel from other countries for their civil nuclear power reactors.

Finally, and perhaps most importantly, the UN General Assembly sent out an unambiguous signal of the broad international support for a production cut-off on 16 December 1993, when it adopted by consensus a resolution recognizing that 'a non-discriminatory, multilateral and internationally and effectively verifiable treaty banning the production of fissile material for nuclear

---

[85] See note 69.

[86] *Arms Control Reporter* (note 82), sheet 608.D.9.

[87] White House Press Release, 5 Oct. 1993; Lynn Davis, US Undersecretary of State for International Security Policy, Prepared written statement submitted to the House Foreign Affairs Committee, 10 Nov. 1993, p. 8; Li, D., Ambassador of the People's Republic of China to the USA, 'Foreign policy and arms control: the view from China', *Arms Control Today*, Dec. 1993, p. 9; Smith, R. J., 'China planning a nuclear test, US aides say', *Washington Post*, 17 Sep. 1993, p. A1.

[88] CD document CD/PV.666, 25 Jan. 1994, p. 5; see also Lippman (note 74), p. A31; Senior Clinton Administration officials, Background briefing on a Comprehensive Test Ban Treaty (note 73), p. 11.

[89] *SIPRI Yearbook 1993* (note 1), p. 91.

[90] Conference on Disarmament, Final Record of the Six Hundred and Sixty-First Plenary Meeting, Geneva, CD document CD/PV.661, 17 Aug. 1993, p. 4.

[91] The White House, Office of the Press Secretary, 'Non-Proliferation and Export Control Policy', 28 Sep. 1993. In a letter dated 9 Oct. 1993, Yeltsin expressed support for Clinton's UN proposal.

weapons or other nuclear explosive devices would be a significant contribution to nuclear non-proliferation in all its aspects'.[92]

Before a fissile material production cut-off convention can be finalized, a number of important issues must be addressed: how HEU for naval nuclear reactors should be covered by the convention; how it can be determined that tritium-producing reactors are not also producing plutonium; how extensive the verification regime should be; assuming that the IAEA is responsible for safeguarding nuclear facilities in the declared nuclear states,[93] how the increased demands on the IAEA will be funded; and whether the verification arrangements for declared and threshold nuclear weapon states should be the same as those for non-nuclear weapon states.

In early 1994 the CD appointed Canadian Ambassador Gerald Shannon as a special co-ordinator for proposals on a fissile material cut-off convention.[94] Shannon reported to the CD on 31 March 1994 that 'a preponderant majority view exists among delegations that the Conference on Disarmament is the most appropriate international forum to negotiate such a treaty' but that this was not a 'unanimous view'. (According to some US officials,[95] China opposed the initiation of negotiations on a ban at the CD.) However, Shannon said, 'there are a substantial number of states which believe that the process of negotiation of a cut-off treaty could be at least launched [at the CD] while we negotiate a Comprehensive Test Ban Treaty. This could be achieved through the establishment, at the appropriate time, of an Ad Hoc Committee at the CD'. He added that he would hold consultations with interested delegations when the 1994 session resumes in May, 'with a view to determining an appropriate mandate' to establish a committee to negotiate a cut-off.[96]

A convention would provide a number of important benefits. First, it would stop the buildup of fissile material and thus limit the number of warheads that could be produced by threshold states such as India and Pakistan. Second, it would help the nuclear weapon states fulfil their obligations under NPT Article VI to end the 'nuclear arms race' and would also make the overall non-proliferation regime less discriminatory. Finally, the convention along with its associated safeguards could reduce the likelihood of theft or diversion of plutonium or HEU in Russia.

[92] Official Records of the General Assembly, Resolutions and Decisions, 48th Session, Resolution 48/75, Part L, pp. 120–21.

[93] As of 31 Dec. 1992, the 5 declared nuclear weapon states had more than 230 civil nuclear reactors; 'Nuclear power reactors in the world', IAEA, Reference Data Series No. 2, pp. 10–11.

[94] Johnson, R., 'Test ban talks set in CD', Disarmament Times, vol. 17, no. 1 (Feb. 1994), p. 1.

[95] Private conversations held in late Mar.–early Apr. 1994 with the author.

[96] Progress report of Ambassador Gerald E. Shannon, Special Coordinator on ban of production of fissile material for nuclear weapons or other nuclear explosive devices, to the Conference on Disarmament, 31 Mar. 1994, Geneva, pp. 1–2.

Weapon-grade plutonium production

The United States

Between 1945 and 1988, the US Government produced 89 tonnes of weapon-grade plutonium and 13 t of reactor-grade plutonium, according to the DOE.[97] Currently, that plutonium is stored as follows: 11 t at the Hanford site near Richland, Washington; 0.5 t at the Idaho National Engineering Laboratory near Idaho Falls, Idaho; 4.0 t at Argonne National Laboratory-West near Idaho Falls; 2.6 t at Los Alamos National Laboratory, New Mexico; 12.9 t at the Rocky Flats plant near Denver, Colorado; 2.1 t at the Savannah River site near Aiken, South Carolina; and the balance divided between the Pantex plant near Amarillo, Texas and the nuclear weapons still in the stockpile.[98] (As an estimate, if one assumes that there are 6000 plutonium pits at Pantex with about 4 kg of plutonium each, it would leave Pantex with 24 t and the stockpile with 44.9 t.)

Russia

In 1993 the Clinton Administration told Congress that it does not believe that any of the five declared nuclear weapon states are now separating plutonium for weapon purposes. However, they pointed out that Russia still has three dual-purpose production reactors in operation, two at Tomsk and one at Krasnoyarsk, that provide heat and electricity to their respective communities. The Administration noted that 'these reactors are making plutonium that may be weapons grade and appear to be reprocessing the spent fuel, which cannot be stored indefinitely. However, we do not believe the recovered plutonium is being used for nuclear weapons'.[99] Russian Ministry of Atomic Energy (MINATOM) officials say that the aluminium-clad uranium fuel used by their plutonium production reactors corrodes quickly in storage pools and the plutonium must be separated for safety reasons.

In January 1992 Yeltsin said that these reactors would be shut down before the year 2000.[100] In a development that may result in the cessation of Russian plutonium production even earlier, Russian Prime Minister Viktor Chernomyrdin and US Vice-President Al Gore agreed during a December 1993 meeting that the USA would help conduct an economic and technical feasibility study to explore the options of converting these three reactors to use fuels that would not require reprocessing (e.g., zirconium-clad fuel that is easier to

---

[97] This number was provided in the Openness Press Conference Fact Sheets, US Department of Energy, 7 Dec. 1993, pp. 21–41. However, the DOE number may be low, *inter alia*, because it apparently does not take into account the blending of super-grade with fuel-grade plutonium and bartering plutonium with the UK; see Cochran, T. B., Arkin, W. M., Norris, R. S. and Hoenig, M. M., *Nuclear Weapons Databook, Vol. II* (Ballinger: Cambridge, Mass., 1987), pp. 66–67, 75; Norris, R. S., Burrows, A. S. and Fieldhouse, R. W., *British, French, and Chinese Nuclear Weapons* (Westview Press: Boulder, Colo., 1994).

[98] Openness Press Conference Fact Sheets (see note 97), pp. 21–41.

[99] Energy and Water Development Appropriations for 1994, House Subcommittee on Energy and Water Development, Part 6 (US Government Printing Office: Washington, DC, 1993), p. 1313.

[100] *SIPRI Yearbook 1993* (note 1), p. 91.

store) or shutting down the reactors and providing alternative sources of power.[101] On 16 March 1994, US Energy Secretary Hazel O'Leary and MINATOM Director Viktor Mikhailov announced that the DOE would help conduct a study to determine how to replace Russia's remaining dual-purpose plutonium-producing reactors with alternative energy sources (i.e., gas turbines fuelled by natural gas to replace the two reactors at Tomsk-7 and a coal-fired power plant to replace the reactor at Krasnoyarsk-26). O'Leary and Mikhailov signed a protocol saying that:

Russia, within one year after creation of an alternate source of energy, would cease production and chemical separation of weapons-grade plutonium. The Russian side noted that both of these cessation and compliance provisions must be met and that the agreement would require that each side permit inspection of its relevant plutonium production facilities as well as the storage sites for the plutonium produced by the reactors in Tomsk and Krasnoyarsk.

They also announced 'their intention to host reciprocal inspections by the end of 1994 to facilities containing plutonium removed from nuclear weapons' (i.e., Pantex and Tomsk-7).[102]

Disposal of plutonium from dismantled warheads

Under the START treaties and the unilateral initiatives taken by Presidents Bush, Gorbachev and Yeltsin, tens of thousands of nuclear warheads are scheduled for dismantlement in the next two decades. Consequently, the USA and Russia are each expected to have at least 50 t of weapon-grade plutonium in excess of any military needs. Thus, they are now confronted with the daunting challenge of determining how to manage and dispose of this surplus plutonium. Their decisions will have important implications for non-proliferation and the environment. Only several kilograms of plutonium are necessary to build a bomb. In addition, plutonium, which has a half-life of about 24 000 years, is one of the most toxic substances on earth.

In response to a 1992 request from Brent Scowcroft, then President Bush's National Security Adviser, the US National Academy of Sciences (NAS) released the findings of its study on the management and disposition options for plutonium in January 1994. NAS found that the two most promising alternatives for long-term plutonium disposition were: (a) to transform the plutonium into intensely radioactive spent fuel by using it as fuel in nuclear reactors; or (b) to mix it with high-level waste and then vitrify it with molten glass to create large glass logs. Both of these options would result in forms from which the plutonium would be difficult to recover for weapon use. The study

---

[101] NAS (note 13), p. 100. Executive Summary, Management and Disposition of Excess Weapons Plutonium, Committee on International Security and Arms Control, National Academy of Sciences (National Academy Press: Washington, DC, 1994), p. 9; Allen, V., 'US, Russia to discuss closing plutonium plants', Reuter, 31 Jan. 1994; Smith, R. J., 'Gore delegations signs 22 accords with Moscow', Washington Post, 17 Dec. 1993, p. A3.

[102] For the text of the protocol, see appendix 16A; see also Lockwood, D., 'US, Russia, reach agreement for plutonium site inspections', Arms Control Today, Apr. 1994, p. 22.

also noted, however, that neither of these options could be implemented for at least 10 years and stressed the need for improvements in transparency, security and safeguards in the interim period.[103] While the findings have not been officially endorsed by the US Government, the NAS report is considered to be the most authoritative study on this subject to date in the USA.

Thus far, MINATOM has not expressed any interest in either of the two options recommended by NAS. Instead, it sees plutonium as a valuable economic asset and has expressed interest in using plutonium from dismantled warheads to fuel civilian reactors to produce energy.[104] Some officials at MINATOM have said that after storing plutonium from dismantled warheads for at least a decade, they eventually intend to use the plutonium to fuel three 'BN-800' liquid-metal fast breeder reactors, which would become operational some time after the turn of the century at the Mayak complex in the southern Urals (also referred to as Chelyabinsk-65). Preliminary construction on these reactors began in 1984 but was halted in 1987 because of local opposition in the wake of the Chernobyl reactor accident and probably also because of a lack of funding. (Beloyarsk, which currently has an operational BN-600 breeder reactor, has also been discussed as a site for a possible fourth BN-800.)[105]

US officials have tried to discourage MINATOM from pursuing the breeder reactor route for a number of reasons.[106] First, the breeder reactor fuel cycle process could produce more plutonium than it would consume, raising concerns about nuclear proliferation.[107] In addition to the potential for increasing plutonium levels, MINATOM's plan could cause security problems because it would require prolonged storage while the new reactors were built. Moreover, breeder reactors using MOX fuel (a blend of plutonium oxide and uranium oxide) are not economically competitive with light water reactors using LEU. In any case, it seems unlikely that MINATOM will be able to find the funds to build these breeder reactors or to complete a fabrication plant at Chelyabinsk-65 to provide MOX fuel for these reactors.[108]

Civilian stocks of plutonium

Today the stocks of civilian plutonium are several times larger than military stocks and are increasing at a much faster rate (by approximately 60–70 t per year). Although reactor-grade plutonium usually has a different isotopic composition from weapon-grade plutonium, it can still be used to make nuclear

[103] NAS (note 13), pp. 1–2.

[104] See, for example, the testimony of General William Burns, 9 Mar. 1993, in *Disposing of Plutonium in Russia*, Committee on Governmental Affairs, US Senate, 103rd Congress (US Government Printing Office: Washington, DC 1993), pp. 20–21; Lippman, T. W., 'Russia thinks plutonium from arms has commercial value, Congress told', *Washington Post*, 10 Mar. 1994, p. A24.

[105] Cochran, T. B., and Norris, R. S., *Russian/Soviet Nuclear Warhead Production Complex*, Nuclear Weapons Databook Working Papers 93-1, 8 Sep. 1993, pp. 60–61, 129; Norris, R. S., 'The Soviet nuclear archipelago', *Arms Control Today*, Jan./Feb. 1992, p. 31.

[106] See, for example, the testimony of General William Burns (note 104), p. 21.

[107] *Proliferation Threats of the 1990s* (note 48), p. 145; Cochran *et al.* (note 97), p. 60.

[108] Cochran *et al.* (note 105), pp. 44, 60.

weapons.[109] While most of these civilian stocks are in the form of radioactive spent fuel from the world's power reactors and it is difficult to extract plutonium from spent fuel, it becomes much easier to separate this plutonium as the radioactivity of the spent fuel decays over the decades after it leaves the reactor. According to the NAS study, approximately 130 t of plutonium have been separated from spent fuel for reuse as civilian reactor fuel, of which about 80–90 t remain in storage in separated form.[110] Nearly all of the separated plutonium in storage is found at four principal sites: La Hague and Marcoule in France, Sellafield in Britain and Chelyabinsk in Russia.[111]

Japan and a number of European countries, including Belgium, Germany and Switzerland, have contracts with these reprocessing plants to have plutonium separated from their spent fuel. Most of the decisions to initiate these civil plutonium programmes were made in the 1970s. In recent years it has become clear that the supply of uranium is larger and nuclear power is far less popular and prevalent than was anticipated when these decisions were made. As a result, some countries are beginning to question the economic wisdom of their civil plutonium programmes.

On 27 September 1993, in conjunction with President Clinton's address to the UN General Assembly, the Clinton Administration announced a new nonproliferation initiative stating: 'The United States does not encourage the civil use of plutonium and, accordingly, does not itself engage in plutonium reprocessing for either nuclear power or nuclear explosive purposes'. In addition, the USA called for a dialogue to explore 'means to limit the stockpiling of plutonium from civil nuclear programs'.[112] Despite these statements, the Clinton Administration has not yet put strong political pressure on Japan and Western Europe to terminate their civil plutonium programmes. In any case, support for a plutonium fuel cycle remains strong in Japan and Western Europe (particularly in France) as well as in Russia.

The United Kingdom

On 15 December 1993, the British Environment Secretary announced to the House of Commons that British Nuclear Fuels Ltd (BNFL), a state-owned company, would begin operating the thermal-oxide reprocessing plant (THORP) at Sellafield in 1994. It has already received shipments of spent fuel from Japan.[113] A number of environmental groups and non-proliferation analysts criticized the decision to open THORP, arguing that the plant is environmentally unsound and that it does not make sense to increase the world's

[109] NAS (note 13), p. 4; Office of Technology Assessment (OTA), *Technologies Underlying Weapons of Mass Destruction* (US Government Printing Office: Washington, DC, 1993), pp. 132–33; Mark, J. C., *Reactor Grade Plutonium's Explosive Properties* (Nuclear Control Institute: Washington, DC, Aug. 1990).
[110] NAS (note 13), p. 4; see also Albright, D., Berkhout, F. and Walker, W., SIPRI, *World Inventory of Plutonium and Highly Enriched Uranium 1992* (Oxford University Press: Oxford, 1993).
[111] OTA (note 109), p. 132.
[112] The White House (note 91), p. 2.
[113] Stevenson, R. W., 'Britain approves nuclear-fuel unit', *New York Times*, 16 Dec. 1993, p. A12; Robinson, E., 'Britain to start up plutonium-producing plant', *Washington Post,* 16 Dec. 1993, p. A48.

stockpile of nuclear weapon-usable plutonium, especially when cheaper sources of energy are available. In the first week of March 1994, the British High Court dismissed a challenge from the environmental group Greenpeace to stop THORP from becoming operational, clearing the way for the facility to begin reprocessing plutonium.[114]

Japan

Japan has invested a substantial amount of money in developing a plutonium fuel cycle. It has already received shipments of reprocessed plutonium from La Hague and has a contract with Sellafield for additional shipments. Japan plans to use MOX fuel in light water reactors and is scheduled to begin operating its $5 billion 'Monju' breeder reactor in the spring of 1994.[115] In addition, it plans to finish construction on a major plutonium reprocessing facility at Rokkasho-mura sometime between 2000 and 2005.[116]

In February 1994, however, it was reported that Japan may postpone a number of follow-on plutonium projects for many years. Monju was originally intended to be the first of a series of breeder reactors, but apparently because of its high cost, the construction of a second breeder reactor, planned to begin immediately, will now be delayed until at least 2000. Furthermore, Japan has not yet found a site for the second breeder reactor. Reportedly, the completion of a second reprocessing plant has now been delayed from 2010 to 2030.[117]

VII. The Safe and Secure Dismantlement Talks

The failed Soviet coup in August 1991 underlined the potential nuclear weapon-related dangers attending the breakup of the USSR and the need to accelerate the arms control process. As a result, US and Russian arms control efforts began to focus increasingly on rapid implementation measures to consolidate former Soviet nuclear weapons in Russia, to strengthen central control over those weapons and to improve their physical security and safety.

In his September 1991 initiative on tactical nuclear weapons, President Bush proposed that the USA and the USSR explore 'joint technical cooperation on the safe and environmentally responsible storage, transportation, dismantling and destruction of nuclear warheads'. He also called for the two states to discuss ways in which 'existing arrangements for the physical security and safety of nuclear weapons could be enhanced'. On 5 October 1991, then Soviet President Mikhail Gorbachev acknowledged that Moscow was amenable to such discussions. In November 1991 the US Congress passed the Soviet Nuclear Threat Reduction Act, which gave the DOD the authority to transfer up to $400 million to facilitate 'the transportation, storage, safeguarding, and

---

[114] Smith, M., 'Thorp N-plant given go-ahead by High Court', *Financial Times*, 5/6 Mar. 1994, p. 1.
[115] Sanger, D. E., 'Japan, bowing to pressure, defers plutonium projects', *New York Times*, 22 Feb. 1994, p. 2.
[116] OTA (note 109), p. 132. Japan already has a pilot reprocessing plant at Tokai.
[117] Sanger (note 115), p. 2.

destruction of nuclear and other weapons in the Soviet Union . . . and to assist in the prevention of weapons proliferation'.[118] In 1992 Congress passed the Former Soviet Union Demilitarization Act, again authorizing the transfer of up to $400 million to the Nunn–Lugar funding and broadening the scope of the programmes for which the money may be used to include defence industry conversion and military-to-military contacts.[119] In 1993 Congress approved the Cooperative Threat Reduction Act, authorizing $400 million in new money for the programme, and expanding the portfolio to include assistance in restoring the environment of former military sites and programmes to provide housing for former military personnel.[120] As a result of these initiatives, a new arms control forum, now called the Safe and Secure Dismantlement (SSD) Talks, emerged to facilitate US efforts to help denuclearize and demilitarize the former USSR. The US DOD now refers to this programme as 'Cooperative Threat Reduction'.

In 1993 the USA held SSD Talks on a bilateral basis with Belarus, Kazakhstan, Russia and Ukraine. By the end of the year, the USA had reported to Congress proposed obligations of $789.54 million for assistance to these four former Soviet republics. Of this amount, a total of $111.5 million had actually been obligated through signed contracts.[121] Of the money that was spent on assistance, about 93 per cent went to Russia, 4 per cent to Belarus, and 3 per cent to general support and assessment activities. Ukraine and Kazakhstan did not receive any assistance in 1993 because they did not sign the necessary agreements until December 1993.

Russia

The USA and Russia signed an 'umbrella agreement' on 17 June 1992 establishing the legal framework for the transfer of Nunn–Lugar assistance. (The umbrella agreement includes, *inter alia*, partial diplomatic immunity and exemptions from taxes and customs for the US contractors providing services and equipment.)[122] Since then, the USA and Russia have signed more than 10 'implementing agreements' for various assistance projects. As of the end of 1993, the Clinton Administration had notified Congress of $441.5 million pledged to Russia, of which $103.5 million had actually been obligated through signed contracts.

Almost all of the equipment that was delivered to former Soviet republics in 1993 under the Nunn–Lugar programme went to Russia. It consisted primarily of: armoured blankets to protect warheads during transit and storage and emergency response equipment to enhance Russia's capability to respond to a

---

[118] *Congressional Record*, 27 Nov. 1991, p. S18798.

[119] *Congressional Record*, 1 Oct. 1992, p. H10281.

[120] *Congressional Record*, 10 Nov. 1993, pp. H9251–H9252.

[121] *Department of Defense Provides Assistance to the Former Soviet Union*, News Release, Office of the Assistant Secretary of Defense (Public Affairs), 24 Nov. 1993, p. 1; US Security Assistance to the Former Soviet Union, Factfile, *Arms Control Today*, Jan./Feb. 1994, pp. 32–33.

[122] The US Nunn–Lugar legislation stipulates that the programmes to 'the extent feasible draw upon US technology and expertise, especially from the private sector of the United States'.

nuclear weapons accident that could occur during the transport of warheads to storage and dismantlement facilities.

Of the implementing agreements signed in 1993, probably the two most important ones were for assistance in dismantling strategic nuclear weapons and in building a storage facility for fissile material extracted from dismantled warheads. The agreement on strategic nuclear arms elimination, signed on 26 August 1993 in Moscow, commits the USA to provide up to $130 million to assist Russia in dismantling its strategic weapons. The equipment that the USA plans to provide for weapon dismantlement includes mobile cranes, plasma cutters (special torches) and bulldozers for ICBM elimination; shears to cut up SLBM tubes; and guillotines, dump trucks, and fork lifts and tractors for heavy bomber dismantlement. In addition, US assistance will ensure the supply of special railroad cars to transport liquid fuel from retired ballistic missiles as well as incinerators to burn the fuel.

On 2 September 1993 the USA and Russia signed an implementing agreement committing the USA to provide up to $75 million worth of assistance in building a fissile material storage facility in Russia. This facility will store plutonium recovered from dismantled warheads. Some Russian officials had told the USA that, if they did not have a new storage facility by 1997, they would have to slow the pace of their warhead dismantlement programme.[123] The Clinton Administration had hoped that Russia would break ground for the new facility in the spring of 1994,[124] but since a location has not yet been selected this projection appears optimistic. Russia originally indicated that it wanted to build the new facility at Tomsk, but after a tank of nuclear waste exploded there on 6 April 1993, local opposition to the project increased.

The funding for the facility will help pay for such items as blast resistant doors; heating, ventilation and air conditioning; electrical power generation; a physical security system; and fire alarm and suppression systems. When this project was first conceived, it was the US understanding that all plutonium extracted from dismantled warheads would be stored at one site. In addition to ensuring that the facility would have state-of-the-art technology, having a single site would facilitate US efforts to monitor and account for excess plutonium in Russia. (The US–Russian umbrella agreement stipulates that representatives of the US Government 'shall have the right to examine the use of any material, training or other services provided [by the USA], if possible at sites of their location or use'.)[125]

[123] Kelley, J. E., Director-in-Charge, International Affairs Issues, National Security and International Affairs Division, Soviet Nuclear Weapons, *US Efforts to Help Former Soviet Republics Secure and Destroy Weapons*, GAO/T-NSIAD-93-5, 9 Mar. 1993, p. 7.

[124] Comptroller of the Department of Defense, *Quarterly Report on Program Activities to Facilitate Weapons Destruction and Non-Proliferation in the Former Soviet Union*, 29 Sep. 1993; Gordon, M., 'Nuclear arsenal: a huge ex-Soviet legacy hard to remove', *New York Times*, 1 Dec. 1993, p. A16.

[125] Office of Technology Assessment (OTA), *Dismantling the Bomb and Managing Nuclear Materials* (US Government Printing Office: Washington, DC, Sep. 1993), p. 183.

Belarus

Belarus signed an umbrella agreement with the USA on 22 October 1992 and has since signed five implementing agreements. These include $25 million for environmental cleanup, $20 million for defence conversion and retraining, $16.26 million to develop export controls, $5 million for emergency response equipment and $2.3 million for the establishment of a government-to-government communications link to transmit data and notifications related to the INF and START treaties. As of the end of 1993, the USA had pledged a total of $76 million in Nunn–Lugar assistance to Belarus. Of this, just under $4 million worth of assistance was delivered in the form of emergency response equipment, including protective suits and boots, and dosimeters.

Ukraine

Ukraine signed an umbrella agreement with the USA on 25 October 1993.[126] On 4 December 1993 in Kiev, Ukraine signed two implementing agreements with the USA: $135 million for strategic nuclear arms elimination; and $2.26 million for the development of export controls. On 18 December in Washington, Ukraine signed three additional implementing agreements: $2.4 million for a government-to-government communications link; $5 million for emergency response equipment; and $7.5 million for assistance in controlling civil fissile materials. As of the end of 1993, the USA had earmarked a total of $177 million for Ukraine, but no assistance was delivered during the course of the year.

Kazakhstan

Kazakhstan signed the umbrella agreement and five implementing agreements with the USA on 13 December 1993[127] in Almaty (Alma-Ata) consisting of: $70 million for strategic nuclear weapon elimination (dismantlement of SS-18 silos); $5 million for emergency response equipment; $2.3 million for the establishment of a government-to-government communications link; $2.26 million to develop export controls; and $5 million for assistance in controlling civil fissile materials. As of the end of 1993, the USA had pledged a total of $85 million to Kazakhstan, but no assistance was delivered during the year.

Future priorities for the SSD Talks

Congress appropriated $400 million in FY 1994 for the Nunn–Lugar programme and the Clinton Administration has requested an additional $400

---

[126] Ukraine, however, did not provide the USA with the diplomatic note required for the umbrella agreement to enter into force until early Jan. 1994. US Arms Control and Disarmament Agency (ACDA), *Annual Report to the Congress, 1993* (forthcoming).

[127] ACDA (note 126); Smith, R. J., 'Kazakhstan ratifies nuclear control pact, will get US aid', *Washington Post*, 14 Dec. 1993, p. A20; Berke, R. L., 'Prodded by Gore, Kazakhstan signs arms accord', *New York Times*, 14 Dec. 1993, p. A15.

million for FY 1995. The DOD has said that it will continue to emphasize assistance for the elimination of strategic offensive arms, noting that the money earmarked thus far is only sufficient to help implement the START I Treaty but not START II. In addition, the DOD says that 'the planned Russian storage facility for fissile material from dismantled nuclear weapons, and the environmentally safe destruction of Russian chemical weapons . . . may require a sustained and multiyear effort if they are to succeed'.[128]

The Russian–US HEU Agreement[129]

On 18 February 1993, the USA signed an agreement with Russia to purchase, over a 20-year period, 500 tonnes of highly enriched uranium (HEU) extracted from dismantled nuclear warheads.[130] The HEU would be blended down to LEU in Russia and then transported to the USA. The USA would later resell the material to nuclear power plants both in the USA and abroad.

The HEU Agreement is estimated to be worth $11.9 billion, but the prices will be negotiated each year by the executive agents, to reflect US inflation and changes in international market conditions. The executive agent for the USA will be the US Enrichment Corporation (USEC), a quasi-governmental organization,[131] and the executive agent for Russia will be MINATOM, whose Techsnabexport department will have responsibility for carrying out the transaction.

The USA has stipulated that the HEU Agreement cannot be implemented until after Russia has worked out mutually acceptable revenue-sharing arrangements with Belarus, Kazakhstan and Ukraine. The Trilateral Statement on how to divide the proceeds with Ukraine was signed by Russia, Ukraine and the USA on 14 January 1994, and the Rada appeared to tacitly accept this agreement in a resolution passed on 3 February 1994 (see section II above). The question of Belarus' and Kazakhstan's share of the proceeds, while less contentious, had not been settled by early 1994. During President Clinton's 15 January 1994 visit to Minsk, the Belarussian Government said that it would like to receive a share of the proceeds, an estimated $50 million.[132] Kazakh President Nazarbayev said in January 1994 that Kazakhstan should receive $1

---

[128] Aspin (note 27), p. 44.

[129] For an in-depth look at the HEU agreement see Bukharin, O., 'Weapons to fuel', *Science & Global Security,* vol. 4, no. 2 (1994), pp. 189–212; Bukharin, O., 'Soft landing for bomb uranium', *Bulletin of the Atomic Scientists,* Sep. 1993, pp. 44–49; Office of Technology Assessment, *Dismantling the Bomb and Managing Nuclear Materials* (US Government Printing Office: Washington, DC, 1993), pp. 137–43.

[130] For the text of the Agreement, see appendix 16A.

[131] The USEC was established by the Energy Policy Act of 1990 (P.L. 102-486), designating 1 July 1993 as the start-up date for assuming responsibility of the US Department of Energy's uranium enrichment activities. Congress created the USEC as a government corporation, a transitional step towards the goal of fully privatizing it as a commercial business.

[132] 'Belarus requests compensation for nuclear weapons', *RFE/RL Military Notes,* 17 Jan. 1994, p. 3. (Since all the strategic weapons based in Belarus are SS-25 ICBMs, which will not have their warheads dismantled, it is unclear whether Belarus should be compensated.)

billion in compensation for the HEU contained in warheads on Kazakh territory.[133]

Under the terms of the HEU Agreement, USEC will purchase 500 t of HEU converted to 15 260 t of LEU over a 20-year period: 10 t of HEU (equivalent to approximately 310 t of LEU) per year for five years and 30 t of HEU (equivalent to approximately 930 t of LEU) each year thereafter for the following 15 years.

Benefits of the HEU Agreement

If implemented, the HEU Agreement will produce a number of benefits. First, it would provide an incentive for Belarus, Kazakhstan and Ukraine to transfer the nuclear warheads on their territory to Russia—a development that would clearly have very positive implications for the START treaties and the NPT. Second, it would give Russia incentives to dismantle many of its strategic nuclear warheads (which it is not required to do under the START or any other legally binding treaties) and to accelerate the pace of its warhead dismantlement. It will also reduce Russia's storage requirements for fissile material recovered from dismantled warheads. Third, the Agreement would help alleviate nuclear proliferation concerns that excess HEU in Russia could fall into the wrong hands in Russia or 'leak out' to foreign countries such as Iran or Iraq. Fourth, at a time when Russia's economy is particularly precarious, the Agreement would provide Russia with hard currency for converting its defence industries into civilian ones, enhancing the safety of nuclear power plants, cleaning up polluted areas, and building and operating facilities for the conversion of HEU to LEU.[134]

VIII. Nuclear weapon-free zones

The Treaty of Tlatelolco[135]

The 1967 Treaty for the Prohibition of Nuclear Weapons in Latin America,[136] the Treaty of Tlatelolco, predates the NPT. As of 1 February 1994 it had 27 Latin American and Caribbean parties that have made a commitment not to test, use, manufacture, produce or acquire nuclear weapons.[137] It also created a regional organization to ensure compliance, the Agency for the Prohibition of Nuclear Weapons in Latin America (known by its Spanish acronym OPANAL). The Treaty will enter into force for the entire region when all

---

[133] 'Kazakhstan wants compensation for weaponry', *RFE/RL Military Notes*, 25 Jan. 1994.

[134] The HEU Agreement stipulates that Russia must use a 'portion of the proceeds' for these purposes.

[135] This section draws heavily on: Redick, J. R., 'Argentina–Brazil nuclear non-proliferation initiatives', *Programme for Promoting Nuclear Non-Proliferation, Issue Review*, no. 3 (Jan. 1994), p. 2; and from 'Argentina and Chile bring into force the Treaty for the Prohibition of Nuclear Weapons in Latin America and the Caribbean', US Arms Control and Disarmament Agency (ACDA), Office of Public Information, Fact Sheet, 1 Mar. 1994. See also annexe A, footnotes to the table of parties.

[136] In 1990 OPANAL decided that the name of the Treaty should include 'and the Caribbean', but as of early 1994 this had still not come into effect.

[137] For the list of parties, see annexe A in this volume.

eligible countries have signed and ratified the Treaty and its two additional protocols and have concluded comprehensive safeguards agreements with the IAEA. Many nations, however, have individually waived this condition for universal adherence and brought the Treaty into force for their respective territories.

In 1992 Argentina, Brazil and Chile proposed a series of amendments to the verification clauses of the Treaty, stating that they would implement the Treaty once these amendments were adopted. The amendments changed the verification procedures so that the IAEA now has the sole responsibility for conducting special inspections. Subsequently, Chile endorsed this proposal and the OPANAL General Conference approved the changes on 26 August 1992.

Argentina's Senate approved the Treaty with the amendments in March 1993 and its Chamber of Deputies followed suit in November 1993. Chile's Congress ratified the amendments to the Treaty in late November 1993. In a decision not to wait for Brazil, both Argentina and Chile formally acceded to the Treaty (Argentina on 18 January and Chile on 28 January 1994).[138] Although the Brazilian Chamber of Deputies adopted the amendments in the autumn of 1993, the Senate had not done so as of early 1994 owing in part to a domestic corruption scandal. Cuba has announced its intention to accede to the Treaty 'when all the other states of the region have done so'.

The Treaty of Rarotonga

Eight members of the South Pacific Forum signed the Treaty of Rarotonga in 1985. The Treaty bans the manufacture, acquisition, possession, stationing and testing of any nuclear explosive device in the South Pacific Nuclear Free Zone. The accord is now in force for 11 of the 15 members of the Forum.[139]

An African nuclear weapon-free zone

South Africa's decision to join the NPT in 1991 opened the door for a nuclear weapon-free zone on the African continent. In April 1993 the Organization of African Unity (OAU) Experts Group met in Harare, Zimbabwe, to initiate the process of drafting a nuclear weapon-free zone treaty. The Experts Group is scheduled to meet two more times in 1994 and plans to have a final treaty text ready for signature by June 1994, in time for the next OAU summit meeting.[140]

IX. Conclusions

In 1993 numerous important initiatives were taken to advance the nuclear arms control agenda, but there was little follow-through producing concrete

[138] 'Argentina, Chile accede to NWFZ treaty', *Arms Control Today*, Jan./Feb. 1994, p. 33.
[139] ACDA (note 126). For the list of parties, see annexe A in this volume.
[140] ACDA (note 126).

results. The START II Treaty was signed but did not enter into force. There was a strong drive to negotiate a multilateral CTBT, but negotiations were deferred until 1994. The international community pushed for a ban on the production of fissile material for weapons, but it appears that negotiations for such a ban may not begin for at least a year or two. A number of 'Nunn–Lugar agreements' for funding assistance for weapon dismantlement were signed by the USA and former Soviet republics to help denuclearize the former USSR, but little assistance was actually delivered in 1993.

This lack of follow-through, particularly with respect to the START I and START II treaties, raises some serious questions for future nuclear arms control and non-proliferation efforts. If the two major nuclear weapon powers are unable to bring the START treaties into effect, it will be more difficult for them to make the case at the 1995 NPT Review and Extension Conference that they are fulfilling their obligations under Article VI to bring an end to the nuclear arms race 'at an early date'. Furthermore, if Ukraine ultimately becomes a new member of the 'nuclear club', this would undermine confidence in the general effectiveness of international non-proliferation efforts. Thus, the new nuclear arms control agenda of non-proliferation could be undermined if the world fails to finish the old agenda.

With an eye towards the NPT Review and Extension Conference, the top priorities in 1994 must be: to complete the CTBT; bring the START I and START II treaties into force; and make progress on a convention to ban the production of fissile material for nuclear weapons. Although this is a full agenda, it should not preclude renewed efforts to take three more initiatives. First, the USA and Russia should agree to a warhead dismantlement regime with reciprocal monitoring. Second, the nuclear weapon states should openly exchange data on the levels of their nuclear stockpiles, including data on their stockpiles of fissile material, with verification arrangements to confirm these declarations. Third, these states, particularly the USA and Russia, should not only de-target their ICBMs[141] but also separate their warheads from all or at least most of their land-based missiles so that it would be impossible to launch those ICBMs quickly.

In many cases the unit of account in nuclear arms control negotiations seems to be shifting from throw-weight, launchers and warheads to dollars, Deutschmarks and yen. This new approach merits some reflection. Although the new deals (e.g., Nunn–Lugar agreements, the HEU Agreement and the Trilateral Statement) appear to be mutually beneficial and should generally be encouraged in the future, the West must be careful not to send the wrong signals to potential nuclear weapon proliferators.

---

[141] On 14 Jan. 1994, the USA and Russia agreed to de-target their strategic ballistic missiles by 30 May 1994. While this measure is significant in a symbolic sense, it cannot be verified confidently and can be reversed in a matter of minutes. (A British–Russian De-Targeting Agreement was signed on 15 Feb. 1994.)

Appendix 16A. Documents on nuclear arms control

US–RUSSIAN HIGHLY ENRICHED URANIUM AGREEMENT (HEU AGREEMENT)

Washington, DC, 18 February 1993

The Government[s] of the United States of America and the Russian Federation, hereafter referred to as the Parties:

Desiring to arrange the safe and prompt disposition for peaceful purposes of highly enriched uranium resulting from the reduction of nuclear weapons in accordance with existing agreements in the area of arms control and disarmament,

Reaffirming their commitment to ensure that the development and use of nuclear energy for peaceful purposes are carried out under arrangements that will further the objectives of the Treaty on the Non-Proliferation of Nuclear Weapons of July 1, 1968,

Affirming their commitment to ensure that nuclear material transferred for peaceful purposes pursuant to this Agreement will comply with all applicable non-proliferation, material accounting and control, physical protection, and environmental requirements, have agreed as follows:

Article I: Purpose

The Parties shall cooperate in order to achieve the following objectives:

1. The conversion as soon as practicable of highly enriched uranium (HEU) extracted from nuclear weapons resulting from the reduction of nuclear weapons pursuant to arms control agreements and other commitments of the parties which is currently estimated at approximately 500 metric tons in the Russian Federation, having an average assay of 90 percent or greater of the uranium isotope 235 into low enriched uranium (LEU) for use as fuel in commercial nuclear reactors. For purposes of this Agreement, LEU shall mean uranium enriched to less than 20 percent in the isotope 235; and

2. The technology developed in the Russian Federation for conversion of HEU resulting from the reduction of nuclear weapons in the Russian Federation may be used for conversion of United States EU in the United States of America; and

3. The establishment of appropriate measures to fulfil the non-proliferation, physical security protection, nuclear material accounting and control, and environmental requirements of the Parties with respect to HEU and LEU subject to this Agreement.

Article II: Implementing Contracts and Agreements

1. The Parties, through their Executive Agents, shall within six months from entry into force of this Agreement seek to enter into an initial implementing contract to accomplish the objectives set forth in Article I of this Agreement. The Parties may conclude additional implementing contracts or agreements pursuant to this Agreement, as required. For any purchase, the Executive Agents shall negotiate terms (including price), which shall be subject to approval by the Parties.

2. It is the intent of the Parties that the initial implementing contract shall provide for *inter alia:*

(i) The purchase by the United States Executive Agent of LEU converted from HEU at facilities in the Russian Federation and sale of the LEU for commercial purposes. The United States will provide information to the Russian Federation on all commercial disposition of such LEU;

(ii) Initial delivery of LEU converted from HEU extracted from nuclear weapons resulting from the reduction of nuclear weapons pursuant to arms control agreements and other commitments of the parties by October 1993, if possible;

(iii) Conversion of no less than 10 metric tons having an average assay of 90 percent or greater of the uranium isotope 235 in each of the first five years, and, in each year thereafter, conversion of no less than 30 metric tons of HEU having an average assay of 90 percent or greater of the uranium isotope 235; however, specific amounts will be stipulated in the first and subsequent implementing contracts;

(iv) The participation of the U.S. private sector and of Russian enterprises;

(v) The allocation among the United States

of America, private sector firms of the United States of America, the Russian Federation, and Russian enterprises of any proceeds or costs arising out of activities undertaken pursuant to any implementing contract;

(vi) The use by the Russian Federation side of a portion of the proceeds from the sale of LEU converted from HEU for the conversion of defense enterprises, enhancing the safety of nuclear power plants, environmental clean-up of polluted areas and the construction and operation of facilities in the Russian Federation for the conversion of HEU to LEU;

(vii) By agreement of the Parties an equivalent amount of HEU can substitute for the corresponding amount of LEU planned for purchase by the United States Executive Agent.

Article III: Executive Agents

Each Party shall designate an executive agent to implement this Agreement. For the United States side the executive agent shall be the Department of Energy. For the Russian side the Executive Agent shall be the Ministry of the Russian Federation of Atomic Energy. After consultation with the other Party, either Party has the right to change its executive agent upon 30 days written notice to the other Party. If a government corporation is established under United States law to manage the uranium enrichment enterprise of the Department of Energy, it is the intention of the United States Government to designate that corporation as the Executive Agent for the United States side.

Article IV: Priority of Agreement

In case of any inconsistency between this Agreement and any implementing contracts or agreement, the provisions of this Agreement shall prevail.

Article V: Additional Measures

1. The Executive Agent of the Russian Federation shall ensure that the quality of LEU derived from HEU subject to this Agreement is such that it is convertible to LEU usable in commercial reactors. Specifications shall be agreed upon in the process of negotiating the initial and subsequent implementing contracts.

2. The conversion of HEU subject to this Agreement shall commence as soon as possible after the entry into force of the initial implementing contract.

3. The Parties shall, to the extent practicable, seek to arrange for more rapid conversion of HEU to LEU than that provided for in Article II (2) (iii).

4. The United States of America shall use LEU acquired pursuant to this Agreement and its implementing contracts and agreements, when subject to United States jurisdiction and control, for peaceful purposes only.

5. HEU and LEU acquired by the United States of America pursuant to this Agreement, and implementing contracts and agreements related to it, shall be subject to safeguards in accordance with the November 19, 1977 Agreement between the United States of America and the International Atomic Energy Agency (IAEA) for the Application of Safeguards in connection with the Treaty for the Non-Proliferation of Nuclear Weapons.

6. The Parties shall maintain physical protection of HEU and LEU subject to this Agreement. Such protection shall, at a minimum, provide protection comparable to the recommendation set forth in IAEA document INFCIRC/225/REV.2 concerning the physical protection of nuclear material.

7. If the Parties enter into an agreement for cooperation concerning the peaceful uses of nuclear energy, nuclear material acquired by the United States of America pursuant to this Agreement and its implementing contracts and agreements, when subject to U.S. jurisdiction or control, shall be subject to the terms and conditions of the Agreement for cooperation.

8. The activities of the United States Government under this Agreement, or any implementing contract or agreement shall be subject to the availability of United States Government funds.

9. In the event the United States Government does not have funds available for implementation of this Agreement, the Executive Agent of the Russian Federation reserves the option to obtain funding for implementation of this Agreement from any private U.S. company.

10. Prior to the conclusion of any implementing contract, the Parties shall establish transparency measures to ensure that the objectives of this Agreement are met, including provisions for nuclear material accounting and control and access, from the time that HEU is made available for conversion until it is converted into LEU. Specific transparency measures shall be established in the same

time frame as the negotiation of the initial implementing contract, and shall be executed by a separate agreement.

11. Prior to the conclusion of any implementing contract, the Parties shall agree on appropriate governing provisions for entry and exit, liability, and status of personnel, exemptions for taxes and other duties, and applicable law.

12. The Executive Agent of the United States shall use the LEU converted from HEU in such a manner so as to minimize disruptions in the market and maximize the overall economic benefit for both parties. This Agreement shall have no effect on contracts between Russian enterprises and United States companies for the delivery of uranium products which are currently in force and consistent with United States and Russian law.

13. This Agreement places no limitations on the right of the Russian Federation to dispose of LEU derived from HEU extracted from nuclear weapons resulting from the reduction of nuclear weapons pursuant to arms control agreements and other commitments of the Parties beyond the specific commitments set forth herein.

Article VI: Entry into Force, Duration and Amendments

1. This Agreement shall enter into force upon signature and shall remain in force until the full amount of HEU provided for in paragraph 1 of Article 1 is converted into LEU, delivered, and supplied to commercial customers.

2. Each Party may propose amendments to this Agreement. Agreed amendments shall enter into force upon signature and shall remain in force so long as this Agreement remains in force.

3. Each Party shall have the right to terminate this Agreement upon 12 months written notification to the other Party.

Done at Washington this 18th day of February 1993, in duplicate in the English and Russian languages, both texts being equally authentic.

For the United States of America:
William Burns

For the Russian Federation:
Viktor Mikhailov

Source: US Department of Energy.

1993 RESOLUTION OF THE UKRAINIAN PARLIAMENT ON RATIFICATION OF THE START I TREATY AND THE LISBON PROTOCOL

Kiev, 18 November 1993

On ratification of the Treaty Between the Union of Soviet Socialist Republics and the United States of America on the Reduction and Limitation of Strategic Offensive Arms signed in Moscow on July 31, 1991 and of the Protocol to it signed in Lisbon on behalf of Ukraine on May 23, 1992

The Verkhovna Rada [Parliament] of Ukraine resolves:

To ratify on behalf of Ukraine, successor state to the former USSR, the Treaty Between the Union of Soviet Socialist Republics and the United States of America on the Reduction and Limitation of Strategic Offensive Arms (hereinafter referred to as the Treaty), signed in Moscow on 31 July 1991, which includes the following documents, integral parts of the Treaty:

– Memorandum of Understanding on the Establishment of the Data Base Relating to the Treaty;

– Protocol on Procedures Governing the Conversion or Elimination of the Items Subject to the Treaty;

– Protocol on Inspections and Continuous Monitoring Activities Relating to the Treaty;

– Protocol of Notifications Relating to the Treaty;

– Protocol on ICBM and SLBM Throw-weight Relating to the Treaty;

– Protocol on Telemetric Information Relating to the Treaty;

– Protocol on the Joint Compliance and Inspection Commission Relating to the Treaty;

– Agreed Statements Annex;

– Terms and Definitions Annex;

– Protocol to the Treaty, signed on behalf of Ukraine in Lisbon on 23 May 1992 (except Article V).

with the following reservations to the Treaty and the documents that form an integral part thereof:

1. In accordance with the Vienna Convention on Succession of States in Respect of State Property, Archives State Debts of 1983 and in accordance with the Law of Ukraine On the Enterprises, Institutions and Organizations of Union Subordination Located on the

Territory of Ukraine, of 10 September 1991, as well as with the Fundamental Directions of the Foreign Policy of Ukraine, all assets of the strategic and tactical nuclear forces deployed in Ukraine, including their nuclear warheads, are the state property of Ukraine.

2. Ukraine does not regard Article V of the Lisbon Protocol as binding for Ukraine.

3. Having become the owner of the nuclear weapons inherited from the former USSR, Ukraine will exercise administrative control over the strategic nuclear forces deployed on its territory.

4. Having suffered the grave consequences of the Chernobyl nuclear disaster, the people of Ukraine realize their great responsibility before the peoples of the world that nuclear war not be unleashed from Ukrainian territory. Hence Ukraine will undertake appropriate measures to prevent the use of nuclear weapons deployed on its territory.

5. As the state-owner of nuclear weapons, Ukraine shall move towards non-nuclear status and will gradually get rid of the nuclear weapons deployed on its territory, provided that guarantees of its national security are extended to it, whereby the other nuclear states will assume obligations never to use nuclear weapons against Ukraine, never to use conventional armed forces against it and never to resort to threat by force, to respect the territorial integrity and inviolability of borders of Ukraine, and to refrain from economic pressure as a means of resolving any disputes.

6. The reduction and further elimination of strategic nuclear weapons deployed on the territory of Ukraine will be carried out in accordance with the Treaty on the Reduction and Limitation of Strategic Offensive Arms of 31 July 1991 and Article II of the Lisbon Protocol so that 36 percent of delivery vehicles and 42 percent of warheads will be subject to elimination. This does exclude the possibility of the elimination of any additional launchers and warheads in accordance with procedures that may be determined by Ukraine.

7. Ukraine shall fulfil its obligations under the Treaty within the timescale provided for, on the basis of the legal, technical, financial, organizational, and other considerations, to ensure nuclear and environmental safety and security. Taking into account the current economic crisis in Ukraine, the implementation of these obligations shall be possible only on condition that sufficient international financial and technical assistance be provided.

8. Entry into force of the Treaty and its implemenetation will not give the member states of this Treaty any grounds to seek any unilateral advantages for any entities of theirs on high-technology markets, in science and technology exchanges and in cooperation in the field of the application of nuclear energy for peaceful purposes and in the use of missile technologies which can affect Ukraine's national interests.

9. If the nuclear warheads, deployed on the territory of Ukraine, are dismantled and destroyed outside its territory, Ukraine will exercise direct control over this process in order to ensure the non-use of the nuclear component of these nuclear warheads for the production of new nuclear weapons.

10. The conditions and schedule for transfer of the nuclear warheads to be dismantled and destroyed shall be determined in a relevant agreement or agreements providing for the return to Ukraine of components of nuclear weapons for their use for peaceful purposes, or their value will be compensated.

The conditions for compensation shall also apply to the tactical nuclear weapons withdrawn from Ukrainian territory to Russia in 1992.

11. Proceeding from the fact that Ukraine did not directly negotiate the Treaty, it is recommended that the President of Ukraine and the Government of Ukraine conduct negotiations with the relevant states and international organizations on the following:

1) international guarantees of Ukraine's national security;

2) the conditions of economic, financial, scientific and technical assistance in the implementation of the obligations under the Treaty;

3) guarantee period [*harantiynyy*] and manufacturer's [*avtorskyy*] servicing of nuclear warheads and missile complexes;

4) revision of conditions of inspection activity financing under the Treaty;

5) the possibility of utilizing silos for peaceful purposes under reliable control;

6) conditions of the use of weapons-grade fissile materials removed from the nuclear weapons in the course of their elimination;

7) guarantees of fair compensation for the material value of the components of nuclear weapons.

12. It is recommended that the President of Ukraine approve the timetable for elimination of the strategic offensive arms determined by

this Resolution, and ensure control over its implementation.

13. It is recommended that the Cabinet of Ministers of Ukraine open a special budget line for costs incurred by fulfilment of the obligations of Ukraine under this Treaty in drafting Ukraine's budget for 1994.

Ukraine will exchange the instruments of ratification only after the conditions, set forth in Articles 5, 6, 7, 9, 10, and 11 above, are implemented.

The Verkhovna Rada of Ukraine expresses its hope that the nuclear states which are not Parties to the Treaty will join the efforts of Ukraine and other legal successor states of the former USSR, as well as the United States, and will begin the reduction of their nuclear arsenals.

Entry into force of the Treaty and its implementation will open the prospect of resolution by the Verkhovna Rada of the issue of accession to the Non-Proliferation Treaty of 1 July 1968.

Chairman of the Verkhovna Rada of Ukraine [Ivan Plyushch]

Sources: The Ukrainian Parliament; and Foreign Broadcast Information Service, 'Supreme Council START I Ratification Resolution' in FBIS-SOV-93-222, 19 Nov. 1993, pp. 45–47.

TRILATERAL STATEMENT BY THE PRESIDENTS OF THE UNITED STATES, RUSSIA AND UKRAINE

Moscow, 14 January 1994

Presidents Clinton, Yeltsin and Kravchuk met in Moscow on January 14. The three Presidents reiterated that they will deal with one another as full and equal partners and that relations among their countries must be conducted on the basis of respect for the independence, sovereignty and territorial integrity of each nation.

The three Presidents agreed on the importance of developing mutually beneficial, comprehensive and cooperative economic relations. In this connection, they welcomed the intention of the United States to provide assistance to Ukraine and Russia to support the creation of effective market economies.

The three Presidents reviewed the progress that has been made in reducing nuclear forces. Deactivation of strategic forces is already well underway in the United States, Russia and Ukraine. The Presidents welcomed the ongoing deactivation of RS-18s (SS-19s) and RS-22s (SS-24s) on Ukrainian territory by having their warheads removed.

The Presidents look forward to the entry into force of the START I Treaty, including the Lisbon Protocol and associated documents, and President Kravchuk reiterated his commitment that Ukraine accede to the Nuclear Non-Proliferation Treaty as a non-nuclear-weapon state in the shortest possible time. Presidents Clinton and Yeltsin noted that entry into force of START I will allow them to seek early ratification of START II. The Presidents discussed, in this regard, steps their countries would take to resolve certain nuclear weapons questions.

The Presidents emphasized the importance of ensuring the safety and security of nuclear weapons pending their dismantlement.

The Presidents recognize the importance of compensation to Ukraine, Kazakhstan and Belarus for the value of the highly-enriched uranium in nuclear warheads located on their territories. Arrangements have been worked out to provide fair and timely compensation to Ukraine, Kazakhstan and Belarus as the nuclear warheads on their territory are transferred to Russia for dismantling.

Presidents Clinton and Yeltsin expressed satisfaction with the completion of the highly-enriched uranium contract, which was signed by appropriate authorities of the United States and Russia. By converting weapons-grade uranium into uranium which can only be used for peaceful purposes, the highly-enriched uranium agreement is a major step forward in fulfilling the countries' mutual non-proliferation objectives.

The three Presidents decided on simultaneous actions on the transfer of nuclear warheads from Ukraine and delivery of compensation to Ukraine in the form of fuel assemblies for nuclear power stations.

Presidents Clinton and Yeltsin informed President Kravchuk that the United States and Russia are prepared to provide security assurances to Ukraine. In particular, once the START I Treaty enters into force and Ukraine becomes a non-nuclear-weapon state party to the Nuclear Non-Proliferation Treaty (NPT), the United States and Russia will:

– Reaffirm their commitments to Ukraine, in accordance with the principles of the CSCE Final Act, to respect the independence and sovereignty and the existing borders of CSCE member states and recognize that border changes can be made only by peaceful and consensual means; and reaffirm their obligation to refrain from the threat or use of force against the territorial integrity or political independence of any state, and that none of their weapons will ever be used except in self-defense or otherwise in accordance with the Charter of the United Nations;

– Reaffirm their commitment to Ukraine, in accordance with the principles of the CSCE Final Act, to refrain from economic coercion designed to subordinate to their own interest the exercise by another CSCE participating state of the rights inherent in its sovereignty and thus to secure advantages of any kind;

– Reaffirm their commitment to seek immediate UN Security Council action to provide assistance to Ukraine, as a non-nuclear-weapon state party to the NPT, if Ukraine should become a victim of an act of aggression or an object of a threat of aggression in which nuclear weapons are used; and

– Reaffirm, in the case of Ukraine, their commitment not to use nuclear weapons against any non-nuclear-weapon state party to the NPT, except in the case of an attack on themselves, their territories or dependent territories, their armed forces, or their allies, by such a state in association or alliance with a nuclear weapon state.

Presidents Clinton and Yeltsin informed President Kravchuk that consultations have been held with the United Kingdom, the third depositary state of the NPT, and the United Kingdom is prepared to offer the same security assurances to Ukraine once it becomes a non-nuclear-weapon state party to the NPT.

President Clinton reaffirmed the US commitment to provide technical and financial assistance for the safe and secure dismantling of nuclear forces and storage of fissile materials. The United States has agreed under the Nunn-Lugar program to provide Russia, Ukraine, Kazakhstan and Belarus with nearly USD 800 million in such assistance, including a minimum of USD 175 million to Ukraine. The US Congress has authorized additional Nunn-Lugar funds for this program, and the United States will work intensively with Russia, Ukraine, Kazakhstan and Belarus to expand assistance for this important purpose. The United States will also work to promote rapid implementation of the assistance agreements that are already in place.

ANNEX

The three Presidents decided that, to begin the process of compensation for Ukraine, Russia will provide to Ukraine within 10 months fuel assemblies for nuclear power stations containing 100 tons of low-enriched uranium. By the same date, at least 200 nuclear warheads from RS-18 (SS-19) and RS-22 (SS-24) missiles will be transferred from Ukraine to Russia for dismantling. Ukrainian representatives will monitor the dismantling of these warheads. The United States will provide USD 60 million as an advance payment to Russia, to be deducted from payments due to Russia under the highly-enriched uranium contract. These funds would be available to help cover expenses for the transportation and dismantling of strategic warheads and the production of fuel assemblies.

All nuclear warheads will be transferred from the territory of Ukraine to Russia for the purpose of their subsequent dismantling in the shortest possible time. Russia will provide compensation in the form of supplies of fuel assemblies to Ukraine for the needs of its nuclear power industry within the same time period.

Ukraine will ensure the elimination of all nuclear weapons, including strategic offensive arms, located on its territory in accordance with the relevant agreements and during the seven-year period as provided by the START I Treaty and within the context of the Verkhovna Rada statement on the non-nuclear status of Ukraine. All SS-24s on the territory of Ukraine will be deactivated within 10 months by having their warheads removed.

Pursuant to agreements reached between Russia and Ukraine in 1993, Russia will provide for the servicing and ensure the safety of nuclear warheads and Ukraine will cooperate in providing conditions for Russia to carry out these operations.

Russia and the United States will promote the elaboration and adoption by the International Atomic Energy Agency of an agreement placing all nuclear activities of Ukraine under IAEA safeguards, which will allow the unimpeded export of fuel assemblies from Russia to Ukraine for Ukraine's nuclear power industry.

Source: *Arms Control Today*, Jan.–Feb. 1994, pp. 21–22.

1994 RESOLUTION OF THE UKRAINIAN PARLIAMENT ON RATIFICATION OF THE START I TREATY AND THE LISBON PROTOCOL

Kiev, 3 February 1994

On the implementation by the President of Ukraine and the Government of Ukraine of the recommendations contained in the para. 11 of the Resolution of the Verkhovna Rada of Ukraine 'On the Ratification of the Treaty between the Union of Soviet Socialist Republics and the United States of America on the Reduction and Elimination of Strategic Offensive Arms' signed in Moscow on July 31, 1991, and Protocol to it signed in Lisbon on behalf of Ukraine on May 23, 1992.

The Verkhovna Rada [Parliament] of Ukraine:
– taking into account the concrete measures taken by the President and the Government of Ukraine during November 1993–January 1994 concerning implementation of provisions of the Resolution of the Verkhovna Rada of November 18, 1993;
– proceeding from the results of the meeting of the Presidents of Ukraine, the United States of America and the Russian Federation in Moscow on January 14, 1994, as well as of the Trilateral Statement and the Annex thereto signed by them;
– taking into account the fact that Ukraine has received the assurances on the side of the Presidents of USA and Russia about their readiness to provide Ukraine with the guarantees of the national security after entry into force of the START-I Treaty and accession of Ukraine to the Treaty on the non-proliferation of nuclear weapons (NPT) as a non-nuclear-weapon state, as well as bearing in mind the obligations on the side of the United States and Great Britain toward Ukraine to respect independence, sovereignty and existing boundaries, to refrain from the threat by force or its use against territorial integrity or political independence, to refrain from economic pressure and the commitment not to use any weapons against Ukraine;
– taking into consideration the confirmation by the Presidents of Ukraine, the USA and Russia that their relations will be built on the basis of respect of independence, sovereignty and territorial integrity of each state, as well as the confirmation of their

readiness to provide assistance in the establishment of the effective market economy in Ukraine;
– recognizing the fact that the United States of America assured Ukraine in providing technical and financial assistance for the safe and secure dismantlement of the nuclear weapons and storing of fissionable material, as well as contributing to the fast realization of the already existing agreements in connection with such an assistance;
– taking into account, that in accordance with the Protocol 'On the Procedure of the Control over the Elimination of Nuclear Munitions Transferred from the Territory of Ukraine to the Industrial Enterprises of the Russian Federation' the representatives of the Ministry of Defence of Ukraine will realize control over the dismantlement and elimination of the strategic nuclear charges on the territory of Russia, that will exclude the reuse of the components of these charges for their original purpose;
– taking also into account the obligation of Russia to provide for the servicing and safety of nuclear charges;
– proceeding from the fact that Ukraine will get the fair compensation for the cost of highly-enriched uranium and other components of all the nuclear weapons, the owner of which is Ukraine;
– taking into consideration the arrangement on providing Ukraine with fair and timely compensation for the cost of highly-enriched uranium on the Russian Federation and the United States of America while nuclear warheads are being withdrawn from Ukraine to Russia for dismantlement and that measures on withdrawal and providing compensation to Ukraine are simultaneous;
– proceeding from the fact that the United States of America, the Russian Federation and Ukraine will steadily comply with the arrangements contained in the Trilateral Statement and the Annex thereto, and with the existing agreements among them and with those which will be concluded concerning the nuclear weapons deployed on the territory of Ukraine;
– considering that the above mentioned facilitates the implementation of the conditions and reservations which were made in the Resolution of November 18, 1993,

RESOLVES:
1. Bearing in mind the concrete measures taken by the President and the Government of Ukraine on the implementation of the provi-

sions of the Resolution of the Verkhovna Rada of November 18, 1993, the meeting steps on behalf of the USA and Russia, to remove the restriction in respect of the Article V of the Protocol to the START-I Treaty signed in Lisbon on May 23, 1993.

2. To instruct the Government of Ukraine to realize the exchange of the instruments of ratification on the START-I Treaty and to intensify the activities on concluding specific international agreements resulting from the reservations contained in the Resolution of the Verkhovna Rada of Ukraine on the Ratification of the START-I Treaty.

Chairman of the Verkhovna Rada of Ukraine

Source: Press Release, Permanent Mission of Ukraine to the United Nations, New York, 3 Feb. 1994.

US–RUSSIAN JOINT STATEMENT ON INSPECTION OF FACILITIES CONTAINING FISSILE MATERIALS REMOVED FROM NUCLEAR WEAPONS

Moscow, 16 March 1994

President Clinton and President Yeltsin, during their meeting in Moscow on January 14, 1994, agreed that the proliferation of weapons of mass destruction and their missile delivery systems represents an acute threat to international security in the period following the end of the Cold War. They declared the resolve of their countries to cooperate actively and closely with each other, and also other interested states, for the purpose of preventing and reducing this threat.

The Presidents agreed to establish a joint working group to consider steps to ensure the transparency and irreversibility of the process of reduction of nuclear weapons, including the possibility of putting a portion of fissionable materials under International Atomic Energy Agency safeguards. Particular attention would be given to materials released in the process of nuclear disarmament and steps to ensure that these materials would not be used again for nuclear weapons.

In furtherance of the Presidents' agreement, the Department of Energy and the Ministry of Atomic Energy of the Russian Federation announced their intention to host reciprocal inspections by the end of 1994 to facili-

ties containing plutonium removed from nuclear weapons. In preparation for these inspections, technical experts will meet to define the procedures for inspecting plutonium that has been removed from nuclear weapons. An initial meeting of technical experts will be held within two months from this date. The two sides intend to conclude an agreement on the means of confirming the plutonium and highly enriched uranium inventories from nuclear disarmament. These inspections will be an important step in the process of establishing a world-wide control regime for fissile materials.

Done in Washington, DC, on March 16, 1994, in English and Russian language texts.

[Hazel O'Leary, Secretary of the US Department of Energy]

For the United States Department of Energy

[Viktor Mikhailov, MINATOM Director]

For the Ministry of the Russian Federation for Atomic Energy

Source: US Department of Energy.

PROTOCOL OF THE MEETING BETWEEN THE UNITED STATES AND THE RUSSIAN FEDERATION ON THE REPLACEMENT OF RUSSIAN PLUTONIUM PRODUCTION REACTORS

Washington, DC, 16 March 1994

To further the agreements reached by Vice President Gore and Prime Minister Chernomyrdin on December 16, 1993, and by Presidents Clinton and Yeltsin on January 14, 1994, delegations of the U.S. and the Russian Federation met on March 14–16, 1994, to agree on a plan for replacement of plutonium production reactors with alternate energy sources. The sides stressed the historic importance of this task and their desire to avoid the risks associated with weapons-grade fissile material.

The Russian side proposed that, upon approval by the Government of the Russian Federation, the heads of the Russian and U.S. governments enter into a mutual agreement to cease military use of plutonium separated after the date of the agreement. This agreement would include provisions for compliance. Further, the Russian side proposed that Russia, within one year after creation of an alternate source of energy, would cease production and chemical separation of weapons-grade plutonium. The Russian side noted that both of these cessation and compliance provisions must be met and that the agreement would require that each side permit inspection of its relevant plutonium production facilities as well as the storage sites for the plutonium produced by the reactors in Tomsk and Krasnoyarsk.

The Russian side considers it possible to perform conversion work on the Tomsk and Krasnoyarsk-26 reactors in order to terminate the production of weapons-grade plutonium. The U.S. side will consider participating in this work if Russia obtains financing.

In working group discussions the Russian delegation described specific options to meet the heat and power needs of Tomsk and Krasnoyarsk which would permit the reactors to be shut down. The Russian side indicated that these options are at different stages of development. Further work is necessary for the projects to be considered for external financing.

For Tomsk, the sides agreed that development of combined heat and power stations based on aeroderivative gas turbines fueled by natural gas is the preferred option to replace the heat and power provided by the Tomsk reactors. The Russian side stated that pre-feasibility analyses have been completed. It proposed that the next step be a full feasibility study which would develop additional analyses necessary to proceed with financing the project. The U.S. Department of Energy stated that it is prepared to assist in securing financing for the completion of a feasibility study that would examine fully the gas turbine option and the potential for cost-effective improvements in energy efficiency.

For Krasnoyarsk, the sides agreed that the alternate energy facility needed to provide electricity and district heat for Krasnoyarsk-26 is a new coal-fired power plant which is being built south of the city. The sides agreed to undertake two parallel efforts. The first element would be the completion of a pre-feasibility study on finishing the coal-fired facility. This pre-feasibility study would be completed by the middle of May 1994. The second element would be a review and revision of an existing Russian feasibility study that had been completed prior to the start of construction. The U.S. side will make recommendations to meet the requirements of

Western financial institutions and private sector investment and recommendations to attract means of financing as soon as possible. The Russian side agreed to update its feasibility study to reflect these recommendations.

The sides agreed that a Joint Steering Committee would be convened to select the participants to implement the provisions of this Protocol, monitor progress, and identify and resolve problems. A report on the implementation of the provisions of this Protocol will be completed by the third meeting of Joint U.S.–Russian Commission on Economic and Technological Cooperation.

Done in Washington, DC, on March 16, 1994, in English and Russian language texts.

[Hazel O'Leary, Secretary of the US Department of Energy]

For the United States Department of Energy

[Viktor Mikhailov, MINATOM Director]

For the Ministry of the Russian Federation for Atomic Energy

———

Source: US Department of Energy.

PROTOCOL ON HIGHLY ENRICHED URANIUM TRANSPARENCY ARRANGEMENTS IN FURTHERANCE OF THE MEMORANDUM OF UNDERSTANDING OF SEPTEMBER 1, 1993

Washington, DC, 18 March 1994

The Department of Energy of the United States of America and the Ministry of Atomic Energy of the Russian Federation, hereinafter referred to as the Parties of the Executive Agents,

In accordance with Article VI of the Memorandum of Understanding Between the Government of the United States of America and the Government of the Russian Federation Relating to Transparency and Additional Arrangements Concerning the Agreement Between the Government of the United States of America and the Government of the Russian Federation Concerning the Disposition of Highly Enriched Uranium Extracted from Nuclear Weapons, dated September 1, 1993, hereinafter referred to as the Memorandum of Understanding (MOU),

Have agreed as follows:

Article I

Purpose

1. For the purposes of ensuring that the highly enriched uranium (HEU) subject to the Agreement is extracted from nuclear weapons and that this same HEU enters the oxidation facility and is oxidized therein; that the declared quantity of HEU is blended down to low enriched uranium (LEU); and that the LEU delivered to the United States of America is fabricated into fuel for commercial nuclear reactors, the Parties shall have the right to implement transparency and access arrangements at the following facilities:

(a) Ural Electrochemical Integrated Enterprise (UEIE), Sverdlovsk-44, Russia; the Tomsk chemical processing and conversion facility (Tomsk) at which HEU metal is oxidized prior to shipment to UEIE; and any other facility at which operations subject to the MOU and this Protocol are performed.

(b) Portsmouth Gaseous Diffusion Plant (Portsmouth), Piketon, Ohio; Nuclear fuel fabrication facilities in the United States to include Westinghouse in Columbia, South Carolina; General Electric in Wilmington, North Carolina; Babcock and Wilcox in Lynchburg, Virginia; Combustion Engineering in Hematite, Missouri; Siemens in Richland, Washington; and any other facility at which operations subject to the MOU and this protocol are performed.

2. All references to uranium, HEU and LEU in this Protocol, are understood to mean uranium, HEU and LEU subject to the MOU.

Article II

Implementation

To provide a means to promote the objectives and the implementation of the MOU and continually improve transparency measures, the Executive Agents hereby establish a Transparency Review Committee (TRC) which shall convene no later than 21 days following the request of either party, unless otherwise agreed. Within the framework of the TRC, the Parties may:

1. consider questions concerning the implementation and effectiveness of transparency measures;

2. discuss and agree upon changes or additional measures or procedures to promote the purposes of the MOU and this Protocol; and

3. resolve, by mutual agreement, any other relevant issues regarding the implementation of the MOU.

Article III

Transparency Measures

The provisions of this Article are without prejudice to any rights under existing or future transparency agreements.

1. The United States side shall have the right to perform the following monitoring activities at Tomsk:

(a) Visual monitoring, by means of physical presence, of HEU metal at the point where such metal is fed into the oxidation process,

(b) Visual monitoring, by means of physical presence, of the HEU oxide as it is withdrawn from the oxidation process, and

(c) Visual monitoring, by means of physical presence, of the HEU oxide at the storage and shipping areas where it is prepared for shipment to UEIE.

2. With respect to the monitoring activities set forth in paragraph 1 of this Article, the Parties shall agree upon applicable procedures within the TRC, consistent with the MOU. An Agreement on such procedures shall be concluded during the first session of the TRC, unless otherwise agreed.

3. The United States side shall have the right to perform monitoring activities at the following locations at UEIE:

(a) the location at which HEU is received;

(b) oxidation feed and withdrawal locations for uranium subject to the MOU;

(c) fluoridation feed and withdrawal locations for uranium subject to the MOU; and

(d) all areas where LEU is being transferred from a technological cylinder to a 30B cylinder.

4. With respect to the locations listed in paragraph 3 of this Article, the Parties shall further agree upon applicable procedures within the TRC, consistent with the MOU. An Agreement on such procedures shall be concluded during the first session of the TRC, unless otherwise agreed.

5. In the event that the Russian side proposes or uses other sites for the processing of HEU, then the Parties shall agree within the TRC upon transparency measures for such sites, consistent with the MOU.

6. The Russian side shall have the right to perform monitoring activities at:

(a) the relevant receiving, storage, feed and withdrawal areas, the 30B cylinder filling area, and other processing areas at Portsmouth; and

(b) the receipt and storage area for sealed UF6 cylinders, the receipt area for sealed containers or uranium powder or pellets, and the shipping area containing serialised fuel assemblies packaged for shipment and sealed, or powder or pellets in sealed shipping containers, at U.S. fuel fabrication facilities.

7. With respect to the locations listed in paragraph 6 of this Article, the Parties shall further agree upon applicable procedures, within the TRC, consistent with the MOU.

8. The monitoring of the content of U-235 in the material being processed is among the major parameters of monitoring for both Parties.

9. Each Party shall endeavor to make additional familiarization visits, at the earliest possible time, to the facilities specified in Article I, in order to enable the Parties to understand fully each other's facilities, processes, and monitoring environment. The teams for the familiarization visits shall have no more than 10 individuals. During these familiarization visits, the Parties shall have the right to observe the other Party's activities at all locations specified in paragraphs 3 and 6 of this Article.

10. Contract representatives shall have the right to perform the activities agreed upon pursuant to the MOU and paragraphs 3, 5, and 6 of this Article, in addition to any activities performed pursuant to the implementing contract. The Russian Federation shall have the right to have contract representatives continuously present within the U.S. Portsmouth, Ohio facility and the United States shall have the right to have contract representatives continuously present within the UEIE facility.

11. Each Party shall have the right to conduct monitoring visits in accordance with the MOU.

(a) The monitoring Party shall notify the monitored Party of its intent to conduct monitoring visits at least 30 days prior to such a visit.

(b) The monitored Party shall facilitate monitoring visits and grant entry into the monitored facility upon the arrival of the monitoring team.

(c) Each monitoring team shall consist of: for UEIE, no more than 10 individuals; for Tomsk, no more than 7 individuals.

12. The Parties shall seek to establish mutually acceptable MC&A systems for UEIE and for Portsmouth at the earliest

possible time, within the TRC, or through other channels.

13. If any LEU subject to the MOU is reexported to a third country, the United States side will require that such re-export be subject to International Atomic Energy Agency safeguards and to peaceful use assurances in the recipient country. Questions arising from transparency of reexports should be discussed in the TRC.

Article IV

Procedures

1. The Parties shall, within the TRC, develop not later than six months after entry into force of this Protocol, unless otherwise agreed, specific additional detailed measures and procedures for implementing the rights and obligations contained in the MOU and this Protocol, including, as appropriate, additional measures regarding permanent contract representatives, monitoring visits, analytical measurements, sampling, declarations and reports. These detailed measures and procedures shall be incorporated as annexes to this Protocol.

2. The monitored Party shall provide personal protective equipment.

3. Permanent contract representatives and visiting monitors shall have the right throughout the entire period of monitoring to be in communication with their embassy and their home country.

4. Each Party shall be responsible for the costs of its monitoring, including monitoring visits, and contract representation activities in the territory of the monitored Party.

Article V

Entry into Force and Amendment

1. This Protocol shall enter into force upon signature and remain in force as long as the MOU remains in force. This Protocol may be amended by the written agreement of the Parties.

2. If changes or additions are proposed in the TRC and the Parties are unable to reach agreement on such changes or additions within one year from the date of the opening of the TRC wherein such changes or additions were proposed, then each Party may so report to its government and then each government may decide, upon consultation with the other government, not to issue delivery orders, under the implementing contract. Deliveries or delivery orders may be resumed, in accordance with the implementing contract, upon resolution of issues raised

by such proposals.

3. Upon entry into force of this Protocol, deliveries of the LEU, in accordance with the implementing contract, to the United States of America may commence.

DONE at Washington, D.C., in two copies, this 18th day of March, 1994, in the English and Russian languages, each text being equally authentic.

FOR THE DEPARTMENT OF ENERGY
OF THE UNITED STATES OF AMERICA:

FOR THE MINISTRY OF ATOMIC
ENERGY OF THE RUSSIAN
FEDERATION:

_____

Source: US Department of Energy.

17. The Chemical Weapons Convention: institutionalization and preparation for entry into force

THOMAS STOCK

I. Introduction

The Convention on the Prohibition of the Development, Production, Stockpiling and Use of Chemical Weapons and on their Destruction was opened to all states for signature on 13 January 1993 in Paris at an international conference hosted by the French Government.[1] A resolution establishing the Organisation for the Prohibition of Chemical Weapons (OPCW) and the Text on the Establishment of a Preparatory Commission (PrepCom) was approved by the Conference. The PrepCom held its inaugural session in The Hague, on 8 February 1993.[2] A Provisional Technical Secretariat (PTS) was set up to assist the PrepCom in its work.

The Chemical Weapons Convention (CWC) is complex, and full and effective implementation of all of its provisions is essential. At least two years are required from opening of the CWC for signature to prepare for its entry into force. The PrepCom is currently establishing procedures for the CWC verification regime, developing a budget and setting up the OPCW infrastructure, including its rules and procedures. There is great hope that this process will be a success, but there is some cause for pessimism.

The establishment of the OPCW represents a unique challenge; the only comparable organization with a mandate for implementing a treaty verification regime is the International Atomic Energy Agency (IAEA), which was established more than 35 years ago.[3]

This chapter provides an overview of the establishment of the international machinery for the CWC in the first year after its opening for signature. One component of the implementation process calls for states parties to undertake national implementation, and the efforts of a number of states to do so are presented. The CWC can enter into force 180 days after 65 states have ratified their signatures and deposited their instruments of ratification but no earlier than two years after its opening for signature (i.e., early 1995). By the end of

---

[1] The CWC was signed by 130 of the more than 150 states which sent representatives to Paris; its text is reproduced in SIPRI, *SIPRI Yearbook 1993: World Armaments and Disarmament* (Oxford University Press: Oxford, 1993), pp. 735–56.

[2] The PrepCom was established under Appendix I of the Convention, which calls for such a commission 'for the purpose of carrying out the necessary preparations for the effective implementation'. See Conference on Disarmament document CD/1170, 26 Aug. 1992, p. 179.

[3] Dorn, W. A. and Rolya, A., 'The Organisation for the Prohibition of Chemical Weapons and the IAEA: a comparative overview', *IAEA Bulletin*, no. 3 (1993), pp. 44–47.

1993 only four states, Fiji, Mauritius, the Seychelles and Sweden, had ratified the CWC. As of 10 December 1993, the number of signatory states had increased to 154 (see table 17.1). The road between signature and ratification may be long and difficult owing to the practical consequences of the CWC obligations for each state party.

The CWC provides incentives for ratification; states which have not ratified the Convention at the time of the first Conference of the states parties will be unable to hold a seat on the OPCW Executive Council for the first one or two years after entry into force. In addition, only citizens of states which have ratified the CWC may be employed in the OPCW.

The long-term goal is universal adherence, but a number of states have not yet signed either for political or practical reasons. For some Middle East countries, especially the members of the Arab League, a precondition for adherence is a commitment to nuclear disarmament by Israel, including the creation of a zone free of weapons of mass destruction.[4] Some of the countries in the Middle East, such as Libya and Syria, are alleged to have chemical weapon (CW) programmes. Iraq is already obliged to destroy its CW stockpiles under UN Security Council Resolution 687, the cease-fire agreement which ended the 1991 Persian Gulf War.[5] Outside the region, other small states may not have signed owing to practical reasons such as the cost of contributing to the CWC infrastructure, including the PrepCom. North Korea, which is alleged to have a CW programme, has also not signed.

When the CWC negotiations were concluded in 1992 there was great enthusiasm which culminated in the Paris Conference. The final stages of the negotiations had involved compromises, and the PrepCom was concerned that some signatory states would attempt to reopen discussion under the pretext of elaborating detailed procedures. In addition, there were questions about a number of issues including: the participation of signatory states; the readiness to make financial contributions for the PrepCom; the possible shortage of manpower to fill positions in the PTS; the process of elaborating particular procedures; the co-operation of the chemical industry; and the experience which states were gaining in preparation for national implementation.

The following discussion provides an overview of the successes and difficulties encountered in building up the PrepCom and the PTS and suggests sources of additional information; it also outlines the main trends related to industry involvement, national implementation and the ratification process.

II. The Preparatory Commission for the OPCW

The major tasks for the PrepCom prior to entry into force of the CWC are *inter alia*: (a) setting operational procedures for the verification regime, (b) drafting the budget for the organization, and (c) establishing the infrastruc-

---

[4] However, some Arab League members—e.g., Algeria, Kuwait, Mauritania, Morocco, Oman, Tunisia and Yemen—have already signed the CWC.

[5] The text of the resolution is reproduced in SIPRI, *SIPRI Yearbook 1992: World Armaments and Disarmament* (Oxford University Press: Oxford, 1992), pp. 525–30.

ture and rules of procedure for the OPCW. The Text on the Establishment of a Preparatory Commission, which was attached to the CWC, lists some 40 separate tasks for the PrepCom. For 1993 the PrepCom was: (*a*) to achieve drafts of the procedures and requirements for implementation of verification provisions, including identification of requirements for inspection equipment and collecting of declaration data; (*b*) to arrive at a preliminary estimate for the size, structure and cost of the Technical Secretariat (TS) for the period immediately after entry into force; (*c*) to work out the information management system for the organization; (*d*) to assist in promoting and facilitating the ratification process; (*e*) to establish rules and procedures for staffing; and (*f*) to prepare an outline for the training programme for future inspectors.

During the *first Plenary Meeting*, in February 1993, the PrepCom decided to organize its work in: (*a*) Plenary Meetings, (*b*) Working Groups A and B,[6] and (*c*) Expert Groups, mandated by the Working Groups. (Figure 17.1 presents the structure of the PrepCom at the end of 1993.) Each Expert Group elected a chairman.[7] The Working and Expert Groups address various issues during the intersessional period between Plenary Meetings, which are held approximately every two to three months. A majority of PrepCom members constitutes a quorum for Plenary Meetings. All decisions must be taken by consensus, but if consensus is not achievable within 24 hours, a two-thirds majority for matters of substance and a simple majority for questions of procedure are recommended. Each signatory state is entitled to participate at all three levels of activity (Plenary Meeting, Working Groups and Expert Groups). It became evident shortly after establishment of the PrepCom that for many states this poses a problem with respect to manpower and expertise. In addition, the decreasing percentage of signatory states participating in the 1993 Plenary Meetings made it difficult to obtain a quorum; most new signatories after the Paris Conference were small countries that were unable to participate.[8] In an effort to reverse the negative trend with regard to participation, the Deputy Executive Secretary of the PTS visited Brussels in the summer of 1993 to discuss future participation in the Plenary Meetings with the 24 signatory states not represented in The Hague.

[6] The PrepCom established Working Group A to assist it with budgetary and administrative matters, and Working Group B (which began work following the second Plenary Meeting in April 1993) to assist in verification, technical co-operation and assistance matters. Ambassador Luis Alberto Villamizar of Colombia chaired Working Group A; Counsellor Sylwin Gizowski of Poland chaired Working Group B. See Preparatory Commission for the Organisation for the Prohibition of Chemical Weapons, 'Draft report of the Preparatory Commission', PREPCOM/I/CRP.10, 12 Feb. 1993, pp. 4–7. A Credentials Committee was also established in accordance with the rules and procedures for all sessions. It examines credentials of newly accredited representatives to the PrepCom.

[7] The chairman is responsible for smooth and effective discharge of mandated activities, for timely submission of reports and for maintenance of effective consultation with signatories. All Expert Groups are open-ended and meet in The Hague.

[8] Eleven member states which attended the second Plenary Meeting did not attend the third Plenary Meeting (Albania, Bangladesh, Belarus, the Holy See, Mali, Mauritius, Namibia, Nepal, Papua New Guinea, Yemen and Zambia).

Table 17.1. Signatory status of the Chemical Weapons Convention as of 10 December 1993

State	Date of signature	State	Date of signature
States which have signed the CWC			
Afghanistan	14 Jan.	France	13 Jan.
Albania	14 Jan.	Gabon	13 Jan.
Algeria	13 Jan.	Gambia	13 Jan.
Argentina	13 Jan.	Georgia	14 Jan.
Armenia	19 Mar.	Germany	13 Jan.
Australia	13 Jan.	Ghana	14 Jan.
Austria	13 Jan.	Greece	13 Jan.
Azerbaijan	13 Jan.	Guatemala	14 Jan.
Bahrain	24 Feb.	Guinea	14 Jan.
Bangladesh	14 Jan.	Guinea-Bissau	14 Jan.
Belarus	14 Jan.	Guyana	6 Oct.
Belgium	13 Jan.	Haiti	14 Jan.
Benin	14 Jan.	Holy See	14 Jan.
Bolivia	14 Jan.	Honduras	13 Jan.
Brazil	13 Jan.	Hungary	13 Jan.
Brunei Darussalam	13 Jan.	Iceland	13 Jan.
Bulgaria	13 Jan.	India	14 Jan.
Burkina Faso	14 Jan.	Indonesia	13 Jan.
Burundi	15 Jan.	Iran	13 Jan.
Cambodia	15 Jan.	Ireland	14 Jan.
Cameroon	14 Jan.	Israel	13 Jan.
Canada	13 Jan.	Italy	13 Jan.
Cape Verde	15 Jan.	Japan	13 Jan.
Central African Republic	14 Jan.	Kazakhstan	14 Jan.
Chile	14 Jan.	Kenya	15 Jan.
China	13 Jan.	Korea, South	14 Jan.
Colombia	13 Jan.	Kuwait	27 Jan.
Comoros	13 Jan.	Kyrgyzstan	22 Feb.
Congo	15 Jan.	Laos	12 May
Cook Islands	14 Jan.	Latvia	6 May
Costa Rica	14 Jan.	Liberia	15 Jan.
Côte d'Ivoire	13 Jan.	Liechtenstein	21 July
Croatia	13 Jan.	Lithuania	13 Jan.
Cuba	13 Jan.	Luxembourg	13 Jan.
Cyprus	13 Jan.	Madagascar	15 Jan.
Czech Republic	14 Jan.	Malawi	14 Jan.
Denmark	14 Jan.	Malaysia	13 Jan.
Djibouti	28 Sep.	Maldives	1 Oct.
Dominica	2 Aug.	Mali	13 Jan.
Dominican Republic	13 Jan.	Malta	13 Jan.
Ecuador	14 Jan.	Marshall Islands	13 Jan.
El Salvador	14 Jan.	Mauritania	13 Jan.
Equatorial Guinea	14 Jan.	Mauritius	14 Jan.[b]
Estonia	14 Jan.	Mexico	13 Jan.
Ethiopia	14 Jan.	Micronesia	13 Jan.
Fiji	20 Jan.[a]	Moldova	13 Jan.
Finland	14 Jan.	Monaco	13 Jan.

State	Date of signature	State	Date of signature
Mongolia	14 Jan.	Senegal	13 Jan.
Morocco	13 Jan.	Seychelles	15 Jan.[c]
Myanmar	14 Jan.	Sierra Leone	15 Jan.
Namibia	13 Jan.	Singapore	14 Jan.
Nauru	13 Jan.	Slovak Republic	14 Jan.
Nepal	19 Jan.	Slovenia	14 Jan.
Netherlands	14 Jan.	South Africa	14 Jan.
New Zealand	14 Jan.	Spain	13 Jan.
Nicaragua	9 Mar.	Sri Lanka	14 Jan.
Niger	14 Jan.	Swaziland	23 Sep
Nigeria	13 Jan.	Sweden	13 Jan.[d]
Norway	13 Jan.	Switzerland	14 Jan.
Oman	2 Feb.	Tajikistan	14 Jan.
Pakistan	13 Jan.	Thailand	14 Jan.
Panama	16 June	Togo	13 Jan.
Papua New Guinea	14 Jan.	Tunisia	13 Jan.
Paraguay	14 Jan.	Turkey	14 Jan.
Peru	14 Jan.	Turkmenistan	12 Oct.
Philippines	13 Jan.	Uganda	14 Jan.
Poland	13 Jan.	Ukraine	13 Jan.
Portugal	13 Jan.	United Arab Emirates	2 Feb.
Qatar	1 Feb.	United Kingdom	13 Jan.
Romania	13 Jan.	United States	13 Jan.
Russian Federation	13 Jan.	Uruguay	15 Jan.
Rwanda	17 May	Venezuela	14 Jan.
Saint Lucia	29 Mar.	Viet Nam	13 Jan.
Saint Vincent and	20 Sep.	Yemen	8 Feb.
the Grenadines		Zaire	14 Jan.
Samoa (Western)	14 Jan.	Zambia	13 Jan.
San Marino	13 Jan.	Zimbabwe	13 Jan.
Saudi Arabia	20 Jan.		

States which have not signed the CWC

Angola	Chad	Libya	Taiwan
Andorra	Egypt	Mozambique	Tanzania
Antigua and Barbuda	Grenada	St Kitts and Nevis	Tonga
Bahamas	Iraq	Sao Tome and Principe	Trinidad and
Barbados	Jamaica	Solomon Islands	Tobago
Belize	Jordan	Somalia	Tuvalu
Bhutan	Korea, North	Sudan	Uzbekistan
Bosnia and Herzegovina	Lebanon	Suriname	Vanuatu
Botswana	Lesotho	Syria	Yugoslavia

[a] Ratification and deposit date 20 Jan. 1993.
[b] Ratification and deposit date 9 Feb. 1993.
[c] Ratification and deposit date 7 Apr. 1993.
[d] Ratification and deposit date 17 June 1993.

Source: 'List of signatures to and ratifications of the CWC as of 10 December 1993', PC-V/INF.2, 10 Dec. 1993.

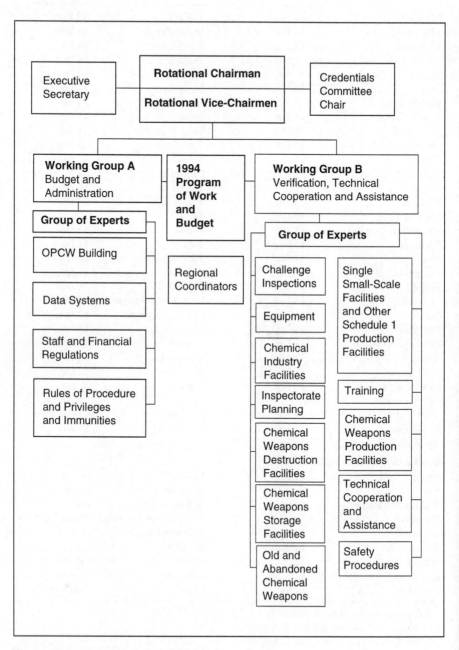

Figure 17.1. Structure of the Preparatory Commission

Note: Based on *The CWC Chronicle*, Henry L. Stimson Center, Washington, DC, vol. 1, no. 4 (Oct. 1993), p. 2; 'Report of the Commission', PC-V/12, 17 Dec. 1993.

Table 17. 2. Attendance at 1993 Plenary Meetings of the Preparatory Commission

Plenary Meeting	Date	Number of signatory states which attended	Number of signatory states	Rate of attendance
First	8–12 Feb.	92	137	67
Second	19–22 Apr.	89	142	63
Third	28 June–2 July	80	146	55
Fourth	27 Sep.–1 Oct.	82	150	55
Fifth	13–17 Dec.	81	154	53

Sources: 'Draft report of the Preparatory Commission', PREPCOM/I/CRP.10, 12 Feb. 1993; 'Report of the Preparatory Commission', PREPCOM/II/9, 22 Apr. 1993; 'Report of the Preparatory Commission', PC-III/11, 2 July 1993; 'Report of the Preparatory Commission', PC-IV/23, 1 Oct. 1993; 'Report of the Commission', PC-V/12, 17 Dec. 1993.

At the time of the *first Plenary Meeting*, 137 states had signed the CWC,[9] and 92 of these states attended the first session. (Table 17.2 presents an overview of the attendance at all 1993 Plenary Meetings.)

Limitations on access to the work of the PrepCom, including that of the PTS, created problems for those excluded from the Plenary Meetings (e.g., the scientific community, non-governmental organizations (NGOs), etc.). The PrepCom meets in closed sessions, as mandated by the Rules of Procedure.[10] Only reports from the Expert Groups, Working Groups and official documents from the Plenary Meetings are available on request to certain NGOs, research institutes and industry associations. During 1993 several PrepCom delegations[11] proposed opening the Plenary Meetings to the concerned community, but a decision to change the Rules of Procedure was not taken, although the issue is under consideration. The success of the implementation efforts of the PrepCom is heavily dependent on active participation by signatory states. However, the NGOs, the scientific and disarmament community, chemical industry and trade associations also have a role to play. The text of the CWC recognizes the need to remain abreast of scientific progress and technical change,[12] and the scientific expertise and knowledge of those outside the CWC infrastructure (i.e., the PrepCom and the PTS) are needed.

[9] Between the first Plenary Meeting and Dec. 1993 the following states became signatories: Armenia, Bahrain, Djibouti, Dominica, Guyana, Kyrgyzstan, Laos, Latvia, Liechtenstein, Maldives, Nicaragua, Panama, Rwanda, Saint Lucia, Saint Vincent and the Grenadines, Swaziland, and Turkmenistan.

[10] See rule 32 in 'Rules of Procedure of the Preparatory Commission for the Organisation for the Prohibition of Chemical Weapons', PREPCOM/II/8, 22 Apr. 1993, p. 11.

[11] The Australian delegation vigorously promoted the idea of making Plenary Meetings public. The draft decision, prepared by Australia, met opposition from two Western delegations and several delegations from developing countries. See Institute for Defense and Disarmament Studies, 'Public access', *Arms Control Reporter* (IDDS: Brookline, Mass., 1994), sheet 704.B.559, Jan. 1994.

[12] CWC, Article VIII, paragraph 21, (h); Conference on Disarmament document CD/1170 (note 2), appendix, p. 29.

Organizational aspects

During its *first Plenary Meeting,* on 8–12 February 1993, the PrepCom adopted Provisional Rules of Procedure[13] and elected a chairman for the first six months.[14]

At the *second Plenary Meeting,* on 19–22 April 1993, the PrepCom,[15] the Executive Secretary,[16] and Working Groups A and B presented reports.[17] The Rules of Procedure for the PrepCom, which had been prepared by Working Group A, were adopted.[18]

The question of whether languages other than English would be used in the Expert Groups[19] was raised by several delegations led by France.[20] Other delegations argued that full interpretation service would significantly add to the annual budget. The Chairman of the PrepCom noted that the 1993 budget provided for interpretation services only for Working Groups and Plenary Meetings.[21] It was decided that interpretation services would be made available to Expert Groups on a case-by-case basis.[22]

The *third Plenary Meeting* took place on 28 June–2 July 1993. The PrepCom then actively functioned at all three levels: the Plenary Meetings, the Working Groups and the Experts Groups,[23] with the Expert Groups as the driving force. As the number of Expert Groups increased, so did the workload for signatory state delegations.[24] The PTS also continued to grow owing to its

[13] 'Provisional Rules of Procedure of the PrepCom for the OPCW', PREPCOM/I/2, 8 Feb. 1993.

[14] Under the Rules and Procedures, the chairmanship rotates every 6 months among the 5 regional groups (Africa, Asia, Eastern Europe, Latin America and the Caribbean, and Western European and Other States) in alphabetical order starting with the African Group. Ambassador E. A. Azikiwe of Nigeria was Chairman for the first 6 months. Representatives from Chile, Hungary, Iran, Tunisia and the USA were elected Vice-Chairmen. The Vice-Chairmen are to represent each of the 5 regional groups.

[15] 'Report of the Preparatory Commission', PREPCOM/II/9, 22 Apr. 1993.

[16] 'Report of the Executive Secretary for the period from the first to the second session of the Preparatory Commission (11 February to 18 April 1993)', PREPCOM/II/3, 19 Apr. 1993.

[17] 'Report of Working Group A', PREPCOM/II/WGA/2, 22 Apr. 1993; 'Report of Working Group B', PREPCOM/II/WGB/1, 20 Apr. 1993. A report on the submission of formal credentials to the Credentials Committee was also received: 'Report on the credentials of representatives of Member States of the Preparatory Commission for the Organisation for the Prohibition of Chemical Weapons', PREPCOM/I/3/Add.1, 22 Apr. 1993.

[18] See PREPCOM/II/8 (note 10).

[19] See PREPCOM/II/9 (note 15), pp. 11–13.

[20] Herby, P. and Robinson, J. P., 'Building the Organisation for the Prohibition of Chemical Weapons: progress in The Hague, quarterly review no. 2', *Chemical Weapons Convention Bulletin,* no. 20 (June 1993), p. 5.

[21] The budget for 1993 contained $2.4 million for conference service.

[22] See PREPCOM/II/9 (note 15), p. 4.

[23] The Plenary Meetings noted an increase in the number of reports and recommendations from Expert Groups. The following statistics were presented at the fourth Plenary Meeting: first Plenary Meeting: 0 Expert Group reports, 1 recommendation; second Plenary Meeting: 12 Expert Group reports, 14 recommendations; third Plenary Meeting: 19 Expert Group reports, 24 recommendations; fourth Plenary Meeting: 16 Expert Group reports, 100 recommendations. See 'Report of the Executive Secretary for the period from the third to the fourth session of the Preparatory Commission (28 June to 26 September)', PC-IV/10, 27 Sep. 1993.

[24] In the intersessional period, four Working Group A Expert Groups conducted activities on: (*a*) staff regulations and rules, (*b*) privileges and immunities agreement with the host government, (*c*) financial regulations and rules, (*d*) data system, and (*e*) OPCW permanent building requirements). Eight Working Group B Expert Groups dealt with: (*a*) safety procedures, (*b*) chemical engineers, (*c*) inspection team composition, (*d*) technical co-operation and assistance, (*e*) analytical chemistry, (*f*) industry declarations, (*g*) equipment, and (*h*) training. Approximately 650 000 pages of official documents were distributed in

recruitment of specialists from national delegations. One consequence of this was that the number of experts able to chair Expert Groups decreased, which led to greater demands on the PTS.

Working Groups A and B presented reports.[25] Only the report on Safety Procedures[26] from a Working Group B Expert Group was adopted by the meeting; other groups were recommended to continue their work. The Executive Secretary presented his report on the interpretation service problem.[27] Approval was given for an October 1993 meeting between the Expert Group on Chemical Industry Facilities (Working Group B) and chemical industry representatives.[28] A new PrepCom chairman was elected for the next six months.[29]

The Executive Secretary asked all signatory states to supply information by the end of August 1993 on the number of installations which might have to be declared under the CWC to facilitate planning for inspections and the size of the future Inspectorate and to prepare the budget for 1994.[30]

The *fourth Plenary Meeting* was held on 27 September–1 October 1993. The PrepCom[31] delivered a report, as did Working Groups A and B.[32] A new chairman was elected for Working Group A.[33]

The *fifth Plenary Meeting* took place on 13–17 December 1993. The reports of Working Groups A and B were presented[34] and a new PrepCom chairman was elected for February–August 1994.[35] The Plenary Meeting adopted a $29.71 million budget for 1994.[36]

---

the intersessional period. See 'Report of the Executive Secretary for the period from the second to the third session of the Preparatory Commission (22 April to 25 June 1993)', PC-III/5, 25 June 1993.

[25] 'Report of Working Group A', PC-III/A/2, 30 June 1993; 'Report of Working Group B', PC-III/B/2, 30 June 1993. The report of the Credentials Committee was also received.

[26] 'Report of the Preparatory Commission', PC-III/11, 2 July 1993, p. 5.

[27] 'Report on Language Services by the Executive Secretary', PC-III/6, 28 June 1993. Full language interpretation service for Expert Group meetings would add at least $1 450 000 to the budget in the first year. The Executive Secretary promised to provide a provisional solution for the remainder of 1993 and to prepare a long-term solution for the 1994 budget.

[28] See PC-III/11 (note 26).

[29] Ambassador Sirous Nasseri of Iran with Vice-Chairmen from Chile, Japan, Romania, Tunisia and the USA; see PC-III/11 (note 26), p. 6.

[30] 'Note by the Executive Secretary', PC-III/4, 15 June 1993. Based on the CWC definitions, information was requested on: (*a*) old and abandoned CW locations; (*b*) chemical weapons production facilities (CWPFs); (*c*) CW storage facilities; (*d*) CW destruction facilities (existing or planned); and (*e*) Schedule 1, 2 and 3 facilities and plant sites as well as other production plant sites. By the end of 1993, only 22 signatory states had supplied information on the number of facilities they are likely to declare on entry into force of the CWC.

[31] 'Report of the Preparatory Commission', PC-IV/23, 1 Oct. 1993.

[32] 'Report of Working Group A', PC-IV/A/2, 30 Sep. 1993; 'Report of Working Group B', PC-IV/B/12, 1 Oct. 1993. Also received were PC-IV/10 (note 23) , and 'Report on the Credentials of Representatives of Member States of the Preparatory Commission for the Organisation for the Prohibition of Chemical Weapons', PC-IV/19, 30 Sep. 1993.

[33] Working Group A was then chaired by Alberto E. Doja of Argentina.

[34] 'Report of Working Group A', PC-V/A/7, 15 Dec. 1993; 'Report Working Group B', PC-V/B/10, 15 Dec. 1993. The Credentials Committee submitted its 'Report on the credentials of representatives of Member States', PC-V/11, 16 Dec. 1993.

[35] Ambassador Grigory V. Berdennikov of Russia was elected.

[36] The Commission budget is calculated in Dutch guilders. All estimates are based on an exchange-rate of Df. 1.90 for July 1993, using the UN exchange-rate system. For the 1994 budget $18.12 million was approved for Part I and $11.59 million for Part II. See the discussion of the Expert Group on the 1994 Programme of Work and Budget in the section 'Matters of substance' below. See also 'Report of the Commission', PC-V/12, 17 Dec. 1993, pp. 6–7, and annex 1, attachments A and B, pp. 16–23.

In response to a debate in the PrepCom about geographical balance in the PTS which began at the *fourth Plenary Meeting*,[37] the Executive Secretary presented a breakdown by nationality of the top PTS employee categories.[38] The Executive Secretary also reported on several errors in the certified copies of the CWC,[39] and it was decided that a final report would be submitted to the *sixth Plenary Meeting*. The December meeting approved the schedule for Expert Group meetings for January–March 1994 and a tentative list of tasks.[40] The *sixth Plenary Meeting* was scheduled for 11–15 April 1994.

A Headquarters Agreement between the PrepCom and the Host State (the Netherlands) establishing the legal status, privileges and immunities of the PrepCom, its Executive Secretary and the PTS staff members was signed on 8 December 1993; it serves as a point of departure for the future Headquarters Agreement for the OPCW.[41]

Matters of substance

At the *first Plenary Meeting* in February 1993, Working Group A established Expert Groups on: (*a*) the 1993 programme of work, (*b*) rules and procedures; (*c*) privileges and immunities, (*d*) financial regulations and rules, (*e*) staff regulations and rules, (*f*) the OPCW building, and (*g*) a draft budget for 1993 (the Group later dealt with the 1994 budget). At the *third Plenary Meeting,* on 28 June–2 July 1993, the Expert Groups presented their first detailed reports.[42]

The *fourth Plenary Meeting* adopted Staff Regulations for the PTS, including financial regulations,[43] and PrepCom Financial Regulations, which entered into force on 1 October 1993.[44] Upon completion of the work on Privileges

[37] 'Statement by the Mexican Delegation', PC-IV/23 (note 31), pp. 12–13.

[38] The survey showed that of 24 top professional positions in the PTS, 11 are filled by citizens from the Western European and Other States category. In addition, it was strongly reiterated that apart from geographical considerations it is important that recruited staff meet the highest standards of efficiency, professional competence and integrity. See 'Note by the Executive Secretary on the breakdown of nationalities for professional and higher categories represented at the Provisional Technical Secretariat as of 14 December 1993', PC-V/A/6, 14 Dec. 1993.

[39] 'Note by the Executive Secretary: errors in the certified copy of the Convention', PC-V/5, 26 Nov. 1993; 'Note by the Executive Secretary: additional errors in the certified copy of the Convention', PC-V/5/Add.1, 10 Dec. 1993.

[40] See PC-V/12 (note 36), annex 2, pp. 24–36.

[41] 'Report of Executive Secretary: retrospective on 1993', PC-V/6, 13 Dec. 1993, p. 9.

[42] For the reports from Working Group A, see PREPCOM/II/WGA/2 (note 17); PC-III/A/2 (note 25); PC-IV/A/2 (note 32); PC-V/A/7 (note 34).

[43] Group of Experts on Staff and Financial Regulations, 'Third report on staff regulations', PC-IV/A/WP.5, 16 Aug. 1993, appendix, pp. 3–20. Staff Regulations and Rules were drafted in May; see Group of Experts on Staff Regulations, 'Report on staff regulations', PC-III/A/WP.6, 7 May 1993. It was recommended that they be checked for consistency against the Executive Secretary Staff Regulations and be used when hiring professional staff such as inspectors. See Group of Experts on Staff and Financial Regulations, 'Fourth report: staff regulations and rules', PC-V/A/WP.5, 17 Nov. 1993.

[44] See PC-IV/23 (note 31), p. 4; Group of Experts on Staff and Financial Regulations, 'Third report on financial regulations', PC-IV/A/WP.4, 16 Aug. 1993 and PC-IV/A/WP.4/Corr.1, 19 Aug. 1993. Draft provisional financial regulations were presented in Apr. 1993; see Group of Experts on Financial and Staff Regulations, 'Second report on financial regulations', PC-III/A/WP.2, 29 Apr. 1993. Later work is reported in Group of Experts on Staff and Financial Regulations, 'Fourth report: financial regulations and rules', PC-V/A/WP.6, 17 Nov. 1993. At the fifth Plenary Meeting the PrepCom approved the establishment of a Finance Group of experts from member states on budgetary and administrative matters to start work in early 1994.

and Immunities,[45] the Executive Secretary was authorized to sign the Headquarters Agreement between the PrepCom and the Netherlands.[46]

The Data System Expert Group outlined its requirements for the OPCW's Information Management System (IMS)[47] at the *fourth Plenary Meeting* which were adopted as the OPCW IMS System.[48] The *fifth Plenary Meeting* asked this group to finalize work on declaration requirements and report to the relevant Expert Groups. Finland, Russia and the UK described their national data bases, as Iran and the USA had done earlier.[49] Hungary demonstrated an advanced computer system tailored to the tasks of the future TS, including declaration requirements.[50]

The report by the OPCW Building Expert Group to the *third Plenary Meeting* had outlined the type of building needed by the OPCW and established a Specialist Task Force[51] composed of experts from signatory states. The Netherlands' bid to host the OPCW had been predicated on a three- to five-year life span for the PrepCom (whereas the mandate calls for OPCW operations to begin in February 1995). Since the building offered by the Netherlands will not be available until 1996, alternative possibilities had to be investigated.[52] In December 1993 the PrepCom decided that the OPCW Laboratory should be functional before entry into force of the CWC.[53] A permanent site for the OPCW headquarters building has not yet been found.

The 1994 Programme of Work and Budget Expert Group presented the final draft of the 1994 budget and work programme to the *fifth Plenary Meeting* in

[45] Combined Group of Experts on the Rules of Procedure and Privileges and Immunities, 'Report on privileges and immunities', PC-III/A/WP.8, 12 May 1993.

[46] 'Draft Agreement between the Kingdom of the Netherlands and the Preparatory Commission for the Organisation for the Prohibition of Chemical Weapons concerning the Headquarters of the Commission', PC-IV/A/WP.6, annex, 26 Aug. 1993, pp. 3–13.

[47] Group of Experts on Data Systems, 'Initial report', PC-III/A/WP.1, 28 Apr. 1993. The IMS system will serve as a comprehensive computerized system suitable for the OPCW and capable of handling internal information as well as information from states parties, including required declarations.

[48] Expert Group on Data Systems, 'Report: second session', PC-IV/A/WP.3, 6 Aug. 1993. After the Nov. 1993 meeting further recommendations on IMS system design, functionality, cost factors, manpower requirement and the format for industrial declarations and security aspects were presented; see Expert Group on Data Systems, 'Third report', PC-V/A/WP.7, 12 Nov. 1993.

[49] USA, 'Chemical Weapons Convention information management system prototype', Discussion Paper, Preparatory Commission for the OPCW, Data Systems Expert Group, PC-III/A/WP.1 (note 47), appendix II, pp. 1–3; 'Note Verbale from the Embassy of the Islamic Republic of Iran in The Hague, addressed to the Provisional Technical Secretariat of the Preparatory Commission for the Organisation for the Prohibition of Chemical Weapons dated 3 August 1993', PC-IV/A/WP.2, 4 Aug. 1993; Finland, 'Perspectives for the construction of an information system for the OPCW', PC-III/A/WP.1 (note 47), appendix III; PTS, 'Automatic data processing at the Provisional Technical Secretariat of the Preparatory Commission for the Organisation for the Prohibition of Chemical Weapons', PC-III/A/WP.1 (note 47), appendix I.

[50] 'Poland: Regional Seminar on National Authority and national implementation measures for the Chemical Weapons Convention, Warsaw, Poland, 7–8 December 1993', PC-V/A/WP.9, 15 Dec. 1993.

[51] Group of Experts on OPCW Building, 'Second interim report', PC-III/A/WP.7, 12 May 1993.

[52] Recommendations and findings concerning the OPCW building were presented at the fifth Plenary Meeting; see Group of Experts on the OPCW Building, 'Fourth interim report', PC-V/A/WP.4, 11 Nov. 1993, which addresses (*a*) interim accommodation of the PTS and later the TS; (*b*) suitability of the location of alternative OPCW building sites; (*c*) programme of the requirements for the OPCW building; (*d*) financial, legal and other implications of the OPCW building options; and (*e*) consultations on interim and permanent accommodation arrangements.

[53] Office space and equipment storage are to be located at the TNO-PML facilities. TNO is the Dutch Institute for Applied Scientific Research of the Netherlands. See PC-V/12 (note 36), p. 3.

December 1993.[54] The group had the demanding task of planning for 1994, the year when most preparation for the future work of the OPCW must be completed if the CWC enters into force in 1995. The PTS directed the Expert Group to outline a budget based on the assumptions that: (a) 65 states will deposit instruments of ratification by 18 July 1994, ensuring that the CWC can enter into force by January 1995; (b) the USA and Russia will deposit their instruments of ratification prior to entry into force, as will the states with the large majority of declarable facilities; and (c) the bilateral US–Russian agreement[55] will enter into force. Budget year 1994 was divided into two parts: phase I—fulfilment of ongoing PTS obligations; and phase II—activities related to the organization and work of the TS, which will start 180 days before entry into force (18 July 1994 or later, depending on the date of deposit of the 65th instrument of ratification). If there are fewer than 65 ratifications, the PTS will continue as currently.[56]

Working Group B on Verification and Technical Co-operation and Assistance began work during the April 1993 *second Plenary Meeting*; it focused on: (a) tasks related to verification, (b) inspection team composition, (c) inspection safety procedures, (d) industry declarations, (e) inspector training requirements, (f) OPCW laboratory requirements, and (g) tasks related to implementation of the provisions on technical co-operation and assistance.[57] By the time of the *third Plenary Meeting*, 9 Expert Groups had begun work.[58] At both the *fourth Plenary Meeting*[59] and the December meeting 10 Working Group B Expert Groups reported on their activities.[60] The work of the Expert Groups and their major achievements during 1993 are discussed below.

A draft of the initial sections of the OPCW Safety and Health Policy Document was prepared by the Safety Procedures Expert Group,[61] and was presented as the OPCW Health and Safety Manual in November 1993.[62] The structure of a Health and Safety Unit was outlined taking into account OPCW health and safety guidelines as regards equipment, workplace exposure, environmental standards and decontamination procedures.

---

[54] Group of Experts on Programme of Work and Budget, 'Final report', PC-V/A/WP.3, 18 Nov. 1993; Group of Experts on Programme of Work and Budget, 'Corrigendum', PC-V/A/WP.3/Corr.1, 10 Dec. 1993. A first draft of the 1994 programme of work and budget was presented to the fourth Plenary Meeting; see 'Initial Report of Expert Group on 1994 Programme of Work and Budget', PC-IV/A/WP.7, 10 Sep. 1993.

[55] The 'Agreement between the United States of America and the Union of Soviet Socialist Republics on Destruction and Non-Production of Chemical Weapons and on Measures to Facilitate the Multilateral Convention on Banning Chemical Weapons' is reproduced in SIPRI, *SIPRI Yearbook 1991: World Armaments and Disarmament* (Oxford University Press: Oxford, 1991), pp. 536–39.

[56] The financial contribution of the states parties to Part II of the budget is to be paid when so decided by the PrepCom or not later than 30 days after receiving a request by the Executive Secretary; see also note 36.

[57] See PREPCOM/II/WGB/1 (note 17).

[58] See PC-III/B/2 (note 25).

[59] See PC-IV/B/12 (note 32), pp. 6–7.

[60] However, despite the fact that the number was not changed, the Expert Groups were not always the same; different subjects sometimes required new groups.

[61] Combined Group of Experts on Safety Procedures, 'Initial report', PC-III/B/WP.1, 21 May 1993.

[62] Expert Group on Safety Procedures, 'Second report', PC-V/B/WP.11, 19 Nov. 1993.

The Chemical Engineers Expert Group[63] presented an interim report in May 1993 on requirements for inspection procedure and activities for four types of facilities.[64]

At the *third Plenary Meeting* examples of 10 different types of inspection teams, their size and composition were given in a report by the Expert Group on Inspection Team Composition.[65] Later a new Expert Group on Inspectorate Planning recommended full-time inspectors supplemented by temporary (on-call) inspectors for the Inspectorate.[66] Inspection priorities for the period after entry into force and regional inspectorate offices were also discussed.

The Expert Group on Analytical Chemists recommended in June 1993 that the OPCW establish a centrally controlled quality-assurance and quality-control programme based on international practice.[67] The OPCW was advised to perform regular proficiency testing of its network of approved laboratories and field activities and to assign to the OPCW Laboratory the role of co-ordinating analytical activities.[68]

In June 1993 the Expert Group on Industry Declarations presented formats and detailed requirements for declarations under Article VI of the CWC in 31 charts.[69] Further work was recommended on the handling of: (*a*) 'low concentrations' of scheduled chemicals, if they are by-products, and (*b*) 'aggregate national data' for the production of Schedule 3 chemicals. It was suggested that the same procedure for declaration and verification be used for facilities producing chemicals under Schedules 2 or 3 for consumption by both captive and non-captive use. In July 1993 the Chemical Industry Facilities Expert Group presented guidelines for inspection and draft declaration formats for Schedule 2 and 3 facilities;[70] the risk a Schedule 2 plant site may present to the CWC and its intent was also addressed. Recommendations on declaration formats and a revised draft Model Facility Agreement for Schedule 2 facilities were later tabled.[71] Work on the Inspection Manual, on standardized declaration forms and on model agreements for industry facilities continued.[72]

---

[63] Combined Group of Experts, 'Chemical engineers: initial report', PC-III/B/WP.2, 21 May 1993.

[64] The facilities were: single small-scale facility, other Schedule 1 production facilities, Schedule 2 facilities and CW production facilities.

[65] Combined Group of Experts, 'Inspection team composition: report', PC-III/B/WP.3, 28 May 1993.

[66] Expert Group on Inspectorate Planning, 'Initial report', PC-IV/B/WP.3, 16 July 1993; and PC-IV/B/WP.3/Rev.1, 29 Sep. 1993.

[67] Combined Group of Experts, 'Analytical chemists: report', PC-III/B/WP.7, 15 June 1993.

[68] The group recommended that signatories be asked to provide spectra and other analytical data on relevant chemicals under the CWC in order for them to be included in the OPCW analytical data base.

[69] Combined Group of Experts on Industrial Declarations, 'Report', PC-III/B/WP.8, 16 June 1993.

[70] Expert Group on Chemical Industry Facilities, 'Initial report', PC-IV/B/WP.5, 23 July 1993.

[71] Expert Group on Chemical Industry Facilities, 'Second report', PC-V/B/WP.2, 8 Oct. 1993; and PC-V/B/WP.2/Corr.1, 23 Nov. 1993.

[72] In addition consultations by the chairman were carried out on unresolved questions such as recycled chemicals, waste disposal, changes to annual production, facilities that have produced Schedule 1 chemicals since 1 Jan. 1946 for purposes not related to CW, and facilities which produce BZ for purposes not prohibited under the CWC, with regard to industrial declarations. Further elaboration is needed as regards low concentrations of Schedule 2 and 3 chemicals produced as by-products and aggregate national data for Schedule 3 chemicals. See Combined Expert Group on Industrial Declarations, 'Report of informal consultations conducted by the chairman of the group in connection with outstanding issues related to industrial declarations', PC-V/B/WP.15, 1 Dec. 1993.

The Technical Co-operation and Assistance Expert Group[73] drafted a Model Agreement on the procurement and provision of emergency, humanitarian and supplementary assistance for use by the OPCW and states parties[74] which was approved by the PrepCom. The need to assist National Authorities[75] in their implementation of the CWC and the organizing of regional seminars was reiterated. In December 1993, further support was recommended from the PTS for the training of personnel from National Authorities.[76] Recommendations were made for stockpiling protective equipment for assistance, for exchange of equipment and information on protection, for establishment of guidelines for a Voluntary Fund, for a data bank on protection against chemical weapons and for a Draft Model Agreement on the Procurement of Assistance.

The Expert Group on Equipment presented the requirements and functions of an OPCW Laboratory and its responsibilities to future designated laboratories.[77] It recommended that the OPCW Laboratory be relatively small and focus on primary functions.[78] A list of equipment for use in inspections was compiled in August 1993.[79] By March 1994 the Laboratory should be functioning at minimum capability, and at full capability by entry into force minus one month at the latest.[80]

The Expert Group on Training[81] addressed the training needed for the Inspectorate, the Verification Division of the PTS (later the Technical Secretariat under the OPCW) and the National Authorities and chose a three-module training approach.[82] A decision about whether inspectors will be offered employment before or after undergoing training must be made soon as it will have a significant impact on the planning process. Signatory states are to submit information on planned national training courses and facilities for on-site inspection training, a component of the training process.[83] The modules for implementing the General Training Scheme (GTS) were further developed.[84]

---

[73] Combined Group of Experts, 'Technical co-operation and assistance: initial report', PC-III/B/WP.4, 28 May 1993; Group of Experts on Technical Co-operation and Assistance, 'First interim report', PC-IV/B/WP.6, 9 Aug. 1993.

[74] See PC-IV/23 (note 31), p. 12.

[75] Article VII of the CWC (see note 1) defines the National Authority as 'the national focal point for effective liaison with the Organization and other States Parties'.

[76] Expert Group on Technical Co-operation and Assistance, 'Second interim report', PC-V/B/WP.16, 3 Dec. 1993.

[77] Expert Group on Equipment, 'Initial report', PC-III/B/WP.9, 18 June 1993.

[78] See PC-III/B/2 (note 25), p. 5.

[79] Expert Group on Equipment, 'First interim report', PC-IV/B/WP.7, 13 Aug. 1993.

[80] Expert Group on Equipment, 'Second interim report', PC-V/B/WP.7, 26 Oct. 1993.

[81] Group of Experts: Training, 'Interim report', PC-III/B/WP.10, 18 June 1993.

[82] Module 1, Basic: general foundation course (basic information concerning the CWC); Module 2, Specialities: courses for specialists and courses for different skills and techniques; and Module 3, Inspection Training: practical training courses.

[83] In Aug. the Executive Secretary presented an overview of 12 national inspector-training programmes. The following countries conduct or plan to conduct such courses: Austria, Finland, France, Germany, Mexico, the Netherlands, Poland, Romania, South Africa, Sweden, Switzerland and the UK. See 'Information to member states on national inspector training programmes', PC-IV/B/2, 4 Aug. 1993. In Oct. 1993 an update was presented on offers from various countries—Australia, Austria, Canada, Finland, Germany, the Netherlands, South Africa and the UK—which have previously organized training courses for inspectors. See 'Information to member states on national inspector training programmes', PC-V/B/4, 18 Oct. 1993.

[84] Expert Group on Training, 'Second interim report', PC-IV/B/WP.8, 13 Aug. 1993.

By the *fifth Plenary Meeting*[85] the content of the training modules had been finalized.[86] The PrepCom adopted guidelines for cost-sharing between states parties and the TS for implementing the General Training Scheme. Criteria and procedures for certification of national training programmes and selection criteria for inspector trainees remain to be established.[87]

The Expert Group on Chemical Weapons Storage Facilities proposed formats for initial declarations, and guidelines for inspections, for the inclusion of simulant-filled munitions defined as chemical weapons and for national aggregate quantities of toxic chemicals and their precursors.[88] The PrepCom agreed at the *fourth Plenary Meeting* that the reference to 'munitions' in Part IV(A) of the Verification Annex of the CWC[89] should apply to both filled and unfilled ammunition.[90] The Group further developed formats for declaration of national aggregates of mixtures of chemicals.[91] At the *fifth Plenary Meeting* the recommendation was adopted that in declaring chemical weapons all locations including storage facilities and storage facilities at CW destruction and temporary holding areas must be included. During the CWC transitional period the Executive Secretary should approve the arrangements between the OPCW and states parties for inspection of chemical weapons at destruction facilities.[92]

The Expert Group on Chemical Weapons Destruction Facilities identified categories of inspection equipment.[93] Work continues on the declaration formats for general and detailed annual plans for destruction, destruction criteria and methods, guidelines for inspection procedures, criteria to assess the completeness of destruction and accommodation of the destruction processes in facilities that produce Schedule 2 chemicals.[94]

---

[85] Expert Group on Training, 'Third interim report', PC-V/B/WP.8, 22 Oct. 1993.

[86] In order to resolve issues related to inspector and inspection assistant training, informal meetings were held. See Expert Group on Training, 'Report of informal meetings conducted by the chairman of the group in connection with outstanding issues related to inspector/inspection assistant candidate training', PC-V/B/WP.18, 10 Dec. 1993. In addition, the Executive Secretary sent a questionnaire to all signatory states in Dec. 1993 to compile information on national offers for training courses and for future PTS planning purposes. See 'Note by the Executive Secretary: preparation of training programme for inspectors/inspection assistants of OPCW: questionnaire', PC-V/B/11, 16 Dec. 1993.

[87] The following countries offered courses: for Module M1, Basic Course: France, the Netherlands, Russia and the UK; for Module M2, Specialist Application Courses: Finland, France, Germany, Switzerland and the UK; for Module M3, Inspection Training: France, Germany, Russia and South Africa. In addition, India and the USA will conduct Module 1 courses; the USA is willing to conduct Module 2 courses on the CW stockpile, destruction and former production facilities.

[88] Expert Group on Chemical Weapons Storage Facilities, 'Initial report', PC-IV/B/WP.2, 9 July 1993.

[89] Annex on Implementation and Verification (Verification Annex), Part IV(A), Section A, paragraphs 1(c)(iii) and 1(c)(iv), Conference on Disarmament document CD/1170 (note 2), p. 88.

[90] See PC-IV/23 (note 31), 1 Oct. 1993, p. 11.

[91] Expert Group on Chemical Weapons Storage Facilities, 'Third interim report', PC-V/B/WP.13, 26 Nov. 1993.

[92] See Verification Annex, Part IV(A), paragraphs 50 and 51 of the CWC, Conference on Disarmament document CD/1170 (note 2), annex 2, pp. 100–1.

[93] Expert Group on Chemical Weapons Destruction Facilities, 'Initial report', PC-IV/B/WP.1, 9 July 1993.

[94] Expert Group on Chemical Weapons Destruction Facilities, 'Interim report', PC-V/B/WP.17, 3 Dec. 1993.

The format of declarations and inspection activities for initial and systematic inspections of Chemical Weapons Production Facilities (CWPFs) was elaborated.[95] This Expert Group also studied: (a) closure and inactivation of these facilities, (b) permitted maintenance activities, (c) risk assessment of closed facilities, and (d) model facility agreements.[96]

The Expert Group on Single Small Scale Facilities and other Schedule 1 Production Facilities outlined declaration requirements and guidelines for inspection activities.[97] Work is still needed on inspection equipment, instrumentation for monitoring and model agreements.[98]

In August 1993 the Expert Group on Challenge Inspection addressed the various challenge inspection issues, including the designation and selection of inspectors and inspection assistants, the inspection mandate, confidentiality and required equipment.[99] The group later focused on securing the site, managed access, and sampling and analysis.[100] No significant progress was made.

The Expert Group on Old and Abandoned Chemical Weapons[101] met first in November 1993 and recommended that the Executive Secretary request information on old CW from signatories.[102] At the request of the Group, the Executive Secretary presented an evaluation of the financial and manpower implications of the two possible interpretations related to the verification of old CW produced between 1925 and 1946.[103] Work remains to define 'capability' or 'usability' for these old weapons and to set up inspection procedures for this category.

Financial aspects

The PrepCom is financed on a modified UN scale of assessments with individual contributions by signatories in a range from 0.01 to 25 per cent of the total budget.[104] The contributions will later be deducted from contributions by states parties to the budget of the OPCW.[105] The largest annual contribution will be from the USA: 25 per cent, equivalent to $8.6 million for 1994.[106]

---

[95] See PC-IV/B/12 (note 32), pp. 14–16.

[96] Expert Group on Chemical Weapons Production Facilities, 'Interim report', PC-V/B/WP.6, 15 Oct. 1993.

[97] 'Expert Group on Single Small-Scale Facilities and other Schedule 1 Production Facilities', PC-IV/B/WP.4, 16 July 1993.

[98] See PC-IV/B/12 (note 32), pp. 6–7.

[99] Expert Group on Challenge Inspections, 'Initial report', PC-IV/B/WP.10, 27 Aug. 1993.

[100] Expert Group on Challenge Inspection, 'First interim report', PC-V/B/WP.12, 19 Nov. 1993.

[101] Expert Group on Old and Abandoned Chemical Weapons, 'First report', PC-V/B/WP.14, 26 Nov. 1993.

[102] 'Note by the Executive Secretary: request for information on old chemical weapons', PC-V/B/6, 7 Dec. 1993.

[103] 'Note by the Executive Secretary: verification regime for old chemical weapons produced between 1925 and 1946', PC-V/B/9, 11 Dec. 1993.

[104] On the scale of assessments, 0.01 per cent equals $2205.

[105] The issue of financial contributions is sensitive; signatories must pay to an international organization for a convention not yet in force.

[106] This figure relates only to Part I of the 1994 budget; $5.5 million are allocated for Part II of the 1994 budget. See PC-V/12 (note 36).

After the *first Plenary Meeting* a provisional budget of $1.8 million was approved for 1 February–30 April 1993; the *second Plenary Meeting* adopted a final budget of $8.84 million for 1993 with contributions adjusted to reflect the then 142 signatories.[107] At that time more than $2 million had been provided by various governments.[108] As of mid-April 1993 only 26 signatory states had paid their contributions;[109] by mid-September the number had increased to 59.[110] As of 10 December 1993, just prior to the *fifth Plenary Meeting*, 67 states had paid their contribution in full or in part.[111] Figured on the agreed assessment scale from the *second Plenary Meeting*, the remaining 75 signatories are responsible for approximately 12 per cent of the total. (Assessments for 12 new signatories which signed after the *second Plenary Meeting* were made in December.[112])

In March 1993 Viet Nam[113] informed the PTS that it could not afford to participate in PrepCom activities and thus did not need to pay its assessment.[114] In June 1993 Lithuania followed suit.[115] While this did not have a major financial impact on the PrepCom budget, it is perhaps representative of the attitude of some of the smaller signatory states and potentially worrisome.

Owing to the fact that some states paid more than their assessment and that the PrepCom had a lower level of expenditure than expected, the financial situation at the end of 1993 was quite good. Those signatory states which had not made their financial contributions by the end of 1993 were asked to do so by the Executive Secretary at the request of the PrepCom.

Remaining tasks

At the December 1993 *fifth Plenary Meeting* the Executive Secretary spoke positively of the achievements of 1993 and pointed to issues which remained to be resolved. He noted that 'it will be necessary for some Expert Groups, particularly those dealing with CW-related site-oriented activities, to continue their work into the early part of 1994'.[116]

In 1994 the PrepCom needs to concentrate on: (*a*) building the OPCW infrastructure, (*b*) preparing the 1995 Programme of Work and Budget, (*c*) continuing to develop detailed procedures for implementing the CWC at entry into

---

[107] Of the first year's budget some $5.15 million were allocated for personnel costs, $2.41 million for conference service and $1.28 million for other services (e.g., communications, computers, travel, etc.).

[108] The countries were: Australia, Bulgaria, Denmark, Finland, New Zealand, Norway, Sweden and the USA. France, Germany, Spain and the UK announced immediate contributions.

[109] See PREPCOM/II/3 (note 16), p. 8.

[110] See PC-IV/10 (note 23), p. 10.

[111] See PC-V/6 (note 41), p. 16.

[112] Their total assessment was $10.610; see 'Assessment of new member states', PC-V/8, 10 Dec. 1993.

[113] The assessment for Viet Nam for the first year's budget was $887.54.

[114] *The CWC Chronicle*, Henry L. Stimson Center, Washington, DC, vol. 1, no. 2 (May 1993), p. 2.

[115] See letter to the PrepCom PTS from 1 June 1993 in 'Note Verbale from the Ministry of Foreign Affairs of Lithuania and the Proposal by the Executive Secretary to deal with the Matter', PC-IV/13, 27 Sep. 1993.

[116] See PC-V/6 (note 41), p. 3.

force, (d) assisting states in their national implementation efforts, and (e) urging non-signatory states to join the CWC.[117]

In 1994 the Expert Groups will have to focus much more on verification issues *inter alia* developing: detailed procedures (in particular confidentiality measures), formats, guidelines, inspection manuals, procedures for procuring equipment and the establishing of training courses. The first training courses are scheduled for mid-August 1994; they will take a two-fold approach, using both the training courses offered by the signatory states and the PTS training programme. At least 140 candidate inspectors will need to be hired.

The PrepCom, its Working Groups and Expert Groups in The Hague have established an intensive working regime, and the first year of work can be deemed a success. However, some issues are highly political,[118] and these were sometimes veiled as purely technical discussions. No significant progress has been made as regards challenge inspection, and the Expert Group on Equipment and Safety Procedures has encountered disagreement from signatory states with respect to the scope of challenge inspections.

III. The Provisional Technical Secretariat

On 11 February 1993, at the *first Plenary Meeting*, the PrepCom established the PTS to assist it in its activities.[119] The PTS is also the nucleus of the future permanent OPCW Technical Secretariat. Ian Kenyon of the UK was appointed Executive Secretary of the PTS for a 24-month term.[120] After intense consultations with signatory state delegations, Kenyon proposed that the PTS structure include a Deputy Executive Secretary and five divisions[121] (the structure of the

---

[117] See PC-V/6 (note 41), p. 20.

[118] No progress has been made on challenge inspections. The sensitive issue of economic and technological development including the free trade of chemicals for purposes not prohibited by Article XI of the CWC is one of the problems which the Expert Group on Technical Co-operation and Assistance faces. It is seen by some countries (e.g., Iran) as a way to abolish the Australia Group.

[119] See PREPCOM/I/CRP.10 (note 6), p. 5. The decision was adopted in accordance with paragraph 8(c) of the 'Text on the Establishment of a Preparatory Commission'; see Conference on Disarmament document CD/1170 (note 2), p. 180.

[120] The Executive Secretary will serve until 10 Feb. 1995. The appointment can be renewed for an additional 12 months, but ends 30 days after the Director-General of the OPCW assumes his post. PREP COM/I/CRP.10 (note 6), pp. 5–6, outlines the role: 'The Executive Secretary shall: (a) administer work programmes and budgets approved by the Preparatory Commission; (b) direct and manage the Secretariat in its work in implementing such programmes and budgets; and (c) in matters of staff appointments, make recommendations to the Preparatory Commission on appointments to senior management positions (Grade D-1, Principal Officer equivalent and above), and directly appoint all other necessary staff (subject only to appropriate reporting to and liaison with the Preparatory Commission), in both cases, in accordance with the principles contained in Article VIII, paragraph 44 of the Convention'.

[121] The divisions are: Verification, Administrative, Legal, External Relations, and Technical Co-operation and Assistance. At the first Plenary Meeting the Executive Secretary recommended the following persons to head the divisions: John Gee (Australia), Verification; Félix C. Calderón (Mexico), Legal; Robert Howard (USA), Administrative; and Sergey Batsanov (Russia), External Relations. Howard later declined the position and was replaced by Reuben Lev (USA). In Mar. the PTS was expanded by appointments including a Special Assistant to the Executive Secretary; a Head of Declarations and Confidentiality in the Verification Division; Heads of Industry A and B in the Verification Division; and a Government Relations Officer in the External Relations Division. In early June Li Chang-he (China) was appointed Deputy Executive Secretary. The Head of the Administration Division also assumed his post. Other appointments included: the Head of Personnel in the Administration Division; the Industry Relations Officer and the Head of Public Affairs and Media in the External Relations Division; the Deputy

PTS as of December 1993 is presented in figure 17.2) At the end of February 1993 the PTS moved into offices in The Hague.[122]

By 12 January 1994, 78 specialists from 34 nations were employed in the PTS on contract basis.[123] It is envisaged that 120 staff members will work in the PTS by the end of Phase I (July 1994); by the end of Phase II (just prior to entry into force of the CWC) 225 staff members should be employed.[124]

In April 1993 the PTS began publishing a newsletter, the *OPCW Synthesis*,[125] which is distributed to signatory states, industry and other NGOs to inform them about the activities of the PrepCom and primarily those of the PTS. Since the *third Plenary Meeting*, the PTS External Relations Division has provided information to the press and other interested persons who are not allowed to take part in Plenary Meetings.

During 1993 the PTS increasingly realized that there is growing interest within the scientific community to support the work in The Hague. In November a meeting was held in The Hague between the Sussex–Harvard Programme on CBW Armament and Arms Limitation and the PTS to discuss an International Information Project.[126] SIPRI's CBW project has also established a special relationship for co-operation with the PTS and the PrepCom.[127]

IV. National implementation

Effective implementation of the CWC also requires its national implementation—'translation' into the national legal systems of the states parties. Many countries have indicated that they intend to ratify the CWC quickly,[128] but states face many technical, industrial, political and legal problems in their preparation for national implementation.

Article VII of the Convention makes clear that national implementation is entirely dependent on individual states parties. There are two components of national implementation: (*a*) implementing necessary legislation, and (*b*) setting up the National Authority. National implementation regimes will vary

---

Legal Adviser in the Legal Affairs Division; the Technical Co-Operation Officer and the Article X Assistance Officer in the Technical Co-operation and Assistance Division; and the Inspection Training Officer and CW Officer in the Verification Division. The Budget and Finance Officer was also appointed. The appointment of the Head of the Division on Technical Co-operation and Assistance in Sep. completed recruitment for senior management positions in the PTS.

[122] The address is: Provisional Technical Secretariat for the Organisation for the Prohibition of Chemical Weapons, Laan van Meerdervoort 51A, 2517 AE The Hague, The Netherlands.

[123] *OPCW Synthesis*, no. 6 (12 Jan. 1994).

[124] In addition, 140 inspectors and inspection assistants will be needed—the minimum number required to carry out verification activities immediately after entry into force of the CWC.

[125] *OPCW Synthesis*, no. 1 (1 Apr. 1993). Five issues of the newsletter *OPCW Synthesis* were published in 1993.

[126] *OPCW Synthesis*, no. 5 (23 Nov. 1993).

[127] See PC-V/6 (note 41), p. 8.

[128] In order to be informed about implementation activities, the Executive Secretary sent a note to all signatory states in Aug. requesting information on: (*a*) progress on establishing the National Authority; (*b*) ratification procedure; (*c*) whether implementing legislation will be adopted before or after ratification; and (*d*) problems in the ratification procedure. See 'Note by the Executive Secretary', PC-IV/3, 19 Aug. 1993. By Dec. 1993, only 20 signatory states had replied.

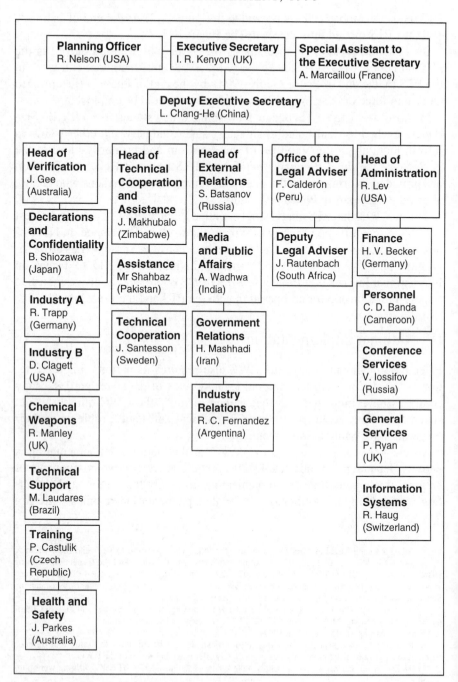

Figure 17.2. The Provisional Technical Secretariat

Note: Based on *The CWC Chronicle*, Henry L. Stimson Center, Washington, DC, vol. 1, no. 4 (Oct. 1993), p. 4; *OPCW Synthesis*, no. 7 (12 Apr. 1994); 'Note by the Executive Secretary on the breakdown of nationalities for professional and high categories represented at the Provisional Technical Secretariat as of 14 December 1993', PC-V/17/6, 14 Dec. 1993.

from state to state. The size and nature of each National Authority will depend on: (*a*) possession or non-possession of CW, (*b*) possession or non-possession of CWPFs, (*c*) the potential for the chemical industry of a state to produce CW, (*d*) the nature of its chemical industry, and (*e*) the already existing regulatory framework for its chemical industry. The extent of a state's obligations will determine whether a National Authority must be created or whether an existing governmental agency can perform the required tasks.

A state which ratifies the CWC before its entry into force but which has not completed all preparatory work at the time of ratification will still be able to finalize its implementation efforts. A state which ratifies the CWC after it has entered into force will have to complete all necessary national implementation measures prior to ratification.[129]

There is no way to predict which countries will ratify the CWC in 1994, but the two main possessors, Russia and the USA, appear to intend to do so.

In November 1993 *US* President Bill Clinton submitted the CWC to the Senate and urged ratification early in the next session of Congress.[130] The US National Authority will have two components: a formal inter-agency, decision-making body and an executive office, the Office of the National Authority. The National Security Council staff will chair the National Authority and the US Arms Control and Disarmament Agency (ACDA) will serve as the office. ACDA will be responsible for compiling declarations and reports, liaison with the OPCW and administrative support for US implementation activities.[131]

In *Russia* the Presidential Committee on Matters Pertaining to the Chemical and Biological Weapons, established in 1992, is dealing with the problems related to implementation of the CWC.

The following examples illustrate how some other signatory states are preparing for national implementation.

Argentina has established a preparatory commission for the National Authority which is to conclude its analysis of the requirements for its National Authority by the end of July 1994.[132]

Australia prepared model legislation for incorporating the CWC into domestic law in connection with its CW Regional Initiative (CWRI).[133] The model was made available to the PrepCom in September 1993 and has been presented to states participating in the CWRI as an example of preparation for

---

[129] Rautenbach, J., 'Some legal aspects of national implementation of the Chemical Weapons Convention', Seminar on National Implementation organized by the PTS, 18 Dec. 1993.

[130] 'Senate urged to ratify ban on chemical arms', *Washington Post*, 26 Nov. 1993, p. A20.

[131] 'Chemical Weapons Convention: White House fact sheet', *Wireless File* (United States Information Service, US Embassy: Stockholm, 26 Nov. 1993), pp. 4–5.

[132] Written answer from the Argentine Embassy in The Hague, 29 Nov. 1993.

[133] The CWRI was proposed by Prime Minister Robert Hawke in 1988 to promote regional support for the CWC as only 3 states (Australia, Indonesia and Myanmar) in the South-East Asian and South Pacific region were members of the CD negotiations in Geneva and hence full participants in the CWC. See Australia, 'Illustrative model legislation for the incorporation of the Chemical Weapons Convention into domestic law, explanatory memorandum', PC-IV/A/WP.10, 28 Sep. 1993.

national implementation.[134] The Chemical Weapons (Prohibition) Bill 1993,[135] Australia's domestic legislation, was introduced in to Parliament on 16 December 1993. As early as 1989 the Department of Foreign Affairs and Trade established a national secretariat to serve as the nucleus of the future National Authority. The draft legislation calls for the creation of a Chemical Weapons Convention Office.

By December 1993 the text of the CWC was being studied by the *Brazilian* Congress after approval by the External Relations Commission.[136] Ratification is expected in the second half of 1994. An Expert Group chaired and co-ordinated by the Ministry of External Relations is examining requirements for a National Authority and will serve as the nucleus of a National Authority.[137]

Bulgaria, an East European country in transition and with no chemical production activities which fall under Schedules 1, 2 and 3, has set up an inter-agency governmental commission to prepare for establishment of its National Authority and to draft the necessary legislation.[138]

The *Czech Republic* established a Preparatory Commission in September 1993, and it is envisaged that the process of ratification will be finalized in the second half of 1994.[139]

Cuba informed the PrepCom in October 1993[140] that in 1991 it had established a Working Group under the responsibility of the Ministry of Foreign Affairs, which is examining the requirements for the Cuban National Authority.

Denmark will complete the ratification procedure in July 1994, and the Ministry of Foreign Affairs will act as the National Authority.[141]

By the end of 1993 *the Netherlands* had nearly completed drafting its implementation legislation. Ratification is expected by the end of 1994.[142]

New Zealand, a leading member of the CWRI, is investigating national implementation requirements and will designate its Ministry of Foreign Affairs and Trade as its National Authority.[143]

---

[134] Appropriate adjustments must, of course, be made to the constitutional and legislative requirements of individual states.

[135] 'Chemical weapons (prohibition) bill 1993', cat. no. 93 4685 0, Parliament of the Commonwealth of Australia, The Senate, 1993. Australia ratified the CWC and deposited its instrument of ratification on 6 May 1994.

[136] Written answer from the Brazilian Embassy in The Hague, 20 Dec. 1993.

[137] 'Installation of Brazilian National Authority under CPCW', paper presented to the Seminar on National Implementation, 18 Dec. 1993, The Hague.

[138] The envisaged documents are: Law on CWC Ratification, Panel Code Amendment Law, Law on the Prohibition of Chemical Weapons, Follow-up Governmental Ordinance. See Bulgaria, 'Preparation for national implementation of the Chemical Weapons Convention', Presentation by the Delegation of Bulgaria to the OPCW Preparatory Commission at a Seminar on National Implementation, 18 Dec. 1993, The Hague.

[139] Written answer from the Czech Republic Embassy in The Hague, 9 Dec. 1993; 'Activities of the Czech Republic in Preparing for the Implementation of the Convention', PC-V/B/WP.9, 5 Nov. 1993.

[140] Cuba, 'Some considerations on the process of establishing the National Authority in the states signatory to the Convention on Chemical Weapons: the Cuban experience', PC-V/A/WP.1, 6 Oct. 1993.

[141] Written answer from the Danish Ministry of Foreign Affairs, 5 Nov. 1993.

[142] Written answer from the Netherlands Ministry of Foreign Affairs, 22 Oct. 1993.

[143] Paper on National Implementation, presented to the Seminar on National Implementation, 18 Dec. 1993, The Hague.

A new law was introduced in the *Norwegian* Parliament in February 1994 to serve as the basis for all national implementation measures so that ratification of the CWC can follow parliamentary approval.[144]

Poland has set up an inter-ministry group of experts to prepare legislative, administrative and technical measures for implementation.[145]

South Africa[146] has taken a different approach and extended its legislation to biological and nuclear weapons and missiles as well as chemical weapons. Its September 1993 Non-Proliferation of Weapons of Mass Destruction Bill establishes a supervisory authority, the Council for Non-Proliferation of Weapons of Mass Destruction, which will also act as its National Authority.

Sweden ratified the CWC in June 1993 and presented its implementation legislation to the PrepCom. Swedish law requires that international treaties be incorporated into domestic law by a legislative act. Sweden informed the PrepCom about its envisaged Inspection Act and the establishment of its National Authority.[147] The National Authority will fall under the Ministry for Foreign Affairs.

Turkey established a CWC working group in 1993 incorporating technical and legal experts from various ministries. It is envisaged that the National Authority will be an independent body which will also handle other international control regime obligations. The draft act for this authority was presented to Parliament at the end of 1993.[148]

In the *United Kingdom* the CWC was presented to Parliament in October 1993.[149] The Department of Trade and Industry will be responsible for the National Authority.[150]

In December 1993 a seminar on national implementation was held in The Hague for states to trade national implementation experiences and to inform the PrepCom of problems faced by states in the implementation and ratification process.[151] Experts from 56 countries discussed issues related to implementation, the status of ratification preparation in individual countries, legal aspects related to implementation and the basic functions of the National Authority.[152] A group of legal experts, supported by the PTS, presented a

---

[144] Written answer from the Norwegian Ministry of Foreign Affairs, 16 Feb. 1994. Norway ratified the CWC on 11 Mar. 1994 and deposited its instrument of ratification on 7 Apr. 1994.

[145] Paturej, K., 'Preparation in Poland towards implementation of the CWC', Regional Seminar on National Authority and National Implementation Measures for the Chemical Weapons Convention, Warsaw, 7–8 Dec. 1993.

[146] Republic of South Africa, 'Non-proliferation of weapons of mass destruction bill', [B 99B-93(GA)].

[147] Sweden, 'Proposed Swedish legislation for the implementation of the Chemical Weapons Convention', PC-IV/A/WP.9, 28 Sep. 1993.

[148] 'Preparatory work undertaken in Turkey for implementation of CWC', paper presented to the Seminar on National Implementation, 18 Dec. 1993, The Hague.

[149] '8 October 1993', *Chemical Weapons Convention Bulletin*, no. 22 (Dec. 1993), p. 20.

[150] Written answer from the British Embassy in The Hague, 25 Oct. 1993.

[151] See *OPCW Synthesis* (note 123).

[152] During the Seminar on National Implementation, The Hague, the Netherlands, 18 Dec. 1993, the PrepCom presented 'A brief handbook on the implementation of the CWC for non-possessor states without a declarable chemical industry' and 'Tasks of the National Authorities of non-CW-possessor states parties'.

study on the legal aspects of national implementation.[153] In December 1993 a regional seminar[154] on the National Authority and National Implementation Measures for the CWC was held in Warsaw for signatory states from the Eastern European Group.[155] Further regional seminars are planned for 1994.

Preparation for national implementation is clearly well under way. It has become apparent that simply copying a model *in toto* will not work; each country must study its own situation and estimate what it needs to meet its obligations under the Convention. In 1994 the PTS will need to play a more active role. The PTS can provide a 'bridging' function by making positive implementation experiences available to signatory countries and by advising and supporting countries which face difficulties.

The necessary 65 ratifications for entry into force of the CWC in 1995 must be achieved by late spring 1994. The ratification scenario of late 1993 may be quite different from the reality of 1994. The communication which the PTS has established with signatory states will have to intensify in order for it to remain informed about the ratification process in individual countries.

Ratification by the two largest CW possessors, Russia and the USA, is crucial if the CWC is to be credible.[156] Planning for the Inspectorate is based on the supposition that both countries will ratify the CWC prior to its entry into force and that the bilateral destruction agreement[157] will have begun to be implemented.[158] Both countries have reaffirmed their support for the CWC,[159] encouraging signs that both will ratify. Russia, however, is having severe difficulties in establishing its destruction programme, not least financially.[160] The ratification debate is also not expected to be easy in either Moscow or Washington. If the CWC enters into force in 1995 without either Russia or the USA, its significance will be diminished. There will be a negative impact on the readiness of smaller countries to ratify the CWC, and the PrepCom budget will suffer since Russia and the USA are significant contributors.

V. The chemical industry and the CWC

Although the chemical industry, the main 'target' of the Convention, is already subject to international regulation and intrusive national supervision in

[153] Kellman, B. *et. al.*, *Manual for National Implementation of the Chemical Weapons Convention* (No publisher: Chicago, Dec. 1993).

[154] The seminar was organized in co-operation with the PTS, the Ministry of Foreign Affairs of Poland, the Polish Chamber of Chemical Industry and CIECH Ltd.

[155] States represented were: Albania, Azerbaijan, Belarus, Bulgaria, Croatia, the Czech Republic, Estonia, Hungary, Latvia, Poland, Romania, the Russian Federation, Slovakia and Ukraine. See PC-V/A/WP.9 (note 50).

[156] Herby, P., 'Building the chemical disarmament regime', *Arms Control Today*, Sep. 1993, pp. 14–19.

[157] See note 55.

[158] If both countries ratify, the costs and manpower required for verification under the CWC will be reduced significantly.

[159] 'Joint Statement by the President of the Russian Federation and the President of the United States on Non-Proliferation of Weapons of Mass Destruction and Means of Their Delivery', FBIS-SOV-94-010, 14 Jan. 1994, pp. 16–17.

[160] See chapter 9 in this volume.

many countries, the only reliable data currently available with regard to scheduled chemicals are from the chemical industry itself.

The concerns still being raised about the active involvement of the chemical industry in the implementation process must be settled before entry into force of the CWC. The main challenge in implementing the CWC with respect to the concerns of the chemical industry is to achieve a balance between the CWC's declaration and verification obligations and the existing regulatory and declaratory mechanisms. Industry is concerned that as more information is required, the risk will increase that proprietary information will be lost.[161]

The chemical industry, which actively supported the CWC negotiations, voiced increasing concern during the first months of the PrepCom's work about various aspects of implementation, in particular as regards the exacting reporting requirements and the limited opportunities for the chemical industry to follow and take part in the work of the Expert Groups.[162] The Expert Group on Chemical Industry Facilities invited representatives from industry to an October 1993 meeting in The Hague to discuss these concerns and to reopen dialogue.[163] The meeting focused on the effect of entry into force on the international chemical industry and the re-establishment of a working relationship between the PTS, the Expert Groups and the chemical industry.[164] Among the issues discussed were: confidentiality; in-plant inspection, operations and safety; and preparation for entry into force.[165] The chemical industry recommended user-friendly facility agreements and minimizing plant disruption during inspections.[166] The protection of confidential business information is still one of the main concerns of industry. As a consequence of the meeting, the PTS was requested to provide more information to the chemical industry about the work of the PrepCom and to publish regular updates on specific topics. The *fifth Plenary Meeting,* in December 1993, scheduled a second joint meeting with industry representatives in April 1994.[167]

Individual countries, such as the USA,[168] have established special mechanisms to inform their chemical industry about developments related to the CWC implementation process. An August 1993 US Office of Technology

[161] Carpenter, W. D. and Zeftel, L., 'Implications of the chemical weapons treaty for the U.S. chemical industry', *The ASA Newsletter,* 93-6, no. 39 (9 Dec. 1993), pp. 1, 6–7.

[162] Ember, L. R., 'Chemical arms treaty makes unprecedented demands of industry', *Chemical & Engineering News,* vol. 71, no. 23 (7 June 1993), pp. 7–18.

[163] The meeting was attended by representatives from 39 countries and international chemical industry associations. See 'Note by the Executive Secretary, Group of Experts & Industry Representatives Meeting, 6–7 October 1993', PC-IV/4, 3 Sep. 1993.

[164] Ember, L. R., 'Chemical industry offers its expertise for implementing chemical arms pact', *Chemical & Engineering News,* vol. 71 no. 44 (1 Nov. 1993), pp. 21–22.

[165] Combined Expert Group on Chemical Industry Facilities and Industry Representatives, 'Panel discussion: effect on the chemical industry of the Chemical Weapons Convention, 6–7 Oct. 1993, Report', PC-V/B/WP.1, 3 Nov. 1993.

[166] See PC-V/B/WP.1 (note 165), p. 5.

[167] The meeting was held in The Hague on 6–7 Oct. 1993. See PC-V/B/WP.1 (note 165).

[168] US Arms Control and Disarmament Agency (ACDA), *Chemical Weapons Convention Update for Industry,* no. 1 (ACDA: Washington, DC, Sep. 1993); *Chemical Weapons Convention Update for Industry,* no. 2 (ACDA: Washington, DC, Nov. 1993); US Congress, Office of Technology Assessment (OTA), *The Chemical Weapons Convention: Effects on the U.S. Chemical Industry,* OTA-BP-ISC-106 (US Government Printing Office: Washington, DC, Aug. 1993).

Assessment study on the effect the CWC will have on the US chemical industry[169] recommends that industry be given adequate information in order for its concerns about intrusive verification procedures to be allayed. In other countries the 'national preparatory working groups' extensively involve chemical industry. Most national chemical manufacturing associations (e.g., those in Germany, Japan, the UK and the USA) are actively informing industry.

In October 1993 a PTS-organized seminar on national trial inspections, with participants from 44 countries,[170] shared past experiences with national and multinational trial inspections, and the participants were able to draw conclusions about the inspection provisions under the CWC.[171]

In the remainder of 1994 the chemical industry must be more involved in the work of the Expert Groups to alleviate its concerns about the detailed declaration requirements, inspection provisions for chemical industry facilities and possible loss of confidential business information. The chemical industry must be better informed about developments in The Hague and the objectives of the CWC. This is a task for both the PTS and individual signatory states. Verification will not function without the support of the chemical industry.

VI. Conclusions

A crucial phase in chemical disarmament began in 1993 when the CWC was opened for signature. There has been overwhelming support for the CWC; 154 states had become signatories and 4 states had ratified the Convention by the end of 1993. States which have refrained from signing have done so for political and technical reasons. The step from signature to entry into force of the CWC is large owing to the requirement for 65 ratifications.

The establishment of the OPCW PrepCom and the PTS as the nucleus of the future Technical Secretariat is the first step in institutionalizing the chemical disarmament process. The financial cost of this process will be significant and the need for highly qualified experts great.

The decreasing participation of signatory states in the work of the PrepCom is an area of major concern. Many of the 154 signatories are small countries with a limited governmental infrastructure, especially as regards disarmament and arms control; the choice to invest limited resources and manpower in the Expert and Working Groups can be difficult.[172]

The scientific community and the NGOs played a positive supporting role during the CWC negotiations and are trying now to continue to support the process of implementing the Convention. Their expertise is certainly impor-

---

[169] See US Congress, OTA (note 168); see also chapter 9 in this volume.

[170] For an in-depth evaluation of national trial inspections, see also Trapp, R., SIPRI, *Verification under the Chemical Weapons Convention: On-Site Inspection in Chemical Industry Facilities*, SIPRI Chemical & Biological Warfare Studies, no. 14 (Oxford University Press: Oxford, 1993).

[171] Provisional Technical Secretariat for the Organisation for the Prohibition of Chemical Weapons, *Seminar on National Trial Inspections, 2 Oct. 1993, The Hague: Summary of Proceedings*, Occasional Papers no. 1 (PTS for the OPCW: The Hague, 1993).

[172] 'Ian R. Kenyon discusses strategies for implementing chemical arms treaty', *Chemical & Engineering News*, vol. 71, no. 49 (6 Dec. 1993), pp. 10–19.

tant in the national implementation undertakings. The signs that the PTS and the PrepCom are willing to become more open to this community are encouraging, although there is room for improvement. The greatest challenge is that 154 signatory states are now involved in the process of negotiating the details and procedures for implementing the verification framework under the CWC and establishing the organizational structures of the OPCW. This is a substantial change from the relatively small group of countries and experts which negotiated the CWC at the Geneva Conference on Disarmament.

18. Biological weapon and arms control developments

ERHARD GEISSLER

I. Introduction

The potential proliferation of biological and toxin weapon (TW) capability is currently perceived as a major concern. A US congressional inquiry into the threat posed by chemical weapons (CW) and biological weapons (BW) noted:

The chemical and biological threat has increased in terms of widespread proliferation, technical diversity, and probability of use. The threat is now truly global (rather than bipolar) proliferation; technological developments have broadened the spectrum and increased the diversity of potential chemical and biological weapons; and the volatility of the world political environment has probably lowered the threshold and increased the potential for use of these weapons.[1]

Biological and toxin weapon proliferation and possible measures to strengthen the 1972 Convention on the Prohibition of the Development, Production and Stockpiling of Bacteriological (Biological) and Toxin Weapons and on their Destruction (BWC)[2] have been the subject of numerous recent publications.[3]

Although the USA and other Western countries in the past conducted extensive biological defence research programmes (BDRPs) in response to a perceived Soviet BW threat, one of the lessons of the 1991 Persian Gulf War was

---

[1] *Countering the Chemical and Biological Weapons Threat in the Post-Soviet World*, Report of the Special Inquiry into the Chemical and Biological Threat of the Committee on Armed Services, House of Representatives, 102nd Congress, 2nd session (US Government Printing Office: Washington, DC, 1993), p. 69.

[2] The text of the BWC is reproduced in Geissler, E. and Woodall, J. P. (eds), SIPRI, *Control of Dual-Threat Agents: The Vaccines for Peace Programme*, SIPRI Chemical & Biological Warfare Studies, no. 15 (Oxford University Press: Oxford, 1994), pp. 243–45.

[3] See, for example, US Congress, Office of Technology Assessment (OTA), *Proliferation of Weapons of Mass Destruction: Assessing the Risks*, OTA-ISC-559 (US Government Printing Office: Washington, DC, Aug. 1993); US Congress, OTA, *Technologies Underlying Weapons of Mass Destruction*, OTA-BP-ISC-115 (US Government Printing Office: Washington, DC, Dec. 1993); Roberts, B. (ed.), *Biological Weapons: Weapons of the Future?* (Center for Strategic and International Studies: Washington, DC, 1993); Zilinskas, R. A. (ed.), *The Microbiologist and Biological Defense Research: Ethics, Politics, and International Security*, Annals of the New York Academy of Sciences, vol. 666 (New York Academy of Sciences: New York, N.Y., 1992). This topic was also discussed at several conferences in 1993, including a meeting of the Pugwash Study Group on implementation of the Chemical Weapons Convention and the BWC (Meselson, M. and Robinson, J. P., 'Report', 1st Workshop of the Pugwash Study Group on the Implementation of the Chemical and Biological Weapons Conventions, Geneva, Switzerland, 8–9 May 1993, *Pugwash Newsletter*, July 1993, pp. 21–24); MOSCON 93 (a segment of which focused on improving the BWC); the Third Workshop on Verification of Arms Reduction organized by the Geneva International Peace Research Institute (Stroot, J. P., *Verification After the Cold War: Broadening the Process* (VU University Press: Amsterdam, forthcoming); and a Wilton Park Conference (Latter, R., *Curbing Biological Weapons Proliferation*, Wilton Park Arms Control Seminar IV (Her Majesty's Stationery Office: London, Nov. 1993).

that troops were not prepared to meet a possible BW attack: 'if Iraq had used biological warfare agents that were available to it, such as anthrax and botulinum toxin, there could have been enormous fatalities and the Army's medical treatment system could have been overtaxed'.[4] In the aftermath of the Persian Gulf War, the US Army established a new organization, the Chemical and Biological Defence Agency (CBDA), to target BW issues. George Friel, the Commanding General of the CBDA, has stated that biological weapons represent 'the last major threat to a deployed force'.[5] According to Friel 'the biological threat has been recently singled out as the one major threat that still poses the ability for catastrophic effects on a theatre-deployed force'.

The US Department of Defense (DOD) increased its budget request for fiscal year (FY) 1994; $170.8 million was requested for the Biological Defense Program, a 54 per cent increase. Additional substantial increases are projected for the years ahead, a large part of which will be spent to develop biological integrated detection systems for rapid detection and identification of BW and TW agents.[6] In addition, on 26 March 1993 the US Department of the Army decided to construct and operate a new BW defence test complex, the Life Sciences Test Facility, at Dugway Proving Ground in Utah.[7]

Concern continues about the potential for the misuse of activities which are permitted under the BWC owing to the fact that 'offensive work can be conducted under the guise of defensive preparations . . . since both activities require the same basic know-how and laboratory techniques at the R&D stage [and] *intent cannot be inferred directly from capability*'.[8]

Even prophylactic and protective activities such as the development of vaccines against dual-threat agents (DTAs)[9] can have a dual nature. Such activities can be carried out both to provide protection against enemy attack and to protect personnel developing biological and toxin weapons or troops preparing to disseminate BW. However, proposals to make such activities transparent under national[10] or international[11] control have thus far been rejected.[12] Pro-

---

[4] US General Accounting Office, *Chemical and Biological Defense: U.S. Forces Are Not Adequately Equipped to Detect All Threats*, GAO/ NSIAD-93-2 (US General Accounting Office: Washington, DC, Jan. 1993), particularly p. 1.

[5] Roose, J .G ., 'Chem-bio defense agency will tackle 'last major threat to a deployed force"', *Armed Forces Journal*, Dec. 1992, p. 10.

[6] *Inside the Army*, 12 Apr. 1993, quoted in *Chemical Weapons Convention Bulletin*, no. 20 (June 1993), p. 18.

[7] *Chemical Weapons Convention Bulletin*, no. 21 (Sep. 1993), p. 21.

[8] See OTA-ISC-559 (note 3), pp. 7, 36, 39; emphasis given in original.

[9] DTAs are pathogens and toxins which are not only natural enemies of people, animals and plants but can also be used for hostile purposes as BW and TW agents; see Geissler, E., 'Vaccines for Peace: an international program of development and use of vaccines against dual-threat agents', *Politics and the Life Sciences*, vol. 11, no. 2 (Aug. 1992), pp. 231–43.

[10] A bill to require that all Federal Research, Development, Testing and Evaluation of the Use of Biological Agents in the Development of Defenses against Biological Warfare be Conducted by the Director of the National Institutes of Health, and for Other Purposes, H.R. 5241, introduced in the US House of Representatives by W. Owens, 100th Congress, 2nd session, 11 Aug. 1988, reproduced in Geissler and Woodall (note 2), pp. 261–63.

[11] See Geissler (note 9).

[12] Pearson, G., 'Vaccines for biological defence: defence considerations', in Geissler and Woodall (note 2), pp. 151–62; see also Hinds, J., Huxsoll, D., Richardson, B. and other representatives of the US DOD, in *Global Spread of Chemical and Biological Weapons*, Hearings before the Committee on Gov-

posals by Finland,[13] France,[14] Austria and Ireland[15] that states parties provide information about the vaccination programmes for their armed forces have also not been approved. The lack of a verification regime for the BWC creates additional cause for concern.

II. Alleged development, possession and/or use of BW and TW agents

The danger of proliferation of BW and TW agents and of related equipment and technology is real, as the example of the Iraqi biological and toxin weapon programme has demonstrated.[16] Fear of proliferation is not exaggerated. In addition to Iraq,[17] which is subject to the obligations of United Nations Security Council Resolution 687,[18] several countries are regarded by Jane's Consultancy Services[19] and other sources as 'possessors' (allegations about Russia are addressed in the following discussion) or 'potential possessors' of BW agents (China,[20] India, Israel, North Korea,[21] South Africa,

ernmental Affairs and its Permanent Subcommittee on Investigations, US Senate (US Government Printing Office: Washington, DC, 1990).

[13] Second Review Conference of the Parties to the Convention on the Prohibition of the Development, Production and Stockpiling of Bacteriological (Biological) and Toxin Weapons and on their Destruction, *Summary Record of the 5th Meeting,* BWC/CONF.II/SR.5, 19 Sep. 1986, p. 5.

[14] See Second Review Conference (note 13), *Summary Record of the 8th Meeting,* BWC/CONF.II/SR.8, 22 Sep. 1986, p. 7.

[15] *Ad Hoc* Meeting of Scientific and Technical Experts from States Parties to the Convention on the Prohibition of the Development, Production and Stockpiling of Bacteriological (Biological) and Toxin Weapons and on Their Destruction, *Report,* BWC/CONF.II/EX/2, Attachment, Proposal by Ireland and Austria on agenda item 4 (a), 21 Apr. 1987, p. 30.

[16] Tucker, J. B., 'Lessons of Iraq's biological warfare programme', *Arms Control,* vol. 14, no. 3 (Dec. 1993), pp. 229–71.

[17] According to *Middle East Watch,* Iraq has stockpiled BW since 1986; see 'Iraqi "genocide"', *The Independent,* 2 Jan. 1993, p. 13.

[18] UNSCOM's activities in 1993 are discussed in chapter 19 in this volume.

[19] Reed, J., 1993: *Defence Exports, Current Concerns,* A Jane's Special Brief (Jane's Consultancy Services: Coulsdon, Surrey, UK, 1993).

[20] According to then President Bush 'it is highly probable that China has not eliminated its BW program since becoming a party to the Convention in 1984'; *Report given by President Bush on Adherence and Compliance,* 19 Jan., quoted in *Chemical Weapons Convention Bulletin* no. 19 (Mar. 1993), p. 17. The USA believed that China conducts BW research at two ostensibly civilian-run research centres; see Smith, R. J. 'China may have revived germ weapons program, U.S. officials say', *Washington Post,* 24 Feb. 1993, p. A4; see also *International Herald Tribune,* 25 Feb., 1993. This claim was denied by the Chinese Foreign Ministry spokesman; see 'China denies germ weapons program', *Washington Post,* 26 Feb., 1993.

[21] The Russian Foreign Intelligence Service provided a US Senate Committee with information that 'North Korea is performing applied military-biological research', possibly for sale to Middle East countries. According to the report 'work is being performed [on] inducers of malignant anthrax, cholera, bubonic plague and smallpox. Biological weapons are being tested on [North Korea's] island territories'. See Tisdall, S., 'West rushes to stop Korean atom bomb: Russia also alerts US to threat of biological weapons', *The Guardian,* 27 Feb., 1993. These claims have also been made by South Korean authorities, who estimated that North Korea's ability to wage biochemical warfare ranks third in the world. See 'North's biochemical warfare capability estimated', Seoul KBS-1 Radio Network, 27 Sep. 1993 (in Korean), in Foreign Broadcast Information Service, *Daily Report–East Asia (FBIS-EAS)* FBIS-EAS-93-185, 27 Sep. 1993, p. 20. North Korea denies these allegations; see 'North denies BW program', Pyongyang Korean Central Broadcasting Network, 3 Oct. 1993 (in Korean), in FBIS-EAS-93-190, 4 Oct. 1993, p. 14; 'Further on South's "anti-DPRK campaign"', Pyongyang KCNA, 5 Oct. 1993 (in English), in FBIS-EAS-93-191, 5 Oct. 1993, p. 13. The US Central Intelligence Agency (CIA) informed the Senate Governmental Affairs Committee on 27 Aug. 1993 that there is 'almost no information on

Syria),[22] 'developers' (Libya[23]) or 'potential developers' (Iran,[24] Taiwan[25]) of BW agents, or 'capable' (Belarus), 'potentially capable' (Pakistan) or 'possibly capable' (South Korea) of developing such weapon agents. Some of these allegations are also made in a Russian intelligence report.[26]

It has to be emphasized, however, that it is impossible for an independent observer to evaluate these claims. Usually no other sources are given for such allegations than 'intelligence reports' or the like which are impossible to verify. In addition, because of the dual-threat nature of BW and TW agents and of the dual-use nature of the related know-how, technology and equipment it might well be that a state is alleged to be a 'possessor' or 'developer' of BW agents simply because facilities on its territory are dealing with DTAs for genuinely peaceful or defensive purposes.

The former Soviet Union, Russia and the new independent states

Additional details concerning previous Soviet BW and TW activities became available in 1993.[27] According to one report:[28]

after the [BW] Convention was signed, highly promising developments in the BW areas re-energized the USSR . . . In the middle of 1970s, a strictly secret Research and Technology Committee was formed under the Central Administration of Microbiology Industry, where leading Soviet scientists ware designated to work.

Production tasks were offered to a large industrial complex, *'Biopreparat'*, which had production facilities all over the country . . . Eighteen R&D Institutes having 25 thousand staff, 6 plants, and a large warehouse in Siberia were included into the System . . . Each group at Biopreparat was assigned a specific task. The Institute in Kol'tsovo near Novosibirsk worked on the lethal virus of haemorrhagic fever and on Venezuela [equine] encephalitis. Experiments needed for testing plague and malignant anthrax were conducted in Obolensk. In Leningrad, experiments were

---

whether Pyongyang seeks to build biological weapons. Nevertheless, North Korea—if it desires—has the capability to develop classic biological agents such as anthrax, plague, or yellow fever', *Chemical Weapons Convention Bulletin*, no. 22 (Dec. 1993), p. 13.

[22] According to then President Bush 'it is highly probable that Syria is developing a biological warfare agent'; see *Report given by President Bush* (note 20); Syria is not a state party to the BWC.

[23] The US CIA informed the Senate Governmental Affairs Committee on 27 Aug. 1993 that 'Libya's BW program is in the research and development phase and has not produced any BW weapons', *Chemical Weapons Convention Bulletin*, no. 22 (Dec. 1993), p. 13.

[24] According Bush 'Iran probably has produced biological warfare agents and apparently has weaponized a small quantity of these agents'; see *Report given by President Bush* (note 20). In a hearing before the US Senate Governmental Affairs Committee the newly confirmed Director of the CIA, James Woolsey, declared on 24 Feb. 1993 that biological weapons 'if not already in production, probably are not far behind' in Iran. See 'Woolsey on proliferation', *Arms Sales Monitor*, no. 19 (15 Mar. 1993).

[25] President Bush stated: 'there is some evidence to indicate that Taiwan may continue to maintain the BW program it was assessed as possessing in the 1970s'; see *Report given by President Bush* (note 20); see also Smith, R. J., 'China may have revived germ weapons program, U.S. officials say', *Washington Post*, 24 Feb. 1993, p. A4.

[26] 'A new challenge after the "cold war": the proliferation of weapons of mass destruction', Report by the Foreign Intelligence Service of the Russian Federation, Moscow, 1993.

[27] Leitenberg, M., 'The conversion of biological warfare research and development facilities to peaceful uses', in Geissler and Woodall, (note 2), pp. 77–105.

[28] Leskov, S., 'The plague and the bomb', *Izvestia*, 26 June 1993 (in Russian), translated by V. Kogan; see also Leitenberg (note 27).

conducted on tularaemia, and methods of increasing the military effectiveness of BWs were being developed.[29]

The Virological Center of the Microbiological Research Institute Sagorsk (now Sergiyev-Posad) is said to have been 'working with spotted fever agents . . . with agents of Venezuelan equine encephalomyelitis, and some other arboviruses'.[30]

Substantial information on Soviet BW activities was provided by Vladimir Pasechnik, who before he defected to Great Britain was Director of the Leningrad (now St Petersburg) Institute for Ultrapure Biological Preparations at the Biopreparat complex.[31] Pasechnik's credibility is perhaps questionable since, for example, he claims to have learned of the existence of the 1972 BWC only after his defection to the West,[32] although several papers dealing with it were published in the former Soviet Union in the 1980s. According to Pasechnik, approximately 400 scientists developed bacteria for antidote-resistant BW at the Institute for Ultrapure Biological Preparations. British, Russian and US experts who conducted an investigation there in October 1992 found that the institute was 'only indirectly connected in the most general way' with BW activities.[33] This information is corroborated by that given in Russia's 1992 confidence-building report.[34] However, according to *Newsweek*, 'a second official higher in Biopreparat than Pasechnik defected to the United States' in 1992 and testified 'that offensive-biological weapons work continued inside the Biopreparat system even after Yeltsin's edict'.[35]

Although President Boris Yeltsin in 1992 ordered the cessation of all activities in violation of the BWC,[36] no information was given in the confidence-building information (see below) submitted by Belarus, Russia, Ukraine[37] and Kyrgyzstan[38] as to whether BW and TW had been stockpiled prior to March 1992 or whether any such stockpiles have since been destroyed. According to

[29] See Leskov (note 28).

[30] Makhlay, A. A., interview in 'TV crew visits, films "secret" virological center', Moscow Tele-radiokompaniya Ostankino Television First Program Network, 17 Feb. 1993, (in Russian), in Foreign Broadcast Information Service, *Daily Report–Central Eurasia, (FBIS-SOV),* FBIS-SOV-93-038, 1 Mar. 1993, pp. 35–36. Neither the name of the institute nor its precise location was given in the interview. The fact that Makhlay was introduced as 'director' and that video footage showed a sign reading 'Moscow 68 km' indicate that the facility is the Virology Center of the CIS United Forces Scientific Research Institute for Microbiology which was already declared in the 1985 Soviet report. More information on the agents studied in the several departments of the Army's Institute of Microbiology are provided in the 1992 Russian report, DDA/4-92/BWIII/Add.3, 22 Sep. 1992, pp. 32–90, particularly pp. 35–36.

[31] Pasechnik, V., Interview on BBC 2, *News Night,* 21 Jan. 1993; see also Gertz, B., 'Russia has biological weapons, defector says', *Washington Times,* 22 Jan. 1993, p. 9; Urban, M., 'The cold war's deadliest secret', *The Spectator,* 23 Jan. 1993, pp. 9–10.

[32] See Pasechnik (note 31).

[33] See Stock, T., 'Chemical and biological weapons: developments and proliferation', SIPRI, *SIPRI Yearbook 1993: World Armaments and Disarmament* (Oxford University Press: Oxford, 1993), pp. 259–92, especially p. 288.

[34] See DDA/4-92/BWIII/Add.3 (note 30), particularly p. 39.

[35] Barry, J., 'Planning a plague?', *Newsweek,* 1 Feb. 1993, pp. 20–22.

[36] See Stock (note 33), p. 287.

[37] Office of Disarmament Affairs (ODA) document ODA/9-93/BWIII.

[38] Office of Disarmament Affairs (ODA) document ODA/9-93/BWIII/Add.1.

Academician Anatoly Kuntsevich, Russia had no BW stockpiles.[39] The head of the Russian Defence Ministry Biological Defence Directorate, N. T. Vasilyev, has declared: 'We only had experimental samples . . . which were tested in laboratory and *field conditions*. Individual lines were set up, which could have been used in wartime for the production of these specific cocktails. However, no biological weapons were produced or stockpiled in our country'.[40] Of course, quite large 'samples' are necessary to carry out field experiments, and quite large samples must have been released in Sverdlovsk to account for an anthrax epidemic there which caused at least 65 deaths (see below).

Doubts about the strict adherence of Russia and other Commonwealth of Independent States (CIS) countries to the BWC still seem to be justified. According to the British Government 'there has been a series of exchanges over the last two years between the United Kingdom, the United States and Russia . . . about the Russian biological weapons programme. These exchanges took place on a confidential basis' and are not published.[41] In addition to the 1992 visit to the Institute for Ultrapure Biological Preparations[42] experts from the UK and the USSR visited a facility at Berdsk, near Novosibirsk, where it was suspected that work was being conducted on the development of BW weapons, and a facility at Pokrov, near Moscow, where it was suspected that BW research was being carried out.[43]

Japanese biological warfare operations during World War II

A study of newly discovered records of the Imperial Japanese Army by Yoshiaki Yoshimi revealed hitherto unknown information about Japanese bacterial warfare operations against China. Diaries from the Strategy Section of the Japanese General Staff Headquarters and from the Medical Affairs Section of the Army Ministry showed that aircraft operations took place in the Changde region in November 1941 and that mice with plague-infected fleas had been released in Guangxin in August 1942.[44] Documents found in China by Masataka Mori revealed that, in March 1942, 300 Chinese died of plague in Yiwu, a small village approximately 2030 km south-west of Shanghai, after a Japanese plane dropped plague-carrying fleas.[45]

BW operations had also been planned for March 1942 on the Bataan peninsula of the Philippines using approximately 10 tons of microbial bombs.

[39] See *Countering the Chemical and Biological Weapons Threat* (note 1), p. 16.

[40] See Makhlay (note 30); emphasis added.

[41] Hogg, D., 'Biological weapons', written answers to questions, *Hansard*, 27 Jan. 1993, p. 705.

[42] See Stock (note 33), p. 288.

[43] *New York Times*, 1 Dec. 1993, quoted in *Chemical Weapons Convention Bulletin*, no. 22 (Dec. 1993), p. 20.

[44] Kyodo, 30 Dec. 1993 in FBIS-EAS-93-249, 30 Dec. 1993, quoted in *Chemical Weapons Convention Bulletin*, no. 23 (Mar. 1994), p. 19.

[45] AP (Tokyo), 'Japanese spread plague, files say', *Stars and Stripes*, Jan. 1993.

In addition, BW operations were slated for Australia, Burma, Hawaii and other Pacific islands and for India.[46]

An exhibition about Unit 731, Japan's leading BW facility, and its involvement in the Japanese BW programme from 1932 to 1945 is touring Japan.[47]

III. The threat of terrorism using BW

There is increasing concern that BW and TW agents might be used by terrorists, including 'state-sponsored' terrorists, or for sabotage purposes.[48] The threat of terrorism using BW 'may be much higher now than it was at the time of the [Gulf] war'.[49] According to the US Special Inquiry into the Chemical and Biological Threat, 'in rear areas, used against unprotected military and civilian personnel, and because of the large areas that may be covered with small amounts of agents and the large number of casualties that may be produced, biological weapons may truly deserve the appellation "poor man's atomic bomb"'.[50]

The magnitude of a BW terrorist threat is well described by the OTA's assessment that 'a given quantity of certain lethal micro-organisms would probably kill even more people if spread effectively by human agents than if by a missile'.[51]

In 1993 it was disclosed that Joseph Stalin considered assassinating Joseph Broz Tito using BW agents in an act of state-sponsored terrorism. Plans were prepared to murder Tito by disseminating plague bacteria at a reception.[52]

New information came to light in 1993 about the assassination of Bulgarian writer and dissident Georgiy Markov—a state-sponsored act of biological terrorism which was actually carried out. Former KGB General Oleg Kalugin admitted that the assassination was conducted on orders from former Bulgarian President Todor Zhivkov. The Soviet KGB provided a device similar to a fountain pen which propelled a small pellet filled with the TW agent ricin. It was fitted into an umbrella and operated from its handle. The contaminated pellet was able to penetrate the skin and to dissolve quickly leaving no trace. Using this device Markov was attacked by Bulgarian secret agents in September 1978 at a bus stop in London and died four days later.[53]

---

[46] *Daily Telegraph*, 29 Nov. 1993, quoted in *Chemical Weapons Convention Bulletin*, no. 23 (Mar. 1994), p. 14.

[47] *The Independent*, 20 Aug. 1993, quoted in *Chemical Weapons Convention Bulletin*, no. 22 (Dec. 1993), p. 11.

[48] US Congress, OTA, *Technology Against Terrorism: Structuring Security*, OTA-ISC-511 (US Government Printing Office, Washington, DC, Jan. 1992), particularly pp. 29–31, 35–44.

[49] Kupperman, R. H. and Smith, D. M., 'Coping with biological terrorism', in Roberts (note 3), pp. 35–46, particularly p. 36.

[50] *Countering the Chemical and Biological Weapons Threat* (note 1), p. 9.

[51] OTA-ISC-559 (note 3), p. 3.

[52] Wolkogonow, D., 'The assassination which did not take place: how the Soviet agent Max prepared a terrorist attack against Tito', *Izvestia*, 11 June 1993, p. 7 (in Russian); Womack, H., 'Stalin "planned to kill Tito by infecting him with the plague"', *The Independent*, 12 June 1993.

[53] Edgington, E., 'I organized Markov's execution: They tried the poison on a horse. It died. Then a prisoner. He lived. Then they went for the real target . . . Soviet spymaster on his role in killing of a dissident', *Mail on Sunday*, 4 Apr. 1993, p. 8. See also 'Further on release', ITAR-TASS, 1 Nov. 1993 (in

IV. Unusual outbreaks of disease

The Sverdlovsk anthrax accident

In 1993 additional information about the 1979 Sverdlovsk anthrax outbreak was released.[54] Although some Russian officials continue to claim that tainted meat was the true cause of the epidemic in Sverdlovsk (now Ekaterinburg),[55] a Russian–US expert team headed by Matthew Meselson which visited Ekaterinburg do not agree.[56] The group reported that a series of 42 necropsies, representing a majority of the fatalities of the anthrax epidemic that occurred in Sverdlovsk, consistently revealed pathological lesions diagnostic of inhalational anthrax. These data led to the conclusion 'that these patients died because of inhalation of aerosols containing *B. anthracis*'.[57]

There are still numerous questions about the outbreak. Was it caused by a leak in the filter system or by an explosion (presumably between 6 and 8 a.m. on 2 April 1979)? Why did new cases of anthrax occur over a period of more than a month? Why were children not infected during the outbreak, and what kind of activities had been conducted in military complex 19 where the outbreak occurred? It is possible that R&D, production and testing of anthrax vaccine were being carried out, which is permitted under the BWC.[58]

Anthrax outbreak in Zimbabwe

An unusual anthrax epidemic in the final months of the Zimbabwe civil conflict in 1979–80 involving over 10 000 persons and resulting in 82 deaths led to suspicion that it was caused by the deliberate spread of *Bacillus anthracis*.[59] The outbreak was unusual in that it affected only Blacks and did not follow typical patterns. In addition, the media in Zimbabwe are said to have reported that the Rhodesian military used anthrax, cholera and CW agents during hos-

English), in FBIS-SOV-93-209, 1 Nov. 1993, p. 5. Later, however, Kalugin emphasized that the headline of the article in *Mail on Sunday*, 'I organized Georgi Markov murder', is incorrect. See 'Former KGB official describes UK questioning', *Izvestia*, 6 Nov. 1992, 1st edn, p. 2 (in Russian), in *FBIS-SOV-93-214*, 8 Nov. 1993, pp. 10–11.

[54] See Stock (note 33), p. 287.

[55] Academician P. N. Burgasov, interview, in Pashkov, A., 'Generals and anthrax', video report, Moscow Russian Television Network, 16 Sep. 1993 (in Russian).

[56] Miller, S. K., 'Secret samples reveal truth about anthrax', *New Scientist*, 20 Mar. 1993, p. 4; Meselson, M., 'New evidence on the 1979 Soviet anthrax epidemic', *ASA Newsletter*, 93-2 (8 Apr. 1993), pp. 1, 5.

[57] Abramova, F. A. *et al.*, 'Pathology of inhalational anthrax in 42 cases from the Sverdlovsk outbreak of 1979', *Proceedings of the National Academy of Sciences, USA*, vol. 90 (Mar. 1993), pp. 2291–94.

[58] Hilts, P. J., 'U.S. and Russian researchers tie anthrax deaths to Soviets', *New York Times*, 15 Mar. 1993, p. A6; Heylin, M., 'New study links anthrax deaths to Soviet military', *Chemical & Engineering News*, vol. 71, no. 1443 (22 Mar. 1993), p. 7; Credeur, A., 'Cover-up of Russian anthrax outbreak like a spy novel', *LSU* [Louisiana State University] *Today*, vol. 9, no. 30 (2 Apr. 1993), pp. 1, 4, 6; Pashkov (note 55).

[59] Nass, M., 'Anthrax epizootic in Zimbabwe, 1978–1980: due to deliberate spread?', *Physicians for Social Responsibility Quarterly*, vol. 2, no. 6 (Dec. 1992), pp. 198–209; 'Rhodesia's chemical warfare against freedom fighters? Scientists to probe anthrax epidemic', *Zimbabwe Herald*, 25 Jan. 1993, p. 1.

tilities.[60] The current Government of Zimbabwe sanctioned a study to determine the origin of the outbreak.[61]

Hantavirus Pulmonary Syndrome

In the south-western United States there was an outbreak of a lethal respiratory disease in 1993.[62] By the end of November 1993, 45 cases of the syndrome had been reported in 12 states (mainly in Arizona and New Mexico) with 27 deaths.[63] Using one of the most powerful modern genetic techniques, the polymerase chain reaction, scientists at the Centers for Disease Control and Prevention, Fort Collins, Colorado, and the US Army Medical Research Institute of Infectious Diseases (USAMRIID), Fort Detrick, Maryland, were able within weeks to discover that the disease was caused by a hitherto unknown hantavirus—pulmonary syndrome hantavirus.[64] The virus was obviously spread by the contaminated urine of deer mice (*Peromyscus maniculatus*) the population of which increased rapidly in early 1993.[65]

As the agent causing the syndrome had been unknown, it is not yet perceived as a DTA although there has been speculation that the virus might have escaped from USAMRIID or other US Army facilities.[66] Another hantavirus which causes Korean haemorrhagic fever is known to be a DTA. The outbreak of hantavirus pulmonary syndrome is an example of the threat of emerging diseases[67] and indicates the need for a system of global biological security[68] including the establishment of a global epidemiological surveillance system (see below). While frightening, the outbreak also demonstrates the efficiency of molecular biotechniques to identify pathogens, thus providing a means of protection against DTAs.

---

[60] 'Anthrax outbreak in Zimbabwe: a case of biological warfare?' *geneWATCH*, vol. 8, no. 5-6 (1993), p. 4; Garrett, B. C., 'A cloud over Zimbabwe: 1978–80 anthrax outbreak', *ASA Newsletter*, 93-1 (10 Feb. 1993), pp. 8, 20.

[61] Council for Responsible Genetics, 'Widespread anthrax outbreak linked to possible biological warfare: definitive investigation being planned', Cambridge, Mass., 3 Feb. 1993; 'Alleged use of BW in Rhodesia', *Trust and Verify*, no. 35 (Jan./Feb. 1993), p. 3.

[62] 'Mystery epidemic fatal to 11 in southwest is linked to rodent urine', *Washington Post*, 5 June 1993, p. A5.

[63] Altman, L. K., 'Virus that caused deaths in New Mexico is isolated', *New York Times*, 21 Nov. 1993, p. 24; Hughes, J. M., *et al.*, 'Hantavirus pulmonary syndrome: an emerging infectious disease', *Science*, vol. 262 (5 Nov. 1993), pp. 850–51.

[64] Marshall, E., 'Hantavirus outbreak yields to PCR', *Science*, vol. 262 (5 Nov. 1993), pp. 832–36.

[65] Nichol, S. T. *et al.*, 'Genetic identification of a hantavirus associated with an outbreak of acute respiratory illness', *Science*, vol. 262 (5 Nov. 1993), pp. 914–17; Stone, R., 'The mouse–piñon nut connection', *Science*, vol. 262 (5 Nov. 1993), p. 833.

[66] 'Were four corners victims biowar casualties?', *Scientific American*, vol. 269, no. 5 (1993), p. 8; Wakefield, J., 'Federal researchers untangle web spun by newly emerged pathogens', *US Medicine*, Mar. 1994, pp. 2, 16–17.

[67] Lederberg, J., Shope, R. E. and Oaks, Jr, S. C. (eds), *Emerging Infections: Microbial Threats to Health in the United States* (National Academy Press: Washington, DC, 1992); Morse, S. (ed.), *Emerging Viruses* (Oxford University Press: Oxford, 1993).

[68] Geissler, E., Calderón, F. C. and Woodall, J. P., 'From BVI to VFP: towards a system of global biological security', in Geissler and Woodall (note 2), pp. 219–39; Geissler, E., 'Towards a system of global biological security' (part I), *ASA Newsletter*, no. 94-1 (10 Feb. 1994), pp. 1, 12–13; Geissler, E., 'Towards a system of global biological security' (part II), *ASA Newsletter*, no. 94-2 (7 Apr. 1994), pp. 1, 10–11.

V. Destruction of smallpox virus stockpiles

Smallpox (variola) virus is one of the most likely candidates for use as a BW agent,[69] and it has been considered militarily significant since 1925[70] and earlier.[71]

After the successful eradication of smallpox virus,[72] in 1980 the World Health Organization (WHO) decided that 'smallpox vaccination is no longer justified. Because vaccination may result in serious complications, which are occasionally fatal, no one except investigators at special risk should be vaccinated in any country' and recommended that 'smallpox vaccination should be discontinued in every country except for investigators at special risk'.[73]

In 1986 the WHO *Ad Hoc* Committee on Orthopox Infections emphasized that smallpox vaccination of military personnel should also be terminated.[74] Because smallpox virus is a putative BW agent, the WHO recognized that 'a country's resumption of vaccination against smallpox would now be interpreted as a sign that it might be considering the use of variola virus for aggressive purposes'.[75] In fact, because of the successful eradication of smallpox virus it became the first 'single-threat agent'.[76] It is claimed that Canada and the USA continue to vaccinate their troops against smallpox,[77] as did presumably the former Soviet Union (at least until the end of 1991).[78]

Following the introduction of genetic engineering methods which allowed the sequencing of the complete smallpox genome, the WHO *Ad Hoc* Committee on Orthopox Infections proposed[79] that the remaining smallpox virus stocks—in the Centers for Disease Control (CDC), Atlanta, Georgia, and the Research Institute for Viral Preparations, Moscow—be destroyed by 31 December 1993 unless serious objections were raised by the international health

[69] Schopp, W., 'Eine potentielle biologische Waffe: Pockenvirus' ['A potential biological weapon: smallpox'], eds W. Dosch and P. Herrlich, *Ächtung der Giftwaffen. Naturwissenschaftler warnen vor Chemischen und Biologischen Waffen [Abolishing Toxic Weapons: Natural Scientists Warn of Chemical and Biological Weapons]* (Fischer Taschenbuch Verlag: Frankfurt am Main, 1985), pp. 167–71.

[70] *Denkschrift der Heeres-Sanitäts-Inspektion des Reichswehrministeriums über die Verwendung von Krankheitskeimen als Kampfmittel im Kriege [Memorandum of the Army Sanitation Inspection of the Reich's War Ministry on the Use of Disease Germs as Weapon Agents in War]* (Berlin, 1925), p. 10, RH-12-9/v.27, Bundes-Militärarchiv, Freiburg, Breisgau.

[71] Poupard, J. A., Miller, L. A. and Granshaw, L., 'The use of smallpox as a biological weapon in the French and Indian war of 1763', *ASM News*, vol. 55, no. 3 (1989), pp. 122–24.

[72] Fenner, F., 'The WHO global smallpox eradication programme: vaccine supply and variola virus stocks', in Geissler and Woodall (note 10), pp. 185–202.

[73] World Health Organization, *The Global Eradication of Smallpox*, Final Report of the Global Commission for the Certification of Smallpox Eradication (World Health Organization: Geneva, 1980); see also Fenner, A. et al., *Smallpox and its Eradication* (World Health Organization: Geneva, 1988), pp. 1264–66.

[74] *Weekly Epidemiological Record*, vol. 61 (1986), p. 289.

[75] Fenner et al. (note 72), p. 1341.

[76] Fenner (note 72), p. 185.

[77] Mahy, B. W. J., Contribution to the round table 'Smallpox virus: the final steps toward eradication', IXth International Congress of Virology, Glasgow, Scotland, 11 Aug. 1993, recorded and produced by Q.E.D. Recording Services: New Barnet, Hertfordshire, UK, 1993.

[78] Dalrymple, J. M., 'DoD-sponsored virus vaccine development: an investigator's perspective', in Zilinskas (note 3), pp. 202–17, particularly p. 212.

[79] Mahy, B. W. J., Esposito, J. J. and Venter, J. C., 'Sequencing the smallpox virus genome', *ASM News*, vol. 57, no. 11 (Nov. 1991), pp. 577–80.

community. This proposal was discussed in a round table on 11 August 1993 at the IXth International Congress of Virology in Glasgow, Scotland.[80] Some participants favoured immediate destruction because:

the continued existence of smallpox virus stocks in Russia and the United States . . . represent a potential military hazard from any terrorist group that succeeded in gaining access to the virus. Recent political uncertainty in several parts of the world, including the former Soviet Union and its satellite countries, has re-emphasized this danger. Destruction of the remaining smallpox virus stocks would eliminate this potential weapon, consistent with the aims of the International Biological and Toxic Weapons Convention of 1972.[81]

Those taking the opposite view argued, 'we should be much more alarmed by the thought of smallpox virus being destroyed than by the smallpox virus being studied responsibly and expertly in one or two laboratories', because additional research on the virus is necessary to understand virus infections fully, because smallpox virus is to be regarded as a 'prime candidate for becoming . . . a re-emerging infectious agent', and for other reasons.[82] The matter of whether and when destruction will be recommended by the WHO is expected to be decided at a May 1994 meeting of the World Health Assembly. The disarmament point of view would favour the destruction of this dangerous virus, and it is to be hoped that the governments of Russia and the USA will follow such a recommendation.

VI. The status of the BWC

Participation in the BWC

Adherence to the BWC has continued to increase at a steady rate. In 1993 five states acceded or succeeded to the Convention: the Czech Republic, Estonia, the Maldives, Slovakia and Suriname. In addition it became known that Croatia had become a state party as a successor state of Yugoslavia effective October 1991.[83] As of 31 December 1993, 131 states were states parties to the BWC.[84]

Kazakhstan and Uzbekistan, which have inherited CBW facilities and test ranges, respectively, from the former Soviet military complex,[85] have not yet acceded to the BWC.

---

[80] See Roundtable (note 77).

[81] Mahy, B. et al., 'The remaining stocks of smallpox virus should be destroyed', *Science*, vol. 262 (19 Nov. 1993), pp. 1223–24.

[82] Joklik, W. K. et al., 'Why the smallpox virus stocks should not be destroyed', *Science*, vol. 262 (19 Nov. 1993), pp. 1225–26.

[83] Institute for Defense and Disarmament Studies, 'BWC member update, 31 December', *Arms Control Reporter* (IDDS: Brookline, Mass.), sheet 701.B.121, Jan. 1994; M. Cassandra, UN Center for Disarmament Affairs, personal communication to the author, Mar. 1994.

[84] For a list of parties, see annexe A in this volume.

[85] See OTA-ISC-559 (note 3), p. 77

Information exchange as a confidence-building measure

Seven rounds of information exchange have taken place thus far, two after the 1991 Third Review Conference of the BWC which improved and amended the measures instituted at the Second Review Conference.[86] However, participation in the confidence-building measures (CBMs) has not improved significantly. The number of states which have participated in the information exchange at least once rose from 49 in 1991 to 58 in 1993 (see table 18.1). In the two rounds which took place after the Third Review Conference only nine additional states participated in the exchange: Iraq (1993),[87] Jordan (1992), South Korea (1992), Kyrgyzstan (1993), Malta (1992), Nicaragua (1993), Slovenia (1993), South Africa (1993) and Tunisia (1992). Only 12 states provided information in all seven rounds: Belarus, Canada, Denmark, Finland, Germany, the Netherlands, Norway, the Russian Federation, Ukraine, Sweden, the UK and the USA.[88]

It is difficult to understand why states parties which participated in the meetings of the *Ad Hoc* Group of Governmental Experts to Identify and Examine Potential Verification Measures from a Scientific and Technical Standpoint (VEREX), discussed below, did not contribute to the CBMs (see table 18.2).

At the Third Review Conference and at VEREX it was proposed that an implementation or oversight committee to monitor the CBMs on a regular basis be created, but this has not been done. States parties might consider whether the mandate of the Organisation for the Prohibition of Chemical Weapons (OPCW) could be extended to embrace identical functions in respect to BW and TW as well as CW as proposed *inter alia* by Nicholas Sims.[89]

Information on facilities and R&D programmes

Although much information was provided during the 1992 and 1993 information exchanges on research centres and national BDRPs, the provision of details on R&D activities including vaccine programmes was limited and was

---

[86] Lundin, S. J., Stock, T. and Geissler, E., 'Chemical and biological warfare and arms control developments in 1991', SIPRI, *SIPRI Yearbook 1992: World Armaments and Disarmament* (Oxford University Press: Oxford, 1992), pp. 147–82, particularly pp. 177–78.

[87] See chapter 19 in this volume.

[88] Of the 39 reports provided in 1993, 1 is in Chinese, 27 in English, 1 in French, 4 in Russian and 5 in Spanish. The report provided by Iraq was not given in one of the authentic languages of the BWC, in contradiction of the agreed modality. As evaluation of the reports might be facilitated by availability of an English version the proposal is repeated here that the UN Centre for Disarmament Affairs (formerly ODA) be requested by states parties to translate forthcoming reports into English. See Geissler E. (ed.), *Strengthening the Biological Weapons Convention by Confidence-Building Measures*, SIPRI Chemical & Biological Warfare Studies, no. 10 (Oxford University Press: Oxford, 1990), p. 135.

[89] Sims, N. A., 'Endogenous development of the multilateral treaty regime (MTR) flowing from the BWC: proposals for special conferences and for a continuous central capability', eds. E. Geissler and R. H. Haynes, *Prevention of a Biological and Toxin Arms Race and the Responsibility of Scientists*, (Akademie Verlag: Berlin, 1991), pp. 443–69; Sims, N. A., 'Control and co-operation in biological defence research: national programmes and international accountability', in Geissler and Woodall (note 2), pp. 56–66.

Table 18.1. Participation in the confidence-building measures

	1987	1988	1989	1990	1991	1992	1993
States parties submitting reports	19	23	21	31	41	37	39
Total no. of states submitting reports	19	25	27	36	49	53	58

restricted to merely mentioning agents covered by the programmes and other general information.

As long as it is not possible to verify the information, even the restricted information which is provided is of limited value. A typical example is the information given and withheld, respectively, by the former Soviet Union and by the Russian Federation. In 1987 the Soviet Union reported on five facilities controlled by the Ministry of Defence, located in Aralsk, Kirov, Leningrad (now St Petersburg), Sverdlovsk (now Ekaterinburg) and Zagorsk (now Sergiyev-Posad). In addition, 14 other facilities were reported which are claimed not to be funded by the Ministry of Defence. They include the All-Union Scientific Research Institute of Molecular Biology in Kol'tsovo, Novosibirsk Region, and the Research Institute for Applied Microbiology, Obolensk, Moscow Region. In 1987 both facilities were said to be funded only by the Ministry of the Medical and Microbiology Industry.[90]

This information contradicts US claims that the USSR had at least seven BW facilities, including those in Omutninsk, Aksu, Pokrov, Berdsk, Penza, Kurgan and Malta.[91] In 1992 it was reported that 'US intelligence officials said they have found more than 20 sites in the former Soviet Union for germ-warfare work'.[92] One of these additional facilities was claimed to be the Leningrad (now St Petersburg) All-Union Scientific Institute for Ultrapure Preparations mentioned above.

In 1992 the Russian Federation reported that in addition to the five military facilities mentioned in 1987 the institutes located in Kol'tsovo and Obolensk were funded at least partially by the High Command of CIS United Armed Forces. This report and the report provided in 1993 do not explicitly mention any of the other facilities referred to in US publications including the Institute for Ultrapure Biological Preparations at St Petersburg. However, it is shown on a diagram attached to the 1992 report indicating at least co-operation with the armed forces. In fact, according to a press interview given by General Valentin Yevstigneyev on 2 December 1992, the Institute for Ultrapure

---

[90] 'Information by the USSR in pursurance of the accords reached at the second Review Conference of the Parties to the Convention on the Prohibition of the Development, Production and Stockpiling of Bacteriological (Biological) and Toxin Weapons and on their Destruction, and in keeping with the decisions and recommendations of the Special Meeting of Scientific and Technical Experts from the Participating States', Moscow, Oct. 1987; see also Geissler (note 88), pp. 88–89.

[91] See Geissler (note 88), p. 84.

[92] 'Yeltsin commits to germ warfare ban', *Washington Post*, 17 Apr. 1992, quoted in Leitenberg (note 27).

Table 18.2. States which participated in the confidence-building measures and in VEREX

	CBMs							VEREX			
	1987	1988	1989	1990	1991	1992	1993	I	II	III	IV
Argentina					•	•	•	•	•	•	•
Australia	•		•			•	•	•	•	•	•
Austria			•		•	•	•	•	•	•	•
Belarus[a]	•	•	•	•	•	•	•				
Belgium		•				•		•	•		
Bolivia								•			
Brazil					•		•	•	•	•	•
Bulgaria		•	•	•	•	•	•	•	•	•	•
Canada	•	•	•	•	•	•	•				•
Chile			•	•				•	•	•	•
China			•	•	•	•	•	•	•	•	•
Cuba					•	•	•	•	•	•	•
Cyprus					•	•	•				
Czech Republic[b]	•	•	•	•		•		•	•	•	•
Denmark	•	•	•	•	•	•		•	•		
Ecuador			•			•		•			
Ethiopia								•			
Finland	•	•	•	•	•	•	•	•	•	•	•
France				•	•	•	•	•	•	•	•
Germany[c]	•	•	•	•	•	•	•	•	•	•	•
Greece			•	•				•	•	•	•
Hungary	•				•	•	•	•	•	•	•
Iceland					•		•				
India								•	•	•	•
Indonesia								•	•	•	•
Iran								•	•	•	•
Iraq						•		•	•	•	•
Ireland		•		•	•		•	•	•	•	•
Italy			•	•	•		•	•	•	•	•
Japan		•			•	•	•	•	•	•	•
Jordan						•					
Kenya								•	•		
Korea, North				•							
Korea, South						•	•	•	•		•
Kyrgyzstan						•					
Luxembourg										•	
Malta					•			•			
Mexico			•			•		•	•	•	•
Mongolia			•	•		•	•				
Netherlands	•	•	•	•	•	•	•	•	•	•	•
New Zealand	•	•	•	•		•	•	•	•	•	•
Nicaragua						•					
Nigeria								•	•	•	
Norway	•	•	•	•	•	•	•	•	•	•	•
Oman										•	•
Pakistan								•	•	•	•

	CBMs							VEREX			
	1987	1988	1989	1990	1991	1992	1993	I	II	III	IV
Panama					•			•			
Peru					•	•		•	•		
Philippines					•			•	•		
Poland	•	•			•			•	•	•	•
Portugal				•	•			•			
Qatar					•						
Romania					•		•	•	•	•	•
Russia[a]	•	•	•	•	•	•	•	•	•	•	
Senegal					•			•			
Slovakia[b]	•	•		•	•	•		•	•	•	
Slovenia						•					
South Africa						•			•	•	•
Spain	•	•	•	•	•	•	•	•	•	•	•
Sri Lanka								•	•	•	•
Sweden	•	•	•	•	•	•	•	•	•	•	•
Switzerland		•	•	•	•	•		•	•	•	•
Thailand				•		•		•	•	•	•
Togo	•										
Tunisia						•					
Turkey				•		•		•			
Ukraine[a]	•	•	•	•	•	•	•				
United Kingdom	•	•	•	•	•	•	•	•	•	•	•
USA		•	•	•	•	•	•	•	•	•	•
Venezuela								•	•		
Yugoslavia					•	•		•			
Zimbabwe								•			

[a] Included in the report of the USSR in 1987–91.
[b] Until 1992 included in the report of Czechoslovakia and in the report of the Czech and Slovak Federal Republic, respectively.
[c] Until 1990, the then two German states reported separately.

Biological Preparations 'did not have direct assignments from the Ministry of Defence [whereas] certain work that interested us was being conducted there'.[93]

Hence numerous questions remain to be answered. For example, it is unclear to what extent these declared facilities were part of the offensive Soviet/Russian BW programme or whether they were involved in defensive (i.e., permitted) activities only. There are not only questions about the information provided by Russia since the USA, for example, claims that other states are also not submitting full information on programmes and facilities

[93] Interview with General Valentin Yevstigneyev, quoted in *Chemical Weapons Convention Bulletin*, no. 19 (Mar. 1993), p. 11.

directly related to the BWC. It is essential to be able to verify the information provided and to evaluate whether comprehensive information has been given.

Although the amendment of the CBMs by *inter alia* a request to report on BW programmes and facilities represents a major step forward, there are still significant shortcomings in this respect. Form A, part 2 of the National Biological Defence Research and Development Program Declaration requests *inter alia* that a state party 'provide a declaration . . . for each facility, both governmental and non-governmental, which has a substantial proportion of its resources devoted to the national biological defence research and development program' without defining what 'a substantial proportion' is. In addition, the report fails to take into account the fact that activities directly related to the BWC and subject to interpretation could be conducted at a few laboratories in a large research centre and be funded by the military. Nevertheless, such funding would be relatively small in comparison to that for work unrelated to the BWC.

Further evaluation of the CBMs has been made elsewhere.[94] Following improvement and amendment, the CBMs now provide a significant amount of information (including much that is superfluous). Their confidence-building value is limited, however, because of the low overall participation in the information exchange and the incompleteness of numerous reports. It is strongly recommended therefore that the CBMs not only be continued but also further improved and made legally binding, especially until a BWC verification regime has entered into force.

VII. The *Ad Hoc* Meetings of Governmental Experts

One of the major loopholes in the BWC is the lack of a verification regime. Because of the *dual-threat* nature of BW and TW agents and of the *dual-use* nature of the associated know-how, equipment and technology, the approach used for CW weapons cannot simply be copied, and verification of compliance with the BWC will presumably never be complete.[95] Independent of this, BWC verification is additionally complicated by questions such as: 'Who pays the high cost of verification? Will poor, developing countries refuse to participate? Will they drop out of the treaty? Will additional nations not join? With the appearance of new nations and the newly gained independence of others, might they choose not to accede to the BWC because of the hassle and expense?'[96]

Adequate verification is inevitable, however, and the Third Review Conference therefore agreed to convene an *Ad Hoc* Group of Governmental Experts to Identify and Examine Potential Verification Measures from a Scientific and Technical Standpoint. The group was to identify measures which could deter-

[94] Geissler, E., 'Confidence-building information from the parties to the Biological Weapons Convention', in Strout (note 3).

[95] Moodie, M., 'Arms control programs and biological weapons', in Roberts (note 3), pp. 47–57.

[96] Huxsoll, D., 'The U.S. Biological Defense Research Program' in Roberts (note 3), pp. 58–67, particularly p. 65.

mine whether a state party to the BWC is engaged in prohibited activities either with regard to agents, weapons or means of delivery.

It was agreed at the Third Review Conference that the following main criteria should guide the *Ad Hoc* Group in its examination of potential verification measures:

Their strengths and weaknesses based on, but not limited to, the amount and quality of information they provide, and fail to provide;
Their ability to differentiate between prohibited and permitted activities;
Their ability to resolve ambiguities about compliance;
Their technology, material, manpower and equipment requirements;
Their financial, legal, safety and organizational implications; [and]
Their impact on scientific research, scientific co-operation, industrial development and other permitted activities; and their implications for the confidentiality of commercial proprietary information.[97]

The mandate of the Group was restricted, however, to evaluation of the feasibility of a BW verification regime. The Group was asked to complete its work by the end of 1993 and to provide all states parties with a consensus report on its work, taking into account the views expressed during the course of its sessions.

In 1992 and 1993 a total of four sessions were held.[98] At most 53 states parties participated in the sessions (see table 18.2) together with an observer representing the WHO. In addition, an observer representing the United Nations Industrial Development Organization (UNIDO) took part in VEREX I.[99]

Identification and examination of verification measures: VEREX

At VEREX I and II[100] the *Ad Hoc* Group identified, compiled and described a set of potential verification measures which could determine whether a state party is engaged in prohibited activities. The group followed a 'measure-oriented' approach and identified and compiled measures not according to prohibited activities but rather in terms of the specific nature of the measures themselves.

[97] Final Document of the Third Review Conference of the Parties to the Convention on the Prohibition of the Development, Production and Stockpiling of Bacteriological (Biological) and Toxin Weapons and on their Destruction, Part II, *Final Declaration*, BWC/CONF.III/23, 27 Sep. 1991, p. 17.

[98] VEREX I, identification of measures, 30 Mar.–10 Apr. 1992; VEREX II, examination of measures, 23 Nov.–4 Dec. 1992; VEREX III, evaluation of measures, 24 May–4 June 1993; and VEREX IV, preparation of a consensus report, 13–24 Sep. 1993.

[99] Tóth, T., Geissler, E. and Stock, T., 'Verification of the BWC', in Geissler and Woodall (note 2), pp. 67–76.

[100] *Ad Hoc* Group of Governmental Experts to Identify and Examine Potential Verification Measures from a Scientific and Technical Standpoint, 'Summary of the work of the *Ad Hoc* Group for the period 30 March to 10 April 1992', BWC/CONF.III/VEREX/2, 13 Apr. 1992; *Ad Hoc* Group of Governmental Experts to Identify and Examine Potential Verification Measures from a Scientific and Technical Standpoint, 'Summary of the work of the *Ad Hoc* Group for the period 23 November to 4 December 1992', BWC/CONF.III/VEREX/4, 8 Dec. 1992.

Table 18.3. Potential BWC verification measures

Off-site measures
Information monitoring
Surveillance of publications
Surveillance of legislation
Data on transfers and transfer requests and on production
Multilateral information sharing
Exchange visits

Data exchange
Declarations (including notifications, data on transfers and transfer requests and on production)

Remote sensing
Surveillance by satellite
Surveillance by aircraft
Ground-based surveillance

Inspections
Sampling and identification
Observation
Auditing

On-site measures
Exchange visits
International arrangements

Inspections
Interviewing
Visual inspections (including observation and surveillance by aircraft)
Identification of key equipment
Auditing
Sampling and identification
Medical examination

Continuous monitoring
By instruments (including ground-based surveillance)
By personnel

Source: *Ad Hoc* Group of Governmental Experts to Identify and Examine Potential Verification Measures from a Scientific and Technical Standpoint, *Report*, BWC/CONF.III/VEREX/9, Geneva, 1993, pp. 132–33.

A total of 21 measures were identified and divided into two major categories: off-site and on-site measures (see table 18.3).[101]

Within the two major groups the measures were clustered into subcategories such as information monitoring, data exchange, remote sensing and inspections for the off-site category; and exchange visits, inspections, and continuous monitoring for the on-site category (see tables 18.3 and 18.4). It was at the level of these subcategories that the possibly differing requirements of various types of prohibition were taken into account. The identified measures were further categorized according to their relevance to the phases of development, acquisition or production, and stockpiling of BW and TW.

[101] BWC/CONF.III/VEREX/2 (note 100), p. 18.

Table 18.4. Illustrative examples of combinations of potential BWC verification measures

---

Combination A
Declarations + multilateral information sharing + satellite surveillance + visual inspection

Combination B
Information monitoring (surveillance of publications + surveillance of legislation + data on transfers, transfer requests and production + multilateral information sharing + exchange visits)

Combination C
One-site inspection (interviewing + visual inspections, identification of key equipment + auditing + sampling and identification)

Combination D
Declarations + multilateral information sharing + on-site visual inspection

Combination E
Declarations + information monitoring

Source: *Ad Hoc* Group of Governmental Experts to Identify and Examine Potential Verification Measures from a Scientific and Technical Standpoint, *Report*, BWC/CONF.III/VEREX/9, Geneva, 1993, pp. 5, 273.

The identified measures vary in their degree of intrusiveness.[102] In addition, the value of some measures must be considered not only from a scientific but also from a political point of view since many prohibited activities are similar to those which are permitted. It is thus highly probable that they will be the subject of scientific and political debate and that concerns will be expressed by industry about commercial proprietary information. Although the US Biotechnology Industry Organization and the US Manufacturers Association expressed 'grave concern' in a joint report regarding the vulnerability of confidential proprietary information,[103] a BWC verification regime may interfere far less with industry interests than in the field of CW since industrial companies do not appear particularly interested in dealing with DTAs.[104]

Several identified measures are closely related to CBMs which were agreed at the Second and Third Review Conferences and depend, for example, on the declaration of facilities. However, such measures may provide incomplete information even if declarations become mandatory. Ground-based surveillance, sampling and identification, observation, exchange visits, inspections, and the like would give a false sense of security if confined only to declared facilities and if, for example, the British and German governments were to continue *not* 'to identify links between the Ministry . . . and the contractors engaged on extramural research'.[105] While the reason for such decisions is

---

[102] For a discussion of these measures, see Tóth, Geissler and Stock (note 99).

[103] Fox, J. I., 'Impacting biological weapons', *Biotechnology*, vol. 11, no. 9 (Sep. 1993), p. 979.

[104] Geissler, E., 'Arms control, health care and technology transfer under the Vaccines for Peace programme', in Geissler and Woodall (note 2), pp. 10–39, particularly p. 19.

[105] Pearson, G., 'Answer to a parliamentary question', *Hansard*, written answers, 20 July, quoted in *Chemical Weapons Convention Bulletin*, no. 21 (Sep. 1993), p. 23.

understandable,[106] excluding non-governmental facilities involved in activities directly related to the BWC from verification measures would significantly undermine any verification attempts. A prerequisite for efficient verification of compliance with the BWC is that *all* facilities carrying out activities directly related to the BWC be declared and made subject to verification measures.

Further evaluation of verification measures

At VEREX III[107] the advantages and disadvantages of possible application of the 21 verification measures identified above was re-evaluated in terms of the kind of quantitative and qualitative information which a particular measure would provide, how it would answer questions about compliance and how it would be possible to differentiate between legitimate and illegitimate activities, taking into account the state of the art in the various areas of science and technology.

The evaluation of the potential verification measures revealed that no single measure would be effective to distinguish conclusively between activities permitted or prohibited by the BWC. The *Ad Hoc* Group therefore proceeded to evaluate these measures in combination. They realized that a combination of several measures could have a synergistic effect compared to their value singly (see table 18.4).

The group also discussed experiences gained from trial inspections carried out by the Netherlands, Canada and the UK at a large vaccine facility and at a pharmaceutical pilot plant.[108] Concern has been expressed occasionally that certain verification measures may lead to the loss of commercial proprietary information. These inspections showed *inter alia* that commercial confidentiality did not obstruct the effective conduct of inspections.[109]

In addition, the experts considered a study on Q-fever, a disease caused by a DTA. This study, carried out in Switzerland, indicated that the inspection scheme used can identify a violation of the BWC with a high degree of reliability.

During VEREX III a statement was made by the non-aligned and other developing countries participating in the meeting requesting the identification

---

[106] According to Defence Procurement Minister Jonathan Aitken 'Universities would prefer us not to disclose whether they are receiving Ministry of Defence funds for research and development projects in order to protect their academic researchers assigned to the projects from potentially violent extremists', 'Answer to a parliamentary question', *Hansard,* written answers, 20 July, quoted in *Chemical Weapons Convention Bulletin,* no. 21 (Sep. 1993), p. 23.

[107] *Ad Hoc* Group of Governmental Experts to Identify and Examine Potential Verification Measures from a Scientific and Technical Standpoint, 'Summary of the work of the *Ad Hoc* Group for the period 24 May to 4 June 1993', BWC/CONF.III/VEREX/6, 8 June 1993.

[108] A second 'practice compliance inspection' at a large pharmaceutical manufacturing site has been carried out in the UK by a team from Canada, the Netherlands and the UK with a US observer. *Disarmament Bulletin* (winter 1993), quoted in *Chemical Weapons Convention Bulletin,* no. 23 (Mar. 1994), p. 15.

[109] In addition to these trial inspections, the American Society of Microbiology was involved in several evaluations of the impact and limitations of verification measures. See Atlas, R. M. and Goldberg, M., 'Biological warfare: examining verification strategies', *ASM News,* vol. 59, no. 8 (1993), pp. 393–96. US delegation contributions to VEREX are based in part on the results of these studies.

of potential verification measures 'which . . . should be the least intrusive as possible, while still reliable and capable of deterring any States Parties from engaging in or being involved with activities which run counter to the object and purpose of the Convention'.[110] As these countries had referred to 'their legitimate interests in the field of biotechnological development for peaceful purposes' the *Ad Hoc* Group examined potential verification measures not only in terms of their impact on scientific research, industrial development and other activities permitted by the Convention but also with regard to the scientific co-operation which is called for in the BWC. In that context, the participants recalled Article X of the BWC which calls for peaceful co-operation in the field of microbiology (and biotechnology) and stressed that the provisions of the BWC should not be used to impose restrictions and/or limitations on the exchange of equipment, materials, and scientific and technological information for peaceful purposes.

During its final session (VEREX IV) the *Ad Hoc* Group elaborated a final consensus report.[111] Although quite different views were expressed with respect to recommendations to use intrusive measures, which were opposed by China, India and the USA while Australia, Canada, France, Germany, the Netherlands and the UK might well have supported stronger language,[112] consensus was reached. The experts:

concluded that potential verification measures as identified and evaluated could be useful to varying degrees in enhancing confidence, through increased transparency, that States Parties were fulfilling their obligations under the BWC. While it was agreed that reliance could not be placed on any single measure to differentiate conclusively between prohibited and permitted activity and to resolve ambiguities about compliance, it was also agreed that the measures could provide information of varying utility in strengthening the BWC.

The *Ad Hoc* Group came to the conclusion that 'some measures in combination could provide enhanced capabilities by increasing, for example, the focus and improving the quality of information, thereby improving the possibility of differentiating between prohibited and permitted activities and of resolving ambiguities about compliance'.[113]

Although it was recognized that a number of further scientific and technical questions remain to be addressed, such as identity of agents, types and quantities, the final conclusion was reached that from the scientific and technical standpoint, 'some of the potential verification measures [identified] would contribute to strengthening the effectiveness and improve the implementation of the Convention, also recognizing that appropriate and effective verification could reinforce the Convention'.

---

[110] See BWC/CONF.III/VEREX/6 (note 107), pp. 173–74.

[111] *Ad Hoc* Group of Governmental Experts to Identify and Examine Potential Verification Measures from a Scientific and Technical Standpoint, *Report*, BWC/CONF.III/VEREX/9, Geneva, 1993.

[112] *Chemical Weapons Convention Bulletin*, no. 22 (Dec. 1993), p. 17.

[113] See *Report* (note 111), p. 9.

The special conference

The consensus report was transmitted by the chairman of the *Ad Hoc* Group to the states parties to the BWC. The UN General Assembly First Committee adopted without vote a resolution commending the work of VEREX and asking the Secretary-General 'to render the necessary assistance . . . should the Depositary Powers be requested by a majority of States to convene a conference' to consider developing a BWC verification regime.[114] After considering the report, a majority of states parties have asked the depositary governments (Russia, the UK and the USA) to convene a conference to examine the report and decide on further action with regard to verification of the BWC. The special conference will be held on 19 September–7 October 1994 in Geneva. It is expected that the conference will consider whether adding BWC compliance measures would require an additional protocol or an amendment to the BWC and how intrusive such measures could be.[115] It is also expected that the conferees will seek to complete work on a proposal for a verification regime well in advance of the 1996 Fourth Review Conference.[116]

VIII. Implementation of Article X

Article X of the BWC requests states parties to facilitate and to participate 'in the fullest possible exchange of equipment, materials and . . . information for the use of bacteriological (biological) agents and toxins for peaceful purposes'. In addition, Article X requests that the 'convention shall be implemented in a manner designed to avoid hampering the economic or technological development of the states parties . . . or international cooperation in the field of peaceful bacteriological (biological) activities'. The Third Review Conference had re-emphasized 'the increasing importance of Article X, especially in the light of recent scientific and technological developments in the field of biotechnology, bacteriological (biological) agents and toxins with peaceful applications'.[117] Likewise the VEREX participants stressed that verification measures should not interfere with the implementation of Article X (see above).

The Third Review Conference therefore called 'upon the Secretary-General of the United Nations to propose for inclusion on the agenda of a relevant United Nations body, not later than 1993, a discussion and examination of the means of improving institutional mechanisms in order to facilitate the fullest possible exchange of equipment, materials and scientific and technological information regarding the use of bacteriological (biological) agents and toxins for peaceful purposes'.[118] While additional countries, including Russia,[119] have

[114] *Disarmament Times*, vol. 26, no. 6 (23 Nov. 1993), p. 3.
[115] Lacey, E. J., interview, *Arms Control Reporter*, sheets 701.B.120–21, Jan. 1994.
[116] See Lacey (note 115).
[117] See BWC/CONF.III/23 (note 97), p. 21.
[118] See BWC/CONF.III/23 (note 97), p. 22.
[119] Presidential Directive, 'On the introduction of controls on the export from the Russian Federation of pathogens, their genetic variations, and fragments of genetic material, which could be used in the

established export controls on DTAs and dual-use biotechnological equipment[120] in implementing Article III of the BWC—which calls for the prevention of the transfer of BW agents and technology—formal measures to contribute to implementation of Article X have not been taken by the Secretary-General or by states parties. Two proposals have been discussed and further elaborated by non-governmental organizations (NGOs), the Vaccines for Peace (VFP) programme and the Biesenthal Vaccine Initiative (BVI), and the Global Program for Monitoring Emerging Diseases (ProMED).

The Vaccines for Peace programme and the Biesenthal Vaccine Initiative

In order to promote peaceful international co-operation in the biosciences, especially between industrialized and developing countries, and to counter reservations about military R&D on and production of vaccines, the Vaccines for Peace programme was been proposed as an international programme for the development and use of vaccines against DTAs to be administered by the WHO.[121] The VFP proposal, which was welcomed by the Third Review Conference,[122] was evaluated by experts in biotechnology, defence, diplomacy, international development, medicine, molecular biology and vaccinology from Australia, France, Germany, Hungary, India, Peru, Russia, Sweden, the UK and the USA and by representatives or observers from the WHO, UNIDO and the UN Office for Disarmament Affairs (now the UN Centre for Disarmament Affairs) in Biesenthal, Germany, on 9–14 September 1992.[123]

In the Biesenthal Consensus[124] the participants at the workshop agreed that a modified VFP programme should be established. A Steering Committee was formed under the chairmanship of Professor Jack Melling to establish a schedule for its implementation; it decided to designate the modified programme the Biesenthal Vaccine Initiative.[125]

Key objectives of the BVI include:

* strengthening the BWC through implementation of Article X and increased mutual transparency in activities related to the Convention,

* prevention of diseases, especially in developing countries,

* enhancement of peaceful international co-operation in molecular medicine and biotechnology and prevention of misuse,

---

creation of bacteriological (biological) and toxic weapons', Russian Federation President's directive no. 711-rp, 17 Nov. 1992, *Rossiyskiye Vesti* (Moscow), 5 Dec. 1992, p. 3 (in Russian).

[120] See Geissler (note 104), pp. 28–30.

[121] Geissler, E., 'Biological and toxin weapons: the renewed threat, with comments by Stefan Noreen of the Swedish mission to the UN', NGO Committee on Disarmament Forum at the UN (2 Feb. 1989). Transcript. (New York: NGO Committee on Disarmament, 1989); 'The international control of biological weapons' (interview), *geneWATCH*, vol. 6, no. 1 (1989), pp. 1–4; Geissler (note 9).

[122] See BWC/CONF.III/23 (note 97), p. 23.

[123] Geissler and Woodall (note 2).

[124] 'Biesenthal Consensus' in Geissler, E., 'Strengthening the Biological Weapons Convention by the Biesenthal Vaccine Initiative', ed. G. T. Tzotzos, *Biotechnology R&D Trends: Science Policy for Development,* Annals of the New York Academy of Sciences, vol. 700 (1993), pp. 43–52, particularly pp. 50–51.

[125] BVI Steering Committee, 'Biesenthal Vaccine Initiative: Mission Statement' (note 124), pp. 51–52.

* conversion, where appropriate, of biological warfare (BW) facilities to peaceful purposes under civilian control,
* increasing world capacity to produce vaccines, [and]
* expanding participation in the BWC and its confidence-building measures.[126]

In 1993, the BVI Steering Committee started activities designed to support conversion of former Soviet BW facilities and proposed to the European Commission, Directorate General (DG) XII, to make use of the VFP programme for conversion of former Soviet BW facilities funded by the International Science and Technology Centre.

The global Programme for Monitoring Emerging Diseases

Referring to earlier proposals to establish a global programme of epidemiological surveillance for the early detection of emerging diseases[127] it was recommended at the XIIth Kühlungsborn Colloquium in Kühlungsborn, Germany, in 1990 to make use of such a programme for strengthening the Convention.[128] This proposal was favourably acknowledged by the Third Review Conference.[129] In addition, the establishment of an international Biological Hazards Early Warning Program was proposed to investigate 'any unusual outbreaks of diseases to determine whether they are of natural origin, or are instead the products of laboratory development and attributable to accident or design'.[130]

The proposal to set up a global surveillance system was further elaborated[131] and discussed at the Biesenthal Workshop on the VFP programme.[132] The participants at that conference recommended 'that a convergent initiative be mounted to implement the Global Epidemiological Surveillance System. In this connection the steering committee [of the Biesenthal Vaccine Initiative, see above] should be encouraged to interface with groups developing this System'.[133]

A Steering Committee was set up, chaired by Professor Stephen S. Morse of Rockefeller University. Under the auspices of the Federation of American Sci-

---

[126] See note 124.

[127] See Miller, J. A., 'Diseases for our future: global ecology and emerging viruses', *BioScience*, vol. 39 (1990), pp. 509–17; Morse, S. S. and Schluederberg, A., 'Emerging viruses: the evolution of viruses and viral diseases', *Journal of Infectious Diseases*, vol. 162 (1990), pp. 1–7.

[128] Wheelis, M. L., 'The role of epidemiology in strengthening the Biological Weapons Convention', in Geissler and Haynes (note 90), pp. 277–83.

[129] See BWC/CONF.III/23 (note 97), p. 22.

[130] Zilinskas, R. A., 'Confronting biological threats to international security: a biological hazards early warning program', in Zilinskas (note 3), pp. 146–76, particularly p. 146.

[131] Morse, S., 'Epidemiologic surveillance for investigating chemical or biological warfare and for improving human health', *Politics and the Life Sciences*, vol. 11, no. 1 (Feb. 1992), pp. 28–29; Wheelis, M., 'Strengthening biological weapons control through global epidemiological surveillance' [with commentaries and response], *Politics and the Life Sciences*, vol. 11, no. 2 (Aug. 1992), pp. 179–97.

[132] Morse, S. S., 'Vaccines for public health: can Vaccines for Peace help in the war against disease?', in Geissler and Woodall (note 2), pp. 168–75; Wheelis, M., 'The Global Epidemiological Surveillance System and Vaccines for Peace: complementary initiatives in public health and weapon control', Geissler and Woodall (note 2), pp. 176–81.

[133] See note 124, p. 51.

entists (FAS) a meeting of the Steering Committee was held in New York on 24 February 1993. At the meeting, a Mission Statement was finalized.[134] The Steering Committee met again on 4 June 1993,[135] again under the auspices of the FAS. At the June meeting the title of the proposed global surveillance system was changed from the Global Epidemiological Surveillance System to the Program for Monitoring Emerging Diseases (ProMED). The change was made to indicate that ProMED will not deal with routine surveillance of common infectious diseases but will evaluate unusual outbreaks, such as the 1993 hantavirus outbreak in south-western USA (see above).[136]

The ProMED project, now chaired by Professor Morse and Dr Barbara Rosenberg, got under way with an international conference in Geneva on 11–12 September 1993, co-sponsored by the FAS and the WHO. The conference was attended by 60 experts who formed working groups to draft plans for a global programme. A report is planned to be released which will include *inter alia* 'the designation of appropriate sentinel facilities, plans for a communications network, recommendations for a response mechanism to provide assistance in controlling disease outbreaks, and a proposal for the organizational management, oversight and financial support of the global program'.[137]

IX. Conclusions

The mere existence of the 1972 BWC is not sufficient to abolish the BW and TW threat, although the results of the three Review Conferences held so far have contributed to political strengthening of the Convention. The introduction of CBMs by the Second Review Conference and their improvement and amendment by the Third Review Conference were major steps forward in strengthening the BWC, but they are not sufficient. This view is substantiated by the fact that there is reason to believe that the BW and TW threat has increased in the 1970s and 1980s. While it is to be welcomed that the number of states parties to the BWC and the number of states participating in the CBMs increased in 1993, there are indications that the number of states suspected of being possessors or developers of BW and TW agents has not decreased.

The BW and TW threat has grown both because of geopolitical and scientific developments. On the other hand, developments in molecular biotechnology have also contributed to mankind's ability to deal with pathogens, including DTAs, as demonstrated in 1993 by the rapid identification of a new type of virus responsible for the outbreak of a deadly disease in the USA. That outbreak was simultaneously a reminder that civilians and troops are not only

---

[134] 'Mission Statement of the Federation of American Scientists (FAS) Project on the Global Control of Emerging Infectious Diseases', reprinted in Geissler and Woodall (note 2), annexe E, pp. 259–60.

[135] Geissler, E., Calderón, F. and Woodall, J. P., 'From BVI to VFP: towards a system of global biological security', in Geissler and Woodall (note 2), pp. 219–39, particularly p. 234.

[136] See Geissler, Calderón and Woodall (note 135), pp. 223–36.

[137] Morse, S. S. and Rosenberg, B. H., 'FAS responds to growing infectious disease problem with proposed global surveillance and response program', and Rosenberg, B., 'The contemporary problem of emerging diseases' in *F.A.S. Public Interest Report*, vol. 46, no. 6 (Nov./Dec. 1993), pp. 1–5.

threatened by the hostile use of biological agents and toxins in war but also as a consequence of natural processes or, as also revealed in 1993, by possible terrorist activities.

The lack of government activity related to implementation of Article X of the BWC, which calls for peaceful co-operation in microbiology (and biotechnology), has been able to be compensated for by the further elaboration of international programmes intended to evaluate unusual outbreaks of disease, to quickly identify their causes and to provide vaccines to protect against DTAs.

A significant step towards further strengthening of the BWC was the successful conclusion of VEREX and the adoption of a consensus report by the *Ad Hoc* Group of Governmental Experts to Identify and Examine Potential Verification Measures from a Scientific and Technical Standpoint. The report identifies 21 measures which, preferably in certain combinations, 'could be useful to varying degrees in enhancing confidence . . . that States Parties were fulfilling their obligations under the BWC'.

No less important is the fact that within weeks of release of the report a majority of the states parties to the BWC requested the convening of a special conference to examine it and to decide on further action with regard to verification of compliance with the BWC. This conference, scheduled for September 1994, will hopefully pave the way for adoption of a verification regime, thus contributing significantly to prevention of biological and toxin warfare.

19. UNSCOM: activities in 1993

TIM TREVAN

I. Introduction

Under the terms of the 1991 Persian Gulf War cease-fire resolution,[1] the United Nations Special Commission on Iraq (UNSCOM) is mandated to identify and eliminate Iraq's weapons of mass destruction and long-range ballistic missile capability and to undertake 'ongoing' monitoring and verification of Iraq's obligation not to reacquire such capabilities. For nuclear weapons, UNSCOM assists and co-operates with the International Atomic Energy Agency (IAEA) in the implementation of this task. Previous chapters in *SIPRI Yearbooks* have reported on UNSCOM activities in 1991 and 1992;[2] this chapter charts developments from December 1992 to early 1994.[3]

The chapter also assesses the degree of Iraq's compliance with its obligations under section C of Security Council Resolution 687[4] and the obstacles, mainly political, raised by Iraq. It records the political developments in 1993 from the confrontational stance taken by Iraq in the first half of 1993 to the more co-operative attitude adopted after a crisis in relations in July. The effect of these political developments on UNSCOM's ability to exercise its immunities, privileges and facilities, and hence to conduct its mandate effectively, is also discussed, as are the achievements of 1993 and the issues remaining to be addressed before UNSCOM can report to the Security Council that it has fulfilled its mandate.

II. Status of implementation as of December 1992

UNSCOM reported to the UN Security Council on 17 December 1992 that:

despite progress in many areas, no major breakthrough has been achieved which could make it possible to change the conclusion of the previous report to the Security Council. The most important developments have taken place in the areas of destruction of proscribed items and information on missile programmes and use. Neverthe-

---

[1] United Nations Security Council document S/RES/687 (1991), 3 Apr. 1991; for the text of the resolution, see SIPRI, *SIPRI Yearbook 1992: World Armaments and Disarmament* (Oxford University Press: Oxford, 1992), appendix 13A, pp. 525–30.

[2] Ekéus, R., 'The United Nations Special Commission on Iraq', *SIPRI Yearbook 1992* (note 1), pp. 509–30; Ekéus, R., 'The United Nations Special Commission on Iraq: activities in 1992', SIPRI, *SIPRI Yearbook 1993: World Armaments and Disarmament* (Oxford University Press: Oxford, 1993), pp. 691–703.

[3] In doing so, it draws heavily on the reports of the Executive Chairman to the Security Council, in particular the biennial reports for 1993 submitted in accordance with the requirements of UN Security Council Resolution 699 (1991), 17 June 1991, contained in UN Security Council documents S/25977, 21 June 1993 and S/26910, 21 Dec. 1993.

[4] See note 1.

less, much remains to be done. The main areas which require action before the Commission will be in a position to report to the Security Council that Iraq is in substantial compliance with its obligations are as follows:

– acceptance and implementation by Iraq of all the Commission's privileges and immunities, including ensuring the safety and security of UNSCOM personnel and property, the operation of and landing rights for UNSCOM aircraft and non-obstruction of the Commission's logistics and aerial surveillance flights;

– unconditional acknowledgement by Iraq of its obligations under Council resolutions 707 and 715 (1991);

– provision by Iraq of the documentation necessary to substantiate the data contained in its declarations and to provide the Commission with a full picture of its foreign procurement networks and suppliers;

– supplementation and revision of Iraq's declarations to the point where, in the view of the Commission, they constitute the full, final and complete disclosures required under resolution 707 (1991) and the initial declarations required under the plans for ongoing monitoring and verification adopted by resolution 715 (1991);

– the initiation and smooth functioning of the plans for ongoing monitoring and verification to ensure that Iraq does not reacquire the weapons proscribed to it.[5]

Early 1993 found Iraq still refusing to acknowledge its obligations under Security Council Resolutions 707 and 715[6] and the plans for ongoing monitoring and verification. Iraq maintained its earlier position on the plans approved under Resolution 715 for ongoing monitoring and verification, namely that both Resolution 715 and the plans were arbitrary, contrary to international law and such as to undermine the UN Charter.[7]

Iraq's disclosure of its proscribed weapon programmes fell short of the full, final and complete disclosure required by Resolution 707, and its initial declarations about its current dual-purpose capabilities (required by the plans for ongoing monitoring and verification)[8] still contained major shortcomings which needed to be rectified if they were to form the basis for a definitive material balance of Iraq's past weapons of mass destruction programmes and for effective monitoring and verification of compliance. The information provided was tailored to what Iraqi authorities believed UNSCOM already knew,

---

[5] 'Third status report on the activities of the Special Commission submitted by the Executive Chairman in accordance with UN Security Council Resolution 699 (1991)', UN Security Council document S/24984, 17 Dec. 1992.

[6] UN Security Council documents S/RES/707 (1991), 15 Aug. 1991 and S/RES/715 (1991), 11 Oct. 1991.

[7] First stated in the letter of 19 Nov. 1991 from then Iraqi Minister for Foreign Affairs, Ahmed Hussein, to the President of the Security Council. By letter, dated 28 Oct. 1992 from the Iraqi Foreign Minister to the Secretary-General. Iraq reiterated its opposition to Resolutions 707 and 715, by stating that: 'It is . . . essential for the Council to conduct a radical review, on the basis of justice and fairness, of the terms and provisions of these two resolutions'. In the statements to the Security Council on 23 Nov. (UN Security Council document S/PV.3139, Resumption 1) and 24 Nov. 1992 (UN Security Council document S/PV.3139, Resumption 2), Deputy Prime Minister of Iraq Tariq Aziz said: 'There is a need for all the measures and the provisions of the no longer necessary Security Council's resolutions to be drastically reviewed'.

[8] The UNSCOM plan is contained in UN Security Council document S/22871/Rev.1, 2 Oct. 1991, and the IAEA plan is contained in UN Security Council documents S/22872/Rev.1, 20 Sep. 1991 and S/22872/Rev.1/Corr.1, 10 Oct. 1991. They were adopted under Security Council Resolution 715 on 11 Oct. 1991 and were intended to enter into force immediately upon adoption by the Security Council.

rather than constituting a frank and open disclosure. One set of declarations, concerning the legal and administrative actions taken by Iraq to give effect to its obligations arising from Resolutions 687 and 707 and the plans for ongoing monitoring and verification, had never been submitted. Furthermore, Iraq had refused to divulge information indicating the names of foreign companies from which it purchased equipment and materials. Accurate information on suppliers was essential for UNSCOM to establish a material balance for proscribed items and, with the IAEA and the Sanctions Committee, to devise a workable and realistic mechanism for export and import controls as required by paragraph 7 of Resolution 715.

Iraq also continued to fail to respect certain of UNSCOM's inspection rights either totally, as with the case of overflights of Baghdad, partially or intermittently. The concern was that in such circumstances UNSCOM could not be sure that it had accounted for all of Iraq's banned capabilities and could not ensure that Iraq would not reacquire such capabilities, especially after a possible lifting of the oil embargo or the sanctions. Consequently, UNSCOM's efforts in 1993 were dedicated largely to forcing Iraq to acknowledge the plans for ongoing monitoring and verification and to present better accounts of its past programmes and suppliers, supported by credible documentary evidence.

III. Political developments in 1993

Attempts in the first half of 1993 to elicit fuller information on chemical weapon (CW) and biological weapon (BW) issues met with unco-operative responses. Iraq denied ever using CW. It refused to turn over the missile-firing records that were essential if UNSCOM were to verify Iraqi claims to have accounted for all the Soviet-supplied Scud missiles. In addition, Iraq still refused to hand over data on its supplier network.

On 31 January 1993, the Iraqi Government officially informed the Executive Chairman of UNSCOM in writing[9] that Iraq considered the new arrangement of interim monitoring (IMT1a/UNSCOM 48) at the Ibn Al Haytham Missile Research and Design Centre to be conducted under Resolution 687. UNSCOM understood this to mean that Iraq would prevent this inspection team, or any other team, from operating under the terms of the plan approved under Resolution 715. Iraq made similar statements in respect of subsequent interim monitoring activities[10] (IMT1b/UNSCOM 54, IMT1c/UNSCOM 57)

[9] Correspondence between the Government of Iraq and the UN Special Commission.

[10] On 1 Apr. 1993, when General Amer Mohammad Rashid al Ubeidi, Director of the Iraqi Military Industrialization Corporation, met the second interim monitoring team, reading from prepared notes and stressing that this was the official Iraqi position on the issue of monitoring, he is reported by the UN Chief Inspector to have said: 'Iraq accepted the first monitoring team to the Ibn Al Haytham Centre in accordance with resolution 687. However, it appears from the modalities of the monitoring team that the Special Commission is trying to overlap in a discreet fashion Iraqi obligations under resolution 687 and resolution 715. This is very clever. Iraq knows that, using Iraqi co-operation under resolution 687, the Special Commission wants to assert Iraqi obligations under resolution 715. Iraq is fully aware of this effort. If the objective of the Special Commission is to make sure that no prohibited activities are going on, prohibited items are destroyed and Iraq has no capability to reactivate proscribed programmes, Iraq

and maintained this position despite assurances by UNSCOM that if Iraq co-operated, its legitimate concerns would be met and UNSCOM's activities would be carried out in a manner which was not unduly intrusive.[11]

On 14 February 1993, Iraq provided a second set of declarations entitled 'Updated Monitoring Information, Report No. 2'. These added little to the first set of such declarations provided in June 1992.

In the period April–June 1993 a problem arose as a result of Iraq's position on this key issue. It at first concerned the removal of certain precursor chemicals and production equipment from the Al Fallujah sites to Al Muthanna for destruction there. This rapidly became intertwined with two other issues: the installation of remote-controlled monitoring cameras at two rocket-engine test stands, and the issue of 'dialogue' between Iraq, on the one hand, and UNSCOM and the IAEA or the Security Council, on the other.

The fundamental underlying issue for Iraq was its desire to see an end to the first phase of implementation of its obligations under section C of Resolution 687—the identification and elimination of proscribed weapons and weapon programmes—and for this to be followed by implementation by the Security Council of paragraph 22 of the resolution (i.e., the lifting of the oil embargo) before proceeding to ongoing monitoring and verification activities). Iraq objected to the destruction of the chemicals and equipment on the grounds that they could be redeployed (despite their obvious and direct connection with the CW programme) and to the installation of the cameras on the grounds that this would constitute ongoing monitoring and verification under Resolution 715, a resolution which Iraq had not yet accepted and whose terms, according to Iraq,[12] were still the subject of discussion between Iraq and the Security Council. Instead, Iraq proposed that action on each of these items await the conclusion of a dialogue on all outstanding issues between it and UNSCOM and the IAEA.[13] In fact, Iraq sought a dialogue in order to negotiate away its difficulties with ongoing monitoring and verification and to obtain early lifting of the oil embargo, whereas the resolutions and the plans made no provision for any negotiation of Iraq's obligations or UNSCOM's rights.

These developments led to the Security Council issuing a statement on 18 June 1993,[14] demanding that Iraq accede to the removal and destruction of the chemicals and equipment in question and cease its obstruction of the installation of the cameras. Iraq acceded to the removal and destruction of the

has no objections as this is part of resolution 687. However, if the objective is to start a *de facto* implementation of resolution 715 without Special Commission testament to the Security Council that Iraq is in full compliance with resolution 687 and without implementing paragraph 22 of that resolution, Iraq will not welcome this mission. The monitoring missions would not be welcome. But, even in this case, Iraq will still co-operate with the Special Commission to see the true objectives of these missions and to explore the intentions of the Special Commission. Iraq told the Special Commission that resolution 715 could only be discussed in connection with the implementation of paragraph 22 of resolution 687. You should never think or believe that it could be done otherwise.' UNSCOM internal reporting.

[11] First offered by the Special Commission in draft form to the Iraqi side during discussions held in New York in Mar. 1992.

[12] Official correspondence from the Iraqi Ministry for Foreign Affairs, dated 8 June 1993.

[13] Various letters from senior Iraqi Government officials to the UN Special Commission during the period 29 Apr. to 21 June 1993.

[14] Circulated as UN Security Council document S/25970, 18 June 1993.

chemicals and equipment but continued to refuse to allow installation of the cameras. In order to resolve this impasse, the Executive Chairman visited Baghdad in July 1993. The result of this visit was a report[15] which recorded UNSCOM and Iraqi position papers, UNSCOM's comments on Iraq's position paper and conclusions reflecting their common understanding.

In its paper, Iraq stated for the first time its readiness to comply with the provisions of the plans for ongoing monitoring and verification as contained in Resolution 715. Both sides agreed to hold high-level technical talks in New York. One of the prime subjects would be the nature and implementation of ongoing monitoring and verification. All outstanding issues, including the activation of the cameras, were to be addressed. In the meantime, the cameras were to be installed, tested and maintained. UNSCOM would send inspectors to the two test sites as and when it wished, and Iraq would inform UNSCOM of each rocket test sufficiently in advance for UNSCOM to send personnel to observe the test.

The first round of high-level technical talks took place in New York from 31 August to 10 September 1993 and resulted in a joint report.[16] This was the first time such a joint report had been submitted to the Security Council, indicating a greater degree of common ground than previously. During these talks, UNSCOM explained to Iraq precisely what ongoing monitoring and verification would entail and Iraq appeared to accept most of the methods planned to be used. Its prime concerns related to how the intrusive rights and privileges of UNSCOM, being extended indefinitely into the future, would be implemented so as not to endanger the safety of the Iraqi leadership, infringe on Iraq's sovereignty or hinder its economic or technical development. For UNSCOM and the IAEA, key questions were identified, the answers to which were necessary if they were ever to be in a position to conclude the identification phase of their operations. Most of these key questions related to foreign suppliers and technical advice although, in the CW area, some questions related to past production levels.

It was agreed at the end of the high-level technical talks to conduct a further round of high-level talks in Baghdad shortly thereafter in order to resolve all outstanding issues. Iraq promised, in this second round, to provide answers to all the questions identified but not answered during the New York talks. However, UNSCOM stipulated that there would be no second round unless the monitoring cameras were activated. Before this happened, an incident occurred when Iraq delayed the installation of gamma-detection sensors on board one of UNSCOM's helicopters. This dispute was quickly resolved upon the return of General Amer Mohammad Rashid al Ubeidi[17] to Baghdad from the New York talks, but this delay resulted in the campaign of survey flights having to be reduced. Furthermore, Iraq did not agree immediately to the activation of the monitoring cameras—agreement was only forthcoming on 23 September 1993, activation taking place on 25 September 1993.

---

[15] Circulated as UN Security Council document S/26127, 21 July 1993.
[16] Circulated as UN Security Council document S/26451, 16 Sep. 1993.
[17] Director of Iraq's Military Industrialization Corporation; see note 10.

The activation of the cameras and the conduct of the gamma-detection surveys permitted the second round of the high-level talks to proceed. A small advance team was sent to Baghdad on 27 September 1993 in order to elicit from the Iraqi side the responses to the questions identified in New York. While Iraq was immediately forthcoming on some of these, most answers were not given before the arrival of the Executive Chairman on 1 October as Iraq sought to place conditions on the handing over of the information (i.e., that UNSCOM should declare the information adequate before even seeing it).

After intensive discussions on all outstanding issues, Iraq provided answers to the key questions identified in New York. Iraq handed over a more detailed account of its past CW production and, for the first time, details on the suppliers of critical equipment or materials in each of the categories, including those who provided technical advice. Iraq's earlier accounts of its past CW production had blatantly failed to take into account past disposal of CW. In Baghdad, Iraq gave for the first time an account of CW production which addressed the obvious shortfalls of earlier declarations.

However, in exchange for this information, Iraq sought to have the information treated as solely confidential to UNSCOM and requested a statement from UNSCOM that Iraq was now fully in compliance with section C of Resolution 687 less the future monitoring aspects thereof. UNSCOM could not give this latter statement; it rather worded the report[18] with caveats relating to adequate verification of the newly received information. The newly provided information needed to be verified, assessed and confirmed by UNSCOM staff in New York before UNSCOM could state that Iraq had discharged its obligation, in compliance with paragraphs 8 and 9(a) of Resolution 687, to provide the information necessary to constitute full, final and complete disclosures of its past programmes—an essential condition for the proper planning of ongoing monitoring and verification.

This did not fully satisfy Iraq, which still sought a definitive statement from UNSCOM and the IAEA to the effect that Iraq was now in full compliance with its obligations. In particular, it sought a statement that UNSCOM was fully satisfied with the newly provided data. In recognition that UNSCOM might need some time to study, verify and assess the new data, Iraq instead accepted a further round of talks in New York.

During this Baghdad round, Iraq also submitted to UNSCOM a further set of declarations in relation to ongoing monitoring and verification and declarations concerning sites that should be subject to baseline inspections under the monitoring regime (table 19.1 lists the inspections carried out in 1993). UNSCOM discussed these declarations with Iraq and how they could be improved to bring them in line with the requirements of the plan.[19] UNSCOM also undertook, upon the delegation's return to New York, to create a standardized reporting format to facilitate Iraq's reporting and UNSCOM's use of

---

[18] Circulated as UN Security Council document S/26571, 12 Oct. 1993.
[19] UN Security Council document S/22871/Rev.1 (note 8).

Table 19.1. The 1993 UNSCOM inspection schedule, in-country dates

Type of inspection/date	Team
Nuclear	
22–27 Jan. 1993	IAEA17/UNSCOM 49
3–11 Mar. 1993	IAEA18/UNSCOM 52
30 Apr.–7 May 1993	IAEA19/UNSCOM 56
25–30 June 1993	IAEA20/UNSCOM 58
23–28 July 1993	IAEA21/UNSCOM 61
1–9 Nov. 1993	IAEA22/UNSCOM 64
Chemical	
18 June 1992–ongoing	CDG/UNSCOM 38
6–18 Apr. 1993	CW10/UNSCOM 55
27–30 June 1993	CW11/UNSCOM 59
19–22 Nov. 1993	CW12/UNSCOM 65
Biological	
11–18 Mar. 1993	BW3/UNSCOM 53
Ballistic Missiles	
25 Jan.–23 Mar. 1993	IMT1a/UNSCOM 48
12–21 Feb. 1993	BM15/UNSCOM 50
22–23 Feb. 1993	BM16/UNSCOM 51
27 Mar.–17 May 1993	IMT1b/UNSCOM 54
5–28 June 1993	IMT1c/UNSCOM 57
10–11 July 1993	BM17/UNSCOM 60
23 Aug.–27 Sep. 1993	BM18/UNSCOM 62
28 Sep.–1 Nov. 1993	BM19/UNSCOM 63
Special Missions	
12–18 Mar. 1993	
14–20 Mar. 1993	
19–24 Apr. 1993	
4 June–5 July 1993	
15–19 July 1993	
25 July–5 Aug. 1993	
9–12 Aug. 1993	
10–24 Sep. 1993	
27 Sep.–1 Oct. 1993	
1–8 Oct. 1993	
5 Oct. 1993–16 Feb. 1994	
2–10 Dec. 1993	
2–16 Dec. 1993	

Source: UN Security Council document S/26910, 21 Dec. 1993.

the data provided. However, UNSCOM informed Iraq that, as these declarations had not yet been made formally under Resolution 715, they could not be accepted by UNSCOM as fulfilment of Iraq's reporting obligations. Once Iraq acknowledged its obligations under Resolution 715 and the plans approved thereunder, Iraq would need to submit the required declarations formally under and in accordance with the resolution.

A further round of talks took place in New York on 15–30 November 1993, comprising high-level technical talks and, during the second week, parallel political talks.[20] In the technical talks UNSCOM informed Iraq that, at that stage, the information available in all areas had been deemed credible and that UNSCOM would deploy its best efforts to expedite the process of verifying the information with a view to arriving at a definitive conclusion. In subsequent working groups, Iraq provided information, supplementary to that provided in the previous round in Baghdad, on its past proscribed programmes and on sites, equipment and materials to be monitored pursuant to the plans for ongoing monitoring and verification. Discussions were held on alternative means of verification, on a process to address past difficulties in verification and on how ongoing monitoring and verification would be implemented.

During the political talks the Deputy Prime Minister of Iraq, Tariq Aziz, met the Executive Chairman and held consultations with members of the Security Council. Following these consultations, Iraq announced[21] that the 'Government of Iraq has decided to accept the obligations set forth in resolution 715 (1991) and to comply with the provisions of the plans for ongoing monitoring and verification as contained therein'. In welcoming this development, UNSCOM requested that Iraq submit as soon as possible consolidated declarations under Resolution 715 and the plans for ongoing monitoring and verification. In response to this request, Iraq submitted to UNSCOM a statement[22] confirming that previous Iraqi declarations were to be considered to have been made under Resolution 715 and its plans.

While this statement addressed the question of the legal status of Iraq's earlier declarations, it did not address the problems arising from the declarations' inadequacies, inadequacies that UNSCOM will have to take up with Iraq before it can fully implement its plan for ongoing monitoring and verification. UNSCOM's current evaluation of Iraq's declarations is that they are credible but still incomplete. The quantities for imports and production declared by Iraq are within UNSCOM's estimate range. However, verification has been rendered difficult as Iraq claims that all relevant documentation about its past programmes has been destroyed. It is hoped that the alternative means of verification noted above will help overcome this problem.

UNSCOM received no declaration from Iraq concerning the legal and administrative measures it had taken to give effect to the relevant resolutions. These are clearly required before any determination is made that Iraq is in compliance with its reporting requirements.

In conclusion, in 1993 there were major positive developments at the political level. Iraq acknowledged its obligations under Resolution 715 and the plans approved thereunder. It stated that its earlier declarations in relation to future monitoring were made under and in conformity with Resolution 715

[20] A full report of this round is to be found in UN Security Council document S/26825, and Corr.1, 1 Dec. 1993.

[21] Letter from the Minister for Foreign Affairs of Iraq to the President of the Security Council, dated 26 Nov. 1993, UN Security Council document S/26811, annex, 26 Nov. 1993.

[22] Enclosure II of UN Security Council document S/26825 (note 20).

and the plans, and it undertook to co-operate with UNSCOM in the implementation of the plans in order to arrive, at the earliest feasible time, at the stage where both UNSCOM and the IAEA will be in a position to report to the Security Council that Iraq is, in their view, meeting all the requirements of section C of Resolution 687.

IV. Immunities, privileges and facilities

In early 1993, UNSCOM encountered further problems with Iraq in the conduct of its mandate, particularly regarding the exercise of its immunities, privileges and facilities and the security of its personnel and property. At the start of a joint nuclear, chemical and biological documentation search in December 1992 (CBW3/UNSCOM 47, IAEA16/UNSCOM 47), Iraqis were observed leaving a site with documentation during an inspection and against the wishes of the inspectors. Also in December 1992, Iraq prevented UNSCOM from conducting an aerial inspection of two sites on the outskirts of Baghdad.[23] In January 1993, Iraq sought to deny UNSCOM the use of its own aircraft to transport personnel and equipment into and from Iraq out of and to Bahrain.[24] In February 1993, Iraq threatened to shoot down a helicopter providing supporting overhead surveillance for an inspection team (BM16/UNSCOM 51) if the aircraft did not leave the vicinity of the site.[25]

These events fitted into a general pattern of Iraqi conduct. Iraq, through its conduct in the latter part of 1992 and the early part of 1993, consistently demonstrated its desire to limit UNSCOM's inspection rights and operational capabilities through seeking to place restrictions on inspectors in the course of their work. While many of these Iraqi actions took place during the course of inspections under Resolution 687, there was no doubt that they formed part of a long-term campaign to establish a practice for the conduct of inspections which would severely restrict the rights provided in the plans for ongoing monitoring and verification and relevant Security Council resolutions. Iraq was clearly seeking to assert the right to interpret how the resolutions should be implemented.

In that campaign Iraq made attempts: to restrict the scope of inspections and information gathering; to restrict access and impose delays on inspections; to restrict the exercise of UNSCOM's aerial rights; to impose limits on the duration, size and composition of inspections; to require advance notice of inspection activities; and to limit the right to take photographs. The incidents varied in seriousness. Some might not have been significant had they not been part of a general trend. However, when taken together, these incidents added up to a major impediment which would have effectively impeded credible ongoing monitoring and verification. This attempt by Iraq to define the terms under which ongoing monitoring and verification would be conducted further under-

---

[23] Reported to the Security Council in UN Security Council document S/24984, 17 Dec. 1992.
[24] Reported in UN Security Council document S/25172*, 2 Mar. 1993.
[25] Reported in UN Security Council document S/25977 (note 3).

lined the need to obtain from Iraq its formal acknowledgement of its obligations under Resolution 715, so that there could be no doubt as to what was to be implemented and how.

However, after the visit of the Executive Chairman to Iraq in July 1993, the situation improved considerably. As noted above, in November 1993 Iraq accepted Resolution 715 and the plans approved thereunder. The most recent inspections, including the largest and most intensive yet conducted by UNSCOM (BM19/UNSCOM 63), have passed without incident and with Iraq extending all the facilities requested by the inspection teams. In December 1993 UNSCOM conducted gamma-radiation detection surveys, using equipment mounted on helicopters, over municipal Baghdad[26]—one year after a similar mission to take aerial photographs was blocked by Iraq.[27] Indeed, Iraq has now assured UNSCOM[28] that it intends to assist it in any way possible to facilitate smooth implementation of ongoing monitoring and verification in order to arrive as soon as possible at the joint objective[29] held by UNSCOM and Iraq: to be in a position where UNSCOM and the IAEA can report in good conscience that Iraq has fulfilled the requirements set forth in paragraph 22 of Resolution 687 for the lifting of the oil embargo.

V. Operational developments

Chemical weapons

In the CW area, activities focused on destruction and were centred around two sites—Al Muthanna, the principal CW-production and storage site designated by UNSCOM as the prime site for destruction activities, and Muhammadiyat, a CW storage site west of Baghdad.

Operations at Muhammadiyat commenced on 21 February 1993 involving the transport of stable, filled munitions to Al Muthanna (21 250-gauge bombs and 9 DB0 cluster bombs) and on-site destruction of unstable munitions (101 250-gauge bombs and 5 500-gauge bombs). The quantities of unfilled munitions remaining at Muhammadiyat are: 5127 250-gauge bombs, 1094 DB2 cluster bombs and 58 DB0 cluster bombs.

At Al Muthanna an incinerator, built by Iraq to UNSCOM design specifications, became operational on 5 November 1992. It operates at temperatures in excess of 1100°C. During the third week of March 1993, a combustion-efficiency monitoring system was installed to monitor performance by continuously measuring concentrations of the combustion gases. Mustard gas is destroyed either by direct injection into the furnace or in a toluene/benzene/diesel mix. Some of the mustard gas has polymerized, complicating the process of extraction and destruction. By December 1993 all but a few 155-mm

---

[26] Reported in UN Security Council document S/26910 (note 3).
[27] Reported in UN Security Council document S/24984 (note 5).
[28] Private discussions.
[29] Reported in UN Security Council document S/26825 (note 20).

mustard gas-filled artillery shells had been destroyed. The remainder were in poor condition and will require an alternative means of destruction.

The neutralization of nerve agents by hydrolysis, also at Al Muthanna, continued. In early February 1993, hydrolysis of the bulk stocks of the nerve agent sarin (GB) was completed, followed shortly after by the completion of the explosive incineration of 122-mm sarin-filled rockets on 14 February 1993.[30] On 22 April the destruction of the remaining sarin from the Al Hussein (Scud) warheads was completed.[31] A small amount of tabun (GA) remains to be destroyed.

Destruction of precursors, CW agents and munitions was to have been completed by March/April 1994. The provisional deadline for completing the tasks of the Chemical Destruction Group is set at mid-1994. Numbers of items destroyed at Al Muthanna, as of 6 December 1993, are listed in table 19.2 as absolute figures.[32] However, there is some uncertainty as to the exact amounts of agent actually destroyed because of various factors such as leakage from containers and deterioration of agent prior to destruction.

In addition to the destruction activities noted above, five inspections conducted chemical activities, either as dedicated CW inspections or in conjunction with other tasks. One investigated allegations of CW use by the Iraqi Government against opposition forces in the Southern Marshes (CW12/ UNSCOM 65). This inspection was constituted at short notice[33] to investigate persistent reports of such CW use. Initially, the team assembled as a fact-finding mission and visited Iran to clarify allegations from persons claiming to have witnessed the incident, specifically to obtain an exact location of the site at which the alleged CW attack took place. Upon obtaining this information, the team returned to Bahrain for further preparations[34] and entered Iraq on 19 November 1993.

The inspection team conducted a thorough inspection of the site and took a large number of soil, water, flora and fauna samples for laboratory analysis. The team also inspected the area around the site of the alleged attack. Vehicles, boats and helicopters were used in this survey. During the inspection the team did not find any immediate evidence of CW use. One unexploded munition was discovered at the site, but it was in too dangerous a condition for the team to take samples from it. Consequently, a second team of explosive demolition experts from UNSCOM's Chemical Destruction Group at Al Muthanna was dispatched to the site on 25 November 1993 and concluded that this munition was not a CW munition but a high-explosive rocket-propelled grenade. It was destroyed by these experts.

[30] Reported in 'United Nations Security Council oversees destruction of Iraqi rockets filled with nerve agent sarin', *United Nations Press Release*, no. IK/139, 24 Feb. 1993.

[31] Reported in 'United Nations Security Council completes destruction of nerve agent sarin in Iraq: work continues', *United Nations Press Release*, no. IK/144, 22 Apr. 1993.

[32] Internal UNSCOM reporting.

[33] Reported in 'Security Council investigating allegations of CW use by Iraq', *United Nations Press Release*, no. IK/156, 17 Nov. 1993.

[34] Reported in 'Security Council's team concludes on-site investigation of alleged CW use in Iraq', *United Nations Press Release*, no. IK/157, 22 Nov. 1993.

Table 19.2. Status of chemical destruction at Al Muthanna, as of 6 April 1994

Items	Quantity destroyed to date
Munitions and sub-components	
122-mm rocket and warhead	319
122-mm rocket warhead	6 454
122-mm rocket motor[a]	1 056
122-mm rocket propellant[a]	16 995
122-mm rocket motor tube[a]	11 239
155-mm projectile (empty)	12
155-mm projectile (mustard)	12 786
155-mm projectile (WP)	45
Al Hussein warhead (GB/GF)	16
Al Hussein warhead (empty)	13
R400 bomb	337
R400 tail fin assembly[a]	804
250-gauge bomb (oil filled)	5 176
250-gauge bomb (polymust,[b] partial)	713
250-gauge bomb (empty)	12
250-gauge bomb (WP)	8
500-gauge bomb (oil filled)	4
500-gauge bomb (polymust,[b] partial)	948
500-gauge bomb (GA, partial)	2
DB 2 bomb (unfilled)	1 115
DB 0 bomb (unfilled)	61
CW agents (in litres)	
Mustard gas	398 046
GA (tabun) nerve agent	21 365
GB/GF nerve agent	61 633
Key pecursors (in litres)	
DF	14 600
D4	121 675
Thio-diethyleneglycol	153 980
Phosphorous oxychloride	344 800
Thionyl chloride	169 980
Phosphorous trichloride	415 000
Immediate precursors (in litres)	
Isopropyl alcohol	250 483
Cyclohexanol/isopropyl alcohol	5 200
Dichlorethane	4 120
Di-isopropylamine	30 000
Morpholine	10 000
Chlorobenzaldehyde	41 800
Other chemicals (in litres)	
Ethylchlorohydrine	1 900
Monoethyleneglycol	49 600
Malonnitrile	200
Ethanol	112 700

Items	Quantity destroyed to date
Thiololpolysulphide	60
Propanol 2	405
3-hydroxy 2-methyl piperdine	50
Hydrogen sulphide	160
Methanol	42 000
Toluene	10 800
Pyridine	19 000
Other chemicals (in kilograms)	
Dimethylamine·HCl	238 500
Sodium cyanide	180 000
Potassium cyanide	3000
KH fluoride	450 000
Sodium fluoride	135 000
Arsenic trioxide	1 850
HF	7 000
Mandelic acid	1 650
Triethanolamine	511
Methyldichloride	2 250
Glycolic acid	50
Diethylaminoethanol thiol HCL	10
2-ethylaminoethanol	180
Chloracetic acid	2 500
Dimethylamine	7 210
Methyl iodide	2 000
KF	600
$CH_3ClOONa$	250
$AlCl_3$	2 800
KI	3 000
$AsCl_3$	75
2, 4 dichlorophenol	2 250
Trichlorophenol	150
Other	
Bulk storage container (2 tonne)	32
White phosphorus (barrels)	648

[a] Munition sub-component
[b] Polymerized mustard agent
Source: Internal reporting from the Chemical Destruction Group to UNSCOM, New York.

In the course of this investigation, UNSCOM also obtained a number of documents, which were subjected to forensic examination. Analysis of these documents and the samples found no evidence to support the claims that CW had been used.[35]

[35] Reported in 'No trace of chemical agent found in samples from southern Iraq', *United Nations Press Release*, no. IK/165, 28 Feb. 1994.

Another inspection (CW11/UNSCOM 59) was able to allay concerns that a bomb observed during inspection activities might have been developed for delivery of CW or BW. It was, in fact, a failed prototype for a CW bomb. In other inspection activities, considerable time was devoted to the development of an updated inventory of CW-production equipment at the Al Muthanna site, seminars were held with the Iraqi representatives to clarify gaps in Iraq's account of its past CW programme, reports of hidden CW caches were investigated and document searches were conducted. While no evidence of hidden CW was found, UNSCOM was unable to conclude a definitive material balance for the CW programme because Iraq continued to fail to provide full accounting for the precursors imported.

Biological weapons

Further BW inspections were also conducted. In addition to inspecting the bomb referred to above (CW11/UNSCOM 59), inspection activities assisted in identifying additional facilities to be included in the plan for ongoing monitoring and verification (BW3/UNSCOM 53). Recommendations were made on the form and nature of monitoring required at these sites. As with the CW issues, seminars were held with the Iraqi side to attempt to clarify details of Iraq's past BW programmes.

Ballistic missiles

Efforts related to ballistic missiles concentrated on three main aspects: trying to establish a definitive material balance for the Scud missiles supplied by the former Soviet Union; trying to account for Iraq's production capacity in the ballistic missile area; and establishing an interim monitoring regime for Iraq's dual-capable missile facilities. This last effort was necessary because of Iraq's refusal, noted above, until 26 November 1993 to acknowledge its obligations under the plans for ongoing monitoring and verification.

One inspection (BM15/UNSCOM 50) had as its main objectives to record serial numbers of specific machinery and to obtain raw materials for analysis to help determine the Iraqi supplier network and to assess the capabilities of certain establishments and facilities in Iraq including the Nasr [Victory] State Establishment, the Al Yawm Al Azim facility and the Technical Corps for Special Projects (TECO) test stand at Zaafaraniyah. It also supervised the destruction of the dies and moulds at Taji used or intended for use in proscribed missile activities.

A subsequent inspection (BM16/UNSCOM 51) checked specific information that items proscribed by Resolution 687 were present in an area west of Baghdad. The items were reported to be related to ballistic missiles with a range greater than 150 km and their associated vehicles. Three undeclared sites, suspected of concealing them, were thoroughly inspected at short notice—a large military ammunition production plant and two military units—

fully integrating helicopter and high-altitude surveillance aircraft with the ground inspection. No proscribed items or activities were observed by the inspection.

However, during the inspection a serious breach of UNSCOM's aerial-surveillance rights occurred. A helicopter was initially prevented from establishing aerial surveillance over one site. Iraqi officials employed repeated and open threats of force to impede the helicopter's mission. On one occasion, this threat was aggravated by Iraqi personnel aiming and training their anti-aircraft guns on the helicopter. These actions on the part of Iraq put UNSCOM personnel in real danger and constituted a gross violation of UNSCOM's rights and immunities. This serious incident was reported by the Executive Chairman to the Security Council on 24 February 1993.[36]

An inspection on 28 September–1 November 1993 also investigated reports concerning suspect, prohibited activities in Iraq and the continued concealment of proscribed items, notably missiles, and verified information provided by Iraq on its past prohibited activities, especially on the operational use of missiles with a range greater than 150 km. This was the largest inspection to date (BM19/UNSCOM 63). In addition to previous inspection procedures, it required the use of new inspection techniques since much of the information to be checked by the team referred to underground storage for prohibited items. Ground-penetrating radar (GPR) mounted on helicopters was used to increase the effectiveness of the survey of areas to be inspected. The GPR was custom-designed to maximize its capability to detect prohibited items, especially missiles, missile launchers and possible 'hide sites'. Two additional helicopters were deployed to Iraq to support the inspection. The primary mission of these helicopters was to conduct GPR surveys. They also performed aerial inspection of specific sites and provided an additional means of securing sites to be inspected including, as necessary, at night using forward-looking infra-red radar (FLIR).

During its deployment, this team inspected more than 30 sites and areas. Altogether, 28 GPR missions were flown, totalling more than 56 hours of flying time. No undeclared prohibited items or activities were identified.

Iraq's failure until 26 November 1993 to acknowledge its obligations under Resolution 715 was a major factor preventing the initiation of long-term monitoring by UNSCOM of Iraq's activities. In the meantime, Iraq was actively pursuing missile-related activities that are covered by the ongoing monitoring and verification plan, to include the establishment of a dedicated missile research and design centre north-west of Baghdad.

This facility, the Ibn Al Haytham Missile Research and Design Centre, was established by Iraq on 4 April 1992 as the main centre for research and design activity in Iraq involving ballistic missiles not prohibited by Resolution 687. This centre is not only involved in the maintenance of existing permitted missile systems, but also in the design of new missile systems, including the Ababil 100 with a range close to 150 km. The centre employs many of the

---

[36] Informal written report to members of the Security Council, not circulated as a public document.

scientists and technicians that were involved in the proscribed ballistic missile programmes prior to the Gulf War and adoption of Resolution 687.

In the absence of Iraq's acknowledgement of Resolution 715, interim monitoring (IMTa/UNSCOM 48) of the centre was initiated by UNSCOM to track Iraqi ballistic missile programmes to ensure that no proscribed activity was taking place. The focus of the first mission was liquid-propulsion systems and related technologies. Based upon the results of this mission, which in part highlighted the significant amount of continuing activity in Iraq in the field of solid propulsion, UNSCOM dispatched to Iraq a new team of interim monitors (IMT1b/UNSCOM 54), which continued the monitoring of the Ibn Al Haytham Centre and initiated interim monitoring of facilities associated with solid propulsion and related technologies. A third missile interim monitoring team (IMT1c/UNSCOM 57)assessed existing Iraqi capabilities in the area of precision machining related to ballistic missile production, in particular gyroscope devices and liquid-fuel engine manufacture.

These interim monitoring inspections provided the comprehensive technical assessments of current Iraqi missile programmes (including research, development and production capabilities) needed for planning and implementation of ongoing monitoring and verification activities in the missile area.

The final major activity in the area of missiles concerned the installation of remote-controlled camera monitoring systems at certain missile test stands in Iraq. On 6 June 1993, UNSCOM informed Iraq[37] of its intention to install remote-controlled camera systems at two missile-engine test stands, Al Yawm Al Azim and Al Rafah. The purpose of these cameras was to verify that no prohibited activities were taking place at these test stands. The camera system was designed to monitor activities continuously and to record all tests at those locations. Iraq responded that it would not accept any monitoring activities and would insist that UNSCOM limit itself to inspection activities under Resolution 687. On 18 June 1993, the President of the Security Council, on behalf of the Security Council, stated that Iraq must accept installation by UNSCOM of monitoring devices at the test stands (see section III above).

Even after this statement by the Security Council, Iraq continued its obstruction of the installation of the cameras. On 5 July 1993, after the initial installation team had spent over a month in Iraq awaiting a change in the Iraqi position which would allow the team to proceed with its mission, it was instructed by the Executive Chairman to withdraw. As an interim measure UNSCOM, after having informed the Security Council, dispatched a team to Iraq on 10 July 1993 (BM17/UNSCOM 60) to seal the relevant equipment and facilities at both sites so as to ensure that they were not used until the cameras had been installed. The Iraqi authorities blocked this team from carrying out its mission.

Pursuant to the arrangements agreed during the Executive Chairman's July 1993 visit to Iraq on the monitoring of missile tests, on 25 July 1993 UNSCOM dispatched a small technical team to Baghdad to install the camera

---

[37] Orally and by letter, during meetings in Baghdad.

systems at the Al Yawm Al Azim and Al Rafah sites. The installation and testing of the cameras were completed on 3 August 1993. As part of the interim arrangements, UNSCOM sent a number of missile experts to Baghdad to observe any missile tests that Iraq might declare to UNSCOM (BM18/UNSCOM 62). These experts also performed detailed engineering surveys of test facilities at Al Yawm Al Azim, Al Rafah and five other test stands capable of missile and rocket-engine tests.

After the first round of high-level talks in New York, the Government of Iraq informed UNSCOM that it had agreed to the activation of the camera systems at Al Rafah and Al Yawm Al Azim. On 25 September 1993, the cameras were activated. Since then they have operated on a continuous basis. The cameras are arranged in a manner that enables UNSCOM to assess whether a test was of a prohibited missile, engine or motor. In accordance with operating procedures established by UNSCOM, these camera systems provide constant coverage of the missile test stands at Al Rafah and Al Yawm Al Azim. Missile test monitoring handbooks, to include engineering baselines for the test sites, check-lists and reporting forms for the Iraqis, were developed. An upgrade of the camera systems to include radio links and improved lenses was undertaken from 2 to 10 December 1993.

Nuclear weapons

The IAEA, with the assistance and co-operation of UNSCOM, conducted a further six inspections in Iraq during the course of 1993. Activities focused on the removal and reprocessing of nuclear fuels, ensuring full accounting for Iraq's holdings of other nuclear materials, identification of installations, equipment and materials which need to be monitored, and sampling of Iraq's water courses as part of a monitoring regime designed to observe any activity at nuclear plants. In addition, the Special Commission, using prototype technology provided by the Government of France, conducted aerial surveys using gamma-radiation sensors mounted on UNSCOM helicopters. Furthermore, the IAEA held high-level discussions with Iraq to clarify certain outstanding issues relating to Iraq's past nuclear programme.

In the high-level discussions, Iraq provided information on foreign technical advice received in relation to centrifuge enrichment of uranium and on the procurement of equipment and materials, in particular maraging steel, from foreign sources.

The IAEA reported that the fresh fuel for the IRT 5000 reactor has been transferred to Russia and transformed, through isotopic dilution, into uranium enriched to slightly less than 20 per cent U-235.[38] This material is now in a storage facility in Russia under IAEA safeguards pending its resale. The French material testing reactor (MTR) type plates and the Russian-origin fuel pins removed from Iraq in June 1992 remain in storage at the IAEA Laboratory in Seibersdorf, Austria. The irradiated fuel was removed from Iraq in two

---

[38] UN Security Council documents S/25983, 21 June 1993 and S/26897, 20 Dec. 1993.

shipments by the Russian Ministry of Atomic Energy and a US subcontractor, under close IAEA supervision. The subcontractor supplied casks capable of withstanding an aeroplane crash into which the fuel was repackaged for shipment. The material was flown out of Iraq in an Antonov-124 directly to Yekaterinburg in the Russian Federation from where it will be transferred to Chelyabinsk for reprocessing. After dilution, the residual materials will be available for resale under the supervision of the IAEA for use in peaceful nuclear activities.

Most of the remaining slurries containing natural uranium from the Al Jezira site have been recovered—some 59 drums—and has been transferred to a storage site at location C at Al Tuwaitha, under IAEA supervision.

While the IAEA reports that the nuclear materials subject to safeguards inspection prior to the Gulf War have long since been accounted for, it also reports that efforts to confirm independently the quantities of nuclear material not subject to safeguards inspection have not been completely successful. Considerable effort has been expended to develop an internally consistent picture of how the nuclear materials from different origins had been used. However, the IAEA is not yet confident that all nuclear materials have been declared and presented.

Concerning dual-purpose items to be monitored, Iraq provided the IAEA at the end of January 1993 with a revised list of items subject to ongoing monitoring and verification which existed or had existed since 1 January 1989 in Iraqi Atomic Energy Commission (IAEC) facilities, universities and state establishments which supported the IAEC programme. However, Iraq indicated that some items might have been omitted from the list, either through oversight or because they were not thought to be covered by Annex 3 of the IAEA plan for ongoing monitoring and verification[39] and that future declarations might include additional items. A further set of declarations was received in the autumn of 1993, the accuracy and completeness of which are being verified by the IAEA.

The first special Aerial Inspection Team (AIT) mission which focused on detection of gamma emissions was flown on 10–25 September 1993. Owing to some early obstruction on the part of Iraq, flights did not begin until 15 September and, consequently, the coverage of the mission was considerably reduced. Partial surveys were conducted at Al Tuwaitha, Al Atheer and Al Jezira. Gamma signals were detected from multiple points at all sites. Preliminary analysis indicates the usefulness of this technique in identifying specific locations warranting more detailed ground inspections. Use will be made of this gamma-detection capability in the future.

The second such aerial inspection using the gamma-detection equipment was flown on 2–15 December 1993. During this mission more extensive coverage of previously covered sites was accomplished and additional sites surveyed.

---

[39] Contained in UN Security Council document S/22872/Rev.1 and Corr.1 (note 8).

Aerial surveillance

Aerial-surveillance activities continued using both U-2 aircraft (a total of 186 missions flown as of 10 December 1993) and helicopter platforms (335 target missions now flown). Helicopter missions continue to be flown in support of ground inspections and to provide a time-series photographic record of sites which need monitoring under the plans for ongoing monitoring and verification. Additional sensors (gamma-detection, FLIR and GPR) have been mounted on to the helicopters for specific missions to give them greater monitoring and detection capability. The gamma-detection sensors and the GPR required the helicopters to operate in a new mode—one of survey. The object of gamma detection is to map background radiation levels as a reference against which to judge future gamma surveys and to identify any unusual sources of radiation which might require immediate investigation. The object of the GPR is to search for underground chambers or hidden items. Such missions have been flown in and around Baghdad and in central, western and north-western Iraq. Iraq has withdrawn its previous objections to flights within the area which it had claimed to constitute the limits of Baghdad.

VI. Issues and priorities for the future

UNSCOM will be able to report to the Security Council that Iraq is in substantial compliance with its obligations and that the plans for ongoing monitoring and verification to ensure that Iraq does not reacquire the weapons proscribed to it have been initiated and are smoothly functioning only when Iraq fulfils certain obligations. Iraq must supplement and revise its declarations to the point where, in the view of UNSCOM, they conform with the full, final and complete disclosures required under Resolution 707 and of initial declarations required under the plans for ongoing monitoring and verification. In regard to the former, supplementation by supporting documentary evidence clearly provides the most satisfactory solution. However, UNSCOM has discussed with Iraq alternative means whereby it might assist UNSCOM in verifying adequately its various declarations.

Iraq will also need to establish a track record of accepting and co-operating in the implementation of all aspects of the plans, including compliance with UNSCOM's privileges and immunities as required for effective and efficient monitoring and verification, ensuring the safety and security of personnel and property, landing rights for aircraft and non-obstruction of inspections and logistics.

On the basis of Iraq's revised declarations, UNSCOM must draw up a list of sites which should be subject to baseline inspections to assess how each site should be monitored and with what frequency. For each site a monitoring and verification protocol will need to be compiled, containing the information on the site essential for effective monitoring and the details of the monitoring and verification activities to be conducted at the site in question. Once these have been prepared in draft, baseline inspections can proceed and final drafts of the protocols can be submitted by the inspection teams to the Executive Chairman for approval.

In addition, UNSCOM, the IAEA and the Sanctions Committee established pursuant to Resolution 661[40] are required, in accordance with paragraph 7 of Resolution 715, to develop a mechanism for monitoring any future sales of supplies by other countries to Iraq of items relevant to section C of Resolution 687 and other relevant resolutions, including Resolution 715 and the plans approved thereunder.

Further activities are planned in each of the weapon categories. Destruction activities currently focus on CW, CW precursors and CW-production equipment at Al Muthanna. Preparations for the implementation of the plans for ongoing monitoring and verification are under way and proposals for the potential form of an export/import control regime after the lifting of sanctions have been discussed. There will be a shift of emphasis towards: verifying definitively Iraq's accounts of its past programmes and its supplier networks; preparations for and operations under ongoing monitoring and verification; and further elaboration of the proposals for import and export monitoring.

The priorities for UNSCOM are now: (a) verification and supplementation of Iraq's declarations at a level acceptable to UNSCOM; (b) the initiation of monitoring inspections; (c) drafting a mechanism for export/import monitoring; (d) the establishment of practice and precedent in the exercise of UNSCOM's privileges, immunities and facilities necessary for effective and efficient implementation of the plan for ongoing monitoring and verification; and (e) completion of the destruction activities related to Iraq's former CW programme at Al Muthanna.

---

[40] UN Security Council document S/RES/661 (1990), 6 Aug. 1990.

Annexes

Annexes

Annexe A. Major multilateral arms control agreements

RAGNHILD FERM

For the arms control agreements prior to 1982, see Goldblat, J., SIPRI, *Agreements for Arms Control: A Critical Survey* (Taylor & Francis: London, 1982); for the Treaty of Rarotonga, see SIPRI, *World Armaments and Disarmament: SIPRI Yearbook 1986* (Oxford University Press: Oxford, 1986), pp. 509–19; and for the CFE Treaty, see SIPRI, *SIPRI Yearbook 1991: World Armaments and Disarmament* (Oxford University Press: Oxford, 1991), pp. 461–74.

I. Summaries of the agreements

Protocol for the prohibition of the use in war of asphyxiating, poisonous or other gases, and of bacteriological methods of warfare (Geneva Protocol)

Signed at Geneva on 17 June 1925; entered into force on 8 February 1928.

Declares that the parties agree to be bound by the above prohibition, which should be universally accepted as part of international law, binding alike the conscience and the practice of nations.

Antarctic Treaty

Signed at Washington, DC, on 1 December 1959; entered into force on 23 June 1961.

Declares the Antarctic an area to be used exclusively for peaceful purposes. Prohibits any measure of a military nature in the Antarctic, such as the establishment of military bases and fortifications, and the carrying out of military manœuvres or the testing of any type of weapon. Bans any nuclear explosion as well as the disposal of radioactive waste material in Antarctica, subject to possible future international agreements on these subjects.

At regular intervals consultative meetings are convened to exchange information and hold consultations on matters pertaining to Antarctica, as well as to recommend to the governments measures in furtherance of the principles and objectives of the Treaty. A Protocol on the protection of the Antarctic environment was signed on 4 October 1991.

Treaty banning nuclear weapon tests in the atmosphere, in outer space and under water (Partial Test Ban Treaty—PTBT)

Signed at Moscow on 5 August 1963; entered into force on 10 October 1963.

Prohibits the carrying out of any nuclear weapon test explosion or any other nuclear explosion: (*a*) in the atmosphere, beyond its limits, including outer space, or under water, including territorial waters or high seas; (*b*) in any other environment if such explosion causes radioactive debris to be present outside the territorial limits of the state under whose jurisdiction or control the explosion is conducted.

Treaty on principles governing the activities of states in the exploration and use of outer space, including the moon and other celestial bodies (Outer Space Treaty)

Signed at London, Moscow and Washington, DC, on 27 January 1967; entered into force on 10 October 1967.

Prohibits the placing into orbit around the earth of any objects carrying nuclear weapons or any other kinds of weapons of mass destruction, the installation of such weapons on celestial bodies, or the stationing of them in outer space in any other manner. The establishment of military bases, installations and fortifications, the testing of any type of weapons and the conduct of military manœuvres on celestial bodies are also forbidden.

Treaty for the prohibition of nuclear weapons in Latin America (Treaty of Tlatelolco)

Signed at Mexico, Distrito Federal, on 14 February 1967; entered into force on 22 April 1968.

Prohibits the testing, use, manufacture, production or acquisition by any means, as well as the receipt, storage, installation, deployment and any form of possession of any nuclear weapons by Latin American countries.

The parties should conclude agreements with the IAEA for the application of safeguards to their nuclear activities.

Under *Additional Protocol I* the extra-continental or continental states which, *de jure* or *de facto*, are internationally responsible for territories lying within the limits of the geographical zone established by the Treaty (France, the Netherlands, the UK and the USA) undertake to apply the statute of military denuclearization, as defined in the Treaty, to such territories.

Under *Additional Protocol II* the nuclear weapon states (China, France, Russia, the UK and the USA) undertake to respect the statute of military denuclearization of Latin America, as defined and delimited in the Treaty, and not to contribute to acts involving a violation of the Treaty, nor to use or threaten to use nuclear weapons against the parties to the Treaty.

In 1990 the General Conference of the Agency for the Prohibition of Nuclear Weapons in Latin America decided that the official name of the Treaty should be changed by adding the words 'and the Caribbean'; in 1991, it decided to modify the wording of Article 25, paragraph 2, which determines which states may become parties to the Treaty; and, in 1992, it decided that Articles 14, 15, 16, 19 and 20, dealing with verification of compliance (in particular, with special inspections) should be replaced by a new text.

Treaty on the non-proliferation of nuclear weapons (NPT)

Signed at London, Moscow and Washington, DC, on 1 July 1968; entered into force on 5 March 1970.

Prohibits the transfer by nuclear weapon states, to any recipient whatsoever, of nuclear weapons or other nuclear explosive devices or of control over them, as well as the assistance, encouragement or inducement of any non-nuclear weapon state to manufacture or otherwise acquire such weapons or devices. Prohibits the receipt by non-nuclear weapon states from any transferor whatsoever, as well as the manufacture or other acquisition by those states of nuclear weapons or other nuclear explosive devices.

Non-nuclear weapon states undertake to conclude safeguard agreements with the International Atomic Energy Agency (IAEA) with a view to preventing diversion of nuclear energy from peaceful uses to nuclear weapons or other nuclear explosive devices.

The parties undertake to facilitate the exchange of equipment, materials and scientific and technological information for the peaceful uses of nuclear energy and to ensure that potential benefits from peaceful applications of nuclear explosions will be made available to non-nuclear weapon parties to the Treaty. They also undertake to pursue negotiations in good faith on effective measures relating to cessation of the nuclear arms race at an early date and to nuclear disarmament, and on a treaty on general and complete disarmament.

Twenty-five years after the entry into force of the Treaty (1995), a conference shall be convened to decide whether the Treaty shall continue in force indefinitely or shall be extended for an additional fixed period or periods.

Treaty on the prohibition of the emplacement of nuclear weapons and other weapons of mass destruction on the seabed and the ocean floor and in the subsoil thereof (Seabed Treaty)

Signed at London, Moscow and Washington, DC, on 11 February 1971; entered into force on 18 May 1972.

Prohibits emplanting or emplacing on the seabed and the ocean floor and in the subsoil thereof beyond the outer limit of a 12-mile seabed zone any nuclear weapons or any other types of weapons of mass destruction as well as structures, launching installations or any other facilities specifically designed for storing, testing or using such weapons.

Convention on the prohibition of the development, production and stockpiling of bacteriological (biological) and toxin weapons and on their destruction (BW Convention)

Signed at London, Moscow and Washington, DC, on 10 April 1972; entered into force on 26 March 1975.

Prohibits the development, production, stockpiling or acquisition by other means or retention of microbial or other biological agents, or toxins whatever their origin or method of production, of types and in quantities that have no justification of pro-phylactic, protective or other peaceful purposes, as well as weapons, equipment or means of delivery designed to use such agents or toxins for hostile purposes or in armed conflict. The destruction of the agents, toxins, weapons, equipment and means of delivery in the possession of the parties, or their diversion to peaceful purposes, should be effected not later than nine months after the entry into force of the Convention.

Convention on the prohibition of military or any other hostile use of environmental modification techniques (Enmod Convention)

Signed at Geneva on 18 May 1977; entered into force on 5 October 1978.

Prohibits military or any other hostile use of environmental modification techniques having widespread, long-lasting or severe effects as the means of destruction, damage or injury to states party to the Convention. The term 'environmental modification techniques' refers to any technique for changing—through the deliberate manipulation of natural processes—the dynamics, composition or structure of the Earth, including its biota, lithosphere, hydrosphere and atmosphere, or of outer space. The understandings reached during the negotiations, but not written into the Convention, define the terms 'widespread', 'long-lasting' and 'severe'.

Convention on prohibitions or restrictions on the use of certain conventional weapons which may be deemed to be excessively injurious or to have indiscriminate effects ('Inhumane Weapons' Convention)

Signed at New York on 10 April 1981; entered into force on 2 December 1983.

The Convention is an 'umbrella treaty', under which specific agreements can be concluded in the form of protocols.

Protocol I prohibits the use of weapons intended to injure by fragments which are not detectable in the human body by X-rays.

Protocol II prohibits or restricts the use of mines, booby-traps and similar devices.

Protocol III restricts the use of incendiary weapons.

South Pacific Nuclear Free Zone Treaty (Treaty of Rarotonga)

Signed at Rarotonga, Cook Islands, on 6 August 1985; entered into force on 11 December 1986.

Prohibits the manufacture or acquisition by other means of any nuclear explosive device, as well as possession or control over such device by the parties anywhere inside or outside the zone area described in an annex. The parties also undertake not to supply nuclear material or equipment, unless subject to IAEA safeguards, and to prevent in their territories the stationing as well as the testing of any nuclear explosive device. Each party remains free to allow visits, as well as transit, by foreign ships and aircraft.

Under Protocol 1, France, the UK and the USA would undertake to apply the treaty prohibitions relating to the manufacture, stationing and testing of nuclear explosive devices in the territories situated within the zone, for which they are internationally responsible.

Under Protocol 2, China, France, the UK, the USA and the USSR would undertake not to use or threaten to use a nuclear explosive device against the parties to the Treaty or against any territory within the zone for which a party to Protocol 1 is internationally responsible.

Under Protocol 3, China, France, the UK, the USA and the USSR would undertake not to test any nuclear explosive device anywhere within the zone.

Treaty on Conventional Armed Forces in Europe (CFE Treaty)

Signed at Paris on 19 November 1990; entered into force provisionally on 17 July 1992 and definitively on 9 November 1992.

Sets ceilings on five categories of military equipment (battle tanks, armoured combat vehicles, artillery pieces, combat aircraft and attack helicopters) in an area stretching from the Atlantic Ocean to the Ural Mountains (the ATTU zone). The CFE-1A Agreement, limiting personnel strength of conventional armed forces in the same area, was signed at Helsinki on 10 July and entered into force simultaneously with the CFE Treaty.

II. Status of the implementation of the major multilateral arms control agreements, as of 1 January 1994

Number of parties

1925 Geneva Protocol	132	Seabed Treaty	92
Antarctic Treaty	41	BW Convention	131
Partial Test Ban Treaty	123	Enmod Convention	62
Outer Space Treaty	94	'Inhumane Weapons' Convention	41
Treaty of Tlatelolco	25	Treaty of Rarotonga	11
Additional Protocol I	4	Protocol 1	0
Additional Protocol II	5	Protocol 2	2
Non-Proliferation Treaty	163	Protocol 3	2
NPT safeguards agreements (non-nuclear weapon states)	98	CFE Treaty	30

Notes

1. The Russian Federation, constituted in 1991 as an independent sovereign state, has confirmed the continuity of international obligations assumed by the Union of Soviet Socialist Republics (USSR).

2. The Federal Republic of Germany and the German Democratic Republic merged into one state in 1990. The dates of entry into force of the treaties listed in the table for the united Germany are the dates previously given for FR Germany.

3. The Yemen Arab Republic and the People's Democratic Republic of Yemen merged into one state in 1990. According to a statement by the united Yemen state, all agreements which either state has entered into are in force for Yemen. The dates of entry into force of the treaties listed in the table for Yemen are the earliest dates previously given for either of the former Yemen states.

4. Czechoslovakia split into two states on 1 January 1993, the Czech Republic and Slovakia. Both states have succeeded to all agreements in this list to which Czechoslovakia was a party.

5. The table records year of ratification, accession or succession.

6. The Partial Test Ban Treaty, the Outer Space Treaty, the Non-Proliferation Treaty, the Seabed Treaty and the BW Convention provide for three depositaries—the governments of the UK, the USA and the USSR. For these agreements, the dates indicated are the earliest dates on which countries deposited their instruments of ratification, accession or succession—whether in London, Washington or Moscow. The dates given for other agreements (for which there is only one depositary) are the dates of the deposit of the instruments of ratification, accession or succession with the relevant depositary, except in the case of the 1925 Geneva Protocol, where the dates refer to the date of notification by the depositary.

7. The 1925 Geneva Protocol, the Partial Test Ban Treaty, the Outer Space Treaty, the Non-Proliferation Treaty, the Seabed Treaty, the BW Convention, the Enmod Convention and the 'Inhumane Weapons' Convention are open to all states for signature.
The Antarctic Treaty is subject to ratification by the signatories and is open for accession by UN members or by other states invited to accede with the consent of all the contracting parties whose representatives are entitled to participate in the consultative meetings provided for in Article IX.
The Treaty of Tlatelolco is open for signature by all the Latin American republics; all other sovereign states situated in their entirety south of latitude 35° north in the western hemisphere; and (except for a political entity the territory of which is the subject of an international dispute) all such states which become sovereign, when they have been admitted by the General Conference; Additional Protocol I—by 'all extra-continental or continental states having *de jure* or *de facto* international responsibility for territories situated in the zone of application of the Treaty', that is, France, the Netherlands, the UK and the USA; Additional Protocol II—by 'all powers possessing nuclear weapons', that is, China, France, the UK, the USA and the USSR.
The Treaty of Rarotonga is open for signature by members of the South Pacific Forum; Protocol 1—by France, the UK and the USA; Protocol 2—by China, France, the UK, the USA and the USSR; Protocol 3—by China, France, the UK, the USA and the USSR.
The CFE Treaty was negotiated and signed in 1990 by NATO and WTO countries. In 1992 the former Soviet republics (except Estonia, Latvia and Lithuania) with territory in the ATTU zone signed the Agreement on the Principles and Procedures of Implementation of the CFE Treaty (Tashkent Agree-

ment), confirming the allocation of TLE on their territories. Also in 1992 the NATO states and Armenia, Azerbaijan, Belarus, Bulgaria, Czechoslovakia, Georgia, Hungary, Kazakhstan, Moldova, Poland, Romania, Russia and Ukraine signed the Final Document of the Extraordinary Conference of the States Parties to the CFE Treaty (Oslo Document), making these states parties to the modified CFE Treaty.

8. Key to abbreviations used in the table:

S	Signature without further action
PI, PII	Additional Protocols to the Treaty of Tlatelolco
P1, P2, P3	Protocols to the Treaty of Rarotonga
CP	Party entitled to participate in the consultative meetings provided for in Article IX of the Antarctic Treaty
SA	Nuclear safeguards agreement in force with the International Atomic Energy Agency as required by the Non-Proliferation Treaty or the Treaty of Tlatelolco, or concluded by a nuclear weapon state on a voluntary basis.

9. Footnotes with summaries of the most important reservations/declarations given in connection with the signing, ratification, accession or succession of a treaty are listed at the end of the table and are grouped separately under the heading for the respective agreements. Not all reservations for all treaties are given. The texts of the statements contained in the footnotes have been abridged, but the wording is close to the original version.

10. A complete list of UN member states and year of membership appears in section III.

State	Geneva Protocol	Antarctic Treaty	Partial Test Ban Treaty	Outer Space Treaty	Treaty of Tlatelolco	Non-Proliferation Treaty	Seabed Treaty	BW Convention	Enmod Convention	'Inhumane Weapons' Convention	Treaty of Rarotonga	CFE Treaty
Afghanistan	1986		1964	1988		1970 SA	1971	1975	1985	S		
Albania	1989					1990		1992				
Algeria	1992		S	1992			1992		1991			
Angola	1990¹											
Antigua and Barbuda	1988		1988	1988	1983¹	1985	1988		1988			
Argentina	1969	1961 CP	1986	1969	S²		1983¹	1979	1987	S		
Armenia						1993						1992
Australia	1930¹	1961 CP	1963	1967		1973 SA	1973	1977	1984	1983	1986	
Austria	1928	1987	1964	1968		1969 SA	1972	1973	1990	1983		
Azerbaijan						1992						1992
Bahamas			1976	1976	1977¹	1976	1989	1986				

State	Geneva Protocol	Antarctic Treaty	Partial Test Ban Treaty	Outer Space Treaty	Treaty of Tlatelolco	Non-Proliferation Treaty	Seabed Treaty	BW Convention	Enmod Convention	'Inhumane Weapons' Convention	Treaty of Rarotonga	CFE Treaty
Bahrain	1988[1]					1988		1988				
Bangladesh	1989[1]		1985	1986		1979 SA		1985	1979			
Barbados	1976[2]			1968	1969[1]	1980		1973				
Belarus	1970[3]		1963	1967		1993	1971	1975	1978	1982		1992
Belgium	1928[1]	1960 CP	1966	1973		1975 SA	1972	1979	1982	S		1991
Belize					S	1985		1986				
Benin	1986		1964	1986		1972	1986	1975	1986	1989[1]		
Bhutan	1979		1978			1985 SA		1978				
Bolivia	1985		1965	S	1969[1]	1970	S	1975	S			
Bosnia and Herzegovina										1993		
Botswana			1968			1969	1972	1991				
Brazil	1970	1975 CP	1964	1969[1]	1968[3]		1988[2]	1973	1984			

Country										
Brunei					1985 SA		1991			1991
Bulgaria	1934[1]	1978	1963	1967	1969 SA	1971	1972	1978	1982	
Burkina Faso	1971		S	1968	1970		1991			
Burma see: Myanmar										
Burundi			S	S	1971	S	S			
Cambodia	1983[4]				1972	S	1983			
Cameroon	1989		S	S	1969	S				
Canada	1930[1]	1988	1964	1967	1969 SA	1972[3]	1972	1981	S	1991
Cape Verde	1991		1979		1979	1979	1977	1979		
Central African Rep.	1970		1964	S	1970	1981	S			
Chad			1965		1971					

State	Geneva Protocol	Antarctic Treaty	Partial Test Ban Treaty	Outer Space Treaty	Treaty of Tlatelolco	Non-Proliferation Treaty	Seabed Treaty	BW Convention	Enmod Convention	'Inhumane Weapons' Convention	Treaty of Rarotonga	CFE Treaty
Chile	1935[1]	1961 CP	1965	1981	1974[4]			1980				
China	1952[5]	1983 CP		1983	PII: 1974[5]	1992[1]	1991[4]	1984		1982[2]	P2: 1989 P3: 1989	
Colombia		1989	1985	S	1972[1] SA	1986	S	1983				
Congo						1978	1978	1978				
Cook Islands											1985	
Costa Rica			1967		1969[1] SA[14]	1970 SA	S	1973				
Côte d'Ivoire	1970		1965			1973 SA	1972	S				
Croatia			1992			1992	1993	1993		1993		
Cuba	1966	1984		1977			1977	1976	1978	1987		
Cyprus	1966		1965	1972		1970 SA	1971	1973	1978	1988[3]		
Czech Republic	1993	1993	1993	1993		1993 SA	1993	1993	1993	1993		1993

Denmark	1930	1965	1964	1967		1969 SA	1971	1973	1978	1982		1991
Dominica					1993	1984			1992			
Dominican Rep.	1970		1964	1968	1968[1] SA[14]	1971 SA	1972	1973				
Ecuador	1970	1987 CP	1964	1969	1969[1] SA[14]	1969 SA		1975		1982		
Egypt	1928		1964	1967		1981[2] SA		S	1982	S		
El Salvador	S		1964	1969	1968[1] SA[14]	1972 SA		1991				
Equatorial Guinea	1989		1989	1989		1984	1992	1989				
Estonia	1931					1992		1993				
Ethiopia	1935		S	S		1970 SA	1977	1975	S			
Fiji	1973[1]		1972	1972		1972 SA		1973			1985	
Finland	1929	1984 CP	1964	1967		1969 SA	1971	1974	1978	1982		

State	Geneva Protocol	Antarctic Treaty	Partial Test Ban Treaty	Outer Space Treaty	Treaty of Tlatelolco	Non-Proliferation Treaty	Seabed Treaty	BW Convention	Enmod Convention	'Inhumane Weapons' Convention	Treaty of Rarotonga	CFE Treaty
France	1926[1]	1960 CP		1970	PI: 1992[6] PII: 1974[7]	1992 SA[3]		1984		1988[4]		1992
Gabon			1964			1974		S				
Gambia	1966		1965	S		1975 SA	S	S				
Georgia												1992
Germany	1929	1979 CP	1964	1971		1975[4] SA	1975	1983[1]	1983	1992		1991
Ghana	1967		1963	S		1970 SA	1972	1975	1978			
Greece	1931	1987	1963	1971	1975[1]	1970 SA	1985	1975	1983	1992		1992
Grenada	1989					1975		1986				
Guatemala	1983	1991	1964		1970[1] SA[14]	1970 SA	S	1973	1988	1983		
Guinea						1985	S					
Guinea-Bissau	1989		1976	1976		1976	1976	1976				

Guyana			S			1993		S			
Haiti			S	S	1969[1]	1970		S		S	
Holy See	1966			S		1971[5] SA			S	S	
Honduras			1964	S	1968[1] SA[14]	1973 SA	S	1979			
Hungary	1952	1984	1963	1967		1969 SA	1971	1972	1978	1982	1991
Iceland	1967		1964	1968		1969 SA	1972	1973	S	S	1991
India	1930[1]	1983 CP	1963	1982			1973[5]	1974[2]	1978	1984	
Indonesia	1971		1964	S		1979[6] SA		1992			
Iran	1929		1964	S		1970 SA	1971	1973	S		
Iraq	1931[1]		1964	1968		1969 SA	1972	1991	S		
Ireland	1930[6]		1963	1968		1968 SA	1971	1972[3]	1982	S	

State	Geneva Protocol	Antarctic Treaty	Partial Test Ban Treaty	Outer Space Treaty	Treaty of Tlatelolco	Non-Proliferation Treaty	Seabed Treaty	BW Convention	Enmod Convention	'Inhumane Weapons' Convention	Treaty of Rarotonga	CFE Treaty
Israel	1969[7]		1964	1977								
Italy	1928	1981 CP	1964	1972		1975[7] SA	1974[6]	1975	1981	S[5]		1992
Jamaica	1970		1991	1970	1969[1] SA[14]	1970 SA	1986	1975				
Japan	1970	1960 CP	1964	1967		1976[8] SA	1971	1982	1982	1982		
Jordan	1977[8]		1964	S		1970 SA	1971	1975				
Kazakhstan												1992
Kenya	1970		1965	1984		1970		1976				
Kiribati						1985 SA					1986	
Korea, North	1989[1,9]	1987				1985 SA		1987	1984			
Korea, South	1989[1]	1986 CP	1964	1967		1975[9] SA	1987	1987	1986[1]			
Kuwait	1971[10]		1965	1972		1989		1972	1980			

Laos	1989	1965	1972	1970			1978	1983
Latvia	1931			1992 SA	1992			1993
Lebanon	1969	1965	1969	1970 SA	S	1975	S	
Lesotho	1972		S	1970 SA	1973	1977		
Liberia	1927	1964		1970	S	S	S	
Libya	1971[11]	1968	1968	1975 SA	1990	1982		
Liechtenstein	1991			1978[10] SA	1991	1991		1989
Lithuania	1933			1991 SA				
Luxembourg	1936	1965	S	1975 SA	1982	1976	S	S	1992
Madagascar	1967	1965	1968[2]	1970 SA	S	S		
Malawi	1970	1964		1986 SA	S	S	1978	

State	Geneva Protocol	Antarctic Treaty	Partial Test Ban Treaty	Outer Space Treaty	Treaty of Tlatelolco	Non-Proliferation Treaty	Seabed Treaty	BW Convention	Enmod Convention	'Inhumane Weapons' Convention	Treaty of Rarotonga	CFE Treaty
Malaysia	1970		1964	S		1970 SA	1972	1991				
Maldives	1966					1970 SA		1993				
Mali			S	1968		1970	S	S				
Malta	1964		1964			1970 SA	1971	1975				
Mauritania			1964			1993						
Mauritius	1970		1969	1969		1969 SA	1971	1972	1992			
Mexico	1932		1963	1968	1967[1,8] SA	1969[11] SA	1984[7]	1974[4]		1982		
Moldova												1992
Monaco	1967											
Mongolia	1968[12]		1963	1967		1969 SA	1971	1972	1978	1982		
Morocco	1970		1966	1967		1970 SA	1971	S	S	S		

Country											
Mozambique						1990					
Myanmar (Burma)			1963	1970		1992		S		S	
Namibia						1992					
Nauru						1982 SA					1987
Nepal	1969		1964	1967		1970 SA	1971	S			
Netherlands	1930[13]	1967 CP	1964	1969	PI: 1971 SA[15]	1975 SA	1976	1981	1983[2]	1987[6]	1991
New Zealand	1930[1]	1960 CP	1963	1968		1969 SA	1972	1972	1984	1993	1986
Nicaragua	1990		1965	S	1968[1,9] SA[14]	1973 SA	1973	1975	S	S	
Niger	1967		1964	1967		1992	1971	1972	1993	1992	
Nigeria	1968[1]		1967	1967		1968 SA		1973		S	
Niue											1986

State	Geneva Protocol	Antarctic Treaty	Partial Test Ban Treaty	Outer Space Treaty	Treaty of Tlatelolco	Non-Proliferation Treaty	Seabed Treaty	BW Convention	Enmod Convention	'Inhumane Weapons' Convention	Treaty of Rarotonga	CFE Treaty
Norway	1932	1960 CP	1963	1969		1969 SA	1971	1973	1979	1983		1991
Oman								1992				
Pakistan	1960		1988	1968				1974	1986	1985		
Panama	1970		1966	S	1971[1] SA	1977	1974	1974				
Papua New Guinea	1980[1]	1981	1980	1980		1982 SA		1980	1980		1989	
Paraguay	1933[14]		S		1969[1] SA[14]	1970 SA	S	1976				
Peru	1985	1981 CP	1964	1979	1969[1] SA[14]	1970 SA		1985				
Philippines	1973		1965	S		1972 SA	1993	1973		S		
Poland	1929	1961 CP	1963	1968		1969 SA	1971	1973	1978	1983		1991
Portugal	1930[1]		S			1977 SA	1975	1975	S	S		1992

Qatar	1976					1989	1974	1975				
Romania	1929[1]	1971[1]	1963	1968		1970 SA	1972	1979	1983	S[7]		1992
Russia	1928[15]	1960 CP	1963	1967	PII: 1979[10]	1970 SA[12]	1972	1975	1978	1982	P2: 1988 P3: 1988	1992
Rwanda	1964		1963	S		1975	1975	1975				
Saint Kitts and Nevis	1989					1993		1991				
Saint Lucia	1988				S	1979 SA		1986	1993			
Saint Vincent and the Grenadines					1992	1984 SA					1986	
Samoa, Western			1965			1975 SA					1986	
San Marino			1964	1968		1970		1975				
Sao Tome and Principe						1983	1979	1979	1979			
Saudi Arabia	1971			1976		1988	1972	1972				

State	Geneva Protocol	Antarctic Treaty	Partial Test Ban Treaty	Outer Space Treaty	Treaty of Tlatelolco	Non-Proliferation Treaty	Seabed Treaty	BW Convention	Enmod Convention	'Inhumane Weapons' Convention	Treaty of Rarotonga	CFE Treaty
Senegal	1977		1964			1970 SA	S	1975				
Seychelles			1985	1978		1985	1985	1979				
Sierra Leone	1967		1964	1967		1975	S	1976	S	S		
Singapore			1968	1976		1976 SA	1976	1975				
Slovakia	1993	1993	1993	1993		1993 SA	1993	1993	1993	1993		1993
Slovenia			1992			1992	1992	1992		1992		
Solomon Islands	1981					1981 SA	1981	1981	1981		1989	
Somalia			S	S		1970	1973	S				
South Africa	1930[1]	1960 CP	1963	1968		1991 SA	1987	1975				
Spain	1929[16]	1982 CP	1964	1968		1987 SA	1987	1979	1978	1993		1992
Sri Lanka	1954		1964	1986		1979 SA		1986	1978			

Country										
Sudan	1980		1966			1973 SA	S			S
Suriname			1993		1977[1] SA[14]	1976 SA		1993		
Swaziland	1991		1969			1969 SA	1971	1991		
Sweden	1930	1984 CP	1963	1967		1970 SA	1972	1976	1984	1982
Switzerland	1932	1990	1964	1969		1977[10] SA	1976	1976[5]	1988	1982
Syria	1968		1964	1968		1969 SA		S	S	
Taiwan			1964	1970		1970	1972	1973		
Tanzania	1963		1964			1991	S	S		
Thailand	1931		1963	1968		1972 SA		1975		
Togo	1971		1964	1989		1970	1971	1976		S
Tonga	1971		1971	1971		1971 SA	1971	1976		

State	Geneva Protocol	Antarctic Treaty	Partial Test Ban Treaty	Outer Space Treaty	Treaty of Tlatelolco	Non-Proliferation Treaty	Seabed Treaty	BW Convention	Enmod Convention	'Inhumane Weapons' Convention	Treaty of Rarotonga	CFE Treaty
Trinidad and Tobago	1962		1964	S	1970[1] SA[14]	1986 SA						
Tunisia	1967		1965	1968		1970 SA	1971	1973	1978	1987		
Turkey	1929		1965	1968		1980[13] SA	1972	1974	S[3]	S		1992
Tuvalu						1979 SA					1986	
Uganda	1965		1964	1968		1982		1992	S			
UK	1930[1]	1960 CP	1963	1967	PI: 1969[11] PII: 1969[11]	1968 SA[14]	1972	1975	1978	S		1991
Ukraine		1992	1963	1967			1971	1975	1978	1982		1992
United Arab Emirates								S				
Uruguay	1977	1980[2] CP	1969	1970	1968[1] SA[14]	1970 SA	S	1981	1993			
USA	1975[17]	1960 CP	1963	1967	PI: 1981[12] PII: 1971[13] SA[15]	1970 SA[15]	1972	1975	1980	S[8]		1992

Uzbekistan					1992			1993	
Venezuela	1928	1965	1970	1970[1] SA[14]	1975 SA		1978		
Viet Nam	1980[1]		1980		1982 SA	1980[8]	1980	1980	S
Yemen	1971[18]	1979	1979		1979	1979	1979	1977	
Yugoslavia	1929[19]	1964	S		1970[16] SA	1973[9]	1973		1983
Zaire		1965	S		1970 SA		1977	S	
Zambia		1965	1973		1991	1972			
Zimbabwe					1991		1990		

The 1925 Geneva Protocol

[1] The Protocol is binding on this state only as regards states which have signed and ratified or acceded to it. The Protocol will cease to be binding on this state in regard to any enemy state whose armed forces or whose allies fail to respect the prohibitions laid down in it. Australia withdrew its reservation to the Protocol in 1986, New Zealand in 1989, Bulgaria, Chile and Romania in 1991. In 1991, Canada and the UK withdrew their reservations only with regard to the right to retaliate in case of an attack by bacteriological weapons.

[2] In notifying its succession to the obligations contracted in 1930 by the UK, Barbados stated that it considered the reservations made by the UK to be withdrawn.

[3] In 1970 at the UN, Byelorussia submitted a note which stated that 'it recognizes itself to be a party' to the Protocol. However, it did not notify the depositary.

[4] In a note to the depositary of 30 Sep. 1993, Cambodia stated that it regarded itself bound by the Protocol to which the coalition government of Democratic Kampuchea acceded in 1983.

[5] In 1952 the People's Republic of China issued a statement recognizing as binding upon it the 1929 accession to the Protocol in the name of China. It considers itself bound by the Protocol on condition of reciprocity on the part of all the other contracting and acceding powers.

[6] Ireland does not intend to assume, by this accession, any obligation except towards the states having signed and ratified this Protocol or which shall have finally acceded thereto, and should the armed forces or the allies of an enemy state fail to respect the Protocol, Ireland would cease to be bound by the said Protocol in regard to such state. In 1972, Ireland withdrew these reservations.

[7] The Protocol is binding on Israel only as regards states which have signed and ratified or acceded to it. The Protocol shall cease to be binding on Israel as regards any enemy state whose armed forces, or the armed forces of whose allies, or the regular or irregular forces, or groups or individuals operating from its territory, fail to respect the prohibitions which are the object of the Protocol.

[8] Jordan undertakes to respect the obligations contained in the Protocol with regard to states which have undertaken similar commitments. It is not bound by the Protocol as regards states whose armed forces, regular or irregular, do not respect the provisions of the Protocol.

[9] The Democratic People's Republic of Korea (North Korea) does not exclude the right to exercise its sovereignty *vis-à-vis* a contracting party which violates the Protocol in its implementation.

[10] In case of breach of the prohibition laid down in this Protocol by any of the parties, Kuwait will not be bound, with regard to the party committing the breach, to apply the provisions of this Protocol.

[11] The Protocol is binding on Libya only as regards states which are effectively bound by it and will cease to be binding on Libya as regards states whose armed forces, or the armed forces of whose allies, fail to respect the prohibitions which are the object of this Protocol.

[12] In the case of violation of this prohibition by any state in relation to Mongolia or its allies, Mongolia shall not consider itself bound by the obligations of the Protocol towards that state. This reservation was withdrawn in 1990.

[13] As regards the use in war of asphyxiating, poisonous or other gases and of all analogous liquids, materials or devices, this Protocol shall cease to be binding on the Netherlands with regard to any enemy state whose armed forces or whose allies fail to respect the prohibitions laid down in the Protocol.

[14] This is the date of receipt of Paraguay's instrument of accession. The date of the notification by the depositary government 'for the purpose of regularization' is 1969.

[15] The Protocol only binds the USSR in relation to the states which have signed and ratified or which have definitely acceded to the Protocol. The Protocol shall cease to be binding on the USSR in regard to any enemy state whose armed forces or whose allies *de jure* or *de facto* do not respect the prohibitions which are the object of this Protocol. In 1992 the Russian President stated that Russia withdrew its reservation concerning the possibility of using biological weapons.

[16] For Spain the Protocol is binding, *ipso facto,* without special agreement with respect to any other state accepting and observing the same obligation, that is, on condition of reciprocity. This reservation was withdrawn in 1992.

[17] The Protocol shall cease to be binding on the USA with respect to use in war of asphyxiating, poisonous or other gases, and of all analogous liquids, materials, or devices, in regard to any enemy state if such state or any of its allies fail to respect the prohibitions laid down in the Protocol.

[18] In case any party fails to observe the prohibition under the Protocol, the People's Democratic Republic of Yemen will consider itself free of its obligation. This reservation appears to be valid for the united Yemen, unless it states otherwise.

[19] The Protocol shall cease to be binding on Yugoslavia in regard to any enemy state whose armed forces or whose allies fail to respect the prohibitions which are the object of the Protocol.

The Antarctic Treaty

[1] Romania stated that the provisions of Article XIII, para. 1 of the Treaty were not in accordance with the principle according to which multilateral treaties whose object and purposes concern the international community, as a whole, should be open for universal participation.

[2] In acceding to the Treaty, Uruguay proposed the establishment of a general and definitive statute on Antarctica in which the interests of all states involved and of the international community as a whole would be considered equitably. It also declared that it reserved its rights in Antarctica in accordance with international law.

The Outer Space Treaty

[1] Brazil interprets Article X of the Treaty as a specific recognition that the granting of tracking facilities by the parties to the Treaty shall be subject to agreement between the states concerned.

[2] Madagascar acceded to the Treaty with the understanding that under Article X of the Treaty the state shall retain its freedom of decision with respect to the possible installation of foreign observation bases in its territory and shall continue to possess the right to fix, in each case, the conditions for such installation.

The Treaty of Tlatelolco

[1] The Treaty is in force for this country due to a declaration, annexed to the instrument of ratification in accordance with Article 28, para. 2, which waived the requirements for the entry into force of the Treaty, specified in para. 1 of that Article. (Colombia made this declaration subsequent to the deposit of ratification, as did Nicaragua and Trinidad and Tobago.)

[2] On signing the Treaty, Argentina stated that it understands Article 18 as recognizing the rights of parties to carry out, by their own means or in association with third parties, explosions of nuclear devices for peaceful purposes, including explosions which involve devices similar to those used in nuclear weapons. On 18 Jan. 1994 Argentina deposited its instruments of ratification of the amended text of the Treaty and waived the requirements for the entry into force of the Treaty laid down in Article 28.

[3] On signing the Treaty, Brazil stated that, according to its interpretation, Article 18 of the Treaty gives the signatories the right to carry out, by their own means or in association with third parties, nuclear explosions for peaceful purposes, including explosions which involve devices similar to those used in nuclear weapons. This statement was reiterated at the ratification. Brazil has not waived the requirements for the entry into force of the Treaty laid down in Article 28. The Treaty is therefore not yet in force for Brazil.

[4] When ratifying the Treaty, Chile did not waive the requirements for the entry into force of the Treaty laid down in Article 28. On 18 Jan. 1994 Chile ratified the amendments to the Treaty and waived the requirements for its entry into force.

[5] On signing Protocol II, China stated, *inter alia*: China will never use or threaten to use nuclear weapons against non-nuclear Latin American countries and the Latin American nuclear weapon-free zone; nor will China test, manufacture, produce, stockpile, install or deploy nuclear weapons in these countries or in this zone, or send its means of transportation and delivery carrying nuclear weapons to cross the territory, territorial sea or airspace of Latin American countries. China maintains that, in order for Latin America to become a nuclear weapon-free zone, all nuclear weapon states, and particularly the superpowers, must: (*a*) undertake not to use or threaten to use nuclear weapons against the Latin American countries and the Latin American nuclear weapon-free zone; (*b*) dismantle all foreign military bases in Latin America and refrain from establishing new bases there; and (*c*) prohibit the passage of any means of transportation and delivery carrying nuclear weapons through Latin American territory, territorial sea or airspace.

[6] On signing Protocol I, France made the following reservations and interpretative statements: The Protocol, as well as the provisions of the Treaty to which it refers, will not affect the right of self-defence under Article 51 of the UN Charter; the application of the legislation referred to in Article 3 of the Treaty relates to legislation which is consistent with international law; the obligations under the Protocol shall not apply to transit across the territories of the French Republic situated in the zone of the Treaty, and destined to other territories of the French Republic; the Protocol shall not limit, in any way, the participation of the populations of the French territories in the activities mentioned in Article 1 of the Treaty, and in efforts connected with the national defence of France; the provisions of Articles 1 and 2 of the Protocol apply to the text of the Treaty as it stands at the time when the Protocol is signed by France, and consequently no amendment to the Treaty that might come into force under Article 29 thereof would be binding on France without the latter's express consent. On ratifying Protocol I, France reiterated its statement made upon signature, and added that it did not consider the zone described in

Article 4, paragraph 2, of the Treaty as established in accordance with international law; it could not, therefore, agree that the Treaty should apply to that zone.

[7] On signing Protocol II, France stated that it interprets the undertaking contained in Article 3 of the Protocol to mean that it presents no obstacle to the full exercise of the right of self-defence enshrined in Article 51 of the UN Charter; it takes note of the interpretation of the Treaty given by the Preparatory Commission for the Denuclearization of Latin America and reproduced in the Final Act, according to which the Treaty does not apply to transit, the granting or denying of which lies within the exclusive competence of each state party in accordance with the pertinent principles and rules of international law; it considers that the application of the legislation referred to in Article 3 of the Treaty relates to legislation which is consistent with international law. The provisions of Articles 1 and 2 of the Protocol apply to the text of the Treaty as it stands at the time when the Protocol is signed by France. Consequently, no amendment to the Treaty that might come into force under the provision of Article 29 would be binding on France without the latter's express consent. If this declaration of interpretation is contested in part or in whole by one or more contracting parties to the Treaty or to Protocol II, these instruments would be null and void as far as relations between France and the contesting state or states are concerned. On depositing its instrument of ratification of Protocol II, France stated that it did so subject to the statement made on signing the Protocol. In 1974, France made a supplementary statement to the effect that it was prepared to consider its obligations under Protocol II as applying not only to the signatories of the Treaty, but also to the territories for which the statute of denuclearization was in force in conformity with Article 1 of Protocol I.

[8] On signing the Treaty, Mexico said that if technological progress makes it possible to differentiate between nuclear weapons and nuclear devices for peaceful purposes, it will be necessary to amend the relevant provisions of the Treaty, according to the procedures established therein.

[9] Nicaragua stated that it reserved the right to use nuclear energy for peaceful purposes such as the removal of earth for the construction of canals, irrigation works, power plants, and so on, as well as to allow the transit of atomic material through its territory.

[10] The USSR signed and ratified Protocol II with the following statement:

The USSR proceeds from the assumption that the effect of Article 1 of the Treaty extends, as specified in Article 5 of the Treaty, to any nuclear explosive device and that, accordingly, the carrying out by any party to the Treaty of explosions of nuclear devices for peaceful purposes would be a violation of its obligations under Article 1 and would be incompatible with its non-nuclear status. For states parties to the Treaty, a solution to the problem of peaceful nuclear explosions can be found in accordance with the provisions of Article V of the Non-Proliferation Treaty and within the framework of the international procedures of the IAEA. The signing of the Protocol by the USSR does not in any way signify recognition of the possibility of the force of the Treaty being extended beyond the territories of the states parties to the Treaty, including airspace and territorial waters as defined in accordance with international law. With regard to the reference in Article 3 of the Treaty to 'its own legislation' in connection with the territorial waters, airspace and any other space over which the states parties to the Treaty exercise sovereignty, the signing of the Protocol by the USSR does not signify recognition of their claims to the exercise of sovereignty which are contrary to generally accepted standards of international law. The USSR takes note of the interpretation of the Treaty given in the Final Act of the Preparatory Commission for the Denuclearization of Latin America to the effect that the transport of nuclear weapons by the parties to the Treaty is covered by the prohibitions in Article 1 of the Treaty. The USSR reaffirms its position that authorizing the transit of nuclear weapons in any form would be contrary to the objectives of the Treaty, according to which, as specially mentioned in the preamble, Latin America must be completely free from nuclear weapons, and that it would be incompatible with the non-nuclear status of the states parties to the Treaty and with their obligations as laid down in Article 1 thereof.

Any actions undertaken by a state or states parties to the Treaty which are not compatible with their non-nuclear status, and also the commission by one or more states parties to the Treaty of an act of aggression with the support of a state which is in possession of nuclear weapons or together with such a state, will be regarded by the USSR as incompatible with the obligations of those countries under the Treaty. In such cases the USSR reserves the right to reconsider its obligations under Protocol II. It further reserves the right to reconsider its attitude to this Protocol in the event of any actions on the part of other states possessing nuclear weapons which are incompatible with their obligations under the said Protocol. The provisions of the articles of Protocol II are applicable to the text of the Treaty of Tlatelolco in the wording of the Treaty at the time of the signing of the Protocol by the Soviet Union, due account being taken of the position of the USSR as set out in the present statement. Any amendment to the Treaty entering into force in accordance with the provisions of Articles 29 and 6 of the Treaty without the clearly expressed approval of the USSR shall have no force as far as the USSR is concerned.

In addition, the USSR proceeds from the assumption that the obligations under Protocol II also apply to the territories for which the status of the denuclearized zone is in force in conformity with Protocol I of the Treaty.

[11] When signing and ratifying Protocol I and Protocol II, the UK made the following declarations of understanding: In connection with Article 3 of the Treaty, defining the term 'territory' as including the territorial sea, airspace and any other space over which the state exercises sovereignty in accordance with 'its own legislation', the UK does not regard its signing or ratification of the Protocols as implying recognition of any legislation which does not comply with the relevant rules of international law. The Treaty does not permit the parties to carry out explosions of nuclear devices for peaceful purposes unless and until advances in technology have made possible the development of devices for such explosions which are not capable of being used for weapon purposes. The signing and ratification by the UK could not be regarded as affecting in any way the legal status of any territory for the international relations of which the UK is responsible, lying within the limits of the geographical zone established by the Treaty. Should any party to the Treaty carry out any act of aggression with the support of a nuclear weapon state, the UK would be free to reconsider the extent to which it could be regarded as committed by the provisions of Protocol II. In addition, the UK declared that its undertaking under Article 3 of Protocol II not to use or threaten to use nuclear weapons against the parties to the Treaty extends also to territories in respect of which the undertaking under Article I of Protocol I becomes effective.

[12] The USA ratified Protocol I with the following understandings: The provisions of the Treaty made applicable by this Protocol do not affect the exclusive power and legal competence under international law of a state adhering to this Protocol to grant or deny transit and transport privileges to its own or any other vessels or aircraft irrespective of cargo or armaments; the provisions of the Treaty made applicable by this Protocol do not affect rights under international law of a state adhering to this Protocol regarding the exercise of the freedom of the seas, or regarding passage through or over waters subject to the sovereignty of a state, and the declarations attached by the United States to its ratification of Protocol II apply also to its ratification of Protocol I.

[13] The USA signed and ratified Protocol II with the following declarations and understandings: In connection with Article 3 of the Treaty, defining the term 'territory' as including the territorial sea, airspace and any other space over which the state exercises sovereignty in accordance with 'its own legislation', the ratification of the Protocol could not be regarded as implying recognition of any legislation which does not, in the view of the USA, comply with the relevant rules of international law. Each of the parties retains exclusive power and legal competence, unaffected by the terms of the Treaty, to grant or deny non-parties transit and transport privileges. As regards the undertaking not to use or threaten to use nuclear weapons against the parties, the USA would consider that an armed attack by a party, in which it was assisted by a nuclear weapon state, would be incompatible with the party's obligations under Article 1 of the Treaty. The definition contained in Article 5 of the Treaty is understood as encompassing all nuclear explosive devices; Articles 1 and 5 of the Treaty restrict accordingly the activities of the parties under para. 1 of Article 18. Article 18, para. 4 permits, and US adherence to Protocol II will not prevent, collaboration by the USA with the parties to the Treaty for the purpose of carrying out explosions of nuclear devices for peaceful purposes in a manner consistent with a policy of not contributing to the proliferation of nuclear weapon capabilities. The USA will act with respect to such territories of Protocol I adherents, as are within the geographical area defined in Article 4, para. 2 of the Treaty, in the same manner as Protocol II requires it to act with respect to the territories of the Parties.

[14] Safeguards agreements under the Non-Proliferation Treaty cover the Treaty of Tlatelolco.

[15] Safeguards agreements under Protocol I.

The Non-Proliferation Treaty

[1] China stated that the nuclear weapon states should undertake: (*a*) not to be the first to use nuclear weapons at any time and under any circumstances; (*b*) not to use or threaten to use nuclear weapons against non-nuclear weapon countries or nuclear-free zones; and (*c*) support the establishment of nuclear weapon-free zones, respect the status of such zones and assume corresponding obligations. All states that have nuclear weapons deployed outside of their boundaries should withdraw all those weapons back to their own territories. China also declared that it regards the signing and ratification of the NPT by Taiwan in the name of China as illegal and null and void.

[2] Egypt stated that since it was embarking on the construction of nuclear power reactors, it expected assistance and support from industrialized nations with a developed nuclear industry. It called upon nuclear weapon states to promote research and development of peaceful applications of nuclear explosions in order to overcome all the difficulties at present involved therein. Egypt also appealed to these states to exert their efforts to conclude an agreement prohibiting the use or threat of use of nuclear weapons against any state, and expressed the view that the Middle East should remain completely free of nuclear weapons.

[3] An agreement between France, the European Atomic Energy Community (Euratom) and the IAEA for the application of safeguards in France had entered into force in 1981. The agreement covers nuclear material and facilities notified to the IAEA by France.

[4] FR Germany declared that it reaffirmed its expectation that the nuclear weapon states would intensify their efforts in accordance with the undertakings under Article VI of the Treaty, as well as its understanding that the security of FR Germany continued to be ensured by NATO; it stated that no provision of the Treaty may be interpreted in such a way as to hamper further development of European unification; that research, development and use of nuclear energy for peaceful purposes, as well as international and multinational co-operation in this field, must not be prejudiced by the Treaty; that the application of the Treaty, including the implementation of safeguards, must not lead to discrimination of the nuclear industry of FR Germany in international competition; and that it attached vital importance to the undertaking given by the USA and the UK concerning the application of safeguards to their peaceful nuclear facilities, hoping that other nuclear weapon states would assume similar obligations.

[5] The Holy See stated, *inter alia*, that the Treaty will attain in full the objectives of security and peace and justify the limitations to which the states party to the Treaty submit, only if it is fully executed in every clause and with all its implications.

[6] On signing the Treaty, Indonesia stated, *inter alia*, that it attaches great importance to the declarations of the USA, the UK and the USSR affirming their intention to provide immediate assistance to any non-nuclear weapon state party to the Treaty that is a victim of an act of aggression in which nuclear weapons are used. Of utmost importance, however, is not the action *after* a nuclear attack has been committed but the guarantees to prevent such an attack. Indonesia trusts that the nuclear weapon states will study further this question of effective measures to ensure the security of the non-nuclear weapon states. On depositing the instrument of ratification, Indonesia expressed the hope that the nuclear countries would be prepared to co-operate with non-nuclear countries in the use of nuclear energy for peaceful purposes and implement the provisions of Article IV of the Treaty without discrimination. It also stated the view that the nuclear weapon states would observe the provisions of Article VI of the Treaty relating to the cessation of the nuclear arms race.

[7] Italy stated that nothing in the Treaty was an obstacle to the unification of the countries of Western Europe; it noted full compatibility of the Treaty with the existing security agreements; it noted further that when technological progress would allow the development of peaceful explosive devices different from nuclear weapons, the prohibition relating to their manufacture and use shall no longer apply; it interpreted the provisions of Article IX, para. 3 of the Treaty, concerning the definition of a nuclear weapon state, in the sense that it referred exclusively to the five countries which had manufactured and exploded a nuclear weapon or other nuclear explosive device prior to 1 Jan. 1967, and stressed that under no circumstance would a claim of pertaining to such category be recognized by Italy for any other state.

[8] Japan declared that it urged a reduction of nuclear armaments and a comprehensive ban on nuclear testing; appealed to all states to refrain from the threat or use of force involving either nuclear or non-nuclear weapons; expressed the view that peaceful nuclear activities in non-nuclear weapon states party to the Treaty should not be hampered and that Japan should not be discriminated against in favour of other parties in any aspect of such activities. It also urged all nuclear weapon states to accept IAEA safeguards on their peaceful nuclear activities.

[9] The Republic of Korea (South Korea) took note of the fact that the depositary governments of the three nuclear weapon states had made declarations in June 1968 to take immediate and effective measures to safeguard any non-nuclear weapon state which is a victim of an act or an object of a threat of aggression in which nuclear weapons are used.

[10] Liechtenstein and Switzerland stated that activities not prohibited under Articles I and II of the Treaty include, in particular, the whole field of energy production and related operations, research and technology concerning future generations of nuclear reactors based on fission or fusion, as well as production of isotopes. Liechtenstein and Switzerland define the term 'source or special fissionable material' in Article III of the Treaty as being in accordance with Article XX of the IAEA Statute, and a modification of this interpretation requires their formal consent; they will accept only such interpretations and definitions of the terms 'equipment or material especially designed or prepared for the processing, use or production of special fissionable material', as mentioned in Article III of the Treaty, that they will expressly approve; and they understand that the application of the Treaty, especially of the control measures, will not lead to discrimination of their industry in international competition.

[11] On signing the Treaty, Mexico stated, *inter alia*, that none of the provisions of the Treaty shall be interpreted as affecting in any way whatsoever the rights and obligations of Mexico as a state party to the Treaty of Tlatelolco. It is the understanding of Mexico that 'at the present time' any nuclear explosive device is capable of being used as a nuclear weapon and that there is no indication that 'in the near future' it will be possible to manufacture nuclear explosive devices that are not potentially nuclear weapons. However, if technological advances modify this situation, it will be necessary to amend the relevant provisions of the Treaty in accordance with the procedure established therein.

[12] The agreement provides for the application of IAEA safeguards in Soviet peaceful nuclear facilities designated by the USSR.

[13] Turkey underlined the non-proliferation obligations of the nuclear weapon states, adding that measures must be taken to meet adequately the security requirements of non-nuclear weapon states.

[14] This agreement, signed by the UK, Euratom and the IAEA, provides for the submission of British non-military nuclear installations to safeguards under IAEA supervision.

[15] This agreement provides for safeguards on fissionable material in all facilities within the USA, excluding those associated with activities of direct national security significance.

[16] Yugoslavia stated, *inter alia*, that it considered a ban on the development, manufacture and use of nuclear weapons and the destruction of all stockpiles of these weapons to be indispensable for the maintenance of a stable peace and international security; it held the view that the chief responsibility for progress in this direction rested with the nuclear weapon states, and expected these states to undertake not to use nuclear weapons against the countries which have renounced them as well as against non-nuclear weapon states in general, and to refrain from the threat to use them.

The Seabed Treaty

[1] Argentina stated that it interprets the references to the freedom of the high seas as in no way implying a pronouncement of judgement on the different positions relating to questions connected with international maritime law. It understands that the reference to the rights of exploration and exploitation by coastal states over their continental shelves was included solely because those could be the rights most frequently affected by verification procedures. Argentina precludes any possibility of strengthening, through this Treaty, certain positions concerning continental shelves to the detriment of others based on different criteria.

[2] Brazil stated that nothing in the Treaty shall be interpreted as prejudicing in any way the sovereign rights of Brazil in the area of the sea, the sea-bed and the subsoil thereof adjacent to its coasts. It is the understanding of Brazil that the word 'observation', as it appears in para. 1 of Article III of the Treaty, refers only to observation that is incidental to the normal course of navigation in accordance with international law.

[3] Canada declared that Article I, para. 1, cannot be interpreted as indicating that any state has a right to implant or emplace any weapons not prohibited under Article I, para. 1, on the sea-bed and ocean floor, and in the subsoil thereof, beyond the limits of national jurisdiction, or as constituting any limitation on the principle that this area of the sea-bed and ocean floor and the subsoil thereof shall be reserved for exclusively peaceful purposes. Articles I, II and III cannot be interpreted as indicating that any state but the coastal state has any right to implant or emplace any weapon not prohibited under Article I, para. 1 on the continental shelf, or the subsoil thereof, appertaining to that coastal state, beyond the outer limit of the sea-bed zone referred to in Article I and defined in Article II. Article III cannot be interpreted as indicating any restrictions or limitation upon the rights of the coastal state, consistent with its exclusive sovereign rights with respect to the continental shelf, to verify, inspect or effect the removal of any weapon, structure, installation, facility or device implanted or emplaced on the continental shelf, or the subsoil thereof, appertaining to that coastal state, beyond the outer limit of the sea-bed zone referred to in Article I and defined in Article II.

[4] China reaffirmed that nothing in this Treaty shall be interpreted as prejudicing in any way the sovereign rights and the other rights of the People's Republic of China over its territorial sea, as well as the sea area, the seabed and subsoil thereof adjacent to its territorial sea.

[5] India stated that as a coastal state, India has, and always has had, full and exclusive rights over the continental shelf adjoining its territory and beyond its territorial waters and the subsoil thereof. It is the considered view of India that other countries cannot use its continental shelf for military purposes. There cannot, therefore, be any restriction on, or limitation of, the sovereign right of India as a coastal state to verify, inspect, remove or destroy any weapon, device, structure, installation or facility, which might be implanted or emplaced on or beneath its continental shelf by any other country, or to take such other steps as may be considered necessary to safeguard its security. The accession by India to the Treaty is based on this position.

[6] Italy stated, *inter alia*, that in the case of agreements on further measures in the field of disarmament to prevent an arms race on the sea-bed and ocean floor and in their subsoil, the question of the delimitation of the area within which these measures would find application shall have to be examined and solved in each instance in accordance with the nature of the measures to be adopted.

[7] Mexico declared that no provision of the Treaty can be interpreted to mean that a state has the right to emplace nuclear weapons or other weapons of mass destruction, or arms or military equipment of any type, on the continental shelf of Mexico. It reserves the right to verify, inspect, remove or destroy any weapon, structure, installation, device or equipment placed on its continental shelf, including nuclear weapons or other weapons of mass destruction.

[8] Viet Nam stated that no provision of the Treaty should be interpreted in a way that would contradict the rights of the coastal states with regard to their continental shelf, including the right to take measures to ensure their security.

[9] In 1974, the Ambassador of Yugoslavia transmitted to the US Secretary of State a note stating that in the view of the Yugoslav Government, Article III, para. 1, of the Treaty should be interpreted in such a way that a state exercising its right under this Article shall be obliged to notify in advance the coastal state, in so far as its observations are to be carried out 'within the stretch of the sea extending above the continental shelf of the said state'.

The BW Convention

[1] FR Germany stated that a major shortcoming of the BW Convention is the absence of any provisions for verifying compliance with essential obligations. The right to lodge a complaint with the UN Security Council is an inadequate arrangement. Furthermore, the establishment of an independent international committee of experts able to conduct impartial investigations when doubts arise as to whether the Convention is being complied with would be a welcome development.

[2] India reiterated its understanding that the objective of the Convention is to eliminate biological and toxin weapons, thereby excluding completely the possibility of their use, and that the exemption with regard to biological agents or toxins, which would be permitted for prophylactic, protective or other peaceful purposes, would not in any way create a loophole in regard to the production or retention of biological and toxin weapons. Also any assistance which might be furnished under the terms of the Convention would be of a medical or humanitarian nature and in conformity with the UN Charter.

[3] Ireland considers that the Convention could be undermined if the reservations made by the parties to the 1925 Geneva Protocol were allowed to stand, as the prohibition of possession is incompatible with the right to retaliate, and that there should be an absolute and universal prohibition of the use of the weapons in question. Ireland notified the depositary government for the Geneva Protocol of the withdrawal of its reservations to the Protocol, made at the time of accession in 1930. The withdrawal applies to chemical as well as to bacteriological (biological) and toxin agents of warfare.

[4] Mexico considers that the Convention is only a first step towards an agreement prohibiting also the development, production and stockpiling of all chemical weapons, and notes the fact that the Convention contains an express commitment to continue negotiations in good faith with the aim of arriving at such an agreement.

[5] Switzerland made the following reservation: Owing to the fact that the Convention also applies to weapons, equipment or means of delivery designed to use biological agents or toxins, the delimitation of its scope of application can cause difficulties since there are scarcely any weapons, equipment or means of delivery peculiar to such use; therefore, Switzerland reserves the right to decide for itself what auxiliary means fall within that definition.

The Enmod Convention

[1] It is the understanding of the Republic of Korea (South Korea) that any technique for deliberately changing the natural state of rivers falls within the meaning of the term 'environmental modification techniques' as defined in Article II of the Convention. It is further understood that military or any other hostile use of such techniques, which could cause flooding, inundation, reduction in the water-level, drying up, destruction of hydrotechnical installations or other harmful consequences, comes within the scope of the Convention, provided it meets the criteria set out in Article I thereof.

[2] The Netherlands accepts the obligation laid down in Article I of the Enmod Convention as extending to states which are not party to the Convention and which act in conformity with Article I of this Convention.

[3] On signing the Convention, Turkey declared that the terms 'widespread', 'long-lasting' and 'severe effects' contained in the Convention need to be more clearly defined, and that so long as this clarification was not made, Turkey would be compelled to interpret for itself the terms in question and, consequently, reserved the right to do so as and when required. Turkey also stated its belief that the difference between 'military or any other hostile purposes' and 'peaceful purposes' should be more clearly defined so as to prevent subjective evaluations.

The 'Inhumane Weapons' Convention

[1] The accession of Benin refers only to Protocols I and III of the Convention.

[2] On signing the Treaty, China stated that the Convention fails to provide for supervision or verification of any violation of its clauses, thus weakening its binding force. The Protocol on mines, booby traps and other devices fails to lay down strict restrictions on the use of such weapons by the aggressor on the territory of the victim and to provide adequately for the right of a state victim of an aggression to defend itself by all necessary means. The Protocol on incendiary weapons does not stipulate restrictions on the use of such weapons against combat personnel.

[3] Cyprus declared that the provisions of Article 7, para. 3b, and Article 8 of Protocol II of the Convention will be interpreted in such a way that neither the status of peace-keeping forces or missions of the UN in Cyprus will be affected nor will additional rights be, *ipso jure*, granted to them.

[4] France ratified only Protocols I and II. On signing the Convention France stated that it regretted that it had not been possible to reach agreement on the provisions concerning the verification of facts which might be alleged and which might constitute violations of the undertakings subscribed to. It therefore reserved the right to submit, possibly in association with other states, proposals aimed at filling that gap at the first conference to be held pursuant to Article 8 of the Convention and to utilize, as appropriate, procedures that would make it possible to bring before the international community facts and information which, if verified, could constitute violations of the provisions of the Convention and the Protocols annexed thereto. Reservation: Not being bound by the 1977 Additional Protocol I to the Geneva Conventions of 1949, France considers that para. 4 of the preamble to the Convention on prohibitions or restrictions on the use of certain conventional weapons, which reproduces the provisions of Article 35, para. 3, of Additional Protocol I, applies only to states parties to that Protocol. France will apply the provisions of the Convention and its three Protocols to all the armed conflicts referred to in Articles 2 and 3 common to the Geneva Conventions of 1949.

[5] Italy stated its regret that no agreement had been reached on provisions that would ensure respect for the obligations under the Convention. Italy intends to undertake efforts to ensure that the problem of the establishment of a mechanism that would make it possible to fill this gap in the Convention is taken up again at the earliest opportunity in every competent forum.

[6] The Netherlands made the following statements of understanding: A specific area of land may also be a military objective if, because of its location or other reasons specified in Article 2, para. 4, of Protocol II and in Article I, para. 3, of Protocol III, its total or partial destruction, capture, or neutralization in the prevailing circumstances offers a definitive military advantage; military advantage mentioned in Article 3, para. 3 under c, of Protocol II, refers to the advantage anticipated from the attack considered as a whole and not only from isolated or particular parts of the attack; in Article 8, para. 1, of Protocol II, the words 'as far as it is able' mean 'as far as it is technically able'.

[7] Romania stated that the provisions of the Convention and its Protocols have a restricted character and do not ensure adequate protection either to the civilian population or to the combatants as the fundamental principles of international humanitarian law require.

[8] The USA stated that it had strongly supported proposals by other countries to include special procedures for dealing with compliance matters, and reserved the right to propose at a later date additional procedures and remedies, should this prove necessary, to deal with such problems.

III. List of UN member states and year of membership

As of 1 January 1994, there were 184 UN member states. The countries marked with an asterisk are also members of the Conference on Disarmament (CD).

Afghanistan, 1946
Albania, 1955
*Algeria, 1962
Andorra, 1993
Angola, 1976
Antigua and Barbuda, 1981
*Argentina, 1945
Armenia, 1992
*Australia, 1945
Austria, 1955
Azerbaijan, 1992
Bahamas, 1973
Bahrain, 1971
Bangladesh, 1974
Barbados, 1966
Belarus, 1945
*Belgium, 1945
Belize, 1981
Benin, 1960
Bhutan, 1971
Bolivia, 1945
Bosnia and Herzegovina, 1992
Botswana, 1966
*Brazil, 1945
Brunei Darussalam, 1984
*Bulgaria, 1955
Burkina Faso (formerly
  Upper Volta), 1960
Burma (see Myanmar)
Burundi, 1962
Byelorussia (see Belarus)
Cambodia (Kampuchea), 1955
Cameroon, 1960
*Canada, 1945
Cape Verde, 1975
Central African Republic,
  1960
Chad, 1960
Chile, 1945
*China, 1945
Colombia, 1945
Comoros, 1975
Congo, 1960
Costa Rica, 1945
Côte d'Ivoire, 1960
Croatia, 1992
*Cuba, 1945
Cyprus, 1960
Czech Republic, 1993

Denmark, 1945
Djibouti, 1977
Dominica, 1978
Dominican Republic, 1945
Ecuador, 1945
*Egypt, 1945
El Salvador, 1945
Equatorial Guinea, 1968
Eritrea, 1993
Estonia, 1991
*Ethiopia, 1945
Fiji, 1970
Finland, 1955
*France, 1945
Gabon, 1960
Gambia, 1965
Georgia, 1992
*Germany, 1973
Ghana, 1957
Greece, 1945
Grenada, 1974
Guatemala, 1945
Guinea, 1958
Guinea-Bissau, 1974
Guyana, 1966
Haiti, 1945
Honduras, 1945
*Hungary, 1955
Iceland, 1946
*India, 1945
*Indonesia, 1950
*Iran, 1945
Iraq, 1945
Ireland, 1955
Israel, 1949
*Italy, 1955
Ivory Coast (see Côte
  d'Ivoire)
Jamaica, 1962
*Japan, 1956
Jordan, 1955
Kazakhstan, 1992
*Kenya, 1963
Korea, Dem. People's Rep. of
  (North Korea), 1991
Korea, Rep. of (South Korea),
  1991
Kuwait, 1963
Kyrgyzstan, 1992

Lao People's Democratic
  Republic, 1955
Latvia, 1991
Lebanon, 1945
Lesotho, 1966
Liberia, 1945
Libya, 1955
Liechtenstein, 1990
Lithuania, 1991
Luxembourg, 1945
Macedonia, Former
  Yugoslav Rep. of, 1993
Madagascar, 1960
Malawi, 1964
Malaysia, 1957
Maldives, 1965
Mali, 1960
Malta, 1964
Marshall Islands, 1991
Mauritania, 1961
Mauritius, 1968
*Mexico, 1945
Micronesia, 1991
Moldova, 1992
Monaco, 1993
*Mongolia, 1961
*Morocco, 1956
Mozambique, 1975
*Myanmar (formerly Burma),
  1948
Namibia, 1990
Nepal, 1955
*Netherlands, 1945
New Zealand, 1945
Nicaragua, 1945
Niger, 1960
*Nigeria, 1960
Norway, 1945
Oman, 1971
*Pakistan, 1947
Panama, 1945
Papua New Guinea, 1975
Paraguay, 1945
*Peru, 1945
Philippines, 1945
*Poland, 1945
Portugal, 1955
Qatar, 1971
*Romania, 1955

*Russia, 1945[a]
Rwanda, 1962
Saint Kitts (Christopher) and
  Nevis, 1983
Saint Lucia, 1979
Saint Vincent and the
  Grenadines, 1980
Samoa, Western, 1976
San Marino, 1992
Sao Tome and Principe, 1975
Saudi Arabia, 1945
Senegal, 1960
Seychelles, 1976
Sierra Leone, 1961
Singapore, 1965
Slovakia, 1993
Slovenia, 1992
Solomon Islands, 1978

Somalia, 1960
South Africa, 1945
Spain, 1955
*Sri Lanka, 1955
Sudan, 1956
Suriname, 1975
Swaziland, 1968
*Sweden, 1946
Syria, 1945
Tajikistan, 1992
Tanzania, 1961
Thailand, 1946
Togo, 1960
Trinidad and Tobago, 1962
Tunisia, 1956
Turkey, 1945
Turkmenistan, 1992
Uganda, 1962

*UK, 1945
Ukraine, 1945
United Arab Emirates, 1971
Upper Volta (see Burkina Faso)
Uruguay, 1945
*USA, 1945
Uzbekistan, 1992
Vanuatu, 1981
*Venezuela, 1945
Viet Nam, 1977
Yemen, 1947
*Yugoslavia, 1945[b]
*Zaire, 1960
Zambia, 1964
Zimbabwe, 1980

[a] In December 1991 Russia informed the UN Secretary-General that it was continuing the membership of the USSR in the Security Council and all other UN bodies.

[b] A claim by Yugoslavia (i.e., Serbia and Montenegro) in 1992 to continue automatically the membership of the former Yugoslavia was not accepted by the UN General Assembly. It was decided that Yugoslavia should apply for membership. Until an application is accepted, Yugoslavia is barred from participating in the work of UN bodies and in the CD.

Annexe B. Chronology 1993

RAGNHILD FERM

For the convenience of the reader, key words are indicated in the right-hand column, opposite each entry. They refer to the subject-areas covered in the entry. Definitions of the acronyms can be found on page xvii.

3 Jan.	The US–Russian Treaty on Further Reduction and Limitation of Strategic Offensive Arms (START II Treaty), requiring the USA and Russia to reduce their strategic nuclear warheads to 3000–3500 each by 1 Jan. 2003, is signed in Moscow by President Bush and President Yeltsin.	START; USA/Russia
7 Jan.	In a declaration to the United Nations, Iraq declares that it will not allow the UN to transport its personnel into the country using its own aircraft.	Iraq/UN
13 Jan.	As a reaction to the declaration of Iraq (see above), which is considered a violation of UN Security Council Resolution 687 of 3 Apr. 1991, US and British air forces attack military targets in Iraq. (On 14 Jan. the UN Secretary-General declares that the attack is in accordance with UN Security Council resolutions.)	USA, UK/Iraq; UN
13 Jan.	The Convention on the Prohibition of the Development, Production, Stockpiling and Use of Chemical Weapons and on their Destruction (CW Convention) is signed in Paris.	CWC
15 Jan.	In a letter to the UN Secretary-General, the North Atlantic Council confirms that NATO is willing to carry out military operations outside its area for the first time, in the no-fly zone over Bosnia and Herzegovina, should the UN consider such action necessary. The first operation starts in early April.	NATO; UN; Bosnia and Herzegovina
17 Jan.	Iraq agrees to allow UN flights into Iraq on a case-by-case basis. (On 19 Jan. Iraq offers a cease-fire.)	UN; Iraq
17–18 Jan.	US warships launch 40 cruise missiles at military targets outside Baghdad.	USA/Iraq
28 Jan.	The Defence Ministers of India and Russia sign, in New Delhi, an agreement on transfers from Russia to India of military equipment, including long-range missiles.	India/Russia
4 Feb.	Belarus ratifies the 1991 START I Treaty. (On 9 Feb. it deposits its instruments of accession, with the Russian Government, to the Non-Proliferation Treaty as a non-nuclear weapon state.)	Belarus; START; NPT

4 Feb.	ITAR-TASS reports that, according to the Russian Ministry of Defence, all tactical nuclear weapons have been removed from Russian ships and submarines and placed in central storage.	Russia; SNF
5 Feb.	The UN Security Council unanimously adopts Resolution 806, transforming the UN Iraq–Kuwait Observation Mission (UNIKOM) into an armed force capable of preventing small-scale violations of the demilitarized zone between Iraq and Kuwait.	UN; Iraq/Kuwait
9 Feb.	Following inconsistencies discovered during routine inspections, the International Atomic Energy Agency (IAEA) requests North Korea to give inspectors access to additional information. The request is refused.	North Korea/ IAEA
18 Feb.	Russia and the USA sign, in Washington, the HEU Agreement, under the terms of which the USA will purchase over a 20-year period from Russia 500 metric tons of highly enriched uranium (HEU) extracted from dismantled nuclear warheads. Russia agrees to work out mutually acceptable arrangements for sharing the revenues from the sale of HEU with Belarus, Kazakhstan and Ukraine.	Russia/USA; Nuclear weapons
22 Feb.	The UN Security Council unanimously adopts Resolution 808, establishing an international tribunal for the prosecution of persons responsible for serious violations of international humanitarian law committed in the former Yugoslavia.	UN; Yugoslavia
7 Mar.	A Peace Accord is signed in Islamabad by the President of Afghanistan, the leader of one faction of the Hizp-e-Islami and six Mujahideen leaders. The Accord is brokered by Pakistan and is actively supported by Iran and Saudi Arabia.	Afghanistan
12 Mar.	North Korea announces that it will withdraw from the NPT, as from 12 June 1993, to 'defend its supreme interests'. North Korea considers the IAEA request to inspect the two military locations an encroachment of the sovereignty of the country, an interference in its internal affairs and a hostile act. (See *9 Feb.*) In addition it cites the US–South Korean joint military exercise which began a few days before.	North Korea; NPT; IAEA; USA/South Korea
24 Mar.	In a speech to the Parliament, the President of South Africa discloses that South Africa had developed and produced nuclear weapons in the late 1970s. The weapons were dismantled and destroyed before South Africa acceded to the NPT in 1991.	South Africa; Nuclear weapons; NPT

26 Mar.	The UN Security Council unanimously adopts Resolution 814, approving a new UN Peacekeeping Operation for Somalia (UNOSOM II) that will have the authority to use force, if necessary, to disarm factions and ensure delivery of humanitarian aid. UNOSOM II will replace the Unified Task Force (UNITAF), headed by the USA.	UN; Somalia
30 Mar.–1 Apr.	The Nuclear Suppliers Group (NSG), meeting at Lucerne, Switzerland, adopts amendments to its 1977 Guidelines (the London Guidelines) that require IAEA safeguards on all current and future nuclear activities as a condition for any significant new supply commitments to non-nuclear weapon states.	NSG
31 Mar.	The UN Security Council adopts by a vote of 14 to 0 (China abstains from voting) Resolution 816, authorizing member states to take all necessary measures to ensure that only authorized flights take place in the no-fly zone over Bosnia and Herzegovina.	UN; Bosnia and Herzegovina
1 Apr.	The IAEA Board of Governors adopts a resolution confirming that North Korea is in non-compliance with its safeguards obligations under the NPT, and decides to report this to the UN. The USA, Russia and the UK, the depositary states of the NPT, urge North Korea to retract its announced withdrawal from the NPT and to comply fully with its Treaty commitments and safeguards obligations. The claim is rejected by North Korea.	North Korea/IAEA; NPT; UN
2 Apr.	NATO approves sending jet fighters into the southern region of Bosnia and Herzegovina, under UN authority, to ensure respect for the no-fly zone.	NATO; Bosnia and Herzegovina
3–4 Apr.	President Clinton and President Yeltsin meet in Vancouver, Canada. They agree that negotiations on a comprehensive nuclear test ban should start at an early date and reaffirm their determination to strengthen the NPT and give it unlimited duration. The two presidents also agree to explore joint missile defences in accordance with international agreements.	USA/Russia; CTB; NPT; Space weapons
5 Apr.	The WEU Council decides to take part in 'police and customs' operations, in co-operation with Bulgaria, Hungary and Romania, in order to strengthen the 1992 UN embargo against Serbia and Montenegro along the Danube River.	WEU; Yugoslavia
11 May	The UN Security Council adopts by a vote of 13 to 0 (China and Pakistan abstain from voting) Resolution 825, urging North Korea to reconsider its decision to withdraw from the NPT and honour its Treaty obligations.	North Korea; NPT; UN

13 May	The US Defense Secretary announces that the US Strate-gic Defense Initiative Organization (SDIO) has received a new mandate to replace its earlier programme on space-based weapons. It is renamed the Ballistic Missile Defense Organization (BMDO) and its emphasis will shift from strategic to theatre defences against ballistic missiles.	USA; SDI; BMDO
23–28 May	The UN Transitional Authority in Cambodia (UNTAC) conducts elections in Cambodia as provided under the 1991 Paris Peace Accords.	Cambodia; UN
26 May	The CSCE Chairman-in-Office and the UN Secretary-General exchange letters which constitute a framework for co-operation between the UN and the CSCE.	CSCE/UN
3 June	Sweden presents the text of a draft Comprehensive Test Ban Treaty at the Conference on Disarmament. (On *6 Dec.* Sweden presents a revised version which includes a verification protocol.)	Sweden; CD; CTBT
4 June	The UN Security Council adopts by a vote of 13 to 0 (Pakistan and Venezuela abstain from voting) Resolu-tion 836, authorizing the UN Protection Force (UNPROFOR) in Bosnia and Herzegovina, in carrying out its mandate, acting in self-defence, to take necessary measures, including the use of force.	UN; Bosnia and Herzegovina
11 June	After four days of talks with US officials, North Korea suspends its announced withdrawal from the NPT 'as long as it considers necessary'. In a joint statement the USA and North Korea agree on the principles of assurances against the threat and use of force, including nuclear weapons, and on peace and security in a nuclear-free Korean Peninsula, including full-scope safeguards. (See *12 Mar.*)	North Korea/USA; NPT; NWFZ
13 June	Phase II of the implementation of the 1991 Paris Peace Accords on Cambodia, the cantonment and disarmament of the military forces of the four 'factions', begins. (Almost immediately, the Khmer Rouge refuses to co-operate.)	Cambodia
15 June	The CIS Defence Ministers, meeting in Moscow, formally abolish the CIS Joint Armed Forces High Command, established in Dec. 1991. It will be replaced by a Joint Staff for Co-ordinating Military Co-operation with much more limited functions.	CIS
16 June	The UN Security Council unanimously adopts Resolu-tion 841, authorizing a world-wide oil and arms embargo on Haiti.	UN; Haiti

21–22 June	The European Council of heads of state and government of the EC states meets in Copenhagen. The French Prime Minister presents a proposal for a Pact for Stability in Europe (the Balladur Plan). The Pact would be addressed to Central and East European states and would implement principles on borders and minorities, improve co-ordination between existing institutions, and promote stability and political and military security in Europe.	EC; Stability Pact
25 June	The Belgian Government decides that Belgium will take part in the Franco-German Eurocorps, established on 22 May 1992. The formal agreement is signed on *12 Oct.*	Belgium/France/ Germany
26 June	23 US sea-launched cruise missiles attack intelligence headquarters in Baghdad in retaliation for an alleged Iraqi plot to kill former US President Bush during a visit to Kuwait in April.	USA/Iraq
2 July	The Ukrainian Parliament approves the Guidelines for the Foreign Policy of Ukraine, declaring that Ukraine is the owner of all the nuclear weapons on its territory but that it intends to become a non-nuclear weapon state.	Ukraine; Nuclear weapons
3 July	President Clinton announces that the USA is extending its moratorium on nuclear testing at least through Sep. 1994, 'as long as no other nation tests'. If the moratorium is broken by another state, the US Department of Energy will be directed to prepare for additional tests.	Nuclear tests; USA
3 July	A peace agreement mediated by the UN and the Organization of American States (OAS) is signed on Governor's Island, USA, by the exiled Haitian President and the leader of the coup of Sep. 1991.	Haiti
7–9 July	The heads of state and government of the Group of Seven leading industrialized countries (the G7), meeting in Tokyo, reiterate the objectives of universal adherence to the NPT as well as the Treaty's extension in 1995 and nuclear arms reduction.	G7; NPT
13 July	The US Arms Control and Disarmament Agency (ACDA) states that the Clinton Administration supports the 'narrow' interpretation of the 1972 ABM Treaty, i.e., that the Treaty prohibits the development, testing and deployment of sea-based, air-based, space-based and mobile land-based ABM systems.	USA; ABM Treaty
14 July	The UN Security Council unanimously adopts Resolution 851, condemning UNITA for continuing military actions in Angola and urging all states to refrain from providing any form of direct or indirect military assistance to UNITA.	UN; Angola

22 July	The US Department of Defense and the Ministry of Defence of Belarus sign, in Washington, three agreements in which the USA pledges to help Belarus to remove strategic nuclear weapons from Belarus to disposal facilities in Russia.	USA/Belarus; Nuclear weapons
23–24 July	The Association of South-East Asian Nations (ASEAN), meeting in Singapore, agrees to establish an ASEAN Regional Forum for the Asia–Pacific region.	ASEAN
25 July	A peace agreement, brokered by the Organization of African Unity (OAU), the Economic Community of West African States (ECOWAS) and the UN, is signed, in Cotonou, Benin, to end the civil war raging since 1990 in Liberia. On *22 Sep.* the UN Security Council decides to establish an observation mission (UNOMIL) to monitor the peace accord.	Liberia; UN
27 July	A cease-fire agreement, mediated by Russia, is signed in Sochi, Abkhazia, by the President of Georgia and the Abkhazian leader. (The Abkhazian offensive is resumed on *16 Sep.*)	Georgia/ Abkhazia
2 Aug.	The North Atlantic Council, holding a special meeting in Brussels, decides to prepare for undertaking stronger measures including air strikes to support UN Security Council decisions on Bosnia and Herzegovina. The measures will be in support of UNPROFOR.	NATO; Bosnia and Herzegovina; UNPROFOR
4 Aug.	A peace agreement between the Rwandan Government and the Patriotic Front, brokered by the OAU and Tanzania, is signed in Arusha, Tanzania. The two parties call for a UN mission to implement the peace.	Rwanda; UN
9 Aug.	The North Atlantic Council, meeting in Brussels, approves operational options for air strikes in Bosnia and Herzegovina and declares that NATO is prepared to act in co-ordination with the UN, when and if the situation demands.	NATO; UN; Bosnia and Herzegovina
10 Aug.	The Conference on Disarmament decides to give its *Ad Hoc* Committee on a Nuclear Test Ban the mandate to negotiate a Comprehensive Test Ban Treaty (CTBT).	CD; CTBT
18 Aug.	In a letter to the CD Secretary General, Ukraine declares that after the START I Treaty becomes effective 'it will reduce strategic means of delivery inherited from the USSR in accordance with the reduction norm set for the former USSR by the START [I Treaty], that is, roughly by 36 per cent'.	Ukraine; START; CD

24 Aug.	The UN Security Council unanimously adopts Resolution 858, establishing a UN Observer Mission in Georgia (UNOMIG) to verify compliance with the *27 July* cease-fire agreement between Georgia and Abkhazian separatist forces.	UN; Georgia/ Abkhazia
25 Aug.	The USA introduces economic sanctions on China and Pakistan, arguing that both countries, by transferring advanced missile technology, have violated the 1987 Missile Technology Control Regime (MTCR) Guidelines.	USA/China, Pakistan; MTCR
25 Aug.	During a visit to Warsaw, President Yeltsin states that he sympathizes with Poland's desire to join NATO and that this 'would not be counter to Russian interests nor to the pan-European integration process'.	Russia; NATO
27 Aug.	The UN Security Council unanimously adopts Resolution 861, suspending the sanctions imposed against Haiti. See *16 June.*	UN; Haiti
30 Aug.	After 14 months of secret talks, sponsored by Norway, between Israel and PLO officials, an agreement is reached (the Oslo Agreement) on a Declaration of Principles (see *13 Sep.*). On *10 Sep.* Israel and the PLO exchange letters of recognition.	Israel/PLO; Norway
31 Aug.	The withdrawal of Russian troops from Lithuania is completed.	Russia/ Lithuania
1 Sep.	The US Defense Secretary releases the 'Bottom–Up Review' of US defence strategy. It calls for overall force cuts and changing of the mix of forces to respond to the post-cold war security challenges.	USA
3 Sep.	A Russian–Ukrainian summit meeting is held in Massandra, Crimea. The two Presidents sign protocols on procedures for dismantling nuclear warheads. The two leaders reportedly also reach an agreement whereby Ukraine will give up its share of the Black Sea Fleet to Russia in exchange for debt relief. Ukraine later denies having made such a deal.	Russia/Ukraine
7 Sep.	India and China sign, in Beijing, an Agreement on the Maintenance of Peace and Tranquillity along the line of actual control in the India–China border areas.	India/China
13 Sep.	The Declaration of Principles (see *30 Aug.*) is signed in Washington by the Israeli and PLO Foreign Ministers. According to this document Israel will, during a five-year period, withdraw from the Gaza Strip and from the West Bank town of Jericho. A permanent Palestine settlement, based on Security Council Resolutions 242 of 1967 and Resolution 338 of 1973, will be established in the area. The accord is also signed by the US Secretary of State and the Russian Foreign Minister.	Israel/PLO; USA; Russia

14 Sep.	Israel and Jordan sign, in Washington, the Israel and Jordan Initial and Common Agenda, pledging to start negotiations on a comprehensive peace treaty, based on UN Security Council Resolutions 242 and 338.	Israel/Jordan
15 Sep.	The UN Security Council unanimously adopts Resolution 864, imposing an arms and oil embargo against the territory of Angola not controlled by the government unless an effective cease-fire is established and the 1991 Peace Accord is implemented. The Security Council reiterates its demand that UNITA accept unreservedly the results of the democratic elections of 30 Sep. 1992.	UN; Angola
15 Sep.	In a letter to President Clinton and other Western leaders, President Yeltsin sets out his objections to any possible enlargement of NATO to certain new democracies of Central and Eastern Europe and suggests a common security guarantee for these states.	Russia; NATO
17 Sep.	The withdrawal of Russian troops from Poland is completed.	Russia/Poland
17 Sep.	In a letter to the heads of state of several Western countries, President Yeltsin complains that the CFE Treaty prevents Russia from deployment of forces in areas where effective military presence is needed. Therefore, in order to ensure its security, Russia could be forced to take measures 'that wouldn't respond fully to the spirit of the Treaty'. (On *28 Sep.* Russia makes a formal proposal in the Joint Consultative Group.)	Russia; CFE
21 Sep.	Claiming that the Parliament (the Supreme Soviet) has blocked the process of economic and constitutional reform and that the political stalemate would lead to disintegration, President Yeltsin issues a decree declaring the suspension of all legislative, administrative and control functions of the Parliament. He calls for elections to the lower house (State Duma) of a two-chamber Federal Assembly for December.	Russia
23–24 Sep.	The Russian Parliament, in an emergency session, votes to impeach the President. On *27 Sep.* the Parliament building in Moscow (the White House) is sealed off by the President's troops.	Russia
24 Sep.	The leaders of the CIS states, meeting in Moscow, agree to establish collective peacekeeping forces by mid-Oct., numbering c. 25 000 troops. The immediate task is to perform peacekeeping duties along the border between Tajikistan and Afghanistan.	Tajikistan/ Afghanistan; CIS

27 Sep.	In his first address to the UN General Assembly, President Clinton outlines a framework for US efforts to prevent the proliferation of weapons of mass destruction and the missiles that deliver them. The USA will propose a multi-lateral convention prohibiting the production of fissile materials for nuclear weapons and submit US fissile material no longer needed for its deterrent to inspection by the IAEA. He expresses support for a CTBT and calls for nuclear weapon-free zones in southern and eastern Asia, in Africa and in the Middle East.	USA; UN; Nuclear weapons; CTBT; NWFZ; IAEA
27 Sep.–1 Oct.	The fourth ABM Treaty Review Conference, held in Geneva, is attended by Belarus, Russia, Ukraine and the USA. The question of succession to the Treaty was discussed.	ABM Treaty
4 Oct.	President Yeltsin's opponents, under siege in the Parliament building, are forced to surrender to troops loyal to the President.	Russia
5 Oct.	China conducts a nuclear test of c. 60 kt. (This is the first nuclear explosion carried out since 25 Sep. 1992.) In its official statement after the test, the Chinese Government reiterates its intention to take an active part in the CTBT negotiating process to conclude a treaty no later than 1996. In addition, it calls for parallel negotiation by all nuclear-weapon states aimed at concluding an international convention on unconditional no-first-use of nuclear weapons against non-nuclear states and nuclear weapon-free zones.	China; Nuclear test; CTBT; No-first-use; NWFZ
5 Oct.	The UN Security Council unanimously adopts Resolution 872, establishing the UN Assistance Mission for Rwanda (UNAMIR).	UN; Rwanda
7 Oct.	President Clinton orders additional US troops and armoured vehicles to Somalia, bringing the number of US troops deployed in the area to nearly 11 000. The troops will serve under US command.	USA; UN; Somalia
8 Oct.	The UN General Assembly adopts by consensus Resolution 48/1 lifting the economic sanctions imposed on South Africa in 1962. (The oil embargo is lifted on *9 Dec.* when the Transitional Executive Council becomes operational.)	UN; South Africa
13 Oct.	Disturbed by the continued obstruction of the UN Mission in Haiti (UNMIH), the UN Security Council unanimously adopts Resolution 873, stipulating that the economic sanctions imposed on Haiti on *16 June* (and lifted on *27 Aug.*) will be reinstated. (On *16 Oct.* the UN Security Council, in Resolution 875, calls on states to halt and inspect ships travelling towards Haiti to verify their cargoes.)	UN; Haiti

20–21 Oct.	An informal NATO Defence Ministers' meeting is held in Travemünde, Germany. The US Defense Secretary proposes a 'Partnership for Peace' which would allow the Central and East European countries to establish various types of defence-related co-operation agreements with NATO.	NATO; PFP
21 Oct.	As a reaction to the Chinese test on 5 Oct. President Yeltsin states that Russia will not resume nuclear testing but reserves the right to reconsider the decision 'if the situation in this sphere continues to develop unfavourably'.	China; Nuclear test; Russia
25 Oct.	The US Foreign Secretary and the Foreign Minister of Ukraine sign, in Kiev, an umbrella agreement, establishing the legal framework for the transfer of US aid to Ukraine under the Nunn–Lugar programme to facilitate the Safe and Secure Dismantlement (SSD) of nuclear weapons in the former USSR.	Ukraine/USA; SSD
29 Oct.	The US Defense Secretary announces that the Defense Department will carry out the first nuclear policy review in 15 years. It will include a revision of doctrine, force structure, operations and arms control. (This is part of the re-examination of all the US military forces, including the 'Bottom–Up Review' of conventional forces and the new Ballistic Missile Defense. See 13 May and 1 Sep.)	USA; Nuclear weapons
1 Nov.	The Treaty on European Union, signed at Maastricht, the Netherlands, on 7 Feb. 1992, enters into force.	EU
2 Nov.	The Russian Security Council approves a new military doctrine which codifies several new missions for the armed forces and excludes its former pledge not to use nuclear weapons first.	Russia; Nuclear weapons; No-first-use
5 Nov.	The French–German–Belgian Eurocorps (see 25 June) is officially installed in Strasbourg, France. It is estimated to be ready for engagement in Oct. 1995.	France; Germany; Belgium
9 Nov.	President Yeltsin presents a draft constitution for Russia to be submitted for approval in a national referendum held on the same day as the parliamentary elections (12 Dec.). According to this document the new legislature, the Federal Assembly (the Parliament), will be comprised of two chambers: the 178-member Federation Council (upper house) and the 450-member State Duma (lower house). The draft constitution envisages increased powers for the President.	Russia
9 Nov.	The Russian and Chinese Defence Ministers sign, in Beijing, a five-year military co-operation agreement.	Russia/China
16 Nov.	The 1982 United Nations Convention on the Law of the Sea (UNCLOS) enters into force.	UNCLOS

16 Nov.	The members of the Co-ordinating Committee for Multi-lateral Export Controls (COCOM), meeting in The Hague, agree to dissolve the organization no later than 31 Mar. 1994. It will be replaced by a new body that may include Russia, China and possibly other new member states.	COCOM
17 Nov.	The South African Government and the African National Congress (ANC) sign an agreement on an interim consti-tution which will end white minority rule in South Africa.	South Africa; ANC
17 Nov.	At the end of the first phase of the implementation of the CFE Treaty, the two groups of states (NATO and the for-mer WTO) have met their TLE reduction obligations.	CFE
18 Nov.	The Ukrainian Parliament (Rada) takes a decision to ratify the 1991 START I Treaty. However, a 13-point resolution is adopted that Ukraine will exchange instruments of rati-fication only under certain conditions, i.a., that it will not consider itself bound by Article V of the 1992 Lisbon Pro-tocol (which states that Belarus, Kazakhstan and Ukraine shall adhere to the NPT as non-nuclear weapon states 'in the shortest possible time'); and that it will dismantle its nuclear weapons gradually provided it will be given security guarantees by other nuclear weapon states.	Ukraine; START
29 Nov.–3 Dec.	At the Standing Consultative Commission (SCC) the USA proposes that the ABM Treaty parties should clarify the distinction between theatre defence systems and strategic ballistic missile defences.	ABM Treaty; USA
30 Nov.–1 Dec.	The CSCE Council of Foreign Ministers, meeting in Rome, adopts a set of decisions to streamline CSCE struc-tures and mechanisms in order to enhance their effective-ness.	CSCE
1 Dec.	At negotiations held in Geneva, initiated by the UN and mediated by Russia, the conflicting parties in Georgia sign a memorandum of understanding stipulating a cease-fire pending further negotiations.	Georgia/ Abkhazia; UN
2 Dec.	The North Atlantic Council, meeting in Brussels, supports the US proposal for a Partnership for Peace (see *20– 21 Oct.*).	NATO; PFP
12 Dec.	A referendum on the new state constitution as well as elections to the new Federal Assembly (see *9 Nov.*) are held in Russia.	Russia
13 Dec.	The Parliament of Kazakhstan takes a decision to accede to the NPT as a non-nuclear weapon state. (The instru-ments of accession are deposited on *14 Feb. 1994.*) The US Vice President and the President of Kazakhstan sign, in Almaty (Alma-Ata), an umbrella agreement on US aid for the Safe and Secure Dismantlement (SSD) of nuclear weapons in Kazakhstan.	Kazakhstan; NPT; USA/ Kazakhstan; SSD

15 Dec.	The British and Irish Prime Ministers, meeting in London, sign a declaration (the Downing Street Declaration) setting out general principles for holding peace talks on Northern Ireland.	UK/Ireland
16 Dec.	The UN General Assembly adopts over 40 resolutions on disarmament supporting, i.a., a Comprehensive Test Ban Treaty (Resolution 48/70), a prohibition on the production of fissile material for nuclear weapons and other explosive devices (48/75L), and a moratorium on the export of anti-personnel land-mines (48/75K).	UN; CTBT; Nuclear weapons; land-mines

The SIPRI 1993 Olof Palme Memorial Lecture: 'Co-operative Security in Europe: What is Required?'

MIKHAIL S. GORBACHEV

. . .

Bearing in mind all true circumstances, three tasks essentially call for a solution:

First, the modernization and streamlining of peace-building structures in Europe as well as their adjustment to the new premises;

Once again, a need to address the concept of peace-building on the continent has arisen.

French Prime Minister Eduard Balladour has come forward with a plan 'for stability and peace in Europe'. The plan envisages a contractual settlement of the issues relating to national minorities and frontiers, and, accordingly, the conclusion, of a 'pact for stability in Europe'. It could include, along with the EC Twelve, the USA, Canada, Russia, Ukraine, Belarus, Moldova and the Baltic republics.

The French proposal deserves attention. Its implementation would enable to put into effect security guarantees and structures of the European nations within the framework of the CSCE.

Pursuing that goal would naturally require further streamlining of the functions agreed in the consultative bodies of the CSCE.

There has been some progress along these lines. The CSCE Charter was adopted, its competencies were set out more clearly, and the office of the Commissioner for National Minorities was set up. The establishment of the CSCE Secretariat was also concluded. The first Secretary General, an experienced German diplomat, Mr Wilhelm Höynck, was appointed. However, this is only a beginning.

Turning the CSCE into a regional collective security organization, as laid down in the Helsinki Document 1992, has been put off. CSCE mechanisms have not yet

* This is an excerpt from the text of the seventh Olof Palme Memorial Lecture, given by Mikhail S. Gorbachev, Nobel Peace Prize Laureate and President of the International Foundation for Socio-Economic and Political Studies, Moscow. In Oct. 1986, SIPRI's Governing Board decided to arrange an annual public lecture, named after the late Swedish Prime Minister Olof Palme. The lecture is to be delivered in Stockholm by a political leader of international stature or an eminent scholar in order to highlight the need for, and problems of, peace and security, in particular of arms control and disarmament. The lecture is also intended to draw attention to SIPRI's commitment to a future with fewer arms and more freedom. The first annual Olof Palme Memorial Lecture was given in 1987 by the late Willy Brandt, former Chancellor of the Federal Republic of Germany, and subsequent lectures by the late Sergey F. Akhromeyev, Chief of the General Staff, First Deputy Minister of Defence and Marshal of the Soviet Union (1988); Victor F. Weisskopf, Professor Emeritus at the Massachusetts Institute of Technology, USA (1989); Oscar Arias Sánchez, former President of the Republic of Costa Rica and Nobel Peace Prize Laureate (1990); Sir Shridath Ramphal, former Secretary-General of the Commonwealth (1991); and Gro Harlem Brundtland, Prime Minister of Norway (1992).

shown their due efficiency, adequate to the crisis situations arising in the recent years.

I think that time has come to make a decisive step in developing the CSCE system.

Taking this opportunity I would like once again come out with what I repeatedly proposed: to establish within the framework of the CSCE a kind of Security Council which would be provided with competencies, on a regional scale, necessary to maintain peace and adopt operational measures. A Security Council for Europe having full powers to act could pursue preventive diplomacy, regularly bringing its influence to bear upon the development of the situation. Peacekeeping forces should be included under its authority; they could be used to stave off possible crises and to make other rapid responses. Naturally, the United States and Canada should participate in it.

A need to create regional security systems is also being felt in other regions of the world. Here I have in mind the Middle East, Africa and Latin America.

The *second* task, closely related to the first one, is the elaboration and settlement of the legal problems with the aim to create a pan-European legal space. Such an idea was raised for the first time in Paris, at the Conference on the Human Dimension of the CSCE.

So far, CSCE documents, starting with the Helsinki Final Act on, have had the character of a political commitment, not that of an international agreement. Considering the expansion of the scope of tasks for the CSCE to maintain peace, it would be important to give these documents a legal status. If not all CSCE participants are ready to do so, then only those provisions which enjoy general agreement could made legal.

Within the CSCE process some new legally-binding documents could also be worked out chiefly with respect to the minorities rights. A remarkable experience in elaborating and adopting this type of documents has already been gained by the Council of Europe. Perhaps, the time is ripe for expanding the group of nations having the Council conventions?

There is a need to address at the pan-European level such problems as the interrelationship between human rights, the rights of minorities and the right to self-determination, on the one hand, and sovereignty of states and inviolability of frontiers, on the other. For the time being, the handling of these questions is affected by the inadequacy of the adopted norms. Of special significance in this context is the question what judicial or arbitration body would have the right to settle the emerging conflicts. The existing bodies in Europe are not suitable for that.

And, finally, the *third* task is a qualitative improvement of the pan-European economic process.

There is a host of agreements in this domain. Quite interesting and promising projects have been put forward. Let me mention, for example, the Lubbers Plan in the field of energy or the relevant sections of François Mitterrand's concept for a pan-European confederation. However, this is still an outstanding problem.

Pan-European co-operation is said to be hindered by the incompatibility of norms and rules of the work of different economies in the East and West. This is true. But why not embark on a work to bring closer those norms and rules with the aim to elaborate common legal norms? This would also be an important part of building a pan-European legal space.

. . .

About the contributors

Dr Ian Anthony (United Kingdom) is Leader of the SIPRI Arms Transfers and Arms Production Project. He is editor of the SIPRI volumes *Arms Export Regulations* (1991) and *The Future of Defence Industries in Central and Eastern Europe* (1994), and author of *The Naval Arms Trade* (SIPRI, 1990) and *The Arms Trade and Medium Powers: Case Studies of India and Pakistan 1947–90* (1991). He has written or co-authored chapters in the *SIPRI Yearbook* since 1988.

Dr Eric Arnett (United States), an engineer, is Researcher and Co-leader of the SIPRI Military Technology and International Security Project. In 1988–92 he was Senior Programme Associate in the Program on Science and International Security and Director of the Project on Advanced Weaponry in the Developing World at the American Association for the Advancement of Science. His publications include *Sea-Launched Cruise Missiles and U.S. Security* (1991) and *Gunboat Diplomacy and the Bomb: Nuclear Proliferation and the U.S. Navy* (1989). He has written chapters for the *Encyclopedia of the American Military* (1994), *The Diffusion of Advanced Weaponry: Technologies, Regional Implications, and Responses* (1994) and the *SIPRI Yearbook 1993*.

Carl Åsberg (Sweden) is a PhD student at the Department of Peace and Conflict Research, Uppsala University.

Karin Axell (Sweden) is Research Associate and responsible for the Armed Conflicts Data Project at the Department of Peace and Conflict Research, Uppsala University. She is the editor of *States in Armed Conflict 1992* (1993) and co-author of 'Armed conflicts in 1989–92' in the *Journal of Peace Research* (1993).

Nicole Ball (United States) is Director of the Program on Enhancing Security and Development of the Overseas Development Council, Washington, DC. She is the author of *Demobilization and Reintegration of Military Personnel in Africa: The Evidence from Seven Country Case Studies* (1993) and *Pressing for Peace: Can Aid Induce Reform?* (1992). She has contributed chapters to the *Encyclopedia of Arms Control and Disarmament; Military Expenditures in Developing Countries and Donors' Options;* and *Trends and Implications for Arms Control, Proliferation, and International Security in the Changing Global Environment* (all 1993).

Dr Vladimir Baranovsky (Russia) is Leader of the SIPRI Project on Russia's Security Agenda. He holds the position of Senior Researcher at the Institute of World Economy and International Relations (Moscow) where he was Head of the International Security Section (1986–88) and Head of the European Studies Department (1988–92). He is the author of *Political Integration in Western Europe* (1983), *European Community in the International Relations System* (1986) and *Western Europe: Military and Political Integration* (1988), and co-editor of *Western European Integration: Political Aspects* (1985), *The Countries of Southern Europe in the Modern World* (1990), *1992: New Horizons of Western Europe* (1993) (all in Russian) and *In from the Cold: Germany, Russia and the Future of Europe* (1992). He has contributed to a number of joint volumes and journals and to the *SIPRI Yearbook 1993*.

Bengt-Göran Bergstrand (Sweden) is Researcher on the SIPRI World Military Expenditure Project. He is on leave as Senior Researcher from the Swedish National Defence Research Establishment (FOA).

Paul Claesson (United States) is Research Assistant on the SIPRI Peacekeeping and Regional Security Project. He has held positions at SIPRI as Research Assistant on the SIPRI Arms Transfers and Arms Production Project and as editor. He is co-author of the chapter on arms trade and arms production in the *SIPRI Yearbook 1993*.

Agnès Courades Allebeck (France) is on leave as Research Assistant on the SIPRI Arms Transfers and Arms Production Project. Her current field of research is French defence industrial policy. She has also carried out research on the foreign policy of the European Community/European Union. She is the author of chapters in the SIPRI volumes *Arms Export Regulations* (1991) and *Arms Industry Limited* (1993), and has contributed to the *SIPRI Yearbook* since 1989.

Anna De Geer (Sweden) is Research Assistant on the SIPRI Chemical and Biological Warfare Project. She is the author of a forthcoming volume *Chemical Export Control* in the SIPRI Chemical & Biological Warfare Studies.

Richard J. Eisendorf (United States) is Editor of the *Bulletin of Regional Cooperation in the Middle East,* Director of Public Relations at Search for Common Ground, Washington, DC, and Co-Chairman of the Middle East Roundtable of the Society for International Development. In 1992–93 he was an international observer and official for elections held in northern Iraq and Cambodia, and in 1989–90 was Political Analyst for the Foreign Affairs and National Defense Division of the Congressional Research Service.

Ragnhild Ferm (Sweden) is Researcher on the SIPRI Arms Control and Disarmament Project. She has published chapters on nuclear explosions, the comprehensive test ban and arms control agreements, and the annual chronologies of arms control and political events in the *SIPRI Yearbook* since 1982. She is the author of brochures and leaflets on SIPRI research topics in Swedish.

Trevor Findlay (Australia) is Leader of the SIPRI Peacekeeping and Regional Security Project. He was formerly an Australian diplomat with several years' experience in multilateral arms control negotiations. His most recent position was Acting Head of the Peace Research Centre at the Australian National University in Canberra. He was founding Editor of the quarterly journal *Pacific Research* and is the author of *Nuclear Dynamite: The Peaceful Nuclear Explosions Fiasco* (1990), *Peace Through Chemistry: The New Chemical Weapons Convention* (1993) and *Arms Control in the Post-Cold War World: With Implications for Asia-Pacific* (1993).

Professor Erhard Geissler (Germany) is Head of the Bioethical Research Group at the Max Delbrück Center for Molecular Medicine in Berlin-Buch. His main fields of research are radiation biology, microbial genetics, animal cell genetics, tumour virology and bioethics. He is co-editor of *Control of Dual-Threat Agents: The Vaccines for Peace Programme,* SIPRI Chemical & Biological Warfare Studies no. 15 (1994) and co-author of *Wieviel Genetik braucht der Mensch?* [How much genetics do people need?] (1994). He is the author of the SIPRI volume *Biological and Toxin Weapons Today* (1986) and editor of *Strengthening the Biological Weapons Conven-*

tion by Confidence-Building Measures, SIPRI Chemical & Biological Warfare Studies no. 10 (1990).

Dr Bates Gill (United States) is Guest Researcher at SIPRI. He has held the Fei Yiming Chair of Comparative Politics at the Johns Hopkins University Center for Chinese and American Studies, Nanjing, China. He is the author of *The Challenge of Chinese Arms Proliferation: US Policy for the 1990s* (1993), *Chinese Arms Transfers* (1992) and the forthcoming volume *Arming East Asia* (1994).

Mikhail S. Gorbachev (Russia) is President of the International Foundation for Socio-Economic and Political Studies, Moscow, and Head of the International Green Cross. He was awarded the Nobel Peace Prize in 1990. He was General Secretary of the Central Committee of the CPSU (1985–91), Chairman of the Presidium of the Supreme Soviet (1988–90) and President of the Soviet Union in 1990–91. His publications include *Perestroika: New Thinking for Our Country and the World* (1987) and *The August Coup: The Truth and the Lessons* (1991).

Gerd Hagmeyer-Gaverus (Germany) is Researcher on the SIPRI Arms Transfers and Arms Production Project. He was formerly a Researcher at the Centre for Social Science Research at the Free University of Berlin, where he co-authored several research reports. He has contributed to chapters on military expenditure and arms trade in the *SIPRI Yearbook* since 1985.

Birger Heldt (Sweden) is a PhD student and previously responsible for the Armed Conflicts Data Project at the Department of Peace and Conflict Research, Uppsala University. He is co-author of a chapter in *States in Armed Conflict 1989* (1991) and a chapter in the *SIPRI Yearbooks 1991–1993*, editor of *States in Armed Conflict 1990–91* (1992) and co-author of *States in Armed Conflict 1992* (1993).

Dr Richard Kokoski (Canada), a physicist, is Co-leader of the SIPRI Military Technology and International Security Project. He is author of the forthcoming SIPRI volume *Technology and the Proliferation of Nuclear Weapons* (1994), co-editor of *Verification of Conventional Arms Control in Europe: Technological Constraints and Opportunities* (SIPRI, 1990), author of a chapter in the *SIPRI Yearbook 1990* and co-author of a chapter in the *SIPRI Yearbook 1993*.

Steven M. Kosiak (United States) is Senior Analyst at the Defense Budget Project (DBP), Washington, DC. He was previously with the Center for Defense Information and the Office of the Defense Advisor at the US Mission NATO. He is author of the DBP annual analysis of the US defence budget submission, authorization and appropriation, and co-author of a chapter in the SIPRI volume *Arms Industry Limited* (1993) and in a DBP volume *An Affordable Long-Term Defense* (1993).

Dr Zdzislaw Lachowski (Poland) is Researcher on the SIPRI Project on Building a Co-operative Security System in and for Europe. He has been a Researcher at the Polish Institute of International Affairs since 1980, where he dealt with problems of European security and the CSCE process in particular, as well as West European political integration. He has published extensively on these subjects. He is co-editor of *Visions of Europe* (in Polish, 1989), and has contributed to the *SIPRI Yearbook* since 1992.

Dunbar Lockwood (United States) is Senior Research Analyst at the Arms Control Association (ACA), Washington, DC, where he is responsible for monitoring nuclear arms control negotiations and agreements between the USA and the nations of the Commonwealth of Independent States. He has worked at the Center for Defense Information (CDI) as a Senior Analyst. He has written monthly news articles for the ACA journal *Arms Control Today* since 1990. He wrote six issues of the CDI *Defense Monitor* in 1986–90 and is the author of a chapter in *Satanfaust: Das nukleare Erbe der Sowjetunion* [The Fist of the Devil: The Nuclear Heritage of the Soviet Union] (1992) and in the *SIPRI Yearbook 1993*.

Evamaria Loose-Weintraub (Germany) is Research Assistant on the SIPRI World Military Expenditure Project. She was previously Research Assistant on the SIPRI Arms Trade Project. She is co-author of a chapter in the SIPRI volume *Arms Export Regulations* (1991) and has contributed to the *SIPRI Yearbooks 1984–1988* and *1992–1993*. Her current research fields are military expenditure in the Central and East European countries and South American economic development. She is co-author of a chapter in the forthcoming SIPRI Research Report *The Future of the Defence Industries in Central and Eastern Europe* (1994).

Erik Melander (Sweden) is a PhD student at the Armed Conflicts Data Project at the Department of Peace and Conflict Research, Uppsala University. He is co-author of *States in Armed Conflict 1992* (1993).

Dr Kjell-Åke Nordquist (Sweden) is Assistant Professor at the Department of Peace and Conflict Research, Uppsala University. He is co-author of *Casualties of Conflict* (1991), prepared for the Red Cross/Red Crescent Movement's World Campaign for the Protection of Victims of War, and author of *Peace After War: On Conditions for Durable Inter-State Boundary Agreements* (1992) and *Conflicting Peace Proposals: Four Peace Proposals in the Palestine Conflict Appraised* (1985). He has co-authored chapters on major armed conflicts in the *SIPRI Yearbook* since 1990.

Thomas Ohlson (Sweden) is a political scientist and economist, working with the Department of Peace and Conflict Research, Uppsala University. In 1982–87 he was Leader of the SIPRI Arms Trade Project. In 1987–90 he was a Researcher at the Centre for African Studies in Maputo, Mozambique. He edited the SIPRI volume *Arms Production in the Third World* (1986) and is co-author of *Arms Transfers to the Third World, 1971–85* (SIPRI, 1987). He edited *Arms Transfer Limitations and Third World Security* (SIPRI, 1987), and co-authored chapters in the *SIPRI Yearbooks 1982–87*. His recent publications include *The New Is Not Yet Born: Conflict and Conflict Resolution In Southern Africa* (1994) and several articles on Southern Africa.

Dr Adam Daniel Rotfeld (Poland) is the Director of SIPRI and Leader of the SIPRI Project on Building a Co-operative Security System in and for Europe. He has been head of the European Security Department in the Polish Institute of International Affairs, Warsaw since 1978. He was a member of the Polish Delegation to the Conference on Security and Co-operation in Europe (CSCE) and Personal Representative of the CSCE Chairman-in-Office to examine the settlement of the conflict in the Trans-Dniester region (1992–93). He is the author or editor of over 20 studies on European security and the CSCE process. He is co-editor of the SIPRI volume

Germany and Europe in Transition (1991) and *European Security System in Statu Nascendi* (1990, in Polish). He has written chapters for the *SIPRI Yearbook* since 1991.

Dr David Shambaugh (United States) is Senior Lecturer in Chinese Politics at the School of Oriental and African Studies, University of London, and Editor of *The China Quarterly*. He was formerly Lecturer in Political Science at the University of Michigan (1987); Director of the Asia Program of the Woodrow Wilson International Centre for Scholars; Consultant to the Ford Foundation, the US Information Agency and other international organizations in China; visiting scholar at the Chinese Academy of Social Sciences, Beijing University, the China Institute of Contemporary International Relations, the Shanghai Institute of International Studies and the China Institute of International Strategic Studies. He is the author of *Beautiful Imperialist: China Perceives America, 1972–1990* (1991) and *The Making of a Premier: Zhao Ziyang's Provincial Career* (1984), and co-editor of *Chinese Foreign Policy: Theory and Practice* (1994).

Dr John Simpson (United Kingdom) is Professor of International Relations and Director of the Mountbatten Centre of the University of Southampton, and Programme Director of the Programme for Promoting Nuclear Non-Proliferation (PPNN). He is a member of the UN Secretary-General's Advisory Board for Disarmament Matters and co-editor of *Nuclear Non-Proliferation: A Reference Handbook* (1992). His field of research includes weapon acquisition processes, the history of the British nuclear weapon programme and nuclear non-proliferation.

Elisabeth Sköns (Sweden) is Researcher on the SIPRI Arms Transfers and Arms Production Project. She is the author of a chapter in the SIPRI volume *Arms Industry Limited* (1993) and has contributed to most editions of the *SIPRI Yearbook* since 1983.

Dr Thomas Stock (Germany) is Leader of the SIPRI Chemical and Biological Warfare Project and Series Editor of the SIPRI Chemical & Biological Warfare Studies. He is an analytical chemist, with research experience in analytical chemistry and chemical toxicology. He is co-author of chapters in the SIPRI volumes *Verification of Conventional Arms Control in Europe* (1990) and *Non-Production by Industry of Chemical-Warfare Agents: Technical Verification under a Chemical Weapons Convention* (1988), and co-editor of *National Implementation of the Future Chemical Weapons Convention* (1990). He has contributed to the *SIPRI Yearbook* since 1991 and has written extensively on the verification and national implementation of chemical disarmament accords.

Tim Trevan (UK) is Special Advisor to the Executive Chairman of the United Nations Special Commission on Iraq (UNSCOM) and Spokesman for the Commission. He has studied cellular pathology and served with the British diplomatic service in London, Yemen and Geneva, where he participated in the negotiation of the Chemical Weapons Convention. He is the author of *An Assessment of the UNSCOM Verification Process* (1993) and *The UN and Iraq: Verification in the Face of Obstruction* (1993).

Professor Peter Wallensteen (Sweden) has held the Dag Hammarskjöld Chair in Peace and Conflict Research since 1985 and is Head of the Department of Peace and Conflict Research, Uppsala University. He has recently published studies of the operation and reforms of the UN Security Council and is author of *From War to Peace: On Conflict Resolution in the Global System* (1994). He has co-authored chapters in the *SIPRI Yearbook* since 1988.

Siemon T. Wezeman (The Netherlands) is Research Assistant on the SIPRI Arms Transfers and Arms Production Project. He is co-author of the SIPRI Research Report *Arms Watch: SIPRI Report on the First Year of the UN Register of Conventional Arms* (1993).

Dr Erik Whitlock (United States) is Deputy Financial Director for Commonwealth of Independent States (CIS) Operations for a Budapest-based construction firm with significant business activity in Kazakhstan. He has written analyses of Russian economic policy and economic developments in the CIS for the Munich-based Radio Free Europe/Radio Liberty Research Institute. He is the author of a contribution on developments in the emerging post-Soviet economy in *The Demise of the USSR and the First Year of Independence* (forthcoming in 1994).

SIPRI Yearbook 1994

Oxford University Press, Oxford, 1994, 841 pp.
(Stockholm International Peace Research Institute)
ISBN 0-19-829182-5

ABSTRACTS

ROTFELD, A. D., 'Introduction: the search for new security rules and arms control concepts', in *SIPRI Yearbook 1994*, pp. 1–10.

The end of the East–West confrontation initiated a transformation of the international system. This process, however, is still in its infancy. With respect to the arms control element of the fledgling 'new world order' two major agreements signed in 1993 were the US–Russian START II Treaty and the multilateral Chemical Weapons Convention. The attempt to establish principles on which a new international order can be based continues: responding to the growing wave of intra-state conflicts has become a pressing concern. The concept of co-operative security offers a useful basis for facing the challenges ahead. The role of arms control and disarmament and their application in a changing world must be examined critically. The problem of preventing weapon proliferation is another pressing concern. Responding to armed conflicts and other crises offers no easy solutions either, relying on a complex mix of preventive diplomacy and military intervention.

FINDLAY, T., 'Multilateral conflict prevention, management and resolution', in *SIPRI Yearbook 1994*, pp. 13–52.

Multilateral efforts to prevent, manage and resolve international conflict were severely tested in 1993. Quiet successes in Cambodia, Eritrea, Macedonia and El Salvador were overshadowed by failures in Angola, Haiti, Somalia and the former Yugoslavia. United Nations endeavours reached new levels of intensity and complexity, but the world body confronted political, managerial and logistical difficulties that the euphoria of the immediate post-cold war years had ill prepared it for. The UN began a long process of reform and restructuring, while regional organizations struggled to share some of the burden.

CLAESSON, P. and FINDLAY, T., 'Peace-keeping case studies: UNOSOM II, UNTAC and UNPROFOR', in *SIPRI Yearbook 1994*, pp. 62–80.

The largest UN peacekeeping operations to date yielded important lessons in 1993. In Somalia UNOSOM II caused a rethinking of the feasibility of UN peace enforcement in a civil war. UNTAC provided a comprehensive plan to bring peace and democracy to Cambodia via well-managed elections. UNPROFOR was established in the former Yugoslavia as an interim measure and evolved into: a traditional disengagement mission in Croatia; a humanitarian support mission in Bosnia and Herzegovina; and a small observation mission in Macedonia. Failure to negotiate a settlement left UNPROFOR without a traditional peacekeeping role in Bosnia and Herzegovina. The UN lacked the means to back Security Council resolutions and member states were reluctant to commit more forces. UNPROFOR faced impossible demands and criticized the Security Council for treating resolutions as if they were self-executing.

WALLENSTEEN, P. and AXELL, K., 'Major armed conflicts', in *SIPRI Yearbook 1994*, pp. 81–95.

Major armed conflicts were waged in 28 locations in 1993, compared to 29 in 1992. The conflicts in Algeria and Georgia escalated from minor to major armed conflicts during 1993. All the conflicts were internal, and a majority concerned control over territory. Reduced conflict intensity was noted in Bangladesh, Guatemala, India, Myanmar, Peru, the Philippines and Somalia. Three locations—India–Pakistan, Laos and Mozambique—reported for 1992 were removed from the list for 1993. However, Mozambique was the only case in which a peace accord settled the conflict.

EISENDORF, R., 'The Middle East: the peace and security-building process', in *SIPRI Yearbook 1993*, pp. 97–124.

The Arab–Israeli arena has been the site of five major wars and innumerable military operations. The present peace process has come closer than any efforts over the past fifty years to resolving the fundamental Palestinian problem. The agreement reached between Israel and the PLO in September 1993 was negotiated in dramatic secret discussions over eight months in Norway while the official talks in Washington were deadlocked. The year also brought into greater focus Israel's conflicts with Jordan, Lebanon and Syria. Discussions continue on the implementation of the Israel–PLO agreement and resolution on other fronts in the Arab–Israeli conflict.

GILL, B., 'North-East Asia and challenges to multilateral security institutions', in *SIPRI Yearbook 1994*, pp. 149–68.

An assessment of North-East Asia which includes its history, its contemporary developments and its record thus far in developing security institutions highlights the challenges which lie ahead for multilateralism in the sub-region. The challenges and prospects for multilateral security institutions in North-East Asia are considered in three principal sections: a brief historical summary of security relations in North-East Asia; an account of current developments influencing multilateral security in North-East Asia; a review of the past, present and possible future multilateral security efforts in North-East Asia.

FINDLAY, T., 'South-East Asia and the new Asia–Pacific security dialogue', in *SIPRI Yearbook 1994*, pp. 125–47.

With the end of the cold war, the largely successful Cambodian peace process and the growing influence and affluence of the members of the Association of South-East Asian Nations (ASEAN), the security outlook for South-East Asia is relatively bright. The subregion is emerging not only as an economic powerhouse but as a locus of Asia–Pacific regionalism, in both the economic an security fields. With the creation in 1993 of an ASEAN Regional Forum, involving nearly all the states of Asia–Pacific, the region will have for the first time its own regional security dialogue.

BARANOVSKY, V., 'Conflict developments on the territory of the former Soviet Union', in *SIPRI Yearbook 1994*, pp. 169–203.

The former Soviet Union remained the scene of domestic instability and inter-state conflict in 1993, as the process of the economic and political transition continued. Specific conflict-related factors included domestic power struggles, the economic crisis, separatism, controversies over the rights of ethnic minorities and the Soviet military legacy. In the Baltic region, potential conflict-generating issues include: the withdrawal of Russian troops; protecting the civil rights of Russian-speaking populations; territorial issues; and the disposition of Kaliningrad. The conflict in Moldova was reduced, whereas in the Caucasus and Tajikistan large-scale violence continued. Of crucial importance to future conflict developments will be the state of Russian–Ukrainian relations and Russia's role in the 'near abroad'.

ROTFELD, A. D., 'Europe: towards a new regional security regime', in *SIPRI Yearbook 1994*, pp. 205–74.

Europe's security arrangements are still inadequate to the new requirements and challenges. In 1993 tendencies towards integration were dominant in Western Europe with the coming into force of the Maastricht Treaty, a new role for the Western European Union and the beginning of a European common foreign and security policy, while disintegration and division continued in Central and Eastern Europe. There was some progress towards realizing the concept of 'expanded security' for Europe. The attitudes of the West, of Russia and of the Central and Eastern European countries to the expansion of NATO were further clarified, and in spite of caution on the Western side there was a move towards closer relations through the Partnership for Peace. The CSCE acquired new operational structures and legal capacity, took responsibility for eight missions in the Balkan, Baltic and Caucasus areas and pursued the strategy of active preventive diplomacy in different ways.

LOCKWOOD, D., 'Nuclear weapon developments', in *SIPRI Yearbook 1994*, pp. 277–307.

All of the five declared nuclear weapon states continued to deploy, or at least develop, new nuclear weapon systems in 1993. With the possible exception of China, they also continued to retire older nuclear weapons, scale back earlier modernization plans or cancel weapons that were under development. Confronted with weak economies and the difficulty of defining a clear and present security threat, the British, French, Russia and US governments found that they could not justify allocating scarce resources to their respective nuclear weapon programmes at the levels maintained in the recent past.

FERM, R., 'Nuclear explosions, 1945–93', in *SIPRI Yearbook 1994*, pp. 308–13.

In 1993 only one nuclear explosion was conducted—by China, on 5 October. All the other declared nuclear weapon states observed their unilaterally announced test moratoria. Tables show the number of nuclear explosions carried out in 1945–93. With new information released by the US Department of Energy on previously classified US nuclear tests, the figure for the US explosions is higher than in previous *Yearbook* tables. Several Soviet tests, for which exact years were not given, have now been identified by date.

STOCK, T. and DE GEER, A., 'Chemical weapon developments', in *SIPRI Yearbook 1994*, pp. 315–42.

The broad support for the Chemical Weapons Convention (CWC) is manifested by its 154 signatures as of 10 December 1993. The effect of the CWC on the behaviour of states in the chemical weapon (CW) area and on CW proliferation received attention in 1993. Allegations of CW use and of the acquisition or attempted acquisition of a CW capability continued to be made. Such allegations could negatively affect future chemical disarmament or strengthen the will to bring about entry into force of the CWC in 1995. Problems related to the destruction of CW continued. Russia is attempting to complete its initial destruction programme, while alternative destruction technologies are under review in the USA as the cost of destruction steadily increases. The possible release of CW agents during the 1991 Persian Gulf War was debated in 1993, and led to discussion of CW and biological weapon (BW) protection and detection capability. Old, abandoned and dumped chemical weapons are becoming an increasing problem as states realize the cost of destruction and removal of these weapons.

ARNETT, E., 'Military technology: the case of India', in *SIPRI Yearbook 1994*, pp. 343–65.

The Indian military technology base crossed new thresholds in 1993, but for bureaucratic reasons Indian military research and development (R&D) is not progressing as far or fast as some observers once predicted. Indian designs will not soon be competitive with their Western counterparts, and claims that sophisticated conventional or nuclear weapons are inevitably within the grasp of India (or other countries without India's scientific resources) should be viewed with scepticism. The Indian government now realizes that the focus on big projects is flawed and is redirecting R&D toward incremental projects. Unfortunately, long-standing but unpromising projects continue to command scarce resources.

KOKOSKI, R., 'Non-lethal weapons: a case study of new technology developments', in *SIPRI Yearbook 1994*, pp. 367–86.

While the concept of non-lethal weapons is not new, since the Persian Gulf War and with growing technological capabilities there has been a renewed effort to further their development for use in situations where less than lethal force is required or desirable. Newer technologies include high-power microwave weapons capable of disabling unprotected electronic systems, advanced portable lasers for use against sensors and personnel as well as chemical and biological agents capable of degrading the performance of equipment and/or personnel. In 1993 the USA launched new efforts to give a coherent structure to the non-lethal research effort, and in January 1994 a new NATO study group began holding meetings that will focus on non-lethal technologies. Various missions proposed for these weapons include their application as a precursor to or in conjunction with conventional military force, for counter-terrorist and peace-keeping actions, as well as possible uses in the area of law enforcement. Among the important concerns raised by their development is their proliferation and their potential destabilizing effect, perhaps making war more likely in some situations.

BALL, N., BERGSTRAND, B.-G., KOSIAK, S., LOOSE-WEINTRAUB, E., SHAMBAUGH, D. and WHITLOCK, E., 'World military expenditure', in *SIPRI Yearbook 1994*, pp. 389–453.

Military spending is declining in nearly all Western and Eastern industrialized countries—the USA, France, Germany, the UK, Russia, and the Central and East European countries. There is also a clear tendency in most countries to cut arms procurement more rapidly than defence spending in general. One of the few countries not decreasing military spending is China. However, China still surrounds its military spending with great secrecy, and some of the methodological problems related to the study of Chinese spending are examined. A new issue—which is starting to play an increasingly greater role, both in security and economic debate—concerns 'conditionality', the link between foreign aid and military expenditure, and whether such aid should be given to countries with high military spending.

ANTHONY, I., CLAESSON, P., COURADES ALLEBECK, A., SKÖNS, E. and WEZEMAN, S. T., 'Arms production and arms trade', in *SIPRI Yearbook 1994*, pp. 455–502.

Global arms industry output continues to fall. Reductions in production for domestic arms procurement have been most marked in Russia and other countries in Central and Eastern Europe. The combined arms sales by the top 100 arms-producing companies of the OECD and developing countries fell to $168 billion in 1992 (down by $8 billion from 1991). The international flow of major conventional weapons levelled off—at a value of about $22 billion in 1993 (in 1990 US dollars)—after a period of fast decline since 1987. The USA remained the dominant supplier, accounting for 48% of total deliveries. Russia increased its share by about one-third to 21% in 1993. Among the recipients, the share of countries in the Middle East has increased since 1991 as equipment programmes agreed in the wake of the Persian Gulf War have been implemented.

GILL, B., 'Arms production and trade in East Asia', in *SIPRI Yearbook 1994*, pp. 551–62.

At a time in the post-cold war era when the international arms trade is in decline, numerous reports have pointed with concern to an arms buildup or arms race in East Asia. Against the background of these reports, data and analytic interpretations are provided with regard to East Asian arms acquisitions. A presentation of research data includes figures and analysis for East Asia on past and current arms production and procurement, expected future procurement and military expenditure.

SIMPSON, J., 'Nuclear arms control and an extended non-proliferation regime', in *SIPRI Yearbook 1994*, pp. 605–29.

The changes in the nuclear non-proliferation environment since 1991 are analysed by outlining how the nuclear non-proliferation agenda, focused upon six 'threshold states', has been expanded by proliferation threats from 'NPT renegade' states and the breakup of the USSR. The questions of whether or not the established non-proliferation regime can meet these new challenges or whether radical changes to the regime are needed are addressed. The prospects for the 1995 NPT Review and Extension Conference are examined, and the overall status of the nuclear non-proliferation regime is assessed. Evolving conceptual and practical arguments about methods of preventing proliferation are reviewed.

LACHOWSKI, Z., 'Conventional arms control and security co-operation in Europe', in *SIPRI Yearbook 1994*, pp. 565–603.

Despite the unparalleled success of European conventional arms control in the beginning of the decade, the evidence that it is at a cross-roads was reinforced in 1993. Its premises no longer exist. The implementation of the arms control and disarmament agreements continues fairly smoothly, but they fail to address a qualitatively changed situation. A new type of challenge, threat and conflict is facing Europe—the fragmentation of the international system, numerous incidents of local armed hostilities in south-eastern Europe tinted with ethnic, religious and other colours. The functions of arms control are changing: from confrontational to co-operative, from 'militarized' to a more political process, from global to regional. What is lacking at present is a new comprehensive strategy for arms control in Europe. Work in the Forum for Security Co-operation in Vienna is a major attempt to inject stability into a remarkably destabilized environment. By harmonizing conventional arms control and disarmament obligations and elaborating a code of conduct for military security as well as working out new measures and commitments it is creating a normative basis and a framework for a security space in Europe.

LOCKWOOD, D., 'Nuclear arms control', in *SIPRI Yearbook 1994*, pp. 639–72.

A number of positive developments in nuclear arms control highlighted 1993: the USA and Russia signed the START II Treaty; Belarus and Kazakhstan acceded to the Non-Proliferation Treaty as non-nuclear weapon states; fewer nuclear explosions were conducted than in any year since 1959; and the United Nations adopted by consensus for the first time resolutions calling for the negotiation of treaties banning nuclear tests and the production of fissile material for weapons. Despite these accomplishments, 1993 ended with no binding international agreements in force which limit strategic offensive nuclear weapons.

STOCK, T., 'The Chemical Weapons Convention: institutionalization and preparation for entry into force', in *SIPRI Yearbook 1994*, pp. 685–711.

The Chemical Weapons Convention (CWC) was opened to all states for signature on 13 January 1993 in Paris. The international machinery for the CWC, the Preparatory Commission (PrepCom) and the Provisional Technical Secretariat (PTS), began their work in February 1993. At least two years are required from opening of the CWC for signature to prepare for its entry into force. The PrepCom is establishing procedures for the CWC verification regime, developing a budget and setting up the Organisation for the Prohibition of Chemical Weapons (OPCW) infrastructure, including its rules and procedures. States parties must undertake national implementation by implementing necessary legislation and by setting up National Authorities. Some states have begun such efforts. There is a need for the chemical industry to be more involved in the work of the PrepCom Expert Groups and to be given access to more information about the work of the PrepCom. By 10 December 1993, 154 states had signed the CWC and 4 states had ratified the Convention.

TREVAN, T., 'UNSCOM: activities in 1993', in *SIPRI Yearbook 1994*, pp. 000–00.

The UNSCOM is required to identify and eliminate Iraq's weapons of mass destruction and long-range missiles capabilities and, thereafter, monitor Iraq's undertaking not to re-acquire such capabilities. UNSCOM has operated since 1991 in environments varying from outright Iraqi obstruction to reluctant co-operation. Actions have passed from identification to destruction of weapons capabilities. In 1993, a seminal development occurred—Iraq's acceptance long overdue, of the plans for ongoing monitoring and verification approved by the Security Council, setting the scene for monitoring activities and, potentially, a co-operative relationship with Iraq. This chapter charts the political and operational developments in this eventful year for UNSCOM.

GEISSLER, E., 'Biological weapon and arms control developments', in *SIPRI Yearbook 1994*, pp. 713–38.

The biological weapon (BW) and toxin weapon (TW) threat increased in 1993 as did concern about BW and TW proliferation. A significant step towards reduction of these threats was the successful conclusion of the work of the *Ad Hoc* Group of Governmental Experts to Identify and Examine Potential Verification Measures from a Scientific and Technical Standpoint (VEREX) which identified a number of potential verification measures. In consequence, a special conference will be held in September 1994 to decide on further action with regard to verification of the 1972 Biological Weapons Convention. The conference is intended to contribute significantly to more efficient prevention of biological and toxin warfare.

GORBACHEV, M. S., 'Common security in Europe: what is required?', in *SIPRI Yearbook 1994*, pp. 807–808.

Three tasks call for a solution today: first, the modernization of peace-building structures in Europe. Here the plan put forward by French Prime Minister Eduard Balladour deserves attention. Now is also the time to make a decisive step in developing the institutional structure of the CSCE, specifically through the establishment of a CSCE Security Council. Second, clarification of the legal status of CSCE decisions and documents: this might help to alleviate the inadequacy of already adopted norms in dealing with contemporary problems.; and third, a qualitative improvement of the pan-European economic process. In this respect several proposals already put forward by European leaders are worthy of attention.

Errata

SIPRI Yearbook 1993: World Armaments and Disarmament

Page 181, footnote 45, line 1:	Should read: 'The US reservation has come to be known as the Connally Amendment. . . .'
Page 449, table 10.14:	The column heading 'Number of deliveries' should read: 'Share of total deliveries (per cent)'.
Page 569, section on Belarus, line 1:	Should read: 'The USA and Belarus signed an umbrella agreement on 22 October 1992,'.
Page 791, second column	The last entry in the column, 'USSR, 1945' should be deleted from the list of UN member states as of 31 December 1992.

INDEX